The Construction of Preference

Do we really know what we want? Or must we sometimes construct our preferences on the spot, using whatever cues are available – even when these cues lead us astray? One of the main themes that has emerged from behavioral decision research during the past three decades is the view that people's preferences are often constructed in the process of elicitation. This idea is derived from studies demonstrating that normatively equivalent methods of elicitation (e.g., choice and pricing) give rise to systematically different responses. These preference reversals violate the principle of procedure invariance that is fundamental to all theories of rational choice. If different elicitation procedures produce different orderings of options, how can preferences be defined and in what sense do they exist? This book shows not only the historical roots of preference construction but also the blossoming of the concept within psychology, law, marketing, philosophy, environmental policy, and economics. Decision making is now understood to be a highly contingent form of information processing, sensitive to task complexity, time pressure, response mode, framing, reference points, and other contextual factors.

Sarah Lichtenstein is a founder and Treasurer of Decision Research. Her fields of specialization are human judgment, decision making, and risk. She is now retired but continues as an advisor and consultant to Decision Research. She published numerous journal articles and book chapters on topics such as preference reversals and value structuring. She was a Fellow of the American Psychological Association and served on the editorial boards of *Organizational Behavior and Human Performance* and *Acta Psychologica*. She is a coauthor of *Acceptable Risk* (1981).

Paul Slovic is a founder and President of Decision Research and Professor of Psychology at the University of Oregon. He studies human judgment, decision making, and risk. Dr. Slovic has received the Distinguished Contribution Award from the Society of Risk Analysis, the Distinguished Scientific Contribution Award from the American Psychological Association, and the Outstanding Contribution to Science Award from the Oregon Academy of Science. He has received honorary doctorates from the Stockholm School of Economics (1996) and the University of East Anglia (2005). He is a coauthor or editor of eight books, most recently *The Perception of Risk* (2000) and *The Social Amplification of Risk* (2003).

THE CONSTRUCTION
OF PREFERENCE

Edited by

SARAH LICHTENSTEIN

Decision Research

PAUL SLOVIC

Decision Research and
The University of Oregon

CAMBRIDGE UNIVERSITY PRESS
Cambridge, New York, Melbourne, Madrid, Cape Town, Singapore, São Paulo

Cambridge University Press
32 Avenue of the Americas, New York, NY 10013-2473, USA

www.cambridge.org
Information on this title: www.cambridge.org/9780521834285

First published 2006

Printed in the United States of America

A catalog record for this publication is available from the British Library.

Library of Congress Cataloging in Publication Data

The construction of preference / edited by Sarah Lichtenstein, Paul Slovic.
    p.   cm.
Includes bibliographical references and index.
ISBN-13: 978-0-521-83428-5 (hardback)
ISBN-10: 0-521-83428-7 (hardback)
ISBN-13: 978-0-521-54220-3 (pbk.)
ISBN-10: 0-521-54220-0 (pbk.)
1. Choice (Psychology)   I. Lichtenstein, Sarah, 1933–   II. Slovic, Paul, 1938–   III. Title.
BF611.C65   2006
153.8′3 – dc22   2005035966

ISBN-13   978-0-521-83428-5 hardback
ISBN-10   0-521-83428-7 hardback

ISBN-13   978-0-521-54220-3 paperback
ISBN-10   0-521-54220-0 paperback

We dedicate this book to
our grandchildren:

James Loving Lichtenstein
Lela Loving Lichtenstein
Jacinto Slovic
Spencer Slovic
Cameron Slovic
Oblio Mathai

The discussion of the meaning of preference and the status of value may be illuminated by the well-known exchange among three baseball umpires. "I call them as I see them," said the first. "I call them as they are," said the second. The third disagreed, "They ain't nothing till I call them." Analogously, we can describe three different views regarding the nature of values. First, values exist – like body temperature – and people perceive and report them as best they can, possibly with bias (I call them as I see them). Second, people know their values and preferences directly – as they know the multiplication table (I call them as they are). Third, values or preferences are commonly constructed in the process of elicitation (they ain't nothing till I call them). The research reviewed in this article is most compatible with the third view of preference as a constructive, context-dependent process. (Tversky & Thaler, 1990, p. 210)

Contents

Contributors

Dan Ariely is the Luis Alvarez Renta Professor of Management Science at the Sloan School of Management and at the Media Laboratory at MIT

Max H. Bazerman is the Jesse Isidor Straus Professor of Business Administration at Harvard Business School

James R. Bettman is the Burlington Industries Professor of Marketing at The Fuqua School of Business, Duke University

Sally Blount is the Dean of the Undergraduate College and the Abraham L. Gitlow Professor of Management at the New York University Stern School of Business

Jerome R. Busemeyer is a Professor of Psychology and Cognitive Science at Indiana University

Melissa L. Finucane is a Research Investigator for Kaiser Permanente

Baruch Fischhoff is the Howard Heinz University Professor in the Department of Social & Decision Sciences and the Department of Engineering and Public Policy, Carnegie Mellon University

Daniel T. Gilbert is the Harvard College Professor of Psychology at Harvard University

Daniel G. Goldstein is an Assistant Professor of Marketing at the London Business School

Robin Gregory is a Senior Researcher at Decision Research

David M. Grether is a Professor of Economics at the California Institute of Technology

Sara D. Hodges is an Associate Professor of Psychology at the University of Oregon

Keith J. Holyoak is a Professor of Psychology at the University of California, Los Angeles

Christopher K. Hsee is the Theodore O. Yntema Professor of Behavioral Sciences and Marketing at the University of Chicago Graduate School of Business

Sheena S. Iyengar is the Sanford C. Bernstein Associate Professor of Leadership and Ethics at Columbia University

Ryan K. Jessup is a Ph.D. candidate in psychology and cognitive science at Indiana University, Bloomington

Eric J. Johnson is the Norman Eig Professor of Business at Columbia Business School, Columbia University

Joseph G. Johnson is an Assistant Professor of Psychology at Miami University

Daniel Kahneman is the Eugene Higgins Professor of Psychology and Public Affairs at the Woodrow Wilson School, Princeton University

Kristen J. Klaaren is an Associate Professor of Psychology at Randolph-Macon College

Daniel C. Krawczyk is a Postdoctoral Fellow at the University of California, Berkeley

Suzanne J. LaFleur is a Research Scientist and Adjunct Assistant Professor at the School of Family Studies, University of Connecticut

Mark R. Lepper is Albert Ray Lang Professor of Psychology at Stanford University

Sarah Lichtenstein is a Senior Researcher at Decision Research

Douglas J. Lisle is Director of Research for TrueNorth Health Center

George Loewenstein is a Professor of Economics and Psychology at Carnegie Mellon University

Mary Frances Luce is Professor of Marketing at The Fuqua School of Business, Duke University

Donald G. MacGregor is President and Senior Scientist at MacGregor-Bates, Inc.

Douglas MacLean is a Professor of Philosophy at the University of North Carolina, Chapel Hill

Naomi Mandel is an Assistant Professor of Marketing at the W.P. Carey School of Business, Arizona State University

Henry Montgomery is a Professor of Cognitive Psychology at Stockholm University

Stephen M. Nowlis is the AT&T Research Professor of Marketing at the W.P. Carey School of Business, Arizona State University

John W. Payne is the Joseph J. Ruvane, Jr., Professor of Management and Marketing, Professor of Psychology, and Deputy Dean of The Fuqua School of Business, Duke University

Ellen Peters is a Research Scientist at Decision Research

Charles R. Plott is the Edward S. Harkness Professor of Economics and Political Science at the California Institute of Technology

Drazen Prelec is a Professor of Management Science at the Massachusetts Institute of Technology

Matthew Rabin is the Edward G. and Nancy S. Jordan Professor of Economics at the University of California, Berkeley

Daniel Read is a Professor of Behavioral Economics at the Durham Business School, University of Durham

Ilana Ritov is an Associate Professor in the Department of Psychology and School of Education, The Hebrew University

Yuval Rottenstreich is an Associate Professor of Management at The Fuqua School of Business, Duke University

Samuel Sattath works at the Center for Rationality, The Hebrew University

David A. Schkade is the Jerome Katzin Endowed Chair in the Rady School of Management, University of California, San Diego

Jonathan W. Schooler is a Professor of Psychology and the Canada Research Chair in Social Cognitive Science at the University of British Columbia

Eldar Shafir is a Professor of Psychology and Public Affairs at Princeton University

Dan Simon is a Professor of Law at the University of Southern California

Itamar Simonson is the Sebastian S. Kresge Professor of Marketing at the Stanford Graduate School of Business

Paul Slovic is the President of Decision Research and a Professor of Psychology at the University of Oregon

Cass R. Sunstein is the Karl N. Llewellyn Distinguished Service Professor of Jurisprudence at the Law School and the Department of Political Science, University of Chicago

Ola Svenson is a Professor of Psychology and the Director of the Risk Analysis, Social and Decision Unit at Stockholm University

Richard H. Thaler is the Robert P. Gwinn Distinguished Service Professor of Behavioral Science and Economics at the Graduate School of Business, University of Chicago

Amos Tversky (1937–1996) was the Davis Brack Professor of Behavioral Sciences at Stanford University

Elke U. Weber is a Professor of Psychology and Management and the Jerome A. Chazen Professor of International Business at Columbia University

Timothy D. Wilson is the Sherrell J. Aston Professor of Psychology at the University of Virginia

Yiheng Xi is a student in the Department of Management of Organizations, Hong Kong University of Science and Technology

Frank Yu is a Ph.D. candidate at the Graduate School of Business at the University of Chicago

Robert B. Zajonc is a Professor of Psychology at Stanford University

Jiao Zhang is a Ph.D. candidate in behavioral science at the Graduate School of Business, University of Chicago

Preface

Cass R. Sunstein

According to the most prominent view in contemporary social science, human beings "have" preferences, and their choices are a product of those preferences. If people are going to select an ice cream flavor, or a television set, or a political candidate, they will consult a kind of internal preference menu, and their choices will result from that consultation. This approach to human behavior dominates economics; it also plays a large role in many other fields, including political science, law, and sociology.

But are people's preferences really elicited, rather than constructed, by social situations? This is an empirical question. Over the last decades, a great deal of progress has been made in answering it. Sometimes people prefer A to B *and* B to A, depending on how the options are framed. If people are told, "Of those who undergo this medical procedure, 90% are still alive after 5 years," they are far more likely to agree to the procedure than if they are told, "Of those who undergo this procedure, 10% are dead after 5 years." Framing matters for ordinary consumer choices as well as for unusual medical decisions. Most consumers might prefer a small television to a medium-sized one when choosing among the two, but if a large television is added to the set of options, many consumers will favor the medium-sized one over the small one. The same point applies to jury determinations. Other things being equal, a jury is far more likely to convict a defendant on a charge if that charge can be characterized as falling in the middle of a set of possibilities.

Or consider questions from the important domain of regulatory policy: Do ordinary people "have" preferences about their own willingness to pay to eliminate a mortality risk of 1/100,000 or to save members of an endangered species? It turns out that people's decisions are greatly affected by amounts that are initially mentioned to them – so much so as to make it possible for analysts to "construct" an extraordinarily wide range of possible amounts.

According to standard economic theory, default rules shouldn't much matter to what people will do, at least if they can easily contract around those rules; people who "prefer" to contract around default rules will do exactly that. But growing evidence suggests that default rules, both private and public, help to construct people's preferences. Suppose that an employer automatically assumes that employees want to devote a certain percentage of their wages to savings in a retirement plan, while allowing employees to "opt out" of the plan if they do so explicitly. If the employer so assumes, there will be far more participation in retirement plans than if the employer assumes that employees do not want to participate in that plan unless they say otherwise.

The point is immensely important. If default rules help to construct preferences, then the standard analysis of such rules, in both economics and law, turns out to be badly mistaken.

All of these examples suggest that if their goal is to predict human behavior, analysts will blunder if they assume that people have preferences that predate framing, default rules, and social interactions. Sometimes preferences are surprisingly labile. This point also unsettles the widely held view that the role of private and public institutions is to "respect" or "satisfy" preferences. If preferences are constructed, then institutions cannot refer to acontextual preferences at all.

To be sure, there are limits to the process of construction. Some televisions just won't sell; most of the time, people are unlikely to want 80% of their wages to go into savings. It would be an overstatement to say of preferences, as Gertrude Stein said of Oakland, that "there is no there there." But frequently what is there is far less fixed, and far more malleable, than conventional theory predicts.

This book collects decades of work on central issues involving the construction of preferences. It includes the seminal papers on that topic; it also offers newer work whose implications have yet to be fully unpacked. The result is a fundamental rethinking of central issues in social science, with intriguing lessons for many questions about human behavior and about the role of human institutions in helping to produce it.

Acknowledgments

We are indebted to many people who, over the course of almost half a century, contributed to the construction of preference and the construction of this book. Ward Edwards built the foundation for the field of Behavioral Decision Theory and introduced us to this field and to each other. Paul Hoffman, founding director of the Oregon Research Institute, provided a stimulating research environment in which to conduct our early experiments on preference reversals. Amos Tversky and Danny Kahneman encouraged our work and contributed to it in many important ways, as did Baruch Fischhoff, who helped us think more broadly about "labile values."

We are particularly grateful to the many fine researchers who, with stunning ingenuity, transformed the study of preference reversals into the study of constructed preferences. A sampling of their contributions is included in this book.

We also thank the economists who took our early work seriously enough to criticize it (and sometimes even to attack it). Their skeptical views motivated much of the subsequent psychological research and made it better. The challenges posed by David Grether and Charles Plott were particularly important in this regard.

In developing our ideas on preference reversals and preference construction, we have been supported intellectually and socially by our colleagues at Oregon Research Institute (Lew Goldberg, Leonard Rorer, Robyn Dawes, and Gordon Bechtel) and Decision Research (Robin Gregory, Ellen Peters, Melissa Finucane, Don MacGregor, Terre Satterfield, Robert Mauro, C. K. Mertz, Jim Flynn, and Tony Leiserowitz). Administrative support for this book has been provided by Toni Daniels and Kay Phillips. Special thanks go to Ellen Peters, Robin Gregory, John Payne, and Chris Starmer for their advice on our introductory chapter and to the National Science Foundation, whose Decision Making, Risk, and Management Science Program has provided essential funding for much of the research on preference construction by us and others.[1]

---

[1] Most recently, support for work on this book has come from the National Science Foundation under Grant Nos. 0112158 and 0241313. Any opinions, findings, and conclusions or recommendations expressed in this material are those of the authors and do not necessarily reflect the views of the National Science Foundation.

Finally, we were sustained in the daunting task of acquiring and assembling the 38 chapters of this book by the steady competence and enthusiasm of Leisha Wharfield, ably assisted by Austin Kaiser. We thank them. We also thank Peter Katsirubas of Techbooks for his help and his patience in the final stages of book preparation.

Sarah Lichtenstein
Paul Slovic
Eugene, Oregon
May 2006

1. The Construction of Preference: An Overview

Sarah Lichtenstein and Paul Slovic

This book is a collection of papers and research articles on *preference construction*. The central idea is that in many situations we do not really know what we prefer; we must construct our preferences as the situation arises.

We do, of course, carry a myriad of preferences in our memory. We were born with some of them, such as a fondness for sweets, avoidance of pain, and, perhaps, fear of snakes. Moreover, we spend our lives, particularly in childhood and adolescence, building preferences from our experiences and our wants, needs, and desires. Some of these learned preferences are broad, such as preferring more money to less; others are quite specific, such as liking a particular flavor of ice cream. These well-established preferences are readily available for use.

The need for preference construction arises when our known preferences are insufficient to solve the decision problem that we face. It seems to us that these more difficult situations have one or more of the following three characteristics.[1] First, some of the decision elements may be totally unfamiliar, such as when choosing what to eat from a menu in a foreign language. Second, the choices available to us may present a conflict among our known preferences, so that tradeoffs must be made. For example, suppose you are choosing between two apartments to rent. One has big windows with a great view but a cramped kitchen. The other has no view but a well-arranged, spacious kitchen. You know you prefer good views and large kitchens, but to make this decision you must make a tradeoff between one aspect (view) and the other (kitchens). Often we know our preferences for individual aspects but do not know the tradeoffs between them. Third, we find it difficult to translate our positive and negative feelings into a numerical response, even when our preferences are clear. For example, suppose you find an apartment with a great view and a big kitchen. Now the question is: How much rent are you willing to pay for this apartment? That question may be hard to answer.

Decision researchers rarely study the first problem, unfamiliarity. Indeed, researchers typically take great pains to choose stimuli that are familiar to the study participants. Thus, the emphasis in research on preference construction

---

[1] We thank John Payne for stimulating our thoughts on this.

is on the second problem, tradeoffs, or the third problem, numerical responses, or both. The distinction between these two problems is not always clear. For example, when you find the apartment with the great view and big kitchen, you might reframe the question as: How much more rent are you willing to pay for it than for the apartment with the small kitchen? This involves a tradeoff between money and kitchen space. But the distinction is valuable because one problem focuses on our internal processes in juggling our preferences and the other focuses on the interface between our preferences and our responses.

Decision research would be important but less interesting if we always used the same methods for constructing our preferences. But we do not. This book documents a huge variety of methods, strategies, and ways of thinking or feeling used to construct preferences. Moreover, both the choice of methods and the preferences themselves are determined not only by our knowledge, feelings, and memory but also by many aspects of the decision environment, including how the preference objects are described, how the preference question is posed, and what response is required.

The variability in the ways we construct and reconstruct our preferences yields preferences that are labile, inconsistent, subject to factors we are unaware of, and not always in our own best interests. Indeed, so pervasive is this lability that the very notion of a "true" preference must, in many situations, be rejected.

This book presents much evidence for this view of preference construction. In addition, it addresses a broad range of questions arising from the preference-construction thesis:

- How do we construct preferences? What techniques, mental juggling, or shortcuts do we use?
- What factors, internal and external, influence our preferences? How do these factors affect our choice of construction methods?
- Under what conditions are our construction methods good or bad (i.e., enhancing or detracting from our best interests)?
- How can our construction methods be improved?
- How should the evidence of preference construction be incorporated into theories of decision making?
- What are the personal, ethical, legal, and public-policy implications of the idea that "true" preferences do not exist?

Overview of This Chapter

The organization of this chapter is based on the contents of the other 37 chapters in this book, with a few side excursions. We start with *preference reversals*, that is, the documentation of situations in which, under one circumstance, A is preferred to B, whereas in another, seemingly equivalent, circumstance, B is preferred to A. The preference reversal literature was not the only, nor even the first, precursor to the idea of preference construction, but it strongly influenced our own thinking and generated an enormous literature that is central to preference construction. In addition, it embodies both the difficulties that, as we suggested earlier, are the heart of preference-construction problems. In one circumstance, subjects are presented with a choice between two options, and they must resolve conflicts by making tradeoffs among the aspects in order to choose which option they prefer. In the other circumstance, subjects are presented with just one option (and then, later, the other), and their task is to translate their preference into a numerical response.

The next section of this chapter is a side excursion: the reaction by experimental economists to the findings of preference reversals. Although there is a substantial literature in economics on this topic, we have included only one such paper (Grether & Plott, 1979/Ch. 5) in this book. However, we believe we have a good perspective on the economic literature and so have indulged ourselves by presenting our views in this introductory chapter.

Following that is a brief section, "The Blossoming of Preference Reversals," that is also not paralleled by book chapters. This short section gives a sampling of the variety of stimuli and responses that have been used to show preference reversals. This is just a listing, without theoretical discussion, but its implication should be clear: The situations are so diverse that no single explanation will cover all of them, nor can any one experiment showing the elimination of preference reversals in one situation be taken as refutation of them all.

We then turn to the theories that have been developed to explain preference reversals, both the six theories included in this book (Chs. 6–11) and a few other theories developed around the same time. We end this section with a re-examination of explanations for the original preference reversal finding (i.e., Lichtenstein & Slovic, 1971/Ch. 3).

The next section of this chapter briefly describes the other precursors of the idea of preference construction, including the enormous influence of Herbert Simon (1955, 1956) on the early research on information processing and choice rules, leading to the first (to our knowledge) explicit statement of preference construction by Bettman (1979). Following that is a section describing the five studies (Chs. 12–16) we chose for this book to exemplify the variety of research that has explored aspects of preference construction.

We turn then to theories of preference construction. Five theories are presented here (Chs. 17–21). Because preference construction is now viewed as the core problem in decision making, virtually every current theory of decision making can be considered a theory of preference construction. Additional theories are presented in the next section (Chs. 22–26), which explores the interplay between the use of reason or analysis and the use of affect or emotion in decision making.

The next sections of this chapter and of the book are devoted to three special topics. The first illuminates discrepancies that Gilbert and Wilson (2000/Ch. 30) call miswanting: What we value now may not be reflected in our decisions, and neither our current values nor our decisions may predict what we will value when we later experience the outcomes.

The second topic is a highly applied one: the use of people's reported willingness to pay (e.g., through higher taxes) to measure the economic value to our society of goods or programs that have no markets (e.g., the value of remote wilderness sites). From the perspective of preference construction, these methods, collectively called Contingent Valuation, have deep flaws that are explored here (Chs. 31–33).

The third topic is preference management. Given that our preferences are often labile, how might we manage them for our own good? An additional issue is that other people can influence our preferences by the ways in which the options are presented to us; in many situations this influence is unavoidable. What are the practical and ethical implications of these influences?

THE START OF PREFERENCE REVERSALS

When Paul Slovic, with his new Ph.D., moved from Ann Arbor, Michigan, to Eugene, Oregon, in 1964, he left Ward Edwards' world of decision making, gambles, and Subjectively Expected Utility to enter Oregon Research Institute's (ORI's) milieu, where Paul Hoffman, Lew Goldberg, and Len Rorer were using linear regression techniques to develop quantitative models of cue utilization in judgment (Hoffman, 1960). Combining these influences, Paul started to study how people weighted probabilities and payoffs when evaluating gambles, using the regression techniques pioneered at ORI (and also by Ken Hammond at Colorado; see Hammond, Hursch, & Todd, 1964). To obtain separate utilization weights for probabilities of winning and probabilities of losing, Paul devised the *duplex gamble*, which was depicted by two discs; one showed the probability of winning and the amount to win (otherwise win nothing); the other, the probability of losing and amount to lose (otherwise lose nothing). The gamble was played by spinning the pointers on both discs; the player could win and not lose, lose and not win, win and lose, or neither win nor lose (see Figure 1.1). Across a set of duplex gambles, the experimenter could independently vary the four risk dimensions of the bets: the (stated) amounts to win and lose and the (stated) probabilities of winning and losing. Thus, correlational techniques could be used to analyze the dimension weights underlying people's preferences for playing these gambles.

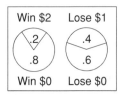

Figure 1.1. Example of a duplex bet.

Sarah Lichtenstein, who joined Paul at ORI in 1966, came from the same background and met the same change in paradigm. Our first major collaboration (Slovic & Lichtenstein, 1968; Ch. 2 is an abridgement) showed the melding of the decision making and judgment approaches: We used duplex bets and linear regression models to examine whether two different response modes, bids (i.e., hypothetical buying and selling prices) and attractiveness ratings, led to systematic changes in the relative importance of the cues (i.e., the four risk dimensions).[2]

We developed a simple two-stage process model: First, decide whether the gamble is attractive or unattractive (the expected values of the gambles ranged from + $3.00 to −$3.00); second, provide a quantitative response (i.e., a rating or a price). For the first stage, we found that the probability of winning received the greatest weight. In this stage, the percentage of variance accounted for by each risk dimension was remarkably similar for rating and for pricing. But there were large response-mode differences in the second stage. For attractive bets, ratings were most influenced by the probability of winning, whereas prices were most influenced by the amount to win. For unattractive bets, no one risk dimension dominated in the rating data, but for prices the amount to lose captured 73% of the total variance accounted for by the linear model. We concluded that the regression weights may reflect beliefs about the relative importance of the risk dimensions and that "change in weights across tasks indicates changing strategies due to subjects' attempts to ease their information-processing problems" (this volume, p. 50).

We then reasoned that, because of the differing information-processing strategies apparently induced by different response modes, we could, with suitably chosen bets, create preference reversals. That is, we could construct pairs of gambles, A and B, such that A would be preferred under one response mode and B under another.

For our first test of this hypothesis, we selected pricing and choice as our two response modes. Prices for attractive bets, we knew, were based on the amount to win. We believed that choices would be based on attractiveness, so that, like the first stage of our 1968 model and like attractiveness ratings, choices would be more influenced by the probability of winning.[3]

Instead of using duplex gambles, which were unfamiliar and thus possibly suspect, we used ordinary two-outcome bets (with the probabilities of winning and losing summing to 1.00). For each pair, one bet, called the $ bet, featured a large amount to win, fostering a large bid, and the other bet, called the P bet, featured a high probability of winning, fostering its choice over the $ bet.

These were the origins of our first preference reversal paper (Lichtenstein & Slovic, 1971/Ch. 3), presenting three experiments. The first and third experiments showed very high rates of the kind of preference reversal we had intended

---

[2] In this 1968 work we *did not* collect any data about the relative importance of gamble attributes in choice. Many subsequent writings (starting with our own, Lichtenstein & Slovic, 1971) are wrong in reporting that we did. We apologize for this error.

[3] Later research has shown that the relationship between choice and rating responses is not this simple. For example, Goldstein and Einhorn (1987) found substantial discrepancies between these two response modes.

to create and very low rates of the opposite, unpredicted reversal (i.e., choosing the $ bet but bidding more for the P bet). For the third experiment, each subject was run individually, the bets were played, and subjects' pay was based on their winnings. At the end of the session, the experimenter interviewed the subjects who had made predicted reversals, trying to get them to change their responses to eliminate the reversals. A previously unpublished excerpt from one such interview is included in this book as an Appendix to Chapter 3.

The second experiment used more, and more varied, pairs of bets to explore the effect of changes in bet attributes on the frequency of preference reversals. We found that the difference between the amounts to lose in the $ bet and the P bet correlated .82 with the number of P-bet choices but was not related to bids (buying prices, in this case), whereas the ratio of the amounts to win in each pair was related ($r = .55$) to bids but not choices. The ranges of probability differences were too small to show any effects.

Our reasoning and results during those early years seemed to us to explain a finding that had puzzled Harold Lindman (1965). His subjects gave bids for a number of gambles and also made paired-comparison choices. He noted a consistent discrepancy between the preference orderings. After discussing these data with us, Lindman (1971) did a more systematic study comparing selling prices and choices and reached much the same conclusions as we had.

Soon after, we were given, through the generosity of Ward Edwards, an exceptional opportunity to replicate our findings in a downtown Las Vegas casino, the Four Queens (Figure 1.2). The experiment was run by John Ponticello, a dealer and pit boss. The subjects were casino patrons risking their own money. In this setting we were able to include bets with negative expected values; we used the mirror images of the positive bets. Thus, for example, the $ bet {2/12 to win 97 chips, 10/12 to lose 11 chips} became {10/12 to win 11 chips, 2/12 to lose 97 chips}. In accord with our 1968 data, we predicted that for bad bets subjects would choose the $ bet (indicating a lesser dislike for it) but offer a larger payment to the dealer to avoid playing the $ bet (indicating a greater dislike for it). Our predictions were strongly confirmed (Lichtenstein & Slovic, 1973/Ch. 4), replicating and extending the earlier findings based on college students.

ECONOMISTS' REACTIONS TO PREFERENCE REVERSALS

The existence of preference reversals presents a formidable challenge to economic theory because a fundamental tenet of economics is that prices and preferences are synonymous. If we prefer A to B, we should be willing to pay more for A. Accordingly, economists David Grether and Charles Plott (1979/Ch. 5) set out not merely to refute our findings, but "to discredit the psychologists' work as applied to economics" (this volume, p. 77). They listed 13 theories or explanations, most of which would, if confirmed, characterize preference

Figure 1.2. The editors in the Four Queens Casino in Las Vegas, Nevada, 1969.

reversals as unimportant artifacts. These included misspecified incentives (no real payoffs) and the fact that the previous researchers were psychologists (who "have the reputation for deceiving subjects," this volume, p. 85). They ran two experiments carefully designed to test all 13 possibilities. Finding a substantial frequency of predicted reversals (e.g., 70% for Experiment I with incentives) and far fewer unpredicted reversals (e.g., 13% in same group), they not only replicated our results but also rejected 12 of their 13 explanations. The data supported only our explanation based on information, processing changes due to changes in response mode.

Grether and Plott (1979/Ch. 5) issued a call-to-arms to economists:

Taken at face value the data are simply inconsistent with preference theory . . . The inconsistency is deeper than the mere lack of transitivity or even stochastic transitivity. It suggests that no optimization principles of any sort lie behind even the simplest of human choices. (this volume, p. 77)

Economists and others responded to this alarm with vigor.[4] One approach was to modify utility theory. Loomes and Sugden (1983) and Fishburn (1985)

---

[4] According to the *Web of Science*, Grether and Plott's article had been cited in about 380 journal articles through February 2005. Our first preference-reversal article (Lichtenstein & Slovic, 1971/Ch. 3) had also been cited about 380 times; one or the other, or both, had been cited in about 600 articles.

explored utility theories without the transitivity assumption, attributing preference reversals to regret. Others focused on the practices, in many experiments,
of having subjects actually play only one gamble, chosen at random, and using
the Becker, DeGroot, and Marschak (1964) method for playing gambles. These
practices can be seen as creating complicated, multistage lotteries. Segal (1988)
suggested giving up the reduction principle (i.e., indifference between a multistage lottery and its single-stage equivalent). Holt (1986) and Karni and Safra
(1987) proposed, instead, to explain preference reversals by retaining the reduction principle but giving up the independence axiom (i.e., only the outcomes
that distinguish two lotteries are relevant to the decision – the axiom that is
belied by the Allais, 1953, paradox). None of these approaches has been successful in explaining preference reversals (see Tversky, Slovic, & Kahneman,
1990/Ch. 8).

Philosophers have scolded economists for their approach to preference
reversals, "whose existence was until quite recently denied by the majority
of economists. Their favorite strategy consisted in trying to explain the phenomenon away as an artifact of the experimental techniques used to observe it"
(Guala, 2000, p. 48). Guala tartly noted that "some of the best experimenters in
economics devoted lots of time and effort to test the functioning of the [Becker–
DeGroot–Marshak] and [Random Lottery Selection] mechanisms – despite the
fact that . . . PR [preference reversals] had been observed *with* and *without* these
elicitation procedures" (p. 50; emphasis in original). In a similar vein, Hausman (1991) titled his essay, "On Dogmatism in Economics: The Case of Preference Reversals." Hausman traced economists' reactions to their reluctance
to abandon a broad and parsimonious theory of rational choice for psychologists' narrower and more complex theories. He concluded that economists'
reactions were hard to defend, creating "unreasonable barriers to theoretical
and empirical progress" (p. 223).

Changing the Task

One way to "explain away" preference reversals that has been used by many
experimenters is to change the task, that is, to give subjects some tasks other
than pricing bets or choosing between them or to change the rules of the game.
We object to this approach because even if preference reversals were eliminated
using the new task or the new rules, that finding would not refute preference
reversals in the original tasks.

Moreover, there is a pattern to the results of these new-task studies: Preference reversals are not eliminated. Instead, predicted reversals decrease and
unpredicted reversals increase. Such a finding is a comfort to economists
because it is the asymmetry between high rates of predicted reversals and low
rates of unpredicted reversals that challenges utility theory; symmetric reversal
rates can be interpreted as utility maximization with error. However, the error
explanation cuts both ways. We propose an alternative hypothesis: Suppose

that, if people never made errors, they would *always* make predicted reversals and *never* make unpredicted reversals. Then, as random errors increase, the rate of predicted reversals will be reduced and the rate of unpredicted reversals will increase. At one extreme is a task with simple, no-loss gambles (e.g., .5 to win $6.50; otherwise nothing) and easy response modes like attractiveness ratings and selling prices (without any selling mechanism specified). For this task, Goldstein and Einhorn (1987) found 93% reversals when the P bet was rated more attractive and only 2% reversals when the $ bet was rated more attractive. At the other extreme, our reversals-with-error hypothesis predicts that complex or confusing tasks will show a more symmetric pattern of reversals, as seen in the following five studies:

Cox and Epstein (1989) converted the pricing task to a kind of choice task. In addition, because of a peculiarity in their pseudo-pricing task, the bets used for pricing were different from the bets used in the plain choice task: For pricing, outcomes were lowered by 1,000 units. Thus, for example, the bet {.50 to win 6,500, .50 to lose 1,000} in choice became {.50 to win 5,500, .50 to lose 2,000}. The authors found equal rates of predicted and unpredicted reversals. In their first experiment, 34% of plain choices were inconsistent with "pricing" choices. Such a high rate of inconsistency between two forms of choice suggests that subjects may have been confused as to whether their pricing responses should reflect their choices (as the game dictated) or should be real prices.

Bostic, Herrnstein, and Luce (1990), with computer presentation and intermixed trials, used three response modes: choice, selling prices, and choice indifference points (i.e., choice between a bet and a sure outcome; the sure outcome is varied between trials until indifference is found). In their second experiment, the narrowing-in on the choice indifference point was well concealed from the subjects (cf. Fischer, Carmon, Ariely, & Zauberman, 1999, who made the narrowing-in obvious, with quite different results). Bostic et al. found the usual preference reversal results for prices versus choices, 81% predicted and 3% unpredicted conditional reversals, but the hidden narrowing-in process apparently increased errors; there were 51% predicted and 22% unpredicted reversals between choices and this kind of certainty equivalence.

Wedell and Bockenholt (1990), using choice and selling price, intermixed trials in which the subject was instructed to imagine that the bet (or the chosen bet) would be played once, 10 times, or 100 times. Again, the results support our reversals-with-error hypothesis; predicted and unpredicted reversal rates were approximately equal.

Cox and Grether (1996) looked at choices, selling prices, second-price sealed bid auctions (for five rounds), and English clock auctions (for five rounds). They found the usual preference reversals for prices and choices (61% predicted, 10% unpredicted) and, for the auctions, decreasing rates of predicted reversals over the five rounds, with increasing (sealed bid) or always high (English clock) rates of unpredicted reversals. The English clock auction was apparently especially difficult for the subjects (the computer lowered the price every 5 seconds): In the first round, two-thirds of all responses were inconsistent with choices; in the fifth round, 45% were. This study is widely cited as showing that market experience reduces preference reversals. We think it shows that these markets induced more errors.[5]

Berg, Dickhaut, and Rietz (2003) used an extremely complex two-stage game and concluded that their data supported the hypothesis that subjects maximized utility with errors. We agree about the errors but believe that the data support our reversals-with-error explanation, not a utility-theory explanation.

We know of only one task that really does eliminate preference reversals. Chu and Chu (1990) required their subjects to engage in arbitrage (the money-pump game). In their second experiment, subjects, run individually, were presented with a single pair of bets; they made a choice and stated a price for each bet. If their responses showed a reversal, they immediately played the money-pump game with the experimenter for one round.[6] They then gave a new choice and new prices to the same bet pair and, if a preference reversal was again shown, they again played the money-pump game for one round. This cycle was continued until the subject did not reverse. The whole process was repeated for two more bet pairs. The subjects learned very quickly, requiring, on average, only 1.8 arbitrage experiences to eliminate their first predicted reversal and only 1.2 arbitrage experiences to eliminate their first unpredicted reversal (if any). Moreover, only 1 of the 40 persons who reversed on the first or second bet pair, and had thus experienced at least one arbitrage, reversed on the third bet pair.

Cherry, Crocker, and Shogren (2003) also found large reductions in rates of reversals (down to about 5%; they did not report predicted and unpredicted reversals separately) using arbitrage once per reversal over 10 pairs of bets. Moreover, they concurrently presented 10 other pairs of bets not subject to arbitrage; with these bets, reversal rates were reduced to about 10%.

These arbitrage results indicate that individuals can learn not to overvalue $ bets if they are repeatedly punished for doing so. Whether these data serve to restore the idea of a "true preference" is open to question. Braga and Starmer

---

[5] The effect of markets on preference reversals may be more complicated than this. Braga and Starmer (2004) compared second-price auctions with second-to-last price auctions. They found that between the first and fifth rounds the second-price auctions greatly reduced predicted reversals and greatly increased unpredicted reversals but the second-to-last priced auctions showed only moderate (e.g., from 82% to 60% in Experiment II) decreases in predicted reversals and no significant increases in unpredicted reversals.

[6] The experimenter (E) owns both bets. E sells the higher-priced bet to the subject (S) for S's stated price. Then E trades bets with S. (This trade is accepted by S because S has indicated a choice-preference for the bet E still owns over the bet S just bought.) Then E buys the lower-priced bet from S for S's stated price. At the end of this sequence, E again owns both bets but S is poorer by the difference between the two prices, having bought the higher-priced bet and sold the lower-priced bet.

(2004) compared this to shocking people every time they bought chocolates. They would stop buying them but they might still like the taste.[7]

Changing the Stimuli

Another method used to "explain away" preference reversals is to use stimuli that are unsuitable for evoking the phenomenon. Schmidt and Hey (2004) used 28 pairs of bets with one (a sure thing), two, or three outcomes. For all pairs, the "safer" bet had a lower variance than the "riskier" bet, but only two of the pairs had the characteristics of P and $ bets (high probability of winning a small amount paired with a low probability of winning a large amount). Nevertheless, they did find some preference reversals, a "considerable fraction" of which they attributed to pricing errors.

Bohm and Lind (1993) used shares in packets of actual Swedish lottery tickets. These stimuli are vastly different from P and $ bets, yet the authors concluded, "Preference reversal was observed, but the frequency was much lower than in earlier experiments" (p. 327).

The stimuli Bohm (1994) used were two used cars, a Volvo, reputed to be dull but reliable (Bohm considered it comparable to a P bet), and an Opel, luxurious but unreliable (for Bohm, comparable to a $ bet). Bohm's 26 subjects made choices and set prices, vying for the cars. He found no preference reversals and concluded, "It is now possible to argue that *preference reversal cannot be seen as a problem for behavior under uncertainty in general as long as preference reversal has not been replicated in non-gambling situations*" (p. 196; emphasis in original). But these automobiles, whatever their reputations, did not have the characteristics that evoke preference reversals (they were actual cars, not attribute descriptions on which the subjects could anchor). And, as we describe later, preference reversals have been found for many nongamble stimuli.

Do Economists Now Accept Preference Reversals?

Behavioral economists such as Richard Thaler, Colin Camerer, George Loewenstein, and Jack Knetsch have long accepted the reality of preference reversals (see, e.g., Tversky & Thaler, 1990). And as behavioral economics has grown, more and more economists agree. Seidl (2002), for example, ended his review of the preference-reversal literature by noting the emergence of the idea of preference construction, adding, "This means that economics is at the verge of a revolution which replaces neoclassical armchair economics with behavioural economics" (p. 646). But not all economists are convinced. For example, Plott (1996) insisted that "the classical preference reversal can be seen as a product of inexperience and lack of motivation, and it goes away with experience in a

---

[7] Note, for example, the interview in the Appendix to Chapter 3. This subject clearly indicated ("it's not worth [it]...I wouldn't be happier," this volume, p. 68) that any change in his responses needed to avoid arbitrage ("Just to make myself look rational," this volume, p. 68) would go against what he felt to be his true preferences.

market setting" (p. 231). In defense of this position he cited only the experiment by Cox and Grether (1996) discussed earlier.

For all the discussion among economists of the power of markets to enforce consistency, they have rarely looked to the literature in marketing or behavioral finance for confirmation of this belief. Were they to do so, they would find considerable evidence of preference lability, including, for example, context effects on in-store purchases that are quite similar to preference reversals (Doyle, O'Connor, Reynolds, & Bottomley, 1999). They would also find important demonstrations of disconnects between fundamental values of commodities and their market prices (e.g., Shiller, 2000).

We do not expect defenses of standard economic theory to cease. Studies purporting to show that the preference-reversal phenomenon is a chimera may well be under way as we write this. We urge the "defenders of the faith" to look at the bigger picture. More than 20 years ago, we (Slovic & Lichtenstein, 1983) made such a plea, but today the big picture is much bigger. It's not just preference reversals between P and $ bets, and it's not just the many other kinds of preference reversals that have been found. The big picture, as documented in this book, is the overwhelming evidence that people often do not have preexisting preferences but must construct them to fit the situation.

THE BLOSSOMING OF PREFERENCE REVERSALS

The original finding of preference reversals has been repeatedly replicated. Moreover, preference reversals have been found with stimuli other than bets and responses other than prices and choices. We will not try to review all this literature; the reader will find many examples in this book. Instead, a brief sampling of the enormous range of these newer findings follows.

Response Mode. Choice is a popular response mode; indeed, some economists treat it like the gold standard (e.g., Cox & Grether, 1996, compared choice with three other modes but did not report comparisons within the others). Shafir (1993) reported several situations for which the option *chosen* by a majority of subjects is the same as the option *rejected* by a majority of other subjects.

Both selling prices (with or without the Becker–DeGroot–Marschak procedure) and buying prices have been shown to produce preference reversals when compared with choice (e.g., Lichtenstein & Slovic, 1971/Ch. 3). Moreover, Birnbaum and Sutton (1992) reported preference reversals between buying and selling prices. Tversky et al. (1990/Ch. 8) obtained reversals with ordinal pricing.

When no details of the pricing procedure are given to subjects, it can be viewed as a kind of certainty matching (p to win $X vs. receive $____ for sure; fill in an amount of money), which has been compared with probability matching (____ to win $X vs. receive $Y for sure; fill in a probability) by

Hershey and Schoemaker (1985) and with a different form of probability matching (_____ to win $X vs. p to win $Y; fill in a probability) by Cubitt, Munro, and Starmer (2004). With double matching, the subject's first match is fed back for a new match on a different attribute (Hershey & Schoemaker, 1985). Fischer et al. (1999) employed six different kinds of matching. All these forms of matching give rise to reversals when compared with choice or with each other.

Ratings of attractiveness are often used to show reversals (e.g., Goldstein & Einhorn, 1987) but are not of interest to economists because they don't usually imply any action. However, ratings of purchase likelihood (also used to show reversals; e.g., Nowlis & Simonson, 1997/Ch. 10) are accepted by consumer researchers as valid predictors of future purchases.

Most preference-reversal studies have compared one kind of response (e.g., pricing) made to stimuli presented one at a time with a different kind of response (e.g., choice) made to pairs of stimuli. But, as Hsee, Loewenstein, Blount, & Bazerman (1999/Ch. 9) have pointed out, the number of stimuli presented at one time need not be confounded with the response mode. Reversals have been found when the number of stimuli was held constant while the response mode was varied (e.g., Goldstein & Einhorn, 1987; Shafir, 1993) and when the response mode was held constant while the number of stimuli was varied (e.g., Hsee, 1996a).

Preference Stimuli. Gambles have never gone out of style; if we had known how many times the six pairs of gambles we used in our original study (Experiment III; see Ch. 3) would appear in print, we might have chosen them with more care. Two-outcome and one-outcome (i.e., no losses) bets are common; multi-outcome bets are rare, but Casey's (1991) first experiment showed reversals using bets with 4 to 20 outcomes.

Mowen and Gentry (1980) translated our six bet pairs into risky new products characterized only by probability of success, profits for successes ($200,000 to $1.6 million), and losses for failures. They found more preference reversals in small groups than with individuals.

Consumer products, from ice cream (Hsee, 1998) to TVs (e.g., Nowlis & Simonson, 1997/Ch. 10), candidates for jobs (e.g., Tversky, Sattath, & Slovic, 1988/Ch. 6; Hsee, 1996a), and job offers (Hsee, Abelson, & Salovey, 1991) are among the many stimuli used to show preference reversals. Cross-category stimuli are pairs made up of two different kinds of stimuli; for example, Irwin, Slovic, Lichtenstein, and McClelland (1993) paired adding a VCR to your TV with improving Denver air quality and found reversals. Time has been used as one stimulus attribute. Tversky et al. (1990/Ch. 8) showed reversals when {receive $X, m years from now} was paired with {receive $Y, n years from now}.

Reversals using stimuli involving dominance have been shown by Goldstein and Einhorn (1987), Hsee et al. (1999/Ch. 9), Birnbaum and Sutton (1992), and Bateman, Dent, Peters, Starmer, and Slovic (2006), who explored in depth the reversals arising from adding a 5-cent loss to a gamble with a chance of winning $9.00.

Judgment Stimuli. Single-stimulus versus paired-stimulus reversals have been shown in judgments of student grade point averages (Slovic & MacPhillamy, 1974), academic performance (Slovic, Griffin, & Tversky, 1990), setting salaries for job candidates (Hsee, 1996a), and generosity (Hsee et al., 1999/Ch. 9). The literature on fairness and the ultimatum game includes reversals (Bazerman, White, & Loewenstein, 1995). Birnbaum (1982) found reversals with judgments of a rape victim's responsibility for the rape, and Kahneman, Ritov, and Schkade (1999/Ch. 31) reported reversals with jury awards of punitive damages. Amiel, Cowell, Davidovitz, and Plovin (2003), comparing choices with matching responses, found reversals for judgments about hypothetical countries differing in income distributions.

Other Violations. All types of preference reversals listed earlier are examples of the violation of *procedure invariance* (Tversky & Kahneman, 1986): When the procedure for eliciting a preference changes, the preference changes. A different kind of procedural change is to limit the time allowed for a decision; Svenson and Edland (1987) found preference reversals with this change. Preference reversals can also arise from violations of other normative principles. May (1954) and Tversky (1969) showed intransitivity, a form of preference reversal. Kahneman and Tversky's (1984) demonstration that preferences can be reversed by changing the wording concerning the fate of 600 people from "400 people will die" to "200 people will be saved" is a famous violation of *description invariance*. This kind of reversal is called a *framing effect* (Tversky & Kahneman, 1981; Kahneman & Tversky, 1984).

Holding both description and procedure (choice) constant but adding a third option to a pair of options can also lead to reversals. Busemeyer, Johnson, and Jessup (this volume, Ch. 11) describe three types of reversals between binary and triadic choices, based on the similarity effect (Tversky, 1972), the attraction effect (also called asymmetric dominance; Huber, Payne, & Puto, 1982), and the compromise effect (Simonson, 1989).

PSYCHOLOGICAL THEORIES OF PREFERENCE REVERSALS

In our first experiments (Lichtenstein & Slovic, 1971/Ch. 3, 1973/Ch. 4), we provided very little theory to explain preference reversals. We said they were due to changes in decision processes or evaluation techniques. We identified the process used in pricing – anchoring and adjustment[8] – but we were vague about choice processes, noting that there may be several different strategies.

Goldstein and Einhorn (1987) presented the first (to our knowledge) psychological theory of preference reversals, called Expression Theory. They assumed that responses to gambles proceeded in three successive stages: (1) an encoding stage, in which the attributes of a gamble are transformed into psychological

---

[8] For an attractive bet, the respondent starts with the amount to win, the anchor, and adjusts downward to take into account the other bet attributes.

attributes such as the utility of the amount to win; (2) an evaluation stage, in which the encoded elements are combined to produce an overall evaluation for each gamble; and (3) an expression stage, in which the overall evaluation is mapped onto the response scale.

Expression Theory, as per its name, attributes preference reversals to the third stage. For choice, Goldstein and Einhorn (1987) assumed that the gamble with the higher evaluation is chosen. For rating and pricing, they proposed that the response is derived from a proportional matching strategy, to wit, finding a response that divides the response scale into two parts, the proportions of which match the proportions in the evaluation scale (i.e., the position of the evaluation relative to the utilities of the worst and best outcomes). Prediction of preference reversals were generated from the fact that the response scale for pricing is larger for $ bets than for P bets (because the amount to win is larger and the scale range is from 0 to amount to win) and from the curvilinearity of utility functions (concave for wins, convex for losses).

Goldstein and Einhorn (1987) tested their theory using four response types, two for single-stimulus presentations, pricing and rating ("How much would you like to play this gamble?"), and two for pairs of bets, choice and price comparisons ("For which . . . would you hold out for the higher price?"). All subjects used all four response types in one experiment using bets with no losses and in a second experiment using bets with both wins and losses. The four response types generated data to observe six kinds of preference reversals; Expression Theory was used to make specific predictions for each type. The data strongly supported their theory for all six kinds of reversals and for bets with and without losses. The most frequent reversals were found between single-stimulus pricing and rating.

Tversky et al. (1988/Ch. 6) found preference reversals between choice and matching for pairs of two-attribute stimuli, such as job candidates with scores on technical knowledge and human relations skills. They attributed the reversals to the prominence effect: The more prominent (or important) attribute will be weighed more heavily in choice than in matching. They then suggested that the prominence effect is an example of the compatibility principle: "The weight of any input component is enhanced by its compatibility with the output" (this volume, p. 105). They developed a class of formal models that express the changes in indifference curves induced by compatibility, the simplest of which is called the contingent weighting model. They used this model to explain not only their choice-matching reversals but also choice-pricing reversals, relying heavily on the data for gambles with wins but no losses reported by Tversky et al. (1990/Ch. 8) and Slovic et al. (1990).

Slovic et al. (1990) presented five experiments illustrating and support-ing the effect of compatibility on several types of preference reversals. They also clarified the relationship between compatibility and prominence. They distinguished two kinds of compatibility: *strategy* compatibility (Fischer & Hawkins, 1993) and *scale* compatibility. Decision strategies and decision tasks may be characterized as qualitative (e.g., dominance or prominence strategies, choice tasks) or quantitative (e.g., contingent weighting strategy, pricing or matching tasks). Strategy compatibility means using a qualitative strategy for qualitative tasks and switching to a quantitative strategy for quantitative tasks. Thus, prominence has its largest effect on choice, whereas scale compatibility, via contingent weighting, shows its effect on pricing and matching.

Schkade and Johnson (1989/Ch. 7) studied the processes that produce preference reversals by using a computer to present the bets. The aspects of the bets were hidden behind labeled boxes and could be viewed only by moving the mouse-driven cursor to the box. When the cursor left a box, that aspect was again hidden. The computer kept track of all cursor movements, including movements near or on the response scale at the bottom of the screen. Their results strongly supported the use of anchoring and adjustment in pricing responses and were consistent with compatibility (Tversky et al., 1988/Ch. 6) but were not consistent, in all respects, with Expression Theory (Goldstein & Einhorn, 1987).

Tversky et al. (1990/Ch. 8) distinguished among three classes of explanations for preference reversals: failure of transitivity (e.g., Loomes & Sugden, 1983), violation of independence or of the reduction axiom (Holt, 1986; Karni & Safra, 1987; Segal, 1988), or failure of procedure invariance, that is, elicitation effects. In their first experiment, subjects priced $ and P bets that had no losses and made three choices for each bet set: between the $ and P bets, between the $ bet and a sure amount, and between the P bet and the same sure amount. In the second experiment the same procedure was followed but the stimuli were: receiving money (e.g., $1,250) immediately, receiving a larger amount (e.g., $1,600) later (e.g., in $1^1/_2$ years), and receiving a much larger amount (e.g., $2,500) much later (e.g., in 5 years). In both experiments they found substantial preference reversals and firmly rejected explanations based on intransitivity and on violations of independence or the reduction axiom. They attributed preference reversals to procedure invariance, more particularly, to compatibility, and most particularly, to the overpricing of $ bets.

A word of caution is in order for the three papers by Tversky, Slovic, and colleagues discussed earlier. These papers reported on a large variety of stimuli and tasks. But when the authors explored P bets and $ bets, they always used bets with no losses (e.g., .50 to win $6.50, otherwise nothing). This design enabled the authors to analyze their data with simple and powerful tests, but it should be used also to moderate or qualify some of their conclusions. For example, "The more important dimension (i.e., probability) is expected to loom larger in choice than in . . . matching" (Slovic et al., 1990, p. 22), but if large losses are included, probability may not be the most important dimension.

Fischer et al. (1999) revisited the prominence effect. The key concept in their theory is what they called the task goal. A task goal is not a fundamental goal, like achieving happiness or money. A task goal is a characteristic of the response generation process: some tasks, such as choice, require the respondent to *differentiate* among the stimuli; other tasks, such as matching, require the respondent to *equate* the stimuli. The authors hypothesized that prominence will have an effect on tasks with differentiation as the task goal but not on tasks requiring equating. In three studies using choice, difference comparisons, and six kinds of matching, they found support for their theory and evidence against competing theories based on compatibility.

Mellers, Ordóñez, and Birnbaum (1992) proposed Change-of-Process Theory to explain preference reversals. They began by assuming the same three stages of response generation as did Goldstein and Einhorn (1987), transforming the bet elements into subjective counterparts, then combining these transformed elements into a single evaluation, and finally, mapping the evaluation on to the response scale. However, in contrast to Goldstein and Einhorn's focus on the third stage, their theory located the source of preference reversals in the second stage, that of combining. Change-of-Process Theory concerns only pricing and rating; it posits that the evaluation is produced by *adding* the subjective elements when rating but by *multiplying* the subjective elements when pricing (like computing expected utility).

Mellers, Ordóñez, and Birnbaum (1992) tested their theory against Expression Theory and Contingent Weighting using one-outcome and two-outcome bets in a between-subjects design. In the first experiment, after 30 practice trials, the subjects either rated or gave buying prices (hypothetical; no bets were played) to 231 win-only bets, a task accomplished in about 1 hour. The second experiment presented 181 bets (after 15 warm-ups) with wins and losses.

Sophisticated analyses of the data from 36 of the Experiment 1 bets and 60 of the Experiment 2 bets indicated support for the Change-of-Process Theory and rejection of Expression Theory and Contingent Weighting.[9] Mellers, Ordóñez, and Birnbaum (1992) apparently did not consider the possibility, which we find compelling, that their results were driven by the huge numbers of stimuli, which might have induced bored subjects to find simplifying strategies that they would not use in the usual experimental settings (Slovic, Lichtenstein, & Edwards, 1965).

Hsee et al. (1999/Ch. 9) emphasized the distinction between evaluation *mode*, either single-stimulus presentation, which they called separate evaluation (SE), or multiple-stimulus presentation, which they called joint evaluation (JE), and evaluation *scale*. They noted that these two task characteristics are frequently confounded in preference-reversal experiments; for example, JE choice is compared with SE pricing. Their work focused on evaluation mode, holding evaluation scale constant. The theory they presented for preference reversals was based on the ease with which attributes can be evaluated. In SE, some attributes are not evaluable and thus have little impact on the response. JE makes these attributes more evaluable, leading to reversals.

---

[9] The unanalyzed bets were included in the design to test the effects of context on the analyzed bets; the effects were minor.

Low evaluability may be due to a subject's lack of familiarity with an attribute (such as a score on a test one does not know much about) but may be found even with such familiar attributes as money or ice cream. Hsee (1998) showed JE /SE reversals for willingness to pay for ice cream sold by two beach vendors, one offering a 10-oz. cup with 8 oz. of ice cream, the other offering a 5-oz. cup with 7 oz. of ice cream. Here, the amount of ice cream is important for pricing but is difficult to evaluate in SE, easy in JE. The less important but highly evaluable attribute that apparently drove SE prices is underfilling/overfilling of the cups.

Hsee et al. (1999/Ch. 9) were careful to note that their theory is not in conflict with other preference reversal theories, which seek to explain a different phenomenon: how responses change when evaluation scales change.

Nowlis and Simonson (1997/Ch. 10) explored preference reversals in numerous studies of consumer preferences for household products (batteries, sunscreen lotions, TVs, and many others). Each option was described by two attributes. One attribute was *comparable*, that is, easy to compare in choice. The other attribute was *enriched*, that is, hard to compare but, in their terms, more informative and meaningful (specifically, the enriched attributes were brand name and country of origin). Their experiments tested 15 hypotheses, in most cases comparing choice with ratings of purchase likelihood, finding repeatedly that products that are superior on the comparable attribute are favored in choice whereas products that are superior on the enriched attribute are favored in ratings.

They based their theory on what they called attribute-task compatibility.[10] Comparable attributes are weighted more in choice for much the same reasons Hsee et al. (1999/Ch. 9) gave for evaluable attributes. Enriched attributes are weighted more in ratings because they are not only "imprecise, ambiguous, and non-quantifiable" (this volume, p. 197), thus impeding their use in choice, but also evoke a "variety of associations, beliefs, and experiences" (this volume, p. 197) that allow a meaningful rating evaluation without the need for cross-product comparisons. We suggest that this theory is incomplete without, and would be clearer with, a more explicit reference to affect (Slovic, Finucane, Peters, & MacGregor, 2002/Ch. 23). To us, the enriched attribute is more laden with affect, thus more readily coded as attractive or unattractive, and thus more easily mapped onto a rating scale than is the comparable attribute.

Busemeyer et al. (this volume, Ch. 11) use Decision Field Theory (DFT) to explain preference reversals. DFT is a theory quite unlike all the others we have discussed. It is a computational model (specifically, an artificial neural network or connectionist model), a microanalysis of the sequence of cognitions leading to a response. For choice, they posit that the responder evaluates, at any one moment in time, only one aspect of the stimuli. Over time, attention shifts stochastically to other aspects, the evaluations of which are integrated with the previous evaluations. Mechanisms of positive self-feedback and lateral

[10] Not to be confused with scale compatibility or strategy compatibility (Fischer & Hawkins, 1993).

inhibition are also assumed, so that gradually, the evaluation of one stimulus increases until it reaches a threshold, at which time a decision is announced.

For single-stimulus responses such as prices, DFT assumes that the responder selects a starting point, a candidate price, and compares that with the stimulus, using the same choice process. If the two evaluations are notably different, so that a threshold is quickly reached, the starting point is adjusted upward or downward as appropriate and the evaluations are repeated. If the evaluations are close, so that neither reaches a threshold, the theory posits a probability that the sequence will end and the currently considered price is given as a response.

The use of DFT to predict the usual kinds of preference reversals has been reported elsewhere (Johnson & Busemeyer, 2005). The chapter in this book (Busemeyer et al., this volume, Ch. 11) reports results for two more unusual situations. The first involves the effects of adding to a pair of options a third, deferred option (i.e., you don't have to choose now; you can keep looking for other options and decide later); the second involves reversals for a bet pair in which the range of options is equated: {.001 to win $16, .9712 to win $4, otherwise zero} versus {.2212 to win $16, .001 to win $4, otherwise zero}.

The power of DFT resides in the fact that the predictions of changes in response are made even though the model parameters and evaluative weights and values are held constant, in contrast to theories that assume changes in weight (e.g., the contingent weighting model, Tversky et al., 1988/ Ch. 6) or evaluation strategies (e.g., differentiating vs. equating, Fischer et al., 1999).

Finally, Busemeyer et al. (this volume, Ch. 11) discuss the neurological evidence relating to one of the central mechanisms of DFT, lateral inhibition. We applaud such efforts to relate the psychology of decision making to the recently emerging focus on decision making in neuroscience.

The profusion of theories to explain preference reversals presents a natural question: Which theory is right? It is nice when one theory is related to another. For example, Tversky et al. (1988/Ch. 6) saw Expression Theory as a "special case of the [most general] contingent model" (this volume, p. 118), and Hsee et al. (1999/Ch. 9) characterized Nowlis and Simonson's (1997/Ch. 10) approach as "an extension of the compatibility principle" (this volume, p. 186). But often these theories address different situations. For example, suppose you were designing a preference-reversal experiment using pairs of job candidates described by two attributes. If you were interested in the prominence effect, you would make the job be technical and the attributes be one that expresses technical skill, the other a less-related skill.[11] If you were interested in scale compatibility, you would make sure that one of the attributes was compatible with one of your response modes and the other was not.[12] For evaluability, the job would be computer analyst and one attribute would be GPA; the

[11] These stimuli were used by Tversky et al. (1988/Ch. 6).
[12] We're not sure whether this has been done with job candidates.

other, the number of programs in an unfamiliar language the candidate has written – and you would use only one response scale.[13] For Nowlis and Simonson's theory (1997/Ch. 10), one candidate would be a Harvard graduate with 2 years of relevant job experience, the other from Podunk University with 10 years of relevant job experience.[14] Each of these experiments will produce preference reversals, but for different reasons. It's possible that all these theories are right in their particular situations.

Indeed, the idea of preference construction implies the *necessity* of multiple theories. In our lives – and in the experimental labs – we face a huge assortment of situations for which a preference must be constructed on the spot. We develop, over time, a variety of different methods or strategies to build our preferences. Different tools in our toolbox will require different explanatory theories. If the situation is novel, we will seize upon whatever hints are available in the stimuli and the response scales. Different hints will also lead to different theories.

One exception to this need for multiple theories is DFT (Busemeyer et al., this volume, Ch. 11). Because it is a theory at a different level of analysis, that is, at the level of microprocesses, it has the potential (not yet realized; perhaps never to be completely realized) to incorporate all the other theories into a unified whole.

What Causes Preference Reversals Between P Bets and $ Bets?

We now turn to a reconsideration of the preference reversals that started this flurry of theorizing: P bets versus $ bets. What causes these reversals? All the theories and all the evidence agree that they are caused by different information-processing strategies.

The theories reviewed here are surprisingly weak about the strategies of choice. Change-of-Process Theory does not apply to choice. Hsee et al. (1999/Ch. 9) proposed that attributes that are difficult to evaluate in SE become more evaluable in choice; Nowlis and Simonson (1997/Ch. 10) similarly assumed that attributes that are easier to compare receive greater weight in choice. Neither theory speaks to how the choice is made, except for the implicit assumption that choice involves between-stimuli comparisons. In contrast, Expression Theory (Goldstein & Einhorn, 1987) assumed that, in choice, each gamble is evaluated separately but they, too, did not elucidate how these evaluations are formed.

The only preference reversal theories that speak directly to information-processing strategies in choice (except for the microprocesses assumed by DFT; Busemeyer et al., this volume, Ch. 11) are the theories that involve the prominence effect. The reasoning by Slovic et al. (1990) is: Qualitative tasks such as choice lead to the use of qualitative strategies such as a lexicographic rule. Prominence is a lexicographic strategy; it will be used in choice when one attribute is more important than the other. Probabilities are more

---

[13] These stimuli were used by Hsee et al. (1999/Ch. 9).
[14] We made up this example.

important than payoffs (when the bets have no losses). Therefore, the probability attribute will dominate choice. The reasoning for Fischer et al. (1999) is similar: Choice requires differentiating. One way to differentiate is on the basis of prominence.

There has been much theorizing about choice outside the preference-reversal literature. Bettman, Luce, and Payne (1998/Ch. 17) have provided a nice summary of the many strategies that have been offered for making choices. Some of these are more relevant for choosing one from many than choosing one from two (e.g., satisficing: pick the first satisfactory option you come across; Simon, 1955). Others are more appropriate to $-bet versus P-bet choice, such as weighted adding (which is tantamount to expected utility), equal weights (Thorngate, 1980), and lexicographic (pick the one that is best on the most important attribute; see Tversky, 1969).

One notable omission from the summary by Bettman et al. (1998/Ch. 17) is the search-for-dominance strategy (Montgomery, 1983): The chooser actively reframes or recodes the bets to achieve dominance. This is a likely strategy for choosing the P bet, which can be reframed as a "sure win."

Affect is another candidate to explain the greater preference for P bets over $ bets in choice than in pricing. Note the discussion of proportion dominance by Slovic et al. (2002/Ch. 23), which called attention to the high degree of affective evaluability associated with certain probabilities. Probabilities have a natural midpoint, .5, below which a probability is "poor" or "bad," and above which it is "good." Payoffs tend to be less clearly associated with affect, leading them to be given less weight in ratings and choices.

Goal-based strategies are also possible. For example, one goal might be to minimize losses. A rule to do this is: If one loss is much bigger than the other, pick the bet with the smaller loss; if not, pick the bet with the higher probability of winning (this is a lexicographic semi-order strategy; Tversky, 1969). Another goal might be reasons: Pick the bet for which you can give the best justification (Shafir, Simonson, & Tversky, 1993/Ch. 22). A third goal might be regret: Pick the bet that will minimize how bad you will feel if you don't win.

In sum, we still do not have a clear understanding about how the choice is made between P bets and $ bets. The fact that, in many studies, P-bet choices hover around 50% suggests that more than one strategy may be involved.

Preference-reversal theories have been much more explicit about single-stimulus responses, including pricing. People price the $ bet higher than the P bet because:

- even if its evaluation is lower than the P-bet evaluation, it receives a higher price in the proportionality judgment because of the larger upper bound of its amount to win (Goldstein & Einhorn, 1987), or
- compatibility with the response scale leads to greater weight placed on the amount to win (Slovic et al., 1990), or
- the combination rule for pricing is multiplicative (Mellers, Ordóñez, and Brinbaum, 1992).

These may be just fancy ways of saying what we know in our hearts is going on: For attractive bets, people start with the amount to win and adjust it downward to take into account the other attributes of the bets. For P bets, they can't go far wrong: The starting point is near the expected value of the bet. But their downward adjustments for the $ bets are inadequate. Call it proportional matching, call it contingent weighting, call it "a natural mechanism for generating compatibility effects" (Slovic et al., 1990, p. 13), we still believe in anchoring and adjustment.

ANTECEDENTS OF PREFERENCE CONSTRUCTION

The research on preference reversals was just one of many lines of research that led to the concept of preference construction. Although the idea of preference construction in decision making evolved quite apart from mainstream psychology, it needn't have done so and was undoubtedly hindered by this isolated development. Construction has played an important role in psychological theorizing at least since Bartlett (1932) highlighted its essential role in memory. For centuries prior to Bartlett, philosophers such as Hobbes, Locke, Hume, and Mill opined that the mind retains faded copies of sensory experiences, linked by associations. The (misguided) notion that stored information consists of ideas suspended in a quiescent state from which they are occasionally aroused was named the "Reappearance Hypothesis" by Neisser (1967). Bartlett demonstrated that organization and change are the rule rather than the exception in memory. In other words, "memory is itself constructive" (p. 311). Building on emerging knowledge in cognitive psychology during the middle of the 20th century, Neisser argued that not only memory but perception and attention as well are "acts of *construction*, which may make more or less use of stimulus information depending on circumstances" (p. 10; emphasis in original). Anticipating what later came to be known as *dual-process theories*, Neisser asserted that "the constructive processes are assumed to have two stages, of which the first is fast, crude, holistic, and parallel while the second is deliberate, attentive, detailed, and sequential" (p. 10).

The early research on judgment (a separate field of psychology before it merged with decision making) was also constructionist, at least implicitly, in that much attention was given to inferences about how people combine information – Using few cues or many? Adding or multiplying? – to arrive at numerical judgments (for a review of this early literature, see Slovic & Lichtenstein, 1971).

More recently, social psychologists have also incorporated construction into their theories (see, e.g., Martin & Tesser, 1992). Wilson and Hodges (1992) referred to the historical view of attitudes as evaluations that are stable over time as "the file drawer analogy" and argued instead, following Tesser (1978), that an attitude at any particular point in time is the result of a constructive process, not merely the reporting of the contents of a mental file. As a result, many attitudes are often unstable and depend on context.

Within the field of decision making, much of the early work (see Edwards, 1954c, 1961) was strongly influenced by traditional utility theory and its variants (e.g., subjectively expected utility theory; Savage, 1954), in which each option is assumed to have an overall utility or subjective value; the decision maker need only select the option that maximizes that person's satisfaction. Thus, much of the early research on probability preferences (Edwards, 1953, 1954a, 1954b), variance preferences (Coombs & Pruitt, 1960), and Bayes' Theorem (Phillips & Edwards, 1966) was not conducive to the development of the idea of preference construction.

An important exception to this trend was the work of Simon (1955), who introduced the idea of *bounded rationality*, centered around the view that decision makers have information-processing capabilities that are subject to limitations of working memory, attention, and computational skill. As a result of these limitations, he insisted, decisions are shaped by the interaction between the properties of the human information-processing system and the properties of task environments (Simon, 1956).

Simon's insights led to a stream of research that is one of the precursors of preference construction: information-processing studies, which used think-aloud techniques, eye-fixations (e.g., Russo & Leclerc, 1994), and other methods (e.g., computer cursor movements; Schkade & Johnson, 1989/Ch. 7) to track the acquisition of information and make inferences about how people arrive, over time, at a decision. This work has been summarized by Svenson (1979, 1996/ Ch. 19). A repeated finding of this research is that people do not search for or use information in ways that are consistent with utility maximization.

A second precursor to preference construction is the literature on choice rules. Starting with Simon's (1955) satisficing rule, Tversky's (1969) lexicographic semi-order, and Tversky's (1972) elimination-by-aspects rule, this literature has elucidated the many ways by which people make choices and studied the effects of stimulus complexity and time pressure on rule use (e.g., Payne, Bettman, & Johnson, 1988). The only reason that we characterize this research as a *precursor* of preference construction, rather than simply *evidence* of preference construction, is that the authors did not, in the early years, use the explicit term, preference construction.

A third precursor to preference construction is the work of Tversky and Kahneman. Their Prospect Theory (Kahneman & Tversky, 1979) can be viewed as belonging in the utility maximization tradition (although with profound changes), but they included in the theory the idea of *editing*, whereby the decision maker sometimes alters an option before evaluating it, so that the mental representations of the options, not the objective states of the world, are the objects of choice. As Kahneman (2003a) has since noted, "This was a large step toward the development of a concept of framing" (p. 727). Framing (Kahneman & Tversky, 1984; Tversky & Kahneman, 1981), that is, the idea that formally inconsequential changes in how options are presented have huge effects on judgments and decisions, is a core element of preference construction.

Perhaps the first explicit discussion of construction in decision making was by Bettman (1979),[15] who proposed that choice heuristics may exist only as fragments or elements including beliefs, evaluations, or combination rules, "which are put together constructively at the time of...making a decision or choice.... The process is reconstructed each time needed, using the elements in memory. Thus rules may differ from one situation to the next, depending on how the fragments or elements are combined" (p. 33). To our knowledge, the notion of construction did not appear again in the decision-making literature until Tversky et al. (1988/Ch. 6) invoked it in response to the body of evidence documenting violations of procedure invariance and demonstrating that people's values and beliefs are often not well defined. In such situations, they remarked, "observed preferences are not simply read off from some master list; they are actually constructed in the elicitation process" (this volume, p. 96).

After that, preference construction rapidly took on an increasingly influential role. By 1992, Payne, Bettman, and Johnson organized their entire review of 9 years of research in behavioral decision making around the concept.

EVIDENCE OF PREFERENCE CONSTRUCTION

There are probably hundreds of articles that could be cited as illuminating the nature of preference construction. We include in this book only a few, because they are recent, they show a variety of effects, and we liked them a lot.

Simon, Krawczyk, and Holyoak (2004/Ch. 12) presented students with two job offers described by four or five attributes and asked the students to rate the importance of each attribute and the desirability of the attribute levels two or three times in the course of making a choice between the job offers. They found that the weights and values changed systematically during the process of decision making, showing increased support for the favored alternative and less support for the other alternative. These shifts are predicted by constraint-satisfaction models of decision making (Simon & Holyoak, 2002), in which decision processes are seen as an effort to achieve cognitive consistency and coherence. The results also lend support to other process theories, especially Montgomery's (1998/Ch. 18) theory based on a search for dominance.

Studies of preference reversals have challenged economic theories of valuation by demonstrating that prices do not necessarily reflect the values revealed by choice or other expressions of preference. Despite this evidence, the equation of price with value is still fundamental to economic analysis. In situations where value is difficult to measure directly, economists have taken comfort in the fact that responses to *changes* in the amount or cost of a commodity are orderly

[15] March (1978) may have a prior claim, but he discussed preference construction only in the context of the ongoing interaction between preferences and actions: "We choose preferences and actions jointly, in part, to discover – or construct – new preferences that are currently unknown" (p. 596); "We find meaning and merit in our actions after they are taken" (p. 601).

and coherent. Ariely, Loewenstein, and Prelec (2003/Ch. 13, 2006/Ch. 14) have mounted a frontal attack on what they termed "the myth of fundamental value." They conducted a series of experiments demonstrating that evaluations of familiar goods and experiences can have a large arbitrary component, yet once a response is given, other responses follow in a consistent and rational manner.

For example, prices assigned to common consumer goods, such as a bottle of wine or a box of chocolates, were strongly conditioned by an arbitrary anchor (the last three digits of the individual's social security number), yet there was order in these arbitrary prices. A wine described as "rare" was consistently priced higher than one described as "average." Their findings led Ariely et al. (2003/Ch. 13) to ask: "How . . . can a pricing decision that is strongly correlated with an individual's social security number reveal a true preference in any meaningful sense of the term?" (this volume, p. 270). Having exposed such *coherent arbitrariness*, they discussed its implications for financial and labor markets. Contingent valuation is another case in point. For example, Gregory, Lichtenstein, Brown, Peterson, and Slovic (1995) found that people generally agreed on the relative value of 12 proposed environmental improvements but the amount they were willing to pay was strongly influenced by differences in the arbitrary "budget units" they were asked to use to express their responses.

Taking these findings as a starting point, Ariely et al. (2006/Ch. 14) posed a more basic question: Do people even have a preexisting sense of whether an experience is good or bad? They showed that individuals will characterize some experiences as either positive or negative, depending on whether they are asked how much they would pay for the experience or how much they would require to be paid. After one such arbitrary response is given, other responses follow in a coherent fashion. Ariely et al. concluded that, rather than indicating the existence of fundamental valuation, correct directional responses to orderly changes in stimuli simply show that people try to behave in a sensible manner when it is obvious how to do so and that coherence of responses serves to disguise just how arbitrary some economic decisions can be.

The work by Ariely et al. (2003/Ch. 13, 2006/Ch. 14) can be seen as illustrating how preferences can be primed by an anchor or by the form of the question asked (willingness to pay vs. willingness to accept). A striking example of priming was provided by Mandel and Johnson (2002/Ch. 15). They created an experimental (hypothetical) Web site for purchasing sofas and cars. The prime was the background, the "wallpaper," of the introductory screen (in the second experiment, the prime also appeared as a sidebar on all other screens). For example, for sofas the wallpaper was fluffy clouds, to prime comfort, or pennies, to prime price. In both experiments, the primes affected product choice, although most subjects said that it did not. These results, the authors noted dryly, "may present significant challenges to consumers" (this volume, p. 299).

The last paper in this section of the book, by Iyengar and Lepper (2000/ Ch. 16), does not provide direct evidence for preference construction. Instead, we view it as a *result* of preference construction. Constructing preferences, in contrast to merely retrieving them, puts a burden on the decision maker, a burden that grows larger as the choice set increases. In three carefully designed experiments, Iyengar and Lepper studied the effects of a limited (i.e., 6) versus an extensive (24 or 30) set of choice options. They found that, in the two studies that measured it, the extensive set was initially more appealing, but in all three studies, the limited set was more motivating or satisfying: In a grocery store jam tasting, more shoppers given the limited set subsequently bought a jar of jam. In a college course, more students who were offered extra credit for a short essay later submitted an essay from a list of 6 topics than from a list of 30 topics – and their essays were of better quality. In a laboratory choice among chocolates, those who chose from among a set of 6 chocolates (vs. 30 chocolates) later were more satisfied with the taste of their chosen chocolate – and they were more likely to take their pay in chocolates rather than dollars. The authors suggested that this deleterious choice overload, which they showed with quite trivial decisions, might be even greater with big, important decisions.

THEORIES OF PREFERENCE CONSTRUCTION

A variety of theoretical concepts have been created to describe and explain preference construction. If preferences are constructed, then decisions are constructed. Thus, these theories of construction constitute theories of decision making; they are more encompassing than the theories designed to explain preference reversals. However, just as many preference-reversal theories are weak in specifying the processes involved in choice, many preference-construction theories completely or mostly neglect the processes involved in the construction of single-stimulus responses (exceptions to this tendency include discussions of the role of memory and affect in decision making; see this volume, Ch. 21 and Chs. 23–25). Thus, both groups of preference theories are essential to provide the broadest view of decision making.

People employ a wide variety of mechanisms to process information – some of which are developed on the spot, in response to the features of the decision task. Gigerenzer and Selten (2001) characterized these process mechanisms (simple search modes, simple stopping rules, and simple decision rules) as components of an "adaptive toolbox" used by boundedly rational individuals to make judgments and decisions. Bettman et al. (1998/Ch. 17) described many of these adaptive mechanisms in the context of consumer decision making. They presented an integrated framework for constructed choice processes based on a mix of cost–benefit considerations and perceptual-like processes involving editing (Kahneman & Tversky, 1979) and framing (Tversky & Kahneman, 1981). Four main goals are seen as motivating these processes: (a) maximizing the accuracy of the choice, (b) minimizing cognitive effort, (c) minimizing the experience of negative emotion when making the choice, and (d) maximizing the ease of justifying the decision.

Montgomery (1998/Ch. 18) presented a theory based on the process of searching for a dominance structure among alternative actions. The key idea in this theory is that the decision maker attempts to structure and restructure information about attributes so that one alternative has at least one clear advantage over all other alternatives, and disadvantages are neutralized or deemphasized. This reconstruction makes the choice self-evident, facilitating action.

A related view of construction based on processes of differentiation and consolidation (Diff Con Theory) was presented by Svenson (1996/Ch. 19). Svenson saw decision making as a kind of conflict resolution in which contradictory goals have to be negotiated and reconciled and a solution constructed. One strategy to resolve decision conflicts is to change the representation of the problem. Svenson's decision maker seeks a sufficiently greater degree of differentiation among alternatives (dominance structuring, Montgomery, 1998/Ch. 18, was, to Svenson, one of many different ways to differentiate). Differentiation is achieved through various pathways: holistic (attending to subtle affective/emotional cues), process (using decision rules that support the decision), and structural (changing attribute importance or other psychological representations of the alternatives). As Svenson pointed out, the same kind of differentiation processes used in the pre-decision stage are often used after a choice has been made to support the decision. Diff Con Theory is a broad theory of choice, capable of encompassing many of the topics addressed in this book, such as the framework presented by Bettman et al. (1998/Ch. 17) and the role of memory, affect, justification, and framing in decision making. Considerable empirical support has been produced for both Search for Dominance Structure and Diff Con theories; Montgomery called for further research to examine the validity of the points on which the theories differ.

Appreciation for the constructive nature of preference was greatly enhanced when Tversky and Kahneman (1981) demonstrated that judgments and decisions could be profoundly influenced by normatively irrelevant differences in the way that information was presented or framed. Although framing effects are powerful, they lack a theoretical basis (Fischhoff, 1983). Steps toward developing such a framework, centered around the concept of *choice bracketing*, were taken by Read, Loewenstein, and Rabin (1999/Ch. 20). A set of choices are said to be bracketed together when they take into account the effect of each choice on all other choices in the set, but not on choices outside the set. When the sets are small, bracketing is narrow; when large, bracketing is broad. Just as in mathematics, where the same equations yield different results depending on how segments of an equation are bracketed, different groupings of choice alternatives may produce different choices (Keren, 1999). Read et al. have paved the way, as Laibson (1999) observed, for future development of a model that provides a theory of bracket formation and a theory of bracket-constrained decision making.

It should be obvious that memory plays an important role in preference as we ask ourselves, "What did I prefer previously in this situation?" and "How well did I like it?" Memories are images that may carry powerful affective or emotional feelings that have a profound effect on preferences and behavior (Slovic et al., 2002/Ch. 23). Yet, despite this evidence, the role of memory in preference construction has received little attention by judgment and decision researchers. Weber and Johnson (this volume, Ch. 21) have begun to remedy this neglect by linking insights about memory from cognitive psychology and social cognition to preference and choice. They argue that properties of memory representation and retrieval may provide a unifying framework for some seemingly disparate preference phenomena. Their *preferences as memory* approach suggests that preferences are neither constructed anew on each occasion nor completely stable and immutable. Besides its relevance to the material in this book on affect, their account relates closely to the discussions of reasons (Shafir, Simonson, & Smith 1993) and priming (Mandel & Johnson, 2002/Ch. 15; Ariely et al., 2003/Ch. 13), as well as to the material on dominance structuring (Montgomery, 1998/Ch. 18), Diff Con Theory (Svenson, 1996/Ch. 19), and miswanting (Chs. 27–30).

AFFECT AND REASON

Long before economists and psychologists began struggling to understand the motives underlying human behavior, philosophers had identified emotion (passion) and reason as the main ingredients. Discussion of the qualities and merits of these two forces gave the upper hand to reason, which became the centerpiece of rationality on which economics was built. The study of decision making, taking its lead from economics, similarly focused on deliberative, analytic thinking and neglected emotional factors. Not that reasons aren't important. Taking heed of the insights of Benjamin Franklin and William James, Shafir, Simonson, and Smith (1993/Ch. 22) discussed the ways in which varied forms of reasons are shaped and molded to resolve conflict and justify choice. They pointed to notions of compatibility and salience to account for differential weightings of reasons that lead the same alternative to be both selected ("Which do you prefer?") and rejected ("Which do you reject?").

But Shafir and colleagues hinted at another ingredient of preference construction, noting the assertion by Zajonc (1980) that choices may *occasionally* (their word, not Zajonc's) stem from affective judgments that preclude a thorough evaluation of the options. Much has changed in the quarter century since Zajonc's radical assertion that affect (a positive or negative feeling state) often comes prior to reason: "We buy the cars we 'like,' choose the jobs and houses we find 'attractive,' and then justify these choices by various reasons" (Zajonc, 1980, p. 155). During this time, social and cognitive psychologists began to integrate affect and reason into what have become known as *dual-process theories* of thinking (Chaiken & Trope, 1999; Sloman, 1996; Stanovich, 1999). This work has caught the attention of judgment and decision researchers, along with exciting theories by neuroscientists such as Damasio (1994) and LeDoux (1996), showing that *both* feelings and reasons are essential to rational behavior.

The study of affective processes in decision making is currently producing a volume of empirical studies not seen since the aftermath of Kahneman and Tversky's pioneering research on heuristic and biases in judgment under uncertainty (Kahneman, Slovic, & Tversky, 1982; Tversky & Kahneman, 1974). An introduction to this work was given by Slovic et al. (2002/Ch. 23), who described many subtle but powerful ways that affect serves as a cue for judgments and decisions. In particular, they introduced the concept of an affect heuristic, by which people judge an object according to how they feel about it. Slovic et al. demonstrated how the affect heuristic leads to an inverse relationship between judgments of risk and benefits; it also leads judgments based on probabilities to differ systematically from judgments based on relative frequencies. They also described the influence of affect on travel preferences, evaluation of life-saving interventions, investment decisions, and youth smoking.

Peters (this volume, Ch. 24) builds on this framework by articulating the functions of affect in preference construction. She argues that affect has four separable roles:

- It can act as information.
- It can serve as a spotlight focusing attention on specific information.
- It can motivate action or extra effort.
- It can serve as a *common currency*, allowing more effective comparisons and tradeoffs.

Zajonc (2001/Ch. 25) has recently contributed further to the dialog on affect and preference that he initiated in 1980. He addressed the mere-exposure paradigm in which an individual is repeatedly exposed to a particular stimulus object. The paradigm simply makes the stimulus accessible to the individual's sensory receptors without requiring any action to be taken and without offering any positive or negative reinforcement. Yet mere exposure creates preferences. With exposure, feelings toward the object become more positive, even when exposures are subliminal. Zajonc put forth an explanation for this phenomenon based on classical conditioning. He noted that nothing bad happens during mere exposure. This absence of noxious or aversive consequences could serve as a safety signal (positive affect), facilitating approach tendencies.

In their discussion of reason-based choice, Shafir, Simonson, and Tversky (1993/Ch. 22) anticipated that reliance on affect might preclude a thorough evaluation of options. They also noted that, when affect is important, an attempt by the decision maker to provide reasons might produce a different, and possibly inferior, decision. Wilson and Schooler (1991) provided evidence for this. Further evidence is provided by Wilson et al. (1993/Ch. 26), who found that people who gave reasons for liking a poster prior to choosing to take it home were subsequently less satisfied with it than those who chose without explicitly considering reasons. In the language of dual-process theorists such as Epstein (1994), giving reasons may interfere with the affective "vibes" that subsequently determine the quality of experience with the object.

Looking ahead to future developments in preference construction, we expect neuroscientists to play an increasing role in delineating the effects of affect and reason. McClure et al. (2004) described a study in which subjects indicated their preferences for the taste of Pepsi versus Coca-Cola while undergoing functional magnetic resonance imagery (fMRI) that monitors blood flow in the brain. When the drinks were unlabeled and subjects used their sense of taste alone to choose a preferred drink, a consistent neural response in the ventromedial prefrontal cortex correlated with their expressed preferences. When subjects were told they were drinking Coke, the hippocampus responded along with the dorsolateral region of the prefrontal cortex, and preference for Coke increased. This finding suggests that different parts of the brain are involved when affect (here, brand name) is evoked.

Not content merely to pioneer the new field of neuromarketing, neuroscientists have also initiated the broader domain of neuro- and neural economics (Glimcher & Rustichini, 2004; Montague & Berns, 2002). Based on the concept of the brain as an economic engine, Montague (2002) argued that the core of neural economics is the assertion that rapid, ongoing economic evaluation is a central function carried out by the nervous systems of mobile creatures, permitting efficient tradeoffs between essential activities, such as drinking water or chasing prey. The nervous system must possess some sort of common currency to make these tradeoffs, and Montague pointed to delivery of the neurotransmitter dopamine as one such common currency. At the psychological level, we propose affect as a candidate for this common currency and look forward to collaboration between psychologists, economists, and neuroscientists to document the workings of these fundamental elements of preference construction. As a step in this direction, Elliott and Dolan (1998) used fMRI to characterize the brain activity underlying the development of preference due to subliminal mere exposure. Their findings of right lateral prefrontal cortex involvement in implicit memory and in preference judgments seems, to us, linked to the recent work of Zajonc (2001/Ch. 25) as well as to the results of the Coke versus Pepsi (McClure et al., 2004) study.

MISWANTING

Even if we constructed our preferences perfectly (which, as this book richly documents, we do not), we will fail to make good decisions if we cannot correctly predict the satisfaction we will experience when we receive the outcome. Kahneman (1994/Ch. 27) has set the stage for discussing this problem by distinguishing between two kinds of rationality. *Logical* rationality demands that our choices be internally consistent and obey some set of formal rules. Intransitive choices and choice/price preference reversals are two examples of the violation of logical rationality. *Substantive* rationality looks beyond our choices to the outcomes; it demands that our decisions be in our best interests. The substantive question on which Kahneman focused was whether choices maximize the (expected) utility of their consequences as these consequences will actually be experienced. This *experienced utility* is distinct from *decision utility*, which is the utility inferred from the decision. Maximizing experienced utility depends on correct forecasting of hedonic experience, which Kahneman called *predicted utility* (see also Kahneman & Snell, 1990).

Numerous studies have explored the inconsistencies between decision utility and experienced utility. Reviews of this work have been presented by Kahneman (1994/Ch. 27), Gilbert and Wilson (2000/Ch. 30), and Hsee, Zhang, and Chen (2004). Kahneman (1994/Ch. 27) considered the case of a sequence of repeated future events (e.g., 8 consecutive days of having a snack); he concluded that people sometimes cannot correctly forecast their changes in preference over the sequence and that, even when they can, they sometimes do not use this information when making decisions now about the future events. Retrospective evaluations of past streams of experience, which serve as a basis for predicted utility, are likewise biased. Global evaluations of a sequence of experiences (e.g., the discomfort experienced during a colonoscopy) appear predictable by a weighted combination of the most extreme affect recorded during the episode and the affect recorded at the end of the episode. Surprisingly, retrospective evaluation is not much affected by the duration of the episode, a phenomenon labeled *duration neglect*.

Hsee and Zhang (2004/Ch. 28) have examined one of the many causes of discrepancy between decision utility and experienced utility: Decisions are often made in JE mode (we choose one from two or more options) whereas our later experience is typically in SE mode (we live with what we chose, not with what we refused). They hypothesized, and reported evidence for, a *distinction bias*. In JE, when two levels of an attribute are only quantitatively different, such as a reward of a large piece of chocolate versus a small piece of chocolate, the utility difference between the levels is enhanced, relative to attributes for which the levels differ qualitatively (because they lie on opposite sides of some reference point), such as an unpleasant task versus a pleasant task. This reference effect occurs neither in SE predicted utility ("How happy will you be with this?") nor in SE experienced utility ("How happy are you with this?"). Thus, choosers selected the unpleasant task with the large reward but experiencers were more happy with the pleasant task and small reward.

Hsee, Zhang, Yu, and Xi (2003/Ch. 29) reported a further problem in achieving substantive rationality: a discrepancy between predicted utility and decision utility. Even when other, nonhedonistic goals (such as trying to maximize someone else's pleasure) are ruled out, people sometimes choose one option but predict greater future satisfaction for the other option. The authors attributed this effect to *lay rationalism*. In making decisions, but not in judging predicted utility, people overweight cold, hard attributes and underweight hot, soft attributes. In a sense, they base their decisions on what they think ought to be important rather than what will give them the most pleasure. Hsee et al. showed three kinds of lay rationalism, *lay economism* (an overemphasis on economic gains), *lay functionalism* (an overemphasis on the primary goal and less emphasis on other attributes that contribute to enjoyment of the outcome), and *lay scientism* (overreliance on hard, objective attributes). For example, they illustrated lay scientism by asking subjects to choose between, and to rate their predicted enjoyment of, two stereo systems differing in sound richness and power. When sound richness was described as an objective attribute and power as a subjective attribute, the percentage of subjects who chose the stereo with the better sound richness was greater than the percentage who rated it higher in predicted enjoyment. But when power was described as objective and sound richness as subjective, the effect reversed – choice then favored the more powerful stereo more than enjoyment ratings did.

Gilbert and Wilson (2000/Ch. 30) observed that much unhappiness has less to do with not getting what we want than with not wanting what we like, a condition they called *miswanting*. Causes of miswanting are many, including imagining the wrong event (mispredicting what stardom or terminal illness actually entails), using the wrong theory of who we are and how well we would like the outcome, misinterpreting our feelings at the time of decision, and overpredicting the intensity and duration of one's future affective reaction. Another biasing factor is *focalism*, the tendency to focus too much on the target event and overlook the many other factors that will influence the nature of the experience. Finally, there is *immune neglect*, a failure to appreciate the assortment of cognitive strategies, tactics, and maneuvers that protect our psychological well-being. Immune neglect causes people to miswant by fearing and avoiding outcomes that will not, in the long run, have much effect on their happiness.

CONTINGENT VALUATION

Societal decisions expressed in laws and regulations rely heavily on the measurement of societal values. These values may often be inferred from markets: More expensive things are, according to economic theory, more valued in our society. But many important resources, such as the giant panda or the maintenance of pristine lakes in remote places, are not on the market. How should we value them? Regulators and policy makers, seeking to determine whether the benefits of their proposals outweigh the costs, have looked to economists for help in assigning dollar values to these nonmarket goods. Economists have obliged in various ways, one of which was to develop methods called Contingent Valuation (CV; see, e.g., Cummings, Brookshire, & Schulze, 1986). In CV, survey respondents are asked to indicate a stated willingness to pay (WTP) for public goods, including goods from which they derive no personal benefit.

CV has been steadily growing in importance for several decades and is used by the Environmental Protection Agency and other state and national bodies.

There is a long history of documented problems with CV. Among these problems are:

- An inordinate number of respondents who either refuse to give a response or who give an absurdly large response. Stevens, Echeverria, Glass, Hager, and More (1991), for example, reported more than 60% refusals.
- A confusion between WTP and willingness to accept (WTA). WTA responses (to the question, "What is the minimum you would demand to give up X?") are known (e.g., Kahneman, Knetsch, & Thaler, 1990) to be unduly larger than WTP responses (to the question, "What is the maximum you would pay to get X?"). This finding alone would cast doubt on the validity of CV methods, but the problem, as discussed by Gregory, Lichtenstein, and Slovic (1993/Ch. 33), is further aggravated when CV practitioners ask for WTP when WTA is appropriate to the situation.
- Preference reversals between WTP based on single-stimulus presentations and WTP based on paired presentations (e.g., Irwin et al., 1993).
- Insensitivity to scope. For example, Toronto residents were willing to pay only slightly more to clean up all the lakes in Ontario than to clean up lakes in a particular region of Ontario (Kahneman & Knetsch, 1992). A study by Desvousges et al. (1992) found that respondents had almost identical WTP values to save 2,000, 20,000, or 200,000 birds from dying in oil ponds.

Kahneman, Ritov, et al. (1999/Ch. 31) analyzed the flaws of CV methods and arrived at a strong conclusion: Stated WTP values do not express economic preferences. Instead, they are best seen as expressions of attitude. The core process of such attitudes is affective valuation, which determines the size and intensity of the emotional response to objects. In this view, WTP is insensitive to the number of birds saved from death in the oil ponds because the dollar value is constructed from the emotional response or attitude toward a prototypical image – an oil-covered bird. Kahneman et al. also used this attitude model to explain punitive damage awards in lawsuits as a function of the outrage felt by the jury toward the defendant.

Hsee and Rottenstreich (2004/Ch. 32) have provided further support for the idea of WTP as an expression of attitude. They examined the problem of scope insensitivity by employing the distinction between analytic and affective thinking embodied in dual-process theories (Chaiken & Trope, 1999; see also Slovic et al., 2002/Ch. 23). They proposed that preferences and WTP values are constructed by two processes, valuation by feeling and valuation by calculation. They showed that when people are induced to rely more on feeling (e.g., by seeing pictures of endangered animals), they are rather insensitive to scope. In contrast, when they are induced to rely more on calculation, they are more sensitive to scope.

Gregory et al. (1993/Ch. 33) recognized the growing evidence that preferences must be constructed, particularly for complex, unfamiliar, nonmarket environmental goods. They urged the designers of CV surveys to function not as archeologists, attempting to uncover what is (not) there, but as architects, working to build a defensible expression of value. They argued that WTP is ill suited to this task and proposed that CV methods be entirely changed from a reliance on WTP to a constructive process for valuation based on multiattribute utility theory.

As far as we can tell, this proposal fell on deaf ears. CV practitioners have responded to the critiques of their methods by continuing to use WTP but making their surveys longer and more detailed (e.g., Bateman et al., 2002). In light of all the evidence for preference construction presented in this book, and most especially in light of the arguments by Kahneman, Ritov, and Schkade (1999/ Ch. 31) that WTP methods elicit attitudes, not economic values, we must renew our plea to CV practitioners and to our government: CV methods are deeply flawed; better methods, based on decision analysis, should be used for forming or informing public policy (Pidgeon & Gregory, 2004).

PREFERENCE MANAGEMENT

We know that other people work hard to influence our preferences. Advertisers, public relations firms, and electoral campaigns are devoted to this effort. Perhaps we should spend more time and effort managing our own preferences. If our preferences are so labile, why not use this lability for our own good? And if social decision makers are controlling our preferences, why not use the knowledge gained from research to improve their decisions on our behalf?

Managing Your Own Preferences

Krantz (1991) has noted that the Talmud asks, "Who is it that is rich?" and answers, "One who is content with his portion." You might, as this quote implies, choose to change your goals and aspiration levels to get more pleasure from your decisions. Likewise, Schwartz (2004) has advocated that people consciously become satisficers (Simon, 1956) rather than maximizers, becoming content with "good enough."

You might reframe the decision problem. L. J. Savage (1954) did so when he considered the Allais (1953) paradox, which involves two bet pairs. The difference between the two pairs lies only in outcomes that are identical within each pair, so that preferences that are based on these outcomes violate the independence axiom (i.e., only outcomes that differ are relevant to the decision) of utility theory. These common outcomes are not obvious as the bets are usually stated (see Table 1.1). Savage reported that his initial preferences were paradoxical (he chose A and D). He then reframed the gambles as numbered lottery tickets (Table 1.1), making the common outcomes in each pair (tickets 12–100) obvious. Savage found that with this new frame one of his preferences changed: "It seems to me that in reversing my preference ... I have corrected an error"

Table 1.1. Two Frames for the Allais Paradox

Choose Between Option A and Option B. Independently, Also Choose Between Option C and Option D.

Original frame

A	$500,000 for sure
B	.10 to win $2,500,000; .89 to win $500,000; .01 to win nothing
C	.11 to win $500,000; .89 to win nothing
D	.10 to win $2,500,000; .90 to win nothing

Savage's (1954) Reframing in Terms of Lottery Tickets

	Ticket Number		
	1	**2–11**	**12–100**
A	$500,000	$500,000	$500,000
B	nothing	$2,500,000	$500,000
C	$500,000	$500,000	nothing
D	nothing	$2,500,000	nothing

(p. 103). The key to successful reframing is just that recognition of error. If both frames seem equally compelling, reframing won't help you manage your preferences.

Payne, Bettman, and Schkade (1999/Ch. 34) addressed the problems of public policy formation, but several of their recommendations, such as sensitivity analysis, might also be used for individual decision making. For an important decision, you might consider, for each aspect in turn, "What if this aspect were a little better or a little worse? Would that change my decision?" This would help you locate the most sensitive aspect for further study.

Schwartz (2004) strongly advocated preference management. He believes that people make too many decisions and urged people to "choose when to choose" (p. 222). He also recommended that you make your decisions non-reversible, so that post-decision thoughts are focused on what Svenson (1996/Ch. 19) called consolidation. Schwartz (p. 227) noted that "wondering whether you would have done better is a prescription for misery," which could be lessened if your choice is irreversible.

What evaluation mode and response scale should you choose when making a decision? Separate evaluation ratings or joint evaluation choice? The research does not indicate a clear answer. On the one hand, joint evaluations make attributes more evaluable (Hsee et al., 1999/Ch. 9), which is good, but as Hsee and Zhang (2004/Ch. 28) have pointed out, your later experience is often a single-stimulus evaluation; separate evaluation during the decision might therefore be a better predictor of later satisfaction.

For many of the effects documented in this book, corrective measures are very difficult. Some effects occur without our awareness, such as the influence of the Web shopping site "wallpaper" shown by Mandel and Johnson

(2002/Ch. 15) or the effect of mere exposure (Zajonc, 2001/Ch. 25); we cannot correct them if we're not aware of them. For other effects, we may be well aware of them but unable to alter them. For example, we have little or no control over the peculiarities of our memory retrieval systems (Weber & Johnson, this volume, Ch. 21). Our inability to accurately predict future satisfaction is resistant to improvement efforts; both Daniel Gilbert and George Loewenstein, who have done extensive research on this topic, confessed to a *New York Times* reporter (Gertner, 2003) that they have had trouble in their own lives correcting for the biases they have documented.

Using Tools To Manage Your Preferences

Sometimes it seems as if we get so upset by economists' resistance to the evidence of preference construction that we forget about another profession that is equally grounded in utility theory and that openly embraces human decision-making faults: *decision analysis*. As one of the founders of decision analysis, Howard Raiffa (1968), noted,

> No one claims that most people *do* behave as they *ought* to behave. Indeed, the primary reason for the adoption of a prescriptive or normative theory ... for choice behavior is the observation that when decision making is left solely to unguided judgment, choices are often made in an internally inconsistent fashion. ... If people always behaved as this prescriptive theory says they ought to, ... we could then just tell people, "Do what comes naturally." (pp. 81–82; emphasis in original)

Decision analysis is a theory-based set of tools for improving decisions. You could use them on your own, by following the "building code" presented by Payne et al. (1999/Ch. 34) or the systematic approach described by Hammond, Keeney, and Raiffa (1999). Or you could hire a decision analyst. That's a costly option usually reserved for large, expensive decisions. But your analyst will put you through the paces, carefully structuring the problem and approaching each preference-assessment task in multiple ways. A skilled analyst won't allow you to avoid the hard tradeoffs, to be overly influenced by aspects that are easy to monetize, to rely only on the most prominent dimension, or to make preference reversals. The analyst will also ensure that you use your heart as well as your mind in the process of constructing your decision (Phillips, 1984). You'll be managing your preferences with knowledgeable help.

Fischhoff (this volume, Ch. 35) recognizes the benefits of decision analysis with its hope for eliciting reflective responses in an active process of preference construction. He endorses it as a cornerstone of a "philosophy of science for reactive measurement" (p. 653), in which analysts help a client review alternative perspectives and confront critical issues, using multiple, converging measures. He contrasts this with a psychophysical model of elicitation of which attitude measurement is an offshoot. This model uses impassive interviewers, standardized questions, minimal clarification, and limited time to think. The appropriate choice of one of these approaches over the other depends, he notes, on the weight given sins of commission (inappropriately influencing people) versus sins of omission (letting them misunderstand their position). The reactive approach need not always be guided by an analyst. For example, Fischhoff describes an interactive DVD designed to help young women make choices about sexual relations.

The practice of decision analysis has evolved and improved in response to the findings of behavioral research (von Winterfeldt, 1999). But it needs to evolve still further in light of the findings on preference construction. Of course, no tool can overcome the problems, noted earlier, arising from influences we are unaware of (e.g., mere exposure) or cannot correct (e.g., memory). However, decision researchers and decision analysts need to develop corrective tools for several of the biasing effects discussed in this book. For example:

Coherent Arbitrariness. Does this effect extend beyond the experiments reported by Ariely et al. (2003/Ch. 13, 2006/Ch. 14)? How can the analyst tell, when the client gives coherent responses A, B, C, and D, that the first one, A, was simply pulled out of the air?

Change During the Decision Process. Simon, Krawczyk, et al. (2004/Ch. 12) presented evidence that preferences change during the process of making a decision. Is the change for the better or the worse? Wilson et al. (1993/Ch. 26) found that giving reasons lowered post-decision satisfaction. This result should worry decision analysts because their techniques for thinking harder about the problem may be quite similar and thus evoke the same biases. It may be some comfort to know that Wilson, LaFleur, and Lindsey (1995) reviewed several studies indicating that experts are less prone to this reasons effect.

Miswanting. Gilbert, Wilson, and their colleagues have begun to study debiasing techniques for some of the causes of the discrepancy between predicted utility and experienced utility (Morewedge, Gilbert, & Wilson, 2005; Norwick, Gilbert, & Wilson, 2005). As this work progresses, it may provide new and valuable tools for decision analysts.

Despite these problems, we believe that decision analysis is the best general-purpose tool for managing our preferences.

Managing the Preferences of Other People

To form public policy, it is necessary to know the preferences of the people. If the people do not have well-established preferences, then the elicitation methods will affect the preferences. None of the aspects of these methods – the framing of the problem, the format, the questions, the response mode – is neutral. Thus policy analysts are put in the position, whether they like it or not, of managing other people's preferences.

Payne et al. (1999/Ch. 34) considered the plight of a government official or marketing manager for a new product who is seeking to understand the preferences of the public regarding environmental decisions or product design. Following the recommendation by Gregory et al. (1993/Ch. 33) to develop means to construct defensible values, they created a set of guidelines for construction, akin to a "building code." They outlined procedures of good preference construction, noting faults that may occur at each stage and suggesting how to mitigate these faults. Much of their discussion centers around the challenging task of measuring values in a world of constructed preferences.

The Ethics of Preference Management. The need or desire of people, groups, or agencies to manage other people's preferences has serious ethical implications. For example, is it ethical for a physician to prolong a colonoscopy beyond the medically needed time without telling the patient, knowing that Redelmeier and Kahneman (1996) have shown that the extra time, with lessened but not absent discomfort, will lower the patient's retrospective overall evaluation of the pain and discomfort? If your answer is a resounding "No," ask yourself if this would be ethical if it could be shown that doing so increases the probability that patients will agree to colonoscopies in future years, thus saving lives. We do not know the answer to this question.

MacLean (this volume, Ch. 36) examines the ethics involved when a physician obtains informed consent from a patient for treatment. He favors a deliberative model, in which the physician and the patient work together to arrive at a decision. Accepting the increasing evidence that patients do not have relevant values that can be uncovered by the patient–physician interaction, he views informed consent as a process of constructing the patient's values.

MacLean also considers several ways to evaluate the adequacy of an informed-consent procedure. *Instrumental* value (e.g., the procedure is good because it allows patients to make decisions consistent with their values) is not applicable because patients don't have the relevant values prior to the procedure. Instead, MacLean argues that the ethical justification for informed consent lies in *pure procedural* value. The essence of this concept is that the procedure itself gives value to the outcome. For example, electing members of Congress by voting is a procedure that has several kinds of value, such as the instrumental value of finding the best qualified person, but the pure procedural value lies in the value accruing to the winner: "The candidate who is elected through a fair voting process is the right candidate for the job precisely because she was chosen this way" (this volume, p. 678). Likewise, the criterion for judging informed consent is to find the procedure that, because of its design and fairness, confers rightness on the decision made.

MacLean's views present a considerable challenge to decision researchers and decision analysts. Is it fairer to present survival rates or death rates to the patient (McNeil, Pauker, Sox, & Tversky, 1982)? For many such framing problems, we suspect that presenting both frames and discussing the reversals is the fairest way. But further research will be needed to more fully illuminate the concept of fairness in information presentation and response mode issues.

Advertisers and political campaigners avidly seek to manage our preferences. We do not know the ethical boundaries of such actions. There is only a thin line between management and manipulation. Are outright lies taboo? How about innuendo? Murray and Häubl (2005) have discussed the implications of some preference-construction effects (e.g., priming and format changes) on the development of online recommendation agents (i.e., programs that interactively elicit shoppers' attribute weights, develop an individualized model of that shopper's preferences, and present product recommendations based on that model). The authors are quite clear that it is in the firm's best interests to develop agents that are trustworthy and do not mislead the customers. But their essay could be read by the unscrupulous as a tutorial on how to snooker customers into buying inferior products while making them happy with their choices.

This opportunity for malevolent manipulation is not unique to Murray and Häubl's (2005) essay or to online shoppers (see, e.g., Hanson & Kysar, 1999a, 1999b). All of the preference-construction effects discussed in this book have the potential for being used to manage our preferences against our best interests. Even if we are aware of these efforts, as Murray and Häubl pointed out, we exaggerate our ability to counteract such influences.

Inevitable Preference Management. In many situations, it is inevitable that other people will manage our preferences. Johnson and Goldstein (2003/ Ch. 37) have examined one such case, defaults. For example, in the United States the default rule for organ donation is that you *are not* a donor unless you specifically ask to be (you opt in). In some other countries, you *are* legally assumed to be a donor unless you specifically ask not to be (you opt out). This difference in defaults, as Johnson and Goldstein have shown, makes a huge difference in the percentage of people who are organ donors; evidently, their preferences have been managed by the default rule. And this management cannot be avoided; unless the country passes a law forbidding all organ donations or a law requiring them for all citizens (neither of which is a feasible alternative), the law must specify a default rule. Which one? Johnson and Goldstein urged further research into the causes of the default effect before deciding, but they noted that most Americans seem to favor organ donation and that increasing rates of donation would save many lives, both arguments for a law that assumes you're a donor unless you opt out.

Sunstein and Thaler (2003/Ch. 38) have expanded these ideas to propose a public policy called Libertarian Paternalism. This policy is deeply rooted in the recognition that (a) we often do not know our preferences and must construct them, and (b) it is inevitable that in many situations others will manage our preferences. The paternalistic part of the policy is their insistence that the management be done for the good of the affected people; the libertarian part is their insistence that this management be done without eliminating freedom of choice.

CONCLUDING REMARKS

We started this chapter with preference reversals and showed how the study of reversals has metamorphized from a curious phenomenon observed with simple gambles in laboratory settings to a method for documenting a broad, encompassing view of human behavior that has come to be known as "the construction of preference." What has emerged is a portrait of human information processing that is rich and complex and relevant to all of the important decisions in life.

Research on preference construction has been varied and imaginative. It has provided ever-expanding insight into how humans think and make decisions.

Even more important, we believe, has been the blossoming of theories of human decision making, well beyond what we could have imagined 35 years ago. These theories are powerful because they are both explicit in the details of our ponderings and broad in scope. Moreover, these theories have increasingly adopted concepts from other areas of psychology, such as memory, emotion, attitudes, and cognition, and from neuroscience. There is even some attention given to individual differences (Levin, 1999; Levin & Hart, 2003; Parker & Fischhoff, 2005; Peters & Slovic, 2000; Stanovich & West, 2000), a topic long neglected in the decision-making literature. We expect that, as this theoretical work continues, we will see more and more links to the rest of psychology in decision-making theories.

Over the same period of time, other fields of psychology have increasingly incorporated the findings and concepts of decision making into their theories. Notably, social psychology has been heavily influenced by the work on heuristics and biases (Kahneman, Slovic, & Tversky, 1982; see, e.g., Nisbett & Ross, 1980). We expect that this kind of integration will also increase. It should now be impossible to write a theoretical treatment of, for example, cognition without any serious discussion of decision making (as Neisser did in 1967).

The practical implications of preference construction are vast. Topics discussed in this book include all manner of personal decisions, marketing and advertising, jurisprudence and juries, informed consent in medical practice, public policy, and the design of decision aids. The ethical problems are just starting to be discussed. We believe all these issues, and more, will receive increased attention in the years to come because, as Caldwell (2004) noted:

Once you stop taking people's expressed preferences at face value, pretty much every single contentious political, economic, sexual, familial, social, and labor issue can be opened up to unpredictable negotiation. (p. 93)

2. Relative Importance of Probabilities and Payoffs in Risk Taking

Paul Slovic and Sarah Lichtenstein

This chapter is concerned with conceptualizing the process by which a person makes decisions about gambles whose probabilities and payoffs are explicitly stated.

Gambles commonly are characterized as multidimensional stimuli. For example, a two-outcome gamble in which one outcome is a gain of some amount of money and the other is a loss can be described by its location on four basic risk dimensions – probability of winning (P_W), amount to win ($\$_W$), probability of losing (P_L), and amount to lose ($\$_L$). The essence of an adequate descriptive theory of risk taking is a thorough understanding of the way in which people go about integrating information from these basic risk dimensions when evaluating gambles.

The influence of these basic risk dimensions is examined here with particular emphasis on two ideas. The first is "importance beliefs." By this is meant that when a person evaluates a bet, he pays more attention to some risk dimensions than to others because he believes that these particular dimensions are most important for his present decision. For example, a person with very little money and great fear of losing it may focus his attention on the amount to lose ($\$_L$) and base his decisions almost exclusively on this dimension, largely disregarding the other information provided in the bet. Such beliefs about the relative importance of the risk dimensions may derive from previous experience, from logical analysis of the decision task, or even from quite irrational fears or prejudices. Importance beliefs, as defined earlier, have been useful for describing and understanding how people combine information in other multidimensional contexts, such as those that occur in clinical judgment or diagnosis (see, e.g., Hammond, Hursch, & Todd, 1964; Hoffman, 1960; Holzberg, 1957; Shepard, 1964). However, this notion has received little or no attention in the area of decision making under risk.

The second concern is with information-processing considerations. Assuming that a person holds strong beliefs about the relative importance of the various risk dimensions, his capacity to employ these beliefs successfully when

This article has been abridged by the authors. The complete version appeared in the *Journal of Experimental Psychology Monograph*, vol. 78, No. 3, Part 2, pp. 1–18. Copyright © 1968 by the American Psychological Association. Adapted with permission.

making decisions may be quite limited. According to Miller (1961), a decision maker under stress may completely neglect some items of information and employ other items according to a priority scheme to reduce information overload. Similarly, the work of Bruner, Goodnow, and Austin (1956) showed that attempts to reduce "cognitive strain" have a very strong influence on information use in decision tasks. Experimental studies demonstrating the influence of information-processing considerations in risk taking include the work of Miller and Meyer (1966) on the structure and number of alternatives available to the decision maker, Herman and Bahrick (1966) on the amount of information a person must encode to evaluate a bet, and Slovic, Lichtenstein, and Edwards (1965) on the effects of boredom on choices among bets. Concern with the decision maker's information-processing capabilities also underlies Simon's (1957) notion of "satisficing" and Toda's (1962) discussion of the decision processes of a "fungus eater."

In summary, the aforementioned considerations lead us to propose that the decision maker may give some dimensions of a gamble considerably more weight than others because he believes that these dimensions are more important for the particular judgment he is making and because his limited information-processing capability forces him to focus on these dimensions and neglect others. The remainder of this chapter attempts to marshal support for these arguments.

DESCRIPTIVE THEORIES AND CONSTRUCTS

A review of the most influential theories and constructs used to describe risk taking will help place the present ideas in perspective. The most popular class of models in this area has been that of the expectation models. The prototype of this class is the expected value (EV) model, which states that the attractiveness of a gamble corresponds to the gamble's mathematical expectation. For the two-outcome gamble offering a chance of gain or loss,

$$EV = P_W \cdot \$_W + P_L \cdot \$_L.$$

This model asserts that when a person chooses among two or more alternative gambles, he maximizes EV.

Since Bernoulli (1738/1954), it has been evident that the EV of a risky course of action is not the sole determiner of its attractiveness for the decision maker. Bernoulli and others proposed that people maximize expected utility (EU) where utility is the subjective value of money. More recently, EU theory has been amended to incorporate the notion that people make decisions on the basis of subjective rather than stated probabilities. According to this amended version, behavior is governed by the subjectively expected utility (SEU) of a gamble (Edwards, 1955). For our exemplary two-outcome gamble,

$$SEU = S(P_W) \cdot U(\$_W) + S(P_L) \cdot U(\$_L),$$

where $S(P)$ and $U(\$)$ represent subjective functions corresponding to stated probabilities and payoffs. . . .

Another influential approach to the understanding of choices among bets has been the study of probability preferences. Probability preferences were first examined by Edwards (1953, 1954a, 1954b), whose Ss made choices among pairs of gambles. Edwards observed consistent tendencies to prefer or avoid long shots (gambles offering a small probability of a large payoff). He also observed consistent choices of bets having specific intermediate probabilities. . . .

Yet another factor thought to be an important determiner of gambling decisions is preference for variance. Theorists such as Fisher (1906) and Allais (1953) have argued that people base their risk-taking decisions not only on expectation but also on the dispersion of a gamble's possible outcomes. Any gamble can be viewed as a probability distribution over the possible outcomes. The mean of this distribution is the gamble's EV. The variance of this distribution has been the most commonly studied index of dispersion. . . .

Although the first experimental study of variance preferences (Edwards, 1954d) concluded that they were less important than probability preferences, studies done since have been interpreted as indicating that variance has rather strong effects (Coombs & Pruitt, 1960; Davidson & Marschak, 1959; Lichtenstein, 1965; Littig, 1962; Royden, Suppes, & Walsh, 1959; Van der Meer, 1963). . . .

To date, probability and variance preferences have been examined in more than 30 studies. Without exception, studies claiming to find such preferences have used gambles whose probabilities and payoffs were highly, if not completely, confounded. This confounding means that patterns of Ss' preferences may be explained not only by recourse to notions of probability and variance preferences but, alternatively, by strategies that involve differential weighting of the basic dimensions of the gambles. . . . The following experiments were designed to permit precise quantitative study of the manner in which responses to gambles change as individual components of a gamble are manipulated.

EXPERIMENT I

Method

To study the relative importance of each component of a gamble, a special type of gamble was constructed in which probabilities of winning and losing, as well as their respective payoffs, could be varied independently. This type of stimulus, called a duplex gamble, is illustrated in Figure 2.1. A duplex gamble is represented by two large discs, each with a pointer on it. The left-hand disc is used for determining winnings. The right-hand disc determines losses. To play, S must spin the pointers on both the winning and

Figure 2.1. Example of a duplex gamble where $P_W = .4$, $\$_W = \$1$, $P_L = .2$, and $\$_L = \$4$.

Table 2.1. List of the 27 Bets Evaluated by Each S

Bet no.	P_W	$\$_W$	P_L	$\$_L$	EV
1	.2	$2	.8	$2	−$1.20
2	.8	1	.2	4	.00
3	.2	1	.8	4	−3.00
4	.8	2	.8	1	+.80
5	.8	2	.4	4	.00
6	.4	4	.4	1	+1.20
7	.8	1	.8	2	−.80
8	.2	2	.4	1	.00
9	.4	1	.4	4	−1.20
10	.2	1	.4	2	−.60
11	.4	2	.4	2	.00
12	.8	2	.2	2	+1.20
13	.8	4	.4	2	+2.40
14	.8	4	.8	4	.00
15	.4	1	.8	1	−.40
16	.4	4	.8	2	.00
17	.4	2	.2	1	−.60
18	.2	4	.4	4	−.80
19	.2	1	.2	1	.00
20	.2	4	.8	1	.00
21	.4	4	.2	4	+.80
22	.4	1	.2	2	.00
23	.2	4	.2	2	+.40
24	.8	1	.4	1	+.40
25	.2	2	.2	4	−.40
26	.4	2	.8	4	−2.40
27	.8	4	.2	1	+3.00

losing discs. This means that he can win and not lose; lose and not win; both win and lose; or neither win nor lose.

A list of the 27 bets used in this study appears in Table 2.1. For these bets, P_W and P_L each occurred three times at each of three levels: .2, .4, and .8; $\$_W$ and $\$_L$ also occurred three times at each of three levels: $1, $2, and $4. The four risk dimensions had zero intercorrelation across bets. The average EV across the set was $0.

Subjects. The Ss were 213 undergraduates, paid for their participation and assigned to four groups. Each group judged the attractiveness of the same bets but did so under different instructions. The Ss did not actually play any of the gambles.

Rating Instructions. The 88 Ss in the rating group were asked to indicate their strength of preference for playing each bet on a bipolar rating scale. Attractive bets were rated between +1 (slight preference for playing) and +5 (strong preference for playing), inclusive. Unattractive bets were rated between −1 (slight preference for not playing) and −5 (strong preference for not playing), inclusive.

Bidding Instructions. Investigators studying gambling decisions have often asked *Ss* to describe their opinion about a gamble's attractiveness by equating it with an amount of money such that they would be indifferent to playing the gamble or receiving the stated amount. These types of responses will be referred to here as "bids." Three different bidding techniques were used in this study. Persons in the first bidding group were asked to state the largest amount of money they would be willing to pay *E* to play each bet. For an undesirable bet, they stated the smallest amount *E* had to pay them before they would play. This procedure has been used previously by Slovic et al. (1965), Lichtenstein (1965), and Coombs, Bezembinder, and Goode (1967). The *Ss* in the second bidding group were given ownership of a ticket to play each gamble. They were asked to state the least amount of money for which they would sell this ticket. For unattractive gambles, they stated the highest amount of money they would pay *E* not to play the gamble. This procedure has been used by Becker, DeGroot, and Marschak (1964), Lindman (1965), Coombs et al. (1967), and Tversky (1967a, 1967b). Following a procedure employed by Coombs et al. (1967), *Ss* in the third bidding group had to state a fair price for a gamble not knowing whether they or *E* owned the right to play it. The maximum allowable bid for an attractive bet, under any instructional set, was $\$_W$, the most money the bet offered to win. The maximum allowable negative bid for an unattractive bet was $\$_L$.

The mean bid across the 27 gambles for the first, second, and third bidding groups was −59, +19, and −5¢, respectively. The relative sizes of these means match the results obtained by Coombs et al. (1967) and reflect a tendency for *Ss* to want to be paid money rather than pay *E*. In other respects the behavior of the 125 *Ss* in the three bidding groups was similar, and their data were combined and designated as that of the bidding groups.

RESULTS

Data Analysis. The primary data analysis consisted of correlating each *S*'s responses with the levels of each risk dimension across the 27 gambles. Because the risk dimensions were themselves uncorrelated, the correlations between risk dimensions and responses are directly proportional to the weights in a linear regression equation characteristic of each *S*. The absolute magnitudes of these correlations thus provide information about the relative importance of each dimension in determining the responses.

A rather unusual model of risky decision making underlies this data-analysis technique, namely,

$$A(G) = \mu + \omega_1 P_W + \omega_2 \$_W + \omega_3 P_L + \omega_4 \$_L,$$

where A(G) is the attractiveness of a gamble and the ωs are weights reflecting the relative importance of each dimension. This model combines, in additive fashion, variables such as P_W and $\$_W$ or P_L and $\$_L$, which are usually thought to combine multiplicatively. In addition, it assumes that the import of probabilities and payoffs is a linear function of their objective values.

The extent to which these assumptions of additivity and linearity are violated by the Ss' behavior was tested in prior work with duplex bets. The Ss made either bidding or rating responses to a complete factorial set of 81 bets (three levels of each of the four risk dimensions) with one replication. Analysis of variance techniques, augmented by Hays' (1963, pp. 406–407) method for partitioning variance, indicated that an average of about 75% of the total response variation was accounted for by a simple weighted combination of the four risk dimensions and less than 1% was due to nonlinear use of these single dimensions. For Ss who rated bets, an additional 1% of the response variance was due to interactions indicating multiplicative combining of P_W and $\$_W$ or P_L and $\$_L$. Under bidding instructions these interactions accounted for about 7% of the variance. Almost all of the remaining variance was error.

The special advantage of the regression technique and the model underlying it is the fact that it permits independent assessment of the relative influence of all four risk dimensions. It is fortunate, therefore, that the model produces a reasonably good fit to this type of data. . . .

Comparison of Bidding and Rating Groups. One of the most important results of this experiment is the finding that, for the groups as a whole, ratings correlated more highly with P_W than with any other dimension, whereas bids correlated most highly with $\$_L$. A multivariate analysis of variance (Vanderplas, 1960) showed the differences between the average weighting profiles of each group to be significant, $p < .001$, $\chi^2(4) = 27$. The generality of the differences between the rating and bidding groups is further illustrated by Table 2.2, which indicates the percentage of Ss within each group for whom a particular risk dimension was most important. Whereas 50% of the Ss in the rating group relied predominantly on P_W, only 18% of the Ss in the bidding group did. Similarly, the percentage of Ss for whom $\$_L$ was most important was 26% in the rating group but 53% in the bidding group.

The differences between rating and bidding seem to illustrate the influence of information-processing considerations on the method by which a gamble is evaluated. Apparently the requirement that Ss evaluate a gamble in monetary units when bidding forces them to attend more to the payoff dimensions – also expressed in terms of dollars – than they do when rating a bet.

The bidding and rating tasks can be conceptualized as involving a two-stage process. In Stage 1 S decides whether the bet is one he would or would not like to play. In Stage 2 he quantifies his first bipolar judgment by indicating the degree to which he likes or dislikes the bet. In an attempt to understand the differences between rating and bidding groups, the importance of the risk dimensions was examined separately within each of these stages.

Table 2.2. Number and Percentage of Ss for Whom a Given
Risk Dimension Was Most Important

	Risk Dimension			
	P_W	$\$_W$	P_L	$\$_L$
Rating group				
Number	44	8	13	23
Percentage	(50)	(09)	(15)	(26)
Bidding group				
Number	23	24	12	66
Percentage	(18)	(19)	(10)	(53)

Note: A χ^2 test indicated that distributions within each group differed
from uniformity at $p < .01$. The distribution for the rating group differed
significantly from that of the bidding group ($p < .01$).

First, every S's response to a given bet was dichotomized into a 0 (if he
found the bet unattractive) or a 1 (if he found the bet attractive). Next, these
dichotomous responses were correlated with the levels of each cue. This provided an index of the importance of each dimension in Stage 1 of the response
process.

Two additional regression analyses were conducted on each S's responses –
one for the subset of bets he found attractive, the other for unattractive bets. The
purpose of each analysis was to determine the importance of each risk dimension in determining responses in Stage 2. Because there was often a low but
nonzero correlation between pairs of risk dimensions within each of these subsets of bets, the correlations between responses and the levels of the dimensions
could not, by themselves, be used to represent the independent importance of
the dimensions. Therefore, Hoffman's (1960) technique was used to determine
the percentage of variance in an S's responses that could be attributed to his
use of each risk dimension after correcting for biases due to nonorthogonality
among the dimensions. . . .

Table 2.3 presents the results of the stage-by-stage analyses. All values have
been transformed into percentage of variance estimates to facilitate comparison.
Part a of the table presents the comparison based on the total set of responses
and represents the combined effect of both Stage 1 and Stage 2. Part b presents
the results of the Stage 1 analysis. The data indicate that the mean weights
for the two groups were remarkably similar at the end of the first stage. For
both groups the most important determiner of the dichotomous (like–dislike)
response was P_W. Thus, the differences found by analysis of the final responses
must have occurred during Stage 2.

The results of the Stage 2 analyses are presented in Part c of Table 2.3. It
is apparent that, when an S in the bidding group found a bet attractive, his
judgment of the relative magnitude of its attractiveness was principally determined by the size of $\$_W$; and when he disliked a bet, $\$_L$ was the primary

Table 2.3. Percentage of Variance Accounted for by Use of the Risk Dimensions During Each Stage of the Response Process

	Risk Dimension			
	P_W	$\$_W$	P_L	$\$_L$
Total response (part a)				
Rating group	24.9	14.1	16.3	18.1
Bidding group	18.0	16.7	12.9	27.2
Stage 1 (part b)				
Rating group	18.6	10.6	12.9	11.7
Bidding group	18.3	10.1	13.5	12.2
Stage 2 (part c)				
Attractive bets				
Rating group	30.2	11.8	12.8	16.7
Bidding group	6.4	49.8	5.3	7.4
Unattractive bets				
Rating group	10.6	13.1	15.8	16.2
Bidding group	4.1	7.9	8.2	54.4

determinant of the degree of dislike. This weighting pattern was characteristic of about 90% of the Ss in the bidding group. For Ss in the rating group, the difference between the method used to estimate degree of attractiveness and that used to determine the degree of unattractiveness was considerably less marked, although there was some tendency for P_W to be used more when quantifying attractiveness.

On the average, categorization of the entire set of bets into attractive and unattractive subsets reduced the variance of the risk dimensions by only 15%. In addition, the mean variances of the risk dimensions within each of the attractiveness categories were virtually identical for the two groups of Ss. Therefore, restriction of range can be discounted as a possible explanation for the group differences shown in Part c of Table 2.3.

Both bids and ratings presumably reflect the same underlying characteristic of a bet – namely, its worth or attractiveness. Why should Ss employ probabilities and payoffs differently when making these related responses? The introspections of one S in the bidding group are especially helpful in providing insight into the type of cognitive process that could lead bidding responses to be overwhelmingly determined by just one payoff factor. This S said,

If the odds were...heavier in favor of winning...rather than losing..., I would pay about 3/4 of the amount I would expect to win. If the reverse were true, I would ask the experimenter to pay me about...1/2 of the amount I could lose.

Note the initial dependence on probabilities in Stage 1 followed in Stage 2 by a complete disregard for any factor other than the winning payoff for attractive bets or the losing payoff for unattractive bets. After deciding he liked a bet, this S used the amount to win, the upper limit of the amount he could bid, as a starting point for his response. He then reduced this amount by a fixed proportion in an attempt to integrate the other dimensions into the response. Likewise, for unattractive bets, he used the amount to lose as a starting point and adjusted it proportionally in an attempt to use the information given by the other risk dimensions. Such adjustments, neglecting to consider the exact levels of the other dimensions, would make the final response correlate primarily with the starting point – one of the payoffs in this case. It seems likely that 90% of the Ss in the bidding group who relied primarily on payoff factors during Stage 2 were using a similar starting point and adjustment procedure. . . .

DISCUSSION

Descriptive theories of risk taking always have been closely linked with normative models. When logical considerations indicated that people should behave according to certain prescribed principles, these principles were incorporated into descriptive models against which performance could be compared. Although it is undeniably valuable to employ normative models as starting points for descriptive theory, preoccupation with normative aspects seems, in this case, to have led to neglect of certain psychological aspects of the risk-taking process. The purpose of the present research was to investigate the usefulness of some neglected psychological variables – in particular, a person's beliefs about the relative importance of probabilities and payoffs and his ability to act on the basis of these beliefs when processing the information contained in the description of a gamble.

These experiments were not designed to test the SEU model. The results do cast doubts, however, on the common interpretation of that model, which regards $S(P)$ as a measure of subjective likelihood and $U(\$)$ as a measure of subjective worth. In Experiment I, the inequalities found among risk dimensions with regard to their influence on the attractiveness of a gamble were often too large to be accounted for by the rather close correspondences between subjective and objective probabilities and between utility and money reported in other studies (Edwards, 1955, 1962; Robinson, 1964; Shuford, 1961; Stevens & Galanter, 1957; Tversky, 1967a, 1967b). The finding that P_W has more import than P_L is particularly critical because it constitutes a violation of the assumption, in the SEU model, that there is just a single probability function, $S(P)$, which is independent of the payoffs. Finally, the discrepancies between ratings and bids for the same bets suggest that the $S(P)$ and $U(\$)$ functions change as a result of changes in response mode. If $S(P)$ and $U(\$)$ functions can be altered drastically by a change in response mode (which seems quite unrelated to subjective worth or subjective likelihood), then surely these functions have been misinterpreted.

The above criticisms should not be construed as implying that the concepts of subjective probability and utility are irrelevant to risky decisions. On the contrary, these concepts belong in the repertoire of factors that influence decisions (and, accordingly, influence regression weights). The authors' objection is to the position that subjective likelihoods and subjective values are the *sole* determiners of decisions....

The picture of the decision-making process that emerges from the present study is one of a person struggling to integrate several sources of information into a single choice or judgment. The decision maker is guided by certain beliefs (e.g., probabilities are more important than payoffs), which he combines with strategies designed to make his task less complex. One such strategy is to subdivide the evaluation of a gamble into two stages. In the first stage, gambles are classified as either attractive or unattractive. In Stage 2, the degree of attractiveness is quantified. When bidding, this quantification seems to proceed as a crude adjustment of $\$_W$ if the bet is attractive or $\$_L$ if the bet is unattractive....

The finding ... that Ss rely more on payoffs when bidding than when rating a bet suggests a possible explanation for some long-puzzling inconsistencies in data bearing on the relationship between objective and subjective probabilities. Dale (1959) found that low probabilities were underestimated and high probabilities were overestimated. On the other hand, when Ss evaluate bets by bidding, the subjective probability functions inferred from these bids have the reverse shape of those found by Dale; that is, a given change in objective probability produces a smaller change in the corresponding subjective probability (Lindman, 1965; Nogee & Lieberman, 1960; Preston & Baratta, 1948; Tversky, 1967a, 1967b). These relatively flat subjective probability functions are exactly what one would expect to find in bidding studies because the introduction of a monetary response mode increases the saliency of the money dimensions and decreases the relative importance of the probabilities.

The overdependence of bids on payoffs also can explain a finding that puzzled Lindman (1965). Lindman had Ss bid for a number of gambles and also make paired-comparison choices among triplets of these gambles. He noted a consistent discrepancy between bids and paired-comparison preference orderings. Examination of the bids indicates that they were ordered almost perfectly according to the larger of the values, $\$_W$ or $\$_L$, whereas the paired-comparison choices, like the ratings and Stage 1 decisions in the present first experiment, were not so dependent on payoffs.

The regression analysis technique used here serves as a convenient overall summary of the influence of each risk dimension on Ss' judgments. Although the results of such analysis may be due to a number of different considerations, two concepts have been emphasized here: (a) the weights may reflect Ss' belief that some of the risk dimensions are more important for, or more relevant to, the task at hand; and (b) change in weights across tasks indicates changing strategies due to Ss' attempts to ease their information-processing problems. The simplicity and descriptive sensitivity of the regression technique should make it useful for studying other aspects of risk-taking behavior such as the effect of display variables, the relationship between risk taking and personality, or the relationship between risk taking and real-life decision making.

ACKNOWLEDGMENTS

This research was supported by Grants MH-O4439 and MH-l2972 from the United States Public Health Service. Portions of this work were presented at the meetings of the Western Psychological Association, San Francisco, May 1967, and the American Psychological Association, Washington, DC, September 1967.

The authors are indebted to Amos Tversky for his criticisms of an earlier version of this chapter.

3. Reversals of Preference Between Bids and Choices in Gambling Decisions

Sarah Lichtenstein and Paul Slovic

Utility theory, in one form or another, has provided the guiding principle for pre-scribing and describing gambling decisions since the 18th century. The expected utility principle asserts that given a choice among gambles, the decision maker will select the one with the highest expected utility.

There are a number of ways other than choosing by which an individual can express his opinions about the utilities of various gambles. Among these are ratings of attractiveness, bids to buy, and bids to sell:

1. Ratings of attractiveness: On an arbitrary scale, S assigns an attractive-ness value to each of a set of bets. For any pair, it is assumed that he prefers the one to which he gives the highest rating.
2. Bids to buy (B bids): E owns a set of bets. For each bet, S indicates the maximum amount of money he would pay to be able to play the bet (see Coombs, Bezembinder, & Goode, 1967; Lichtenstein, 1965). For any pair of bets, it is assumed that he prefers the one for which he bids the most money.
3. Bids to sell (S bids): S owns a set of bets. For each bet, S indicates the minimum amount for which he would sell the right to play the bet (see Becker, DeGroot, & Marschak, 1964; Coombs et al., 1967; Tversky, 1967b). For any pair it is assumed that S prefers the bet for which he demands the most money.

Because utility theory assumes that these different responses are all deter-mined by the same underlying values, it predicts that Ss who are asked to choose one of two bets will choose the one for which they would make the higher bid or to which they would give the higher rating.

In contrast, the view of the present authors is that such decisions do not rely solely on expected utilities. Slovic and Lichtenstein (1968) have demon-strated that a gamble is a multidimensional stimulus whose various attributes have differential effects on individual decision-making behavior. In particular, they presented evidence that choices and attractiveness ratings are determined

Originally published in the *Journal of Experimental Psychology*, vol. 89, pp. 46–55. Copyright © 1971 by the American Psychological Association. Reprinted with permission.

primarily by a gamble's probabilities, whereas bids are most influenced by the amount to be won or lost. Specifically, when Ss found a bet attractive, their bids correlated predominantly with the amount to win; when they disliked a bet, the amount to lose was the primary determiner. It was argued that these differences between ratings and choices on the one hand and bids on the other demonstrated the influence of information-processing considerations on the method by which a gamble is judged. In the bidding task, Ss had to evaluate a gamble in monetary units; this requirement apparently led them to attend more to payoffs when bidding than they did when making choices or ratings.

The notion that the information describing a gamble is processed differently for bids than for choices suggested that it might be possible to construct a pair of gambles such that S would choose one of them but bid more for the other. For example, consider the pair consisting of Bet P (.99 to win $4 and .01 to lose $1) and Bet $ (.33 to win $16 and .67 to lose $2). Bet P has a much better probability of winning but Bet $ offers more to win. If choices tend to be determined by probabilities, whereas bids are most influenced by payoffs, one might expect that Ss would choose Bet P over Bet $, but bid more for Bet $. If such a reversal of orderings were to occur, it would provide dramatic confirmation of the notion that bidding and choice involve two quite different processes, processes that involve more than just the underlying utilities of the gambles. The following three experiments tested this hypothesis.

For all three experiments, the general paradigm was first to present S with a number of pairs of bets. All of the bets had positive expected value and were viewed by Ss as bets they would like to play. Every pair was composed of two bets with the same (or nearly the same) expected value: a "P bet," that is, a bet with a high probability of winning a modest amount and a low probability of losing an even more modest amount, and a "$ bet," that is, a bet with a modest probability of winning a large amount and a large probability of losing a modest amount. For each pair, S indicated which bet he would prefer to play. After S had made all his choices, he then made a bid for each of the bets, which this time were presented one at a time.

EXPERIMENT I

Experiment I was a group study comparing choices with S bids. The Ss were 173 male undergraduates who were paid for participating; there was no actual gambling. The stimuli were 13 two-outcome bets, 6 bets with excellent odds (the P bets) and 7 bets with large winning payoffs (the $ bets). All bets had positive expected values, ranging from $1.40 to $4.45. First these bets were combined into 12 pairs, each of which had one P bet and one $ bet; no bet occurred more than twice. The Ss were asked to pick, for each pair, the bet they would prefer to play. After each choice, Ss indicated how strongly they preferred their chosen bet by marking one of four lines on their answer sheet; the first line was labeled *slight* preference and the fourth was labeled *very strong* preference.

Table 3.1. Bets Used in Experiment I

Pair	P Bet	Expected Value	$ Bet	Expected Value
1	.99 Win $4.00	$3.95	.33 Win $16.00	$3.94
	.01 Lose 1.00		.67 Lose 2.00	
2	.95 Win $2.50	$2.34	.40 Win $ 8.50	$2.50
	.05 Lose .75		.60 Lose 1.50	
3	.95 Win $3.00	$2.75	.50 Win $6.50	$2.75
	.05 Lose 2.00		.50 Lose 1.00	
4	.90 Win $2.00	$1.60	.50 Win $ 5.25	$1.88
	.10 Lose 2.00		.50 Lose 1.50	
5	.80 Win $2.00	$1.40	.20 Win $ 9.00	$1.40
	.20 Lose 1.00		.80 Lose .50	
6	.80 Win $4.00	$3.10	.10 Win $40.00	$3.10
	.20 Lose .50		.90 Lose 1.00	

The instructions suggested that the two intermediate lines might be labeled "moderate" and "strong." After about 1 hour of intervening work, Ss then made bidding responses to 19 singly presented bets. The first 6 bets were intended as practice bets and differed from those used in the paired comparisons. The responses to these bets were not analyzed. The next 13 bets were the same as those used earlier. In the bidding instructions, S was told he owned a ticket to play the bet and was asked to name a minimum selling price for the ticket such that he would be indifferent to playing the bet or receiving the selling price. For both the bidding and choice tasks, Ss knew their decisions were "just imagine."

Because the 12 pairs contained several repetitions of single bets, only the results of a subset of 6 pairs of bets, which contained no bets in common, are presented here; these bets are shown in Table 3.1. The results for the other 6 pairs were virtually identical to these.

Results

The first column of Figure 3.1 shows the results of Experiment I. The top histogram indicates that most Ss varied their choices across bets, choosing the P bet over the $ bet about half the time. This does not mean, however, that the Ss felt indifferent about their choices. The mean strength of preference, when coded 1 (slight), 2, 3, or 4 (very strong), was 2.94, with a standard deviation of .95. Most of the Ss (65%) never used the slight preference rating.

The second histogram in the first column of Figure 3.1 shows that Ss were far more consistent in their bids: 70% of the Ss never bid more for the P bet than for the $ bet with which it had previously been paired.

The proportion of times that the bid for the $ bet exceeded the bid for the P bet, given that the P bet had been chosen from the pair, is called the "proportion of conditional predicted reversals" in Figure 3.1. Of the 173 Ss, 127 (73%) always

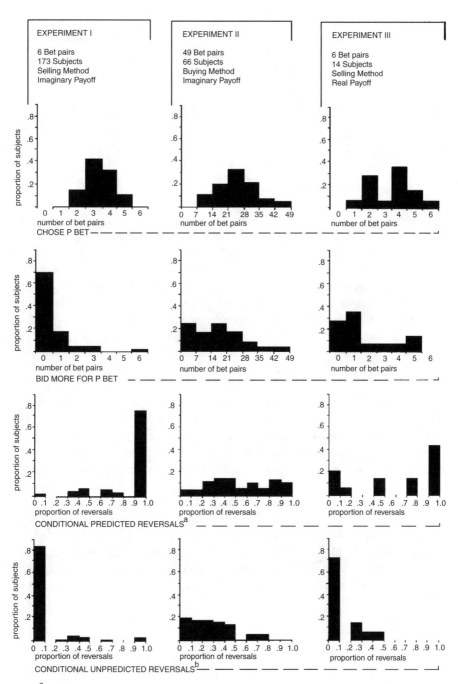

Figure 3.1. Summary of results for three experiments.

Table 3.2. Strength of Preference Rating Given to Choices in Experiment I

	Bid More for:			
	P Bet		$ Bet	
Bet Chosen	$\bar{X}$	SD	$\bar{X}$	SD
P	3.06	.93	3.10	.91
$	2.78	.94	2.78	.91

made this reversal: For every pair in which the P bet was chosen, the $ bet later received a higher bid.

The histogram labeled "conditional unpredicted reversals" shows the proportion of times in which the bid for the P bet exceeded the bid for the $ bet, given that the $ bet had been previously chosen. This latter behavior was not predicted by the authors and is hard to rationalize under any theory of decision making. It might best be thought of as a result of carelessness or changes in S's strategy during the experiment. Unpredicted reversals were rare in Experiment I; 144 Ss (83%) never made them.

The mean strength of preference rating was as high when Ss made reversals as it was when Ss were consistent, as shown in Table 3.2. This finding suggests that reversals could not be attributed to indifference in the choice task.

It is clear that when S bids are compared with choices, reversals occur as predicted. Would the effect also hold for comparisons of choices with B bids? There are certain considerations suggesting that the reversal effect might be diminished, because the effect seems to be largely attributable to a tendency to overbid for $ bets but not for P bets. For example, with the P bet, .99 to win $4 and .01 to lose $1, it is hard to imagine a bid much beyond the expected value of $3.95; whereas with the $ bet, .33 to win $16 and .67 to lose $2, bids greatly exceeding the expected value of $3.94 are common. Because Ss ask to be paid more when selling a bet than they pay to play when buying, the S bid method leads to higher bids than the B bid method (Coombs et al., 1967; Slovic & Lichtenstein, 1968). Therefore, S bidding should act to enhance the amount of differential overbidding and thereby lead to more reversals than B bidding.

EXPERIMENT II

The goals of Experiment II were to test the generality of the reversal phenomenon by using the B bid technique, as well as to study the relationships between various attributes of the bets and the reversal phenomenon by using a larger and more varied set of stimuli.

Method

The Ss were 74 college students run in four groups. No bets were actually played; Ss were paid by the hour. The stimuli were 49 pairs of bets following 11 practice pairs. Contained in these pairs were 88 different single bets. These 88 bets, following 10 practice bets, constituted the bidding stimuli. Results from the practice stimuli were excluded from the analyses. The bets in each pair were equated in expected value. Each P bet had a winning probability from 8/12 to 11/12; the probability of winning for the $ bet ranged from 1/12 to 5/12. The $ bet always had a larger amount to win than the P bet. With few exceptions, the win exceeded the loss in a given bet.

The bets were expressed in dollars and cents; the winning amount ranged from 10¢ to $10, the losing amount from 10¢ to $3.70; the expected value ranged from 10¢ to $3. A typical bet pair looked like this: P bet, 10/12 to win $1.00 and 2/12 to lose $0.20; $ bet, 3/12 to win $9.00 and 9/12 to lose $2.00.

The bets were chosen in an attempt to represent a variety of P bets and $ bets. Thus, the winning amount in the $ bet always exceeded the winning amount in the P bet, but the ratio of the former to the latter ranged from 1.3 to 100. The difference between the amount to lose in the $ bet and the amount to lose in the P bet varied from −$3.00 to $2.80.

The Ss were first briefly instructed in the choice task. They were asked to choose, from each pair, which bet they would prefer to play. After choosing, the Ss turned to the bidding task. Instructions for the buying method of bidding emphasized "the *highest* price you would pay to play it. Ask yourself each time, 'Is that the *most* money I would pay to play that bet?'"

Results

Comparison of the second column with the first column of Figure 3.1 shows there were fewer predicted reversals (Kruskal-Wallis analysis of variance by ranks, $\chi^2 = 82.73$, $p < .01$) and more unpredicted reversals (Kruskal-Wallis analysis of variance by ranks, $\chi^2 = 87.66$, $p < .01$) for B bids (Experiment II) than for S bids (Experiment I). As expected, the B bids in Experiment II were lower, relative to the expected values of the bets, than the S bids in Experiment I. Bids for the P bets averaged 7¢ below expected value in Experiment I, but 44¢ below expected value in Experiment II, $t = 5.97$, $p < .01$. Bids for the $ bets were $3.56 *higher* than expected value in Experiment I, but 40¢ below expected value in Experiment II, $t = 12.98$, $p < .01$. These results indicate that the B bid technique serves to dampen the tendency toward gross overbidding for $ bets and hence to reduce the rate of predicted reversals. In addition, because bids for $ bets are closer in range to bids for P bets in Experiment II, even fairly small fluctuations in bidding could more easily produce an increase in the occurrence of unpredicted reversals, as observed. Nevertheless, 46 of the 66 Ss ($p < .01$) had a higher rate of conditional predicted reversals than conditional unpredicted reversals.

The 49 pairs of bets used in this experiment were constrained by the requirements that all P bets had high probability of winning a modest amount, whereas all $ bets had low to moderate probability of winning a large amount. Nevertheless, there were differences in the degree to which individual pairs of these bets elicited predicted reversals. Despite the constraints, there was sufficient variability within some of the characteristics of the bets to permit analysis of their relationship to Ss' bids and choices. This analysis indicated that the difference between the amount to lose in the $ bet and the amount to lose in the P bet correlated .82 across the 49 bet pairs with the number of Ss who chose the P bet. Thus, when the amount to lose in the $ bet was larger than the amount to lose in the P bet, Ss chose the P bet 73% of the time. But when the reverse was true, the P bet was chosen only 34% of the time. This loss variable had no differential effect on bids.

Variations in amount to win, on the other hand, affected bids but not choices. The amount to win in the $ bet was always larger than the amount to win in the P bet, but the ratio of the two winning amounts varied. This win ratio correlated .55 across the 49 bet pairs with the number of Ss who bid more for the $ bet than for its previously paired P bet. The win ratio did not correlate ($r = -.03$) with the number of Ss who chose the P bet.

These results, that variations in amount to lose affected choices but not bids, whereas variations in amount to win affected bids but not choices, are further evidence that different modes of information processing are used in bidding and choosing.

The probabilities of winning across the 49 bet pairs in Experiment II had very narrow ranges (8/12 to 11/12 in the P bets, 1/12 to 5/12 in the $ bets) and had no differential effects on the frequency of reversals.

The probability of observing a predicted reversal increases both when the probability of S choosing the P bet increases and when the probability of S bidding more for the $ bet increases. This, together with the correlational information presented earlier, implies that the ideal bet pair for observing reversals would have a larger $-bet loss than a P-bet loss (facilitating choice of the P bet) and a large $-bet win relative to the P-bet win (facilitating a larger bid for the $ bet). In fact, in this experiment, the bet pair that had the most predicted reversals (40 of 66 Ss reversed) had just these characteristics: P bet, 9/12 to win $1.10 and 3/12 to lose $.10; $ bet, 3/12 to win $9.20 and 9/12 to lose $2.00.

EXPERIMENT III

The purpose of Experiment III was to test whether the predicted reversals would occur under conditions designed to maximize motivation and minimize indifference and carelessness. Lengthy and careful instructions were individually administered to 14 male undergraduates. The bets were actually played, and Ss were paid their winnings.

Table 3.3. Bets Used in Experiment III

Pair	P Bet	Expected Value	$ Bet	Expected Value
1	35/36 Win 400	386	11/36 Win 1600	385
	1/36 Lose 100		25/36 Lose 150	
2	34/36 Win 250	233	14/36 Win 850	239
	2/36 Lose 50		22/36 Lose 150	
3	34/36 Win 300	272	18/36 Win 650	275
	2/36 Lose 200		18/36 Lose 100	
4	33/36 Win 200	167	18/36 Win 500	175
	3/36 Lose 200		18/36 Lose 150	
5	29/36 Win 200	142	7/36 Win 900	135
	7/36 Lose 100		29/36 Lose 50	
6	32/36 Win 400	350	4/36 Win 4000	356
	4/36 Lose 50		32/36 Lose 100	

The stimuli were the 12 bets, 6 P bets and 6 $ bets, shown in Table 3.3. The probabilities were expressed in thirty-sixths, so that a roulette wheel could be used to play the bets. The amounts to win and lose were shown as points (ranging from 50 to 4,000), and a conversion to money was established such that the minimum win was 80¢ (even for Ss who had a net loss of points) and the maximum win was $8.00. The concept of converting points to money, and the minimum and maximum win, were explained to Ss at the beginning of the experiment. However, the actual conversion curve was not revealed until the experiment was over.

Each S was run individually. After six practice pairs, S chose his preferred bet from each of the six critical pairs three consecutive times, with a different order of presentation and top–bottom alignment each time. The E kept a record of S's choices. After S had responded to each pair twice, this fact was pointed out to him. The E told S that he would see these same six pairs one last time, that E would remind S of which bet he had preferred on each of the first two times, and that E would ask S for his final, binding decision. The E emphasized that his interest was in obtaining S's careful and considered judgments and that S should feel free to change his decision if, by so doing, he would reflect his true feelings of preference for one bet over the other. Then, as S looked at each pair, E would report either "The first two times, you said you would prefer to play Bet A (Bet B); do you still prefer that bet?" or "You chose Bet A once and Bet B once. Which bet do you really want to play?" It was emphasized that this final choice would determine which bet S would actually play.

Following this final round of choices, S was instructed in making S bids. This explanation was far more complex than that used in Experiment I and included all the persuasions discussed by Becker et al. (1964). These instructions were designed to convince S that it was in his best interests to bid for a bet exactly what that bet was worth to him. The S was told that E would choose a counteroffer against which to compare S's price by spinning the roulette wheel and entering the number so obtained in a conversion table specially designed for each bet. The conversion table was a list of the 36 roulette numbers with a counteroffer associated with each number. If the counteroffer was equal to, or greater than, S's previously stated bid, E would buy the bet from S, paying S the amount of the counteroffer. If the counteroffer was smaller than S's price, no sale would be made, and S would play the bet. The counteroffer tables were constructed on the basis of previous bids for similar bets, with a range chosen to include most of the anticipated bids. The values of the counteroffers can influence the expected value of the game as a whole, but they do not affect the optimal response strategy, a fact that was pointed out to Ss.

Further discussion of the technique emphasized two points: (a) The strategy that S should follow to maximize his gain from the game was always to name as his price exactly what he thought the bet was worth to him. (b) A good test of whether S's price was right for him was to ask himself whether he would rather play the bet or get that price by selling it. The price was right when S was indifferent between these two events. The E then presented several (up to 12) practice trials. These practice trials included the complete routine: S stated his selling price, E obtained a counteroffer, and the bet was either sold or played.

The 12 critical bets were then presented three times successively. However, the playing of the critical bets (including selection of a counteroffer) was deferred until S had stated his price for all bets. On the third presentation, while S was studying a particular bet, but before S had stated his price, E told S what his price had been for the first two times and urged him now to reconsider and name the final, binding price to be used later in playing the game.

After these decisions, S played the game. First, he played his preferred bet for each of the six pairs of bets. Then the bids were played, starting with the selection by E of a counteroffer and ending with either sale or play of the bet for all 12 bets. The S kept track of his own winnings or losses of points, which were, at the end, converted to money.

Results

All data analyses were based only on the third, final choices and bids Ss made. Results from these carefully trained and financially motivated Ss give further credence to the reversal phenomenon. As shown in Column 3 of Figure 3.1, six Ss always made conditional predicted reversals, and five Ss sometimes made them. Unpredicted reversals were rare.

Is it possible that the reversals in all three experiments resulted solely from the unreliability of Ss' responses? This hypothesis can be examined by assuming that the probability that S truly prefers the P bet in the choice task is equal to the probability that he truly values the P bet more in the bidding task. Call this single parameter p, and let $p' = 1 - p$. Suppose further that because of unreliability of response, S will report the opposite of his true preference with

Table 3.4. Proportions of Choosing and Bidding Responses

Expected Under the "Null Model":

		Bid More for:		
		P Bet	**$ Bet**	
Bet Chosen:	P	$pr's' + p'rs$ (a)	(b) $pr's + p'rs'$	$pr' + p'r$
	$	(c) $prs' + p'r's$	(d) $prs + p'r's'$	$pr + p'r'$
		$ps' + p's$	$ps + p's'$	1

Observed

Exp. I			Exp. II			Exp. III		
.085 (a)	(b) .425	.510	.261 (a)	(b) .271	.532	.250 (a)	(b) .321	.571
(c) .031	(d) .459	.490	(c) .127	(d) .341	.468	(c) .048	(d) .381	.429
.116	.884	1	.388	.612	1	.298	.702	1

a probability of r ($r' = 1 - r$) in the choice task and will reverse the true order of his bids with a probability of s ($s' = 1 - s$) in the bidding task.

Under this "null model," S will choose the P bet while bidding more for the $ bet if he truly prefers the P bet and responds with his true preference in the choice task but responds with error in the bidding task, or if he truly prefers the $ bet and responds with error in the choice task but truly in the bidding task. The probability of observing this response is thus: $pr's + p'rs'$. The probabilities of all possible responses, constructed in similar fashion, are shown in Table 3.4.

These expected probabilities can be compared with the proportions actually obtained. For each experiment, three of these proportions are independent and yield three equations in the three unknowns, p, r, and s; these equations may be solved for p. In general, if the actual cell proportions are a, b, c, and d as shown in Table 3.4, solving for p yields the equation:

$$pp' = \frac{ad - bc}{(a + d) - (b + c)}.$$

For the three experiments reported here, the obtained values for pp' were .295, .315, and .270, respectively. All of these yield only imaginary solutions for p. However, they are all close to the maximum possible real value for pp', .25, which would imply that $p = .5$. When $p = .5$ is substituted into the expressions in Table 3.4, then regardless of the rates of unreliability, r and s, all the following conditions must hold: (a) All marginals must be equal to .5; (b) Cell a must equal Cell d; (c) Cell b must equal Cell c.

These three conditions are not independent; only the last, that Cell b must equal Cell c, was subjected to statistical test. For the data shown in Table 3.4, McNemar's test for correlated proportions yielded $\chi^2 = 338.27$ for Experiment I, $\chi^2 = 167.29$ for Experiment II, and $\chi^2 = 15.61$ for Experiment III; for all, $p < .01$. Because the "null model" can in no way account for the data, it is reasonable to reject the notion that unreliability of response is the sole determiner of the reversal effects.

Postexperimental Interviews

The Ss in Experiment III who gave predicted reversals were interviewed at the end of the experiment in an effort to persuade them to change their responses. The inconsistency of the responses was explained to S. If S was initially unwilling to change any responses, E's interview comments became more and more directive. If pointing out that S's pattern of responses could be called *inconsistent* and *irrational* did not persuade S, E explained to S a money-pump game by means of which E could systematically and continuously get S to give E points without ever playing the bets.[1] This was intended to illustrate to S the consequences of his responses. After S understood the nature of the money-pump game, he was again urged to resolve the reversal.

Eleven of the 14 Ss were interviewed. Of these, 6 Ss changed one or more responses after only a little persuasion, 3 changed only after the money-pump game was presented to them, and 2 Ss refused to change their responses at all, insisting throughout the interview that their original responses *did* reflect their true feelings about the bets.[2]

Comments by Ss supported the authors' contention that Ss process the bet information differently in the two tasks. Some Ss showed this indirectly, by mentioning only the probabilities when discussing choices while focusing on the amount to win and entirely disregarding the amount to lose when discussing bids.

Other Ss explicitly stated they were using different processing methods in choosing and bidding. For example, one S, L. H., tried to justify his bid for the $ bet of Pair 5 by noting that his bid was less than half of the amount to win. When

---

[1] Paraphrased: Suppose I own both bets and you own some points. You have said that the $ bet is worth X points to you. Are you willing then to buy the $ bet from me for X points? OK, now you own the $ bet and I have X of your points. But you said you really would rather play the P bet than the $ bet. So would you like to trade me the $ bet for the P bet, which you like better? OK, now are you willing to sell me the P bet for Y points, which is what you told me it is worth? OK, now I have both bets back again and also I now have (X − Y) of your points. We are ready to repeat the game by my selling you the $ bet again for X points.

[2] An edited transcript of one of these Ss, not previously published, is shown in the Appendix.

E pointed out to him that his chance of winning was much less than one-half, he replied,

7 against 29 ... I'm afraid I wasn't thinking of the 7 to 29 [the winning odds]. I was thinking of it in terms of relative point value. ... In other words, I looked at the 29 and the 7 [when I was choosing] but as for bidding, I was looking at the relative point value, which gave me two different perspectives on the problem.

Subject L. F. said,

I don't arrive at the evaluation ... quite the same way that I arrive at the preferable bet. And there's some inconsistency there. Now, whether in a particular case this leads to an inconsistency maybe's not too important. It's just that they're two different models. ... I imagine that shows that the models aren't really accurate, but in terms of just betting, they're sound enough. I wouldn't change them.

Subject M. K. said,

You see, the difference was, that when I had to pick between [the P bet] and [the $ bet] I picked the bet which was more sure to produce some points for me. When I was faced with [the $ bet alone], my assessment of what it was worth to me, you know, changed because it wasn't being compared with something.

DISCUSSION

In three experiments, *S*s frequently chose one bet from a pair of bets and subsequently bid more for the bet they did not choose. The frequency of such reversals varied somewhat as experimental conditions changed, but was always far greater than could be explained by unreliability alone. Similar results have recently been found by Lindman (1971).

These reversals clearly constitute inconsistent behavior and violate every existing theory of decision making. For example, subjectively expected utility theory (Edwards, 1955) postulates both a subjective probability function and a subjective worth function, but does not allow either function to change its shape as the response mode changes. Bids and choices should both be predictable from the same functions; reversals are therefore impossible under the model.[3]

The present results imply that attempts to infer subjective probabilities and utility functions from bids or choices should be regarded with suspicion.

---

[3] This statement is not strictly true for B bids. When *S* offers a B bid for the bet, the utility of this bid cannot be directly equated to the expected utility of the bet. Rather, when a bid of b is given to a bet with outcomes X and Y, the utilities of the quantities (X − b) and (Y − b) are relevant. In a choice situation, however, the utilities of X and Y are relevant. Thus, reversals could occur with suitably chosen utility curves (Raiffa, 1968, pp. 89–91). Utility theory does not, however, help one understand why there were *more* predicted reversals in the present study with S bids (where reversals are normatively impossible) than with B bids (where reversals are normatively permitted).

Because these subjective factors are not the sole determiners of decisions, inferences about them are likely to vary from one response mode to the next, because of changes in the decision processes used by Ss.

What are the different decision processes that underlie bids and choices? The mechanisms determining choices are not clear, but it must be kept in mind that in paired comparisons, each attribute of one bet can be directly compared with the same attribute of the other bet. There is no natural starting point, and S may be using any number of strategies to determine his choice. Tversky (1969) has given several examples of such strategies.

In contrast, bidding techniques provide an obvious starting point: the amount to win. Evidence from the present experiments, as well as from the previous study by Slovic and Lichtenstein (1968), indicates that the S who is preparing a bidding response to a bet he sees as favorable starts with the amount to win and adjusts it downward to take into account the other attributes of the bet. The amount to win translates directly into an amount to bid. However, the probabilities of winning and losing, presented in probability units, are more difficult to translate into monetary units. In trying to adjust his bid to take into account this more complex information, S is not very precise. Some Ss simply subtract a constant from the amount to win. Others multiply the amount to win by the probability of winning, entirely disregarding the amount to lose. All such schemes produce bids that are highly correlated with amount to win but poorly reflect the variations in probabilities and amount to lose.

The P bets of the present study offered such high probabilities of winning that their modest winning amounts needed to be adjusted downward only slightly to take the other factors into account when bidding. In contrast, the $ bets offered only a modest chance to win a large amount of money. Thus Ss should have made a sizable downward adjustment of the amount to win when bidding for these bets. Their failure to do so led them to bid more for the $ bet than for the corresponding P bet. This, in turn, led to bids that often did not match their choices. Predicted reversals are thus seen as a consequence of the differing evaluation techniques used in the two tasks.

Is the behavior of Ss who exhibit reversals truly irrational? Tversky (1969) posed a similar question about Ss in whom he had induced systematic intransitivities and for the following reasons answered it in the negative. He noted that it is impossible to reach any definite conclusion concerning human rationality in the absence of a detailed analysis of the cost of the errors induced by the strategies S follows compared with the cost to S of evaluating alternative strategies. The approximations Ss follow to simplify the difficult task of bidding might prove to be rather efficient, in the sense that they reduce cognitive effort and lead to outcomes not too different from the results of optimal strategies. In using such approximations, the decision maker assumes that the world, unlike the present experiments, is *not* designed to take advantage of his approximation methods.

In sum, this study speaks to the importance of information-processing considerations too often neglected by decision theorists. The reversal phenomenon is of interest not because it is irrational but because of the insights it reveals about the nature of human judgment and decision making.

ACKNOWLEDGMENTS

This work was sponsored by the Personnel and Training Research Programs, Psychological Sciences Division, Office of Naval Research, under Contract N00014-68-C-0431, Contract Authority NR 153–311, and by Grants MH-15414 and MH12972 from the United States Public Health Service. We are grateful to Peter Christenson, who was the E in Experiments II and III, and to Leonard Rorer, Lewis Goldberg, and Robyn Dawes for their helpful suggestions.

APPENDIX

This transcript, not previously published, is excerpted from a half-hour post-experimental interview (May 1968) with a subject from Experiment III who is being questioned about the reversal inherent in his bids and choices made to the two bets shown in the following table. The subject chose Bet B over Bet A on three replications. He also bid three times for Bet A and three times for Bet B; these bids are as follows:

	Bet A	Bet B
	11/36 to win 1600 points and 25/36 to lose 150 points	35/36 to win 400 points and 1/36 to lose 100 points
Bids		
First	500	400
Second	650	400
Third	550	400

S: Male college student
E: Sarah Lichtenstein

E: Well, are you satisfied with your bids and your choices?
S: Yeah.
E: Now I want to ask you further about some things. Turn to page 19, will you? It's easier to look at the bet when I talk to you about it. Now, all three times in these paired comparisons you chose Bet B.
S: Right.
E: And you have no doubts in your mind about that?
S: Nope.
E: You also bid on these same bets. Now let me tell you what your bids were on Bet A and Bet B. Bet A is 550 points. Bet B is 400 points. Would you, if you were to do it again, change either of those bids?

S: I certainly wouldn't change B, you know, 35 to 1. A, 550, you said?

E: Yes. Would you change that?

S: I don't know. Actually I had a 1/3, it's really a 1/3 chance of winning. Approximately. So I would say, not really, because 550 is approximately 1/3. I might change it, but nothing drastic, maybe 25 or 50 or so.

E: I see. May I point out to you that you've bid more for Bet A.

S: Yeah, I see that.

E: And yet you would really rather play, given the choice, Bet B. Does that bother you in any way? I mean there's ...

S: No, not really, because I have ... er ... 99 ... you know, what are my chances of losing? I mean I'm talking about Bet B, and they're not very much, in losing, while in Bet A, there's a 2/3 chance I will lose. So I would have no hesitancy whatsoever on that. I would take Bet B every time.

E: You'd take Bet B every time. Well, then, why did you bid less for it?

S: 'Cause I couldn't bid any higher, but I would have. I could have, you know, but this says 400 points, so I bid the highest I could bid.

E: I see. Well, how about the bid for Bet A? Do you have any further feelings about it now that you know that you are choosing one but bidding more for the other one?

S: It's kind of strange, but no, I don't have any feelings at all whatsoever really about it. It's just one of those things. It shows my reasoning process isn't so good, but, other than that, I ... no qualms.

E: No qualms. Okay. Some people would say that that pattern of responses is not a reasonable pattern.

S: Yeah, I could see that.

E: Well, supposing I asked you to make it reasonable. Would you say well it's reasonable now or would you change something?

S: Actually, it is reasonable.

E: Can I persuade you that that is an irrational pattern?

S: No, I don't think you probably could, but you could try.

E: Okay. The reason I would say it's irrational is because you choose Bet B but you value Bet A more.

S: Yeah, I see what you're ...

E: That's contradictory ...

S: Maybe it's just that I like to go with the sure thing.

E: Hmmm. You really prefer Bet B over Bet A, and there's no question in your mind about that.

S: No.

E: You've also made it perfectly clear to me that 400 points is your true value for Bet B. You have not completely convinced me, however, that you wouldn't maybe if I pushed – like I am pushing you, very hard – maybe if I did push, you might be willing to lower that 550 for Bet A, and then you would be in a position, if you lowered it below 400, you would be in a position of saying you preferred Bet B and you value it more, also.

S: But then that wouldn't be right. It wouldn't be right for myself to do that because according to the rules of the game or whatever it's not worth ... it's not worth less.

E: Well, now let me suggest what has been called a money-pump game and try this out on you and see how you like it.

S: Okay.

E: If you think Bet A is worth 550 points, you ought to be willing to give me 550 points if I give you the bet. Does that sound reasonable?

S: If I were to give you ..., yeah, that would be reasonable.

E: So first you have Bet A.

S: Okay.

E: And I have Bet B, and I also have your 550 points. That was reasonable, wasn't it?

S: Yeah.

E: That I should take your 550 points? (both say okay)

E: So, you have Bet A, and I say, "Oh, you'd rather have Bet B wouldn't you?"

S: Yeah. It's a sure thing.

E: Okay, so I'll trade Bet B. Now ...

S: I'm losing money.

E: I'll buy Bet B from you. I'll be generous; I'll pay you more than 400 points. I'll pay you 401 points. Are you willing to sell me Bet B for 401 points?

S: Well, certainly.

E: Certainly. Okay, so you give me Bet B.

S: Um hum.

E: I give you 401 points, and you'll notice that I kept your 550 and ...

S: That's right.

E: I gave you 401.

S: I noticed that immediately.

E: I'm now ahead 149 points.

S: That's good reasoning on my part. (laughs) How many times are we going to go through this?

E: Well, ...

S: Okay, I see your point you're making.

E: You see, you see the point, I can go through it indefinitely if I simply stick to the pattern of responses you have told me. Now that you see that in that money-pump sense that pattern of responses just doesn't ...

S: Doesn't fit.

E: Doesn't fit.

S: It ain't so good.

E: Are you still ... Do you still feel that you would not want to change any of your three responses here?

S: I'd have to think a lot more time on it. But it sounds ... I may change something, yes.

E: What do you think you might change?

S: Well, I'd leave B as it is because...

E: You prefer B in the choice.

S: I prefer, yeah, right. I may either change my mind or take A or I may change my mind on the 550, but I'd say it would take a while. But what would I do, you want to know? I'd really, conservatively, I think the first thing I'd look at is the 550 and think more along those lines and really I don't know.

E: To get yourself out of this hole...

S: Okay.

E: If you just change the 550 and didn't change anything else you'd have to change it down to at most 399.

S: Um hmm. Just to make myself look rational. But, it's not worth, that means I'm willing to part with it for 399 points, and I wouldn't be...

E: You don't really feel that that's a genuine...

S: Yeah, right.

E: Indifference point for you?

S: Yeah, exactly. So maybe I should be looking at B, or change my choice to A.

E: Yeah. Well, how about that? Do you think in all honesty that you could prefer Bet A, be happier playing Bet A than Bet B?

S: No, I wouldn't be happier playing Bet A than Bet B.

E: Which would you be happier playing?

S: Well, I would be happier playing Bet B because I would say I'm a sure winner.

E: Well, I think I've pushed you as far as I know how to push you short of actually insulting you.

S: That's right!

Note. An audio recording of this interview may be found at
www.decisionresearch.org.

4. Response-Induced Reversals of Preference in Gambling: An Extended Replication in Las Vegas

Sarah Lichtenstein and Paul Slovic

In a previous paper, Lichtenstein and Slovic (1971) argued that variations in response mode cause fundamental changes in the way people process information, and thus alter the resulting decisions. Evidence supporting that view came from three experiments in which Ss chose their preferred bets from pairs of bets and later placed monetary values (prices) on each bet separately. In every pair of bets, one, designated the $ bet, featured a large amount to win; the other, called the P bet, featured a large probability of winning. Many Ss, after choosing a P bet, would frequently place a higher price on the $ bet. The authors hypothesized that the following process leads to such reversals of preference. When pricing an attractive bet, Ss use the amount to win as a natural starting point or anchor. Then they adjust downward the amount to win in order to incorporate the other aspects of the bet. This adjustment may be rather crude and insufficient, making the starting point – amount to win – the primary determiner of the response. Thus, the $ bets, with their large winning payoffs, receive higher prices than the P bets. This bias would not be expected in choice responses, where the amount to win does not dominate decisions (Slovic & Lichtenstein, 1968).

The previous study (Lichtenstein & Slovic, 1971) used gambles with positive expected value (EV) exclusively. A more stringent test of the reversal effect was provided in the present study by the inclusion of unattractive (negative-EV) bets. Lindman (1971) reported reversals of preference for both positive- and negative-EV bets using imaginary money, but no real-play situation including negative-EV bets has been studied. It was hypothesized that reversals would occur with negative-EV bets because Ss, when pricing unattractive bets, would use the amount to lose as a starting point and make an adjustment upward in an attempt to account for the other aspects of the bet. If, as with positive-EV bets, this adjustment were rather crude and insufficient, the $ bet, with its large loss, would be underpriced. No such bias was expected in the choice task.

The present chapter describes an expanded replication of the previous experiments in a nonlaboratory real-play setting unique to the experimental literature on decision processes – a casino in downtown Las Vegas.

Originally published in the *Journal of Experimental Psychology*, vol. 101, pp. 16–20. Copyright © 1973 by the American Psychological Association. Reprinted with permission.

METHOD

The game was located in the balcony of the Four Queens Casino. The equipment included a PDP-7 computer, a DEC-339 cathode ray tube (CRT), a playing table, into which were set two keyboards (one for the dealer and one for the player), and a roulette wheel.

The game was operated by a professional dealer who served as E. The Ss were volunteers who understood that the game was part of a research project. Only 1 S could play the game at a time. Anyone could play the game, and the player could stop playing at any time (the dealer politely discouraged those who wanted to play for just a few minutes; a single complete game took 1–4 hr.). Some Ss were recruited through newspaper reports of the project, and some learned of it by watching others play.

All Ss received complete instructions from the dealer, who explained the game and helped S with practice bets until S felt ready to begin play. At the start of the game, S was asked to choose the value of his chips. Each chip could represent 5¢, 10¢, 25¢, $1, or $5, and the value chosen remained unchanged throughout the game. The player was asked to buy 250 chips; if, during the game, more chips were needed, the dealer sold him more. At the end of the game (or whenever the player quit), the player's chips were exchanged for money.

The game was composed of two parts. Part 1 was a paired-comparison task, with 10 pairs of positive-EV and 10 pairs of negative-EV bets. Part 2 was a selling-price task, in which all of the previously presented 40 bets were presented again, one at a time. The 40 bets are shown in Table 4.1. Each negative-EV bet is the mirror image of a positive-EV bet in the same row.

Part 1

Four bets appeared on the CRT, labeled B1 and B2 (for negative-EV, or "bad" bets) and G1 and G2 (for positive-EV, or "good" bets). All four bets had the same absolute EV, but the bad bets shown were never the mirror images of the good bets shown. For example, the bad bets of Row 1 in Table 4.1 were presented with the good bets of Row 2 in Table 4.1, and vice versa.

The player chose one good bet and one bad bet by pushing, on the keyboard in front of him, the buttons labeled BET G1 or BET G2 and BET B1 or BET B2. After this selection, the chosen bad bet was displayed alone on the CRT. The player then selected the roulette numbers he wanted to be designated as winning numbers for that bet. After the player chose his numbers for the bad bet, the dealer spun the roulette wheel and exchanged the appropriate chips with the player. The chosen good bet then appeared on the CRT and was played in a like manner. This continued until 10 bad bets and 10 good bets had been played.

Part 2

The second part of the game used the selling-price technique described by Becker, DeGroot, and Marschak (1964) and used by Lichtenstein and Slovic

Table 4.1. Probabilities and Win–Loss Data for Bets Used

| Positive Expected Value | | | | | | | Negative Expected Value | | | | | |
| P Bet | | | $ Bet | | | Absolute Expected Value | P Bet | | | $ Bet | | |
Prob. of Winning	Win	Lose	Prob. of Winning	Win	Lose		Prob. of Winning	Win	Lose	Prob. of Winning	Win	Lose
7/12	17	7	2/12	97	11	7	5/12	7	17	10/12	11	97
10/12	9	3	3/12	91	21	7	2/12	3	9	9/12	21	91
9/12	10	2	3/12	73	15	7	3/12	2	10	9/12	15	73
8/12	16	11	3/12	94	22	7	4/12	11	16	9/12	22	94
11/12	12	24	2/12	79	5	9	1/12	24	12	10/12	5	79
11/12	10	2	5/12	65	31	9	1/12	2	10	7/12	31	65
10/12	16	2	5/12	48	12	13	2/12	2	16	7/12	12	48
9/12	18	2	3/12	85	11	13	3/12	2	18	9/12	11	85
10/12	20	10	5/12	64	20	15	2/12	10	20	7/12	20	64
8/12	30	15	4/12	95	25	15	4/12	15	30	8/12	25	95

Note: Abbreviations: P = bet featuring a large probability of winning (positive EV) or losing (negative EV); $ = bet featuring a large amount to win (positive EV) or to lose (negative EV).

(1971). This technique is designed to persuade S to report his true subjective value for the bet; any deviations from this strategy, any efforts to "beat the game," necessarily result in a game of lesser value to S than the game resulting when he honestly reports his subjective evaluations.

The CRT displayed one bet at a time, and the player was told that he "owned" that bet. He could either play the bet or sell it back to the dealer. His task, then, was to state a selling price, defined by E as follows:

Your price for the bet depends on how much you want to play the bet. If you like the bet, and want to play it, you would expect the dealer to pay you for it. So your price would be stated like this: "The *dealer must pay me* _____ chips to buy this bet." But if the bet is a bet you do *not* like and do *not* want to play, you should be willing to give the dealer chips in order to avoid playing the bet. So you should state your price like this: "*I will pay the dealer* _____ chips to get rid of this bet." You may also wish, on some bets, to state a price of *no chips*. This would mean that you would *not* demand that the dealer pay you to buy the bet from you, and also you would *not* be willing to pay the dealer to get rid of the bet.

To choose your selling price, first ask yourself whether you like the bet and want to play it. If the bet looks like a good bet to you, you would like either to play the bet or to sell the bet to the dealer and receive chips from him for sure. Your price for the bet should be all three of these things: (a) the *smallest* number of chips for which you would be willing to sell the bet; (b) the number of chips that you think the bet is worth; (c) just that number of chips so that you don't care what the dealer does. If he buys the bet, you'll be happy. If he refuses to buy the bet, you'll be happy to play it. If you think you'd rather play the bet than sell it for a certain number of chips, then that number of chips is the *wrong* price for you. You should raise your price until you don't care whether you sell the bet or play it.

If you think the bet is a bad bet, you must either play it or *pay the dealer* to take it off your hands. Your price for the bet should be both of these things: (a) the *largest* number of chips you would be willing to pay the dealer to avoid playing this bet; (b) just that number of chips so that you don't care whether the dealer buys the bet or not – the dislike you feel at having to play the bet is just exactly balanced by the dislike you feel for having to pay out that many chips to get rid of the bet.

Players sometimes priced a good bet as if it were a bad bet, and vice versa. The dealer sometimes questioned the price if he thought the player had misread the bet or made a careless error, but such prices were not refused. If the player stated a price for the bet that was more than he could win from it, or offered to pay more to avoid the bet than he could lose, E was instructed to refuse the price, explain why it was not acceptable, and let S respond again.

After the player entered his price on the keyboard, the dealer generated a counteroffer by spinning the roulette wheel to generate a random number r (disregarding 0 and 00) and entering that number into the computer, which used the following rule to generate a counteroffer:

$$\text{counteroffer} = \begin{cases} EV + \dfrac{r}{2} - 10, & \text{if } r \text{ is even} \\ EV + \dfrac{r+1}{2} - 10, & \text{if } r \text{ is odd.} \end{cases}$$

If the counteroffer was equal to, or greater than, the player's price, the bet was sold at the price of the counteroffer. If the counteroffer was less than the player's price, the player played the bet, using the playing procedure described earlier. For example, if a player said −10 (*I'll pay 10 chips to avoid playing the bet*), and the counteroffer was −12 (dealer demands 12 chips), the player played the bet; if the counteroffer was −8 (dealer demands 8 chips), the player would pay the dealer 8 chips and not play the bet.

With this set of counteroffers, the player who states the EV of the bet as his price for each bet will maximize his expected winnings. For this strategy, the EV for the entire transaction (pricing and either selling or playing) for a single bet is EV + 2, and the player will play, on the average, half of the bets, while selling half. To assure that the game had, at best, a 0 EV, players were required to pay "entrance fees," giving the dealer 16 chips before each 8 bets.

After the player priced and either played or sold all 40 bets, his remaining chips were exchanged for money and the game was ended.

Subjects
During the 10 weeks the game was in operation, the dealer recorded the start of 86 games. There were 53 completed games, played by 44 different Ss (1 S completed 3 games; 7 Ss completed 2 games). Only data from these 53 completed games were analyzed.

Although Ss were not questioned about themselves (in fact, they did not have to give their true names), a few did volunteer some background information. Seven of the 44 complete-game players worked in Las Vegas as dealers. Others included a chemist, a ticket vendor for a bus line, a computer programmer, a television director, a mathematician, a sheep rancher, a real-estate broker, an Air Force pilot, an engineer, the owner of a small grocery, and several college students. The dealer's impression was that the game attracted a higher proportion of professional and educated persons than the usual casino clientele.

RESULTS

Stakes and Outcomes
Although players could play for chips worth $1 or $5 each, none ever did. For the 53 complete games, 32 were played for 5¢ a chip, 18 for 10¢, and 3 for 25¢. The highest net win was $83.50, the largest loss was $82.75, the mean outcome was −$2.36, and the interquartile range was −$8.40 to +$5.50.

Excluded Data
In the present study, Ss sometimes placed a positive price on one bet and a negative price on the bet with which it had been paired. Because the present authors assume a different process taking place when S views a bet as favorable (and thus gives it a positive price) than when S views a bet as unfavorable (and thus gives it a negative price), no prediction about reversals can be made

Table 4.2. Frequencies of Responses

| Choice | Positive Expected Value | | | Negative Expected Value | | |
| | Higher Price | | | Higher Price | | |
	P	$	Total	P	$	Total
P	44	185[a]	229	190	46	236
$	25	230	255	85[a]	27	112
Total	69	415	484	275	73	348

Note: Abbreviations: P = bet featuring a large probability of winning (positive EV) or losing (negative EV); $ = bet featuring a large amount to win (positive EV) or to lose (negative EV).
[a] Predicted reversals.

when the prices of the two bets in a pair differ in sign. These data were therefore excluded from the reversal analysis. Most exclusions were made from the negative-EV pairs: Out of 530 pairs of responses, 134 had a positive price given to the $ bet and a negative price given to the P bet. A few additional response pairs were excluded because of a positive P-bet price paired with a negative $-bet price, or a price of 0 paired with a negative price. In all, 182 response pairs (30%) were excluded from the negative-EV pairs. From the positive-EV bets, 46 response pairs (7%) were excluded; most of these had a positive price given to the P bet paired with a negative price given to the $ bet.

Reversals

The left half of Table 4.2 shows the 484 sets of responses made to favorable bets. In the choosing task, the P bet was chosen over the $ bet 229 times (47%). The critical question is what happened when the bets of these 229 pairs were presented singly for pricing. The table shows that in 185 instances, the $ bet received the higher price. This is the critical reversal that was predicted: In 81% of those instances in which the P bet was chosen over the $ bet, S priced the $ bet higher.

A few unpredicted reversals also occurred with the favorable bets. Of the 255 instances in which the $ bet was chosen over the P bet, the P bet later received the higher price 25 times (10%).

The right half of Table 4.2 shows the 348 sets of responses made to unfavorable bets. In the choosing task, the $ bet was chosen over the P bet 112 times (32%). For these unfavorable bets, the critical question is what happened when the bets of these 112 pairs were presented singly for pricing. The table shows that in 85 instances, the P bet received the higher price. This is the predicted reversal: In 76% of those instances in which the $ bet was chosen over the P bet, S priced the P bet higher.

Unpredicted reversals were slightly more frequent with the unfavorable bets than with favorable bets. Of the 236 instances in which the P bet was chosen over the $ bet, the $ bet later received the higher price 46 times (20%).

Was this predominance of predicted reversals over unpredicted reversals widespread across Ss? Six Ss chose the $ bet from all favorable pairs. Thus, predicted reversals were impossible; the rate of such reversals was undefined. Five Ss chose the P bet from all favorable pairs, so that unpredicted reversals were impossible. The remaining 33 of the 44 Ss chose at least one $ bet and at least one P bet, so that rates of both types of reversals (predicted and unpredicted) could be computed. Of these 33 Ss, 28 showed a higher rate of predicted reversals than unpredicted reversals (significant by the sign test, $p < .01$). For negative-EV (unfavorable) bets, 29 of the 44 Ss chose at least one $ bet and at least one P bet. Of these 29 Ss, 23 showed a higher rate of predicted reversals than unpredicted reversals (sign test, $p < .01$). These data indicate that the reversal effects shown in Table 4.2 were widespread across Ss.

Because Ss in this and previous experiments were not asked to respond repeatedly to each stimulus, the reliabilities of the two response tasks are not known. However, as discussed in the previous report (Lichtenstein & Slovic, 1971, pp. 52–53), reasonable assumptions about error rates cannot explain results such as those reported here.

DISCUSSION

There is a natural concern that the results of any experiment may not be replicated outside the confines of the laboratory. But the results of this experiment, carried out in a Las Vegas casino, were strikingly similar to the findings of previous experiments based on college students gambling with hypothetical stakes or small amounts of money. The widespread belief that decision makers can behave optimally when it is worthwhile for them to do so gains no support from this study. The source of the observed information-processing bias appears to be cognitive, not motivational.

In addition, this study demonstrates that the observed bias occurs with unfavorable as well as favorable gambles. For positive-EV bets the observed reversal phenomenon, which depends on Ss setting relatively high prices for the high-payoff $ bets, might be interpreted simply as the result of one or two less interesting biases. First, Ss may believe that they gain some advantage by overpricing bets, even though the design of the task precludes this. Second, by setting high selling prices, Ss increased their chances of playing rather than selling the bets. Thus, the results may stem from a predilection for playing rather than selling bets, thereby enjoying more "action."

With negative-EV bets, however, any tendency to overprice the bets, or any effort to increase the probability of playing the bets, would have worked against the reversal effect. But predicted reversals did occur, because Ss tended to underprice (i.e., avoid, by choosing a large negative price) the $ bets.

The overdependence on payoff cues in pricing a gamble suggests a general hypothesis that the compatibility or commensurability between a cue dimension and the required response will affect the importance of the cue in determining the response. Compatibility-induced biases in information processing may appear in many areas of human judgment. For example, one might expect a used-car buyer to give too much weight to the seller's asking price for the car and too little weight to other factors (e.g., condition, mileage, etc.) when selecting his counteroffer. Or, the monetary awards granted by proposal review committees and by juries in personal-injury suits may be overdetermined by the amount of money that the researcher or the plaintiff has requested.

The strain of amalgamating different types of information into an overall decision may often force an individual to resort to judgmental strategies that do an injustice to his underlying system of values. The systematic bias in the pricing responses of the present study is one demonstration of this. Most individuals are unaware of the biases to which their judgments are susceptible. Research that explores the locus of such biases is a necessary precursor to the development of aids to decision making.

ACKNOWLEDGMENTS

This research was supported by the Wood Kalb Foundation, by Grant GS-32505 from the National Science Foundation, and by Grant MH-21216 from the National Institute of Mental Health. We are particularly grateful to the Four Queens Hotel and Casino, Las Vegas, Nevada; to the late Benjamin Goffstein and to Thomas Callahan, the former and present presidents and general managers of the Four Queens Hotel and Casino; to the members and staff of Nevada's State Gaming Commission and its Gaming Control Board; to John Ponticello, our dealer and *E*; and to John Goetsch and Russel Geiseman, our programmers. We would like to acknowledge the support of Ward Edwards, who directed the research project. Lewis R. Goldberg, Amos Tversky, and Daniel Kahneman gave us valuable comments on the manuscript.

5. Economic Theory of Choice and the Preference Reversal Phenomenon

David M. Grether and Charles R. Plott

A body of data and theory has been developing within psychology that should be of interest to economists. Taken at face value the data are simply inconsistent with preference theory and have broad implications about research priorities within economics. The inconsistency is deeper than the mere lack of transitivity or even stochastic transitivity. It suggests that no optimization principles of any sort lie behind even the simplest of human choices and that the uniformities in human choice behavior that lie behind market behavior may result from principles that are of a completely different sort from those generally accepted. This chapter reports the results of a series of experiments designed to discredit the psychologists' works as applied to economics.

The phenomenon is characterized by the following stylized example. Individuals under suitable laboratory conditions are asked if they prefer lottery A to lottery B as shown in Figure 5.1. In lottery A a random dart is thrown to the interior of the circle. If it hits the line, the subject is paid \$0, and if it hits anywhere else, the subject is paid \$4. Notice that there is a very high probability of winning, so this lottery is called the P bet, standing for probability bet. If lottery B is chosen, a random dart is thrown to the interior of the circle, and the subject receives either \$16 or \$0, depending on where the dart hits. Lottery B is called the \$ bet because there is a very high maximum reward. After indicating a preference between the two lotteries, subjects are asked to place a monetary value on each of the lotteries.

Psychologists have observed that a large proportion of people will indicate a preference for lottery A, the P bet, but place a higher value on the *other* lottery, the \$ bet. The following argument will help us see one way in which this behavior violates preference theory. Let w = initial wealth; $(z,1,0)$ = the state in which A is held and the wealth level is z; $(z,0,1)$ = the state in which B is held and the wealth level is z; $(z,0,0)$ = the state in which neither A nor B are held and the wealth level is z; $\$(A)$ and $\$(B)$ are the respective selling limit prices; $\sim$ and $\succ$ indicate indifference and preference, respectively.

Originally published in the *American Economic Review*, vol. 69, pp. 623–628. Copyright © 1979 by the American Economic Association. Reprinted with permission. The original included an Appendix that is not reprinted here.

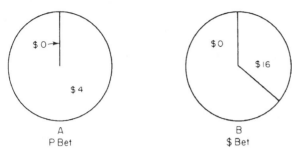

Figure 5.1. Exemplar lotteries.

(1)	$(w + \$(A),0,0) \sim (w,1,0)$	by definition of $\$(A)$
(2)	$(w + \$(B),0,0) \sim (w,0,1)$	by definition of $\$(B)$
(3)	$(w,1,0) \succ (w\ 0,1)$	by the statement of preference of A over B
(4)	$(w + \$(A),0,0) \succ (w + \$(B),0,0)$	by transitivity
(5)	$\$(A) > \$(B)$	by positive "utility value" of wealth

Though (5) follows from the theory, it is not observed.

Notice this behavior is not simply a violation of some type of expected utility hypothesis. The preference measured one way is the *reverse* of preference measured another and seemingly theoretically compatible way. If indeed preferences exist and if the principle of optimization is applicable, then an individual should place a higher reservation price on the object he prefers. The behavior as observed appears to be simply inconsistent with this basic theoretical proposition.

If the results are accepted uncritically and extended to economics, many questions are raised. If preference theory is subject to systematic exception in these simple cases, how many other cases exist? What type of theory of choice can serve as a basis for market theory and simultaneously account for these data? Could such an alternative theory also serve as a basis for welfare economics? Should special extensions of the theory of market choice to other situations, such as crime (Becker, 1968), suicide (Hammermesh & Soss, 1978), marriage (Becker, 1973, 1974), extramarital affairs (Fair, 1978), politics, and so forth, be called into question? How are we to regard cost–benefit measures once we have accepted the fact that the sign of the benefit-minus-cost figure can be *reversed* by simply measuring preference in terms of "most preferred" options rather than in terms of a limit selling or purchase price?

There is little doubt that psychologists have uncovered a systematic and interesting aspect of human choice behavior. The key question is, of course, whether this behavior should be of interest to economists. Specifically, it seems necessary to answer the following: (a) Does the phenomenon exist in situations where economic theory is generally applied? (b) Can the phenomenon be explained by applying standard economic theory or some immediate variant thereof?

This study was designed to answer these two questions. The experiments prior to those reported here were not designed with economics audiences in mind and thus do not answer either question though they are suggestive. In the first section we review the earlier experiments and their shortcomings from an economics point of view. Our experimental design is covered in the second section, and our results are reviewed in the third section. In the end we conclude that the answer to the first question is "yes," and the answer to the second appears to be "no." As reflected in our concluding remarks, we remain as perplexed as the reader who has just been introduced to the problem.

EXISTING EXPERIMENTAL WORK

Experimental results of direct relevance are reported in four papers (Lichtenstein & Slovic, 1971, 1973; Lindman, 1971; Slovic, 1975). The experiments are listed in Table 5.1 beside an array of theories, each of which would either render the experiment irrelevant from an economist's point of view or explain the results in terms of accepted theory. Along with the economic-theoretic explanations, we have listed some psychological-theoretic explanations and some theories that seek to explain the results as artifacts of experimental methods.

Economic-Theoretic Hypotheses

Theory 1: Misspecified Incentives. Almost all economic theory is applied to situations in which the agent choosing is seriously concerned or is at least choosing from among options that in some sense matter. No attempt is made to expand the theory to cover choices from options that yield consequences of no importance. Theories about decision-making costs do suggest that unmotivated choice behavior may be very different from highly motivated choice behavior, but the differences remain essentially unexplored. Thus, the results of experiments in which subjects may be bored, playing games, or otherwise not motivated present no immediate challenges to theory.

On this basis several experiments may be disregarded as applying to economics, even though they may be very enlightening for psychology. In Lichtenstein and Slovic (1971) the first two experiments were made from gambles that involved imaginary money, and in the third, the gambles were for points, the value of which was not revealed until after the choices were made. All experiments by Lindman (1971) involved gambles for "imaginary money." Three of the experiments by Slovic (1975) dealt with the choices among fictitious commodity bundles. The only experiments that cannot be criticized on this ground are Lichtenstein and Slovic (1973), which was conducted on a Las Vegas casino floor for real and binding cash bets, and Experiment 3 of Slovic, in which gambles for values of up to $4 cash or 19 packs of cigarettes were used.

Table 5.1. Coexisting Experimental Results: Relevance and Possibe Explanations

Theoretical Criticism and/or Explanation	Lichtenstein & Slovic (1971) Experiment			Lichtenstein & Slovic (1973)	Lindman (1971)	Slovic (1975) Experiment				This Study Experiment	
	1	2	3			1	2	3	4	1	2
Economic theory											
1. Misspecified incentives	I	I	I	N	I	I	I	N	I	N	N
2. Income effects	N	N	E	?	N	N	N	E	N	N	N
3. Indifference psychological	N	I	I	I	I	I	I	I	I	N	N
4. Strategic responses	E	E	E	E	E	N	N	N	N	E	N
5. Probabilities	I	I	N	?	N	N	N	N	N	N	N
6. Elimination by aspects	N	N	N	N							N
7. Lexicographic semi-order	N	N	N	N						N	N
8. Information processing: Decision costs	E	E	E	?	E	E	E	E	E	N	N
9. Information processing: Response mode, easy justification	E	E	E	E	E	E	E	E	E	E	E
Experimental methods											
10. Confusion and misunderstanding	N	N	N	N	N	N	N	N	N	N	N
11. Frequency low	N	N	N	N	N	N	N	N	N	N	N
12. Unsophisticated subjects	?	?	?	N	?	?	?	?		N	N
13. Experimenters were psychologists	I	I	I	I	I	I	I	I	I	N	N

I = The experiment is irrelevant to economics because of the reason or theory.
N = The experimental results cannot be explained by this reason or theory.
E = The experimental results are consistent with the reason or theory.
? = Data insufficient.

Theory 2: Income Effects. Three different modes of extracting subjects' attitudes have been used in existing experiments. Subjects were asked their preference between pairs[1] of lotteries, they were asked the maximum amount they would pay for the right to play various lotteries, and they were asked the minimum amount for which they would sell various lotteries. Clearly the income position of a subject can differ among these situations and this could account for apparent inconsistencies in preference. In three experiments income effects are of potential importance: Lichtenstein and Slovic (1971), Experiment 3; Lichtenstein and Slovic (1973); and Slovic (1975), Experiment 3.

In Lichtenstein and Slovic (1971), Experiment 3, subjects knew that all the gambles would be played at the end of the experiment. First, the subjects indicated their preferences from among a series of pairs of bets, the most preferred of which was to be played. After these choices, the subjects were given a series of bets for which selling limit prices were extracted by standard techniques (see Becker, DeGroot, & Marschak, 1964). After all choices were made, the relevant bets were played. Because all bets had a positive expected value, subjects had an increasing expected income throughout the experiment. Once one has agreed to play several P bets and expected income has accordingly increased, it is not so surprising that subsequently one is willing to go for riskier but potentially more rewarding gambles. Standard theories of risk taking suggest that risk aversion decreases with income, so as expected income increases, a tendency toward a higher limit selling price (the certainty equivalent for lotteries) would be expected. Thus, the data that show preference reversals are consistent with an "income effect" hypothesis.

In Slovic (1975), Experiment 3, subjects first revealed indifference curves in a cigarette-money space. From this exercise they had an expectation of receiving some cigarettes (up to 19 packs) from lotteries they knew would be played. A preference for a monetary dimension would thus be expected when 2 or 3 days later, subjects were offered a choice between cigarette-money commodity bundles to which they had previously expressed indifference. Again, the "income effect" hypothesis is consistent with the data.

The third case (Lichtenstein & Slovic, 1973) is an experiment conducted on a casino floor. Bets were played as soon as preferences were indicated. The wealth position of the subject at any time depended on the sequence of wins and losses leading up to that time, and these are not reported. Consequently, the relationship between the theory and this experiment cannot be determined.

Theory 3: Indifference. In all experiments except those in Slovic (1975), subjects were required to register a preference among bets. No indications of indifference were allowed. Thus, the preference reversals exhibited in all other experiments could have been due to a systematic resolution of indifference on the

---

[1] Slovic (1975) asked subjects to rank lotteries from sets of different sizes.

part of subjects forced to record a preference. Slovic's results are also consistent with this hypothesis.

Psychological-Theoretic Hypotheses

Theory 4: Strategic Responses. Everyone has engaged in trade and has some awareness of the various distributions of gains that accompany trade. Thus, when asked to name a "selling price," an individual's natural strategic response may be to name a price above any true limit price modulated by what an opponent's preferences are conjectured to be. When asked to name a "buying price," one would tend to understate the values. This strategic reaction to the very words "selling price" may be very difficult to overcome, even though the subject is selling to a passive lottery in which such strategic posturing may actually be harmful.

This theory predicts the reversals of all experiments except those reported by Slovic (1975), in which the words buying and selling were not used. Notice that this theory would predict reversals when selling prices are elicited and fewer reversals, or reversals of the opposite sort, when buying prices are asked for. That is, one can argue that there is little ambiguity about the "value" of a P bet (for example, with probability of .99 win $4 and lose $1 with probability of .01). However, this is not true for the corresponding $ bets (for example, win $16 with probability one-third and lose $2 with probability two-thirds). Thus, any tendency to state selling prices higher than the true reservation prices will primarily affect prices announced for $ bets. This behavior clearly can yield apparent preference reversals of the type reported. The same argument applied to buying prices suggests that there will be a tendency to understate the value of $ bets more than P bets.

Experiment 2 of Lichtenstein and Slovic (1971) used buying prices rather than selling prices. Compared with Experiment 1 (which involved selling prices), Lichtenstein and Slovic report that for Experiment 2 the rate of reversals was significantly lower (significance level at least .01) and the rate of opposite reversals significantly higher (also at least .01). Further, they report that bids for the P bets average $.07 below expected value in Experiment 1, but $.44 below expected value in Experiment 2. Bids for the $ bets were $3.56 higher than expected value in Experiment 1 and $.04 below expected value in Experiment 2. Thus, the data in these two experiments are quite consistent with this theory.

Theory 5: Probabilities. With the exception of Slovic (1975), Experiments 1, 2, and 4, all experiments involved lotteries at some stage. Naturally, if subjective probabilities are not well formed or change during the experiment, consistency among choices is not to be expected. In fact, probabilities in all experiments except Lichtenstein and Slovic (1971), Experiments 1 and 2, were operationally defined, and with the exception of Lichtenstein and Slovic (1973), there was no reason to suspect that they may have changed during the experiment.

Theory 6: Elimination by Aspects. Tversky (1972) developed the elimin-ation-by-aspects model. Let A be a set of "aspects" and let the objects be subsets of A. This theory holds that individuals order the elements of A and then choose from among objects by a lexicographic application of this underlying order. Specifically, the stochastic version holds that an element x of A is chosen at random (perhaps with a probability proportional to its importance), and all objects B, such that $x \notin B$, are then eliminated. The process continued until only one object remains.

This theory runs counter to traditional economic reasoning on two counts. First, the lexicographic application runs directly counter to the principle of sub-stitution (quasi-concavity of utility functions). Second, the random elimination choice process does not sit well with the idea of maximization or "rational" choice.

One implication of the model is a type of moderate stochastic transitivity.[2] The heart of the preference reversal phenomenon was previously shown to be a type of cyclic choice. Such an intransitivity is in violation of the moderate stochastic transitivity property of the model. Thus, the preference-reversal phe-nomenon must be added to Tversky's own work (1969) as situations in which the elimination-by-aspects model does not seem to work.

Theory 7: Lexicographic Semi-order. In a classic paper Tversky (1969) demonstrated that binary choices could cycle in a predictable fashion. The argu-ment used was that choices are made on the basic dimensions of objects, but when for two objects the magnitudes along a dimension become "close," their magnitudes are treated as being equal. Thus, a series of objects x, y, z, and w may be ordered as listed when compared in that order because each is close to those adjacent on a given dimension. Yet, w may be chosen over x because the magnitudes on this dimension are far enough apart to be discernible.

It is difficult to see how this argument can be applied to account for the cycles in the reversal phenomenon. No long chains of binary comparisons were involved. No small magnitude differences, such as those used by Tversky (1969), were present. We suspect that whatever ultimately accounts for the preference reversals will also account for the Tversky intransitivities, but we doubt that it will be the lexicographic semi-order model.

Theory 8: Information Processing – Decision Costs. Individuals have prefer-ences over an attribute space, but the location of an object in this attribute space may not be readily discernible. Resolution of choice problems, which involves locating an object in the attribute space, is a costly, disagreeable activity, so in their attempt to avoid decision costs people tend to adopt the following simple rule. An individual first looks at the "most prominent" dimension or aspect of the object. The magnitude of this aspect, called an "anchor," is used as the value

---

[2] If $P(x, y) \geq 1/2$ and $P(y, z) \geq 1/2$ then $P(x, z) \geq \min [P(x, y), P(y, z)]$.

of the object and is adjusted upward or downward to account for other features. As an empirical generalization the psychologists note that the adjustments are usually inadequate, so the ultimate choice is heavily influenced by the starting point or anchor. Individuals who originally choose the P bet have tended to focus on the probability of winning and inadequately adjust for the low monetary amounts. When asked about selling price or buying price, they naturally focus on dollars first and adjust for the probabilities. Because the adjustments for probabilities are inadequate, the dollar bets tend to be given the higher value. Thus, the "preference-reversal" phenomenon is explained.

This theory is consistent with all experiments where no incentives were used. It is also consistent with the choices from among indifferent objects such as those in the Slovic (1975) study. When incentives are used, however, more effort in decision making is warranted, and the frequency of reversals should go down. Thus, on this theory one might have expected fewer reversals than occurred in the Lichtenstein and Slovic (1973) study, but because no control group (i.e., a group playing the gambles without monetary incentives) existed for this subject pool, the results are inconclusive.

Theory 9: Information Processing – Response Mode and Easy Justification. The anchoring and adjustment mechanism described previously may exist but it may be entirely unrelated to the underlying idea of decision-making costs. Indeed Lichtenstein and Slovic (1971) argue only that "variations in response mode cause fundamental changes in the way people process information, and thus alter the resulting decisions" (p. 16). The view is that of the decision maker "as one who is continually searching for systematic procedures that will produce quick and reasonably satisfactory decisions" (Slovic, 1975, p. 280). On occasion, it is argued that the mechanism is "easy to explain and justify to oneself and to others" (Slovic, 1975, p. 280). The anchoring process described earlier is offered as the mechanism that people adopt. The particular dimension used as an anchor is postulated to be a function of the context in which a decision is being made. Such thinking may not necessarily be contrary to preference theory. Rather, it is as though people have "true preferences" but what they *report* as a preference is dependent on the terms in which the reporting takes place. Certain words or contexts naturally induce some dimensions as anchors whereas others induce other dimensions. The theory is consistent with all observations to date. Details can be found in Slovic.

Experimental Methods

The psychologists whose work we are reporting are careful scientists. Yet a bit of suspicion always accompanies a trip across a disciplinary boundary. In particular, we consider four possible sources of experimental bias.

Theory 10: Confusion and Misunderstanding. In all experiments subjects were trained, rehearsed, and/or tested over procedures and options. In all instances repeated choices were made. In general there is reason to believe there was little confusion or misunderstanding, and in all cases the results hold up even when the responses of potentially confused subjects are removed from the data. However, there is some evidence reported by Lindman (1971) that suggests some type of "learning" takes place with experience. All experimenters reported some very "erratic" choices whereby, for example, a subject offered to pay more for a gamble than the maximum that a favorable outcome would yield.

Theory 11: Frequency Low. If the phenomenon only occurs infrequently or with very few subjects, there may not be a great need for concern or special attention. In fact, however, the behavior is systematic and the rate of reversals is high. Consider, for example, the following results, recalling that a P bet is a lottery with a high probability of winning a modest amount whereas the $ bet has a low probability of winning a relatively large amount of money. The Lichtenstein and Slovic (1971) study found that of 173 subjects indicating a preference for the P bet, 127 (73%) always placed a higher monetary valuation on the $ bet (they called these predicted reversals). On the other hand, the reverse almost never happens. That is, individuals who state that they prefer the $ bet will announce prices that are consistent with their choices. In this same study, for example, 144 subjects *never* made the other reversal (termed unpredicted reversals).

Theory 12: Unsophisticated Subjects. Psychologists tend to use psychology undergraduates who are required to participate in experiments for a grade. With the exception of Lichtenstein and Slovic (1973), the sources of subjects were not made explicit in the studies. If indeed psychology undergraduates were used, one would be hesitant to generalize from such very special populations.

Theory 13: The Experimenters Were Psychologists. In a very real sense, using psychologists as experimenters can be a problem. Subjects nearly always speculate about the purposes of experiments, and psychologists have the reputation for deceiving subjects. It is also well known that subjects' choices are often influenced by what they perceive to be the purpose of the experiment. To give the results additional credibility, we felt that the experimental setting should be removed from psychology.

EXPERIMENTAL DESIGN

Our format was designed to facilitate the maximum comparisons of results between experiments. The gambles used for our experiments (see Table 5.2) were the same ones used by Lichtenstein and Slovic (1971), Experiment 3, where actual cash payoffs were made. They used a roulette wheel to play the gambles and, therefore, all probabilities were stated in thirty-sixths. The random device for our experiments was a bingo cage containing balls numbered 1 to 36. This eliminates the problem of nonoperational probabilities that was raised by Theory 5. All the gambles were of the form: If the number drawn is less than or equal to n, you lose $\$x$, and if the number drawn is greater than n, you win $\$y$.

Table 5.2. Experiment 1: Pairs of Gambles Used in the Experiments

Pairs	Type	Probability of Winning	Amount if Win	Amount if Lose	Expected Value
1	P	35/36	$ 4.00	−$1.00	3.86
	$	11/36	$16.00	−$1.50	3.85
2	P	29/36	$ 2.00	−$1.00	1.42
	$	7/36	$ 9.00	−$ .50	1.35
3	P	34/36	$ 3.00	−$2.00	2.72
	$	18/36	$ 6.50	−$1.00	2.75
4	P	32/36	$ 4.00	−$ .50	3.50
	$	4/36	$40.00	−$1.00	3.56
5	P	34/36	$ 2.50	−$ .50	2.33
	$	14/36	$ 8.50	−$1.50	2.39
6	P	33/36	$ 2.00	−$2.00	1.67
	$	18/36	$ 5.00	−$1.50	1.75

The procedures for both of our experiments were so nearly identical that we shall describe only the first experiment in detail. Only those features of the second experiment that differ from the first will be discussed.

Procedures: Experiment 1

Student volunteers were recruited from economics and political science classes. They were told that it was an economics experiment, that they would receive a minimum of $5, and that the experiment would take no longer than 1 hour. As the subjects arrived, they were randomly divided into two groups. The groups were in separate rooms, and there was no communication between them until after the experiment. Once the experiment was started, subjects were not allowed to communicate with each other, though they were allowed to ask the experimenters questions.

Table 5.3 gives the organization of the experiment. At the start of the experiment the subjects received a set of general instructions that described the nature of the gambles they were to consider and explained how they were to be paid. Throughout the experiments all instructions and other materials handed out were read aloud. The instructions included a sample gamble (not used in the actual experiment): Lose $1 if the number on the ball drawn is less than or equal

Table 5.3. Experiment 1

Parts	Group 1 No Monetary Incentives	Group 2 Monetary Incentives
1	Preferences for pairs (1), (2), (3)	Same
2	Selling prices, all 12 gambles	Same
3	Preferences for pairs (4), (5), (6)	Same

to 12, and win $8 if the number is greater than 12. The way the gambles worked was demonstrated.

Two different monetary incentive systems were used, which together control for Theory 1 and allow Theory 8 to be assessed. In one room (Group 1) subjects were told that they would be asked to make a series of decisions concerning various gambles and that when they were finished they would be paid $7. In the other room (Group 2) subjects were told that at the end of the experiments one of their decisions would be chosen at random (using a bingo cage to determine which one), and their payment would depend on which gamble they chose and on the outcome of that particular gamble. It was explained that they had a credit of $7 and whatever they won or lost would be added to or substracted from that amount. Finally, it was stated that the most they could lose on any of the gambles was $2 so that $5 was the minimum possible payment.[3]

The use of a randomizing device to pick which decision "counted" was intended to reduce the problem of income effects discussed as Theory 2. Strictly speaking, even this procedure does not completely eliminate the possibility of some income effects, but it should reduce their magnitude substantially. Here, there is little opportunity to have a growing expectation of rewards over the course of the experiment.

Part 1 of the experiment was distributed (the subjects were allowed to keep the instructions). This part consisted of three pairs of gambles.[4] For each pair subjects were told to indicate which bet they preferred or if they were indifferent. Subjects were told that if one of these three pairs was chosen at the end of the experiment, the two gambles would be played and that individual payments would be made according to which gamble was listed as preferred. Indifference was allowed, and the subjects were told, "If you check 'Don't care,' the bet you play will be determined by a coin toss." Indifference was thus allowed and operationally defined in conformance with Theory 3.

After all subjects had completed Part 1, the instructions and Part 1 were collected and the instructions for Part 2 were distributed. For Part 2 of the experiments the subjects were asked to give their reservation prices for each of the 12 bets (the order of presentation was randomized). Specifically, subjects were asked "What is the *smallest* price for which you would sell a ticket to the following bet?"[5]

---

[3] This was the only difference in the instructions between the two rooms. In the other room also, a decision was to be chosen randomly at the end of the experiment. However, it was stated that this was just for fun as people often wish to know how much they would have won.

[4] In each pair the bets were referred to as A and B. Assignment of P bets and $ bets to A or B was done randomly. On all materials passed out students were told to write their names, Social Security numbers, and, in the room where payoffs were uncertain, their addresses.

[5] Announced preferences and those inferred from reservation prices should agree, but as this need not be the case with buying prices, no experiments involving buying prices were considered.

To ensure that actual reservation prices were revealed, the method suggested by Becker et al. (1964) was employed. If one of the 12 items were chosen to be played at the end of the experiment, an offer price between $0.00 and $9.99 would be randomly generated, and the subjects would play the gamble if their announced reservation price exceeded the offer price. Otherwise, they would be paid the offer price (in addition to the $7 credit).[6] Thus, our procedures conformed to those used in many other experiments, and the problems raised by Theory 1 were avoided.

To be sure that all subjects fully understood how payments were to be determined, the instructions to Part 2 were rather elaborate. The details included the following: an explanation about why it was in the subjects' best interest to reveal their true reservation prices, a practice gamble, a demonstration of the procedures, and a written test. The correct answers to the test were discussed, and subjects' questions were answered. These procedures were designed to anticipate the problems raised by Theory 10. Subjects were allowed to work on Part 2 at their own pace and were allowed to determine selling prices in whatever order they pleased.

Part 3 was identical to Part 1, except that the remaining three pairs of bets were presented as shown on Table 5.3. Again, for each pair, subjects were asked to indicate a preference for bet A, bet B, or indifference. This procedure controls for a possible order effect implicit in the "cost of decision making" arguments of Theory 8. Once the subject has "invested" in a rule that yields a precise dollar value, then he/she would tend to use it repeatedly when the opportunity arises. Thus, we might expect greater consistency between decisions of Parts 2 and 3 than between those of Parts 1 and 2. After completing this part of the experiment, the subjects were paid as described.

Procedures: Experiment 2

The purpose of this experiment was to test the strategic behavior theory described as Theory 4. The structure of the experiment was identical to that of Experiment 1 with two major exceptions. First, Section 2 of the experiment was replaced at points by a section in which "limit prices" were extracted without references to market-type behavior. Second, subjects were not partitioned according to the method of payment. All subjects were paid with the same procedure as Group 2 in Experiment 1.

The organization of Experiment 2 is shown in Table 5.4. Subjects were randomly divided into two rooms (the same two as used before) and designated as Group 1 and Group 2. Each group received identical instructions, except the order in which the parts were administered was different, as shown in Table 5.4.

Part 2 for Group 1 and Part 4 for Group 2 were identical to Part 2 of Experiment 1. Part 4 for Group 1 and Part 2 for Group 2 consisted of a new section.

---

[6] The offer prices were generated by making three draws (with replacement) from a bingo cage containing balls numbered 0 to 9, these three draws giving the digits of the offer price.

Table 5.4. Experiment 2

Parts	Group 1	Group 2
	Monetary Incentives	
1	Preferences for pairs (1), (2), (3)	
2	Selling prices, all 12 gambles	Dollar equivalents, all 12 gambles
3	Preferences for pairs (4), (5), (6)	
4	Dollar equivalents, all 12 gambles	Selling prices, all 12 gambles

In this new section no words suggestive of market-type activity (for example, selling prices and offer prices) were used. Instead, students were asked to give "the exact dollar amount such that you are indifferent between the bet and the amount of money."

RESULTS

Experiment 1

Table 5.5 summarizes the results for the room in which the subjects' payment was independent of their choices. It is clear that the reversal phenomenon has been replicated: of the 127 choices of P bets, 71 (56%) were inconsistent with the announced reservation prices. By comparison, only 14 (11%) of the 130 choices of $ bets were contradicted by the quoted reservation prices. Allowing the subjects to express indifference appears to have had little effect as indifference was indicated in only 7 (3%) of the 264 choices made.

The propensity to reverse was the same for preferences obtained before and after selling prices for both types of bets. Thus, if asking for selling prices focuses attention on the dollar dimension, it does not stay focused on it. The proportions in which P bets and $ bets were chosen before pricing differed significantly

Table 5.5. Frequencies of Reversals, Experiment 1 (No Incentives)

	Bet	Choices	Reservation Prices		
			Consistent	Inconsistent	Equal
TOTAL	P	127	49	71	7
	$	130	111	14	5
Indifferent		7			
Before giving	P	73	30	39	4
prices	$	56	48	5	3
After giving	P	54	19	32	3
prices	$	74	63	9	2
$n = 44$					

Table 5.6. Frequencies of Reversals, Experiment 1 (With Incentives)

| | Bet | Choices | Reservation Prices | | |
			Consistent	Inconsistent	Equal
TOTAL	P	99	26	69	4
	$	174	145	22	7
Indifferent		3			
Before giving	P	49	15	31	3
prices	$	87	70	12	5
After giving	P	50	11	38	1
prices	$	87	75	10	2
$n = 46$					

from those obtained after the prices (significant at .025 but not at .01). No other statistically significant effects were found.

Table 5.6 shows the corresponding data for the room in which the decisions were made for real money. Clearly (and unexpectedly) the preference-reversal phenomenon is not only replicated, but is even stronger. Seventy percent of the choices of P bets were inconsistent with announced selling prices, whereas reversals occurred for just 13% of the $-bet choices. Choice patterns and reversal rates appear to be the same for choices made before and after obtaining selling prices. The only significant differences between the performance in the two rooms are a higher proportion of selections of the $ bet in the incentive room (easily significant at .01 levels) and also a greater proportion of reversals on P bets (just clears the bar at .05).

We calculated a variety of summary statistics on the prices. The prices for $ bets tended to be higher than the prices for the corresponding P bets and were above their expected values. The distributions are apparently different for the two types of bets. In all 12 cases the mean, median, and estimated standard deviations were greater for the $ bet than for the corresponding P bet. There does not seem to be any systematic difference between the prices quoted in the two rooms. For each of the 12 bets the hypothesis of equal means was rejected only once (the P bet in pair number 2), and the t statistic was just significant at a .05 level. From Table 5.7 one can see that not only were the preference reversals frequent, but also large. The magnitude of the reversals is generally greater for the predicted reversals than for the unpredicted reversals and also tends to be somewhat smaller for the group with incentives "on." Thirty-four individuals (20 in the incentives room and 14 in the other) reversed every time they chose a P bet, and of the 24 individuals who never reversed, 14 of them always chose the $ bet.

Experiment 2
Tables 5.8 and 5.9 summarize the results of Experiment 2. Clearly, the preference-reversal phenomenon has again been replicated, and the strategic

Table 5.7. Experiment 1: Mean Values of Reversals (in Dollars)

	Predicted		Unpredicted	
Bet	Incentives	No Incentives	Incentives	No Incentives
1	1.71	2.49	.40	.79
2	1.45	2.64	.51	.90
3	1.48	1.29	1.00	.25
4	3.31	5.59	3.00	1.83
5	1.52	1.79	.38	1.29
6	.92	1.18	.33	.31

or bargaining behavior explanation shot down. If this explanation had been correct, reversals should have been obtained when using selling prices and not when dollar equivalents were asked for. It is apparent from the tables that this simply is not the case. Further, this theory would have predicted that selling prices should be higher than the monetary equivalents, but this is not true either. The mean selling price exceeded the mean equivalent in only 10 of the 24 cases. Again, in every instance the mean price and dollar amount for a $ bet exceeds the respective means for the corresponding P bet. For each bet, six t tests (testing equality of means within and between rooms) were calculated. Of the 72 tests calculated, the null hypothesis was rejected four times at a significance level of .05 and never at the .01 level. The overall conclusion is that the results obtained using prices and dollar equivalents are essentially the same. In both rooms and by both prices and equivalents, approximately one-half the subjects reversed

Table 5.8. Experiment 2: Selling Prices: Group One

	Bet	Choices	Consistent	Inconsistent	Equal
				Selling Prices	
TOTAL	P	44	8	30	6
	$	72	54	15	3
Indifferent		4			
Preferences before	P	20	5	12	3
prices	$	39	24	12	3
Indifferent		1			
Preferences after	P	24	3	18	3
prices	$	33	30	3	0
Indifferent		3			
				Equivalents	
TOTAL	P	44	4	34	6
	$	72	59	11	2
Indifferent		4			
$n = 20$					

Table 5.9. *Experiment 2: Equivalents: Group Two*

	Bet	Choices	Consistent	Inconsistent	Equal
				Equivalents	
TOTAL	P	44	16	27	1
	$	64	54	9	1
Indifferent		0			
Preferences before	P	22	8	14	0
equivalents	$	32	27	4	1
Preferences after	P	22	8	13	1
equivalents	$	32	27	5	0
				Selling Prices	
TOTAL	P	44	19	22	3
	$	64	51	10	3
$n = 18$					

whenever they chose a P bet. The number of individuals who chose a P bet at least once and never reversed varied between two and four.

CONCLUSION

Needless to say, the results we obtained were not those expected when we initiated this study. Our design controlled for all the economic-theoretic explanations of the phenomenon that we could find. The preference reversal phenomenon, which is inconsistent with the traditional statement of preference theory, remains. It is rather curious that this inconsistency between the theory and certain human choices should be discovered at a time when the theory is being successfully extended to explain choices of nonhumans (see Kagel & Battalio, 1975, 1976).

As is clear from Table 5.1, our design not only controlled for the several possible economic explanations of the phenomena, but also for all but one of the psychological theories considered. Note that all the theories for which we exercised control can be rejected as explanations of the phenomena. Thus, several psychological theories of human choice are also inconsistent with the observed preference reversals. Theory 8 is rejected because reversals do not go down as rewards go up. Theories 6 and 7 are rejected because the original results of Lichtenstein and Slovic (1971) have been replicated.

The one theory that we cannot reject, 9, is in many ways the least satisfactory of those considered because it allows individual choice to depend on the context in which the choices are made. For example, if the mode of response or the wording of the question is a primary determinant of choice, then the way to modify accepted theory is not apparent. Even here, however, we have additional insight. If the questions give "cues" that trigger a mode of thinking, such cues do not linger. The reversals occur regardless of the order in which the questions are asked.

The fact that preference theory and related theories of optimization are subject to exception does not mean that they should be discarded. No alternative theory currently available appears to be capable of covering the same extremely broad range of phenomena. In a sense the exception is an important discovery, as it stands as an answer to those who would charge that preference theory is circular and/or without empirical content. It also stands as a challenge to theorists who may attempt to modify the theory to account for this exception without simultaneously making the theory vacuous.

ACKNOWLEDGMENTS

The financial support supplied by the National Science Foundation and the National Aeronautics and Space Administration is gratefully acknowledged. We wish to express our appreciation to Brian Binger, Elizabeth Hoffman, and Steven Matthews, who served as research assistants.

6. Contingent Weighting in Judgment and Choice

Amos Tversky, Samuel Sattath, and Paul Slovic

The relation of preference between acts or options is the key element of decision theory that provides the basis for the measurement of utility or value. In axiomatic treatments of decision theory, the concept of preference appears as an abstract relation that is given an empirical interpretation through specific methods of elicitation, such as choice and matching. In choice the decision maker selects an option from an offered set of two or more alternatives. In matching the decision maker is required to set the value of some variable to achieve an equivalence between options (e.g., what chance to win $750 is as attractive as 1 chance in 10 to win $2,500?).

The standard analysis of choice assumes procedure invariance: Normatively equivalent procedures for assessing preferences should give rise to the same preference order. Indeed, theories of measurement generally require the ordering of objects to be independent of the particular method of assessment. In classical physical measurement, it is commonly assumed that each object possesses a well-defined quantity of the attribute in question (e.g., length, mass) and that different measurement procedures elicit the same ordering of objects with respect to this attribute. Analogously, the classical theory of preference assumes that each individual has a well-defined preference order (or a utility function) and that different methods of elicitation produce the same ordering of options. To determine the heavier of two objects, for example, we can place them on the two sides of a pan balance and observe which side goes down. Alternatively, we can place each object separately on a sliding scale and observe the position at which the sliding scale is balanced. Similarly, to determine the preference order between options, we can use either choice or matching. Note that the pan balance is analogous to binary choice, whereas the sliding scale resembles matching.

The assumption of procedure invariance is likely to hold when people have well-articulated preferences and beliefs, as is commonly assumed in the classical theory. If one likes opera but not ballet, for example, this preference is likely to emerge regardless of whether one compares the two directly or evaluates them

Originally published in *Psychological Review*, vol. 95, pp. 371–384. Copyright © 1988 by the American Psychological Association. Reprinted with permission.

independently. Procedure invariance may hold even in the absence of precomputed preferences, if people use a consistent algorithm. We do not immediately know the value of 7(8 + 9), but we have an algorithm for computing it that yields the same answer regardless of whether the addition is performed before or after the multiplication. Similarly, procedure invariance is likely to be satisfied if the value of each option is computed by a well-defined criterion, such as expected utility.

Studies of decision and judgment, however, indicate that the foregoing conditions for procedure invariance are not generally true and that people often do not have well-defined values and beliefs (e.g., Fischhoff, Slovic, & Lichtenstein, 1980; March, 1978; Shafer & Tversky, 1985). In these situations, observed preferences are not simply read off from some master list; they are actually constructed in the elicitation process. Furthermore, choice is contingent or context sensitive: It depends on the framing of the problem and on the method of elicitation (Payne, 1982; Slovic & Lichtenstein, 1983; Tversky & Kahneman, 1986). Different elicitation procedures highlight different aspects of options and suggest alternative heuristics, which may give rise to inconsistent responses. An adequate account of choice, therefore, requires a psychological analysis of the elicitation process and its effect on the observed response.

What are the differences between choice and matching, and how do they affect people's responses? Because our understanding of the mental processes involved is limited, the analysis is necessarily sketchy and incomplete. Nevertheless, there is reason to expect that choice and matching may differ in a predictable manner. Consider the following example. Suppose Joan faces a choice between two job offers that vary in interest and salary. As a natural first step, Joan examines whether one option dominates the other (i.e., is superior in all respects). If not, she may try to reframe the problem (e.g., by representing the options in terms of higher order attributes) to produce a dominant alternative (Montgomery, 1983). If no dominance emerges, she may examine next whether one option enjoys a decisive advantage, that is, whether the advantage of one option far outweighs the advantage of the other. If neither option has a decisive advantage, the decision maker seeks a procedure for resolving the conflict. Because it is often unclear how to trade one attribute against another, a common procedure for resolving conflict in such situations is to select the option that is superior on the more important attribute. This procedure, which is essentially lexicographic, has two attractive features. First, it does not require the decision maker to assess the tradeoff between the attributes, thereby reducing mental effort and cognitive strain. Second, it provides a compelling argument for choice that can be used to justify the decision to oneself as well as to others.

Consider next the matching version of the problem. Suppose Joan has to determine the salary at which the less interesting job would be as attractive as the more interesting one. The qualitative procedure described earlier cannot be used to solve the matching problem, which requires a quantitative assessment or a matching of intervals. To perform this task adequately, the decision maker should take into account both the size of the intervals (defined relative to the natural range of variation of the attributes in question) and the relative weights of these attributes. One method of matching first equates the size of the two intervals and then adjusts the constructed interval according to the relative weight of the attribute. This approach is particularly compelling when the attributes are expressed in the same units (e.g., money, percent, test scores), but it may also be applied in other situations where it is easier to compare ranges than to establish a rate of exchange. Because adjustments are generally insufficient (Tversky & Kahneman, 1974), this procedure is likely to induce a relatively flat or uniform weighting of attributes.

The preceding discussion is not meant to provide a comprehensive account of choice or of matching. It merely suggests different heuristics or computational schemes that are likely to be used in the two tasks. If people tend to choose according to the more important dimension, or if they match options by adjusting unweighed intervals, then the two procedures are likely to yield different results. In particular, choice is expected to be more lexicographic than matching; that is, the more prominent attribute will weigh more heavily in choice than in matching. This is the *prominence hypothesis* investigated in the following section.

The discrepancy between choice and matching was first observed in a study by Slovic (1975) that was motivated by the ancient philosophical puzzle of how to choose between equally attractive alternatives. In this study the respondents first matched different pairs of (two-dimensional) options and, in a later session, chose between the matched options. Slovic found that the subjects did not choose randomly but rather tended to select the option that was superior on the more important dimension. This observation supports the prominence hypothesis, but the evidence is not conclusive for two reasons. First, the participants always matched the options prior to the choice; hence, the data could be explained by the hypothesis that the more important dimension looms larger in the later trial. Second, and more important, each participant chose between matched options; hence, the results could reflect a common tie-breaking procedure rather than a genuine reversal of preferences. After all, rationality does not entail a random breaking of ties. A rational person may be indifferent between a cash amount and a gamble but always pick the cash when forced to take one of the two.

To overcome these difficulties we develop in the next section a method for testing the prominence hypothesis that is based entirely on interpersonal (between-subjects) comparisons, and we apply this method to a variety of choice problems. In the following two sections we present a conceptual and mathematical analysis of the elicitation process and apply it to several phenomena of judgment and choice. The theoretical and practical implications of the work are discussed in the final section.

TESTS OF THE PROMINENCE HYPOTHESIS

Interpersonal Tests

We illustrate the experimental procedure and the logic of the test of the prominence hypothesis in a problem involving a choice between job candidates. The participants in the first set of studies were young men and women (ages 20–30 years) who were taking a series of aptitude tests at a vocational testing institute in Tel Aviv, Israel. The problems were presented in writing, and the participants were tested in small groups. They all agreed to take part in the study, knowing it had no bearing on their test scores. Some of the results were replicated with Stanford undergraduates.

Problem 1 (Production Engineer): Imagine that, as an executive of a company, you have to select between two candidates for a position of Production Engineer. The candidates were interviewed by a committee who scored them on two attributes (technical knowledge and human relations) on a scale from 100 (superb) to 40 (very weak). Both attributes are important for the position in question, but technical knowledge is more important than human relations. On the basis of the following scores, which of the two candidates would you choose?

	Technical knowledge	Human relations	[N = 63]
Candidate X	86	76	[65%]
Candidate Y	78	91	[35%]

The number of respondents (N) and the percentage who chose each option are given in brackets on the right side of the table. In this problem, about two thirds of the respondents selected the candidate who has a higher score on the more important attribute (technical knowledge).

Another group of respondents received the same data except that one of the four scores was missing. They were asked "to complete the missing score so that the two candidates would be equally suitable for the job." Suppose, for example, that the lower left value (78) were missing from the table. The respondent's task would then be to generate a score for Candidate Y in technical knowledge so as to match the two candidates. The participants were reminded that "Y has a higher score than X in human relations, hence, to match the two candidates Y must have a lower score than X in technical knowledge."

Assuming that higher scores are preferable to lower ones, it is possible to infer the response to the choice task from the response to the matching task. Suppose, for example, that one produces a value of 80 in the matching task (when the missing value is 78). This means that X's score profile (86, 76) is judged equivalent to the profile (80, 91), which in turn dominates Y's profile (78, 91). Thus, a matching value of 80 indicates that X is preferable to Y. More generally, a matching response above 78 implies a preference for X; a matching response below 78 implies a preference for Y; and a matching response of 78 implies indifference between X and Y.

Formally, let (X_1, X_2) and (Y_1, Y_2) denote the values of options X and Y on Attributes 1 and 2, respectively. Let V be the value of Y_1 for which the options are matched. We show that, under the standard assumptions, X is preferred to Y if and only if $V > Y_1$. Suppose $V > Y_1$, then (X_1, X_2) is equivalent to (V, Y_2) by matching, (V, Y_2) is preferred to (Y_1, Y_2) by dominance, hence, X is preferred to Y by transitivity. The other cases are similar.

We use the subscript 1 to denote the primary, or the more important, dimension and the subscript 2 to denote the secondary, or the less important, dimension – whenever they are defined. If neither option dominates the other, X denotes the option that is superior on the primary dimension and Y denotes the option that is superior on the secondary dimension. Thus, X_1 is better than Y_1, and Y_2 is better than X_2.

Let C denote the percentage of respondents who chose X over Y, and let M denote the percentage of people whose matching response favored X over Y. Thus, C and M measure the tendency to decide according to the more important dimension in the choice and in the matching tasks, respectively. Assuming random allocation of subjects, procedure invariance implies $C = M$, whereas the prominence hypothesis implies $C > M$. As was shown earlier, the two contrasting predictions can be tested by using aggregate between-subjects data.

To estimate M, we presented four different groups of about 60 respondents each with the data of Problem 1, each with a different missing value, and we asked them to match the two candidates. The following table presents the values of M derived from the matching data for each of the four missing values, which are given in parentheses.

	1. Technical knowledge	2. Human relations
Candidate X	32% (86)	33% (76)
Candidate Y	44% (78)	26% (91)

There were no significant differences among the four matching groups, although M was greater when the missing value was low rather than high ($M_L = 39 > 29 = M_H$) and when the missing value referred to the primary rather than to the secondary attribute ($M_1 = 38 > 30 = M_2$). Overall, the matching data yielded $M = 34\%$ compared with $C = 65\%$ obtained from choice ($p < .01$). This result supports the hypothesis that the more important attribute (e.g., technical knowledge) looms larger in choice than in matching.

In Problem 1, it is reasonable to assume – as stated – that for a production engineer, technical knowledge is more important than human relations. Problem 2 had the same structure as Problem 1, except that the primary and secondary attributes were manipulated. Problem 2 dealt with the choice between candidates for the position of an advertising agent. The candidates were characterized by their scores on two dimensions: creativity and competence. One-half of the participants were told that "for the position in question, creativity is more important than competence," whereas the other half of the participants were told the opposite. As in Problem 1, most participants (65%, $N = 60$) chose according to the more important attribute (whether it was creativity or competence) but only 38% ($N = 276$) of the matching responses favored X over Y. Again, M was higher for the primary than for the secondary attribute, but all four values of M were smaller than C. The next two problems involve policy choices concerning safety and the environment.

Problem 3 (Traffic Accidents): About 600 people are killed each year in Israel in traffic accidents. The ministry of transportation investigates various programs to reduce the number of casualties. Consider the following two programs, described in terms of yearly costs (in millions of dollars) and the number of casualties per year that is expected following the implementation of each program.

	Expected number of casualties	Cost	[N = 96]
Program X	500	$55M	[67%]
Program Y	570	$12M	[33%]

Which program do you favor?

The data on the right side of the table indicate that two-thirds of the respondents chose Program X, which saves more lives at a higher cost per life saved. Two other groups matched the cost of either Program X or Program Y so as to make the two programs equally attractive. The overwhelming majority of matching responses in both groups (96%, $N = 146$) favored the more economical Program Y that saves fewer lives. Problem 3 yields a dramatic violation of invariance: $C = 68\%$ but $M = 4\%$. This pattern follows from the prominence hypothesis, assuming the number of casualties is more important than cost. There was no difference between the groups that matched the high ($55M) or the low ($12M) values.

A similar pattern of responses was observed in Problem 4, which involves an environmental issue. The participants were asked to compare two programs for the control of a polluted beach:

Program X: A comprehensive program for a complete clean-up of the beach at a yearly cost of $750,000 to the taxpayers.
Program Y: A limited program for a partial clean-up of the beach (that will not make it suitable for swimming) at a yearly cost of $250,000 to the taxpayers.

Assuming the control of pollution is the primary dimension and the cost is secondary, we expect that the comprehensive program will be more popular in choice than in matching. This prediction was confirmed: $C = 48\%$ ($N = 104$) and $M = 12\%$ ($N = 170$). The matching data were obtained from two groups of respondents who assessed the cost of each program so as to match the other. As in Problem 3, these groups gave rise to practically identical values of M.

Because the choice and the matching procedures are strategically equivalent, the rational theory of choice implies $C = M$. The two procedures, however, are not informationally equivalent because the missing value in the matching task is available in the choice task. To create an informationally equivalent task we modified the matching task by asking respondents, prior to the assessment of the missing value, (a) to consider the value used in the choice problem and indicate first whether it is too high or too low, and (b) to write down the value that they consider appropriate. In Problem 3, for example, the modified procedure read as follows:

	Expected number of casualties	Cost
Program X	500	?
Program Y	570	$12M

You are asked to determine the cost of Program X that would make it equivalent to Program Y. (a) Is the value of $55M too high or too low? (b) What is the value you consider appropriate?

The modified matching procedure is equivalent to choice not only strategically but also informationally. Let C^* be the proportion of responses to Question (a) that lead to the choice of X (e.g., "too low" in the preceding example). Let M^* be the proportion of (matching) responses to Question (b) that favor option X (e.g., a value that exceeds $55M in the preceding example). Thus, we may view C^* as choice in a matching context and M^* as matching in a choice context. The values of C^* and M^* for Problems 1–4 are presented in Table 6.1, which yields the ordering $C > C^* > M^* > M$. The finding $C > C^*$ shows that merely framing the question in a matching context reduces the relative weight of the primary dimension. Conversely, $M^* > M$ indicates that placing the matching task after a choice-like task increases the relative weight of the primary dimension. Finally, $C^* > M^*$ implies a within-subject and within-problem violation of invariance in which the response to Question (a) favors X and the response to Question (b) favors Y. This pattern of responses indicates a failure, on the part of some subjects, to appreciate the logical connection between Questions (a) and (b). It is noteworthy, however, that 86% of these inconsistencies follow the pattern implied by the prominence hypothesis.

In the previous problems, the primary and the secondary attributes were controlled by the instructions, as in Problems 1 and 2, or by the intrinsic value of the attributes, as in Problems 3 and 4. (People generally agree that saving lives and eliminating pollution are more important goals than cutting public expenditures.) The next two problems involved benefit plans in which the primary and the secondary dimensions were determined by economic considerations.

Table 6.1. *Percentages of Responses Favoring the Primary Dimension Under Different Elicitation Procedures*

	Dimensions		Choice	Information Control		Matching	
	Primary	Secondary	(C)	C*	M*	(M)	θ
Problem:							
1. Engineer	Technical knowledge	Human relations	65	57	47	34	.82
N			63	156	151	267	
2. Agent	Competence	Creativity	65	52	41	38	.72
N			60	155	152	276	
3. Accidents	Casualties	Cost	68	50	18	4	.19
N			105	96	82	146	
4. Pollution	Health	Cost	48	32	12	12	.45
N			104	103	94	170	
5. Benefits	1 year	4 years	59			46	.86
N			56			46	
6. Coupons	Books	Travel	66			11	.57
N			58			193	
Unweighted mean			62	48	30	24	

C = percentage of respondents who chose X over Y; M = percentage of respondents whose matching responses favored X over Y; C^* = percentage of responses to Question (a) that lead to the choice of X; M^* = percentage of matching responses to Question (b) that favor option X.

Problem 5 (Benefit Plans): Imagine that, as a part of a profit-sharing program, your employer offers you a choice between the following plans. Each plan offers two payments, in 1 year and in 4 years.

	Payment in 1 year	Payment in 4 years	[N = 36]
Plan X	$2,000	$2,000	[59%]
Plan Y	$1,000	$4,000	[41%]

Which plan do you prefer?

Because people surely prefer to receive a payment sooner rather than later, we assume that the earlier payment (in 1 year) acts as the primary attribute, and the later payment (in 4 years) acts as the secondary attribute. The results support the hypothesis: $C = 59\%$ ($N = 56$) whereas $M = 46\%$ ($N = 46$).

Problem 6 resembled Problem 5 except that the employee was offered a choice between two bonus plans consisting of a different combination of coupons for books and for travel. Because the former could be used in a large chain of bookstores, whereas the latter were limited to organized tours with a particular travel agency, we assumed that the book coupons would serve as the primary dimension. Under this interpretation, the prominence effect emerged again: $C = 66\%$ ($N = 58$) and $M = 11\%$ ($N = 193$). As in previous problems, M was

Table 6.2. Percentages of Respondents ($N = 101$) Who Chose Between Matched Alternatives ($M = 50\%$) According to the Primary Dimension (After Slovic, 1975)

	Dimensions			
Alternatives	Primary	Secondary	Choice Criterion	C
1. Baseball players	Batting average	Home runs	Value to team	62
2. College applicants	Motivation	English	Potential success	69
3. Gifts	Cash	Coupons	Attractiveness	85
4. Typists	Accuracy	Speed	Typing ability	84
5. Athletes	Chin-ups	Push-ups	Fitness	68
6. Routes to work	Time	Distance	Attractiveness	75
7. Auto tires	Quality	Price	Attractiveness	67
8. TV commercials	Number	Time	Annoyance	83
9. Readers	Comprehension	Speed	Reading ability	79
10. Baseball teams	% of games won against first place team	% of games won against last place team	Standing	86
Unweighted mean				76

C = percentage of respondents who chose X over Y.

greater when the missing value was low rather than high ($M_L = 17 > 3 = M_H$) and when the missing value referred to the primary rather than the secondary attribute ($M_1 = 19 > 4 = M_2$). All values of M, however, were substantially smaller than C.

Intrapersonal Tests

Slovic's (1975) original demonstration of the choice-matching discrepancy was based entirely on an intrapersonal analysis. In his design, the participants first matched the relevant option and then selected between the matched options at a later date. They were also asked afterward to indicate the more important attribute in each case. The main results are summarized in Table 6.2, which presents for each choice problem the options, the primary and the secondary attributes, and the resulting values of C. In every case, the value of M is 50% by construction.

The results indicate that, in all problems, the majority of participants broke the tie between the matched options in the direction of the more important dimension as implied by the prominence hypothesis. This conclusion held regardless of whether the estimated missing value belonged to the primary or the secondary dimension, or whether it was the high value or the low value on the dimension. Note that the results of Table 6.2 alone could be explained by a shift in weight following the matching procedure (because the matching always preceded the choice) or by the application of a common tie-breaking procedure (because for each participant the two options were matched). These explanations, however, do not apply to the interpersonal data of Table 6.1.

On the other hand, Table 6.2 demonstrates the prominence effect within the data of each subject. The value of C was only slightly higher (unweighted mean: 78) when computed relative to each subject's ordering of the importance of the dimensions (as was done in the original analysis), presumably because of the general agreement among the respondents about which dimension was primary.

THEORETICAL ANALYSIS

The data described in the previous section show that the primary dimension looms larger in choice than in matching. This effect gives rise to a marked discrepancy between choice and matching, which violates the principle of procedure invariance assumed in the rational theory of choice. The prominence effect raises three general questions. First, what are the psychological mechanisms that underlie the choice-matching discrepancy and other failures of procedure invariance? Second, what changes in the traditional theory are required to accommodate these effects? Third, what are the implications of the present results to the analysis of choice in general and the elicitation of preference in particular? The remainder of this chapter is devoted to these questions.

The Compatibility Principle

One possible explanation of the prominence effect, introduced earlier in this chapter, is the tendency to select the option that is superior on the primary dimension, in situations where the other option does not have a decisive advantage on the secondary dimension. This procedure is easy to apply and justify because it resolves conflict on the basis of qualitative arguments (i.e., the prominence ordering of the dimensions) without establishing a rate of exchange. The matching task, on the other hand, cannot be resolved in the same manner. The decision maker must resort to quantitative comparisons to determine what interval on one dimension matches a given interval on the second dimension. This requires the setting of a common metric in which the attributes are likely to be weighted more equally, particularly when it is natural to match their ranges or to compute cost per unit (e.g., the amount of money spent to save a single life).

It is instructive to distinguish between qualitative and quantitative arguments for choice. Qualitative, or ordinal, arguments are based on the ordering of the levels within each dimension, or on the prominence ordering of the dimensions. Quantitative, or cardinal, arguments are based on the comparison of value differences along the primary and the secondary dimensions. Thus, dominance and a lexicographic ordering are purely qualitative decision rules, whereas most other models of multiattribute choice make essential use of quantitative considerations. The prominence effect indicates that qualitative considerations loom larger in the ordinal procedure of choice than in the cardinal procedure of matching, or equivalently, that quantitative considerations loom larger in matching than in choice. The prominence hypothesis, therefore, may be construed as an example of a more general principle of compatibility.

The choice-matching discrepancy, like other violations of procedure invariance, indicates that the weighting of the attributes is influenced by the method of elicitation. Alternative procedures appear to highlight different aspects of the options and thereby induce different weights. To interpret and predict such effects, we seek explanatory principles that relate task characteristics to the weighting of attributes and the evaluation of options. One such explanation is the compatibility principle. According to this principle, the weight of any input component is enhanced by its compatibility with the output. The rationale for this principle is that the characteristics of the task and the response scale prime the most compatible features of the stimulus. For example, the pricing of gambles is likely to emphasize payoffs more than probability because both the response and the payoffs are expressed in dollars. Furthermore, noncompatibility (in content, scale, or display) between the input and the output requires additional mental transformations, which increase effort and error, and reduce confidence and impact (Fitts & Seeger, 1953; Wickens, 1984). We shall next illustrate the compatibility principle in studies of prediction and similarity and then develop a formal theory that encompasses a variety of compatibility effects, including the choice-matching discrepancy and the preference-reversal phenomenon.

A simple demonstration of scale compatibility is shown in the following experiment. The subjects ($N = 234$) were asked to predict the judgments of an admission committee of a small, selective college. For each of 10 applicants the subjects received two items of information: a rank on the verbal section of the Scholastic Aptitude Test (SAT) and the presence or absence of strong extracurricular activities. The subjects were told that the admission committee ranks all 500 applicants and accepts about the top fourth. Half of the subjects predicted the rank assigned to each applicant, whereas the other half predicted whether each applicant was accepted or rejected.

The compatibility principle implies that the numerical data (i.e., SAT rank) will loom larger in the numerical prediction task, whereas the categorical data (i.e., the presence or absence of extracurricular activities) will loom larger in the categotical prediction of acceptance or rejection. The results confirmed the hypothesis. For each pair of applicants, in which neither one dominates the other, the percentage of responses that favored the applicant with the higher SAT was recorded. Summing across all pairs, this value was 61.4% in the numerical prediction task and 44.6% in the categorical prediction task. The difference between the groups is highly significant. Evidently, the numerical data had more impact in the numerical task, whereas the categorical data had more impact in the categorical task. This result demonstrates the compatibility principle and reinforces the proposed interpretation of the choice-matching discrepancy in which the relative weight of qualitative arguments is larger in the qualitative method of choice than in the quantitative matching procedure.

In the previous example, compatibility was induced by the formal correspondence between the scales of the dependent and the independent variables. Compatibility effects can also be induced by semantic correspondence, as illustrated in the following example, taken from the study of similarity. In general, the similarity of objects (e.g., faces, people, letters) increases with the salience of the features they share and decreases with the salience of the features that distinguish between them. More specifically, the contrast model (Tversky, 1977) represents the similarity of objects as a linear combination of the measures of their common and their distinctive features. Thus, the similarity of a and b is monotonically related to

$$\theta f(A \cap B) - g(A \triangle B).$$

where $A \cap B$ is the set of features shared by a and b, and $A \triangle B = (A - B) \cup (B - A)$ is the set of features that belongs to one object and not to the other. The scales f and g are the measures of the respective feature sets.

The compatibility hypothesis suggests that common features loom larger in judgments of similarity than in judgments of dissimilarity, whereas distinctive features loom larger in judgments of dissimilarity than in judgments of similarity. As a consequence, the two judgments are not mirror images. A pair of objects with many common and many distinctive features could be judged as more similar, as well as more dissimilar, than another pair of objects with fewer common and fewer distinctive features. Tversky and Gati (1978) observed this pattern in the comparison of pairs of well-known countries with pairs of countries that were less well known to the respondents. For example, most subjects in the similarity condition selected East Germany and West Germany as more similar to each other than Sri Lanka and Nepal, whereas most subjects in the dissimilarity condition selected East Germany and West Germany as more different from each other than Sri Lanka and Nepal. These observations were explained by the contrast model with the added assumption that the relative weight of the common features is greater in similarity than in dissimilarity judgments (Tversky, 1977).

Contingent Tradeoff Models

To accommodate the compatibility effects observed in studies of preference, prediction, and judgment, we need models in which the tradeoffs among inputs depend on the nature of the output. In the present section we develop a hierarchy of models of this type, called contingent tradeoff models. For simplicity, we investigate the two-dimensional case and follow the choice-matching terminology. Extensions and applications are discussed later. It is convenient to use $A = a,b,c,\ldots$ and $Z = z,y,x,\ldots$ to denote the primary and the secondary attributes, respectively, whenever they are properly defined. The object set S is given by the product set $A \times Z$, with typical elements az, by, and so on. Let $\geq_c$ be the preference relation obtained by choice, and let $\geq_m$ be the preference relation derived from matching.

As in the standard analysis of indifference curves (e.g., Varian, 1984, Ch. 3), we assume that each $\geq_i$, $i = c, m$, is a weak order, that is, reflexive, connected, and transitive. We also assume that the levels of each attribute are consistently ordered, independent of the (fixed) level of the other attribute. That is,

$$az \geq_i bz \text{ iff } ay \geq_i by \quad \text{and} \quad az \geq_i ay \text{ iff } bz \geq_i by, i = c, m.$$

Under these assumptions, in conjunction with the appropriate structural conditions (see, e.g., Krantz, Luce, Suppes, & Tversky, 1971, Ch. 7), there exist functions F_i, G_i, and U_i, defined on A, Z, and $Re \times Re$, respectively, such that

$$az \geq_i by \text{ iff } U_i[F_i(a), G_i(z)] \geq U_i[F_i(b), G_i(y)], \tag{1}$$

where U_i, $i = c, m$, is monotonically increasing in each of its arguments.

Equation 1 imposes no constraints on the relation between choice and matching. Although our data show that the two orders do not generally coincide, it seems reasonable to suppose that they do coincide in unidimensional comparisons. Thus, we assume

$$az \geq_c bz \text{ iff } az \geq_m bz \quad \text{and} \quad az \geq_c ay \text{ iff } az \geq_m ay.$$

It is easy to see that this condition is both necessary and sufficient for the monotonicity of the respective scales. That is,

$$F_c(b) \geq F_c(a) \text{ iff } F_m(b) \geq F_m(a) \quad \text{and} \quad G_c(z) \geq G_c(y) \text{ iff } G_m(z) \geq G_m(y). \tag{2}$$

Equations 1 and 2 define the general contingent tradeoff model that is assumed throughout. The other models discussed in this section are obtained by imposing further restrictions on the relation between choice and matching. The general model corresponds to a dual indifference map, that is, two families of indifference curves, one induced by choice and one induced by matching. A graphical illustration of a dual map is presented in Figure 6.1.

We next consider a more restrictive model that constrains the relation between the rates of substitution of the two attributes obtained by the two elicitation procedures. Suppose the indifference curves are differentiable, and let RS_i denote the rate of substitution between the two attributes (A and Z) according to procedure $i = c, m$. Thus, $RS_i = F\sqrt{G_i}$, where F_i, and G_i, respectively, are the partial derivatives of U_i with respect to F_i and G_i. Hence, $RS_i(az)$ is the negative of the slope of the indifference curve at the point az. Note that RS_i is a meaningful quantity, even though F_i, G_i, and U_i are only ordinal scales.

A contingent tradeoff model is proportional if the ratio of RS_c to RS_m is the same at each point. That is,

$$RS_c(az)/RS_m(az) = \text{constant}. \tag{3}$$

Recall that in the standard economic model, the foregoing ratio equals 1. The proportional model assumes that this ratio is a constant, but not necessarily 1. The indifference maps induced by choice and by matching, therefore, can be mapped into each other by multiplying the RS value at every point by the same constant.

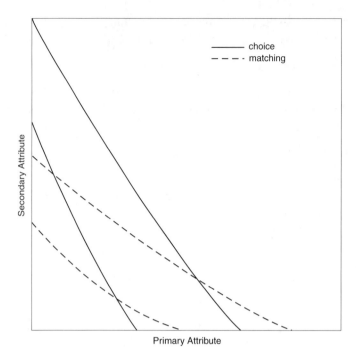

Figure 6.1. A dual indifference map induced by the general model (Equations 1 and 2).

Both the general and the proportional model impose few constraints on the utility functions U_i. In many situations, preferences between multiattribute options can be represented additively. That is, there exist functions F_i and G_i defined on A and Z, respectively, such that

$$az \geq_i by \text{ iff } F_i(a) + G_i(z) \geq F_i(b) + G_i(y), \ i = c, m, \tag{4}$$

where F_i and G_i are interval scales with a common unit. The existence of such an additive representation is tantamount to the existence of a monotone transformation of the axes that maps all indifference curves into parallel straight lines.

Assuming the contingent tradeoff model, with the appropriate structural conditions, the following cancellation condition is both necessary and sufficient for additivity (Equation 4; see Krantz et al., 1971, Ch. 6):

$$ay \geq_i bx \quad \text{and} \quad bz \geq_i cy \text{ imply } az \geq_i cx, \ i = c, m.$$

If both proportionality and additivity are assumed, we obtain a particularly simple form, called the contingent weighting model, in which the utility scales F_c, F_m and G_c, G_m are linearly related. In other words, there is a monotone transformation of the axes that simultaneously linearizes both sets of indifference curves. Thus, if both Equations 3 and 4 hold, there exist functions F and G

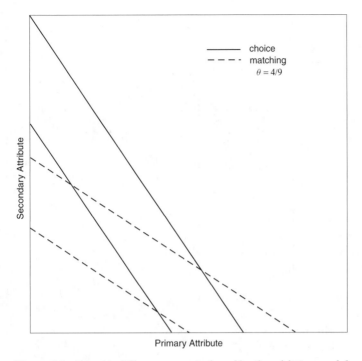

Figure 6.2. A dual indifference map induced by the additive model (Equation 4).

defined on A and Z, respectively, and constants $\alpha_i \beta_i$, $i = c, m$, such that

$$az \geq_i by \ \text{ iff } \ \alpha_i F(a) + \beta_i G(z) \geq \alpha_i F(b) + \beta_i G(y)$$
$$\text{iff } \ F(a) + \theta_i G(z) \geq F(b) + \theta_i G(y), \tag{5}$$

where $\theta_i = \beta_i / \alpha_i$. In this model, therefore, the indifference maps induced by choice and by matching are represented as two sets of parallel straight lines that differ only in slope $-\theta_i$, $i = c, m$ (see Figure 6.2). We are primarily interested in the ratio $\theta = \theta_c / \theta_m$ of these slopes.

Because the rate of substitution in the additive model is constant, it is possible to test proportionality (Equation 3) without assessing local RS_i. In particular, the contingent weighting model (Equation 5) implies the following interlocking condition:

$$ax \geq_c bw, \ dw \geq_c cx, \quad \text{and} \quad by \geq_m az \ \text{imply} \ dy \geq_m cz,$$

and the same holds when the attributes (A and Z) and the orders ($\geq_c$ and $\geq_m$) are interchanged. Figure 6.3 presents a graphic illustration of this condition. The interlocking condition is closely related to triple cancellation, or the Reidemeister condition (see Krantz et al., 1971, 6.2.1), tested by Coombs, Bezembinder, and Goode (1967). The major difference between the assumptions is that the present interlocking condition involves two orders rather than one. This condition says,

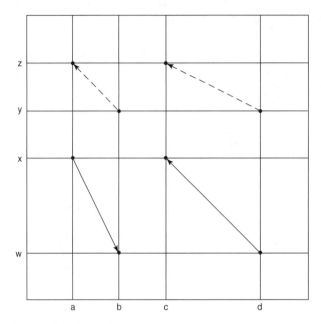

Figure 6.3. A graphic illustration of the interlocking condition where arrows denote preferences.

in effect, that the intradimensional ordering of A-intervals or Z-intervals is independent of the method of elicitation. This can be seen most clearly by deriving the interlocking condition from the contingent weighting model. From the hypotheses of the condition, in conjunction with the model, we obtain

$$F(a) + \theta_c G(x) \geq F(b) + \theta_c G(w) \quad \text{or} \quad \theta_c[G(x) - G(w)] \geq F(b) - F(a)$$
$$F(d) + \theta_c G(w) \geq F(c) + \theta_c G(x) \quad \text{or} \quad F(d) - F(c) \geq \theta_c[G(x) - G(w)]$$
$$F(b) + \theta_m G(y) \geq F(a) + \theta_m G(z) \quad \text{or} \quad F(b) - F(a) \geq \theta_m[G(z) - G(y)].$$

The right-hand inequalities yield

$$F(d) - F(c) \geq \theta_m[G(z) - G(y)] \quad \text{or} \quad F(d) + \theta_m G(y) \geq F(c) + \theta_m G(z),$$

hence $dy \geq_m cz$ as required.

The interlocking condition is not only necessary but also sufficient, because it implies that the inequalities

$$F_i(d) - F_i(c) \geq F_i(b) - F_i(a) \quad \text{and} \quad G_i(z) - G_i(y) \geq G_i(x) - G_i(w)$$

are independent of $i = c, m$, that is, the two procedures yield the same ordering of intradimensional intervals. But because F_c and F_m (as well as G_c and G_m) are interval scales, they must be linearly related. Thus, there exist functions F and G and constants α_i, β_i such that

$$az \geq_i by \text{ iff } \alpha_i F(a) + \beta_i G(z) \geq \alpha_i F(b) + \beta_i G(y).$$

Thus, we have established the following result.

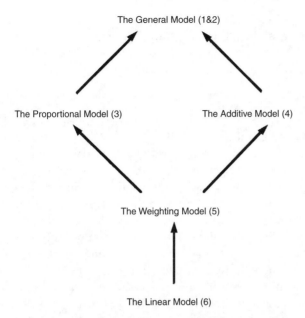

The General Model (1&2)

The Proportional Model (3)   The Additive Model (4)

The Weighting Model (5)

The Linear Model (6)

Figure 6.4. A hierarchy of contingent preference models. (Implications are denoted by arrows.)

Theorem: Assuming additivity (Equation 4), the contingent weighting model (Equation 5) holds iff the interlocking condition is satisfied.

Perhaps the simplest, and most restrictive, instance of Equation 5 is the case where A and Z are sets of real numbers and both F and G are linear. In this case, the model reduces to

$$az \geq_i by \text{ iff } \alpha_i a + \beta_i z \geq \alpha_i b + \beta_i y \qquad (6)$$
$$\text{iff } a + \theta_i z \geq b + \theta_i y, \; \theta_i = \beta_i/\alpha_i, \; i = c, m.$$

The hierarchy of contingent tradeoff models is presented in Figure 6.4, where implications are denoted by arrows.

In the following section we apply the contingent weighting model to several sets of data and estimate the relative weights of the two attributes under different elicitation procedures. Naturally, all the models of Figure 6.4 are consistent with the compatibility hypothesis. We use the linear model (Equation 6) because it is highly parsimonious and reduces the estimation to a single parameter $\theta = \theta_c/\theta_m$. If linearity of scales or additivity of attributes is seriously violated in the data, higher models in the hierarchy should be used. The contingent weighting model can be readily extended to deal with more than two attributes and methods of elicitation.

The same formal model can be applied when the different preference orders $\geq_i$ are generated by different individuals rather than by different procedures. Indeed, the interlocking condition is both necessary and sufficient for representing the (additive) preference orders of different individuals as variations in the weighting of attributes. (This notion underlies the INDSCAL approach to multidimensional scaling, Carroll, 1972.) The two representations can be naturally combined to accommodate both individual differences and procedural variations. The following analyses focus on the latter problem.

APPLICATIONS

The Choice-Matching Discrepancy

We first compute $\theta = \theta_c/\theta_m$ from the choice and matching data, summarized in Table 6.1. Let $C(az, by)$ be the percentage of respondents who chose az over by, and let $M(az, by)$ be the percentage of respondents whose matching response favored az over by. Consider the respondents who matched the options by adjusting the second component of the second option. Because different respondents produced different values of the missing component (y), we can view $M(az, b)$ as a (decreasing) function of the missing component. Let y be the value of the second attribute for which $M(az, by) = C(az, by)$.

If the choice and the matching agree, $\bar{y}$ should be equal to y, whereas the prominence hypothesis implies that $\bar{y}$ lies between y and z (i.e., $|z - y| \geq |z - \bar{y}|$). To estimate θ from these data, we introduce an additional assumption, in the spirit of probabilistic conjoint measurement (Falmagne, 1985, Ch. 11), which relates the linear model (6) to the observed percentage of responses:

$$M(az, b\bar{y}) = C(az, by) \text{ iff}$$
$$(a + \theta_m z) - (b + \theta_m \bar{y}) = (a + \theta_c z) - (b + \theta_c y) \text{ iff} \tag{7}$$
$$\theta_m(z - \bar{y}) = \theta_c(z - y).$$

Under this assumption we can compute

$$\theta = \theta_c/\theta_m = (z - \bar{y})/(z - y),$$

and the same analysis applies to the other three components (i.e., $\bar{a}$, $\bar{b}$, and $\bar{z}$).

We applied this method to the aggregate data from Problems 1 to 6. The average values of θ, across subjects and components, are displayed in Table 6.1 for each of the six problems. The values of $\theta = \theta_c/\theta_m$ are all less than unity, as implied by the prominence hypothesis. Note that θ provides an alternative index of the choice-matching discrepancy that is based on Equations 6 and 7 – unlike the difference between C and M that does not presuppose any measurement structure.

Prediction of Performance

We next use the contingent weighting model to analyze the effect of scale compatibility observed in a study of the prediction of students' performance, conducted by Slovic, Griffen, and Tversky (1990). The subjects ($N = 234$) in this study were asked to predict the performance of 10 students in a course (e.g., History) on the basis of their performance in two other courses (e.g., Philosophy and English). For each of the 10 students, the subjects received a grade in one course (from A to D) and a class rank (from 1 to 100) in the other course. One-half of the respondents were asked to predict a grade, and the other half were asked to predict class rank. The courses were counterbalanced across respondents. The compatibility principle implies that a given predictor (e.g., grade in Philosophy) will be given more weight when the predicted variable is expressed on the same scale (e.g., grade in History) than when it is expressed on a different scale (e.g., class rank in History). The relative weight of grades to ranks, therefore, will be higher in the group that predicts grades than in the group that predicts ranks.

Let (r_i, g_j) be a student profile with rank i in the first course and grade j in the second. Let r_{ij} and g_{ij} denote, respectively, the predicted rank and grade of that student. The ranks range from 1 to 100, and the grades were scored as $A+ = 10$, $A = 9 \ldots D = 1$. Under the linear model (Equation 6), we have

$$r_{ij} = \alpha_r r_i + \beta_r g_j \quad \text{and} \quad g_{ij} = \alpha_g r_i + \beta_g g_j.$$

By regressing the 10 predictions of each respondent against the predictors, r_i and g_j, we obtained for each subject in the rank condition an estimate of $\theta_r = \beta_r / \alpha_r$, and for each subject in the grade condition an estimate of $\theta_g = \beta_g / \alpha_g$. These values reflect the relative weight of grades to ranks in the two prediction tasks. As implied by the compatibility hypothesis, the values of θ_g were significantly higher than the values of θ_r, $p < .001$ by a Mann-Whitney test.

Figure 6.5 represents each of the 10 students as a point in the rank $\times$ grade plane. The slopes of the two lines, θ_r and θ_g, correspond to the relative weights of grade to rank estimated from the average predictions of ranks and grades, respectively. The multiple correlation between the inputs (r_j, g_j) and the average predicted scores was .99 for ranks and .98 for grades, indicating that the linear model provides a good description of the aggregate data. Recall that in the contingent weighting model, the predicted scores are given by the perpendicular projections of the points onto the respective lines, indicated by notches. The two lines, then, are orthogonal to the equal-value sets defined by the two tasks. The figure shows that grades and ranks were roughly equally weighted in the prediction of grades ($\theta_g = 1.06$), but grades were given much less weight than ranks in the prediction of ranks ($\theta_r = .58$). As a consequence, the two groups generated different ordering of the students. For example, the predicted rank of Student 9 was higher than that of Student 8, but the order of the predicted grades was reversed. Note that the numbered points in Figure 6.5 represent the design, not the data. The discrepancy between the two orderings is determined jointly by the angle between the lines that is estimated from subjects' predictions and by the correlation between the two dimensions that is determined by the design.

These data suggest a more detailed account based on a process of anchoring and adjustment (Slovic & Lichtenstein, 1971; Tversky & Kahneman, 1974). According to this heuristic, the subject uses the score on the compatible attribute (either rank or grade) as an anchor and adjusts it upward or downward on

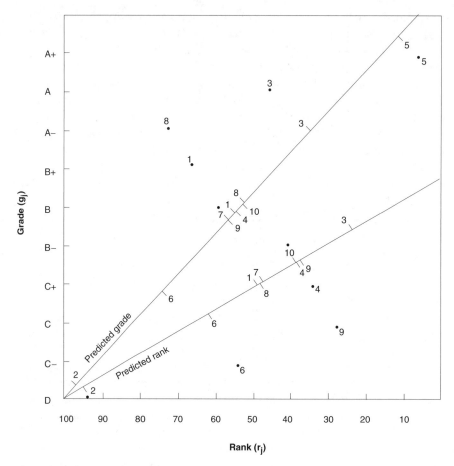

Figure 6.5. Contingent weighting representation of predicted ranks and grades. (The dots characterize the input information for each of the 10 students. The slopes of the two lines correspond to the relative weight of grades to ranks in the two prediction tasks.)

the basis of the other score. Because adjustments are generally insufficient, the compatible attribute is overweighted. Although the use of anchoring and adjustment probably contributes to the phenomenon in question, Slovic et al. (1990) found a significant compatibility effect even when the subject only predicted which of the two students would obtain a higher grade (or rank), without making any numerical prediction that calls for anchoring and adjustment.

Preference Reversals

The contingent weighting model (Equation 5) and the compatibility principle can also be used to explain the well-known preference reversals discovered by Lichtenstein and Slovic (1971; see also Slovic and Lichtenstein, 1968, 1983). These investigators compared two types of bets with comparable expected values – an

H bet that offers a high probability of winning a relatively small amount of money (e.g., 32/36 chance to win \$4) and an L bet that offers a low probability of winning a moderate amount of money (e.g., 9/36 chance to win \$40). The results show that people generally choose the H bet over the L bet (i.e., $H >_c L$) but assign a higher cash equivalent to the L bet than to the H bet (i.e., $C_L > C_H$, where C_L and C_H are the amounts of money that are as desirable as L and H, respectively). This pattern of preferences, which is inconsistent with the theory of rational choice, has been observed in numerous experiments, including a study conducted on the floor of a Las Vegas casino (Lichtenstein & Slovic, 1973), and it persists even in the presence of monetary incentives designed to promote consistent responses (Grether & Plott, 1979).

Although the basic phenomenon has been replicated in many studies, the determinants of preference reversals and their causes have remained elusive heretofore. It is easy to show that the reversal of preferences implies either intransitive choices or a choice-pricing discrepancy (i.e., a failure of invariance), or both. To understand this phenomenon, it is necessary to assess the relative contribution of these factors because they imply different explanations. To accomplish this goal, however, one must extend the traditional design and include, in addition to the bets H and L, a cash amount X that is compared with both. If procedure in variance holds and preference reversals are due to intransitive choices, then we should obtain the cycle $L >_c X >_c H >_c L$. If, on the other hand, transitivity holds and preference reversals are due to an inconsistency between choice and pricing, then we should obtain either $X >_c L$ and $C_L > X$, or $H >_c X$ and $X > C_H$. The first pattern indicates that L is *overpriced* relative to choice, and the second pattern indicates that H is *underpriced* relative to choice. Recall that $H >_c X$ refers to the choice between the bet H and the sure thing X, whereas $X > C_H$ refers to the ordering of cash amounts.

Following this analysis, Tversky, Slovic, and Kahneman (1990) conducted an extensive study of preference reversals, using 18 triples (H, L, X) that cover a wide range of probabilities and payoffs. A detailed analysis of response patterns showed that, by far, the most important determinant of preference reversals is the overpricing of L. Intransitive choices and the underpricing of H play a relatively minor role, each accounting for less than 10% of the total number of reversals. Evidently, preference reversals represent a choice-pricing discrepancy induced by the compatibility principle: Because pricing is expressed in monetary units, the payoffs loom larger in pricing than in choice.

We next apply the contingent weighting model to a study reported by Tversky et al. (1990) in which 179 participants (a) chose between six pairs consisting of an H bet and an L bet, (b) rated the attractiveness of all 12 bets, and (c) determined the cash equivalent of each bet. To provide monetary incentives and assure the strategic equivalence of the three methods, the participants were informed that a pair of bets would be selected at random and that they would play the member of the pair that they had chosen, or the bet that they had priced or rated higher. The present discussion focuses on the relation between pricing and rating, which can be readily analyzed using multiple regression. In general, rating resembles choice in favoring the H bets, in contrast to pricing that favors the L bets. Note that in rating and pricing each gamble is evaluated separately, whereas choice (and matching) involve a comparison between gambles. Because the discrepancy between rating and pricing is even more pronounced than that between choice and pricing, the reversal of preferences cannot be explained by the fact that choice is comparative, whereas pricing is singular. For further discussions of the relation between rating, choice, and pricing, see Goldstein and Einhorn (1987) and Schkade and Johnson (1989).

We assume that the value of a simple prospect (q, y) is approximated by a multiplicative function of the probability q and the payoff y. Thus, the logarithms of the pricing and the rating can be expressed by

$$\theta_i \log y + \log q, i = r, p, \tag{8}$$

where θ_r and θ_p denote the relative weight of the payoff in the rating and in the pricing tasks, respectively. Note that this model implies a power utility function with an exponent θ_i. The average transformed rating and pricing responses for each of the 12 bets were regressed, separately, against $\log q$ and $\log y$. The multiple correlations were .96 and .98 for the ratings and the pricing, respectively, indicating that the relation between rating and pricing can be captured, at least in the aggregate data, by a very simple model with a single parameter.

Figure 6.6 represents each of the 12 bets as a (numbered) point in the plane whose coordinates are probability and money, plotted on a logarithmic scale. The rating and pricing lines in the figure are perpendicular to the respective sets of linear indifference curves (see Figure 6.2). Hence, the projections of each bet on the two lines (denoted by notches) correspond to their values derived from rating and pricing, respectively. The angle between these lines equals the (smaller) angle between the intersecting families of indifference curves. Figure 6.6 reveals a dramatic difference between the slopes: $\theta_r = 2.7$, $\theta_p = .75$, hence $\theta = \theta_p / \theta_r = .28$. Indeed, these data give rise to a negative correlation ($r = -.30$) between the rating and the pricing, yielding numerous reversals of the ordering of the projections on the two lines. For example, the most extreme L bet (No. 8) has the lowest rating and the highest cash equivalent in the set.

The preceding analysis shows that the compatibility principle, incorporated into the contingent weighting model, provides a simple account of the well-known preference reversals. It also yields new predictions, which have been confirmed in a recent study. Note that if preference reversals are caused primarily by the overweighting of payoffs in the pricing task, then the effect should be much smaller for nonmonetary payoffs. Indeed, Slovic et al. (1990) found that the use of nonmonetary payoffs (e.g., a dinner for two at a very good restaurant or a free weekend at a coastal resort) greatly reduced the incidents of preference reversals. Furthermore, according to the present analysis, preference reversals

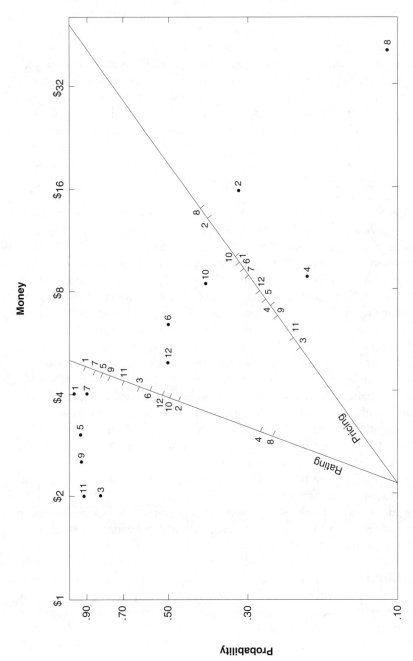

Figure 6.6. Contingent weighting representation of rating and pricing. (The dots characterize the six *H* bets and six *L* bets denoted by odd and even numbers, respectively, in logarithmic coordinates. The slopes of the two lines correspond to the weight of money relative to probability in rating and pricing.)

are not limited to risky prospects. Tversky et al. (1990) constructed riskless options of the form ($x, t) that offers a payment of $x at some future time, t (e.g., 5 years from now). Subjects chose between such options and evaluated their cash equivalents. The cash equivalent (or the price) of the option ($x, t) is the amount of cash, paid immediately, that is as attractive as receiving $x at time t. Because both the price and the payment are expressed in dollars, compatibility implies that the payment will loom larger in pricing than in choice. This prediction was confirmed. Subjects generally chose the option that paid sooner and assigned a higher price to the option that offered the larger payment. For example, 83% of the subjects ($N = 169$) preferred $2,500 in 5 years over $3,550 in 10 years, but 71% assigned a higher price to the second option. Thus, the replacement of risk by time gives rise to a new type of reversals. Evidently, preference reversals are determined primarily by the compatibility between the price and the payoff, regardless of the presence or absence of risk.

We conclude this section with a brief discussion of alternative accounts of preference reversals proposed in the literature. One class of comparative theories, developed by Fishburn (1984, 1985) and Loomes and Sugden (1982, 1983), treats preference reversals as intransitive choices. As was noted earlier, however, the intransitivity of choice accounts for only a small part of the phenomenon in question; hence, these theories do not provide a fully satisfactory explanation of preference reversals. A different model, called expression theory, has been developed by Goldstein and Einhorn (1987). This model is a special case of the contingent model defined by Equation 1. It differs from the present treatment in that it focuses on the expression of preferences rather than on the evaluation of prospects. Thus, it attributes preference reversals to the mapping of subjective value onto the appropriate response scale, not to the compatibility between the input and the output. As a consequence, this model does not imply many of the compatibility effects described in this chapter, such as the contingent weighting of grades and ranks in the prediction of students' performance, the marked reduction in preference reversals with nonmonetary payoffs, and the differential weighting of common and of distinctive features in judgments of similarity and dissimilarity.

A highly pertinent analysis of preference reversals based on attention and anchoring data was proposed by Schkade and Johnson (1989). Using a computer-controlled experiment in which the subject can see only one component of each bet at a time, these investigators measured the amount of time spent by each subject looking at probabilities and at payoffs. The results showed that in the pricing task, the percentage of time spent on the payoffs was significantly greater than that spent on probabilities, whereas in the rating task, the pattern was reversed. This observation supports the hypothesis, suggested by the compatibility principle, that subjects attended to payoffs more in the pricing task than in the rating task.

The relation between preference reversals and the choice-matching discrepancy was explored in a study by Slovic et al. (1990). Subjects matched 12 pairs of

H and *L* bets by completing the missing probability or payoff. The overall percentage of responses that favored *H* over *L* was 73% for probability matches and 49% for payoff matches. (For comparison, 76% preferred *H* over *L* in a direct choice.) This result follows from scale compatibility: The adjusted attribute, either probability or money, looms larger than the nonadjusted attribute. However, the pattern differs from the prominence effect described earlier, which produced relatively small differences between the matches on the primary and the secondary attributes and large differences between choice and matching (see, e.g., Problem 1). This contrasts with the present finding of large differences between probability and payoff matches, and no difference between probability matches and choice. Evidently, preference reversals are induced primarily by scale compatibility, not by the differential prominence of attributes that underlies the choice-matching discrepancy. Indeed, there is no obvious reason to suppose that probability is more prominent than money or vice versa. For further examples and discussions of elicitation biases in risky choice, see Fischer, Damodaran, Laskey, and Lincoln (1987) and Hershey and Schoemaker (1985).

DISCUSSION

The extensive use of rational theories of choice (e.g., the expected utility model or the theory of revealed preference) as descriptive models (e.g., in economics, management, and political science) has stimulated the experimental investigation of the descriptive validity of the assumptions that underlie these models. Perhaps the most basic assumption of the rational theory of choice is the principle of invariance (Kahneman & Tversky, 1984) or extensionality (Arrow, 1982), which states that the relation of preference should not depend on the description of the options (description invariance) or on the method of elicitation (procedure invariance). Empirical tests of description invariance have shown that alternative framing of the same options can lead to different choices (Tversky & Kahneman, 1986). The present studies provide evidence against the assumption of procedure invariance by demonstrating a systematic discrepancy between choice and matching, as well as between rating and pricing. In this section we discuss the main findings and explore their theoretical and practical implications.

In the first part of the chapter we showed that the more important dimension of a decision problem looms larger in choice than in matching. We addressed this phenomenon at three levels of analysis. First, we presented a heuristic account of choice and matching that led to the prominence hypothesis; second, we related this account to the general notion of input–output compatibility; and third, we developed the formal theory of contingent weighting that represents the prominence effect as well as other elicitation phenomena, such as preference reversals. The informal analysis, based on compatibility, provides a psychological explanation for the differential weighting induced by the various procedures.

Although the prominence effect was observed in a variety of settings using both intrapersonal and interpersonal comparisons, its boundaries are left to be explored. How does it extend to options that vary on a larger number of attributes? The present analysis implies that the relative weights of any pair of attributes will be less extreme (i.e., closer to unity) in matching than in choice. With three or more attributes, however, additional considerations may come into play. For example, people may select the option that is superior on most attributes (Tversky, 1969, Experiment 2). In this case, the prominence hypothesis does not always result in a lexicographic bias. Another question is whether the choice-matching discrepancy applies to other judgmental or perceptual tasks. The data on the prediction of students' performance indicate that the prominence effect is not limited to preferential choice, but it is not clear whether it applies to psychophysics. Perceived loudness, for example, depends primarily on intensity and to a lesser degree on frequency. It could be interesting to test the prominence hypothesis in such a context.

The finding that the qualitative information about the ordering of the dimensions looms larger in the ordinal method of choice than in the cardinal method of matching has been construed as an instance of the compatibility principle. This principle states that stimulus components that are compatible with the response are weighted more heavily than those that are not, presumably because (a) the former are accentuated, and (b) the latter require additional mental transformations that produce error and reduce the diagnosticity of the information. This effect may be induced by the nature of the information (e.g., ordinal vs. cardinal), by the response scale (e.g., grades vs. ranks), or by the affinity between inputs and outputs (e.g., common features loom larger in similarity than in dissimilarity judgments). Compatibility, therefore, appears to provide a common explanation for many phenomena of judgment and choice.

The preceding discussion raises the intriguing normative question as to which method, choice or matching, better reflects people's "true" preferences. Put differently, do people overweigh the primary dimension in choice, or do they underweigh it in matching? Without knowing the "correct" weighting, it is unclear how to answer this question, but the following study provides some relevant data. The participants in a decision-making seminar performed both choice and matching in the traffic-accident problem described earlier (Problem 3). The two critical (choice and matching) questions were embedded in a questionnaire that included similar questions with different numerical values. The majority of the respondents (21 out of 32) gave inconsistent responses that conformed to the prominence hypothesis. After the session, each participant was interviewed and confronted with his or her answers. The subjects were surprised to discover that their responses were inconsistent, and they offered a variety of explanations, some of which resemble the prominence hypothesis. One participant said, "When I have to choose between programs I go for the one that saves more lives because there is no price for human life. But when I match the programs I have to pay attention to money." When asked to reconsider their answers, all respondents modified the matching in the direction of the choice, and a few reversed the original choice in the direction of the matching. This observation suggests that choice and matching are both biased in opposite directions, but it may reflect a routine compromise rather than the result of a critical reassessment.

Real-world decisions can sometimes be framed either as a direct choice (e.g., should I buy the used car at this price?) or as a pricing decision (e.g., what is the most I should pay for that used car?). Our findings suggest that the answers to the two questions are likely to diverge. Consider, for example, a medical decision problem where the primary dimension is the probability of survival, and the secondary dimension is the cost associated with treatment or diagnosis. According to the present analysis, people are likely to choose the option that offers the higher probability of survival with relatively little concern for cost. When asked to price a marginal increase in the probability of survival, however, people are expected to appear less generous. The choice-matching discrepancy may also arise in resource allocation and budgeting decisions. The prominence hypothesis suggests that the most important item in the budget (e.g., health) will tend to dominate a less important item (e.g., culture) in a direct choice between two allocations, but the less important item is expected to fare better in a matching procedure.

The lability of preferences implied by the demonstrations of framing and elicitation effects raises difficult questions concerning the assessment of preferences and values. In the classical analysis, the relation of preference is inferred from observed responses (e.g., choice, matching) and is assumed to reflect the decision maker's underlying utility or value. But if different elicitation procedures produce different orderings of options, how can preferences and values be defined? And in what sense do they exist? To be sure, people make choices, set prices, rate options, and even explain their decisions to others. Preferences, therefore, exist as observed data. However, if these data do not satisfy the elementary requirements of invariance, it is unclear how to define a relation of preference that can serve as a basis for the measurement of value. In the absence of well-defined preferences, the foundations of choice theory and decision analysis are called into question.

ACKNOWLEDGMENTS

This work was supported by Contract N00014-84-K-0615 from the Office of Naval Research to Stanford University and by National Science Foundation Grant 5ES-8712-145 to Decision Research. The article has benefited from discussions with Greg Fischer, Dale Griffin, Eric Johnson, Daniel Kahneman, and Lennart Sjöberg.

7. Cognitive Processes in Preference Reversals

David A. Schkade and Eric J. Johnson

Decision makers can reveal their preferences for alternatives using different methods or *response modes*. For example, a decision maker might choose between two alternatives or match them by adjusting a feature of the first so that it is equally as preferred as the second. According to normative theories of choice, preference orderings should be invariant across response modes, a property called *procedure invariance* (Tversky, Sattath, & Slovic, 1988). Empirically, however, different response modes can reveal very different preferences. The most well-known inconsistencies are demonstrations that preferences for simple gambles differ systematically across response modes (Slovic & Lichtenstein, 1983). Because these *preference reversals* are contrary to the most basic principles of rational choice, they have drawn substantial attention from both economists and psychologists.

The theories that have been proposed for preference reversal posit psychological mechanisms that could create different evaluations of the same gambles in different response modes. These theories have generally been tested through the extent to which they account for empirical patterns of inconsistent responses. By this standard, most of the proposed theories achieve some success, accounting for reversals in at least one pair of response modes. This research has largely used the characteristics of stimuli to manipulate these hypothesized psychological mechanisms. More recent research has studied these mechanisms through process tracing measures (Johnson, Payne, & Bettman, 1988) or by introducing choices involving riskless outcomes and then analyzing response patterns to reveal the influence of intransitivity and the tendency to overprice or underprice certain types of options (Tversky, Slovic, & Kahneman, 1990).

In this chapter, we take a process tracing approach. Instead of focusing exclusively on the results of the elicitation process, we also study additional indicators of psychological processes. To do this, we observe evidence of the intervening mental events as decision makers form responses to preference assessment questions, through a computer-based experimental methodology that records information acquisition and other process tracing data. By

This article has been abridged by the editors. Reprinted from *Organizational Behavior and Human Decision Processes*, vol. 44, pp. 203–231. Copyright © 1989 with permission from Elsevier.

relating these process measures to the occurrence of preference reversals, we provide new insights concerning their underlying causes. We first review existing research and theories, and then present the results of process tracing experiments on two of the most studied types of reversals, pricing versus choice and pricing versus attractiveness ratings. In a third experiment, we manipulate anchors to further explore their possible role in producing reversals. Finally, the results of the three studies are integrated, and implications for theory and future research are discussed....

PREFERENCE-REVERSAL THEORIES

In the first explanation proposed for preference reversals, Lichtenstein and Slovic (1971) hypothesized that decision makers arrive at prices through a process of *anchoring and adjustment*. Specifically, the decision maker first considers how it would feel to obtain the greater amount, G, with certainty and then adjusts downward to account for the probability of winning, P, and the size of the lesser amount, L. If adjustments of this type are insufficient (e.g., Tversky & Kahneman, 1974), prices would be biased toward gambles with large amounts to win ($ bets). The authors suggested several different possible ways that choices could be made, but assumed that none was predominant. An anchoring and adjustment process could also produce reversals when both responses are judgments. For example, the observed pattern of pricing versus rating reversals would be generated if rating anchors were based on the probability of winning, producing higher anchors for P bets than for $ bets. Thus, for anchoring and adjustment to produce reversals between two judgments, the order of anchors for P and $ bets would have to reverse across response modes. Anchoring and adjustment may also be a significant determinant of related inconsistencies between probability and certainty equivalents in utility assessment (Johnson & Schkade, 1989) and is thought to be widespread in judgment tasks (Lopes, 1982; Tversky & Kahneman, 1974).

Tversky et al. (1988) distinguish between tasks requiring ordinal responses (e.g., choice) and those requiring cardinal responses (e.g., pricing, matching). The authors propose a *prominence hypothesis* – that the more important dimension receives greater weight in ordinal than in cardinal response modes. For example, if the probability of winning (P) is the most important dimension for gambles, then P bets (which are dominant on this dimension) will be more preferred in choice relative to pricing. This differential weighting appears to be quite robust, in both risky and riskless contexts.

Tversky et al. (1988) also discuss a related phenomenon they call the *compatibility principle*: Attributes that are more easily mapped onto the response scale are given greater weight in the evaluation process. Thus, payoffs may be weighted more heavily than probabilities in pricing because both payoffs and the pricing response share the same dollar scale. Similarly, the authors argue that probabilities may be weighted more heavily in rating because they map more easily onto the rating scale than do dollar payoffs.[1]

Goldstein and Einhorn (1987) suggest in their Expression Theory that in judgment modes, such as pricing and rating, decision makers use a proportional matching strategy between a mental evaluation dimension and the external response scale. First, they assume that the evaluation process is the same for all response modes. This evaluation, denoted U(gamble), is on a mental "utility" scale and is arrived at through some unspecified process, prior to the expression stage. In choice, it is assumed that the gamble with the highest evaluation is then chosen. For judgment, the response is determined by a process of matching the proportional distance from the utility of the greater payoff, $U(G)$, to U(gamble), relative to the distance from $U(G)$ to the utility of the lesser payoff, $U(L)$, with the distance from the top of the response scale (T) to the response (R), relative to the distance from the top to the bottom of the scale (B):

$$\frac{U(G) - U(\text{gamble})}{U(G) - U(L)} = \frac{T - R}{T - B}.$$

(1)

In pricing, the top of the scale is G and the bottom is L, whereas for rating, the top and bottom are the best and worst possible ratings, respectively. Disparities between the ranking of evaluations and responses are the result of the difference in curvature of the utility and response scales. Thus, it is the expression of the preference, rather than the way it is determined, that may lead to reversals.

To summarize, although these various explanations[2] for preference reversal are based on diverse cognitive mechanisms, they all explain at least some of the characteristic response inconsistencies (e.g., overpricing the $ bet and rating the P bet higher). We now further examine the processes underlying preference reversals by exploring the relationship between process tracing measures and reversals in analyses of pricing-choice (Experiment 1) and pricing-rating (Experiment 2) reversals.

EXPERIMENT 1: PRICING VERSUS CHOICE

In this first experiment we examine indications of the cognitive processes underlying the classic preference reversals between pricing and choice, using stimuli similar to those in previous research. We first describe our computer-based data

---

[1] Probabilities are more compatible with the rating scale than payoffs for at least three reasons: (1) the upper and lower bounds on probabilities are constant across gambles, like those for the rating scale, whereas those for payoffs change from gamble to gamble; (2) there are clear "best" and "worst" values for both probabilities and the rating scale, in contrast to payoffs, where you can always be better off by adding additional amounts; and (3) probabilities and rating points are both in some sense unitless, whereas dollar payoffs have clearly expressed units that require some (probably effortful) translation into rating points.

[2] Loomes and Sugden (1983) also proposed a possible explanation for reversals. However, it applies only to certain narrowly defined situations and, in particular, does not address reversals involving ratings. Thus, we will not discuss it further here.

collection methodology, then discuss differences in process measures between pricing and choice, and finally analyze the relationships between these measures and reversals.

The pricing-choice preference-reversal task really consists of three separate responses, in which a decision maker must: (1) set a price for the P bet, (2) set a price for the $ bet, and (3) make a choice between the P and $ bets. Reversals could result from processes in any or all of these three responses. For example, a decision maker might overprice the $ bet, underprice the P bet, or use an inappropriate choice strategy. When we observe a reversal, we know that an inconsistency has occurred but cannot easily tell, from outcome data alone, if the locus of the effect is in pricing the P bet, pricing the $ bet, or in making a choice between them.

By observing detailed measures of the judgment and choice processes that occur during each response, we hope to isolate the sources of these reversals. Previous process tracing work on decision making has found certain types of measures to be related to various judgment and choice phenomena. For example, Russo and Dosher (1983) found that dimensional information acquisition patterns were associated with higher error rates than were interdimensional patterns, and Johnson and Schkade (1989) found greater inconsistencies between preferences assessed using probability and certainty equivalents when subjects used heuristic rather than expectation strategies. We will concentrate on four classes of such measures (total time, attention to stimulus features, patterns of information acquisition, response activity), recording them for each of the component responses. These measures will be described in detail in the following section.

METHOD

Stimuli

Eight pairs of two-payoff gambles were used. Five of these were drawn directly from the standard set of items first used by Lichtenstein and Slovic (1971), and a sixth was modified slightly. Two similar pairs were added (Table 7.1). Each pair consisted of a P bet and a $ bet, and payoffs ranged from a loss of $3 to a gain of $20. The gambles in a given pair were matched on expected value, ranging from $1.35 to $5.50, with an average of $3.19.

Procedure

Sixteen paid MBA students participated in individual 1-hour sessions. Subjects evaluated every gamble in both response modes, which were separated by an unrelated task. In pricing, subjects were told to assume that they owned the gamble and were asked to specify a selling price that made them indifferent between playing the gamble and selling it. In choice, they were told to assume that they would receive and play the gamble they selected. Response mode order and gamble order were randomized.

Table 7.1. Stimuli

Pair	Type	EV[a]	P	G	L
1	P	5.50	33/36	6.00	0.00
	$	5.54	13/36	18.00	−1.50
2	P	4.55	32/36	5.50	−3.00
	$	4.44	8/36	20.00	0.00
3	P	3.86	35/36	4.00	−1.00
	$	3.85	11/36	16.00	−1.50
4	P	3.50	32/36	4.00	−0.50
	$	3.44	8/36	19.00	−1.00
5	P	2.72	34/36	3.00	−2.00
	$	2.71	18/36	6.50	−1.00
6	P	2.33	34/36	2.50	−0.50
	$	2.39	14/36	8.50	−1.50
7	P	1.67	33/36	2.00	−2.00
	$	1.75	18/36	5.00	−1.50
8	P	1.42	29/36	2.00	−1.00
	$	1.35	7/36	9.00	−0.50

[a] EV = expected value.

Gambles were presented as decision trees on an IBM PC-AT, using the *Mouselab* software package (Johnson, Payne, Schkade, & Bettman, 1988). Information is acquired through a hand-controlled pointing device called a "mouse." When a screen first appears, payoff and probability values are hidden behind labeled boxes that can be "opened" to reveal their contents by moving the cursor into a box (Figure 7.1). When the cursor leaves a box, it closes to again conceal its information. Pricing responses are indicated by moving a pointer along the response scale. The pointer is initiated by moving the cursor to the desired location and then pressing a mouse button. Choices are indicated by moving the cursor into the appropriate box and pressing a mouse button (Figure 7.2). Subjects were first familiarized with the use of a mouse in responding and searching for information and then completed three practice trials prior to the experimental stimuli for each response mode.

Total Time

We are interested in the time required to make these decisions for two reasons: First, it provides an approximate measure of overall effort. Second, it allows us to examine specific ideas about the choice and judgment response modes. For example, some theories of choice (see Abelson & Levi, 1985; Schoemaker, 1982) and specific theories of preference reversals (Goldstein & Einhorn, 1987) suggest that choice consists mainly of two evaluation judgments, one for each gamble. If this is true, we might expect the time required to make a choice to be larger than the time required to make a single judgment.

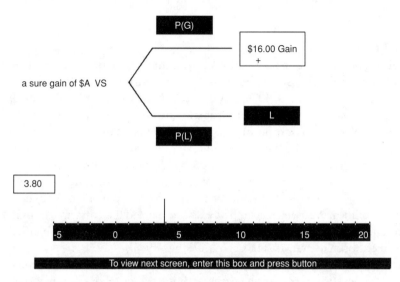

What value for S would make you indifferent?

Figure 7.1. Computer display for pricing task.

Attention Measures

The amount of attention given to a stimulus feature may be related to its salience or importance (e.g., Fiske, 1980; Taylor & Fiske, 1981) and the way it is processed (e.g., Just & Carpenter, 1976; Russo & Dosher, 1983). For instance, Russo and Rosen (1975) found that alternatives with higher utilities received greater attention. If the attention given to an item of information is related to its importance, then measures such as the proportion of total time spent on

Figure 7.2. Computer display for choice task.

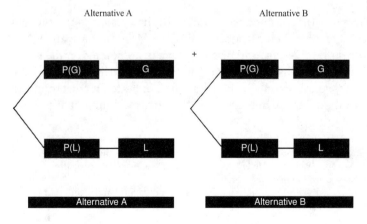

various problem elements should vary across gambles or response modes. The *Mouselab* system recorded the duration for which each feature of the display was accessed.[3]

Search Measures

The pattern of information acquisitions during the course of a decision has been a primary measure used in process tracing research (e.g., Bettman & Kakkar, 1977; Bettman & Zins, 1979; Payne, 1976; Russo & Rosen, 1975). One reason for this is that different decision strategies are often characterized by different patterns of search. For example, if subjects calculated expected value by directly weighting payoffs by their probabilities of occurrence, we might expect them to look at a payoff and its associated probability in close proximity (e.g., the probability of winning and the amount to win). In contrast, this strategy would produce fewer shifts in attention between the two payoffs or between the two probabilities. Previous research has also connected the pattern of search with differences in performance (e.g., Johnson et al., 1988; Johnson & Schkade, 1989; Rosen & Rosenkoetter, 1976; Russo & Dosher, 1983).

We refer to shifts in attention from one problem element to another as *transitions*. To measure information search activity, the number of transitions between all possible pairs of boxes was recorded. We also examined a transition index suggested by Payne and Braunstein (1978) that compares the number of transitions (within a gamble) between a payoff and its probability (an *outcome* transition) to the number of transitions (within a gamble) between two payoffs or two probabilities (a *dimensional* transition).[4] The index is calculated as

$$\text{Search index} = \frac{\text{outcome transitions} - \text{dimensional transitions}}{\text{outcome transitions} + \text{dimensional transitions}}. \qquad (2)$$

This index approaches +1 for an exclusively outcome-oriented strategy (e.g., expected value) and −1 for a heavily dimensional strategy (e.g., lexicographic).

Response Measures

A class of measures that has not been widely studied concerns the process by which subjects generate their response. Using the *Mouselab* software, when gambles first appear on the screen in pricing, there is no pointer on the scale. In pilot testing we found that subjects did not simply move directly to the scale location corresponding to their final response, but often made a number of adjustments to the initial pointer position. We analyzed the initial pointer

---

[3] However, very brief exposures, such as those that occur when the cursor incidentally opens one box on its way to another, are too short to produce a meaningful mental representation (Card, Moran, & Newell, 1983). We therefore excluded from analysis all acquisitions of less than 150 milliseconds' duration (Russo & Dosher, 1983).

[4] A third type of within-gamble transition, those between a probability and a different payoff (e.g., $P \rightarrow L$), is excluded from this index.

placements because if they differ systematically from the final response, they may indicate anchors. In addition, pilot testing indicated that subjects often made cursor movements near the scale without moving the pointer itself, perhaps mentally simulating possible response values. We therefore also recorded the amount of time for which the cursor was within one-half inch of the scale as an additional indicator of response activity. These movements may capture important aspects of the response generation process such as those implied by anchoring and adjustment or Expression Theory.

Statistical Analysis

For each gamble pair, subjects gave three responses (prices for both the P and $ bets and a choice). Unless otherwise noted, process measures were analyzed using repeated measures analysis of variance, with response mode, gamble type (nested within pricing), and gamble pair as within-subject factors, and a random blocking factor for subjects. To test differences related to the presence of reversals, a covariate that indicated whether a trial was involved in a reversal was added. Measures scaled as proportions were analyzed using a variance-stabilizing arcsin transformation (Winer, 1971, p. 400).

RESULTS

Our results replicate both the pattern of reversals (Table 7.2) and the aggregate prices and choices observed in previous studies (Goldstein, 1984; Grether & Plott, 1979; Lichtenstein & Slovic, 1971, 1973; Tversky et al., 1988). For example, (1) P bets were slightly preferred in choice, whereas $ bets were strongly preferred in pricing; (2) P bets were priced just below expected value (mean = $3.00), whereas $ bets were highly overpriced, relative to expected value (mean = $5.91); and (3) the asymmetry of reversals was highly significant (McNemar's Q test, $p < .001$). Thus, our use of the *Mouselab* methodology did not change the basic pattern of results associated with preference reversals.

Process Differences Between Response Modes

What processes underlie these reversals in preference? We organize our results into three sections: First, we describe overall patterns observed in the

Table 7.2. Response Patterns: Experiment 1

		Choice		
		P Bet	**$ Bet**	**Total**
Pricing	P bet > $ bet	.09 [a]	.06	.15
	$ bet > P bet	.45	.40	.85
	TOTAL	.54	.46	$n = 125$ [b]

[a] Entries are response proportions.
[b] Three ties on price are excluded.

measures, concentrating on processing differences between the two response modes. Second, we relate these differences to the occurrence of reversals. Finally, we examine how well the process differences together account for the frequency of reversals.

Total Time. If choice consists of two component judgments, we might expect the time required to choose between the two gambles to be greater than the time required to make a single judgment. However, choosing between two gambles required significantly less time than generating a price for even a *single* gamble, $F(1, 356) = 7.21, p < .01$. It took an average of 32.05 seconds for subjects to make a choice, but an average of 36.80 seconds *per gamble* to generate a price. Thus, it seems unlikely that choice consists simply of a comparison of two judgments of overall evaluation. In addition, it took longer to generate prices for $ bets (an average of 40.12 seconds) than for P bets (33.47 seconds), $F(1, 356) = 11.81$, $p < .001$.

Attention. Payoffs (G, L) were accessed longer than probabilities in both response modes. However, the proportion of time spent looking at payoffs (relative to probabilities) was significantly greater in pricing (56% of the search time spent on P, Q, G, and L) than in choice (51%), $F(1, 356) = 3.82, p < .05$. This result is consistent with the prominence hypothesis, which predicts that the payoff (dollar) dimension will be more heavily weighted in pricing. It also matches the results of Slovic and Lichtenstein (1968) and Lichtenstein and Slovic (1971), in which prices correlated more highly with payoffs than with probabilities and vice versa in choices.

Search Patterns. Search patterns are of interest because they can often reflect the processes used in integrating information (Payne, Braunstein, & Carroll, 1978). In choice subjects made frequent transitions between the two gambles, an average of 3.19 per choice (17.6% of all transitions). If choice simply consisted of the sequential evaluations of one alternative and then the next, we would expect only one such transition. Transitions within gambles are more outcome-oriented in choice[5] (+.25) than in pricing (+.04), $F(1, 356) = 31.52, p < .0001$.

Response Generation. Another clear difference between the two response modes is that subjects spent much more time indicating a response in pricing than in choice. A large part of this time was spent in the response scale making adjustments to the position of the pointer. Although subjects spent an average of only 1.92 seconds in the boxes that indicate a choice, they spent an average of 6.60 seconds adjusting the response scale in pricing. This difference is highly significant, $F(1, 356) = 162.80, p < .0001$. In contrast, pilot testing showed that asking subjects to simply indicate a given value on the scale took just 1 to 2 seconds.

In fact, the time spent in the scale may substantially underestimate the total time spent considering possible responses in pricing. Informal observation and an analysis of the search patterns showed that subjects spent significant amounts

[5] The search index in choice excluded between-gamble transitions to make it comparable with the index in pricing.

of time moving the cursor along the scale in the region immediately above the response scale, perhaps to simulate possible responses. If this time is included, we find that subjects spent an average of 11.07 seconds, or over 30% of their time, considering possible responses. This significant amount of time spent in and around the response scale is consistent with both anchoring and adjustment and Goldstein and Einhorn's (1987) focus on the expression phase.

What are subjects doing during this time? To investigate this we constructed two measures: The first was the response location at which their adjustment began, as indicated by the spot where the pointer first appeared on the response scale. In addition to this *starting point* measure, we calculated the distance, or *adjustment*, from this starting point to the final response. Starting points were quite different for $ and P bets: The average starting point for $ bets ($6.10) was much higher than that for P bets ($3.19), $F(1, 230) = 68.12, p < .0001$. In addition, subjects made small but significant downward adjustments for both P and $ bets (an average of $0.19 in each case), $p < .05$.

Summary. Together, these four sets of measures indicate that choice and pricing seem to involve quite different processes. Choice is the quicker process, with a significant number of comparisons made between gambles. Choosing between two gambles takes less time than generating a price for even a single gamble. Pricing is characterized by greater attention to the payoff information, whereas in choice there is increased emphasis placed on probabilities. Finally, a distinguishing feature of pricing strategies is a fairly long period of response generation in which subjects seem to use the scale to simulate various responses. Also, the starting points for this process differ for the two types of bets.

These differences between response modes are intriguing and may have implications for theories of preference reversals. Before considering these implications, however, we must identify a relationship between process measures and reversals. To do this, we next examine differences in these measures for responses involved in a reversal and those that are consistent.[6]

Differences Between Reversals and Consistent Responses

Total Time. There are several reasons that the time for reversal trials might be different than that for nonreversals. If reversals are caused by a lack of motivation, for example, we might expect them to have trials of shorter duration. Similarly, if calculating expected value helped prevent reversals, such calculations might take longer than informal heuristic processes. However, there is no systematic difference between the time taken for consistent and reversal trials.

Attention. The amount of attention to probabilities relative to payoffs is strongly related to reversals. When subjects give consistent responses, they

---

[6] The "unpredicted" reversals that occur when the P bet gets a higher price but the $ bet is chosen are infrequent and did not differ significantly from consistent responses on process measures. Thus, in both Experiment 1 and Experiment 2 they were treated as consistent responses in the reversal analyses that follow.

spend about the same proportion of time accessing probabilities in choice (45%) and in pricing (46%). However, when they commit reversals, they spend relatively more time on probabilities in choice (52%) than in pricing (43%), $F(1, 356) = 8.77, p < .01$.

The locus of this effect appears to be in choice and is different for each bet type. In P bets, there is a significant correlation between reversals (1 = reversal, 0 = consistent) and the proportion of time spent looking at the probability of winning ($r = .28, p < .01$). In $ bets increased attention to the amount to win and the amount to lose both led to more consistent responses ($r = -.15, p < .10$ and $-.21, p < .05$, respectively). None of the corresponding correlations in pricing are significant. This increased attention to the high probability of winning in the P bet is consistent with lexicographic or elimination strategies that have been found to produce choice intransitivities (e.g., Tversky, 1969).

Search Patterns. The pattern of information search is also related to reversals. In choice, the search index is more outcome-oriented (.34) for reversals than for consistent responses (.17), whereas in pricing there is essentially no difference (.07 vs. .02). This interaction is marginally significant, $F(1, 356) = 2.73$, $p < .10$. A key component of this effect is transitions between the probability of winning and the amount to win in the P bet in choice, which have a significant correlation with reversals ($r = .24, p < .01$).

Response Generation. In pricing, starting points are more extreme for reversals than for consistent responses. For P bets, reversals are associated with lower starting points ($2.99) than are consistent responses ($3.34), but for $ bets, reversals are associated with higher starting points ($6.76) than are consistent responses ($5.59). Because starting points for the two bets are significantly further apart for reversals, $F(1, 230) = 4.30, p < .05$, it is less likely that sufficient adjustments will be made to yield a higher price for the P bet. There are no significant differences between reversals and consistent responses in the amount of adjustment.

What drives these starting points? One possibility is that gamble elements that are more compatible with the response scale play a bigger role in determining starting points. To examine this, we computed the partial correlation of each gamble element with starting points, controlling for the other elements (Table 7.3). For reversals, the amount to win, G, was by far the most important determinant of starting points, whereas for consistent responses, all three elements received substantial weight. This helps to explain the larger difference between P- and $-bet starting points for reversals, because the amount to win is much larger in $ bets than in P bets. Further, if adjustments away from these starting points are sometimes insufficient (e.g., Tversky & Kahneman, 1974), G may be given greater weight in responses because of its key role in determining starting points (and particularly so for reversals).

We have identified several systematic differences in process measures between reversals and consistent responses. However, to what extent do these differences together predict reversals? To assess the joint predictive ability of

Table 7.3. Starting Points as a Function of Gamble
Elements for Consistent and Reversal Trials: Experiment 1

	Consistent	Reversal
G	.553***	.485***
L	.301***	.126
P	.185*	.035

Note: Entries are partial correlations between starting points and
each gamble element, controlling for the other two elements. The
probabilities of winning and losing are perfectly correlated, and
thus the results for P contain the same information as those for Q.
*p < .05; ***p < .001.

the process measures, we next examine how well a set of individually important process variables can predict the occurrence of reversals. This will also give
indications of whether they reflect the same or different aspects of reversals.

Predicting Reversals with Process Measures

To assess the joint effect of the process measures discussed earlier, we focused
on a set of attention, search, and response variables found to be related to reversals in the preceding analysis. Five variables were analyzed: (1) the difference
between response modes in the proportion of time spent looking at probabilities;
(2) the proportion of time in choice spent looking at the probability of winning
in the P bet; (3) the search index in choice; (4) the relative position of starting
points for the P and \$ bets; and (5) whether adjustments away from the start-
ing points were in the same direction for both bets (adjustments in the same
direction would tend to reinforce differences in starting points). A dichotomous
response variable (1 if reversal, 0 if consistent) was regressed on these five variables[7] (Table 7.4). The overall model fit was highly significant, $F(5, 122) = 8.84$,
$p < .0001$, $R^2 = .266$.

The signs of the coefficients are consistent with our earlier analyses of process differences between reversals and consistent responses, indicating that no
substantial multicollinearity is present. The low correlations between the variables further support this conclusion (Table 7.4). It appears that processes that
occur in choice as well as those in pricing are related to reversals (cf. Tversky
et al., 1990).

The preceding analysis is correlational, as none of the predictors were experimentally manipulated. However, the process measures do precede the response
temporally, and it is more likely that the processes caused the reversal rather
than the converse. Thus, reversals appear to be predictable, in part, on the basis
of observed measures of judgment and choice processes.

[7] We also estimated the analogous logistic regression model using maximum likelihood. This
   model yielded similar results: $\chi^2(5) = 40.21$, $p < .001$, pseudo $R^2 = .23$, and all coefficients have
   the same sign and relative significance. We present the linear model for simplicity.

Table 7.4. *Process Regression Results: Experiment 1*

Variable	Coefficient	t	$p(t)$
X_1 Difference in PQ time proportion	.591	2.35	.020
X_2 Proportion of P time, choice	1.035	2.56	.012
X_3 Search index, choice	.137	1.62	.108
X_4 Starting point order	.212	4.13	.001
X_5 Direction of adjustment	.158	2.03	.044

Correlation Matrix of Independent Variables				
	X_1	X_2	X_3	X_4	X_5
X_1					
X_2	.359				
X_3	−.076	.134			
X_4	−.054	−.029	.156		
X_5	.043	.018	−.100	−.035	

Note: X_1 = proportion of time on probabilities in choice − proportion of time on probabilities in pricing. X_2 = proportion of time on probability of winning in P bet, choice. X_3 = search index in choice. X_4 = 1, if \$-bet starting point > P-bet starting point; 0, if they are equivalent; or −1, if \$-bet starting point < P-bet starting point. X_5 = 1, if direction of adjustment same for both bets; or 0, otherwise.

DISCUSSION: EXPERIMENT 1

The story told by these data is largely a tale of two processes, one operating in choice and the other in pricing. Although pricing and choice strategies are related, process measures indicate that they differ in several key respects. These include the amount of time to respond, relative attention to probabilities and payoffs, and response activity. These observations strengthen the view that choice and judgment processes are quite different.

Along with the story of two different processes comes a story of at least two potential causes of reversals. Pricing is characterized by a high level of activity in generating a scale response and greater attention to payoffs. The pattern of starting points and subsequent movements within the scale is consistent with the use of an anchoring and adjustment strategy. Moreover, these starting points appear to be heavily influenced by the greater payoff, G, suggesting a relationship between the choice of starting points and the compatibility of gamble elements with the response scale.

The second potential cause of reversals originates in choice, in which transition and attention data suggest that choice strategies may be related to the frequency of reversals. Although we cannot yet characterize these strategies as clearly as we would like, one possibility is that subjects use some sort of expectation-type strategy such as expected value. This would be consistent with the outcome-oriented search patterns and the fairly even division of choices between P and $ bets. Another possibility is an elimination-type strategy that searches within outcomes. This would produce the process differences that we have observed to be related to reversals that cannot be explained by an expectation strategy, including the significant number of intergamble transitions and the increased attention to probabilities. Whatever the ultimate characterization of the choice process may be, our results suggest that elements of both choice and judgment strategies play a role in reversals.

Although we have characterized reversals as arising from differences between choice and judgment, there are other kinds of reversals that involve only judgments (e.g., pricing vs. rating). Do similar process differences underlie reversals between judgments? We might expect that two types of judgment would show fewer process differences than pricing and choice, yet previous research has found even more frequent systematic reversals between judgments. To explore these issues, we next conducted a process tracing study of reversals between pricing and rating, using an approach similar to that in Experiment 1.

EXPERIMENT 2: PRICING VERSUS RATING

METHOD

The stimuli and procedure are the same as in Experiment 1, with two exceptions: Choice was replaced by ratings of attractiveness on a scale of 0 to 100 (gambles were rated individually), and the two separate individual sessions for each subject (one for each response mode) were conducted at least 3 days apart. All process measures collected for pricing, including activity associated with the response scale, were also recorded in rating. Twelve paid MBA students participated.

In both pretesting and Experiment 1, subjects spent a substantial amount of time moving the cursor along the response scale without switching to the pointer. To better capture this behavior, we modified the software to record cursor movements occurring in the region within one-half inch of the scale in the same fashion as pointer movements in the scale. Therefore, in Experiment 2 we used the point at which the cursor initially entered the region immediately above the scale as the response starting point.

For each gamble pair, subjects gave four responses (prices and ratings for both P and $ bets). Process measures were analyzed as in Experiment 1, with the exception that response mode and the type of bet were fully crossed.

RESULTS

Our results replicate the pattern of reversals (Table 7.5) and the aggregate prices and ratings observed in previous studies (e.g., Goldstein & Einhorn, 1987; Johnson et al., 1988; Tversky et al., 1988). For example, (1) P bets were rated

Table 7.5. Response Patterns: Experiment 2

		Rating		
		P Bet	$ Bet	Total
Pricing	P bet > $ bet	.09[a]	.02	.11
	$ bet > P bet	.70	.19	.89
	TOTAL	.79	.21	$n = 87$[b]

[a] Entries are response proportions.
[b] Nine ties on price and/or rating are excluded.

much higher (mean = 74.0) than $ bets (mean = 59.9); (2) P bets were priced just below expected value (mean = $3.14), whereas $ bets were highly overpriced relative to expected value (mean = $6.77); and (3) the asymmetry of reversals was highly significant (McNemar's Q test, $p < .001$). Again, the *Mouselab* methodology did not alter the basic nature of the phenomenon.

Process Differences Between Response Modes

Because pricing and rating are both judgments, we might expect few process differences between them. Our results indicate that, although they are more similar than pricing and choice, there are also significant differences. As in Experiment 1, we look at total time, attention and search measures, and response generation.

Total Time. Time to respond differs both by response mode and type of gamble. Subjects took less time to rate a gamble (an average of 26.89 seconds) than to generate a price (34.53 seconds), $F(1, 358) = 11.07, p < .001$. Also, $ bets again took longer (34.30 seconds) than P bets (29.11 seconds), $F(1, 358) = 54.48$, $p < .0001$.

Attention. The proportion of time spent on probabilities is significantly higher in rating (54%) than in pricing (43%), $F(1, 358) = 44.85, p < .0001$. Like the corresponding result in Experiment 1, this is consistent with the idea that problem elements that are most easily mapped onto the response scale get greater consideration.

Search. Because both ratings and prices require overall evaluations of the gamble, we might expect that they would have similar patterns of search and that search would be primarily outcome-oriented. However, this is not the case. Using the same search index as in Experiment 1, we found that search patterns in pricing (−.204) were significantly more dimensional than those in rating (+.005), $F(1, 358) = 35.28, p < .0001$.

Response Generation. As in Experiment 1, subjects spent almost a third of the total time (32.6%) in and around the pricing response scale, and a similar pattern occurred in rating (30.8%). One difference between response modes was that in pricing more of this time was spent in the scale, adjusting the pointer, whereas in rating more of this time was spent near the scale, $F(1,363) = 19.47$, $p < .001$.

In pricing, starting points[8] were again higher for \$ bets (\$7.17) than for P bets (\$3.72), $F(1, 170) = 59.56, p < .0001$. These starting points were again significantly higher than final responses, indicating downward adjustment by an average of \$.49, $F(1, 170) = 20.19, p < .001$. However, in rating, starting points were higher for P bets (67.8) than for \$ bets (58.2), $F(1, 170) = 13.97, p < .001$. These starting points were lower than final responses, indicating upward adjustment by an average of 3.95, $F(1, 170) = 30.80, p < .0001$. Thus, although subjects appear to be using similar response mechanisms in both pricing and rating, the relative location of the starting points and direction of the adjustments differ.

Summary. These two judgment modes, pricing and rating, show clear similarities, but also important differences. The most striking similarities are the large amount of time spent in and around the response scale and the frequent use of what appears to be an anchoring and adjustment strategy. However, the starting points and direction of adjustments differ between pricing and rating. Other differences include greater attention to payoffs than to probabilities in pricing but the opposite in rating, more dimensional search in pricing, and somewhat less total time per gamble for rating. To explore the relationship of these measures to reversals, we next analyze differences between responses involved in a reversal and those that are consistent.

Differences Between Reversals and Consistent Responses

Total Time. As before, our interest in total time results, in part, from possible motivational explanations for the reversal phenomenon. Shorter times for reversal trials would be consistent with the notion that reversals result from a lack of effort or carelessness on the part of decision makers. If anything, the opposite seems to be true in this study, because those trials that resulted in consistent responses took less time (29.17 seconds) than those that resulted in reversals (33.17 seconds), $F(1, 358) = 5.57, p < .02$. As in Experiment 1, this difference is small in pricing. However, in rating, consistent responses took much less time (21.29 seconds) than reversals (30.11 seconds), $F(1, 358) = 10.63, p < .001$.

Attention. Recall that in Experiment 1, we found significant relationships between the proportion of time spent examining probabilities and the tendency to commit a reversal. In comparing choices to prices, most of the effect occurred in choice. In this study of two judgment modes there is no significant relationship between reversals and the proportion of time spent examining probabilities, despite the large difference between pricing and rating on this measure.

Search. Experiment 1 also showed a relationship between the type of search and whether subjects committed a reversal. However, this relationship occurred

---

[8] Recall that starting points are now defined as the point of entrance into the near-scale region, in contrast to Experiment 1, where the initial pointer position was used.

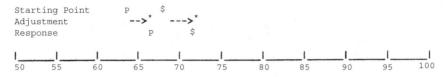

Rating, Consistent Responses

Rating, Reversals

Pricing, Consistent Responses

Pricing, Reversals

* Adjustment significantly different from zero, p <.05.

Figure 7.3. Starting points, adjustments, and final responses for consistent and reversal trials.

in choice and not in pricing. In this study there is no significant relationship between search patterns and the frequency of reversals.

Response Generation. Although we have not found relationships between reversals and either search or attention measures in comparing the two judgments, starting points and the amount and direction of adjustments are strongly related to reversals. Figure 7.3 shows the starting points, adjustments, and responses for each combination of response mode and gamble type, shown separately for consistent and reversal trials. First, in addition to the results for

Table 7.6. **Starting Points as a Function of Gamble Elements: Experiment 2**

	Pricing		Rating	
	Consistent	Reversal	Consistent	Reversal
G	.171	.386***	.502***	.310***
L	.073	.099	.470***	.239**
P	−.026	.096	.445***	.560***

$**p < .01; ***p < .001.$

response mode and item type noted earlier, the starting points differ for consistent and reversal trials, primarily because the ordering of P bets and $ bets in the rating task is reversed. This crossover interaction of reversal with type of bet is highly significant, $F(1, 170) = 34.25$, $p < .0001$. In pricing, there is no significant relationship between starting points and reversals. Second, the amount of adjustment differs for the four decisions during reversals and consistent responses. For example, in rating, P bets show much more adjustment during reversals than during consistent responses.

Why do these differences occur? One hypothesis consistent with that advanced for prices in Experiment 1 is that the selection of starting points reflects heavier consideration of one gamble element over the others. According to the compatibility account, the greater payoff, G, would be most salient in pricing, and the probability of winning, P, in rating. As in Experiment 1, we computed the partial correlation of each gamble element with starting points, controlling for the other elements (Table 7.6). The results are consistent with the compatibility hypothesis: Starting points in consistent trials seem to give similar weights to all gamble elements. In contrast, for reversal trials, G is the only important determinant of starting points in pricing, whereas P is by far the most significant determinant of starting points in rating.

Predicting Reversals with Process Measures

As in Experiment 1, to assess the joint effect of the process measures discussed earlier, we focused on a set of attention, search, and response variables found to be related to reversals in the preceding analysis. Eight variables were analyzed: (1) total time in rating, (2) the proportion of time in and around the response scale in P bets, (3) the relative position of starting points for the P and $ bets in pricing, (4) the relative position of starting points for the P and $ bets in rating, and (5–8) the amount of adjustment for each combination of bet type and response mode. A dichotomous response variable (1 if reversal, 0 if consistent) was regressed on these variables[9] (Table 7.7). The time in and around the response scale and the amount of adjustment for $ bets in rating were dropped because of a lack of significance. The overall model fit was highly significant, $F(6, 89) = 11.34$,

---

[9] We also estimated the analogous logistic regression model using maximum likelihood. This model yielded similar results.

Table 7.7. Process Regression Results: Experiment 2

Variable	Coefficient	t	p(t)
X_1 Total time in rating	.012	3.97	.000
X_2 Starting point order, pricing	.102	1.83	.070
X_3 Starting point order, rating	.271	5.98	.000
X_4 Adjustment, P bet, pricing	.041	2.56	.012
X_5 Adjustment, $ bet, pricing	−.019	−1.41	.161
X_6 Adjustment, P bet, rating	.017	4.21	.000

Correlation Matrix of Independent Variables

	X_1	X_2	X_3	X_4	X_5	X_6
X_1						
X_2	−.007					
X_3	.198	−.059				
X_4	−.119	.016	−.405			
X_5	.116	.063	.153	.484		
X_6	.060	−.193	.038	.137	.193	

Note: X_1 = average time for a rating response. X_2 = 1, if $-bet starting price > P-bet starting price; 0, if they are equivalent; or −1, if $-bet starting price < P-bet starting price. X_3 = 1, if P-bet starting rating > $-bet starting rating; 0, if they are equivalent; or −1, if $-bet starting rating > P-bet starting rating. X_4 = starting point − response, P bet, pricing. X_5 = starting point − response, $ bet, pricing. X_6 = response − starting point, P bet, rating.

$p < .0001$, $R^2 = .433$. As might be expected from Figure 7.3, variables from the rating task were the most significant predictors of reversals. Again, the occurrence of reversals appears to be predictable, in part, by measures of judgment processes.

DISCUSSION: EXPERIMENT 2

In Experiment 1 we saw a contrast between two very different processes operating in pricing (a judgment task) and choice. In Experiment 2 it appears that the two judgment tasks, pricing and rating, share largely similar strategies of generating a starting point and then adjusting it to arrive at a response. Although there are some differences (greater attention to payoffs in pricing but to probabilities in rating, pricing took somewhat longer, information search more dimensional in pricing), these are not related to reversals.

The process differences between pricing and rating that are related to reversals concern the way subjects use information to generate responses. Although the strategies used in rating and pricing seem quite similar, the roles of the gamble elements are different: Starting points in pricing are influenced heavily by the greater payoff, G, and in rating by the probability of winning, P. This results in higher starting points for $ bets than for P bets in pricing, but the opposite in rating. Moreover, this tendency is much stronger for reversals than for consistent responses. Thus, pricing and rating appear to use the same strategy "subroutine" but give it different inputs to process. However, the mental information of information observed here does not appear to be commutative (i.e., the order in which items of information enter the process affects the outcome): The information that influences the starting point early in the process gets greater weight in determining the response than the information that later influences the adjustment. One cognitive mechanism that could produce this overweighting is anchoring and (insufficient) adjustment.

If the selection of starting points does play a role in reversals, then we may be able to influence the frequency of reversals through a starting point manipulation. For example, when the manipulation reflects the naturally occurring starting points observed in Experiments 1 and 2, we should see a similar pattern of reversals. In contrast, when the manipulated starting points are opposite from the natural starting points, we should see a reduced frequency of reversals. In the next experiment, we directly manipulate starting points to further examine their role in producing reversals.

EXPERIMENT 3: ANCHOR MANIPULATION

METHOD

The stimuli and procedure are identical to those used in Experiment 2. In addition, there are four within-subjects experimental conditions in which starting points were manipulated. Twenty-seven paid MBA students were first required to decide whether their response was less than, equal to, or greater than a given value before the response scale appeared (Figure 7.4). Starting points were

Figure 7.4. Computer display for anchor manipulation.

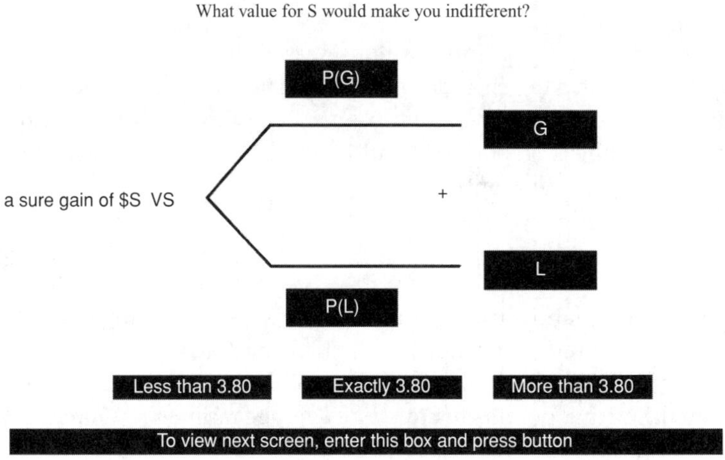

Table 7.8. Response Patterns: Experiment 3

		Rating				
		$A_p > A_\$$		$A_\$ > A_p$		
Pricing		$P > \$$	$\$ > P$	$P > \$$	$\$ > P$	
$A_p > A_\$$	$P > \$$	.37	.02	.22	.14	.37
	$\$ > P$	.46	.15	.30	.34	.63
$A_\$ > A_p$	$P > \$$	.06	.00	.00	.02	.04
	$\$ > P$	.75	.19	.56	.42	.96
		.82	.18	.54	.46	$n = 202$

Note: Entries are response proportions in the given cell. A_p refers to the anchor for the P bet, etc. P > $ means the response was higher for the P bet. The 14 ties on price, rating, or both are excluded. Responses predicted by anchoring and adjustment in each quadrant are underlined.

manipulated by systematically varying this value. The scale then appeared with the pointer already placed at the starting point value: Subjects were not free to choose the initial pointer placement.

Each gamble was assigned a "high" and a "low" starting point. High starting points were at about the 75th percentile of the response range, and low starting points at about the 25th percentile. The starting points were matched so that when the P bet had a high starting point for a given response mode, its corresponding $ bet had a low starting point, or vice versa, yielding four starting point combinations (Table 7.8). When the starting point in rating is higher for the P bet than for the $ bet, and vice versa in pricing, we expect the greatest frequency of the "usual" reversals (i.e., P bet preferred in rating and $ bet preferred for pricing should be most frequent in the lower left quadrant). However, when the starting point in rating is higher for the $ bet than for the P bet, and vice versa in pricing, we expect the lowest frequency of the usual reversals (i.e., the upper right quadrant).

The assignment of starting points to items was varied so that a subject received two of the eight pairs in each of the four starting point conditions, and across subjects, every pair appeared in every condition. Thus, for each response mode, each subject responded to all 16 gambles: 8 with high starting points and 8 with low starting points.

RESULTS

The starting point manipulation had large and significant effects in the predicted directions on both prices and ratings. In pricing, high starting points generated an average price of $5.30 and low starting points $3.94, $F(1, 396) = 22.03$, $p < .001$. In rating, high starting points generated an average rating of 70.7 and low starting points 58.6, $F(1, 396) = 46.39$, $p < .001$.

If the starting point manipulation had no effect, the same rate of reversals should occur with all four combinations of pricing and rating starting points. However, as predicted, there are large differences. The rate of reversals is highest in the quadrant predicted by anchoring and adjustment (75%), lower and roughly equal in the main diagonal quadrants (46% and 56%), and lowest in the upper right quadrant (30%; Table 7.8). These differences are significant, $F(3, 179) = 7.74, p < .001$. In the upper right quadrant, the asymmetry in reversals just achieves significance[10] (McNemar's $Q = 4.27, p = .04$). Thus, a simple starting point manipulation reduced the previously observed frequency of reversals (70% in Experiment 2) by more than half. Further, the pattern of reversals in the lower left quadrant is virtually identical to that observed in Experiment 2 without a starting point manipulation (cf. Table 7.5), whereas the patterns in other quadrants are substantially different. This result lends additional credence to the idea that starting point order plays an important role in reversals in the absence of a starting point manipulation.

DISCUSSION: EXPERIMENT 3

Although response patterns, relative to those in Experiment 2, change in the direction predicted by anchoring and adjustment, the absolute frequencies are not fully consistent with this as a single explanation. In the main diagonal quadrants, an anchoring and adjustment model predicts no significant asymmetry in reversals, and in the upper right quadrant, a significant asymmetry in the opposite direction from the usual reversals (Table 7.8). Neither of these predictions is supported, as the majority of reversals in all four quadrants are of the usual kind. In neither response mode could the starting point manipulation completely overcome strong ambient tendencies to prefer the P bet in rating and the $ bet in pricing, although the shifts are highly significant and in the predicted direction.

GENERAL DISCUSSION

In these experiments we have seen that measures of judgment and choice processes bear strong relationships to preference reversals. In part, these relationships are connected to fundamental process differences between judgment and choice. We find that in choice (compared with judgment), subjects take much less time, use different patterns of information search, and often employ strategies that make comparisons between the two alternatives. In contrast, in the judgment modes, pricing and rating, subjects often use a strategy focused on the response scale in which a starting point is selected and then adjusted to arrive at the response. Our results show that there are also systematic

---

[10] Contrast this result with the McNemar's Q of 85.04, $p < .0001$, for the other three quadrants combined.

relationships between detailed process measures of such mechanisms and the frequency of reversals. The most important of these are indicators of anchoring and adjustment activity and differential attention to probabilities and payoffs. In particular, the degree to which starting points are influenced by payoffs in pricing and probabilities in rating is a key factor.

Overall, our results are consistent with an explanation that relates starting points, anchoring and adjustment, and compatibility (see Tversky et al., 1988). In pricing and rating, many subjects seem to generate responses by making a series of adjustments on or near the response scale. The starting point for this process seems to depend on the values of the gamble elements as well as the response mode. One explanation for the differential influence of gamble elements on starting points is their compatibility with the response scale. Because payoffs are more compatible with pricing's dollar response scale than are probabilities, G is the most influential element,[11] leading to higher starting points for $ bets than for P bets. In contrast, probabilities are more compatible with the rating scale than are dollar payoffs, giving P the most influence in determining starting points in rating. If we assume that the starting points we observe are indicative of anchors, an obvious mechanism suggests itself: Because adjustments are often insufficient, the natural consequences are higher ratings for P bets but higher prices for $ bets – the standard pattern of reversals.

This account also addresses reversals that occur between judgment and choice. Together with the slight preference for the P bet in choice that has been observed in this study and others, the strong majority preferences for the $ bet in pricing and the P bet in rating produced by the compatibility-anchoring mechanism would give rise to pricing-choice and rating-choice reversals. Further, under this explanation the frequency of reversals should be greatest between rating and pricing (where compatibility and thus anchoring work in opposite directions across response modes) and least frequent between rating and choice (where the P bet is preferred in both cases, but to differing degrees). This is exactly the pattern that has been observed in this study and others (Goldstein & Einhorn, 1987; Tversky et al., 1988). This account is also consistent with the importance of overpricing the $ bet found by Tversky et al. (1990).

Our data seem, in some ways, to agree with the focus on generating responses suggested by Expression Theory. In the judgment tasks, pricing and rating, subjects spent almost a third of their time in and around the response scale. On the other hand, our account also departs from Expression Theory in some ways. We find that choice and judgment processes are quite different and that choice does not seem to consist mainly of two component evaluation judgments.

---

[11] Because G is both larger in magnitude and varies more than L, it probably receives the bulk of the subjective weight attributed to the payoff dimension. This is also consistent with the findings of Slovic and Lichtenstein (1968) and Lichtenstein and Slovic (1973) that for "favorable" bets like those in this study the amount to win tends to be the most important element, whereas for "unfavorable" bets the amount to lose tends to be more important.

Moreover, the evaluation process differs somewhat (e.g., starting points) across bet types as well. These results seem inconsistent with Expression Theory's assumption that the process by which the "basic evaluation" is determined is the same for all response modes and gamble types.

Although several more ambitious attempts to manipulate the frequency of reversals have failed (e.g., large incentives, extensive instructions, group contexts), a simple starting point manipulation was sufficient to cut the rate of reversals by more than half. However, although Experiment 3 demonstrates that starting points are sufficient to change the pattern of reversals, it does not show that anchors are necessarily the causal mechanism that produces reversals in other experiments. Unfortunately, we cannot tell whether the processes that produce reversals in other experiments are also themselves altered by this manipulation. Doing so would require a more complete observation of anchors than that provided by our starting points. Thus, more direct inferences about the underlying causes of preference reversal based on this result must await future research. At the same time, it is encouraging that anchoring, coupled with insufficient adjustment, also provides an explanation for a similar judgment inconsistency in the assessment of utilities using simple lotteries (see Johnson & Schkade, 1989).

Process tracing, by itself, is not necessarily the answer to discovering the causes of judgment and choice phenomena. Many of the measures that we have gathered are not related to reversals (even when they differ between response modes). Rather, specific measures suggested by prior theory (e.g., compatibility, anchoring and adjustment) seem to be the most informative. A major obstacle to using process data is identifying appropriate measures at an appropriate level of analysis. The "rich" data provided by process methods can often be overwhelming rather than informative. Theories that address judgment and choice phenomena at a process level can help by identifying specific process measures on which to focus and task or stimulus characteristics that might affect the rate of reversals. Finally, studies that combine process tracing with input–output models should prove valuable in establishing an understanding of these phenomena across different judgment tasks.

ACKNOWLEDGMENTS

This work was supported in part by a research fellowship to the first author from the IBM Corporation. We thank John Payne, Amos Tversky, Sarah Lichtenstein, Maya Bar-Hillel, Paul Slovic, Don Kleinmuntz, and Lynda Kilbourne for helpful comments.

8. The Causes of Preference Reversal

Amos Tversky, Paul Slovic, and Daniel Kahneman

Axiomatic theories of choice introduce preference as a primitive relation, which is interpreted through specific empirical procedures such as choice or pricing. Models of rational choice assume a principle of procedure invariance, which requires strategically equivalent methods of elicitation to yield the same preference order. Thus, if the decision maker prefers A to B, then the cash equivalent, or minimum selling price, of A should exceed that of B. However, there is a substantial body of evidence showing that the price ordering of risky prospects is systematically different from the choice ordering, contrary to standard theories of choice.

The effect of elicitation method on preference between gambles was first observed by Slovic and Lichtenstein (1968) who found that both buying and selling prices of gambles were primarily determined by the payoffs, whereas choices between gambles (and ratings of their attractiveness) were primarily influenced by the probabilities of winning and losing. Slovic and Lichtenstein reasoned that, if the method used to elicit preferences affected the weighting of the gambles' components, it should be possible to construct pairs of gambles such that the same individual would choose one member of the pair but set a higher price for the other. Lichtenstein and Slovic (1971, 1973) demonstrated such reversals in a series of studies, one of which was conducted on the floor of the Four Queens Casino in Las Vegas with experienced gamblers playing for real money.

The preference-reversal phenomenon involves a pair of gambles of comparable expected value. One gamble (the H bet) offers a high probability of winning a modest sum of money; the other gamble (the L bet) offers a low probability of winning a relatively large amount of money. These bets were also called the P bet and the $ bet, respectively. For example,

H bet: 28/36 chance to win $10

L bet: 3/36 chance to win $100.

Reprinted from *The American Economic Review*, vol. 80, pp. 204–217. Copyright © 1990 by the American Economic Association. Reprinted with permission.

When offered a choice between the two options, most subjects choose the H bet over the L bet. However, when asked to state their lowest selling price, the majority state a higher price for the L bet than for the H bet.

There have been three waves of studies of preference reversal (PR). The first included the original experiments of Slovic and Lichtenstein (1968), Lichtenstein and Slovic (1971, 1973), and the study of Lindman (1971). The second wave of studies, conducted during the late 1970s and early 1980s, consisted of critical replications and attempts to eliminate PRs by procedural variations and by increased incentives. A particularly careful replication was performed by Grether and Plott (1979), who designed a series of experiments "to discredit the psychologists' work as applied to economics" (p. 623). Grether and Plott generated a list of 13 objections and potential artifacts that would render the PR phenomenon irrelevant to economic theory. Their list included poor motivation, income effects, strategic responding, and the fact that the experimenters were psychologists (which might have led the respondents to be suspicious and behave peculiarly). Grether and Plott attempted to eliminate PR by careful experimental procedures, including a special incentive system, but the effect was hardly diminished. Further studies by Hamm (1984), Pommerehne, Schneider, and Zweifel (1982), and Reilly (1982) led to similar conclusions. PR was also observed by Mowen and Gentry (1980) in both individual and group choices concerning product development, by Knez and Smith (1991), who allowed their subjects to trade bets in an experimental market, and by Berg, Dickhaut, and O'Brien (1985), who introduced arbitrage. See also Slovic and Lichtenstein (1983).

The robustness of PRs led to the third wave of articles, which attempted to explain the phenomenon rather than eliminate it. Three classes of models for PR were introduced: (a) nontransitive choice models were developed independently by Loomes and Sugden (1982, 1983) and by Fishburn (1984, 1985); (b) response bias models were proposed by Tversky, Sattath, and Slovic (1988), and by Goldstein and Einhorn (1987); and (c) generalized utility models, which maintain transitivity but abandon the independence axiom, were applied to PR by Holt (1986) and Karni and Safra (1987). The three families of models respectively attribute PR to violations of transitivity, procedure invariance, or the independence axiom. Violations of these principles have been observed in other contexts, but their contributions to PR have not been assessed. The present chapter provides such assessment. To accomplish this goal, we extend the traditional experimental design, introduce an ordinal payoff scheme, and develop a new diagnostic analysis to determine the causes of PR.

Diagnostic Analysis

Let C_H and C_L denote, respectively, the cash equivalent (or minimum selling price) of H and L, and $\succ$ and $\approx$ denote strict preference and indifference, respectively. (The elicitation of cash equivalents is discussed in the next section.) A standard PR is said to occur when H is preferred to L, but L is priced higher than H, that is, $H \succ L$ and $C_L > C_H$. Note that $\succ$ refers to preference between options, whereas $>$ refers to the ordering of cash amounts. We assume that the two relations are consistent in the sense that $X > Y$ implies $X \succ Y$; more money is preferred to less. We now show that PR implies either intransitivity or a failure of procedure invariance, or both. Procedure invariance holds whenever the decision maker prefers a bet B to a cash amount X if and only if his or her selling price for B exceeds X; that is, $B \succ X$ iff $C_B > X$. In particular, invariance implies that $C_B = X$ iff $B \approx X$. If invariance holds, PR entails the following cycle:

$$C_H \approx H \succ L \approx C_L \succ C_H,$$

where the two inequalities are implied by PR and the two equivalences follow from invariance.

Because procedure invariance is commonly taken for granted, many authors have interpreted PR as an instance of intransitivity. The finding that strategically equivalent methods of elicitation yield systematically different preferences (see, for example, Tversky et al., 1988) suggests that PR may be caused by a failure of procedure invariance, not of transitivity. Two types of discrepancy between choice and pricing could produce PR: overpricing of L and underpricing of H. *Overpricing* of L is said to occur if the decision maker prefers the price over the bet when offered a choice between them (i.e., $C_L \succ L$). *Underpricing* of H is said to occur if the decision maker prefers the bet over its price in a direct choice (i.e., $H \succ C_H$). The two other forms of a choice-pricing discrepancy – underpricing of L and overpricing of H – produce a nonstandard pattern of reversals. Note that overpricing and underpricing merely identify the sign of the discrepancy between pricing and choice; the labels do not imply that the bias resides in the pricing.

If PR is due to an intransitivity, it should be observable in binary choice data without the use of a pricing task. On the other hand, choice could be transitive if PR is due to overpricing of L or to underpricing of H. To find out whether PR is caused by intransitivity or by noninvariance, we extend the usual experimental design to include an option of receiving X for sure. In this design, the decision maker provides three choices (H-L, H-X, L-X) and two assessments of price (C_H and C_L). The relevant data for diagnosing the sources of PR consists of all patterns of preferences satisfying

$$H \succ L \text{ and } C_L > X > C_H.$$

These are the patterns that exhibit PR and satisfy the condition that X lies between the two prices. Note that for any PR pattern it is possible to select a cash amount X that falls between the two prices stated by a given individual. For an experiment, however, it is more convenient to determine X in advance and to restrict the analysis to all PR patterns in which the prices stated by the subject straddle the predetermined value of X. The critical data, then, are the observed choices between X and H and between X and L. Ignoring ties, there are four possible response patterns.

(1)   *Intransitivity*: $L \succ X$ and $X \succ H$, yielding $L \succ X \succ H \succ L$.
(2)   *Overpricing of L (OL)*: $X \succ H$ and $X \succ L$, yielding $C_L \succ X \succ L$.
(3)   *Underpricing of H (UH)*: $H \succ X$ and $L \succ X$, yielding $H \succ X \succ C_H$.
(4)   *Both OL and UH*: $H \succ X$ and $X \succ L$, yielding $H \succ X > C_H$ and $C_L \succ X \succ L$.

Note that the present diagnostic procedure classifies all test patterns according to whether they violate transitivity but not invariance (pattern 1) or invariance but not transitivity (patterns 2, 3, and 4) because no test pattern can violate both. The relative frequencies of these patterns can be used to test PR models that assume invariance but not transitivity (for example, the regret theory of Loomes & Sugden, 1982) against models that assume transitivity but not invariance (for example, the contingent weighting model of Tversky et al., 1988). The relative incidence of violations of transitivity and invariance could be different in a more elaborate diagnostic procedure (involving more than three options), which yields patterns of preference that can violate transitivity and invariance at once. The preceding discussion is summarized as follows.

Any pattern of preferences that satisfies the test conditions ($H \succ L$ and $C_L > X > C_H$) and monetary consistency ($X > Y$ implies $X \succ Y$) obeys the following propositions:

(a)   Either transitivity or invariance ($B \succ X$ iff $C_B > X$) is violated.
(b)   Intransitivity holds iff $L \succ X \succ H$, yielding pattern 1.
(c)   Overpricing of L occurs iff $X \succ L$, yielding patterns 2 or 4.
(d)   Underpricing of H occurs iff $H \succ X$, yielding patterns 3 or 4.

This analysis provides a simple method for the diagnosis of all preference patterns satisfying the test condition according to the implied cause of PR. The applications of this method to experimental data are described in Studies 1 and 2.

Elicitation Procedures
The preceding analysis provides an effective method for diagnosing PR, assuming preferences and selling prices are observable. Such data are routinely elicited in experiments and surveys, and are normally taken at face value – provided the results are reproducible and the respondents have no reason to conceal or misrepresent their preferences. Nevertheless, students of choice favor elicitation procedures that are incentive compatible. Becker, DeGroot, and Marschak (1964) devised such a scheme for the elicitation of cash equivalents, which has often been used in PR studies. In this procedure, called the BDM scheme, the subject states a selling price for a gamble. An offer is then generated by some random process. The subject receives the offer if it exceeds the stated selling price and plays the gamble if the stated price exceeds the offer.

Recently, Holt (1986) and Karni and Safra (1987) pointed out that the justification of the BDM scheme and of similar procedures assumes the independence axiom of expected utility theory. If this axiom fails, the stated price of a bet is no longer equal to its cash equivalent; hence, the presence of PR in some experiments can be attributed to violations of independence. In particular, Holt argued that the usual payoff schemes in which the subject plays only one bet, selected at random, assume independence among the subject's responses. This argument, however, invokes the independence axiom in a sequential setup where no systematic violations of this axiom have been observed. Moreover, Tversky and Kahneman (1986) showed that the common violations of independence and substitution generally disappear when the choice is presented in a sequential form. This finding undermines the empirical basis of Holt's argument. Karni and Safra analyzed the actual lottery induced by the BDM scheme and showed that a generalized utility model with a nonlinear (probability) weighting function can explain the observed discrepancy between choice and stated prices in this scheme. According to this interpretation, PR data do not reflect inconsistent preferences because the choices and the pricing do not involve the same bets. Consequently, PR can be explained by a model that satisfies transitivity and invariance, but not independence. In a closely related development, Segal (1988) suggested that PR may be produced by a failure of the reduction axiom, which reduces a two-stage lottery to the equivalent one-stage lottery. The preceding accounts, however, cannot explain the basic finding that the same pattern of PR obtained under the BDM scheme (for example, Grether & Plott, 1979) is equally prevalent in experiments that do not use any incentive-compatible elicitation scheme (for example, Lichtenstein & Slovic, 1971) and therefore do not invoke the independence or the reduction axioms. If PR is caused by a failure of these axioms, the frequency of reversals should increase when the BDM scheme is used, contrary to fact.

As noted by Karni and Safra (1987), there may be no incentive-compatible scheme for the elicitation of selling prices that does not rely on the independence axiom. To demonstrate PRs, however, it is not necessary to elicit the actual selling prices; it is sufficient to establish their *order*. The ordering of selling prices can be obtained under weaker conditions, as demonstrated by the following incentive-compatible procedure, which we call the ordinal payoff scheme. The subject is first presented with each bet separately and asked to state its lowest selling price. The subject is then presented with pairs of bets and asked to select the preferred prospect in each pair. Subjects know that one of these pairs will be selected at random at the end of the session and that a random device will determine whether they play the bet they preferred in the choice task or the bet they priced higher. Because the prices are merely used to order the bets within each pair, choice and pricing are strategically equivalent. A reversal then amounts to an inconsistency in which the subject expresses in the choice task a preference for playing the H bet and in the pricing task a preference for playing the L bet. To rationalize this pattern within a generalized (nonindependent) utility model, it is necessary to assume that subjects prefer an even chance to play *either* H or L over the option of playing H, *and* over the option of playing L. Such a mixed strategy, however, could explain random reversals, but not systematic ones. The presence of systematic reversals in the ordinal

Table 8.1. The Monetary Bets Used in Study 1[a]

	Triple	1	2	3	4	5	6
Set							
	H	(0.97,4)	(0.81,2)	(0.94,3)	(0.89,4)	(0.94,2.5)	(0.92,2)
I	L	(0.31,16)	(0.19,9)	(0.50,6.5)	(0.11,40)	(0.39,8.5)	(0.50,5)
	X	(3.85)	(1.50)	(2.75)	(3.25)	(2.40)	(1.85)
	H	(0.97,100)	(0.81,50)	(0.94,75)	(0.89,100)	(0.94,65)	(0.92,50)
II	L	(0.31,400)	(0.19,225)	(0.50,160)	(0.11,1000)	(0.39,210)	(0.50,125)
	X	(95)	(40)	(70)	(80)	(60)	(45)
	H	(0.78,10)	(0.69,7)	(0.86,3)	(0.94,4)	(0.92,12)	(0.89,11)
III	L	(0.08,100)	(0.17,40)	(0.19,13)	(0.03,150)	(0.06,175)	(0.08,135)
	X	(8)	(5.50)	(2.75)	(3.75)	(10)	(9)

[a] The pair (P, X) denotes a bet that offers a probability P to win $X and nothing otherwise, and (X) denotes $X for sure. The probabilities were expressed as multiples of $1/36$.

payoff scheme, therefore, cannot be explained by violations of independence or of the reduction axiom.

STUDY 1 (MONETARY BETS)

The participants in the studies reported in this chapter (unless specified otherwise) were recruited by ads in the University of Oregon newspaper. The number of men and women was roughly the same, and their median age was 22 years. The studies were run in a class setting, and participants were paid for participation. One hundred and ninety-eight individuals (called the main group) participated in the main part of Study 1.

We constructed 18 triples that consisted of a high-probability bet (*H*), a low-probability bet (*L*), and a cash amount (*X*), with roughly the same expected value. The 18 triples were divided into 3 sets of 6 triples each, displayed in Table 8.1. Set I included relatively small bets like those used in previous studies, without negative outcomes. Set II was obtained by multiplying all payoffs in Set I by a factor of 25. Set III was a mixture of small and large bets including a few long shots. The options were presented in written form. All probabilities were expressed as multiples of $1/36$ (for example, $11/36$ to win $16.00) and interpreted with reference to a roulette wheel with 36 numbered sectors. Within each set, the respondents first assessed the cash equivalent for each of the 12 bets and then chose between the options of each triple: *H* versus *L*, *H* versus *X*, *L* versus *X*. The order of the options within each set was randomized. The order of the sets was I, II, III for half of the participants, and III, II, I for the others. As part of the general instructions, the participants were asked to imagine that one pair of bets would be selected at random, and they would have a chance to play either the bet they had chosen or the bet for which they had stated a higher cash equivalent.

152 A. Tversky, P. Slovic, and D. Kahneman

Table 8.2. *Percentage of Preferences for All Subjects in Study 1*

	Triple	1	2	3	4	5	6	Mean
Set								
	$H \succ L$	83	68	71	71	73	62	71
I	$C_H > C_L$	26	22	30	33	17	14	24
	PR	59	53	45	41	59	49	51
	$H \succ L$	91	86	77	84	82	70	82
II	$C_H > C_L$	54	48	46	47	48	32	46
	PR	38	44	36	41	40	44	41
	$H \succ L$	81	68	74	74	81	79	76
III	$C_H > C_L$	38	21	39	38	58	46	40
	PR	48	48	42	39	29	36	40
	$H \succ L$	67	75	62	67	62	56	65
I$_\$$	$C_H > C_L$	44	18	22	44	12	9	25
	PR	32	60	51	36	50	49	46

To investigate the effect of monetary incentives, we ran an additional group of subjects whose payoffs were contingent on their responses. These subjects ($N = 179$) evaluated only Set I.[1] They received the same instructions as the main group, but were told that 15% of the participants, selected at random would actually play one bet determined as follows. A pair of bets would be selected at random, and the chosen subjects would play the bet that they had favored either in the choice or in the pricing task. Because each subject plays at most one bet, this procedure defines a compound lottery in which the probability of winning a prize is considerably smaller than in the original bet. Exactly the same compound lottery, however, is induced by the choice and by the pricing. Assuming invariance, therefore, there is no reason for reversals in the ordinal payoff scheme.

Results

Table 8.2 presents, for each (H, L) pair, the percentage of subjects who chose H over L ($H \succ L$), the percentage of subjects who priced H above L ($C_H > C_L$), and the percentage of subjects who exhibited PR ($H \succ L$ and $C_L > C_H$). Only the subjects ($N = 179$) who had no missing data were included in this analysis. Because no indifference was allowed in choice, we excluded tied prices from the analysis. Their inclusion, of course, would have inflated the PR rate. The I$_\$$ data refer to the subjects who evaluated Set I with monetary incentives.

The PR phenomenon is clearly evident in Table 8.2. Overall, H is chosen over L in 74% of the cases, but C_H exceeds C_L in only 34% of the cases. Nearly half of the response patterns are inconsistent and the standard reversals (45%) are

---

[1] These subjects also rated the attractiveness of all 12 bets; the analysis of the rating data was reported by Tversky et al. (1988).

overwhelmingly more frequent than the nonstandard ones (4%). Table 8.2 also shows that there are no major differences among three sets of gambles that span a wide range of payoffs. Furthermore, the use of monetary incentives in the $I_\$$ condition had no systematic effect on the prevalence of PR, in agreement with previous studies (see, for example, Slovic & Lichtenstein, 1983). The overall percentage of PR with real payoffs is 46% (Set $I_\$$) compared with an overall rate of 44% without payoffs (Sets I, II, III).

The hypothesis that subjects prefer mixtures was tested by presenting 42 Stanford students with the six pairs of H and L bets from Set I. They were told that one-third of the participants, selected at random, would play one of their chosen bets. For each pair, they were given three options: (a) select the H bet, (b) select the L bet, and (c) let the experimenter select between H and L at random. None of the responses favored the mixed strategy.

The results of Study 1 cannot be explained as a failure of the independence axiom, or of the reduction axiom, for two reasons. First, this account assumes that the subjects favor a mixed strategy, contrary to the responses of the Stanford students. Second, even if – contrary to these data – we assume that subjects adopt a mixed strategy, the standard and the nonstandard reversals should have been equally frequent. We conclude that PR is not an elicitation artifact caused by nonindependence; hence, it must violate either transitivity or procedure invariance.

Having established the validity of PR, we turn now to the diagnostic analysis described earlier. Unlike the preceding discussion that was based only on the price ordering, the following analysis assumes that the stated prices C_H and C_L are the actual cash equivalents of H and L. We shall address this assumption in the next section. The diagnostic analysis is based on the data of all subjects from the main group who completed all tasks. About half of the PR patterns in Sets I, II, and III met the test condition $C_L > X > C_H$, yielding 620 individual patterns of preference that satisfied

$$H \succ L \text{ and } C_L > X > C_H.$$

These data were classified into four types according to the observed relation of X to L and to H, and the distribution of the four types is presented in Table 8.3. The data show that only 10% of the preference patterns are intransitive and 90% exhibit noninvariance. Among the noninvariant patterns, the overpricing of L is much more common than the underpricing of H. Further evidence for this conclusion comes from a study by Bostic, Herrnstein, and Luce (1990), who used a series of successive choices to determine, for each subject, a cash amount X that is indifferent to a given bet. They found that this cash amount was roughly the same as the stated price for H bets and substantially below it for L bets. That is, $X = C_H$ and $X < C_L$, as entailed by the overpricing of L.

Discussion

The high incidence of PR (45%) obtained using the ordinal payoff scheme indicates that PR cannot be explained by a generalized utility model, as

Table 8.3. *Distribution of Response Patterns in Study 1*

Pattern	N	Percent	Diagnosis
(1) $L \succ X, X \succ H$	62	10.0	Intransitivity
(2) $X \succ L, X \succ H$	406	65.5	Overpricing of L (OL)
(3) $L \succ X, H \succ X$	38	6.1	Underpricing of H (UH)
(4) $H \succ X, X \succ L$	114	18.4	Both OL and UH
TOTAL	620	100	

proposed by Holt (1986), by Karni and Safra (1987), and by Segal (1988). Recall that these authors provided no direct evidence for this proposal; they only showed that PR could be consistent with transitivity and invariance if independence (or the reduction axiom) is discarded. The data refute this interpretation. The present analysis demonstrates that abandoning independence or the reduction axiom is neither necessary nor sufficient to account for PR. The results summarized in Table 8.3 show that the PRs observed in Study 1 are produced primarily by the failure of procedure invariance. The finding that 90% of test patterns violated this condition rules out all models of PR that assume procedure invariance, including regret theory (Loomes & Sugden, 1982, 1983). Because this theory attributes all PR to intransitivity, it entails that 100% of the test patterns in Table 8.3 should be intransitive. The fact that only 10% of the test patterns conformed to this prediction indicates that regret theory does not provide an adequate explanation of PR.

This conclusion does not imply that intransitivity plays no role in PR. Loomes, Starmer, and Sugden (1989) have demonstrated that the cycle $H \succ L \succ X \succ H$, implied by regret theory, is significantly more frequent than the opposite cycle $L \succ H \succ X \succ L$. The present study confirmed this result; the observed frequencies of the two cycles were 132 and 44, respectively (see Appendix 1). It is noteworthy that the incidence of intransitivity reported by these investigators (15–20%) is higher than that observed in the present study, but the rates of PR are roughly the same. Although the difference in the incidence of intransitivity does not affect our main conclusion regarding the prevalence of noninvariance, it raises the question as to whether the present methodology underestimates the contribution of intransitivity of PR. Because the ordinal payoff scheme requires, in effect, the ranking of all bets, it might induce intransitive subjects to behave transitively. But if our procedure reduces the number of cycles, it should also reduce the incidence of PR. In fact, the PR rate in the present study is slightly higher than in other studies. Moreover, the finding that the rate of PR is generally insensitive to the payoff scheme makes this possibility even less likely. Finally, Appendix 1 shows that the percentage of cycles that satisfy the test condition (10%) is higher than the percentage of cycles among PR patterns that do not satisfy the test condition (5.2%). The available evidence, therefore, does not support the hypothesis that the present diagnostic procedure underestimates intransitivity, although this possibility cannot be ruled out.

It could be argued that the subjects in Study 1 did not state their actual selling prices but rather some monotone transformation of these prices because only their order – not the actual values – is relevant to the present payoff scheme. The subjects, however, had no strategic or any other reason to transform their prices. Moreover, the present procedure discourages such transformation because the subject has to evaluate each bet separately, without knowing how it will be paired. Stating the cash equivalent of each bet, as requested, is obviously the simplest way to achieve a ranking without having to remember the responses to previous bets. Indeed, the standard deviations (across subjects) of observed prices in Study 1 did not exceed those obtained from comparable bets in studies that used the BDM scheme (for example, Bostic et al., 1990), contrary to what might be expected if our subjects reported monotone transformations of their selling prices. As in other studies, the standard deviations were considerably smaller for H bets than for L bets.

In contrast to the present design, where each bet was priced separately and the subject did not know which bets would be paired, Cox and Epstein (1989) employed a different procedure in which the subject priced each pair of H and L bets concurrently and then played the higher-priced bet. This procedure allows the subject to generate a price ordering by comparing the two bets without performing the more difficult task of assessing their actual selling prices. Indeed, Cox and Epstein acknowledged (on the basis of the subjects' responses) that their procedure did not elicit proper cash equivalents. Because the bets were framed differently in choice and in pricing (by translating all outcomes), many response patterns were inconsistent (32%), but the reversals were random rather than systematic.

Scale Compatibility

Why do people overprice the low-probability high-payoff bets? Following Tversky et al. (1988), we interpret this finding as an instance of a more general principle of compatibility: The weight of any aspect (for example, probability, payoff) of an object of evaluation is enhanced by compatibility with the response (for example, choice, pricing). The effect of scale compatibility is illustrated in a study by Slovic, Griffin, and Tversky (1990). Participants predicted the 1987 market value of 12 companies (taken from *Business Week* top 100) on the basis of their 1986 market value (in billions of dollars) and their rank (among the top 100) with respect to 1987 profits. One-half of the subjects predicted 1987 market value in billions of dollars, whereas the other half predicted the company's rank with respect to its 1987 market value. As implied by compatibility, each predictor was given more weight when the criterion was expressed on the same scale (for example, money, rank). As a consequence, the relative weight of the 1986 market value was twice as high for those who predicted in dollars than for those who predicted the corresponding rank. This effect produced many reversals of judgment in which one company was ranked above another but the order of their predicted value was reversed.

Because the selling price of a bet is expressed in dollars, compatibility entails that the payoffs, which are expressed in the same units, will be weighted more heavily in pricing than in choice. (Because the payoffs are much larger in the L bets than in the H bets, the major consequence of a compatibility bias is overpricing of L bets.) To accommodate violations of procedure invariance, Tversky et al. (1988) developed a family of models in which the weighting of attributes is contingent on the method of elicitation. The simplest model of this type, called the contingent weighting model, assumes that the bet $B = (P, X)$ is chosen over $B' = (P', X')$ iff

$$\log P + \alpha \log X > \log P' + \alpha \log X'$$

and that B is priced above B iff

$$\log P + \beta \log X > \log P' + \beta \log X'.$$

This loglinear form represents the ordering of bets according to both choice and pricing by a multiplicative probability-value model with a power function for gains. In this representation, procedure invariance entails $\beta = \alpha$, whereas compatibility implies $\beta > \alpha$. Slovic et al. (1990) applied this model to the choice and the price ordering from Study 1 and assessed α and β separately for each subject. In accord with compatibility, β exceeded α for 87% of the subjects ($N = 179$), indicating greater risk aversion in choice than in pricing.

The role of compatibility in PR was investigated in two additional studies reported by Slovic et al. (1990). In the first study, subjects were presented with six pairs of H and L bets. Three pairs involved monetary payoffs as in Study 1, and three pairs involved nonmonetary outcomes, such as a 1-week pass for all movie theaters in town or a dinner for two at a good restaurant. If PRs are primarily a result of the compatibility of prices and payoffs, which are both expressed in dollars, their incidence should be substantially reduced by the use of nonmonetary outcomes. This prediction was confirmed: The percentage of choice of H over L was roughly the same in the monetary (63%) and the nonmonetary bets (66%), but the percentage of cases in which $C_L > C_H$ was substantially greater in the former (54%) than in the latter (33%), and the overall incidence of PR decreased significantly from 41% to 24%.

A second study by Slovic et al. (1990) investigated reversals in a matching task. This experiment employed the 12 pairs of H and L bets from Sets I and II, described in Table 8.1. In each pair, one value – either a probability or a payoff – was missing, and the subjects were asked to set the missing value so that they would be indifferent between the two bets. Consider, for example, the bets $H = (0.92, \$50)$ and $L = (0.50, \$125)$ from Set II, Table 8.1. If we replace the 0.5 probability in L by a question mark, the subject is asked in effect "What chance to win \$125 is equally attractive as a 0.92 chance to win \$50?" The value set by the subject implies a preference between the original bets. If the value exceeds 0.50, we infer that the subject prefers H to L, and if the value is less than 0.50, we reach the opposite conclusion. Using all four components as missing values, the authors obtained the preferences inferred from matching either the probability or the payoff of each bet. Because compatibility applies to matching, not only to pricing, the attribute on which that match is made is expected to be weighted more heavily than the other attribute. As a consequence, the inferred percentage of preference for H over L should be higher for probability matches than for payoff matches. Indeed, the overall percentage of preference for H over L derived from probability matches (73%) was significantly higher than that derived from payoff matches (49%).

The matching data suggest an additional factor, besides scale compatibility, that might contribute to PR. In an extensive comparison of choice and matching, Tversky et al. (1988) have shown that the more prominent attribute of options looms larger in choice than in matching. Thus, the choice order is more lexicographic than that induced by matching. If probability is perceived by subjects as more important than payoffs, as suggested by the finding that the rating of bets is dominated by probability (Goldstein & Einhorn, 1987; Slovic & Lichtenstein, 1968), then the prominence effect may contribute to PR over and above the effect of scale compatibility. This could help explain the robustness of PR, as well as the similarity between the choice data and the preferences derived from probability matches. Note that in pricing and payoff matches, both compatibility and prominence enhance the PR effect, whereas in probability matches, they operate in opposite directions (see Slovic et al., 1990).

STUDY 2 (TIME PREFERENCES)

According to compatibility, reversals of preference are not restricted to risky prospects; they should also occur in other situations in which decision makers both choose and price options with a monetary component. In the next study, we test this prediction in the context of time preferences. Consider a delayed payment of the form (X, T) that offers a payment of X, T years from now. Following the design of Study 1, we constructed four triples of options that consisted of a long-term prospect L (for example, $2,500, 5 years from now), a short-term prospect S (for example, $1,600, 1.5 years from now), and an immediate payment X (for example, $1,250 now).

One hundred and sixty-nine subjects participated in the study. One-half of the subjects first chose between the three pairs of options (S vs. L, S vs. X, L vs. X) in each triple. The order of the pairs was randomized across triples. Following the choice, these subjects priced each of the S and L options by stating "the smallest immediate cash payment for which they would be willing to exchange the delayed payment." The other subjects performed the choice and pricing tasks in the opposite order. There were no systematic differences between the groups, so their data were combined.

The upper part of Table 8.4 presents the four triples of options employed in this study. The lower part of the table includes, for each triple, the percentage of subjects who chose S over L ($S \succ L$), the percentage of subjects who priced S above L ($C_S > C_L$), and the percentage of PR patterns ($S \succ L$ and $C_L > C_S$). Table 8.4 reveals a massive amount of PR. Overall, the short-term option (S) was

Table 8.4. The Options Used in Study 2 and the Respective Percentage of Preferences. The Pair (X, T) Denotes the Option of Receiving $X, T Years From Now, and (X) Denotes an Immediate Cash Payment

Triple	1	2	3	4	Mean
S	(1600, 1.5)	(1600, 1.5)	(2500, 5)	(1525, 0.5)	
L	(2500, 5)	(3550, 10)	(3550, 10)	(1900, 2.5)	
X	(1250)	(1250)	(1250)	(1350)	
$S \succ L$	57	72	83	83	74
$C_S > C_L$	12	19	29	40	25
PR	49	56	57	46	52

chosen over the long-term option (L) 74% of the time, but was priced higher only 25% of the time, yielding more than 50% PR patterns.

Note that in the pricing task each option is evaluated singly, whereas choice involves a comparison between options. The observed reversals, therefore, are consistent with an alternative hypothesis that payoffs are weighted more heavily in a singular than in a comparative evaluation. To test this hypothesis, we replicated the study in a new group of 184 subjects, with one change. Instead of pricing the options, the subjects were asked to rate the attractiveness of each option on a scale from 0 (not at all attractive) to 20 (extremely attractive). If PR is controlled, in part at least, by the nature of the task (singular vs. comparative), rating and pricing should yield similar results. On the other hand, if PR is produced primarily by the compatibility between payoffs and prices, rating and choice should yield similar results. The data reveal no discrepancy between choice and rating. Overall, S was chosen over L 75% of the time (as in the original study) and the rating of S exceeded the rating of L in 76% of the cases, in accord with procedure invariance. Only 11% of the patterns exhibited PR.

We also applied the diagnostic analysis to the results of Study 2. Recall that the relevant test data consisted of all patterns of the form

$$S \succ L \text{ and } C_L > X > C_S.$$

These are the patterns that exhibit PR, and the immediate payment of $X falls between the two cash equivalents. These data were classified into four types according to the observed relation of X to L and to S. The distribution of the four types is presented in Table 8.5 along with the appropriate diagnoses. The table shows that the major determinant of PR in delayed payments is the overpricing of the long-term prospect (L) and that the underpricing of the short-term prospect (S) and the intransitivity of $\succ$ play a relatively minor role (see also Appendix 2). Evidently, payoffs are weighted more heavily in pricing than in choice.

GENERAL DISCUSSION

The PR phenomenon has been demonstrated in numerous studies but its causes have not been established. The present chapter attempts to determine these

Table 8.5. Distribution of Response Patterns in Study 2

Pattern	N	Percent	Diagnosis
(1) $L \succ X, X \succ S$	16	15.4	Intransitivity
(2) $X \succ L, X \succ S$	57	54.8	Overpricing of L (OL)
(3) $L \succ X, S \succ X$	12	11.5	Underprincing of S (US)
(4) $S \succ X, X \succ L$	19	18.3	Both OL and US
TOTAL	104	100	

causes by comparing several accounts that attribute PR to violations of transitivity, procedure invariance, independence, or the reduction axiom. To assess the relative contributions of these effects we extend the standard experimental design, employ an ordinal payoff scheme, and introduce a new diagnostic analysis. The results appear quite clear.

First, PR cannot be attributed to violations of the independence or the reduction axioms and therefore cannot be rationalized by a generalized (nonindependent) utility model, as proposed by Holt (1986), Karni and Safra (1987), and Segal (1988). Note that the basic PR pattern does not involve these axioms, which are only needed to justify payoff procedures such as the BDM scheme. If PR were caused by nonindependence, or by a failure of the reduction axiom, it should be observed in the BDM scheme but not in the present ordinal scheme or in experiments where the payoffs are not contingent on the subject's responses. The finding that PR is no more frequent in the BDM scheme, which assumes independence, than in elicitation procedures that do not assume this axiom, rules out nonindependence as a viable explanation of PR. Evidently, the effect of response mode (for example, choice, pricing) cannot be explained by the payoff scheme.

If PR does not represent a violation of independence or of the reduction axiom, it must be the result of either intransitivity or a failure of procedure invariance. The diagnostic procedure indicates that only 10% of PR patterns are intransitive, whereas the remaining 90% represent noninvariance. Because Fishburn's (1984, 1985) skew-symmetric bilinear model and Loomes and Sugden's (1982, 1983) regret theory assume procedure invariance and attribute all PR to intransitivity, they do not provide an adequate account of PRs. It is also noteworthy that regret theory is consistent with the predominant direction of the (relatively small percentage of) intransitive triples observed in Study 1, but is not consistent with the pronounced intransitivity of choices between gambles demonstrated by Tversky (1969).

The overpricing of the low-probability high-payoff bets emerges from the present analysis as the major cause of PR. The results of Bostic et al. (1990) provide further support for this conclusion. We have interpreted the overpricing of long shots as an effect of scale compatibility: Because the prices and the payoffs are expressed in the same units, payoffs are weighted more heavily in pricing than in choice. Compatibility also implies new PRs in other domains, such as time preferences. Study 2 shows that when faced with a choice between delayed payments, people frequently select the short-term prospect but assign a higher cash equivalent to the long-term prospect. Other consequences of compatibility have been confirmed in other studies showing (a) that the prevalence of PR is substantially reduced by using nonmonetary payoffs and (b) that the matched attribute is weighted more heavily than the other attribute in a matching task. Further evidence on the role of compatibility in PR, based on attention and anchoring data, is presented by Schkade and Johnson (1989). We conclude that scale compatibility explains, at least in part, the primary cause of PR, namely, the overpricing of L bets. It should be noted, however, that compatibility does not explain several secondary effects commonly observed in PR studies, including the occurrence of systematic intransitivities and the occasional underpricing of H bets.

Experimental studies of choice challenge the classical analysis of decision making. Violations of the independence axiom of expected utility theory have attracted much attention. In addition, a growing body of empirical evidence questions the assumption of invariance, which is essential to the theory of rational choice. In particular, alternative framings of the same options (for example, in terms of gains vs. losses or in terms of survival vs. mortality) produce inconsistent preferences (Tversky & Kahneman, 1986), and alternative elicitation procedures (e.g., choice, pricing) give rise to reversal of preferences (Tversky et al., 1988). These results confirm the conclusion of Grether and Plott (1979):

> Taken at face value the data are simply inconsistent with preference theory and have broad implications about research priorities within economics. The inconsistency is deeper than the mere lack of transitivity or even stochastic transitivity. It suggests that no optimization principles of any sort lie behind the simplest of human choices and that the uniformities in human choice behavior which lie behind market behavior may result from principles which are of a completely different sort from those generally accepted. (p. 623)

Indeed, the failures of description invariance (framing effects) and procedure invariance (elicitation effects) pose a greater problem for rational choice models than the failure of specific axioms, such as independence or transitivity, and they demand descriptive models of much greater complexity. Violations of description invariance require an explicit treatment of the framing process, which precedes the evaluation of prospects (Kahneman & Tversky, 1979). Violations of procedure invariance require context-dependent models (for example, Tversky et al., 1988) in which the weighting of attributes is contingent on the method of elicitation. These developments highlight the discrepancy between the normative and the descriptive approaches to decision making, which many choice theorists (see Machina, 1987) have tried to reconcile. Because invariance – unlike independence or even transitivity – is normatively unassailable and descriptively incorrect, it does not seem possible to construct a theory of choice that is both normatively acceptable and descriptively adequate.

APPENDIX 1 – DISTRIBUTION OF RESPONSE PATTERNS IN STUDY 1

	1	2	3	4	5	6	Total
	$C_L > X > C_H$	$C_H > X > C_L$	$C_L > C_H > X$	$C_H > C_L > X$	$X > C_L > C_H$	$X > C_H > C_L$	
1. $X > H, H > L, X > L$	406	142	154	2	203	427	1334
2. $H > X, L > H, L > X$	81	8	61	0	13	25	188
3. $X > H, L > H, L > X$	62	8	15	0	25	22	132
4. $H > X, L > H, X > L$	20	4	7	0	2	11	44
5. $X > H, L > H, X > L$	81	10	17	1	32	26	167
6. $H > X, H > L, L > X$	38	11	33	0	13	11	106
7. $X > H, H > L, L > X$	158	15	54	1	52	19	299
8. $H > X, H > L, X > L$	114	114	89	2	22	128	469
TOTAL	960	312	430	6	362	669	2739

APPENDIX 2 – DISTRIBUTION OF RESPONSE PATTERNS IN STUDY 2

	1	2	3	4	5	6	Total
	$C_L > X > C_S$	$C_S > X > C_L$	$C_L > C_S > X$	$C_S > C_L > X$	$X > C_L > C_S$	$X > C_S > C_L$	
1. $X > S, S > L, X > L$	57	14	63	5	32	65	236
2. $S > X, L > S, L > X$	19	0	59	1	4	1	84
3. $X > S, S > L, L > X$	16	1	10	1	4	1	33
4. $S > X, L > S, X > L$	1	2	7	0	4	4	18
5. $X > S, L > S, X > L$	14	3	9	0	2	3	31
6. $S > X, S > L, L > X$	12	2	24	3	5	1	47
7. $X > S, L > S, L > X$	9	1	12	1	2	2	27
8. $S > X, S > L, X > L$	19	11	42	8	12	18	110
TOTAL	147	34	226	19	65	95	586

ACKNOWLEDGMENTS

Support for this research was provided by Contract N00014-84-K-0615 from the Office of Naval Research and by grant no. 89-0064 of the Air Force Office of Scientific Research to Stanford University, by the Air Force Office of Scientific Research and by NSF grant no. SES-8712145 to Decision Research. We thank Mark Layman for his valuable assistance in the analysis of the data. The chapter has benefited from discussions with Edi Karni and Eldar Shafir. We are grateful to Graham Loomes for many helpful comments.

9. Preference Reversals Between Joint and Separate Evaluations of Options: A Review and Theoretical Analysis

Christopher K. Hsee, George Loewenstein, Sally Blount, and Max H. Bazerman

In normative accounts of decision making, all decisions are viewed as choices between alternatives. Even when decision makers appear to be evaluating single options, such as whether to buy a particular car or to go to a certain movie, they are seen as making implicit tradeoffs. The potential car owner must trade off the benefits of car ownership against the best alternative uses of the money. The potential moviegoer is not just deciding whether to go to a movie but also between going to a movie and the next best use of her time, such as staying home and watching television.

At a descriptive level, however, there is an important distinction between situations in which multiple options are presented simultaneously and can be easily compared and situations in which alternatives are presented one at a time and evaluated in isolation. We refer to the former as the joint evaluation (JE) mode and to the latter as the separate evaluation (SE) mode. We review results from a large number of studies that document systematic changes in preferences between alternatives when those alternatives are evaluated jointly or separately. We show that these JE/SE reversals can be explained by a simple theoretical account, which we refer to as the *evaluability hypothesis*.

JE/SE reversals have important ramifications for decision making in real life. Arguably, all judgments and decisions are made in JE mode, in SE mode, or in some combination of the two. For example, most people in the market for a new car engage in JE; they assemble a number of options before deciding among them. In contrast, academic researchers typically select the research projects they work on sequentially – that is, one at a time. Very few academics, at least of our acquaintance, collect multiple research project options before deciding among them. Sometimes, the same decision is made in both modes. For example, a prospective home purchaser might initially be shown a series of houses that are on the market (JE), but, if she rejects all of these options, she will subsequently confront a series of accept/reject decisions as houses come on the market (SE). The research we review shows that preferences elicited in JE may be dramatically different from those elicited in SE. Thus, for instance,

Originally published in *Psychological Bulletin*, vol. 125, pp. 576–590. Copyright © 1999 by the American Psychological Association Reprinted with permission.

the type of house that the prospective homeowner would buy in the JE phase of the search may be quite different from what she would buy in the SE phase.

In fact, most decisions and judgments fall somewhere between the extremes of JE and SE. For example, even when the prospective home buyer is in the second phase of the search – being presented with homes one at a time as they come on the market – she is likely to make comparisons between the current house being evaluated and previous houses she has seen. Strictly speaking, therefore, the distinction between JE and SE should be viewed as a continuum.[1] Most of the studies reviewed in this article involve the two extremes of the continuum.

At a theoretical level, JE/SE reversals constitute a new type of preference reversal that is different from those that have traditionally been studied in the field of judgment and decision making. To appreciate the difference, one needs to distinguish between evaluation scale and evaluation mode, a distinction originally made by Goldstein and Einhorn (1987).[2] Evaluation scale refers to the nature of the response that participants are asked to make. For example, people can be asked which option they would prefer to accept or reject, for which they would pay a higher price, with which they would be happier, and so forth. Evaluation mode, on the other hand, refers to JEs versus SEs, as defined earlier. In the traditionally studied preference reversals, the tasks that produce the reversal always involve different evaluation scales; they may or may not involve different evaluation modes. Of those reversals, the most commonly studied is between choosing (which is about selecting the more acceptable option) and pricing (which is about determining a selling price for each option; e.g., Lichtenstein & Slovic, 1971; Tversky, Sattath, & Slovic, 1988). Other preference reversals that involve different evaluation scales include, but are not limited to, those between rating attractiveness and pricing (e.g., Mellers, Chang, Birnbaum, & Ordóñez, 1992), choosing and assessing happiness (Tversky & Griffin, 1991), selling prices and buying prices (e.g., Irwin, 1994; Kahneman, Knetsch, & Thaler, 1990; Knetsch & Sinden, 1984; see also Coursey, Hovis, & Schulze, 1987), and accepting and rejecting (e.g., Shafir, 1993; see Birnbaum, 1992; Payne, Bettman, & Johnson, 1992, for reviews).

Unlike those conventionally studied preference reversals, the JE/SE reversal occurs between tasks that take place in different evaluation modes – joint versus separate. They may or may not involve different evaluation scales. The original demonstration of JE/SE reversal was provided by Bazerman, Loewenstein,

---

[1] SE refers both to (1) situations where different options are presented to and evaluated by different individuals so that each individual sees and evaluates only one option, and to (2) situations where different options are presented to and evaluated by the same individuals at different times so that each individual evaluates only one option *at a given time.* The former situations are pure SE conditions. The latter situations involve a JE flavor because individuals evaluating a later option may recall the previous option and make a comparison.

[2] Goldstein and Einhorn (1987) refer to the evaluation mode as the response method and to the evaluation scale as the worth scale.

and White (1992). Participants read a description of a dispute between two neighbors and then evaluated different potential resolutions of the dispute. The dispute involved splitting either sales revenue or a tax liability associated with the ownership of a vacant lot between the neighbors' houses. Participants were asked to take the perspective of one homeowner and to evaluate various possible settlements. Each settlement was expressed in terms of both a payoff (or liability) to oneself and a payoff (or liability) to the neighbor. Across outcomes, the authors varied both the absolute payoff to oneself and whether the neighbor would be receiving the same as or more than the respondent. As an example, consider the following two options:

Option J: $600 for self and $800 for neighbor
Option S: $500 for self and $500 for neighbor

(For ease of exposition, we consistently use the letter *J* to denote the option that is valued more positively in JE and the letter *S* to denote the other option.) In JE, participants were presented with pairs of options, such as the one previously listed, and asked to indicate which was more acceptable. In SE, participants were presented with these options one at a time and asked to indicate on a rating scale how acceptable each option was. These two modes of evaluation resulted in strikingly different patterns of preference. For example, of the two options previously listed, 75% of the participants judged J to be more acceptable than S in JE, but 71% rated S as more acceptable than J in SE.

In a study reported by Hsee (1996a), participants were asked to assume that as the owner of a consulting firm, they were looking for a computer programmer who could write in a special computer language named KY. The two candidates, who were both new graduates, differed on two attributes: experience with the KY language and undergraduate grade point average (GPA). Specifically,

	Experience	**GPA**
Candidate J:	Has written 70 KY programs in last 2 years	3.0
Candidate S:	Has written 10 KY programs in last 2 years	4.9

The study was conducted at a public university in the Midwest where GPA is given on a 5-point scale. In the JE condition, participants were presented with the information on both candidates. In the SE condition, participants were presented with the information on only one of the candidates. In all conditions, respondents were asked how much salary they would be willing to pay the candidate(s). Thus, the evaluation scale in this study was held constant across the conditions, that is, willingness to pay (WTP), and the only difference lay in evaluation mode. The results revealed a significant JE/SE reversal ($t = 4.92$, $p < .01$): In JE, WTP values were higher for Candidate J ($Ms = \$33.2K$ for J and $\$31.2K$ for S); in SE, WTP values were higher for Candidate S ($Ms = \$32.7K$ for S and $\$26.8K$ for J). Because the evaluation scale was identical in both conditions, the reversal could only have resulted from the difference in evaluation mode.

Although other types of preference reversal have attracted substantial attention in both the psychology and economics literature, JE/SE reversals, which are as robust a phenomenon and probably more important in the real world, have received much less attention to date. The studies documenting JE/SE reversals have not been reviewed systematically. Our chapter attempts to fill that gap.

In the next section, we propose a theoretical account of JE/SE reversals that we call the evaluability hypothesis and present empirical evidence for this hypothesis. Then, in the third section, we review other studies in the literature that have documented JE/SE reversals in diverse domains and show that the evaluability hypothesis can account for all of these findings. In the section that follows, we examine how our explanation differs from explanations for conventional preference reversals. We conclude with a discussion of implications of the evaluability hypothesis beyond preference reversals.

THEORETICAL ANALYSIS

In this section, we present a general theoretical proposition called the evaluability hypothesis and apply it to explain JE/SE reversal findings, including those discussed earlier and many others that are reviewed in the next section. This hypothesis was first proposed by Hsee (1996a) and has also been presented in somewhat different forms by Loewenstein, Blount, and Bazerman (1993) in terms of attribute ambiguity, by Hsee (1993) in terms of reference dependency of attributes, and by Nowlis and Simonson (1994) in terms of context dependency of attributes.

The basic idea of the evaluability hypothesis can be summarized as follows. Some attributes (such as one's GPA) are easy to evaluate independently, whereas other attributes (such as how many programs a candidate has written) are more difficult to evaluate independently. In SE, difficult-to-evaluate attributes have little impact in differentiating the evaluations of the target options, so that easy-to-evaluate attributes are the primary determinants of the evaluations of the target options. In JE, people can compare one option with the other. Through this comparison, difficult-to-evaluate attributes become easier to evaluate and hence exert a greater influence. Easy-to-evaluate attributes do not benefit as much from JE because they are easy to evaluate even in SE. This shift in the relative impact of the two attributes, if sufficiently large, will result in a JE/SE reversal.

In the next section we provide a detailed account of the evaluability hypothesis. We first discuss what we mean by evaluability and show how it affects the evaluations of options varying on only one attribute. Then we extend our analysis to JE/SE reversals.

The Evaluability of an Attribute

Suppose that there are two options, A and B, to be evaluated, that they vary on only one attribute, and that their values on the attribute are a and b, respectively. Assume here, and in all of the subsequent examples in this chapter, that people care about the attribute on which A and B vary, that the attribute has a monotonic function (i.e., either larger values are always better or smaller values are always better), and that people know which direction of the attribute is more desirable (i.e., know whether larger values or smaller values are better). For example, consider two applicants to an MBA program who are identical on all relevant dimensions except that Applicant A has a Graduate Management Admission Test (GMAT) score of 610, and Applicant B has a GMAT score of 590.

Will Applicant A be evaluated more favorably than Applicant B? Let us first consider JE and then consider SE. In JE, the applicants are presented side by side to the same evaluators. In this case, we propose that Applicant A will always be favored over Applicant B. The reason is simple: In JE people compare one option against the other, and, given that people know which direction of the attribute is more desirable, they can easily tell which candidate is better.

In SE, each of the two applicants is evaluated by a group of evaluators who are not aware of the other applicant. Will Applicant A also be favored over Applicant B in SE? The answer is more complex; it depends on the *evaluability* of the attribute – whether the attribute is difficult or easy to evaluate independently. The evaluability of an attribute further depends on the type and the amount of information the evaluators have about the attribute. Such information, which we call the *evaluability information*, refers to the evaluator's knowledge about which value on the attribute is evaluatively neutral, which value is the best possible, which is the worst possible, what the value distribution of the attribute is, and any other information that helps the evaluator map a given value of the attribute onto the evaluation scale.

The crux of the evaluability hypothesis is that the shape of the evaluability function of an attribute is determined by the evaluability information that evaluators have about the attribute. The evaluability function can vary from a flat line to a fine-grained monotonic function. Depending on the shape of the function, one can predict whether two given values on the attribute (say a GMAT score of 610 and one of 590) will result in reliably different evaluations. There are many types of evaluability information people may have about an attribute. For illustrative purposes, we examine three alternative scenarios.

Scenario 1: When the evaluators have no evaluability information (except that greater numbers on the attribute are better). In SE of this case, any value on the attribute is extremely difficult or impossible to evaluate. That is, people have no idea whether a particular value is good or bad, let alone how good or how bad it is. We assume that the value will be evaluated, on average, as neutral, although it may be accompanied by a large variance. The evaluation function for the attribute will then be a flat line, as in Figure 9.1. In other words, those who see one option will give it roughly the same evaluation as those evaluating the other option. For example, suppose that the two applicants mentioned earlier are evaluated in SE by individuals who know nothing about GMAT scores other than greater numbers are better. Then those evaluating Applicant A will have about the same impression of that applicant as those evaluating Applicant B.

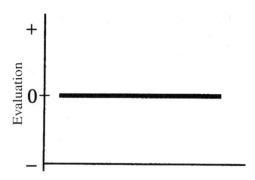

Figure 9.1. The evaluation function of an attribute when there is no evaluability information.

We should note in passing that, in reality, people rarely possess no evaluability information about an attribute. For example, even people who know nothing about the range or distribution of GMAT scores may assume, on the basis of their knowledge of other tests, that GMAT scores should not be negative and that a score of 0 must be bad. As a result, the evaluation function is seldom absolutely flat.

Scenario 2: When the evaluators know the neutral reference point (i.e., the evaluative zero-point) of the attribute. In this case, the evaluation function of the attribute in SE approximates a step function, as depicted in Figure 9.2. Any values above the reference point are considered good, and any values below the reference are considered bad.

In this case, whether two attribute values will result in different evaluations in SE depends on whether they lie on the same side of the neutral reference point or straddle it. If the attribute values lie on the same side of the reference point, they will receive similar evaluations. If the attribute values are on opposite sides of the reference point (or one of the values coincides with the reference point), then the one above the reference point will be evaluated more favorably than the other. For example, suppose that the individuals who evaluate the two applicants are told that the average GMAT score of applicants is 500, which they interpret as the neutral reference point (i.e., neither good nor bad). Then the two candidates will both be evaluated as good and will not be differentiated. On the other hand, if the evaluators are told that the average GMAT score is 600, then Applicant A (scored 610) will be evaluated as good and Applicant B (scored 590) as bad.[3]

---

[3] Unless otherwise specified we assume in this chapter that people evaluating Option A and people evaluating Option B in SE have the same evaluability information. For example, we assume that those evaluating Applicant A and those evaluating Applicant B have the same knowledge about GMAT scores.

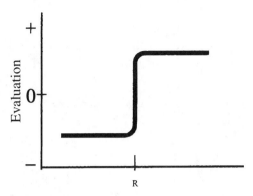

Figure 9.2. The evaluation function of an attribute when there is neutral reference point information (R).

Again, the preceding analysis is oversimplified. In reality, even if the evaluators only know the neutral reference point of the attribute, they will make speculations about the size and the meaning of the unit on the attribute. For example, people who are told that the average GMAT score is 600 may assume that a score like 601 is not very much different from 600 and not very good and that a score like 700 is quite different from 600 and must be quite good. As a result, the evaluation function is more likely to be S-shaped, rather than a strict step function.

Scenario 3: When the evaluators are aware of the best possible and worst possible values of the attribute. In this scenario, the attribute is relatively easy to evaluate. The evaluation function will be monotonically increasing, as depicted in Figure 9.3. The general slope of the evaluation function, however, will be inversely related to the size of the range between the best and the worst values (e.g., Beattie & Baron, 1991; Mellers & Cooke, 1994).

In this condition, any two values on the attribute will create different impressions and result in different evaluations, The size of the difference depends on the size of the range between the best and the worst values. For example, Applicant A (with a score of 610) and applicant B (with a score of 590) will be evaluated more differently if the evaluators are told that GMAT scores range from 550 to 650 than if they are told that GMAT scores range from 400 to 800. Qualifying the range effect. Beattie and Baron (1991) found that the range manipulation affected only the evaluations of unfamiliar stimuli. Consistent with the evaluability hypothesis, this finding suggests that providing or varying range information affects only the evaluation of attributes that would otherwise be hard to evaluate, namely, those for which the evaluators do not already have clear knowledge about the range or other evaluability information.

Again, in reality, the evaluation function in this condition will not be as linear as the one depicted in Figure 9.3. For example, people who are told that most applicants' GMAT scores range from 400 to 800 may treat the midpoint

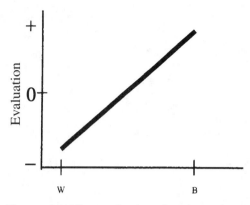

Figure 9.3. The evaluation function of an attribute when there is information about its worst value (W) and best value (B).

of the range, 600, as the neutral reference point. As a consequence, the evaluation function will be somewhat S-shaped, with its slope particularly steep around 600.

Evidence for the Preceding Analysis: The Score Study

According to the preceding analysis, the evaluation function of an attribute varies predictably, depending on the evaluability information that people have. To test this proposition, we asked college students ($N = 294$) recruited from a large midwestern university to evaluate a hypothetical applicant to a university. In different experimental conditions, we varied evaluability information to see whether different applicant test scores would lead to different evaluations as a function of evaluability information.

The questionnaire for this study included 12 between-subject versions. They constituted 3 Evaluability Conditions × 4 Score Conditions. In all versions, respondents were asked to imagine that they worked for the admissions office of a university, that their job was to evaluate prospective students' potential to succeed in college, and that they had just received the application of a foreign student named Jane. Participants were further told that Jane had taken an Academic Potential Exam (APE) in her country, that students in Jane's country are on average as intelligent as American students, that APE is a good measure of one's potential to succeed in college, and that the higher an APE score, the better.

Corresponding to the three scenarios discussed in the previous section, the three evaluability versions for this study were (a) no information, (b) average score information, and (c) score range (i.e., best and worst score) information. The no-information version read:

You have no idea of the distribution of APE scores. You don't know what the average APE score, what the best APE score, or what the worst APE score is.

Table 9.1. Mean Evaluations of the Applicant in the Score Study

	Score of Applicant			
Evaluability	1,100	1,200	1,300	1,400
No information	5.13$_a$	5.20$_a$	5.54$_a$	5.84$_a$
Average score information only	4.56$_a$	4.71$_a$	6.40$_b$	6.84$_b$
Score range information	3.04$_a$	3.98$_b$	6.52$_c$	8.30$_d$

Note: The ratings were made on a scale ranging from 0 (*extremely poor*) to 10 (*extremely good*). Means in the same row that do not share subscripts are significantly different from each other.

The average-score version read:

You don't have a clear idea of the distribution of APE scores. You know that the average APE score is 1,250, but you don't know what the best APE score or what the worst APE score is.

The score-range version read:

You don't have a clear idea of the distribution of APE scores. You know that the best APE score is 1,400 and the worst APE score is 1,100, but you don't know what the average APE score is.

Each of the three evaluability versions was crossed with four versions of Jane's APE score: 1,100, 1,200, 1,300, and 1,400, respectively. For example, the 1,100-version read:

Jane scored 1,100 on APE. The admissions office requires that you give a rating to each applicant even if you don't have all the information. Given what you know, how would you rate Jane's potential to succeed in college? Circle a number below:

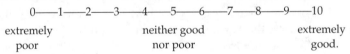

0——1——2——3——4——5——6——7——8——9——10

extremely　　　　　　　neither good　　　　　　　extremely
poor　　　　　　　　　　nor poor　　　　　　　　　good.

The results, summarized in Table 9.1, lend support to the preceding analysis. In the no-information condition, the four scores formed almost a flat line, $F(3, 96) = 1.51$, *ns*. Planned comparisons indicate that the difference between any two score conditions was insignificant, suggesting that different scores created similar impressions. There is, however, a statistically insignificant yet distinctively positive slope across the four scores. This arises probably because, even without any explicitly given evaluability information, the respondents used their knowledge about other tests to speculate on the missing information.

In the average-score condition, the four scores formed an S-shaped function, with a steeper slope around the neutral reference point (the average score of 1,250). An F test across the four score conditions revealed a significant effect, $F(3, 96) = 15.55$, $p < .01$. Planned comparisons indicate that score 1,100 and score 1,200 were not evaluated significantly different, nor were scores 1,300 and 1,400, but either of the first two scores was judged significantly different from either of the latter two.

In the score-range condition, the four scores formed a steep upward slope, $F(3, 97) = 73.83, p < .001$. Planned comparisons show that each score was evaluated as significantly different from every other score in the predicted ordering. Note that the data are also indicative of an S shape, suggesting that the respondents may have treated the midpoint of the range as a reference point and considered scores above this point to be generally good and scores below that point to be bad.

In sum, the findings of this study show that the evaluation function of an attribute can migrate from a flat line to a steeply sloped function depending on the evaluability information the evaluators have.

Elaboration

Several points deserve elaboration here. First, whether an attribute is easy or difficult to evaluate is not an intrinsic characteristic of the attribute. It is determined by the evaluability information the evaluators have about the attribute. Thus, the same attribute can be easy to evaluate in one context and for one group of evaluators but difficult to evaluate in another context or for outer evaluators. For example, GMAT score is an easy-to-evaluate attribute for people familiar with the meaning of the score, its distribution, and so forth, but a difficult-to-evaluate attribute for other people.

Second, an attribute can be difficult to evaluate even if its values are precisely given and people perfectly understand its meanings. For example, everybody knows what money is and how much a dollar is worth, but the monetary attribute of an option can be difficult to evaluate if the decision maker does not know the evaluability information for that attribute in the given context. Suppose, for instance, that a person on a trip to a foreign country has learned that a particular hotel room costs $50 a night and needs to judge the desirability of this price. If the person is not familiar with the hotel prices of that country, it will be difficult for him to evaluate whether $50 is a good or bad price. To say that an attribute is difficult to evaluate does not imply that the decision maker does not know its value but means that the decision maker has difficulty determining the *desirability* of its value in the given decision context.

Finally, attributes with dichotomous values – such as whether a job candidate for an accountant position has a certified public accountant (CPA) license or not, or whether a vase being sold at a flea market is broken or not – are often easy to evaluate independently. People often know that these attributes have only two alternative values, and, even in SE when evaluators see only one value of the attribute (e.g., either with or without a CPA license), they know whether the value is the better or worse of the two. This is a special case of the situation where the evaluator has full knowledge of the evaluability information about the attribute. In several of the studies to be reviewed in the following sections, the easy-to-evaluate attribute is of this type.

Evaluability and JE/SE Reversals

So far, we have discussed only the evaluability of a single attribute. In this section, we extend our analysis to options involving a tradeoff across two attributes and explore how the evaluation hypothesis explains JE/SE reversals of these options.

Consider two options, J and S, that involve a tradeoff across Attribute x and Attribute y:

	Attribute x	Attribute y
Option J:	x_J	y_J
Option S:	x_S	y_S

where $x_J > x_S$ and $y_J < y_S$ (> denotes better than and < denotes worse than).

According to the evaluability hypothesis, JE/SE reversals occur because one of the attributes is more difficult to evaluate than the other, and the relative impact of the difficult-to-evaluate attribute increases from SE to JE. Specifically, suppose that Attribute x is relatively difficult to evaluate independently and Attribute y is easy to evaluate independently. In SE, because Attribute x is difficult to evaluate, x_J and x_S will receive similar evaluations; as a result, this attribute will have little or no effect in differentiating the desirability of one option from that of the other. Because Attribute y is easy to evaluate, y_J and y_S will be evaluated differently; consequently, the evaluations of J and S in SE will be determined mainly by the values of Attribute y. Because $y_S > y_J$, S will tend to be evaluated more favorably than J. In JE, in contrast, people can easily compare the two options on an attribute-by-attribute basis (e.g., Russo & Dosher, 1983; Tversky, 1969). Through this comparison, people can easily tell which option is better on which attribute, regardless of whether the attribute is difficult or easy to evaluate in SE. Thus, both attributes will affect the evaluations of the target options.

The preceding analysis indicates that, compared with SE, the effect of the difficult-to-evaluate attribute relative to that of the easy-to-evaluate attribute increases in JE. In other words, the difficult-to-evaluate attribute (x) benefits more from JE than the easy-to-evaluate attribute (y). If Option S is favored in SE, and if Attribute x is important enough and/or the difference between x_J and x_S is large enough, then a JE/SE reversal will emerge, such that Option J will be favored over Option S in JE.

Evidence for the Preceding Analysis: Hiring Study and Compact Disc Changer Study

Consider the hiring study (Hsee, 1996a) discussed earlier, involving a candidate with more KY programming experience and one with a higher GPA. Participants in this experiment were all college students, who knew which GPA values are good and which are bad, but they were unfamiliar with the criterion of KY programming experience. Thus, these participants had clear evaluability information for the GPA attribute but not for the KY-programming experience attribute. By definition, GPA was an easy-to-evaluate attribute, and KY programming experience was a relatively difficult-to-evaluate attribute.

To assess whether our judgment of evaluability concurred with participants' own judgment, Hsee (1996a) asked those in each SE condition, after they had made the WTP judgment, to indicate (a) whether they had any idea of how good the GPA of the candidate they had evaluated was and (b) whether they had any idea of how experienced with KY programming the candidate was. Their answers to each question could range from 1 (*I don't have any idea*) to 4 (*1 have a clear idea*). The results confirmed our judgment that GPA was easier to evaluate than KY experience. The mean rating for GPA, 3.7, was significantly higher than the mean rating of 2.1 for KY experience ($t = 11.79$, $p < .001$).

According to the evaluability hypothesis, the difficult-to-evaluate attribute has a greater impact relative to the easy-to-evaluate attribute in JE than in SE. This is indeed what happened in the hiring study. As summarized earlier, the results indicate that the evaluations of the candidates in SE were determined primarily by the GPA attribute, and the evaluations in JE were influenced more heavily by the KY-experience attribute. It suggests that JE enabled the participants to compare the two candidates directly and thereby realize that the lower-GPA candidate had in fact completed many more programs than had the higher-GPA candidate.[4]

In most studies that demonstrate JE/SE reversals, whether an attribute is difficult or easy to evaluate independently is assumed. In the compact disc (CD) changer study described in the next paragraph, the evaluability of an attribute was manipulated empirically.[5] As mentioned earlier, the evaluability hypothesis asserts that JE/SE reversals occur because one of the attributes of the stimulus objects is difficult to evaluate in SE, whereas the other attribute is relatively easy to evaluate. If this is correct, then a JE/SE reversal can be turned on or off by varying the relative evaluability of the attributes.

To test this intuition, the CD changer study was designed as follows: It involved the evaluations of two CD changers (i.e., multiple compact disc players):

	CD capacity	THD
CD Changer J:	Holds 5 CDs	.003%
CD Changer S:	Holds 20 CDs	.01%

[4] It should be noted that the distinction between difficult-to-evaluate and easy-to-evaluate attributes is different from that between proxy and fundamental attributes in decision analysis (e.g., Fischer, Damodaran, Laskey, & Lincoln, 1987). A proxy attribute is an indirect measure of a fundamental attribute – a factor that the decision maker is ultimately concerned about; for example, cholesterol level is a proxy attribute of one's health. A proxy attribute can be either easier or more difficult to evaluate than its fundamental attribute. For example, for people familiar with the meaning and the value distribution of cholesterol readings, the cholesterol attribute can be easier to evaluate than its fundamental attribute, health; for people unfamiliar with cholesterol numbers, it can be very difficult to evaluate.
[5] This study was originally reported by Hsee (1996a).

It was explained to every participant that total harmonic distortion (THD) was an index of sound quality. The smaller the THD, the better the sound quality.

The study consisted of two evaluability conditions: difficult/easy and easy/easy. In the difficult/easy condition, participants received no other information about THD than described previously. As verified in subsequent questions (discussed later), THD was a difficult-to-evaluate attribute, and CD capacity was a relatively easy-to-evaluate attribute. Although most people know that less distortion is better, few know whether a given THD rating (e.g., .01%) is good or bad. On the other hand, most have some idea of how many CDs a CD changer could hold and whether a CD changer that can hold 5 CDs (or 20 CDs) is good or not. In the easy/easy condition, participants were provided with information about the effective range of the THD attribute. They were told, "For most CD changers on the market, THD ratings range from .002% (best) to .012% (worst)." This information was designed to make THD easier to evaluate independently. With this information, participants in the SE conditions would have some idea where the given THD rating fell in the range and hence whether the rating was good or bad.

In each of the evaluability conditions, participants (202 students from a large public university in the Midwest) were either presented with the information about both CD changers and evaluated both of them (JE) or presented with the information about one of the options and evaluated it alone (SE). In all conditions, the dependent variable was WTP price.

To ensure that the evaluability manipulation was effective, Hsee asked participants in the two SE conditions, after they had indicated their WTP prices, (a) whether they had any idea of how good the THD rating of the CD changer was and (b) whether they had any idea of how large its CD capacity was. Answers to those questions ranged from 1 to 4, greater numbers indicating greater evaluability. The results confirmed the effectiveness of the evaluability manipulation. Mean evaluability scores for THD and CD capacity in the difficult/easy condition were 1.98 and 3.25, respectively, and in the easy/easy condition were 2.53 and 3.22. Planned comparisons revealed that evaluability scores for THD increased significantly from the difficult/easy condition to the easy/easy condition ($t = 2.92, p < .01$), but those for CD capacity remained the same.

The main prediction for the study is that a JE/SE reversal was more likely to emerge in the difficult/easy condition than in the easy/easy condition. The results, summarized in Table 9.2, confirmed this prediction: In the difficult/easy condition, there was a significant JE/SE reversal ($t = 3.32, p < .01$), and the direction of the reversal was consistent with the evaluability hypothesis, implying that the difficult-to-evaluate attribute (THD) had a lesser relative effect in SE than in JE, and the easy-to-evaluate attribute (CD capacity) had a greater relative effect. In the easy/easy condition, the reversal disappeared ($t < 1$, ns).

The fact that increasing the evaluability of the difficult-to-evaluate attribute could eliminate the JE/SE reversal supports the evaluability hypothesis. It suggests that what drives this type of preference reversal is differential evaluability between the attributes.

Table 9.2. Mean Willingness-to-Pay Values in the CD
Changer Study

Evaluability and Evaluation Mode	CD Changer J	CD Changer S
Difficult/easy		
Joint	$228	$204
Separate	$212	$256
Easy/easy		
Joint	$222	$186
Separate	$222	$177

Note: CD = compact disc.

Summary

In this section, we first introduced the notion of evaluability and then used it to account for JE/SE reversals. The evaluability hypothesis, as our analysis shows, is not a post hoc speculation but a testable theory. First of all, the concept of evaluability was defined independently of the JE/SE-reversal effect, which it subsequently explained. Moreover, we presented evidence of independent measures of evaluability and showed that participants' judgments of evaluability coincided with ours and predicted the observed reversals. Finally, in one study we empirically manipulated evaluability and demonstrated that this manipulation could turn the JE/SE reversal on or off in the direction predicted by the evaluability hypothesis.

REVIEW AND EXPLANATION OF JE/SE REVERSALS

JE/SE reversals have been documented in diverse contexts. All of the findings involve pairs of options where one option is favored in JE and the other is favored in SE. Within this shared structure, JE/SE reversals can be classified into three types. In one type, the two options belong to the same category (e.g., both options are CD players), they share well-defined attributes (e.g., sound quality and CD capacity), and they involve explicit tradeoffs along those attributes. All of the examples shown so far are of this type. In the second type of JE/SE reversal, the options also belong to the same category (just as in the first type), but they do not share well-defined attributes and do not involve explicit tradeoffs. In the third type of JE/SE reversal, the options are from different categories. In what follows, we provide examples of each type of reversal and show how the evaluability hypothesis can be used to explain the finding.

JE/SE Reversals for Options From the Same Category and With Explicit Tradeoffs

All of the JE/SE reversals discussed so far belong to this type. Here, the two options are from the same category (e.g., both are job candidates for a programmer position), and they involve an explicit tradeoff along two attributes (e.g., GPA and programming experience). For this type of reversal, the evaluability hypothesis provides a straightforward explanation. In the previous section, we already examined how the evaluability hypothesis explains the result of the programmer-hiring study.

The same analysis can be applied to Bazerman et al.'s (1992) self-neighbor study. Recall that in JE of this study the option that would give $600 to oneself and $800 to the neighbor (Option J) was favored over the option that would give $500 to both oneself and the neighbor (Option S), but in SE the pattern was reversed. The two options can be interpreted as involving a tradeoff across the following two attributes:

	Payoff to self	Equality between self and neighbor
Option J:	$600	Unequal
Option S:	$500	Equal

Payoffs to self, we believe, were difficult to evaluate in SE because, lacking a comparison, respondents would not know how good a given settlement was. In contrast, whether or not the amount awarded to self was equal to the amount awarded to the neighbor was easy to evaluate. Most people, we surmise, would find an unequal treatment (especially when it is in favor of the other party) highly unattractive and would find an equal treatment neutral or positive. That is why the rank order of the two options in SE was determined primarily by the equality (equal versus unequal treatment) attribute. In JE, the payoff-to-self attribute was made easier to evaluate by the fact that the decision maker could compare the two values directly. On the other hand, the equality attribute, which was already easy to evaluate in SE, would not benefit as much from JE. That is why the payoff-to-self attribute loomed larger and led to a reversal in JE.

Bazerman, Schroth, Shah, Diekmann, and Tenbrunsel (1994) obtained similar preference reversals with hypothetical job offers for MBA students that differed in terms of payoffs to oneself and equality or procedural justice in the company.[6] Blount and Bazerman (1996) showed inconsistent evaluations of absolute versus comparative payoffs in recruiting participants for an experiment. These findings can be analyzed in the same way as Bazerman et al.'s (1992) preference-reversal findings.[7]

Interested in tradeoffs between absolute amount of income and temporal trend of income, Hsee (1993) solicited joint and separate evaluations of two

---

[6] Even in SE of these studies, the participants (who were MBA students) should have some idea of the distribution information for the salary attribute, and therefore, the salaries were not difficult to evaluate in its absolute sense. However, we suggest that JE provided more information about the salary attribute than SE, and, consequently, the salaries may have been even *more easy* to evaluate in JE than in SE.

[7] Bazerman, Tenbrunsel, and Wade-Benzoni (1998) had an alternative explanation for these results, which we discuss later.

hypothetical salary options, one with a higher absolute amount but a decreasing trend over a fixed 4-year period (Option J) and the other with a lower absolute amount but an increasing trend (Option S). The results revealed a JE/SE reversal: In JE, respondents slightly preferred the higher absolute-salary option, but in SE, the increasing-trend option was favored. Again, this result can be explained by evaluability. In SE, the absolute amount of earnings was difficult to evaluate, but whether the salary increased or decreased over time would elicit distinct feelings: People feel happy with improving trends and feel dejected with worsening trends, as shown in numerous recent studies (e.g., Ariely, 1998; Hsee & Abelson, 1991; Hsee, Salovey, & Abelson, 1994; Kahneman, Fredrickson, Schreiber, & Redelmeier, 1993; Loewenstein & Prelec, 1993; Loewenstein & Sicherman, 1991). In JE, the difference in absolute amount of earnings between the options became transparent and therefore loomed larger.

In a more recent study, Hsee (1996a) observed a JE/SE reversal in WTP for two consumer products. Participants were asked to assume that they were a music major looking for a music dictionary in a used book store. They were provided the information about and indicated their WTP for either both or one of the following dictionaries:

	# of entries	Any defects?
Dictionary J:	20,000	Yes, the cover is torn; otherwise it's like new.
Dictionary S:	10,000	No, it's like new.

In JE, Dictionary J received higher WTP values, but in SE, Dictionary S enjoyed higher WTP values. The evaluability hypothesis also provides a ready explanation for the results. In SE, most respondents, who were not familiar with the evaluability information of music dictionary entries, would not know how to evaluate the desirability of a dictionary with 20,000 (or 10,000) entries. In contrast, even without something to compare it to, people would find a defective dictionary unappealing and a new-looking dictionary appealing. Therefore, we believe that the entry attribute was difficult to evaluate in SE and the defect attribute relatively easy to evaluate. This explains why in SE the rank order of WTPs for the two dictionaries was determined by the defect attribute. In JE, it was easy for people to realize that Dictionary J was twice as comprehensive, thus prompting them to assign a higher value to that dictionary.

Lowenthal (1993) documented a similar JE/SE reversal in a rather different context. Interested in voting behavior, she created hypothetical congressional races between candidates who were similar except for two dimensions. For example, consider the following two candidates:

	Jobs to be created	Personal history
Candidate J:	5,000 jobs	Convicted of misdemeanor
Candidate S:	1,000 jobs	Clean

In JE, participants voted for Candidate J, but, when asked to evaluate the candidates separately, participants rated Candidate S more favorably. For most respondents, who knew little about employment statistics, whether a candidate could bring 5,000 jobs or 1,000 jobs would be difficult to evaluate in isolation, but a candidate convicted of a misdemeanor would easily be perceived as unappealing and a candidate with a clean history as good. The direction of the reversal observed in the study is consistent with the evaluability hypothesis, suggesting that the personal history attribute had a greater impact in SE, and the job attribute loomed larger in JE.

JE/SE Reversals for Options From the Same Category but Without Explicit Tradeoffs

Sometimes, JE/SE reversals occur with options that do not present explicit tradeoffs between attributes. Instead, one option apparently dominates the other.

In a recent study, Hsee (1998) asked students to imagine that they were relaxing on a beach by Lake Michigan and were in the mood for some ice cream. They were assigned to either the JE or the SE condition. Those in the JE condition were told that there were two vendors selling Haagen Dazs ice cream by the cup on the beach. Vendor J used a 10-oz. cup and put 8 oz. of ice cream in it, and Vendor S used a 5-oz. cup and put 7 oz. of ice cream in it. Respondents saw drawings of the two servings and were asked how much they were willing to pay for a serving by each vendor. Respondents in each SE condition were told about and saw the drawing of only one vendor's serving, and they indicated how much they were willing to pay for a serving by that vendor.

Note that, objectively speaking, Vendor J's serving dominated Vendor S's, because it had more ice cream (and also offered a larger cup). However, J's serving was underfilled, and S's serving was overfilled. The results revealed a JE/SE reversal: In JE, people were willing to pay more for Vendor J's serving, but in SE, they were willing to pay more for Vendor S's serving.

In another experiment, Hsee (1998) asked participants to indicate their WTP prices for one or both of the following dinnerware sets being sold as a clearance item in a store:

	Set J	Set S
	(includes 40 pcs)	(includes 24 pcs)
Dinner plates:	8, in good condition	8, in good condition
Soup/salad bowls:	8, in good condition	8, in good condition
Dessert plates:	8, in good condition	8, in good condition
Cups:	8, 2 of which are broken	
Saucers:	8, 7 of which are broken	

Note that Set J contained all the pieces contained in Set S, plus 6 more intact cups and 1 more intact saucer. Again, there was a JE/SE reversal. In JE, respondents were willing to pay more for Set J. In SE, they were willing to pay more for Set S, although it was the inferior option.

Although the options in these studies do not involve explicit tradeoffs along well-defined attributes, the findings can still be accounted for by the evaluability hypothesis. In the ice cream study, the difference between the two servings can be reinterpreted as varying on two attributes: the absolute amount of ice cream a serving contained and whether the serving was overfilled or underfilled. Thus, the two servings can be described as follows:

	Amount of ice cream	Filling
Serving J:	8 oz.	Underfilled
Serving S:	7 oz.	Overfilled

In SE, it was probably difficult to evaluate the desirability of a given amount of ice cream (7 oz. or 8 oz.), but the filling attribute was easier to evaluate: An underfilled serving was certainly bad and an overfilled serving good. According to the evaluability hypothesis, the filling attribute would be the primary factor to differentiate the evaluations of the two servings in SE, but in JE, people could see that Serving J contained more ice cream than Serving S and make their judgments accordingly. The results are consistent with these predictions.

To see how the evaluability hypothesis applies to the dinnerware study, let us rewrite the differences between the dinnerware sets as follows:

	# of intact pieces	Integrity of the set
Set J:	31	Incomplete
Set S:	24	Complete

In SE, the desirability of a certain number of intact pieces (31 or 24) was probably rather difficult to evaluate (especially for students who were unfamiliar with dinnerware). On the other hand, the integrity of a set was probably much easier to evaluate: A set with broken pieces was certainly undesirable, and a complete set was desirable. Thus, the evaluability hypothesis would expect the intact set (S) to be favored in SE. In JE, the respondents could easily compare the sets and thereby would realize that Set J dominated Set S. Again, the results are consistent with these expectations.

JE/SE Reversals for Options From Different Categories

In the studies reviewed so far, the options to be evaluated are always from the same category. JE/SE reversals have also been found between the evaluations of apparently unrelated options.

Kahneman and Ritov (1994) observed a JE/SE reversal in an investigation of what they called the headline method. They presented participants with headlines describing problems from different categories and asked them how much they were willing to contribute to solving these problems. Consider the following, for example:

Problem J: Skin cancer from sun exposure common among farm workers.
Problem S: Several Australian mammal species nearly wiped out by
                   hunters.

It was found that in JE, respondents were willing to make a greater contribution to Problem J, and in SE, they were willing to make a greater contribution to Problem S.

In a more recent study, Kahneman, Ritov, and Schkade (1999) studied people's reactions to two problems:

Problem J: Multiple myeloma among the elderly.
Problem S: Cyanide fishing in coral reefs around Asia.

Again, there was a JE/SE reversal: In JE, people considered the disease issue (J) to be more important and also expected greater satisfaction from making a contribution to that issue. In SE, however, the reverse was true.

In an experiment conducted by Irwin, Slovic, Lichtenstein, and McClelland (1993), respondents were asked to evaluate problems such as:

Problem J: Improving the air quality in Denver.
Problem S: Adding a VCR to your TV.

When asked to select in pairwise comparisons between those options (JE), respondents overwhelmingly opted for improving the air quality. When those options were presented separately (SE), most respondents were willing to pay more for upgrading their TV.

The main difference between these effects and the JE/SE reversals reviewed previously is that in these studies, the stimulus options are from unrelated categories. For example, in Kahneman et al.'s (1999) study, multiple myeloma is a human health problem, and cyanide fishing is an ecological problem.

Our explanation of these results requires both norm theory (Kahneman & Miller, 1986) and the evaluability hypothesis. Take Kahneman et al.'s (1999) study, for example. In SE, the absolute importance of either problem is difficult to evaluate independently. People do not have much preexisting evaluability information for either multiple myeloma or cyanide fishing. According to norm theory, when evaluating an object, people often think about the norm of the category to which the object belongs and judge the importance of that object relative to the category norm. More specifically, norm theory suggests that, when evaluating multiple myeloma, participants would evoke the norm of the human health problem category, and, when evaluating cyanide fishing, they would evoke the norm of the ecological-problem category. These evoked category norms essentially served as the evaluability information for judging the importance of each problem in SE. According to Kahneman et al., multiple myeloma is unimportant relative to the typical or normative human health problem, and cyanide fishing is important relative to the typical or normative ecological problem.

In summary, the differences between Problems J (multiple myeloma) and S (cyanide fishing) in Kahneman et al.'s (1999) study can be considered as varying on two attributes: their absolute importance and their relative importance within their respective category.

	Absolute importance	Relative importance within category
Problem J:	Hard to evaluate	Unimportant
Problem S:	Hard to evaluate	Important

The absolute importance of each problem is difficult to judge independently, but the relative importance of each problem within its given category (i.e., relative to the category norm) is easy to evaluate. That explains why cyanide fishing was considered more important in SE.

In JE, people could compare one problem with the other, and, through this comparison, they would recognize that a human health problem (J) must be more important than an ecological problem (S), hence assigning a higher WTP value to multiple myeloma.

A similar analysis can be applied to Kahneman and Ritov's (1994) farmer/mammal study and Irwin et al.'s (1993) VCR/air quality study.[8]

The evaluability hypothesis and norm theory are not rival explanations. Instead, they complement each other to explain the aforementioned findings. Norm theory describes how category norms are evoked. The evaluability hypothesis describes how differential evaluability information can lead to JE/SE reversals. The linkage between the two theories is that, in all of the studies discussed in this section, the evaluability information is the category norm of the option under evaluation.

Note that the structure of the problems discussed earlier is indeed quite similar to that of the ice cream study analyzed in the previous section. In the ice cream study, the absolute amount of ice cream is difficult to evaluate independently, but the amount of ice cream relative to the cup size is easy to evaluate. In Kahneman et al.'s (1999) health/ecological problem study, the absolute importance of each problem is difficult to evaluate independently, but the importance of each problem relative to the norm of its given category is easy to evaluate. More generally, the absolute value of an option is often hard to evaluate independently, but its relative position within a given category is usually easier

---

[8] There is another possible interpretation of Irwin et al.'s (1993) results. When making a choice between worse air pollution in Denver and upgrading their own appliance, people may have felt it would be selfish to benefit themselves trivially at the expense of *all* Denver residents. When they were asked to put a monetary value on clean air, no such direct tradeoff is implied, and they may have thought about the benefit of clean air to only themselves.

to evaluate because the category serves as the evaluability information. As a result, a high-position member in a low category is often valued more favorably than a low-position member in a high category.

Another study pertinent to the preceding proposition is reported by Hsee (1998). Students were asked to assume that they had received a graduation gift from a friend and to judge the generosity of the gift giver. For half of the students, the gift was a $45 wool scarf from a department store that carried wool scarves ranging in price from $5 to $50. For the other half of the students, the gift was a $55 wool coat from a department store that carried wool coats ranging in price from $50 to $500. Even though the $55 coat was certainly more expensive, those receiving the scarf considered their gift giver to be significantly more generous. These results can be explained in the same way as the ice cream study and the health/ecological problem study. The absolute price of a gift ($45 or $55) is difficult to evaluate in SE. However, whether the given gift is at the low end or high end of its respective product category is easy to evaluate in SE. The $45 scarf is at the top of the scarf category, and the $55 coat is near the bottom of the coat category. Therefore, the scarf appears more expensive and its giver more generous.

Summary

In this section, we have reviewed recent research findings that document JE/SE reversals in diverse domains of decision making. They include JE/SE reversals between options that involve explicit tradeoffs along well-defined attributes (e.g., the programmer hiring study), between options that belong to the same category but do not involve explicit tradeoffs (e.g., the ice cream study), and between options that come from unrelated categories (e.g., the health/ecological problem study). We have shown that the evaluability hypothesis provides a simple and unifying explanation for all of these seemingly unrelated findings.

In the next section, we discuss how the evaluability hypothesis differs from existing explanations of conventionally studied preference reversals.

EVALUABILITY AND OTHER EXPLANATIONS FOR PREFERENCE REVERSALS

Although the term *preference reversal* can be used to describe many documented violations of normative axioms, such as Allais's Paradox (Allais, 1953) and intransitivity (e.g., May, 1954; Tversky, 1969), the concept of preference reversal gained its recognition in decision research with the P-bet/$-bet research of Lichtenstein and Slovic (1971) and subsequently of Grether and Plott (1979). The P bet offers a high likelihood of winning a small amount of money, whereas the $ bet offers a low probability of winning a larger amount of money. The P bet is often preferred when participants are asked to make a choice between the two bets, and the $ bet is favored when participants are asked to indicate a minimum selling price for each bet. The standard explanation for this type of preference reversal is the compatibility principle (Slovic, Griffin, & Tversky, 1990). According to this principle, the weight given to an attribute is greater when it matches the evaluation scale than when it does not. For example, attributes involving monetary values, such as monetary payoff, loom larger if preferences are elicited in terms of price rather than in terms of choice. This principle serves as a compelling explanation for the choice–pricing preference reversal and many other related choice–judgment reversals (see Schkade & Johnson, 1989, for process data that support the scale compatibility explanation of choice–pricing reversals). The compatibility principle is concerned with preference reversals involving different evaluation scales as opposed to those with different evaluation modes.

Another type of commonly studied preference reversal occurs between choice and matching (Tversky et al., 1988; for more recent studies, see Coupey, Irwin, & Payne, 1998). For example, consider a study by Tversky et al. (1988) involving two hypothetical job candidates for a production engineer position: Candidate A had a technical score of 86 and a human relations score of 76; Candidate B had a technical score of 78 and a human relations score of 91. In choice, participants were asked to choose between the two candidates, and most chose Candidate A. In matching, participants were presented with the same alternatives, but some information about one of the candidates was missing. The participants' task was to fill in that information to make the two alternatives equally attractive. Typically, the values respondents filled in implied that they would have preferred Candidate B had the information not been missing. To explain the preference reversal between choice and matching, Tversky et al. proposed the prominence principle, which states that the most prominent attribute in a multiattribute choice set is weighted more heavily in choice than in matching. In the previous example, technical score was apparently the more important attribute, and, according to the prominence principle, it loomed larger in choice than in matching. Fischer and Hawkins (1993) extended the prominence principle by contending that the most prominent attribute looms larger in qualitative tasks (e.g., choice and strength-of-preference judgment) than in quantitative tasks (e.g., value-matching and monetary-equivalent value judgments).

Although the prominence principle provides a good explanation for the standard choice–matching preference reversal, it does not readily apply to JE/SE reversals studied in the present research. In the choice–matching paradigm, both the choice task and the matching task are carried out in the JE mode, and the prominence principle explains how the relative weight of the attributes varies between tasks that involve different evaluation scales. JE/SE reversals, on the other hand, can take place even if the evaluation scale is held constant (e.g., about willingness to pay), and therefore they cannot be explained by theories that focus on differential evaluation scales. In addition, the prominence principle relies on difference in attribute prominence for preference reversals to occur. However, our research shows that a JE/SE reversal can be turned on or off even if the relative prominence of the attributes remains constant (e.g., in the CD-changer experiment previously reviewed). It suggests that for tasks that differ in evaluation modes, differential evaluability alone is sufficient to induce a preference reversal. The evaluability hypothesis is not, therefore, an alternative explanation to the prominence or compatibility principle; instead, they seek to explain different phenomena.

Mellers and her associates (Mellers, Chang, et al., 1992; Mellers, Ordóñez, & Birnbaum, 1992) have a change-of-process theory to account for preference reversals between tasks involving different evaluation scales. It asserts that people using different evaluation scales (e.g., ratings versus prices) adopt different cognitive models when evaluating alternative risky options, thus leading to preference reversals between those options. Like the compatibility and the prominence principles, the change-of-process theory also relies on difference in evaluation scales to explain preference reversals and hence does not apply to the JE/SE reversals explored in the present research.

Recently, Bazerman, Tenbrunsel, and Wade-Benzoni (1998) provided another explanation for some of the JE/SE reversals reviewed earlier, which they termed the want/should proposition. In the series of studies involving options varying on payoffs to self and equality or fairness (e.g., Bazerman et al., 1992, 1994), Bazerman et al. (1998) suggest that the payoff attribute is a should attribute (i.e., a factor the respondents think they should consider) and the equality attribute is a want attribute (i.e., a factor that the respondents want to consider). They then explain these JE/SE reversals by proposing that should attributes loom larger in JE and want attributes loom larger in SE. That is presumably because SE gives decision makers greater leeway to do what they are motivated to do rather than what they feel they should do: This proposition is consistent with the elastic justification notion posited in Hsee (1995, 1996b).

We agree with Bazerman et al. (1998) that the want/should proposition is an appealing alternative explanation for the JE/SE reversals in those studies. However, it lacks several ingredients of a general explanation for JE/SE reversals. First, it is often difficult to know a priori which attributes are should attributes and which are want attributes. For example, in the programmer-hiring study, it is difficult to identify a priori whether GPA is the should attribute and programming experience is the want attribute, or vice versa. Further, the want/should proposition is silent about why a JE/SE reversal can be turned on or off by evaluability manipulation. Nevertheless, the want/should proposition provides a possible explanation for JE/SE reversals involving tradeoffs between monetary payoffs and fairness. Further research is needed to determine whether those findings are caused by the want/should difference, by differential attribute evaluability, or by a combination of the two.

Nowlis and Simonson (1997) documented robust preference reversals between a choice task and a rating task. In one experiment, for example, participants in the choice condition were presented with multiple products varying in price and brand and asked to choose one. Participants in the rating condition were also presented with those multiple products simultaneously and asked to rate their purchase intention on a rating scale. For the choice group, low-price/low-quality products (e.g., a $139 Goldstar microwave oven) were preferred; in the rating group, high-price/high-quality products (e.g., a $179 Panasonic microwave oven) were favored. These observations resemble the traditional choice–judgment reversal where the main difference between choice and judgment lies in evaluation scale, not evaluation mode. Nowlis and Simonson also showed that the preference reversal was not mitigated even when the participants were given information about the price range of the product, e.g., that the prices of microwaves range from $99 to $299. This result is not inconsistent with our research. Unlike attributes such as THD, which are extremely difficult to evaluate, the price of a microwave is familiar to most people. Adding range information to an already familiar attribute, especially when the range is very large ($99 to $299) relative to the difference between the original stimulus values ($139 and $179), may in fact decrease, rather than increase, the impact of the attribute (e.g., Mellers & Cooke, 1994).

Nowlis and Simonson's work is complementary to our research. Their findings corroborate most traditional choice–judgment preference-reversal studies by showing that a difference in evaluation scale alone is sufficient to produce preference reversals. Their work further indicates that evaluation-scale-based preference reversals are different from JE/SE reversals and cannot be readily explained by the evaluability hypothesis. Nowlis and Simonson explained their results in terms of compatibility between type of response (choice versus rating) and type of attribute (comparative versus enriched). Their explanation is an extension of the compatibility principle (Slovic et al., 1990).

We conclude this section with two caveats. First, we have made a clear distinction between evaluation mode and evaluation scale and have shown that a JE/SE reversal can occur even if the evaluation scale is held constant. However, evaluation mode and evaluation scale are often naturally confounded in real-world decision making. When people are called on to decide which of two options to accept (i.e., a choice task), they are inevitably in the JE mode, comparing the two options side by side. In other words, choice is a special case of JE. On the other hand, when people consider how much they are willing to sell an item for, they are typically in the SE mode, focusing primarily on the target item alone (although they need not be). In this example, choice is confounded with JE, and pricing is confounded with SE. As a result, explanations for these reversals require a combination of the evaluability hypothesis and traditional theories for the evaluation scale effect, such as compatibility and prominence.

Second, the present article focuses only on one type of inconsistency between JE and SE – preference reversal. In a JE/SE reversal, the desirability of one option *relative* to the other changes between the evaluation modes. Hsee and Leclerc (1998) recently explored another type of JE/SE inconsistency where the desirability of *both* options changes between the evaluation modes, although their relative desirability remains unchanged, so there is no preference reversal. Specifically, they found that the desirability of low-quality products increased from SE to JE, whereas the desirability of high-quality products decreased from SE to JE. Those findings are not driven by differential attribute evaluability and are beyond the realm of this chapter (see Hsee & Leclerc, 1998, for details).

IMPLICATIONS OF THE EVALUABILITY HYPOTHESIS

Although the evaluability hypothesis is proposed originally to explain JE/SE reversals, it is potentially a more general theory. It describes how people make judgments and decisions when they do or do not have sufficient evaluability information. As such, the evaluability hypothesis has implications for phenomena beyond preference reversals. To illustrate, let us examine how this hypothesis explains why people are sometimes grossly insensitive to normatively important variables.

In a dramatic demonstration of this insensitivity, Desvousges et al. (1992, as cited by Kahneman et al., 1999) asked respondents how much they were willing to pay to save x number of migrating birds dying in uncovered oil ponds every year. X varied across different groups of respondents; it was either 2,000, 20,000, or 200,000. Normatively speaking, the number of bird deaths (x) should be an important determinant of respondents' WTP, but it had little effect. Mean WTP was about the same ($80, $78, and $88, respectively) for saving 2,000 birds, 20,000 birds, or 200,000 birds. This apparent anomalous result is highly consistent with the evaluability hypothesis. In the Desvousges et al. (1992) study, respondents had no evaluability information about bird death tolls, making this attribute extremely difficult to evaluate independently. According to the evaluability hypothesis, an attribute would have no power to differentiate the evaluations of the target options if the evaluators have no evaluability information about the attribute; the evaluation function in this condition resembles a flat line. That is why WTP values were virtually the same for the different bird-death conditions. This result is very similar to the finding in the no-information condition of the previously described score study, whereas ratings for the foreign student were virtually the same among the different score conditions.

Although it was not tested in the Desvousges et al. (1992) study, the evaluability hypothesis would predict that if the three bird-death conditions had been evaluated by the same group of participants in a JE mode, or if the respondents had received more evaluability information about endangered birds, then the bird-death numbers would have had a greater effect on WTP. Consistent with this prediction, Frederick and Fischhoff (1998) observed much greater scale sensitivity in a within-subject study, in which respondents were asked to evaluate several goods that differed in scale, than in a between-subjects design, in which different participants evaluated each of the goods.

The evaluability hypothesis can also explain why people in SE are often insensitive to variation in the value they are actually concerned about and sensitive only to variation in the proportion of that value to a certain base number. For example, suppose that there are two environmental protection programs:

Program J is designed to save birds in a forest where there are 50,000 endangered birds; it can save 20% of these birds.

Program S is designed to save birds in a forest where there are 5,000 endangered birds; it can save 80% of these birds.

Although Program J can save 10,000 birds (i.e., 20% × 50,000), whereas Program S can save only 4,000 birds (i.e., 80% × 5,000), chances are that Program S will be favored in SE. This example is a variant of Fetherstonhaugh, Slovic, Johnson, and Friedrich's (1997) finding that programs expected to save a given number of lives received greater support if the number of lives at risk was small than if it was large (see also Baron, 1997b, and Jenni & Loewenstein, 1997, for similar results). Baron (1997b) showed that the high sensitivity to relative (rather than absolute) risk was most pronounced in studies using a between-subjects (SE) design and was mitigated in a study using a JE mode. This finding is consistent with the evaluability hypothesis.

Note that the structure of the options in the previous example is parallel to that in the ice cream study. The actual number of birds the program can save is like the actual amount of ice cream; it is the main value of concern. The size of the forest is like the size of the cup; it is a base number. The proportion of birds a program can save is like the filling attribute; it reflects the relationship between the value of concern and the base number. As in the ice cream study, the evaluability hypothesis predicts that, in SE, Program S would be considered more favorably than Program J. The reason is simple: The actual value of concern – in this case, how many birds the program can save – is difficult to evaluate independently. In contrast, the proportion attribute – whether a program can save 20% or 80% of the birds in a forest – is relatively easy to evaluate; 20% seems small, and 80% seems large.

Another finding that may be related to evaluability is the observation by Fox and Tversky (1995) that the ambiguity aversion effect (the tendency to prefer gambles with known probabilities to those with unknown probabilities) occurred only in JE and not in SE. Fox and Tversky interpreted their results as showing that ambiguity aversion is an inherently comparative phenomenon, a hypothesis they called comparative ignorance. However, their findings can also be explained in terms of evaluability. Like many other attributes reviewed earlier, whether a gamble is ambiguous or not may be easier to evaluate in JE than in SE. Fox and Tversky sought to demonstrate that the effect was specific to ambiguity by showing (in their Study 5) that such a reversal did not occur with two gambles that differed in their probability of winning rather than ambiguity (one had a high probability of winning and the other had a small probability of winning). However, this result is consistent with an evaluability interpretation because there is no reason to think that probability was particularly difficult to evaluate, even in SE. Ambiguity aversion may, in fact, be an inherently comparative phenomenon, but it is only one of many attributes that receive greater weight in JE than in SE.

Marsh (1984) summarizes a variety of findings from the Dr. Fox studies of student evaluation, in which students gave higher reaching ratings to slick lecturers who presented little substance than to duller lecturers who covered material in depth. Marsh argues that the findings may reflect a process that is quite analogous to the evaluability hypothesis:

Finally, I would like to suggest a counter-explanation for some of the Dr. Fox findings. . . . Some instructor characteristics such as expressiveness and speech clarity can be judged in isolation because a frame of reference has probably been established through prior experience, and these characteristics do influence student ratings. For other characteristics such as content coverage, external frames of reference are not so well defined . . . If students were asked to compare high and low content lectures . . . I predict that their responses would more accurately reflect the content manipulation. (p. 745)

Let us conclude this chapter with a discussion of a rather metaphysical question: Which evaluation mode is better – joint or separate?

The long-standing advice for people to always consider the alternatives in decision making (e.g., Baron, 1988; Janis & Mann, 1977) implies that JE is always better than SE. However, we believe that the answer is not that simple. We agree that, in most cases, JE is better because it makes explicit the tradeoffs underlying the options. This point is particularly evident if we consider the ice cream and the dinnerware studies (Hsee, 1998), where JE led to a preference for the objectively dominant option, and SE led to a preference for the objectively inferior option.

The idea that JE is better than SE is consistent with previous findings, showing that people often arrive at better decisions if they have considered alternatives than if they have not. For example, Frisch and Jones (1993) conducted a retrospective study in which participants reported a recent decision that resulted in either a very bad outcome or a very good outcome. Participants then responded to a battery of questions about the decision processes that had led to each of these decisions. Although acknowledging that good decisions can result in bad outcomes and vice versa, their study was premised on the idea that, on average, good decisions tend to result in better outcomes than do bad decisions. The single strongest difference in process between decisions that turned out well and decisions that turned out badly was whether participants had considered alternative courses of action before deciding.

However, JE is not unconditionally better than SE. In JE, people may be overly sensitive to the difference between the alternative options on a certain attribute, whereas this difference may not even be detectable in SE. If the ultimate consumption of an option is in the SE mode, then the preference elicited in JE may be inconsistent with one's actual consumption experience.

The preceding point has important implications for discrepancies between decision and experience utilities (e.g., Kahneman & Snell, 1990, 1992). It is probably not difficult for us to recall times when we decided to choose one option over another, but we ended up being unhappy with the option we chose and would probably be happier had we chosen the forgone option. Such decision–experience inconsistencies permeate consumer decisions, career decisions, and marital decisions, to name just a few. There have been a number of explanations for these inconsistencies, including, for example, changing tastes (March, 1978), inability to predict adaptation (Loewenstein & Frederick, 1997), differential arousal states (Loewenstein, 1996), and the prominence and the compatibility principles (Tversky & Griffin, 1991).

We believe that JE/SE reversals should be added to the list of important sources of discrepancies between decision utility and experience utility. At the time of the decision, an individual is typically exposed to all possible alternatives, and so the evaluation mode is JE. At the time of experiencing the consequence of the option one has chosen, the individual is usually in SE. For example, when people buy a piano in a musical instrument store, there are typically myriad models for them to compare and choose from (JE). However, after they buy a piano, and when they use it at home – that is, play it, look at it, and so forth – they are exposed mostly to that particular piano alone (SE). Just as different attributes have different relative impact in JE than in SE, so will these attributes have different relative impact in the decision phase than in the consumption phase.

To illustrate, consider an audio store that carries two models of loudspeakers of equal price. One model looks attractive, and the other looks ugly. The ugly-looking model has a slightly lower distortion level and thus sounds slightly better. For most nonaudiophile consumers, the appearance of a speaker is easy to evaluate independently, and its sound quality is not. The sound quality of a speaker can only be appreciated when it is compared directly with another speaker. When consumers are in the store and are making a purchase decision, they are typically in JE; they can easily compare one model against the other. Through the comparison, the difference in sound quality becomes salient. In this situation, many people may end up buying the better-sounding but ugly-looking model. However, once people have purchased a set of speakers and brought them home, they are usually in the SE mode; they enjoy (or suffer with) whatever they have bought and do not actively compare it with the forgone alternative. In SE, the difference in sound quality between the ugly and the attractive models may not make any difference in one's consumption experience, but the difference in appearance may. Thus, people who bought the ugly model may not enjoy its sound quality any more than those who bought the good-looking model, but the former group of consumers may be constantly bothered by the ugly appearance of the speakers they bought.[9] The moral of this example is that when making decisions, people may put too much weight on difficult-to-evaluate attributes and may be too concerned with differences between options on those attributes that will make little or no difference in SE, hence little or no difference in actual consumption experience.

Shafir (2002) argues that the distinction between joint and separate evaluation has even wider implications. He proposes that guidelines and policies arise from joint evaluation of alternative scenarios, but events in the real world, to which these guidelines and policies are supposed to apply, usually present themselves one at a time. Because of inconsistencies between joint and separate evaluation, these guidelines and policies may not optimally serve these events in the real world.

In short, people make judgments and decisions in one of two primary evaluation modes – joint or separate. Our research shows that evaluations in these modes can yield inconsistent preferences. In addition, as just discussed, people do not always evaluate objects in the mode that is most likely to result in the best consumption experience. Which mode people use depends on whether they have a ready alternative with which to compare. When there is an available alternative option, people often naturally engage in JE. When no alternatives are present, people do not automatically think of alternatives (e.g., Gettys, Pliske, Manning, & Casey, 1987; Legrenzi, Girotto, & Johnson-Laird, 1993), and they engage in SE. Which mode is better for the consumer is a different issue. It depends on the goal people intend to achieve through the decision. If the goal is to choose the objectively most valuable option, then JE is probably better. If the goal is to choose the option that will optimize one's consumption experience, and if consumption takes place in SE, then SE may prove better.

ACKNOWLEDGMENTS

This article has benefitted from our discussions with the following people (in alphabetical order of their last names): Donna Dreier, Scott Jeffrey, Danny Kahneman, Josh Klayman, Rick Larrick, Joe Nunes, Itamar Simonson, Ann Tenbrunsel, Kimberly Wade-Benzoni, and Frank Yates.

---

[9] Two qualifications about this example: First, sometimes people may also find themselves in JE during the consumption phase, when, for example, their neighbor happens to have bought the alternative model and they can easily compare theirs with their neighbor's. However, we believe that in most circumstances, the evaluation mode at the consumption phase is much closer to the SE end on the JE/SE continuum than is the evaluation mode at the purchase phase. Second, our analysis here applies mainly to decisions whose main purpose is to optimize consumption experience. However, sometimes the decision maker has other goals in mind, and/or the construct of consumption experience does not capture the whole scope of costs and benefits of an option. Under those circumstances, our analysis may not apply.

10. Attribute-Task Compatibility as a Determinant of Consumer Preference Reversals

Stephen M. Nowlis and Itamar Simonson

Consumer preferences can be formed in different ways. In some cases, buyers directly compare alternatives across various attributes and choose the one they most prefer. In other situations, consumers evaluate each option separately and then pick the one that is judged most favorably. It has traditionally been assumed in marketing and decision research that preferences are invariant across such preference formation and elicitation methods (Tversky, Sattath, & Slovic, 1988). For example, the proportion of consumers who indicate (in a rating task) a higher purchase likelihood for Brand A than for Brand B is expected to be similar to the proportion of consumers who prefer Brand A over B in a choice task. Accordingly, marketing researchers have employed a variety of techniques for assessing and predicting consumer preferences, such as choice, rating, ranking, and matching (e.g., Urban & Hauser, 1993).

A question that naturally arises is whether alternative preference elicitation tasks generate the same preferences or whether they lead to systematically different preferences or "preference reversals." Tversky et al. (1988) demonstrate a systematic discrepancy between choice and value-matching whereby an alternative that is superior on the more prominent dimension (and significantly inferior on a second dimension) is more likely to be preferred in choice. Prior research also examines the differences between judgment and choice (e.g., Billings & Scherer, 1988; Ganzach, 1995; Montgomery, Selart, Gärling, & Lindberg, 1994; Payne, 1982) as well as between attribute- and attitude-based preferences (Sanbonmatsu & Fazio, 1990; Sanbonmatsu, Kardes, & Gibson, 1991). In particular, several studies document systematic preference reversals between choice and ratings (e.g., Bazerman, Loewenstein, & White, 1992; Fischer & Hawkins, 1993; Goldstein & Einhorn, 1987).

In this research, we examine preference reversals between two classes of preference elicitation tasks: those that are based primarily on direct alternative comparisons and those that involve separate evaluations of individual options. We propose that attributes on which consumers can compare options relatively easily and precisely (e.g., option A costs $50 more than option B,

Reprinted with permission from *Journal of Marketing Research*, vol. 34, pp. 205–218. Copyright © 1997 by the American Marketing Association. The original publication included an Appendix that is not published here.

option A has feature X and option B does not), referred to hereafter as *comparable* attributes, tend to be relatively more important in comparison-based tasks (e.g., choice). Conversely, attributes that are more difficult to compare but are more meaningful and informative when evaluated on their own (e.g., brand name, country of origin), referred to hereafter as *enriched* attributes, tend to receive relatively greater weight when preferences are formed on the basis of the evaluation of individual options (e.g., purchase likelihood ratings). Consequently, options that excel on comparable attributes are expected to be preferred more in comparison-based tasks, and those that excel on enriched attributes should be preferred more in tasks that involve separate alternative evaluations. Our main focus here is on preference reversals between choice and purchase likelihood ratings, which are among the most common tasks used to measure consumer preferences, but we show that the same phenomena generalize to other tasks that involve either direct comparison of options or separate evaluations. We also demonstrate that the preference reversals generalize to different types of comparable and enriched attributes.

This research could have significant theoretical and practical implications. In particular, a finding that options with advantages on comparable dimensions (e.g., lower prices) and/or disadvantages on enriched dimensions (e.g., inferior brand names) are preferred more in comparison-based tasks (e.g., choice) than in tasks that involve evaluations of individual options (e.g., ratings) could improve our understanding of (1) the characteristics of preference elicitation tasks and attributes that affect consumer preferences and (2) the role of the compatibility between the tasks and the attributes in determining preferences. For practitioners, a systematic tendency to prefer high-perceived-quality brands when evaluated individually would have a variety of implications for issues such as the measurement of consumer preferences and intentions, store display format (e.g., high-quality brands could benefit more than low-quality brands from end-of-aisle displays), distribution, and advertising.

We begin with a review of prior research regarding preference reversals and present the analysis that leads to the prediction of preference reversals between comparison-based tasks and those involving evaluations of individual options. We then report the results of eight studies that examine the factors that cause the preference reversals and explore alternative explanations. We conclude with a discussion of the theoretical and practical implications of the findings.

ATTRIBUTE-TASK COMPATIBILITY AND CONSUMER PREFERENCE REVERSALS

We propose that consumer preference reversals across different preference elicitation tasks are related to the compatibility between the task and attribute characteristics. There is a great deal of prior research regarding the effect of preference elicitation format on preferences, much of which relates to the *preference-reversal* phenomenon (e.g., Lichtenstein & Slovic, 1971) and the prominence and compatibility principles proposed by Tversky et al. (1988). The preference reversal phenomenon, which should be distinguished from the more general concept of preference reversals between tasks, refers to the observation that people tend to choose a gamble with a higher probability of winning a relatively small amount of money, yet they indicate a higher selling price for a gamble (assuming they owned it) that offers a smaller probability of winning a larger amount. Goldstein and Einhorn (1987) and other researchers further demonstrate that people are more likely to prefer a high-probability, low-payoff gamble (over a low-probability, high-payoff gamble) when rating the overall attractiveness of the gambles than when choosing between them.

Tversky et al. (1988) contrast choice with a matching task in which subjects enter a missing value for one of two options to make the two equally attractive. The two options were constructed such that one was superior on the more prominent dimension and greatly inferior on the less prominent dimension. These authors demonstrate that the option that is superior on the prominent attribute is more likely to be preferred in choice. Building on these results, they propose the *prominence hypothesis*, according to which the more prominent attribute receives greater weight in choice than in matching. That is, prominence, as conceptualized by Tversky et al., refers specifically to the comparison between choice and matching, and it does not lead to any predictions with respect to differences between choice and ratings.

Tversky et al. (1988) and Slovic, Griffin, and Tversky (1990) further propose the *scale compatibility hypothesis*, according to which the weight of a stimulus attribute is enhanced by its compatibility with the task (or response mode), and suggest that compatibility is partially responsible for both the preference-reversal phenomenon (i.e., choice versus pricing of gambles) and the choice-matching discrepancy. For example, a gamble's payoff is stated in terms of dollars and is therefore more compatible with a pricing task (in which the gamble's selling price also is stated in terms of dollars) than with choice. Unlike prominence, the concept of compatibility also could have implications for the comparison between choice and ratings (e.g., Schkade & Johnson, 1989; Tversky et al., 1988). Currently, however, there is no well-defined theory of the properties that define compatibility, though Slovic et al. (1990) suggest some conditions that contribute to compatibility effects. So far, demonstrations of the compatibility hypothesis involve situations in which the inputs (or attributes) and outputs (or responses) were in the same or very similar measurement units (e.g., the input and output were students' class rank, the input was monetary payoff, and the output was monetary price), in which the basis of compatibility is more than just that both the attribute values (e.g., prices) and the responses (e.g., attractiveness ratings) are numerical. However, the concept of compatibility between input and response (or task) may not be limited to situations in which inputs and outputs are in the same units.

Fischer and Hawkins (1993, p. 583) extend prior work on both prominence and compatibility and introduce the following *strategy compatibility hypothesis:* "Qualitative preference tasks are more likely than quantitative tasks to evoke preference for the alternative that is superior with respect to the most important attribute." They examine this hypothesis using different preference elicitation tasks, including choice and attractiveness ratings. The strategy compatibility hypothesis implies, for example, that if quality is more important than price, then higher-quality brands will be preferred more in choice (a qualitative task) than in purchase likelihood ratings. This is a significant extension, which does not follow directly from the prominence hypothesis (Tversky et al., 1988) and is based on several additional assumptions. In particular, Fischer and Hawkins (1993, p. 583) assume that "quantitative response tasks evoke quantitative strategies in which the decision maker makes tradeoffs between value attributes." However, whereas a matching task involves a quantitative strategy and requires trading off one attribute for another, it is less clear that rating tasks involve more quantitative strategies than choice. Furthermore, as noted by Fischer and Hawkins, the finding that the more prominent dimension of gambles, probability, is more important in ratings than in choice (e.g., Goldstein & Einhorn, 1987) is inconsistent with the strategy compatibility hypothesis. Also, as Fischer and Hawkins indicate, the strategy compatibility hypothesis cannot account for their findings that (1) choice and strength of preference (a quantitative task) produced similar preferences, and (2) the prominent attribute was more important in attractiveness ratings (though less important than in choice) than in matching or pricing tasks, even though the strategy compatibility hypothesis makes no distinction among different quantitative tasks.

Finally, recent investigations explore the differences between tasks in which alternatives are evaluated jointly and those in which each option is considered separately (Hsee, 1996a; see also Hsee, Loewenstein, Blount, & Bazerman, 1999; Mellers & Cooke, 1996). Hsee (1996a) suggests that if two options involve a tradeoff between two attributes and one of the attributes is hard to evaluate independently whereas the other is easy, then the former attribute will have a lower weight in the separate than in the joint evaluation. This proposition, and a similar prediction made by Nowlis and Simonson (1994), are examined subsequently.

Next, we examine the role of the compatibility between the characteristics of preference elicitation tasks and those of the attributes of considered options in generating preference reversals. Our main focus is on preference tasks that are used most often to elicit consumer preferences – choice and ratings – and on the key attributes that consumers consider – price and quality. However, this research demonstrates that the analysis generalizes to other tasks and attributes with similar characteristics.

Attribute Comparability and Enrichment as Determinants of Consumer Preference Reversals

To examine the effect of attribute-task compatibility on consumer preferences, consider the following example of a generic two-option set, representing two tiers of brand quality and price.

A Generic Two-Tier Set of Color Televisions: Choice Versus Ratings

Color television A	Color television B
Brand: Sony	Brand: Magnavox
Price: $309	Price: $209

Task (choice or ratings):
Choice: Which of the two televisions would you buy?
Purchase likelihood rating: Indicate on the scale below how likely
   you would be to buy Television A (followed by B)

First, consider the choice task. Although there is more than one way to choose from a set of two options that are described on two attributes, there is a great deal of evidence that within-attribute comparisons play a key role in choice processes (e.g., Russo & Dosher, 1983; Schkade & Johnson, 1989). Furthermore, a straightforward way to resolve a binary choice problem (with two differentiating attributes) is to compare intervals on the two attributes, with the resolution derived being based on whether the advantage (or benefit) of an option on one dimension outweighs its disadvantage (or cost) on the other dimension. For example, when faced with the set of televisions, consumers can choose by comparing the difference between the Sony and Magnavox brands with the price difference of $100.

The critical role of comparisons in choice processes suggests that attribute importance could be influenced by attribute comparability. Prior research offers evidence that supports this proposition. Slovic and MacPhillamy (1974) investigated situations in which two alternatives had attributes in common (i.e., both alternatives offered different values on the same dimension) and attributes that were unique to each option (i.e., each option had a feature that was not offered by the other option). They found that in choice, common attributes on which the two options could be compared directly received greater weight than did noncommon attributes (see also Markman & Medin, 1995). This finding can be extended to suggest that, of the attributes on which all alternatives have values, those that produce precise and unambiguous differences tend to be relatively more important than attributes that do not lend themselves as well to comparisons. Furthermore, greater diagnosticity of an input tends to enhance its weight and the likelihood that it will be used (e.g., Lynch, Marmorstein, & Weigold, 1988), which again suggests that attributes that produce precise and unambiguous comparisons are likely to receive greater weight in choice.

In particular, prices and brand names are likely to differ in terms of how easily and effectively they can be compared. Prior research indicates that it is easier to compare numerical information, such as prices, than verbal information, such as brand names (Viswanathan & Narayanan, 1994), and that direct comparisons are more common with numeric data and absolute evaluations (e.g., "this person has excellent qualifications") are more common with verbal data (Huber, 1980). Furthermore, price differences are precise, unambiguous, and easy to compute. Familiar brand names, conversely, are often enriched, qualitative cues that represent a variety of associations, beliefs, and experiences (e.g., Aaker, 1991; Keller, 1993). Consequently, differences between brands are likely to be imprecise, ambiguous, and nonquantifiable. This analysis suggests that the weight of brand names (prices) will tend to be lower (higher) in choice and other comparison-based tasks relative to tasks in which within-attribute comparisons play a less important role.

Consider next a purchase likelihood rating task (as illustrated in the color television example). To construct a rating, the respondent, for example, can evaluate the attractiveness of each attribute value and combine these evaluations in some fashion. Here, consumers do not have the benefit of comparisons with other externally available options, and they need to rely on prior knowledge to assess the attractiveness of the provided absolute values. Although consumers often have a great deal of knowledge and can consider options to which they were exposed previously (e.g., Biehal & Chakravarti, 1983; Sujan, 1985), such information is likely to be less salient and influential than the externally available attribute values of another option in the choice set under consideration.

This analysis suggests that more comparable attributes (e.g., the price of a television), which are expected to receive greater weight in comparison-based tasks, tend to be less meaningful and useful when evaluated on their own without the benefit of comparisons. Furthermore, a price may not be helpful when forming an overall evaluation, because it is difficult with a single option to see the tradeoff between brand name and price (e.g., the portion of the price due to a superior brand such as Sony). Conversely, though brand names tend to be less comparable, the richness of brand associations suggests that a brand name can be a powerful cue in a rating task, and consumers might be able to form a meaningful evaluation of a brand even without comparing it with another brand. Therefore, relative to choice, a rating task is expected to enhance the weight of brand names and diminish the weight of prices.

More generally, we propose that two characteristics of attributes determine their relative weights in choice and ratings: More comparable dimensions tend to receive greater weight in comparison-based tasks, whereas more enriched

Table 10.1. Attribute-Task Compatibility and Attribute Importance

	Type of Attribute	
Task Type	Comparable (e.g., Price in Dollars)	Enriched (e.g., Brand Name)
Comparison-based (e.g., choice)	Attribute compatible with task and receives greater weight	Attribute incompatible with task and receives less weight
Separate evaluations (e.g., ratings)	Attribute incompatible with task and receives less weight	Attribute compatible with task and receives greater weight

attributes that can be interpreted easily on their own tend to receive greater weight in tasks that involve separate option evaluations. In Table 10.1, we summarize the relationships between the type of preference elicitation task and the type of attribute.

This analysis leads to the prediction that there will be preference reversals between choice and purchase likelihood ratings, such that low-quality, low-price brands will be preferred more in choice.

H_1:   Consumers are more likely to prefer a low-price, low-perceived-quality brand over a high-price, high-perceived-quality brand (both with the same features) when making choices rather than separate ratings of purchase likelihood.

STUDIES OF THE ROLE OF ATTRIBUTE-TASK COMPATIBILITY AS A DETERMINANT OF CONSUMER PREFERENCE REVERSALS

Overview of the Experiments

We tested H_1 and additional hypotheses (discussed subsequently) regarding the role of attribute-task compatibility in consumer preference reversals in a series of eight experiments. A total of 1,590 respondents participated across the eight studies, with between 70 and 400 respondents per study. Respondents included both visitors to a popular science museum (52%) and students enrolled in marketing courses (48%). The museum respondents, who received $2 for their participation, were between 18 and 80 years of age and represented a wide range of demographic characteristics. Respondents indicated their preferences for the two options presented in each product category, using one of several preference elicitation tasks (as described subsequently). They were told that there were no right or wrong answers and that they should consider only their personal preferences.

In the following sections, we present several hypotheses and describe the manner in which they were tested. We begin with the test of H_1, regarding preference reversals between choice and purchase likelihood ratings involving options that differ in price and (perceived) brand quality.

Table 10.2. Preference for High- and Low-Tier Brands (Test of H_1):
Share of Low-Tier Brands (%)[a]

Study	Choice	Ratings	Number of Product Categories in Which H_1 was in the Expected Direction[b]
1	50	35	5/5
2	47	34	7/7
3	47	33	7/7
4	58	48	6/7
5	44	32	7/7
6	52	30	7/7
7	63	35	11/11

[a] The share of the high-tier brand can be calculated as 100% minus the share of the low-tier brand.

[b] For example, in Study 1, five of the five tested categories were in the expected direction.

Preference Reversals Involving Options Varying in Price and Brand Quality

We tested H_1 in seven separate studies, which also examined hypotheses discussed subsequently. In each product category designed to test H_1, respondents evaluated a high-quality, high-price (i.e., high-tier) brand and a low-quality, low-price (low-tier) brand.[1] Respondents in one task chose between the two brands in each product category. In a second task, respondents rated their likelihood of purchasing each of the two brands considered in the choice task. Ratings of purchase likelihood were on a 0 (very unlikely to buy) to 20 (very likely to buy) scale. Between 5 and 11 product categories were tested in each study, including batteries, cameras, sunscreen lotion, microwave ovens, cordless telephones, and hotels. To make the choice and purchase likelihood data comparable, the ratings were converted to ordinal data (e.g., Montgomery et al., 1994). For example, cases in which Brand A received a higher purchase likelihood rating than did Brand B were coded as a choice of Brand A. Ties in purchase likelihood ratings were excluded.

As shown in Table 10.2, the results of the seven studies provide strong support for H_1, demonstrating a systematic preference reversal whereby low-tier options are preferred more in choice than in purchase likelihood ratings, whereas high-tier options are preferred more in ratings. Although the magnitude of the preference reversals in individual studies varied between 10% and 28%, which reflects the influence of such factors as the particular attributes

[1] The high- and low-perceived-quality brand names for this and subsequent studies were pretested in a pilot study with 51 visitors to the science museum. Each brand name was rated in terms of overall quality and performance, using 1-to-10 scales. In all product categories, the designated high-quality brands were rated significantly higher than were the low-quality brands, $p < .01$.

and attribute values selected for each category, the direction of the results was consistent with H_1 in 50 of the 51 tests (across the seven studies).

In addition to examining the percent difference in option shares across tasks, we tested H_1 and the other hypotheses presented subsequently with logit models, in which choices (or converted ratings) were modeled as a function of independent dummy variables, representing (1) the type of option (e.g., high- versus low-tier), (2) the tasks (e.g., choice versus ratings), (3) the attribute type (where relevant), (4) the interactions among tasks, options, and attribute types, and (5) option-specific dummy variables that capture the mean tendency to select each alternative (e.g., Guadagni & Little, 1983).[2] Consistent with H_1, in each of the seven studies separately, the coefficient of the interaction between the task (choice versus ratings) and option type (low- versus high-tier) was statistically significant, $p < .01$ in each study.

In summary, the results of seven studies in which H_1 was tested demonstrate a systematic preference reversal, whereby high-price, high-perceived-quality brands are preferred more in ratings of purchase likelihood than in choice.[3] These results are consistent with the proposition that more enriched attributes (e.g., brand name) receive greater weight in preference elicitation tasks involving separate option evaluations, whereas more comparable attributes (e.g., price) receive greater weight in comparison-based tasks. However, to provide a more complete test of this general proposition, we need to show the following:

1. The preference reversals between choice and ratings are not limited to options that differ in price and quality and extend to other comparable and enriched attributes;
2. The preference reversals involving options that differ in price and quality can be eliminated by making price information less comparable or by making brand quality information more comparable;
3. The preference reversals are not limited to choice and ratings and extend to other preference elicitation tasks in which options are compared directly or evaluated separately;
4. Alternative explanations do not offer better accounts for the observed preference reversals; and
5. Decision process measures support the assumption that brand names loom larger in ratings, whereas prices play a greater role in choice.

In the following sections, we report the results of investigations in which these tests were conducted. We begin by examining other enriched and comparable attributes besides brand name and price.

[2] More detailed information about the logit models and results in each study as well as the product category-specific (%) differences between tasks can be obtained from the authors.
[3] Similar systematic preference reversals between choices and purchase likelihood ratings were obtained in a separate study, in which respondents in the choice condition also had the option of rejecting both brands and going to another store.

Preference Reversals with Other Comparable and Enriched Attributes

Comparable attribute: Unique features. Product and service alternatives often offer different features.[4] Consider the following simplified example, in which one television brand is associated with relatively lower perceived quality but offers a feature that the other television brand does not (assuming that price and other product features are the same for both options):

A Generic Two-Tier Set of Color Televisions: Brand Name Versus Unique Features

Color television A	Color television B
Brand: Sony	Brand: Magnavox
Features	Features
	Hi-fi stereo

Task (choice or ratings):
Choice: Which of the two televisions would you buy?
Purchase likelihood rating: Indicate on the scale below how likely
  you would be to buy Television A (followed by B)

As illustrated in this example, the fact that one option offers a feature that the other option does not tends to be salient and unambiguous when the two options are compared directly. A consumer faced with this choice can detect readily that the Magnavox television offers hi-fi stereo, whereas the Sony television does not. Conversely, when rating (separately) the purchase likelihood of the Magnavox and Sony televisions, the hi-fi stereo feature is less salient, because it is just one of several features that each television offers or does not offer, and it has no special status as the differentiating feature. Accordingly, differentiating product features are expected to receive greater weight in choice than in ratings, whereas enriched attributes such as brand name are expected to receive relatively greater weight in ratings (as explained previously). This differential weighting of features and brand names in choice and ratings suggests that there will be preference reversals between the two tasks, whereby an alternative with superior features and an inferior brand name will be more preferred in choice.

H_2:   Consumers are more likely to prefer a low-perceived-quality brand with an additional feature over a high-perceived-quality brand without the feature (both with the same price) when making choices rather than separate ratings of purchase likelihood.

We tested H_2 in three studies, with five to seven product categories per study. Again, respondents either made a choice or rated their likelihood of purchasing each of the two alternatives (on a 0–20 scale). The choice set in each category

---

[4] We focus here only on features that are either present or absent, and the discussion does not apply to features, such as colors, that have different possible values.

Table 10.3. *Preference for Brands With or Without Unique Features (Test of H_2): Share of Lower-Quality Brands With Extra Feature (%)*[a]

Study	Choice	Ratings	Number of Product Categories in Which H_2 was in the Expected Direction
1	53	38	5/5
2	57	43	7/7
3	58	50	7/7

[a] The share of the higher-quality brand is calculated as 100% minus the share of the low-quality brand.

included a low-quality brand that had a distinctive product feature and a high-quality brand that did not offer that feature, with both brands having the same price and other features. For example, in the cordless telephone category, the Cobra brand had (in addition to several common features) "full 10-channel capability for reduced interference," a feature that Sony did not offer, with both brands priced at $69. Similarly, in the microwave oven category, Goldstar but not Panasonic offered a "turntable for more even cooking" (both priced at $179).

As shown in Table 10.3, the results of the three studies support H_2. The share of the low-quality brand with the additional feature was consistently higher in choice than in ratings, and this result was in the expected direction in all 19 tests. The logit analysis showed, for each of the three studies separately, that the coefficient testing this effect was statistically significant, $p < .05$.

Enriched attribute: Country of origin. Next, we test whether the preference reversals extend to a different type of an enriched attribute. Country of origin is often an important cue that provides a great deal of information (e.g., Hong & Wyer, 1990), but comparisons of country of origin (e.g., a Japanese-made versus Taiwanese-made camcorder) tend to be fuzzy and imprecise. Therefore, for the same reasons outlined previously, we expect that products with relatively superior country of origin and higher price will be preferred more often in purchase likelihood ratings than in choice.[5]

H_3:   Consumers are more likely to prefer a product with a lower price and relatively inferior country of origin over a high-price, superior country-of-origin product (both with the same features) when making choices rather than separate ratings of purchase likelihood.

The option sets used to test H_3 included one alternative made in a country that is associated with higher-quality products and higher prices and a second

[5] This test was proposed by Wilfried Vanhonacker in a seminar at the Hong Kong University of Science and Technology.

alternative made in a country that is associated with lower-quality products and lower prices.[6] For example, in the category of cameras, subjects evaluated a camera made in Japan that cost \$169 and a camera made in Korea that cost \$109. Both brands also offered a common set of product features. The test was replicated in seven categories, including cordless telephones and microwave ovens.

Consistent with H_3, the share of the brands with the less reputable country of origin and lower price was, on average, 9% higher (46% versus 37%) in the choice task compared with their implied share in the rating task. The direction of this result was consistent across all seven product categories. The logit analysis showed that the coefficient testing this effect was statistically significant, $t = 2.4, p < .01$.

In summary, the results demonstrate that the preference reversals are not limited to options that differ in price and brand quality, and similar reversals are observed when either price is replaced with product features or brand name is replaced with country of origin. These findings are consistent with the notion that preference reversals between choice and purchase likelihood ratings are obtained whenever the differentiating dimensions include an enriched attribute and a comparable attribute.

Next, we examine whether the preference reversals can be eliminated by changing the nature of the attributes, such as using qualitative price descriptions or numeric brand quality indicators, while keeping the same underlying dimensions of price and quality. If these reversals are indeed eliminated, that provides strong evidence that the nature of the attributes is a key factor controlling these phenomena.

Eliminating the Preference Reversals Using Enriched Price Values or Comparable Quality Values

The finding that the preference reversals generalize to other enriched and comparable attributes suggests that a critical determinant of these reversals is the characteristics of the differentiating attributes (comparable versus enriched). If this conjecture is true, then it should be possible to eliminate the preference reversals simply by making prices less comparable and more enriched *or* by making brand quality more comparable and less enriched (without changing the other attribute). We first consider the case in which dollar prices are made less comparable and more enriched.

Replacing Dollar Prices With Qualitative Descriptions. If a consumer is evaluating two options that differ in terms of brand names and dollar prices, we expect preference reversals to occur between ratings and choice because

---

[6] The more and less reputable countries of origin for this study were pretested in a pilot study with 38 students. Each country of origin was rated in terms of its ability to produce high-quality brands that perform well, using 1 to 10 scales. In all product categories, the designated more reputable country of origin was rated significantly higher than was the less reputable country of origin, $p < .01$.

brand names are more compatible with ratings and prices are more compatible with choice (as per H_1). However, if dollar prices (e.g., $29) are replaced with qualitative price values (e.g., "very high price," "average price"), then both prices and brand names are more compatible with ratings than with choice, because both attributes are now enriched. Therefore, the asymmetry between attributes is eliminated, and the preference reversals between the tasks no longer should occur.

H_4:   The discrepancy between purchase likelihood ratings and choice, per H_1, will be eliminated when prices in dollars are replaced with verbal price descriptions.

We tested H_4 by manipulating the price information, using dollar or verbal values. For example, in the microwave oven category, respondents evaluated either a Goldstar brand priced at $129 and a Panasonic priced at $189 or a Goldstar with a price described as "low" and a Panasonic with a "moderate" price. The verbal descriptions of the prices were selected using a comparison of the prices in dollars with the price ranges in the relevant categories, as reported in *Consumer Reports*. Respondents evaluated alternatives in seven product categories, including color televisions, batteries, and wristwatches.

First, consistent with H_1, the preference reversals were observed in all seven categories when dollar prices were provided, and the coefficient from the logit analysis that tested this effect was statistically significant (an average difference of 13% between tasks, $p < .01$). However, when dollar prices were replaced with verbal price descriptions, there was only a 1% average difference in preference share between the choice and ratings tasks, with no consistent pattern across the product categories. The logit analysis showed that the coefficient testing this effect was not statistically significant, $p > .5$.

In summary, consistent with H_4, the preference reversals were eliminated when dollar prices were replaced with verbal descriptions, because both differentiating attributes (brand names and prices) were enriched. Next, we examine whether the preference reversals are eliminated when brand names are replaced with more comparable and less enriched quality indicators.

Replacing Brand Names With Numeric Quality Ratings.   Brand names often serve as important indicators of quality (e.g., Aaker, 1991). Similarly, *Consumer Reports* quality ratings are used by consumers to assess product quality. However, in the context of this research, there are two key differences between brand names and numeric quality ratings, namely, the latter are more comparable and less enriched. Therefore, if brand names are replaced by quality ratings, then both of the differentiating attributes – prices and quality ratings – are more compatible with choice than with ratings, and hence no preference reversals should be observed.

H_5:   The preference reversals between purchase likelihood ratings and choice, as predicted in H_1, will be eliminated when brand names are replaced with numeric quality ratings.

We tested H_5 in a manner similar to H_4, except that in this case we described options with either brand names or *Consumer Reports* quality ratings. The high-quality brand names were replaced by relatively high *Consumer Reports* quality ratings, and the low-quality brand names were replaced by low-quality ratings. The quality ratings were selected on the basis of the attractiveness ratings of the brands in the pilot study (described previously). Respondents evaluated alternatives in seven product categories, including cordless telephones, cameras, and toasters.

Consistent with H_1, when the options were described with brand names, the preference reversals were observed in all seven categories, and the coefficient from the logit model that tested this effect was significant (an average difference of 14% between tasks, $p < .01$). However, when brand names were replaced with quality ratings, there was only a 2% difference in preference share between the choice and ratings tasks, with no consistent pattern across the product categories. The coefficient in the logit analysis that tested this effect was not statistically significant, which is consistent with H_5, $p > .5$.

In summary, the results indicate that the preference reversals between choice and ratings can be controlled by manipulating the comparability or enrichment of the differentiating attributes. Combined with the previous finding that the preference reversals generalize to other enriched and comparable dimensions, this evidence lends strong support to the proposition that the nature of the attribute information plays a key role in the observed preference reversals. Next, we examine the other key determinant of the reversals, the preference elicitation task, and test whether the reversals generalize to other tasks that are based on either direct option comparisons or separate evaluations of options.

Preference Reversals Between Other Comparison-Based and Separate Evaluation Tasks

Comparison-Based Task: Strength of Preference. A strength-of-preference task, in which consumers are asked to indicate the degree to which they prefer one option relative to another, is likely to involve direct attribute comparisons between the alternatives, similar to choice (e.g., Fischer & Hawkins, 1993; Mellers, Chang, Birnbaum, & Ordóñez, 1992). Accordingly, using the same arguments presented previously, we would expect brand names to have lower weight and price to have greater weight in a strength-of-preference task compared with a purchase likelihood rating task.

H_6:   Consumers are more likely to prefer an option that is superior on a comparable attribute (e.g., a low-price, low-perceived-quality brand) over an option that is superior on an enriched attribute (e.g., a high-price, high-perceived-quality brand) when rating their strength of preference between these options than when making separate ratings of purchase likelihood.

To test H_6, we asked respondents to evaluate high- and low-tier brands by choosing between them, rating them in terms of purchase likelihood, or rating them in terms of strength of preference. Thus, H_6 was tested by comparing ratings of strength of preference with ratings of purchase likelihood, whereas H_1 was tested by comparing choices with ratings of purchase likelihood. Strength of preference was rated on a 19-point scale, from 9 on one end (to indicate strong preference for alternative A) to 9 on the other side of the scale (to indicate strong preference for alternative B). We tested seven product categories, including batteries, cameras, and sunscreen lotion.

Consistent with H_6, the results of the logit analysis indicated that the difference between the two tasks was in the expected direction and was statistically significant, $t = 2.4$, $p < .01$. Low-tier brands were preferred, on average, 10% more often in the strength-of-preference task than in the purchase likelihood ratings, with six of the seven tests in the expected direction. And consistent with H_1, when the response modes were either choices or ratings of purchase likelihood, the low-tier brands were preferred 10% more often in the choices than the ratings. This result was observed in six of the seven product categories, and the coefficient from the logit model that tested this effect was statistically significant, $t = 2.4$, $p < .01$. These findings suggest that the preference reversals generalize to other comparison-based tasks. Next, we examine preference reversals between choice and another task that involves separate option evaluations to test whether the reversals generalize to other tasks besides ratings.

Separate Evaluation Task: Choosing Whether to Purchase an Individual Option. A task that combines some of the characteristics of choice and purchase likelihood ratings involves asking consumers to indicate for each brand separately whether they would buy it (assuming they needed the product) or look for another option. Because consumers evaluate options separately, we expect this task (relative to choice) to favor options that are superior on enriched attributes.

H_7:   Consumers are more likely to prefer an option that is superior on a comparable attribute (e.g., a low-price, low-perceived-quality brand) over an option that is superior on an enriched attribute (e.g., a high-price, high-perceived-quality brand) when making direct choices between them as opposed to making separate decisions of whether to purchase each option.

To test H_7, respondents either chose between high- and low-tier brands or indicated for each brand separately whether they would buy it. For example, in the microwave ovens category, subjects saw a low-tier oven and were asked whether they would "(a) Buy this microwave oven, or (b) Not buy this microwave oven and go to another store"; then they were asked the same questions regarding the high-tier oven. Seven product categories were tested, including batteries, cordless telephones, and televisions.

Consistent with H_7, the share of the low-tier brands was, on average, 15% higher among respondents who made choices than when they made separate decisions regarding each option, and this pattern was observed in all seven product categories. The coefficient from the logit model that tested this hypothesis was statistically significant, $t = 2.6$, $p < .01$.

In summary, the results demonstrate that the preference reversals are not limited to choice and purchase likelihood ratings, and they are observed with other comparison-based and separate-evaluation tasks. These findings provide further support to the notion that, when options differ on an enriched attribute and a comparable attribute, systematic preference reversals occur between tasks that are comparison-based and those that involve separate alternative evaluations.

An Alternative Explanation Based on the Context Dependency or Evaluability of Attributes

The findings presented so far are consistent with the notion that the observed preference reversals are determined by the compatibility between the differentiating attributes and the preference elicitation tasks. However, a related but different explanation for these reversals is that they occur because of differences in the information available in comparison-based and separate-evaluation tasks. In particular, this account suggests that continuous attributes such as price are less important in separate evaluations than in comparison-based tasks because they cannot be evaluated effectively out of context (i.e., separately), which leads to preference reversals. For example, the fact that a roll of Bounty paper towels costs 99¢ may not be helpful when rating that product because the consumer has difficulty interpreting the price out of context – that is, without knowing how it compares with other brands on the market. Such an account is proposed by Nowlis and Simonson (1994), who suggest that "context-dependent" attributes (e.g., prices) receive lower weights in ratings than in choice. Similarly, Hsee (1996a) focuses on the "evaluability" of attributes and proposes that, when one attribute is difficult to evaluate or interpret independently (e.g., the number of entries in a dictionary) and a second attribute is easy (e.g., a new dictionary has a stain on the cover), then the former attribute receives lower weight and the latter receives greater weight in separate evaluations.

An implication of this alternative explanation is that the discrepancy between separate and joint evaluations should be reduced or eliminated if consumers are shown the same information, using the same presentation format in the two tasks. To test this prediction, the two considered options in a particular category could be displayed together, in ratings as in choice, such that the options are rated consecutively and consumers can see one option when rating the other. A second testable prediction derived from the Nowlis and Simonson (1994) and Hsee (1996a) accounts is that providing information that makes it easy to evaluate attribute values should decrease or eliminate the preference reversals. In particular, if indeed the factor that drives the reversals is the difficulty of evaluating certain attributes (e.g., prices) separately, then providing information about the range of market values on these attributes should reduce or eliminate the cause of the preference reversals.

In contrast, the explanation advanced here suggests that rating both options in a category consecutively and providing information about the values of attributes that are difficult to assess independently will not reduce and actually could increase the magnitude of preference reversals. Specifically, we propose that the key determinant of the preference reversals between joint and separate evaluations is the compatibility between attributes and preference elicitation tasks, not the knowledge or evaluability of attribute values. For example, brand names are less compatible with comparison-based tasks such as choice, because differences between brand names tend to be ambiguous and imprecise. Conversely, brand names are more compatible with purchase likelihood ratings, because brand names can provide a great deal of information, and brand evaluations are often highly accessible in memory (e.g., Alba, Hutchinson, & Lynch, 1991). The reverse is true for prices, which produce precise and unambiguous differences in choice (e.g., "Sony costs $100 more than Magnavox"), whereas the cost of one attribute (e.g., the Sony brand) in terms of another (e.g., price) is ambiguous and difficult to detect in separate evaluations. Therefore, rating two options in a category one after the other and providing information that makes it easy to evaluate attribute values separately is not expected to reduce the magnitude of preference reversals, because it does not change the differential compatibility of enriched and comparable attributes with tasks involving joint or separate evaluations. Rather, information about the market range of comparable attributes (e.g., price) is expected to make these attributes more salient, which is likely to have a greater effect on the task that is compatible with the attribute (e.g., choice) and might have little or no effect on a task in which comparable attributes are less useful. This, in turn, can lead to even larger preference reversals.

H_8:   The preference reversals between choice and purchase likelihood ratings (per H_1) still will hold if consumers in the rating task are presented with both alternatives from the choice task one below the other and rate them consecutively.

H_9:   Providing information about the range of values of comparable attributes (price and product features) will increase the magnitude of preference reversals between choice and ratings.

To test H_8 we used the same method employed for testing H_1, except that the two options in each category either were presented in the rating task one below the other (as in the choice task) and rated consecutively or were separated by options from six other categories. We tested H_9 in a study in which three factors were manipulated in a 2 (response mode was either choice or rating of purchase likelihood) × 2 (the alternatives in each product category were either a high-price, high-quality brand and a low-price, low-quality brand or a high-quality brand and a low-quality brand with a unique feature) × 3 (respondents received additional information about prices, features, or neither) between-subjects design. Respondents in all tasks evaluated alternatives in seven product categories, including batteries, cordless telephones, and microwave ovens.

In the provided information conditions, respondents received information about (1) the range of market prices in the category "according to *Consumer Reports*," to enable them to assess specific prices relative to that range, or (2) how common or unique particular product features were, which was used to inform respondents that the feature that differentiated the two options in each category was relatively unique. To ensure that respondents paid attention to the provided information, they were given a short test in which they were asked to rate how expensive or unique particular prices or features were relative to other products on the market. For example, in the microwave oven category, respondents were told that the typical price range for ovens was $99 (typical lowest price) to $299 (typical highest price), and they then were asked to rate (on a 1–10 scale) how expensive the prices of $109, $129, $189, and $209 were; the two ovens that were evaluated subsequently in the choice and rating tasks were priced at $139 and $179.[7] In the provided feature information, respondents were given information about the uniqueness of several features, including the one that differentiated the options that were subsequently evaluated (e.g., "turntable for more even cooking" is offered by 10% of the microwave ovens on the market). An examination of the responses to these tests indicated that 99% (98%) of the respondents in the information conditions evaluated the test prices (features) consistent with that information. Respondents next made choices or ratings, which can be compared with the control (no provided attribute information) condition. The provided information, the manipulation check, and the evaluated alternatives in each category (in both the choice and rating tasks) all were presented on the same page, so that the provided information would be salient and fresh in the respondents' minds when they formed their preferences. Because the two options in each category were rated consecutively, this study provided an additional test of H_8.

In the study designed specifically to test H_8 (and H_1), the low-tier brands were preferred, on average, 11% more in choice than in ratings of purchase likelihood, which was similar to the discrepancy between choice and ratings of separated options (10%). Therefore, the preference reversals were observed even when the options appeared, in ratings like in choice, one below the other on the same page. The logit analysis showed that the coefficient testing H_8 was statistically significant, $t = 2.6$, $p < .01$.

---

[7] In three of the seven product categories, the prices of the target (evaluated) set were in the middle of the provided price range, two categories were closer to the low end, and two wore closer to the high end.

Consistent with H_9, when respondents were given information on market prices, the magnitude of the preference reversals increased from 12% (the share of the low-tier was 44% in choice versus 32% in ratings) to 20% (52% versus 32%). The preference-reversal magnitude increased in six of the seven categories. The interaction testing this effect in the logit model was statistically significant, $t = 2.0$, $p < .05$. Similarly, when respondents were given information about product features, the magnitude of the preference reversals increased from 8% (58% versus 50%) to 18% (71% versus 53%). This increase was observed in six of the seven categories. The coefficient of the interaction from the logit analysis that tested this effect was statistically significant, $t = 2.3$, $p < .01$. Note also that these results provide further support for H_8, because the preference reversals were observed even though the options in the rating task were presented together on the same page.

In summary, the results are inconsistent with the explanation of the preference reversals that are based on differential attribute evaluability. If, indeed, the cause was the difficulty of evaluating attribute values (e.g., prices) in isolation, then evaluating the two options in each category consecutively or providing information about the market range of these attributes should have decreased or eliminated the preference reversals. However, consecutive option ratings did not affect the preference reversal, and providing information almost doubled, rather than eliminated, the preference-reversal magnitude. Therefore, even when consumers are provided with the information needed for a meaningful evaluation of individual attribute values such as prices, they do not use that information unless the task requires them to do so, perhaps because they do not recognize the difficulty of evaluating such values out of context. Next, we examine more closely the decision processes underlying the observed preference reversals.

Differential Attribute Processing in Choice and Purchase Likelihood Ratings

The explanation for the preference reversals that we propose can be investigated further using think-aloud protocols (e.g., Ericsson & Simon, 1980), which could provide insights into the manner in which brand names, prices, and features are processed in choice and ratings. An important difference between the two tasks relates to the role of comparisons. There are likely to be more within-attribute comparisons in choice (e.g., comparing the prices of Brands A and B), simply because in a rating task options are evaluated separately whereas choice typically involves comparisons of two or more options (e.g., Billings & Scherer, 1988). Although consumers might use their prior knowledge about other alternatives in the same category when rating a particular option, it is unlikely to be as salient and produce the same level of comparisons as the externally provided options in the choice task.

A less obvious difference is the proposition that in a choice task consumers can compare the intervals on two attributes directly (hereafter, interattribute comparisons) to determine whether the benefit on one dimension justifies the cost on the other, whereas in a rating task it is more difficult to determine how one attribute value affects another. In particular, in choice consumers can compare the cost or worth of brand names in terms of prices and features, whereas such an interattribute comparison is less likely to be performed in ratings. Note that interattribute comparisons can be performed in both tasks. In a rating task, consumers could indicate that "$X is a good price for brand Y" or that an inferior brand's quality is offset by superior features. In choice between two options, as we suggested, consumers also could contrast the intervals on two attributes, for example, by saying that the difference between the brands does not justify the price difference or that the feature difference compensates for the brand name difference.

We also propose that comparing brand names is more difficult than comparing prices and features, which suggests that, in a choice task, there should be fewer brand comparisons than there are price or feature comparisons. Finally, our analysis suggests that brand names will be more important in ratings whereas prices and unique features will be more important in choice. Previous research has shown that the order in which attribute information is acquired and evaluated can be used as a measure of attribute importance (e.g., Heeler, Okechuku, & Reid, 1979; Simonson, Huber, & Payne, 1988). Contrasting the order in which attributes are considered in choice and ratings is complicated by the fact that in choice both options are considered simultaneously, whereas in ratings they are evaluated separately. However, it is possible to compare the two tasks in terms of whether brand names are considered before or after prices and unique features in the decision process (focusing on the first time that each attribute is mentioned). Our analysis suggests that brand names will be considered before prices and unique features more often in ratings than in choice. That leads to H_{10}, H_{11}, and H_{12}, which we tested using think-aloud protocols.

H_{10}:   There will be more interattribute comparisons in choice than in ratings of purchase likelihood.

H_{11}:   In a choice task, there will be fewer brand comparisons than price or feature comparisons.

H_{12a}:   Brand names will be considered before prices more often in ratings than in choice.

H_{12b}:   Brand names will be considered before unique features more often in ratings than in choice.

To test these hypotheses, two factors were manipulated in a 2 (response mode was either choice or rating of purchase likelihood) × 2 (the alternatives in each product category were either a high-price, high-quality brand and a low-price, low-quality brand or a high-quality brand and a low-quality brand with a unique feature) between-subjects design. Before starting the task, subjects received instructions on how to think aloud and were given one practice problem. We emphasized that there were no right or wrong answers. Five product categories were tested, including several of the option sets that were used in earlier studies. The protocols were analyzed by two independent judges. The interjudge reliability was 90%, and disagreements were resolved by discussion. The judges were asked to identify (1) all cases in which the decision process included interattribute comparisons, such as "$200 is good for a Sony" or "The difference between Sony and Magnavox is not worth $100," and (2) all instances of brand, price, and feature comparisons in choice, such as "Sony is much better than Magnavox," "This one is $100 more expensive than the other one," and "Sony does not have hi-fi stereo." A different judge counted the number of cases in which brand names were mentioned before or after prices and unique features.

As suggested by H_{10}, the protocols of the respondents indicated that they used explicit comparisons relating brands and prices in 24% of the choices compared with 14% of the ratings, $t = 1.7$, $p < .05$. And respondents made comparisons that involved brand names and features in 23% of the choices compared with 3% of the ratings, $t = 4.1$, $p < .01$. Consistent with H_{11}, there were on average .71 price comparisons and .66 feature comparisons per choice compared with just .36 brand comparisons per choice, t (brand-price) $= 4.9$, $p < .01$ and t (brand-feature) $= 4.1$, $p < .01$.

H_{12} suggests that brand names will be considered before prices or unique features more often in ratings than in choice. With respect to the brand-price order (H_{12a}), brand names were mentioned before prices in 69% of the ratings compared with 59% of the choices, $t = 1.4$, $p < .10$. In the problems in which options differed in terms of brand names and unique features (H_{12b}), brand names were mentioned before the unique features in 81% of the ratings compared with 59% of the choices, $t = 3.2$, $p < .01$.

In summary, the results lend support to our assumptions regarding process and attribute importance differences between choice and rating tasks. Specifically, the findings suggest that choices are characterized by more interattribute comparisons, which is consistent with the notion that choice makes the relations between attributes more salient. Furthermore, consistent with the proposition that brand comparisons are more difficult to make, respondents in the choice task were significantly more likely to compare prices and features than they were to compare brands. In addition, the results suggest that brand names received more weight in ratings than in choice, though this effect was only marginally significant when the other differentiating attribute was price.

Implications of the Preference Reversals for Consumer Attribute Sensitivity in Choice and Ratings

A potentially important implication of the observed preference reversals is that comparison-based tasks are more sensitive than are separate evaluation tasks to the differences between options in terms of price and features (see, e.g., Fischer, 1995). In other words, changes in the price or features of one alternative relative to another are expected to generate relatively greater preference changes in choice than in ratings. Conversely, consumers who evaluate alternatives separately are expected to rely primarily on brand names and to have difficulty assessing the cost of brand names in terms of price and features. Consequently, ratings should be relatively insensitive to changes in prices and features.

H_{13a}:   A change in the feature difference between two considered options will have a larger effect on preference shares in a comparison-based task (choice) than in a separate-evaluation task (ratings).

H_{13b}:   A change in the price difference between two considered options will have a larger effect on preference shares in a comparison-based task (choice) than in a separate-evaluation task (ratings).

We tested H_{13} by manipulating the price or feature differences between the two considered options in each category. This enabled us to contrast the choice and ratings in terms of the effect of these changes on preference shares. Specifically, two factors were manipulated in a 2 (response mode was either choice or rating of purchase likelihood) × 5 (option sets) between-subjects design. The five set designs included (1) a high-quality brand and a low-quality brand offered at a "moderate" price difference (the control condition), (2) the brands offered at a larger price difference, (3) the brands offered at a smaller price difference, (4) additional product features added to the low-quality brand, and (5) additional product features added to the high-quality brand.

In conditions 2 and 3, the price difference between the brands was increased by 75% or reduced by 75%, respectively, such that the lower-quality brand always was priced lower (to avoid dominance). For example, in the control condition for microwave ovens, subjects evaluated a Goldstar oven priced at $129 and a Panasonic oven priced ($60 higher) at $189 (with the same product features). In the second condition, the price of the Panasonic was raised to $234 (for a difference in price between the brands of $105 = 1.75 [$60]). In the third condition, the price of the Goldstar was raised to $174 (for a difference in price between the brands of only $15 =.25 [$60]).[8]

As an example of the conditions in which product features were added to the brands, in the microwave oven category, the product features "turntable for more even cooking, programmable cooking settings, and browning function" were added to the existing features of either the high- or low-quality brand. In these conditions, the prices were kept the same as in the control condition (e.g., $129 for the Goldstar oven and $189 for the Panasonic oven). Respondents

---

[8] In five of the product categories (including microwave ovens), the price difference between the brands was made larger or smaller by increasing the prices of the high-quality or low-quality brands, respectively. In the other six categories, the price difference was made larger or smaller by decreasing the prices of the low-quality or high-quality brands, respectively.

in all tasks evaluated alternatives in 11 product categories, including cordless telephones, compact disc players, hotels, and sunscreens.

To test H_{13a} and H_{13b}, we used a measure of share variability, which calculates the average effect on choice shares of (1) adding product features (to either the high- or low-quality brand) and (2) changing price (either large or small price difference). For example, for the microwave oven category, in the choice task, the low-tier brand (Goldstar) received a choice share of 63% in the control condition, a share of 74% when it had additional product features, and a share of 31% when the high-tier brand (Panasonic) offered the additional features. Therefore, in this case, the measure of share variability in choice for product features was 22% ($[(74\% - 63\%) + (63\% - 31\%)]/2$). When the response mode was ratings, the Goldstar brand received a preference share of 24% in the control condition, a share of 48% when it had additional product features, and a share of 18% when the Panasonic brand offered the features, for a measure of variability of 15% ($[24\% + 6\%]/2$). Therefore, in this case, the measure of variability was 7% ($22\% - 15\%$) lower in ratings than in choice. Consistent with H_{13a}, the measure of share variability resulting from changes in feature differences was lower by an average of 9% ($24\% - 15\%$), across the 11 product categories, in ratings compared with choice. The direction of this result was consistent across 10 of the 11 product categories, and the coefficient from the logit analysis testing this effect was statistically significant, $t = 2.9$, $p < .01$.

Similarly, consistent with H_{13b}, the measure of share variability for changes in price differences was lower by an average of 10% ($21\% - 11\%$) in the rating task compared with choice. The direction of the results was consistent across all 11 product categories. The coefficient from the logit model testing this effect was statistically significant, $t = 2.5$, $p < .01$. These results demonstrate that choices are more sensitive than ratings are to differences between options in terms of prices and product features.

DISCUSSION

In this research, we examine the effect on consumer preferences of the compatibility between the preference elicitation task and the attributes that differentiate the alternatives. Consistent with our theoretical analysis, we demonstrate systematic preference reversals and explore alternative explanations for these phenomena. In this section, we summarize and interpret the findings and explore their theoretical and practical implications.

Overview of the Findings and Their Theoretical Implications

Building on previous research (e.g., Slovic & MacPhillamy, 1974), we propose that the importance of an attribute in a particular preference elicitation task is influenced by the compatibility between the attribute and the task. Specifically, attributes that produce clear and unambiguous comparisons tend to be more important in comparison-based tasks, whereas enriched and less comparable dimensions tend to be more important in evaluations of individual options. Accordingly, we expect options with advantages on comparable dimensions to be preferred more in comparison-based tasks and options with advantages on enriched dimensions, whose values are informative and meaningful even without the benefit of comparisons, to be preferred more in tasks involving separate evaluations.

We examine these basic propositions in six ways. We first demonstrate systematic preference reversals between choice and purchase likelihood ratings with alternatives that differ in terms of price and brand names. Second, building on our theoretical analysis, we show that these reversals generalize to additional tasks and attributes and that one can predict the conditions under which such reversals are likely to occur. Third, we establish that the preference reversals can be eliminated by changing the comparability or enrichment of attributes, as predicted by our analysis. Fourth, think-aloud protocols reveal that choices are more likely than are ratings to involve interattribute comparisons and comparisons involving prices and features than brand names, which supports the idea that the reversals are due to the ease with which attributes can be compared in different preference elicitation formats. Fifth, we find support for the explanation of the preference reversals that is based on attribute-task compatibility when contrasting it with alternative explanations for the results. And sixth, we demonstrate an implication of our explanation, that choices are more sensitive than are purchase likelihood ratings to changes in prices and features.

As hypothesized, the high-price, high-perceived-quality brands had systematically smaller shares in choice than in purchase likelihood ratings, and this effect was observed across numerous product categories and studies. Although the absolute size of this reversal did vary because of such factors as the product category, attributes, and specific attribute values, it occurred across seven studies in the predicted direction in 50 of 51 cases. These findings also are consistent with those derived from other studies. Horsky and Nelson (1992) show, in the context of a study about car purchases, that price tends to have significantly greater weight in choices than in preferences derived from Linmap. Similarly, a recent unpublished study by IntelliQuest demonstrates that the weight of price in preferences derived from a choice task is significantly greater (about double in magnitude) than is the weight of price derived on the basis of a conjoint procedure that involves self-explicated weights and ratings. Also, Bazerman et al. (1992) show that dollar values (salary bonuses) are more important in choice than in ratings.

Although choice and purchase likelihood ratings are particularly important in the measurement of consumer preferences, our theoretical analysis applies to any pair of preference elicitation tasks in which one is comparison based and the other involves separate evaluations. We test this proposition in two ways. First, we examine another comparison-based task, strength-of-preference ratings, and show that there were systematic preference reversals between the preferences elicited from that task and those derived from purchase likelihood ratings. Second, we replace the rating task with a task in which respondents indicated for each option separately whether they would choose it. Consistent with our analysis regarding the role of direct comparisons, systematic preference reversals were observed between the (standard) choice task and this separate-choice task.

In addition to demonstrating that the preference reversals generalize to different tasks, it is also important to show that they generalize to other attributes that differ in terms of comparability and enrichment. Specifically, we test two comparable attributes, price and product features, which were expected to receive greater weight in choice than in ratings. We also test two less-comparable, enriched attributes, brand name and country of origin, which were expected to receive greater weight in ratings. In all cases, the predicted preference reversals were observed, such that brands associated with superior features, lower prices, inferior brand names, or inferior country of origin were preferred more in choice than in ratings. Furthermore, we show that changing the comparability of attribute values has a predictable effect on the presence or absence of the preference reversals. Specifically, when dollar prices were replaced with qualitative price descriptions and brand names were replaced by quality ratings, the pattern of systematic preference reversals between choice and ratings was eliminated.

Finally, given the evidence that different preference elicitation tasks lead to systematically different preferences, a question that naturally arises is, Which preferences are "right"? This question, however, has no clear answer. Both comparison-based and individual evaluation tasks are associated with error for the same reason that consumers do not have well-articulated preferences for specific attribute values, though this limitation manifests itself differently in the two task types. In individual option evaluations, attribute importance is influenced by the ease of evaluating each attribute by itself, and consumers have difficulty using interattribute comparisons. In comparison-based tasks, conversely, the tendency to evaluate options that are based to a large extent on the immediate context (i.e., the choice set under consideration) leads to a variety of context effects that are inconsistent with value maximization (e.g., Huber, Payne, & Puto, 1982; Simonson & Tversky, 1992). In addition, comparison-based tasks could be more likely than separate evaluation tasks to involve simplifying decision rules that ignore much of the available information (e.g., Lindberg, Gärling, & Montgomery, 1989b). Therefore, both types of tasks are associated with biases, and neither task produces "true" preferences (see also Payne, Bettman, & Johnson, 1992). It should be noted, though, that a direct choice between alternatives has the advantage in that it represents the task that consumers typically perform in the marketplace, whereas ratings of attractiveness or purchase likelihood are more common in the laboratory than in actual purchase decisions. Consequently, it might be easier to learn from choice tasks about the behavior of consumers in their natural environment.

Practical Implications and Directions for Research

The findings of this research have implications for the measurement of consumer preferences and for marketers' pricing, merchandising, distribution, and communications strategies. Purchase likelihood ratings and choice commonly are used to measure and predict buyers' preferences. Given the systematic discrepancy between the preferences elicited by these tasks, marketing researchers face the problem of deciding which of these and other methods they should employ (see also Huber, Wittink, Fiedler, & Miller, 1993). For example, if ratings of purchase likelihood are used to predict the performance of a new product, then the results will tend to underestimate the share of less expensive alternatives. The optimal solution to this problem appears to involve measuring preferences using a task and context that are most similar to those that buyers actually will face in the marketplace. In most cases consumers choose among alternatives, which suggests that a comparison-based measure like choice would be more appropriate. However, in other situations consumers face a decision of whether to buy a single available option (Dhar, 1997) or whether they need to form overall ratings of individual alternatives before choosing among them, in which case an individual evaluation task might be more appropriate.

With respect to pricing, this research suggests that consumers' price sensitivity depends on the manner in which their preferences are formed. If alternatives are evaluated individually, because of the manner in which they are displayed, the difficulty of making comparisons, the fact that there is only one available option, or for other reasons, then consumers will tend to be less price (and feature) sensitive than if preferences involve a direct comparison of alternatives. For example, consider the demand for the pioneering product in a category, before other brands are introduced. In this case, buyers are likely to be relatively sensitive to brand names but insensitive to prices, not merely because early adopters are inherently more brand sensitive and less price sensitive, but because of the importance of these attributes when consumers evaluate a single option.

The findings of the present research also have implications for marketers' merchandising strategies. In particular, they suggest that alternatives that excel on easily compared attributes (e.g., a low-price product) appear more attractive when they are displayed next to alternatives that are relatively inferior on these dimensions (but, for a boundary condition, see Simonson, Nowlis, & Lemon, 1993). For example, private-label brands are likely to gain a greater share if they are placed just next to the corresponding national brands, which are typically more expensive. Indeed, many retailers display their store brands next to the national brands, often with an explicit suggestion to compare prices. Conversely, products with a main advantage on dimensions that are complex, qualitative, and difficult to compare are likely to perform better if presented in a manner that makes it more difficult for buyers to make comparisons with competing options. Therefore, for example, it is expected that high-quality brands will benefit more than low-quality brands from an end-of-aisle display.

This research further suggests a factor that should be taken into consideration when designing brand distribution and communications strategies. One of the important decisions that companies face is whether to sell their products using distribution channels that offer competing products. Benneton and Mary Kay, for example, elected to sell their products through their own stores and sales force, respectively. Similarly, many companies have a policy of not using dealers that offer competing product lines. Conversely, other companies, including many prestigious brands, employ distribution channels that do offer other brands. Although decisions on distribution channels depend on many factors, the present research suggests one reason why high-tier brands can benefit more than can low-tier brands from an exclusive distribution channel. With respect to communications, the same argument suggests that brands that are superior on attributes that can be efficiently compared will benefit most from comparative ads, and vice versa.

Future research might further investigate the practical and theoretical implications of the observed preference reversals and of the impact of the role of attribute-task compatibility. For example, this research suggests that alternative preference elicitation methods, such as those used in conjoint measurement, can lead to systematically different preferences. However, in the present research there were only two options in each category, whereas conjoint applications typically involve numerous options. Therefore, future research could examine whether similar reversals occur with more than two options and whether the preferences derived from conjoint analysis are indeed sensitive to whether options are evaluated separately or jointly. Additional research also might consider how consumer satisfaction or regret differs depending on whether consumers form their preferences with comparison-based or separate evaluation tasks. For example, it is recommended that satisfaction ratings be done relative to competition (e.g., Hauser, Simester, & Wernerfelt, 1994). Our research suggests that the relative weights of comparable and enriched dimensions in determining overall satisfaction judgments could be influenced by whether comparative or absolute ratings are used.

Finally, future research could examine other attribute characteristics, besides comparability and enrichment, that moderate the impact of attributes on different preference elicitation tasks, as well as the conditions under which attributes become more or less comparable or enriched. For example, using Nelson's (1970) distinction between search and experience attributes (or products), we might expect experience attributes to be relatively more enriched. Furthermore, research on decisions involving noncomparable alternatives (e.g., Johnson, 1984) might provide insights into the manner in which consumers compare enriched attributes in comparison-based tasks. The findings of such research will enhance our understanding of the manner in which the preference elicitation task and the characteristics of considered alternatives combine to influence consumer preferences.

ACKNOWLEDGMENTS

This chapter has benefited from the suggestions of Greg Allenby, Scott Hawkins, Debbie McInnis, Amos Tversky, and *Journal of Marketing Research* reviewers.

11. Preferences Constructed From Dynamic Microprocessing Mechanisms

Jerome R. Busemeyer, Joseph G. Johnson, and Ryan K. Jessup

THE COMPUTATIONAL MODELING APPROACH

Decision researchers have struggled for a long time with the fact that preferences are highly changeable and vary in complex ways across contexts and tasks. For example, reversals have been observed when preferences are measured using binary versus triadic choice sets or when preferences are measured by choice versus price methods. Several theoretical approaches have been developed to understand this puzzling variability in preferences. One approach is to modify the classic utility model by allowing the weights or values that enter the utility function to change across contexts or tasks. For example, Tversky, Sattath, and Slovic (1988) believe that the decision weights for attributes change across choice versus price tasks. A second approach is to use different heuristic rules to form preferences, depending on task and context. For example, Payne, Bettman, and Johnson (1993) propose that decision makers switch from compensatory to noncompensatory types of rules when the number of options increases or as time pressure increases. Both of these approaches are well established and have made a large impact on decision research.

This chapter presents a computational approach to understanding how preferences change across contexts and tasks. According to this approach, preferences are constructed from a dynamic process that takes decision contexts as inputs and generates task responses as outputs. Computational models are formed by a collection of microprocessing units, each of which performs an elementary cognitive or affective evaluation. These simple microprocessing units are interconnected to form a recurrent dynamical system whose emergent behavior becomes fairly complex. The goal of a computational approach is to use a common set of parameters and processing assumptions to explain changes in preferences across contexts and tasks. One can view the computational approach as a microanalysis that provides dynamic mechanisms for deriving the global properties posited by other approaches. Later in this chapter, we show how a computational model can explain preference reversals induced by changes in context or changes in tasks; such reversals have been previously explained by modifying decision weights across preference tasks or switching strategies across context and time pressure manipulations.

Although there are many different types of computational models, we focus on a class known as connectionist or artificial neural network models. These models are designed to form a bridge between cognition and neuroscience (Grossberg, 1982; Rumelhart & McClelland, 1986). Later in this chapter, we identify possible neural substrates associated with the elementary processes posited in some computational models.

DECISION FIELD THEORY

Several computational models (artificial neural network or connectionist) have been recently developed for preferential choice (Grossberg & Gutowski, 1987; Guo & Holyoak, 2002; Holyoak & Simon, 1999; Levin & Levine, 1996; Usher & McClelland, 2004). These theories vary in terms of their neural plausibility versus applicability to mainstream decision research. Here, we focus on our own model, known as decision field theory (DFT), which was designed to find an effective balance between these two goals.[1] DFT has two major parts, one describing how choices are made (Busemeyer & Townsend, 1993; Diederich, 1997; Roe, Busemeyer, & Townsend, 2001) and the second describing how quantities (e.g., prices) are matched to options (Busemeyer & Goldstein, 1992; Johnson & Busemeyer, 2005; Townsend & Busemeyer, 1995).

Choice Process

According to DFT, the decision maker deliberates over each course of action by thinking about possible events and feeling the anticipated consequences of alternative actions. At each moment, different events come to mind, and the affective reactions to the consequences of each action are evaluated and compared. These comparisons are accumulated over time to form a preference state, representing the integration of all the preceding affective reactions produced by thinking about each event during deliberation. This deliberation process continues until the accumulated preference for one action reaches a threshold, which determines the choice and the deliberation time of the decision.

This sequential sampling process is illustrated for three options in Figure 11.1, with each trajectory representing the cumulative preference for an action.[2] The horizontal axis represents deliberation time, and the vertical axis indicates the state of preference for each action at each moment in time. In this figure, action A eventually reaches the threshold first, and is chosen after T = 69 time steps. The *threshold bound* for the decision process, symbolized by θ, is the key parameter for controlling speed and accuracy tradeoffs. Impulsive individuals may tend to

---

[1] The name "decision field theory" reflects the influence of Kurt Lewin's earlier "psychological field theory."

[2] In the binary choice case, there would only be two trajectories, one for each option.

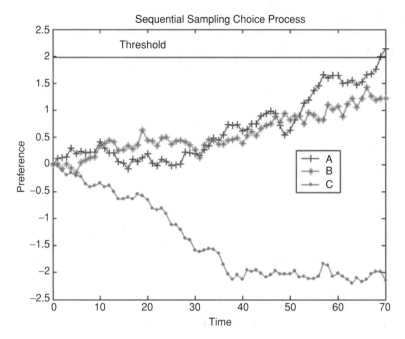

Figure 11.1. Illustration of (simulated) sequential sampling decision process for a choice among three alternatives.

have lower thresholds, whereas perspicacious individuals may tend to exhibit higher thresholds.[3]

The dynamical system used to generate this deliberation process is presented next. The inputs into the dynamic system are the affective evaluations, symbolized as m_{ij}, of the possible consequences of a decision. At any moment in time, the decision maker is assumed to attend to one of the possible events or attributes leading to consequences for each action. Thus, the inputs to the dynamic system fluctuate from one moment (time t) to another moment (time $t + h$) as the decision maker's attention switches from one possible event or attribute to another. To formalize these ideas, we define $W_j(t)$, for all attributes j as stochastic variables, called the *attention weights*, which fluctuate across time. The weighted value for each option i within a set of n options at time t is:

$$U_i(t) = \Sigma_j\, W_j(t) \cdot m_{ij} + \varepsilon_i(t). \qquad (1)$$

The error term, $\varepsilon_i(t)$, is a stochastic variable with a mean of zero representing the influence of irrelevant features (e.g., in an experiment, these are features

---

[3] The race-to-threshold stopping rule applies to optional stopping time decision tasks, under which the decision maker controls the timing of the decision. For fixed stopping time decision tasks, when there is an externally determined stopping time, we assume that the sequential sampling process continues until the appointed time, and the option with the maximum preference state at that time is chosen.

that are outside of an experimenter's control). The previous equations look like the classic weighted utility model, but unlike the classic model, the attention weights are stochastic rather than deterministic (see Fischer, Jia, & Luce, 2000, for a closely related model). The mean values of the attention weights correspond to the deterministic weights used in the classic weighted utility model. Comparisons among weighted values of the options produce what are called *valences*. A positive valence for one option indicates that the option has an advantage under the current focus of attention, and a negative valence for another option indicates that the option has a disadvantage under the current focus of attention. The valence for each option i within a set of n options is formed by comparing the weighted value for option i with the average of the other $(n - 1)$ options:

$$v_i(t) = U_i(t) - U_g(t), \tag{2}$$

where $U_g(t) = \Sigma_{k \neq i} U_k(t)/(n - 1)$. Valence is closely related to the concept of advantages and disadvantages used in Tversky's (1969) additive difference model. Note, however, that the additive difference model assumed complete processing of all features, whereas the present theory assumes a sequential sampling process that stops when a threshold is crossed. Finally, the valences are integrated over time to form a *preference state* for each action. This is a recursive network, with positive self-recurrence within each unit and negative lateral inhibitory connections between units. Positive self-feedback is used to integrate the valences produced by an action over time, and lateral inhibition produces negative feedback from other actions. The preference state for option i from a set of n options evolves according to the linear dynamic system:

$$P_i(t + h) = s \cdot P_i(t) + v_i(t + h) - \Sigma_{k \neq i} s_{ik} \cdot P_k(t). \tag{3}$$

Conceptually, the new state of preference is a weighted combination of the previous state of preference and the new input valence.

Inhibition is also introduced from the competing alternatives. We assume that the strength of the lateral inhibition connection (s_{ik}) is a decreasing function of the dissimilarity between a pair of alternatives. For example, if two options A and C are more dissimilar than options B and C, then the lateral inhibition between A and C would be smaller than that between options B and C, or $s_{AC} < s_{BC}$. Lateral inhibition is commonly used in artificial neural networks and connectionist models of decision making to form a competitive system in which one option gradually emerges as a winner dominating over the other options (cf. Grossberg, 1988; Rumelhart & McClelland, 1986). As shown later in this chapter, this concept serves a crucial function for explaining several paradoxical phenomena of preferential choice.

In summary, a decision is reached by the following deliberation process. As attention switches from one event or attribute to another over time, different affective values are probabilistically selected, these values are compared across options to produce valences, and finally these valences are integrated into preference states for each option. This process continues until the preference for one option exceeds a threshold criterion, at which point in time the winner is chosen. Formally, this is a Markov process; matrix formulas have been mathematically derived for computing the choice probabilities and distribution of choice response times (for details, see Busemeyer & Diederich, 2002; Busemeyer & Townsend, 1992; Diederich & Busemeyer, 2003). Alternatively, Monte Carlo computer simulation can be used to generate predictions from the model.

Dynamic Value-Matching Model

A somewhat different model is needed for single-stimulus responses. The basic idea of the matching model is that a price or probability equivalent is selected by a series of covert comparisons. Consider the problem of finding the price equivalent of a gamble. In this case, the decision maker needs to find the price that makes her indifferent between the price and the gamble. We assume that the search for the price equivalent starts near the middle of the range of feasible payoffs (the midpoint between the minimum and maximum payoffs of the gamble). This candidate price is then inserted into the DFT choice process for choosing between the gamble and the candidate price. If the candidate price is too low, so that the preference state of the gamble first crosses the threshold, then the price is incremented a small amount; if the candidate price is too high, so that the choice process favors the candidate price over the gamble, then the price is decremented a small amount. However, if the candidate price is approximately equal in value to the gamble, then the preference states will linger around zero or the neutral state. Each time this occurs there is a probability r that the process exits and reports the candidate price. Markov chain theory is used to determine the distribution of probabilities generated by the search process (see Busemeyer & Townsend, 1992; Johnson & Busemeyer, 2005; for the mathematical derivations). Note that the only new parameter introduced by the matching model is the exit rate, r, for reporting indifference when entering the neutral state.

PREFERENCE REVERSALS

Now we shall apply the preceding computational modeling approach to some important findings concerning preference reversals from the decision-making literature. Two different types of preference reversals are analyzed here: reversals of preferences across binary versus triadic choice contexts and reversals of preferences between choices and prices.

Reversals Between Binary and Triadic Choices

Preferences revealed by binary versus triadic choice procedures exhibit three very robust types of preference reversals. The similarity effect (Tversky, 1972) refers to the effect of adding a new competitive option to form the triadic set, an option that is highly similar to one of the original binary choice options. The attraction effect (Huber, Payne, & Puto, 1982) refers to the effect of adding an option dominated by one of the first two to form the triadic set. The compromise effect (Simonson, 1989) refers to the effect of adding a new extreme option to form the triadic set, thus turning one of the original binary choice options into a compromise between two extremes.

First, consider a classic example, described by Tversky (1972), of a preference reversal produced by the similarity effect. When given a choice between a rock music album versus a classical music album (say by Beethoven), suppose the latter is more frequently chosen, indicating a preference for the Beethoven album over the rock album. However, when another classical music album (say by Mozart) is added to form a set of three options {rock, Beethoven, Mozart}, then the classical Mozart album steals choices away from the classical Beethoven album, making the rock album more popular than the Beethoven album. Thus adding a similar option (the classical Mozart album is similar to the classical Beethoven album) reverses the preference orders obtained from the binary versus triadic choice measures.

Next consider an example of a preference reversal produced by the attraction effect (see, e.g., Table 2 from Simonson, 1989). When people were asked to make a binary choice between cars varying in miles per gallon (mpg) and quality of ride, brand B (24 mpg, 83 rating on ride quality) was more frequently chosen (61%) over brand A (33 mpg, 73 rating on ride quality). However, when a third option D (33 mpg, 70 rating on ride quality) was added to the choice set, then brand A was chosen most often (62%). Thus, adding a dominated option (A dominates D) reversed the preference order revealed by binary and triadic choices.

Finally, consider an example of a preference reversal produced by the compromise effect (see, e.g., Table 3 of Simonson, 1989). When people were asked to make a binary choice between batteries varying in expected life and corrosion rate, brand B (12 hrs, 2%) was more frequently chosen (66%) over brand C (14 hrs, 4%). However, when a third option A (16 hrs, 6%) was added to the choice set then brand C was chosen more often (60%) relative to option B. Thus adding an extreme option A, which turns option C into a compromise, reversed the preference orders obtained between the binary and triadic choice methods.

These three preference reversals are puzzling and difficult to explain. Tversky (1972) proposed the elimination-by-aspects model to account for the similarity effect. However, the attraction effect cannot be explained by the elimination-by-aspects model. Later Tversky and Simonson (1993) proposed the componential context model, which uses the concept of loss aversion to account for the attraction and compromise effects. Roe et al. (2001) proved that loss aversion prevents the componential context model from accounting for the similarity effect. A strategy-switching model which assumes that decision makers switch from compensatory (e.g., weighted average) to noncompensatory (e.g., lexicographic) strategies with increasing choice set size cannot account for the compromise effect. Thus, a comprehensive account of all three effects has eluded decision researchers.

Roe et al. (2001) demonstrated that DFT was able to account for all three effects using a single set of principles and a single set of parameters.[4] DFT does not require the concept of loss aversion to account for the attraction and compromise effects. Instead, these effects are emergent properties of the dynamics produced by the lateral inhibitory system that forms a competition between options. An interesting a priori prediction from this theory is that increasing deliberation time should increase the size of the attraction and compromise effects (see Roe et al., 2001). Empirical support for this prediction was reported in experiments by Dhar, Nowlis, and Sherman (2000).

Recently, Dhar and Simonson (2003) reported new challenging findings on the attraction and compromise effects. They examined how these two effects changed when decision makers were given the additional option of deferring their decision (they could refuse to choose one of the available options). In a consumer purchasing setting, this would correspond to a consumer deciding not to buy a product from the current store and instead continuing to search for a (possibly better) product somewhere else. Surprisingly, they found that allowing people to defer the choice had opposite effects on the attraction versus the compromise effects – it increased the size of the attraction effect, but it decreased the size of the compromise effect. They concluded that these findings suggest that a different mechanism operates for attraction and compromise effects. This conclusion seems to run counter to the DFT explanation, which asserts that both effects are emergent properties of the lateral inhibitory network.

To examine this new empirical challenge in more detail, we generated predictions from DFT after including a simple assumption concerning the deferred choice option. All the options, including the option to defer, are treated in exactly the same manner: The preference state for each option evolves over time in a race according to Equation 3, and the first option to reach the threshold wins the race and determines the choice. Thus, the deferred choice option is selected whenever its preference state reaches the threshold bound before the other options in the choice set.

This representation requires specifying the attribute values that would be expected by choosing the deferred choice option. In other words, if a consumer decided to wait and look for another option, what attribute values would the decision maker expect to find after this search? The simplest assumption, which was used in the present application, is that the expected value of an attribute for the deferred choice is just the average of the presented attribute values. For example, suppose an individual is shown two extreme options: one that has good quality (say 4 on a 5-point scale) but is economically poor (say 1 on a

---

[4] Usher and McClelland (2004) proposed an alternative connectionist model that also can account for all three findings using a common set of principles and parameters.

5-point scale) and another that has poor quality (say 1 on a 5-point scale) but is economically good (4 on a 5 point-scale). Then the expected attribute value of deferring for quality is the average (2.5 on the 5-point scale) of these two extremes, and the same holds for the expected value for economy (also 2.5 on a 5-point scale).

Although we could work out the mathematical solution for generating predictions under this new condition, we decided it may be easier if we simply used a computer simulation to generate the model predictions.[5] We simulated 100,000 choice trials for each of eight conditions in a 2 (binary vs. triadic choice) × 2 (attraction vs. compromise choice set) × 2 (inclusion vs. exclusion of a deferred choice option) factorial design. It is important to note that exactly the *same* model parameters were used to compute predictions for all eight conditions; only the attribute values, m_{ij}, change across conditions in accordance with the descriptions of the choice alternatives. The results of the simulation were analyzed according to the methods used by Dhar and Simonson (2003).

First, consider the attraction effect. Define A as the dominating option (target), D as the dominated decoy, B as the other competitive option, and N as the no choice or deferred choice option. When the deferred choice is excluded, the attraction effect is defined as the difference $\Pr[A]\{A,B,D\}] - \Pr[A]\{A,B\}]$, where $\Pr[A]\{A,B,D\}]$ denotes the probability of choosing A from the set $\{A, B, D\}$. As can be seen in Table 11.1a, the model correctly predicts a preference reversal in accordance with the attraction effect: Option B is chosen most frequently in the binary choice but the dominating option A is chosen most frequently in the triadic choice. Adding the dominated option D increased the preference for option A by 11%. When the deferred choice is included, the attraction effect is defined as the difference $\Pr[A]\{A,B,D,N\}] - \Pr[A]\{A,B,N\}]$. As can be seen in Table 11.1a, the attraction effect increased in size to 21% when the deferred option is included, which is in accord with the results reported by Dhar and Simonson (2003).

Next, consider the compromise effect. Define A as one extreme option, B as the other extreme option, C as the intermediate or compromise option between A and B, and once again N is the deferred choice option. When the deferred choice is excluded, the compromise effect is defined as the difference

$$\Pr[C|\{B, C\}] - \frac{\Pr[C|\{A, B, C\}]}{\Pr[C|\{A, B, C\}] + \Pr[B|\{A, B, C\}]}.$$

As shown in Table 11.1b, the DFT model predicts a preference reversal in accord with the compromise effect in this case: Option B is chosen most frequently in the binary choice, but the compromise option C is chosen more frequently than B in the triadic choice. The compromise effect size is 7% under this condition. When the deferred choice is included, the compromise

[5] The MATLAB code for the computer simulation is available from the authors.

Table 11.1. Predictions for the Probability of Choice From Decision Field
Theory for (a) the Attraction Effect, and (b) the Compromise Effect

(a)

	No Deferred Choice Option		With Deferred Choice Option	
Option	Binary	Triadic	Binary	Triadic
A: Target	0.43	0.54	0.29	0.50
B	0.57	0.45	0.33	0.36
D: Decoy	–	0.00	–	0.00
N: Deferral	–	–	0.38	0.14
Effect Size		0.11		0.21

(b)

	No Deferred Choice Option		With Deferred Choice Option	
Option	Binary	Triadic	Binary	Triadic
A	–	0.27	–	0.24
B	0.54	0.35	0.29	0.27
C: Target	0.45	0.38	0.26	0.25
N: Deferral	–	–	0.45	0.25
Effect size		0.07		0.01

effect is defined as the difference

$$\frac{\Pr[C|\{B,C,N\}]}{\Pr[C|\{B,C,N\}]+\Pr[B|\{B,C,N\}]} - \frac{\Pr[C|\{A,B,C,N\}]}{\Pr[C|\{A,B,C,N\}]+\Pr[B|\{A,B,C,N\}]}.$$

Under this condition, the DFT model no longer predicts a preference reversal.
Moreover, as shown in Table 11.1b, the size of the compromise effect shrinks to
nearly zero under this condition. In accordance with Dhar and Simonson (2003),
the model predicts that the compromise effect *decreases* when the deferred choice
option is included.

In summary, DFT correctly predicts the opposing effects of the ability to defer
choice on the sizes of the attraction and compromise effects.[6] This was accomplished simply by allowing the preference state for the deferred choice option
to compete in the race along with the preference states for the other options.
Although one must be cautious when verbalizing the emergent behavior of a
complex computational model, we can try to interpret how this happens.

---

[6] Although these predictions are dependent on the parameter values used here, similar results
were obtained with variations in the parameter values and so the predictions are reasonably
robust.

First consider the attraction effect. For the binary choice, it is difficult to decide between the two competing options A and B, and according to the model, this decision takes a long time. In this case, the deferred choice often wins and "steals choice probability" from both A and B. For the triadic choice condition, the addition of the dominating option bolsters option A, and according to the model it is rapidly selected before the deferred choice option can have an effect. Thus, the increase in the size of the attraction effect occurs because the probability of choosing option A is lowered in the binary choice when the deferred choice option is allowed.

Next consider the compromise effect. For the binary choice, the relative probability for choosing option B remains near 50%; for the triadic choice, it takes time for the lateral inhibitory system to generate a bias favoring the compromise option. That is, the system becomes more vulnerable to the effects of the deferred choice option. Thus, the decrease in the size of the compromise effect results from the choice probability being taken away from the compromise by the deferred choice option. This explanation is in agreement with the conclusions from Dhar and Simonson (2003).

Preference Reversals Between Choice and Prices

A second robust type of reversal is obtained when preferences are measured by different elicitation methods; the most common of these are reversals between choices and pricing methods. The classic example was discovered by Lichtenstein and Slovic (1971) in a study examining two types of gambles that were approximately equal in expected value: a "P bet" that produced a very high probability of winning a small amount, and a "$ bet" that produced a relatively low probability of winning a large amount. When asked which gamble they would choose, the P bet is chosen slightly but systematically more often by participants; but when asked to give a price equivalent to each gamble, the $ bet is more frequently given a higher price. These results were repeated by Lindman (1971) and later replicated under various conditions by Grether and Plott (1979). The findings were also replicated by Lichtenstein and Slovic (1973) in Las Vegas gambling casinos using real stakes.

A popular explanation for this reversal was provided by Tversky et al. (1988). According to their theory, the weight given to the attributes of the decision vary contingent on the type of task. In the choice task, more weight is given to the most prominent dimension, which tends to be probability in choice tasks. In the price task, more weight is given to the dollar amount because it is compatible with the response mode. This shift in weights produces changes in the utilities for the gambles depending on the task, causing the preferences to reverse.

There are a couple of problems with this explanation. One is that preference reversals between choice and prices occur even when the prominence effect is eliminated by using gambles with equally likely outcomes (Ganzach, 1996). Another is that preference reversals also occur between buying and selling prices (Birnbaum & Sutton, 1992), even though the compatibility effect should operate in the same manner for these two preference measurement methods.

An alternative explanation for preference reversals between choice and prices, based on the concept of anchoring and adjustment, was proposed first by Lichtenstein and Slovic (1971) and later by other researchers (Goldstein & Einhorn, 1987; Schkade & Johnson, 1989). To be concrete, consider the following two gambles from Slovic, Griffin, and Tversky (1990): For the P bet, you win $4 with probability 35/36, otherwise nothing; for the $ bet, you win $16 with probability 11/36, otherwise nothing. When asked to report a price for a gamble, perhaps individuals start at some anchor and then adjust toward the true indifference point. Assuming the anchor is midway between the minimum and maximum payoff, the anchor for the P bet becomes $2 and the anchor for the $ bet becomes $8.[7] The observed preference reversals may simply result from insufficient adjustments from these initial anchors. According to this view, revealed preference reversals do not necessarily imply changes in underlying utilities depending on the task. Instead, the reversals observed in the measurements may simply reflect the dynamic processes used to generate the responses in the two tasks.

One important limitation with anchoring and adjustment models is the lack of a well-specified mechanism for determining the amount of adjustment. Consider for example the following pair of gambles: Gamble A wins $16 with probability .001, $4 with probability .9712, otherwise zero; gamble B wins $16 with probability .2212, $4 with probability .001, otherwise zero. Gamble A is very nearly the same as the P bet, and gamble B is very nearly the same as the $ bet. In this case, however, the range is equated across the two gambles, and so the two gambles have identical anchors (both are anchored at $8). Lacking a theory for the size of the adjustment, there is no basis for predicting preference reversals for this pair of gambles.

The dynamic matching model described earlier was designed for this purpose. The dynamic adjustment mechanism of the matching model is strongly influenced by the variance of a gamble: The rate of adjustment toward the true indifference point decreases with increases in the variance of a gamble (see Johnson & Busemeyer, 2005, for details). Note that the variance of gamble B (also the $ bet) is much larger than the variance of gamble A (also the P bet), and therefore more rapid adjustments will occur for the latter.

To examine the predictions of the matching model for the pair of gambles A and B described earlier, the following simple assumptions were made. We set the values in Equation 1, m_{ij}, equal to the outcome values, and the probabilities of the

[7] We assume anchoring in the middle of the payoff range for simplicity, to illustrate that biased anchors are not necessary to produce the basic result. However, it could be that participants anchor on, for example, the maximum payoff of each gamble (see Johnson & Busemeyer, 2005, for implications of various anchors).

Table 11.2. Decision Field Theory Predictions for
Choices and Prices

	A: Low Variance	B: High Variance
EV(gamble)[a]	3.90	3.54
Variance(gamble)	0.58	44.30
Pr(choice)	0.58	0.42
Pr(higher price)	0.29	0.71
Mean $	4.14	5.10
Median $	3.61	4.43
Variance $	0.77	3.41

[a] EV = expected value.

attention weights were assigned directly from the stated outcome probabilities. The threshold bound for the choice process was set equal to three, the variance of irrelevant dimensions was set to zero, and the exit rate for the matching process was set to $r = .02$. Using these parameters we computed the choice probabilities and the distribution of prices from the matching model (using the Markov chain derivations described by Johnson & Busemeyer, 2005). The results are shown in Table 11.2.

The first row of Table 11.2 shows the expected values of each gamble; under the present simplifying assumptions, these are also the true indifference points. The second row shows the variance of the payoffs produced by each gamble, and the last row shows the variance of the prices. Comparing these two rows, we see that the variance of the prices is ordered according to the variance of the gambles. The third row indicates the probability of choosing each gamble, and the fourth row indicates the probability that the price for one gamble exceeds the other. Comparing these two rows one can see that gamble A is chosen more frequently (.58), but the price for gamble B is more frequently greater (.71). Furthermore, the mean and median prices are higher for gamble B compared with gamble A. Thus, the matching model predicts a preference reversal even when the range of the gambles is held constant because of the dynamic mechanism used to make price adjustments for each gamble. This provides it with an important advantage over other anchoring and adjustment models.

Johnson and Busemeyer (2005) reviewed a broad range of preference-reversal phenomena; they demonstrated that the matching model is able to explain the major findings, including other reversals between choices versus prices, as well as reversals between probability versus certainty equivalents and between buying versus selling prices. As we have done here, Johnson and Busemeyer used the same parameters, model assumptions, and evaluative mechanism (e.g., weights and values) across all applications. We do not wish to argue that changes in decision weights across tasks never occur. Instead, we think it is important to first check whether or not preference reversals can be explained by a response mechanism before claiming changes in weights across tasks.

CONNECTIONS WITH NEUROSCIENCE

This section briefly reviews some literature from neuroscience that provides additional support for computational models. Perhaps the most interesting support comes from Ratcliff, Cherian, and Segraves (2003), who found that a diffusion process could predict remarkably well the neural firing rates of cells that were related to behavior in a choice task in the macaque. These authors conclude that the noisy information accumulation process posited by diffusion models such as DFT may have direct neural correlates, as evidenced also by others (e.g., Gold & Shadlen, 2001). A more general overview of the anatomical structures implicated by computational models is offered by Busemeyer, Townsend, and Stout (2002). The remainder of this section focuses on the operation of one key mechanism: lateral inhibition.

According to DFT, lateral inhibition is critical for bolstering the dominant option in the attraction effect and enhancing the intermediate option in the compromise effect. The locus of this lateral inhibition may lie within the basal ganglia, which have been implicated in decision behavior through their feedback loops to key cortical areas (Middleton & Strick, 2000). Moreover, Schultz et al. (1995) observed that dopaminergic neurons afferent to the basal ganglia fire in concert with reliable predictors of reward (see also Gold, 2003, and Hollerman & Schultz, 1998). Together these findings support the notion that the basal ganglia have an important function in decision behavior.

Knowledge of the basal ganglia architecture should enhance our understanding of the cortical loops and lateral inhibition. In particular, we are concerned with two substructures in the basal ganglia, the globus pallidus internal segment (GPi) and the striatum. In cortico-striatal loops, the axons from the cortex enter into the basal ganglia via the striatum, which then projects to GPi, which in turn projects to the cortical area from which it arose. Ordinarily, GPi inhibits cortical activity due to its reliance on GABA, an inhibitory neurotransmitter. However, striatal neurons may act to inhibit GPi, thus releasing the cortex to engage in a specified activity (Bar-Gad & Bergman, 2001). Furthermore, extensive connectivity and communication within the striatum produces lateral inhibition (Bar-Gad & Bergman, 2001; Wickens & Oorschot, 2000).

Several clusters of striatal nuclei, each perhaps representing a different action (or reward), synapse onto GPi neurons (Wickens & Oorschot, 2000). Because the striatum consists of lateral inhibitory networks, all the potential actions compete against one another for selection, and only one action can be selected at a time. This competition causes all of the clusters of nuclei to mutually inhibit one another below baseline, preventing any one option (represented by the clusters of nuclei) from crossing the threshold of activation. However, when one activity is chosen, the corresponding nuclei inhibit the respective GPi neurons, freeing the cortex to engage in the selected activity.

As stated before, one must be cautious when trying to interpret the behavior of a complex computational model, and perhaps one should be even more wary of interpreting neural activity in terms of behavior. But if we take the preceding analysis of activity and overlay it with the concept of an attraction effect, we might be able to produce a viable picture of neural activation occurring during attraction-based preference reversal.

Consider the dyadic choice between A and B, where independent clusters of neurons code both options within the striatum. Although both achieve some degree of preference, assume option B is preferred most often. However, when option D, an option dominated by option A, is added to the choice set, a preference reversal occurs. Again, three different clusters of neurons within the striatum code the three different options. In this case, because options A and D are similar, and option A dominates option D, the clusters of nuclei coding option A within the striatum will consistently inhibit the neurons coding option D because of A's superiority (i.e., the salient rewards of A will consistently supersede those of D). Furthermore, as option D becomes more inhibited by the lateral GABAergic connections from A, it releases option A to inhibit both option D and other options (e.g., option B) to a greater extent. One might cautiously surmise that because option B is less similar (than is option A) to option D, it will not benefit from option D's weakness as much as option A does, perhaps due to less overall lateral communication. Thus, option A will receive less and less inhibition from the competing options coded in the striatum and will eventually surpass a threshold of activation. This will result in GABAergic afferents inhibiting the GPi neurons that restrain the selection of option A, hence freeing the cortex to engage in the selection of option A.

CONCLUSIONS

The goal of the current chapter has been to inform the reader of the efficacy of computational modeling, specifically within the domain of preferential decision making. Using one particular computational model, DFT, we have illustrated how this approach can provide a parsimonious alternative explanation for the volatility of expressed preferences. The key mechanisms of DFT were briefly introduced; these include momentary shifts in attention to possible future events (or attributes in a consumer choice context), affective evaluation under the current focus of attention, and dynamic integration of these affective reactions. This theory was successfully applied to two key types of preference reversals or situations where task and/or context effects produce changes in preference structures. Finally, tentative links to a young but growing literature on the neuroscience of decision making were presented for a popular component of computational models (lateral inhibition), suggesting an additional degree of plausibility (i.e., neurological).

The microlevel analysis afforded by computational models can result in global behavior similar to more traditional approaches, such as contingent weighting or strategy-switching – but computational modeling is not simply another "language," or framework for representing traditional decision theories. Rather, this approach involves distinct departures from typical algebraic utility equations.

First, computational models represent cognition (here, deliberation) as the concurrent operation of several interdependent processing units, such as units that track the momentary preference for a course of action or consumer choice option. The collective operation of these units defines the deliberation process. Thus, whereas some other approaches suggest processing assumptions based on the nature of the algebraic formulations, computational modeling details these processes precisely.

Second, the majority of computational models (including the one presented here) are dynamic, meaning they specify how deliberation proceeds over time. In this manner, computational models can provide insight into the evolution of preference during a decision, including effects such as speed-accuracy tradeoffs or the effect of time pressure. This is in stark contrast to static approaches that provide only a calculation of some values (e.g., utilities) which in turn determine final measures (e.g., discrete choices).

Finally, a significant advantage of computational models is the retention of stable underlying evaluations, such as weights and values, by using a common set of parameters and assumptions across applications of the model. Although we do not claim that importance weights and/or subjective values *never* change across tasks or contexts, we have shown how this need not be the default explanation for robust empirical trends.

In sum, computational modeling provides a powerful tool to decision researchers who are interested in elucidating the nature of human information processing underlying overt decisions. This approach suggests that the deliberation and response processes, rather than the evaluative mechanism, may be responsible for context-dependent construction of preference. The examples included herein demonstrate how this shift in focus – from tweaking weights and values to a more thorough understanding of the nature of deliberation – can perform at least as well as traditional approaches in explaining complex and puzzling human behavior.

12. Construction of Preferences by Constraint Satisfaction

Dan Simon, Daniel C. Krawczyk, and Keith J. Holyoak

A central tenet of classical theories of rational choice is that people harbor a stable, well-defined, and discernable order of preferences, and have computational skills that enable them to choose the courses of action that maximize their preferences. A paradigmatic example of a classical theory is multiattribute decision theory, which prescribes that the utility of a choice is equivalent to the sum of its preferences, that is, the sum of the weighted values of its attributes (Edwards & Newman, 1982; Keeney & Raiffa, 1976).

Research has challenged the axiom of preference invariance. Rather than being stable, well- defined, and discernable, preferences have been shown to be constructed (Markman, Zhang, & Moreau, 2000; Slovic, 1995); to some degree, they are labile, reversible, and obscure (for a review, see Payne, Bettman, & Johnson, 1992). Preference invariance is violated under different descriptions of essentially the same options (Tversky & Kahneman, 1986), when different modes of elicitation are invoked (Lichtenstein & Slovic, 1971), and when options are presented in different contexts (Shafir, Simonson, & Tversky, 1993). Various process theories claim that preferences are reconstructed to create dominance

ask to a point of commitment (Janis & Mann, 1977; , 1992; for a review, see Brownstein, 2003). These ent with cognitive dissonance theory, which posits e exclusively a postcommitment phenomenon (see mon & Holyoak, 2002).

ent with theories that posit restructuring for dom- ed that they do not follow from a general psycho- al evidence supporting them is rather limited. The ed from a methodology that measures values, but ould be challenged for using sequential measure- the natural flow of the decision process (Russo, , Meloy, & Medvec, 1998). One general theoret- lain certain forms of preference construction is nstraint satisfaction (Holyoak & Thagard, 1989; Rumelhart & McClelland, 1986; Thagard, 1989).

Science, vol. 15, pp. 331–336. Copyright © 2004 by the ited with permission.

Connectionist networks perform constraint satisfaction by applying a relaxation algorithm that settles the network into a stable state in which asymptotic activation levels define a set of coherent variables. Bidirectional links enable units that "go together" to become highly active and to collectively inhibit their rivals, thus becoming increasingly *coherent* with the emerging decision (coherence implies a state in which positively related variables are similarly activated). Evidence of constraint-satisfaction processing has been obtained in inference-based judgments (Holyoak & Simon, 1999; Read & Marcus-Newhall, 1993; Simon, Pham, Le, & Holyoak, 2001; Spellman, Ullman, & Holyoak, 1993), probabilistic judgments (Simon, Snow, & Read, 2004), and analogical reasoning (Spellman & Holyoak, 1992). Work on legal decision making (Holyoak & Simon, 1999) has shown that coherence shifts in one decision task can trigger allied shifts in a subsequent decision task involving similar underlying issues.

The objective of the present study was to examine constraint-satisfaction processing in a realistic preference-based choice task and to determine whether coherence (or dominance) is achieved by restructuring the preferences – their values, weights, or both. The experimental design allowed direct, within-subjects measurement of changes in preferences.

EXPERIMENT 1

Experiment 1 was designed to determine whether people's assessments of a variety of attributes systematically shift to favor one choice over another. The experiment involved a choice between job offers, and was designed to emulate the type of decision task to which multiattribute decision-making theory is most readily applied.

Method
Participants. Participants were 80 undergraduates at the University of California, Los Angeles (UCLA), who took part in the experiment to partially fulfill a course requirement for an introductory psychology class. Participants were run in groups ranging from one to three persons.

Materials. Two instruments were used. The first was a baseline test that was presented before participants learned about the job offers. In this five-page instrument, called "Waiting For a Job Offer," participants were told to imagine that they were about to graduate from college and were interviewing for a job in the field of marketing. While waiting to receive an offer, they were asked to state their evaluation of job-related features "that might be included in job offers." The booklet contained 11 statements describing a variety of job attributes that participants were to judge on a 10-point scale from −5 (*highly undesirable*) to +5 (*highly desirable*). Our focus was on eight attributes, one high and one low, on four dimensions: commute, office, vacation, and salary. Each of the eight attributes appeared in one of the 11 statements (three were used as distractor statements relating to aspects of job choice not tested in the second instrument of the experiment). After completing the desirability task, participants were asked to rate the importance of each of the four dimensions, assuming that they were included in a job offer. Each dimension was delimited by values that corresponded to its high and low attributes. The importance ratings were made on a 9-point scale ranging from 0 (*no weight*) to 8 (*maximum weight*). The order of statements for both the desirability and importance tasks was counterbalanced to control for order effects.

In the second instrument, called "Choosing Your Next Job," participants were told that they had received job offers from two large department store chains, called Bonnie's Best ("BB") and Splendor. The companies were described as being similar in size, reputation, stability, and opportunities for promotion. Participants were also informed that they had met with key personnel at the two companies and found them both to be stimulating and pleasant.

The jobs differed in several key aspects. Four attributes were ascribed to each job such that each offer had two positive attributes and two negative attributes. The commute to Splendor was short (18 min), and Splendor offered a private office, but it also paid a low salary ($600 less than the industry's average of $40,000) and offered minimal time off for vacation. The four attributes varied in the opposite manner for BB: It offered a higher salary ($40,800) and superior vacation package, but the commute to its offices was longer (40 min), and it offered only a cubicle. The eight attributes contained in the offers were the same ones that had been tested in the baseline measure. In an effort to manipulate participants' decisions in favor of a particular choice, one job was described as being located in a fun part of town with good shopping and restaurants ("good-location" attribute), and the other was located in a dull, industrial part of town ("bad-location" attribute).

In the second instrument, participants were asked to report their choice between the offers and their confidence in that choice (on a scale from 0 to 5, with 5 representing maximal confidence), and were then asked for desirability evaluations for the eight attributes and importance evaluations for the four dimensions. The questions eliciting the preferences and weights were the same as those in the first instrument, except that they were worded in terms of the job offers. The order of questions was varied, as was the presentation order of the job offers.

Design and Procedure

Across two between-subjects conditions, we varied which company was associated with the good-location attribute. For half of the participants, BB had the good-location attribute, whereas Splendor had the bad-location attribute, and for the other half of the participants, the reverse was true. All participants completed the experiment in two phases. In the first phase, they completed the baseline test. After this booklet was collected, they completed a 5- to 10-min unrelated reasoning task. In the second phase (the post-test), participants received a booklet containing the job offers and the second instrument.

RESULTS

The data were initially analyzed to determine whether the manipulation of overall attribute goodness (inclusion of the good- or bad-location attribute) was predictive of the decision. The manipulation was effective, as 92% of participants in the good-Splendor condition decided in favor of the Splendor offer, and 72% of participants in the bad-Splendor condition decided in favor of the BB offer, $\chi^2(1, N = 80) = 33.80, p < .001$. Confidence in the decisions was high, with means of 4.20 for BB choosers and 4.13 for Splendor choosers (with 5 representing maximum confidence). These means were not significantly different, $p > .05$. The phenomenon of high decision confidence despite the inherent ambiguity of the input parallels findings for legal decision making (Holyoak & Simon, 1999; Simon et al., 2001) and provides evidence for a constraint-satisfaction process.

To test whether participants' assessments of the different attributes shifted to fit with their decision, we first analyzed the desirability data after linearly rescaling all desirability ratings to range from -1 to 1. (This transformation was performed so that we could later multiply the desirability ratings with the importance ratings using a comparable scale.) To measure participants' overall evaluation of the desirability of the attributes of each job choice, we converted the ratings obtained into values that we call S *scores*, which provide an index of desirability for the Splendor job. The S score was computed by summing the average rating for the eight attributes (excluding location, which would create a confounding), reversing the scale for the attributes favoring BB (see Holyoak & Simon, 1999, for a similar coherence analysis). High S scores indicate strong preferences for Splendor's positive attributes and low preference for BB's positive attributes, and low S scores indicate the opposite.

Mean desirability ratings were compared using a 2 (decision group) × 2 (test phase) mixed-model analysis of variance (ANOVA), which revealed a highly significant interaction between decision group and phase, $F(1, 78) = 18.73$, $p < .001$. The rated desirability of the composite of Splendor attributes was higher at the post-test than the baseline test for Splendor choosers, whereas the rated desirability of the composite of Splendor attributes was lower at the post-test than the baseline test for BB choosers.

We then tested for differences between the importance ratings for the attributes before and after the decision. Prior to running statistical tests, we rescaled the importance data such that the data ranged from 0 to 1, with 0 representing lowest possible importance. This was done to compute a composite utility measure, as described in the next paragraph. The analysis of the importance ratings was performed by running a separate mixed-model ANOVA for each attribute, with decision group as a between-subjects variable and phase as a within-subjects variable. These analyses revealed significant interactions for the office attribute, $F(1, 78) = 7.42, p < .01$; the commute attribute, $F(1, 78) = 11.15, p < .01$; and the vacation attribute, $F(1, 78) = 6.56, p < .05$. Post hoc Newman-Keuls tests revealed that ratings of the attributes that were favorable

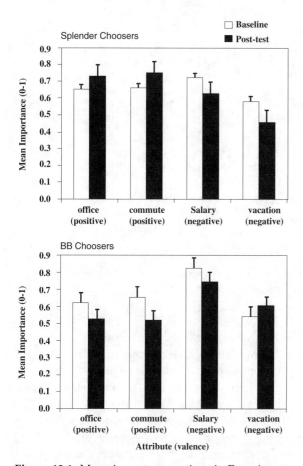

Figure 12.1. Mean importance ratings in Experiment 1. Ratings for each of the four attributes at the baseline test and the post-test are shown separately for participants who chose the job offer from Splendor (top panel) and for participants who chose the job offer from BB (bottom panel).

for Splendor choosers (office and commute) differed reliably between the two decision groups at the post-tests ($p < .01$), but not at the baseline tests. Overall, the results indicate that for all attributes except salary, the importance ratings of the two decision groups diverged from the baseline to the post-test, with means generally increasing for those traits that were desirable attributes of the chosen job and decreasing for those traits that were undesirable attributes of the chosen job (see Figure 12.1).

To provide an integrated measure of coherence using both desirability of attributes and importance weights, we computed the product of attribute desirability (scaled from -1 to 1) and attribute importance (scaled from 0 to 1) to

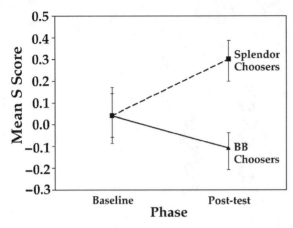

Figure 12.2. Mean integrated S scores (desirability multiplied by importance value for each attribute) for both decision groups at each test phase in Experiment 1. High S scores indicate ratings favorable to a decision for Splendor (see the text).

make an *integrated S score*. This integrated S score provides an analogue of utility as it is conventionally defined in multiattribute utility theory. A mixed-model ANOVA with decision group as a between-subjects variable and test phase as a within-subjects variable revealed a highly significant interaction between decision group and phase, $F(1, 78) = 26.80$, $p < .001$. This analysis of integrated S scores yielded the same basic trends as were observed for the desirability scores alone, and the differences were somewhat more reliable (see Figure 12.2).

Finally, we determined whether attribute assessments changed as a coherent set by looking for positive correlations among the various attribute shifts that accompanied the decision. A correlational analysis using Cronbach's alpha was carried out on the S scores (not integrated S scores) for the four critical attributes and the decision (represented by 0 for BB choosers and 1 for Splendor choosers). A Cronbach's alpha of near 0 would indicate no correlation between the decision and the desirability of the set of attributes, and an alpha of 1 would indicate the highest possible correlation. This analysis revealed that the overall positive correlations were low at the baseline test (Cronbach's $\alpha = -.22$), but they were considerably higher at the post-test (Cronbach's $\alpha = .48$). Thus, it appears that the overall mean shifts discussed earlier were accompanied by correlational shifts among the attributes.

EXPERIMENT 2

The goal of Experiment 2 was to assess whether the coherence shifts observed in Experiment 1 are a postcommitment phenomenon or whether they occur prior to the point of commitment to a final decision. It has often been claimed that the point of commitment (i.e., a declaration of a "final decision") is psychologically critical to triggering dissonance reduction. According to Festinger (1964), "Dissonance-reduction processes do not automatically start when a decision is made. Simply making a decision is not enough. The decision must have the effect of committing the person" (p. 42; see also Gollwitzer & Bayer, 1999; Kiesler, 1971; Wicklund & Brehm, 1976). In contrast, constraint-satisfaction models imply that coherence shifts begin prior to the point of commitment and in fact drive the decision-making process.

Method

Participants. Participants were 80 UCLA undergraduates who were recruited as in Experiment 1.

Materials, Design, and Procedure

The baseline test instrument was presented in a five-page booklet and was identical to that used in Experiment 1, with the exception that the long commute was changed from 40 to 35 min (the same change was made in the other instruments).

The second and third instruments were presented together in a single 10-page booklet. To determine whether participants would demonstrate coherence shifts in the absence of any manipulation that would lead them to choose one option over the other, we removed the location manipulation used in Experiment 1. The other main difference from Experiment 1 was the addition of a section of text presented alongside the description of the job offers. This text, designed to delay the point of commitment, stated that a large corporation named Punch was considering buying out either BB or Splendor, and a buy-out would eliminate all new jobs in the respective company. The instructions advised the participants to consider the offers, but to delay their final decision until the situation was clarified. After the descriptions of the job offers were presented, the instructions read: "At this stage you are still waiting to hear about the decision by Punch and are suspending your own decision. However, you may have a feeling about the aspects included in the two job offers." Ratings of desirability and importance were then obtained with the questions framed in terms of the job offers. Finally, at the end of this second instrument (interim phase), the instructions stated: "Even though you are still waiting to learn about Punch's decision, you may have a preliminary leaning toward either one of the two offers. Please indicate your preliminary leaning. Remember that you will still be free to make any decision you like after you are told about Punch's plans." After indicating their preliminary leaning, participants were asked to rate their confidence in it on a scale from 1 (*low confidence*) to 5 (*high confidence*). The preliminary leaning was obtained after ratings of desirability and importance so that eliciting a leaning could not itself cause any coherence shift at the interim phase.

After completing the second instrument, participants were informed that the possible buy-out would not occur, and they were instructed to go ahead and make their choice between the two offers. Participants were reminded that they were free to make any decision regardless of their previous responses. The third and final phase of the experiment (the post-test), which was essentially identical to the post-test used in Experiment 1, was then administered.

Results

The data were initially tabulated to determine the number of participants who had decided in favor of each of the two offers and whether participants had switched decisions from the interim to final decision. A total of 44 participants tentatively chose BB in the interim phase, whereas 36 chose Splendor. Four participants who were leaning toward BB in the interim phase switched their final decision to Splendor and were dropped from all subsequent analyses. The confidence in the decisions was generally high, with means of 3.48 for tentative BB choosers, 3.44 for tentative Splendor choosers, 3.70 for final BB choosers, and 3.50 for final Splendor choosers. None of these means differed reliably.

We then tested for coherence shifts using the desirability scores. As in Experiment 1, this analysis was performed after first converting all of the ratings to a standard range of -1 to 1. S-score data were analyzed using a 2×3 mixed-model ANOVA, which revealed a significant interaction between decision and test phase, $F(2, 148) = 9.62$, $p < .001$. Post hoc Newman-Keuls tests revealed that for BB choosers, both the interim mean S score ($M = -.22$) and the post-test score ($M = -.27$) were significantly lower than the baseline score ($M = -.07$), but the interim and post-test scores did not differ reliably. These differences suggest that the BB choosers shifted toward liking BB more and Splendor less both prior to and after they had committed to a decision, but not before the offers were made. The pattern revealed by Newman-Keuls tests was less clear for Splendor choosers. For them, mean S scores increased from the baseline test ($M = .06$) to the interim test ($M = .07$) to the post-test ($M = .11$); however, these differences did not reach significance, $p > .05$. Further Newman-Keuls tests revealed that the two decision groups differed significantly at all phases of the experiment.

As in Experiment 1, we tested for differences among the importance ratings in each phase of the experiment by running a separate mixed-model ANOVA for each attribute, with decision as a between-subjects variable and phase as a within-subjects variable. These analyses revealed a significant interaction for the commute attribute, $F(2, 148) = 5.80$, $p < .01$. The office attribute approached, but did not reach, significance, $F(2, 148) = 2.72$, $p = .06$. There were no significant interactions for either the salary or the vacation attribute. Overall, the results of Experiment 2 were less robust than those of Experiment 1. Nonetheless, the general trends of the importance ratings indicated that the ratings of the two decision groups gradually diverged from the baseline to the interim to the post-test, with means generally increasing for those traits that were desirable attributes of the chosen job and generally decreasing for those traits that were

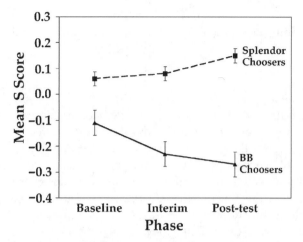

Figure 12.3. Mean integrated S scores (desirability multiplied by importance value for each attribute) for both decision groups at each test phase in Experiment 2. High S scores indicate ratings favorable to a decision for Splendor.

undesirable attributes of the chosen job, though these patterns were absent for BB choosers on the salary and vacation attributes.

To further assess coherence shifts, we again calculated integrated S scores by taking the product of desirability and importance. Figure 12.3 depicts the resulting mean integrated S scores. A 2×3 mixed-model ANOVA revealed a significant interaction between decision group and test phase, $F(2, 148) = 14.49$, $p < .001$. Post hoc Newman-Keuls tests identified patterns similar to those observed for the desirability scores alone. For BB choosers, both the interim mean S score ($M = -.23$) and the post-test score ($M = -.27$) were significantly lower than the baseline score ($M = .-11$), but the interim and post-test scores did not differ reliably. These differences suggest that the BB choosers shifted toward valuing BB more and Splendor less both prior to and after they had committed to a decision, but not before the offers were made. For Splendor choosers, the post-test score ($M = .11$) was significantly higher than both the baseline and interim scores; however, the change from the baseline test ($M = .07$) to the interim test ($M = .08$) was not reliable. As in the analysis of desirability alone, the two decision groups differed significantly at each phase of the experiment.

Also as in Experiment 1, a correlational analysis was carried out using Cronbach's alpha to determine whether there were positive correlations among the decision and the supporting attributes. At the baseline test, there were few positive correlations (Cronbach's $\alpha = -.58$). At the interim test, however, this changed, and the correlations overall became positive (Cronbach's $\alpha = .13$). At the post-test, the correlations increased again (Cronbach's $\alpha = .28$), indicating that increased coherence among the desirability scores accompanied the overall attribute shifts.

GENERAL DISCUSSION

The present study demonstrates that preferences used in decision making are not fixed, as assumed by classic theories of rational choice, but rather are reconstructed in the course of decision making (cf. Janis & Mann, 1977; Montgomery, 1983; Russo et al., 1996, 1998; Svenson, 1992). Our principal finding is that as people processed the decision task, their preferences for the attributes of the alternative that was ultimately chosen increased while their preferences for the attributes of the to-be-rejected choice decreased. These results constitute a violation of the axiom of preference invariance (though they do not provide evidence of preference reversals). In general, both the reported values of the attributes (ratings of desirability) and their weights (ratings of importance) shifted to make one alternative dominate the other. The most robust coherence shifts involved the product of these two factors (a close analogue to the overall utility of a choice as defined in multiattribute decision theory). Other dynamic models of decision making (e.g., decision field theory; Busemeyer & Townsend, 1993) predict divergence of the choice options, but not changes in assessments of the attributes underlying them. The present evidence that the attributes themselves are reevaluated (before the point of commitment) thus provides evidence for constraint satisfaction over other dynamic accounts. These findings cannot be attributed to differences in methods used to elicit or describe the options, nor to variations in context (cf. Slovic, 1995; Tversky & Kahneman, 1986). Rather, the reconstruction of preferences seems to be the natural outcome of the very process of decision making.

As we have found in previous studies that tested decisions involving high-level reasoning (Holyoak & Simon, 1999; Simon et al., 2001), evidence integration (Simon, Snow, & Read, 2004), and social reasoning (Read, Snow, & Simon, 2003), decisions were accompanied by coherence shifts and high levels of confidence. This suggests that constraint-satisfaction processing provides a good explanation for a broad range of decision-making tasks. Experiment 1 demonstrated that the introduction of one piece of strong evidence (the good-location/bad-location manipulation) triggers changes in the evaluation of unrelated attributes (cf. Holyoak & Simon, 1999, Experiment 3). This finding is reminiscent of classical perceptual phenomena associated with the ambiguous Necker cube, for which a shift in the interpretation of one portion of the figure causes shifts in the interpretation of all other portions. Our results indicate that a variation in one attribute not only determines the decision (which would be entirely rational), but also causes a global coherence shift involving changes in preferences for other logically unrelated attributes. Experiment 2 provided evidence that preference changes occur both before and after the point of commitment, as has been found for other types of decisions (Phillips, 2002; Simon et al., 2001) and using different methodological designs (Russo et al., 1996, 1998).

The magnitudes of the shifts observed in these studies were smaller than those observed in our previous work with legal cases (Holyoak & Simon, 1999; Simon et al., 2001). One reason for this difference is that the arguments that figured in the studies of legal decision making were more abstract and ambiguous. Moreover, many of the legal issues involved competing attributes (e.g., alternative precedents), either of which might reasonably be viewed as superior. In contrast, the attributes involved in the present study varied monotonically in goodness (e.g., a higher or a lower salary), thus effectively blocking cardinal reversals of preference.

Although our findings challenge the descriptive validity of formal decision-making theories, they do not challenge their normative or prescriptive value. Following the procedure implied by multiattribute decision theory may assist decision makers in gaining insights into their values and goals, help people communicate about their respective values and goals (Baron, 2000; Edwards & Fasolo, 2001), and perhaps serve as a benchmark for identifying whether and how far one's preferences actually shifted in the course of making a decision. At the same time, constraint satisfaction provides an adaptive psychological mechanism that enables people to construct dominance and thus reach confident decisions in complex cases.

ACKNOWLEDGMENTS

This research was supported by National Science Foundation Grants SES-0080424 and SES-0080375.

13. "Coherent Arbitrariness": Stable Demand Curves Without Stable Preferences

Dan Ariely, George Loewenstein, and Drazen Prelec

Economic theories of valuation generally assume that prices of commodities and assets are derived from underlying "fundamental" values. For example, in finance theory, asset prices are believed to reflect the market estimate of the discounted present value of the asset's payoff stream. In labor theory, the supply of labor is established by the tradeoff between the desire for consumption and the displeasure of work. Finally, and most importantly for this chapter, consumer microeconomics assumes that the demand curves for consumer products – chocolates, CDs, movies, vacations, drugs, and so forth – can be ultimately traced to the valuation of pleasures that consumers anticipate receiving from these products.

Because it is difficult, as a rule, to measure fundamental values directly, empirical tests of economic theory typically examine whether the effects of *changes* in circumstances on valuations are consistent with theoretical prediction – for example, whether labor supply responds appropriately to a change in the wage rate, whether (compensated) demand curves for commodities are downward sloping, or whether stock prices respond in the predicted way to share repurchases. However, such "comparative static" relationships are a necessary but not sufficient condition for fundamental valuation (e.g., Summers, 1986). Becker (1962) was perhaps the first to make this point explicitly when he observed that consumers choosing commodity bundles randomly from their budget set would nevertheless produce downward-sloping demand curves.

In spite of this ambiguity in the interpretation of demand curves, the intuition that prices must in some way derive from fundamental values is still strongly entrenched. Psychological evidence that preferences can be manipulated by normatively irrelevant factors, such as option "framing," changes in the "choice context," or the presence of prior cues or "anchors," is often rationalized by appealing to consumers' lack of information about the options at stake and the weak incentives operating in the experimental setting. From the standpoint of economic theory, it is easy to admit that consumers might not be very good at

Originally published in *The Quarterly Journal of Economics*, vol. 118, pp. 73–105. Copyright © 2003 by the President and Fellows of Harvard College and the Massachusetts Institute of Technology. Reprinted with permission.

predicting the pleasures and pains produced by a purchase, especially if the purchase option is complex and the choice hypothetical. It is harder to accept that consumers might have difficulty establishing how much they value each individual bit of pleasure or pain in a situation where they can experience the full extent of this pleasure or pain just before the pricing decision.

In this chapter we show that consumers' absolute valuation of experience goods is surprisingly arbitrary, even under "full information" conditions. How-ever, we also show that consumers' *relative* valuations of different amounts of the good appear orderly, as if supported by demand curves derived from funda-mental preferences. Valuations therefore display a combination of arbitrariness and coherence that we refer to as "coherent arbitrariness."

Our findings are consistent with an account of revealed preference, which posits that valuations are initially malleable but become "imprinted" (i.e., pre-cisely defined and largely invariant) after the individual is called upon to make an initial decision.[1] Prior to imprinting, valuations have a large arbitrary com-ponent, meaning that they are highly responsive to both normative and nonnor-mative influences. Following imprinting, valuations become locally coherent, as the consumer attempts to reconcile future decisions of a "similar kind" with the initial one. This creates an illusion of order, because consumers' coherent responses to subsequent *changes* in conditions disguise the arbitrary nature of the initial, foundational choice.

EXPERIMENT 1: COHERENTLY ARBITRARY VALUATION OF ORDINARY PRODUCTS

Our experiments take an old trick from the experimental psychologists' arsenal – the anchoring manipulation – and use it to influence valuation of products and hedonic experiences with normatively irrelevant factors. In a famous early demonstration of anchoring, Tversky and Kahneman (1974) spun a wheel of fortune with numbers that ranged from 0 to 100, asked subjects whether the number of African nations in the United Nations was greater than or less than that number, and then instructed subjects to estimate the actual figure. Estimates were significantly related to the number spun on the wheel (the "anchor"), even though subjects could clearly see that the number had been generated by a purely chance process.[2] This and many other anchoring studies seemed to show that people lack preexisting subjective probability distributions over unknown quantities.

---

[1] The idea that preferences are not well defined but become articulated in the process of making a decision is consistent with a large body of research on what decision researchers refer to as "constructed preferences" (e.g., Slovic, 1995, and Hoeffler & Ariely, 1999).

[2] For recent studies of anchoring, see, for example, Chapman and Johnson (1999), Jacowitz and Kahneman (1995), Strack and Mussweiler (1997), and Epley and Gilovitch (2001).

The vast majority of anchoring experiments in the psychological literature have focused on how anchoring corrupts subjective judgment, not subjective valuation or preference. Because valuation typically involves judgment, however, it is not surprising that valuation, too, can be moved up or down by the anchoring manipulation. Johnson and Schkade (1989) were the first to demonstrate this experimentally. They showed that asking subjects whether their certainty equivalent for a lottery is above or below an anchor value influences subsequently stated certainty equivalents. Green, Jacowitz, Kahneman, and McFadden (1998) and Kahneman and Knetsch (1993) found the same effect with judgments of willingness to pay (WTP) for public goods; higher values in the initial Yes/No question led to higher subsequent WTP.

Our first experiment replicates these results with ordinary consumer products. The first class meeting of a market research course in the Sloan School MBA program provided the setting for the study. Fifty-five students were shown six products (computer accessories, wine bottles, luxury chocolates, and books), which were briefly described without mentioning market price. The average retail price of the items was about $70. After introducing the products, subjects were asked whether they would buy each good for a dollar figure equal to the last two digits of their Social Security number. After this Accept/Reject response, they stated their dollar maximum WTP for the product. A random device determined whether the product would in fact be sold on the basis of the first, Accept/Reject, response or the second, WTP, response (via the incentive-compatible Becker-Degroot-Marschak procedure, 1963). Subjects understood that both their Accept/Reject response and their WTP response had some chance of being decisive for the purchase and that they were eligible to purchase at most one product.

In spite of the realism of the products and transaction, the impact of the Social Security number on stated WTP was significant in every product category. Subjects with above-median Social Security numbers stated values from 57% to 107% greater than did subjects with below-median numbers. The effect is even more striking when examining the valuations by quintiles of the Social Security number distribution, as shown in Table 13.1. The valuations of the top quintile subjects were typically greater by a factor of *three*. For example, subjects with Social Security numbers in the top quintile were willing to pay $56 on average for a cordless computer keyboard, compared with $16 on average for subjects with bottom quintile numbers. Evidently, these subjects did not have, or were unable to retrieve, personal values for ordinary products.

Alongside this volatility of absolute preference we also observed a marked stability of relative preference. For example, the vast majority of subjects (> 95%) valued a cordless keyboard more than a trackball and the highly rated wine more than the lower-rated wine. Subjects, it seems, did not know how much they valued these items, but they did know the relative ordering within the categories of wine and computer accessories.

Table 13.1. Average Stated Willingness to Pay Sorted by Quintile of the Sample's Social Security Number Distribution

Quintile of SS# Distribution	Cordless Trackball	Cordless Keyboard	Average Wine	Rare Wine	Design Book	Belgian Chocolates
1	$ 8.64	$16.09	$ 8.64	$11.73	$12.82	$9.55
2	$11.82	$26.82	$14.45	$22.45	$16.18	$10.64
3	$13.45	$29.27	$12.55	$18.09	$15.82	$12.45
4	$21.18	$34.55	$15.45	$24.55	$19.27	$13.27
5	$26.18	$55.64	$27.91	$37.55	$30.00	$20.64
Correlations	.415	.516	.328	.328	.319	.419
	$p = .0015$	$p < .0001$	$p = .014$	$p = .0153$	$p = .0172$	$p = .0013$

Note: The last row indicates the correlations between Social Security numbers and WTP (and their significance levels).

COHERENT ARBITRARINESS

The sensitivity of WTP to anchors suggests that consumers do not arrive at a choice or at a pricing task with an inventory of preexisting preferences and probability distributions, which is consistent with a great deal of other psychological evidence (Drolet, Simonson, & Tversky, 2000; Kahneman & Miller, 1986; Payne, Bettman, & Johnson, 1993). Rather than specific WTP values for products, consumers probably have some range of acceptable values. If a give-or-take price for a product falls outside this range, then the purchase decision is straightforward: "Don't Buy" if the price is above the range, and "Buy" if the price is below the range. But, what if the stated price falls within the WTP range, so that the range does not determine the decision, one way or the other? We do not know much about how a choice in such a case might be made. We do know that if the situation demands a choice, then the person will in fact choose, that is, will either purchase or not purchase. We assume that this "foundational" choice then becomes a part of that person's stock of decisional precedents, ready to be invoked the next time a similar choice situation arises (Gilboa & Schmeidler, 1995).

To relate this discussion to our actual experiment, suppose that a subject with a Social Security number ending with 25 has an a priori WTP range of $5 to $30 for wine described as "average" and $10 to $50 for the "rare" wine. Both wines, therefore, might or might not be purchased for the $25 price. Suppose that the subject indicates, for whatever reason, that she would be willing to purchase the average bottle for $25. If we were to ask her a moment later whether she would be willing to purchase the "rare" bottle for $25, the answer would obviously be "yes," because from her perspective this particular "choice problem" has been solved and its solution is known: If an average wine is worth at least $25, then a rare wine must be worth more than $25! Moreover, when the subject is subsequently asked to provide WTP values for the wines, then that problem, too, is now substantially constrained: The prices will have to be ordered so that both prices are above $25 and the rare wine is valued more.

There are many psychological details that we are not specifying. We do not say much about how the choice is made if the price falls within the range, nor do we propose a psychological mechanism for the anchoring effect itself. There are several psychological accounts of anchoring, and for our purposes it is not necessary to decide between them (Epley & Gilovich, 2001; Mussweiler & Strack, 2001a). The substantive claims we do make are the following: First, in situations in which valuations are not constrained by prior precedents, choices will be highly sensitive to normatively irrelevant influences and considerations such as anchoring. Second, because decisions at the earlier stages are used as inputs for future decisions, an initial choice will exert a normatively inappropriate influence over subsequent choices and values. Third, if we look at a series of choices by a single individual, they will exhibit an orderly pattern (coherence) with respect to numerical parameters like price, quantity, quality, and so on.[3]

Behaviorally then, consumers in the marketplace may largely obey the axioms of revealed preference; indeed, according to this account, a person who remembered all previous choices and accepted the transitivity axiom would never violate transitivity. However, we cannot infer from this that these choices reveal true preferences. Transitivity may only reflect the fact that consumers *remember* earlier choices and make subsequent choices in a fashion that is consistent with them, not that these choices are generated from preexisting preferences.

VALUATION OF NOVEL PAIN EXPERIENCES

If preferences and valuations at a moment in time are largely inferences that a person draws from the history of his or her own previous decisions, a natural question that arises is whether the inference has a narrow scope (restricted only to very similar previous choices) or whether the scope is more general. For example, if I go on record as being willing to pay $25 for a wine, will that only influence my subsequent WTP for wine, for a broader range of items or experiences, or

---

[3] Another research literature, on "evaluability," is also relevant here. "Evaluability" has been identified as the cause of preference reversals that arise when options are evaluated either jointly (within-subject) or separately (between-subjects). Hsee, Loewenstein, Blount, and Bazerman (1999) explain these reversals by assuming that it is more difficult to evaluate some attributes separately than jointly, depending on whether the attributes have well-established standards. For example, subjects in one study were asked to assess two political candidates, one who would bring 1,000 jobs to the district and the other who would bring 5,000 jobs to the district but had a driving-under-the-influence (DUI) conviction. When the candidates were evaluated separately, the first candidate was judged more favorably, presumably because the employment figure was hard to evaluate. However, when the candidates were compared side-by-side, people indicated that the employment difference more than compensated for the DUI conviction and gave their preference to the second candidate.

even for pleasures generally? The broader the scope of inferences, the more will previous choices constrain any future choice. If purchases of specific products and services function as precedents, not just for those same items but also for the general valuation of pleasure (including here the avoidance of discomfort), then an adult consumer should have accumulated an inventory of previous choices sufficient to stabilize his or her dollar valuation of hedonic experiences.

In the next five experiments, we address the question of whether consumers do indeed enter the laboratory with a stable, preexisting valuation of pleasure and pain. In each experiment, subjects stated their willingness to accept (WTA) pains of different durations (induced by a loud noise played over headphones) – in exchange for payment. Subjects were initially exposed to a sample of the noise and then asked whether – hypothetically – they would be willing to experience the same noise again in exchange for a payment of magnitude X (with X varied across subjects). Their actual WTAs were then elicited for different noise durations.

We used this artificial hedonic "product" for several reasons. First, we were able to provide subjects with a sample of the experience before they made subsequent decisions about whether to experience it again in exchange for payment. They therefore entered the pricing phase of the experiment with full information about the experience they were pricing. Second, we wanted to avoid a situation in which subjects could solve the pricing problem intellectually, without drawing on their own sensory experience. Annoying sounds have no clear market price, so our subjects could not refer to similar decisions made outside the laboratory as a basis for their valuations. Third, we wanted to make the money stakes in this decision comparable to the stakes in routine consumer expenditures. The plausible range of values for avoiding the annoying sounds in our experiments ranges from a few cents to several dollars. Fourth, with annoying sounds it is possible to re-create the same hedonic experience repeatedly, permitting an experiment with repeated trials. Prior research shows that with annoying sounds, unlike many other types of pleasures and pains, there is little or no satiation or sensitization to repeated presentations (Ariely & Zauberman, 2000).

EXPERIMENT 2: COHERENTLY ARBITRARY VALUATION OF PAIN

The goal of Experiment 2 was to test (1) whether valuation of annoying sounds was susceptible to an anchoring manipulation; (2) whether additional experience with the sounds would erode the influence of the anchor; and (3) whether valuation would be sensitive to a within-subject manipulation of the duration of the annoying sound, thus demonstrating coherence with respect to this attribute.

One hundred and thirty-two students from the Massachusetts Institute of Technology participated in the experiment. Approximately half were undergraduates, and the rest were MBA students or, in a few cases, recruiters from large investment banks. Subjects were randomly assigned to six experimental conditions. The experiment lasted about 25 minutes, and subjects were paid according to their performance as described in the next few paragraphs.

At the beginning of the experiment, all subjects listened to an annoying, 30-second sound delivered through headphones. The sound was a high-pitched scream (a triangular wave with frequency of 3,000 Hz), similar to the broadcasting warning signal.

The main experimental manipulation was the anchor price, which was manipulated between subjects at three levels: an anchor price of 10¢ (low anchor), an anchor price of 50¢ (high anchor), and no anchor (no anchor). Subjects in the low-anchor [high-anchor] condition first encountered a screen that read:[4]

In a few moments we are going to play you a new unpleasant tone over your headset. We are interested in how annoying you find it to be. Immediately after you hear the tone, we are going to ask you whether you would be willing to repeat the same experience in exchange for a payment of 10¢ [50¢].

Subjects in the no-anchor condition listened to the sound but were not given any external price and were not asked to answer any hypothetical question.

Before the main part of the experiment started, subjects were told that they would be asked to indicate the amount of payment they required to listen to sounds that differed in duration but were identical in quality and intensity to the one they had just heard. Subjects were further told that on each trial the computer would randomly pick a price from a given price distribution. If the computer's price was higher than their price, the subject would hear the sound and also receive a payment corresponding to the price that the computer had randomly drawn. If the computer's price was lower than their price, they would neither hear the sound nor receive payment for that trial. Subjects were told that this procedure ensured that the best strategy is to pick the minimum price for which they would be willing to listen to the sound, not a few pennies more and not a few pennies less. The prices picked by the computer were drawn from a triangle distribution ranging from 5¢ to 100¢, with the lower numbers being more frequent than the higher numbers. The distribution was displayed on the screen for subjects to study and, importantly, the distribution was the same for all subjects.

After learning about the procedure, subjects engaged in a sequence of nine trials. On each trial, they were informed of the duration of the sound they were valuing (10, 30, or 60 seconds) and were asked to indicate their WTA for the sound. The three durations were presented either in an increasing (10 seconds, 30 seconds, 60 seconds) or decreasing order (60 seconds, 30 seconds, 10 seconds). In both cases, each ordered sequence repeated itself three times, one after the other. After each WTA entry, the computer asked subjects whether they were

---

[4] In a different study (Ariely, Loewenstein, & Prelec, 2002) we tested whether the order in which subjects received the sample and the anchor made a difference. It did not.

willing to experience the sound for that price minus 5¢ and whether they would experience it for that price plus 5¢. If subjects did not answer "no" to the first question and "yes" to the second, the computer drew their attention to the fact that their WTA was not consistent with their responses and asked to them to reconsider their WTA price.

After finalizing a WTA value, subjects were shown their price along with the random price drawn from the distribution. If the price specified by the subject was higher than the computer's price, the subject did not receive any payment for that trial and continued directly to the next trial. If the price set by the subject was lower than the computer's price, the subject heard the sound over the headphones, was reminded that the payment for the trial would be given to them at the end of the experiment, and then continued to the next trial. At the end of the nine trials, all subjects were paid according to the payment rule.

Results

A set of simple effect comparisons revealed that average WTA in the high-anchor condition ($M = 59.60$) was significantly higher than average WTA in either the low-anchor condition ($M = 39.82$), $F(1, 126) = 19.25, p < .001$, or the no-anchor condition ($M = 43.87$), $F(1, 126) = 12.17, p < .001$.[5] WTA in the low-anchor condition was not significantly different from WTA in the no-anchor condition, $p = .37$. Because subjects in the high-anchor condition specified higher WTAs, they naturally listened to fewer sounds ($M = 2.8$) than subjects in the low-anchor and no-anchor conditions ($Ms = 4.5$ and 4.1), $F(1, 126) = 14.26, p < .001$. High-anchor subjects also earned significantly less money on average ($M = \$1.53$) than those in the no-anchor condition and the low-anchor condition ($Ms = \$2.06$ and $\$2.16$), $F(1, 126) = 7.99, p < .005$.

Although there was a significant drop in WTA values from the first to the second replication, $F(1, 252) = 17.54, p < .001$, there was no evidence of convergence of WTA among the different anchor conditions. Such convergence would have produced a significant interaction between the repetition factor and the anchoring manipulation, but this interaction was not significant.[6]

WTA values were highly sensitive to duration in the expected direction, $F(2, 252) = 294.46, p < .001$ (for more discussion of sensitivity to duration see

[5] For the purpose of statistical analysis, responses above 100¢ (7.7%) were truncated to 101¢ (the highest random price selected by computer was 100¢, so responses above 101¢ were strategically equivalent). Repeating the analyses using untruncated values did not qualify any of the findings.
[6] A variety of different tests of convergence produced similar results. First, we carried out an analysis of variance in which we took only the first and last trial as the repeated measure dependent variable. Again, the interaction between trial (first versus last) and the anchoring manipulation was nonsignificant. We also estimated the linear trend of WTA over time for each subject. The estimated trends were decreasing, but the rate of decline did not differ significantly between the two anchoring conditions.

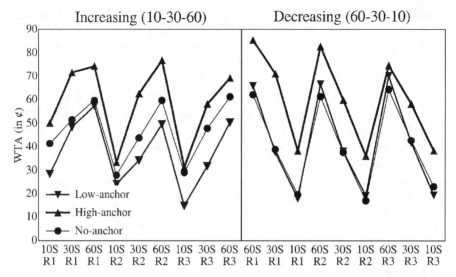

Figure 13.1. Mean WTA for the nine trials in the three anchor conditions. The panel on the left shows the increasing condition (duration order of 10, 30, and 60 seconds). The panel on the right shows the decreasing condition (duration order of 60, 30, and 10 seconds).

Ariely and Loewenstein, 2000, and Kahneman, Wakker, & Sarin, 1997). The mean price for the 10-second sound ($M = 28.35$) was significantly lower than the mean price for the 30-second sound ($M = 48.69$), $F(1, 252) = 169.46, p < .001$, and the mean price for the 30-second sound was lower than the mean price for the 60-second sound ($M = 66.25$), $F(1, 252) = 126.06, p < .001$.

Figure 13.1 provides a graphical illustration of the results thus far. First, the vertical displacement between the lines shows the powerful effect of the anchoring manipulation. Second, despite the arbitrariness revealed by the effect of the anchoring manipulation, there is a strong and almost linear relationship between WTA and duration. Finally, there is no evidence of convergence between the different conditions across the nine trials.

Figure 13.2 provides additional support for the tight connection between WTA and duration. For each subject, we calculated the ratio of WTA in each of the durations to each of the other durations and plotted these separately for the three conditions. As can be seen in the figure, the ratios of WTAs are stable and independent of condition (there are no significant differences by condition).

In summary, Experiment 2 demonstrates arbitrary but coherent pricing of painful experiences, even when there is no uncertainty about the nature or duration of the experience. Neither repeated experience with the event, nor confrontation with the same price distribution, overrode the effect of the initial anchor.

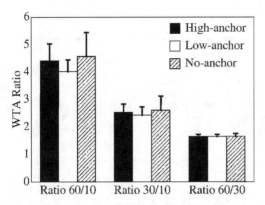

Figure 13.2. Mean of individual WTA ratios for the different durations across the different conditions. Error bars are based on standard errors.

EXPERIMENT 3: RAISING THE STAKES

Experiment 3 was designed to address two possible objections to the previous procedure. First, it could be argued that subjects might have somehow believed that the anchor was informative, even though they had experienced the sound for themselves. For example, they might have thought that the sound posed some small risk to their hearing and might have believed that the anchor roughly corresponded to the monetary value of this risk. To eliminate this possibility, Experiment 3 used subjects' own Social Security numbers as anchors. Second, one might be concerned that the small stakes in the previous experiment provided minimal incentives for accurate responding, which may have increased the arbitrariness of subjects' responses and their sensitivity to the anchor. Experiment 3, therefore, raised the stakes by a factor of ten. In addition, at the end of the experiment, we added a question designed to test whether the anchor-induced changes in valuation carry over to tradeoffs involving other experiences.

Ninety students from the Massachusetts Institute of Technology participated in the experiment. The procedure closely followed that of Experiment 2, except that the stimuli were 10 times as long: The shortest stimulus lasted 100 seconds, the next lasted 300 seconds, and the longest lasted 600 seconds. The manipulation of the anchor in this experiment was also different. At the onset of the experiment, subjects were asked to provide the first three digits of their Social Security number and were instructed to turn these digits into a money amount (e.g., 678 translates into $6.78). Subjects were then asked whether, hypothetically, they would listen again to the sound they just experienced (for 300 seconds) if they were paid the money amount they had generated from their Social Security number.

In the main part of the experiment, subjects had three opportunities to listen to sounds in exchange for payment. The three different durations were again ordered in either an increasing set (100 seconds, 300 seconds, 600 seconds) or

Table 13.2. Events Ranked in Experiment 3

	The Event	Mean Rank
1	Missing your bus by a few seconds	4.3
2	Experiencing 300 seconds of the same sound you experienced	5.1
3	Discovering you purchased a spoiled carton of milk	5.2
4	Forgetting to return a video and having to pay a fine	5.4
5	Experiencing a blackout for an hour	5.8
6	Having a blood test	6.0
7	Having your ice cream fall on the floor	6.0
8	Having to wait 30 minutes in line for your favorite restaurant	6.2
9	Going to a movie theater and having to watch it from the second row	6.7
10	Losing your phone bill and having to call to get another copy	7.3
11	Running out of toothpaste at night	8.1

Note: The different events that subjects were asked to order-rank in terms of their annoyance, at the end of Experiment 3. The items are ordered by their overall mean ranked annoyance from the most annoying (lower numbers) to the least annoying (high numbers).

a decreasing set (600 seconds, 300 seconds, 100 seconds). In each trial, after they indicated their WTA, subjects were shown both their own price and the random price drawn from the distribution (which was the distribution used in Experiment 2 but multiplied by 10). If the price set by the subject was higher than the computer's price, subjects continued directly to the next trial. If the price set by the subjects was lower than the computer's price, subjects received the sound and the money associated with it (the amount set by the randomly drawn number), and then continued to the next trial. This process repeated itself three times, once for each of the three durations.

After completing the three trials, subjects were asked to rank order a list of events in terms of how annoying they found them (for a list of the different tasks, see Table 13.2). At the end of the experiment, subjects were paid according to the payment rule.

Results

The three digits entered ranged from 041 (translated to $0.41) to 997 (translated to $9.97), with a mean of 523 and a median of 505. Figure 13.3 compares the prices demanded by subjects with Social Security numbers above and below the median. It is evident that subjects with lower Social Security numbers required substantially less payment than subjects with higher numbers (Ms = $3.55 and $5.76), $F(1, 88) = 28.45$, $p < .001$. Both groups were coherent with respect to duration, demanding more payment for longer sounds, $F(2, 176) = 92.53$, $p < .001$. As in the previous experiment, there was also a small but significant interaction between anchor and duration, $F(2, 176) = 4.17$, $p = .017$.

If subjects have little idea about how to price the sounds initially and hence rely on the random anchor in coming up with a value, we would expect

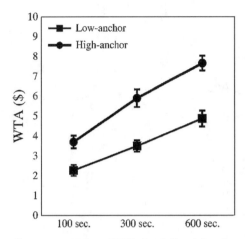

Figure 13.3. Mean WTA (in dollars) for the three annoying sounds. The data are plotted separately for subjects whose three-digit anchor was below the median (low anchor) and above the median (high anchor). Error bars are based on standard errors.

responses to the initial question to be relatively close to the anchor, regardless of whether the duration was 100 seconds or 600 seconds. However, having committed themselves to a particular value for the initial sound, we would expect the increasing duration group to then adjust their values upward, whereas the decreasing group should adjust their anchor downward. This would create a much larger discrepancy between the two groups' valuations of the final sound than existed for the initial sound. Figure 13.4 shows that the prediction is supported. Initial valuations of the 600-second tone in the decreasing order condition ($M = \$5.16$) were significantly larger than initial valuations of the 100-second tone in the increasing order condition ($M = \$3.78$), $t(88) = 3.1$, $p < .01$, but the difference of $1.38 is not very large. In the second period, both groups evaluated the same 300-second tone, and the valuation in the increasing condition was greater than that of the decreasing condition ($Ms = \$5.56$ and $\$3.65$), $t(88) = 3.5$, $p < .001$. By the final period, the two conditions diverged dramatically, with WTA being much higher in the increasing condition compared with the decreasing condition ($Ms = \$7.15$ and $\$2.01$), $t(88) = 9.4$, $p < .0001$.

We now turn to the rank ordering of the different events in terms of their annoyance (see Table 13.2). Recall that we wanted to see whether the same anchor that influenced subjects' pricing would also influence the way they evaluated the sounds independently of the pricing task. The results showed that the rank ordering of the annoyance of the sound was not influenced by either the anchor, $F(1, 86) = 1.33$, $p = .25$, or the order, $F(1, 86) = 0.221$, $p = .64$. In fact, when we examined the correlation between the rank ordering of

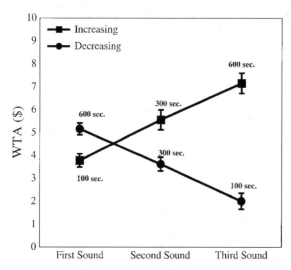

Figure 13.4. Mean WTA (in dollars) for the three annoying sounds. The data are plotted separately for the increasing (100 seconds, 300 seconds, 600 seconds) and the decreasing (600 seconds, 300 seconds, 100 seconds) conditions. Error bars are based on standard errors.

the annoyance of the sound and the initial anchor, the correlation was slightly negative (-0.096), although this finding was not significant, $p = .37$.

In summary, Experiment 3 demonstrates that coherent arbitrariness persists even with randomly generated anchors and larger stakes. In addition, the last part of Experiment 3 provides some evidence that the effect of the anchor on pricing does not influence the evaluation of the experience relative to other experiences.

EXPERIMENT 4: COHERENTLY ARBITRARY VALUATIONS IN THE MARKET

We now consider the possibility that the presence of market forces could reduce the degree of initial arbitrariness or facilitate learning over time. Earlier research that compared judgments made by individuals who were isolated or who interacted in a market found that market forces did reduce the magnitude of a cognitive bias called the "curse of knowledge" by approximately 50% (Camerer, Loewenstein, & Weber, 1989).

To test whether market forces would reduce the magnitude of the bias, we exposed subjects to an arbitrary anchor (as in the second experiment), but then elicited the WTA values through a multiperson auction, rather than using the Becker-Degroot-Marschak (1963) procedure. Our conjecture was that the market would not reduce the bias, but would lead to a convergence of prices within specific markets. Earlier research found that subjects who had bid on gambles in an auction similar to ours adjusted their own bids in response to the market price, which carried information about the bids of other market participants (Cox & Grether, 1996). Relying on others' values can be informative in some purchase settings, but in these markets other participants had been exposed to the same arbitrary anchor. Moreover, having experienced a sample of the noise, subjects had full information about the consumption experience, which makes the valuations of others prescriptively irrelevant.

Fifty-three students from the Massachusetts Institute of Technology participated in the experiment, in exchange for a payment of $5 and earnings from the experiment. Subjects were told that they would participate in a marketplace for annoying sounds and that they would bid for the opportunity to earn money by listening to annoying sounds. They participated in the experiment in groups, varying in size from 6 to 8 subjects. The experiment lasted approximately 25 minutes.

The design and procedure were very similar to Experiment 2, but we increased the high anchor to $1.00 (instead of 50¢) and used an auction rather than an individual-level pricing procedure. As in the second experiment, the sound durations were 10, 30, or 60 seconds, subjects were given three opportunities to listen to each of these sounds, and the order of the durations was manipulated between subjects. In the increasing condition, durations were presented in the order 10, 30, 60 seconds (repeated three times), and in the decreasing condition the durations were in the order 60, 30, 10 seconds (also repeated three times). All subjects first experienced 30 seconds of the same annoying sound that was used in the second experiment. Next, the bidding procedure was explained to the subjects as follows:

On each trial, the experimenter will announce the duration of the sound to be auctioned. At this stage every one of you will be asked to write down and submit your bid. Once all the bids are submitted, they will be written on the board by the experimenter, and the three people with the lowest bids will get the sound they bid for and get paid the amount set by the bid of the fourth lowest person.

Subjects were then asked to write down whether, in a hypothetical choice, a sum of X (10¢ or 100¢, depending on their condition) would be sufficient compensation for them to listen to the sound again. At this point the main part of the experiment started. On each of the nine trials, the experimenter announced the duration of the sound that was being auctioned; each of the subjects wrote a bid on a piece of paper and passed it to the experimenter, who wrote the bids on a large board. At that point, the three lowest bidders were announced, and they were asked to put on their headphones and listen to the sound. After the sound ended the subjects who "won" the sound received the amount set by the fourth lowest bid.

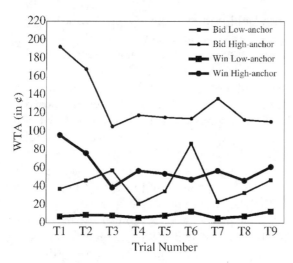

Figure 13.5. Mean bids (WTA) and mean payment as a function of trial and the two anchor conditions.

Results

The general findings paralleled those from the previous experiments. In the low-anchor condition, the average bids were 24¢, 38¢, and 67¢ for the 10-, 30-, and 60-second sounds, respectively (all differences between sound durations are significant within a condition), and in the high-anchor condition, the corresponding average bids were 47¢, $1.32, and $2.11. Overall, mean WTA in the low-anchor condition was significantly lower than WTA in the high-anchor condition, $F(1, 49) = 20.38, p < .001$. The difference in the amount of money earned by subjects in the two conditions was quite stunning: The mean payment per sound in the high-anchor condition was $.59, whereas the mean payment in the low-anchor condition was only $.08.

The main question that Experiment 4 was designed to address is whether the WTA prices for the low- and high-anchor conditions would converge over time. As can be seen from Figure 13.5, there is no evidence of convergence, whether one looks at mean bids or the mean of the prices that emerged from the auction.

Although the bids and auction prices in the different conditions did not converge to a common value, bids *within* each group did converge toward that group's arbitrary value. Figure 13.6, which plots the mean standard deviation of bids in the eight different markets for each of the nine trials, provides visual support for such convergence. To test whether convergence was significant, we first estimated the linear trend in standard deviations across the nine rounds separately for each group. Only one of the eight within-group trends was positive (0.25), and the rest were negative (ranging from 20.76 to 214.89). A two-tailed t test of these eight estimates showed that they were significantly negative, $t(7) = 2.44, p < .05$.

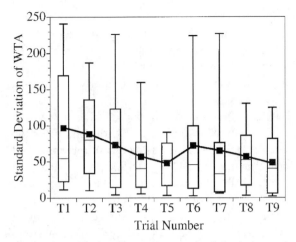

Figure 13.6. The within-group standard deviations of the bids (WTA), plotted as a function of trial.

In summary, Experiment 4 demonstrates that coherent arbitrariness is robust to market forces. Indeed, by exposing people to others who were exposed to the same arbitrary influences, markets can strengthen the impact of arbitrary stimuli, such as anchors, on valuation.

EXPERIMENT 5: THE IMPACT OF MULTIPLE ANCHORS

According to our account of preference formation, the very first valuation in a given domain has an arbitrary component that makes it vulnerable to anchoring and similar manipulations. However, once individuals express these somewhat arbitrary values, they later behave in a fashion that is consistent with them, which constrains the range of subsequent choices and renders them less subject to nonnormative influences. To test this, Experiment 5 exposed subjects to three different anchors instead of only one. If the imprinting account is correct, then the first anchor should have a much greater impact on valuations compared with later ones. On the other hand, if subjects are paying attention to anchors because they believe they carry information, then all anchors would have the same impact as the initial one (similarly, Bayesian updating predicts that the order in which information arrives is irrelevant).

At the end of the pricing part of the experiment, we gave subjects a direct choice between an annoying sound and a completely different unpleasant stimulus. We did this to see whether the influence of the anchor extends beyond prices to qualitative judgments of relative aversiveness.

Forty-four students from the Massachusetts Institute of Technology participated in the experiment, which lasted about 25 minutes. The experiment followed a procedure similar to the one used in Experiment 2, with the following adjustments. First, there were only three trials, each lasting 30 seconds. Second, and most important, in each of the three trials subjects were introduced to a new sound with different characteristics: a constant high-pitched sound (the same as in Experiment 2), a fluctuating high-pitched sound (which oscillated around the volume of the high-pitched sound), or white noise (a broad-spectrum sound). The important aspect of these sounds is that they were qualitatively different from each other, but similarly aversive.

After hearing each sound, subjects were asked if, hypothetically, they would listen to it again for 30 seconds in exchange for 10¢, 50¢, or 90¢ (depending on the condition and the trial number). Subjects in the increasing conditions answered the hypothetical questions in increasing order (10¢, 50¢, 90¢), and subjects in the decreasing conditions answered the hypothetical questions in decreasing order (90¢, 50¢, 10¢). Each of these hypothetical questions was coupled with a different sound. After answering each hypothetical question, subjects went on to specify the smallest amount of compensation (WTA) they would require to listen to 30 seconds of that sound. The same Becker-Degroot-Marschak (1963) procedure used in Experiment 2 determined whether subjects heard each sound again and how much they were paid for listening to it.

After the three trials, subjects were asked to place their finger in a vise (see Ariely, 1998). The experimenter closed the vise slowly until the subject indicated that he or she just began to experience the pressure as painful – a point called the "pain threshold." After the pain threshold was established, the experimenter tightened the vise an additional 1 mm (a quarter-turn in the handle) and instructed the subject to remember the level of pain. Subjects then experienced the same sound and answered the same anchoring question that they had been asked in the first trial. They were then asked if they would prefer to experience the same sound for 30 seconds or the vise for 30 seconds.

Results

Figure 13.7 displays mean WTAs for the three annoying sounds and the two anchoring orders. With respect to the first bid, the low anchor generated significantly lower bids ($M = 33.5$¢) than the high anchor ($M = 72.8$¢), $F(1, 42) = 30.96$, $p < .001$. More interesting is the way subjects reacted to the second bid, which had the same anchor (50¢) for both conditions. In this case, we can see that there was a carryover effect from the first bid, so that the mean WTA price for the sound in the increasing condition ($M = 43.5$¢) was lower than the sound in the decreasing condition ($M = 63.2$¢), $F(1, 42) = 6.03$, $p < .02$. The most interesting comparison, however, is the WTA associated with the third sound. For this sound, subjects in both conditions had been exposed to the same three anchors, but the effects of the initial anchor and the most recent anchor (preceding the final stimulus) were in opposition to each other. In the increasing condition, the initial anchor was 10¢, and the most recent anchor was 90¢. In the decreasing condition, the initial anchor was 90¢, and the most recent anchor was 10¢. If the most recent anchor is stronger than the initial anchor, then WTA in the increasing condition should be higher than the one in the decreasing condition. If the initial anchor is stronger than the most recent anchor, as predicted by the imprinting

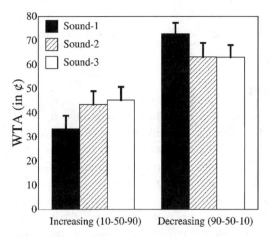

Figure 13.7. Mean WTA (in cents) for the three annoying sounds. In the increasing condition the order of the hypothetical questions was 10¢, 50¢, and 90¢, respectively. In the decreasing condition the order of the hypothetical questions was 90¢, 50¢, and 10¢, respectively. Error bars are based on standard errors.

account, then WTA in the decreasing condition should be higher than WTA in the increasing condition. In fact, WTA was higher in the decreasing condition compared with the increasing condition ($Ms = 63.1$¢ and 45.3¢), $F(1, 42) = 5.82$, $p < .03$. Thus, the initial anchor has a stronger effect on WTA than the anchor that immediately preceded the WTA judgment, even though the initial anchor had been associated with a qualitatively different sound.

Another way to examine the results of Experiment 5 is to look at the binary responses to the hypothetical questions (the anchoring manipulation). In the first trial, the proportion of subjects who stated that they would be willing to listen to the sound they had just heard for X¢ was different, but not significantly so, across the two anchor values (55% for 10¢ and 73% for 90¢, $p > .20$ by χ^2 test). The small differences in responses to these two radically different values supports the idea that subjects did not have firm internal values for the sounds before they encountered the first hypothetical question. On the third trial, however, the difference was highly significant (41% for 10¢ and 82% for 90¢, $p < .001$ by χ^2 test). Subjects who were in the increasing-anchor condition were much more willing to listen to the sound, compared with subjects in the decreasing-anchor condition, indicating that they were sensitive to the change in money amounts across the three hypothetical questions. Consistent with the imprinting account proposed earlier, subjects acquired a stable internal reservation price for the sounds.

The response to the choice between the sound and vise pain revealed that subjects in the increasing-anchor condition had a higher tendency to pick the sound (72%), compared with the decreasing-anchor condition (64%), but this difference was not statistically significant, $p = .52$. These results again fail to support the idea that the anchor affects subjects' evaluations of the sound relative to other stimuli.

EXPERIMENT 6: MONEY ONLY?

The previous experiments demonstrated arbitrariness in money valuations. Neither of the follow-up studies (in Experiments 3 and 5), however, found that the anchoring manipulation affected subsequent choices between the unpleasant sounds and other experiences. This raises the question of whether these null results reflect the fact that the effects of the anchor are narrow or rather that the coherent arbitrariness phenomenon arises only with a relatively abstract response dimension, like money. To address this issue, we conducted an experiment that employed a design similar to that of Experiments 2 through 4 but which did not involve money. Because Experiments 2 through 4 had all demonstrated coherence on the dimension of duration, in Experiment 6 we attempted to demonstrate arbitrariness with respect to duration.

Fifty-nine subjects were recruited on the campus of the University of California at Berkeley with the promise of receiving $5.00 in exchange for a few minutes of their time and for experiencing some mildly noxious stimuli. After consenting to participate, they were first exposed to the two unpleasant stimuli used in the experiment: a small sample of an unpleasant-tasting liquid composed of equal parts Gatorade and vinegar, and an aversive sound (the same as used in Experiments 2 through 4). They were then shown three containers of different sizes (1 oz., 2 oz., and 4 oz.), each filled with the liquid they had just tasted and were asked to "Please answer the following hypothetical question: Would you prefer the middle-size drink or X minutes of the sound?" where X was 1 minute for half the subjects and 3 minutes for the other half (the anchor manipulation). After the initial anchoring question, subjects were shown three transparent bottles with different drink quantities in each (1 oz., 2 oz., and 4 oz.). For each of the three drink quantities, subjects indicated whether they would prefer to drink that quantity of liquid or endure a sound of duration equal to 10 seconds, 20 seconds, 30 seconds, and so forth, up to 8 minutes. (The specific instructions were: "On each line, please indicate if you prefer that duration of the sound to the amount of the drink. Once you have answered all the questions the experimenter will pick one of the lines at random, and you will be asked to experience the sound described on that line or the drink depending on your preference in that line.") To simplify the task, the choices were arranged in separate blocks for each drink size and were arranged in order of duration.

Results

Revealing arbitrariness with respect to tone duration, the anchoring manipulation had a significant effect on tradeoffs between the sound's duration and drink quantity, $F(1, 57) = 24.7, p < .0001$. The mean maximum tone duration at which subjects preferred the tone to the drink (averaging over the three drink

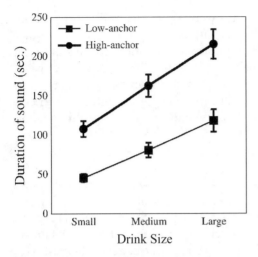

Figure 13.8. Mean maximum duration at which subjects prefers tone to drink. Error bars are based on standard errors.

sizes) was 82 seconds in the 1-minute anchor condition and 162 seconds in the 3-minute anchor condition. Revealing consistency with respect to tone duration, however, subjects were willing to tolerate longer sound durations when the other option involved a larger drink size, $F(2, 114) = 90.4$, $p < .0001$ (see Figure 13.8).

The experiment demonstrates that arbitrariness is not limited to monetary valuations (and, less importantly, that coherence is not an inherent property of duration).[7] In combination with the results of the add-on components of

---

[7] In a discussion of the arbitrary nature of judgments in "contingent valuation" research, Kahneman, Schkade, and Sunstein (1998) and Kaheman, Ritov, and Schkade (1999) point out a similarity to some classical results in psychophysical scaling of sensory magnitude. The well-known "ratio scaling" procedure (Stevens, 1975) asks subjects to assign positive numbers to physical stimuli (e.g., tones of different loudness) in such a manner that the ratio of numbers matches the ratio of subjectively perceived magnitudes. Sometimes the subjects are told that a reference tone has a certain numerical value (e.g., 100) which is also called "the modulus," whereas in other procedural variants, subjects have no reference tone and are left to assign numbers as they please. In the latter case, one finds typically that the absolute numbers assigned to a given physical stimulus have little significance (are extremely variable across subjects), but the ratios of numbers are relatively stable (across subjects). Kahneman et al. (1998, 1999) point out that the money scale used in WTP is formally an unbounded ratio scale, like the number scale used in psychophysics, and hence should inherit the same combination of arbitrary absolute but stable relative levels. However, unlike the psychophysical setting in which the response modulus is truly arbitrary (the subjects do not come to the experiment knowing what a 100-point loudness level is), the WTP response scale is not at all arbitrary. Subjects should know what a dollar is worth in terms of other small pleasures and conveniences. If we had asked subjects to evaluate the sounds in terms of uninterpreted "points" rather than dollars, then we would have duplicated the psychophysical procedure of scaling without a modulus, but in that case, of course, the results would be predictable and uninteresting. In any case, the results of Experiment 6 show that exactly the same pattern of coherent arbitrariness can be obtained with well-defined attributes such as duration and drink size.

Experiments 3 and 5, it suggests that the web of consistency that people draw from their own choices may be narrow. Thus, for example, a subject in our first experiment with a high Social Security number who priced the average wine at $25 would almost surely price the higher quality wine above $25. However, the same individual's subsequent choice of whether to trade the higher quality wine for a different type of good might be relatively unaffected by her pricing of the wine, and hence by the Social Security number anchoring manipulation.

GENERAL DISCUSSION

The main experiments presented here (Experiments 2–4) show that when people assess their own willingness to listen to an unpleasant noise in exchange for payment, the money amounts they specify display the pattern that we call "coherent arbitrariness." Experiment 1 demonstrated the pattern with familiar consumer products, and Experiment 6 showed that the pattern is not restricted to judgments about money. Coherent arbitrariness has two aspects: coherence, whereby people respond in a robust and sensible fashion to noticeable changes or differences in relevant variables, and arbitrariness, whereby these responses occur around a base level that is normatively arbitrary.

Our main focus up to this point was to demonstrate the coherent arbitrariness phenomenon and test whether it is reduced or eliminated by repeated experience, market forces, or higher stakes. Next, we discuss a variety of other phenomena that may be interpreted as manifestations of coherent arbitrariness.

Contingent Valuation

The clearest analogy to our research comes from research on contingent valuation, in which people indicate the most they would be willing to pay for a public benefit (e.g., environmental improvement). Of particular relevance to coherent arbitrariness is the finding that people's WTP for environmental amenities is remarkably unresponsive to the scope or scale of the amenity being provided (Kahneman & Knetsch, 1992). For example, one study found that WTP to clean one polluted lake in Ontario was statistically indistinguishable from WTP to clean all polluted lakes in Ontario (Kahneman & Knetsch, 1992).

Importantly, insensitivity to scale is most dramatic in studies that employ between-subjects designs. When scope or scale is varied within-subject, so that a single person is making judgments for different values, the valuations are far more responsive to scale (see Kahneman, Ritov, & Schkade, 1999; Kahneman et al., 1998).

This effect has even been observed in a study that examined intuitive pricing of common household items. Frederick and Fischhoff (1998) elicited WTPs for two different quantities of common market goods (e.g., toilet paper, applesauce, and tuna fish) using both a between-subjects design (in which respondents valued either the small or large quantity of each good) and a within-subject design (in which respondents valued both the small and large quantity of each good). The difference in WTP was in the right direction in both designs, but it was much greater (2.5 times as large) in the within-subject condition, which explicitly manipulated quantity. This held true even for goods such as toilet paper, for which the meaning of the quantity description (number of rolls) should have been easy to evaluate. Frederick and Fischhoff (p. 116) suggest that this would be a common finding for valuation studies generally – that "valuations of any particular quantity [of good] would be sensitive to its relative position within the range selected for valuation, but insensitive to which range is chosen, resulting in insensitive (or incoherent) values across studies using different quantity ranges." In fact, the tendency for within-subject manipulations to produce larger effects than between-subjects manipulations is a common phenomenon (e.g., Fox & Tversky, 1995; Kahneman & Ritov, 1994; Keren & Raaijmakers, 1988).

Financial Markets

Like the price one should ask to listen to an aversive tone, the value of a particular stock is inherently ambiguous. As Shiller (1998) comments, "Who would know what the value of the Dow Jones Industrial Average should be? Is it really 'worth' 6,000 today? Or 5,000 or 7,000? Or 2,000 or 10,000? There is no agreed-upon economic theory that would answer these questions" (p. 1315). In the absence of better information, past prices (asking prices, prices of similar objects, or other simple comparisons) are likely to be important determinants of prices today. In a similar vein, Summers (1986) notes that it is remarkably difficult to demonstrate that asset markets reflect fundamental valuation. It is possible to show that one or more predictions of the strong markets theory are supported, but "the verification of one of the theory's predictions cannot be taken to prove or establish a theory" (p. 594). Thus, studies showing that the market follows a random walk are consistent with fundamental valuation, but are insufficient to demonstrate it; indeed, Summers presents a simple model in which asset prices have a large arbitrary component, but are nevertheless serially uncorrelated, as predicted by fundamental valuation.

Although the overall value of the market or of any particular company is inherently unknowable, the impact of particular pieces of news is often quite straightforward. If Apple was expected to earn $X in a particular year but instead earned $2X, this would almost unquestionably be very good news. If IBM buys back a certain percentage of its own outstanding shares, this has straightforward implications for the value of the remaining shares. As Summers (1986) points out, the market may respond in a coherent, sensible fashion to such developments even when the absolute level of individual stocks, and of the overall market, is arbitrary.

Labor Markets

In the standard account of labor supply, workers intertemporally substitute labor and leisure with the goal of maximizing utility from lifetime labor, leisure, and consumption. To do so optimally, they must have some notion of how much they value these three activities, or at least of how much they value them relative to one another. Although it is difficult to ascertain whether labor supply decisions have an element of arbitrariness, due to the absence of any agreed-upon benchmark, there is some evidence of abnormalities in labor markets that could be attributed to arbitrariness. Summarizing results from a large-scale survey of pay-setting practices by employers, Bewley (1998) observes that "Nonunion companies seemed to be isolated islands, with most workers having little systematic knowledge of pay rates at other firms. Pay rates in different nonunion companies were loosely linked by the forces of supply and demand, but these allowed a good deal of latitude in setting pay" (p. 485). Wage earners, we suspect, do not have a good idea of what their time is worth when it comes to a trade-off between consumption and leisure and do not even have a very accurate idea of what they could earn at other firms. Like players in the stock market, the most concrete datum that workers have with which to judge the correctness of their current wage rate is the rate they were paid in the past. Consistent with this reasoning, Bewley continues, "Though concern about worker reaction and morale curbed pay cutting, the reaction was to reduction in pay relative to its former level. The fall relative to levels at other firms was believed to have little impact on morale, though it might increase turnover" (p. 485). In other words, workers care about changes in salary but are relatively insensitive to absolute levels or levels relative to what comparable workers make in other firms. This insensitivity may help to explain the maintenance of substantial interindustry wage differentials (see Dickens & Katz, 1987; Krueger & Summers, 1988; Loewenstein & Thaler, 1989). Similarly, coherent arbitrariness is supported by the quip that a wealthy man is one who earns $100 more than his wife's sister's husband.

Criminal Deterrence

Imagine an individual who is contemplating committing a crime, whether something as minor as speeding on a freeway or something as major as a robbery. To what extent will such an individual be deterred by the prospect of apprehension? Research on criminal deterrence has produced mixed answers to this question, with some studies finding significant negative effects of probability or severity of punishment on crime and others reaching more equivocal conclusions. These studies have employed different methodologies, with some examining cross-sectional differences in crime and punishment across states and others examining changes over time. Coherent arbitrariness has important implications for these studies. Like many other types of cost–benefit calculations, assessing the probabilities and likely consequences of apprehension is difficult, as is factoring such calculations into one's decision-making calculus. Thus, this is a domain characterized by value uncertainty where one might expect to observe the coherent arbitrariness pattern. Coherent arbitrariness, in this case, would mean that people would respond sensibly to well-publicized *changes* in deterrence levels but much less to absolute levels of deterrence (for a discussion of similar results in civil judgments, see Sunstein,

Kahneman, Schkade, & Ritov, 2002). We would predict, therefore, that one should find short-term deterrence effects in narrowly focused studies that examine the effect of policy changes, but little or no deterrence effects in cross-sectional studies. This is, indeed, the observed pattern. Interrupted time series studies have measured sizable reactions in criminal behavior to sudden, well-publicized increases in deterrence (Ross, 1973; Sherman, 1990), but these effects tend to diminish over time. The implication that we draw is that the prevailing level of criminal activity does not reflect any underlying fundamental tradeoff between the gains from crime and the costs of punishment.

FINAL COMMENTS

Our experiments highlight the general hazards of inferring fundamental valuation by examining individuals' responses to change. If all one observed from our experiment was the relationship between valuation and duration, one might easily conclude that people were basing their WTA values on their fundamental valuation for the different stimuli. However, the effect of the arbitrary anchor shows that, although people are adjusting their valuations in a coherent, seemingly sensible fashion to account for duration, they are doing so around an arbitrary base value. Moreover, this effect does not diminish as subjects gain more experience with the stimulus or when they provide valuations in a market context.

A key economic implication of coherent arbitrariness is that some economic variables will have a much greater effect than others. When people recognize that a particular economic variable, such as a price, has changed, they will respond robustly but when the change is not drawn to their attention, they will respond more weakly, if at all. This point was recognized early on by the economist John Rae (1834), who noted that:

When any article rises suddenly and greatly in price, when in their power, they are prone to adopt some substitute and relinquish the use of it. Hence, were a duty at once imposed on any particular wine, or any particular sort of cotton fabric, it might have the effect of diminishing the consumption very greatly, or stopping it entirely. Whereas, were the tax at first slight, and then slowly augmented, the reasoning powers not being startled, vanity, instead of flying off to some other objects, would be apt to apply itself to them as affording a convenient means of gratification. (p. 374)

The speed at which an economic variable changes is only one of many factors that will determine whether it is visible to individuals – whether it "startles" the reasoning powers, as Rae expressed it. Other factors that can make a difference are how the information is presented, for example, whether prices of alternative products are listed in a comparative fashion or are encountered sequentially (see Russo & Leclerc, 1991) and whether prices are known privately or discussed. Thus, for example, large salary differentials may be easier to sustain in a work environment in which salary information is not discussed. In sum, changes or differences in prices or other economic conditions will have a much greater impact on behavior when people are made aware of the change or difference than when they are only aware of the prevailing levels at a particular point in time.

These results challenge the central premise of welfare economics that choices reveal true preferences – that the choice of A over B indicates that the individual will in fact be better off with A rather than with B. It is hard to make sense of our results without drawing a distinction between "revealed" and "true" preferences. How, for example, can a pricing decision that is strongly correlated with an individual's Social Security number reveal a true preference in any meaningful sense of the term? If consumers' choices do not necessarily reflect true preferences, but are to a large extent arbitrary, then the claims of revealed preferences as a guide to public policy and the organization of economic exchange are weakened. Market institutions that maximize consumer sovereignty need not maximize consumer welfare.

As many economists have pointed out (e.g., Sen, 1982), the sole psychological assumption underlying ordinal utility is that people will behave consistently. Our work suggests that ordinal utility may, in fact, be a valid representation of choices under specific, albeit narrow, circumstances, without revealing underlying preferences, in any nonvacuous sense of "preference." When people are aware of changes in conditions, such as the change in price in the example just given, they will respond in a coherent fashion that mimics the behavior of individuals with fixed, well-defined preferences. However, they will often not respond reasonably to new opportunities or to hidden changes in old variables, such as price or quality. The equilibrium states of the economy may therefore contain a large arbitrary component, created by historical accident or deliberate manipulation.

ACKNOWLEDGMENTS

We thank Colin Camerer, Shane Frederick, John Lynch, James Bettman, and Birger Wernerfelt for helpful comments and suggestions. We are also grateful for financial support to Ariely and Prelec from the Sloan School of Management, to Loewenstein from the Integrated Study of the Human Dimensions of Global Change at Carnegie Mellon University (NSF grant No. SBR-9521914), and to Loewenstein and Prelec from the Center for Advanced Study in the Behavioral Sciences (NSF grant No. SBR-960123 to the Center, 1996–1997).

14. Tom Sawyer and the Construction of Value

Dan Ariely, George Loewenstein, and Drazen Prelec

In a famous passage of Mark Twain's novel, *Tom Sawyer*, Tom is faced with the unenviable job of whitewashing his aunt's fence in full view of his friends who will pass by shortly and whose snickering promises to add insult to injury. When his friends do show up, Tom applies himself to the paintbrush with gusto, presenting the tedious chore as a rare opportunity. Tom's friends wind up not only paying for the privilege of taking their turn at the fence, but deriving real pleasure from the task – a win–win outcome if there ever was one. In Twain's words, Tom "had discovered a great law of human action, without knowing it – namely, that in order to make a man or a boy covet a thing, it is only necessary to make the thing difficult to attain."

There are no mysteries in what painting a fence entails. Hence, Tom's "law" challenges the intuition that whether a familiar activity or experience is pleasant or unpleasant is a self-evident matter – at least to the person participating in that activity. If true, Tom's law would pose a fundamental challenge to economics. In a world where people don't reliably know what they like, it cannot be assumed that voluntary trades will improve well-being or that markets will increase welfare.

Recent research by psychologists and behavioral economists suggests that Twain's notions about human nature may be on the mark, at least in some situations (Frederick & Fischhoff, 1998; Hsee, Loewenstein, Blount, & Bazerman, 1999; Kahneman, Ritov, & Schkade, 1999; Slovic, 1995; Sunstein, Kahneman, Schkade, & Ritov, 2002). In a set of previous experiments that document a phenomenon we (Ariely, Loewenstein, & Prelec, 2003) labeled "coherent arbitrariness," we showed that valuations of goods and experiences have a large arbitrary component – "arbitrariness." Yet, after one valuation has been made, people provide subsequent valuations that are scaled appropriately relative to the first – "coherence." In one study that illustrates the concept, we sold consumer products ranging in value from $10 to $100 (computer equipment, wine bottles, chocolate boxes, books) to postgraduate business students. Students were presented with one product at a time and were asked whether they would buy it for a price obtained by converting the last two digits of their Social

Reprinted from the *Journal of Economic Behavior & Organization*, vol. 60, pp. 1–10. Copyright © 2006, with permission from Elsevier.

Security number (an essentially random identification number) into a dollar figure – e.g., 34 became $34. After this yes/no response, which we intended to serve as an "anchor" for their later responses (Chapman & Johnson, 1999; Johnson & Schkade, 1989), we elicited their maximum willingness to pay for the product, using a standard incentive-compatible procedure.

Although students were reminded that the Social Security number is a random quantity conveying no information, those who happened to have high Social Security numbers were willing to pay much more for the products. For example, students with Social Security numbers in the bottom 20% of the Social Security number distribution priced on average a 1998 Cotes du Rhone wine at $8.64, whereas those with Social Security numbers in the top 20% of the distribution priced on average the same bottle at $27.91. Because the assignment of Social Security numbers to students is random, we can regard the two groups as identical with respect to their underlying tastes and knowledge of wine. Evidently, the same person can value a given item at $10 or at $30, depending on historical accidents, such as answering questions about randomly generated prices.

If consumers' valuations of goods are so malleable, then why does one observe stable demand curves in the marketplace? A second aspect of the study provides a clue. If one looks across the different goods that were sold, one can see that, although absolute values were surprisingly malleable, subjects did seem to have a sensible idea of the relative values of the different goods. For example, because the information that was provided about the wine (based on *The Wine Advocate* magazine) made it obvious which wine was superior, all students priced the relatively fancy bottle of wine – the 1996 Hermitage Jaboulet "La Chapelle" – higher than the 1998 Cote du Rhone. The students did not know how much they valued either bottle, as demonstrated by the effect of the arbitrary Social Security number, but they did know that the superior wine was worth more than the inferior wine, and they priced them accordingly. A researcher who looked at our data but did not know about the Social Security number manipulation would conclude that these consumers were behaving perfectly in line with economic theory – the more valuable products were indeed priced higher than the less valuable ones. But the effect of the Social Security number manipulation shows that valuations, in fact, incorporated a high degree of arbitrariness.

Although the effect of the arbitrary Social Security number on valuations was dramatic, one could argue that the result crucially exploited subjects' uncertainty about what the goods were worth, either to them or in the market (for resale perhaps). A stronger test required an experience that could not be traded, but that could be experienced, and hence fully understood, before the valuation task. For this purpose, many of the experiments reported in the same paper elicited subjects' willingness to accept compensation in exchange for listening to aversive sounds delivered to subjects through headphones. The benefit of using sounds is that subjects can be given a sample that provides full information about the experience. In an experiment representative of several reported in the paper, we told subjects that they were about to hear an unpleasant sound played over headphones and asked them to consider, hypothetically, whether they would be willing to listen to the sound for 300 seconds in exchange for an amount that they composed from the last three digits of their social security number (e.g., 287 = $2.87). After hearing a sample of the sound and making this hypothetical choice, subjects then stated the smallest amount of money they would accept to actually hear the sound for 100, 300, and 600 seconds. After each response, they endured the sound and received payment if their stated minimum fell below a randomly drawn price for that duration. Even in such a transparent setting, we found that valuations followed the "coherently arbitrary" pattern: Subjects demanded about one and a half times as much to hear the 300-second sound as to hear the 100-second sound, and half again more to hear the 600-second sound. However, subjects with lower ending Social Security numbers demanded much less compensation than those with higher numbers.

These results showed that individuals did not seem to have a preexisting personal dollar value for ordinary products and experiences. Taking these findings as a starting point, the present chapter asks a more basic question: *Do people even have a preexisting sense of whether an experience is good or bad?* Tom's law suggests that they do not – that the exact same experience can be desired or avoided, depending on context and presentation. The three experiments presented here show that individuals can be made to exogenously classify some experiences as either positive or negative, depending on whether the preceding question asked them if they would pay or needed to be paid for the experience in question. Experiment 1 demonstrates the basic effect of Tom's law. The results of Experiment 2 show, further, that after one such arbitrary response is given (as either positive or negative), other responses follow in a seemingly coherent fashion. Finally, to rule out two competing explanations – that the effect can be attributed to the demands of the situation or that subjects use the form of the initial anchoring question to infer the quality of the experience – Experiment 3 demonstrates that Tom's law holds even when the random assignment of individuals to either the "pay" or "be paid" conditions was made transparent (the assignment was set by the last digit of their Social Security number, and both possibilities were presented on the elicitation form).

EXPERIMENT 1

The purpose of the first experiment was to test whether there are experiences that individuals can perceive as either positive or negative. The study was conducted with 146 undergraduate students enrolled in a marketing class at the University of California at Berkeley. At the end of class, respondents were told that, in a week's time, their professor (Ariely, whom they were familiar with) would be conducting a 15-minute poetry reading from Walt Whitman's "Leaves of Grass." Half of the respondents (N = 75) were then asked whether,

Table 14.1. Desire to Listen to a Free Poetry Reading in Experiment 1[a]

Accept Group	
Would you attend the recital for $2?	59% say Yes
Would you attend the recital for Free?	8% say Yes
Pay Group	
Would you pay $2 to attend the recital?	3% say Yes
Would you attend the recital for Free?	35% say Yes

[a] The top panel summarizes the results for the participants who were first asked whether they will accept $2 to listen to poetry. The bottom panel summarizes the results for the participants who were first asked whether they will pay $2 to listen to poetry.

hypothetically, they would be willing to pay $2 to listen to their professor recite poetry. The other half of the respondents (N = 71) were asked whether, hypothetically, they would be willing to accept $2 to listen to their professor recite poetry. After answering one of these hypothetical questions, all respondents were told that the poetry reading scheduled for the following week was going to be free and were asked to indicate if they wanted to be notified via email about its location and time. The goal of this question was to test whether the initial hypothetical question affected whether respondents viewed the experience as positive (meaning that they would like to attend if it was free) or negative (meaning that they would prefer not to attend if it was free).

The results in Table 14.1 show that the poetry reading did not have great appeal: Only 3% of the respondents were willing to pay $2 to listen to Ariely recite poetry. However, most (59%) respondents were willing to endure the recital if they were paid $2. More important for our purpose was the response to the second question. The percentage of respondents willing to attend the free poetry recitation was 35% when they had first been asked if they would pay to attend the recital, but only 8% when they had first been asked whether they would attend the recital in exchange for pay, $t(144) = 4.0, p < .001$. The first response clearly influences whether individuals view the experience as positive or negative.

EXPERIMENT 2

Experiment 2 (conducted with a large undergraduate class at MIT) was designed to replicate Experiment 1 while also examining consistency within an individual across responses. Half of the respondents (N = 91) were first asked whether, hypothetically, they would be willing to pay $10 to listen to Professor Ariely recite poetry for 10 minutes, followed by a request to indicate their monetary valuations for 1, 3, and 6 minutes of poetry reading. The other half (N = 73) were first asked whether, hypothetically, they would be willing to accept $10 to listen to Professor Ariely recite poetry for 10 minutes, followed by a request to

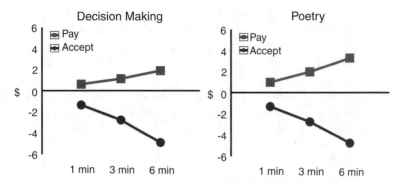

Figure 14.1. Experiment 2: Willingness to pay/accept money in US$ for different durations of experiment participation (left) and poetry (right) as a function of whether the hypothetical question was for paying (squares) or accepting payment (circles).

indicate the minimum they would be willing to accept for 1, 3, and 6 minutes of poetry reading. After indicating their prices, respondents were asked similar questions about their willingness to participate in a study of decision making, which was described to them by giving an example of the Wason card selection task. Subjects who had been asked about their willingness to pay to listen to poetry in the first part of the study were in this part of the experiment asked about their hypothetical willingness to accept $10 for a 10-minute participation in such a study. Subjects who had been asked about their willingness to accept compensation to listen to poetry were asked about their hypothetical willingness to pay $10 for a 10-minute participation in such a study. After this initial hypothetical question, subjects were asked to indicate their monetary valuations for participating in such a study for 1, 3, and 6 minutes.

As is evident from Figure 14.1, valuations were strongly influenced by the initial question. Individuals in the pay condition were, on average, willing to pay for the experience, whereas individuals in the accept payment condition, on average, required compensation to undergo the same experience. Furthermore, respondents consistently indicated higher sums of money for longer durations, whether it was a matter of paying for or being paid for the experience. Respondents did not have a preexisting sense of whether the poetry reading (or participating in a decision-making experiment) was a good or bad experience, but they knew that either way, "more" of the experience warranted greater payment.

EXPERIMENT 3

Our third and final experiment addresses the concern that the subjects might have taken the initial question as a cue about the quality or value of the poetry reading event. To that end we modified the procedure in two ways. First, before providing any response, subjects heard a 1-minute sample of poetry reading from their professor (the experiment took place at a large undergraduate class at MIT). Direct exposure to a sample of the experience should logically diminish the significance of any indirect cues. Second, the instructions made explicit that there were two different conditions and that the assignment to one or the other condition was random.

The experiment began with the professor announcing that in a few days he would be conducting a reading of poetry from Walt Whitman's "Leaves of Grass." For about a minute, he read the first few verses of "Whoever you are holding me now in hand."

> Whoever you are holding me now in hand,
> Without one thing all will be useless,
> I give you fair warning before you attempt me further,
> I am not what you supposed, but far different.
>
> Who is he that would become my follower?
> Who would sign himself a candidate for my affections?
> The way is suspicious, the result uncertain, perhaps destructive,
> You would have to give up all else, I alone would expect to be your sole and
>   exclusive standard,
> Your novitiate would even then be long and exhausting,
> The whole past theory of your life and all conformity to the lives around you
>   would have to be abandon'd,
> Therefore release me now before troubling yourself any further, let go your
>   hand from my shoulders,
> Put me down and depart on your way.

After reading the sample the professor added:

The full reading will last fifteen minutes. The number of seats is fixed, but I would like to get something close to a full house. I am not sure how many of you are interested in attending this, so I have developed a scheme for allocating the seats to those who are most interested in the reading.

The scheme was explained on the instruction sheet. Subjects were first asked to write down the last digit of their Social Security number. If the number was odd, they were asked to answer the first question from the two questions shown later in this paragraph. If the number was even, they were asked to answer the second question from the two questions shown later in paragraph. Both questions were printed on the same page, one immediately above the other. In the first question (odd digits only), they first inserted the last digit of their Social Security number into the sentence: "Would you attend the poetry reading for a payment of $___?" and then answered it with either a Yes or a No. They also answered the same question with the dollar value increased by 50¢ and decreased by 50¢. In the second question (even digits only), they inserted the last digit of their Social Security number into the sentence: "Would you

Table 14.2. Results of Experiment 3[a]

Odd Social Security Number Digit (hypothetical question about being paid to attend) (N = 46)	
% Willing to attend for $ = Soc. Sec. No.	63%
Would attend for free	9%
Mean valuation (st. error)	−$4.46 (.51)

Even Social Security Number Digit (hypothetical question about paying to attend) (N = 35)	
% Willing to pay $ = Soc. Sec. No. to attend	20%
Would attend for free	49%
Mean valuation (st. error)	−$1.13 (.59)

[a] The top panel summarizes the results for participants who were first asked whether they would attend the poetry recital in return for the dollar equivalent of the last digit of their Social Security number. The bottom panel summarizes the results for participants who were first asked whether they would pay the dollar equivalent of the last digit of their Social Security number to attend the poetry recital.

pay $___ in order to attend the poetry reading?" and then answered with a Yes or a No. They also answered the question with a 50¢ increase and decrease.

Subjects then turned to the back page of the questionnaire, which elicited a two-sided demand curve, ostensibly to help the experimenter determine whether he "will need to pay subjects for attending." Here, the format was identical for both groups. Subjects indicated whether they "would attend the recital if paid $10, $9, $8, . . , $1," whether they "would attend the recital if it was for free," and whether they "would pay $1, $2, . . . , $10" to attend the recital. In all, subjects answered 21 pricing questions, which specified their personal value (positive or negative) of the recital to within ±50¢, within the range of +$10 to −$10.

The results are summarized in Table 14.2. On the initial question, a majority of subjects (63%) were willing to attend the recital if paid the dollar equivalent of their digit, but only 20% were willing to pay that equivalent to attend. More importantly, the subsequent valuations of the reading were strongly influenced by the initial question: Of those who initially considered whether they would attend if paid, only 9% were willing to attend for free, in contrast to the 49% who would do so among those who initially considered whether they would pay for the reading, $t(79) = 4.48, p < .0001$. The mean value of the reading was negative for both groups, but much more so for those who had been asked if they would attend for pay, who required on average $4.46 in compensation to attend the reading, as opposed to the $1.13 required by those who were asked if they would pay to attend, $t(79) = 4.28, p < .0001$. Interestingly, in this study the actual digit of the Social Security number had no effect on valuations nor on willingness to attend for free, after controlling for whether the digit was odd or even. It seems that the main effect of the anchoring question was to determine whether the subjects perceived the experience as positive or negative, not *how* positive or negative.

The results of Experiment 3 are consistent with the previous two experiments and effectively rule out an inferential explanation for the "Tom Sawyer" effect. It is hard to imagine how the subject could infer anything about the quality of the poetry reading from a transparently random assignment. The experiment also rules out a demand effect explanation, because any conceivable demand effects would surely be present in exactly the same form across both experimental conditions.

DISCUSSION

Looking around, we see people making a myriad of choices, ranging from the trivial to the profound. People decide whether or not to purchase Big Macs, smoke, run red lights, take vacations in Patagonia, listen to Wagner, slave away at doctoral dissertations, marry, have children, live in the suburbs, vote Republican, and so on. The apparent orderliness in these choices, their stability for a given individual, and the generally correct directional response to changing incentives encourage the belief that the choices are firmly rooted in personal likes and dislikes – in fundamental values.

We suggest, in contrast, that correct directional responses to changing incentives do not provide strong support for fundamental valuation but can follow from the fact that people try to behave in a sensible manner when it is obvious how to do so. If earlier choices are recalled, the next time a similar choice situation arises, decision makers will attempt to behave in a fashion that doesn't violate obvious rules of consistency. If one was willing to pay $X for company Y's stock yesterday, then today's announcement of an unexpectedly profitable quarter should make one willing to pay more than $X. Such a sensible decision-making heuristic, however, tells us nothing about whether yesterday's valuation was reasonable. Economists observe responsiveness to incentives and conclude that individuals are making choices based on fundamental valuation, much as they would if they observed our experiment without awareness of the initial manipulation. However, as Summers (1986) points out in a seminal paper, such responsiveness is a necessary, but not sufficient, condition to establish fundamental valuation. People can respond sensibly to changes in conditions, even when they do so from arbitrary baseline levels.

The degree of coherence and arbitrariness in any set of choices is likely to depend on many factors. Arbitrariness is enhanced by ambiguity in a good or experience. We deliberately selected somewhat ambiguous experiences in the three experiments presented here; clearly, some experiences are unambiguously good or bad. At the same time, many of the most important decisions that people make – about marriage, education, emigration, jobs, and vacations – involve streams of heterogeneous experiences that are arguably even more difficult to assess, and hence are even more vulnerable to arbitrary influences and conventions, than our simple poetry-reading proposition (Ariely & Carmon, 2003). Is a vacation that includes peaceful hours of reading on the beach, delicious meals, but also screaming children, money worries, and stressful transportation a good thing or a bad thing, on balance? This is a difficult question to answer.

Coherence will depend on how easy it is to spot behavioral inconsistencies, which depends in turn on whether numerical scales or indices are available, on how close in time choices are made, and on whether connections among them are obvious. In general, we should expect to see the greatest degree of coherence when an individual who has made an initial choice, and is now faced with a second choice, remembers the first and is aware of how he or she must resolve the second choice so as to be consistent with the first. These requirements are regularly satisfied in a narrow range of decisions, of which financial decisions are perhaps the best example.

But even in highly rationalized financial markets, we have no assurance that the absolute level of prices are "sensible." In financial markets, a stock's value is supposed to reflect individual investors' estimates about that company's expected stream of future dividends, appropriately discounted, but estimates of future dividend streams are inherently uncertain, and there is no agreed-upon discount rate. When we look at short-term fluctuations in prices, we do indeed see stock prices responding appropriately to good or bad news about individual companies or about the economy as a whole. In the long term, however, markets exhibit wide fluctuations that are completely out of line with historical fluctuations in dividend streams, as the economist Robert Shiller has argued persuasively (Shiller, 1998). Day by day, investors can see the coherence in short-term market responses, but nothing signals so clearly whether the market is over- or underpriced as a whole.

The arbitrariness inherent in people's preferences means that decisions can be influenced by nonnormative factors. One such factor is whether the decision maker is exposed to alternatives simultaneously or one at a time (see Hsee et al., 1999). Economics generally assumes that all economic decisions are choices between alternatives. Thus, choosing whether or not to eat out at a restaurant tonight is implicitly a choice between eating at the restaurant versus spending the money in other ways. However, the phenomenon of coherent arbitrariness suggests that whether these choices are implicit or explicit may make a difference.

The distinction between explicitly considering alternative options and not doing so has important implications for empirical, and especially experimental, research in economics. One important design issue, when conducting experiments, is whether to compare different experimental treatments between- or within-subject – whether to expose individual subjects to different treatments or compare treatments across subjects. This decision is often viewed mainly as an issue of time constraints and statistical power. However, considerable research suggests that people can behave quite differently in these two experimental setups. For example, Frederick and Fischhoff (1998) elicited willingness to pay for two different quantities of common market goods (e.g., toilet paper, applesauce, and tuna fish) using both a between-subjects design (in which respondents valued either the small or large quantity of each good) and a within-subject design (in which respondents valued both the small and large quantity of each good). The difference in willingness to pay was in the right direction in both designs, but it was much greater (2.5 times as large) in the within-subject condition, which explicitly manipulated quantity. The usual finding is that within-subject manipulations produce larger effects than between-subjects manipulations (e.g., Fox & Tversky, 1995; Keren & Raaijmakers, 1988), though there are situations in which the opposite occurs.[1]

Why does it matter whether economic decisions are determined by fundamental values? First, coherent arbitrariness violates the basic economic assumptions about how the "general equilibrium" of an economy comes into existence. Modern economics assumes that exogenous consumer preferences interact with "technologies" and initial endowments to produce equilibrium states of the economy – prices and production levels. This analysis falls apart if preferences are themselves influenced by the very equilibrium states that they are presumed to create. Indeed, in the domain of economic decision making, the most salient and potentially powerful anchors may well be the public parameters of the economy itself – the relative prices and scarcities of different commodities. By posting a price for a new product, for instance, a firm invites consumers to consider whether they would purchase at that price and so replicates the anchoring manipulation as conducted in our experiments. If prices and other economic parameters function like public anchors, then consumer tastes no longer exist independently of prices but are *endogenous* to the economy. In that case, the equilibrium price and production levels of the economy are no longer uniquely determined by its physical and human resources and characteristics. Rather, a certain price level may prevail because of collective anchoring, triggered by historical accidents or manipulations.

Second, economics as practiced today is not only a descriptive but also a prescriptive social science. Economists derive the "welfare implications" of alternative policies, such as taxation or trade, in which welfare is defined in terms of the degree to which a policy leads to the satisfaction of individual preferences. Economists have, of course, identified many situations in which free market exchange may not increase welfare (e.g., Schelling, 1978). Such market failures usually arise from interactions between people with asymmetric information

---

[1] Between-subjects experiments produce larger effects than within-subject experiments when the variable being manipulated is something that subjects do not think is normatively appropriate to respond to. Thus, for example, in a study of discrimination, one might get different responses to a Black or White name on a resume if these were presented to separate subjects, but if the same subject saw both, they would be likely to recognize that race was being varied across resumes and, unless they were consciously and deliberately racist, would take efforts to evaluate both similarly.

or from situations in which people do not internalize the costs they impose on each other. The suboptimalities that arise from coherent arbitrariness, in contrast, begin at the level of the individual. If preferences have a large arbitrary component, then even strictly personal consumption choices by fully informed individuals need not maximize welfare.

Moreover, these individual-level effects can be exacerbated by social and market interaction. The literature on information cascades already shows that, when people are uncertain about the quality of consumption goods, initial choices can have big effects on market outcomes. Thus, for example, if a small number of early diners arbitrarily choose new restaurant A over new restaurant B, A can end up packed and B empty. The scope for such effects is enlarged to the degree that people are uncertain about their own preferences. Our research suggests that the degree of uncertainty may be very substantial, even when individuals have relevant experience with the objects of choice.

15. When Web Pages Influence Choice: Effects of Visual Primes on Experts and Novices

Naomi Mandel and Eric J. Johnson

Imagine visiting a commercial Web site that has a rich and colorful graphical background. Is it possible that this background could influence the products you buy? Would these effects occur even if you were knowledgeable about the products offered? Most of our respondents, both experts and novices, tell us that they would be unaffected, but our results suggest otherwise – that even subtle changes in a Web environment can produce changes in the products selected for both expert and novice decision makers.

In this article, we use online experiments to examine how priming affects the construction of preferences (Fischhoff, 1991; Payne, Bettman, & Johnson, 1993; Slovic, 1995) and explore the possibility that priming effects operate through external search as well as internal retrieval. Prior research in priming has demonstrated the resulting increase in accessibility of certain product-related information, suggesting that priming effects are primarily limited to memory-based choice. However, we examine the possibility that priming can change external search, thereby influencing stimulus-based choice. We argue that these effects operate in a manner similar to what Bruner (1957) termed "perceptual readiness" and what Higgins (1996, p. 136) suggests are "goals . . . that produce a readiness to respond to certain goal relevant stimuli."

We also examine how priming might work in the applied setting of online commerce. Because the Internet environment reduces consumer search costs and puts consumers in control of the information they receive, many have argued that the Internet empowers consumers. Indeed, the popular press (e.g., Cortese & Stepanek, 1998) describes the Web as an environment that will improve consumers' decisions. Similarly, some have speculated that the Web induces a state of flow (Hoffman & Novak, 1996) that could diminish or eliminate the effects of unrelated external stimuli. However, this research demonstrates the powerful influence of online atmospherics, in sharp contrast to the media's view that the Web empowers consumers.

A final goal of the current research is the extension of process analysis to Web data in a way that is reminiscent of information search techniques used to test different process theories, such as MouseLab (Johnson, Payne, & Bettman,

1993) or Search Monitor (Brucks, 1988). We argue that the use of such techniques increases sample size, variability in the independent variables, and external validity.

In the remainder of this chapter, we first develop theory that explores the linkages between priming, expertise, searching, and choice. We then present a pretest and two experiments that test our hypotheses. We close by discussing the implication of this work for our understanding of consumer preferences.

THEORETICAL BACKGROUND

The psychology literature has used the term "priming" to refer to several distinct phenomena that share the same underlying mechanism. Exposure to some prior event, the prime, increases the accessibility of information already existing in memory. This increase in accessibility is usually verified by one of three tests. In semantic priming studies (Collins & Loftus, 1975; McKoon & Ratcliff, 1995; McNamara, 1992), subjects decide whether an item such as "dog" is a word or nonword and respond more quickly and accurately when the item is preceded by an associated word, such as "cat." In categorical priming, a person's judgment about a person, product, or object is influenced by the constructs that are activated in an earlier task (Herr, 1989). In feature priming, which we use in our studies, a subject is exposed to a prime that is associated with a particular feature, and this feature is then weighted more heavily in evaluation (Yi, 1990).

Yet, increased accessibility does not always cause the information to be incorporated into subsequent judgment and actions. When certain kinds of information are made accessible, such as stereotypes, they may produce no change in subsequent judgments (Devine, 1989), or they may produce contrast effects (Herr, 1986; Herr, Sherman, & Fazio, 1983; Martin, 1986), in which the resulting judgment is in a direction opposite to that suggested by the prime.

Given the apparent subtlety of the visual primes we use here, which are embedded in the background wallpaper of a Web page, it is unlikely that we will find such a contrast effect in terms of subject reactance. Therefore, we expect this increased accessibility to affect product choice, which we capture in the following hypothesis:

H_1: Subjects will have increased preferences for products that have higher values on the primed attribute.

Alba and Hutchinson (1987) define familiarity as the consumer's number of purchases or experiences with the product class and expertise as the ability to perform product-related tasks successfully. In this study, we examine the moderating roles of both subjective expertise (an individual's perception of his or her own knowledge) and objective expertise (as measured by a quiz; Brucks, 1985).

How are priming's effects moderated by the consumer's level of expertise in the product category? The literature offers two opposing possibilities.

First, expertise might limit the effect of priming. Alba and Hutchinson (1987) have suggested that experts process product information more deeply, whereas novices are more influenced by external factors. Several studies have confirmed that consumers who are inexperienced in the product class are more susceptible to context and response mode manipulations. For example, Coupey, Irwin, and Payne (1998) found that preference reversals between choice and matching tasks are greater when the products are unfamiliar to subjects. Novices have also been found to weigh attributes more heavily when they are made salient through promotion (Wright & Rip, 1980). Finally, Bettman and Sujan (1987) found that in a choice of comparable alternatives (either cameras or computers) priming an attribute such as reliability affected novices' product choices but not those of experts. Therefore, we might expect novices to be more susceptible to the influences of priming than experts.

An alternative hypothesis is that priming indeed affects knowledgeable consumers but through a different route. The key distinction here is how memory-based and external search are used by experts and novices (Alba & Hutchinson, 1987; Hastie & Park, 1986; Johnson & Russo, 1984). Because experts tend to have a surfeit of product knowledge (Brucks, 1985), their preferences may actually be more susceptible to priming than those of novices. Experts are more likely than novices to operate on memory-based evaluations, so they may have more information consistent with the prime available for choice. Consistent with this notion, Chapman and Johnson (1999) have shown that making more information available in memory can increase the effect of anchors, which, they argue, operate through a priming mechanism. Given the two opposing theoretical arguments, we posit two opposing hypotheses:

H_{2a}:   The effect of priming on preferences will be stronger for novices than for experts in the product class; and

H_{2b}:   The effect of priming on preferences will not be moderated by levels of expertise.

The preceding hypotheses do not address the mechanisms that may be involved in any changes in preferences. Even if expertise does not moderate the effect of priming, there may be other mechanisms mediating the effect for both experts and novices. Although Bettman and Sujan (1987) demonstrated that priming could influence the choices of both experts and novices, the authors offered the following as one limitation to their study: "the lack of detailed process measures to determine the microprocessing strategies underlying the observed effects" (p. 146). One purpose of the current chapter is to elucidate such underlying mechanisms.

Many priming researchers have used the increased availability of prime-consistent information in memory to explain their results. However, there is a second possible effect, relevant to external search environments such as these: that primes make certain goals more salient and therefore influence subsequent information search. Biehal and Chakravarti (1986) have shown that brand accessibility can influence the amount of information sought about the brand as well as brand choice. Ratneshwar et al. (1997) showed that subjects demonstrate higher recall and recognition of a product benefit that is made salient. But will individuals more thoroughly search for information about a particular product feature when that feature has been made accessible? To address this question, we examine whether priming influences the consumer's search for information. If priming increases the accessibility of prime-consistent goals, we expect decision makers to pay more attention to prime-consistent information. This leads to the following related hypotheses:

H_3:   Priming will influence the amount of prime-consistent attribute information searched.

This demonstration is important because it would establish that priming influences external as well as internal search.

Because novices depend more on external search, these effects will be stronger for novices than experts. Consequently, we expect these differences in external search to cause observed differences in choice. Therefore, for novices (but not necessarily experts), changes in search should mediate changes in preference. In other words, if the effect of priming operates by making prime-consistent goals more accessible, we expect the resulting differences in search to mediate any observed changes in novices' preferences:

H_4:   For novices, the prime should produce a change in search behavior that mediates the changes in preference.

Experts, in contrast to novices, depend more on memory-based search. Although changes in external search may well occur, we argue that these changes in search, if they occur, will be largely unrelated to changes in choice. Experts will be influenced instead by changes in the accessibility of prime-consistent information in internal memory. Thus, we predict weaker or no mediation for the experts:

H_5:   For experts, the prime may not produce a change in search, and any changes in search will either not mediate or weakly mediate any change in preferences.

We tested these hypotheses with a pretest and two experiments. Experiment 1 assessed the predictions made in Hypotheses 1 and 2, regarding priming's influence on choice and the moderating role of expertise. Experiment 2 replicated the findings of Experiment 1 and tested the predictions of Hypotheses 3 through 5, regarding the interactions between priming, expertise, and search.

PRETEST

In the pretest, we developed Web page backgrounds that primed product attributes in two product categories: cars and sofas. We administered a questionnaire via the World Wide Web in a computer laboratory with 47 subjects. Subjects first read advertisements that differed only in the background wallpaper and then, on a separate page, listed the most important attributes to consider when buying the product.

The two product categories, cars and sofas, were selected because they appealed to both students and nonstudents. Each participant completed the task for both product categories and was randomly assigned to one of two primes for each category. This resulted in a 2 (product, within) × 2 (prime, between) mixed design.

The car Web site contained either a red and orange flamelike background, designed to prime safety, or a green background with small dollar signs, designed to prime price. The sofa Web site contained either a blue background with fluffy clouds, designed to prime comfort, or a green background with embedded pennies, designed to prime price. After examining each ad, subjects proceeded to the next page (containing a neutral gray background and no prime), which asked them to list, in descending order, the four most important attributes to consider when buying a car or sofa. Two independent judges read and categorized the lists of salient attributes.

A categorical analysis of variance (ANOVA) revealed that subjects indeed mentioned primed attributes more frequently than unprimed attributes. In the car task, subjects exposed to the safety prime were more likely than those exposed to price prime to cite safety as important (76% vs. 64%), whereas those exposed to the price prime were more likely than those exposed to the safety prime to cite price as important (82% vs. 52%), $\chi^2(1) = 6.19, p < .01$. Two other features that were frequently mentioned were appearance and fuel efficiency, but these features were equally likely to be mentioned by both treatment groups.

A similar pattern was found for the sofa task. Subjects who saw the comfort prime were more likely than those who saw the price prime to cite comfort as an important feature when buying a sofa (90% vs. 78%), and those who saw price prime were more likely than those who saw comfort prime to cite price (94% vs. 66%), $\chi^2(1) = 7.37, p < .01$. Other features that were frequently mentioned were appearance and durability, but these attributes were equally likely to be mentioned by both treatment groups.

EXPERIMENT 1

Design

The pretest established that visual primes can increase the accessibility of certain attributes. But does priming an attribute increase preference for products that excel on that attribute for both experts and novices? The first experiment tested the effect of priming on preference and choice, and it examined whether expertise would moderate this effect. We employed the same two product classes, cars and sofas, and the same background primes developed in the pretest. Because each subject performed the task for both cars and sofas, product category was a two-level within-subject factor and background prime was a between-subjects factor. Each subject saw only one of two possible primes in a category. On the car Web site, the background on the welcome page was either red and orange with flames (to prime safety) or green with dollars (to prime price). On the sofa Web site, this initial screen was either blue with clouds (to prime comfort) or green with pennies (to prime price). Figures 15.1 and 15.2 show examples of these Web pages for the sofa task. Participants also answered multiple-choice questions about cars and furniture, designed by the experimenters to gain an objective measure of expertise. Using responses to the questions, we divided subjects in two groups, experts and novices.

Method

Seventy-six undergraduate students at a major university completed the 20-minute task in a computer lab in exchange for a $5.00 payment. Before making a choice, subjects first visited a Web page describing a hypothetical shopping site. The page background served as a prime, and subjects' reading was self-paced.

All subjects then went to identical shopping environments with neutral backgrounds that offered two different products within the product category. Each product description contained a picture and links to separate pages that described the product's features. The car features described were the engine, safety, price, and transmission. Both products were on the efficient frontier; the Calabria was a cheaper but less safe sedan, and the Siena was a mini-van that was safer but more expensive.[1] The sofa product page contained the Palisades, an economical but less comfortable sofa, and the Knightsbridge, which was comfortable but expensive. An example of this page is shown in Figure 15.3.

On the next page, subjects were required to make a choice between the two products. In addition, they provided a constant sum measure, which required allocating 100 points between the two products according to preference. Subjects who were primed on price were expected to prefer the cheaper product, whereas subjects who were primed on a quality feature (comfort or safety) were expected to prefer the product that rated higher on that feature. The order of these questions was counterbalanced to prevent a subject's answer on an early question from influencing responses to later questions. Finally, subjects answered questions about their gender, age, and expertise in the product class.

Results

Manipulation Checks. Subjects rated the two cars on safety and price and rated the two sofas on comfort and price to confirm that our product descriptions produced the desired perceptions. Indeed, the Calabria was perceived as

---

[1] Coincidentally, Toyota introduced a minivan called the Sienna several months after this study took place, and thus the fictional minivan's name was changed to Sarina for the second experiment.

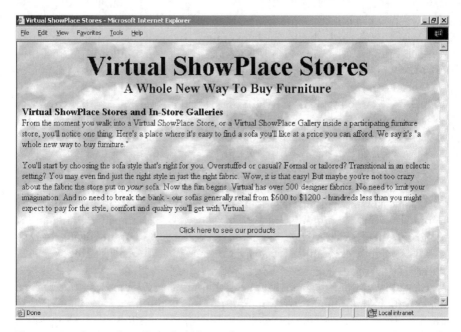

Figure 15.1. Screen for sofa task with comfort prime.

Figure 15.2. Screen for sofa task with price prime.

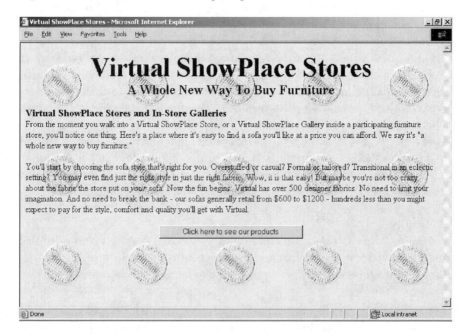

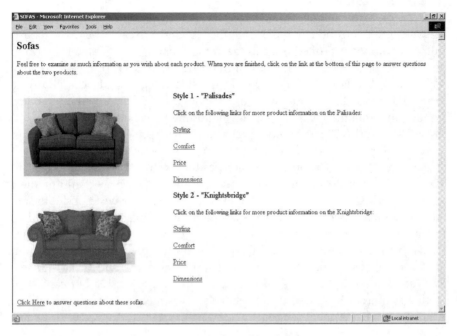

Figure 15.3. Product information screen for sofa task.

a cheaper, $t(138) = 1.78$, $p < .05$, and less safe, $t(138) = 5.31$, $p < .001$, vehicle than the Siena, and the Palisades was perceived as a somewhat cheaper, $t(150) = 1.35$, $p < .10$, and less comfortable sofa, $t(150) = 7.91$, $p < .001$, than the Knightsbridge.[2]

Dependent Measures. In the choice question, subjects were asked to choose the product they would prefer to purchase. A categorical ANOVA, aggregated across both product categories, indicated that subjects who were primed on money were significantly more likely to choose the cheaper, lower-quality product than were those primed on the quality feature (safety or comfort), $\chi^2(1) = 4.84$, $p < .05$. The cheaper car had an average market share of 65.8% among those who had been primed on money and an average market share of 50.0% among those who had been primed on safety. The cheaper sofa had an average market share of 55.8% among those who had been primed on money and an average market share of 38.7% among those who had been primed on comfort. The priming affected choice similarly in the two product categories; the prime × product interaction was not significant, $p > .50$. Also, the prime × expertise interaction was not significant, $p > .50$, indicating that the manipulation similarly affected the choices of both novices and experts.

[2] Because of a minor programming error, we did not receive price ratings from six of the subjects, so these data were excluded from this analysis.

In the constant sum question, subjects were instructed to allocate 100 points between the two products to indicate their preferences. For the car category, subjects who were primed on price gave more points on average ($M = 61.5$) to the cheaper, less safe car than did subjects who were primed on safety ($M = 50.8$), $F(1, 66) = 2.98$, $p < .10$. In the sofa category, subjects who were primed on price gave more points on average ($M = 55.8$) to the cheaper, less comfortable sofa than did those who were primed on comfort ($M = 45.9$), $F(1, 66) = 3.48$, $p < .10$. Therefore, subjects had a stronger preference for the cheaper product when they had viewed a price prime than when they had seen a comfort or safety prime. The order in which products were shown on the page and the order in which questions were presented did not have a significant effect on these findings. Again, the prime × expertise interaction was not significant, indicating that experts were just as susceptible as novices to the manipulation.

Hypothesis 1, which suggested that subjects who were primed on a particular attribute would be more likely to prefer the product that excelled on that attribute, was supported. Somewhat surprisingly, this effect was the same for both experts and novices, inconsistent with Hypothesis 2a but consistent with Hypothesis 2b. Clearly, this result deserves more attention and will be addressed in Experiment 2.

EXPERIMENT 2

Experiment 1 provided supportive evidence that the visual priming of attributes can affect product choice. Intriguing, however, are questions about how this priming occurs, particularly in the face of the somewhat surprising result that experts, like novices, were affected by priming. In the next experiment, we examine the effect of primes on information search, exploring the possibility that primes influence not just the retrieval in memory-based search but external search as well. We demonstrate that these search processes differ for experts and novices, nonetheless producing the same end result.

The results of Experiment 1 suggest an interesting set of possibilities that depend on levels of expertise and the differential effects of priming. Simply put, we posit that both experts' and novices' choices are affected by primes but that these effects have different mechanisms for the experts and novices. Specifically, novices lack much internal product knowledge and rely on the externally provided product information. Here, the effect of priming is primarily in making the feature of price or quality more salient, and it should operate through external search. Thus, for novices, the effect of priming is not necessarily to activate attribute-relevant information in memory but to increase the accessibility of the attribute as a goal. For experts, who have significant product knowledge in memory, the story has the same ending but reaches it by a different path. Here, internal attribute-relevant structures are made accessible by the prime, and it is the internal search of these attributes that produces the change in preferences.

As in Experiment 1, individuals made choices of both cars and sofas after viewing an introductory page containing the prime. Experiment 2 contained several key changes. First, the visual prime was present as a sidebar on every page in the survey, as well as in the wallpaper on the opening page. This gave the site a consistent look and feel and exposed subjects to the prime for longer time periods. Also, subjects were randomly assigned to one of three primes for each category: money, quality, or a plain background. Finally, we measured the number of attributes searched and the amount of time spent looking at attribute information by recording the time when the subject clicked on a hyperlink to retrieve information. We measured entry and exit time for each hyperlink at the user's browser using a JavaScript program that measured the time at the client (as opposed to the server). We also recruited only subjects who had reported modem speeds of 33.6 kilobits per second and higher and who were from the United States.

Method

Design. The experiment used a 2 (product category: cars vs. sofas; within-subject) × 3 (prime: money vs. quality vs. plain; between-subjects) × 2 (order: car task first vs. sofa task first; between-subjects) design. Subjects were 385 Internet users from a panel, who agreed to be contacted for future surveys after filling out an initial sign-up survey. The U.S. panelists represented the current Internet population rather well, with a median age of 29 (just under the population median of between 30 and 34) years and a median income of between $35,000 and $49,999 (which included the population median of $35,225; Bellman, Lohse, & Johnson, 1999). They agreed to participate in the study in exchange for a 1/10 chance to win a $10 phone card and a 1/500 chance to win a $500 prize.

Procedure. On entering the site, subjects viewed some brief instructions and then completed both a car task and a sofa task. Participants viewed an introductory screen containing the background prime and information about the hypothetical commercial site. For the car task, this background was either green with pennies (money prime), red with flames (quality prime), or white (no prime). In addition, this prime was present as a sidebar on all of the other pages in the task. On the next page, subjects viewed the two products in the car category and had the option to link to separate pages to learn information about each car's engine, safety, price, and standard and optional features. The time stamp was recorded each time the participant accessed an attribute page. These time stamps were used to determine whether participants had viewed the attribute information and how long they spent looking at it. Participants then made a choice between the two products and indicated the strength of their preference by distributing a constant sum of 100 points between the two products. On the next page, subjects indicated the importance of safety and price (on a 7-point scale) and rated the two products on safety and price. Participants also completed a car quiz, which gave an objective measure of expertise.

The sofa task was almost exactly the same as the car task, and the subject was again randomly assigned to one of three background primes: blue with clouds (quality), green with pennies (money), or white (plain). Participants had the option to link to attribute pages to learn about the sofa's styling, comfort, price, and dimensions. They then completed choice and constant sum measures and answered a furniture quiz. Finally, after tasks for both categories were completed, subjects answered a funneled series of demand questions and several demographic questions.

Results and Discussion

Manipulation Checks. As expected, participants rated the expensive product choices higher in quality and more expensive than the cheaper product choices. In the car category, subjects rated the Sarina higher than the Calabria on both safety ($M = 5.40$ vs. 4.66), $t(385) = 9.18$, $p < .0001$, and price ($M = 4.89$ vs. 4.47), $t(385) = 6.63$, $p < .0001$. In the sofa category, subjects rated the Knightsbridge higher than the Palisades on both comfort ($M = 5.11$ vs. 4.61), $t(385) = 6.14$, $p < .0001$, and price ($M = 5.15$ vs. 4.28), $t(385) = 10.46$, $p < .0001$.

The individual items on the car quiz were highly intercorrelated (Cronbach $\alpha = .89$), as were the items on the furniture quiz ($\alpha = .87$). These quiz scores were also highly correlated to subjects' own self-ratings of category expertise ($\alpha = .71$ for cars and .75 for sofas). Subjects were divided into three equal groups according to their quiz scores. Furniture experts had higher quiz scores ($M = 9.4$, SD $= .64$) than did moderate subjects ($M = 7.6$, SD $= .49$), who scored higher than novices ($M = 4.7$, SD $= 1.45$). Car experts also had higher quiz scores ($M = 10.9$, SD $= .83$) than did moderate subjects ($M = 8.1$, SD $= 1.16$), who scored higher than novices ($M = 4.3$, SD $= 1.25$). Therefore, we can confidently conclude that three different levels of subject expertise exist in each category.

Analysis of Outliers. Of the 385 subjects, 45 did not browse any product attributes, and these subjects were removed from the analysis. In addition, several subjects were removed for spending an excessive amount of time browsing a single product feature. The mean for all looking times was 13.58 seconds, and the standard deviation was 26.53 seconds. Therefore, we Winsorized the data (Keselman, Lix, & Kowalchuk, 1998; Luce, 1986; Pachella, 1974), defining the outlier cutoff as the mean plus three times the standard deviation, or 93.17 seconds. Twelve subjects had looking times greater than 93.17 seconds, and these were deleted, leaving 328 observations.

Effects of Prime on Choice and Constant Sum. Replicating the results of Experiment 1, choice and constant sum assignments were affected by the background prime. As shown in Figure 15.4, the prime significantly affected market shares of the two products in the choice set. A categorical ANOVA confirmed the main effect of prime on choice, $\chi^2(2) = 26.49$, $p < .001$, and an ANOVA confirmed the overall effect of prime on constant sum assignment, $F(8, 310) = 2.19$, $p < .05$. Planned contrasts revealed that the market share of the cheaper product was significantly higher for those who saw the money prime than for

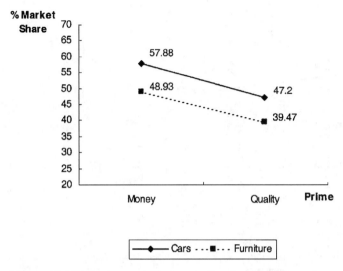

Figure 15.4. Experiment 2: Preference for the cheaper product as a function of prime.

those who saw the quality prime; for cars, $F(1, 310) = 11.16$, $p < .001$; for sofas, $F(1, 310) = 6.80$, $p < .01$. The results in the control condition were quite similar to those in the money prime condition. Therefore, the effects appear to be primarily because of the quality primes and not the money primes.

Consistent with Hypothesis 2b, the effect of priming on choice was not moderated by expertise, as measured by the subject's quiz score, $F(8, 310) = 0.89$, $p > .20$. As in our prior studies, involvement, gender, and task order did not moderate the effect of priming on choice or constant sum assignment.

Effects of Prime on Search and Looking Time. Here, we expected primes to influence the amount of attention paid to the primed attributes, as measured by the number of attributes searched and the amount of time spent looking at attribute information. Our results confirmed Hypothesis 3, that the prime significantly influenced the attention given to prime-consistent attributes. In the car task, subjects primed on safety looked at more safety features ($M = 1.22$ out of 2 possible features) than did those primed on price ($M = 1.03$), $F(8, 285) = 3.92$, $p < .0001$. Subjects primed on price looked at an average of 1.39 price features, whereas those primed on safety looked at 1.28 price features, a difference that was directional but not significant. In the sofa task, subjects primed on comfort looked at an average of 1.24 comfort features, compared with those primed on price, who looked at an average of 0.95 comfort features, $F(8, 285) = 4.83$, $p < .0001$. Meanwhile, those primed on price browsed an average of 1.53 price features, compared with those primed on comfort, who browsed an average of 1.21 price features, $F(8, 285) = 7.39$, $p < .0001$.

We observed a similar pattern for the time spent looking at the attributes, as shown in Figure 15.5. For cars, subjects primed on money looked at price

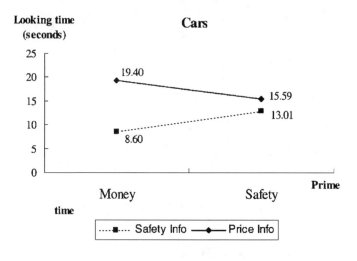

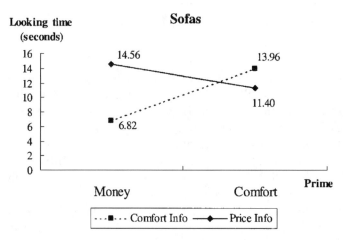

Figure 15.5. Experiment 2: Looking time as a function of prime.

information longer than did those primed on safety, $F(1, 310) = 3.74$, $p < .05$, whereas subjects primed on safety looked at safety information longer than did those primed on money, $F(1, 310) = 5.14$, $p < .05$. For sofas, subjects primed on money looked at price information longer than did those primed on comfort, $F(1, 310) = 10.38$, $p < .001$, whereas subjects primed on comfort looked at comfort information longer than did those primed on money, $F(1, 310) = 10.15$, $p < .001$.[3]

---

[3] In a prior study, not reported here, we examined information acquisition via user logs that record time at the server (rather than the client, as in this study). The results largely replicated the information acquisition analysis that we report here when we analyzed the order of acquisition. However, analysis of time, although directionally correct, suffered from excessive noise due

The Moderating Role of Expertise. The size of priming's effects on both the number of prime-consistent attributes searched and the amount of time spent looking at them depended on the level of expertise, consistent with Hypotheses 4 and 5. In other words, the priming affected the search behavior of novices, but it did not affect the search behavior of experts. Novices were more likely to look at prime-consistent attribute information than prime-inconsistent attribute information. In contrast, experts and moderates were equally likely to look at both primed and nonprimed attributes. This was confirmed by a significant prime × expertise interaction, $F(16, 285) = 2.73$, $p < .0005$. Novices were more likely to look at price information when primed on price in either the car task, $F(1, 274) = 15.97$, $p < .0001$, or the sofa task, $F(1, 274) = 15.84$, $p < .0001$, and more likely to look at quality information when primed on quality in either the car task, $F(1, 274) = 3.85$, $p < .10$, or the sofa task, $F(1, 274) = 16.09$, $p < .0001$. Meanwhile, experts and moderates were equally likely to look at primed and nonprimed attributes, $p > .50$ for all planned contrasts.

Priming also influenced the attribute looking times of novices and experts differently, as demonstrated by a significant prime × expertise interaction, $F(8, 310) = 3.42$, $p < .001$. These results, aggregated across product categories, are shown in Figure 15.6. Consistent with Hypothesis 4, novices who received the money prime spent more time looking at price information and less time looking at quality (safety or comfort) information than did novices who received the quality prime, $F(8, 310) = 5.58$, $p < .0001$. Consistent with Hypothesis 5, there was no significant effect of priming on attribute looking time for individuals of moderate expertise, $F(8, 310) = 0.92$, $p > .50$, or high expertise, $F(8, 310) = 0.87$, $p > .50$.

The Mediating Role of Search. We hypothesized that browsing behavior would mediate the effect of priming on preference for novices (Hypothesis 4) but not for experts (Hypothesis 5). In other words, the relationship between priming and preference would be mediated by external search behavior only for novices, whereas experts would rely more on internal memory search and inference in forming preference. Baron and Kenny (1986) refer to this type of model as "moderated mediation" because the level of expertise moderates the mediational effects of search behavior. To test this model, we used looking time as the mediating variable (as defined by the difference between time spent looking at price information and time spent looking at quality information) and expertise as the moderator. The two measures of search, looking time and number of attributes searched, are highly correlated because an individual must necessarily select an item before spending time looking at it. Not surprisingly, our pattern of results was similar for both measures, and therefore, we present only the looking time results.

to caching and network delays, suggesting that client-side measurement of latencies may be more desirable than server-side measurement in future research. That study also replicated the choice, constant sum, and mediational analysis reported here.

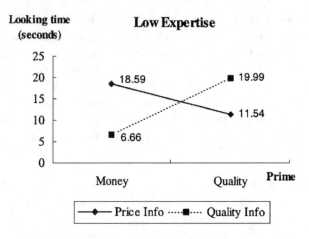

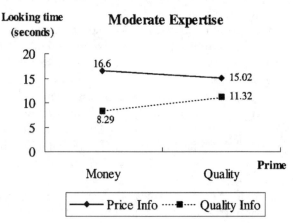

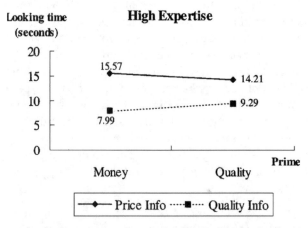

Figure 15.6. Experiment 2: Looking time as a function of prime for varying levels of expertise.

The following relationships were examined following the steps outlined by Baron and Kenny (1986) as necessary to establish mediated moderation: (1) priming influenced preference, as already established, $F(8, 310) = 2.19$, $p < .05$; (2a) priming influenced looking time, $F(8, 301) = 4.24$, $p < .0001$, and looking time influenced preference, $F(1, 300) = 5.55$, $p < .05$; (2b) when looking time was added to Model 1, the effect of priming on preference was reduced, $F(8, 310) = 1.16$, $p > .20$; and (3) finally, the expertise × looking time interaction affected preference, $F(1, 299) = 3.54$, $p < .10$. The presence of this interaction, along with the mediational effects of looking time on the priming-to-preference relation, indicates the existence of moderated mediation.

In other words, mediation occurred only in the low-expertise condition. For low-expertise subjects, priming had a strong effect on looking time, $F(8, 310) = 3.47$, $p < .001$, and when looking time was added to the preference model, it had a significant effect on preference for the cheaper product, $F(1, 283) = 5.66$, $p < .05$, and reduced the effect of priming on preference for the cheaper product, $F(8, 325) = 1.80$, $p < .10$.

In contrast, mediation did not occur for the medium- and high-expertise subjects. Priming had no effect on looking time for medium-expertise, $F(8, 310) = 0.92$, $p > .50$, and high-expertise subjects, $F(8, 310) = 0.87$, $p > .50$. When added to the preference model, looking time did not exhibit a significant effect on preference nor did it reduce the effect of priming for either group of subjects.

Effects of Prime on Attribute Weights and Product Ratings. Despite the observed differences in preference, subjects' ratings of attribute importance were not affected by the primes. The background prime did not affect subjects' stated importance of quality, $F(8, 310) = 1.11$, $p > .50$, or price, $F(8, 310) = 0.32$, $p > .50$, or the difference between the importances of these two attributes, $F(8, 310) = 0.33$, $p > .50$. The product ratings on particular features, such as the safety of the Calabria, also did not differ as a function of the prime, expertise, or their interaction.

Demand Characteristics. As in other experiments, when subjects were asked the purpose of the experiment, not a single individual mentioned the graphics, visuals, pictures, or wallpaper in their responses. On the next page, when they were asked whether they believed that background visuals might have affected their choices, 13.77% of subjects said "yes." However, 9.35% of subjects also agreed that download time might have influenced their choices, and this was not the purpose of our experiment. These effects do not appear to be subliminal; when subjects were asked to recall background wallpaper in an open-ended question, 30 subjects recalled pennies, 25 recalled clouds, and 10 recalled flames.

Discussion. Experiment 2 confirmed that, although visual priming influences choice for both experts and novices, it is accomplished through different mechanisms for these two groups. After viewing the prime, novices are induced to spend more time looking at information related to the primed product feature, which then affects their preferences. However, experts show no differences in looking time as a function of the priming, but they still tend to prefer the product that excels on the primed feature.

What were the experts doing while the novices were searching for information? Although we cannot be sure using our current data, the differences in decision processes we found for experts and novices, combined with the nature of our decision task, put some constraints on possible explanations. First, as Alba and Hutchinson (1987) point out, experts are more likely than novices to make schema-based inferences, allowing them to assume the presence of typical product attributes when this information is not externally available. Therefore, even though our products were hypothetical, the product class is not, and car experts are likely to assume that a typical minivan is safer and more expensive than a typical sedan, without relying on external search. However, when these experts rely on memory rather than external information, they are still likely to use selective processing of attribute information and eliminate brands from consideration on the basis of partial examination of their attributes (Biehal & Chakravarti, 1986). Thus, in response to the prime, experts appear to have selectively considered information in their memories, whereas novices selectively considered external information.

How do we reconcile the unexpected inconsistency between product choice and stated attribute importance? One might suspect reactance to the manipulated background. However, reactance seems unlikely because many subjects recalled the background visuals, but few admitted that the visuals might have affected their responses. Another possibility is that subjects were not conscious of the priming's effect, and thus, they were unable to report it when asked about attribute importance, a result consistent with other research. For example, Bizer and Krosnick (2001) recently found that, whereas increased attitude importance can cause increased attitude accessibility, increased attitude accessibility does not always increase attitude importance. As we have seen, priming may cause increased use of certain attributes, which are then weighted more heavily in choice because of availability, heuristics, and inference. However, it is unlikely that the priming changes the individual's underlying long-term perception of the attribute's importance.

GENERAL DISCUSSION

This research has both applied and conceptual goals. As an applied contribution, it illustrates the potential of the World Wide Web for use in consumer behavior experimentation (Johnson, 2001). In particular, our last study brings together at a fairly economical level a large relevant subject population, producing increased external validity while gathering process data traditionally collected in laboratory settings.

As a conceptual contribution, we demonstrate that visual primes can produce changes in choice, even for experts. We have also suggested that priming affects novices and experts via different routes. For novices, priming effects operate via external search, and these effects mediate the observed changes in preference. For experts, external search remains unchanged and yet their choices are still affected. This finding, although consistent with the idea that experts have richer internal representations of the product class, is inconsistent with the idea that they are less easily swayed by contextual effects.

Although the link between priming, increased accessibility, and judgment has been well documented in both consumer and social psychology, the current work suggests other effects. The first, following from our analysis of novices, is that priming can influence search, which, in turn, influences choice. This result extends the range of the potential influences of priming. Our results with experts are less definitive because we do not directly observe the process that creates changes in choice. However, because we used new brands, unknown to the experts, it is not simply increased accessibility of information about the brands but, perhaps, the use of inferences about the products that are consistent with the prime.

The relationship between priming and expertise is complex and deserves further research. The choices in our studies were hypothetical, and it will be important for future research to demonstrate effects on choices that have greater consequences for subjects. A broader range of primed attributes and products would also lend credibility to these results. Finally, the internal, memory-based process by which priming influences the choices of experts needs to be explored further in future research.

It is important to note that our priming manipulation was not subliminal. All of our subjects could plainly see the background on the first page, and many recalled the wallpaper when asked in the second study. However, an important question is whether or not they were aware of the prime's effect. In fact, most subjects did not think that the wallpaper influenced their choice. Perhaps even more surprisingly, the wallpaper did not change subjects' attribute importance ratings. This lack of awareness suggests that the combination of labile preferences and the fluidity of design in electronic environments may present significant challenges to consumers.

ACKNOWLEDGMENTS

The authors particularly thank the editor, associate editor, and three reviewers for helpful comments, as well as Tory Higgins, Gerald Haübl, and participants at workshops at Ohio State University and Columbia University for useful comments and suggestions. This research has been supported by the Columbia School of Business, the Columbia Center for the Decision Sciences, and the member firms of the Wharton Forum for Electronic Commerce.

16. When Choice Is Demotivating: Can One Desire Too Much of a Good Thing?

Sheena S. Iyengar and Mark R. Lepper

Ne quid nimis. [In all things moderation.]
> – Publius Terentius Afer (Terence), c. 171 B.C. (Bovie, 1992)

It is a common supposition in modern society that the more choices, the better – that the human ability to manage, and the human desire for, choice is infinite. From classic economic theories of free enterprise, to mundane marketing practices that provide customers with entire aisles devoted to potato chips or soft drinks, to important life decisions in which people contemplate alternative career options or multiple investment opportunities, this belief pervades our institutions, norms, and customs. Ice cream parlors compete to offer the most flavors; major fast-food chains urge us to "Have it *our* way."

On the face of it, this supposition seems well supported by decades of psychological theory and research that has repeatedly demonstrated, across many domains, a link between the provision of choice and increases in intrinsic motivation, perceived control, task performance, and life satisfaction (Deci, 1975, 1981; Deci & Ryan, 1985; Glass & Singer, 1972a, 1972b; Langer & Rodin, 1976; Rotter, 1966; Schulz & Hanusa, 1978; Taylor, 1989; Taylor & Brown, 1988). In a typical laboratory study, the intrinsic motivation of participants is compared across two conditions: one in which participants are given a choice among half a dozen possible activities and a second in which participants are told by an experimenter which specific activity to undertake (Zuckerman, Porac, Lathin, Smith, & Deci, 1978). The recurring empirical finding from these studies is that the provision of choice increases intrinsic motivation and enhances performance on a variety of tasks.

Moreover, the positive consequences of choice are often apparent even in contexts where the choice itself is trivial or incidental (Cordova & Lepper, 1996; Dember, Galinsky, & Warm, 1992; Swann & Pittman, 1977). Indeed, many important theories in social psychology, including attribution theory (e.g., Kelley, 1967, 1973), dissonance theory (e.g., Collins & Hoyt, 1972; Cooper & Fazio, 1984; Linder, Cooper, & Jones, 1967), and reactance theory (e.g., Brehm, 1966),

Originally published in the *Journal of Personality and Social Psychology*, vol. 79, pp. 995–1006.

all presume that even purely illusory perceptions of choice will have powerful effects (Langer, 1975; Lefcourt, 1973; Lewin, 1952).

Although prior research has made a compelling case for the psychological benefits of the provision of choice, there remain some potential limitations to this literature. Consider one seemingly trivial, yet potentially important, methodological characteristic of prior studies: that the number of options presented in previous experiments was characteristically small, typically between two and six alternatives. It would appear, then, that what prior research has actually shown is that choice among relatively limited alternatives is more beneficial than no choice at all. Presumably, of course, constraints on the number of options offered in past choice studies were imposed primarily for the sake of convenience; however, real-world situations often provide more than a limited selection, sometimes even an overwhelming number of options. What happens when the range of alternatives becomes larger and the differences among options become relatively small?

Certainly, there are cases when even a vast array of choices may still have beneficial effects. Imagine a group of people who arrive at a new restaurant, for example, all hoping to order their personal favorite dishes. Obviously, the more items offered on the menu, the more satisfied these customers will be, on average. More generally, in preference-matching contexts, in which people enter hoping to find some particular product or service they already know themselves to prefer, larger numbers of options should increase the likelihood that they will be successful in their search.

On the other hand, a growing body of research also suggests that people can have difficulty managing complex choices. To begin with, research has shown that as the attractiveness of alternatives rises, individuals experience conflict and as a result tend to defer decision, search for new alternatives, choose the default option, or simply opt not to choose (Dhar, 1997; Shafir, Simonson, & Tversky, 1993; Shafir & Tversky, 1992). Furthermore, consumer research suggests that as both the number of options and the information about options increases, people tend to consider fewer choices and to process a smaller fraction of the overall information available regarding their choices (Hauser & Wernerfelt, 1990).

In fact, studies show that the selection, evaluation, and integration of information are all clearly affected by the available number of options; this suggests that, as the complexity of making choices rises, people tend to simplify their decision-making processes by relying on simple heuristics (Payne, 1982; Payne, Bettman, & Johnson, 1988, 1993; Timmermans, 1993; Wright, 1975). For instance, a comparison of the decision strategies of people presented with three, six, or nine alternatives revealed that 21% used an elimination strategy in the case of three options, 31% used an elimination strategy in the case of six options, and 77% used an elimination strategy when there were nine options (Timmermans, 1993). The increase in the percentage of participants who used an elimination strategy as the number of alternatives grew was also accompanied by a decrease in the percentage of information used. This sharp decrease in the number of attributes considered as problem complexity increases suggests that information overload may produce a change to a noncompensatory but more efficient decision rule.

The three studies presented in this chapter, therefore, examine for the first time the possibility that there may be differential motivational consequences of encountering contexts that offer a limited (i.e., psychologically manageable), versus an extensive (i.e., psychologically excessive), number of choices. Specifically, the *choice overload* hypothesis underlying these studies is that, although the provision of extensive choices may sometimes still be seen as initially desirable, it may also prove unexpectedly demotivating in the end.

In these studies, limited-choice conditions were operationalized as contexts that offered roughly the same number of options (approximately six) as used in past research (e.g., Zuckerman et al., 1978). In comparison, extensive-choice conditions were operationalized as contexts in which participants would have some reasonably large, but not ecologically unusual, number of options.

In addition, to provide a clear test of the choice overload hypothesis, several additional methodological considerations seemed important. On the one hand, to minimize the likelihood of simple preference matching, care was taken to select contexts in which most participants would not already have strong specific preferences. On the other hand, to minimize the potential importance of effortful information search, care was also taken to select tasks for which "right" and "wrong" choices would be subjective, so that the effort involved in making a choice would be largely a function of personal preferences. Finally, across experiments, we sought to examine this hypothesis in both field and laboratory settings. Using these criteria, then, the present studies tested the hypothesis that having a limited and more manageable set of choices may be more intrinsically motivating than having an overly extensive set of choices.

STUDY 1

In this first field experiment, consumers shopping at an upscale grocery store encountered a tasting booth that displayed either a limited (6) or an extensive (24) selection of different flavors of jam. The two dependent measures of customers' motivation were their initial attraction to the tasting booth and their subsequent purchasing behavior.

METHOD

Participants and Experimental Site

Study 1 involved a field experiment that examined the motivational consequences of limited versus extensive choice in an upscale grocery store (Draeger's Supermarket) located in Menlo Park, California. This grocery store is of particular interest because its salient distinguishing feature is the extraordinary selection it offers, especially when compared with large grocery chains. For instance, Draeger's offers roughly 250 different varieties of mustard, 75 different varieties of olive oil, and over 300 varieties of jam. In addition, because of the regular presence of tasting booths at this store, shoppers are frequently offered sample tastes of the enormous array of available products. As a result, this store provided a particularly conducive environment in which a naturalistic experiment that used tasting booths could be conducted.

On two consecutive Saturdays, neither of which fell on a long holiday weekend, a tasting booth was set up inside the grocery store. Over the course of these two 5-hour experimental periods, the behavior of approximately 754 shoppers was observed. Among the 386 customers present in the store during the hours when the extensive-choice booth was displayed, only 242 actually encountered the display. Among the 368 customers present in the store during the hours when the limited-choice booth was displayed, only 260 actually encountered the display. By observation, the customers who stopped at the booth were typically middle-aged Caucasians; approximately 62% of these customers were women and 38% were men.

Product Selection

Exotic Jams. Before the study, the number of brands and selections within a number of product categories were carefully catalogued. On the basis of the following criteria, the product selected as the experimental stimulus was Wilkin & Sons (Purveyors to Her Majesty the Queen) jams. To control for potential differences that might arise from different types of packaging or advertising, it was necessary to find one brand for which there was a sufficiently large variety to constitute an extensive-choice condition. (In total, Wilkin & Sons has 28 varieties of jams.) In addition, careful attention was given to selecting a product with which most consumers would be familiar, yet not so familiar that preferences would already be firmly established. Hence, to ensure that potential customers would not just reach for the more traditional flavors such as strawberry and raspberry, these common flavors were removed from the set of 28, leaving a choice set of 24 more exotic flavors. Finally, because the dependent measure involved purchasing behavior, a relatively inexpensive product needed to be chosen. The price of Wilkin & Sons jams ranged from $4 to $6.

Jam Preferences Survey. To ensure that the limited-choice set consisted of neither the most preferred nor the least preferred jam flavors, a preliminary survey of 30 Stanford University undergraduates examined individual preferences for the 24 flavors of jam. These students were provided a list of the 24 exotic jam flavors and were asked, "Please read the following list of jams. Put a star next to the two best-sounding jams, in your opinion. Put a check mark next to two good but not excellent-sounding jams, and an X next to the two worst-sounding jams." On the basis of this preliminary survey, kiwi and peach jams were selected to represent the two most preferred jams, black cherry and three-fruits marmalade were selected to represent the moderately tasty jams, and lemon curd and red currant were selected to represent the least preferred jams.

Procedure

Two research assistants, dressed as store employees, invited passing customers to "come try our Wilkin and Sons jams." Shoppers encountered one of two displays. On the table were either 6 (limited-choice condition) or 24 (extensive-choice condition) different jams. On each of two Saturdays, the displays were rotated hourly; the hours of the displays were counterbalanced across days to minimize any day or time-of-day effects.

Initial Testing. Consumers were allowed to taste as many jams as they wished. All consumers who approached the table received a coupon for a $1-discount off the purchase of any Wilkin & Sons jam. Afterwards, any shoppers who wished to purchase the jam needed to go to the relevant jam shelf, select the jam of their choice, and then purchase the item at the store's main cash registers. As a result, regardless of the tasting-booth display encountered by each customer, all potential buyers of Wilkin & Sons products necessarily encountered the entire display of flavors.

An inconspicuous observer recorded the number of customers who approached the table, as well as the number of passers-by who did not stop. A second observer, also unobtrusive, made educated guesses about the ethnicity, age, and gender of each customer who did stop at the tasting booth.

In addition, a random sample of solicitations was tape-recorded and later presented to two independent raters, unaware of both the conditions and hypotheses of the study, who rated each solicitation on a 1 to 5 Likert scale of "friendliness," ranging from *not at all friendly* to *very friendly*. Overall, the average friendliness score was high ($M = 4.5$), and the correlation between the raters was high, $r = .90, p < .0001$. Subsequent analyses on these scores showed that the solicitations did not vary according to condition, $F(1, 99) = .86$, not significant.

Subsequent Purchasing. On the bottom left-hand corner of each discount coupon was a code indicating the condition assignment and gender of each consumer. Other numbers and letters surrounded these codes to lead customers to believe that the code represented a coupon scan number. Coupons could be redeemed over a period of 1 week.

RESULTS

The central aim of Study 1 was to examine whether the number of options displayed affected consumers' initial attraction to or subsequent purchase of the displayed product. As noted, more women than men stopped at the booth; however, there were no gender differences by condition, either for initial attraction or for subsequent purchasing behavior.

Initial Attractiveness of Selections

To what extent does having extensive choice initially seem desirable? Of the 242 customers who passed the extensive-selection display of jams, 60% (145) actually stopped at the booth. In contrast, of the 260 customers who passed the limited-selection display of jams, only 40% (104) stopped. Thus, consumers who encountered the extensive-choice condition were more attracted to the booth than consumers exposed to the limited-choice condition, suggesting that the variety provided in the extensive-choice condition was initially more attractive, $\chi^2(1, N = 502) = 19.89, p < .001.$[1]

One might imagine that consumers who encountered 24 different jams would sample more flavors than would those who encountered 6 different varieties. In fact, however, there were no significant differences, $F(1, 245) = 0.83, ns;$ consumers in the extensive-choice condition sampled an average of 1.50 jams (range = 1–2), whereas consumers in the limited-choice condition sampled an average of 1.38 jams (range = 1–2).

Subsequent Purchasing Behavior

Is the initial attractiveness of extensive choice also reflected in subsequent purchasing behavior? Our findings suggest not: Nearly 30% (31) of the consumers in the limited-choice condition subsequently purchased a jar of Wilkin & Sons jam; in contrast, only 3% (4) of the consumers in the extensive-choice condition did so, $\chi^2(1, N = 249) = 32.34, p < .0001.$ Thus, consumers initially exposed to limited choices proved considerably more likely to purchase the product than consumers who had initially encountered a much larger set of options.

DISCUSSION

These findings are striking. Certainly, they appear to challenge a fundamental assumption underlying classic psychological theories of human motivation and economic theories of rational choice – that having more, rather than fewer, choices is necessarily more desirable and intrinsically motivating. The findings from this study show that an extensive array of options can at first seem highly appealing to consumers, yet can reduce their subsequent motivation to purchase the product. Even though consumers presumably shop at this particular store in part because of the large number of selections available, having "too much" choice seems nonetheless to have hampered their later motivation to buy.

There are, however, several potential limitations to this initial field experiment. To begin with, it is possible that consumers in the limited-choice condition believed that there was something special about the specific six jams displayed, especially after they became aware of the multitude of other options available on the shelf. Such a belief could have made the limited-choice consumers more prone to purchase jam. Consequently, it is worth considering whether the pattern of results would be altered if the limited-choice condition

---

[1] In keeping with current guidelines, because the cell sizes in the present studies were substantial (Siegel, 1956) and because there were more than five times as many subjects as there were cells (Delucchi, 1983), it was not deemed necessary to perform a correction for continuity.

were operationalized such that participants were not aware of the multitude of other options potentially available.

In addition, the contrasting displays of jam may have invited motivationally differing consumer groups. Although the display of 24 jams may have aroused the curiosity of otherwise uninterested passers-by, the display of 6 jams may have appealed to store customers who were more serious about the purchasing of jam. To rule out this possibility, it was necessary to examine the motivational consequences of limited versus extensive choices with a sample of participants who were not given the opportunity to self-select their condition assignment.

Finally, because consumers in both conditions sampled no more than two jam flavors, it is possible that the consumers in the extensive-choice condition felt that they did not have sufficient time to determine their preferences. Although consumers in both conditions were allowed the freedom to peruse and to sample as many of the displayed flavors as they wished, social pressure or time constraints may have prevented them from taking full advantage of this opportunity. Thus, one might question whether the obtained differences in motivation would be eliminated if participants in both conditions were given the opportunity to peruse their options in an unconstrained, nonpublic context.

Study 2 endeavored to address these concerns and to generalize the findings from Study 1 to an educational setting, in which measures of actual performance, as well as choice, could be observed. Thus, in Study 2, participants in the limited-choice condition were not aware of any options beyond those in the limited-choice set. Similarly, careful attention was given to choosing a task that enabled participants to spend as much time as they wished in perusing their choices. Moreover, unlike Study 1, Study 2 employed a yoked design; the limited-choice set was rotated such that for every item encountered by an extensive-choice participant, there was a limited-choice participant who had encountered the same item.

STUDY 2

In Study 2, students in an introductory social psychology class were given the opportunity to write a two-page essay as an extra-credit assignment. Students were given either 6 or 30 potential essay topics on which they could choose to write. Intrinsic motivation was assessed by comparing the percentage of students who completed the assignment across the two conditions and the quality of the essays written in each condition.

METHOD

Participants
One hundred ninety-seven students in an introductory social psychology class at Stanford University served as the participants in this study. The class included 116 women and 81 men. In addition to attending biweekly lectures,

all students were required to attend smaller weekly discussion sections led by five graduate student teaching assistants. The students were divided into 10 discussion sections; each of the five teaching assistants led 2 sections. Sections included anywhere from 8 to 26 students. Four students ultimately dropped the class and were therefore excluded from the analysis.

Procedures

As part of the course, all students were required to watch the movie, *Twelve Angry Men*. Related to this requirement, an extra-credit assignment was offered, and it was the administration of this extra-credit opportunity that provided the context for a naturalistic experiment.

Before Thanksgiving week, extra-credit assignments were distributed to the students. All assignments included the following instructions:

Instead of having section next week, all students will be required to watch a movie being shown in room 40 on Monday, November 25, between 7–9 PM. After watching the movie, you can obtain two extra credit points on your next midterm examination by writing a response paper to the movie. The following is a list of possible questions you can write about. Papers should be approximately one to two pages typed, double spaced, and are due Tuesday, December 3, in class. If you choose to do this assignment, you must circle the paper topic and attach this page to your response paper.

After reading these instructions, students found themselves confronted by either 6 different essay topics (limited-choice condition) or 30 different essay topics (extensive-choice condition). All essay questions dealt with topics related to the material covered in the course. Careful attention was given to selecting essay topics that were comparable in difficulty, and analyses of performance revealed no differences as a function of the specific topic chosen.

In all, there were six different versions of the extra-credit assignment. In addition to the 30-topic assignment, five versions of the 6-topic assignment were created, such that all of the items from the list of 30 were counterbalanced across the five limited-choice assignments.

Students were first informed of the movie requirement during the weekly section meeting before Thanksgiving week. To minimize the possibility that students would notice the different versions, assignments were handed out in the section meetings rather than in class lectures. At this time, the teaching assistants distributed these assignments, with an identical verbal description, reinforcing the information about the opportunity for students to gain two extra points on their next midterm. On no occasion were students led to believe that their essays would be graded. On the contrary, they were explicitly told that their performance on the assignment was irrelevant to the receipt of the two points.

Because each of the five teaching assistants administered two separate sections, one of these two sections was assigned to the limited-choice condition and the other was assigned to the extensive-choice condition. In this way, five sections of students received 6 essay topics and five sections of students received 30. Because the number of students per section varied, it was not possible to assign equal numbers of students to the two conditions. As a result, 70 students were assigned to the limited-choice condition, whereas 123 students were assigned to the extensive-choice condition. No differences were found across the five teaching assistants in terms of assignment completion; students assigned to one teaching assistant were just as likely to do the extra-credit assignment as students assigned to another teaching assistant.

Dependent Measures

Two measures assessed students' subsequent motivation in the two conditions. The first was the percentage of participants who chose to write an essay. The second was the quality of the essays produced.

As previously indicated, the students were told that their performance on these extra-credit assignments would have no effect on their class grades. Nevertheless, it was of interest to determine whether the number of alternatives available might also affect performance quality. Accordingly, two graduate students, unaware of both the participants' choice conditions and the hypotheses of this experiment, graded each of the response papers for both content and form using two 10-point scales, which ranged from *extremely poor* to *excellent*.[2]

When grading for content, two factors were taken into consideration. The first was the accurate depiction and appropriate use of social-psychological concepts. The second was the use of clear examples from the film that related and mapped onto the different social-psychological processes being discussed. The inter-rater correlation for content scores was $r = .70$, $p < .0001$. The form score similarly assessed students' facility on two dimensions. First, each paper was judged on whether it had clear structure (e.g., "Did the introductory paragraph define a hypothesis?"). Second, the papers were evaluated on technical proficiency – spelling, grammar, and the like. The inter-rater correlation for form scores was $r = .89$, $p < .0001$. Because there was considerable agreement across the two graders on both content and form, their ratings were averaged, yielding one content and one form score per student.

RESULTS

Preliminary Analyses

The central point of interest in Study 2 lay, once again, in the comparison of participants' responses across the two experimental conditions of limited versus extensive choice. Because preliminary analyses showed no differences as a function of gender and no interactions between gender and condition on either measure, the data were collapsed across this factor.

---

[2] No actual grade proved lower than a "5," and grades were not restricted to whole numbers.

Assignment Completion

Did the number of choices provided on the instruction sheet actually influence the percentage of students who completed the assignment? Overall, 65% (126) of the students chose to do the assignment. There was, however, a significant effect of condition, $\chi^2(1, N = 193) = 3.93$, $p < .05$. Of the 70 students assigned to the limited-choice condition, 74% turned in the assignment. In contrast, of the 123 students assigned to the extensive-choice condition, only 60% chose to complete the assignment.

Quality of Essays

Were these differences in students' willingness to write an essay also reflected in differences in the quality of these essays? For content, there was a main effect for condition, $F(1, 124) = 4.18$, $p < .05$. On average, students assigned to the limited-choice condition performed slightly, although significantly, better ($M = 8.13$, $SD = 0.95$) than those assigned to the extensive-choice condition ($M = 7.79$, $SD = 0.91$). A similar main effect was found for form, $F(1, 124) = 4.64$, $p < .03$. On average, students in the limited-choice condition scored higher ($M = 8.04$, $SD = 1.33$) than students in the extensive-choice condition ($M = 7.59$, $SD = 1.02$).

Because measures of content and form proved significantly correlated ($r = .52$, $p < .0001$), content and form grades were also averaged to give one overall grade. The condition effect was also significant for this overall measure, $F(1, 124) = 5.65$, $p < .02$, with students in the limited-choice condition receiving higher grades ($M = 8.09$, $SD = 1.05$) than those in the extensive-choice condition ($M = 7.69$, $SD = 0.82$).

One might ask whether the observed differences in motivation or performance could somehow have been driven by differences in students' prior performance in the class. There were, however, no differences in class midterm performance by condition among the students who completed the extra-credit assignments, nor were there differences in midterm performance between those who subsequently did or did not choose to do the assignment.

DISCUSSION

The findings from Study 2 both confirm and expand on the findings from Study 1. The results from both studies suggest that the provision of extensive choices does not necessarily lead to enhanced motivation when compared with contexts that offer a limited array of choices. Quite the opposite seems to be the case. In both studies, people actually seemed to prefer to exercise their opportunity to choose in contexts where their choices were limited, and, in Study 2, they even performed better in such limited-choice contexts.

Particularly counterintuitive, from the perspective of traditional models, is the finding that the same choice selected from a limited-choice set can lead to better performance than if the same option had been selected from an extensive-choice set. Interestingly, in contrast to prior studies, the measure of performance in the present experiment was designed to reflect intrinsic motivation. Because none of the participants thought that their essays would be evaluated, the quality of the paper they wrote should have been primarily a function of their personal interest and motivation.

Thus, the results of Studies 1 and 2 support the hypothesis that extensive-choice contexts may be initially more appealing but are subsequently more likely to hamper people's intrinsic motivation. Although these field experiments provide compelling empirical evidence to support this hypothesis, they shed little light on the mediating mechanisms underlying choice overload. What, then, are the processes that produce the decreases in subsequent motivation exhibited in contexts that offer extensive choices?

One possibility is that people encountering overly extensive choices use a choice-making heuristic that necessarily leads them to feel less committed to exercising their preferences. Previous research has argued that limited-choice contexts invite people to engage in rational optimization – to try to decide which option in a set is the single best one for them. By contrast, choosers in extensive-choice contexts may endeavor to balance the tradeoffs between accuracy and effort, adopting simplifying heuristic strategies that are much more selective in their use of available information (Christensen-Szalanski, 1978, 1980; Payne et al., 1988, 1993). Consequently, extensive-choice contexts may invite people merely to "satisfice" – to stop when they find any choice that seems acceptable (Mills, Meltzer, & Clark, 1977; Simon, 1955, 1956). In other words, when people have "too many" options to consider, they simply strive to end the choice-making ordeal by finding a choice that is merely satisfactory, rather than optimal. Doing otherwise would demand more effort than seems justified by the prospective increase in utility or satisfaction. Hence, one might predict that people who encounter extensive choices should report making a less informed decision and should be more likely to opt for a default choice (Hauser & Wernerfelt, 1990; Payne, 1982; Shafir, Simonson, & Tversky 1993; Shafir & Tversky, 1992). Similarly, choosers opting to satisfice in extensive-choice contexts should also report being less confident of their choices and less likely to expect to be satisfied with their particular choices.

A contrasting possibility is that choosers in extensive-choice contexts may actually feel more committed to the choice-making process; that is, that they may feel more responsible for the choices they make because of the multitude of options available. These enhanced feelings of responsibility, in turn, may inhibit choosers from exercising their choices, out of fear of later regret. In other words, choice makers in extensive-choice contexts might feel more responsible for their choices given the potential opportunity of finding the very best option, but their inability to invest the requisite time and effort in seeking the so-called best option may heighten their experience of regret with the options they have chosen. If so, choosers in extensive-choice contexts should perceive the choice-making process to be more enjoyable given all the possibilities available. They should at the same time, however, find it more difficult and frustrating given the potentially overwhelming and confusing amount of information to be considered.

Study 3, therefore, sought both to provide an instantiation of the phenomenon of choice overload in a controlled laboratory setting and to supplement the findings from the last two studies by including a number of measures designed to test the two opposing hypotheses outlined earlier. To test the first hypothesis – that people encountering extensive choices tend to use a satisficing heuristic, whereas people encountering limited choices tend to use an optimizing heuristic – Study 3 examined choosers' expectations regarding the choices they had made.

As before, after participants had encountered either a limited array or an extensive array of options in this study, they were asked to make a choice. Unlike the prior two studies, however, before being given the opportunity to sample the selection they had made, choosers' expectations about this choice were assessed. Participants provided predictions about how satisfied they would be with their stated preference – whether they expected the choice they made to be merely "satisfactory" or "among the best." Participants also indicated whether they had chosen a default option and reported how well informed they felt about the choice they had made. To test the second hypothesis – that people in extensive-choice contexts feel more responsible for the choices they make – several affect items were added to Study 3. Specifically, after making their choices, but before sampling their choices, participants were asked to provide ratings of their enjoyment, difficulty, and frustration during the choice-making process. Later, after sampling their choices, they provided ratings of satisfaction and regret.

Finally, Study 3 also included a no-choice control condition. Inclusion of this third group allowed us to examine whether differences between the limited- and extensive-choice groups were the result of increases in motivation among limited-choice participants and/or decreases in motivation among extensive-choice participants.

STUDY 3

In Study 3, participants initially made a selection from either a limited array or an extensive array of chocolates. Subsequently, participants in the experimental groups sampled the chocolate of their choosing, whereas participants in the control group sampled a chocolate that was chosen for them. Participants' initial satisfaction with the choosing process, their expectations concerning the choices they had made, their subsequent satisfaction with their sampled chocolates, and their later purchasing behavior served as the four main dependent measures in this study.

Conceptually, then, the design of Study 3 involved three groups: limited choice, extensive choice, and a no-choice control condition. Because it seemed important to control for the number of alternatives presented across the choice and no-choice conditions, half of the participants in the no-choice conditions were shown the same 6 choices as participants in the limited-choice condition, whereas the other half were shown the full array of 30 choices, as were participants in the extensive-choice condition.

Because the choice-condition participants and their no-choice counterparts were treated identically up through the administration of the first set of dependent measures, analyses of these measures will involve only comparisons of those exposed to limited displays versus those exposed to extensive displays. Once participants had been given either their own selection or an arbitrarily assigned chocolate to taste, however, comparisons of limited-choice and extensive-choice participants to those in the no-choice control condition then became relevant.

METHOD

Participants

One hundred thirty-four students from Columbia University were randomly assigned to one of three conditions. There were 33 participants in the limited-choice condition, 34 participants in the extensive-choice condition, and 67 participants in the no-choice condition. This sample included 63% women and 37% men. The ethnic distribution of the participants was 55% Caucasian, 25% Asian, 5% Latino, 4% African American, and 11% other.

To eliminate any participant who might have an aversion to chocolate, all potential participants were prescreened on the basis of two questions. First, all potential participants were asked, "Do you like chocolate?" Only those who responded "yes" to this item were then recruited to be participants in this study. Second, participants were asked, "How often do you eat Godiva chocolates?" Responses were coded as "never," "occasionally," or "frequently." Because it was believed that high familiarity with Godiva flavors and varieties might confound a participant's behavior within this study, only those participants who responded "never" or "occasionally" were recruited for this study. Approximately 92% of all potential participants met these two criteria and were invited to be part of the study.

Instruments

Decision-Making Measures. A questionnaire was designed to examine participants' affective responses to the choice-making process and their expectations after making a choice. To prevent participants' responses from being biased by the outcome of their choices, we asked them to complete the questionnaire after they had chosen which chocolates they wished to sample, but before they had been given the opportunity to sample their choice. All items called for ratings on a Likert scale ranging from 1 (*not at all*) to 7 (*extremely*).

To test the hypothesis that people encountering extensive choices can expe-rience the choice-making process as both enjoyable and overwhelming, the questionnaire examined participants' perceptions of the choice-making pro-cess. Specifically, participants were asked about the extent to which they felt the choice-making process had been enjoyable ("How much did you enjoy mak-ing the choice?"), difficult ("Did you find it difficult to make your decision of which chocolate to pick?"), or frustrating ("How frustrated did you feel when making the choice?"). They also predicted how satisfied they would be if they had the opportunity to sample their chosen chocolate ("How satisfied do you think you will be if you sample this chocolate?").

To evaluate whether people encountering limited choices are more likely to optimize (i.e., to seek the very best option) whereas people encountering exten-sive choices are more likely to satisfice (i.e., to accept any satisfactory option), two items were created to examine participants' expectations regarding their choices. To measure perceived satisficing, we asked participants to provide rat-ings for, "How confident are you that this chocolate will satisfy you?" To exam-ine perceived optimizing, we asked "How confident are you that this chocolate will be among the best you've ever had?" Similarly, to evaluate whether people in an extensive-choice context feel less informed and are therefore more prone to choose a default option, we also asked participants, "Do you feel that you made a well-informed decision on the chocolate you picked?" and, "Is this a chocolate that you would normally pick?"

Sample-Satisfaction Measures. The satisfaction measures were designed to inquire about participants' overall satisfaction with their sampled chocolates. Specifically, these questions assessed participants' actual satisfaction with the chocolate they had consumed, their regrets about the chocolate they had tasted, and their satisfaction with the number of choices they had been given. Exper-imental participants reported their satisfaction with their chosen samples, of course, whereas control participants reported their satisfaction with a choco-late that had been chosen for them.

To test the hypothesis that participants exposed to extensive choices would be less satisfied with their choices than participants exposed to limited choices, three items examined participants' satisfaction with their sampled chocolates: "How satisfied were you with the chocolate you tasted?"; "How much did you enjoy the sample you tasted?"; and "How tasty was the chocolate you sampled?" All responses were given on Likert scales, ranging from 1 (*not at all*) to 7 (*extremely*).

Similarly, to test whether any potential decrease in satisfaction among people encountering overly extensive choices would be accompanied by an increase in regret, two items were included to measure regret: "How much do you regret eating the chocolate you tasted?" and "Do you think that there were chocolates on the table that tasted much better?" Both items were answered on 7-point Likert scales, ranging from 1 (*no, not at all*) to 7 (*yes, completely*).

Because one can only infer through behavioral measures in Studies 1 and 2 whether 30 or 24 choices actually constituted an overly extensive choice set, Study 3 included a manipulation check in which participants were asked their perceptions about the number of choices provided. Specifically, participants were asked: "When initially given the task to pick a chocolate from the display, do you think the selection should have included more kinds of chocolates?" Responses were given on a 7-point Likert scale, with 1 labeled *I felt that I had too few to choose from*, 4 labeled *I had the right number of choices to choose from*, and 7 labeled *No, I had too many to choose from*.

Demographic Measures. At the conclusion of the experiment, all participants completed a brief demographics questionnaire. This questionnaire inquired about participants' age, ethnicity, gender, and affiliation with Columbia University.

Experimental Procedures

As participants entered the laboratory, the experimenter directed them to sit at a round table on which there was one of two different displays of chocolates. In the limited-choice display, participants encountered one row of 6 different flavors of Godiva chocolates; in the extensive-choice display, participants encountered 30 different chocolates, arranged in five rows of 6. Next to each chocolate was a label indicating its "official" Godiva name (e.g., "Grand Marnier Truffle"). When designating the composition of the five rows, careful attention was given to ensuring that similar flavors were not in the same row (e.g., a Strawberry Cordial would not be assigned to the same group as the Raspberry Cordial). In those conditions in which participants encountered only six chocolates, the five groups were rotated such that for every chocolate encountered in the extensive-choice display there was a possibility of the same chocolate being encountered in the limited-choice display.

The experimenter gave participants the following cover story for the study: "We're doing a marketing research study that examines how people select chocolates. What I would like you to do is take a look at the names of the chocolates and the chocolates themselves, and tell me which one you would buy for yourself." All participants then proceeded to choose the chocolate they would wish to have.

Because prior research suggests that people making a choice among four alternatives sometimes take less time than people making a selection between two (Hendrick, Mills, & Kiesler, 1968; Kiesler, 1966), the amount of time spent deciding which chocolate to sample was also recorded in this study. Once the participants pointed to a chocolate, they were asked to complete the decision-making measures described earlier.

Next, participants encountered the manipulation of choice. In the two choice conditions, the experimenter offered the participants the opportunity to sample the chocolate they had chosen. In contrast, in the no-choice condition, the participants were not permitted to sample the chocolate they had chosen but were instead told, "We have some sample chocolates that have been chosen for you at random. These are [e.g.,] 'Milk Chocolate Truffles.'" The experimenter then opened a box containing eight identical chocolates, which were not of the participants' choosing, and asked the participants to take one. As in prior studies (Zuckerman et al., 1978), we used a yoked design, so that the same chocolates chosen by participants in the choice conditions were the ones offered to participants in the no-choice condition.

After sampling the chocolate, participants completed the sample satisfaction measures and the demographics questionnaire described previously. Next, the experimenter led the participant to believe that the experiment had concluded, saying, "Thanks. We appreciate your time. You can go see the manager for your compensation in room three."

In the payment room, a second experimenter, unaware of the condition assignments, greeted the participants. This experimenter offered the subject a choice of receiving a payment of either $5 or a box containing four Godiva chocolates ordinarily priced at $5: "As you know, your compensation is $5 for being in the study. You can choose between getting $5 in cash or a box of Godiva chocolates that is worth $5. Which one would you like for participating in the survey?" Boxes bearing the emblem of Godiva were visible to the participants as they walked into the room. The number of participants who opted for the box of chocolates constituted the final dependent measure.

One potential problem with these experimental procedures is that although the first experimenters were unaware of the hypotheses underlying the study, they were necessarily aware of the experimental manipulations. As a result, one might reasonably wonder whether the experimenters might vary their behavior across conditions. Therefore, all experimental sessions were videotaped, and 40 sessions (10 from each choice condition and 20 from the no-choice condition) were randomly selected for coding by external raters. Two raters unaware of the hypotheses and the experimental manipulations rated the friendliness of the two experimenters across the 40 sessions on a 5-point Likert scale. There was considerable agreement across the two raters ($r = .69, p < .0001$), and their responses were therefore averaged. This average friendliness score ($M = 2.86$, $SD = 0.78$) did not vary by condition, $F(2, 36) = .01$, ns, and there were no interactions between condition and experimenter, $F(2, 36) = .22$, ns.

RESULTS

Preliminary Analyses

Our primary aim in Study 3 was to examine differences in satisfaction, purchasing behavior, and related measures across limited-choice, extensive-choice, and no-choice conditions. Before turning to these central issues, however, we first examined the effects of gender and ethnicity on these various measures. No significant differences were observed on any of the dependent variables as a function of these factors. Nor were there any significant interactions between these two factors and experimental conditions. Hence, the data were collapsed across these demographic variables.[3]

Finally, preliminary analyses also provided an empirical examination of two key presumptions underlying our main analyses. As should be expected, for those measures obtained before the introduction of the choice manipulation, there were no significant interactions between the size of the choice set and participants' later receipt of their own selection or an arbitrary alternative. Similarly, as predicted, there were no significant differences on measures obtained after the choice manipulation between no-choice participants previously exposed to a limited versus an extensive set of available alternatives. Data for the relevant measures were therefore collapsed, as appropriate, across these factors.

Manipulation Checks

Choosing Time. As one might assume, the amount of time spent deciding which chocolate to sample varied significantly by condition, $F(1, 131) = 77.02$, $p < .0001$. Contrary to some prior findings (Hendrick et al., 1968; Kiesler, 1966), participants spent significantly more time (in seconds) deciding which chocolate to sample when there were 30 chocolates ($M = 24.36$, $SD = 12.99$) than they did when there were only six ($M = 8.91$, $SD = 6.02$). However, it should be noted that, unlike this study, previous studies compared choosing times across much smaller choice sets of only two versus four alternatives.

Perception of Choices. Similarly, we examined participants' responses to the question concerning whether they felt the number of choices available was too few, just right, or too many. Here again, there was a significant effect for the number of options presented, $F(1, 132) = 43.68$, $p < .0001$. Participants who encountered 30 chocolates reported feeling that they had been given "too many" ($M = 4.88$, $SD = 1.20$), whereas participants who encountered 6 chocolates reported feeling that the number of alternatives was "about right" ($M = 3.61$, $SD = 1.01$). These data provide direct evidence for our assumption that 30 chocolates would seem an overly extensive choice set.

Decision-Making Measures

Satisficing Versus Optimizing. Were participants in the extensive-choice condition more apt to satisfice, and were participants in the limited-choice condition more apt to optimize? We find no empirical evidence to support such a hypothesis. Contrary to prior predictions (Mills et al., 1977), participants' confidence that they had chosen a satisfactory chocolate versus one of the very best chocolates did not vary as a function of the number of chocolates displayed. The results revealed no differences by condition for questions regarding goals of

[3] Preliminary analyses also asked whether certain chocolates were more preferred than the rest. Although no chocolate was universally chosen, there were four chocolates that were never selected. An examination of the frequency distribution reveals that none of the 30 chocolates was selected more than 12.7% of the time and that the specific choices did not differ by condition.

either satisficing, $F(1, 94) = 0.15$, *ns*, or optimizing, $F(1, 94) = 0.09$, *ns*. Instead, a within-subject analysis of variance (ANOVA) suggested that both the limited- and extensive-choice participants were predictably more confident that their chocolate selection would satisfy them ($M = 5.67$, $SD = 1.21$) than that it would be among the best they had ever had ($M = 4.16$, $SD = 1.59$), $F(1, 190) = 54.75$, $p < .0001$.

Nor were there any differences in anticipated satisfaction. Results indicate that baseline predictions of likely satisfaction did not vary by condition, $F(1, 132) = 0.61$, *ns*, suggesting that participants did not perceive the number of available alternatives to be an important variable in their expected satisfaction with their choices.

In addition, we observed no differences by condition in participants' reports of how informed they felt about their choices or in their tendency to choose default options. Both extensive-choice and limited-choice participants reported being moderately well informed ($M = 4.55$, $SD = 1.39$), $F(1, 132) = 0.14$, *ns*. Likewise, there were no differences in participants' responses to the question of whether they chose a chocolate that they would normally pick, $F(1, 132) = 0.24$, *ns*.

Desirability of Choosing. Is it possible for people to experience extensive choices as being both more enjoyable and more overwhelming? Consistent with the findings of Study 1, participants encountering the extensive options ($M = 6.02$, $SD = 0.75$) reported enjoying the decision-making process significantly more than participants who encountered limited options ($M = 4.72$, $SD = 1.36$), $F(1, 132) = 47.01$, $p < .0001$. Yet, participants offered extensive choices ($M = 4.45$, $SD = 1.79$) also reported finding the decision-making process to be more difficult than did participants offered more limited choices ($M = 3.30$, $SD = 1.49$), $F(1, 132) = 16.38$, $p < .0001$. Likewise, extensive-choice participants ($M = 3.10$, $SD = 1.77$) also reported finding the decision-making process to be more frustrating than did limited-choice participants ($M = 2.24$, $SD = 1.72$), $F(1, 123) = 7.61$, $p < .007$.

Interestingly, there was no significant correlation between the extent to which participants reported enjoying decision-making and the extent to which they found the decision process to be difficult ($r = .11$, *ns*) or frustrating ($r = .11$, *ns*). How difficult participants found the decision-making process, however, was correlated with the extent to which they found the process to be frustrating ($r = .36$, $p < .0001$). Thus, it appears that people can indeed find choosing among too many alternatives to be both enjoyable and overwhelming.

Subsequent Satisfaction

Five questions assessed participants' actual subsequent satisfaction with the particular sample chocolate they were given to taste. Three of these items (i.e., tastiness, enjoyment, and satisfaction) assessed subjective enjoyment directly. Because these questions proved significantly correlated with one another (average $r = .62$, $p < .0001$) and the pattern of results was similar across the three, a composite enjoyment measure was derived by averaging across these three items for each participant. Two other items assessed participants' feelings of regret about the chocolate they had tasted. These two items also proved significantly correlated ($r = .41$, $p < .0001$) and were combined into a composite regret measure. Finally, because these two composite measures (i.e., "enjoyment" and "regret") proved to be highly related ($r = -.55$, $p < .0001$), a single overall sample-satisfaction score was created for each participant by averaging these components (with regret scores, of course, being coded negatively). It should be noted that the three items that constitute the satisfaction measure were converted into z scores before averaging, as were the two items constituting the regret measure.

A one-way ANOVA on these overall satisfaction scores yielded significant differences among conditions, as in the prior studies, $F(1, 122) = 28.02$, $p < .0001$. Tukey comparisons further showed that, in keeping with the results from Studies 1 and 2, participants in the limited-choice condition were significantly more satisfied ($M = 6.28$, $SD = 0.54$) with their sampled chocolates than were participants in the extensive-choice condition ($M = 5.46$, $SD = 0.82$). Tukey comparisons further revealed that on this measure, participants in both choice groups reported themselves to be more satisfied with their chosen chocolates than did no-choice participants ($M = 4.92$, $SD = 0.98$), who had been given samples of chocolates they had not selected.

Purchasing Behavior

Finally, as in the previous studies, we also examined the effects of limited versus extensive choices on participants' ultimate purchasing behavior. Once again, the results demonstrated the significant advantages of a relatively small choice set, $\chi^2(2, N = 134) = 21.84$, $p < .0001$. In particular, participants in the limited-choice condition (48%) were significantly more likely to choose chocolates as compensation, compared with participants in both the extensive-choice condition (12%), $\chi^2(1, N = 67) = 10.78$, $p < .001$, and the no-choice condition (10%), $\chi^2(1, N = 100) = 18.06$, $p < .0001$, which, on this behavioral measure, clearly did not differ from one another.

GENERAL DISCUSSION

In 1830, Alexis de Tocqueville (1830/1969) commented that, "In America I have seen the freest and best educated of men in circumstances the happiest to be found in the world; yet it seemed to me that a cloud habitually hung on their brow, and they seemed serious and almost sad even in their pleasures" (p. 536). More than 100 years later, we are confronted by an empirical instantiation of what some have referred to as "the tyranny of choice" (Schwartz, 2000).

The three studies described in this chapter demonstrate for the first time the possibility that, although having more choices might appear desirable, it may sometimes have detrimental consequences for human motivation. Studies 1, 2, and 3 provide compelling empirical evidence that the provision of extensive choices, though initially appealing to choice makers, may nonetheless undermine choosers' subsequent satisfaction and motivation. Study 1 showed that although more consumers were attracted to a tasting booth when the display included 24 flavors of jam rather than 6, consumers were subsequently much more likely to purchase jam if they had encountered the display of only 6 jams. Study 2 revealed that students in an introductory college-level course were more likely to write an essay for extra credit when they were provided a list of only 6, rather than 30, potential essay topics. Moreover, even after having chosen to write an essay, students wrote higher-quality essays if their essay topic had been picked from a smaller rather than a larger choice set. Finally, Study 3 demonstrated that people reported enjoying the process of choosing a chocolate more from a display of 30 than from a display of 6. However, despite their greater initial enjoyment in the extensive-display condition, participants proved more dissatisfied and regretful of the choices they made and were subsequently considerably less likely to choose chocolates rather than money as compensation for their participation.

But what are the mediating mechanisms underlying this phenomenon of choice overload? Contrary to the predictions of our first hypothesis, we found no empirical support in Study 3 for the theory that choosers in extensive-choice contexts are more likely to use a satisficing heuristic, whereas choosers in a limited-choice context are more likely to use an optimizing heuristic. Instead, at least in this study, choosers in both extensive-choice contexts and limited-choice contexts tended to report using a satisficing heuristic. Nor were there any differences in participants' reports of their anticipated satisfaction with the selections they had made, their feelings of having made an informed choice, or their tendency to opt for a default choice.

Consistent with our second hypothesis, however, we did find considerable empirical support for the theory that choosers in extensive-choice contexts enjoy the choice-making process more – presumably because of the opportunities it affords – but also feel more responsible for the choices they make, resulting in frustration with the choice-making process and dissatisfaction with their choices. Indeed, participants in the extensive-choice condition reported experiencing the decision-making process as being simultaneously more enjoyable, more difficult, and more frustrating. Later, after actually sampling their chocolates, extensive-choice participants reported being more dissatisfied and having more regret about the choices they had made than did limited-choice participants. This greater dissatisfaction and regret exhibited by extensive-choice participants may be the consequence of an initial greater tendency to disengage from the choice-making process, which later results in the choosers' inability to use the psychological processes for the enhancement of the attractiveness of their own choices (see Gilovich & Medvec, 1995). Even more compelling, participants in the extensive-choice condition were actually less likely to opt for chocolates rather than money as their compensation than were their limited-choice counterparts, and they did not differ in this respect from participants in the no-choice control condition.

How can there be so much dissatisfaction in the face of so much opportunity? More than providing a conclusive answer to this question, the present findings raise a number of questions of both theoretical and practical relevance that are worth considering in future research.

Perhaps it is not that people are made unhappy by the decisions they make in the face of abundant options but that they are instead unsure – that they are burdened by the responsibility of distinguishing good from bad decisions. Interviews with several hundred U.S. citizens suggest that modern Americans are uneasy about their current life decisions – that they do not seem to know whether they are doing the right things with their lives, or even what those "right things" are (Bellah, Madsen, Sullivan, Swindler, & Tipton, 1985). Our findings demonstrate that the offer of overly extensive choices in relatively trivial choice-making contexts can have significant demotivating effects, but perhaps the phenomenon of choice overload may be further exacerbated in contexts (such as decisions about major stock purchases or alternative medical treatments) in which (a) the costs associated with making the "wrong" choice, or even beliefs that there are truly "wrong" choices, are much more prominent, and/or (b) substantial time and effort would be required for choosers to make truly informed comparisons among alternatives. In the present studies, care was taken to select tasks for which "right" and "wrong" choices would be subjective and for which the effort involved in making a choice would be largely a function of personal preferences. If one were to compare the present contexts with those in which the choosers perceived there to be significantly "better" and "worse" choices, in domains of personal significance, we might expect even more substantial choice overload effects.

Indeed, whether choosers perceive their choice-making task to be a search for the "objectively best" option, or a search for the one option most reflective of their personal preferences, may fundamentally influence their very preference for choosing. Although prior research has indicated that people will necessarily be intrinsically motivated to make their own choices, the more choosers perceive their choice-making task to necessitate expert information, the more they may be inclined not to choose, and further, they may even surrender the choice to someone else – presumably more expert (e.g., de Charms, 1968; Deci & Ryan, 1985; Langer & Rodin, 1976; Lepper, 1983; Malone & Lepper, 1987; Schulz, 1976; Taylor, 1989; Zuckerman et al., 1978). In Schwartz's (1994) terms, one important paradox confronting the modern world is that as the freedom of individuals expands, so too does their dependence on institutions and other people.

Similarly, if the identity of the choice recipient were varied, we might observe variation in the experience of choice overload among the choosers. Prior research has shown that, when confronted by choices that are anticipated to result in regret, choosers experience decision aversion more so when making choices for others – even when the others exhibit no preferences – than when making choices for themselves (Beattie, Baron, Hershey, & Spranca, 1994). In the three present studies, we did not systematically vary the identity of the choice recipients. Consistent with the results of Beattie and his colleagues, we might expect that if we were to compare choosers making choices for themselves with choosers making choices for others, the latter would show greater choice overload effects in extensive-choice contexts.

Perhaps the experience of choice overload is accompanied by the use of more decision rules that are affective rather than cognitive. Contrary to recent findings by Dhar and Nowlis (1999), the results from our studies suggest that even when a choice-making situation involves an approach–approach conflict, the provision of choices with uniquely good features does not appear to minimize decision aversion. Being confronted by a plethora of options, each possessing unique attributes, may instead simultaneously attract and repel choice makers. One wonders then: Do people use affective experiences aroused by choosing as a heuristic for deciding how they ultimately feel about the product? If not such an affective "bleedover," then what else might be accounting for these effects?

Moreover, even when choices are self-generated, it is possible that overly extensive choices may have demotivating consequences. Because people seem to enjoy extensive-choice contexts more than limited-choice contexts, they may sometimes prefer to make available to themselves many more choices than they can possibly handle. Hence, it would be of considerable theoretical interest to examine the effects of extensive-choice contexts that are self-generated, rather than externally generated as in the present studies.

Finally, it is worth considering attributes of contexts in which the provision of extensive choices does not lead to choice overload. To minimize the likelihood of simple preference matching in the present studies, we selected specific choice-making tasks and prescreened our participant population to ensure that they would not already have strong specific preferences. We all know people who, when confronted by an extraordinary variety of options, know exactly what they want. Is this certainty in preference the result of arduously developed and maintained expertise? The ultimate paradox might be that the only circumstance in which choosers are truly comfortable with extensive choices is when, because of the chooser's previous experience, these choices are perceived as limited in number. Therefore, the precise number of options that would be considered reasonable, as opposed to excessive, may vary as a function of both the chooser's perception of their choice-making goals and their prior expertise with the subject of choice.

Having unlimited options, then, can lead people to be more dissatisfied with the choices they make. Although such a finding may seem counterintuitive to social psychologists long schooled in research on the benefits of choice, the commercial world seems already to know what experimental psychologists are just now discovering. Several major manufacturers of a variety of consumer products have been streamlining the number of options they provide customers. Proctor & Gamble, for example, reduced the number of versions of its popular

Head and Shoulders shampoo from 26 to 15, and they, in turn, experienced a 10% increase in sales (Osnos, 1997). Indeed, even to many of today's humorists, this phenomenon seems already well known. Consider Bill Watterson's (1996) portrayal of one particularly exasperated grocery shopper:

Look at this peanut butter! There must be three sizes of five brands of four consistencies! Who demands this much choice? I know! I'll quit my job and devote my life to choosing peanut butter! Is "chunky" chunky enough or do I need EXTRA chunky? I'll compare ingredients! I'll compare brands! I'll compare sizes and prices! Maybe I'll drive around and see what other stores have! So much selection, and so little time! (p. 107)

ACKNOWLEDGMENTS

We gratefully acknowledge the cooperation and assistance of Draeger's Grocery Store located in Menlo Park, California, for generously offering their store as a field site for conducting Study 1. Similarly, Study 2 could not have occurred without the cooperation and support of Claude Steele at Stanford University who generously allowed his introductory social psychology course to be used as a forum for conducting this field experiment. Further, we would like to thank the numerous graduate students in the Department of Psychology at Stanford University and undergraduate research assistants who generously dedicated their time and effort to help conduct these studies.

17. Constructive Consumer Choice Processes

James R. Bettman, Mary Frances Luce, and John W. Payne

Consumer choices concerning the selection, consumption, and disposal of products and services can often be difficult and are important to the consumer, to marketers, and to policy makers. As a result, the study of consumer decision processes has been a focal interest in consumer behavior for over 30 years (e.g., Bettman, 1979; Hansen, 1972; Howard & Sheth, 1969; Nicosia, 1966). One can infer from recent trends in the nature and structure of the marketplace that the importance of understanding consumer decision making is likely to continue. Rapid technological change, for instance, has led to multitudes of new products and decreased product lifetimes. In addition, new communications media, such as the World Wide Web, have made enormous amounts of information on options potentially available (Alba et al., 1997). Further, consumers are often asked to make difficult value tradeoffs, such as price versus safety in purchasing an automobile, environmental protection versus convenience in a variety of goods, and quality of life versus longevity in complex health care decisions.

How do consumers cope with the decisions they must make, some of which involve difficult tradeoffs and uncertainties? One approach to studying consumer decisions has been to assume a rational decision maker with well-defined preferences that do not depend on particular descriptions of the options or on the specific methods used to elicit those preferences. Each option in a choice set is assumed to have a utility, or subjective value, that depends only on the option. Finally, it is assumed that the consumer has ability or skill in computation that enables calculation of which option will maximize his or her received value and selects accordingly. This approach to studying consumer decisions, often attributed to economists and called rational choice theory, has contributed greatly to the prediction of consumer decisions.

Over the past 25 years, an alternative, information-processing approach to the study of consumer choice (e.g., Bettman, 1979) has argued that rational choice theory is incomplete and/or flawed as an approach for understanding how consumers actually make decisions. The information-processing approach endorses *bounded rationality* (Simon, 1955), the notion that decision makers have limitations on their capacity for processing information. Such limitations

This article has been abridged by the editors. The complete version appeared in the *Journal of Consumer Research*, vol. 25, pp. 187–217. Copyright © University of Chicago Press 1998.

include limited working memory and limited computational capabilities. In addition, decision makers are characterized by perceptions attuned to changes rather than absolute magnitudes and diminishing sensitivity to changes to stimuli (Tversky & Kahneman, 1991). More generally, behavior is shaped by the interaction between the properties of the human information-processing system and the properties of task environments (Simon, 1990).[1]

The notions of bounded rationality and limited processing capacity are consistent with the growing belief among decision researchers that preferences for options of any complexity or novelty are often constructed, not merely revealed, in making a decision (Bettman, 1979; Bettman & Park, 1980; Payne, Bettman, & Johnson, 1992; Slovic, 1995; Tversky, Sattath, & Slovic, 1988). People often do not have well-defined preferences; instead, they may construct them on the spot when needed, such as when they must make a choice. Thus, consumer preference formation may be more like architecture, building some defensible set of values, rather than like archaeology, uncovering values that are already there (Gregory, Lichtenstein, & Slovic, 1993).

The idea of constructive preferences denies that individuals simply refer to a master list of preferences in memory when making a choice and also asserts that preferences are not necessarily generated by applying some invariant algorithm such as a weighted adding model (Tversky et al., 1988). Rather than one invariant approach to solving choice problems, consumers appear to utilize a wide variety of approaches, often developed on the spot. Consumers may also develop problem representations on the spot by structuring or restructuring the available information (Coupey, 1994). One important property of this constructive viewpoint is that preferences will often be highly context dependent. In addition, because decision approaches are developed on the fly, processing will be highly sensitive to the local problem structure. This implies that processing approaches may change as consumers learn more about problem structure during the course of making a decision.

Why are preferences constructive? One reason individuals may construct preferences is that they lack the cognitive resources to generate well-defined preferences for many situations (March, 1978). A second important reason is that consumers often bring multiple goals to a given decision problem.

Preferences are not always constructed; people do have firm and stable preferences for some objects. For example, the first author has a well-defined

---

[1] For a recent comparison of these alternative perspectives on decision making, see McFadden (1999). As McFadden notes, economists vary in terms of the degree to which they believe rational choice theory describes actual decision behavior. A middle ground adopted by some economists is that individuals have a consistent set of preferences but that such preferences become known by the individual (are "discovered") only through thought and experience (Plott, 1996). In a similar vein, Lucas (1986) has argued that economists tend "to focus on situations in which the agent can be expected to 'know' or to have learned the consequences of different actions so that his observed choices reveal stable features of his underlying preferences" (p. S402).

and highly positive value for chocolate. In such cases, consumers may simply retrieve these previously formed evaluations from memory and select the option with the highest evaluation (i.e., affect referral; Wright, 1975).

People are most likely to have well-articulated preferences when they are familiar and experienced with the preference object, and rational choice theory may be most applicable in such situations. Even in such cases, however, situational factors may intrude; although a consumer has a strong preference for chocolate, he or she may sometimes order another dessert. The probability that prior preferences will be retrieved from memory and used will depend on their relative accessibility and diagnosticity, among other factors (Feldman & Lynch, 1988). Also, preferences may be more constructive to the degree that the decision problem is complex or stressful.

As noted earlier, an important implication of the constructive nature of preferences (and evidence for such construction) is that choices often are highly contingent on a variety of factors characterizing decision problems, individuals, and the social context. For example, the following are some of the major conclusions from research on consumer decision making:

1.   Choice among options depends critically on the goals of the decision maker. The option that is selected will depend on the extent to which the consumer's goals are minimizing the cognitive effort required for making a choice, maximizing the accuracy of the decision, minimizing the experience of negative emotion during decision making, maximizing the ease of justifying the decision, or some combination of such goals.

2.   Choice among options depends on the complexity of the decision task. Options that are superior on the most prominent attribute are favored as the task becomes more complex because the use of simple decision processes increases with task complexity.

3.   Choice among options is context dependent. The relative value of an option depends not only on characteristics of that option, but also on the characteristics of other options in the choice set.

4.   Choice among options depends on how one is asked; strategically equivalent methods for eliciting preferences can lead to systematically different decisions.

5.   Choice among options depends on how the choice set is represented (framed) or displayed, even when the representations would be regarded as equivalent by the decision maker on reflection. A key issue in framing is whether the outcomes are represented as gains or losses, with losses affecting decisions more than corresponding gains.

Thus, constructive processing generally implies contingent choices. However, the fact that a choice is contingent need not imply that the processing was constructive, that is, developed on the spot. For example, a consumer may have a well-established, but contingent, preference for hot chocolate on a cold day and a cold soda on a warm day; such a preference is not constructive.

The constructive view of consumer decision making raises fundamental theoretical issues. It is clearly not sufficient to respond "it depends" when asked to describe consumer choices. A major purpose of this chapter, therefore, is to provide a conceptual framework for understanding constructive consumer choice. This framework then allows us to accomplish the two other major goals of the chapter: (1) reviewing consumer decision research with the framework serving as an organizing device, and (2) using this review to find gaps in our knowledge that suggest new research directions. The remainder of the chapter is structured as follows: We begin with a discussion of the nature of consumer decision tasks and decision strategies as necessary background for presenting the proposed framework; then we present the conceptual framework, provide a selective review of the literature on consumer decision making, and enumerate proposed areas for new research.

CONSUMER DECISION TASKS AND DECISION STRATEGIES

Decision Tasks and the Consumer Information Environment

A typical consumer choice, such as the simplified automobile choice task illustrated in Table 17.1, involves a set of alternatives, each described by some attributes or consequences. The set of alternatives can vary in size from one choice to the next, with some choices involving as few as two options and others potentially involving many more (in some cases the two options may be simply to either accept or reject an alternative). The attributes may vary in their potential consequences, their desirability to the consumer, and the consumer's willingness to trade off less of one attribute for more of another. For example, a consumer may be fairly certain about the values of some of the attributes (e.g., horsepower) but be more uncertain about others (e.g., reliability). The consumer may not have information for all of the options on some attributes (e.g., reliability information would not be available for a new model). In addition, some attributes, such as safety, may be difficult for consumers to trade off; making tradeoffs requires possibly accepting a loss on such an attribute,

Table 17.1. An Example of a Consumer Decision Task

Car	Reliability	Price	Safety	Horsepower
A	Worst	Best	Good	Very poor
B	Best	Worst	Worst	Good
C	Poor	Very good	Average	Average
D	Average	Poor	Best	Worst
E	Worst	Very poor	Good	Best

Note: Attributes are scored on 7-point scales ranging from best to worst, with best indicating the most desirable value for the attribute and worst indicating the least desirable value.

with potentially threatening consequences. Finally, some choices may not cor-respond to the previous example, in which all options are from the same product category. Individuals can be faced with choices in which the attributes defining the options may differ, such as deciding whether to spend money on a vacation or on a new stereo. Such choices have been called noncomparable (Bettman & Sujan, 1987; Johnson, 1984). The difficulty of the choice problem faced by the consumer will increase with more options and attributes, with increased uncer-tainty about the values of the attributes, if there are more attributes that are difficult to trade off and if the number of shared attributes is smaller, among other factors.

We previously discussed some general properties of consumer decision tasks. One of the most important findings from prior consumer research is that the same individual may use a variety of different strategies when making deci-sions. A great deal of research has focused on characterizing such strategies, their properties, and the factors influencing their usage. In the next section we provide a brief overview of consumer decision strategies and their properties. We examine the determinants of strategy use in a later section.

Consumer Decision Strategies

Characteristics of Decision Strategies. We begin by considering four pri-mary aspects that characterize choice strategies: the total amount of information processed, the selectivity in information processing, the pattern of processing (whether by alternative [brand] or by attribute), and whether the strategy is compensatory or noncompensatory.

First, the amount of information processed can vary a great deal. For exam-ple, an automobile choice may involve detailed consideration of much of the information available about each of the available cars, as implied by most ratio-nal choice models, or it may entail only a cursory consideration of a limited set of information (e.g., repeating what one chose last time).

Second, different amounts of information can be processed for each attribute or alternative (selective processing), or the same amount of information can be processed for each attribute or alternative (consistent processing). For example, suppose a consumer considering the cars in Table 17.1 decided that safety was the most important attribute, processed only that attribute, and chose car D, with the best value on that attribute. This choice process would involve highly selective processing of attribute information (because the amount of informa-tion examined differs across attributes) but consistent processing of alternative brand information (because one piece of information is considered for each car). The fact that working memory capacity is limited effectively requires selec-tive attention to information. In general, the more selective consumers are in processing information, the more susceptible their decisions may be to factors that influence the salience of information, some of which may be irrelevant.

Third, information may be processed primarily by alternative, in which multiple attributes of a single option are processed before another option is considered, or by attribute, in which the values of several alternatives on a single attribute are examined before information on another attribute is considered. For example, a consumer might engage in attribute processing by examining the price of each of the five cars, concluding that car B was the most expensive, car A was the least expensive, and car C had a very good price. However, the consumer could process in an alternative-based fashion by examining the reliability, price, safety, and horsepower of car A to form an overall valuation of that car. Many standard models of decision making (e.g., weighted adding) assume alternative-based processing, although attribute-based processing is often easier (Tversky, 1972).

Finally, an important distinction among strategies is the degree to which they are compensatory. A compensatory strategy is one in which a good value on one attribute can compensate for a poor value on another. A compensatory strategy thus requires explicit tradeoffs among attributes. Deciding how much more one is willing to pay for very good rather than average reliability in a car involves making an explicit tradeoff between reliability and price, for example. Frisch and Clemen (1994), among others, have argued that making tradeoffs is an important aspect of high-quality, rational decision making. In a noncompensatory strategy, a good value on one attribute cannot make up for a poor value on another. If a consumer decides to choose the safest car, then car D will be chosen regardless of its high price and regardless of the high ratings for car B on reliability or car E for horsepower.

Specific Decision Strategies. There are many different decision strategies, and these strategies can be characterized by the previously discussed aspects of choice processing. One classic decision strategy is the weighted adding strategy. Assume that the consumer can assess the importance of each attribute and assign a subjective value to each possible attribute level. Then the weighted adding strategy consists of considering one alternative at a time, examining each of the attributes for that option, multiplying each attribute's subjective value times its importance weight (e.g., multiplying the subjective value of average reliability in a car times the importance of a car's reliability), and summing these products across all of the attributes to obtain an overall value for each option. Then the alternative with the highest value would be chosen. Weighted adding is therefore characterized by extensive, consistent (not selective), alternative-based, and compensatory processing. Because weighted adding is extensive, compensatory, and involves explicit tradeoffs, it is often considered to be more normatively accurate than heuristics that do not possess these characteristics (Frisch & Clemen, 1994). Weighted adding, however, potentially places great demands on consumers' working memory and computational capabilities. Nevertheless, weighted adding is the decision model that underlies many of the techniques used by market researchers to assess preferences.

The lexicographic strategy provides a good contrast to weighted adding: The alternative with the best value on the most important attribute is simply selected (assuming that there are no ties on this attribute). If a consumer thought that reliability was the most important attribute for cars, he or she could use a lexicographic strategy, examine reliability (and no other information) for all five cars, and choose car B. The lexicographic strategy involves limited, attribute-based, noncompensatory processing that is selective across attributes and consistent across alternatives.

Satisficing is a classic strategy in the decision-making literature (Simon, 1955). Alternatives are considered sequentially, in the order in which they occur in the choice set. The value of each attribute for the option currently under consideration is considered to see whether it meets a predetermined cutoff level for that attribute. If any attribute fails to meet the cutoff level, processing is terminated for that option, the option is rejected, and the next option is considered. For example, car A might be eliminated very rapidly because it has the worst level of reliability. The first option that passes the cutoffs for all attributes is selected. If no option passes all the cutoffs, the levels can be relaxed and the process repeated. One implication of satisficing is that which option is chosen can be a function of the order in which the options are processed. The satisficing strategy is alternative-based, selective, and noncompensatory. The extent of processing will vary depending on the exact values of the cutoffs and attribute levels.

Elimination by aspects combines elements of both the lexicographic and satisficing strategies. Elimination by aspects eliminates options that do not meet a minimum cutoff value for the most important attribute. This elimination process is repeated for the second most important attribute, with processing continuing until a single option remains (Tversky, 1972). In our car example, suppose that the consumer's two most important attributes were reliability and safety, in that order, and that the cutoff for each was an average value. This consumer would first process reliability, eliminating any car with a below-average value (cars A, C, and E). Then the consumer would consider safety for cars B and D, eliminating car B. Hence, car D would be selected. Elimination by aspects is attribute-based, noncompensatory, and the extensiveness and selectivity of processing will vary depending on the exact pattern of elimination of options.

The equal weight strategy, a variation on weighted adding, considers all of the alternatives and all of the attribute values for each alternative. However, processing is simplified by ignoring information about attribute weights. A value is obtained for each alternative by summing all of the attribute values for that option, and the alternative with the highest value is selected. The equal weight strategy is thus a special case of weighted adding if unit weights are assumed. The equal weight strategy has often been advocated as a highly accurate simplification (Dawes, 1979). Processing is extensive, consistent, alternative-based, and compensatory.

The majority of confirming dimensions strategy was first described by Russo and Dosher (1983). Alternatives are processed in pairs, with the values of the two alternatives compared on each attribute, and the alternative with a majority of winning (better) attribute values is retained. The retained option is then compared with the next alternative from the choice set, and this process of pairwise comparison continues until all the alternatives have been evaluated and one option remains. This strategy is a simplified case of a more general model of choice, additive difference (see Tversky, 1969, for a presentation of the additive difference model and a discussion of the relationship between additive difference and adding models). Processing is extensive, consistent, attribute-based, and compensatory.

Alba and Marmorstein (1987) proposed that consumers may evaluate and choose alternatives using counts of the number of good or bad features characterizing the alternatives. Consumers develop cutoffs for specifying good and bad features, and depending on the consumer's focus (i.e., good features, bad features, or both), different versions of the strategy could be developed. Note that this strategy can be seen as a voting rule applied to multiattribute choice, where each attribute has one vote. Weber, Goldstein, and Barlas (1995) provide evidence consistent with such a strategy, noting that encoding of such outcomes is often simple. For example, whether an outcome is a gain or a loss may have a larger impact on preferences than the actual magnitude of the outcome. The amount and selectivity of processing for this strategy, as well as whether it is compensatory or noncompensatory, will depend on the variant of the rule used. Processing is alternative-based for all variants, however.

Consumers also use combinations of strategies. A typical combined strategy has an initial phase in which some alternatives were eliminated and a second phase where the remaining options are analyzed in more detail (Payne, 1976; see Beach's, 1990, image theory for further analysis of the role of elimination or screening processes in decision making). One frequently observed strategy combination is an initial use of elimination by aspects to reduce the choice set to two or three options followed by a compensatory strategy, such as weighted adding, to select among those remaining.

The strategies presented thus far have been those most commonly addressed in consumer research; they range from weighted adding to more heuristic strategies, such as elimination by aspects, that process information in a more selective and noncompensatory fashion. However, recent work utilizing more perceptual approaches (e.g., Simonson & Tversky, 1992) has suggested decision heuristics that are relational and perceptual. Such heuristics emphasize the ratings of a given option relative to other alternatives. For example, one heuristic of this type might examine dominance relationships among pairs of alternatives and use such information to make a choice (e.g., the choice of an asymmetrically dominating option; Huber, Payne, & Puto, 1982). Another exemplar might assess relative tradeoffs between pairs of options on pairs of attributes, compare these tradeoff rates, and use these comparisons as inputs to a choice (e.g., tradeoff contrast; Simonson & Tversky, 1992). Finally, a consumer might compare the relative advantages and disadvantages of an option to those of other options (e.g., compromise effects; Simonson & Tversky, 1992). For other work on relational heuristics, see Drolet (1997).

Tversky and Simonson (1993) propose a model called the componential context model that includes these types of relational heuristics as special cases. Specifically, they define

$$V_B(x, S) = \sum_{i=1}^{n} \beta_i v_i(x_i) + \theta \sum_{y \in S} R(x, y),$$

where $V_B(x, S)$ is the value of option x given a choice set S and background context B, β_i is the weight of attribute i, $v_i(x_i)$ is the utility of the value x_i of option x on attribute i, $R(x, y)$ is the relative advantage of option x over option y, and θ is the weight given to the relative advantage component of the model. The relative advantage term is obtained by taking utility differences between the two options on each attribute and combining them. This model is compensatory, consistent, and has both alternative-based and attribute-based components. It is difficult to assess the amount of processing for this model; for the small problems typically used in this research stream (e.g., three options and two dimensions), the relative advantage component may be assessed essentially perceptually, with little effort. For larger problems where direct perceptual assessment may not be feasible, the amount of processing could be extensive, although simpler versions could certainly be specified (e.g., only examine the relative advantage term for the two attributes with the largest weights). We will return to issues in specifying the processes implied by this model. For another model of relative advantage combining absolute and comparative components, see Shafir, Osherson, and Smith (1989, 1993).

Table 17.2 provides a summary of the properties of the previously considered strategies. Note that one can make inferences about the types of strategies consumers use by observing such characteristics as the amount, selectivity, and degree of alternative-based versus attribute-based processing.

Table 17.2. Characteristics of Decision Strategies

Strategy[a]	Amount of Information Processed	Selective (S) vs. Consistent (C)	Attribute-Based (AT) vs. Alternative-Based (AL)
WADD	Extensive	C	AT
LEX	Limited	S	AL
SAT	Variable	S	AL
EBA	Variable	S	AT
EQW	Extensive	C	AL
MCD	Extensive	C	AT
FRQ	Variable	Variable	AL
CCM	Variable	C	Both AT, AL

[a] WADD = weighted adding; LEX = lexicographic; SAT = satisficing; EBA = elimination by aspects; EQW = equal weight; MCD = majority of confirming dimensions; FRQ = frequency of good and/or bad features; CCM = componential context model.

We have argued earlier that consumer choices are constructive and have briefly noted some of the major findings from research on consumer decision making. In the next section we attempt to provide an integrated framework that can explain such contingent choice patterns.

AN INTEGRATED FRAMEWORK FOR CONSTRUCTIVE CHOICE PROCESSES

Payne (1982) reviewed two major frameworks for understanding contingent choice: a cost–benefit (accuracy–effort) approach and a perceptual approach. The basic premise of the accuracy–effort approach is that each decision strategy can be characterized by its accuracy and the effort it requires in any given situation. Decision makers select strategies in a situation based on some compromise between the desire to make an accurate decision and the desire to minimize cognitive effort. Because the accuracy and effort characteristics generally differ across strategies for a given decision environment and across environments for a given strategy, strategy usage will vary depending on the properties of the decision task.

The perceptual framework is usually associated with the work of Tversky and Kahneman; they prefer explanations of constructive decision making based on principles of human perception. For example, Kahneman and Tversky (1979) argue that our perceptions are attuned to noticing changes rather than absolute magnitudes of stimuli and that outcomes will naturally be coded as gains and losses relative to some reference point. They also argue that different ways of framing a problem may lead to different choices, much like the effect of taking different perspectives on perception; that subjects are often unaware of the effects of framing; and that such effects are likely to persist in the same way that perceptual illusions persist (Tversky & Kahneman, 1981, 1986). Thus, incentives may be less effective for problems involving perceptual factors than for problems involving accuracy–effort tradeoffs. Finally, Simonson and Tversky (1992) explicitly invoke the analogy to perceptual contrast effects in motivating their tradeoff contrast results.

Although the accuracy–effort and perceptual frameworks, considered separately, can each account for some findings in constructive choice, we believe that an integrated framework that extends each approach and then combines the two approaches is both possible and would be extremely useful. The key to integrating the approaches is to note that the perceptual approach has much to say about which aspects of a choice task are noticed and how tasks are represented, and the accuracy–effort approach is well suited for considering how consumers utilize the information they notice to attain their goals. Thus, the two approaches complement each other by providing insights into different aspects of the decision process. In addition to integrating them, each approach can be extended in important ways. For example, we propose that the goals considered in the accuracy–effort approach be augmented by including goals for minimizing the experience of negative emotion during decision making and for maximizing the ease with which a decision can be justified. We propose extending the perceptual approach by considering some perceptual processes as choice heuristics whose properties and use could be examined in a manner similar to other heuristics. We call our integrated framework a choice goals framework. . . .

A Choice Goals Framework

In this section we outline the basic postulates of our framework for understanding constructive decision making. Similar to Bettman's (1979) outline for an information-processing theory of consumer choice, we consider what consumers are trying to accomplish (goals), what influences the information they attend to and how it is perceived or encoded, and what factors affect the heuristics consumers utilize to combine information and make a decision. . . .

Consumer Goals. Choices are made to achieve goals. Bettman (1979) instantiated this notion by postulating that a consumer making a decision has a goal hierarchy, often developed constructively on the spot, specifying the goals and subgoals he or she must attain. More recently, interpretive research on consumer behavior has focused on what choices and consumer possessions *mean* to consumers (Belk, 1988). Thus, it is critical to characterize a consumer's goals for a particular task when trying to ascertain why his or her choice processes take a certain form.

A fruitful level of analysis for developing an explanatory framework is to examine consumers' metagoals for choice processing. Examples of such metagoals are maximizing the accuracy of a decision, minimizing the cognitive effort required for the decision, minimizing the experience of negative emotion while making the decision, or maximizing the ease with which a decision can be justified. Note, however, that the usefulness of a choice goal framework is compromised if too many goals are postulated, such as a different goal for each decision. To gain explanatory power, we focus on the limited subset of such goals postulated earlier and examine the degree to which such goals can explain observed constructive decision making.

The selection of these particular goals is not arbitrary; we believe that as a set they capture many of the most important motivational aspects relevant to decision making. Historically (e.g., in the rational choice approach), accuracy was the first goal considered; the goal of making a choice was considered to be maximizing utility. Simon (1955) and others were instrumental in bringing effort-related goals to bear on understanding choice in response to the realization that humans have limited processing capacity, as previously discussed. Computational problems are not the only factors that make choices difficult, however. Humans are emotional beings, and choices can involve wrenching tradeoffs. Thus, we believe that the goal of minimizing experienced negative emotion is important in some situations. Finally, humans are also social beings, and one of the most decision-relevant characteristics of the social context is that decisions are often evaluated, either by others or by oneself. Hence, the decision maker often must be able to justify a decision to others or to himself or herself.

We argue that different subsets of these goals are relevant in different situations. We will specify further some of the many problem characteristics that influence a decision when various goals are relevant. For example, irreversible decision problems that are very important to oneself or one's spouse may evoke goals for increased accuracy, minimizing negative emotion, and increased ease of justification. The relative weight placed on various goals will also reflect the individual's ability to obtain timely and unambiguous feedback on his or her performance relative to these goals. In general, effort feedback is much easier to obtain than accuracy feedback. The individual usually has a very good notion about how hard he or she is working and thus has timely and unambiguous feedback on effort, whereas feedback on accuracy is often delayed and ambiguous (Einhorn, 1980). The consumer also can assess his or her emotional state fairly easily. Finally, feedback on ease of justification is often immediate but can be ambiguous, because what makes for a good explanation in a given situation may not be clear. Reasonable justifications may be easier to predict in situations where the choice task is relatively simple with limited information, because the options for justification are more limited. Thus, the ability to obtain timely and relatively unambiguous feedback on effort and emotion may make those goals particularly salient in many situations. However, there has not been nearly enough research on the factors determining the relative salience of goals in choice situations....

Attention, Information Selectivity, and Perceptual Interpretation. As noted earlier, the fact that consumers have limited processing capacity means that they generally cannot process all of the available information in a particular situation. Hence, selectivity is necessary, and which information is selected for processing can have a major impact on choice. Put another way, it is critical to understand the determinants of the focus of attention, because many contingent choice effects are brought about by making salient different aspects of the choice environment.

Based on the psychology of attention, we know that there are two major types of attention, voluntary and involuntary (Kahneman, 1973). Voluntary attention describes when attention is devoted to information that is perceived to be relevant to current goals (i.e., is labeled as "diagnostic" in Feldman and Lynch's (1988) accessibility–diagnosticity framework). Individuals will devote more effort to examining information they believe will help them attain whichever goals are more heavily weighted in that situation.

Attention also may be captured involuntarily by aspects of the environment that are surprising, novel, unexpected, potentially threatening, or extremely perceptually salient, thus exemplifying one aspect of accessibility in the Feldman and Lynch (1988) framework. For example, changes and losses may be particularly salient (Kahneman & Tversky, 1979), and particular problem representations may make certain aspects stand out and gain involuntary attention.

Thus, attention and selectivity can be influenced both by goal-driven and more involuntary perceptual factors (for a similar distinction, see Tversky, 1977).

The effects of goals and perceptual factors can go beyond attention. For example, preexisting goals can lead to motivated reasoning and distortion of the meaning of new information (Kunda, 1990; Russo, Medvec, & Meloy, 1996). In addition, aspects of the environment that capture involuntary attention may also set in motion perceptual interpretations and behavioral responses (e.g., interpreting a loud noise as a threat and the corresponding orienting response). As we discuss further in the next section, we believe that particularly salient aspects of the choice task can at times not only capture attention but also suggest certain types of heuristics. For example, simple problem displays that make asymmetric dominance visually transparent may make heuristics that are based on relational properties of the options more accessible and thus more likely to be used. We believe that the connection of both goal-driven and more perceptual processes to selectivity and interpretation is a critical factor enabling a more integrated framework for understanding constructive consumer choice....

Choice Heuristics. First, we assume that individuals have a repertoire of strategies for solving decision problems, perhaps acquired through experience or training. Different consumers may vary in terms of the strategies they possess; for example, many children's processing deficits may be due to lack of knowledge of appropriate strategies (John & Whitney, 1986; Roedder, 1981; Roedder, Sternthal, & Calder, 1983).

Second, different strategies vary in their advantages and disadvantages with respect to accomplishing different goals in a given situation. That is, different strategies will be more or less accurate, effortful, emotionally wrenching, or easy to justify in a given choice environment. For example, the weighted adding strategy may tend to be accurate, effortful, and potentially more emotionally difficult because it requires making tradeoffs, which may be emotion laden in some situations. It is less clear how weighted adding would fare in terms of ease of justification; its thorough processing would aid justification, but the many subjective tradeoffs required could hinder justification. Elimination by aspects, on the other hand, may be easy to explain and defend (Tversky, 1972), avoids emotion-laden tradeoffs, and varies in its effort and accuracy depending on characteristics of the choice task.

Third, the advantages and disadvantages for a given strategy will be affected by individual differences in computational skills and expertise in the choice domain, both of which can affect how easily and accurately a heuristic can be implemented (Stanovich & West, 1998). For example, the ability to analyze and select the most relevant information improves with expertise (Alba & Hutchinson, 1987; Russo & Leclerc, 1994; West, Brown, & Hoch, 1996); with increased expertise a consumer might be more able to evaluate the safety of a car, for instance.

Fourth, the relative advantages and disadvantages for a particular strategy may differ from one environment to another. For example, a strategy that is more accurate in one environment may be less accurate in another, or different information presentation formats may make certain strategies more or less effortful to implement (for a classic example of such format effects, see Russo, 1977).

Finally, given the array of possible approaches and their relative advantages and disadvantages for a given situation, we assume that the consumer selects the approach that best meets his or her goals for that situation. Thus, consumers may select different approaches in different situations as their goals, the constraints of the situation, and/or their knowledge change (for a discussion of the potential infinite regress problem of "deciding how to decide how to decide . . . ," see Payne, Bettman, & Johnson, 1993, pp. 107–108). . . .

[The authors then review the literature of consumer choice, focusing on three topics: the tradeoff between accuracy and effort, the minimization of negative emotion, and the maximization of ease and justification.]

DISCUSSION

We have now presented a framework for constructive consumer choice and have attempted to review the literature on consumer decision making in light of that framework. However, there are several issues that still remain. First, there are some areas of research that we feel we cannot yet do a good job of explaining within our framework. Second, some broad generalizations about the literature have become apparent that point to large gaps in our knowledge. Third, we discuss the conditions under which constructive choices are likely to be adaptive (i.e., intelligent, if not optimal, responses to task demands). Finally, we consider the implications of a constructive view of consumer choice for measuring preferences, one of the most crucial applied problems in consumer research.

Findings That Our Framework Cannot Fully Explain

Two areas of research pose problems for our framework, framing effects and preferences over time. It is clear that different ways of framing a problem can lead to different choices (Tversky & Kahneman, 1986). For example, Levin and Gaeth (1988) show that labeling beef as 75% lean results in more favorable evaluations than referring to it as 25% fat, especially before tasting it. Mellers, Schwartz, and Cooke (1998) suggest that such framing manipulations influence the salience of the good and bad features of outcomes. Different frames clearly can make gains or losses more salient, and differential reactions to gains and losses underlie many framing effects (e.g., Puto, 1987; Shiv, Edell, & Payne, 1997; Tversky & Kahneman, 1981). Thus, frames may have an emotional component, and we have argued earlier that avoidance of losses may help satisfy the goal of minimizing negative emotion (Luce, Payne, & Bettman, 1999). More generally, framing effects suggest that "people choose, in effect, between descriptions of options rather than between the options themselves" (Tversky, 1996, p. 7).

The framework presented in this chapter can make some inroads into explaining such effects, arguing that a frame makes certain aspects both more perceptually salient (involuntary attention) and less effortful to process. In addition, people may fail to transform problems into a single canonical representation that would avoid framing effects due to limits on intuitive computation, even in simple problems (Kahneman & Tversky, 1984). People tend to accept the frame presented in a problem and evaluate options in terms of the reference point suggested by that frame, a concept clearly related to the concreteness principle mentioned earlier. The choice goals framework, however, is silent on why losses loom larger than equivalent gains (loss aversion).

A topic related to research on framing that our framework does not address in sufficient detail is the nature of problem representations. Our framework tends to consider problem representations as given by the structure of the task (see Coupey, 1994, and Lynch, Chakravarti, & Mitra, 1991, for exceptions). However, our framework should be extended to address the principles governing how representations are formed. For example, individuals may construct representations that minimize cognitive load, perhaps by using relevant analogies. Depending on the goodness of the analogy, this can be an efficient solution, although individuals may not consider alternative representations once they have one that seems reasonable (Legrenzi, Girotto, & Johnson-Laird, 1993). When no appropriate analogy exists, the consumer must construct a representation. We speculate that the representation formed will depend on what is most salient in the choice environment (due to both voluntary and involuntary attention), but very little is known about this process.

A second area of research that is problematic for our model focuses on choices that have consequences over time. Simonson (1990), for example, shows that whether one chooses items for future consumption on multiple occasions by making a combined choice all at one time or separately on each occasion has a systematic influence on choices. In particular, choices made all at one time increase the amount of variety in the choices. Read and Loewenstein (1995) provide a model and theoretical account of this phenomenon based on time contraction (consumers compress future time intervals when making combined choices and hence overestimate the effect of satiation) and choice bracketing (combined choices are framed together as a portfolio, whereas the separate choices are viewed more independently). As another example of choices over time, Wertenbroch (1998) argues that consumers exert self-control in consumption by rationing their purchase quantities (e.g., buying only a single pack of cigarettes at a time to help cut down on their smoking; see Hoch & Loewenstein, 1991, for other work on self-control). Again, some aspects of these results can be understood in terms of our framework, particularly the Wertenbroch results. The consumer appears to be trading off increased acquisition effort for increased long-run accuracy. However, there are also tradeoffs between long-run and short-run accuracy (i.e., the consumer wanting a cigarette now but knowing it is bad for him or her in the long run).

These two areas of research (framing and choice over time) reveal gaps that our framework still cannot fill. In both cases, perceptual principles seem involved to some extent (e.g., diminishing sensitivity to changes and loss aversion in framing and time contraction in the choices over time). Thus, research that attempts to buttress the perceptual aspects of the choice goals framework is needed.

Some Generalizations From Reviewing Constructive Consumer Choice

In reviewing the literature on constructive consumer choice, we have drawn many generalizations about specific topic areas.... However, two broader generalizations have also emerged: (1) task differences between research based on accuracy–effort ideas (e.g., task difficulty issues) and research based on perceptual notions (e.g., asymmetric dominance and other relationships among options), and (2) the lack of research on the dynamics of constructive choice.

First, striking task differences became apparent between research based on the accuracy–effort and perceptual approaches. Research based on accuracy–effort concerns generally considers larger, more complex problems and focuses more heavily on process than on outcome. Conversely, research from the perceptual perspective relies more on small, relatively simple problems and focuses on outcomes rather than process. These differences are very understandable; for example, to observe process one must have problems of some complexity. Otherwise, there will be either no process to observe or the process will be so constrained that it will be trivial and invariant across conditions. Also, studies interested in observing process often restrict information gathering so that each piece of information examined can be observed (e.g., by using computerized information acquisition programs). At the other extreme, perceptual studies often make all information available simultaneously.

We believe that these differences in tasks across types of studies have major consequences. For example, the use of simple problems and simultaneous presentation in perceptual research makes relational aspects much more salient, for example, hence making context effects and an ease of justification goal more prevalent. Thus, one large gap in the literature could be addressed by research that attempts to unconfound the conceptual approach from problem type. For example, research on context effects could be carried out with larger, more complex problems. Researchers using a perceptual framework could also attempt to enumerate the types of relational heuristics consumers might use and try to observe the processes involved in implementing such heuristics (this would also require more complex problems). Accuracy–effort researchers, in contrast, might attempt to analyze relational heuristic properties and how their usage varies depending on typical accuracy–effort variables, such as time pressure, problem size, and so on.

A second broad generalization that is readily apparent is that there is very little work on choice dynamics. This is true at two levels. First, there is a need for work on how the focus of attention changes constructively over the course of a decision. Verbal protocols taken during choice processes reveal a complex dynamic course, with various aspects being noticed, which then cause shifts in processing, which then lead to different aspects being noticed, and so on (see, e.g., Payne et al., 1993, pp. 175–176). However, we are not aware of any research in consumer choice that attempts to model the detailed, changing focus of attention over the course of a choice episode. To really understand how choice is constructed "on the fly," analysis at this level of detail seems necessary. Second, there is little research on sequences of choices over time. Without studying such sequences and the interactions among choices and their outcomes over time, it is difficult to observe how representations change or how learning occurs at the process level, for example. Third, people may have limited ability to predict to-be-experienced utility (Kahneman, 1994). Consequently, people may seek to maximize the accuracy of a choice but instead experience later disappointment or regret due to a failure to consider how their tastes might change over time. Hence, a second broad gap in research is studying various facets of choice dynamics.

When Will Constructive Choice Be Adaptive?

One issue we have not yet addressed is when constructive choices will be adaptive. Although being adaptive is hard to define, we generally mean making intelligent, if not necessarily optimal, choices. We believe that consumers are often adaptive in this sense but that such adaptivity is not universal. There is some evidence, for example, that consumers' responses to time pressure are adaptive. However, many factors can lead to failures in adaptivity, including lack of knowledge of appropriate strategies, difficulties in assessing properties of the choice task, overreliance on the most salient factors in the task environment, overgeneralization of heuristic strategies, and difficulties in implementing strategies. We also believe that certain kinds of failures are more likely than others. For example, overreliance on the most salient surface properties of the task can be particularly problematic if such properties capture consumers' attention but are not related to consumers' underlying values. In such a case, choices will likely not be adaptive. As a broad generalization, we believe lack of adaptivity is often more prevalent in studies based on perceptual notions, partly because such studies enhance perceptual salience and are often designed to specifically document biases in choice. It is clear, however, that much more research is needed on the extent and determinants of consumer adaptivity. One major problem in conducting such research will be to develop defensible measures for the goodness of a consumer's choice.

Assessment of Preferences in a Constructive World

In a constructive world, preferences differ depending on a wide variety of factors, as reviewed earlier. What does this imply for the assessment of preferences, which is a major focus of market research? We believe that the answer to this question depends on the goal of the analyst. One possible goal is that the analyst wishes to be able to predict the consumer's preferences to be able to predict market response. Context matching is the recommended approach for prediction purposes. In implementing context matching, the analyst attempts to determine the relevant factors that might influence preferences in the consumer's environment and then match the values of those factors in the measurement environment (Simmons, Bickart, & Lynch, 1993; Wright & Kriewall, 1980). For example, such factors as the number of options and attributes, the context provided by competing options, interattribute correlations, time pressure, response mode, and others can affect choices. The environment in which preferences are elicited should try to approximate the consumer's environment on all of these factors, particularly if the consumer has little familiarity with the decision. Context matching thus demands a thorough knowledge of the properties of consumer choice environments. In some cases, factors may differ systematically across environments (e.g., the set of available options may vary from store to store or from region to region). In that case, measurements may need to be taken for each of the major variants of the choice environment and then aggregated based on the relative frequency of these variants. Thus, context matching seems appropriate, even if potentially difficult, for prediction, which may be the goal in many market research applications.

However, in some situations we may wish to aid consumers as they construct their preferences (e.g., when measuring values for environmental goods or when helping a consumer select a college). For example, consumers are increasingly being asked to make choices among or to provide values for environmental goods, such as cleaning up a lake, preventing deaths of animals, or decreasing levels of pollution. Environmental goods are often unfamiliar and often involve difficult tradeoffs. In such situations we want to help consumers achieve a "defensible" expression of their preferences (Gregory et al., 1993) or to help them develop preferences by considering the implications of those preferences and how to manage them (e.g., to reduce regret; Simonson, 1992; Slovic, 1995). Thus, an important area for future research is developing guidelines for a good preference-construction process and doing empirical research to document that such guidelines are indeed effective. Such guidelines might include ensuring consideration of multiple viewpoints and options, using multiple response modes (Huber, Wittink, Fiedler, & Miller, 1993), and requiring explicit tradeoffs. For an example of such guidelines, see Payne, Bettman, and Schkade (1999).

We have sought to convey the constructive nature of consumer choice in this chapter. We have also tried to communicate an integrated framework for understanding such behavior. Finally, throughout this chapter we have attempted to identify gaps requiring future research.... We are excited that a broad array of intriguing research opportunities remains, and we believe that understanding consumer decision processes will continue to be a major focus of consumer behavior research and theory.

ACKNOWLEDGMENTS

This research was supported by grants from the Decision, Risk, and Management Science Program of the National Science Foundation and from the Environmental Protection Agency.

18. Decision Making and Action: The Search for a Dominance Structure

Henry Montgomery

INTRODUCTION

There is a close link between decision making and action. By making a decision a person commits herself to act in a certain way. However, in behavioral decision research, the link between decision making and action is largely neglected. The reason may be that decision making primarily is seen as a question of forming preferences, that is, a question of finding the better or best alternative. However, in contrast to decisions preferences are not necessarily linked to actions. An individual may prefer alternative x to alternative y without committing herself to any action. That is, the alternatives in preferences need not be action alternatives (e.g., preferences among articles of consumption), which always is true in a decision situation (e.g., in decisions to buy an article of consumption).

As a consequence of a large number of empirical findings, the presumed synonymy between preferences and decisions or choices has become problematic. First, it has been found that preferences in a nonchoice context may be inconsistent with people's choices (Lichtenstein & Slovic, 1971; Slovic & Lichtenstein, 1983; Tversky, Sattath, & Slovic, 1988). Second, it has been shown that people's preferences may be practically unrelated to people's actions; (Lindberg, Gärling, & Montgomery, 1990; Montgomery, 1993; Rohrman & Borcharding, 1988). That is, people do not necessarily enact an alternative that they prefer. The reason may be that the preference has been formed without making a decision to enact the preferred alternative.

These research findings emphasize the necessity to distinguish between preferences and decisions. In this chapter, a decision-making theory – search for dominance structure (SDS) theory (Montgomery, 1983, 1989) – is presented that highlights this distinction, as well as how pre-decisonal processes prepare the decision maker for action. The latter feature of the theory contrasts with assumptions in other theories of decision making and action control. After having presented SDS theory, I review empirical data that bear on the validity of the theory. Thereafter, I compare SDS theory with other approaches to decision

Originally published in M. Kofta, G. Weary, and G. Sedek (Eds.), *Personal Control in Action*, pp. 279–298. Copyright © 1998 by Plenum Press. Reprinted with permission.

making that invite discussion of how SDS should be developed or changed. Finally, I use the literature reviewed in this chapter as a platform for discussing relationships between decision making and action.

SDS THEORY

Decision-Making Phases

SDS theory describes the cognitive process that starts when an individual faces a decision conflict between a number of alternatives and ends when a decision is made. Each alternative is experienced in terms of its attractiveness on a number of subjectively defined dimensions or attributes. The key idea in the theory is that the decision maker attempts to structure and restructure given information about attributes in such a way that one alternative becomes the self-evident choice. More precisely, the decision maker attempts to find a dominance structure, that is, a cognitive structure in which the to-be-chosen alternative dominates other alternatives on relevant attributes. In a dominance structure the to-be-chosen alternative has at least one clear advantage to other alternatives, and all disadvantages, if any, of that alternative are neutralized or deemphasized.

The search for a dominance structure is assumed to go through four phases, namely pre-editing, finding a promising alternative, dominance testing, and dominance structuring. Figure 18.1 shows how the process is organized in terms of the four phases.

In the pre-editing phase, which typically occurs early in the decision process, the decision maker attempts to simplify the decision problem by selecting those alternatives and attributes that should be included in the representation of the decision situation.

In the finding-a-promising-alternative phase the decision maker finds a candidate for his or her final choice. An alternative that is more attractive than other alternatives on an important attribute may be selected as a promising alternative. When a promising alternative has been found the decision maker has formed a preference, albeit a temporary one, for a particular alternative. The question now arises as to whether the decision maker can decide to choose this alternative. This question is dealt with in subsequent phases of the decision-making process.

The dominance testing phase implies that the decision maker tests whether a promising alternative dominates the other alternatives. These tests could be more or less systematic or exhaustive. If the promising alternative is found to be dominant, it is chosen and the decision process ends.

If, on the other hand, a violation of dominance is found, the decision maker continues to the dominance structuring phase. In this phase the decision maker attempts to neutralize or counterbalance the disadvantage(s) found for the promising alternative. These attempts are based on various operations.

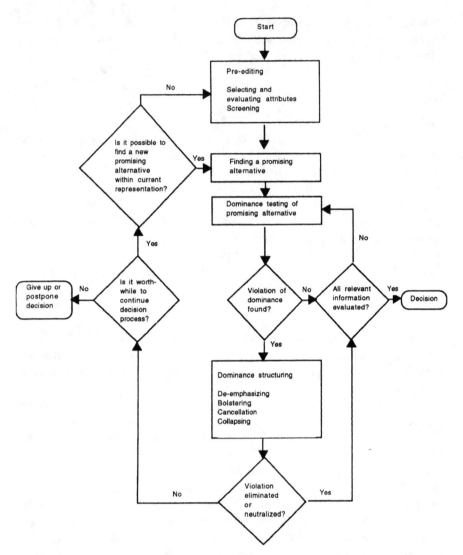

Figure 18.1. The search for a dominance structure theory of decision making.

The decision maker may deemphasize a disadvantage by arguing that the probability of the disadvantage is very low and that it could be controlled or avoided in one way or another. Another possibility is to bolster the advantages of the promising alternative and in this way indirectly deemphasize the disadvantages. In the cancellation operation the decision maker attempts to find dominance by canceling a disadvantage by relating it to an advantage that has some natural connection to the disadvantage in question. Finally, the decision maker may find a dominance structure by collapsing two or more attributes into a new, more comprehensive attribute.

If the decision maker fails to find a dominance structure he or she may go back to a previous phase and make a new start in the search for dominance or he or she may postpone the decision, if possible.

SDS Theory and Action

To decide is to commit oneself to follow a line of action. The commitment means that the decision maker is ready to defend the decision and stick to it in the face of adverse circumstances. This means that there will be a certain degree of consistency in the decision maker's pattern of behavior. It may be speculated that such a consistency will promote the individual's possibility to reach his or her long-term goals even if the defense of the decision may involve a biased view of the external world.

This view of decision making suggests that it will be important for the individual in his or her pre-decisional processes to build up a basis that may promote post-decisional commitment. In line with this suggestion, Montgomery (1989) assumed that SDS theory portrays the decision-making process as a preparation for action. The search for a dominance structure implies that the decision maker prepares himself or herself for coping with problems that may arise when implementing a tentatively chosen alternative. In other words, a dominance structure implies that the decision maker has access to counterarguments to any drawbacks of the chosen alternative that have been considered in the decision-making process. In this way, the decision maker will have resources to maintain his or her commitment to the chosen line of action.

SDS Theory and Mind-Sets

SDS theory deviates from other theories that assume that pre-decisional processes involve a careful and impartial weighing of pros and cons of different choice alternatives (Edwards, 1954c; Festinger, 1957; Gollwitzer, Heckhausen, & Ratajczak, 1990). In a series of recent papers, Gollwitzer and his associates argued that pre-decisional processes are characterized by a deliberative mind-set, which is expected to foster a relatively evenhanded and accurate appraisal of evidence (e.g., Gollwitzer, Heckhausen, & Ratajezah, 1990; Taylor & Gollwitzer, 1996). These theorists offer a contrasting view of the post-decisional phase, where people plan to implement a chosen alternative. This phase is characterized by an implemental mind-set, in which the individual musters motivation, resources, and cognition that favor the achievement of chosen goals.

SDS theory's view of pre-decisional processes is similar to mind-set theory's view of post-decisional processes. Dominance structuring may be seen as an implemental activity. The decision maker "runs" the tentatively chosen alternative and looks for possibilities of solving problems associated with its implementation. However, in contrast to mind-set theory, the implemental activities in dominance structuring are provisional. Their purpose is not purely implemental but also concerned with testing the feasibility of the tentatively chosen alternative, which occurs in the dominance-testing phase. That is, SDS theory states that if the decision maker does not succeed in constructing a dominance structure, he or she abandons the promising alternative. In this way, the search for a dominance structure affords a "window of realism" (Taylor & Gollwitzer, 1996), the size of which is negatively related to the decision maker's motivation to stick to the promising alternative.

The distinction between deliberative and implemental mind-sets is strongly supported by empirical data (Gollwitzer, 1990). The same is true for the similar distinction between state and action orientation (Kuhl, 1992). However, the support for the assumption that pre-decisional processes are primarily deliberative is indirect and meager. For example, Taylor and Gollwitzer (1996) asked subjects to report their recent thoughts related to an unsolved personal problem and found that subjects divided their attention about equally between positive and negative consequences of a change decision. Obviously, the request to think of an unsolved problem may have stimulated subjects to answer in a way that is consonant with this request, for example, by listing an equal amount of positive and negative consequences. Moreover, subjects' sensitivity to the demand characteristics of their task may have been further accentuated by the fact that subjects were asked to make retrospective rather than concurrent reports on their thoughts (Ericsson & Simon, 1980). In the following section, I will review data that may give a clearer picture of the nature of pre-decisional processes and their compatibility with SDS theory and, hence, the notion that decision making can be seen as preparation for action.

EMPIRICAL VALIDITY OF SDS THEORY

I now discuss a body of research findings that are all related to, or compatible with, the key idea of SDS theory, namely, the notion of decision making as a search for a "good" structure that makes one alternative the self-evident choice. Some of this research deals with limited aspects of the decision-making process, whereas other findings highlight the decision process as a whole. The research findings also vary with respect to how explicitly they assume that a "good" decision-making structure is a dominance structure. The review includes research that clearly supports SDS theory but also data that are less supportive or that even appear to be at odds with the theory.

Pre-Editing

There is ample evidence for the hypothesis that decision makers attempt to simplify a given decision problem by focusing on a limited subset of attributes (Svenson, 1979), by rounding off information about attribute levels (Kahneman & Tversky, 1979), and by screening out alternatives that fall short on important attributes (Beach, 1990). However, these research findings belong to those that illustrate a limited aspect of SDS theory and that also support other decision-making models, such as prospect theory (Kahneman & Tversky, 1979) and image theory (Beach, 1990).

Finding and Defending a Promising Alternative

Research that has examined decision making as a process across time has shown that before an alternative is definitely chosen it draws more attention than other alternatives and is judged as more and more attractive compared with its competing alternatives (Dahlstrand & Montgomery, 1984; Lewicka, 1997; Montgomery & Svenson, 1989; Sedek, Kofta, & Tyszka, 1993). The tendency to an increasing attractiveness gap between chosen and nonchosen alternatives as time proceeds has been demonstrated in a number of additional experimental studies (Beckmann & Kuhl, 1984; Mann, Janis, & Chaplin, 1969; Tyszka & Wielochovski, 1991). The same phenomenon has also been found in research on decision making in naturalistic contexts, such as career decisions (Soelberg, 1967), various decisions in people's private lives (Blom Kemdal & Montgomery, 1997), residential choices (Lindberg et al., 1990), and in a case study of a military decision (Montgomery, 1997).

It seems safe to conclude that pre-decisional processes often deviate from the picture of an impartial decision maker who carefully weighs pros against cons before making his or her decision. On the contrary, we are faced with the picture of a deeply committed decision maker who attempts to prove that a particular alternative definitely is better than its competing alternatives. The validity of this picture is further substantiated in studies of the decision-making processes of depressed people (Lewicka, 1997) and persons who have undergone learned helplessness training (Sedek et al., 1993). In line with the assumption that persons in this precondition lack cognitive resources or motivation to build up support for a to-be-chosen alternative, it was found that they examined choice alternatives in a more balanced and impartial manner than was true for nondepressed or no-helplessness-training control subjects (Lewicka, 1997; Sedek et al., 1993).

Existence of Dominance Structures

The fact that the decision maker manages to increase the support for the chosen alternative does not necessarily mean that the alternative dominates its rivals. Montgomery (1994), however, found strict dominance or close to strict dominance for the chosen alternative in a great majority of think-aloud protocols collected in a previous study of housing choices (Montgomery & Svenson, 1989). In the same vein, Lindberg, Gärling, and Montgomery (1989a) found that when information was missing about choice alternatives, subjects tended to bolster (enhance) the value of inferred aspects of the finally chosen alternative in such a way that more than 90% of the inferences supported or did not speak against the finally chosen alternative. Other studies have identified dominance structures in post-decisional justifications in a political discourse (Axelrod, 1976; Biel &

Montgomery, 1986; Gallhofer & Saris, 1989) and in justifications of professorial appointments (Montgomery & Hemlin, 1991).

Dominance-Structuring Operations

Many of the process tracing studies that concerned the validity of SDS theory did not closely examine the particular operations that led to the representation supporting the finally chosen alternative. However, the overall pattern in the think-aloud protocols analyzed by Montgomery and Svenson (1989) suggests that subjects would rather deemphasize the value of nonchosen alternatives than bolster the value of the chosen alternative. On the other hand, rating data collected in other studies suggest the opposite pattern, that is, more bolstering than deemphasizing (Lewicka, 1997; Sedek et al., 1993), as also was true in Lindberg et al.'s study (1989a) of inferences of missing information about choice alternatives. Lindberg et al.'s (1990) naturalistic field study (interviews) of persons looking for a new home evidenced a combined usage of bolstering and deemphasizing operations. The data suggested that to facilitate the choice of a new home, attributes favoring the new dwelling were seen as more important (bolstering), whereas attributes favoring the old dwelling were perceived as less important (deemphasizing).

In a reanalysis of the think-aloud data previously analyzed by Montgomery and Svenson (1989) on choices between homes, Montgomery (1994) found support for the cancellation operation (canceling disadvantages by relating them to advantages that have some natural connection with the disadvantage). For example, a long traveling time to downtown (disadvantage) was seen as providing an opportunity to relax during the journey (advantage). The realism of the collapsing operation (collapsing of two or more attributes to a more comprehensive attribute) is supported by studies showing that housing choices could be predicted from the respondents' beliefs about how the alternatives relate to various general life values, such as freedom and security (e.g., Lindberg, Gärling, & Montgomery, 1988, 1989c). We also found that at least 50% of the choice situations were associated with dominance structures on the level of life values (e.g., a chosen alternative is seen as better than or equal to its competitors with respect to freedom, security, family, etc.), whereas on the level of attributes (e.g., size, location, standard) pure dominance structures were rare (Garvill, Gärling, Lindberg, & Montgomery, 1991). The fact that subjects' choices appear to have been guided by life values suggests that dominance structures on this level may have facilitated the respondents' choices.

It may be concluded that there exists empirical support for each of the four dominance-structuring operations (i.e., deemphasizing, bolstering, cancellation, and collapsing). In addition, recent evidence suggests that dominance structures may also be attained by changing the external situation, that is, with a more direct link to overt action than is assumed in the dominance-structuring operations described earlier. Montgomery (1993) reported data showing that decision makers may not accept negative information about a promising alternative, but instead figure out actions that will improve the alternative. Other studies have shown that the individual may also intervene in the external world before the decision, to increase the support for a promising alternative (Blom Kemdal & Montgomery, 1997; Willén, 1994).

Preferences Versus Choices

SDS theory assumes that our preferences should be backed up more by dominance structuring when we anticipate a decision and engage in the search of support for the promising alternative. Hence, SDS theory implies that options should be less differentiated in attractiveness with no requirements to choose compared with a situation where subjects are to make a choice between the same options. This prediction has been only partially validated. It is supported by think-aloud data in terms of an evaluation index that was calculated for each alternative from the number of positive and negative evaluations of the alternative on specific attributes (Montgomery, Selart, Gärling, & Lindberg, 1994; Selart, Montgomery, Romanus, & Gärling, 1994) whereas ratings of specific attributes (e.g., size or cost of housing alternatives) and more general values (life values) associated with the options (e.g., health or freedom) gave mixed support (Garvill et al., 1991; Lindberg, Gärling, & Montgomery, 1989b). Attractiveness on the level of life value is assumed to result from the collapsing operation because life values are assumed to integrate attractiveness on specific attributes. In line with our prediction, we found a greater mean difference between life value ratings of chosen and nonchosen options than between life value ratings of preferred and nonpreferred options (preference ratings). However, there was no difference between the two tasks with respect to the proportion of cases where the chosen or preferred alternative was dominant on the level of life values (Garvill et al., 1991). On the other hand, approximately 50% of the choice situations included an alternative that was already dominant on the level-of-life values before subjects were asked to make a choice. Evidently, in these cases there was no need to restructure information to attain dominance, but of course there are still 50% of the choice situations that have a nondominant structure.

In a series of studies, SDS theory was used as a point of departure for elucidating the nature of the so-called prominence effect (Montgomery, Gärling, Lindberg, & Selart, 1990; Montgomery et al., 1994). This effect concerns the case where a choice has to be made between two alternatives that are described on two attributes (e.g., effectiveness and painfulness of two medical treatments). The effect implies that the more important attribute (e.g., effectiveness) looms larger in the choice than in a task where subjects have matched the two alternatives to be equally attractive. That is, in choices between two options judged as equally attractive, subjects tend to choose the option that is superior on the more important attribute (e.g., a treatment that is more effective but also more painful; Slovic, 1975; Tversky et al., 1988). SDS theory predicts that in the choice situation subjects will attempt to restructure the given alternative in such a way that one of the alternatives will be seen as clearly better. In the present case this could mean that subjects, to attain dominance, emphasize differences between alternatives on the prominent attribute and deemphasize differences on the nonprominent attribute. This prediction was indeed confirmed in think-aloud data collected from choices between two alternatives compared with think-aloud data from preference judgments of the same alternative with no choice requirement (Montgomery et al., 1994). It was also predicted from SDS theory that there would be no prominence effect for preference judgments because in this task subjects would not need to restructure the alternatives to be able to make a choice. However, also in preference judgments, subjects tended to emphasize the prominent attribute more than they did in the matching task (see also Fischer & Hawkins, 1993; Selart, 1996; Selart et al., 1994). Obviously, SDS theory does not seem able to explain the prominence effect, although the theory itself was supported by the think-aloud data obtained for choices.

Dominance Violations and Dominance Structuring

A straightforward prediction from SDS theory is that if a promising alternative does not dominate a competing alternative, then the decision maker will restructure available information to attain dominance. If, on the other hand, the promising alternative is dominant, there is no reason to restructure the information. In Garvill et al.'s (1991) study these predictions were only partially borne out when ratings of levels of life values associated with choice housing alternatives were compared between dominated and nondominated choice sets. In line with the predictions it was found that in the nondominated choice sets subjects tended to increase the differentiation between the alternatives when making the choice, whereas there was no such tendency in the dominated choice sets. In a recent study of real-life decision processes concerning career choices (Svenson & Hill, 1997), it was found that subjects who experienced goal conflicts (i.e., dominance violations) tended to reverse the conflict into an advantage favoring the chosen alternative. In line with SDS theory, it can be concluded that decision makers encountering a dominance violation may increase the differential support for the to-be-chosen alternative. However, the resulting cognitive structure may either fall short of strict dominance or be changed more than is needed to attain dominance.

Other studies have demonstrated that decision-making strategies seem to be sensitive to dominance structures or close-to-dominance structures in given information. That is, when one option dominates another one, subjects tend to choose the former rather than a third alternative that is not dominant (Ariely & Wallsten, 1995; Huber, Payne, & Puto, 1982; Tyszka, 1983), and they are less interested in looking for additional options or additional information about the given options (Bockenholt, Albert, Aschenbrenner, & Schmalhofer, 1991; Shafir, Simonson, & Tversky, 1993). Thus, in line with SDS theory, it appears that subjects do less to make a decision when dominance is at hand. Also in line with SDS theory, Ariely and Wallsten (1995) reported data that are compatible with the notion that subjects restructure (or categorize) close-to-dominance as being equivalent to dominance. Ariely and Wallsten coined the term "subjective dominance" to denote how decision makers conceive of close-to-dominance.

DEVELOPING AND CONSTRAINING SDS THEORY: A COMPARISON WITH OTHER APPROACHES TO DECISION MAKING

By and large, it appears that SDS theory is congruent with process data on human decision making. In particular, many observations are in line with the key idea in the model that the decision maker attempts to structure and restructure given information about attributes in such a way that one alternative becomes the self-evident choice. Data also support the existence of decision-making stages and operations that are largely in line with the model. Apparently, the findings reviewed earlier are sufficiently encouraging to justify using SDS theory as a platform for further theory development on the nature of human decision making. However, the fact that some predictions from the model have been unsuccessful invites thinking about how the model may be developed or changed. In the following section, I discuss two approaches to decision making that invite a discussion of how SDS theory may be modified or constrained.

Dominance Structuring or Differentiation?

The concept of dominance is central in the two final stages of SDS theory. In the dominance-testing phase the decision maker will react differently depending on whether he or she finds dominance or not. In the dominance-structuring phase he or she attempts to attain dominance. However, as noted previously, in both contexts empirical data suggest that subjects do not make a clear distinction between dominance and what may be interpreted as close-to-dominance. Moreover, it might be conjectured that in situations when a dominating alternative is only marginally better than its rivals, decision makers want to increase the differentiation between the alternatives to have a safety margin against preference reversals in the post-decision future (Svenson, 1992). In other words, it may be questioned whether the attainment of a dominance structure is a necessary and sufficient condition for getting to the decision point. Still, dominance as such seems to be an important decision criterion also in cases when one might expect the decision maker to look for more information before making the final decision (Bockenholt et al., 1991; Shafir, Simonson, & Tversky, 1993).

In his differention and consolidation theory of decision making (Diff Con theory), Svenson (1992, 1996) suggested that when a sufficiently high degree of differentiation, rather than dominance, between a chosen and nonchosen alternative is at hand, then the decision maker is ready to make a decision. The rationale for this decision criterion is to choose an alternative that can withstand threats that may appear in the post-decision future. Differentiation may be achieved by three processes, namely, holistic differentiation (which includes matching to previous prototypical decision situations), process differentiation (using decision rules that support the decision), and structural differentiation (which includes changes in the representation of attractiveness, attribute importance, facts, or the decision problem as a whole). Diff Con theory posits that these subprocesses continue after the decision to consolidate the support for the chosen alternative.

Diff Con theory implies that dominance is neither a sufficient nor a necessary decision criterion. The notion of sufficient differentiation offers a more flexible, but also a more loosely defined, decision criterion. However, the problems with validating predictions from SDS theory regarding the role of dominance could be handled, I think, by introducing subjective dominance, rather than strict dominance as the decision criterion. Ariely and Wallsten (1995) define subjective dominance as "a perceived relationship in which a certain difference on some dimension, although noticeable, is considered unimportant and the values on this dimension are considered to be subjectively equal, while simultaneously all other dimensions are clearly perceived as better for one of the items" (p. 224). Subjective dominance differs from strict dominance by excluding cases where a strictly dominating alternative is only slightly better than its competitors on favorable attributes. In this situation the decision maker will view the alternatives as being practically the same. Subjective dominance also differs from strict dominance by including cases when one alternative has a decisive advantage, although it is not strictly dominant. However, the notion of subjective dominance implies that SDS theory comes closer to Diff Con theory inasmuch as a more vaguely defined decision criterion is introduced. That is, the well-defined notion of dominance is replaced by the less well-defined notion of subjective dominance.

There are a number of reasons for keeping (subjective) dominance as a decision criterion. First, as discussed earlier, empirical studies show that decision makers are very sensitive to dominance relations. Second, as also discussed previously, people appear to have access to dominance structures in a variety of situations. Third, and most important, having access to a dominance structure implies that the decision maker has built up a cognitive basis for acting in line with the decision, that is, to implement the decision. This is because a dominance structure implies that a counterargument is available against any drawback that may be associated with the chosen alternative in the decision maker's representation of the decision problem. Hence, if a drawback that has been taken into account in a dominance structure emerges after the decision is made, the decision maker will be able to defend his or her decision and continue implementing it (Montgomery, 1989). Svenson (1992) himself assumes that an important aim of differentiation is to defend the decision against future threats. Obviously, this goal is facilitated by having access to a dominance structure in the post-decision phase.

Another important difference between SDS theory and Diff Con theory, besides the role of dominance, is that the former model stresses that differentiation is accomplished by a kind of structuring, that is, dominance structuring, whereas Diff Con theory regards structuring as one of several possible ways of attaining differentiation. SDS theory regards the other types of differentiation as subordinate to structuring. By using different decision rules (rule differentiation) the decision maker changes his or her representation of the decision situation (e.g., using the conjunctive rule means that attribute levels are classified as acceptable or not), which in turn is equivalent to or facilitates dominance structuring. Similarly, what Svenson (1992, p. 154) calls holistic differentiation leads either to a decision or to the finding of a promising alternative, which in turn may provide an input to the dominance structuring phase.

Further research is needed to evaluate the validity of the two theories on these discrepant points.

SDS Theory and Naturalistic Decision Making

SDS theory starts out from a general model of human decision making that for many years has been prevalent in behavioral decision-making research. In recent years doubts have been raised about the applicability of this model to decision making in a naturalistic context (e.g., Klein, Orasanu, Calderwood, & Zsambok, 1993). The criticism has concerned the following assumptions: (1) that decision making involves a choice among several options, (2) that choice is equivalent to conflict resolution, (3) that decision problems are represented in terms of attributes or dimensions, and (4) that the description of decision making is restricted to mental processes and structures. An alternative picture has emerged in which decision making is seen as (1) typically involving just one option, which has to be accepted or not (Beach & Lipshitz, 1993); (2) being largely automatic and being based on recognition of prototypical choice situations (Klein, 1993a); (3) involving attempts to use available information to form coherent stories or scenarios (Beach, 1990; Cohen, Freeman, & Wolf, 1996; Pennington & Hastie, 1993a); and (4) taking place in a dynamic environment with which the decision maker interacts (Brehmer, 1990; Orasanu & Connoly, 1993, Rasmussen, 1993). This picture simultaneously plays down the idea of decision making as conflict resolution between alternative courses of action and the idea that decision making can be studied under well-controlled laboratory conditions.

What are the implications of this picture of naturalistic decision making for SDS theory? Admittedly, in previous research I have overestimated the role of conflict resolution in decision making. Decisions do not differ from preference judgments in this respect as much as I thought. Our own research (e.g., Garvill et al., 1991; Montgomery, 1994) illustrates that people often have access to ready-made cognitive structures that relieve them from the burden of solving conflicts. On the other hand, SDS theory definitely deals with conflict resolution. However, even if it is true that human decision making very often does not involve conflict resolution, in the sense assumed by researchers in behavioral decision making, these situations still exist and people's decisions in these situations may be of great importance for themselves and for other people.

Actually, researchers advocating a naturalistic approach to decision making have reserved a niche for SDS theory in situations involving conflicts between different goals (Cohen, 1993; Klein, 1993b; Lipshitz, 1993).

The holistic and dynamic aspects of human decision making, which could be difficult to study in the laboratory, definitely pose a challenge to SDS theory. However, I regard SDS theory as having taken a step in that direction inasmuch as (1) dominance structures can be seen as good "gestalts," and (2) the theory's ambition to understand the link between decision making and action may facilitate further modeling on how decision makers interact with the external world.

ACTING AND DECIDING – HOW MAY THEY BE RELATED?

The literature reviewed in the present chapter shows that the concept of action is prominent in current research on decision making. In this final section, I discuss, in the light of this literature, how action may be related to decision making.

Preparation for Action

SDS theory, as well as Diff Con theory, stresses the link between pre-decisional processes and the commitment to act in line with the chosen alternative in post-decisional processes. Both theories assume that pre-decisional processes aim at building up a firm ground for defending the to-be-chosen alternative in a post-decisonal future. The validity of this assumption is backed up by empirical support for the four phases of SDS theory as well as for the differentiation assumption in Diff Con theory. It seems clear that people, in their decision-making processes, often manage to increase the cognitive support for the to-be-chosen alternative, which in turn means that later on it will become easier to defend that alternative. That the pre-decisonal process indeed may be oriented toward facilitating ensuing action is shown by the finding that decision makers may not accept the character of given alternatives, but instead try to figure out how they could improve the to-be-chosen alternative (Montgomery, 1993). On the other hand, it appears that research is lacking on the extent to which decision makers in post-decisional processes actually employ the support built up in pre-decisional processes to defend their decision.

Interventions in the External World

The earlier formulations of SDS theory focused on the decision maker's cognitive processes. However, on his or her way to the decision, the individual may also intervene in the external world to increase the support for the to-be-chosen alternative (Blom Kemdal & Montgomery, 1997; Willén, 1994). Similarly, naturalistic decision theories stress that decision makers interact with a dynamic environment, although the research in this tradition does not seem to be concerned with the support that pre-decisional action may give to the final decision.

Thoughts as Actions

The empirical support for dominance structuring is not unequivocal. In general, the support is stronger when think-aloud data rather than quantitative ratings were used. Think-aloud data also differentiate more clearly between preferences and choices than do rating data. It may be speculated that think-aloud reports reflect an internal argumentation process. In line with the view of thinking advanced in so-called rhetoric psychology (Billig, 1991), dominance structuring may be analogous to arguing with a defender of a competing alternative. Assuming that the argumentation process primarily is expressed in words, it follows that verbal data will reflect this process more closely than is the case for ratings.

A stress on the rhetorical and argumentative character of thinking implies that thinking may be seen as a kind of acting. Just as is the case in conflicts between individuals acting in the external world, the individual decision maker uses his or her thoughts as weapons against an opponent. In this fight the individual may be more or less successful, which will be manifested in the choice or the rejection of a tentatively chosen alternative.

The Control of the Control

SDS theory and Diff Con theory may be seen as models of how the individual attempts to control his or her thinking when confronted with a decision problem. The decision maker avoids certain thoughts and entertains others in his or her search for a "good gestalt." But what controls the control? To be sure, the individual does not have unlimited freedom to construct any degree of differentiation or any kind of dominance structure. Obviously, the makeup of the individual as well as of his or her environment provides constraints for differentiation or dominance structuring. Moreover, within these constraints the individual at any given moment may be further limited by his or her perspective on the choice situation (Montgomery, 1994). For example, the choice between giving money or not to a beggar will be experienced differently from an ego-protective or altruistic perspective.

However, as suggested by Kant (1785/1959), the individual may have some freedom to choose the principles (i.e., the perspective) he or she will follow. In other words, the individual will be free to decide how to decide. Knowledge of how people make such metadecisions may provide a deeper understanding of how people control their actions.

ACKNOWLEDGMENTS

This chapter was supported by a grant from the Swedish Council for Research in the Humanities and Social Sciences. I thank Ola Svenson for his comments on a previous draft.

19. Pre- and Post-Decision Construction of Preferences: Differentiation and Consolidation

Ola Svenson

Making a decision is often a kind of conflict resolution in which contradictory goals have to be negotiated and reconciled and a solution constructed. This conflict resolution is highly dependent on problem, context, and individual factors, which obscure and often make it hard to find regularities in human decision processes. The present chapter discusses how regularities in human decision making can be found through empirical research despite these confounding factors. To meet this purpose, Differentiation and Consolidation (Diff Con) theory is presented as a framework for process studies of decision making.

Decision making can be studied using either structural or process approaches (Abelson & Levi, 1985; Svenson, 1979). In its pure form, a structural approach relates choices and ratings to input variables (e.g., the maximum amount that can be gained, the variability across alternatives in gains and/or probabilities). Psychological intervening variables are derived from psychological theory and behavioral patterns in decision tasks. However, no attempts are made in structural approaches to assess the psychological process at different stages from problem presentation to final decision.

In process approaches the researcher follows and draws conclusions about the psychological process from problem presentation to decision by collecting process tracing measures, such as information search, think-aloud protocols, and other measures, at a minimum of two different moments of time in the decision process. Hypotheses and theories based on process data can later be tested in other process or structural studies.

It is possible to distinguish four different stages in the development of decision making research during the last 50 years. In his seminal paper on decision making, Ward Edwards (1954c) said virtually nothing about the psychological processes leading to a decision. Decisions were primarily modeled as if they followed a subjective expected utility rule and as if they followed basic assumptions of decision theory, such as transitivity and consistency. This first stage in

The present chapter is adapted from *Organizational Behavior and Human Decision Processes*, vol. 65, Ola Svenson, "Decision Making and the Search for Fundamental Psychological Regularities: What Can Be Learned from a Process Perspective?" pp. 252–267. Copyright 1996, with permission from Elsevier.

the evolution of human decision-making research represents a purely structural approach to decision research.

The second stage of this evolution was already going on or followed very quickly when demonstrations of behavior inconsistent with the postulates and predictions of the theory started to appear (e.g., Coombs, 1958; May, 1954; Papandreou, 1953). However, the mediating processes leading to a decision were still largely ignored. For a long time this second-stage perspective dominated decision research; thus, a massive research literature now tells us the limits of the subjective expected utility model in describing and predicting human decision making (Einhorn & Hogarth, 1981; Slovic, Fischhoff, & Lichtenstein, 1977). In fact, most of contemporary research still uses the utility model elaborated in different ways as a theoretical and empirical research reference (Dawes, 1998; Payne, Bettman, & Johnson, 1992; Yates, 1990).

Quite soon, however, one could find researchers who acted as precursors to later developments and who saw the human decision maker as an information processor with limited capabilities, which, in turn, could explain the deviations from theoretical expectations (e.g., Miller, 1956; Simon, 1955). These researchers argued that these limitations were essential in describing and predicting human decisions. This can be seen as the third stage in the evolution of decision research. One of the limitations of the human decision maker is the restricted number of entities that can be handled by working memory at one moment in time. This necessitates sequential processing in more complex decisions and encouraged process tracing studies of decision making.

It took a long time before process tracing studies gained any general recognition, and they were hard to publish in regular journals, as reflected in Svenson's (1979) coverage of the existing literature up to the late 1970s. Payne (1976), who worked in Simon's department, has been one of the most prominent U.S. process-oriented decision researchers through the years. In Europe, Svenson (1973, 1974, 1979), Montgomery (Montgomery & Svenson, 1989), Tyszka (Tyszka, 1985; Tyszka & Wielochovski, 1991), and van Raaij (1977), among others, performed early process tracing decision-making studies.

In essence, this third stage explored the decision-making process and found evidence for a sequence of rules different from the subjective expected utility principle. For example, it was recognized that often alternatives were eliminated by using some cut-off criterion on one or several attributes and that compensatory rules were used more toward the end of the process (Svenson, 1979). The representation of the decision alternatives was always assumed to be stable within uncertainty limits in this stage. A similar development occurred within structural approaches (Tversky, 1972).

The fourth stage included assumptions of changes of representations to solve decision conflicts, which could be seen as a step toward a more (living) system-oriented perspective. However, the idea of changing representations of decision problems was not completely new in the decision research literature. Shepard

(1964) suggested that the solution of a decision problem could be achieved through a change of the attractiveness representations of the decision alternatives. He proposed that decision makers actively construct a possible solution to a decision problem through changing weights of different attributes.

This theme was followed up by researchers both in the structural approach as editing (Kahneman & Tversky, 1979) and in a more developed form in the process approach as a continuous influence of decision rules on changes of the representation system to meet rule requirements (Svenson, 1979). Payne (1982) called the process of adapting decision rules to the structure of a problem contingent decision behavior, and Montgomery (1983) selected the rule of dominance as the guiding principle for the changes of the representation system. Beach (1990) presented image theory of decision making and Payne, Bettman, and Johnson (1993) developed the process perspective on decision making further. Toward the turn of the century, constraint satisfaction, which implies changes of representations of alternatives, was presented as an approach to model decision processes (Holyoak & Simon, 1999). The different approaches in the fourth stage put different emphasis on adaptive selection of rules and restructuring of decision problems, but they were all more or less open to both alternatives. Diff Con theory (Svenson, 1992, 2003) explicitly models both adaptive use of decision rules and restructuring of decision problem representations.

THE SEARCH FOR REGULARITIES

One of the major goals in psychological science is to find regularities (or invariants; Simon, 1990). Even though preferences have been found so variable, both structural and process approaches have revealed many regularities or lawful relations in the past. The Allais (1953) Paradox, framing effects (Tversky & Kahneman, 1981), and the fact that preference judgments and choices do not correspond (Slovic, 1975; Slovic, Griffin, & Tversky, 1990) all refer to regularities found in structural approaches. Shafir and LeBoeuf (2002) summarized regularities in terms of deviations from normative models found in structural approaches. Process approaches have detected regularities such as the use of different types of decision rules in succession (noncompensatory in the first part of a decision followed by compensatory processing; e.g., Ford, Schmitt, Schechtman, Hults, & Doherty, 1986; Svenson, 1979), the relation of the information search pattern to the attribute x alternative representation (Payne, 1976), and how value conflicts can be solved in important decisions (Svenson & Hill, 1997). The present chapter contends that a process perspective on human decision making is essential for the further exploration of regularities of human decision making. The methods used in this exploration may be derived both from structural and process approaches as long as the underlying theory models decision making as a psychological process. In the present context, Svenson's (1992, 2003) Diff Con theory of human decision making will be used as a framework in the search for regularities in human decision making.

A PROCESS APPROACH TO PRE- AND POST-DECISION PROCESSES

Most process studies of decision making focus on pre-decision information-gathering and -processing patterns. However, Svenson (1992) has advocated that decision research should also cover post-decision processes as an important phase for understanding human decision making. Earlier work by Festinger (1964) had addressed this issue but without using a decision theoretical representation system focusing on the post-decision stage. Janis and Mann (1977) were interested in pre- and post-decision processes, but again without defining either decision rules or a decision theoretic representation system. Frey (1981, 1986) studied post-decision information selection from a social psychological standpoint. In the present chapter, both pre- and post-decision processes will be treated as important components in human decision making.

Introduction to Diff Con

Diff Con theory (Svenson, 1992, 2003) proposes that the goal of a decision process is not just to fulfill one or several decision rules but also to create an alternative that is sufficiently superior compared with its competitor(s) through restructuring and application of one or several decision rules. The structuring and restructuring principles are performed in congruence with decision rules, usually not in congruence with one rule only (e.g., subjectively expected utility or dominance) but in relation to different rules contingent on the situation and the person in that situation. This process is named differentiation. The corresponding post-decision process in support of the chosen alternative is called consolidation. The general framework provided by the Diff Con theory approach to decision making is able to accommodate different existing decision models as subprocesses or special cases (Svenson, 1992) and will therefore be used here as an organizing principle. Note that most contemporary structural or static decision theories do not consider degree of differentiation or what may be called preference strength, as pointed out by Busemeyer and Townsend (1993) in their presentation of decision field theory. With both representation and rules depending on context and amenable to flexible adaptation to reach a decision, process approaches can help us understand why preferences are often so variable and hard to predict.

Levels of Decision Making

Diff Con theory distinguishes four different types of decision problems that elicit different psychological processes. The first level of decision processes includes the many quick and largely automatic and unconscious decisions (Shiffrin & Schneider, 1977; Svenson, 1990, 1992) so common in daily life. Such decisions are also called recognition-primed decisions by Klein (1989) and can be identified as an exemplar model in decision making (Estes, 1994). When such decisions are made, no direct reference is needed to attractiveness. It is simply known from earlier experience (including attractiveness evaluations) what decision should be made in a particular situation. To illustrate, as a habit you may buy milk in a green container of a certain design. But you do not think about the quality of that milk every time you make your choice in your local store. Nor do you use your affective/emotional system to get a feeling for the preferred choice. Instead, you use the perceptual cues of the milk container without any reference to your milk preferences at the moment of choice. E. R. Smith (1992) provides an excellent exposition of exemplar-based models in social psychology that can be applied to this kind of decision making.

Decisions made with reference to one or a few attractiveness attributes favoring the chosen candidate belong to Level 2 decisions. Such decision problems do not involve any conflicts between attributes, and the solution is quite obvious. Decisions driven by affect also belong to this level and may be as quick as Level 1 decisions. Metastrategic considerations and referrals to habits belong to this category only if attractiveness plays a role in those decisions (Fiske & Pavelchak, 1986). Kunreuther and Hogarth (1993) studied post-decision justifications and found many instances of metarules in their verbal protocols. Such metarules can immediately tell a decision maker what to do. Svenson and Fischhoff (1985) treated metastrategies and lower-level decision making from different perspectives.

Usually, when we think of decision making as a process we refer to choices between alternatives with goal conflicts. Some attributes favor one alternative and other attributes another alternative. Such decisions are grouped in the Level 3 category. Most of the existing decision research literature treats problems at this level. The difference between repeated and unique decisions was elaborated by Lopes (1981), Keren and Wagenaar (1987), and Keren (1991a); decisions at Level 3 that are repeated may become transformed to Level 2 or Level 1 decisions.

In real-life decision making, the search and creation of decision alternatives play – or should play – a significant role. However, almost no decision research has treated this problem (Fischhoff, 1996). In Level 4 decisions, the set of decision alternatives is not fixed, nor is the set of attributes that characterize them. Problem solving therefore constitutes an important subprocess in decision making at this level. Keeney (1992) contrasts Level 3 and Level 4 decisions and calls the former "alternative-focused thinking" and the latter "value-focused thinking" in decision making (Mintzberg, Raisinghani, & Thoret, 1976).

It is important to point out that decision makers often use processes at different levels in the same decision process. Lower-level processes are also nested within higher-level decision processes as subprocesses of the latter.

As mentioned earlier, most decision research has been focused on Level 3 decision problems (some of which may be seen as Level 2 problems; Abelson & Levi, 1985; Einhorn & Hogarth, 1981; Keeney, 1992; Kleindorfer, Kunreuther, & Schoemaker, 1993; Payne et al., 1992; Yates, 1990). Comparatively less attention has been given to Level 1 and Level 4 decision problems (but see, e.g., Keller & Ho, 1988; Klein, 1989). In principle, the Diff Con theory framework includes all levels of decision making both in their own right and as components in higher-level processes. However, the focus here will be on Level 3 decisions as the prototype decision problem.

THE DIFF CON THEORY FRAMEWORK

The purpose of a decision process is to select one of two or more decision alternatives. Diff Con theory emphasizes that this is achieved in a *differentiation* process, which over time separates the alternatives until one alternative reaches a degree of differentiation from the others that is sufficient for a decision. The differentiation variable is a hypothetical construct that is related to attractiveness measures and decision rule support (Svenson, 1992). Diff Con theory assumes that sufficient differentiation protects the decision maker from external (e.g., poor outcome) and internal (e.g., change of own values) threats to the preference of the chosen alternative. Other factors, such as cognitive (e.g., gestalt factors; Helson, 1933) and motivational factors (e.g., need for dissonance reduction; Festinger, 1957) are essential for differentiation and consolidation.

The goal in Diff Con theory is to achieve differentiation in a balanced way in which pros and cons together contribute to a sufficient degree of differentiation. Early contributors, such as Wald (1950), also assumed that decisions were made following sufficient separation of an alternative as a result of processing the available information.

Diff Con theory assumes that a minimization-of-effort principle is at work (e.g., Beach & Mitchell, 1978; Payne et al., 1993). It is assumed that retrospectively questioning a chosen alternative or changing it generally requires energetic effort, which a decision maker wants to minimize. However, pre-decision differentiation also requires energetic effort, which leads to a readiness to learn from decisions and routinize them if they are repeated (Lopes, 1981). The contrast and accentuation effects (Kreuger & Rothbart, 1990) illustrate how differentiation of alternatives can be used in category learning, which, in turn, can be related to decision processes. Following a decision, several threats against the choice appear (losing the good aspects of the nonchosen alternative, stuck with the poor aspects of the chosen alternative, unpredicted events, new perspectives on the decision in retrospect, etc.), which have to be handled. Diff Con theory assumes that one way of handling, for example, disappointment, regret (Loomes & Sugden, 1982), or dissonance (Festinger, 1964) is to continue differentiating the chosen alternative after the decision. This is called *consolidation*. Other ways of handling the post-decision phase include active management of the outcome of a decision and a series of new decisions and actions.

Representation of Decision Alternatives

In Diff Con theory, decision alternatives can be described in holistic, matrix (alternatives × attributes) or nonmatrix representations. Nonmatrix representations include images, scenarios, or alternatives with aspects (cues) that are not naturally ordered on attributes shared by the alternatives (e.g., a gift of a fruit tree vs. a painting). Images are mental representations of physical objects or scenes and other (e.g., symbolic) representations. They consist of aspects such as sounds, smells, ideas, and words and can also contain other images. When the time dimension enters an image and it becomes dynamic, this is called a scenario. To illustrate, two job alternatives may first be represented in a matrix representation with numbers for salary, travel time, and length of vacation. Then the information may be transformed to visual or mental images. When the decision maker starts thinking about future possible conversations at the jobs and imagining entering a crowded train to go to one of the jobs, the representations have changed into scenario representations. Scenarios can consist of other scenarios, images, and aspects. All kinds of representations used by Diff Con include aspects, and therefore the representations of aspects will be elaborated further.

A decision problem presents a set of alternatives (e.g., houses for sale). Each alternative is described by *aspects* (e.g., 150 m^2). Sometimes, the aspects can be ordered on *attributes* (e.g., house size). *Physical* attributes may be represented by *perceived* attributes (e.g., one house may be seen as larger than another of the same size), which, in turn, are related to *attractiveness*. The attractiveness of each aspect consists of both *cognitive/evaluative* and *affective/emotional* components. Either of these components may not be monotonically related to attractiveness (e.g., a really big house may be expensive to maintain or it may evoke a "rattle around inside" feeling); thus, the overall attractiveness may or may not be monotonically related to an attribute (Svenson, 1979).

Whether or not the aspects are ordered on attributes, the aspects or attributes relate to a set of cognitive/evaluative goals (Keeney, 1992) and to affective/emotional reactions and goals (Svenson, 2003). The importance of an aspect or attribute reflects its potential relative contribution to fulfillment of the decision maker's goals. Note that the different alternatives in a decision problem need not be represented in the same way. To illustrate, one alternative can be represented by a set of numbers (e.g., a new job offer) and another by a set of scenarios (e.g., the old job).

A fundamental characteristic of attractiveness representations is their variability. Thus, there is no true point estimate of the attractiveness of an aspect that can be assumed strictly invariant over time. There is always a variation of attractiveness caused by, for example, the variability of the stream of environmental inputs and the decision maker's own inner processes, including uncertainty about goals and unstable mappings of the goals onto the decision problem. Decision makers' uncertainty about how to represent their own values and goals in a decision problem has been elaborated by, for example, Fischhoff, Slovic, and Lichtenstein (1980), Fischhoff (1991), and Slovic (1995). Some of this uncertainty lies in the fact that people do not know what they will like in the future (Kahneman & Snell, 1992). Different ways of framing the same decision problem can elicit different perspectives. A decision maker vacillating between different perspectives can elicit different goals and introduce quite sizeable variability in attractiveness (Montgomery, 1994; Shepard, 1964; Tversky & Kahneman, 1981). Perceived uncertainty about facts or the outcome of a decision also contributes to and affects the uncertainty of the attractiveness of decision alternatives. According to Diff Con, all sources of uncertainty can be exploited by the decision maker in structuring and restructuring decision problem representations to reach a final decision.

Identifying Decision Alternatives, Goal Elicitation, and Editing

When a decision problem appears, the decision maker undertakes a process of identifying the alternatives, eliciting goals, and editing the information. This process is assumed to be governed by *markers* telling the decision maker where to start. Markers can be perceptual or cognitive and relate to the goal structure and the representation of the decision problem. To exemplify, the nomination of one attribute as most important can be governed by some marker so that the aspects on that attribute are compared first. A marker can be, for example, the label of an attribute (e.g., costs) or the aspects on an attribute (e.g., a very high or low value). It is assumed that markers are very important and may explain important parts of otherwise puzzling behavior. Svenson (1983, 1985) found that, in ratings of total risk as a function of varying risk levels over a year, the longest exposure time with a constant risk served as a marker, and the process started with the corresponding risk level during that period of time. Otherwise, the length of the longest period was totally neglected in forming the final judgment. *Editing* is also initiated by markers and essential to reduce the effort. It is a crucial activity in a decision process and will be elaborated in a later section (Abelson & Levi, 1985; Coupey, 1994; Kahneman & Tversky, 1979; Ranyard, 1989; Tversky & Kahneman, 1992). Identification of alternatives may concern selection among several given ones, as in most laboratory studies. However, in many real-life situations, decision problems evolve, as when one encounters one alternative at a time that has to be accepted or rejected (Fischhoff, 1996) or when a situation requires the creation of new alternatives. *Screening* is a process in which some alternatives are eliminated early (Beach, 1990), for example, because they do not satisfy some criterion level on one or more screening attributes.

The goals elicited by the decision maker for a decision depend on the decision maker, situational components, and the decision problem itself. The active creation and restructuring of alternatives, selection, and editing processes are all performed in accordance with the goals elicited and applied to the decision problem. The goals include apparent aspects of the decision situation but also intentions and goals at higher levels as well, such as schemas about how to behave, the goal of minimizing effort, or what to strive for in life. The result of the editing process, in turn, may affect the relative importance of different goals at lower levels active in the ongoing decision process.

Selection of a Reference and/or a Preliminary Choice Alternative

A reference decision alternative can be selected in a Level 1 quick process involving a classification without any evaluative component at the time. This alternative may serve in determining aspiration levels (Dembo, 1931) or as an anchor in other respects. It may also be derived in more elaborate and deliberate processes. A selection of a preliminary (Beach, 1990; Montgomery, 1983) alternative can also involve a quick holistic association or other more deliberate processes.

The preliminary choice in unfamiliar or more complex situations follows or is contingent on the identification of the set of decision alternatives. Sometimes, the number of alternatives are reduced first in a screening process using a noncompensatory rule such as the conjunctive rule (Svenson, 1979). The preliminary choice candidate is selected from this set ("consideration set" in marketing research) and is later tested in the differentiation process. Levin and Jasper (1993) suggested that the attribute(s) used in the earlier elimination stages as screening attributes can be just as important later in the differentiation process. This contrasts with Beach's (1990) view. Montgomery (1994) emphasized that a preliminary or finally chosen decision alternative is seen from a generally positive "inside" perspective as contrasted with the "outside" perspective of the nonchosen alternatives. In applied settings there may often be just one new alternative that is considered; the decision therefore concerns a choice between the status quo alternative and just one other alternative (Kahneman, Knetsch, & Thaler, 1990; Samuelson & Zeckhauser, 1988; Schweitzer, 1994; Svenson, 1990).

Differentiation Leading to a Decision

The differentiation of the preliminary chosen alternative from its competitor(s) may be successful or it may fail. However, according to the theory, the probability of an alternative being chosen is higher than its competitors if it is selected as the preliminary choice. This is implied by the fact that differentiation attempts to support the first preliminary choice in a biased (from a normative decision theoretic perspective) way, favoring that candidate, as shown by Russo and colleagues (Russo, Medvec, & Meloy, 1996; Russo, Meloy, & Medvec, 1998; Russo, Meloy, & Wilks, 2000). Empirical evidence for this can also be found in studies by Shafir and Tversky (Shafir, 1993; Shafir & Tversky, 1992), in which more and neutral information increases differentiation. However, if the preliminary alternative cannot be sufficiently differentiated despite its favored position, it will be replaced by another candidate, which then becomes the next focus of the differentiation process. There are three kinds of differentiation processes in Diff Con theory: holistic, process, and structural differentiation. Svenson (1992, 2003) has provided full accounts of differentiation processes and therefore the presentation here will be short.

Holistic Differentiation. Holistic differentiation is quick and may be experienced by the decision maker as something like a classification process (not readily available for conscious control or awareness) of the preferred alternative.

The process may be both totally separated from any attractiveness or goal considerations at the moment (Level 1 decisions), such as many habits, or it may involve affective/emotional factors elicited instantaneously, as in some Level 2 decisions (Zajonc, 1980). Holistic differentiation may lead to a degree of differentiation that is sufficient for a final choice. However, it may also be part of more complex differentiation processes (e.g., in selecting a preliminary alternative).

Process Differentiation. Process differentiation includes the use of one or more decision rules (e.g., the conjunctive rule, the additive difference rule; Beach, 1990; Svenson, 1979, 1992), the elicitation of which depends on the individual, the context, and the structure of the decision problem. The frequently reported initial use of the conjunctive rule in the screening of the alternatives to reduce the number of options belongs to this category of differentiation. Changing the criterion limits on different attributes, in rules using such criteria, is another and related kind of process differentiation. To exemplify, a conjunctive rule can be applied with successively stricter criteria of rejection in the early stages of a decision process to reduce the set of possible alternatives. Decision makers may not be consciously aware of the rules they use. So, when asked about what rules were applied to reach a decision, the answer can be reasonably adequate, post hoc rationalization or "I don't know."

In later stages of the differentiation process, the preliminary choice can be tested against other alternatives with different decision rules. Note that in most decision research, decision rules are typically formulated so that they predict a choice of one alternative if the rule identifies this alternative as superior to the other alternatives. The size of the difference between the alternatives is of no consequence for the choice according to these theories. This contrasts with Diff Con theory, which requires that a sufficiently superior alternative is chosen. Therefore, application of an additional decision rule can give further support (arguments) for a preliminary choice, adding to the total level of differentiation. Instead of predicting only processes that are used for elimination or denial of conflicts in a decision situation, Diff Con theory assumes that a pattern of pros and cons for a chosen alternative may also lead to a satisfactory decision.

Structural Differentiation. Structural differentiation refers to changes in psychological representations of decision alternatives. All such changes are made to meet the requirements of one or several decision rules. To illustrate, let one of the decision rules, activated in a decision problem, be a lexicographic rule in which the size of the attractiveness difference on the most important attribute favoring the preliminary choice determines the choice. If this difference is small, then structural differentiation should make that difference sufficiently large to motivate a choice. This can be done through upgrading the chosen alternative on that attribute, downgrading the nonchosen, or both. Changes on other attributes, if any, are irrelevant in this example and can go either way. If the restructuring on the decisive attribute is insufficient, another decision rule can be activated (e.g., sufficient advantage on two or three most important attributes for a weighed attractiveness difference rule).

Structural differentiation processes are of different kinds, depending on which parts of the structure are the targets (e.g., goals, attractiveness, facts). Different kinds of processes are assumed to take place concurrently and to be contingent on each other, and can be divided into the following categories (Svenson, 1992).

Attractiveness restructuring concerns the attractiveness of aspects and is governed by decision rules setting the goals for the process. The restructuring is made possible through uncertainty about attractiveness, uncertainty in goal elicitation, or uncertainty about the relative importance of different goals. These uncertainties can be kept fuzzy by the decision maker and used in negotiating the structure before the decision.

Attribute importance restructuring refers to changes in the importance of an attribute. For example, differentiation when using a weighed additive difference rule can be performed by changing the relative importance among the attributes so that attributes favoring the hypothetical choice attain more importance (weight).

Facts restructuring refers to changes in the perceived reality to support the preliminary choice alternative to a greater extent. A decision maker selecting and citing facts that are biased toward supporting the hypothetical choice reflects facts restructuring, as does systematic memory or rounding errors of facts, making them more supportive after than before a decision (e.g., hindsight effects; Fischhoff, 1975).

Problem restructuring implies using available facts and/or searching for new facts for an alternative way of representing the decision problem. This may involve new attributes that support a preliminary choice and/or the creation of new alternatives. Problem restructuring includes Level 4 decision processes in which new alternatives can also be created and old ones thoroughly modified. This kind of restructuring may give further support to a preliminary choice alternative but it may also eliminate it from the set of possible alternatives.

Post-Decision Consolidation

Post-decision consolidation is performed in processes similar to those in the pre-decision phase. Following a decision, the decision maker has now lost the opportunity of choice, the unique good aspects of the rejected alternative(s) are gone, and the decision maker is stuck with the bad aspects of the chosen alternative. This is not a desirable state. In response to this, processes corresponding to pre-decision differentiation take over in what is now called post-decision consolidation. In some cases, in particular, when decisions have been quick and perhaps immature, post-decision consolidation supporting the decision may be a late substitute for pre-decision processes (Svenson, 1992). In other cases, the decision maker may depreciate positive aspects of the chosen alternative during the decision process, perhaps to anticipate post-decision regret (and end up with a pleasant post-decision surprise). In such cases pre-decision differentiation may seem relatively weaker (but still sufficient), and post-decision consolidation may seem relatively stronger.

The same kinds of differentiation processes (holistic, process, and structural) as presented in the pre-decision phase can also be used in the post-decision consolidation phase. However, some decision rules, such as the conjunctive rule, may be less frequent after the decision than before because of its pre-decision screening character. Note that it is also possible to split the post-decision phase into (1) post-choice, (2) implementation, and (3) post-outcome stages. Lewin, Dembo, Festinger, and Sears (1944) suggested two different phases: (1) goal setting, which corresponds to decision, and (2) goal striving, which corresponds to the implementation phase (see also Gollwitzer, Heckhausen, & Steller, 1990).

Among other things, attractiveness restructuring is likely to depend on the pattern of aspects in a decision problem. If, for example, the preliminary cho-sen alternative is initially far better on the most important attribute, there is less need to consolidate on that attribute than if it is just barely superior. If the second most important attribute also supports the chosen alternative, then there is less need to consolidate than if it conflicts with the chosen option. If the attractiveness difference is sufficient on the most important attribute, there is room for attention to and consolidation of the second most important attribute. Some studies (Shamoun & Svenson, 2002; Svenson, Ortega Rayo, Sandberg, Svahlin, & Andersen, 1994) indicate that advantageous aspects on less impor-tant attributes may be changed so that they give less, but still sufficient, sup-port for a preliminary or chosen alternative, in this way perhaps approaching a gestalt of a preferred alternative. This may be the result of consolidation toward a typical gestalt for the chosen alternative involving both supporting and con-tradicting aspects, which are all changed to retain some kind of compensatory pattern and an overall support for the chosen alternative.

Post-decision processes have been studied within the cognitive dissonance approach using holistic judgments of decision alternatives or information search tracing (Brehm, 1956; Festinger, 1957, 1964; Frey, 1986; Greenwald, 1980). Zakay and Tsal (1993) studied post-decision confidence and structured possi-ble sources affecting the degree of (overall) confidence following a decision. Joseph, Larrick, Steele, and Nisbett (1992) have combined decision theory with dissonance theory. Simon and Holyoak (2002) modeled decision processes as a striving toward cognitive consistency and coherence (Simon, Krawczyk, & Holyoak, 2004; Simon, Pham, Le, & Holyoak, 2001).

PROCESS STUDIES OF DECISION MAKING WITH A DIFF CON PERSPECTIVE

In a process study, a structure is measured at least twice in search of changes of the structure over time. Because we are interested in human decision mak-ing, our focus is on mental representation structures. Diff Con describes how such structures are constructed and reconstructed in a decision process. Since the original version of Diff Con was published in 1992, an increasing number of researchers have shown interest in a process perspective on human decision making, and many of the results obtained are relevant for Diff Con theory. An illustration of the growing interest in process approaches is provided by Brownstein's (2003) review of research on pre-decision processes (he did not cover post-decision processes). A number of studies have illustrated pre-decision differentiation in terms of early rejection of alternatives and the selection of one preliminary choice alternative, and the following successive differentiation in terms of attractiveness statements (e.g., Bettman, Johnson, & Payne, 1991; Ford et al., 1986; Kleinmuntz, 1963; Montgomery & Svenson, 1989; Svenson, 1974, 1979). This regularity in decision processes can be found in different paradigms using a variety of methods.

Early studies within the Diff Con framework focused on post-decision consolidation processes. First, they showed that post-decision structural consolidation occurs regularly (Benson & Svenson, 1992; Benthorn, 1994; Svenson & Benthorn, 1992; Svenson & Malmsten, 1991; Svenson et al., 1994). Second, in accordance with the predictions of Diff Con (Svenson, 1992), aspects on the first and/or second most important attributes are predominantly used in post-decision consolidation. Third, the work within the Diff Con framework drew attention to individual differences in the degree of importance ascribed to the attributes (Benthorn, 1994; Svenson & Benthorn, 1992; Svenson & Hill, 1997). To find regularities in decision processes, it is necessary to aggregate data across decision makers according to each person's judgment of the importance of an attribute, even when this means aggregating across different attributes. In this way regularities in processes can be found. Fourth, early research showed that uninteresting and noninvolving decision problems may not lead to post-decision consolidation, whereas interesting and more involving problems do (Benthorn, 1994). The importance of involvement in a decision for differentiation and consolidation has surfaced repeatedly (Svenson et al., 1994) in later projects. Involvement has traditionally been regarded as one of several factors affecting a decision process (Verplanken & Svenson, 1997). However, involvement can be both an antecedent and a result of the decision problem. Involvement as a possible result of the decision process was illustrated by Shamoun (2004), who found that after a decision individuals reporting less differentiated decisions tended to judge their involvement in the task higher than individuals reporting more differentiated decisions.

Fifth, researchers have brought attention to the importance of justification of a decision (e.g., Kunda, 1990). To our surprise, we found that consolidation could not be related to a need to justify a decision to other people (Svenson et al., 1994). Sixth, aspect attractiveness restructuring has been easier to demonstrate than attribute importance restructuring (N. Malmsten, personal communication, January 16, 1996). However, in some situations attractiveness and attribute importance restructuring were both significant and appeared at the same time (Salo, 2000). Seventh, decision outcome feedback speeds up post-decision consolidation processes (Svenson & Malmsten, 1996), and time pressure seems to weaken differentiation and/or immediate consolidation (Benson, 1993).

There are different structures or patterns of attractiveness in different decision problems, and there are also different ways in which differentiation and consolidation can be performed (Svenson & Shamoun, 1997). One particularly interesting structure that has concerned decision researchers over the years is value conflict on the most important attributes; that is, when the attractiveness of an aspect on one important attribute clearly favors one alternative and an aspect on another important attribute a competing alternative. Thus, any choice will include a disadvantage on an important attribute. Svenson and Hill (1997) found that over a period of months a very important personal decision's main disadvantage was completely restructured into a significant advantage above what would be needed for dominance. To illustrate, an uninteresting profession can change to an interesting one (even before the training in the profession has started), and a poor salary can change to a good salary. This result was replicated and expanded (Salo & Svenson, 2001; Shamoun & Svenson, 2002). Lundberg and Svenson (2000) showed that after a choice, former counterindicative aspects were instead seen as giving support to a chosen alternative in investment decisions.

Patient decision making was studied by Feldman-Stewart and collaborators, who followed patient decision-making processes about alternative treatments for prostate cancer. The study used a Diff Con approach and followed differentiation in patient decision-aiding processes over time (Feldman-Stewart, Brundage, Van Manen, & Svenson, 2004).

A few studies have investigated consolidation in experimental group settings. To exemplify, Eisele (2000) found no differences in attractiveness restructuring between single individual decisions and restructuring of decisions made in a group (of three members – either a majority or a consensus decision). Eisele used hypothetical decisions, but Hammarberg and Svenson (2000) investigated more important decisions (involving outcomes of about $450) and found that, for majority decisions (three member groups), the members of the majority did not consolidate their decisions. However, participants who were in a minority position (those who gave up their own preferred alternative) consolidated their own preferred alternative and not the group's choice. Lindecrantz (2001) showed that state-oriented decision makers (Kuhl & Beckman, 1994) took longer to differentiate and consolidate than action-oriented decision makers, but that both groups reached the same degree of consolidation toward the end of the differentiation/consolidation process. Carlson and Klein Pearo (2004) showed that evaluation of aspects before a decision weakened the restructuring of those aspects in a subsequent decision process.

Simon et al. (2001) found that decision makers who judged their agreement with different arguments for, neutral, or against a decision changed their judgments of the arguments in coherence with their preliminary choices. This was done when the decision makers were asked to delay their decisions and when they were asked to memorize the decision problem afterwards. Phillips (2002) wanted to find out if only attractiveness values are restructured or if process differentiation in terms of a change of a conjunctive-rule acceptance criterion also played a role in differentiation and/or consolidation. His results indicated that distortion of attractiveness values in favor of a preliminary choice took place predominantly in the differentiation phase before the final decision was made. The change of acceptance criterion level occurred mainly in the post-decision consolidation phase. This is an interesting result, but it needs to be followed up and replicated.

Decision rules, structuring, and restructuring assume fundamental psychological structures and processes for their execution. This opens up the question of how to model the processes executing the processing of information and restructuring in a psychological model. In decision research, this problem interested Payne and his colleagues (Payne et al., 1993) when they studied repetitive decision tasks. Harte, Westenberg, and van Someren (1994) reviewed 23 think-aloud studies of judgment and decision making, mainly nonrepetitive tasks. They found that only four of the studies used some kind of psychological process model when presenting results. Oswald Huber (1989) made an early but unrecognized theoretical contribution when he modeled cognitive processes in decision-making processes. Holyoak and Simon (1999) used constraint satisfaction to describe the bidirectional adaptation of mental representations of a decision problem and the decision maker's preliminary decision. In this way, they connected decision processes to psychological processes of constraint satisfaction theory developed in the fields of cognition and social psychology. Diff Con theory has not yet been committed to any single theoretical psychological perspective and is therefore still open to, and attempts to, integrate different fundamental psychological theoretical approaches, such as constraint satisfaction, perceptual gestalt, motivational theory, and dissonance theory.

CONCLUDING REMARKS

To a large extent, decision making, as we define it, is the art of conflict resolution, that is, conflicts among inner goals and between one's own and others' goals, conflicts concerning how to evaluate alternatives in relation to competing goals, and so on. Half a century of research has complicated, widened, and deepened our knowledge about the decision processes operative in solving these conflicts.

Starting from a predominantly structural research paradigm, decision research now also encompasses a process perspective, in which decision problems are constructed and reconstructed to enable a decision maker to make a final choice. Diff Con theory attempts to provide a framework that is not only wide enough to accommodate much of contemporary research, but that also imposes some organization on a field that has tended to outgrow most developments of classical decision theory. Diff Con theory also has a not-yet-utilized potential for linking the constructed reality in the post-decision with future decisions. I hope that perspectives such as Diff Con theory will contribute to a process unifying a field that otherwise threatens to become too disparate for the effective convergence of research findings. Expected utility models played this unifying role for a long time, but it seems that those models now must be replaced by alternative frameworks.

ACKNOWLEDGMENTS

This chapter was supported by a grant from the Swedish Council for Research in the Humanities and Social Sciences, the Swedish Work Environment Fund, and the Swedish Nuclear Power Inspectorate. The author thanks Anders Biel, Anne Edland, Joke Harte, Baruch Fischhoff, Gideon Keren, Sarah Lichtenstein, John W. Payne, and Paul Slovic for valuable comments and discussions relating to the issues covered here.

20. Choice Bracketing

Daniel Read, George Loewenstein, and Matthew Rabin

> If we do not accustom ourselves to look upon war, and the single campaigns in a war, as a chain which is all composed of battles strung together, one of which always brings on another; if we adopt the idea that the taking of a certain geographical point, the occupation of an undefended province, is in itself anything; then we are very likely to regard it as an acquisition which we may retain; and if we look at it so, and not as a term in the whole series of events, we do not ask ourselves whether this possession may not lead to greater disadvantages hereafter.
>
> von Clausewitz, *On War* (1832/1992)

INTRODUCTION

The consequences of choices can rarely be fully appreciated in isolation. Even seemingly trivial decisions, such as whether or not to indulge in dessert, save small amounts of money, or purchase lottery tickets, can have profound cumulative effects on our physical and material well-being. When we make choices without considering these effects, we can do to ourselves what the bad general can do to his army – make a series of local choices that each appear to be advantageous but which collectively lead to a bad global outcome.

In this chapter we introduce the concept of *choice bracketing*, a term that designates the grouping of individual choices together into sets. A set of choices are *bracketed together* when they are made by taking into account the effect of each choice on all other choices in the set, but not on choices outside of the set. When the sets are small, containing one or very few choices, we say that bracketing is *narrow*, whereas when the sets are large, we say that it is *broad*. Broad bracketing allows people to consider all the hedonic consequences of their actions, and hence promotes utility maximization. Narrow bracketing, on the other hand, is like fighting a war one battle at a time with no overall guiding strategy, and it can have similar consequences.

Originally published in the *Journal of Risk and Uncertainty*, vol. 19, pp. 171–197. Copyright ©1999 by Kluwer Academic Publishers. Reprinted with permission.

To illustrate the effects of choice bracketing, consider the decision to smoke or abstain. If choices are made one cigarette at a time, the expected pleasure from each cigarette can easily seem to outweigh its trivial health consequences, so lighting up may appear to be the best choice. But if 7,300 single-cigarette choices (1 year's worth for a pack-a-day smoker) are combined, the health consequences may appear less trivial and might well outweigh the pleasure. The individual who makes 7,300 individually inconsequential decisions to smoke, therefore, makes an aggregate choice that might have been rejected had all the decisions been bracketed together. Whether someone who likes cigarettes ends up as a lifetime smoker may thus depend in part on how she brackets her choices.

In recent years, the distinction between narrow and broad bracketing, under the guise of different more-or-less synonymous labels, has been a frequent object of research. Simonson (1990) used *sequential* and *simultaneous* choice; Kahneman and Lovallo (1993) used *narrow* and *broad decision frames*; Herrnstein and Prelec (1992a, 1992b) used *isolated* and *distributed* choice; Rachlin (1995) used decision making based on *acts* and *patterns*; and Heyman (1996) used *local* and *overall* value functions. Thaler (1999) argues that many choice errors are the result of *myopic loss aversion*, which he contrasts with more global forms of utility maximization. All of these researchers have used these terms in the way that we use choice bracketing – to distinguish between choices made with an eye to the local consequences of one or a few choices (narrow bracketing) or with an eye to the global consequences of many choices (broad bracketing).

We argue that bracketing effects are central to understanding a great deal of human choice. Moreover, the distinction between broad and narrow bracketing is one that is often overlooked, even by economists. Economic theory assumes that people bracket broadly by maximizing well-defined global utility functions. Yet, specific economic analyses often rationalize puzzling behavior by showing how it is rational within narrow brackets. For instance, most formal models of risk attitudes assume that they are defined over aggregate wealth levels, and hence that consumers judge each risky choice according to the impact it will have on aggregate long-term risk. Yet, specific economic analyses of activities that involve risk, such as insurance purchases, treat consumers' individual decisions as if they were the only decisions that they make.

An example is Cicchetti and Dubin's (1994) analysis of consumers' purchases of insurance to protect themselves against the possibility of malfunctions in their home telephone wiring. The authors explain the frequency of purchases of wiring insurance, which is actuarially extremely unfair, using a standard account of risk aversion as the desire to avoid variation in wealth. In their data set, people pay 45 cents each month to insure against an expected loss of 26 cents a month, reflecting a 1/200 chance of losing $55. Looked at from the narrow month-by-month frame, by either the consumers themselves or the readers of the article, such risk aversion may seem reasonable. But from the perspective of risk to lifetime consumption power, the magnitude of the risk these people are facing is miniscule. Risk aversion over such small stakes makes sense *only* if we think of each choice in isolation, which is precisely how such examples are presented by authors. Consumers seem to bracket the decision narrowly, which is why they purchase the insurance. But economists also adopt narrow brackets when analyzing those choices, without recognizing that they are violating a bedrock assumption of economics.

In what follows, we provide a broad review of bracketing phenomena. First we elaborate on the concept of choice bracketing by placing it in the context of two other varieties of *choice partitioning*: outcome editing and joint versus separate evaluation of alternatives. We then provide a rough classification of bracketing effects and document these with many examples, both from related existing literature and some new research of our own. Following that, we offer some hypotheses concerning why and when people bracket narrowly rather than broadly. We then examine the normative question of when narrow or broad bracketing leads to superior decisions. We show that, although broad bracketing should and perhaps typically does produce better decisions, there are some situations in which narrow bracketing is better. Our concluding comments are made in the last section.

CHOICE BRACKETING IN CONTEXT

Choice bracketing can be distinguished from two closely related forms of choice partitioning. *Outcome editing* refers to whether the outcomes associated with a particular alternative are aggregated or segregated. *Joint versus separate evaluation* refers to whether the alternatives of a particular choice are evaluated one at a time or comparatively. After defining choice bracketing, we elaborate on each of these other types of partitioning effects.

Choice Bracketing

Consider the choices: $\{x_1, y_1\}$ and $\{x_2, y_2\}$. Under narrow bracketing, each choice is made separately. Under broad bracketing, a choice is made between the four possible alternative-pairs of the two choices – that is, from the set $\{x_1 x_2, x_1 y_2, y_1 x_2, y_1 y_2\}$. A bracketing effect occurs whenever the outcomes chosen under narrow bracketing differ from those chosen under broad bracketing. For instance, if x is chosen over y for both narrowly bracketed choices, then bracketing matters if anything other than $x_1 x_2$ is chosen under broad bracketing. The special, but common, case of *temporal bracketing* applies when the sequencing of choices is important. In narrow temporal bracketing, the individual first chooses between x_1 and y_1 (subscripts now designate time) without consideration of the subsequent choice between x_2 and y_2, and then chooses between x_2 and y_2. Again, bracketing effects occur when narrow bracketing leads to a different final outcome than broad bracketing. In practice, choices are usually made sequentially, and therefore most bracketing effects are probably cases of temporal bracketing.

Choice bracketing is illustrated by responses to the following classic problem from a study by Tversky and Kahneman (1981):

Imagine that you face the following pair of concurrent decisions. First examine both decisions, then indicate the options you prefer:
Decision (I) Choose between:

A.   a sure gain of $240 [84 percent].
B.   25% chance to gain $1000, and 75% chance to gain nothing [16 percent].

Decision (II) Choose between:

C.   a sure loss of $750 [13 percent].
D.   75% chance to lose $1000, and 25% chance to lose nothing [87 percent] (p. 454).

When the two choices were presented in this way, a large majority of subjects chose A and D. This is because people are loss averse – a loss of x is far more aversive than a gain of x is pleasurable – and because they give disproportionate weight to outcomes that are certain relative to those that are uncertain (Kahneman & Tversky, 1979). Consequently, subjects were risk averse when making Choice I (they chose the sure gain) and risk seeking when making Choice II (they chose the uncertain loss). When B and C are combined, however (giving a 25% chance to gain $250 and a 75% chance to lose $750), they dominate outcomes A and D (a 25% chance to gain $240 and a 75% to lose $760). Tversky and Kahneman's subjects apparently bracketed the two choices separately and treated each choice as if it had no connection to the other. That they would want something different if they had bracketed broadly was demonstrated when the outcomes from each choice pair were explicitly combined: Nobody chose the dominated AD pair.

Outcome Editing

Outcome editing (Kahneman & Tversky, 1979; Thaler, 1985) refers to how outcomes (or attributes) are integrated or segregated when their utility is evaluated. If an alternative has multiple outcomes, such as a compensation package that includes both a long-term raise in salary and a bonus, decision makers can either evaluate each outcome separately and then compute the value of the alternative as the sum of these separate values, or they can first combine the outcomes and then compute the value of the composite outcome. Imagine an alternative x with two attributes, r and s. In a simple case, integrated outcomes are first combined and then valued, as in $v(r + s)$, whereas segregated outcomes are first valued and then added, $v(r) + v(s)$. The hedonic consequences of the set of outcomes can vary depending on which editing procedure is used.

The distinction between choice bracketing and outcome editing can be illustrated using the example from Tversky and Kahneman (1981) described earlier.

Decision makers can either treat each choice in isolation (narrow bracketing) or combine them (broad bracketing). Broad bracketing confronts the decision maker with four alternatives: AC, AD, BC, and BD. Within these alternatives, the individual outcomes can be segregated or integrated. Thus, under broad bracketing the alternative AD could be expressed in a segregated form:

a sure gain of $240, combined with a 25% chance to lose $1,000 and 75% chance to lose nothing,

or in an integrated form:

a 25% chance to lose $760 and a 75% chance to gain $240.

Choice bracketing and outcome editing are close relatives and, in many cases, such as the example just presented, the distinction depends on the point at which editing occurs. If the effect reported by Tversky and Kahneman (1981) is due to a failure to transform the problem into the four-alternative representation, then it is a bracketing effect. If people do achieve that representation, but then fail to integrate the outcomes, then it is an illustration of outcome editing. Many problems, such as this one, may turn out to be ambiguous concerning when the editing occurs. We suggest, however, that for the problem previously described and for the great majority of other situations revealing a failure to integrate outcomes across choices, the problem is not that decision makers combine the choices into a composite choice and then fail to integrate the outcomes (i.e., broad bracketing followed by outcome segregation), but that the decision maker views each choice as a separate choice to be evaluated on its own merits (narrow bracketing). As will be seen in many of the following examples, when experimenters turn separate choices into single choice, subjects readily integrate the outcomes.

Joint Versus Separate Evaluation of Alternatives

A third type of partitioning effect, which Hsee, Lowenstein, Blount, and Bazerman (1999) refer to as *joint* versus *separate* evaluation, occurs between the alternatives offered within a single choice rather than between choices. Separate evaluation occurs when each alternative in a choice is first evaluated without reference to its neighbors, and then one of the alternatives is chosen based on the outcome of these evaluations. In joint evaluation, people choose between alternatives by making explicit comparisons between them. Numerous studies show that whether people evaluate alternatives jointly or separately can have a major impact on choice (e.g., Kahneman & Ritov, 1994; Nowlis & Simonson, 1997). In one study (Hsee, 1996a), for example, participants were asked to assume that, as the owner of a consulting firm, they were looking for a computer programmer who could write in a special computer language – KY language. The two candidates, who were both new graduates, differed on two attributes: experience with the KY language and undergraduate grade point average (GPA) (on a 5-point scale):

	Experience	GPA
Candidate J:	70 KY programs in last 2 years	3.0
Candidate S:	10 KY programs in last 2 years	4.9

In the joint evaluation condition, participants were presented with the information on the two candidates as previously listed. In the separate evaluation condition, participants were presented with the information on only one of the candidates. In all conditions, respondents were asked what salary they would be willing to pay the candidate(s). The result revealed a significant preference reversal between the two modes of evaluation: The salary offered to candidate J was higher ($Ms = \$33.2k$ for J and $\$31.2k$ for S) in joint evaluation, but lower in separate evaluation ($Ms = \$32.7k$ for S and $\$26.8k$ for J). Because the evaluation scale was identical in both conditions, the reversal could only have resulted from the difference in evaluation mode.

A REVIEW OF BRACKETING EFFECTS

Bracketing effects occur because broad bracketing facilitates the consideration of choice factors that are either not perceived or given relatively less weight in narrow bracketing. These include the following choices.

Emergent properties. Alternatives can combine into options that have features that are not part of the alternatives taken by themselves. Sets of options that give rise to such gestalts are more likely to be recognized in broad bracketing.

Adding-up effects. Alternatives that are chosen repeatedly have trivial or even nonnoticeable costs or benefits when considered individually. When choices are bracketed together, however, the aggregated costs or benefits can exceed a threshold so that they play a greater role in choice.

Taste change. What we choose now can change our tastes and thus influence what we will want in the future. When choices are bracketed together, we are more likely to recognize how a choice of one alternative will influence our desire for future alternatives. Taste change effects are specific to temporal bracketing.

Tradeoffs. When making many choices between multidimensional alternatives, it may be possible to find "integrative solutions" in which the good parts of some alternatives compensate for the bad parts of others. Again, these tradeoffs are easier to see when choices are bracketed together.

These factors embrace what we believe to be the majority of bracketing effects. They are not, however, mutually exclusive, and even in the examples we discuss later there is scope for controversy about where they fit into the framework. The first two factors are the most general, and describe the "essential" differences between broad and narrow bracketing. Broad bracketing reveals global patterns and magnifies local consequences that can be missed or ignored under narrow bracketing. Taste change can be viewed either as a special kind of emergent property that unfolds over time or as an adding-up effect involving endogenous changes. Tradeoffs are also emergent properties, but these are unique to situations in which choices involve allocating limited resources to alternatives. In the remainder of this section we elaborate on these four factors and give examples of their operation.

Emergent Properties

When combined, alternatives can have set-level or emergent features that do not exist as features of any single alternative. An illustrative emergent feature is representativeness. A representative sample (the result of a sequence of sampling decisions) has properties that reflect those of its population, yet no single element in the sample can be said to be representative, nor can the representativeness of the sample be inferred from one element. Analogously, in some situations, the outcome of many choices must be combined for emergent features to be recognized, and this can only be accomplished through broad bracketing.

We consider three ways in which broad bracketing can highlight properties of alternatives that might otherwise not be apparent. First, people often prefer sets of goods (e.g., clothes, books, movies) that are diverse rather than homogeneous. They are more likely to pay attention to this diversity when they bracket multiple choices together (e.g., by purchasing several books in one trip to the bookstore) than when they bracket them separately (e.g., in a series of single-book purchases). Second, people like to have their pleasures and pains distributed over time in specific ways: They like to spread them out rather than to get them all at once, and they like things to improve over time rather than to get worse. They can only know which choices will achieve these goals when they schedule many experiences simultaneously. Finally, people like to avoid risk – especially the risk of loss – and one way to reduce risk is to combine many risky choices. Consequently, the attractiveness of a portfolio of gambles, when perceived with the benefit of broad bracketing, may be greater than the sum of the attractiveness of its constituents.

Diversity. When making many separate choices between goods, people tend to choose more diversity when the choices are bracketed broadly than when they are bracketed narrowly. This was first demonstrated by Simonson (1990), who gave students their choice of one of six snacks during each of three successive weekly class meetings. Some students chose all three snacks in the first week (broad bracketing; Simonson called this simultaneous choice), although they didn't receive their chosen snack until the appointed time. Other students chose each snack on the day that they were to receive it (narrow bracketing; sequential choice). Under broad bracketing, fully 64% chose a different snack for each week, as opposed to only 9% under narrow bracketing. In a follow-up study using supermarket scanner data, Simonson and Winer (1992) showed that consumers displayed an analogous pattern; they chose proportionally more rare flavors when they bought several containers of yogurt than when they bought only one or two. In other words, those who bought one or two containers at a time restricted themselves to their favorites (e.g., strawberry and blueberry), but if they chose several at once they "spread their wings" a bit and chose more novel items like piña colada and vanilla.

Read and Loewenstein (1995) replicated Simonson's diversification effect; they called it the *diversification bias* for snacks in several experiments. In one study conducted at two adjacent houses on Halloween, they presented trick-or-treaters with two piles of candy bars. Children in the broad-bracketing condition were told to "take two candies – whichever two you like." Those in the narrow-bracketing condition were told to take one candy, then were given the same choice when they came to the second house. The broad-bracketing children always chose two different candies, whereas more than half of the narrow-bracketing children chose the same candy at both houses. Other studies (Read, Loewenstein & Kalyanaraman, 1999; Read, Van den Ouden, Trienekens, & Antonides, 1999) have demonstrated the diversification bias for choices of lottery tickets and audio tracks.

Scheduling Future Experiences: The Desire for Improvement and Spreading. When experiences are distributed over time, the utility of each experience is influenced by what has gone before and what is to come. Improving sequences are experienced as a series of gains, whereas declining sequences are experienced as a series of losses. Like diversity, improvement is a gestalt property of experiences that is not apparent under narrow bracketing. Indeed, when people schedule experiences one at a time, they typically choose to have the best experiences as soon as possible and to delay the worst ones, thus ending up with a declining sequence. Loewenstein and Prelec (1993), for example, asked one group to choose between having dinner at a fine French restaurant on a Friday in 1 or 2 months. Most chose to have the French dinner in 1 month. Another group was asked whether they preferred to eat at home on Friday in 1 month and at the French restaurant on Friday in 2 months or to consume the two meals in reverse order, with the French dinner first. The majority now wanted the French dinner in 2 months. For both groups, dinner at home was the most likely alternative to the French dinner, but it was only when the two dinners were expressed as a sequence that the desire for improvement became a basis for decision.

Loewenstein and Prelec (1993) also described a second common preference for sequences: a desire for spreading multiple desirable or undesirable experiences out over time. For example, most people do not want to consume two fine meals on successive evenings or to receive two pieces of bad news on the same day. Linville and Fischer (1991) attribute this to a limited capacity for coping with bad experiences or appreciating good ones. As with the desire for improvement, the desire for spreading only applies when scheduling more than one activity.

We investigated the role of bracketing in the scheduling of pleasant and unpleasant experiences. Subjects were asked to schedule four activities over two weekends, one unpleasant and one pleasant gardening task, and one unpleasant and one pleasant reading task. In the narrow bracketing condition, they scheduled the reading and gardening tasks separately, whereas in the broad bracketing condition the two decisions were combined. The task was described in the following way:

Imagine that on the next two Saturdays you must plan when to do some reading and some gardening. On one Saturday you will spend two tedious hours reading the Pennsylvania driver's manual in preparation for your licensing exam. On the other Saturday you will spend two pleasant hours reading a new novel by your favorite author.

In addition to reading, on one Saturday you will spend two boring hours weeding dandelions from your garden. On the other Saturday you will spend two enjoyable hours planting flower bulbs.

As expected, a majority of narrow bracketing subjects chose an improving sequence for both activities. They thus ended up weeding and reading the driver's manual on the first Saturday and then planting flowers and reading a novel on the second Saturday. Broad bracketing subjects, however, who were exposed to both scheduling decisions before they made any choices, spread out the good and bad by taking one pleasant and one unpleasant task for each Saturday. Spreading, which was a feature that could emerge only from the combination of two alternatives, was seen as an option only under narrow bracketing.

Risk Aggregation. When several positively valued but risky gambles are combined, the perceived risk from the super-gamble can be less than the risk from any individual gamble. Consequently, a decision maker who refuses a single gamble may nonetheless accept two or more identical ones. This is especially true when the risks from the different gambles are uncorrelated or (even better) negatively correlated, but even when risks are positively (but imperfectly) correlated, a portfolio of individually unacceptable gambles can be quite attractive. Thus, decision makers may accept several gambles when they are bracketed broadly, but reject them if they are bracketed narrowly.

Risk aggregation, in this context, was first discussed by Samuelson (1963), who asked a colleague if he would accept equal odds to win $200 or lose $100. The colleague refused but stated that he would accept 100 such bets.[1] This pattern of preference is driven by a combination of *loss aversion* (people's extreme distaste for losses) and narrow bracketing. Imagine that Samuelson's colleague had a loss-averse piecewise-linear value function with a slope of 1 in the domain of gains, but a slope of 2.5 in the domain of losses. Although he would refuse a single bet – because $.5 \times 2.5 \times -(100) + .5 \times 200 = -25$ – he would have

---

[1] Samuelson's (1963) paper has stimulated a lively ongoing debate, as well as empirical research. See, for example, Lopes (1981, 1996); Tversky and Bar-Hillel (1983); Redelmeier and Tversky (1992); Wedell and Bockenholt (1990, 1994); Keren and Wagenaar (1987); and Keren (1991b).

willingly played a portfolio of two bets because their value would be .25 × 2.5× (−200) + .5 × 100 + .25 × 400 = 25. Bracketing many choices together can, therefore, transform undesirable prospects into desirable ones.

Thaler (1999) adapted Samuelson's question for a course on decision making that he taught to 25 executives from a single firm, including its Chief Executive Officer (CEO). When Thaler asked the non-CEO executives whether they would accept a project for their division that offered an even chance of losing $1 million or gaining $2 million, only three stated that they would. However, when the CEO was asked whether he would like his subordinates to undertake the project, he enthusiastically nodded. The CEO, unlike his subordinates, was in a position to bracket all of the "gambles" together. He realized that if they were all accepted, the profits would most likely be stupendous, and there was almost no chance of any loss at all. Although this difference in preference may be due to factors other than loss aversion, such as the reluctance of the subordinates to make a decision that would prematurely end their careers, it is consistent with a large body of similar evidence in contexts where such considerations are absent (see Kahneman and Lovallo, 1993).

In another application of the same idea, Benartzi and Thaler (1995) attributed the equity premium puzzle – the low rate of return for bonds relative to stocks – to *myopic loss aversion*, which is their term for a combination of narrow bracketing and loss aversion shown by investors who invest in fixed income securities in preference to equities despite the much higher historical rate of return to equities.[2] Benartzi and Thaler argue that investors dislike stocks because they look at their portfolios frequently – perhaps once a month – even though the average investor is saving for a distant retirement. Over brief periods, stock prices are almost as likely to fall as to rise. For loss-averse investors, the falls will be extremely painful and the rises only mildly enjoyable, so the overall experience might not be worth undertaking. By this logic, if people could resist looking at their portfolios for longer periods – that is, bracket their investment choices more broadly – the likelihood that they would see such losses would diminish, and the clear benefits of stocks would emerge. Although we can never be sure that U.S. investors during this period had correct expectations about the scale of risk, Gneezy and Potters (1997) and Thaler, Tversky, Kahneman, and Schwartz (1997) have conducted experiments that support Benartzi and Thaler's interpretation. In Thaler et al.'s (1997) study, for example, subjects made investment decisions between stocks and bonds at frequencies that simulated either eight times a year, once a year, or once every 5 years. Subjects in the two long-term conditions invested the large majority of their funds in stocks, whereas those in the frequent evaluation condition invested the majority in bonds.

---

[2] Since 1925, equities have consistently outperformed bonds by a wide margin: Stocks have had an average annual real return of 7%, whereas bonds have averaged less than 1%.

Adding-Up Effects

Bracketing effects due to adding up occur when the perceived costs of alternatives accumulate at a different rate than their benefits. The costs or benefits from a single act may be so low as to fall below a threshold of consideration, whereas the cumulative costs or benefits of many such acts can be momentous. Consider, for example, the health consequences of one cigarette, the girth added by one slice of cake, or the effects on one's grades of a single decision to "skip class." In each of these examples, the anticipated cumulative benefit from indulging on multiple occasions seems to increase much more slowly than the cumulative costs. We suspect, for example, that the magnitude of the anticipated pleasure from 100 desserts does not even approach 100 times the pleasure from a single dessert, whereas the anticipated growth in your waistline is (if anything) greater than that from a single dessert. The same is true for cigarettes and skipping class. If people bracket narrowly and consider the costs and benefits of a single action, then the balance of costs and benefits will likely favor the benefits, whereas if they bracket broadly the balance can be reversed.

The failure to take tiny but cumulative effects into account has been implicated in many apparently suboptimal patterns of choice. Sabini and Silver (1982), for example, attribute procrastination to a combination of narrow bracketing and the apparently trivial amount of work that can be accomplished on a project in a short period:

> Imagine you have two days to write a paper. You believe it will take about six hours. To avoid being rushed, you decide to get to work. . . . Now suppose you had to decide what to do for the next five minutes – either work on the paper or play one game of pinball. . . . In the short run, five minutes of pinball is far more pleasurable than five minutes of paper writing, and after all, how much of a paper can you do in five minutes? Pinball is the obvious choice. The game is over so you must decide about the next five minutes. The situation is only trivially changed, so you will reach the same result. Once you've fragmented your night into five minute intervals, you may be doomed to play until you run out of money, the machine breaks, or someone meaner than you wants to play. . . . One of the ways of being irrational and procrastinating is to act on rational calculations for intervals that are irrationally short. . . . A model that would capture rational action must not only show how means are fit to goals, but also how appropriate intervals for calculation are picked. (p. 133)

Sabini and Silver's (1982) discussion highlights another context in which bracketing effects have received considerable attention – that of self-control (see, e.g., Ainslie, 1992; Heyman, 1996; Rachlin, 1995). Heyman's view is typical in that he suggests that self-control (in this case, avoiding or recovering from addiction) can be accomplished by putting preference "under the control of global value functions." The problem of addiction is considered in the next section. For now, we note only that those global value functions are equivalent to the "appropriate intervals" for utility calculation described by Sabini and Silver: Only when those intervals are large is self-control possible.[3]

Another consequence of narrow bracketing is the *peanuts effect*, in which repeated and seemingly inconsequential transactions can add up to significant total expenditures. Markowitz (1952) argued that the value function for money, both in the domain of gains and losses, is S-shaped. The initial flat segment reflects the observation that small amounts of money are treated as peanuts – that is, underweighted or ignored. Because people view $1.00 as peanuts, a large fraction would prefer, for example, a 0.1 chance of $10 over $1 for sure, but would also prefer $100 for sure over a 0.1 chance of $1,000. A consequence of this underweighting of small money amounts is that people may spend disproportionate amounts on trivial items. Two dollars may not seem like much for the daily cappuccino, nor $5 for a hot lunch, but the pleasure/cost calculus can look different if these expenditures are aggregated over time and especially if we consider alternative uses for the money. Personal financial advisors often advise clients to keep track of expenses over some period (e.g., a week or month). They report that many clients are surprised at what a large fraction of the total results from very small expenditures. Rent-to-own companies capitalize on this effect by offering people durable goods, such as computers or stereos, for "only" $25 per week over a period of 3 years or more (Swagler & Wheeler, 1989; Walden, 1990).

The "pennies a day" technique for eliciting charitable donations also plays on the peanuts effect (Gourville, 1998).[4] Many organizations, such as public radio stations, plead for contributions by reminding potential donors that it will only cost them a small amount per day, perhaps "no more than a cup of coffee." When many days are aggregated, however, the opportunity cost of a large amount of money may seem greater than the benefit from the good in

---

[3] We should be cautious about implicating narrow bracketing in all failures of self-control. Smoking, overeating, and procrastination have all been explained by researchers as resulting from hyperbolic time-discounting (Ainslie, 1992; Laibson, 1997; Loewenstein & Prelec, 1992; O'Donoghue & Rabin, 1997, 1999; Read & Van Leeuwen, 1998). In these models, the pursuit of immediate gratification does not arise because people fail to recognize the global consequences of their actions, but rather because they have different preferences at different times: Right now, they care equally about (say) next Monday and next Tuesday, but come next Monday, they care much more about Monday than Tuesday. Because hyperbolic discounting has been so firmly established by behavioral evidence (e.g., Kirby, 1997), determining whether bracketing is also implicated in these phenomena is difficult. Hence, hyperbolic discounting tells us that broad bracketing itself is not always sufficient to induce good long-run behavior: Even when people do bracket broadly, often they cannot control themselves sufficiently and behave as if they are bracketing narrowly. All dieters, for instance, know that small lapses add up (one dieter's expression is "a moment on the lips, a lifetime on the hips"), yet they face a constant and often losing battle to prevent lapses from occurring.

[4] Gourville does not, in fact, attribute the pennies-a-day phenomenon to peanuts effects, but rather to mental accounting conventions that cause pennies-a-day expenditures to be classified into mental accounts containing small items.

question; imagine the response to the plea that your donation will cost "only $350 dollars per year, no more than the cost of a small refrigerator."

Taste Change

Taste change occurs when choosing an option at one time affects that option's future utility and hence the likelihood of choosing it again. Bracketing is important because if individuals bracket narrowly, taking each choice separately, they will not take into account these *internalities* (Herrnstein, Loewenstein, Prelec, & Vaughan, 1993) – that is, effects of earlier choices on the utilities associated with later choices. Herrnstein (1982; Herrnstein & Prelec, 1992a) argues that the tendency to ignore internalities, which he calls *melioration*, can account for a wide range of suboptimal patterns in repeated choice. The most important taste change effects are *habit formation* and *satiation*.

Habit Formation. If choosing an option increases its utility in future encounters, then a habit is being formed. Many acquired tastes are unpleasant when they are first encountered, but become more attractive than their alternatives once they have been tried a few times. For many, caviar, opera, and exercise fit this description. To recognize that the early displeasure will be repaid by later pleasure, one has to bracket early experiences together with later ones. If we bracket narrowly, therefore, we will never acquire these tastes.[5]

Just as narrow bracketing can prevent people from forming good habits, it might also lead them to form bad habits and become addicted (e.g., Herrnstein & Prelec, 1992b; Heyman, 1996). If we define x as taking a drug and y as abstaining, then harmful addiction occurs when the individual repeatedly takes a drug $(x, x, x, \dots)$ but would be better off not taking it $(y, y, y, \dots)$. Although taking the addictive drug in the first period decreases the utility obtained from both taking it (due to habituation) and not taking it (due to withdrawal) in the second period, it actually increases the value of taking the drug relative to that of not taking it. That is, in the second period neither x nor y is as good as they were, but x is preferred more strongly to y than it was in the first period. Addiction can result from narrow bracketing when the effects of taking a drug on one's future preferences and well-being are ignored. According to Heyman (1996),

When preference is under the control of the overall value functions [broad bracketing] ... just the right amount of drug will be consumed, which may be moderate amounts or none. ... However, when preference is under the control of local value functions

---

[5] A second situation in which melioration can lead to suboptimal choices is when the choice of an option decreases its utility in the future. Ideally, in such circumstances, people should ration – that is, reduce their consumption of – that option to take account of its marginal cost on future choices. However, consistent with melioration with narrow bracketing, Herrnstein and Prelec (1992a) argue that people tend to ignore or underweight negative internalities. As a consequence, they will tend to overconsume highly attractive, but rapidly satiating rewards.

[narrow bracketing], drug use will increase. . . . Thus, a switch from overall to local value functions, in someone with a history of heavy drug use, will trigger a relapse or an increase in drug consumption beyond that which was intended. (p. 571)

Although it is difficult to demonstrate that real-world cases of harmful addiction result from narrow bracketing, experiments in stylized addiction-like settings have shown that the choice behavior of both humans and animals more closely approaches the optimum when choices are bracketed broadly. In a prototypical study, subjects make sequential choices between pairs of alternatives whose payoffs depend on which alternatives were chosen before. Just as with real addiction, the payoff to both alternatives x and y are negatively related to the number of times x has been chosen in the past, yet, regardless of the choice history, on every trial the payoff is greater for x than for y. If y is chosen every time, however, the subject gets the highest overall payoff, whereas if x is chosen every time, the subject gets the lowest payoff. Alternative x is like a drug, which is always better than anything else but which gets less enjoyable with repeated consumption and simultaneously worsens the quality of every other aspect of life. To recognize the "trap," the experimental subject (and the addict) has to recognize the interdependence between the choice of x and the returns to both x and y (cf. Ainslie, 1975, 1992). Manipulations that increase awareness of the internality (e.g., Herrnstein et al., 1993) reduce the frequency of x choices. The experiments most directly pertinent to choice bracketing have been conducted by Kudadjie-Gyamfi and Rachlin (1996). Their subjects made choices like those just described, except that one group made the choices in clusters of three, whereas control groups made nonclustered choices. Kudadjie-Gyamfi and Rachlin anticipated that the clustered choice group would treat each choice in a cluster as part of a single set (i.e., they would bracket broadly) whereas the nonclustered groups would treat each choice in isolation. As predicted, when the choices were clustered, subjects were more likely to choose the y alternative, and they obtained a significantly higher payoff.

Tradeoffs Across Choices

When two parties negotiate over many issues simultaneously they can look for integrative agreements, which are settlements in which one party concedes on a dimension that it values less than the other in exchange for a reciprocal concession on a dimension that it values more. A union, for instance, may be willing to concede on wage increases (which management values more) in exchange for job security (which the union values more). In this way both sides end up with an agreement that they prefer to the one which would have come from making separate concessions on wages and job security. Integrative agreements are possible only when more than one issue is negotiated simultaneously. Analogously, individual decision makers can reach integrative agreements with themselves if they take into account the possibility of tradeoffs across the many choices that they face. Just as with union and management, such an intrapersonal integrative solution can only be reached if the decision maker brackets more than one choice together.

In this section we examine cases that illustrate the impact of bracketing on the exploitation of opportunities for intrapersonal tradeoffs. First, we look at how people trade off the amount of the time they spend working across days that offer different wage rates; then we examine how people trade off across categories of consumption; and finally we consider people's notions of a just division of resources and how they allocate resources between different people who value those resources differently.

Tradeoff Between Labor and Leisure. Many workers, such as salespeople, fishermen, academics, and artists, daily choose how much time to spend working and how much time relaxing. Moreover, the return to each hour of work varies from day to day. On some days there are many fish, whereas on other days there are few. Likewise, artists and academics have days when the Muse is resident and days when she is painfully absent. In such situations, the most efficient way for workers to organize their time is to work long hours when the return to time spent is high and take leisure when the return is low. This commonsensical integrative solution to the work-hour problem is the prediction of basic economic theory.[6]

Camerer, Babcock, Loewenstein, and Thaler (1997) tested this prediction in a study of the daily work-hour decisions of New York City cab drivers. Cab drivers can decide when to quit work each day and also face wage rates that are relatively stable during the span of a day but which fluctuate, and are largely uncorrelated, across days. The authors found that, contrary to economic theory, drivers quit early on good days and worked late on bad days. The drivers seemed to have adopted the strategy of working each day until they made a fixed amount of money (perhaps enough to pay for cab rental and living expenses plus a "little extra") and then quitting. This pattern suggests that the cab drivers are making their labor supply decision "one day at a time," which is almost the worst possible earning strategy. The authors calculated that if the cabbies had worked the same total number of hours, but allocated equal hours to each day, they would have increased their net take-home pay by about 10%

---

[6] The basic economic theory of labor supply predicts that the supply response to a change in wage depends on the relative strength of the income effect and the substitution effect. The income effect captures the intuition that, as people become wealthier, they tend to work less because they have less need to earn money (their marginal utility of consumption is lower). The substitution effect captures the intuition that when wages are high, there is an incentive to work longer hours because the return (in terms of consumption) per hour worked is high. If a particular worker gets a permanent wage increase, according to this theory, whether he will supply more or less labor depends on the relative strength of the income and substitution effects. When wages fluctuate from day to day, however, as is true in a small number of occupations, the theory makes a strong prediction: People should work longer hours on high-wage days and quit early on low-wage days. This is because any one day's wage has a negligible effect on wealth, so there should be no wealth effect, and the substitution effect should dominate. The worker who behaves in this way can maximize earnings while minimizing total hours worked.

and that if they had optimized by working longer hours on good days and shorter hours on bad days, they would have earned about 20% more.

Tradeoffs Across Purchase Categories. Another area in which there is a well-documented tendency to think narrowly, and thus fail to make optimal tradeoffs across choices, is household and mental budgeting. Budgeting involves earmarking money for specific categories of expense. A household, for instance, might allocate fixed portions of its income to utilities, transportation, food, and clothing. The money so earmarked is spent on that category of expense and on nothing else. Budgeting can be a useful shortcut for ensuring that vital expenses are met, but if budget boundaries are too restrictive – that is, if there is a reluctance to transfer money from one account to another – they can prevent the decision-making unit, whether household or individual, from making beneficial tradeoffs.

A budget contains three elements: a category of expense, an amount budgeted, and a fiscal period. Accounting conventions dictate that money in the account be spent only on that category and within that fiscal period. A series of experiments by Heath and Soll (1996) demonstrate that people are quite strict about their budgets. Money saved in one category will be recycled into that category: Money saved on free theater tickets, for example, is used to buy more entertainment, such as CDs or sports tickets. The specificity of such budgets can be striking: Subjects in a study conducted by O'Curry (1995) reported that they would use a categorywide reduction in beer prices to buy better quality beer. As Heath and Soll (1996) observe, because budget decisions are made relative to categories, they can lead to simultaneous feelings of wealth ("I didn't spend all my clothing allowance, so now I can buy that gaudy hat") and poverty ("but I've spent enough on books this week").

Research into household budgeting has focused on how people use categories, and no one has investigated how choices are influenced by changing the scope of the mental account. We might expect, for example, that if people could be induced to keep an "entertainment and clothing" account, then shoes and theater tickets would become substitutes. We investigated this prediction by manipulating another aspect of the budget – the fiscal period. The fiscal period demarcates the interval during which a particular budget allocation is to be used. Two groups of Carnegie Mellon students responded to the following question:

Imagine that you are a poor student, and you set aside $25 per week [$100 per month] for entertainment. It is the last day of the week [7th of the month] and you have already spent $25 on entertainment. Tonight there is a concert that you would like to attend, but the tickets cost $15. Will you go?

In terms of the consequences to the student, the fiscal period is just window-dressing. The student attending the concert has spent more than planned, but will have enjoyed a concert. Changing the fiscal period, however, had the expected effect. Students were more likely to attend the concert if their fiscal period was 1 month rather than 1 week (39% vs. 8%), $\chi^2(1) = 7.7$, $p < .005$. At least in this case, budgeting decisions were altered by changing the domain of choices bracketed within a budget.

Fair Divisions. Bracketing also seems important in understanding what people think is a fair allocation of resource. In particular, narrow bracketing of resource-allocation decisions – that is, allocation on a case-by-case basis – is likely to lead to more equal, but less efficient, splits of resources than broad bracketing. Suppose that $10 worth of money or other goods must be split between two people. How would the average person, acting as a third party, decide to split the surplus between the two? One possible allocation rule is to give it all to the poorer person, or (for nonmoney goods) to the one who values the goods more. But research shows that, rather than maximizing the total welfare gain of the two individuals, disinterested people often prefer an allocation that equalizes welfare gains (Yaari & Bar-Hillel, 1984). Because people who value a resource less require more of it to increase their utility by a given amount, equalizing welfare gains typically implies that more of any given resource should be allocated to those who value it less.

Although we have no comment on the moral soundness of this Rawlsian maximin criterion as an ultimate principle of justice, its implications can be strikingly different depending on whether the allocation decisions are bracketed narrowly or broadly. Imagine, for example, that the same two people are the subject of repeated allocation decisions and that our goal is to maximize the minimum welfare gain that will result from these decisions. Imagine further that the goods being allocated are just as often more valued by one party as the other party. If we bracket very few decisions together, it is most likely that for each allocation the best (maximin) decision will be to maximize the sum of the two parties' benefits.

For example, suppose that we have to make two allocation decisions for two people, Johnny and Keanu. The first is to distribute 12 grapefruits and the second is to distribute 12 avocados. Johnny values grapefruits twice as much as Keanu, and Keanu values avocados twice as much as Johnny. If we bracket narrowly, the maximin criterion would lead us to first give 4 grapefruits to Johnny and 8 to Keanu, and then to give 8 avocados to Johnny and 4 to Keanu – equating their benefits in each separate distribution. If we bracket broadly, however, we would give all the grapefruits to Johnny and all the avocados to Keanu. Both ways of allocating gives equal welfare gains to both, but those gains are 50% greater under broad bracketing. If one imagines larger numbers of individual allocation decisions, it becomes clear that maximizing the addition to total welfare on each choice is likely to be the best policy even if one wants to pursue the maximin criterion in the aggregate.[7]

[7] Observe that treating an individual allocation decision in isolation is something of a fiction; every choice of allocation to two people is surely concatenating some additional resources to resources they already have, so that a maximin criterion should designate that we give all the resources to the person most in need – and be virtually impervious to any additional efficiency or distributional arguments.

DETERMINANTS OF BRACKETING

In the previous section, we summarized the results of numerous studies that document the important consequences of bracketing choices narrowly or broadly. We did not directly address what causes people to bracket the way they do, in part because very few studies have addressed this question. Undoubtedly, many bracketing choices result from a wide range of subtle and unconscious factors that influence the way we categorize the world. For example, putting on one's shoes could be construed as: putting on each of two shoes; putting on a pair of shoes; part of getting dressed; part of preparing to leave the house; or, perhaps somewhat far-fetched, part of furthering one's career. Our lack of insight into the factors that influence bracketing even in mundane choices suggests that developing a theory of how people bracket is a crucial direction for future research. Despite our comparative ignorance on this issue, we provide a preliminary analysis of four factors that we suspect are important.

Cognitive Capacity Limitations. Cognitive limitations – in perception (Miller, 1956), attention (Kahneman, 1973), memory (Baddeley, 1986), analytical processing (Simon, 1957), and so forth – are one important determinant of bracketing. Such limitations sharply constrain our ability to simultaneously consider multiple decisions. As the number of choices – or the number of alternatives per choice – increases, the cognitive cost of broad bracketing will undergo a combinatorial explosion. To take an abstract example, narrowly bracketing two choices $\{x_1, y_1\}$ and $\{x_2, y_2\}$ involves two binary comparisons; broadly bracketing the choice so that it is made between the composite alternatives $\{x_1 x_2, x_1 y_2, y_1 x_2, y_1 y_2\}$ involves at least three and as many as six binary comparisons. If there are three choices, the composite choice can involve up to 28 binary comparisons. This does not take into account the resources needed to evaluate what will rapidly become exceedingly complex alternatives.

Cognitive Inertia. Cognitive limitations are probably very important in the real world and even in some experimental demonstrations of bracketing. In Tversky and Kahneman's (1981) twin-gamble dominance violation illustration, described earlier, subjects might not integrate the gambles (despite being advised that the decisions are concurrent) because doing so would be cognitively taxing. But not all bracketing effects can be explained in this way. Many are due simply to the fact that people usually deal with problems in the way that they are presented to them. If choices come to them one at a time, they will bracket them narrowly, and if choices come to them collectively, they will bracket more broadly.

This was elegantly illustrated by Redelmeier and Tversky (1992) in the domain of gambles. Given a choice, people will usually prefer a larger number of gambles (assuming they have a positive expected value and are independent) to a smaller number (e.g., Keren & Wagenaar, 1987). Their study involved two groups, each of whom chose between five or six gambles. Most of the first group, who made a direct choice, took six gambles. A second group made two choices. First, they chose between zero gambles or five. Most chose the five. Then they were offered one more gamble, which amounted to a choice between the original five gambles or six gambles. Most refused the sixth gamble. Indeed, the proportion taking the sixth gamble was identical to that taking a single gamble when the choice was between one or zero. The second group had bracketed narrowly, by treating the single gamble choice as separate from the earlier choice of five gambles. Only when the choices were explicitly bracketed together, as they were in the first group, did subjects recognize that the five gambles influenced the desirability of the sixth.

In a modification of Redelmeier and Tversky's (1992) study, we asked 143 Carnegie Mellon students to:

Imagine that on each of 5 days you will be allowed to choose between the following:

A.   50–50 chance of losing $25 or winning $40; or
B.   Do not gamble.

The students then made separate choices for each day. In the narrow bracketing condition, subjects chose for only the first day, whereas in the broad bracketing condition subjects made the decision for all 5 days. All subjects knew that they would be making five choices, so the only difference between groups was that single-day subjects would have more flexibility in their choices because they weren't precommitted to a pattern of gambles. They did not, however, take this view. Although 50% of the broad-bracketing subjects gambled on the first day, only 32% of the narrow-bracketing subjects did, $\chi^2(1) = 4.57$, $p < .05$. Note that cognitive limitations cannot account for results such as these. Rather, the difference between broad and narrow bracketing apparently involves a shift in viewpoint and not more processing power.

Narrow bracketing attributable to cognitive inertia may also contribute to the embedding effect (Kahneman & Knetsch, 1992) – the tendency for respondents in contingent valuation studies to report approximately equal willingness to pay to correct problems that differ dramatically in scope. Respondents, for example, might agree to pay as much to clean the pollution from one lake in Ontario as to clean all of the lakes in Canada. In a verbal protocol study, Schkade and Payne (1994) found that when people estimate their willingness to pay to correct a particular environmental problem, they spend almost no time thinking about other uses for the money. Rather, they take the problem as it comes and think about how much they can afford to pay in general and do not think about things like what proportion of their scarce resources they can spend on this cause as opposed to other causes. When respondents in Schkade and Payne's study were reminded that there were other causes as well, many indicated that their earlier statements of willingness to pay were too high.

Preexisting Heuristics. Bracketing decisions can also be determined by socially acquired heuristics and decision rules. For example, in our work-oriented society, it is common to divide the week into two intervals of unequal length – the work-week and the weekend; periods of eating are labeled "meals," and food intake occurring between these designated times is referred to as "snacking"; and so on. All of these conventions, many or most of which exist for good reasons, influence the way that people bracket decisions.

In a study that illustrates both the arbitrariness and consequentiality of such divisions, we asked visitors to the Pittsburgh International Airport to state how much fattening bread pudding they would want during a week-long conference in Ohio:

You are attending a conference at a hotel in Ohio for a week (Monday morning through Monday morning). You eat all your meals at the conference hotel. The specialty of the hotel dining room is New Orleans Bread Pudding, which is delicious, but heavy on the fat and calories. However, you can have the bread pudding with dinner at no extra cost.

Broad bracketing respondents were induced to make the entire week's choices together by being asked "On which day(s), if any, would you like to eat a bread pudding?" They then checked off their decision for each day. The remaining respondents were induced to bracket more narrowly. Again, they made separate decisions for each day, but this time the week was divided into two subperiods: weekdays and weekend. Subjects chose to eat many more puddings when they were broken down into weekdays and weekend days (.57 per day) than when the days of the week were expressed as one block (.35 per day), $t(44) = 4.00$, $p < .05$.

Motivated Bracketing. People sometimes adopt a particular bracket to accomplish some goal – most typically to overcome problems of self-control. Much of social guidance regarding bracketing is clearly motivated to counteract otherwise tempting misbehavior. For example, abstinent alcoholics are instructed to take it "one day at a time," presumably because taking it one year at a time makes their task seem overly daunting.[8] Narrow bracketing may also facilitate self-control when people are budgeting time, money, or calories. Eating only 14,000 calories per week is a rule that is much easier to fudge on than 2,000 calories per day, even if, or perhaps precisely because, the former allows for more flexible and thus efficient scheduling. Those who get the urge to binge, for example, might be able to persuade themselves that today is the beginning of a new week. Similarly, spending is much easier to restrict on an entertainment budget of $10 per day rather than $70 per week, and spending 2 hours with one's child per day is more difficult to shirk on than spending at least 14 hours per week.[9] This might be one reason why the taxi drivers in Camerer

---

[8] By contrast, not-yet-addicted drug users are urged to take a broader view of their drug use – lest each day of drug use appear to have inconsequential costs.

[9] Thaler and Shefrin's (1981) emphasis on the relationship between mental accounting and the self-control problems in their planner-doer model reflects this insight. See Laibson (1994) for a simple principal-agent model along these lines that is also suggestive of budgeting as a self-control mechanism.

et al.'s (1997) study employed a daily earnings target; if they had, for example, picked a weekly target they might have been tempted to quit early on any given day while assuring themselves that they could make up the deficiency later in the week.

Because narrow bracketing can make goals seem easier to attain, it can also increase motivation. This may be an additional reason for a lot of seemingly short-sighted behavior, such as that shown by the cab drivers. By setting a goal of earning a fixed amount per day, they had something realistic to work toward. Indeed, such a feasible performance-based goal may have enabled them to get more work done in less time than an alternative strategy such as "work 8 hours per day." Anthony Trollope (1883/1980) attributed his remarkable productivity to a work schedule that explicitly recruited severe narrow-bracketing in the service of long-term goals:

When I have commenced a new book, I have always prepared a diary, divided into weeks, and carried on for the period which I have allowed myself for the completion of the work. In this I have entered, day by day, the number of pages I have written, so that if at any time I have slipped into idleness for a day or two, the record of that idleness has been there, staring me in the face, and demanding of me increased labour, so that the deficiency might be supplied. . . . In the bargains I have made with publishers I have . . . undertaken always to supply them with so many words, and I have never put a book out of hand short of the number by a single word. (p. 119)

Trollope's strategy was exactly the same as the one used by the cab drivers. On days when he was very productive he was able to quit early, and on days when the writing was slow he worked longer hours – or else, as indicated in the text, paid a price. Trollope produced at least three major novels a year, many of which are still widely read, while successfully holding a responsible position in the English postal service. It is difficult to fault him for bracketing too narrowly.

Broad bracketing can also serve motivational purposes. Both Rachlin's (1995) and Heyman's (1996) accounts of self-control and addiction are based on the premise that broad bracketing leads to superior choices and that people have some control over the type of brackets they adopt. Ainslie and Haslam (1992) likewise posit that people may use broad bracketing of choices as a self-control device:

Imagine a person on a weight-reducing diet who has been offered a piece of candy. The person knows that the calories in one piece of candy will not make any noticeable difference in weight, and yet he is apt to feel that he should not eat the candy. What would it cost him? Common experience tells us: his expectation of sticking to the diet. He will face many chances to eat forbidden foods, and if he sees himself eating this one, it will not seem likely to him that he will refuse the others. (p. 188)

By bracketing dieting choices together, and by viewing rejection or acceptance of the single piece of candy as a larger choice between diet versus no diet, this person increases the chance of adherence to his diet. Although the evidence is not clear concerning whether bracketing as a framing strategy is a successful means of self-control, the widespread existence of rigid rules of conduct and the explicit claims that these rules are self-control devices suggest that it has some beneficial effect.

IS BROAD BRACKETING ALWAYS BETTER
THAN NARROW BRACKETING?

The underlying premise of this chapter is that broad bracketing usually leads to better outcomes than narrow bracketing. By "better" we mean that people will usually gain more happiness from making the choices dictated by the broader bracketing than the narrow one. An examination of the studies cited earlier should make this clear: People who buy stocks will be wealthier than those who buy bonds; dieters who bracket their dining decisions broadly will eat fewer desserts than those who consider each day separately; and consumers who bracket all their purchases together without setting up inviolable budgets will be able to make efficient tradeoffs across purchase categories. The general principle is that broad bracketing allows people to pursue maximization of their global well-being. However, broad bracketing is not an unalloyed good, and there may be cases where it is actually better to bracket narrowly. We see at least four caveats to the broader-is-better view of bracketing.

First, as is no doubt clear from many of our examples, choices made under broad bracketing often involve putting up with small discomforts or annoyances to achieve long-term gains. For example, people who invest all of their retirement funds in stocks, as they might do if they bracket broadly, may be wealthier when they retire, but at the cost of ongoing anxiety during the intervening period. A priori, it is impossible to determine whether the expected gain is adequate compensation for the anxiety. Likewise, for cab drivers to attempt to bracket more broadly – for example, by attempting to maximize their weekly earnings while minimizing hours driven – might require more self-control and more careful record-keeping, burdens, which could offset the benefits derived from greater efficiency. To be able to determine whether broadly or narrowly bracketed choices are better in a particular situation, we need some way of comparing the overall or total utility (Kahneman, Wakker, & Sarin's, 1997, term) of a lifetime of small annoyances against the big gains from broad bracketing. Ironically, it may turn out that narrow bracketing is sometimes better because it enables us to take little annoyances into account (such as the pain of record keeping) that have a significant effect on total utility but which can be ignored when one takes the long view.

The second caveat is that, because broad bracketing facilitates the consideration of factors that are given little weight during narrow bracketing, it can exacerbate errors people make in anticipating the role these factors play in their experienced well-being. A possible case in point is the diversification bias, already discussed. Although people like diversity when they choose sets of goods, it is by no means certain that they are always more satisfied with diverse experiences. That is, diversity may influence their choices, but not the pleasure they get from what they choose. In one study, Read and Loewenstein (1995) found that people who chose a diverse set of snacks under broad bracketing often wanted to change their minds if given a chance – and usually changed their minds in the direction of less diversity. In another study, Read, Van den Ouden, et al. (1999) found that people who chose more variety, whether under broad or narrow bracketing, retrospectively evaluated their choices as being less enjoyable than did those who chose less variety, suggesting that the tendency to diversify under broad bracketing may lead people to make poor choices. We suggest that the larger principle is that broad bracketing can lead to superior choices only when there are genuine and important preference interactions between alternatives. Broad bracketing will be worse than narrow bracketing when it leads people to either exaggerate trivial preference interactions or to imagine nonexistent ones.

The third caveat to the superiority of broad bracketing has already been discussed under the heading of "motivated bracketing." When people have self-control problems, broad bracketing might undermine the motivation to embark on a long chain of difficult choices. Broad bracketing, in this situation, can make the task seem overwhelming. In such cases, treating each choice in isolation may be the best strategy. In negotiation, this is known as a "salami tactic" (Fisher, 1969), in which a big problem is sliced up like a salami and dealt with one slice at a time. Salami tactics are one way that a planner can convince a doer (to use Thaler and Shefrin's, 1981, terminology) to undertake a long series of connected choices that would seem unpalatable if they had to make them all at once. Many self-control programs, such as Alcoholics Anonymous, emphasize the importance of taking small steps toward the goal of recovery. Although it may be feasible to desist from drinking for a single day, the prospect of not drinking for the rest of one's life might be so alarming that it becomes a reason to drink rather than to abstain. Of course, these examples are not straightforward cases of the superiority of narrow bracketing. The decision to undertake the task in the first place, and then to bracket each choice separately, is made by an "executive" decision maker who presumably brackets broadly to begin with but then uses the salami strategy to get its untrustworthy self to accomplish the task.

The fourth and final problem with broad bracketing is that it is not free. As we have already observed, there are cognitive costs involved with attempting to integrate many choices together, and these costs have to be balanced against the benefits of broad bracketing. For trivial everyday decisions, and perhaps for not-so-trivial but complicated ones, it may be that the costs exceed the benefits or that broad bracketing simply exceeds the individual's cognitive capacities. When narrow bracketing is inevitable, whether due to cognitive constraints or other reasons, a natural follow-up question is whether people employ decision rules that are "constrained optimal" – that is, optimal given their narrow bracketing of choices. In the domain of risky choice, for example, if people do bracket narrowly, then it will be optimal for them to be virtually risk neutral over moderate-stake gambles; a very simple heuristic – to always maximize expected return except on huge gambles – would make people better off than the (more complicated) procedures they actually do use on their narrowly bracketed choices. Similarly, New York City cab drivers could be better off driving a fixed number of hours each day rather than aiming for a fixed level of take-home pay.

CONCLUDING COMMENTS

Bracketing is different from other familiar sources of decision suboptimalities in that it seems to play an interactive or enabling role. Many established causes of decision errors exert an influence only under narrow bracketing. Loss aversion, for example, would have little impact on decision making if people aggregated multiple decisions together. This is because loss aversion matters only for decisions that can lead to either gains or losses. But in many domains, the likelihood that any individual decision will shift the decision maker from one side of the divide to the other is exceedingly small. Hence, it is often not loss aversion alone, but the combination of loss aversion and narrow bracketing, that causes problems. This is illustrated by the case of Samuelson's colleague. If he played 100 gambles, the marginal effect of any single gamble on the overall payoff would be negligible, and the likelihood that by itself it would make a winning portfolio into a losing one is essentially zero.

Narrow bracketing generally shifts people's attention from the macro level to the micro level – a level at which many of the most pernicious patterns of decision making seem to occur. Many researchers claim that dieters and drug addicts are defeated by small, but frequent, indulgences (Herrnstein & Prelec, 1992a, 1992b). Others have argued that lapses of morality rarely happen all at once, but more typically involve a series of cascading misbehaviors (e.g., Lifton, 1990). Narrow bracketing exacerbates problems like these by shifting attention from the big picture to localized, isolated decisions – from the campaign that is our life to the skirmish that is today.

ACKNOWLEDGMENTS

We are grateful to Colin Camerer, Erik Eyster, Drazen Prelec, Shane Frederick, and Richard Thaler for useful comments on an earlier draft, and to Baruch Fischhoff, Chuck Manski, and two anonymous referees for very thorough comments. The chapter was completed while Read was visiting the Rotterdam Institute for Business Economic Studies, and Loewenstein and Rabin were visiting

the Center for Advanced Study in the Behavioral Sciences. We acknowledge
support from NSF grants # SBR-960123 (to the Center), support for Loewenstein
from the Center for Integrated Study of the Human Dimensions of Global
Change at Carnegie Mellon University, and support for Rabin from the Sloan,
MacArthur, and Russell Sage Foundations.

21. Constructing Preferences From Memory

Elke U. Weber and Eric J. Johnson

Our memories define who we are and what we do. Aside from a few preferences hardwired by evolution, they also define what we like and how we choose. The increasingly more hierarchical coding of experience in memory makes a gourmet out of a gourmand. Grieving as a process of letting go of departed loved ones involves the extinction of associations between them and a host of daily encountered stimuli that serve as constant reminders of their absence. Memory processes in the construction of value and preference even have a utility of their own. We savor the memory and anticipation of pleasant choice options and may delay choice to lengthen the pleasurable experience (Loewenstein, 1988). Yet, despite this wealth of evidence of the involvement of memory processes in preference and choice, their role in preference construction has largely been ignored in existing models of judgment and decision making (Johnson & Weber, 2000; Weber, Goldstein, & Barlas, 1995).

In this chapter, we argue that our view of preference changes if conceptualized explicitly as the product of memory representations and memory processes. We draw on insights about the functions and operations of memory provided by cognitive psychology and social cognition to show that memory plays a crucial role in preference and choice. Economics and behavioral decision research have traditionally been silent on the nature and role of memory processes in preference formation, preferring to treat preference and choice in an "as-if" fashion as mathematical transformations and integrations of the features of choice objects, taking inspiration from psychophysics rather than cognitive psychology. Recently, however, a number of researchers have started to highlight the influence of implicit memory processes (Arkes, 2001) and (multiple) memory representations (see Arkes, 2001; Reyna, Lloyd, & Brainerd, 2003, for a similar discussion). Much of this work has concentrated on inferential processes, such as the notable computational memory process model MINERVA-DM designed to explain probabilistic inference and judgment (Dougherty, Gettys, & Ogden, 1999; Dougherty, Gronlund, & Gettys, 2003), and work on false memories (Reyna & Lloyd, 1997). Within research on preference and choice, image theory (Beach & Mitchell, 1987) has been a pioneer in assigning an important role to memory matching processes, as has naturalistic decision making (Klein, Orasanu, Calderwood, & Zsambok, 1993), which emphasizes recognition priming and the Brunswikian notions of functionalism and representative design (Hammond, 1990). Recent work on decision modes (Ames, Flynn, & Weber, 2004; Weber, Ames, & Blais, 2005; Weber & Hsee, 2000) has documented that choice processes based on recognition of a class of decision situations for which a prescribed best action or production rule exists are just as prevalent as computational choice processes.

In this chapter, we examine memory processes in preference construction and choice at a more "micro" and process-oriented level than previous investigations into the role of memory processes, but at a level that is cognitive and functional, rather than computational. We suggest that a consideration of properties of memory representation and retrieval can provide a unifying explanatory framework for some seemingly disparate preference phenomena.

PREFERENCES AS FUNCTIONAL RELATIONSHIPS

Current formal representations of preferences within behavioral decision research map external stimuli to their internal experience, such as prospect theory's value function (Kahneman & Tversky, 1979) and von Neumann-Morgenstern (1947) utilities. Similarly, indifference functions describe equivalent levels of hedonic value or utility generated by combinations of different levels of two or more external attributes, such as reference-dependent prospect theory (Tversky & Kahneman, 1991) or standard models of consumer choice (Varian, 1999). This theoretical framework has had a long and important history within economics and psychology. Functional mapping representations of preference have been obviously useful and are particularly amenable to mathematical formalization. They make the following explicit assumptions about the nature of preference in formal axioms and implicit assumptions about the psychology of preferences:

Stability. The mappings between choice attributes and utility are usually assumed to remain constant over time and across measurement procedures, a property often referred to as procedure invariance (Tversky, Sattath, & Slovic, 1988).

Continuity. Almost all representations of preferences use continuous functions to portray the mapping between all attribute levels and utility (in a utility function) or between combinations of attributes (in an indifference curve). Discontinuities do not exist within the defined range of experience.

Precision. Because value, utility, and tradeoff functions are represented by lines, the mappings are infinitely precise. A given level of income, for example, generates an infinitely resolvable and precise amount of utility. For two attributes, an exact equivalence between differing amounts of each attribute can be calculated.

Decision researchers over the last 20 to 30 years have questioned these assumptions. The first property to be challenged, based on changes in preference revealed by different response modes, was stability. Preferences were characterized as "labile," because they often seemed to vary across response modes (Lichtenstein & Slovic, 1971), leading to the indexing of utility functions. By the early 1990s, researchers were starting to examine situations where preferences might not exist at all, but had to be constructed in response to preference tasks (Fischhoff, 1991; Payne, Bettman, & Johnson, 1992; Slovic, 1995). As an as-if model of preference and choice, the functional relationship framework is naturally moot on the issue of preference construction, that is, it cannot make predictions about systematic differences in the construction process as a function of variables not included in the model that, nevertheless, have been shown to influence the choice process.

It may be best to appreciate the functional relationships framework as a metaphor that has yielded important insights into decision and choice but that, like any metaphor, is incomplete, highlighting some aspects of the phenomena under study, but letting others reside in the shadows. We suggest that it may be useful to conceptualize preferences under a different metaphor, in particular as the output of the human memory and inference system, because there is little reason that knowledge related to preferences should not possess the properties and characteristics of other types of knowledge. This focus might illuminate characteristics of preferences (as memories) that might be hidden from other vantage points. Our purpose is to lend some unifying theoretical structure to the now widely held view that preferences are often labile and constructed and to suggest possible components of this constructive process. To do so, we adopt some well-documented, high-level properties of human memory and apply them to preference formation. The preferences-as-memory (PAM) approach suggests that preferences are neither constructed from first principles anew on each occasion nor completely stable and immutable.

Conceptualizing preference as the product of memory processes and memory representations predicts systematic deviations from the functional account. Where functional approaches assume stability, PAM suggests that preferences may differ as a function of differences in short-term accessibility as the result of priming. Where functional accounts assume continuity and precision, the discrete nature of memory episodes and the presence of excitatory and inhibitory processes in memory (i.e., recalling one aspect of a choice situation may enhance or inhibit recollection of other aspects) suggest that preference can be discontinuous and lumpy, and can take on different values in a path-dependent fashion. In contrast to the functional account's idea of precision, PAM suggests that memory and thus preference is reactive, that is, the very act of assessing a preference can change it.

PREFERENCES AS MEMORY (PAM)

The PAM framework assumes that decisions (or valuation judgments) are made by retrieving relevant knowledge (attitudes, attributes, previous preferences, episodes, or events) from memory to determine the best (or a good) action. This process is functionally equivalent to constructing predictions about one's experience of the consequences of different actions, that is, what Kahneman and collaborators (Kahneman & Snell, 1990; Schkade & Kahneman, 1998) call predicted utility. Rather than accessing the equivalent of stable, continuous, and infinitely resolvable utility and indifference curves, we suggest that people make an attempt to retrieve past reactions and associations to similar situations. It is in the nature of human memory that such retrieval attempts do not always generate a single and precise answer. Because retrieval depends on prior encoding, memory representation, memory query, situational context, and prior attempts at retrieval, the results may vary.

A small but important number of robust empirical properties of the human memory system may play a role in the process of constructing predicted utility. We focus on three aspects of the process: (a) memory interrogation, that is, the queries posed to memory; (b) the accessibility of information in memory that is relevant to the queries; and (c) memory representation, that is, the structure of memory, which reflects the structure of the world and our task environments in a Brunswikian fashion.

INTERROGATING MEMORY

A major assumption of PAM's account of how utility predictions (and thus preferences) are generated is that people consult their memory (or the external environment) with a series of component queries about the attributes of choice alternatives, in particular, their merits or liabilities. When asked to pick their preferred CD from a choice set of three, for example, people consult their memory about previous experiences with the same or similar CDs. Because it helps with evidence generation and integration, these queries are typically grouped by valence; for example, memory is first queried about what I like about a given CD, and only after no additional positive attributes are generated may a query about negative attributes ensue. We also assume that most tasks suggest a natural way to the order in which queries are posed. Being asked to pick one CD out of three triggers queries about positive attributes first, whereas being asked to reject one of those CDs naturally triggers queries about each CD's negative attributes first (Shafir, Simonson, & Tversky, 1993). A home-owner asked to provide a selling price for her house will first consult her memory about positive features of the house before considering downsides, whereas a potential buyer may pose these queries in the opposite order (Birnbaum & Stegner, 1979). Because of interference processes, described later, the order in which queries are posed is important; that is, it affects the answers provided by memory and thus preference.

We do not assume that such queries are explicit or conscious, although they can be. Instead, we assume that they occur without conscious effort and as a natural part of automatic preference-construction processes. In this sense all decisions are reason based, to borrow Shafir, Simonson, and Tversky's (1993) term. The major difference between that work and ours is that we imbed our order-of-queries-based explanation into a broader theory about memory structure and memory processes. We emphasize the measurement and manipulation of reasons as a diagnostic tool and assert that the type, valence, and number of reasons obtained depend systematically on the valuation or choice task (e.g., pick vs. reject, buying vs. selling) and the accessibility of relevant information in memory. Recent work by McKenzie and colleagues (e.g., McKenzie & Nelson, 2003) suggests that different semantic frames that might be seen as logically equivalent (e.g., a glass being half-full or half-empty) linguistically transmit different information. A PAM interpretation of this view is that different frames lead the decision maker to generate different queries (e.g., "Where did the contents of the glass come from?" vs. "What happened to the other half of the glass's contents?"). Also relevant is work by Fischer and colleagues (Fischer, Carmon, Ariely, & Zauberman, 1999) suggesting that different response modes have different goals. A PAM interpretation hypothesizes that different goals naturally evoke different queries or different orders in which queries are posed.

MEMORY ACCESSIBILITY

Priming

Social cognition and memory research have demonstrated that the presentation of a stimulus can produce a short-term, transient increase in the accessibility of the same stimulus and related concepts (see Higgins and Kruglanski, 1996, for a review). In this phenomenon, called priming, previous activation of a memory node affects later accessibility, resulting in both shorter reaction times and greater likelihood of retrieval. A recent field experiment (North, Hargreaves, & McKendrick, 1999) linked priming and revealed preference. A supermarket where wine was sold played equally pleasant music with either strongly stereotypical French or German cultural associations on alternative days and measured the amount of wine that was sold from each country of origin. French wines sold more strongly on the days French music was played, and German wines sold more briskly when German music was played. Type of music accounted for almost a quarter of the variance in wine sales, even though respondents were unaware that the music affected their choice, with a majority denying such an effect. Priming also produced differences in behavior in a study by Bargh, Chen, and Burrows (1996), who primed (in an "unrelated experiments" paradigm) constructs such as "politeness" or "being elderly." When primed with the construct elderly (by being given an adjective rating task that involved adjectives related to the construct), for example, respondents walked away from the experiment more slowly than those who were not so primed. Walking speed was not mediated by other possible factors, such as a change in mood, and the priming effect again appeared to occur without awareness. In an important application of priming, Siegel, Krank, and Hinson's (1987) work on classical conditioning mechanisms in physical addictions suggests that the best predictor of continued abstinence after a rehab program is physical relocation (even to non-drug-free environments), because relocation removes the environmental cues associated with previous drug use that elicit withdrawal symptoms in recovering addicts.

Mandel and Johnson (2002) examined the effects of priming on consumer choice by selectively priming particular product attributes by using the background ("wallpaper") of the initial page of an online-shop Web site. Preliminary studies had shown that a background of a blue sky with clouds primed the attribute "comfort" while leaving the accessibility of other attributes unchanged. When deciding between different couches, respondents who had seen this background on the initial store Web page were more likely than control subjects to choose a more comfortable but more expensive couch over a less comfortable but cheaper couch. Similar results were shown for other primes and products.

Priming also has the potential to explain semantic framing effects reported in the behavioral decision literature, such as Levin and Gaeth's (1988) studies of differential preference for fried ground beef described as either "being 90% lean" or "containing 10% fat," Bell and Loftus' (1989) study of differential speed estimates provided for a car observed in a videotaped car accident depending on whether respondents were asked to estimate the speed of the car when it "hit" versus "smashed into" the parked truck, and McKenzie's work described earlier. In these studies, the details of the way in which fat content, traveling speed, or glass contents were described primed different components of the objects' representation in memory. These differences in short-term activation resulted in different answers to explicit evaluative questions, despite identical sensory information.

Memory Is Reactive

When you listen to a CD on your stereo, the fact that you have accessed this string of 1s and 0s does not change the music recorded on the disk. This is not true of human memory. "Tests of memory are not neutral events that merely assess the state of a person's knowledge; tests also change or modify memories. . . . Changes can be positive, aiding later retentions, or negative, causing forgetting, interference, and even false recollection" (Roedinger & Guynn, 1996, p. 225). Negative effects fall into the category of interference effects, which are mostly limited to short time spans. Here we concentrate on positive effects, namely, how access can both increase short-term accessibility and change the long-term content of memory. The picture that emerges is that memory, and therefore preferences, are reactive to measurement. By analogy to Heisenberg's uncertainty principle, the measurement can influence the behavior of the object under observation.

Short-Term Effects. Studies of anchoring suggest that memory accessibility and preference can be changed by asking a prior question, even if the answer to this question should be irrelevant to subsequent tasks. Chapman and Johnson (1999) asked a group of students if their selling price for a gamble was greater or less than the last four digits of their Social Security number, converted into a price. Although normatively irrelevant, this comparative judgment influenced their selling prices for the gamble, despite respondents' denial of any such effect. Contemporary accounts of anchoring attribute this effect to a short-term increase in the accessibility of information in memory. The Selective Accessibility Model (Strack & Mussweiler, 1997) and the Anchoring as Activation (Chapman & Johnson, 1999) perspective suggest that, despite its substantive irrelevance, an anchor makes anchor-consistent information more accessible and therefore more likely to be included in a subsequent judgment. Chapman and Johnson (2002) reviewed a large body of empirical evidence supporting this interpretation (Chapman & Johnson, 1994, 1999; Mussweiler & Strack, 2001b; Mussweiler, Strack, & Pfeiffer, 2000; Strack & Mussweiler, 1997) and found information consistent with the anchor to be more accessible than inconsistent information, as revealed by reaction time differences. For anchoring to occur, the anchor must be used in a preliminary judgment (and not just be present). Anchoring can be enhanced by increasing the knowledge base relevant to the judgment. Finally, asking people to consider other judgments can debias anchoring. Although accessibility may not be sufficient to explain all anchoring effects (Epley & Gilovich, 2001), accessibility-mediated anchoring effects are strong and robust, and persist in the presence of significant accuracy incentives, experience, and market feedback (Ariely, Loewenstein, & Prelec, 2003).

Long-Term Effects. Queries about possible choice options seem to not only generate short-term changes in the accessibility of related information, but also actually to change memory representation in a more permanent fashion. Students asked prior to election day whether they intended to vote predicted that they would do so in numbers greater than the actual voting percentage later observed for comparable control-group subjects who were not asked that question (Greenwald, Carnot, Beach, & Young, 1987). More interestingly, answering the question affirmatively increased students' subsequent actual voting behavior, months after the initial question had been posed and without any conscious memory of ever having answered it. Hirt and Sherman (1985) term this widely replicated phenomenon the self-correcting nature of errors in prediction. In the context of consumer choice, Morwitz and collaborators (Fitzsimons & Morwitz, 1996; see also Morwitz, 1997; Morwitz, Johnson, & Schmittlein, 1993; Morwitz & Pluzinski, 1996) have demonstrated that measuring purchase intentions can change purchases. Actual purchases of a personal computer increased by about one-third as the result of answering a single purchase intent question several months previously. Just as we can induce "false memories" in people (e.g., of being lost as a child in a shopping mall; Loftus & Pickrell, 1995), we can induce "false preferences" in people by asking them for behavioral intentions in ways that will result in a biased answer, capitalizing on such things as social desirability or wishful thinking. Such effects cannot be explained by conscious attempts at consistency over time, as explicit memories of prior measurement episodes typically do not exist.

Interference and Inhibition

If priming increases accessibility, other tasks or events can affect memory accessibility negatively. The classic memory phenomenon of inhibition or interference is illustrated by the following example. Imagine you have just moved and have not yet completely committed your new telephone number to memory. You try to have the newspaper delivered to your new address and are asked for your new phone number. You almost had it recalled when the customer service representatives reads out your old number, asking you if that is it. You now find it impossible to recall the new number.

Although 80 years of research on interference effects have produced a plethora of explanations and theoretical mechanisms, they all share a common idea: When one component of a memory structure is recalled, the recall of others components that could have been response competitors is temporarily suppressed. Inhibition as the result of prior recall of related and competing material is one of the oldest and most developed memory phenomena (see Anderson & Neely, 1996, for a review of theories and results). Interference effects have been shown in many different experimental paradigms, including the effect of new material on the recall of old (retroactive interference) and the effect of old material on new (proactive interference). Interference has been shown to occur for both semantic and episodic memory and for verbal as well as nonverbal materials, such as visual stimuli and motor skills. Recent studies have demonstrated conditions under which implicit memory also shows interference effects (Lustig & Hasher, 2001).

Are there functional advantages to memory processes such as priming or inhibition? Like other species, humans did not evolve to ponder and analyze, but to act in ways that maximize survival and inclusive fitness. The effective use of heuristics documented by Payne, Bettman, and Johnson (1990) and Gigerenzer, Todd, and The ABC Group (1999) suggest that humans are probably wired to pick a good action/option quickly. Excitatory and inhibitory memory activation processes facilitate the fast emergence of a response/action/decision that, in the past, has been associated with a successful outcome. Task goals and choice context determine the focus of attention, which translates into a series of implicit queries of external and internal knowledge bases, often executed in a task-specific order. Queries, in turn, result in increased activation (priming) of response-consistent information and decreased activation (inhibition) of response-inconsistent information. Russo and colleagues' (Carlson & Russo, 2001; Russo, Meloy, & Medvec, 1998; Russo, Meloy, & Wilks, 2000) evidence of very early pre-decision polarization and bias in the exploration of choice alternatives in favor of an initially selected alternative is also consistent with a strategic semantic priming and inhibition explanation. An early focus on one choice alternative (perhaps because it scored highly on an attribute that was randomly examined first) will result in greater accessibility of features consistent with it and reduced accessibility of features inconsistent with it.

Memory interference may help explain established phenomena in the behavioral decision literature and provide predictions for other effects. The basic idea is that the natural and sequential order of different queries used in the process of constructing preference or other judgments produces interference, in the sense that the responses to earlier queries inhibit possible responses to later queries. Reyna et al. (2003) suggested, for example, that interference can occur between verbatim, gist, and procedure representations. Hoch (1984, 1985) examined interference in the prediction of preferences and purchase intentions. Respondents were asked to provide reasons why they would or would not buy a consumer product in the future. Hoch counterbalanced the order of the two tasks in a between-subjects design, arguing that the first task caused interference with the second. Consistent with this hypothesis and the PAM framework, he found that the first task generated more reasons than the second. Respondents were more likely to predict that they would purchase the item when they generated reasons for buying it first, even though everyone answered both types of questions. To demonstrate that this effect was due to memory interference, Hoch separated the reasons-generation task in time from the judgment of purchase intention. Consistent with the fact that interference is a transient phenomenon, he no longer found an effect of reasons-generation on purchase intentions.

Although not motivated by a PAM (and, in particular, memory interference) perspective, several studies have manipulated the natural order of queries, often in an attempt to debias judgments. Koriat, Lichtenstein, and Fischhoff (1980) argued that, when asked for a confidence judgment in a general knowledge forced-choice quiz, people naturally ask first why their choice is correct and only then examine reasons why their choice might be wrong. A PAM interpretation suggests that this order will inhibit generation of con-reasons, leading to a biased ratio of pro/con evidence and thus overconfidence. The interference account suggests that overconfidence occurs because people naturally generate pro-reasons first, not necessarily because they have a motivational stake in generating more pro- than con-reasons. Consistent with this explanation, Koriat et al. showed that asking people to generate reasons why an answer might be wrong before generating reasons why the answer might be right diminished overconfidence. Similarly, asking respondents in anchoring studies to first generate reasons why an anchor might be irrelevant minimized anchoring bias (Chapman & Johnson, 1999; Mussweiler et al., 2000). Current research being conducted in our lab suggests that a similar decomposition of judgment and choice tasks into a series of component queries, combined with interference processes (by which the answers to earlier queries inhibit the answers to later queries), may be responsible for such phenomenon as loss aversion and time discounting.

THE STRUCTURE OF REPRESENTATIONS

To better predict how memory processes affect accessibility and preferences, we need a fuller understanding of the structure of memory representations that are relevant to preference construction. Not all knowledge is interconnected. For reasons of cognitive economy, concepts vary in their degree of interconnectedness, which reflects, at least in part, the natural co-occurrence of concepts in our daily experience in natural environments (Sherman, McMullen, & Gavanski, 1992). Most commodities (e.g., a house you plan to buy) have rich, highly structured, strongly hierarchical representations. Currencies (e.g., money, time), on the other hand, another important category in trades and other transactions, probably have a very different (more impoverished, flatter, and less connected) representation. Memory theorists argue that the number of connections between a concept node and associated subordinate nodes determines the likelihood of retrieval of any given subordinate node, a phenomenon sometimes called the fan effect (Anderson & Reder, 1999; Reder & Anderson, 1980) or cue overload (Anderson & Spellman, 1995). The basic intuition is that for a given memory cue, the probability that associated information is retrieved is a diminishing function of the number of connected nodes. Thus, ceteris paribus, memory cues with many associates will result in less recall of any one associate than cues with fewer associates. The hierarchical structure of human memory representation is probably an adaptive response to this constraint. To recall rich sets of facts, people organize this information into hierarchies of information and subinformation, a hallmark of expertise. A hierarchical category structure ensures that only a manageable number of relevant items are interconnected at any given level. Consider the category "mug." It may consist of subcategories such as coffee mug and beer mug, with each subcategory containing fewer links than a representation without subcategories. Properties of the category as a whole (mugs have handles and are heavier and larger than cups) are associated with the higher-level category, producing a more efficient representation, less prone to cue overload. We hypothesize that representations of currencies, such as money or time, differ from the hierarchical representations of commodities such as mugs. The nonhierarchical representation and nonsystematic patterns of connections for currencies, and in particular for functional properties of currencies (e.g., "things to do with $100 or 5 hours of time") lead to impaired retrieval. Imagine you were asked to name an approximate price for the following objects (possible responses are in parentheses): a newsstand copy of *Time* magazine ($2.95), a vending machine can of Diet Coke ($1.00), and a round-trip airline ticket from Los Angeles to Chicago ($400). Introspection and pilot testing in our lab indicates that this is a fairly easy task. Respondents name prices that they feel confident about within 2 to 3 seconds. Now consider the opposite task, naming something that costs $2.95, $1.00, or $400, respectively. Introspection and pilot data indicate this is a much harder task, requiring much more time, presumably because of the hypothesized asymmetry in memory connectivity as the result of the structure of memory. For Western respondents, chances are that any commodity that has a price-tag associated with it has a hierarchical structure. On the other hand, we don't have natural (or even easily generated ad hoc) categories of the kind "things to buy with $400."

Other evidence of this commodity/currency retrieval asymmetry comes from statements made while generating buying versus selling prices in endowment effect experiments conducted in our lab. Although people in both the buying and selling condition easily generate many statements (both good and bad) about the mug, statements about good or bad attributes of the money they could receive or keep are much less frequent, and mentions of alternative uses of the money are almost nonexistent.

Differences in the structure of memory for different classes of trading objects may lie at the root of other phenomena in decision research, such as people's failure to attend sufficiently to the opportunity costs of their choices or actions (Thaler, 1999). Although it may be easy to generate a large number of reasons for the purchase of a particular vacation home, the structure of memory for currencies and their uses makes it very hard to generate alternative uses for the required purchase price. A deeper understanding of the way in which people organize and cluster their knowledge about the world may be helpful in modeling behavior in many preference and choice tasks. The current inability of behavioral decision researchers to provide ex ante predictions about such things as the reference point(s) used in a given task (Fischhoff, 1983) or about the number and type of mental accounts used seriously curtails our ability to apply our most popular behavioral models. We suggest that experimental paradigms and procedures designed to reveal the organization and structure of memory in a particular content domain may help with such predictions.

Many behavioral decision models use similarity (e.g., between choice outcomes, between presented outcomes and some memory referent) as a variable in their predictions, typically without specifying how such similarity could or should be assessed. Judgment heuristics such as representativeness (Tversky & Kahneman, 1974) make implicit use of the category structure of human knowledge, including people's ability to generate and use ad hoc categories ("feminist bank tellers"). A better understanding of the organization and structure of preference-related knowledge and memory will lend greater predictive power to such models.

CAVEATS

Alternative Theories

We do not (necessarily) conceive of the PAM interpretations of the behavioral decision research phenomena discussed in this chapter as alternative explanations to those offered previously by others, but instead as a cognitive process-level account of the essence of other explanations or descriptions (e.g., myopia or hyperbolic discounting to describe time discounting). What does a cognitive process-level account add to high-level descriptive labels such as myopia or loss aversion? First, we hope that PAM explications of such constructs will provide unifying theory across disparate phenomena. For example, similarities in effects between temporal discounting and loss aversion have been noted as a curious phenomenon (Prelec & Loewenstein, 1991). A PAM account of those two classes of effects may show that this similarity in effects is the result of similarity in fundamental memory processes in preference construction. Second, process-level explanations are of crucial importance when addressing the normative status of violations of traditional preference models and in designing effective interventions. Understanding the causes of loss aversion would help us characterize it as either a decision error in generating predicted utility or as a valid factor in predicting utility. Further, if we choose to change elicitation procedures, a process-level explanation will be helpful in engineering better alternatives.

In other cases, PAM accounts of phenomena *are* offered as alternative explanations that differ from others accounts (e.g., a desire for self-consistency to explain priming effects), by postulating that the phenomena can occur without the awareness of the decision maker. An implicit null hypothesis of the PAM theoretical structure is that many phenomena that may seem motivational are actually sufficiently explained by basic cognitive processes. The PAM framework does not exclude the possibility that motivational variables may play important roles. It simply tries to see how far it can get without them.

Level of Analysis

The PAM framework outlined in this proposal is intended as much more than simply a metaphor; rather, it is a process-level account, albeit one at a relatively high level of abstraction. It is probably premature to worry about the precise nature of memory microprocesses involved in preference formation. Thus, we do not address relevant theoretical controversies within each of the areas of memory research on which we drew in this chapter to explain preference phenomena. In the case of priming, theoretical accounts range from spreading activation (Anderson, 1983; Collins & Loftus, 1975) to connectionist models (Ratcliff & McKoon, 1997). Interference effects (Postman & Underwood, 1973) have been explained in two ways, the first of which is known as the cue-overload principle (Watkins & Tulving, 1978; Watkins & Watkins, 1975), which is related to research on fan effects (Anderson & Reder, 1999; Reder & Anderson, 1980). This approach emphasizes that new information competes with old for associations in memory. More recent accounts describe interference as occurring from a process of selective retrieval with the explicit inhibition of competing material, sometimes called negative priming (Anderson & Neely, 1996; Milliken, Joordens, Merikle, & Seiffert, 1998). Later stages of a PAM research program may usefully revisit these distinctions, in light of data that may speak to one or more of them. Much of the memory literature that we reviewed and utilized falls into the growing category of implicit memory. Although space constraints prevent us from reviewing the explicit/implicit memory distinction, it is the unconscious and automatic nature of the PAM processes that provides their appeal. Finally, we think that developments in cognitive neuroscience over the next couple of years will inform the PAM perspective and further theoretical developments and research in future years.

Affect and Memory

The PAM framework might, at first sight, appear to be overly cognitive, a "cold" model of decision making. However, this claim would be based on an artificial dichotomy between memory and affect, whereas in reality the two concepts are closely intertwined. First, affect determines what is recalled. Information consistent with basic or core emotions (Russell, 2002) is more available in memory (Forgas, 1995; Johnson & Tversky, 1983). Second, affect is often recalled or generated from memory. In addition to retrieving the factual event information, cognition often delivers feelings, either through explicit or implicit retrieval or mental simulation, in what Russell (2002) terms the virtual reality hypothesis. People have been shown to use both task-related and task-misattributed affect as information when making judgments and choices (Loewenstein, Weber, Hsee, & Welch, 2001; Schwarz & Clore, 1983). Current work in our lab explores the relationship between affect induction and PAM framework memory processes in preference construction, to see whether recently reported affect-related moderation of endowment effects (Lerner, Small, & Loewenstein, 2004) can be explained as priming effects and affect-consistent recall or whether nonmemory processes need to be invoked. Complex preference and choice phenomena like loss aversion and time discounting may well have multiple, independent determinants. However, parsimony dictates that we should search for the smallest number of necessary explanatory processes.

SIGNIFICANCE, IMPLICATIONS, AND APPLICATIONS

A better understanding of the cognitive process underlying preference construction serves several functions. Process explanations help to understand when predictions of utility are accurate predictors of experienced utility. Knowing why and how different preference elicitation methods lead to different predictions will help with the design of effective preference elicitation procedures, that is, interventions that produce "better" outcomes from either a societal or individual perspective. In addition, a memory-process orientation provides insights into how and why effects such as loss aversion, time discounting, and tradeoff difficulty may vary across people, domains, and decision context. Work in our lab currently examines developmental changes in preference (e.g., in the degree of loss aversion) as the result of known changes in susceptibility to interference with age (Anderson & Craik, 2000). A better understanding of the relationship between memory processes and preference may lead to the design of interventions that minimize socially harmful consequences of changes in memory performance on preference and choice (e.g., increased susceptibility to persuasion and advertising) in older populations.

ACKNOWLEDGMENTS

This paper reports work supported by the National Science Foundation under Grant No. SES-0352062. Any opinions, findings, and conclusions or recommendations expressed in this material are those of the authors and do not necessarily reflect the views of the National Science Foundation. We thank the National Science Foundation for their support.

22. Reason-Based Choice

Eldar Shafir, Itamar Simonson, and Amos Tversky

The result is that peculiar feeling of inward unrest known as *indecision*. Fortunately it is too familiar to need description, for to describe it would be impossible. As long as it lasts, with the various objects before the attention, we are said to *deliberate*; and when finally the original suggestion either prevails and makes the movement take place, or gets definitively quenched by its antagonists, we are said to decide . . . in favor of one or the other course. The reinforcing and inhibiting ideas meanwhile are termed the *reasons* or *motives* by which the decision is brought about.

– William James (1890/1981)

My way is to divide half a sheet of paper by a line into two columns; writing over the one *Pro*, and over the other *Con*. Then, during three or four days' consideration, I put down under the different heads short hints of the different motives, that at different times occur to me for or against the measure. When I have thus got them all together in one view, I endeavor to estimate the respective weights . . . find at length where the balance lies. . . . And, though the weight of reasons cannot be taken with the precision of algebraic quantities, yet, when each is thus considered, separately and comparatively, and the whole matter lies before me, I think I can judge better, and am less liable to make a rash step; and in fact I have found great advantage for this kind of equation, in what may be called *moral* or *prudential algebra*.

– Benjamin Franklin, 1772 (cited by Bigelow, 1887)

INTRODUCTION

The making of decisions, both big and small, is often difficult because of uncertainty and conflict. We are usually uncertain about the exact consequences of our actions, which may depend on the weather or the state of the economy, and we often experience conflict about how much of one attribute (e.g., savings) to trade off in favor of another (e.g., leisure). To explain how people resolve such conflict, students of decision making have traditionally employed either formal models or reason-based analyses. The formal modeling approach, which is commonly used in economics, management science, and decision research,

Reprinted from *Cognition*, vol. 49, pp. 11–36, Copyright © 1993, with permission from Elsevier.

411

412 E. Shafir, I. Simonson, and A. Tversky

typically associates a numerical value with each alternative and characterizes choice as the maximization of value. Such value-based accounts include normative models, like expected utility theory (von Neumann & Morgenstern, 1947), as well as descriptive models, such as prospect theory (Kahneman & Tversky, 1979). An alternative tradition in the study of decision making, characteristic of scholarship in history and the law, and typical of political and business discourse, employs an informal, reason-based analysis. This approach identifies various reasons and arguments that are purported to enter into and influence decision, and explains choice in terms of the balance of reasons for and against the various alternatives. Examples of reason-based analyses can be found in studies of historic presidential decisions, such as those taken during the Cuban missile crisis (e.g., Allison, 1971), the Camp David accords (Telhami, 1990), or the Vietnam War (e.g., Berman, 1982; Betts & Gelb, 1979). Furthermore, reason-based analyses are commonly used to interpret "case studies" in business and law schools. Although the reasons invoked by researchers may not always correspond to those that motivated the actual decision makers, it is generally agreed that an analysis in terms of reasons may help explain decisions, especially in contexts where value-based models can be difficult to apply.

Little contact has been made between the two traditions, which have typically been applied to different domains. Reason-based analyses have been used primarily to explain nonexperimental data, particularly unique historic, legal, and political decisions. In contrast, value-based approaches have played a central role in experimental studies of preference and in standard economic analyses. The two approaches, of course, are not incompatible: reason-based accounts may often be translated into formal models, and formal analyses can generally be paraphrased as reason-based accounts. In the absence of a comprehensive theory of choice, both formal models and reason-based analyses may contribute to the understanding of decision making.

Both approaches have obvious strengths and limitations. The formal, value-based models have the advantage of rigor, which facilitates the derivation of testable implications. However, value-based models are difficult to apply to complex, real-world decisions, and they often fail to capture significant aspects of people's deliberations. An explanation of choice based on reasons, on the other hand, is essentially qualitative and typically vague. Furthermore, almost anything can be counted as a "reason," so that every decision may be rationalized after the fact. To overcome this difficulty, one could ask people to report their reasons for decision. Unfortunately, the actual reasons that guide decision may or may not correspond to those reported by the subjects. As has been amply documented (e.g., Nisbett & Wilson, 1977), subjects are sometimes unaware of the precise factors that determine their choices and generate spurious explanations when asked to account for their decisions. Indeed, doubts about the validity of introspective reports have led many students of decision making to focus exclusively on observed choices. Although verbal reports and introspective accounts can provide valuable information, we use "reasons" in the present chapter to describe factors or motives that affect decision, whether or not they can be articulated or recognized by the decision maker.

Despite its limitations, a reason-based conception of choice has several attractive features. First, a focus on reasons seems closer to the way we normally think and talk about choices. When facing a difficult choice (e.g., between schools or jobs) we try to come up with reasons for and against each option – we do not normally attempt to estimate their overall values. Second, thinking of choice as guided by reasons provides a natural way to understand the conflict that characterizes the making of decisions. From the perspective of reason-based choice, conflict arises when the decision maker has good reasons for and against each option or conflicting reasons for competing options. Unlike numerical values, which are easy to compare, conflicting reasons may be hard to reconcile. An analysis based on reasons can also accommodate framing effects (Tversky & Kahneman, 1986) and elicitation effects (Tversky, Sattath, & Slovic, 1988), which show that preferences are sensitive to the ways in which options are described (e.g., in terms of gains or losses) and to the methods through which preferences are elicited (e.g., pricing versus choice). These findings, which are puzzling from the perspective of value maximization, are easier to interpret if we assume that different frames and elicitation procedures highlight different aspects of the options and thus bring forth different reasons to guide decision. Finally, a conception of choice based on reasons may incorporate comparative considerations (such as relative advantages, or anticipated regret) that typically remain outside the purview of value maximization.

In this chapter, we explore the logic of reason-based choice and test some specific hypotheses concerning the role of reasons in decision making. The chapter proceeds as follows. The first section considers the role of reasons in choice between equally attractive options. The second section explores differential reliance on reasons for and against the selection of options. The third section investigates the interaction between high and low conflict and people's tendency to seek other alternatives, whereas the fourth section considers the relation between conflict and the addition of alternatives to the choice set. The fifth section contrasts the effect of a specific reason for choice with that of a disjunction of reasons. The next section explores the role that irrelevant reasons can play in the making of decisions. Concluding remarks are presented in the last section.

CHOICE BETWEEN EQUALLY ATTRACTIVE OPTIONS

How do decision makers resolve the conflict when faced with a choice between two equally attractive options? To investigate this question, Slovic (1975) first had subjects equate pairs of alternatives and later asked them to make choices between the equally valued alternatives in each pair. One pair, for example, was gift packages consisting of a combination of cash and coupons. For each pair, one component of one alternative was missing, as shown in the following table, and subjects were asked to determine the value of the missing component that would render the two alternatives equally attractive. (In the following example, the value volunteered by the subject may be, say, $10.)

	Gift package A	Gift package B
Cash	–	$20
Coupon book worth	$32	$18

A week later, subjects were asked to choose between the two equated alternatives. They were also asked, independently, which dimension – cash or coupons – they considered more important. Value-based theories imply that the two alternatives – explicitly equated for value – are equally likely to be selected. In contrast, for this choice between gift packages, 88% of the subjects who had equated these alternatives for value then proceeded to choose the alternative that was higher on the dimension that the subject considered more important.

As Slovic (1975, 1990) suggests, people seem to be following a choice mechanism that is easy to explain and justify: Choosing according to the more important dimension provides a better reason for choice than, say, random selection or selection of the right-hand option. Slovic (1975) replicated this pattern in numerous domains, including choices between college applicants, auto tires, baseball players, and routes to work. (For additional data and a discussion of elicitation procedures, see Tversky et al., 1988.) All the results were consistent with the hypothesis that people do not choose between the equated alternatives at random. Instead, they resolve the conflict by selecting the alternative that is superior on the more important dimension, which seems to provide a compelling reason for choice.

REASONS PRO AND CON

Consider having to choose one of two options or, alternatively, having to reject one of two options. Under the standard analysis of choice, the two tasks are interchangeable. In a binary choice situation it should not matter whether people are asked which option they prefer or which they would reject. Because it is the options themselves that are assumed to matter, not the way in which they are described, if people prefer the first they will reject the second, and vice versa.

As suggested by Franklin's opening quote, our decision will depend partially on the weights we assign to the options' pros and cons. We propose that the positive features of options (their pros) will loom larger when choosing, whereas the negative features of options (their cons) will be weighted more heavily when rejecting. It is natural to select an option because of its positive features and to reject an option because of its negative features. To the extent that people base their decisions on reasons for and against the options under consideration, they are likely to focus on reasons for choosing an option when deciding which to choose and to focus on reasons for rejecting an option when deciding which to reject. This hypothesis leads to a straightforward prediction: Consider two options, an *enriched* option, with more positive and more negative features, and an *impoverished* option, with fewer positive and fewer negative features. If positive features are weighted more heavily when choosing than when rejecting and negative features are weighted relatively more when rejecting than when choosing, then an enriched option could be both chosen and rejected when compared with an impoverished option. Let P_c and P_r denote, respectively, the percentage of subjects who choose and who reject a particular option. If choosing and rejecting are complementary, then the sum $P_c + P_r$ should equal 100. On the other hand, according to our hypothesis, $P_c + P_r$ should be greater than 100 for the enriched option and less than 100 for the impoverished option. This pattern was observed by Shafir (1993). Consider, for example, the following problem, which was presented to subjects in two versions that differed only in the bracketed questions. One-half of the subjects received one version, the other half received the other. The enriched option appears last, although the order presented to subjects was counterbalanced.

Problem 1 (n = 170): Imagine that you serve on the jury of an only-child sole-custody case following a relatively messy divorce. The facts of the case are complicated by ambiguous economic, social, and emotional considerations, and you decide to base your decision entirely on the following few observations. [To which parent would you award sole custody of the child?/Which parent would you deny sole custody of the child?]

	Award	Deny
Parent A: average income		
average health		
average working hours		
reasonable rapport with the child		
relatively stable social life	36%	45%
Parent B: above-average income		
very close relationship with the child		
extremely active social life		
lots of work-related travel		
minor health problems	64%	55%

Parent A, the impoverished option, is quite plain – with no striking positive or negative features. There are no particularly compelling reasons to award or deny this parent custody of the child. Parent B, the enriched option, on the other hand, has good reasons to be awarded custody (a very close relationship with the child and a good income), but also good reasons to be denied sole custody (health problems and extensive absences due to travel). To the right of the options are the percentages of subjects who chose to award and to deny custody to each of the parents. Parent B is the majority choice both for being awarded custody of the child and for being denied it. As predicted, $P_c + P_r$ for parent B ($64 + 55 = 119$) is significantly greater than 100, the value expected if choosing and rejecting were complementary, $z = 2.48$, $p <$ .02. This pattern is explained by the observation that the enriched parent (parent B) provides more compelling reasons to be awarded as well as denied child custody.

This pattern has been replicated in hypothetical choices between monetary gambles, college courses, and political candidates (Shafir, 1993). For another example, consider the following problem, presented to half the subjects in the "prefer" and to the other half in the "cancel" version.

Problem 2 (n = 172):
Prefer: Imagine that you are planning a week vacation in a warm spot over spring break. You currently have two options that are reasonably priced. The travel brochure gives only a limited amount of information about the two options. Given the information available, which vacation spot would you prefer?
Cancel: Imagine that you are planning a week vacation in a warm spot over spring break. You currently have two options that are reasonably priced, but you can no longer retain your reservation in both. The travel brochure gives only a limited amount of information about the two options. Given the information available, which reservation do you decide to cancel?

	Prefer	Cancel

Spot A: average weather
    average beaches
    medium-quality hotel
    medium-temperature water
    average nightlife
	33%	52%

Spot B: lots of sunshine
    gorgeous beaches and coral reefs
    ultra-modern hotel
    very cold water
    very strong winds
    no nightlife
	67%	48%

The information about the two spots is typical of the kind of information we have available when deciding where to take our next vacation. Because it is difficult to estimate the overall value of each spot, we are likely to seek reasons on which to base our decision. Spot A, the impoverished option, seems unremarkable yet unobjectionable on all counts. On the other hand, there are obvious reasons – gorgeous beaches, an abundance of sunshine, and an ultra-modern hotel – for choosing spot B. Of course, there are also compelling reasons – cold water, winds, and a lack of nightlife – why spot B should be rejected. We suggest that the gorgeous beaches are likely to provide a more compelling reason when we choose than when we reject, and the lack of nightlife is likely to play a more central role when we reject than when we choose.

Indeed, spot B's share of being preferred and rejected exceeds that of spot A ($P_c + P_r, = 67 + 48 = 115$), $p < .05$. These results demonstrate that options are not simply ordered according to value, with the more attractive selected and the less attractive rejected. Instead, it appears that the relative importance of options' strengths and weaknesses varies with the nature of the task. As a result, we are significantly more likely to end up in spot B when we ask ourselves which we prefer than when we contemplate which to cancel (67% vs. 52%), $z = 2.83$, $p < .001$.

One of the most basic assumptions of the rational theory of choice is the principle of procedure invariance, which requires strategically equivalent methods of elication to yield identical preferences (see Tversky et al., 1988, for discussion). The choose–reject discrepancy represents a predictable failure of procedure invariance. This phenomenon is at variance with value maximization, but is easily understood from the point of view of reason-based choice: reasons for choosing are more compelling when we choose than when we reject, and reasons for rejecting matter more when we reject than when we choose.

CHOICE UNDER CONFLICT: SEEKING OPTIONS

The need to choose often creates conflict: We are not sure how to trade off one attribute relative to another or, for that matter, which attributes matter to us most. It is a commonplace that we often attempt to resolve such conflict by seeking reasons for choosing one option over another. At times, the conflict between available alternatives is hard to resolve, which may lead us to seek additional options or to maintain the status quo. Other times, the context is such that a comparison between alternatives generates compelling reasons to choose one option over another. Using reasons to resolve conflict has some nonobvious implications, which are addressed later. The present section focuses on people's decision to seek other alternatives; the next section explores some effects of adding options to the set under consideration.

In many contexts, we need to decide whether to opt for an available option or search for additional alternatives. Thus, a person who wishes to buy a used car may settle for a car that is currently available or continue searching for additional models. Seeking new alternatives usually requires additional time and effort, and may involve the risk of losing the previously available options. Conflict plays no role in the classical theory of choice. In this theory, each option x has a value $v(x)$ such that, for any offered set, the decision maker selects the option with the highest value. In particular, a person is expected to search for additional alternatives only if the expected value of searching exceeds that of the best option currently available. A reliance on reasons, on the other hand, entails that we should be more likely to opt for an available option when we have a convincing reason for its selection and that we should be more likely to search further when a compelling reason for choice is not readily available.

To investigate this hypothesis, Tversky and Shafir (1992a) presented subjects with pairs of options, such as bets varying in probability and payoff, or student apartments varying in monthly rent and distance from campus, and had subjects choose one of the two options or, instead, request an additional option, at some cost. Subjects first reviewed the entire set of 12 options (gambles or apartments) to familiarize themselves with the available alternatives. In the study of choice between bets some subjects then received the following problem:

Conflict:
Imagine that you are offered a choice between the following two gambles:

(x) 65% chance to win $15
(y) 30% chance to win $35

You can either select one of these gambles or you can pay $1 to add one more gamble to the choice set. The added gamble will be selected at random from the list you reviewed.

Other subjects received a similar problem except that option y was replaced by option x', to yield a choice between the following:

Dominance:

(x) 65% chance to win $15
(x') 65% chance to win $14

Subjects were asked to indicate whether they wanted to add another gamble or select between the available alternatives. They then chose their preferred gamble from the resulting set (with or without the added option). Subjects were instructed that the gambles they chose would be played out and that their payoff would be proportional to the amount of money they earned minus the fee they paid for the added gambles.

A parallel design presented choices between hypothetical student apartments. Some subjects received the following problem:

Conflict:
Imagine that you face a choice between two apartments with the following characteristics:

(x) $290 a month, 25 minutes from campus
(y) $350 a month, 7 minutes from campus

Both have one bedroom and a kitchenette. You can choose now between the two apartments or you can continue to search for apartments (to be selected at random from the list you reviewed). In that case, there is some risk of losing one or both of the apartments you have found.

Other subjects received a similar problem except that option y was replaced by option x', to yield a choice between the following:

Dominance:

(x) $290 a month, 25 minutes from campus
(x') $330 a month, 25 minutes from campus

Note that in both pairs of problems the choice between x and y – the *conflict* condition – is nontrivial because the xs are better on one dimension and the ys are better on the other. In contrast, the choice between x and x' – the *dominance* condition – involves no conflict because the former strictly dominates the latter. Thus, although there is no obvious reason to choose one option over the other in the conflict condition, there is a decisive argument for preferring one of the two alternatives in the dominance condition.

On average, subjects requested an additional alternative 64% of the time in the conflict condition and only 40% of the time in the dominance condition, $p < .05$. Subjects' tendency to search for additional options, in other words, was greater when the choice among alternatives was harder to rationalize than when there was a compelling reason and the decision was easy.

These data are inconsistent with the principle of value maximization. According to value maximization, a subject should search for additional alternatives if and only if the expected (subjective) value of searching exceeds that of the best alternative currently available. Because the best alternative offered in the dominance condition is also available in the conflict condition, value maximization implies that the percentage of subjects who seek an additional alternative cannot be greater in the conflict than in the dominance condition, contrary to the observed data.

It appears that the search for additional alternatives depends not only on the value of the best available option, as implied by value maximization, but also on the difficulty of choosing among the options under consideration. In situations of dominance, for example, there are clear and indisputable reasons for choosing one option over another (e.g., "This apartment is equally distant and I save \$40!"). Having a compelling argument for choosing one of the options over the rest reduces the temptation to look for additional alternatives. When the choice involves conflict, on the other hand, reasons for choosing any one of the options are less immediately available, and the decision is more difficult to justify (e.g., "Should I save \$60 a month or reside 18 minutes closer to campus?"). In the absence of compelling reasons for choice, there is a greater tendency to search for other alternatives.

CHOICE UNDER CONFLICT: ADDING OPTIONS

An analysis in terms of reasons can help explain observed violations of the principle of independence of irrelevant alternatives, according to which the preference ordering between two options should not be altered by the introduction of additional alternatives. This principle follows from the standard assumption of value maximization and has been routinely assumed in the analysis of consumer choice. Despite its intuitive appeal, there is a growing body of evidence that people's preferences depend on the context of choice, defined by the set of options under consideration. In particular, the addition and removal of options from the offered set can influence people's preferences among options that were available all along. Whereas in the previous section we considered people's tendency to seek alternatives in the context of a given set of options, in this section we illustrate phenomena that arise through the addition of options and interpret them in terms of reasons for choice.

A major testable implication of value maximization is that a nonpreferred option cannot become preferred when new options are added to the offered set. In particular, a decision maker who prefers y over the option to defer the choice should not prefer to defer the choice when both y and x are available. That the "market share" of an option cannot be increased by enlarging the offered set is known as the *regularity condition* (see Tversky & Simonson, 1993). Contrary to regularity, numerous experimental results indicate that the tendency to defer choice can increase with the addition of alternatives. Consider, for instance, the degree of conflict that arises when a person is presented with one attractive option (which he or she prefers to deferring the choice), compared with two competing alternatives. Choosing one out of two competing alternatives can be difficult: The mere fact that an alternative is attractive may not in itself provide a compelling reason for its selection, because the other option may be equally attractive. The addition of an alternative may thus make the decision harder to justify and increase the tendency to defer the decision.

A related phenomenon was aptly described by Thomas Schelling (personal communication), who tells of an occasion in which he had decided to buy an encyclopedia for his children. At the bookstore, he was presented with two attractive encyclopedias and, finding it difficult to choose between the two, ended up buying neither – this, despite the fact that had only one encyclopedia been available he would have happily bought it. More generally, there are situations in which people prefer each of the available alternatives over the status quo but do not have a compelling reason for choosing among the alternatives and, as a result, defer the decision, perhaps indefinitely.

The phenomenon described by Schelling was demonstrated by Tversky and Shafir (1992a) in the following pair of problems, which were presented to two groups of students ($n = 124$ and 121, respectively).

High conflict:
Suppose you are considering buying a compact disk (CD) player, and have not yet decided what model to buy. You pass by a store that is having a 1-day clearance sale. They offer a popular SONY player for just $99, and a top-of-the-line AIWA player for just $169, both well below the list price. Do you:

(*x*) buy the AIWA player.	27%
(*y*) buy the SONY player.	27%
(*z*) wait until you learn more about the various models.	46%

Low conflict:
Suppose you are considering buying a CD player, and have not yet decided what model to buy. You pass by a store that is having a 1-day clearance sale. They offer a popular SONY player for just $99, well below the list price. Do you:

(y) buy the SONY player.	66%
(z) wait until you learn more about the various models.	34%

The results indicate that people are more likely to buy a CD player in the latter, *low-conflict*, condition than in the former, *high-conflict*, situation, $p < .05$. Both models – the AIWA and the SONY – seem attractive, both are well priced, and both are on sale. The decision maker needs to determine whether she is better off with a cheaper, popular model or with a more expensive and sophisticated one. This conflict is apparently not easy to resolve and compels many subjects to put off the purchase until they learn more about the various options. On the other hand, when the SONY alone is available, there are compelling arguments for its purchase: It is a popular player, it is very well priced, and it is on sale for 1 day only. In this situation, having good reasons to choose the offered option, a greater majority of subjects decide to opt for the CD player rather than delay the purchase.

The addition of a competing alternative in the preceding example increased the tendency to delay decision. Clearly, the level of conflict and its ease of resolution depend not only on the number of options available, but on how the options compare. Consider, for example, the following problem, in which the original AIWA player was replaced by an inferior model ($n = 62$).

Dominance:
Suppose you are considering buying a CD player, and have not yet decided what model to buy. You pass by a store that is having a 1-day clearance sale. They offer a popular SONY player for just $99, well below the list price, and an inferior AIWA player for the regular list price of $105. Do you:

(x') buy the AIWA player.	3%
(y) buy the SONY player.	73%
(z) wait until you learn more about the various models.	24%

In this version, contrary to the previous *high-conflict* version, the AIWA player is dominated by the SONY: It is inferior in quality and costs more. Thus, the presence of the AIWA does not detract from the reasons for buying the SONY, it actually supplements them: The SONY is well priced, it is on sale for 1 day only, *and* it is clearly better than its competitor. As a result, the SONY is chosen more often than before the inferior AIWA was added. The ability of an asymmetrically dominated or relatively inferior alternative, when added to a set, to increase the attractiveness and choice probability of the dominating option is known as the asymmetric dominance effect (Huber, Payne, & Puto, 1982). Note that in both the *high-conflict* and the *dominance* problems subjects were presented with two CD players and an option to delay choice. Subjects' tendency to delay, however, is much greater when they lack clear reasons for buying either player than when they have compelling reasons to buy one player and not the other, $p < .005$.

The previously discussed patterns violate the regularity condition, which is assumed to hold so long as the added alternatives do not provide new and relevant information. In the earlier scenario, one could argue that the added options (the superior player in one case and the inferior player in the other) conveyed information about the consumer's chances of finding a better deal. Recall that information considerations could not explain the search experiments of the previous section because there subjects reviewed all the potentially available options. Nevertheless, to test this interpretation further, Tversky and Shafir (1992a) devised a similar problem, involving real payoffs, in which the option to defer is not available. Students ($n = 80$) agreed to fill out a brief questionnaire for $1.50. Following the questionnaire, one-half of the subjects were offered the opportunity to exchange the $1.50 (the default) for one of two prizes: a metal Zebra pen (henceforth, Zebra), or a pair of plastic Pilot pens (henceforth, Pilot). The other half of the subjects were only offered the opportunity to exchange the $1.50 for the Zebra. The prizes were shown to the subjects, who were also informed that each prize regularly costs a little over $2.00. On indicating their preference, subjects received their chosen option. The results were as follows: 75% of the subjects chose the Zebra over the payment when the Zebra was the only alternative, but only 47% chose the Zebra *or* the Pilot when both were available, $p < .05$. Faced with a tempting alternative, subjects had a compelling reason to forego the payment: The majority took advantage of the opportunity to obtain an attractive prize of greater value. The availability of competing alternatives of comparable value, on the other hand, did not present an immediate reason for choosing either alternative over the other, thus increasing the tendency to retain the default option. Similar effects in hypothetical medical decisions made by expert physicians are documented by Redelmeier and Shafir (1993).

In the earlier study the addition of a competing alternative was shown to increase the popularity of the default option. Recall that the popularity of an option may also be enhanced by the addition of an inferior alternative. Thus, in accord with the asymmetric dominance effect, the tendency to prefer x over y can be increased by adding a third alternative z that is clearly inferior to x but not to y (see Fig. 22.1). The phenomenon of asymmetric dominance was first demonstrated by Huber, Payne, and Puto (1982) in choices between hypothetical options. Wedell (1991) reports similar findings using monetary gambles. The following example involving real choices is taken from Simonson and Tversky (1992). One group ($n = 106$) was offered a choice between $6 and an elegant Cross pen. The pen was selected by 36% of the subjects, and the remaining 64% chose the cash. A

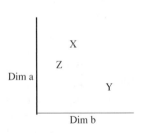

Figure 22.1. A schematic representation of asymmetric dominance. The tendency to prefer X over Y can be increased by adding an alternative, Z, that is clearly inferior to X but not to Y.

second group ($n = 115$) was given a choice among three options: $6 in cash, the same Cross pen, and a second pen that was distinctly less attractive. Only 2% of the subjects chose the less attractive pen, but its presence increased the percentage of subjects who chose the Cross pen from 36% to 46%, $p < .10$. This pattern again violates the regularity condition discussed earlier. Similar violations of regularity were observed in choices among other consumer goods. In one study, subjects received descriptions and pictures of microwave ovens taken from a "Best" catalogue. One group ($n = 60$) was then asked to choose between an Emerson priced at $110 and a Panasonic priced at $180. Both items were on sale, one-third off the regular price. Here, 57% chose the Emerson and 43% chose the Panasonic. A second group ($n = 60$) was presented with these options along with a $200 Panasonic at a 10% discount. Only 13% of the subjects chose the more expensive Panasonic, but its presence increased the percentage of subjects who chose the less expensive Panasonic from 43% to 60%, $p < .05$.[1]

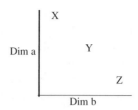

Figure 22.2. A schematic representation of extremeness aversion. Option Y is relatively more popular in the trinary choice, when both X and Z are available, than in either one of the binary comparisons, when either X or Z is removed.

Simonson and Tversky (1992) have interpreted these observations in terms of "tradeoff contrast." They proposed that the tendency to prefer an alternative is enhanced or hindered depending on whether the tradeoffs within the set under consideration are favorable or unfavorable to that alternative. A second cluster of context effects, called *extremeness aversion*, refers to the finding that, within an offered set, options with extreme values are relatively less attractive than options with intermediate values (Simonson, 1989). For example, consider two-dimensional options x, y, and z, such that y lies between x and z (see Fig. 22.2). Considerations of value maximization imply that the middle alternative, y, should be relatively less popular in the trinary choice than in either one of the binary comparisons (y compared to x, or y compared to z). Extremeness aversion, on the other hand, yields the opposite prediction because y has small advantages and disadvantages with respect to x and to z, whereas both x and z have more extreme advantages and disadvantages with respect to each other. This pattern was observed in several experiments. For example, subjects were shown five 35-mm cameras varying in quality and price. One

---

[1] These effects of context on choice can naturally be used in sales tactics. For example, Williams-Sonoma, a mail-order business located in San Francisco, used to offer a bread-baking appliance priced at $279. They later added a second bread-baking appliance, similar to the first but somewhat larger and priced at $429 – more than 50% higher than the original appliance. Not surprisingly, Williams-Sonoma did not sell many units of the new item. However, the sales of the less expensive appliance almost doubled. (To the best of our knowledge, Williams-Sonoma did not anticipate this effect.)

group ($n = 106$) was then given a choice between two cameras: a Minolta X-370 priced at $170 and a Minolta 3000i priced at $240. A second group ($n = 115$) was given an additional option, the Minolta 7000i priced at $470. Subjects in the first group were split evenly between the two options, yet 57% of the subjects in the second group chose the middle option (Minolta 3000i), with the remaining divided about equally between the two extreme options. Thus, the introduction of an extreme option reduced the "market share" of the other extreme option, but not of the middle option. Note that this effect cannot be attributed to information conveyed by the offered set because respondents had reviewed the relevant options prior to making their choice.

We suggest that both tradeoff contrast and extremeness aversion can be understood in terms of reasons. Suppose a decision maker faces a choice between two alternatives, x and y, and suppose x is of higher quality whereas y is better priced. This produces conflict if the decision maker finds it difficult to determine whether the quality difference outweighs the price difference. Suppose now that the choice set also includes a third alternative, z, that is clearly inferior to y but not to x. The presence of z, we suggest, provides an argument for choosing y over x. To the extent that the initial choice between x and y is difficult, the presence of z may help the decision maker break the tie. In the pen study, for example, the addition of the relatively unattractive pen, whose monetary value is unclear but whose inferiority to the elegant Cross pen is apparent, provides a reason for choosing the Cross pen over the cash. Similarly, in the presence of options with extreme values on the relevant dimensions, the middle option can be seen as a compromise choice that is easier to defend than either extreme. Indeed, verbal protocols show that the accounts generated by subjects while making these choices involve considerations of asymmetric advantage and compromise; furthermore, asymmetric dominance is enhanced when subjects anticipate having to justify their decisions to others (Simonson, 1989). It is noteworthy that the arguments leading to tradeoff contrast and extremeness aversion are comparative; they are based on the positions of the options in the choice set, hence they cannot be readily translated into the values associated with single alternatives.

Tversky and Simonson (1993) have proposed a formal model that explains the earlier findings in terms of a tournament-like process in which each option is compared against other available options in terms of their relative advantages and disadvantages. This model can be viewed as a formal analog of the preceding qualitative account based on reasons for choice. Which analysis – the formal or the qualitative – proves more useful is likely to depend on, among other things, the nature of the problem and the purpose of the investigation.

DEFINITE VERSUS DISJUNCTIVE REASONS

People sometimes encounter situations of uncertainty in which they eventually opt for the same course of action, but for very different reasons, depending on how the uncertainty is resolved. Thus, a student who has taken an exam may decide to take a vacation, either to reward herself in case she passes or to console herself in case she fails. However, as shown in the following illustration, the student may be reluctant to commit to a vacation while the outcome of the exam is pending. The following problem was presented by Tversky and Shafir (1992b) to 66 undergraduate students.

Disjunctive version:
Imagine that you have just taken a tough qualifying examination. It is the end of the fall quarter, you feel tired and run-down, and you are not sure that you passed the exam. In case you failed you have to take the exam again in a couple of months – after the Christmas holidays. You now have an opportunity to buy a very attractive 5-day Christmas vacation package in Hawaii at an exceptionally low price. The special offer expires tomorrow, while the exam grade will not be available until the following day. Would you:

(a) buy the vacation package.	32%
(b) not buy the vacation package.	7%
(c) pay a $5 nonrefundable fee in order to retain the rights to buy the vacation package at the same exceptional price the day after tomorrow – after you find out whether or not you passed the exam.	61%

The percentage of subjects who chose each option appears on the right. Two additional versions, called *pass* and *fail*, were presented to two different groups of 67 students each. These two versions differed only in the expression in brackets.

Pass/fail versions:
Imagine that you have just taken a tough qualifying examination. It is the end of the fall quarter, you feel tired and run-down, and you find out that you [passed the exam./failed the exam. You will have to take it again in a couple of months – after the Christmas holidays.] You now have an opportunity to buy a very attractive 5-day Christmas vacation package in Hawaii at an exceptionally low price. The special offer expires tomorrow. Would you:

	Pass	Fail
(a) buy the vacation package.	54%	57%
(b) not buy the vacation package.	16%	12%
(c) pay a $5 nonrefundable fee in order to retain the rights to buy the vacation package at the same exceptional price the day after tomorrow.	30%	31%

The data show that more than half of the students chose the vacation package when they knew that they passed the exam, and an even larger percentage chose the vacation when they knew that they failed. However, when they did not know whether they had passed or failed, less than one-third of the students chose the vacation and 61% were willing to pay $5 to postpone the decision until the following day, when the results of the exam would be known.[2] Once the outcome of the exam is known, the student has good – albeit different – reasons for taking the trip: Having passed the exam, the vacation is presumably seen as a reward following a hard but successful semester; having failed the exam, the vacation becomes a consolation and time to recuperate before a reexamination. Not knowing the outcome of the exam, however, the student lacks a definite reason for going to Hawaii. Notice that the outcome of the exam will be known long before the vacation begins. Thus, the uncertainty characterizes the actual moment of decision, not the eventual vacation.

The indeterminacy of reasons for going to Hawaii discourages many students from buying the vacation, even when both outcomes – passing or failing the exam – ultimately favor this course of action. Tversky and Shafir (1992b) call the previously discussed pattern of decisions a *disjunction effect*. Evidently, a disjunction of different reasons (reward in case of success or consolation in case of failure) is often less compelling than either definite reason alone. A significant proportion of the students were willing to pay, in effect, for information that was ultimately not going to affect their decision – they would choose to go to Hawaii in either case – but that promised to leave them with a more definite reason for making that choice. The willingness to pay for noninstrumental information is at variance with the classical model, in which the worth of information is determined only by its potential to influence decision.

People's preference for definite as opposed to disjunctive reasons has significant implications in cases where the option to defer decision is not available. Consider the following series of problems presented by Tversky and Shafir (1992b) to 98 students.

Win/lose version:
Imagine that you have just played a game of chance that gave you a 50% chance to win $200 and a 50% chance to lose $100. The coin was tossed and you have [won $200/lost $100]. You are now offered a second identical gamble: 50% chance to win $200 and 50% chance to lose $100. Would you:

	Won	Lost
(a) accept the second gamble.	69%	59%
(b) reject the second gamble.	31%	41%

The students were presented with the *win* version of this problem, followed a week later by the *lose* version, and 10 days after that by the following version, which is a disjunction of the previous two. The problems were embedded among

[2] An additional group of subjects ($n = 123$) were presented with both the fail and the pass versions, and asked whether or not they would buy the vacation package in each case. Two-thirds of the subjects made the same choice in the two conditions, indicating that the data for the disjunctive version cannot be explained by the hypothesis that those who like the vacation in case they pass the exam do not like it in case they fail, and vice versa. Note that although only one-third of the subjects made different decisions depending on the outcome of the exam, more than 60% of the subjects chose to wait when the outcome was not known.

other, similar problems so that the relation between the various versions was not transparent. Subjects were instructed to treat each decision separately.

Disjunctive version:
Imagine that you have just played a game of chance that gave you a 50% chance to win $200 and a 50% chance to lose $100. Imagine that the coin has already been tossed, but that you will not know whether you have won $200 or lost $100 until you make your decision concerning a second, identical gamble: 50% chance to win $200 and 50% chance to lose $100. Would you:

(a) accept the second gamble.   36%
(b) reject the second gamble.   64%

The data show that a majority of subjects accepted the second gamble after having won the first gamble, and a majority also accepted the second gamble after having lost the first gamble. However, the majority of subjects rejected the second gamble when the outcome of the first was not known. An examination of individual choices reveals that approximately 40% of the subjects accepted the second gamble both after a gain in the first and after a loss. Among these, however, 65% rejected the second gamble in the disjunctive condition, when the outcome of the first gamble was not known. Indeed, this response pattern (accepting in both conditions but rejecting in the disjunction) was the single most frequent pattern, exhibited by 27% of all subjects. This pattern, which violates Savage's (1954) sure-thing principle, cannot be attributed to unreliability (Tversky & Shafir, 1992b).

The students were offered a gamble with a positive expected value and an even chance of a nontrivial loss. Different reasons were likely to arise for accepting the second gamble depending on the outcome of the first. In the *win* condition, the decision maker is already up $200, so even a loss on the second gamble leaves him or her ahead overall, which makes this option quite attractive. In the *lose* condition, on the other hand, the decision maker is down $100. Playing the second gamble offers a chance to "get out of the red," which for many is more attractive than accepting a sure $100 loss. In the *disjunctive* condition, however, the decision maker does not know whether she is up $200 or down $100; she does not know, in other words, whether her reason for playing the second gamble is that it is a no-loss proposition or, instead, that it provides a chance to escape a sure loss. In the absence of a definite reason, fewer subjects accept the second gamble.

This interpretation is further supported by the following modification of the problem, in which both outcomes of the first gamble were increased by $400 so that the decision maker could not lose in either case.

Imagine that you have just played a game of chance that gave you a 50% chance to win $600 and a 50% chance to win $300. Imagine that the coin has already been tossed, but that you will not know whether you have won $600 or $300 until you make your decision concerning a second gamble: 50% chance to win $200 and 50% chance to lose $100.

A total of 171 subjects were presented with this problem, equally divided into three groups. One group was told that they had won $300 on the first gamble, a second group was told that they had won $600 on the first gamble, and the third group was told that the outcome of the first gamble – $300 or $600 – was not known (the disjunctive version). In all cases, subjects had to decide whether to accept or to reject the second gamble which, as in the previous problem, consisted of an even chance to win $200 or lose $100. The percentage of subjects who accepted the second gamble in the $300, $600, and disjunctive versions, were 69%, 75%, and 73%, respectively. (Recall that the corresponding figures for the original problem were 59%, 69%, and 36%; essentially identical figures were obtained in a between-subjects replication of that problem.) In contrast to the original problem, the second gamble in this modified problem was equally popular in the disjunctive as in the nondisjunctive versions. Whereas in the original scenario the second gamble amounted to either a no-loss proposition or a chance to avoid a sure loss, in the modified scenario the second gamble amounts to a no-loss proposition regardless of the outcome of the first gamble. The increased popularity of the second gamble in the modified problem shows that it is not the disjunctive situation itself that discourages people from playing. Rather, it is the lack of a specific reason that seems to drive the effect: When the same reason applies regardless of outcome, the disjunction no longer reduces the tendency to accept the gamble.

As illustrated earlier, changes in the context of decision are likely to alter the reasons that subjects bring to mind and, consequently, their choices. Elsewhere (Shafir & Tversky, 1992) we describe a disjunction effect in the context of a one-shot prisoner's dilemma game, played on a computer for real payoffs. Subjects ($n = 80$) played a series of prisoner's dilemma games, without feedback, each against a different unknown player. In this setup, the rate of cooperation was 3% when subjects knew that the other player had defected and 16% when they knew that the other had cooperated. However, when subjects did not know whether the other player had cooperated or defected (the standard version of the prisoner's dilemma game) the rate of cooperation rose to 37%. Thus, many subjects defected when they knew the other's choice – be it cooperation or defection – but cooperated when the other player's choice was not known. Shafir and Tversky (1992) attribute this pattern to the different perspectives that underlie subjects' behavior under uncertainty as opposed to when the uncertainty is resolved. In particular, we suggest that the reasons for competing are more compelling when the other player's decision is known and the payoff depends on the subject alone than when the other's chosen strategy is uncertain and the outcome of the game depends on the choices of both players.

The previous "disjunctive" manipulation – which has no direct bearing from the point of view of value maximization – appears to influence the reasons for decision that people bring to mind. Another kind of manipulation that seems to alter people's reasons without bearing directly on options' values is described in what follows.

NONVALUED FEATURES

Reasons for choice or rejection often refer to specific features of the options under consideration. The positive features of an option typically provide reasons for choosing that option and its negative features typically provide reasons for rejection. What happens when we add features that are neither attractive nor aversive? Can choice be influenced by features that have little or no value?

Simonson and his colleagues have conducted a number of studies on the effects of nonvalued features and tested the hypothesis that people are reluctant to choose alternatives that are supported by reasons that they do not find appealing. In one study, for example, Simonson, Nowlis, and Simonson (1993) predicted that people would be less likely to choose an alternative that was chosen by another person for a reason that does not apply to them. Berkeley business students ($n = 113$) were told that, because of budget cuts and to save paper and duplicating costs, a questionnaire that they will receive was designed for use by two respondents. Thus, when subjects had to enter a choice, they could see the choice made by the previous "respondent" and the reason given for it. The choices and reasons of the previous respondents were systematically manipulated. One problem, for example, offered a choice between attending the MBA programs at Northwestern University and UCLA. In one version of the questionnaire, the previous respondent had selected Northwestern and provided the (handwritten) reason, "I have many relatives in the Chicago area." Because this reason does not apply to most subjects, it was expected to reduce their likelihood of choosing Northwestern. In a second version, no reason was given for the choice of Northwestern. As expected, those exposed to an irrelevant reason were less likely to choose Northwestern than subjects who saw the other respondent's choice but not his or her reason (23% vs. 43%), $p < .05$. It should be noted that both Northwestern and UCLA are well known to most subjects (Northwestern currently has the highest ranked MBA program; the UCLA program is ranked high and belongs to the same UC system as Berkeley). Thus, it is unlikely that subjects made inferences about the quality of Northwestern based on the fact that another respondent chose it because he or she had relatives in Chicago.

In a related study, Simonson, Carmon, and O'Curry (1994) showed that endowing an option with a feature that was intended to be positive but, in fact, has no value for the decision maker can reduce the tendency to choose that option, even when subjects realize that they are not paying for the added feature. For example, an offer to purchase a collector's plate – that most did not want – if one buys a particular brand of cake mix was shown to lower the tendency to buy that particular brand relative to a second, comparable cake mix brand (from 31% to 14%), $p < .05$. Choosing brands that offer worthless bonuses was judged (in a related study) as more difficult to justify and as more susceptible to criticism. An analysis of verbal protocols showed that a majority of those who failed to select the endowed option explicitly mentioned not needing the added feature. It should be noted that sale promotions, such as the one involving the collector's plate offer, are currently employed by a wide range of companies, and there is no evidence that they lead to any inferences about the quality of the promoted product (e.g., Blattberg & Neslin, 1990).

The previously cited manipulations all added "positive," albeit weak or irrelevant, features, which should not diminish an option's value, yet they apparently provide a reason against choosing the option, especially when other options are otherwise equally attractive. Evidently, the addition of a potentially attractive feature that proves useless can provide a reason to reject the option in favor of a competing alternative that has no "wasted" features.

CONCLUDING REMARKS

People's choices may occasionally stem from affective judgments that preclude a thorough evaluation of the options (cf. Zajonc, 1980). In such cases, an analysis of the reasons for choice may prove unwarranted and, when attempted by the decision maker, may actually result in a different, and possibly inferior, decision (Wilson & Schooler, 1991). Other choices, furthermore, may follow standard operating procedures that involve minimal reflective effort. Many decisions, nonetheless, result from a careful evaluation of options, in which people attempt to arrive at what they believe is the best choice. Having discarded the less attractive options and faced with a choice that is hard to resolve, people often search for a compelling rationale for choosing one alternative over another. In this chapter, we presented an analysis of the role of reasons in decision making and considered ways in which an analysis based on reasons may contribute to the standard quantitative approach based on the maximization of value. A number of hypotheses that derive from this perspective were investigated in experimental settings.

The reasons that enter into the making of decisions are likely to be intricate and diverse. In the preceding sections we have attempted to identify a few general principles that govern the role of reasons in decision making and thus some of the fundamental ways in which thinking about reasons is likely to contribute to our understanding of the making of decisions. A reliance on the more important dimensions – those likely to provide more compelling reasons for choice – was shown in the first section to predict preferences between previously equated options. The notions of compatibility and salience were summoned in the next section to account for the differential weighting of reasons in a choice versus a rejection task. Reasons, it appears, lend themselves to certain framing manipulations that are harder to explain from the perspective of value maximization. Then, manipulating the precise relationships between competing alternatives was shown to enhance or reduce conflict, yielding decisions that were easier or more difficult to rationalize and justify. Providing a context that presents compelling reasons for choosing an option apparently increases people's tendency to choose that option, whereas comparing alternatives that render the aforementioned reasons less compelling tends to increase people's tendency to maintain the status quo or search for other alternatives. The ability of the context of decision to generate reasons that affect choice was further discussed next, where the addition and removal of competing alternatives was interpreted as generating arguments for choice based on comparative considerations of relative advantages and compromise. The relative weakness of disjunctive reasons was discussed in the next section, including a number of studies that contrasted people's willingness to reach a decision based on a definite reason for choice with their reluctance to arrive at a decision in the presence of uncertainty about which reason is actually relevant to the case at hand. The last section reviewed choice situations in which the addition of purported reasons for choosing an option, which subjects did not find compelling, was seen to diminish their tendency to opt for that option, even though its value had not diminished.

The nature of the reasons that guide decision, and the ways in which they interact, await further investigation. There is evidence to suggest that a wide variety of arguments play a role in decision making. We often search for a convincing rationale for the decisions that we make, whether for interpersonal purposes, so that we can explain to others the reasons for our decision, or for intrapersonal motives, so that we may feel confident of having made the "right" choice. Attitudes toward risk and loss can sometimes be rationalized on the basis of common myths or clichés, and choices are sometimes made on the basis of moral or prudential principles that are used to override specific cost–benefit calculations (cf. Prelec & Herrnstein, 1991). Formal decision rules, moreover, may sometimes act as arguments in people's deliberations. Thus, when choosing between options x and z, we may realize that, sometime earlier, we had preferred x over y and y over z and that, therefore, by transitivity, we should now choose x over z. Montgomery (1983) has argued that people look for dominance structures in decision problems because they provide a compelling reason for choice. Similarly, Tversky and Shafir (1992b) have shown that detecting the applicability of the sure-thing principle to a decision situation leads people to act in accord with this principle's compelling rationale. Indeed, it has been repeatedly observed that the axioms of rational choice that are often violated in nontransparent situations are generally satisfied when their application is transparent (e.g., Tversky & Kahneman, 1986). These results suggest that the axioms of rational choice act as compelling arguments, or reasons, for making a particular decision when their applicability has been detected, not as universal laws that constrain people's choices.

In contrast to the classical theory that assumes stable values and preferences, it appears that people often do not have well-established values and that preferences are actually constructed – not merely revealed – during their elicitation (cf. Payne, Bettman, & Johnson, 1992). A reason-based approach lends itself well to such a constructive interpretation. Decisions, according to this analysis, are often reached by focusing on reasons that justify the selection of one option over another. Different frames, contexts, and elicitation procedures highlight different aspects of the options and bring forth different reasons and considerations that influence decision.

The reliance on reasons to explain experimental findings has been the hallmark of social psychological analyses. Accounts of dissonance (Wicklund & Brehm, 1976) and self-perception (Bem, 1972), for example, focus on the reasons that people muster in an attempt to explain their counterattitudinal behaviors. Similarly, attribution theory (Heider, 1980) centers around the reasons that people attribute to others' behavior. These studies, however, have primarily focused on post-decisional rationalization rather than pre-decisional conflict. Although the two processes are closely related, there are nevertheless some important differences. Much of the work in social psychology has investigated how people's decisions affect the way they think. The present chapter, in contrast, has considered how the reasons that enter into people's thinking about a problem influence their decision. A number of researchers have recently begun to explore related issues. Billig (1987), for example, has adopted a rhetorical approach to understanding social psychological issues, according to which "our inner deliberations are silent arguments conducted within a single self" (p. 5). Related "explanation-based" models of decision making have been applied by Pennington and Hastie (1988, 1992) to account for judicial decisions, and the importance of social accountability in choice has been addressed by Tetlock (1992). From a philosophical perspective, a recent essay by Schick (1991) analyzes various decisions from the point of view of practical reason. An influential earlier work is Toulmin's (1950) study of the role of arguments in ethical reasoning.

In this chapter, we have attempted to explore some of the ways in which reasons and arguments enter into people's decisions. A reason-based analysis may come closer to capturing part of the psychology that underlies decision and thus may help shed light on a number of phenomena that remain counterintuitive from the perspective of the classical theory. It is instructive to note that many of the experimental studies described in this chapter were motivated by intuitions stemming from a qualitative analysis based on reasons, not from a value-based perspective, even if they can later be interpreted in that fashion. We do not propose that accounts based on reasons replace value-based models of choice. Rather, we suggest that an analysis of reasons may illuminate some aspects of reflective choice and generate new hypotheses for further study.

ACKNOWLEDGMENTS

This research was supported by U.S. Public Health Service Grant No. 1-R29-MH46885 from the National Institute of Mental Health, by Grant No. 89-0064 from the Air Force Office of Scientific Research, and by Grant No. SES-9109535 from the National Science Foundation. The chapter was partially prepared while the first author participated in a Summer Institute on Negotiation and Dispute Resolution at the Center for Advanced Study in the Behavioral Sciences and while the second author was at the University of California, Berkeley. Funds for support of the Summer Institute were provided by the Andrew W. Mellon Foundation. We thank Robyn Dawes for helpful comments on an earlier draft.

23. The Affect Heuristic

Paul Slovic, Melissa L. Finucane, Ellen Peters,
and Donald G. Macgregor

INTRODUCTION

This chapter introduces a theoretical framework that describes the importance of affect in guiding judgments and decisions. As used here, *affect* means the specific quality of goodness or badness (a) experienced as a feeling state (with or without consciousness) and (b) demarcating a positive or negative quality of a stimulus. Affective responses occur rapidly and automatically – note how quickly you sense the feelings associated with the stimulus word "treasure" or the word "hate." We shall argue that reliance on such feelings can be characterized as the *affect heuristic*. In this chapter we trace the development of the affect heuristic across a variety of research paths followed by ourselves and many others. We also discuss some of the important practical implications resulting from ways that this heuristic affects our daily lives.

BACKGROUND

Although affect has long played a key role in many behavioral theories, it has rarely been recognized as an important component of human judgment and decision making. Perhaps befitting its rationalistic origins, the main focus of descriptive decision research has been cognitive, rather than affective. When principles of utility maximization appeared to be descriptively inadequate, Simon (1956) oriented the field toward problem-solving and information-processing models based on bounded rationality. The work of Tversky and Kahneman (1974; Kahneman, Slovic, & Tversky, 1982) demonstrated how boundedly rational individuals employ heuristics such as availability, representativeness, and anchoring and adjustment to make judgments and how they use simplified strategies such as elimination by aspects to make choices (Tversky, 1972). Other investigators elaborated the cognitive strategies underlying judgment and choice through models of constructed preferences (Payne, Bettman,

This chapter has been abridged and revised by the editors. The complete version appeared in T. Gilovich, D. Griffin, & D. Kahneman (Eds.), *Heuristics and biases: The psychology of intuitive judgment* (pp. 397–420), New York. Copyright © Cambridge University Press 2002. Reprinted with permission.

& Johnson, 1993; Slovic, 1995), dominance structuring (Montgomery, 1983), and comparative advantages (Shafir, Osherson, & Smith, 1989, 1993). In 1993, the entire volume of the journal *Cognition* was dedicated to the topic of reason-based choice, in which it was argued that "Decisions... are often reached by focusing on reasons that justify the selection of one option over another" (Shafir, Simonson, & Tversky, 1993, p. 34). Similarly, a state-of-the-art review by Busemeyer, Hastie, and Medin (1995) was titled "Decision Making from a Cognitive Perspective." In keeping with its title, it contained almost no references to the influence of affect on decisions.

Despite this cognitive emphasis, the importance of affect is being recognized increasingly by decision researchers. A limited role for affect was acknowledged by Shafir, Simonson, and Tversky (1993), who conceded that "People's choices may *occasionally* stem from affective judgments that preclude a thorough evaluation of the options" (p. 32, emphasis added).

A strong early proponent of the importance of affect in decision making was Zajonc (1980), who argued that affective reactions to stimuli are often the very first reactions, occurring automatically and subsequently guiding information processing and judgment. According to Zajonc, all perceptions contain some affect. "We do not just see 'a house': We see a *handsome* house, an *ugly* house, or a *pretentious* house" (p. 154). He later adds, "We sometimes delude ourselves that we proceed in a rational manner and weight all the pros and cons of the various alternatives. But this is probably seldom the actual case. Quite often 'I decided in favor of X' is no more than 'I liked X'.... We buy the cars we 'like,' choose the jobs and houses we find 'attractive,' and then justify these choices by various reasons" (p. 155).

Affect also plays a central role in what have come to be known as *dual-process* theories of thinking, knowing, and information processing. As Epstein (1994) has observed, "There is no dearth of evidence in every day life that people apprehend reality in two fundamentally different ways, one variously labeled intuitive, automatic, natural, non-verbal, narrative, and experiential, and the other analytical, deliberative, verbal, and rational" (p. 710).

One of the characteristics of the experiential system is its affective basis. Although analysis is certainly important in some decision-making circumstances, reliance on affect and emotion is a quicker, easier, and more efficient way to navigate in a complex, uncertain, and sometimes dangerous world. Many theorists have given affect a direct and primary role in motivating behavior. Epstein's (1994) view on this is as follows:

The experiential system is assumed to be intimately associated with the experience of affect,... which refer[s] to subtle feelings of which people are often unaware. When a person responds to an emotionally significant event... the experiential system automatically searches its memory banks for related events, including their emotional accompaniments.... If the activated feelings are pleasant, they motivate actions and thoughts anticipated to reproduce the feelings. If the feelings are unpleasant, they motivate actions and thoughts anticipated to avoid the feelings. (p. 716)

Also emphasizing the motivational role of affect, Mowrer (1960a, 1960b) conceptualized conditioned emotional responses to images as prospective gains and losses that directly "guide and control performance in a generally sensible adaptive manner" (1960a, p. 30). He criticized theorists who postulate purely cognitive variables such as expectancies (probabilities) intervening between stimulus and response, cautioning that we must be careful not to leave the organism at the choice point "lost in thought." Mowrer's solution was to view expectancies more dynamically (as conditioned emotions such as hopes and fears) serving as motivating states leading to action.

One of the most comprehensive and dramatic theoretical accounts of the role of affect in decision making is presented by the neurologist, Antonio Damasio (1994), in his book *Descartes' Error: Emotion, Reason, and the Human Brain*. Damasio's theory is derived from observations of patients with damage to the ventromedial frontal cortices of the brain that has left their basic intelligence, memory, and capacity for logical thought intact but has impaired their ability to "feel" – that is, to associate affective feelings and emotions with the anticipated consequences of their actions. Close observation of these patients combined with a number of experimental studies led Damasio to argue that this type of brain damage induces a form of sociopathy (Damasio, Tranel, & Damasio, 1990) that destroys the individual's ability to make rational decisions, that is, decisions that are in his or her best interests. Persons suffering this damage became socially dysfunctional, even though they remain intellectually capable of analytical reasoning.

Commenting on one particularly significant case, Damasio (1994) observes:

The instruments usually considered necessary and sufficient for rational behavior were intact in him. He had the requisite knowledge, attention, and memory; his language was flawless; he could perform calculations; he could tackle the logic of an abstract problem. There was only one significant accompaniment to his decision-making failure: a marked alteration of the ability to experience feelings. Flawed reason and impaired feelings stood out together as the consequences of a specific brain lesion, and this correlation suggested to me that feeling was an integral component of the machinery of reason. (p. xii)

In seeking to determine the neural underpinnings of rational behavior, Damasio argues that thought is made largely from images, broadly construed to include sounds, smells, real or imagined visual impressions, ideas, and words. A lifetime of learning leads these images to become "marked" by positive and negative feelings linked directly or indirectly to somatic or bodily states (Mowrer and other learning theorists would call this conditioning): "In short, *somatic markers are . . . feelings generated from secondary emotions*. These emotions and feelings *have been connected, by learning, to predicted future outcomes of certain scenarios*" (Damasio, 1994, p. 174; emphasis in original). When a negative somatic marker is linked to an image of a future outcome it sounds an alarm. When a positive marker is associated with the outcome image, it becomes a beacon of incentive. Damasio concludes that somatic markers increase the accuracy and efficiency of the decision process and their absence degrades decision performance.

Damasio tested the somatic marker hypothesis in a decision-making experiment in which subjects gambled by selecting cards from any of four decks. Turning each card resulted in the gain or loss of a sum of money, as revealed on the back of the card when it was turned. Whereas normal subjects and patients with brain lesions outside the prefrontal sectors learned to avoid decks with attractive large payoffs but occasional catastrophic losses, patients with frontal lobe damage did not, thus losing a great deal of money. Although these patients responded normally to gains and losses when they occurred (as indicated by skin conductance responses immediately after an outcome was experienced) they did not seem to learn to *anticipate* future outcomes (e.g., they did not produce normal skin conductance responses when contemplating a future choice from a dangerous deck). In other words, they failed to show any proper anticipatory responses, even after numerous opportunities to learn them.

Despite the increasing popularity of affect in research programs and recent attempts to acknowledge the importance of the interplay between affect and cognition, further work is needed to specify the role of affect in judgment and decision making. The ideas articulated below are intended as a step toward encouraging the development of theory about affect and decision making and demonstrating how such a theory can be tested.

The basic tenet of this chapter is that images, marked by positive and negative affective feelings, guide judgment and decision making. Specifically, it is proposed that people use an affect heuristic to make judgments. That is, representations of objects and events in people's minds are tagged to varying degrees with affect. In the process of making a judgment or decision, people consult or refer to an "affect pool" containing all the positive and negative tags consciously or unconsciously associated with the representations. Just as imaginability, memorability, and similarity serve as cues for probability judgments (e.g., the availability and representativeness heuristics), affect may serve as a cue for many important judgments. Using an overall, readily available affective impression can be far easier – more efficient – than weighing the pros and cons or retrieving from memory many relevant examples, especially when the required judgment or decision is complex or mental resources are limited. This characterization of a mental shortcut leads to labeling the use of affect a "heuristic."

EMPIRICAL EVIDENCE

Manipulating Preferences Through Controlled Exposures

The fundamental nature and importance of affect has been demonstrated repeatedly in a remarkable series of studies by Robert Zajonc and his colleagues (see, e.g., Zajonc, 1968). The concept of stimulus exposure is central to all of these studies. The central finding is that, when objects are presented to an individual repeatedly, the *mere exposure* is capable of creating a positive attitude or preference for these objects.

In the typical study, stimuli such as nonsense phrases, or faces, or Chinese ideographs are presented to an individual with varying frequencies. In a later session, the individual judges these stimuli on liking, or familiarity, or both. The more frequent the prior exposure to a stimulus, the more positive the response. A meta-analysis by Bornstein (1989) of mere-exposure research published between 1968 and 1987 included over 200 experiments examining the exposure–affect relationship. Unreinforced exposures were found to reliably enhance affect toward visual, auditory, gustatory, abstract, and social stimuli.

Winkielman, Zajonc, and Schwarz (1997) demonstrated the speed with which affect can influence judgments in studies employing a subliminal priming paradigm. Participants were primed through exposure to a smiling face, a frowning face, or a neutral polygon presented for 1/250 of a second, an interval so brief that there is no recognition or recall of the stimulus. Immediately following this exposure, an ideograph was presented for 2 seconds, following which the participant rated the ideograph on a scale of liking. Mean liking ratings were significantly higher for ideographs preceded by smiling faces. This effect was lasting. In a second session, ideographs were primed by the "other face," the one not associated with the stimulus in the first session. This second priming was ineffective because the effect of the first priming remained.

It is not just subliminal smiles that affect our judgment. La France and Hecht (1995) found that students accused of academic misconduct who were pictured as smiling received less punishment than nonsmiling transgressors. Smiling persons were judged as more trustworthy, good, honest, genuine, obedient, blameless, sincere, and admirable than nonsmiling targets.

The perseverance of induced preferences was tested by Sherman, Kim, and Zajonc (1998), who asked participants to study Chinese characters and their English meanings. Half of the meanings were positive (e.g., beauty), half were negative (e.g., disease). Then participants were given a test of these meanings followed by a task in which they were given pairs of characters and were asked to choose the one they preferred. Participants preferred characters with positive meaning 70% of the time. Next, the characters were presented with neutral meanings (desk, linen) and subjects were told that these were the "true" meanings. The testing procedure was repeated and, despite learning the new meanings, the preferences remained the same. Characters that had been initially paired with positive meanings still tended to be preferred.

These various studies demonstrate that affect is a strong conditioner of preference, whether or not the cause of that affect is consciously perceived. They also demonstrate the independence of affect from cognition, indicating that there may be conditions of affective or emotional arousal that do not necessarily require cognitive appraisal. This affective mode of response, unburdened by cognition and hence much faster, has considerable adaptive value....

Image, Affect, and Decision Making

... Slovic and colleagues at Decision Research embarked on a research program designed to test whether introducing a hazardous facility into a region might stigmatize that region and cause people to avoid going there to recreate, retire, or do business. Believing self-report to be unreliable ("If they build it, will you not come?"), research on stigmatization was conducted through a number of empirical studies designed to examine the relationship between imagery, affect, and decision making. After conducting these studies, we learned that they fit closely with a large body of existing theory and research, such as the work of Damasio, Mowrer, and Epstein described earlier.

Several empirical studies have demonstrated a strong relationship between imagery, affect, and decision making. Many of these studies used a word-association technique. This method involves presenting subjects with a target stimulus, usually a word or very brief phrase, and asking them to provide the first thought or image that comes to mind. The process is then repeated a number of times, say three to six, or until no further associations are generated. Following the elicitation of images, subjects are asked to rate each image they give on a scale ranging from very positive (e.g., +2) to very negative (e.g., −2), with a neutral point in the center. Scoring is done by summing or averaging the ratings to obtain an overall index.

This imagery method has been used successfully to measure the affective meanings that influence people's preferences for different cities and states (Slovic et al., 1991) as well as their support or opposition to technologies such as nuclear power (Peters & Slovic, 1996). Subsequent studies have found affect-laden imagery elicited by word associations to be predictive of preferences for investing in new companies on the stock market (MacGregor, Slovic, Dreman, & Berry, 2000) and predictive of adolescents' decisions to take part in health-threatening and health-enhancing behaviors such as smoking and exercise (Benthin et al., 1995).

Evaluability

The research with images points to the importance of affective impressions in judgments and decisions. However, the impressions themselves may vary not only in their valence but in the precision with which they are held. It turns out that the precision of an affective impression substantially affects judgments....

Hsee (1996a, 1996b, 1998) has developed the notion of *evaluability* to describe the interplay between the precision of an affective impression and its meaning or importance for judgment and decision making. Evaluability is illustrated by an experiment in which Hsee asked people to assume they were music majors looking for a used music dictionary. In a joint-evaluation condition, participants were shown two dictionaries, A and B (see Table 23.1), and asked how much they would be willing to pay for each. Willingness to pay was far higher for Dictionary B, presumably because of its greater number of entries. However, when one group of participants evaluated only A and another group

Table 23.1. Attributes of Two Dictionaries in Hsee's Study

	Year of Publication	Number of Entries	Any Defects?
Dictionary A	1993	10,000	No, it's like new
Dictionary B	1993	20,000	Yes, the cover is torn; otherwise it's like new

Source: Adapted from Hsee (1998). Copyright © 1998 by John Wiley & Sons Limited. Reproduced with permission.

evaluated only B, the mean willingness to pay was much higher for Dictionary A. Hsee explains this reversal by means of the *evaluability principle*. He argues that, without a direct comparison, the number of entries is hard to evaluate, because the evaluator does not have a precise notion of *how good* or *how bad* 10,000 (or 20,000) entries is. However, the defects attribute is evaluable in the sense that it translates easily into a precise good/bad response and thus it carries more weight in the independent evaluation. Most people find a defective dictionary unattractive and a like-new one attractive. Under joint evaluation, the buyer can see that B is far superior on the more important attribute, number of entries. Thus, number of entries becomes *evaluable* through the comparison process.

According to the evaluability principle, the weight of a stimulus attribute in an evaluative judgment or choice is proportional to the ease or precision with which the value of that attribute (or a comparison on the attribute across alternatives) can be mapped into an affective impression. In other words, affect bestows meaning on information (cf. Mowrer, 1960a, 1960b; Osgood, Suci, & Tannenbaum, 1957), and the precision of the affective meaning influences our ability to use information in judgment and decision making. Evaluability can thus be seen as an extension of the general relationship between the variance of an impression and its weight in an impression-formation task (Mellers, Richards, & Birnbaum, 1992)....

Proportion Dominance

In situations that involve uncertainty about whether we will win or lose or that involve ambiguity about some quantity of something (i.e., how much is enough), there appears to be one information format that is highly evaluable, leading it to carry great weight in many judgment tasks. This is a representation characterizing an attribute as a proportion or percentage of something, or as a probability. At the suggestion of Chris Hsee (personal communication), we shall refer to the strong effects of this type of representation as *proportion dominance*....

Proportion dominance, linked to notions of affective mapping and compatibility, provides an explanation for the anomalous finding that adding a small loss to a gamble that previously had no losing outcome increases its attractiveness (Bateman, Dent, Peters, Starmer, & Slovic, 2006). Consider the gamble 7/36 to win $9, otherwise nothing. Such gambles are typically rated as rather unattractive prospects, being judged primarily on the basis of their mediocre probability of winning. The payoff carries little weight in the judgment. Early explanations centered around compatibility (Slovic, Griffin, & Tversky, 1990): The probability 7/36 is readily coded and mapped onto a rating scale of attractiveness, whereas a $9 payoff may be harder to map on a rating scale because its attractiveness depends on what other payoffs are available.

According to this explanation, if we make a gamble's payoff more compatible with the attractiveness rating, we would presumably enhance the weight given to payoff in the rating response mode. Bateman et al. (2006) did this in an experiment focusing on the gamble 7/36 to win $9. To make the payoff more compatible with regard to the scale of attractiveness, they added a small loss (5¢) to the gamble:

> 7/36 win $9
> 29/36 lose 5¢

... The results exceeded expectations. The gamble with no loss had the lower attractiveness rating (mean = 9.4 on a 0–20 scale). Adding a 5¢ loss led to a much higher attractiveness rating (mean = 14.9)....

Would adding a small loss to the gamble enhance its attractiveness in choice as it did in rating? Bateman et al. addressed this question by asking 96 University of Oregon students to choose between playing a gamble and receiving a gain of $2. For half of the students, the gamble was 7/36 win $9; for the others, the gamble had the 5¢ loss. Whereas only 33.3% chose the $9 gamble over the $2, 60.8% chose the $9–5¢ gamble over the $2.

The curious finding that adding a small loss to a gamble increases its rated attractiveness, explained originally as a compatibility effect, can now be seen to fit well with the notions of affective mapping and evaluability. According to this view, a probability maps relatively precisely onto the attractiveness scale because probability has a lower and upper bound (0 and 1) and a midpoint below which a probability is "poor" or "bad" (i.e., has worse than an even chance) and above which it is "good" (i.e., has a better than even chance). People know where a given value, such as 7/36, falls within the bounds, and exactly what it means – "I'm probably not going to win." In contrast, the mapping of a dollar outcome (e.g., $9) onto the attractiveness scale is diffuse, reflecting a failure to know how good or bad or how attractive or unattractive $9 is. Thus, the impression formed by the gamble offering $9 to win with no losing payoff is dominated by the relatively precise and unattractive impression produced by the 7/36 probability of winning. However, adding a very small loss to the payoff dimension brings the $9 payoff into focus and thus gives it meaning. The combination of a possible $9 gain and a 5¢ loss is a *very attractive* win/loss ratio, leading to a relatively precise mapping onto the upper end of the scale....

Proportion dominance surfaces in a powerful way in a very different context, the life-saving interventions studied by Fetherstonhaugh, Slovic, Johnson, and Friedrich (1997), Baron (1997b), Jenni and Loewenstein (1997), and Friedrich et al. (1999). For example, Fetherstonhaugh et al. found that people's willingness to intervene to save a stated number of lives was determined more by the proportion of lives saved than by the actual number of lives that would be saved. However, when two or more interventions were directly compared, number of lives saved become more important than proportion saved. Thus, number of lives saved, standing alone, appears to be poorly evaluable, as was the case for number of entries in Hsee's music dictionaries. With a side-by-side comparison, the number of lives became clearly evaluable and important, as also happened with the number of dictionary entries.

Slovic (2000a), drawing on proportion dominance and the limited evaluability of numbers of lives, predicted (and found) that people, in a between-groups design, would more strongly support an airport-safety measure expected to save 98% of 150 lives at risk than a measure expected to save 150 lives. Saving 150 lives is diffusely good, hence only weakly evaluable, whereas saving 98% of something is clearly very good because it is so close to the upper bound on the percentage scale and hence is readily evaluable and highly weighted in the support judgment. Subsequent reduction of the percentage of 150 lives that would be saved to 95%, 90%, and 85% led to reduced support for the safety measure, but each of these percentage conditions still garnered a higher mean level of support than did the save-150-lives condition (see Table 23.2).

Turning to a more mundane form of proportion dominance, Hsee (1998) found that an overfilled ice cream container with 7 oz. of ice cream was valued more highly (measured by willingness to pay) than an underfilled container with 8 oz. of ice cream. This "less is better effect" reversed itself when the options

Table 23.2. Proportion Dominance and Airport Safety. Saving a Percentage of 150 Lives Receives Higher Support Ratings Than Does Saving 150 Lives

	Potential Benefit				
	Save 150 Lives	Save 98%	Save 95%	Save 90%	Save 85%
Mean support[a]	10.4	13.6	12.9	11.7	10.9
Median[a]	9.8	14.3	14.1	11.3	10.8
% of ratings > 13	37	75	69	35	31

[a] Entries in these rows describe mean and median responses to the question: "How much would you support this proposed measure to purchase the new equipment?" They were also told, "Critics argue that the money spent on this system could be better spent enhancing other aspects of airport safety." The response scale ranged from 0 (would not support at all) to 20 (very strong support). An overall ANOVA resulted in $F_{4,200} = 3.36$, $p = .01$. The save 98% and save 95% conditions were both significantly different from the save-150-lives condition at $p < .05$, Tukey HSD test. Source: Slovic, 2000a. Copyright © 2000 Roger Williams University School of Law. Reprinted with permission.

were juxtaposed and evaluated together. Thus, the proportion of the serving cup that was filled appeared to be more evaluable (in separate judgments) than the absolute amount of ice cream.

Insensitivity to Probability

Outcomes are not always affectively as vague as the quantities of money, ice cream, and lives that were dominated by proportion in the earlier experiments. When consequences carry sharp and strong affective meaning, as is the case with a lottery jackpot or a cancer, the opposite phenomenon occurs – variation in probability often carries too little weight. As Loewenstein, Weber, Hsee, and Welch (2001) observe, one's images and feelings toward winning the lottery are likely to be similar whether the probability of winning is one in 10 million or one in 10,000. They further note that responses to uncertain situations appear to have an all-or-none characteristic that is sensitive to the *possibility* rather than the *probability* of strong positive or negative consequences, causing very small probabilities to carry great weight. This, they argue, helps explain many paradoxical findings such as the simultaneous prevalence of gambling and the purchasing of insurance. It also explains why societal concerns about hazards such as nuclear power and exposure to extremely small amounts of toxic chemicals fail to recede in response to information about the very small probabilities of the feared consequences from such hazards. Support for these arguments comes from Rottenstreich and Hsee (2001), who show that, if the potential outcome of a gamble is emotionally powerful, its attractiveness or unattractiveness is relatively insensitive to changes in probability as great as from .99 to .01.

Midcourse Summary

We can now see that the puzzling finding of increased attractiveness for the gambles to which a loss was appended is part of a larger story that can be summarized as follows:

1. Affect, attached to images, influences judgments and decisions.
2. The evaluability of a stimulus image is reflected in the precision of the affective feelings associated with that image. More precise affective impressions reflect more precise meanings (i.e., greater evaluability) and carry more weight in impression formation, judgment, and decision making.
3. The anomalous findings from the experiments with gambles, ice cream preferences, and life-saving interventions suggest that without a context to give affective perspective to quantities of dollars, ice cream, and lives, these quantities may convey little meaning. Amounts of anything, no matter how common or familiar or intrinsically important, may in some circumstances not be evaluable.
4. Probabilities or proportions, on the other hand, often are highly evaluable, reflecting the ease with which people recognize that a high

probability of a desirable outcome is good and a low probability is bad. When the quantities or outcomes to which these probabilities apply are affectively pallid, probabilities carry much more weight in judgments and decisions. However, just the opposite occurs when the outcomes have precise and strong affective meanings – variations in probability carry too little weight.

The Affect Heuristic in Judgments of Risk and Benefit. Another stream of research that, in conjunction with many of the findings reported earlier, led us to propose the affect heuristic had its origin in the early study of risk perception reported by Fischhoff, Slovic, Lichtenstein, Reid, and Combs (1978). One of the findings in this study and numerous subsequent studies was that perceptions of risk and society's responses to risk were strongly linked to the degree to which a hazard evoked feelings of dread (see also Slovic, 1987). Thus, activities associated with cancer are seen as riskier and more in need of regulation than activities associated with less dreaded forms of illness, injury, and death (e.g., accidents).

A second finding in the study by Fischhoff, Slovic, Lichtenstein, et al. (1978) has been even more instrumental in the study of the affect heuristic: the finding that judgments of risk and benefit are negatively correlated. For many hazards, the greater the perceived benefit, the lower the perceived risk and vice versa. Smoking, alcoholic beverages, and food additives, for example, tend to be seen as very high in risk and relatively low in benefit, whereas vaccines, antibiotics, and X-rays tend to be seen as high in benefit and relatively low in risk. This negative relationship is noteworthy because it occurs even when the nature of the gains or benefits from an activity is distinct and qualitatively different from the nature of the risks. That the inverse relationship is generated in people's minds is suggested by the fact that risk and benefits generally tend to be positively (if at all) correlated in the world. Activities that bring great benefits may be high or low in risk but activities that are low in benefit are unlikely to be high in risk (if they were, they would be proscribed).

A study by Alhakami and Slovic (1994) found that the inverse relationship between perceived risk and perceived benefit of an activity (e.g., using pesticides) was linked to the strength of positive or negative affect associated with that activity. This result implies that people base their judgments of an activity or a technology not only on what they *think* about it but also on what they *feel* about it. If they like an activity, they are moved to judge the risks as low and the benefits as high; if they dislike it, they tend to judge the opposite – high risk and low benefit.

Alhakami and Slovic's (1994) findings suggested that use of the affect heuristic guides perceptions of risk and benefit as depicted in Figure 23.1. If so, providing information about risk should change the perception of benefit and vice versa (see Figure 23.2). For example, information stating that risk was low for some technology should lead to more positive overall affect that would, in turn, increase perceived benefit. Indeed, Finucane, Alhakami, Slovic, and Johnson

(2000) conducted this experiment, providing four different kinds of information designed to manipulate affect by increasing or decreasing perceived risk and increasing or decreasing perceived benefit. In each case there was no apparent logical relation between the information provided (e.g., information about risks) and the nonmanipulated variable (e.g., benefits). The predictions were confirmed. When the information that was provided changed either the perceived risk or the perceived benefit, an affectively congruent but inverse effect was observed on the nonmanipulated attribute, as depicted in Figure 23.2. These data support the theory that risk and benefit judgments are causally determined, at least in part, by the overall affective evaluation.

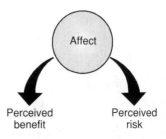

Figure 23.1. A model of the affect heuristic explaining the risk/benefit confounding observed by Alhakami and Slovic (1994). Judgments of risk and benefit are assumed to be derived by reference to an overall affective evaluation of the stimulus item. Source: Finucane et al. (2000). Copyright © 2000 by John Wiley & Sons Limited. Reproduced with permission.

The affect heuristic also predicts that using time pressure to reduce the opportunity for analytic deliberation (and thereby allowing affective considerations freer rein) should enhance the inverse relationship between perceived benefits and risks. In a second study, Finucane et al. (2000) showed that the inverse relationship between perceived risks and benefits increased greatly under time pressure, as predicted. These two experiments with judgments of benefits and risks are important because they support the contention by Zajonc (1980) that affect influences judgment directly and is not simply a response to a prior analytic evaluation. . . .

Judgments of Probability, Relative Frequency, and Risk

The affect heuristic has much in common with the model of *risk as feelings* proposed by Loewenstein et al. (2001) and with dual process theories put forth by Epstein (1994), Sloman (1996), and others. . . .

To demonstrate the influence of the experiential system, Denes-Raj and Epstein (1994) showed that, when offered a chance to win a prize by drawing a red jelly bean from an urn, subjects often elected to draw from a bowl containing a greater absolute number, but a smaller proportion, of red beans (e.g., 7 in 100) than from a bowl with fewer red beans but a better probability of winning (e.g., 1 in 10). For these individuals, images of 7 winning beans in the large bowl appeared to dominate the image of 1 winning bean in the small bowl.

We can characterize Epstein's subjects as following a mental strategy of *imaging the numerator* (i.e., the number of red beans) and neglecting the denominator (the number of beans in the bowl). Consistent with the affect heuristic, images of winning beans convey positive affect that motivates choice.

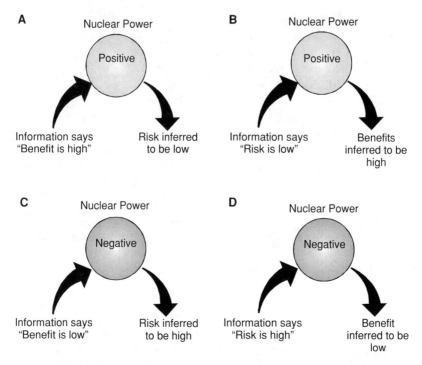

Figure 23.2. Model showing how information about benefit (A) or information about risk (B) could increase the overall affective evaluation of nuclear power and lead to inferences about risk and benefit that coincide affectively with the information given. Similarly, information could decrease the overall affective evaluation of nuclear power as in C and D. Source: Finucane et al. (2000). Copyright © 2000 by John Wiley & Sons Limited. Reproduced with permission.

Although the jelly bean experiment may seem frivolous, imaging the numerator brings affect to bear on judgments in ways that can be both nonintuitive and consequential. Slovic, Monahan, and MacGregor (2000) demonstrated this in a series of studies in which experienced forensic psychologists and psychiatrists were asked to judge the likelihood that a mental patient would commit an act of violence within 6 months after being discharged from the hospital. An important finding was that clinicians who were given another expert's assessment of a patient's risk of violence framed in terms of relative frequency (e.g., "Of every 100 patients similar to Mr. Jones, 10 are estimated to commit an act of violence to others") subsequently labeled Mr. Jones as more dangerous than did clinicians who were shown a statistically equivalent risk expressed as a probability (e.g., "Patients similar to Mr. Jones are estimated to have a 10% chance of committing an act of violence to others").

Not surprisingly, when clinicians were told that "20 out of every 100 patients similar to Mr. Jones are estimated to commit an act of violence," 41% would refuse to discharge the patient. But when another group of clinicians was given the risk as "patients similar to Mr. Jones are estimated to have a 20% chance of committing an act of violence," only 21% would refuse to discharge the patient. Similar results have been found by Yamagishi (1997), whose judges rated a disease that kills 1,286 people out of every 10,000 as more dangerous than one that kills 24.14% of the population.

Unpublished follow-up studies by Slovic showed that representations of risk in the form of individual probabilities of 10% or 20% led to relatively benign images of one person, unlikely to harm anyone, whereas the equivalent frequentistic representations created frightening images of violent patients (example: "Some guy going crazy and killing someone"). These affect-laden images likely induced greater perceptions of risk in response to the relative-frequency frames.

Although frequency formats produce affect-laden imagery, story and narrative formats appear to do even better in that regard. Hendrickx, Vlek, and Oppewal (1989) found that warnings were more effective when, rather than being presented in terms of relative frequencies of harm, they were presented in the form of vivid, affect-laden scenarios and anecdotes. Sanfey and Hastie (1998) found that, compared with respondents given information in bar graphs or data tables, respondents given narrative information more accurately estimated the performance of a set of marathon runners. Furthermore, Pennington and Hastie (1993b) found that jurors construct narrative-like summations of trial evidence to help them process their judgments of guilt or innocence.

Perhaps the biases in probability and frequency judgment that have been attributed to the availability heuristic may be due, at least in part, to affect. Availability may work not only through *ease* of recall or imaginability, but because remembered and imagined images come tagged with affect. For example, Lichtenstein, Slovic, Fischhoff, Layman, and Combs (1978) invoked availability to explain why judged frequencies of highly publicized causes of death (e.g., accidents, homicides, fires, tornadoes, and cancer) were relatively overestimated and underpublicized causes (e.g., diabetes, stroke, asthma, tuberculosis) were underestimated. The highly publicized causes appear to be more affectively charged, that is, more sensational, and this may account both for their prominence in the media and their relatively overestimated frequencies.

Further Evidence

The studies described earlier represent only a small fraction of the evidence that can be marshaled in support of the affect heuristic. Although we have developed the affect heuristic to explain findings from studies of judgment and decision making (e.g., the inverse relationship between perceived risks and benefits), one can find related proposals in the literature of marketing and social cognition. For example, Wright (1975) proposed the *affect-referral heuristic* as a mechanism by which the remembered affect associated with a product influences subsequent choice of that product (see also Pham, 1998).

Attitudes have long been recognized as having a strong evaluative component (see, e.g., Thurstone, 1928, or Edwards, 1957). Pratkanis (1989) defined attitude as "a person's evaluation of an object of thought" (p. 72). He went on to propose that attitudes serve as heuristics, with positive attitudes invoking a favoring strategy toward an object and negative attitudes creating disfavoring response. More specifically, he defined the *attitude heuristic* as the use of the evaluative relationship as a cue for assigning objects to a favorable class or an unfavorable class, thus leading to approach or avoidance strategies appropriate to the class. Pratkanis described numerous phenomena that could be explained by the attitude heuristic, including halo effects not unlike the consistency described earlier between risk and benefit judgments (Finucane et al., 2000). Other important work within the field of social cognition includes studies by Fazio (1995) on the accessibility of affect associated with attitudes and by Schwarz and Clore (1988) on the role of affect as information.

Returning to the recent literature on judgment and decision making, Kahneman and colleagues have demonstrated that responses as diverse as willingness to pay for the provision of a public good (e.g., protection of an endangered species) or a punitive damage award in a personal injury lawsuit seems to be derived from attitudes based on emotion rather than on indicators of economic value (Kahneman & Ritov, 1994; Kahneman, Schkade, & Sunstein, 1998).

Hsee and Kunreuther (2000) have demonstrated that affect influences decisions about whether or not to purchase insurance. In one study, they found that people were willing to pay twice as much to insure a beloved antique clock (that no longer works and cannot be repaired) against loss in shipment to a new city than to insure a similar clock for which "one does not have any special feeling." In the event of loss, the insurance paid $100 in both cases. Similarly, Hsee and Menon (1999) found that students were more willing to buy a warranty on a newly purchased used car if it was a beautiful convertible than if it was an ordinary looking station wagon, even if the expected repair expenses and cost of the warranty were held constant.

Loewenstein et al. (2001) provided a particularly thorough review and analysis of research that supports their *risk-as-feelings hypothesis*, a concept that has much in common with the affect heuristic. They presented evidence showing that emotional responses to risky situations, including feelings such as worry, fear, dread, or anxiety, often diverge from cognitive evaluations and have a different and sometimes greater impact on risk-taking behavior than do cognitive evaluations. Among the factors that appear to influence risk behaviors by acting on feelings rather than cognitions are background mood (e.g., Isen, 1993; Johnson & Tversky, 1983), the time interval between decisions and their outcomes (Loewenstein, 1987), vividness (Hendrickx et al., 1989), and evolutionary preparedness. Loewenstein et al. invoked the evolutionary perspective to explain why people tend to react with little fear to certain types of objectively dangerous stimuli that evolution has not prepared them for, such as guns, hamburgers, automobiles, smoking, and unsafe sex, even when they recognize the threat at a cognitive level. Other types of stimuli, such as caged spiders, snakes, or heights, which evolution may have prepared us to fear, evoke strong visceral responses even when we recognize them, cognitively, to be harmless.

Individual differences in affective reactivity also are informative. Damasio relied on brain-damaged individuals, apparently lacking in the ability to associate emotion with anticipated outcomes, to test his somatic-marker hypothesis. Similar insensitivity to the emotional meaning of future outcomes has been attributed to psychopathic individuals and used to explain their aberrant behaviors (Hare, 1965; Patrick, 1994). Using the Damasio card-selection task, Peters and Slovic (2000) found that normal subjects who reported themselves to be highly reactive to negative events made fewer selections from decks with large losing payoffs. Conversely, greater self-reported reactivity to positive events was associated with a greater number of selections from high-gain decks. Thus, individual differences in affective reactivity appear to play a role in the learning and expression of risk-taking preferences.

THE DOWNSIDE OF AFFECT

Throughout this chapter we have made many claims for the affect heuristic, portraying it as the centerpiece of the experiential mode of thinking, the dominant mode of survival during the evolution of the human species. But, like other heuristics that provide efficient and generally adaptive responses but occasionally lead us astray, reliance on affect can also deceive us. Indeed, if it was always optimal to follow our affective and experiential instincts, there would have been no need for the rational/analytic system of thinking to have evolved and become so prominent in human affairs.

There are two important ways that experiential thinking misguides us. One results from the deliberate manipulation of our affective reactions by those who wish to control our behaviors. The other results from the natural limitations of the experiential system and the existence of stimuli in our environment that are simply not amenable to valid affective representation. Both types of problems are discussed next.

Manipulation of Affect in Our Daily Lives

Given the importance of experiential thinking, it is not surprising to see many forms of deliberate efforts being made to manipulate affect to influence our judgments and decisions. Consider, for example, some everyday questions about the world of entertainment and the world of consumer marketing:

1.   Question: Why do entertainers often change their names?
     Answer: To make them affectively more pleasing. One wonders whether the careers of John Denver, Sandra Dee, and Judy Garland would have been as successful had they performed under their real names – Henry Deutschendorf, Alexandra Zuck, and Frances Gumm.

> Students of *onomastics*, the science of names, have found that the intellectual products of persons with less attractive names are judged to be of lower quality (Erwin & Calev, 1984; Harari & McDavid, 1973), and some have even asserted that the affective quality of a presidential candidate's name influences the candidate's chances of being elected (Smith, 1997).

2. Question: Why do movies have background music? After all, can't we understand the events we are watching and the dialog we are hearing without music?
   Answer: Music conveys affect and thus enhances meaning even for common human interactions and events.

3. Question: Why are all the models in the mail-order catalog smiling?
   Answer: To link positive affect to the clothing they are selling.

4. Question: Why do packages of food products carry all those little blurbs such as "new," "natural," "improved," or "98% fat free"?
   Answer: These are *affective tags* that enhance the attractiveness of the product and increase the likelihood it will be purchased, much as adding "Save 98%" increased the attractiveness of saving 150 lives.

Clearly, entertainers and marketers of consumer products have long been aware of the powerful influence of affect. Perhaps no corporate entities have more zealously exploited consumers' affective sensitivities than the tobacco companies. A recent ad for Kool Natural Lights, for example, repeats the word "natural" 13 times in a single half-page advertisement (Brown & Williamson Tobacco Company, 1999). The attractive images of rugged cowboys and lush waterfalls associated with cigarette ads are known to all of us. Indeed, affective associations between cigarettes and positive images may begin forming in children as young as 3 years old (Fischer, 1991). As Epstein (1994) observes, "Cigarette advertising agencies and their clients are willing to bet millions of dollars in advertising costs that the...appeal of their messages to the experiential system will prevail over the verbal message of the Surgeon General that smoking can endanger one's life, an appeal directed at the rational system" (p. 712). Through the workings of the affect heuristic, as explicated by Finucane et al. (2000), we now have evidence suggesting that cigarette advertising designed to increase the positive affect associated with smoking will quite likely depress perceptions of risk. The factual (impassionate) appeal by the Surgeon General will likely have little effect.

Attempts at affective manipulation often work directly on language. Communicators desiring to change attitudes toward stigmatized technologies, for example, created "nukespeak" to extol the virtues of "clean bombs" and "peacekeeper missiles," whereas promoters of nuclear power coined a new term for reactor accidents: "excursions." Genetically modified food has been promoted as "enhanced" by proponents and "Frankenfood" by opponents.

Manipulation of attitudes and behavior by persuasive argumentation is often quite effective, but at least it tends to be recognized as an attempt to persuade. Manipulation of affect is no less powerful but is made more insidious by often taking place without our awareness. It is unlikely that Hsee's subjects recognized that what they were willing to pay for the used music dictionary was determined far more by the torn cover than by the more important dimension, number of entries.

Legal scholars such as Hanson and Kysar (1999a, 1999b), paying close attention to research on affect and other judgment heuristics, have begun to speak out on the massive manipulation of consumers by the packaging, marketing, and public relations practices of manufacturers. Such manipulation, they argue, renders ineffective three primary forms of legal control over dangerous products – warning requirements, product liability suits, and regulation of advertising. Hanson and Kysar (2001) point to the need for new regulatory strategies that would take into account the full liability of manufacturers who manipulate consumers into purchasing and using hazardous products.

Failures of the Experiential System: The Case of Smoking

Judgments and decisions can be faulty not only because their affective components are manipulable, but also because they are subject to inherent biases of the experiential system. For example, the affective system seems designed to sensitize us to small changes in our environment (e.g., the difference between 0 and 1 deaths) at the cost of making us less able to appreciate and respond appropriately to larger changes (e.g., the difference between 570 deaths and 670 deaths). Fetherstonhaugh et al. (1997) referred to this insensitivity as *psychophysical numbing*.

Similar problems arise when the outcomes that we must evaluate change very slowly over time, are remote in time, or are visceral in nature. The irrationality of decisions to smoke cigarettes provides dramatic examples of these types of failure (Slovic, 2000a, 2001). Despite the portrayal of beginning smokers as "young economists" rationally weighing the risks of smoking against the benefits when deciding whether to initiate that activity (e.g., Viscusi, 1992), recent research paints a different picture. This account (Slovic, 2001) shows young smokers acting experientially in the sense of giving little or no thought to risks or to the amount of smoking they will be doing. Instead, they go with the affective impulses of the moment, enjoying smoking as something new and exciting, a way to have fun with their friends. Even after becoming "regulars," the great majority of smokers expect to stop soon, regardless of how long they have been smoking, how many cigarettes they currently smoke per day, or how many previous unsuccessful attempts they have experienced. Only a fraction actually quit, despite many attempts. The problem is nicotine addiction, a condition that young smokers recognize by name as a consequence of smoking but do not understand experientially until they are caught up in it. . . .

The failure of the experiential system to protect many young people from the lure of smoking is nowhere more evident than in the responses to a survey question that asks smokers: "If you had it to do all over again, would you start smoking?" More than 85% of adult smokers and about 80% of young smokers (ages 14–22) answer "no" (Slovic, 2001). Moreover, the more individuals perceive themselves to be addicted, the more often they have tried to quit, the longer they have been smoking, and the more cigarettes they are smoking per day, the more likely they are to answer "no."

We can now address a central question posed by Viscusi (1992): "At the time when individuals initiate their smoking activity, do they understand the consequences of their actions and make rational decisions?" (p. 11). Viscusi went on to define the appropriate test of rationality in terms of "... whether individuals are incorporating the available information about smoking risks and are making sound decisions, given their own preferences" (p. 12).

The data indicate that the answer to Viscusi's question is "no." Most beginning smokers lack the experience to appreciate how their future selves will perceive the risks from smoking or how they will value the tradeoff between health and the need to smoke. This is a strong repudiation of the model of informed rational choice. It fits well with the findings indicating that smokers give little conscious thought to risk when they begin to smoke. They appear to be lured into the behavior by the prospects of fun and excitement. Most begin to think of risk only after starting to smoke and gaining what to them is new information about health risks.

These disturbing findings underscore the distinction that behavioral decision theorists now make between decision utility and experienced utility (Kahneman, 1994; Kahneman & Snell, 1992; Loewenstein & Schkade, 1999). Utility predicted or expected at the time of decision often differs greatly from the quality and intensity of the hedonic experience that actually occurs.

CONCLUSION

We hope that this rather selective and idiosyncratic tour through a mélange of experiments and conjectures has conveyed the sense of excitement we feel toward the affect heuristic. This heuristic appears at once both wondrous and frightening: wondrous in its speed, subtlety, sophistication, and ability to "lubricate reason"; frightening in its dependency on context and experience, allowing us to be led astray or manipulated, inadvertently or intentionally, silently and invisibly.

It is sobering to contemplate how elusive meaning is, due to its dependence on affect. Thus, the forms of meaning that we take for granted and on which we justify immense effort and expense toward gathering and disseminating "meaningful" information may be illusory. We cannot assume that an intelligent person can understand the meaning of and properly act on even the simplest of numbers such as amounts of money, not to mention more esoteric measures or statistics, unless these numbers are infused with affect.

Contemplating the workings of the affect heuristic helps us appreciate Damasio's (1994) contention that rationality is not only a product of the analytical mind, but of the experiential mind as well:

> The strategies of human reason probably did not develop, in either evolution or any single individual, without the guiding force of the mechanisms of biological regulation, of which emotion and feeling are notable expressions. Moreover, even after reasoning strategies become established . . . their effective deployment probably depends, to a considerable extent, on a continued ability to experience feelings. (p. xii)

Ironically, the perception and integration of affective feelings, within the experiential system, appears to be the kind of high-level maximization process postulated by economic theories since the days of Jeremy Bentham. These feelings form the neural and psychological substrate of utility. In this sense, the affect heuristic enables us to be rational actors in many important situations. But not in all situations. It works beautifully when our experience enables us to anticipate accurately how we will like the consequences of our decisions. It fails miserably when the consequences turn out to be much different in character than we anticipated.

The scientific study of affective rationality is in its infancy. It is exciting to contemplate what might be accomplished by future research designed to help humans understand the affect heuristic and employ it beneficially.

ACKNOWLEDGMENTS

Financial support for the writing of this chapter was provided by the National Science Foundation under grant SES 9876587.

24. The Functions of Affect in the Construction of Preferences

Ellen Peters

A major theme that emerges from judgment and decision-making research is that we frequently do not know our own "true" value for an object or situation (e.g., how much we value a consumer good or better air quality). In such cases we appear to construct our values and preferences "on the spot" when asked to form a particular judgment or to make a specific decision (Payne, Bettman, & Schkade, 1999; Slovic, 1995). The present chapter focuses on the role of affect and the affect heuristic in the construction of preferences and extends earlier work on the affect heuristic by explicating four proposed functions of affect in the construction process.

Recent research has developed and tested theories of judgment and decision making that incorporate affect as a key component in a process of constructing values and preferences. Within these theories, integral affect (positive and negative feelings about a stimulus) and incidental affect (positive and negative feelings such as mood states that are independent of a stimulus but can be misattributed to it) are used to predict and explain a wide variety of judgments and decisions ranging from choices among jelly beans to life satisfaction and valuation of human lives (Kahneman, Schkade, & Sunstein, 1998; Schwarz & Clore, 1983; Slovic, Finucane, Peters, & MacGregor, 2002).

THE FUNCTIONS OF AFFECT IN CONSTRUCTING JUDGMENTS AND DECISIONS

Mild incidental affect and integral affect are ubiquitous in everyday life. Imagine finding a quarter lying on the sidewalk (a mild positive mood state is induced) or considering whether you will have a bowl of oatmeal or a chocolate croissant for breakfast (mild positive and negative integral affective feelings are experienced). These feelings can have an impact on the processing of information and, thus, what is judged or decided. Research in this area has begun to delineate some of the various ways that affect alters how we process information.

Most recent research in affect has considered its informational value. That is, at the moment of judgment or choice, decision makers consult their feelings about a target or option and ask, "How do I feel about this?" (Schwarz & Clore, 2003). These feelings then act as information to guide the judgment or decision process. In the present chapter, I argue that affect has four separable roles.

First, it can act as *information* as suggested earlier. Second, it can act as a *spotlight*, focusing us on different information – numerical cues, for example – depending on the extent of our affect. Third, affect can *motivate* us to take action or do extra work. Finally, affect, when present, acts as a *common currency*, allowing us to compare apples to oranges more effectively than when it is absent.

Affect as Information

One of the most comprehensive theoretical accounts of the role of affect and emotion in decision making was presented by the neurologist, Antonio Damasio (1994). In seeking to determine the neural underpinnings of rational behavior in humans, Damasio argued that a lifetime of learning leads decision options and attributes to become "marked" by positive and negative feelings linked directly or indirectly to somatic or bodily states. When a negative somatic marker is linked to an outcome, it acts as information by sounding an alarm that warns us away from that choice. When a positive marker is associated with the outcome, it becomes a beacon of incentive drawing us toward that option. Affect developed through experience thus provides information about what to choose and what to avoid. Damasio claims that we make better quality and more efficient decisions by consulting and being guided by these feelings. Without these feelings, information in a decision lacks meaning and the resulting choice suffers.

Peters, Slovic, and Hibbard (2004) were interested in the processes by which decision makers bring meaning to dry, cold facts. We attempted to influence the interpretation and comprehension of information about health-plan attributes by providing information in a form that can be used easily to evaluate the overall goodness or badness of a health plan. We suggested that more evaluable information is more affective and that decision makers will use this affect as information when interpreting and drawing meaning from numbers relevant to a judgment or choice. For example, in one of the studies, older-adult participants were presented with identical attribute information (quality of care and member satisfaction) about two health plans. The information was presented in bar chart format with the actual score displayed to the right of the bar chart (see Figure 24.1). The information for half of the subjects in each group was supplemented by the addition of affective categories (i.e., the category lines plus affective labels that placed the health plans into categories of poor, fair, good, or excellent). The attribute information was designed such that Plan A was good on both attributes whereas Plan B was good on quality of care but fair on member satisfaction. The specific scores for quality of care and member satisfaction were counterbalanced across subjects such that, for half of the subjects, the average quality-of-care scores were higher; for the other half, average member satisfaction scores were higher. We predicted and found that affective categories influenced the choices. Specifically, older adults preferred health plan A more often when the categories were present (Plan A was always in the good affective category when the categories were present).

456

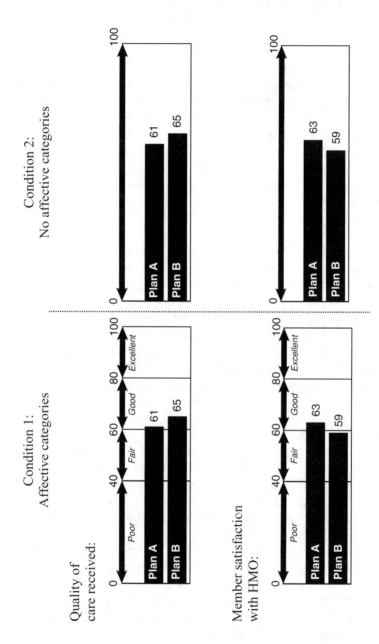

Condition 1:
Affective categories

Quality of
care received:

Member satisfaction
with HMO:

Condition 2:
No affective categories

Figure 24.1. Example of affective categories in health-plan choice.

In a second study, we found that choices of older adults with high deliberative ability (high speed of processing) were influenced less by the presence versus absence of affective categories than were choices of older adults with low deliberative ability. The results suggest that adults with high deliberative efficiency are better able to compare information and derive evaluative meaning from the data. This finding is consistent with research by Salthouse (1992) demonstrating that faster processing is associated with greater working memory capacity. However, for adults with low deliberative efficiency, affective categories appear to provide more information and influence the evaluative meaning. A third study provided direct evidence of the affective basis of this manipulation by demonstrating that decision makers accessed their feelings about the health plan highlighted by affective categories (e.g., Plan A in Figure 24.1) faster than their thoughts in the presence but not the absence of the evaluability manipulation.

Affect also appears to act as information in the construction of prices. Peters, Slovic, and Gregory (2003) demonstrated that buying and selling prices for real-play and hypothetical lottery tickets were constructed through a process guided in part by affect. For example, in their Study 2, buyers made offers for a lottery ticket with a real 5% chance to win a real $100; buyers with more positive feelings about having a ticket offered twice as much for it. Sellers of a lottery ticket in the same study required twice as much in payment for their ticket if they had more negative feelings about not having a ticket. In four studies, buyers and sellers appeared to anchor on salient numerical values and then to adjust from those anchors based on these affective considerations. Affect, in other words, appeared to be information used to determine the extent of adjustment from an initial anchor. Peters, Slovic, Hibbard, and Tusler (2006) also linked affect to the adjustment process in a very different context. Specifically, they found that decision makers who were asked to estimate the number of fatalities in the United States each year from various causes of death anchored on a provided number (the actual number of deaths from a different disease) and then appeared to adjust based on the extent of their worry about the disease under consideration. These findings are important in that they are the first to link affect as a possible mechanism underlying the adjustment process.

The interested reader can find additional examples of the role of affect as information in some of the excellent work on discrete emotions and mood (Connolly & Zeelenberg, 2002; Lerner & Keltner, 2000; Mellers, Schwartz, Ho, & Ritov, 1997; Schwarz & Clore, 2003). Affect has also been shown to act as information to influence perceptions of risk (Constans & Mathews, 1993; Johnson & Tversky, 1983; Loewenstein, Weber, Hsee, & Welch, 2001; Peters & Slovic, 1996; Rottenstreich & Hsee, 2001; Wright & Bower, 1992). Decision makers appear to consult their affective feelings and use them as information in judgment and decision processes. Affect as information thus acts as a substitute for the assessment of other specified target attributes in judgment (Kahneman, 2003c).

Without affect, information appears to have less meaning and to be weighed less in judgment and choice processes.

Affect as a Spotlight

Considerably less work has been done on the other three proposed functions of affect in the construction of preferences. Peters et al. (2003) proposed that affect plays a role as a lens or spotlight in a two-stage process. First, the quality of affective feelings (e.g., weak vs. strong or positive vs. negative) focuses the decision maker on different information. Then, that information (rather than the feelings themselves) is used to guide the judgment or decision. Although the impact of incidental feelings has been shown to function as a spotlight in memory and judgment (e.g., mood-congruent biases on memory; Bower, 1981), little research has examined how feelings about a target might alter what information becomes salient.

Peters et al. (2003) proposed that affect may influence the numerical anchors used by buyers and sellers in the construction of monetary valuations. In their Study 2, for example, buyers who reported low positive affect toward having a lottery ticket appeared to anchor on a price of zero more than buyers who reported greater positive affect toward the lottery ticket; buyers high in positive affect seemed to anchor more often on the expected value. Sellers, on the other hand, who reported low compared with high negative affect toward giving up their ticket appeared more likely to anchor on the expected value response and less likely to anchor on the winning amount of the lottery. The level of affect toward an object seems to make different numerical cues more salient.

Depending on how strongly we feel about an object, we may focus on different information. Alhakami and Slovic (1994) demonstrated that the negative correlation between perceived risk and perceived benefit is mediated by affect. In other words, decision makers with positive affect toward a technology tend to perceive it as high in benefit and low in risk; the reverse happens if decision makers have a negative affect about it. Although this effect has been interpreted in terms of the role of affect as information (Slovic et al., 2002), it may be related to affect's role as a spotlight. The affect-as-spotlight hypothesis predicts that decision makers who have positive feelings about a technology will spend more time looking at its benefits and will remember them better whereas they spend less time looking at its risks and will remember them less well. It predicts the reverse for technologies that they do not like (e.g., less time spent considering and poorer memory for its benefits).

Affect as a Motivator of Behavior

In a third role for affect, it appears to function as a motivator of behavior. Classical theories of emotion include, as the core of an emotion, a readiness to act and the prompting of plans (Frijda, 1986). Lerner, Small, and Loewenstein (2004), for example, studied the impact of experimentally induced emotion states of sadness and disgust on prices set by buyers and sellers in a real-play market. In particular, they linked prices with the action tendencies resulting from these incidental emotion states (i.e., disgust and "an implicit action tendency to expel current objects and avoid taking in anything new," p. 5). Although affect is a much milder experience compared with a full-blown emotion state, recent research has demonstrated that we tend to automatically classify stimuli around us as good or bad and that this tendency is linked to behavioral tendencies. Stimuli classified as good elicit a tendency to approach whereas those classified as bad elicit avoidance tendencies (Chen & Bargh, 1999). Incidental mood states also motivate behavior as people tend to act to maintain or attain positive mood states (Isen, 2000).

Affect appears to be linked not only to automatic tendencies to act but also with the extent of deliberative effort decision makers are willing to put forth. Participants in Peters et al.'s (2003) real-play Study 2 compared with their hypothetical-play Study 1 had stronger feelings about their lottery tickets and showed more evidence of having calculated an expected value (40% of Study 2 first-time buyers gave the expected value as their response compared with 10% in Study 1). In addition, half of Study 1 participants gave the same buying price as their earlier selling price compared with only 3% of participants in the real-play Study 2. Thus, real play seemed to motivate buyers and sellers to work harder, and the motivating effect of real play was mediated by affect.

Affect as Common Currency

Affect is simpler in some ways than thoughts (see Figure 24.2). Affect comes in two "flavors," positive and negative; thoughts include more, and more complex, cost–benefit and other tradeoffs (Trafimow & Sheeran, 2004). Several theorists have suggested that, as a result, affect plays a role as a common currency, allowing decision makers to compare apples with oranges (Cabanac, 1992). Montague and Berns (2002) link this notion to "neural responses in the orbitofrontal-striatal circuit which may support the conversion of disparate types of future rewards into a kind of internal currency, that is, a common scale used to compare the valuation of future behavioral acts or stimuli" (p. 265). By translating more complex thoughts into simpler affective evaluations, decision makers can compare and integrate good and bad feelings rather than attempting to make sense out of a multitude of conflicting logical reasons.

In the health-plan choice studies of Peters, Slovic, and Hibbard (2004), affective categories were hypothesized to act as overt markers of affective meaning in choices. If this is the case, then these overt markers should help participants to consider relevant information (that is not considered as much when affective categories are not present) such that they can apply that information to a complex judgment. Thus, affective categories should influence not just the choice of a health plan, as shown in previous studies, but it should help decision makers to take into account more information and be more sensitive to variation in information.

We conducted an initial test of this hypothesis. Participants were asked to judge a series of eight health plans one at a time on a 7-point attractiveness scale ranging from 1 = *extremely unattractive* to 7 = *extremely attractive*. For each health

Figure 24.2. Affect is simpler than thoughts. ROSE IS ROSE Copyright © 2003. Reprinted by permission of United Feature Syndicate, Inc.

plan, they received information about cost and two quality attributes presented with numerical scores (e.g., Plan A scored 72 out of 100 points when members of the health plan rated the "ease of getting referrals to see a specialist"). The eight health plans represented a 2 × 2 × 2 design of low and high scores on each of the three attributes; eight versions were constructed using a Latin square design. Participants who received the quality information with affective categories (poor, fair, good, excellent) took into account more information in their judgments and showed significantly greater sensitivity to differences in quality among the plans. Thus, providing information in a more affective format appeared to help these judges better integrate important quality information into their judgments.

HOW DO YOU KNOW IT'S AFFECT?

The study of affect and emotion is relatively new to the science of judgment and decision making. Decision makers appear to consult the feelings they experience as they consider a target or option. The experienced feelings can be relevant or irrelevant to the judgment or decision at hand but influence the construction of preferences either way.

A question that frequently arises, however, is how do you know it's affective feeling as opposed to more cognitive thought? After all, a decision maker may have good and bad thoughts as well as good and bad feelings about an object. In the present section, I consider how a researcher might measure affect, examine affect in relation to its functions, and differentiate it from more cognitive thoughts. No one method can "prove" the affective basis of a judgment or decision. However, by using multiple methods to measure and manipulate affect, we can provide converging evidence that is more consistent with an affective as opposed to a cognitive story.

Self-Report Measures

Peters and Slovic (2006) examined various measures of affect based on different conceptualizations. Affect can be: (1) a holistic reaction to an object that is derived from spontaneous images of the objects, (2) bipolar or unipolar in structure, and finally, (3) based on discrete emotional evaluations (e.g., angry, happy) or more general valenced evaluations (e.g., good, bad). They recommended that further research with affective self-reports include the holistic, unipolar, discrete emotion (HUE) evaluative measures developed in their paper in combination with a holistic bipolar valenced evaluation measure. Bradley and Lang (1994) developed the Self-Assessment Manikin as a nonverbal pictorial technique to directly measure the pleasure, arousal, and dominance associated with a person's affective reactions to stimuli. They thought that the body-based characters would be less problematic than scales such as the HUE that require more verbalization and thus may draw more on cognitive thoughts. Each of these measures relies on self-reported feelings about an object or the decision maker's internal state; these feelings can then be examined in relation to a judgment or decision thought to be constructed at least in part through affect. For example, a modified version of the HUE scale was used successfully by Peters et al. (2003) to examine the relation between affect and prices. In that study, they asked how participants felt about having or not having a lottery ticket. Researchers who are interested in the experienced feelings evoked by a stimulus could ask instead "how does it make you feel?" Asking the question in this way focuses more directly on the experienced affect hypothesized to be important to the affect heuristic rather than on the affective component of attitude ("how do you feel about it?").

Individual Differences

Other research has focused on individual differences in affect (both self-reported and physiological) and posited that if a hypothesized relation exists between the individual-difference measure and choices, then affect is at least one of the mechanisms underlying that choice process. For example, greater self-reported reactivity to negative events predicted faster learning of the likelihood of losing in a task (Zinbarg & Mohlman, 1998). Peters and Slovic (2000) demonstrated that college students high in negative reactivity learned to choose fewer high-loss options, whereas those high in positive reactivity learned to choose more high-gain options. In an unpublished study, Peters and Mauro

found that individual differences in physiological reactions (heart rate) in anticipation of a choice were associated with choices among decks of cards that differed in the amount of gains, losses, and expected values. Bechara, Damasio,
Damasio, and Anderson (1994) had similar physiological findings with non-
brain-damaged adults; in their study, the presence of anticipatory skin conductance responses was associated with good choices in their Iowa Gambling Task.
Patients with bilateral damage to the ventromedial prefrontal cortex showed
abnormal emotional reactions, did not develop these anticipatory responses,
and made bad choices overall in this task and in life.

Accessibility

Kahneman (2003c) argued that the accessibility of information was a determinant of what information most influenced a judgment or choice. For example, if a
stereotype was particularly accessible and salient (e.g., Linda the feminist bank
teller), then the representativeness heuristic would be evoked and similarity
with the stereotype would guide subsequent judgments. Affect may also guide
judgments and choices more when it is more accessible. Verplanken, Hofstee,
and Janssen (1998) found that participants could make affective evaluations
of brand names and countries faster than cognitive evaluations, suggesting
that the affect-based evaluations were more "accessible" and therefore were
more likely to be the basis of those attitudes. Peters, Slovic, and Hibbard (2004)
modified this technique to examine the possible affective basis of health-plan
choices made more evaluable through affective categories. We hypothesized
that participants would respond faster with affective evaluations than cognitive
evaluations of choice options in the presence versus the absence of evaluability. A finding that affective feelings are more quickly accessible than cognitive
thoughts in the presence of affective categories would be consistent with affect
underlying evaluability's effect on choice.

Without affective categories, participants accessed feelings about the options
more slowly than thoughts; mean reaction times (RTs) were 1,545 and 1,460
msecs, respectively. However, as hypothesized, they accessed feelings about the
options faster than thoughts when affective categories were present; mean RTs
were 1,266 and 1,382 msecs, respectively, $F(1, 76) = 4.9, p < .05$, for the interaction
of the categories manipulation with feelings versus thoughts. The interaction of
thoughts versus feelings with the affective-categories manipulation remained
significant, $F(1, 70) = 4.2, p < .05$, after controlling for the valence of the response
and the order (asking thoughts first or feelings first). These results provided the
first direct test of the role of affect in evaluability. Not only were the affect
items accessed more quickly but they predicted choices among the health plans
significantly better than the thought items.

Experimental Manipulations

Each of the previous methods employed to examine the how-do-you-
know-it's-affect question has focused on measuring affect. Affect can also be

experimentally manipulated. In one study, incidental affect (i.e., positive and negative moods) was induced and misattributed as integral affect toward a lottery ticket (Peters, Västfjäll, & Starmer, 2006). Compared with those in a negative mood, positive-mood buyers were willing to pay more for a ticket and positive-mood sellers required a greater minimum payment in exchange for their ticket; these findings were mediated by self-reported affect toward the ticket. Mood also influenced perceptions of the likelihood of winning the lottery such that positive-mood sellers perceived their chances of winning the lottery as higher than negative-mood sellers. Lerner and her colleagues have also manipulated discrete-emotion states such as anger and fear and demonstrated important relations with judgments (e.g., Lerner, Gonzalez, Small, & Fischhoff, 2003).

IS AFFECT RATIONAL?

Emotion's influence on decision making can be one of overwhelming power and control (he was overcome with fear; she was filled with grief; both are incapable as decision makers). Damasio, on the other hand, argues that affect increases the accuracy and efficiency of the decision process, and its absence (e.g., in the brain-damaged patients) degrades decision performance. Affect is rational in the sense that some level of affect is necessary for information to have meaning so that decisions can be made. However, affect's role is nuanced. It sometimes may help and other times hurt decision processes. Which occurs will depend on how affect influences the information processing that takes place in the construction of preferences and how that particular influence matches whatever processing will produce the best decision in that situation. In other words, the presence of affect does not guarantee good or bad decisions, only different information processing.

ACKNOWLEDGMENTS

Many thanks to Daniel Västfjäll, Sarah Lichtenstein, Robin Gregory, Paul Slovic, and David Trafimow for comments on a previous draft of this chapter as well as many enjoyable discussions on the topic of affect and decision making. Preparation of this chapter was supported in part by the National Science Foundation under Grant Nos. SES-0111941, SES-0339204, and SES-0241313. Any opinions, findings, and conclusions or recommendations expressed in this material are those of the author and do not necessarily reflect the views of the National Science Foundation.

25. Mere Exposure: A Gateway to the Subliminal

Robert B. Zajonc

Preferences constitute one of the fundamental sources of social and individual stability and change. They give our lives direction and our actions meaning. They influence ideological values, political commitments, the marketplace, kinship structures, and cultural norms. They are sources of attachment and antagonism, of alliance and conflict. No species would evolve if it could not actively discriminate between objects, events, and circumstances that are beneficial and those that are harmful.

Preferences are formed by diverse processes. Some objects, by their inherent properties, induce automatic attraction or aversion. Sucrose is attractive virtually at birth, whereas bitter substances – quinine, for example – are universally aversive. Preferences may also be established by classical or operant conditioning. If a child is rewarded when she sits in a particular corner of the crib, that corner will become a preferred location for her. An office worker whose colleagues notice his new tie will develop a preference for similar ties. Preferences can also be acquired by virtue of imitation, a social process that emerges in fashions. Preferences also arise from conformity pressures. In economics, preference is regarded as the product of rational choice – a deliberate computation that weighs the pros and cons of alternatives.

But among the many ways in which preferences may be acquired, there is one that is absurdly simple, much simpler than rational choice. I discuss here this very primitive way – conscious and unconscious – of acquiring preferences, namely, the mere repeated exposure of stimuli, and I explain the process whereby repeated exposure leads to the formation of preferences.

THE MERE-REPEATED-EXPOSURE PHENOMENON

The repeated-exposure paradigm consists of no more than making a stimulus accessible to the individual's sensory receptors. There is no requirement for the individual to engage in any sort of behavior, nor is he or she offered positive or

Originally published in *Current Directions in Psychological Science*, vol. 10, pp. 224–228. Copyright © 2001 by the American Psychological Society. Reprinted with permission from Blackwell Publishing Ltd.

negative reinforcement. The exposures themselves are sometimes so degraded that the individual is not aware of their occurrence. Their effects are measured by the resulting changes in preference for the object. In contradiction to some early contentions (Birnbaum & Mellers, 1979; Lazarus, 1982), it can now be claimed that no cognitive mediation, rational or otherwise, is involved in these effects.

It is well known that words with positive meanings have a higher frequency of usage than words with negative meanings (Zajonc, 1968). The relationship holds over all parts of speech. Not only is *good* (5,122 occurrences in a random sample of 1,000,000 English words) more frequent than *bad* (1,001), and *pretty* (1,195) more frequent than *ugly* (178), but also *on* (30,224) is more frequent than *off* (3,644), *in* (75,253) is more frequent than *out* (13,649), and even *first* (5,154) is more frequent than *last* (3,517). In fact, the words in nearly every semantic category, and even letters and numbers, show a strong correlation between ratings for preference and frequency of usage, and not only words but all kinds of stimuli have been found to increase in attractiveness with repeated exposures. This seemingly innocent finding (Zajonc, 1968) has stimulated decades of research on the relation between cognition and affect.

Obviously, the first question to ask is that of causality, that is, whether we are more likely to seek out positive than negative experiences, and therefore favor positive stimuli, or whether aspects of the world that we experience often acquire thereby positive valence. The finding that frequently occurring numbers and letters are better liked than less frequent numbers and letters favors the latter possibility. It has been demonstrated that the mere repeated exposure of a stimulus is entirely sufficient for the enhancement of preference for that stimulus. This mere-repeated-exposure effect is found in a variety of contexts, for a wide assortment of stimuli, using diverse procedures, and among both humans and nonhuman animals. In the extreme, an exposure effect was obtained prenatally (Rajecki, 1974). Tones of two different frequencies were played to two sets of fertile chicken eggs. When the hatched chicks were then tested for their preference for the tones, the chicks in each set consistently chose the tone that was played to them prenatally. Similarly, one group of rats was exposed to music by Schönberg and another to music by Mozart to see if they could acquire corresponding preferences. They did, slightly favoring the latter composer. And Taylor and Sluckin (1964) found that domestic chicks that were exposed either to their conspecific age peers or to a matchbox preferred the object to which they were previously exposed.

The earliest explanation of the effect was offered by Titchener. It proposed a virtual tautology, namely, that we like familiar objects because we enjoy recognizing familiar objects. But Titchener's hypothesis had to be rejected because in numerous studies, the enhancement of preferences for objects turned out not to depend on individuals' subjective impressions of how familiar the objects were (Wilson, 1979).

SUBLIMINAL INDUCTION OF AFFECT

The cumulative results lead to the inescapable conclusion that the changes in affect that accompany repeated exposures do not depend on subjective factors, such as the subjective impression of familiarity, but on the objective history of exposures (Zajonc, 2000). Even when exposures are subliminal, and subjects have no idea that any stimuli at all have been presented, those subliminal stimuli that are flashed frequently are liked better than those flashed infrequently (Murphy, Monahan, & Zajonc, 1995; Zajonc, 1980).[1] In fact, exposure effects are more pronounced when obtained under subliminal conditions than when subjects are aware of the repeated exposures.

ABSENCE OF AVERSIVE EVENTS
AS AN UNCONDITIONED STIMULUS

Careful experiments have ruled out explanations of this phenomenon based on ease of recognition, an increased perceptual fluency, or subjective familiarity. But mere-exposure effects cannot take place in a total vacuum. What, then, is the process that induces preferences by virtue of exposures? One possibility that cannot be ruled out is that we have here a form of conditioning, unique to be sure, but nevertheless a form that features the essential conditioning factors. The classical paradigm of classical conditioning requires that the conditioned stimulus (CS) be followed by an unconditioned stimulus (US), preferably within 500 ms. The paradigm also requires that this joint occurrence be repeated several times in very much the same form. It is taken as given that the US has an innate capacity of eliciting the unconditioned response (UR). Thus, a dog will salivate (UR) when presented with food (UC), and if a bell is rung (CS) during the dog's feeding time, then after several repetitions of this joint event, the bell alone will make the dog salivate. The elicitation of salivation by the bell alone is evidence that conditioning has been successful and salivation has become a conditioned response (CR). Although the connection between the response and the US is innate, the new relationship between the CS and the CR is acquired.

In the mere-repeated-exposure paradigm, the repeatedly exposed stimuli can be viewed as CSs. We can also think of the preference response as the CR. But where is the US? The mere-exposure paradigm requires that no positive or negative consequences follow exposures. And no response other than maintaining sensory access to the exposed stimulus is required of the participant. But just because the experimenter does not provide a US does not mean that there is no event that, from the point of view of the participant, could constitute a US. In fact, there is such an event. Contiguous with exposures (i.e., the presentations of the CS) are events characterized by a conspicuous absence of noxious

---

[1] The fact that the stimuli were actually below participants' awareness was tested by a forced-choice method developed by Eriksen (1980).

or aversive consequences. Hence, the very absence of a noxious consequence could well act as a US. The absence of aversive consequences constitutes a safety signal that is associated with the CS. As in classical conditioning, after several CS–US occurrences, in which the US is simply the fact that the individual does not suffer any untoward experiences, the CR – an approach tendency – becomes attached to the CS, now communicating that the current environment is safe.

On the initial presentations, when the stimulus is novel, both avoidance and approach responses are elicited, and the tendency to explore (approach) is tentative. But because the aftermath of the CS is invariably benign, avoidance and escape drop out to leave only approach responses. It is thus that positive affect can be attached to a stimulus by virtue of mere repeated exposures. Some forms of imprinting (Zajonc, 2000) can be conceptualized in the very same manner.

REPEATED EXPERIENCES AS A SOURCE OF POSITIVE AFFECT

How can we inquire into the dynamics of this conditioning paradigm in which even the CS is inaccessible to awareness and the very presence of the US is a matter of conjecture? We can assume that the absence of an aversive event that engenders approach behavior to the exposed object generates positive affect. Therefore, because a condition such as an absence of an aversive event is diffuse and unattached to any particular object in the immediate environment, not only should the exposed object become more attractive, but the overall affective state of the individual should become more positive. We should expect an enhancement of the individual's general affect and mood state just by virtue of the repeated exposures themselves. Monahan, Murphy, and I (Monahan, Murphy, & Zajonc, 2000) inquired into the effects of sheer stimulus repetition by subliminally exposing two groups to Chinese ideographs. One group was exposed to 5 ideographs, five times each in random order. The other group was exposed to 25 different ideographs, each shown but once. All exposures lasted 4 ms. Following the exposures, the participants in the repeated-exposures condition were in better moods and felt more positive than the participants who were exposed to 25 different ideographs.

Thus, repetitions of an experience in and of themselves are capable of producing a diffuse positive affective state. And if that is one of the consequences of repeated exposures, then the changed mood, although diffuse and unspecific, could well become attached to stimuli that are presented just afterward. Previous research has demonstrated that repeated exposures enhance preferences for the exposed stimuli. The exposures can also generate positive affect in response to additional stimuli that are similar in form or substance – even though they were not previously exposed. But if the affect generated by repetition of exposures is diffuse and nonspecific, then any stimulus, if it follows a benign repetition experience, would become infused with positive affect. In a new experiment (Monahan et al., 2000), we again presented 5 stimuli five times each to one group

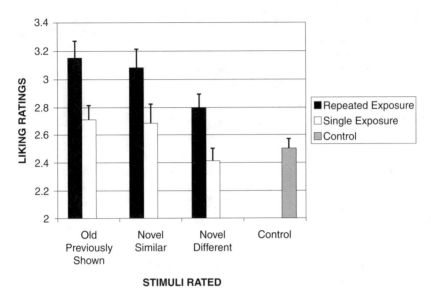

Figure 25.1. Preferences for diverse stimuli as a function of exposure condition (adapted from Monahan, Murphy, & Zajonc, 2000). Copyright © 2000 by the American Psychological Society. Reprinted with permission from Blackwell Publishing Ltd.

of participants and 25 different stimuli once each to another group. Afterward, however, instead of measuring the participants' overall mood, we asked them to rate three categories of stimuli: Chinese ideographs that were previously shown, Chinese ideographs that were similar to those previously shown but novel, and totally distinct stimuli – random polygons. In all cases, the group that was exposed to repeated ideographs rated the stimuli more positively than the group exposed to 25 ideographs one time each. Also in all cases, the ratings of the repeated-exposure group were more positive than those obtained from a control group that had not experienced any prior exposures of the stimuli (see Figure 25.1).

THE INDEPENDENCE OF AFFECT AND COGNITION

This array of findings supports not only the proposition that affect may be elicited without a prior cognitive appraisal, but also the contention that affect and cognition may well be independent processes, because in the context of exposure effects, prototypical cognition is measured by recognition memory, whereas prototypical affect is measured by preference judgments. (For a more detailed discussion of the distinction, see Zajonc, 2000, pp. 46–47.) When I first published this hypothesis (Zajonc, 1980), claiming that affective reactions may precede cognitive reactions and thus require no cognitive appraisal, there was no neuroanatomical or neurophysiological evidence to support it.

Eventually, however, LeDoux (1996), Zola-Morgan, Squire, Alvarez-Royo, and Clower (1991) and other investigators published results confirming the original hypothesis that affect and cognition, although participating jointly in behavior, are separate psychological and neural processes that can be influenced independently of one another. Especially important is the work of Zola-Morgan and his colleagues, who have conducted experiments with monkeys, showing that lesions to the amygdala (a brain structure that is responsive to affective qualities of stimulation) impair emotional responsiveness but leave cognitive functions intact, whereas lesions to the hippocampus (a brain structure that plays an important role in memory) impair cognitive functions but leave emotional responsiveness intact.

Other neuroanatomical studies have confirmed that affect can be induced unconsciously. Thus, Elliott and Dolan (1998), taking PET (positron emission tomography) measures, examined preference acquisition as a function of subliminal repeated exposures and inquired into the neuroanatomical correlates of these effects. They found that different regions of the brain were activated during subjects' affective reactions and memory judgments. Recognition judgments were localized in the frontopolar cortex and the parietal areas, whereas preference reactions showed right lateral frontal activation. This finding that recognition and preference are associated with different brain structures further supports the hypothesis that cognition and affect are independent systems.

Given the independence of affect, we can explain why it is that repeated-exposure effects are clearer and stronger when the exposures are subliminal than when subjects are aware of them. If a given process depends on cognitive appraisal, different individuals will access different cognitive content and attach different meanings to the same stimuli. Hence, the between-participants variability in reactions will be increased. If cognitive processes are not involved in a behavior, however, affective influences, which are necessarily less diverse than cognitive influences, will dominate the behavior, yielding a more homogeneous array of reactions.

CONCLUSION

The mere-exposure effect, when viewed as classical conditioning with the US consisting of the absence of aversive consequences, is a very simple yet effective process for acquiring behavioral tendencies of adaptive value. The mere-exposure effect provides a flexible means of forming selective attachments and affective dispositions, with remarkably minimal investment of energy, even when exposures are not accessible to awareness.

The consequences of repeated exposures benefit the organism in its relations to the immediate animate and inanimate environment. They allow the organism to distinguish objects and habitats that are safe from those that are not, and they are the most primitive basis of social attachments. Therefore, they form the basis for social organization and cohesion – the basic sources of psychological and social stability. Imprinting effects manifest substantial permanence. It remains to be demonstrated, however, how permanent are preferences induced by mere repeated exposures, under supraliminal and subliminal coditions. It is also not yet known if repeated-exposure effects are more readily established in younger than in older organisms and what processes can reverse or extinguish them.

ACKNOWLEDGMENT

I am grateful to Hazel Markus for her helpful suggestions.

26. Introspecting About Reasons Can Reduce Post-Choice Satisfaction

Timothy D. Wilson, Douglas J. Lisle, Jonathan W. Schooler,
Sara D. Hodges, Kristen J. Klaaren, and Suzanne J. LaFleur

> He who deliberates lengthily will not always choose the best.
>
> – Goethe

Introspection is often considered a uniquely human capability. Other species possess sophisticated cognitive and communicative skills (e.g., Premack & Premack, 1983; Ristau & Robbins, 1982), but as far as we know, we are the only species that thinks *about* its thoughts and feelings. Given the possibly unique status of our ability to self-reflect, it is tempting to view self-reflection as a uniformly beneficial activity. This assumption has been made, at least implicitly, by theorists in several areas of psychology. Many forms of psychotherapy view introspection as an integral part of the healing process, and some decision theorists argue that reflection about a choice will lead to better decision making (e.g., Janis & Mann, 1977; Koriat, Lichtenstein, & Fischhoff, 1980; Raiffa, 1968). Similarly, Langer (1978, 1989) has argued that we would be better off in most contexts if we were more "mindful" and contemplative about our actions.

Introspection and self-reflection undoubtedly can be very useful, with the ability to superimpose reason and discretion on otherwise impulsive actions. There is no reason to assume that introspection is always beneficial, however, and in fact, there may be times when it is best to avoid too much of it. There is a growing literature documenting the drawbacks of self-reflection and rumination. Morrow and Nolan-Hoeksema (1990) found that people who ruminated about a negative mood were less successful in improving their moods than people who performed a distracting task. Schooler and Engstler-Schooler (1990) found that people who verbalized their memories for nonverbal stimuli, such as faces, had an impaired memory for these stimuli, whereas Schooler, Ohlsson, and Brooks (1993) found that people who tried to verbalize solutions to insight problems performed more poorly than people who did not.

We have been concerned with the possible harmful effects of a different kind of introspection – namely, thinking about the reasons for one's feelings. Thinking about reasons can be disruptive, we suggest, for the following reasons. People often have difficulty verbalizing exactly why they feel the way they do about an attitude object. The reasons that come to mind are ones that are accessible in memory and sound plausible, even if they are not completely accurate (Nisbett & Wilson, 1977). For example, when looking at a painting by Monet, people might have a generally positive reaction. When thinking about *why* they feel the way they do, however, what comes to mind and is easiest to verbalize might be that some of the colors are not very pleasing and that the subject matter, a haystack, is rather boring. If so, people might adopt, at least temporarily, the more negative attitude implied by their reasons. We have found evidence in several studies for just this sequence of events. When people are asked why they feel the way they do about something, they often change their attitudes in the direction of the attitude implied by their reasons (for reviews, see Wilson, 1990; Wilson, Dunn, Kraft, & Lisle, 1989; Wilson & Hodges, 1992).

Even if people do not know exactly why they feel the way they do, it might seem that they would focus only on reasons that were consistent with their initial feelings. Why, for example, would people think of negative attributes of the Monet painting if their initial reaction were positive? As noted by Benjamin Franklin (1950), "So convenient a thing it is to be a reasonable creature, since it enables one to find or make a reason for every thing one has a mind to do." Undoubtedly such a justification process can and does occur. We simply suggest, that under some circumstances, the reasons that are most accessible and plausible do not correspond perfectly with people's initial affect, leading to attitude change. This is particularly likely to occur when people are not very knowledgeable about the attitude object, when their initial feelings and beliefs about the attitude object are inconsistent (Erber, Hodges, & Wilson, 1995; Millar & Tesser, 1989), and when a contrary reason happens to be salient or accessible (Salancik, 1974; Seligman, Fazio, & Zanna, 1980; for a more in-depth discussion of this issue, see Wilson, Dunn, et al., 1989; Wilson & Schooler, 1991).

The fact that thinking about reasons can change people's attitudes does not demonstrate that it is in any way deleterious to reflect in this manner. In fact, it might even be argued that people's new attitudes are more informed and less impulsive and thus advantageous in some respects. We suggest, however, that the attitude change following introspection about reasons can have negative consequences. We assume that, left to their own devices, people often form satisfactory preferences and personal choices. People are certainly not perfect information processors, but they often manage to assign weights to the different attributes of alternatives that produce a satisfactory choice (satisfactory to them). People may not be aware of how they are weighting the information, but they often use schemes that are adaptive and functional. The old adage "I may not know why, but I know what I like" probably has more than a grain of truth to it.

If so, what happens when people introspect about why they feel the way they do? This kind of introspection, we suggest, can change an optimal weighting scheme into a less optimal one. When people analyze reasons, they might focus on those attributes of the attitude object that seem like plausible causes of their evaluations (e.g., the color of a painting) but were not weighted heavily before. Similarly, they might overlook attributes that were weighted heavily. As a result of this change in people's weighting scheme, they change their preferences. Assuming that their original preference was fairly optimal, this change in weights might lead to a less optimal preference.

We recently found support for this hypothesis in two studies (Wilson & Schooler, 1991). In one, people who analyzed why they liked or disliked different brands of strawberry jam changed their preferences toward the jams. Consistent with our hypothesis that this change would be in a nonoptimal direction, their preferences corresponded less with expert ratings of the jams than the preferences of control subjects. In a second study, college students who analyzed why they felt the way they did about a series of courses they could take the following semester changed their minds about which courses to take, and these choices corresponded less with expert opinion (student evaluations of the courses) than the choices of control subjects did. These studies suggest that people who analyzed reasons changed their preferences in nonoptimal ways. The criterion of what constituted a "good" decision, however, is open to question. The fact that people's attitudes toward strawberry jams or college courses do not correspond to expert opinion does not mean that these attitudes are dysfunctional for those individuals. If the experts happen to prefer Brand A, but we prefer Brand B, what is the harm? As long as people themselves are happy with their preferences and choices, we have no grounds for criticizing these choices.

There is reason to believe, however, that people will be less satisfied with choices they make after thinking about why they feel the way they do. As we have seen, analyzing reasons can change the way people weight information about a stimulus, thereby changing their preferences. There is also evidence that these new preferences are not very stable, because they are contrary to the way people chronically evaluate stimuli in that domain. We have found, for example, that the attitudes people express after analyzing reasons are poor predictors of their later behavior, behavior that occurs after people have had a chance to reevaluate the stimulus (see Wilson, Dunn, et al., 1989, for a review). One reason for this finding may be that when people analyze reasons, they change the way they weight information about the stimulus, but over time they return to their chronic weighting schemes, essentially reverting to their initial attitudes.

If so, people might come to regret choices that they make immediately after analyzing reasons. Consider the following example: A woman is looking for something to hang over her mantel and goes to a store that sells art posters. She is in a particularly introspective mood and decides to analyze why she feels the way she does about each poster she examines. After doing so, she decides which one she likes best, purchases it, and takes it home. There is a good possibility, we suggest, that the act of analyzing reasons will change this person's mind about which poster to purchase. Trying to verbalize her reasons may highlight features of the posters that were not central to her initial evaluations, leading to a change in her preferences. Put differently, this person is probably not fully aware of how she usually (i.e., chronically) forms evaluations of works of art, leaving her open to the kinds of attitude change we have found in our previous studies. But what will happen over the next few weeks, as she looks at the poster over her mantel? Our suspicion is that the features she focused on when she analyzed reasons would probably no longer be salient. Instead, she would revert to her chronic means of evaluating works of art, possibly causing her to regret her choice.

The present study tested the hypothesis that people who analyze reasons will change their preferences and consumer choices. We predicted that people who analyzed reasons for liking or disliking individual posters would become less happy with their choice of poster over time. We also explored whether the effects of analyzing reasons would be moderated by people's level of knowledge about art, as suggested by a study by Wilson, Kraft, and Dunn (1989). Wilson, Kraft, and Dunn found that people who were unknowledgeable about politics changed their political attitudes after analyzing reasons whereas knowledgeable people did not. Unknowledgeable people were significantly more likely to bring to mind reasons that were evaluatively inconsistent, such that these reasons were more likely to imply an attitude different from their prior one. Knowledgeable people, in contrast, brought to mind reasons that were evaluatively consistent and more likely to reflect their prior attitude. In the present study, we examined whether people's knowledge about art had similar effects.

METHOD

SUBJECTS

Forty-three female undergraduates at the University of Virginia volunteered for a study entitled "Posters" in return for course credit or a payment of $5. We used only females because of their greater availability and to avoid sex differences in preferences for different kinds of posters. In previous studies on the effects of analyzing reasons on attitudes, we have not found sex differences.

MATERIALS

Subjects evaluated five posters. Two had received high ratings in a pre-test: paintings by Monet (*Nymphéas*) and Van Gogh (*Les Irés Saint Rémy*). The other three, which were much less popular in our pre-testing, were of a more contemporary, humorous style: a cartoon of animals rising in a hot air balloon, a photograph of a cat perched on a rope with the caption "Gimme a Break," and a photograph of a cat standing at a fence with the caption "One Step at a Time." All the posters were mounted on cardboard and were either 18 × 24 in. or 20 × 28 in.[1]

PROCEDURE

Subjects, seen individually, were told that the purpose of the experiment was to examine the different kinds of visual effects that people like in pictures and drawings. The experimenter (who was unaware of the purpose of the study or the hypothesized results) explained that "what we're doing now is simply trying to gather some basic information that will help us in later studies." She seated the subject in a chair approximately 3 m from the posters, handed the subjects a questionnaire, and left the room.

Reasons Analysis Manipulation

Subjects were randomly chosen to receive one of two versions of this questionnaire. In the reasons condition, the questionnaire instructed subjects to describe why they liked or disliked each of the five posters, in order to organize their thoughts. They were told that they would not be asked to hand in their answers and were given half a page to describe their reasons for liking each poster. In the control condition, the questionnaire asked subjects for background information about their major and why they had chosen it, why they had decided to attend the University of Virginia, and their career plans.

Dependent Measures

Liking Ratings. If subjects were in the reasons condition, the experimenter picked up their reasons questionnaire when she returned, mentioned that they would not be needing it anymore, and placed it in a trash can. Subjects in both conditions then rated how much they liked each poster on 9-point scales (1 = *dislike very much* and 9 = *like very much*). The experimenter left the room while subjects made these ratings, having instructed them to slide their completed questionnaires through a slot in a covered box to maintain anonymity.

---

[1] The first four subjects in each condition saw a different set of humorous posters: a drawing of penguins, a drawing of hot air balloons, and a photograph of a cat with a different caption. Because these posters were discontinued by the manufacturer, we switched to the humorous posters described in the text for the remaining subjects. The two art posters were identical for all subjects. Liking ratings reported for the humorous posters include only those subjects who saw the second set of posters.

Choice Measure. When the experimenter returned, she said that the experiment was over, gave the subject her credit slip or money, and proceeded to give a mock debriefing, in which she repeated that the purpose of the experiment was to determine what makes people like certain visual effects more than others. She then said:

Before you go, I have a little surprise for you. The professor in charge of this study always likes to give people who participate a little something extra for being in the experiment. This time, he was able to get copies of these posters from the manufacturer, so you get to choose whichever one you like the best to take home.

She then explained that she had to go get an explanation sheet (which subjects expected to receive) and would return shortly. She told the subjects to pick out the poster they wanted from bins that contained several copies of each poster and then left the room. Subjects thus made their choices unobserved by the experimenter. All posters were rolled up so that only their reverse, blank sides were showing. Therefore, when the experimenter returned, she could not tell which ones the subjects had taken (this was determined later by a count of how many posters were left in each bin).

After subjects had made their choices, the experimenter said she had forgotten to give them one final questionnaire, which assessed subjects' educational background in art. (The first eight subjects did not receive this questionnaire.) Finally, they were asked not to tell anyone that they had received a poster as part of the study, because the posters might run out and not be available for future participants.

Post-Choice Liking Measure. At the end of the semester, a different experimenter (unaware of the subjects' condition) called subjects and asked them five questions concerning their satisfaction with their choice of poster: whether they still had it (verified by asking subjects to look at the bottom of the poster and read to the experimenter the name of the manufacturer), whether they had hung it on a wall in their dorm or apartment, whether they planned to keep it when they left school for the summer, how much they now liked the poster on a 10-point scale, and how much money it would take (hypothetically) to buy the poster from them. We called subjects an average of 25 days after they had participated in the experiment (range = 15 to 40).[2] We obtained responses from 40 of the 43 subjects; we could not reach the remaining 3. At the conclusion of the study, we mailed all subjects a written explanation of its true purpose.

[2] These figures do not include the first four subjects in each condition. They were run at the end of the previous semester, and so considerably more time elapsed before they were called ($M = 188$ days). The results of our post-choice satisfaction measure remain significant, with nearly identical p levels, when these subjects are removed from the analyses.

RESULTS

REPORTED LIKING FOR THE POSTERS

As predicted, subjects who thought about their reasons reported different attitudes than control subjects. Consistent with our pre-testing, subjects in the control condition liked the art posters considerably more than the humorous posters. In contrast, subjects who analyzed reasons liked the art posters less than control subjects and liked the humorous posters more (see means in Table 26.1). We tested these differences by entering subjects' mean rating of the art posters and their mean rating of the humorous posters into a 2 (Condition: control vs. reasons analysis) × 2 (Poster Type: art vs. humorous) between-within analysis of variance (ANOVA). This analysis yielded a highly significant Condition × Poster Type interaction, $F(1, 41) = 7.44$, $p < .01$, reflecting the fact that subjects who analyzed reasons rated the art posters lower and the humorous posters higher. The main effect of poster type was also highly significant, $F(1, 41) = 12.99$, $p < .01$, reflecting the fact that, overall, subjects preferred the art posters to the humorous ones. The main effect of condition was not significant, $F(1, 41) = 1.17$, reflecting the fact that analyzing reasons did not cause an across-the-board increase or decrease in liking for the posters.

CHOICE OF POSTER

As predicted, people in the reasons condition were more likely to choose one of the humorous posters to take home than people in the control condition. Among control subjects, 20 of 21 (95%) chose one of the art posters, whereas only 14 (64%) of 22 reasons subjects chose an art poster, $\chi^2(2) = 4.71$, $p < .05$. The percentage choosing each poster is displayed in Table 26.1.[3]

Post-Choice Satisfaction

A factor analysis revealed that the post-choice satisfaction measures could be considered to be two separate variables: the three behavioral-type questions (whether people still had the poster, whether they had hung it, and whether they planned to keep it) and the two subjective questions (how much people

---

[3] The average within-subject correlation between people's liking ratings and choice of poster was .60, which differed significantly from zero, $t(42) = 11.53$, $p < .001$. This correlation did not differ significantly by condition, $t(41) = 1.07$. This result is consistent with our hypothesis that if people act on their attitudes soon after analyzing reasons, their behavior will be consistent with the new attitude that the reasons analysis produced. If behavior is measured at a later point in time, so that people have had a chance to reevaluate the stimulus, then their behavior is likely to be less consistent with the attitude produced by the reasons analysis. See Wilson, Dunn, et al. (1989) for a more complete discussion of this issue and for more evidence bearing on it.

Table 26.1. Reported Liking for the Posters and Percentage of Those Who Chose Each One

Variable and Condition	Art Posters		Humorous Posters		
	A	B	C	D	E
Reported liking[a]					
Control					
M	6.62	7.48	3.88	4.00	3.76
(SD)	(2.18)	(1.66)	(2.32)	(2.72)	(2.64)
Reasons					
M	5.50	6.59	6.17	5.39	4.83
(SD)	(2.67)	(2.84)	(2.35)	(2.45)	(2.50)
Percentage choosing					
Control	33	62	0	0	5
Reasons	23	41	9	18	9

Note: Poster A was the Van Gogh, Poster B was the Monet, Poster C was the cartoon of the balloons, Poster D was the cat with the caption "Gimme a Break," and Poster E was the cat with the caption "One Step at a Time."
[a] The liking ratings were made on 9-point scales, with 1 = *dislike very much* and 9 = *like very much*.

said they liked their poster and their "asking price" if someone wanted to buy it, which we first transformed to a logarithmic scale to reduce the variance). Accordingly, we entered the mean of the three behavioral responses and the mean of the two subjective responses (after converting them to standard scores) into a 2 (Condition: reasons vs. control) × 2 (Type of Measure: behavioral vs. subjective) between-within ANOVA. As predicted, people in the control condition expressed greater satisfaction with their choice than people in the reasons condition (Ms = .26 and −.26, averaging across the behavioral and subjective indexes). The main effect of reasons condition was significant, $F(1, 38) = 5.32$, $p = .02$. The Condition × Type of Measure interaction did not approach significance, $F(1, 38) < 1$, indicating that the magnitude of this effect was not reliably different on the behavioral and the subjective indexes. (In subsequent analyses we therefore averaged across these indexes.)

In Table 26.2 we have broken down the means by both condition and the type of poster people chose. It should be noted that the people who were most dissatisfied with their choice were those who analyzed reasons and chose one of the humorous posters, though the Reasons × Choice interaction was nonsignificant, $F(1, 36) < 1$. Analyses that include Choice as a factor are difficult to interpret, however, given that this factor is a subject self-selection variable and some of the resulting cell sizes are extremely small.

It might be argued that the reasons manipulation reduced post-choice satisfaction because it lowered people's liking for the posters during the experimental session, and this reduced liking persisted for several weeks. Alternatively, we predicted that subjects would be happy with their choice when they made

Table 26.2. Pre- and Post-Choice Ratings of the Posters Chosen

	Art Poster		Humorous Poster	
Rating	Control Condition	Reasons Condition	Control Condition	Reasons Condition
Pre-choice liking[a]				
n	20	14	1	8
M	7.85	8.50	9.00	8.25
Post-choice satifaction[b]				
n	19	14	1	6
M	.23	−.10	−.17	−.45
Adjusted M[c]	.27	−.11	−.24	−.42

[a] Subjects' liking for the poster they chose, with 1 = *dislike very much* and 9 = *like very much*.

[b] The mean of responses to five questions about subjects' satisfaction with their poster, after converting each measure to standard scores.

[c] Adjusted in an analysis of covariance for pre-choice liking.

it but that over time their initial evaluation in the reasons condition would reassert itself, resulting in a change in their liking. The results were consistent with this latter interpretation. First, as already seen, the main effect of the reasons manipulation on people's ratings of the posters at the experimental session was not significant, indicating that the manipulation did not lower satisfaction with the posters at this time. Second, as seen in the top half of Table 26.2, people's pre-choice ratings of the poster they subsequently selected were as high in the reasons condition as in the control condition. In fact, collapsing across type of poster, subjects in the reasons condition rated the poster they chose slightly higher. Finally, to test further the prediction that the differences in post-choice satisfaction were not due to differences in pre-choice liking, we repeated the analysis on the post-choice liking index after adjusting the means for pre-choice liking (see the adjusted means in Table 26.2). The significant effect of reasons condition remained, $t(37) = 2.80$, $p < .01$.

It might also be argued that analyzing reasons reduced people's confidence in their attitudes toward the posters. Thinking about reasons might have muddied the waters, reducing the extent to which people preferred any one poster to another. The reduction in post-choice satisfaction might have stemmed from this bunching together of subjects' preferences; that is, people may have given all the posters similar ratings initially, reducing their eventual satisfaction with the one they chose. To test this bunching hypothesis, we computed a range score for each subject by subtracting her lowest from her highest rating of the posters. The difference between conditions in the mean range was nonsignificant, $t = .94$. Wilson and Schooler (1991) also found that people who analyzed reasons did not have a lower range in their ratings than control subjects. Finally, we have found in several previous studies that people who analyze reasons do not have lower confidence in their preferences than control subjects (Wilson, Dunn, et al., 1989).

Analyses of Subjects' Reasons

A research assistant divided people's responses on the reasons questionnaire into individual reasons and then assigned these reasons to different categories of why people liked or disliked the posters. (Another assistant independently coded a random subset of subjects' questionnaires. He agreed with the first coder's division of the responses into reasons 94% of the time and agreed with her classifications into categories 83% of the time.) Subjects gave an average of 2.85 reasons for liking or disliking each poster. These reasons concerned the colors in the posters (20%), other aspects of the poster content (54%), affective reactions or memories triggered by the poster (e.g., "It conveys a feeling of calmness," "It is a pleasant poster"; 22%), and the artist who painted the picture or took the photograph (3%).

We predicted that when people analyzed reasons, thoughts would come to mind that were inconsistent with their initial affective reactions to the posters. Consistent with this hypothesis, people gave a relatively large number of reasons for liking the humorous posters and relatively few for disliking them, $Ms = 1.95$ versus 0.92, $t(21) = 3.22$, $p < .005$. They gave about the same number of reasons for liking and disliking the art posters, $Ms = 1.59$ versus 1.20, $t(21) < 1$. Given the overwhelming preference for the art posters among control subjects, it is unlikely that these reasons are an accurate reflection of the factors causing subjects' initial evaluations of the posters. Instead, the attributes of the posters that were easiest to verbalize as reasons seem to have been at least partly inconsistent with people's initial reactions. Once people had verbalized these reasons, we predicted that they would adopt the attitude the reasons implied. To address this question, an assistant coded people's reasons according to the attitude toward the posters they implied. (One of the authors coded a subset of the reasons, and his ratings correlated .91 with the assistant's.) Consistent with our hypothesis, the average within-subject correlation between this liking-expressed-in-reasons index and subjects' subsequent liking ratings was very high, mean $r = .93$, $t(21) = 10.74$, $p < .001$. The liking-expressed-in-reasons index was also significantly correlated with people's choice of poster, $r = .58$, $t(21) = 4.24$, $p < .001$.

MODERATING EFFECTS OF KNOWLEDGE ABOUT ART

To see whether level of knowledge about art moderated the results, we performed a median split on the number of art courses people had taken in high school and college.[4] The data about art courses were unavailable for the first

---

[4] Strictly speaking, we measured people's educational experience with art, not their level of knowledge. We use the term *knowledge* to be consistent with previous studies that assessed it with measures of experience (e.g., Wilson, Kraft, & Dunn, 1989; Wood, 1982) and because experience has been found to correlate significantly with knowledge (Davidson, Yantis, Norwood, & Montano, 1985).

Table 26.3. Initial Liking for the Posters, by Level of Knowledge

| | Level of Knowledge | | | |
| | Low | | High | |
Type of Poster	Control Condition	Reasons Condition	Control Condition	Reasons Condition
Art	7.39	5.56	6.25	6.50
Humorous	3.63	6.08	4.17	4.97

Note: The liking ratings were made on 9-point scales, with 1 = dislike very much and 9 = like very much.

eight subjects, and therefore the analyses have reduced power. Nonetheless, the results were generally consistent with the prediction that analyzing reasons would have a greater effect on people who were unknowledgeable about art. On people's initial ratings of the posters, the interaction among reasons condition, poster type, and knowledge was marginally significant, $F(1, 31) = 2.89$, $p = .10$. As expected, those who were low in knowledge showed the same Condition × Poster Type interaction discussed earlier, $F(1, 31) = 7.61$, $p = .01$. (That is, those who analyzed reasons liked the humorous posters more and the art posters less than control subjects; see Table 26.3.) This interaction was not significant among people high in knowledge, $F(1, 31) < 1$. Knowledge did not moderate the effects of analyzing reasons on people's choice of poster, $F(1, 31) < 1$, possibly because this dichotomous dependent measure was of low power.

On the measure of post-choice satisfaction, the effects of the reasons manipulation were most pronounced among unknowledgeable people, $Ms = .21$ and $-.54$ in the control and reasons conditions, respectively. Among people high in knowledge, these means were .14 and $-.02$. Although the Reasons Condition × Knowledge interaction was not significant, $F(1, 29) = 2.33$, $p = .14$, a contrast testing the predicted pattern of results was significant, $F(1, 29) = 8.62$, $p < .01$ (this contrast assigned a weight of -3 to the low knowledge/reasons cell and $+1$ to the other three cells).

Wilson, Kraft, and Dunn (1989) found that when unknowledgeable people analyzed reasons, they were more likely to call to mind a poorly articulated, inconsistent set of beliefs, such that at least some of these reasons were inconsistent with their prior attitude, leading to attitude change. Knowledgeable people, in contrast, called to mind a consistent set of beliefs that better reflected their prior attitude and were less likely to change their attitudes after analyzing reasons. To see whether a similar process occurred in the present study, we computed the same index of evaluative consistency used by Wilson, Kraft, and Dunn (1989). We divided the number of reasons for liking or disliking the posters (whichever was greater) by the total number of reasons people gave, such that the higher this ratio, the more evaluatively consistent the reasons (e.g., if someone gave all negative or all positive reasons, she received a score of 1). Given that our measure of knowledge was people's formal educational experience with art, we expected subjects to differ primarily in their thoughts about the art posters (i.e., there is no reason to expect that taking art courses gives people any more expertise in the genre of humorous posters). Consistent with this reasoning, knowledgeable people showed more evaluative consistency in their reasons about the art posters than control subjects (Ms = .80 and .65, respectively) but did not show any more consistency in their reasons about the humorous posters (Ms = .71 and .73, respectively). A Knowledge × Poster Type ANOVA on the measure of evaluative consistency revealed a nearly significant interaction, $F(1, 16) = 3.62, p = .08$.

DISCUSSION

The present findings add to the mounting body of evidence that thinking about the reasons for one's preferences can alter decision making in nonoptimal ways. Subjects instructed to think about the reasons for their attitudes were more likely to prefer the humorous posters than control subjects and were more likely to choose a humorous poster to take home. After a few weeks had elapsed, however, they were less satisfied with their choice. Consistent with previous findings, these effects were especially pronounced among people who were relatively unknowledgeable about art.

Apparently, the qualities of the art posters that made them appealing to our subject population were relatively difficult to verbalize, whereas positive features of the humorous posters were easy to verbalize, producing a biased sample of reasons. Consistent with this hypothesis, when people analyzed reasons, they verbalized more positive features of the humorous than the art posters and more negative features of the art than the humorous posters. Verbalizing these reasons caused subjects to adopt the attitude they implied, as suggested by the high correlation between the liking-expressed-in-reasons index and subsequent ratings of the posters and by the fact that reasons subjects chose different posters to take home.

We suggest that, over time, people's initial evaluations returned, causing those who analyzed reasons to regret their choice. Once these participants took the poster home, it is unlikely that they continued to analyze reasons every time they looked at it. Consequently, the reasons that were salient at the time they chose the poster – and which appear to have driven their choice – probably faded in memory, and their chronic way of evaluating posters probably returned. We know from the control condition that when people in our subject population do not analyze reasons, they do not particularly like the humorous posters. Therefore, if people in the reasons condition became more like control subjects in that they no longer analyzed reasons, we would expect them to become dissatisfied with their choice.

This explanation, we should note, is consistent with our prior work showing that analyzing reasons reduces attitude–behavior consistency. As noted by Wilson, Dunn, et al. (1989), this reduction in consistency is particularly likely if some interval separates the measure of people's attitude and the measure of their behavior. With such a separation, people's attitudes are likely to be driven by the newly salient information resulting from analyzing reasons, whereas their behavior is likely to be driven by their chronic way of evaluating the stimulus. Similarly, in the present study, people's choice of poster was driven by the reasons they had just brought to mind, but their attitudes several weeks later were probably driven more by their chronic way of evaluating posters.

According to this interpretation, the people who should have been the least happy with their choice are those for whom the reasons manipulation was particularly effective – namely, those in the reasons condition who chose a humorous poster. If the reasons manipulation did not change people's choices, such that they still chose an art poster, there is no reason to assume that they would be unhappy with this choice. The results shown in Table 26.2 are consistent with this line of reasoning, in that post-choice satisfaction was lowest among people in the reasons condition who chose a humorous poster. We acknowledge, however, that it is difficult to test this hypothesis, because it relies on a subject self-selection variable – which poster people chose. Further, including the poster people chose as a factor in the analyses results in extremely small cell sizes (in one case, a cell n of 1; see Table 26.2).

We should emphasize that subject self-selection was not a problem in our primary test of the effects of analyzing reasons on post-choice satisfaction: Those who analyzed reasons were significantly less satisfied, collapsing across their choice of poster. The more fine-grained prediction that people who analyzed reasons and chose a humorous poster would be the least satisfied cannot be addressed definitively, because the relevant findings, though in the predicted direction, are contaminated by self-selection. Thus, the results are consistent with the prediction that analyzing reasons changed people's attitudes temporarily and that their chronic way of evaluating the posters returned, but this explanation needs to be verified more directly by future research.

The fact that analyzing reasons led to a decrease in post-choice satisfaction is particularly impressive in light of the considerable amount of research generated by dissonance theory on post-decisional satisfaction. This research shows that once people make a choice, their liking for the chosen alternative increases to reduce the psychological tension created by the knowledge that they could have chosen other, attractive alternatives (e.g., Brehm, 1956). Despite these internal pressures to like what they chose, subjects who analyzed reasons became more dissatisfied with their choice than control subjects. Our findings are not inconsistent with dissonance research; were it not for pressures to reduce dissonance, subjects in the reasons conditions might have been even more displeased with their choices. The results do suggest, however, that there are limits to the extent to which people can convince themselves that what they chose was the best alternative.

These results, in conjunction with several other recent studies, illustrate that introspection can have unintended negative consequences (Wilson & LaFleur,

1993; Wilson & Schooler, 1991). We cannot emphasize too strongly, however, that we are not making a broadsided attack on introspection and self-reflection. Such an attack is unwarranted for several reasons. First, some affective reactions are very unpleasant, either to the individual experiencing them (e.g., speech anxiety) or to the target of the affect (e.g., racial prejudice). It would be beneficial to alter these reactions, even if only temporarily, by having people examine the reasons that underlie them (Tesser, Leone, & Clary, 1978).

Second, there is evidence that other kinds of self-reflection, such as focusing on one's feelings (without attempting to explain the reasons for them), does not disrupt people's attitudes in the way that analyzing reasons does (Millar & Tesser, 1986; Wilson & Dunn, 1986). Simply focusing on a feeling can strengthen it, whereas recruiting reasons that may not be consistent with one's initial affective reaction can lead to attitude change (see Wilson, Dunn, et al., 1989).

Third, we have examined introspection in a limited set of circumstances. For example, people introspected for a fairly short time in our studies, and it is possible that a more lengthy, in-depth analysis would not have had the same negative consequences (although in a recent study we found that asking people to analyze reasons four times on separate occasions resulted in about the same amount of attitude change as did analyzing reasons only once; Wilson & Kraft, 1993).

Fourth, for analyzing reasons to have negative effects, the reasons that are accessible and plausible to people must conflict with their initial affect. In the present study, the reasons that were most salient – such as the pleasingness of the colors of the posters – happened to conflict with people's initial attitudes. Some stimuli may have a more limited range of plausible reasons, so that people are unlikely to be misled by analyzing these reasons. Attitudes toward a can opener, for example, are probably relatively easy to explain. The pool of plausible reasons for liking a can opener is small, and these reasons probably correspond fairly well to the real reasons people like can openers. Even with more complex stimuli, people will not be misled if the reasons that come to mind match their initial affect – even if those reasons are wrong. For example, if people like a painting, and the most accessible reason for their feelings is that it has nice colors (i.e., a positive reason), they will not change their attitudes toward it, even if the colors had nothing to do with their initial evaluation.

When will people bring to mind reasons that conflict with an initial attitude? Because knowledgeable people have more consistent beliefs, they appear to be less likely to bring to mind reasons that conflict with their prior evaluation of the attitude object. That is, if people have homogeneous beliefs about an attitude object, all of which imply the same attitude, then focusing on a subset of these beliefs when analyzing reasons will not cause attitude change. Unknowledgeable people appear to have a less consistent set of beliefs, increasing the likelihood that when they analyze reasons, thoughts will come to mind that conflict with their prior attitude. Consistent with this view, unknowledgeable people in both the present study and Wilson, Kraft, and Dunn's (1989) expressed reasons that were less evaluatively consistent, and changed their attitudes more, than knowledgeable people (see also Lusk & Judd, 1988). Further, Wilson, Kraft, and Dunn (1989) found that unknowledgeable people were more likely to bring to mind reasons that conflicted with their prior attitude (prior attitudes were not assessed in the present study).

Clearly, more work is needed to specify the conditions under which introspecting about reasons will have deleterious consequences. The present study suggests, however, that unbridled claims about the value of introspection need to be tempered. Janis and Mann (1977), for example, suggested that decisions should always be made analytically and vigilantly and that if they are not, people will be most likely to "undergo unanticipated setbacks and experience postdecisional regret" (p. 11). In contrast, our findings suggest that it is not always advantageous to make decisions vigilantly and that, under some circumstances, those who do will be the ones who experience the most regret. Introspection is undoubtedly a valuable, useful ability, but as with most good things, there are times when it is best done in moderation.

ACKNOWLEDGMENTS

This research was supported by National Institute of Mental Health Grant R01-MH41841. We would like to thank Annette Chiang and Coretta Organ for their expert assistance with the conduct of this research. We also thank Dan Lassiter for his valuable comments on a previous draft of this article.

27. New Challenges to the Rationality Assumption

Daniel Kahneman

INTRODUCTION

The assumption that agents are rational is central to much theory in the social sciences. Its role is particularly obvious in economic analysis, where it supports the useful corollary that no significant opportunity will remain unexploited. In the domain of social policy, the rationality assumption supports the position that it is unnecessary to protect people against the consequences of their choices. The status of this assumption is therefore a matter of considerable interest. This chapter argues for an enriched definition of rationality that considers the actual outcomes of decisions and presents evidence that challenges the rationality assumption in new ways.

The criteria for using the terms "rational" or "irrational" in nontechnical discourse are *substantive:* One asks whether beliefs are grossly out of kilter with available evidence and whether decisions serve or damage the agent's interests. In sharp contrast, technical discussions of rationality generally adopt a *logical* conception, in which an individual's beliefs and preferences are said to be rational if they obey a set of formal rules such as complementarity of probabilities, the sure thing principle, or independence of irrelevant alternatives. In the laissez-faire spirit of modern economics and decision theory, the content of beliefs and of preferences is not a criterion of rationality – only internal coherence matters (Sen, 1993). The methodology of the debate reflects this concern for consistency: In the classic paradoxes of Allais (1953) and Ellsberg (1961), for example, two intuitively compelling preferences are shown to be jointly incompatible with the axioms of expected utility theory, though each preference is unobjectionable on its own. Irrational preferences are diagnosed without having to observe anything that is not a preference.

Some authors have been dissatisfied with the exclusive focus on consistency as a criterion of rationality. Thus, Sen (1990) has written:

Rationality may be seen as demanding something other than just consistency of choices from different subsets. It must, at least, demand cogent relations between aims and objectives actually entertained by the person and the choices that the person makes. This

Originally published in the *Journal of Institutional and Theoretical Economics*, vol. 150, pp. 18–36.

problem is not eliminated by the terminological procedure of describing the cardinal representation of choices as the "utility" of the person, since this does not give any independent evidence on what the person is aiming to do or trying to achieve. (p. 210)

This chapter asks whether there exists a cogent relation between a person's choices and the hedonic consequences of these choices.

In spite of occasional attempts to broaden the scope of the rationality debate in decision theory, the patterns of preference discovered by Allais (1953) and Ellsberg (1961) have been at the center of this debate for several decades. It is often implied that if these paradoxes can be resolved, then economic analysis can safely continue to assume that agents are rational. The focus on paradoxes has indirectly strengthened the rationality dogma: If subtle inconsistencies are the worst indictment of human rationality, there is indeed little to worry about. Furthermore, the preferences that Allais and Ellsberg described do not appear foolish or unreasonable, and lay people as well as many theorists believe they can be defended (Slovic & Tversky, 1974). Indeed, the ambiguous normative status of the Allais and Ellsberg patterns has inspired many attempts to reconcile observed preferences with rationality by adopting a more permissive definition of rational choice (Tversky & Kahneman, 1986).

More recent challenges to the rationality assumption do not lend themselves to such attempts at reconciliation. Numerous experiments illustrate beliefs and preferences that violate a fundamental requirement variously labeled extensionality (Arrow, 1982), consequentialism (Hammond, 1985), or invariance (Tversky & Kahneman, 1986). The same choice problem may evoke different preferences, depending on inconsequential variations in the formulation of options (Tversky & Kahneman, 1986) or in the procedure used to elicit choices (Tversky, Slovic, & Kahneman, 1990). The main method of this research still involves the documentation of pairs of preferences, each acceptable on its own, which jointly violate an axiom of invariance. These inconsistencies are more difficult to rationalize than the classic paradoxes because invariance is a more compelling axiom of rational choice than cancellation or independence (Tversky & Kahneman, 1986). Some examples of this research will be presented in the following discussion.

The present treatment attempts to supplement the logical analysis of preferences by introducing substantive criteria of rationality. Unlike the logical analysis, a substantive criterion is external to the system of preferences. It requires some way of assessing outcomes as they occur, not only as they are conceived at the time of decision. The substantive question on which we focus here is whether choices maximize the (expected) utility of their consequences, as these consequences will actually be experienced. Accurate prediction of future tastes and accurate evaluation of past experiences emerge as critical elements of an individual's ability to maximize the experienced quality of his outcomes. Demonstrated deficiencies in the ability to predict future experiences and to learn from the past emerge as new challenges to the assumption of rationality. More provocatively, the observed deficiencies suggest the outline of a case in favor of some paternalistic interventions, when it is plausible that the state knows more about an individual's future tastes than the individual knows presently. The basis of these developments is an analysis of the concept of utility, which is introduced in the next section.

MULTIPLE NOTIONS OF UTILITY

The term "utility" can be anchored either in the hedonic experience of outcomes or in the preference or desire for that outcome. In Jeremy Bentham's (1823/1996) usage, the utility of an object was ultimately defined in hedonic terms, by the pleasure that it produces. Others have interpreted utility as "wantability" (Fisher, 1918/1968). Of course, the two definitions have the same extension if people generally want that which they will eventually enjoy – a common assumption in discussions of utility. Economic analysis is more congenial to wants and preferences than to hedonic experiences, and the current meaning of utility in economics and decision research is a positivistic version of wantability: Utility is a theoretical construct inferred from observed choices. This definition has been thoroughly cleansed of any association with hedonistic psychology and of any reference to subjective states.

The present analysis starts with two observations. The first is that the methodological strictures against a hedonic notion of utility are a relic of an earlier period in which a behavioristic philosophy of science held sway. Subjective states are now a legitimate topic of study, and hedonic experiences such as pleasure, pain, satisfaction, or discomfort are considered open to useful forms of measurement. The second observation is that it may be rash to assume as a general rule that people will later enjoy what they want now. The relation between preferences and hedonic consequences is better studied than postulated.

These considerations suggest an explicit distinction between two notions of utility. The *experienced utility* of an outcome is the measure of the hedonic experience of that outcome. This is similar to Bentham's (1823/1996) awkward use; the first footnote of his book was properly apologetic about the poor fit of the word "utility" to pleasure and pain, but he found no better alternative. The *decision utility* of an outcome, as in modern usage, is the weight assigned to that outcome in a decision.

The distinction between experienced utility and decision utility opens new avenues for the study of rationality. In addition to the syntactic criterion of consistency, we can now hope to develop a substantive/hedonic criterion for the rationality of a decision: Does it maximize the expectation of experienced utility? Of course, this criterion is not exhaustive, and its adoption implies no commitment to a hedonistic philosophy. As Sen has often pointed out (e.g., Sen, 1987), the maximization of (experienced) utility is not always "what people are trying to achieve." It is surely the case, however, that people sometimes do try to maximize pleasure and minimize pain, and it may be instructive to drop the assumption that they perform this optimization task flawlessly.

Errors in the assignment of decision utility to anticipated outcomes can arise from inaccurate forecasting of future hedonic experience. Correct prediction of future tastes is therefore one of the requirements of rational decision making (March, 1978). Kahneman and Snell (1990) defined the *predicted utility* of an outcome as the individual's beliefs about its experienced utility at some future time. Two sets of empirical questions arise: (1) How much do people know about their future tastes? Is it likely that an objective observer (or a government) could make more accurate predictions than individuals would make on their own behalf? (2) Do people adequately consider the uncertainty of their future tastes in making decisions? Are decision utilities adequately informed by reasoned beliefs about experienced utility?

Additional issues arise because of possible disparities between memory and actual hedonic experience. Outcomes are commonly extended over time, and global evaluations of such outcomes are necessarily retrospective – and therefore subject to errors. Examples of substantial discrepancies between *retrospective utility* and *real-time utility* are discussed later.

The restoration of Bentham's notion of utility as an object of study evidently sets a large agenda for theoretical and empirical investigation. The following sections summarize highlights of what has been learned in early explorations of this agenda. Decision utility, predicted utility, and the relations between real-time and retrospective utility are discussed in turn. The final section reviews possible implications of the findings for the rationality debate.

SOME CHARACTERISTICS OF DECISION UTILITY

Decision utility has long been a topic of study, and much is known about it. The following discussion selectively addresses three research conclusions that are of particular relevance to the issue of rationality, as it is construed in this chapter.

1.   *Carriers of utility.* The main carriers of decision utility are events, not states; in particular, utility is assigned to gains or losses relative to a reference point, which is often the status quo (Kahneman & Tversky, 1979).

2.   *Loss aversion.* Losses loom larger than corresponding gains (Kahneman & Tversky, 1979; Tversky & Kahneman, 1991).

3.   *Framing effects.* The same objective outcomes can be evaluated as gains or as losses, depending on the framing of the reference state (Tversky & Kahneman, 1986).

An early observation that illustrates points (1) and (2) was labeled the isolation effect (Tversky & Kahneman, 1986).

Problem 1: Assume yourself richer by $300 than you are today. You have to choose between
    a sure gain of $100
    50% chance to gain $200 and 50% chance to gain nothing

Problem 2: Assume yourself richer by $500 than you are today. You have to choose between
    a sure gain of $100
    50% chance to lose nothing and 50% chance to lose $200.

It is easily seen that the two problems are extensionally equivalent in terms of wealth: Both offer a choice between a state in which wealth is increased by $400 and a gamble with equal chances to increase current wealth by $300 or by $500. If people spontaneously evaluate options in these terms they will choose the same option in the two problems – but observed preferences favor the sure thing in Problem 1 and the gamble in Problem 2. Because the equivalence of the two problems is intuitively compelling when it is pointed out, the difference between the responses they elicit is a framing effect: An inconsequential feature of the formulation strongly affects preferences. Most important in the present context, the experiment demonstrates that people are content to assign utilities to outcomes stated as gains and losses, contrary to the standard assumption that the carriers of utility are states of wealth.

Figure 27.1 exhibits loss aversion in a schematic value function: The function is steeper in the domain of losses than in the domain of gains. The ratio of the slopes in the two domains, called the loss aversion coefficient, has been estimated as about 2:1 in several experiments involving both risky and riskless options (Tversky & Kahneman, 1991, 1992). Figure 27.2 (from Kahneman, Knetsch, & Thaler, 1991) illustrates the role of a reference point in the evaluation

Figure 27.1. A typical value function.

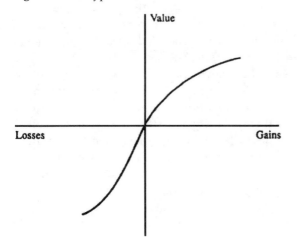

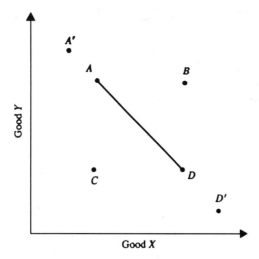

Figure 27.2. Multiple reference points for the choice between A and D.

of a transaction. The choice illustrated in this figure is between a state (Point A) with more of Good Y and a state (Point D) with more of Good X. The hypotheses about the carriers of utility and about framing effects entail that the preference between A and D could differ depending on the current reference point – contrary to a substantial body of economic theory. Consider the choice between A and D from C. This is a positive choice between two gains, in Good X or in Good Y. If the reference is A, however, the two options are framed quite differently. One possibility is to retain the status quo by staying at A. The alternative is to accept a trade that involves the conjunction of a loss in Good Y and a gain in Good X. The C–A interval is evaluated as a gain in the first frame (from C), but the same interval is evaluated as a loss from A. Because of loss aversion, the effect of the C–A difference is expected to be greater in the latter case than in the former. We therefore predict a systematic difference between the preferences in the two frames: If people are indifferent between A and D from C, they should strictly prefer A over D from A (Tversky & Kahneman, 1991).

The predicted result, known as the endowment effect (Thaler, 1980), has been confirmed in several laboratories. Subjects in one condition of an experiment by Kahneman, Knetsch, and Thaler (1990) were offered a choice between a decorated mug (worth about $6 at the University bookstore) and a sum of money; they answered a series of questions to determine the amount of money at which they were indifferent between the two options. Other subjects were first given a mug; they answered similar questions to indicate the amount of money for which they would just agree to exchange it. The subjects had no strategic incentive to conceal their true values. A critical feature of the study is that the choosers in the first group and the mug owners in the second group faced objectively identical options: They could leave the experimental situation owning a new mug or with extra money in their pockets. The analysis of Figure 27.2 applies, however. If the mug is Good Y, the C–A interval (the difference between having a mug and not having one) is evaluated as a gain by the choosers and as a loss by the mug owners. As predicted, the average cash value of a mug was much larger for the owners ($7.12 in one experiment) than for choosers ($3.50). A significant (but somewhat smaller) difference between owners and choosers was observed in a replication by Franciosi, Kujal, Michelitsch, and Smith (1993).

Implications of the endowment effect for various aspects of economic and legal theory have been discussed extensively elsewhere (Ellickson, 1989; Hardie, Johnson, & Fader, 1993; Hovenkamp, 1991; Kahneman et al., 1991). The effect is relevant to the present treatment because it implies that decision utilities may be extremely myopic. The subjects in the mugs experiment made a decision that was to have consequences over the relatively long term: A coffee mug is an object that one may use daily, sometimes for years. The long-term states between which the subjects had to choose – "own this mug" or "not own this mug" – were the same for all subjects. The large difference between the preferences of owners and choosers indicates that these enduring states were not the main object of evaluation. The effective carriers of utility were the transitions that distinguished the experimental treatments: "receive a mug" or "give up your mug." In this experiment, and perhaps in many other situations, people who make decisions about a long-term state appear to use their evaluation of the transition to that state as a proxy.

The results of the mugs experiment present two overlapping challenges to the assumption of rationality. The logical notion of rationality is violated by the inconsistent preferences observed in different representations of the choice between a mug and money. A substantive condition of rationality is violated if the endowment effect is viewed as a costly manifestation of extreme myopia. An agent who routinely uses transient emotions as a proxy for the utility of long-term states is manifestly handicapped in the achievement of good outcomes.

PREDICTED UTILITY: DO PEOPLE KNOW WHAT THEY WILL LIKE?

Although the constancy of underlying tastes is a matter of theoretical debate, the following proposition will not be controversial: The hedonic experience associated with a particular stimulus or with a particular act of consumption is susceptible to large changes over time and over varying circumstances. Some cyclical changes of experienced utility are regular and readily predictable: Ingesting the same food may evoke delight in a state of hunger, disgust in satiation. At the other extreme, radical changes of circumstances produce adaptations and changes of experienced utility that violate common expectations. A well-known psychological study showed that most paraplegics adapt far better than most people would predict and that lottery winners are generally less happy in the long run than the common fascination with lotteries might suggest (Brickman, Coates, & Janoff-Bulman, 1978).

Many decisions explicitly or implicitly involve predictions of future consumption and of future utility (March, 1978). An encyclopedia may not be worth buying if one will not use it, the premium paid for a house with a view may be wasted if the view ceases giving pleasure after a time, and a medical procedure that improves survival chances should perhaps be rejected by a patient who is likely to find life without vocal cords intolerable.

How accurately do people predict their future utility? Most of the evidence about this question is indirect. Thus, it is suggestive that some important results of hedonic research are generally considered counterintuitive (Kahneman & Snell, 1990). The surprises include the striking increase of liking by mere exposure to initially neutral stimuli and some effects of dissonance on tastes. A study of people's intuitions about possible ways to induce a child to like or to dislike a food showed a similar lack of collective wisdom about the dynamics of taste. Dynamic inconsistency may be another manifestation of inaccurate hedonic prediction. For example, Christensen-Szalanski (1984) documented the incidence of cases in which women in labor reversed a long-standing preference for delivery without anesthetics. The reversals could be due to improper discounting of the pain in the initial preferences; they could also reflect an error in the initial prediction of the intensity of labor pains.

Loewenstein and Adler (1995) observed a remarkable result in a study of the endowment effect. They showed subjects a mug engraved with a decorative logo and asked some of these subjects to "imagine that we gave you a mug exactly like the one you can see, and that we gave you the opportunity to keep it or trade it for some money" (p. 931). The subjects then filled out a form indicating their preferences for a range of stated prices, following the procedure of Kahneman et al. (1990). The mean predicted selling price was $3.73. Next, all subjects were given a mug and a second form, which actually provided an opportunity to exchange the mug for cash. The mean selling price for the subjects who had made a prediction a few minutes earlier was $4.89, significantly higher than the predicted value and only moderately lower than the selling price of $5.62 stated by subjects who had not made a prediction. The subjects in this experiment were apparently unable to anticipate that possession of the mug would induce a reluctance to give it up.

Simonson (1990) reported a result that illustrates a failure of hedonic prediction – or perhaps a failure to make such a prediction. Simonson gave students an opportunity to select from a choice set of snacks at the beginning of a class meeting; they received their selections at the end of the class. Subjects in one experimental condition made one choice each week for 3 weeks. In another condition subjects made choices for all 3 weeks at the first session. The choices made by the two groups were strikingly different. Subjects who chose a snack on three separate occasions tended to choose the same snack or a closely similar one every time. In contrast, subjects who chose in advance for 3 weeks tended to pick different items for the different occasions. It is reasonable to view these variety-seeking choices as erroneous: The subjects apparently failed to realize that their current preferences would be restored after a 1-week interval. A further study clarified the nature of the error. Anticipatory choices were less variable when subjects were asked, before indicating a decision, to predict the preferences they would actually have on the subsequent occasions of testing. This finding suggests that the subjects were in fact able to predict their future preferences accurately. In the absence of a special instruction, however, they did not take the trouble to generate a prediction of their future taste before making a decision about future consumption.

Kahneman and Snell (1992) reported an exploratory study of the accuracy of hedonic prediction. They examined predictions of future liking for a food item or a musical piece, under conditions that made a change of attitude likely. In an initial experiment the subjects consumed a helping of their favorite ice cream while listening to a particular piece of music at the same hour on 8 consecutive working days under identical physical conditions. Immediately after each episode they rated how much they had liked the ice cream and the music. At the end of the first session they predicted the ratings they would make on the following day and on the final day of the experiment. This experiment was intended to test the accuracy of hedonic predictions under relatively favorable conditions. We reasoned that student subjects have not only had much experience consuming ice cream and listening to music; they have had experience with repeated consumption of these items and could therefore be expected to anticipate the effect of frequent repetition on their tastes. Other experiments in the series used a stimulus that is less familiar and less popular than ice cream in the student population – plain low-fat yogurt.

The accuracy of hedonic predictions was generally quite poor. A comparison of the average of predictions to the average of the actual ratings revealed some shared failures to anticipate common trends in the hedonic responses. For example, most subjects predicted, after tasting one spoonful of plain low-fat yogurt, that they would assign the same rating to a 6-oz. helping on the next day. In fact, the larger helping was a much worse experience. Most subjects also failed to anticipate the considerable improvement in the attitude toward plain yogurt that occurred (for most of them) with further exposure to that substance. There apparently exists a lay theory of hedonic changes, of mediocre accuracy, which most of our subjects accepted. Another analysis was concerned with individual differences in predictions and in actual hedonic changes. There was substantial variability in both measures, but the correlation between them was consistently close to zero. The data provided no indication that individuals were able to predict the development of their tastes more accurately than they could predict the hedonic changes of a randomly selected stranger.

The results of these studies suggest two conclusions. (1) People may have little ability to forecast changes in their hedonic responses to stimuli (Kahneman & Snell, 1992; Loewenstein & Adler, 1995). (2) Even in situations that permit accurate hedonic predictions, people may tend to make decisions about future consumption without due consideration of possible changes in their tastes (Simonson, 1990). If supported by further research, these hypotheses about the accuracy of predicted utility and about its impact on decision utility would present a significant substantive challenge to the assumption of rationality.

The properties of predicted utility have implication for other domains. Consider the issue of informed consent to an operation that will change the patient's life in some significant way. The normal procedure for consent emphasizes the provision of objective information about the effects of surgery. However, truly informed consent is possible only if patients have a reasonable conception of expected long-term developments in their hedonic responses and if they assign appropriate weight to these expectations in the decision. A more controversial issue arises if we admit that an outsider can sometimes predict an individual's future utility far better than the individual can. Does this superior knowledge carry a warrant, or even a duty, for paternalistic intervention? It appears right for Ulysses' sailors to tie him to the mast against his will if they believe that he is deluded about his ability to resist the fatal call of the sirens.

REAL-TIME AND RETROSPECTIVE UTILITY – DO PEOPLE KNOW WHAT THEY HAVE LIKED?

Retrospective evaluations of the experienced utility of past episodes are undoubtedly the most important source of predictions of the hedonic quality of future outcomes. The experiences of life leave their traces in a rich store of evaluative memories, which is consulted, apparently automatically, whenever a significant object or experience is brought to mind (Zajonc, 1980). The system of affective and evaluative memories may be independent of any ability to recall the incidents that produced an attitude. Thus, people often recognize that they like or dislike a person they have met before, without knowing why. Evaluative memories are immensely important because they contain the individual's accumulated knowledge of stimuli that are to be approached and of others that are to be avoided. Indeed, the only form of utility that people could possibly learn to maximize is the anticipated utility of future memories. Every individual has the lifelong habit of trusting memories of past episodes to guide choices among future outcomes. As we shall see, however, trusted evaluative memories are sometimes deceptive.

Although retrospective evaluations and affective memories define what is learned from the past, they are not the ultimate criterion of experienced utility. Hedonic or affective quality is an attribute of each moment of experience; the sign and intensity of the experience may vary considerably, even over the course of a brief episode, such as drinking a glass of wine. The retrospective evaluation of an extended episode necessarily involves two operations: the recollection of the momentary experiences that constituted the episode and an operation that combines the affect of these moments into a global evaluation. Because both operations are fallible, retrospective evaluations should be viewed with greater distrust than introspective reports of current experience. The effects of defective memory are sometimes painfully obvious: People who care for an elderly parent often observe that they accept their parent's immediate responses to the current situation with normal respect, even as they dismiss most retrospective evaluations as unreliable. The difficulties that arise in summarizing an episode by a global evaluation are more subtle, but no less significant.

There are strong normative intuitions about the correct way to combine the utilities of a continuous series of experiences into a global evaluation. A principle of *temporal integration* has considerable appeal: The utility of an episode extended over time is the integral of momentary hedonic value over the duration of the episode. The justification for temporal integration is the assumption that successive selves should be treated equally, an assumption so compelling that a general case for utilitarianism has been built on it (Parfit, 1984). Even more appealing than temporal integration is the principle of *temporal monotonicity*. Consider two episodes that are preceded and followed by a steady state of hedonic neutrality. Assume that the second episode is obtained by adding an unanticipated period of pain (or pleasure) to the first, prior to the return to the neutral state. The monotonicity principle asserts that the hedonic quality of the added period determines whether the longer episode has higher or lower global utility than the shorter. In other words, adding pain at the end of an episode must make it worse; adding pleasure must make it better.[1]

Several recent studies indicate that retrospective evaluations obey neither temporal integration nor temporal monotonicity. The studies conducted so far have dealt with episodes that were brief and uniform, both in content and in the sign of the hedonic experience, either nonnegative or nonpositive throughout. Several experiments involved controlled exposure to affect-inducing stimuli (films of pleasant or unpleasant content; loud unpleasant sounds; immersion of a hand in painfully cold water). Subjects used an "affect meter" to provide a continuous record of their momentary hedonic response during some of these episodes. Later, they also provided retrospective global evaluations of the "overall discomfort" or "overall pleasure" of the episodes and in some cases chose an episode to which they would be exposed again. In one nonexperimental study (Redelmeier & Kahneman, 1996) patients undergoing a colonoscopy for medical reasons provided reports of pain every 60 seconds, as well as subsequent global evaluations and measures of preference for the entire episode.

The results of these studies support two empirical generalizations. (1) *"The Peak & End Rule"*: Global evaluations are predicted with high accuracy by a

---

[1] The temporal monotonicity principle does not apply if the addition of pain or pleasure to the episode alters hedonic aftereffects, such as relief, afterglow, or the affect associated with subsequent recollection. More generally, the analysis of experienced utility becomes difficult to apply where the consumption of memories plays an important role (Elster & Loewenstein, 1992).

weighted combination of the most extreme affect recorded during the episode and of the affect recorded during the terminal moments of the episode. Here again, as in the context of decision utility, the evaluation of particular moments appears to be used as a proxy for the evaluation of a more extended period of time. (2) *Duration Neglect*: The retrospective evaluation of overall or total pain (or pleasure) is not independently affected by the duration of the episode. In the colonoscopy study, for example, the duration of the procedure varied from 4 to 69 minutes in a sample of 101 patients. Surprisingly, these variations of duration had no significant effect on retrospective evaluations. The ratings of both patients and attending physicians were dominated by the intensity of pain at its worst and by the intensity of discomfort during the last few minutes of the procedure. Duration neglect is not immutable, of course: People can judge the duration of episodes with fair accuracy and will treat this attribute as relevant when their attention is explicitly drawn to it (Varey & Kahneman, 1992). In general, however, affective peaks and endings are more salient than duration in the cognitive representation of events.

Figure 27.3 is taken from a study that examined violations of the rule of temporal monotonicity in a choice between painful episodes (Kahneman, Fredrickson, Schreiber, & Redelmeier, 1993). Paid volunteers expected to undergo three experiences of moderate physical pain during an experimental session. In fact, they had only two trials. In the Short trial the subject held one hand in water at 14°C for 60 seconds, then immediately dried his hand with a towel. In the Long trial, the subject held the other hand in water for a total of 90 seconds. During the first 60 seconds of the Long trial the temperature of the water was 14°C, just as in the Short trial; during the extra 30 seconds the

Figure 27.3. Mean of real-time discomfort measure on Long trial for 11 subjects who indicated little or no decrement of discomfort when temperature changed (thin line), and for 21 subjects who indicated decreased discomfort (thick line).

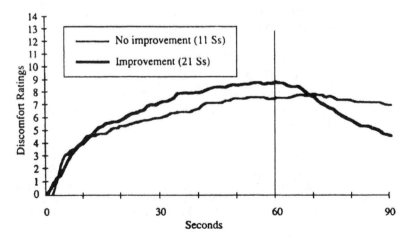

temperature of the water was gradually raised to 15°C, still unpleasant but for most subjects a clear improvement over the initial state. The order of the two trials was varied for different subjects. A few minutes after the second trial, the subjects were reminded that they were due to have another trial and were asked which of the two preceding experiences they chose to repeat.

The curves shown in Figure 27.3 present average momentary ratings of discomfort for the Long trial, separately for two groups of subjects who showed different patterns of response: the majority who indicated decreasing discomfort as the temperature of the water was raised and a minority who reported little change of discomfort. The choices of which trial to repeat were markedly different in these two groups: 17 of the 21 subjects whose discomfort diminished preferred to repeat the Long trial, in violation of temporal monotonicity; only 5 of the 11 subjects whose discomfort did not change preferred the Long trial. The results of both groups conform to the Peak & End rule and exhibit duration neglect. For the minority whose pain did not diminish, the peak and the end of the pain were at the same level (see Figure 27.3) and were the same in the Short and in the Long trials. The Peak & End rule predicts that these subjects should evaluate the two trials alike, a prediction that is confirmed by the nearly even split of preferences. For the larger group of subjects whose pain diminished at the end of the Long trial, the Peak & End rule predicts that this trial should be less aversive than the Short one, and the choice data again confirm the prediction. Overall, about two-thirds of subjects violate dominance in this situation, a robust result that has been replicated with numerous subjects under slightly different conditions.

Additional analyses clarify the mechanism that produces these violations of temporal monotonicity: Most subjects erroneously believed that the coldest temperature to which they had been exposed was not the same in the two trials; their memory of the worst moment of the Long trial was mitigated by the subsequent improvement. Our evidence suggests that episodes are evaluated by a few "snapshots" rather than by a continuous film-like representation (Fredrickson & Kahneman, 1993). The snapshots are in fact montages, which may blend impressions of different parts of the experience. The overall experience is judged by a weighted average of the utility of these synthetic moments.

Other experiments showed that subjects who are given only verbal descriptions of the trials generally prefer the Short one, in accordance with the principle of temporal monotonicity. Telling these subjects that their memory of the Long trial will be more favorable does not diminish their preference for the Short trial. This observation indicates that the participants in the original experiment did not deliberately apply a policy of selecting the experience that would leave them with the most pleasant memory. However, subjects who have had personal experience with the two trials are quite reluctant to abandon their preference for the Long trial, even when the nature of the two trials is carefully explained after the fact. It is evidently not easy to overcome a lifetime habit of trusting one's evaluations of personal memories as a guide to choice.

The studies reviewed in this section have documented a consistent pattern of violations of a compelling normative rule. The axiom of temporal monotonicity is a substantive principle of rationality, a variant of "more is better" formulations of dominance. The violations of this principle have been traced to basic cognitive processes that produce representations and evaluations of episodes. The requirements of substantive rationality are apparently not compatible with the psychology of memory and choice.

The results of the cold-water study illustrate an ethical dilemma that was extensively discussed by Schelling (1984a). The history of an individual through time can be described as a succession of separate selves, which may have incompatible preferences and may make decisions that affect subsequent selves. In the cold-water experiment, for example, the experiencing subject who records momentary affect and the remembering subject who makes retrospective evaluations appear to have conflicting evaluations. Which of these selves should be granted authority over outcomes that will be experienced in the future? The principle of temporal monotonicity assigns priority to the experiencing subject. In the normal conduct of life, however, it is the remembering subject who assumes the all-important role of laying out guidelines for future actions. Is there an ethical justification for favoring one of these evaluations over the other? This question has immediate implications for the application of rules of informed consent in medical practice. Imagine a painful medical procedure that lasts a specified number of minutes and ends abruptly with pain at its peak. We have seen that the physician could probably ensure that the patient will retain a more favorable memory of the procedure by adding to it a medically superfluous period of diminishing pain. Of course, the patient would probably reject the physician's offer to provide an improved memory at the cost of more actual pain. Should the physician go ahead anyway, on behalf of the patient's future remembering self? This dilemma illustrates a class of problems of paternalism that are likely to arise in many policy debates if considerations of experienced utility are assigned the weight they deserve in these debates.

GENERAL DISCUSSION

The standard theory of choice provides a set of conditions for rationality that may be necessary, but are hardly sufficient: They allow many foolish decisions to be called rational. This chapter has argued that it is generally useful and sometimes possible to supplement the logical analysis of decisions by substantive criteria. A substantive analysis provides a more demanding definition of rationality, which excludes some preferences that would pass a test of coherence. The core of a substantive analysis is an independent assessment of the quailty of decision outcomes.

The line between logical and substantive analyses is often fuzzy. For example, the "more is better" rule of dominance is a substantive rule that has the force of a logical principle. A substantive judgment is also implicitly invoked in experimental studies of invariance, where decision makers express conflicting preferences in choice problems that are said to be "the same," "extentionally equivalent," or "not different in any consequential respect." In the mugs experiment, for example, it appears unreasonable for owners and choosers to set very different prices for the same object because the long-term consumption they will derive from it is presumably the same and because long-term considerations carry more weight than the transient affect associated with giving up an object. A criterion of utility experienced over time is implicit in this argument.

The research reviewed in earlier sections was explicit in evaluating decisions by a criterion of experienced utility. Various proxies were used to measure this subjective variable. For example, choices made near the moment of consumption were the criterion in evaluating earlier commitments (Simonson, 1990). In other studies, the adequacy of retrospective evaluations and of the decisions they support was assessed by applying normative rules (e.g., temporal monotonicity) to real-time records of hedonic experience.

The correspondence of experienced utility and decision utility is commonly taken for granted in treatments of choice. Contrary to this optimistic assumption, two obstacles to the maximization of experienced utility have been identified here. First, preliminary findings suggest that people lack skill in the task of predicting how their tastes might change. The evidence for this conclusion is still sketchy, but its significance is clear: It is difficult to describe as rational agents who are prone to large errors in predicting what they will want or enjoy next week. Another obstacle to maximization is a tendency to use the affect associated with particular moments as a proxy for the utility of extended outcomes. This peculiarity in the cognitive treatment of time explains the importance that people attach to the emotions of transactions and may cause other forms of myopia in decision making. The use of moments as proxies entails a neglect of duration in the evaluation of past episodes, which has been confirmed in several studies. These results illustrate one particular form of distortion in evaluative memory; there may be others. Observations of memory biases are significant because the evaluation of the past determines what is learned from it. Errors in the lessons drawn from experience will inevitably be reflected in deficient choices for the future.

The rules that govern experienced utility emerge as an important subject for empirical study. For example, research could address the question of how to maximize experienced utility under a budget constraint. Scitovsky (1976) offered an insightful analysis of this problem in his *Joyless Economy*, where he took the position that the maximization of pleasure is a difficult task, which is performed with greater success in some cultures than in others. The process of hedonic adaptation played a central role in his treatment of "comforts," which suggests that it is pointless to invest resources in objects that quickly lose their ability to give pleasure. Expenditure should be directed to goods and activities that provide recurrent pleasures when appropriately spaced over time. In this light, money may be better spent on flowers, feasts, and vacations than on improved durables. A systematic empirical study of the issues that Scitovsky raised is both possible and necessary.

A deeper understanding of the dynamics of the hedonic response is needed to evaluate the welfare consequences of institutions. For example, the course of income changes over a standard academic career appears designed for a pleasure machine that responds well to gradual increments and treats any losses as highly aversive (Frank, 1992; Kahneman & Varey, 1991; Loewenstein & Sicherman, 1991). Another institution that probably delivers improving outcomes over time is the penal system: The well-being of prison inmates is likely to improve in the course of their sentence, as they gain seniority and survival skills. This arrangement is humane, but perhaps less than efficient in terms of individual deterrence. Suppose, for the sake of a provocative example, that prisoners apply a Peak & End rule in retrospective evaluations of their prison experience. The result would be a global evaluation that becomes steadily less aversive with time in prison, implying a negative correlation between sentence length and the deterrence of individual recidivism. This is surely not a socially desirable outcome. Should shorter periods of incarceration under conditions of increasing discomfort be considered? As this speculative example illustrates, detailed consideration of experienced utility can yield quite unexpected conclusions.

The hedonic criterion of experienced utility is appropriate for some decisions, but it is neither universal nor exhaustive. Rational people may have other objectives than the maximization of pleasure. As Sen (1990) has noted, the rationality of decisions is best assessed in the light of "what the person is aiming to do or trying to achieve" (p. 210). At least in principle, a substantive evaluation of individual decisions can be extended to other criterial objectives, such as the achievement of increased personal capabilities or of a good reputation. As the example of experienced utility illustrates, the investigation of any proposed criterion for decision making must involve three elements: (1) a normative analysis; (2) development of measurement tools for the evaluation of outcomes; and (3) an analysis of ways in which decisions commonly fail by this criterion. Experienced utility is an obvious subject for such a program, but it need not be the only one.

From the point of view of a psychologist, the notion of rationality that is routinely invoked in economic discourse is surprisingly permissive in some respects, surprisingly powerful in others. For example, economic rationality does not rule out extreme risk aversion in small gambles or radical discounting of the near-term future, although these attitudes almost necessarily yield inferior aggregate outcomes. On the other hand, rationality is often taken to be synonymous with flawless intelligence. Thus, a critic of the rationality assumption faces the following well-fortified position: (1) a definition of rationality that appears to be overly permissive in some important respects; (2) a willingness of choice theorists to make the theory even more permissive, as needed to accomodate apparent violations of its requirements; (3) a methodological position that treats rationality as a maintained hypothesis, making it very difficult to disprove; and (4) an apparent readiness to assume that behavior that has not been proved to be irrational is highly intelligent.

In contrast to the many recent attempts to relax the definition of rational choice, the argument of this chapter has been that the definition should be made more restrictive by adding substantive considerations to the logical standard of coherence. There is compelling evidence that the maintenance of coherent beliefs and preferences is too demanding a task for limited minds (Simon, 1955; Tversky & Kahneman, 1986). Maximizing the experienced utility of a stream of future outcomes can only be harder. The time has perhaps come to set aside the overly general question of whether or not people are rational, allowing research attention to be focused on more specific and more promising issues. What are the conditions under which the assumption of rationality can be retained as a useful approximation? Where the assumption of rationality must be given up, what are the most important ways in which people fail to maximize their outcomes?

ACKNOWLEDGMENTS

Presented at the 11th International Seminar on the New Institutional Economics, Wallerfangen/Saar, Germany, June 1993, and at the IEA Conference on Rationality and Economics, Turin, Italy, October 1993. A different version was presented at a Political and Economic Analysis Workshop in Honor of P. Zusman, in Rehovot, Israel, June 1993. The research leading to this chapter was supported by grants from Sloan Foundation, the McArthur Foundation, and the National Science Foundation. I am greatly indebted to Amos Tversky for many discussions of the issue of rationality over the years and for insightful comments on drafts of this chapter. He should not be assumed to have agreed with all I say. Alan Schwartz provided helpful editorial assistance.

28. Distinction Bias: Misprediction and Mischoice Due to Joint Evaluation

Christopher K. Hsee and Jiao Zhang

Suppose that a person is faced with two job offers. She finds one job interesting and the other tedious. However, the interesting job will pay her only $60,000 a year, and the tedious job will pay her $70,000 a year. The person wants to choose the job that will give her the greatest overall happiness. To make that choice, she tries to predict the difference in happiness between earning $60,000 a year and earning $70,000 a year and also to predict the difference in happiness between doing the interesting job and doing the tedious job. Is she able to make these predictions accurately? Is she able to choose the job that will indeed bring her the greater overall happiness?

Consider another example. A person currently lives in a 3,000-square-foot (ft^2) house that is within walking distance to work. He has the option to move to a 4,000-ft^2 house for the same price as his current house, but if he moves there, it will take him an hour to drive to work every day. To decide whether to move, he tries to forecast the difference in happiness between living in the 3,000-ft^2 house and living in the 4,000-ft^2 house and also to forecast the difference in happiness between being able to walk to work and having to drive an hour to work. Is he able to make these predictions accurately? Is he able to make a decision that will give him the greater overall happiness?

More generally, if people are presented with two alternative values of an attribute, are they able to accurately predict the difference these values will make to their happiness? If people are faced with two options involving a tradeoff along two attributes, are they able to choose the option that will bring them the greater overall happiness?

These are fundamental questions about affective forecasting and about choice, and they are among the most enduring and significant questions in psychology. These questions are relevant in a wide range of domains, for example, when people decide which career to pursue, when voters decide which candidate to endorse, when consumers decide which product to purchase, and when policy makers decide which policy to implement.

Traditional economists and decision theorists assume that people know their preferences and that what they choose reveals what is best for them, given the

Originally published in the *Journal of Personality and Social Psychology*, vol. 86, pp. 680–695.

information they have at the time of choice. In reality, this is not the case. In a series of seminal articles, Kahneman and his coauthors (e.g., Kahneman, 2000; Kahneman & Snell, 1990, 1992; Kahneman, Wakker, & Sarin, 1997) have argued that what people predict will make them happy (i.e., *predicted utility*) and what people choose (i.e., *decision utility*) can be systematically different from what actually makes them happy (i.e., *experienced utility*). In other words, people may mispredict and mischoose.

In this chapter, we outline a theory about misprediction and mischoice. As we explain later, the theory indicates that people are likely to overpredict the experiential difference between having an annual salary of $60,000 and having an annual salary of $70,000 and between living in a 3,000-ft^2 house and living in a 4,000-ft^2 house, but they are less likely to overpredict the experiential difference between doing an interesting job and doing a tedious job or between being able to walk to work and having to drive to work. Moreover, our theory suggests that if people are given options that entail a tradeoff between these two types of factors, they may choose an option that does not generate the greatest happiness. For example, people may choose a tedious $70,000 job over an interesting $60,000 job, even if the latter would bring them greater overall happiness.

Misprediction and mischoice may result from a variety of causes. In recent years, many scholars have made significant contributions to the identification of these causes (e.g., Dhar, Nowlis, & Sherman, 1999; Frey & Stutzer, 2002a, 2002b, 2003; Gilbert, Driver-Linn, & Wilson, 2002; Gilbert, Gill, & Wilson, 2002; Gilbert, Pinel, Wilson, Blumberg, & Wheatley, 1998, 2002; Gilbert & Wilson, 2000; Hirt & Markman, 1995; Hsee & Weber, 1997; Kahneman & Snell, 1992; Loewenstein & Schkade, 1999; March, 1994; Markman & Hirt, 2002; Novemsky & Ratner, 2003; Nowlis & Simonson, 1997; Prelec & Herrnstein, 1991; Ratner, Kahn, & Kahneman, 1999; Schkade & Kahneman, 1998; Simonson, 1990; Simonson & Nowlis, 2000; Wilson & Gilbert, 2003; Wilson & Schooler, 1991).

For example, when predicting the impact of an event, people may neglect the power of adaptation and rationalization (e.g., Gilbert et al., 1998; Gilbert, Driver-Linn, & Wilson, 2002), may overlook other events that may influence their lives and dilute the impact of the focal event (e.g., Schkade & Kahneman, 1998; Wilson, Wheatley, Meyers, Gilbert, & Axsom, 2000), and may overweight unique features of the event (e.g., Dunn, Wilson, & Gilbert, 2003; Houston & Sherman, 1995; Kahneman & Tversky, 1979). People may also hold incorrect beliefs about the dynamics of experiences and make inaccurate predictions (e.g., Kahneman & Snell, 1990, 1992; Novemsky & Ratner, 2003). People may overpredict the importance of external rewards such as income and status and underestimate the importance of activities with intrinsic values such as hobbies and socializing with friends (e.g., Frey & Stutzer, 2003). People may overweight attributes that are easy to articulate and underweight other attributes that are important for experience when asked to analyze reasons during the choice phase (e.g., Wilson & Schooler, 1991). People may also base their decisions on principles (e.g., March, 1994; Prelec & Herrnstein, 1991), on rules and heuristics (e.g., Amir & Ariely, in press; Ratner et al., 1999; Simonson, 1990), on lay theory of rationality (e.g., Hsee, Zhang, Yu, & Xi, 2003), or on specious payoffs (e.g., Hsee, Yu, Zhang, & Zhang, 2003). Finally, people may be more or less aroused during decision than during experience and therefore make suboptimal choices (e.g., Gilbert, Gill, and Wilson, 2002; Loewenstein, 1996; Read & van Leeuwen, 1998).

In the present research, we explore another potential cause of misprediction and mischoice: joint versus separate evaluation. In the next section we present our general theory. Then we examine its implications for misprediction involving a single attribute and report empirical evidence. After that, we examine the implications of our theory for mischoice involving multiple attributes and report more empirical evidence. In the General Discussion section we (a) delineate the differences of this research from evaluability and other related research, (b) suggest ways to improve prediction and choice, and (c) examine the implications of our work for research on happiness and subjective well-being.

THEORY

Briefly speaking, we suggest that the evaluation mode in which choices and predictions are made is often different from the evaluation mode in which experience takes place. Choices and predictions are often made in the *joint evaluation* (JE) mode, in which the choosers or predictors compare multiple options or scenarios. On the other hand, the actual experience typically takes place in the *single evaluation* or *separate evaluation* (SE) mode, in which experiencers face only the option or scenario they or others have chosen for them. Because of the JE/SE difference, people in JE may overpredict the experiential difference between alternatives in SE.

Our analysis in this section is built on the evaluability hypothesis proposed by Hsee (1996a) and refined by Hsee, Loewenstein, Blount, and Bazerman (1999). We focus on our current analysis here, and in the General Discussion section we discuss how it is related to and different from the original evaluability hypothesis.

Let us consider the evaluation of a single attribute. Assume that greater values on the attribute are better. Our central proposition is that the evaluation function of the attribute can be systematically different depending on whether the evaluation is elicited in JE or in SE. In JE, people are presented with alternative values (i.e., alternative levels) of the attribute, and people can easily compare these values and discern their differences (e.g., Kleinmuntz & Schkade, 1993; Tversky, 1969). Through the comparison, people can easily differentiate the desirability of the alternative values. Consequently, the evaluation function in JE will be relatively steep and smooth. This JE function is depicted by the solid line in Figure 28.1.

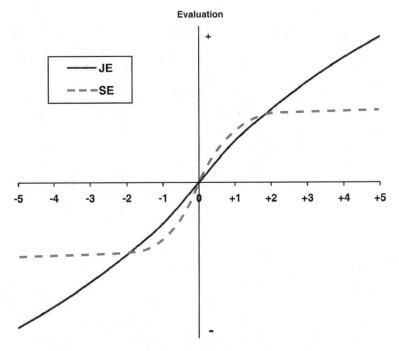

Figure 28.1. Joint-evaluation (JE) curve and separate-evaluation (SE) curve of a hypothetical attribute. The SE curve is flatter than the JE curve in most regions except around zero (or a reference point). Decision utility and predicted utility usually follow the JE curve, and experienced utility typically follows the SE curve.

In SE, different people are presented with different values of the attribute; each person sees only one value and cannot easily compare it with the alternative values.[1] We propose that for most attributes, people do not have a precise idea of how good or how bad an isolated value is and that people in such a situation will crudely code a value as good if it is positive or above a certain reference point or bad if it is negative or below a certain reference point. In other words, people in SE are generally able to tell whether a value is good or bad but are unable to tell exactly how good or how bad it is.

For example, most people would find gaining money good and losing money bad, but they would be relatively insensitive to the size of the gain and the size of the loss. Thus, the resulting evaluation function in SE will be close to a step function: steep around zero or a reference point and flat elsewhere. This SE function, originally proposed by Hsee et al. (1999), is depicted by the dashed

---

[1] Strictly speaking, people make comparisons even in SE, but these comparisons are typically not between explicit alternatives but between the given stimulus and the natural zero point or some implicit norm (for further discussion, see Hsee & Leclerc, 1998).

line in Figure 28.1.[2] (More precisely, the slope of the curves in Figure 28.1 should be steeper in the negative domain than in the positive domain, to reflect loss aversion; Kahneman & Tversky, 1979. However, because loss aversion is not relevant to the thesis we pursue in this chapter, we omitted it from our figure to keep the graphs simple.)

The difference between the JE and the SE functions, as depicted in Figure 28.1, has many potential implications. For example, combining the JE/SE difference and the negative-based prominence effect (Willemsen & Keren, 2002), Willemsen and Keren (2004) predicted and showed that negative features exert a greater influence on SE than on JE.

In the present research, we explore the implications of the JE/SE difference depicted in Figure 28.1 for misprediction and mischoice. We discuss these topics in turn.

MISPREDICTION

Our analysis of JE and SE implies that when people predict how much of a difference two values – for example, two salary levels – will make to their happiness, they are likely to overpredict the difference. We refer to this overprediction effect as the *distinction bias*. Our analysis can also specify when the distinction bias is likely to occur and when it is not. The following is our explanation.

When people predict future experience, especially when they do so before they make a decision, they often compare alternative scenarios or compare the current situation with a future scenario. In other words, the predictors are in JE. On the other hand, when people experience what actually happens, they are in SE. For example, when a realtor takes a home buyer to see different houses on the market, the home buyer will compare these houses and predict whether she will be happier in one house or in another (JE). Even if the realtor shows the home buyer only one house, the home buyer may still engage in JE; she may compare whether she will be happier in the new home or in her current residence. She may say, "The new house has higher ceilings and a bigger kitchen than my current home, and I would feel so much better if I could live in this house." On the other hand, once a person has purchased a home and lives in it, she is mostly in SE of that home alone. Of course, she might occasionally compare her house with others' or with what she could have bought (e.g., Kahneman, 1995; Kahneman & Tversky, 1982; Roese, 1997). However, we consider JE/SE as a continuum, and relatively speaking, the homeowner is less

---

[2] Another factor that influences the shape of the SE curve is whether one uses feelings or calculations to make the evaluation. The more one resorts to feelings, the less sensitive the person is to quantitative variations and the closer the evaluation function is to a step function, which is steep around zero (or a reference point) and flat elsewhere. See Hsee and Rottenstreich (2004) for a detailed exposition of this idea and empirical tests.

likely to engage in JE during the experience phase than during the prediction phase.

We do not intend to imply that people always predict experiences in JE. Instead, we mean that in many cases, especially when people try to make a choice between alternatives, they make predictions in JE. In the present research we focus only on such cases.

We propose that when people in JE make predictions, they are likely to overpredict in some experiences but not in others. Formally, let x_1 and x_2 denote two alternative values of an attribute. The question we want to address is this: Would people in JE overpredict the difference that x_1 and x_2 will make to experience in SE? To answer this question, we only need to compare whether the slope of the JE curve is steeper than the slope of the SE curve around x_1 and x_2. If the JE curve is steeper than the SE curve in the given region, it implies that people in JE are likely to overpredict. If the JE curve is not steeper than SE, it implies that people in JE are not likely to overpredict. For example, in Figure 28.1, if $x_1 = +2$ and $x_2 = +4$, then people in JE are likely to overpredict how much of a difference these values will make in SE. On the other hand, if $x_1 = -1$ and $x_2 = +1$, then people in JE are not likely to overpredict how much of a difference these values will make in SE.

Generally speaking, if x_1 and x_2 are merely *quantitatively different*, that is, if x_1 and x_2 have the same valence or are on the same side of a reference point, then people in JE are likely to overpredict the experiential difference these values will create in SE. On the other hand, if x_1 and x_2 are *qualitatively different*, that is, if x_1 and x_2 involve different valences or one is above the reference point and one below, then people in JE are not likely to overpredict the experiential difference these values will create in SE.

We do not preclude the possibility that people in JE would underpredict the experiential difference between alternative values. We suspect that an underprediction may occur if (a) x_1 and x_2 are qualitatively different and (b) x_1 and x_2 are close to each other relative to other values presented in JE. However, we believe that overprediction is more common. The present research focuses on overprediction.

It is important to note that the unit of analysis in this research is difference, not attribute. When we say qualitative versus quantitative, we mean qualitative versus quantitative differences rather than qualitative versus quantitative attributes. A qualitative difference may come from either a qualitative attribute or a quantitative attribute. For example, whether a job provides health insurance is a qualitative attribute, and the difference between a job with health insurance and one without is a qualitative difference. On the other hand, the return from a stock investment is a quantitative attribute, but the difference between a negative return and a positive return is a qualitative difference. In fact, if one knows the average stock return in a given period, say, 11%, and uses it as the neutral reference point, then for that person even the difference between two nominally positive returns, say, 2% and 20%, is a qualitative difference.[3]

Our analysis provides a simple yet general picture of when people in JE are likely to overpredict and when they are not. For example, people in JE are likely to overpredict the difference in happiness between winning $2,000 in a casino and winning $4,000 in a casino, between living in a 3,000-ft^2 house and living in a 4,000-ft^2 house, and between earning $60,000 a year and earning $70,000 a year. In each example, the difference between the two alternatives is merely quantitative (unless people have acquired a reference that happens to lie between these values). The difference looks salient and distinct in JE, but it actually is inconsequential in SE. This is what we have referred to as the distinction bias.

On the other hand, people in JE are unlikely to overpredict the difference in happiness between winning $1,000 in a casino and losing $1,000 in a casino, between doing an interesting job and doing a tedious job, and between being able to walk to work and having to drive an hour to work. In each case, the difference between the two alternatives is qualitative, and even in SE it will make a considerable difference.

In sum, the distinction bias is likely to occur for merely quantitatively different values but unlikely to occur for qualitatively different values. We now report two studies to demonstrate these effects. Study 1 used hypothetical scenarios; Study 2 involved real experiences.

STUDY 1: POEM BOOK

Method

Respondents (249 students from a large Midwestern university in the United States) were asked to imagine that their favorite hobby is writing poems and that they had compiled a book of their poems and were trying to sell it on campus. Respondents were assigned to one of five conditions, one for JE and four for SE. Those in the JE condition were asked to consider the following four scenarios and assume that one of these scenarios had actually happened to them:

> So far no one has bought your book.
> So far 80 people have bought your book.
> So far 160 people have bought your book.
> So far 240 people have bought your book.

The respondents were encouraged to compare these scenarios and then asked to predict how they would feel in each scenario. They indicated their predicted

---

[3] An attribute may also have multiple reference points; in that case, the difference between values across any of the reference points may be qualitative.

happiness by circling a number on a 9-point scale ranging from 1 (*extremely unhappy*) to 9 (*extremely happy*).

Respondents assigned to each of the four SE conditions were presented with one of the four scenarios, asked to assume that the scenario was what had happened to them, and then asked to indicate their feelings on the same 9-point scale.

Results and Discussion

Before reporting the results, let us first state our predictions. Notice that of the four scenarios, the no-buyer scenario is obviously bad and qualitatively different from the other three scenarios, which are only quantitatively different. These differences are summarized as follows:

0 buyers
} qualitatively different
80 buyers
} only quantitatively different
160 buyers
} only quantitatively different
240 buyers

According to our theory concerning qualitative and quantitative differences, we made the following predictions: First, people in JE would overpredict the difference in happiness between the 80-buyer, the 160-buyer, and the 240-buyer scenarios. Second, people in JE would not (at least were less likely to) over-predict the difference in happiness between the no-buyer and the 80-buyer scenarios.

As summarized in Figure 28.2, the results accorded with our predictions. Let us first concentrate on the 80-buyer, the 160-buyer, and the 240-buyer scenarios. In JE, people thought that they would be significantly happier in the 240-buyer scenario than in the 160-buyer scenario and significantly happier in the 160-buyer scenario than in the 80-buyer scenario (Ms = 8.54, 6.26, and 3.34, respectively), $t(49) > 3$, $p < .001$, in any comparisons. However, in SE, people were virtually equally happy across the three scenarios (Ms = 7.86, 7.57, and 7.14, respectively), $t(97) < 1$, not significant (ns), in any comparisons.

Let us now turn to the no-buyer and the 80-buyer scenarios. Here, people in JE predicted greater happiness in the 80-buyer scenario than in the no-buyer scenario (Ms = 3.34 and 1.66, respectively), $t(49) = 8.20$, $p < .001$, and people in SE of the 80-buyer scenario indeed reported greater happiness than people in SE of the no-buyer scenario (Ms = 7.14 and 2.18, respectively), $t(98) = 16.15$, $p < .001$. In other words, people in JE did not overpredict the difference in happiness between the no-buyer scenario and the 80-buyer scenario; in fact, they even underpredicted the difference.

Consistent with our theory, Study 1 demonstrates that people in JE overpredict the difference two merely quantitatively different events make on SE, but

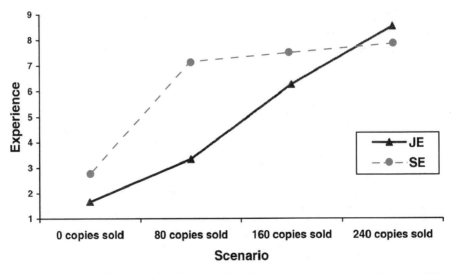

Figure 28.2. Poem book study: Compared with people in separate evaluation (SE), people in joint evaluation (JE) are more sensitive to the differences between the quantitatively different scenarios (the 80-copy, the 160-copy, and the 240-copy scenarios) but less sensitive to the difference between the qualitatively different scenarios (the 0-copy and the 80-copy scenarios).

they do not overpredict the difference two qualitatively different events make on SE.

STUDY 2: WORDS

Method

Study 2 was designed to replicate the findings of Study 1. Unlike Study 1, Study 2 entailed real experiences and included symmetrically positive and negative events.

Respondents (360 students from a large Midwestern university in the United States) were assigned to one of nine conditions: one JE-predicted-experience condition, four SE-real-experience conditions, and four SE-predicted-experience conditions. We included the SE-predicted-experience conditions to test whether the expected inconsistency between JE-predicted experience and SE-real experiences arises from the difference between JE and SE or from the difference between predicted experience and real experience.

Participants in the JE-predicted-experience condition were asked to suppose that the experimenter would give them one of the following four tasks:

Read a list of 10 negative words, such as *hatred* and *loss*.
Read a list of 25 negative words, such as *hatred* and *loss*.
Read a list of 10 positive words, such as *love* and *win*.
Read a list of 25 positive words, such as *love* and *win*.

They were asked to compare the four tasks and to predict how they would feel if they had completed each task. In each of the four SE-real-experience conditions, the respondents were told about only one of the four tasks and asked to actually perform the task and indicate their feelings on completion. In each of the four SE-predicted-experience conditions, the respondents were also told about only one of the four tasks and were then asked to predict their feelings after completing the task. In all the conditions, the respondents gave their answers by circling a number on a 9-point scale ranging from 1 (*extremely unhappy*) to 9 (*extremely happy*).

Results and Discussion

We first describe our predictions. When the four tasks are sorted from the most negative to the most positive, the differences between these tasks can be summarized as follows:

25 negative words
} only quantitatively different
10 negative words
} qualitatively different
10 positive words
} only quantitatively different
25 positive words

Notice that the difference between the 25-negative-word task and the 10-negative-word task is only a matter of degree. Thus, we predicted that people in JE would overpredict the difference in experience between these two tasks. By the same token, we predicted that people in JE would also overpredict the experiential difference between the 25-positive-word task and the 10-positive-word task. On the other hand, the difference between the 10-negative-word task and the 10-positive-word task is a matter of valence. Thus, we predicted that people in JE were unlikely to overpredict the experiential difference between these two tasks.

The results, which we summarize in Figure 28.3, support our predictions. Let us first consider the JE-predicted-experience and the SE-real-experience conditions and focus on the 25-negative-word and the 10-negative-word tasks. In the JE-predicted-experience condition, people predicted significantly greater unhappiness from reading 25 negative words than from reading 10 negative words ($M = 3.33$ vs. 4.00), $t(39) = 3.74$, $p < .001$. However, in the SE-real-experience conditions, those who read 25 negative words reported virtually the same degree of unhappiness as those who read 10 negative words ($M = 4.64$ vs. 4.62; $t < 1$, *ns*).

The same was true for the two positive-word tasks. The JE predictors predicted significantly greater happiness from reading 25 positive words than from reading 10 positive words ($M = 6.73$ vs. 6.03), $t(39) = 4.71$, $p < .001$. However, the SE-real experiencers did not find reading 25 positive words any happier

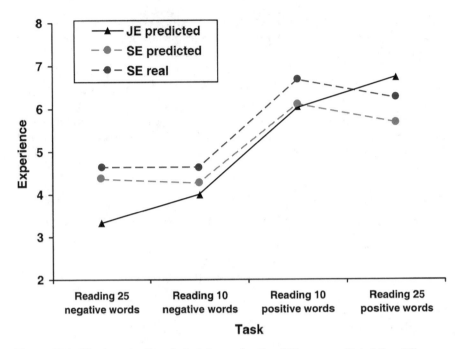

Figure 28.3. Word study: People in joint evaluation (JE) overpredicted the difference in experience between reading 25 negative words and reading 10 negative words, and between reading 10 positive words and reading 25 positive words (both of which are only quantitatively different). However, people in JE did not overpredict the difference between reading 10 negative words and reading 10 positive words (which are qualitatively different).

than reading 10 positive words, $t(80) = 1.23$, *ns*; if anything, the results veered in the opposite direction ($M = 6.27$ for 25 positive words and $M = 6.69$ for 10 positive words).

Finally, we compare the two qualitatively different tasks: reading 10 negative words and reading 10 positive words. The JE predictors rather accurately predicted the difference between these tasks for SE-real experiencers: $M = 4.00$ and 6.03, $t(39) = 5.67$, $p < .001$ in JE, and $M = 4.62$ and 6.69, $t(83) = 5.47$, $p < .001$ in SE.

These results corroborate our proposition that people in JE tend to exhibit the distinction bias when predicting the impact of merely quantitatively different values and not when predicting the impact of qualitatively different values. Indeed, the JE and SE curves formed by the results of this study (Figure 28.3) are remarkably similar to the JE and SE curves proposed by our theory (Figure 28.1).

One may wonder whether the distinction bias could be explained by the fact that the predictors in JE did not do the tasks and had less knowledge about the tasks than the experiencers. The answer is no. As indicated earlier, we also included four SE-predicted-experience conditions. The results are also summarized in Figure 28.3. As the figure shows, the SE-predicted-experience results are similar to the SE-real-experience results and different from the JE-prediction results. This result reinforces our belief that the inconsistency between predicted experience in JE and real experience in SE is due to the JE/SE difference.

So far, we have discussed the implication of the JE/SE difference for misprediction. Before we move to the next section, about mischoice, we submit an important qualification: According to the evaluability hypothesis (Hsee et al., 1999), the JE/SE difference characterized in Figure 28.1 applies only to attributes that are not very easy to evaluate independently. If an attribute is very easy to evaluate independently – in other words, if people have sufficient knowledge about the attribute so that they can easily evaluate the desirability of any of its value in SE – then the SE curve of the attribute will resemble its JE curve, and there will be no JE/SE difference. This proposition is consistent with previous research showing that experts have more stable preferences across situations than novices (e.g., Wilson, Kraft, & Dunn, 1989).

To test the idea that the JE/SE difference will disappear for independently easy-to-evaluate attributes, we ran a study parallel to Study 1 (poem book). The new study was identical to Study 1 except that the key attribute was not how many copies of the book were sold but what grade (A, B, C, or D) a professor assigned to the book. Presumably, students are highly familiar with grades, and grades are an independently easy-to-evaluate attribute. We predicted that the SE result would resemble the JE result. The data confirmed our prediction. In fact, the JE and the SE results were so similar that the two curves virtually coincided with each other.

However, we believe that it is the exception rather than the rule to find an attribute, like grade, that is so independently easy to evaluate that its SE curve will coincide with its JE curve. Most attributes are more or less difficult to evaluate independently, and their JE and SE will differ in the way depicted in Figure 28.1.

MISCHOICE

Our theory also yields implications for choice. We suggested earlier that affective predictions are sometimes made in JE. Here, we suggest that even more often than predictions, choices are made in JE. Choosers typically have multiple options to compare and choose from. On the other hand, experiencers are typically in SE of what they are experiencing. Again, we do not imply that choosers are always in pure JE and experiencers always in pure SE. However, we consider JE/SE as a continuum and believe that in most situations choosers are closer to JE and experiencers are closer to SE. The present research is concerned with these situations.

Because choosers and experiencers are typically in different evaluation modes, they may also have different utility functions. Figure 28.1 describes a typical JE curve and a typical SE curve. These curves may also apply to choosers and experiencers. Specifically, choosers' utility function will resemble the JE curve in Figure 28.1, and experiencers' utility function will resemble the SE curve. In other words, "decision utility" will follow the JE curve, and "experienced utility" will follow the SE curve.

On the basis of this analysis, we predict a potential mischoice, namely, an inconsistency between choice and experience. To show a choice–experience inconsistency, we need at least two options, and these options must involve a tradeoff between at least two attributes. Specifically, suppose that two options involve a tradeoff along two attributes, as follows:

	Attribute X	Attribute Y
Option A	x_1	y_1
Option B	x_2	y_2

Suppose also that x_1 is worse than x_2 qualitatively, and y_1 is better than y_2 only quantitatively. Then a choice–experience inconsistency may emerge, and its direction is such that choosers will prefer Option A, and experiencers will be happier with Option B.

In the context of the salary/job example we introduced earlier, the hypothesis implies that people may choose the tedious $70,000 job but would actually be happier with the interesting $60,000 job. In the context of the home/commuting example, the hypothesis implies that people may choose the 1-hr-drive-away, 4,000-ft^2 house, but would actually be happier with the within-walking-distance, 3,000-ft^2 house. Indeed, in a carefully conducted econometric study, Frey and Stutzer (2003) did secure evidence that people who spend more time commuting are less happy with their lives, even though they have larger homes or higher incomes.

STUDY 3: TASK–REWARD

Method

Unlike Studies 1 and 2, Study 3 featured two options, and these options consisted of a tradeoff along two attributes. Study 3 was designed to achieve three different objectives. First, it sought to replicate the findings of the first two studies concerning the distinction bias in prediction. Second, it sought to show mischoice of multiattribute options and thereby test our hypothesis about choice–experience inconsistency. Finally, it sought to show that people not only make mispredictions and mischoices for themselves but also make mispredictions and mischoices for other people.

Stimuli. The study involved two options. Each required participants to perform a task and enjoy a reward at the same time. In one option, participants were asked to recall a failure in their lives; in the other, they were asked to recall a success in their lives. The reward for the first task was a 15-g Dove chocolate; the reward for the second was a 5-g Dove chocolate. See the following summary:

	Task	**Reward**
Option A	Recall failure	15-g chocolate
Option B	Recall success	5-g chocolate

We selected these stimuli on the basis of the following considerations. First, the recollection of a success was a positive experience, and the recollection of a failure was a negative experience. Therefore, the two tasks differed in valence or quality. Second, the two rewards – the two chocolates – differed only in degree or quantity.

Subjects and Procedures. Participants were 243 students from a large university on the east coast of China. They participated in this study as a class requirement. The study consisted of four between-subjects conditions:

Condition 1 (choosers for self): Participants compared both options, chose one, and experienced it.

Condition 2 (choosers for others): Participants compared both options and chose one for other participants (experiencers who did not make a choice).

Condition 3 (experiencers): Participants were given only the negative-task/ large-reward option and experienced it.

Condition 4 (experiencers): Participants were given only the positive-task/ small-reward option and experienced it.

We describe each condition in greater detail now. In Condition 1, respondents were instructed that their task was to recall and briefly write down a true story in their lives and that in return they could eat a Dove chocolate. (Instructions were in Chinese in all the conditions.) They were told that they could eat the chocolate only while recalling and writing down the event and could not eat it afterward or take it home. They were told that they could choose one of two types of events to recount: either a failure in their lives or a success in their lives. If they chose the former, they could eat a 15-g Dove chocolate, and if they chose the latter, they could eat a 5-g Dove chocolate. They were shown the two types of chocolates. They were then asked to decide which task–reward combination they wanted to choose.

To test whether people would overpredict the impact of either the chocolates or the tasks, we then asked the respondents to separately predict their experience about the tasks and about the chocolates. The task–experience–prediction question asked them to focus on the tasks alone and predict whether they would feel better by doing Task A (recalling and writing down a failure story) or Task B (recalling and writing down a success story). They were asked to indicate their prediction about each task on a 9-point scale ranging from -4 (*extremely unhappy*) to $+4$ (*extremely happy*). The reward–experience–prediction question asked the respondents to focus on the chocolates alone and predict whether they would feel better by eating the 5-g or the 15-g chocolate.

They were asked to indicate their prediction about each chocolate on the same 9-point scale described earlier.

Finally, the respondents were given the chocolate they had chosen and asked to perform the task they had promised to perform. After they had completed the task and eaten the chocolate, they were asked to indicate their overall experience. After that, they were asked two other questions, which assessed their experience about the task and their experience about the chocolate, respectively. Each question asked the respondents to focus on the task alone (the chocolate alone) and indicate how they had felt about performing the task (eating the chocolate). Answers to all the questions were given on the same 9-point rating scale as described earlier.

In Condition 2, the participants were asked to make a choice for other, unidentified students rather than for themselves. Participants were given the same information about the tasks and chocolates as in Condition 1 and were asked to choose one of the task–reward options for the other students. The participants were told, "Whichever option you choose for them is what they will get. They will not know the existence of the other option," implying the experiencer was in pure SE. They were also told, "Your goal is to choose the option that will give them the greatest happiness." They then made a choice. After that, they were asked to predict the other students' experience with the tasks and with the chocolates separately, just as participants in Condition 1 were asked to predict their own experience with the tasks and with the chocolates separately.

In Condition 3, the participants were not given a choice. They were directly asked to recall and briefly write down a failure story and given a 15-g Dove chocolate to eat while performing the task. After they had completed the task and eaten the chocolate, they were asked to indicate their overall experience. After that, they were asked to indicate their experience about the task and their experience about the chocolate separately, as in Condition 1. All the responses were given on the same 9-point scale as described earlier. Condition 4 was identical to Condition 3 except that the respondents recalled and wrote down a success story and got only a 5-g Dove chocolate.

Results

We report our results in two parts. We first report whether choosers mispredicted the impact of the tasks and the impact of the rewards. We then report whether choosers failed to make the experientially optimal choice for themselves and for others.

Mispredictions. According to our theory regarding qualitative and quantitative differences, we expected that choosers would not overpredict the impact of the tasks but would overpredict the impact of the chocolates, because the two tasks differed in valence, and the two chocolates differed only in size.

We tested our predictions in two ways. First, we tested whether choosers mispredicted *others'* experiences. We did so by comparing the predictions of the choosers in Condition 2, who made predictions for others, with the experiences

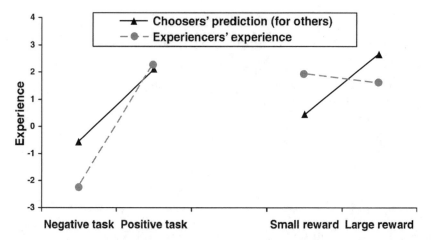

Figure 28.4. Task–reward study: The left panel shows that choosers (for others) did not overpredict the difference in others' experience between doing the positive task and doing the negative task (which are qualitatively different). The right panel shows that the choosers (for others) overpredicted the difference in others' experience between having the small reward and having the large reward (which are only quantitatively different).

of the experiencers in Conditions 3 and 4. Second, we tested whether choosers mispredicted *their own* experiences with tasks and chocolates. We did so by comparing the predictions of the choosers in Condition 1, who made predictions for themselves, with their own subsequent experiences. Figure 28.4 summarizes the results of the first comparison; Figure 28.5 summarizes the results of the second comparison.

Both sets of results confirmed our predictions. As Figure 28.4 shows, choosers in Condition 2 did not overpredict the impact of tasks on others' experience. They predicted that experiencers would be happier with the positive task than with the negative task ($M = 2.13$ vs. -0.58), $t(54) = 5.72$, $p < .001$, and the experiencers (those in Conditions 3 and 4) were indeed happier with the positive task than with the negative task ($M = 2.29$ vs. -2.23), $t(63) = 11.86$, $p < .001$. On the other hand, the choosers grossly overpredicted the impact of the chocolates. They predicted that the larger chocolate would engender greater happiness than the smaller chocolate ($M = 2.67$ vs. 0.47), $t(54) = 6.69$, $p < .001$, but in reality the larger chocolate did not bring any more happiness than the smaller one ($M = 1.65$ vs. 1.94), $t(63) < 1$, *ns*.

Figure 28.5 shows a similar pattern. The choosers in Condition 1 predicted greater happiness with the positive task than with the negative task ($M = 2.17$ vs. -0.96), $t(50) = 8.39$, $p < .001$, and indeed they were happier with the positive task than with the negative task ($M = 2.56$ vs. -1.29), $t(50) = 7.49$, $p < .001$. On the other hand, the choosers predicted greater happiness with the bigger chocolate than with the smaller one ($M = 2.31$ vs. 1.02), $t(50) = 3.96$, $p < .001$, but

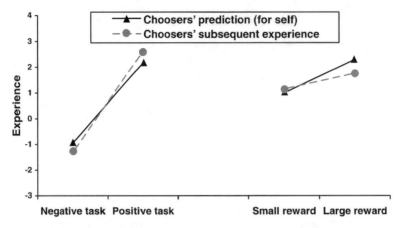

Figure 28.5. Task–reward study: The left panel shows that choosers (for self) did not overpredict the difference in their own subsequent experience between doing the positive task and doing the negative task. The right panel shows that the choosers (for self) overpredicted the difference in their own subsequent experience between having the small reward and having the large reward.

in reality the size of chocolate had no significant effect ($M = 1.75$ vs. 1.11), $t(50) = 1.15$, *ns*.[4]

Mischoice. Because choosers overpredicted the impact of the rewards but not the impact of the tasks, we expected a choice–experience inconsistency in the following direction: The choosers would favor the option with the larger reward, but the experiencers would be happier with the option with the positive task.

Figure 28.6 summarizes the choice data. The left panel shows results for those who chose for themselves (Condition 1). The right panel shows results for those who chose for others (Condition 2). Consistent with our prediction, the majority (65%) of the respondents in both conditions chose the negative-task/large-reward option, $\chi^2(1, N = 55) = 5.25$, $p < .05$, in both conditions.

Figure 28.7 summarizes the experience data. The left panel is the result of those in Conditions 3 and 4 who did not make a choice and therefore were experiencers in pure SE. The right panel is the result of those in Condition 1, who had made a choice for themselves. In stark contrast with the preference revealed by the choice data, both groups of experiencers were happier with the

---

[4] Unlike Conditions 3 and 4, in which the big and small chocolates made no difference in experience, in Condition 1 the big and small chocolates made some difference. This difference occurred perhaps because in Condition 1 the choosers had seen both chocolates, and therefore were not in pure SE. This difference may also have resulted from the fact that the experiencers had made predictions during the choice phase, and their predictions may have influenced their subsequent experiences (e.g., Sherman, 1980; Spangenberg & Greenwald, 1999).

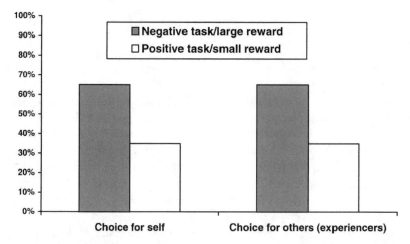

Figure 28.6. Task–reward study: Most choosers chose the negative-task/large-reward option over the positive-task/small-reward option, regardless of whether they made the choice for themselves or for others (pure experiencers).

positive-task/small-reward option than with the negative-task/large-reward option: ($M = 2.41$ vs. -0.71), $t(63) = 7.51$, $p < .001$, for the pure experiencers; ($M = 2.61$ vs. 0.09), $t(50) = 5.61$, $p < .001$, for the choosers. The results in the right panel of Figure 28.7 are particularly noteworthy. These are from people who had made the choice themselves (Condition 1). In the choice phase, most of them opted for the negative-task/large-reward option, but they ended up being less

Figure 28.7. Task–reward study: Both experiencers (who had not made choices) and choosers (who had made choices) were happier with the positive task/small reward than with the negative task/large reward.

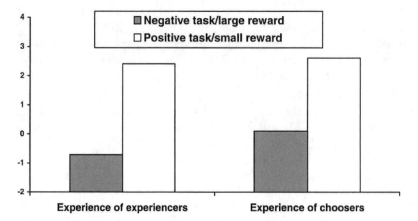

happy than the minority of people who chose the positive-task/small-reward option.[5]

Discussion

Study 3 may be a microcosm of life. In Study 3, most people thought that the bigger chocolate would bring greater happiness and chose to, or asked others to, endure a painful task to obtain the bigger chocolate, yet the bigger chocolate did not bring greater happiness. In real life, many people think that more money would bring greater happiness and choose to, or encourage others to, endure hard work to obtain more money, yet more money may not bring more happiness. In this section, we discuss the implications of Study 3 for misprediction and mischoice and address several potential alternative explanations.

About Mispredictions. The misprediction results secured in this study replicate the misprediction results found in Studies 1 and 2. They show that people in JE are rather accurate in predicting the impact of the difference between something good and something bad but inaccurate in predicting the impact of the difference between a small good thing and a large good thing. In other words, the distinction bias occurs for merely quantitatively different values but not for qualitatively different values.

The misprediction results of this study also extend the previous findings in one important direction: In the previous studies, the predictors in JE were not told that the experiencers would be in pure SE and might have thought that the experiencers would also know the alternatives. Thus, what they were predicting may not have been "how I would feel when I experience Option X if I didn't know about Option Y" but "how I would feel when I experience Option X given that I also know about Option Y." In this study, the respondents in Condition 2 were asked to make predictions for other people, and they were explicitly told that the others would not know the alternative option, implying that the experiencers were in pure SE. Even so, the predictors overpredicted the impact of the rewards. In this sense, the misprediction found in this study is more dramatic than that demonstrated in the previous studies.

About Mischoice. The study reveals two types of mischoices. First, most people fail to choose the experientially optimal option for others. Second, most people fail to choose the experientially optimal option even for themselves. The first finding comes from a comparison between the choices of those who made the choice for others (Condition 2) and the experience of those who did not choose (Conditions 3 and 4). This is a direct test of our theory. The choosers

---

[5] Figure 28.7 reveals another potentially interesting effect: Compared with the experiencers, the choosers seemed happier with the option they had chosen, especially if they had chosen the negative-task/large-reward option. It suggests that people who made the choice themselves may have experienced cognitive dissonance during the experience phase. Brown and Feinberg (2002) have done extensive research on this topic.

(Condition 2) were in JE, and the experiencers (Conditions 3 and 4) were in pure SE.

This finding has potentially important implications for the extensive economic literature on principals and agents. Agents make decisions for principals. For example, lawyers (agents) make legal decisions for their clients (principals); parents (agents) make marital decisions for their children (principals); policy makers (agents) make policy decisions for their constituents (principals; e.g., Shafir, 2002). The agents are the choosers; the principals are the experiencers. Previous literature has identified various reasons why agents may make poor choices: For example, they have different tastes from the principals; they have ulterior motivations. Our theory and data suggest that even if the agents are well intended and have tastes similar to their principals, they may still make poor choices, because the agents are usually in JE and the principals are usually in SE.

In an article on fairness, Kahneman, Knetsch, and Thaler (1986) made a similar point about consumers and theorists. They observed that when consumers judge the fairness of an event, they rarely compare it with other events, but when theorists study fairness, they compare alternative scenarios. Consequently, theorists focus too much on factors that seem salient in comparison but have little influence on consumers' fairness judgment.

The second finding – that people make suboptimal choices for themselves – comes from a comparison between the choices of people who made the choices for themselves and their own subsequent experiences (Condition 1). This result is a less direct test of our theory but is nevertheless intriguing. Here, the experiencers were the choosers themselves, and they had already seen both options when they experienced the chosen option. In this sense, their experience was not in pure SE; they may have had some memory of the foregone option. However, despite the possible memory effect, the respondents were still happier with the positive-task/small-reward option during the experience phase. It suggests that experience is naturally an SE process.

We address a few potential alternative explanations here. First, the choosers had not experienced the task or eaten the chocolate when they made the choice, but the experiencers had done both when they reported their experience and may have acquired more knowledge or developed adaptation. To address this concern, we asked the pure experiencers in Conditions 3 and 4 and the self-choosers in Condition 1 to predict their overall experience right before they started working on the task and eating the chocolate. These are SE predictions. The results were similar to the SE-experience results but in the opposite direction of the choice results: For the pure experiencers, $M = -0.65$ for the negative-task/large-reward option, and $M = 2.52$ for the positive-task/small-reward option; for the self-choosers, $M = 0.24$ for the negative-task/large-reward option, and $M = 2.44$ for the positive-task/small-reward option. These findings suggest that the choice–experience inconsistency is not a result of differential knowledge or adaptation.

Another potential alternative explanation for choice–experience inconsistency is that the choosers based their decision on considerations other than predicted happiness. This explanation implies that the choosers could have accurately predicted that the positive-task/small-reward option would provide better experience, yet for other reasons they chose the negative-task/large-reward option. If this explanation stands, then there should be an inconsistency between what people predict will provide a better experience and what people choose. To test this explanation, we ran another condition ($N = 33$). It was similar to Condition 2 (choice for others), except that the participants were asked to predict which option would make the other participants happier. What we found is that the prediction result was very similar to the choice result: Most (66%) of the respondents predicted that the negative-task/large-reward option would yield greater happiness than the positive-task/small-reward option. Thus, the choice–experience inconsistency in this study is chiefly a result of JE/SE misprediction, not a result of inconsistency between choice and predicted experience.[6]

Other Evidence for Mischoice

Recently, we replicated the result of the task–reward study using very different stimuli (Hsee & Zhang, 2003). The stimuli were two audiovisual episodes. Each episode consisted of a static image and a concurrent steady noise. The noise in the two episodes differed only in degree of loudness, 72 dB and 78 dB, and the images in the two episodes differed in quality, an ugly adult (in the softer noise episode) and a cute baby (in the louder noise episode):

	Noise	Picture
Episode A	72 dB	ugly adult
Episode B	78 dB	cute baby

As in Study 3, participants in the study were assigned to one of four conditions: choosers for self, choosers for others, pure experiencers of the soft-noise/ugly-picture episode, and pure experiencers of the loud-noise/cute-picture episode. The choosers were presented with samples from each episode and asked to compare the samples before making a choice (JE). The pure experiencers were presented with and experienced only one of the episodes (SE).

Because the noises in the two episodes differed only quantitatively, and the images differed qualitatively, we expected the noises to exert a greater impact on

---

[6] There may be another potential alternative explanation. Suppose that most people prefer the negative-task/large-reward option but their preference is very weak, and that a few people prefer the positive-task/small-reward option and their preference is strong. Then most people would choose the negative-task/large-reward option, but the mean experience ratings may be higher for the other option. However, this explanation is not likely for this study. First, there is no reason to believe that those who prefer the negative-task/large-reward option have a weaker preference than those who prefer the positive-task/small-reward option. Second, this explanation is inconsistent with the finding that people in JE overpredicted the impact of the reward but did not overpredict the impact of the tasks.

choice than on experience. The results confirmed our expectation and are very similar to those in Study 3. Both the choosers for self and the choosers for others preferred the soft-noise/ugly-picture option, but both the pure experiencers who had not seen both options and people who had seen both options and made a choice for themselves were happier with the loud-noise/cute-picture option.

This study was a strategic replication of Study 3. The two studies used very different attributes: One used positive and negative life events, and one used pleasant and unpleasant pictures. One used small and large chocolates, and one used loud and soft noises. Despite these differences, the two studies revealed the same pattern of choice–experience inconsistency.

GENERAL DISCUSSION

When people predict the experiential impact of alternative values or choose between alternative options, they are in JE, but people who eventually experience the value or the option are usually in SE. The present research shows that JE and SE can lead to systematically different results. Generally speaking, the utility function of an attribute is flatter in SE than in JE, except around the reference point. When people in JE make predictions or choices, they do not spontaneously adjust for this difference; instead, they project their preferences in JE onto their predictions and choices for experiences in SE. As a result, they overweight differences that seem distinct in JE but are actually inconsequential in SE.

The present research contributes to the existing affective forecasting literature by identifying evaluation mode as a source for overprediction. Furthermore, our research not only accounts for overprediction but also specifies when people do not overpredict. Finally, our research extends the misprediction findings to something that has a behavioral consequence – mischoice.

In the remainder of the chapter, we first discuss the relationship between the present research and several other lines of research we recently conducted. Then we discuss ways to improve prediction and reduce choice–experience inconsistency. Finally, we discuss the implications of this work for research on subjective well-being.

Relationship With Evaluability

The JE/SE analysis we present in this chapter builds on the evaluability hypothesis proposed by Hsee (1996a, 1998, 2000) and Hsee et al. (1999). In fact, the shape of the SE evaluation function depicted in Figure 28.1 is adapted from Hsee et al. (1999). The evaluability hypothesis was developed to explain preference reversals between JE and SE (e.g., Bazerman, Loewenstein, & White, 1992; González-Vallejo & Moran, 2001; Hsee, 1996a, 1998; Kahneman, Ritov, & Schkade, 1999; Moore, 1999; Nowlis & Simonson, 1997; Shafir, 2002; Sunstein, Kahneman, Schkade, & Ritov, 2002). In a typical JE/SE reversal study reported by Hsee (1996a), for example, two job candidates for a computer programming position were evaluated in either JE or SE. The two candidates involved a trade-off along two attributes – experience in a special computer language and grade point average (GPA). In JE, people were willing to pay more for the more experienced candidate; but in SE, people were willing to pay more for the higher GPA candidate. According to the evaluability hypothesis, GPA is independently easier to evaluate for student respondents than is programming experience. Thus, in SE, the respondents based their judgment on GPA. In JE, the respondents could directly compare the two candidates' experience levels. The comparison made the experience attribute easier to evaluate and hence gave it more weight. (For information on other theories of preference reversals, see, e.g., Fischer, Carmon, Ariely, & Zauberman, 1999; Irwin, 1994; Mellers, Chang, Birnbaum, & Ordóñez, 1992; Nowlis & Simonson, 1997; Tversky, Sattath, & Slovic, 1988. For a review, see Hsee, Zhang, & Chen, 2004.)

The original evaluability hypothesis focuses on the difference between independently easy-to-evaluate attributes and independently difficult-to-evaluate attributes. The present research assumes that most attributes are neither impossible to evaluate independently nor perfectly easy to evaluate independently. If an attribute were impossible to evaluate independently, its SE curve would be flat in all regions. If an attribute were perfectly easy to evaluate independently, its SE curve would collapse with its JE curve. For most attributes, which lie between these two extreme cases, the SE curve is flatter than the JE curve in most regions, except around the reference point. This is the case we depict in Figure 28.1 and study in this chapter.

The present research extends the evaluability and JE/SE reversal research in several important directions. First, the original evaluability hypothesis posits that whether or not an attribute has a greater impact on JE than on SE depends on whether the attribute is independently difficult to evaluate. The present research shows that whether or not an attribute has a greater impact on JE than on SE depends on whether the values of the attribute under consideration involve a quantitative difference or a qualitative difference. As Study 1 and Study 2 show, even for the same attribute, values in different regions could have either greater impact in JE than in SE or similar impact between JE and SE, depending on whether these values are quantitatively different or qualitatively different. The concepts of quantitative/qualitative differences add greater specificity and operationalism to the original evaluability hypothesis.

Second, the original evaluability and JE/SE research was not concerned about affective forecasting and did not ask respondents in JE to predict their or other people's feelings in SE. Therefore, the responses of people in JE, though different from those of people in SE, could not be considered biased. The present research is concerned about affective forecasting and asks people in JE to predict their or other people's feelings in SE. Therefore, the predictions of people in JE, which are different from the experiences of people in SE, can be considered biased. This bias has not been demonstrated in the original JE/SE literature.

Finally, the present research extends JE/SE reversal to choice–experience inconsistency. We believe that choice–experience inconsistency is a more important finding than a mere JE/SE reversal. To appreciate this point, let us consider a distinction Kahneman (1994) and others (see also Hammond, 1996a; Hsee et al., 2004; Sen, 1993) have drawn between internal inconsistency and substantive inconsistency of decisions. *Internal inconsistencies* refer to findings that normatively inconsequential manipulations can change people's preferences; they show that preferences are labile. *Substantive inconsistencies* refer to findings that people fail to choose what is best for them; they show that decisions are suboptimal. The JE/SE reversal, as documented in the existing literature, is an internal inconsistency. The choice–experience inconsistency, as studied in the present research, is a substantive inconsistency.

Relationship With Lay Rationalism and Medium Maximization

So far, we have focused on distinction bias as the main cause of choice–experience inconsistency. Here, we mention two other related lines of research we recently conducted: lay rationalism and medium maximization. *Lay rationalism* (Hsee, Zhang, et al., 2003) refers to a tendency to overweight attributes that appear rationalistic, such as quantity and economic value, and downplay attributes that appear subjective. For example, when participants were asked whether they would choose a small chocolate in the shape of a heart or a large chocolate in the shape of a cockroach, most opted for the large one. However, when asked which they would enjoy more, most favored the small one.

Medium maximization (Hsee, Yu, et al., 2003) refers to a tendency to focus on specious immediate payoffs rather than the ultimate consequence of one's action. For example, when participants were asked to choose between a short task that would award 60 points and a long task that would award 100 points and were told that the points had no other use except that with 60 points they could receive a vanilla ice cream and with 100 points they could receive a pistachio ice cream (of equal amount), most chose the long task. However, when asked which type of ice cream they preferred, most favored the one corresponding to the short task (vanilla).

In theory, distinction bias is orthogonal to lay rationalism and medium maximization. Distinction bias is about failure to make accurate predictions and is a result of the JE/SE difference. Lay rationalism and medium maximization are about failure to follow predictions and are not due to the JE/SE difference. In reality, however, these three factors can simultaneously lead to a choice–experience inconsistency. For example, suppose that a person chooses a tedious job that pays $70,000 a year over an interesting job that pays $60,000 a year and that her long-term happiness would actually be higher if she chose the lower paying job. Her decision to choose the higher paying job may result from three possible causes: First, she overpredicts the difference in happiness between the two salaries – an example of distinction bias. Second, she finds it more "rational" to base her choice on salary than on interest – a manifestation of lay rationalism. Finally, she focuses on the immediate payoff rather than the ultimate experiential consequences of her choice – an instance of medium maximization.

Ways to Improve Predictions and Decisions

The following story, from Hsee (2000), suggests a choice–experience inconsistency due to the distinction bias and provides a context in which to explore possible remedies. A person was shopping for a pair of high-end speakers in an audio store. He was particularly interested in one of two equally expensive models. He found the appearance of one model very attractive and compatible with his furniture and the appearance of the other model ugly and incompatible with his furniture. A salesperson encouraged him to compare the sound quality of the two models in a soundproof audition room. Through careful comparisons he found the sound quality of the ugly model slightly but distinctively better, and he bought the ugly model. But soon after he had brought the speakers home, he became so annoyed with their appearance that he relegated these speakers to the basement.

This story implies a choice–experience inconsistency: The person chose to buy the better-sounding/ugly-looking model, but he would probably have been happier had he bought the worse-sounding/good-looking model. This example also supports our theory: The subtle difference in sound quality was only a matter of degree and probably would make no difference in SE experience, but the difference seemed distinct in JE and apparently dictated his choice. This is a classic distinction bias.

How could we minimize the choice–experience inconsistency? To reduce choice–experience inconsistency, choosers not only need to predict their future experiences before making a choice but also need to simulate SE in making predictions. The closer the prediction is to SE, the more accurate it will be.

To illustrate, consider three possible ways the salesperson could have asked the speaker buyer to predict his preference for two sets of speakers:

1. The salesperson puts the two sets of speakers side by side and allows the buyer to easily compare their sound with the push of a button on a remote control. The salesperson asks the buyer, "Compare them carefully. Which set do you enjoy more?" This method is very similar to what the salesperson actually did in the example.

2. The same as No. 1, except that the salesperson gives different instructions: "Focus on one set of speakers first. Study it carefully and think about how much you enjoy it. Write down your overall impression. After that, focus on the other set. Study it carefully and think about how much you enjoy it. Write down your overall impression."

3. The salesperson puts the two sets of speakers in different rooms and prevents the buyer from making direct comparisons. The salesperson first leads the buyer to one room and tells the buyer, "Focus on this set of speakers. Study it carefully and think about how much you enjoy it. Write down your overall impression." The salesperson then sends the buyer away for a cup of tea. Afterward, the salesperson leads the buyer to the other room and repeats the procedure for the other pair of speakers.

Of the three cases, the first is closest to JE, and the last is closest to SE. Specifically, in the first case, both the presentation of the stimuli and the process of prediction are in JE. In the second case, the presentation of the stimuli is still in JE, but the process of prediction is closer to SE. In the last case, both the presentation of the stimuli and the process of prediction are in SE.

We surmise that in the first case, the buyer is least likely to make the correct prediction and least likely to choose the model that will give him the best consumption experience and that in the last case, he is most likely to do so. Unfortunately, the common practice is much more similar to the first case than to the last case. Before making decisions, people either spontaneously engage in, or are encouraged by friends and professionals to engage in, direct comparisons of the choice alternatives. In fact, even decision experts encourage people to do so (e.g., Janis & Mann, 1977). In stark contrast with the traditional view, our advice is to refrain from direct comparison. To make a good prediction and a good choice for something that is to be consumed in SE, people should simulate SE in prediction and in choice.

Of course, we do not mean that people should always avoid JE during choice. Instead, we mean that people should align the evaluation mode of choice with the evaluation mode of consumption. Thus, if the consumption will take place in JE, people should engage in JE in choice. For example, suppose that a person is buying a dress that she will wear to a party, where people will naturally compare each others' dresses. Then she should engage in JE when she makes her purchase decision. If she does not engage in JE and instead she decides whether to buy a particular dress based on how good the dress looks by itself rather than how good the dress looks in comparison with other dresses, then she may fail to buy the dress that would give her the greatest happiness at the party.

Another situation in which one should conduct JE in choice is when the objective of the choice is to maximize some other value than consumption experience, and JE is more likely than SE to identify the option that would maximize that value. For example, suppose that a person working in the admissions office of a college wants to recruit students who have the greatest academic potential. In this case, JE of all applicants is more likely than SE to identify such students, and the person should adopt JE. Generally speaking, if the purpose of one's decision is to maximize consumption experience, and the consumption will take place in SE, then the decision maker should simulate SE when making the decision.

Implications for Happiness Research
For most people, the pursuit of subjective well-being, or broadly defined happiness, is an ultimate goal of life. In recent years, both psychologists and economists have made significant contributions to the understanding of happiness (e.g., Argyle, 1987; Diener, 2000; Diener, Scollon, & Lucas, 2003; Diener, Suh, Lucas, & Smith, 1999; Easterlin, 1974, 2001; Frank, 1997; Frey & Stutzer, 2000, 2002a, 2002b; Kahneman, 2000; Kahneman, Diener, & Schwarz, 1999; Kim-Prieto, Diener, Tamir, Scollon, & Diener, 2005; Myers, 1993; Ryan & Deci, 2001;

Scitovsky, 1976; Seligman, 2002; Seligman & Csikszentmihalyi, 2000; Strack, Argyle, & Schwarz, 1991).

Among other things, the literature has documented three robust findings: First, virtually everyone prefers more money to less money. Second, across generations, when individuals' wealth has steadily increased, happiness has not. Finally, at a given time in a given society, wealthy people are happier than less wealthy people, but the correlation is small. These findings, especially the latter two, have received various explanations, including adaptation and rising aspirations (e.g., Brickman, Coates, & Janoff-Bulman, 1978; Diener et al., 1999; Diener, Tamir, et al., 2003; Easterlin, 2001; Frederick & Loewenstein, 1999; van Praag, 2003).

We offer an additional, and not necessarily alternative, explanation for these findings. First, why do people prefer more money to less money? When choosing whether to have more or less wealth, they are in JE of different wealth scenarios, and so their evaluation curve resembles the generally steeper JE curve in Figure 28.1. More wealth is obviously better.

Second, why has happiness not increased across generations when wealth has? For example, why is the happiness of the average person in the 1990s similar to the happiness of the average person in the 1970s, even though the person in the 1990s possesses more wealth than the person in the 1970s? According to our theory, when people report their happiness, they are mostly in SE of their states, including their financial states, and they do not spontaneously compare across generations. Thus, the wealth-to-happiness function resembles our SE curve in Figure 28.1. Except at very low wealth levels, the evaluation curve is largely flat. (Even if some people do compare their wealth with the wealth of a previous generation, this effect will be a constant and will not make a later generation happier than a previous generation. For example, suppose that some people in the 1990s compared their wealth with that of people in the 1970s and felt happy. Then some people in the 1970s would also have compared their wealth with that of people in the 1950s and also felt happy. Such comparisons, if any, would not make people in the 1990s happier than people in the 1970s.)

Finally, why at a given time in a given society are wealthy people somewhat happier than less wealthy people? That is because at a given time within a given society people may occasionally compare themselves with each other, and therefore their happiness has an element of JE. (For example, people may say, "I feel awful, because my neighbor recently bought a global positioning system for his new Jaguar, but I do not even have enough money to fix the muffler of my old Dodge.") However, we believe that in most situations, people do not engage in such comparisons; instead, they mostly mind their own states and experience their own lives as in SE. This probably is why, even at a given time and within a given society, the correlation between wealth and happiness is rather small.

In a recent article, van Praag (2003) made an insightful distinction between a virtual welfare (happiness) function and a true welfare (happiness) function.

The *virtual welfare function* represents people's evaluations of different fictitious income levels. The *true welfare function* represents people's evaluations of their own income levels. According to van Praag, the virtual welfare function is generally steeper than the true welfare function. This proposition is consistent with ours. In our terms, the virtual welfare function represents JE of alternative income levels and resembles the steeper JE curve in Figure 28.1, and the true welfare function represents SE of people's own incomes and therefore resembles the flatter SE curve in Figure 28.1. Van Praag made another important argument: The virtual welfare function reflects how individuals evaluate different income levels when making a decision and describes the decision utility of incomes. In contrast, the true welfare function reflects how individuals experience their incomes in reality and describes the experienced utility of incomes. This analysis corroborates our assertion that decisions are based on JE of alternative scenarios, and experiences reflect SE of actual outcomes.

Happiness researchers have also tried to determine what factors affect happiness and what factors do not. For example, Easterlin (2003) recently observed that factors such as whether a person is in good or poor health and whether a person is married or widowed have greater effects on happiness than material factors such as income and home size (see also Frey & Stutzer, 2003; McLanahan & Sorensen, 1984; Myers, 1993). These effects may be multiply determined. One likely explanation is differential adaptation: It is more difficult to adapt to poor health or widowhood than to wealth (Easterlin, 2003). Another potential explanation is our analysis on qualitative and quantitative differences. Differences such as whether a person is in good or poor health and whether a person is married or divorced are qualitative and have a significant impact on happiness. On the other hand, differences such as whether a person earns $60,000 or $70,000 a year and whether a person lives in a 3,000- or 4,000-ft^2 home – as long as these differences do not cross a reference point – are merely quantitative and have less impact on happiness. More importantly, our theory suggests that in making decisions, people are more likely to overestimate the impact of factors such as income and home size than to overestimate the impact of factors such as health and marriage. We hope that our theory can help people make better predictions and happier choices.

ACKNOWLEDGMENTS

We thank Ed Diener, Ayelet Fishbach, David Schkade, and Fang Yu for their comments on early versions of this article; Dan Gilbert for comments on early versions of this article that were given outside of the review process; and the University of Chicago and China Europe International Business School for research support.

29. Lay Rationalism and Inconsistency Between Predicted Experience and Decision

Christopher K. Hsee, Jiao Zhang, Frank Yu, and Yiheng Xi

Traditional decision theorists assume that when choosing between options that have the same costs, decision makers analyze which option will deliver the highest expected outcome utility and choose that option. This is a consequentialist utility analysis approach. In reality, people rarely base their decisions strictly on this approach.

In recent years, behavioral decision theorists have proposed that choices are often driven by decision makers' affect toward the choice options (e.g., Frederick, 2002; Hsee & Rottenstreich, 2004; Kahneman, Schkade, & Sunstein, 1998; Loewenstein, 1996; Loewenstein, Weber, Hsee, & Welch, 2001; Rottenstreich & Hsee, 2001; Slovic, Finucane, Peters, & MacGregor, 2002), and that such affect-driven decisions often lead to different choices than the consequentialist utility analysis would prescribe. For example, when choosing between two equally expensive computers, one with a faster processor and the other having a more appealing color, decision makers may focus more on the color of the computers than warranted by a careful consequentialist utility analysis. It appears that decisions are not "cold" enough.

In the present research, we suggest that decisions may be too "cold." Decision makers may give too much weight to "rationalistic" factors by the consequentialist benchmark. Rationalistic factors are attributes, such as economic value, size, quantity, numerical specifications, and functions.[1] At the end of the chapter, we discuss when people overweight rationalistic attributes and when they underweight these attributes, and how to reconcile the present research with research on affect-driven and impulsive decisions. For the time being, we will elaborate on our theory and show that it is possible for decisions to be too cold.

Our research focuses on situations where the choice options have a well-defined consumption period, are predicted to induce different experiences during the consumption period, and do not have any other consequentialist differences (such as differences in future costs or benefits). In such situations, the

---

[1] "Rationalistic" does not mean "rational." The word "rational" is loaded with too many interpretations, and we avoid using this word in this chapter.

Originally published in the *Journal of Behavioral Decision Making*, vol. 16, pp. 257–272. Copyright © 2003 John Wiley & Sons, Ltd. Reproduced by permission of John Wiley & Sons Limited.

consequentialist utility analysis is reduced to a prediction of which option will deliver the best experience during the consumption period. According to this analysis, the decision maker should consider an attribute only to the extent that it affects predicted consumption experience. In other words, the decision makers should predict which option will bring the best consumption experience and base their decisions strictly on their predictions. If people indeed resort to this consequentialist analysis, there should be no inconsistency between predicted experience and decision.

In reality, decision makers may not spontaneously make such predictions, and even if they do, they may not strictly base their decisions on such predictions. We propose that decision makers have a tendency to resist affective influence and to rely on rationalistic attributes to make their decisions. We refer to this tendency as *lay rationalism*. Specifically, if one group of people are asked to predict which option in a choice set will bring the best consumption experience and another group of people are asked to indicate which option they will choose, there may be a *predicted-experience-versus-decision inconsistency*, and the inconsistency will be in a systematic direction: Decision makers give more weight to rationalistic attributes than do experience predictors.

The remainder of the chapter is organized as follows. In the next three sections, we identify and study three specific manifestations of lay rationalism: (a) lay economism (focus on economic values), (b) lay scientism (focus on hard rather than soft attributes), and (c) lay functionalism (focus on main function or objective). Table 29.1 summarizes the general theme of this chapter and the three specific manifestations.

In each section, we present evidence for predicted-experience-versus-decision inconsistencies. Then we discuss the significance and potential problems of using predicted-experience-versus-decision inconsistency to study lay rationalism and suggest alternative methods. We also review the relevant literature and discuss the relationship between our notion of lay rationalism and the literature on rule-based and reason-based choice. We conclude with an integrative framework that reconciles the present research and research on affective and impulsive decisions.

LAY ECONOMISM

Lay economism urges decision makers to focus on economic calculus and choose the option that entails the greatest (perceived) economic gains. Some attributes are more central to economic calculus than others. For example, the size and the price of a pizza are more central to economic calculus than its shape, color, or taste. Lay economism implies that when the choice options involve a tradeoff between an attribute central to economic calculus and another attribute less central to economic calculus but still important for consumption experience, people will assign more weight to the attribute central to economic calculus in their decision than in their prediction of consumption experience.

Table 29.1. A Summary of the Main Propositions

		Decision Makers Tend to Focus on the Following Factors:	Decision Makers Tend to Downplay the Following Factors:
General Thesis	Lay Rationalism	Rationalistic Factors	Hedonistic Factors
Specific manifestations	Lay economism	Total/absolute economic payoff	Factors unrelated to total or absolute economic value but still important for consumption experience, such as trend, social comparision, etc.
	Lay scientism	Hard (objective and unequivocal) attributes	Soft (subjective and malleable) attributes
	Lay functionalism	Primary function or primary objective	Factors unrelated to primary function or objective but still important for consumption experience

This effect has been explored in a study reported by Hsee (1999). Research participants were asked to imagine that they could receive a piece of chocolate as the prize for winning a lottery and could choose either a smaller and less expensive (0.5 oz./$0.50) chocolate that was in the shape of a heart, or a larger and more expensive (2 oz./$2.00) chocolate that was in the shape of a cockroach. A predicted-experience-versus-decision inconsistency emerged: When asked to predict which chocolate they would more enjoy eating, most respondents favored the heart-shaped one, but when asked which one they would choose, most picked the roach-shaped one. We interpret these results as evidence for lay economism.

In this section, we report two other studies. Each examines an instance of lay economism. The first study examines the tendency to focus on absolute economic gains over temporal comparisons. The second study examines the tendency to focus on absolute economic gains over social comparisons.

Dinner Set Study

Respondents (143 students from a Midwestern university in the United States) were asked to imagine that they had won a sweepstakes and could choose one of two prizes, each entitling them to a set of four free dinners. The recipient could consume only one free dinner in each of the following 4 weeks. Each prize specified the monetary values of the dinners they could have and the sequence in which they had to consume these dinners

PRIZE A:

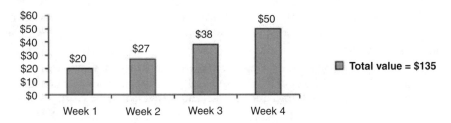

Total value = $135

PRIZE B:

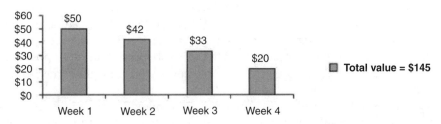

Total value = $145

Figure 29.1. Stimuli for the dinner set study.

in the following 4 weeks. These specifications were conveyed through graphs (Figure 29.1).

Note that the values of individual meals were increasing in Prize A and decreasing in Prize B, but the total value was lower in Prize A than in Prize B. Half of the respondents were asked to predict which set of dinners they would enjoy more in the next 4 weeks, and the other half were asked to indicate which set they would choose.

From the consequentialist utility-analysis perspective, both the total value of the dinners and their temporal sequence are valid cues to predict the enjoyment of these dinners. Specifically, expensive dinners are usually more enjoyable than inexpensive dinners, and improving sequences are usually more enjoyable than decreasing sequences (e.g., Ariely, 1998; Hsee & Abelson, 1991; Kahneman, Fredrickson, Schreiber, & Redelmeier, 1993; Loewenstein & Prelec, 1993). Therefore, from the consequentialist perspective, people should use both of these attributes to predict the enjoyment of each dinner set and choose the one with the greater predicted overall enjoyment. There should be no predicted-experience-versus-decision inconsistency. However, we expected an inconsistency. Because total value is central to economic calculus and temporal sequence is not, we expected that the respondents would give more weight to the total-value attribute in their decision than in their prediction of consumption experience. The results confirmed our expectation. Of the respondents asked to predict enjoyment, only 32% favored the descending, more expensive option (B). But of the respondents asked to choose one set of dinners, 51% opted for that option, $\chi^2(1, N = 143) = 5.30, p = 0.024$.

Office Study

Like temporal sequence, social comparison (i.e., whether one gets more or less than a similar other) also plays an important role in people's experience. However, just as decision makers emphasize absolute economic gains over temporal patterns, decision makers emphasize absolute economic gains over social comparisons. Specifically, suppose that people are faced with two options, one superior on absolute payoff to oneself and the other superior on the relative payoff between self and others. Compared with what people predict would bring the better experience, people will be more likely to choose the option superior on absolute payoff.

This effect was originally demonstrated in a study by Tversky and Griffin (1991). Participants evaluated hypothetical job offers from two companies. One company offered them more money ($35,000) but offered their colleagues even more ($38,000). The other company offered them less salary ($33,000) but offered their colleagues even less ($30,000). When asked to predict feelings, most predicted greater happiness by working at the lower-paying job. But when asked to make a decision, most opted for the higher-paying job.

We interpret these results as evidence for lay economism in decision making. However, these results are susceptible to an alternative explanation: The perceptions of fairness affected only one's feelings at the job, but the money earned from the job could be used long after one left the job. In feeling-predictions respondents were asked only about their feelings at the job, but in decisions respondents may have taken a longer-term perspective.

This kind of alternative explanation is difficult to eliminate altogether in research on predicted-experience-versus-decision inconsistency. Whenever an inconsistency is observed, a critic may always say that the options entail other consequentialist differences than predicted experiences. In this research we try our best to avoid this criticism by using stimuli that do not have other consequentialist differences beyond a specified period. The following study is a replication of Tversky and Griffin (1991) in a context with this intention in mind.

Participants (116 students from a Southern university and a Midwestern university in the United States) were asked to imagine that they planned to work for 1 year before returning to college and had received two offers, which were identical in compensation and workload. The only differences were in office size. The participants read:

Company A gives you a small (100-sq-ft) office and gives another employee (who has similar qualifications to you) an equally small office. Company B gives you a medium size (170-sq-ft) office but gives another employee (who has similar qualifications to you) a large (240-sq-ft) office.

Notice that unlike income from salary, which could be used after one leaves the job, the size of one's office can only be enjoyed at work and has the same "consumption period" as the fairness attribute (colleague's office size). Even so, we replicated Tversky and Griffin's (1991) predicted-experience-versus-decision inconsistency. Of the respondents in the prediction condition, only 34% predicted greater happiness in Company B (with medium office for self and larger office for others), but of the respondents in the decision condition, 57% chose to work at that company, $\chi^2(1, N = 116) = 6.46$, $p = 0.011$. Although an office is not money, it reflects a tangible material benefit, like salary and prize, and is in this sense an economic gain. Therefore, the result of this study supports lay economism.

Discussion of Lay Economism

Lay economism represents a tendency in decision makers to act like a lay economist – to focus on economic calculus, to compare options in terms of economic gains and losses, and to downplay other experience-inducing factors, such as temporal trends and social comparisons. Ironically, what a lay economist would do may be quite the opposite of what a real economist would recommend. No right-minded real economist would say that one should choose the job with a bigger office if one is not happy or that one should choose the more expensive, roach-shaped chocolate if one would not enjoy it. The lay economist may well be more concerned with economic gains and losses than what the real economist would recommend.

LAY SCIENTISM

Lay scientism urges decision makers to base their choice on "hard attributes" rather than "soft attributes." We define hard and soft attributes as follows: When two options differ on a certain attribute, if it is (or perceived to be) objective and unequivocal as to which option is better, then this attribute is a hard attribute. If it is (or perceived to be) subjective and malleable as to which option is better, then it is a soft attribute. For example, the resolution of a digital camera is a hard attribute. Ceteris paribus, a 5-megapixel camera is unequivocally better than a 3-megapixel camera. On the other hand, the taste of a coffee is a soft attribute. It is a matter of personal taste whether one likes the taste of one coffee or the taste of another. The distinction between hard and soft attributes is similar, but not identical, to such other distinctions in the literature as quantitative versus qualitative attributes (e.g., González-Vallejo, Erev, & Wallsten, 1994; Viswanathan & Narayanan, 1994; Yalch & Yalch, 1984), comparable versus enriched attributes (Nowlis & Simonson's, 1997), and search attributes versus experiential attributes (Wright & Lynch, 1995).

Lay scientism implies that people will place more weight on the hard attribute relative to the soft attribute in decision than in prediction of consumption experience. The following study demonstrates this effect.

Stereo Study

Respondents (563 students from two Midwestern universities, two Southern universities and one West Coast university in the United States) were asked to imagine that they were shopping for a stereo system and had narrowed their choices to two equally expensive Sony models. The two models involved a tradeoff between sound richness and power.

To half of the respondents, sound richness was described as a subjective (soft) attribute and power as an objective (hard) attribute. The respondents read,

You listened to both models. You found Sony A's sound richer than Sony B's, and personally you liked Sony A's rich sound. However, Sony B is much more powerful than Sony A: Sony B has 150 watts/channel whereas Sony A has only 50 watts/channel. The power of a stereo is an objective measure. In contrast, whether the sound of a stereo is rich or not is purely subjective.

To the other half of the respondents, sound richness was described as an objective (hard) attribute and power as a subjective (soft) attribute. The respondents read,

On a certain scale (where greater numbers indicate richer sound), Sony A is rated 150, whereas Sony B is rated only 50. However, you listened to both models. You found Sony B's sound "more powerful" than Sony A's, and personally you liked Sony B's powerful sound. The sound richness rating is an objective measure. In contrast, whether a stereo sounds powerful or not is purely subjective.

We expected an inconsistency between predicted enjoyment and decision in both conditions, but in opposite directions. Indeed, in the condition where power was the hard attribute, more people favored the more powerful model in decision than in enjoyment prediction. In the condition where sound richness was the hard attribute, fewer people favored the more powerful model in decision than in predicted enjoyment (see Figure 29.2). An analysis combining both conditions reveals a significant 2 (whether power or sound richness was the hard attribute) × 2 (prediction vs. decision) interaction effect, $\chi^2(1, N = 563) = 5.83, p = .016$.

Discussion of Lay Scientism
Lay scientism reflects the tendency in decision makers to trust hard facts and discount soft preferences. There are two related underlying reasons for this

Figure 29.2. Percentages of respondents favoring the more powerful model.

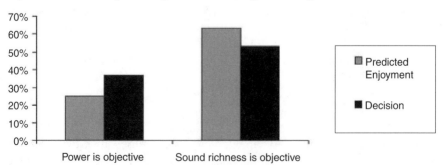

tendency. First, making a decision on the basis of a hard attribute seems more objective and scientific, and hence more justifiable. Second, there is greater certainty in the relative desirability of the choice options on the hard attribute than on the soft attribute; therefore, it is safer to base the decision on the hard attribute.

LAY FUNCTIONALISM

Lay functionalism urges decision makers to focus on the primary objective or function of the choice options and not to be distracted by factors unrelated to the primary objective or function, even if they are still important for consumption experience. For example, the primary objective for going to school is to get an education. Thus, if a student is admitted by two schools, one providing a better education (e.g., Yale) and the other located in a more attractive city (e.g., Hawaii), lay functionalism would advise the student to attend the school that provides the better education. Likewise, the primary function of a pain reliever is to relieve pain. Thus, if a patient has the choice of a more effective pain reliever that tastes bitter or a less effective pain reliever that tastes sweet, lay functionalism would advise the patient to choose the more effective pain reliever. In these situations, lay functionalism seems quite right. Indeed, lay functionalism is often taught by parents to their children and by teachers to their students.

However, in many other situations, choice options may involve attributes that are unrelated to the primary objective or function but are nevertheless very important to the overall consumption experience. In these situations, lay functionalism may lead decision makers to underweight these attributes. The following studies demonstrate this effect.

Television Study

Respondents (94 students from a Midwestern university in the United States) were asked to imagine that they were shopping for a TV on the Internet and were interested in two models that were equally large and equally expensive. They were also told that:

A reliable consumer survey company has rated those TVs on two attributes (picture quality and sound quality) on a scale from 40 (poor) to 100 (perfect). Their ratings are as follows:

	Picture quality	Sound quality
Model A	85	90
Model B	90	75

Presumably, in purchasing a TV, having good picture quality is a more important objective than having good sound quality. This assumption was verified in a pretest where 100% of the 25 respondents considered picture quality as more important than sound quality in purchasing a TV.

From the consequentialist utility-analysis perspective, buyers should base their choice on their prediction of which TV will deliver the better overall consumption experience. However, we expected that people would weigh picture quality more in decision than in prediction of consumption experience and thus exhibit a predicted-experience-versus-decision inconsistency. The results confirmed the prediction. When asked to predict which TV they would enjoy more when using it, only 24% of the respondents picked Model B (the one with the better picture quality), but when asked to make a purchase decision, 45% of the respondents chose Model B, $\chi^2(1, N = 94) = 4.31$, $p = .038$.[2]

Castle-Village Study

This is a replication of the TV study with the priority of objectives empirically manipulated. Respondents (116 students from a Midwestern university in the United States) were asked to imagine they were choosing between two bus tours in Austria, which would take them to see a village and a castle. Half of the respondents were told that their primary objective in joining the tour was to see a castle and the other half were told that their primary objective was to see a village. In the castle-as-primary-objective condition, the expected qualities of the two bus tours, in terms of an informed friend's ratings on 1 (worst) to 10 (best) scales, are as follows:

	Castle	Village
Tour A	6	9
Tour B	8	4

The village-as-primary-goal condition was identical to the castle-as-primary-goal condition except that participants were told that their primary goal was to see the village and the labels of castle and village in the previous display were swapped.

As predicted, in both conditions the option better serving the primary goal was favored more in decision than in predicted enjoyment. Specifically, in the castle-as-primary-goal condition, more people favored the better-castle tour in decision than in predicted enjoyment, but in the village-as-primary-goal condition, fewer people favored the better-castle tour in decision than in predicted enjoyment (see Figure 29.3). When combined, the two conditions yield a significant interaction between objective (castle versus village) and response (predicted enjoyment versus decision), $\chi^2(1, N = 116) = 7.53$, $p = .006$.

---

[2] The reader may wonder why only 24% of the respondents expected greater enjoyment from the better-picture model. That is because the better-picture model was only slightly better in picture (90 versus 85 on the 100-point scale) than the better-sound model, but the better-sound model was considerably better in sound (90 versus 75 on the 100-point scale) than the better-picture model.

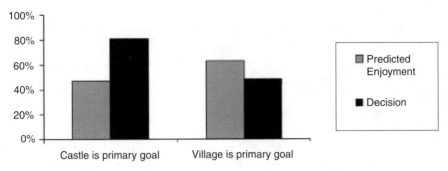

Figure 29.3. Percentages of respondents favoring the better castle tour.

Check Study

A variation of lay functionalism is the belief that in making decisions one should adopt the most efficient path to achieve the main objective and not be distracted by process-related considerations. This study illustrates this effect.

Respondents (136 students from a Midwestern university in the United States) were asked to assume that they had won $1,000 in a lottery conducted by Marshall Field's (a local department store) and that they could choose one of two ways to receive the money:

A.   You go to Marshall Field's downtown. They will give you a beautifully printed check for $1,000, with your name printed on it. You then deposit the check in your bank.

B.   Marshall Field's will directly wire the money to your bank. You don't get to see the check.

Presumably, the primary objective of the decision maker is to get the money. With respect to this objective, Method B is the more efficient option, although Method A yields more incidental pleasures from seeing the check. This assumption was verified in a pre-test where we asked 46 respondents whether seeing the check or efficiency in getting the money was more important to them in this scenario, and 76% of the respondents considered efficiency more important.

Of the respondents asked to predict whether they would feel happier if Method A were used or if Method B were used, only 46% predicted greater happiness if Method B (the more efficient method) were used. Of the respondents asked to choose one method, a significantly higher percentage – 63% – picked B, $\chi^2(1, N = 136) = 4.27, p = .039$.

Discussion of Lay Functionalism and Its Relationship With Lay Economism and Scientism

Lay functionalism represents a tendency in decision makers to be instrumental and functionalist. This tendency may lead decision makers to underweight factors that are important to their consumption experience but do not serve to fulfill their main objective. In a recent study, Chitturi, Raghunathan, and Mahajan (2003) found that when presented with a more functional cell phone and a better-looking cell phone, consumers often choose the more functional model, even though they like the better-looking model more and believe that the better-looking model is more expensive. These intriguing findings are consistent with our results.

Although we have presented the three cases of lay rationalism (lay economism, lay scientism, and lay functionalism) separately, they may share some inherent relationship. Both lay economism and lay scientism seem to stem from a general desire to base one's decision on things that are "real" – that is, substantive, material, and concrete, and not on factors that are ethereal or purely psychological. For example, getting a more expensive meal, getting a bigger office, or getting more wattage feels like a "real" gain, whereas the preference for a worse-to-better dinner sequence, for a fair treatment, or for a rich sound seems ethereal and purely psychological. Furthermore, people may also consider substantive gains as more important than psychological experiences. Therefore, lay economism and lay scientism may also be related to lay functionalism. This analysis suggests a hierarchical structure of the three special cases we have discussed within the general rubrics of lay rationalism.

COMMENTS ON PREDICTED-EXPERIENCE-VERSUS-DECISION INCONSISTENCY AND LAY RATIONALISM

So far, a predicted-experience-versus-decision inconsistency has been viewed as a means to demonstrate lay rationalism. In fact, such an inconsistency is important in its own right. In their seminal work, Kahneman and Snell (1990, 1992; Kahneman, 1994) made a distinction among three types of utilities – decision utility (as revealed by one's choice), experienced utility (feelings with the chosen option), and predicted utility (prediction of experienced utility). One of the most important questions for all decision theorists is when decision utility differs from experienced utility, that is, when people fail to choose the option leading to the best experience.

According to Kahneman and Snell (1990, 1992), there are two possible causes. One is an inconsistency between predicted utility and experienced utility. That is, decision makers may mispredict their experience and consider a less enjoyable option more enjoyable. The other is an inconsistency between predicted utility and decision utility. That is, decision makers may base their choice on factors other than predicted experience.

The last few decades have witnessed a large amount of research on the first type of inconsistency, about predicted and actual experience (e.g., Gilbert, Gill, & Wilson, 2002; Kahneman & Snell, 1990, 1992; Loewenstein & Frederick, 1997; Loewenstein & Schkade, 1999; March, 1978; Schkade & Kahneman, 1998). In contrast, there has been much less research on the second type of inconsistency, about predicted utility and decision utility. The present research, which studies predicted-experience-versus-decision inconsistencies, seeks to fill this gap.

We wish to mention that the predicted-experience-versus-decision inconsistency is not a choice-judgment preference reversal (e.g., Lichtenstein & Slovic, 1971; Slovic & Lichtenstein, 1968). In the choice-judgment preference reversal, choice is a dichotomous selection task and judgment is a numeric rating or value estimation task. In the predicted-experience-versus-decision inconsistency, both the prediction and the decision tasks are dichotomous selections.

Likewise, predicted-experience-versus-decision inconsistency is not a joint-separate evaluation reversal. In a joint-separate evaluation reversal (e.g., Bazerman, Moore, Tenbrunsel, Wade-Benzoni, & Blount, 1999; Hsee, 1996a), joint evaluation requires that two or more choice options are presented simultaneously and separate evaluation requires that only one choice option is presented at a time. In our predicted-experience-versus-decision inconsistency studies, both the prediction and the decision tasks are performed under the joint evaluation mode where the choice options are juxtaposed. Therefore, the predicted-experience-versus-decision inconsistency cannot be explained by theories for choice-judgment or joint-separate evaluation preference reversals.

Finally, we wish to suggest that lay rationalism is more likely to influence decisions that are elicited in joint evaluation than decisions elicited in separate evaluation. In separate evaluations, rationalistic attributes, such as economic value and quantitative specifications, are often difficult to evaluate (see Hsee, 1996a; Hsee, Loewenstein, Blount, & Bazerman, 1999, for further discussions on evaluability). For example, without a direct comparison, most people would not know how good a mini-stereo system is if it has 50 W or if it has 150 W. If one group of people are asked to decide whether they would buy the 50-W model and another group are asked to decide whether they would buy the 150-W model, that is, if the decisions are elicited in separate evaluation, the difference between 50 W and 150 W is unlikely to make a difference. Only in joint evaluation can people recognize the superiority of 150 W over 50 W, and choose the 150-W model. In other words, joint evaluation is a prerequisite for lay rationalism to influence decisions in this case.

OTHER WAYS TO STUDY LAY RATIONALISM

So far, we have used exclusively predicted-experience-versus-decision inconsistency to study lay rationalism. In this section we suggest several other potential methods. One is protocol analysis of what one thinks during the decision-making process. However, once learned and internalized, lay rationalism may operate automatically and may not be articulated in thought elicitations.

Another potential method is priming. For example, research participants may be asked to do an ostensibly unrelated task prior to the main decision-making task and asked to envision a rational economist or a hedonist gourmet in the ostensibly unrelated task. If the manipulation has any effect, its direction will be such that the subsequent decision will be more rationalistic after the economist priming. Moreover, we submit that such a priming manipulation will have a greater effect on decision than on predicted experience. Specifically, suppose that one runs a 3 (priming: accountant, gourmet, or no priming) × 2 (response: decision versus predicted experience) design. Our predictions are that the priming manipulation will have little effect on predicted experience but will have a greater impact on decision and that the decision will be more consistent with the predicted experience after the gourmet priming than after the economist priming. These predictions reflect our belief that predicted experiences are more stable than decisions.

A third method is to manipulate the need for justification. The notion of lay rationalism resonates with social psychological research showing that people like to make decisions in a way that appears justifiable. The desire for justification is documented when one is making a choice for others (e.g., Kray, 2000; Kray & Gonzales, 1999) and when one is expected to explain one's choice to others (e.g., Tetlock & Boettger, 1989; see Kunda, 1990, and Lerner & Tetlock, 1999, for reviews). The desire for justification is also observed when one is making the choice for oneself and is not expected to explain the choice to others (e.g., Bazerman et al., 1999; Bettman, Luce, & Payne, 1998; Hsee, 1995; Shafir, Simonson, & Tversky, 1993; Simonson, 1989; Soman & Cheema, 2001). Likewise, we expect that even if the need for justification is merely internal, decision makers will still try to be rationalistic.

We speculate that the need for self-justification arises not only when one makes the decision but also when one consumes the chosen option, especially if the option turns out to be undesirable. In other words, focusing on rationalistic attributes in decision making is an insurance against *anticipated* need for justification. If decision makers base their choices on rationalist factors, for example, if they base their choices on hard attributes, then even if the outcome turns out to be undesirable in the future, they could at least appease themselves by saying, "I made the best choice I could; it was the objectively best option." If this speculation is valid, then increasing the anticipated need for self-justification should accentuate the desire to resort to rationalistic factors in decision making. In the following study, we illustrate this effect in the case of lay scientism.

Hiring Study
Participants (79 students from a Midwestern university in the United States) were asked to imagine that they worked for the human resource department of a company and were helping the marketing department to fill a position that required two equally important qualifications: one-on-one communication skills and math skills. The respondents then read the following description,

which characterized communication skills as a soft attribute and math skills as a hard attribute:

There are two viable candidates. To assess their communication skills, you interviewed them yourself. To assess their math skills, you gave them a math test. In the interviews, you found Candidate A engaging and warm. Her answers were persuasive. Candidate B's answers were also good, but you did not find them as engaging as Candidate A's and you don't know why you had that feeling. As for the math test (highest score = 100), Candidate A scored 85 and Candidate B scored 95.

We manipulated the need for self-justification as follows. In the low-need-for-self-justification condition, respondents were asked to assume "you will return to school and will leave the company soon. You will probably never find out how well the person you hired performs in the company." In the high-need-for self-justification condition, the respondents were asked to imagine, "you will continue to work in the company and will soon find out how well the person you hired performs. If she does not perform well, you may ask yourself why you hired her instead of the other candidate." In both conditions, respondents were told that no one else would ask them to justify their decision.

The result reveals a significant difference between the two conditions: In the low-need-for-self-justification condition, only 12% of the respondents chose the better-math candidate, but in the high-need-for-self-justification condition, the percentage rose to 30%, $\chi^2(1, N = 79) = 3.87$, $p = .049$. We interpret this result as evidence for our proposition that decision makers give more credence to hard attributes when the need to justify their decisions is high than when the need is low.

GENERAL DISCUSSION

Lay Rationalism and Related Literature

Our research is inspired by prior research suggesting that people base their choices on rules and reasons (e.g., March, 1994; Prelec & Herrnstein, 1991; Simonson, 1989; Simonson & Nowlis, 2000) or easy-to-articulate reasons (e.g., Shafir, Simonson, & Tversky, 1993). Examples of such rules and reasons include "don't waste" (Arkes & Ayton, 1999; Arkes & Blumer, 1985), "seek variety" (e.g., Simonson, 1990), "don't buy stocks from obscure companies" (Barber, Heath, & Odean, 2002), "don't choose the same dish as your friends" (Ariely & Levav, 2000), and "don't pay for delays" (Amir & Ariely, in press), to name just a few. Sometimes, people may choose a rule-consistent option even if they prefer another option. This effect was revealed in a study on variety seeking (Simonson, 1990). Students were asked either to make candy selections for future consumption occasions or to make predictions for their preferences during those occasions. Those in the selection (decision) condition sought more variety than those in the preference-prediction condition. Our present research extends the existing research by focusing on lay rationalism, identifying its three key manifestations (economism, scientism, and functionalism) and documenting systematic inconsistencies between predicted and decision utilities.

Our notion of lay economism is also influenced by Thaler's (1985, 1999) transaction utility theory. According to Thaler, holding the predicted consumption utility and the current price of a product constant, consumers are more likely to purchase the product with a higher reference price. The reference price of a product may be its list price, perceived market price, and so forth. In essence, the transaction utility theory suggests that one's purchase decision is influenced not only by the predicted consumption utility of the product but also by the perceived economic gains or losses in the purchase. Indeed, purchasing something below its reference price is like achieving an economic gain, and purchasing something above its reference price is like suffering an economic loss. The present research on lay economism extends Thaler's original theory by showing that the pursuit of transaction utility is not limited to purchase decisions and can engender a predicted-experience-versus-decision inconsistency.

Another line of research that has inspired ours, especially our lay functionalism notion, is Tversky, Sattath, and Slovic's (1988) work on prominence. The prominence effect refers to the phenomenon that people assign more weight to the most important attribute of choice options when they are asked to make a choice (the choice condition) than when they are asked to fill in a missing attribute value in one of the options so that these options would appear equally attractive (the matching condition). There are at least two explanations for this phenomenon. One is compatiability (e.g., Fischer, Carmon, Ariely, & Zauberman, 1999; Fischer & Hawkins, 1993; Nowlis & Simonson, 1997; Tversky et al., 1988). This explanation is not germane to our research, because it requires one condition to involve a comparative response and the other condition a non-comparative response, but in our research both the decision and the predicted-experience conditions involve comparative choice responses. The other explanation is justification. According to Tversky et al. (1988), to base a decision on the most important attribute "provides a compelling argument for choice that can be used to justify the decision to oneself as well as to others" (p. 372). In this sense, lay functionalism and prominence reflect the same underlying principle.

Our notion of lay scientism may also underline the medium effect. When people make efforts, they often receive a "medium" (e.g., points or money), which they could trade for a desired outcome. Hsee, Yu, Zhang, and Zhang (2003) found that when choosing between options that award a medium, people would base their decisions on the face value of the medium rather than strictly on the desirability of the outcomes. Hsee et al. explain this effect in terms of psychological myopia, a tendency to focus on the immediate reward. Another potential contributor to the medium effect is lay scientism, a tendency to focus on hard attributes. Typically, the desirability of the final outcome is ambiguous but the amount of media (e.g., number of points) is clear.

A main theme of the present research is that decision makers underweight hot factors and overweight cold factors by the consequentialist utility-analysis benchmark. This theme echoes the celebrated work by Wilson and his colleagues. These authors found that people asked to analyze reasons before making a decision are less likely to choose the option they will like later on than people not asked to analyze reasons (e.g., Wilson, Dunn, Kraft, & Lisle, 1989; Wilson, Hodges, & LaFleur, 1995; Wilson & Schooler, 1991). According to Wilson and colleagues, analyzing reasons focuses the decision maker's attention on easy-to-articulate features of the choice options and away from less easy-to-articulate feelings. The present research extends Wilson and colleagues' research in two directions. First, the current research shows that even if they are not explicitly asked to analyze reasons, people may still choose options that are rationalistic but inconsistent with predicted preferences; it suggests that seeking rationalism in decision making is a spontaneous and automatic process. Moreover, the present research not only posits that decision makers focus on rationalistic attributes but also identifies three specific classes of rationalistic attributes.

When Decisions Are Too Hot and When They Are Too Cold

Predicted-experience-versus-decision inconsistency implies that, by the standard of the consequentialist utility analysis, decision makers focus too much on cold factors, such as quantity, money, and goals, and too little on hot factors, such as feelings and experiences. This portrait of decision makers seems at odds with the existing literature on affect-driven decisions (e.g., Hsee & Kunreuther, 2000; Slovic et al., 2002). Some research even portrays the decision makers as myopic, impulsive, or ignorant of important cold considerations (Bazerman et al., 1999; Loewenstein, 1996; Schelling, 1984b; Thaler & Shefrin, 1981).

How can we reconcile these two apparently contradictory models? We propose that the relative validity of the two models depends on the nature of the situation. Imagine two types of situations, A and B, each involving a trade-off between a cold attribute and a hot attribute. In Type A situations, the cold attribute produces other and longer-term consequences than its effect on one's experience during a given consumption period. In Type B situations, both the cold and the hot attributes affect one's experience only during the consumption period. From the consequentialist utility-analysis perspective, decision makers should give more weight to the cold attribute in Type A situations than in Type B situations. In reality, most people do not sufficiently distinguish these two types of situations. Although people may indeed give more weight to the cold attribute in Type A situations than in Type B situations, they may not do so enough. As a result, in Type A situations people may still underweight the cold attribute and in Type B situations they may still overweight the cold attribute.

To appreciate our distinction between Type A and Type B situations, let us consider the following two scenarios:

Type A: A person, who loves apples, especially juicy apples, wins a basket of apples as a free gift at a farm fair. He is given two baskets to choose from. One contains 5 juicy-looking apples and the other contains 20 not very juicy-looking apples. Whichever basket he chooses, he may eat the apples in the basket while he is at the fair or bring them home.

Type B: The same as Scenario A, except that he may eat the apples only while he is at the fair and is not allowed to bring home any remaining apples.

From a consequentialist utility-analysis perspective, the apple lover should give the cold attribute – quantity of apples – more weight in Type A Scenario than in Type B Scenario. In reality, he may not sufficiently distinguish these two scenarios. Although he may indeed give more weight to quantity in Type A Scenario than in Type B Scenario, he may not do so enough. As a result, compared with what the consequentialist utility analysis would recommend, the apple lover may still underweight quantity in Type A Scenario and overweight quantity in Type B Scenario.

Previous research on affect-driven and impulsive decisions mainly concerns Type A situations. The present research mainly concerns Type B situations.

The idea that people do not sufficiently distinguish Type A and Type B situations is consistent with Klayman and Brown's (1993) assertion that rules and heuristics are adapted but not easily adaptable. We believe that lay rationalism is developed to contain affect in Type A situations but they are overgeneralized and used even in Type B situations. This view also echoes Arkes and Ayton's (1999) proposition regarding the sunk-cost fallacy. They argue that the sunk-cost fallacy is a result of overgeneralizing the "don't waste" rule from situations where past investments predict future benefits to situations where past investments do not predict future benefits.

Obviously, we are not merely interested in apple choices. The reason we analyze these situations is that they exemplify important real-life decisions. Consider two stylized examples. In the first, a high school graduate who does not have much savings and needs money to go to college is choosing between two short-term jobs: One pays more (a cold attribute) and the other is more enjoyable (a hot attribute). In the second example, a middle-aged person who has enough savings to live comfortably for the rest of her life and is not interested in giving anybody else her money is choosing between two life-long jobs. Again, one job pays more and the other is more enjoyable. Of the two examples, the first resembles a Type A situation, and the second resembles a Type B situation. From the consequentialist perspective, the person in the first example should pay more attention to the financial aspect of the job offers, and the person in the second example should give more consideration to the enjoyment aspect of the job offers. In reality, although people may do so, they probably do not do so enough. As a result, young and financially needier people do not earn as much as they should and older and financially more secure people do not allow themselves as much enjoyment as they could.

Utility About Consequence and Utility About Decision

We have argued throughout this chapter that decisions can be too rationalistic and cold. However, making a rationalistic decision may itself engender a pleasure; that is, a cold decision may itself create a hot feeling. For example, if a person chooses the option with the greatest economic gain, he may feel happy about the choice per se. A number of behavioral decision theories (e.g., Loewenstein et al., 2001; Luce, Payne, & Bettman, 1999; Mellers, Schwartz, Ho, & Ritov, 1997; Mellers, Schwartz, & Ritov, 1999; Thaler, 1985) have proposed a distinction between two types of utilities in decision making. One is about the consequence of the decision; the other is about the process of decision. Consumption utility is about the consequence of the decision, and the utility from making a rationalistic decision is about the process of decision. To say that a decision is too cold or rationalistic is only from the consequentialist perspective, that is, only in comparison with (predicted) *consumption* utility. Ultimately, whether it is a mistake to choose a rationalist option that does not produce the highest consumption utility depends on how much utility one derives from making such a choice and whether it compensates the loss in consumption utility.

ACKNOWLEDGMENTS

Funding for this project is provided by the University of Chicago Graduate School of Business, National Science Foundation, and China Europe International Business School. Many individuals have provided helpful comments on this research, and we are particularly grateful to the following people (in alphabetical order of their last names): Jennifer Boobar, Boaz Keysar, Josh Klayman, Cade Massey, Ann McGill, Yuval Rottenstreich, Eldar Shafir, Jack Soll, and Dick Thaler.

30. Miswanting: Some Problems in the Forecasting of Future Affective States

Daniel T. Gilbert and Timothy D. Wilson

"It would not be better if things happened to men just as they want."

Heraclitus, *Fragments* (500 B.C.)

INTRODUCTION

Like and *want* are among the first things children learn to say, and once they learn to say them, they never stop. Liking has to do with how a thing makes us feel, and wanting is, simply enough, a prediction of liking. When we say, "I like this doughnut," we are letting others know that the doughnut currently under consumption is making us feel a bit better than before. When we say, "I want a doughnut," we are making an abbreviated statement whose extended translation is something like, "Right now I'm not feeling quite as good as I might be, and I think fried dough will fix that." Statements about wanting tend to be statements about those things that we believe will influence our sense of well-being, satisfaction, happiness, and contentment. Hence, when we say we want something, we are more or less promising that we will like it when we get it.

But promises are easier to make than to keep, and sometimes we get what we say we want and feel entirely unhappy about it. We order a cheeseburger only to find that it looks and smells precisely as cheeseburgers always look and smell, and despite that fact, we have absolutely no interest in eating it. We are perplexed and embarrassed by such mistakes and can only offer cunning explanations such as, "I guess I didn't really want a cheeseburger after all." Dining companions often consider such accounts inadequate. "If you didn't *want* the damned thing, then why did you *get* it?" they may ask, at which point we are usually forced to admit the truth, which is that we just do not know. We only know that it looks exactly like what we said we wanted, we are not going to eat it, and the waiter is not amused.

Although we tend to think of unhappiness as something that happens to us when we do not get what we want, much unhappiness is actually of the

Originally published in J. Forgas (Ed.), *Feeling and thinking: The role of affect in social cognition* (pp. 178–197). Cambridge, UK. Copyright © 2000 Cambridge University Press. Reprinted with the permission of Cambridge University Press.

cheeseburger variety and has less to do with not getting what we want and more to do with not wanting what we like. When wanting and liking are unco-ordinated in this way we may say that a person has *miswanted*. The word sounds odd at first, but if wanting is indeed a prediction of liking, then it, like any pre-diction, can be wrong. When the things we want to happen do not improve our happiness, and when the things we want not to happen do, it seems fair to say that we have wanted badly. Why should this happen to people as clever and handsome as us?

THE FUNDAMENTALS OF MISWANTING

In a perfect world, wanting would cause trying, trying would cause getting, get-ting would cause liking, and this chapter would be missing all the words. Ours is apparently not such a place. How is it possible to get what we want and yet not like what we get? At least three problems bedevil our attempts to want well.

Imagining the Wrong Event

The fundamental problem, of course, is that the events we imagine when we are in the midst of a really good want are not precisely the events we experience when we are at the tail end of a really disappointing get. For instance, most of us are skeptical when we hear movie stars describe how relentless adoration can be a source of suffering or when terminally ill patients insist that a dreaded disease has given their lives deeper meaning. We feel certain that we would be delighted in the first instance and devastated in the second because most of us have no idea what stardom or terminal illness actually entail. When we think of "adoring fans," we tend to envision a cheering throng of admirers calling us back for an encore performance rather than a slightly demented autograph hound peeping through our bedroom window at midnight. When we think of "terminal illness," we tend to envision ourselves wasting away in a hospital bed, connected to machines by plugs and tubes, rather than planting flowers in the hospice garden, surrounded by those we love. Terminal illness is not an event, but a class of events, and each member of the class unfolds in a different way. How much we like an event depends mightily on the details of its unfolding. When the imagined cheeseburger (a half-pound of prime aged beef) is not the experienced cheeseburger (three ounces of rubbery soy), it seems inevitable that our wanting and our liking will be poorly matched.

Given how varied a class of events can be, we might expect people prudently to refrain from directing their wants toward classes ("I don't know if I want a cheeseburger") and direct them instead toward particular, well-understood members of the class ("However, I know I don't want *that* cheeseburger"). Research suggests that people are not always so prudent and that when asked to make predictions about future events, they tend to imagine a particular event while making little provision for the possibility that the particular event they are imagining may not necessarily be the particular event they will be experiencing

(Dunning, Griffin, Milojkovic, & Ross, 1990; Griffin, Dunning, & Ross, 1990; Griffin & Ross, 1991; Lord, Lepper, & Mackie, 1984; Robinson, Keltner, Ward, & Ross, 1995). When our spouse asks us to attend "a party" on Friday night, we instantly imagine a particular kind of party (e.g., a cocktail party in the penthouse of a downtown hotel with waiters in black ties carrying silver trays of hors d'oeuvres past a slightly bored harpist) and then estimate our reaction to that imagined event (e.g., yawn). We generally fail to consider how many different members constitute the class (e.g., birthday parties, orgies, wakes) and how different our reactions would be to each. So we tell our spouse that we would rather skip the party, our spouse naturally drags us along anyhow, and we have a truly marvelous time. Why? Because the party involves cheap beer and hula hoops rather than classical music and seaweed crackers. It is precisely our style, and we like what we previously did not want because the event we experienced (and liked) was not the event we imagined (and wanted to avoid).

Using the Wrong Theory

If imagining the wrong event were the sole cause of miswanting, then we would only miswant objects and experiences when the details of their unfolding were unknown to us. The fact is, people often want – and then fail to like – objects and experiences whose details they know quite well. Even when we know precisely the kind of party our spouse is hauling us to, or precisely the kind of cheeseburger this particular restaurant serves, we may still be surprised to find that we enjoy it a great deal more or less than we had anticipated. For example, Read and Loewenstein (1995) asked subjects to plan a menu by deciding which of several snacks they would eat when they returned to the laboratory on each of three consecutive Mondays (cf. Simonson, 1990). Subjects tended to order a mixed plate that included instances of their favorite snack ("I'll have a Snickers bar on the first two Mondays"), as well as instances of their next favorite ("And tortilla chips on the third Monday"). Alas, when it actually came time to eat the snacks, subjects were not so pleased on the day when they arrived at the laboratory only to find themselves faced with a snack that was . . . well, not their favorite. Their disappointment was perfectly understandable. We *should* be disappointed when we do not get what we like most, and the only thing that seems hard to understand is why subjects wanted something that they knew perfectly well they did not like perfectly well.

Apparently, subjects in this study believed that variety is the spice of life – and in this case, they were wrong (cf. Kahneman & Snell, 1992). A Snickers with every meal is indeed a dull prospect for anyone, but a Snickers once a week is just about right. As such, Snickers lovers are made *less* happy – and not *more* happy – when their weekly Snickers is replaced by a less desirable treat. Because subjects in this study had erroneous theories about their own need for variety over time, they miswanted tortilla chips when they planned their menu. The moral of this ripping yarn about snack foods is that even when people have a perfect idea of what an event will entail (i.e., tortilla chips are deep-fried corn pancakes covered with salt, period), they may still have imperfect ideas about themselves and thus may make imperfect predictions about how they will react to the event. People who can imagine sun, surf, sand, and daiquiris in exquisite detail may still be surprised when their desert island vacation turns out to be a bust – not because they imagined *this* island and ended up on *that* one, but simply because they did not realize how much they require daily structure, intellectual stimulation, or regular infusions of Pop Tarts. Highbrows fall asleep at the ballet, pacifists find themselves strangely excited by a glimpse of world class wrestling, and tough guys in leather jackets are occasionally caught making clucking sounds by the duck pond. To the extent that we have incorrect theories about who we are, we may also have incorrect beliefs about what we will like.

Misinterpreting Feelings

If we could imagine events exactly as they were actually to unfold, and if we had complete and accurate knowledge of our relevant tastes and attitudes, could we necessarily avoid miswanting? Unfortunately not. When we imagine a future event, we normally have an affective reaction to its mental representation (imagining one's spouse happily entwined with the mail carrier usually illustrates this fact convincingly), and we naturally take this affective reaction to the mental representation of the event as a proxy for the affective reaction we might have to the event itself. If the mere thought of a mate's infidelity makes us feel slightly nauseous, then we have every reason to suppose that the real thing would end in an upchuck. Our affective reactions to imaginary events are, in a sense, experiential previews of our affective reactions to the events themselves, and they figure prominently in our predictions of future liking. Few of us need to consult a cookbook to know that we should avoid any event involving liver and maple syrup. That funny feeling right *here* is information enough (see Forgas, 1995; Schwarz, 1990; Schwarz & Clore, 1983).

Wantings, then, are based on three ingredients: the particular details that we imagine when we consider a future event, our beliefs about the ways in which people like us are likely to react to such events, and the "gut reactions" we experience when we imagine the event. Just as the first two of these ingredients can lead us to miswant, so too can the third. How so? The crux of the problem is that the feelings we experience when we imagine a future event are not necessarily or solely caused by that act of imagination. We may feel enormously excited when we contemplate spending next Sunday at the circus, and thus we may drop buckets of money on ringside tickets without realizing that the good news we received about our aging uncle's miraculous recovery from psoriasis just moments before we purchased our ticket has contaminated our affective reaction to the thought of dancing elephants (Wilson & Brekke, 1994). Come Sunday, we may find ourselves bored to tears beneath the big top, wondering why we paid good money to see a herd of clowns in a little car. Our miswanting in this case would not have been a result of having imagined the wrong event

("Oh, I was thinking of a flea circus") nor of having had a false conception of ourselves ("Why did I think I liked men in floppy shoes?"). Rather, we would have miswanted because when we initially thought about the circus we felt excited, and we took that fact as information about the circus rather than as information about Uncle Frank's remission. Feelings do not say where they came from, and thus it is all too easy for us to attribute them to the wrong source.

Experimental demonstrations of this home truth abound. People may mistakenly believe that their lives are empty when, in fact, their gloomy mood is a consequence of rain (Schwarz & Clore, 1983); they may mistakenly believe that a person is attractive when, in fact, their pounding pulse is being caused by the swaying of a suspension bridge (Dutton & Aron, 1974), and so on. Because we cannot always tell if the feelings we are having as we imagine an event are being caused solely by that imagining, we may use these feelings as proxies for future liking and, hence, miswant.

THINKING AND FEELING

We ordinarily experience both thoughts and feelings when we imagine a future event, and these influence our wantings to different extents, under different circumstances, and with different results. Sometimes, our affective reactions to an imagined event provide an excellent basis for wanting, but our cognitive reactions muck things up. This seems to be what happened when Wilson et al. (1993) offered college students a reproduction of an impressionist painting or a poster of a cat with a humorous caption. Before making their choices, some students were asked to think about why they liked or disliked each poster ("deep thinkers") and others were not ("shallow thinkers"). When the experimenters phoned the students later and asked how much they liked their new objet d'art, the deep thinkers were the least satisfied. Presumably, the shallow thinkers used their current affective reaction as the basis for their decision and ended up liking the posters they had chosen. Deep thinkers, on the other hand, had some badly mistaken theories about their own aesthetic preferences ("Now that I think about it, the olive green in the Monet is rather drab, whereas the cat poster is bright and cheery"), and when they allowed these cognitive reactions to overrule their affective reactions, they inevitably miswanted.

At other times, however, our cognitive reactions can provide an excellent basis for our wantings, and our affective reactions may lead us astray. For example, Gilbert, Gill, and Wilson (2002) asked shoppers at a grocery store to write down all the items they had come to buy and allowed some shoppers to retain that list. Next, they asked some shoppers to eat a quarter-pound of blueberry muffins before entering the store. As shoppers exited the store, the experimenters examined their cash register receipts. When shoppers were deprived of their shopping lists, those who had eaten blueberry muffins bought fewer unwanted items than did those who had not eaten any muffins.

Presumably, when these listless shoppers encountered items in the store, they had more positive affective reactions to the items when they were unfed ("The marshmallow cookies look so delicious!") than they did when they were well-fed ("I never want to eat again") and thus were more inclined to buy items that they had not intended to buy. Shoppers who had their lists in hand, however, were unaffected by the blueberry muffins and bought no more unwanted items when they were unfed than when they were well fed. These listful shoppers surely had the same affective reactions as did their listless counterparts, but because they had in hand a copy of *A Theory About What I Will Want in the Future* (a.k.a. a grocery list), they were able to avoid basing their choices on their affective reactions and thus they were able to avoid miswanting.

It seems, then, that feelings sometimes serve us better than theories, and theories sometimes serve us better than feelings. Alas, sometimes neither serves us well at all. Gilbert, Gill, and Wilson (2002) asked college students to predict how much they would enjoy eating a bite of spaghetti the next morning or the next evening. Some of the students were hungry when they made these predictions, others were not. Some students were allowed to think deeply about their predictions, and others were distracted while they made their predictions. When the students were distracted, they relied on their gut feelings to make their predictions, and thus the hungriest students naturally predicted that they would like spaghetti more the next day than did the less hungry students. Notably, the time of day at which the spaghetti was to be eaten made no difference to them at all. When students were allowed to think deeply, however, they relied on their theories to make their predictions, and thus they predicted that they would enjoy spaghetti (which is generally considered a more appropriate dinner than breakfast) more the next evening than they would the next morning. Notably, the students' current hunger made no difference to them at all. Finally, when students were actually brought to the laboratory in the morning or evening and given a bite of spaghetti, neither the extent of their hunger the day before nor the time of day at which the spaghetti was eaten had a measurable influence on their enjoyment of the food. In other words, students relied on their cognitive reactions when they could, their affective reactions otherwise, and in this instance, neither of these reactions to the imagined event enabled them to want correctly.

MISWANTING OVER TIME

What do spaghetti, cheeseburgers, marshmallow cookies, tortilla chips, and Snickers bars have in common? They are objects that can be wanted today and liked tomorrow, but once that liking occurs, they quickly become a trivial bit of personal history that only our thighs remember. Each of these objects can be experienced, but none of these experiences has enduring emotional consequences, and thus none provides an opportunity for us to think about how people might want or miswant in the long run. When we want a bite of pecan pie or a warm shower or a sexy kiss, it is not because we think these things will change us in some significant way, but because we think they will be perfectly lovely for as long as they last. On the other hand, when we want a promotion or a wedding or a college degree, it is not so much because we believe these things will improve our lives at the moment we attain them, but because we think they will provide emotional rewards that will persist long enough to repay the effort we spent in their pursuit. Significant events are supposed to have significant emotional consequences, and the duration of these consequences matters a lot.

If it is difficult to know whether we will be happy 15 minutes after eating a bite of spaghetti, it is all the more difficult to know whether we will be happy 15 months after a divorce or 15 years after a marriage. Gilbert, Pinel, Wilson, Blumberg, and Wheatley (1998) have suggested that people tend to overestimate the duration of their emotional reactions to future events – especially negative events – and that this can lead them to miswant in the long term. For example, Gilbert, Gill, and Wilson (2002) asked assistant professors to predict how happy they would be in general a few years after achieving or failing to achieve tenure at their current university, and they also measured the general happiness of those former assistant professors who had or had not achieved tenure at the same institution. Although assistant professors believed that the tenure decision would dramatically influence their general happiness for many years to come (and hence desperately wanted tenure), the former assistant professors who had not achieved tenure were no less happy than the former assistant professors who had. Similarly, Gilbert, Gill, and Wilson (2002) asked voters in a gubernatorial election to predict how happy they would generally be a month after an election. Voters believed that they would be significantly happier a month after the election if their candidate won than if their candidate lost. As it turned out, a month after the election, the losers and winners were just as happy as they had been before the election (see Brickman, Coates, & Janoff-Bulman, 1978; Taylor, 1983; Taylor & Armor, 1996; Wortman & Silver, 1989).

Do not misunderstand: Those assistant professors who were promoted and those voters whose candidate triumphed were surely happier about the event, and were surely happier for some time after the event, than were those who lost their jobs or who backed the incumbent governor who lost hers. But after just a little while – a much littler while than the assistant professors and voters had themselves predicted – the emotional traces of these events had evaporated (see Suh, Diener, & Fujita, 1996). What might cause people to overestimate the enduring emotional effect of such events?

Focalism: The Invisible Future
When asked how we might feel a year after losing our left hand, we tend to imagine the immediate emotional impact of this calamity ("No more clapping, no more shoe tying – I'd be sad"). What we do *not* do is go on to calculate

the impact of the dental appointments, foreign films, job promotions, freak snowstorms, and Snickers bars that will inevitably fill the year that follows our unhanding. Rather, we naturally focus on the event whose emotional impact we are trying to gauge and then make some provision for the passage of time ("I guess a year later I'd be a little less sad"). But how we will feel in general a year after losing a hand and how we will feel *about* losing a hand a year after the loss are not the same thing. Predicting the latter may be relatively simple, but predicting the former requires that we estimate the combined impact of the focal event and all the nonfocal events that follow it. Put another way, our general happiness some time after an event is influenced by just two things: (a) the event, and (b) everything else. If we estimate that happiness by considering only the event, then we are ignoring some of the most powerful determinants of our future well-being (see Loewenstein & Schkade, 1999; Schkade & Kahneman, 1998).

Wilson, Wheatley, Meyers, Gilbert, and Axsom (2000) demonstrated how focalism (the failure to consider the consequences of nonfocal events when making predictions about the ultimate affective impact of focal events) can give rise to the durability bias and hence promote miswanting. College students were asked to predict their happiness the day after their football team won or lost an important game. Some students were also asked to complete a "future diary" in which they listed the events that they thought would occur in the 3 days after the game. Those students who completed the diary and who were thus most likely to consider the impact of future nonfocal events when making their predictions made less extreme predictions about their general happiness – predictions that turned out to be more accurate when their overall happiness was measured the day after the game.

It seems that merely considering the emotional impact of an event can lead us to overestimate that impact, simply because we do not also consider other impactful events as well. Focalism is an especially vexing problem because avoiding it seems to require that we do the impossible, namely, consider the impact of *every* event before estimating the impact of *any* event. If we think of happiness as a general state that is determined by innumerable events, it does indeed seem likely that no single event will have the power to influence our general happiness for very long. Indeed, those events that seem to make a big difference (e.g., moving to a new country) tend to be those that give rise to many other events, which suggests that the ramifications of an event – that is, the sheer number of experiences it alters – may be the best predictor of its ultimate emotional impact. Although few parents would believe it, the death of a spouse may have more impact than the death of a child, simply because the former produces more changes in one's life than does the latter (see Lehman et al., 1993). In any case, it seems quite clear that focusing on an event can cause us to overestimate the duration of its influence on our happiness and, hence, to miswant.

Immune Neglect: The Invisible Shield

Many shrewd observers of the human condition have remarked on people's extraordinary ability to change the way they feel simply by changing the way they think. When circumstances threaten our psychological well-being, we execute an assortment of cognitive strategies, tactics, and maneuvers that are designed to prevent, limit, or repair the damage (e.g., Festinger, 1957; Freud, 1937; Steele, 1988; Taylor & Brown, 1988; Vaillant, 1993; Westen, 1994). These maneuvers usually have two properties. First, they work like a charm, enabling all of us to be well above average in all the ways that count. Second and more important, we tend not to know we are executing them, and what looks like rationalization to the giggling onlooker feels very much like rational reasoning to us. Taken together, the mechanisms that protect the sources of our psychological well-being (e.g., our sense of competence, integrity, and worth) in the face of assault constitute a psychological immune system that seems to be both powerful and invisible to the person it serves.

If our happiness is, in fact, defended by an invisible shield, then it is easy to see why we overestimate our vulnerability to the slings and arrows of outrageous fortune. Recall that voters in the Gilbert, Gill, and Wilson (2002) study overestimated the duration of their emotional reactions to their candidate's electoral triumph or defeat. Interestingly, voters in that study were also asked to predict how their opinions of the candidates would change once one was elected, and their answers may tell us something about why they overestimated the durability of their emotions. Although voters flatly denied that the outcome of the election would change their opinions of the candidates by even a hair, a month after the election, those voters whose candidate had lost had experienced an unforeseen transformation: Although the new governor had yet to take office, had yet to perform an official act, and had yet to make a substantive speech, those who had voted against him had a significantly higher opinion of him than they had had a month earlier. It seems that those voters overestimated the duration of their disappointment because they did not realize that once they were stuck with a governor whom they had not wanted, their psychological immune systems would help them locate 16 new reasons to like him anyway.

Gilbert, Gill, and Wilson (2002) provided direct experimental evidence of immune neglect: the tendency for people to fail to consider how readily their psychological immune systems will vitiate their despair. Students were given the opportunity to apply for an exciting and lucrative position as an ice-cream taster in a model business. The application process included answering several questions before a video camera while judges watched from another room. The situation was arranged such that if students were rejected, their psychological immune systems would have much more work to do in one condition than the other. Specifically, students in the "difficult rationalization" condition were shown a number of highly relevant questions and were told that while answering these questions they would be observed by a panel of judges, who would then vote on the student's appropriateness for the job. Unless the judges unanimously disapproved of the student, he or she would be offered the job. In the "easy rationalization" condition, students were shown a number of largely irrelevant questions and were told that while answering these questions they would be observed by a single judge who would solely determine whether or not they were offered the job. Students in each condition predicted how they would feel if they were rejected, and how they would feel 10 minutes later. All participants then answered the relevant or irrelevant questions before the video camera and were promptly rejected. Their happiness was measured immediately following the rejection and then again 10 minutes later.

As the top part of Figure 30.1 shows, the students believed they would be much less happy immediately following rejection than they actually turned out to be. But as the bottom part of Figure 30.1 shows, the more interesting effect occurred 10 minutes later. Not only were all the students happier than they expected to be 10 minutes after being rejected, but they were happier when they had been rejected by a solo judge who had heard them answer irrelevant questions than when they had been rejected by a panel of judges who had heard them answer relevant questions. This difference reveals the work of the psychological immune system, which should have found it easier to heal the wounds of rejection in the easy rationalization condition ("One guy doesn't think I'm competent. So what? Maybe I look like his ex-roommate, or maybe he's biased against Southerners, or maybe he just didn't have enough information to go on") than in the difficult rationalization condition ("An entire group of judges agreed on the basis of adequate information that I'm not smart enough to taste ice cream? Yikes!"). The important point is that the students did not *anticipate* this difference, which suggests that when they looked into their emotional futures, they saw only the pain of rejection. What they did not consider was the ease or difficulty with which their psychological immune systems would dispatch their malaise.

Immune neglect can have important interpersonal consequences, too. For example, few of us would expect to come undone if an irritated motorist shouted a few choice words about our parentage as we crossed against the light, but we might well expect to be shocked and dismayed if a good friend did the same. We expect an insulting remark from a stranger to be less painful than an insulting remark from a friend, and thus we might naturally expect the former to have less enduring emotional consequences than the latter. Gilbert, Lieberman, Morewedge, and Wilson (2004) asked pairs of college students to evaluate each other's personalities on the basis of brief autobiographies in which they had explicitly been asked to describe some embarrassing incidents. Some students were told that they would work together as a team later in the experiment ("partners") and others were told that they would never meet ("strangers"). The students were asked to predict how they would feel a few minutes after finding out that the other student had read their autobiography and given them a very negative evaluation, and indeed, they predicted that they would feel worse if the

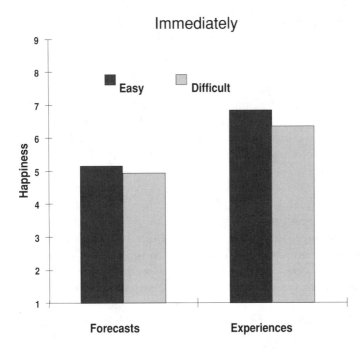

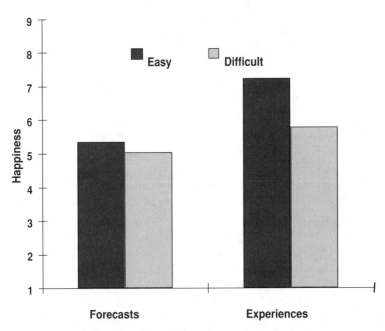

Figure 30.1. Predicted and actual happiness after rejection.

negative evaluation came from their partner than from a stranger. In fact, the students were considerably *happier* after receiving a negative evaluation from their partner than a from a stranger, and they even forgave their partners more readily than they forgave strangers. Why should this have happened?

Once again, the invisibility of the psychological immune system seems to explain these paradoxical results. Most of us find it rather uncomfortable to interact with people we do not like, and so we are highly motivated to like those with whom we must interact (Darley & Berscheid, 1967). Our psychological immune systems work much harder to help us find ways to forgive our partner's transgressions ("My partner probably didn't realize that the embarrassing incident I wrote about in my autobiography was a unique occurrence, and now that I think of it, I'd probably have made the same negative evaluation myself if I were in the same position") than to forgive the transgressions of strangers. The insulted students' psychological immune systems did what they were designed to do by enabling them to feel happy about working with someone who had evaluated them negatively. What is interesting, of course, is that the students were unable to predict this outcome just 10 minutes before it happened. Like most of us, they blithely predicted that a big pain would last longer than a little one, unaware that big pains often evoke remedies that little pains do not. Broken legs hurt so much that they cry out to be fixed, whereas trick knees are often allowed to go on hurting for a lifetime.

Immune neglect can cause us to miswant by causing us to fear and avoid outcomes that will not, in the long run, hinder our happiness. But one ironic consequence of the failure to anticipate the operation of the psychological immune system is that we may inadvertently do things that impair its operation, thereby undermining our own hidden talent for happiness. For example, if given the opportunity to shop at a store that allows customers to return merchandise for any reason and another store at which all sales are final, most of us would patronize the first rather than the second – and we might even be willing to pay a bit more just so we could have the luxury of changing our minds later on. We firmly believe that bridges ought to be there for crossing and recrossing, and our aversion to burning them is probably wise in many respects. But if keeping one's options open is wise in many respects, it is not wise in all respects, because open options have the unfortunate consequence of paralyzing the psychological immune system. As dissonance theorists have long noted, it is the firm commitment to a single course of action that most effectively triggers attempts to justify it.

Gilbert and Ebert (2002) gave college students a short course in black-and-white photography. The students took photographs of their favorite people and places on campus and were then taught how to develop their photographs. After students had printed their two favorite photographs, they were asked to donate one of them to the experimenter's "photography project." Some students were told that the donated photograph would be mailed to England that evening, whereas others were told that the photograph would not be mailed for 5 days.

Students in this latter condition were told that if they changed their minds about which photograph to keep after they made the donation, they could swap the chosen for the donated photograph anytime before it was mailed. When the students' happiness with their photographs was measured 2 days later, those whose decisions were reversible did not like the chosen photograph as much as did those students whose decisions were irreversible. This makes sense inasmuch as these students were probably still in the process of deciding which photograph they would keep, and thus they did not yet have a final outcome with which their psychological immune systems could help them feel happy. But interestingly, 9 days later, the irreversible deciders were *still* happier with their photographs than were the reversible deciders – despite the fact that the reversible deciders' "swapping opportunity" had expired days ago and their unchosen photograph was irrevocably winging its way across the Atlantic. It seems that merely having had a brief opportunity to change their minds prevented reversible deciders from *ever* exercising their hidden talent for happiness.

All of this work on immune neglect leads to one conclusion: Our tendency to neglect the operation of the immune system when anticipating the future can have unhappy consequences. We often want one thing so much more than another that we willingly incur enormous costs in our attempts to avoid the unwanted event. We may spend little time with our children and neglect our hobbies while putting in long hours at the office because we are convinced that keeping our current job will be better than being forced to find a new one. What we fail to realize is that while the thing we wanted to experience is in some ways better than the thing we wanted to avoid, it is probably worse in others, and should we fail to achieve what we wanted, our psychological immune systems will quickly help us locate the ways in which the thing we got was better than the thing we were aiming for. As the man who narrowly missed the opportunity to franchise the first McDonalds restaurant (and hence narrowly missed the opportunity to become a billionaire) noted many decades later, "I believe it turned out for the best" (Van Gelder, 1996). If we do indeed have a greater talent for happiness than we recognize, then our ignorance of this talent may cause us to pay a steeper price for future experiences than we should.

CONCLUSIONS

The naïve psychology of happiness is simple: We want, we try, we get, we like. And then, with the help of television commercials, we want some more. Wants are underwritten by our beliefs about the relation between getting and liking, and in this sense they are prescriptions for action. They tell us what to do with our time by telling us what to aim for and what to avoid, and we allow ourselves to be steered by them because we trust that they are, by and large, correct. Most of us feel certain that if we could experience all the events and only the events we want to experience, happiness would inevitably follow.

The research discussed in this chapter suggests that there are at least two flaws in the naïve analysis of happiness. First, our wants are, like any other prediction, susceptible to error. We may misconstrue events, misunderstand ourselves, misinterpret our feelings – and any of these mistakes can be a cause of miswanting. In short, things do not always feel the way we expect them to feel. Second, even if we could predict how much we would like an event when it happened, we might still be unable to predict how that event would affect us in the long run. One reason is that our general happiness is influenced by a multitude of events. It is impossible to consider all of these influences every time we consider one of them, of course, but unless we do just that, we have little hope of correctly predicting the future states that are their conjoint products. A second reason we have trouble predicting the enduring emotional consequences of an event is that liking does not *follow* from getting so much as it *accommodates* it. Although our initial emotional reaction to an event is usually based on those properties of the event that caused us to aim for it or avoid it in the first place, once a particular outcome is achieved, we have an uncanny ability to reconstrue it in terms of its most sanguine properties. Because we do not recognize how easily we can reconstrue events in this way, we anticipate more enduring reactions than we often have.

"In the world there are only two tragedies," wrote Oscar Wilde (1893). "One is not getting what one wants, and the other is getting it." We all chuckle and nod knowingly when we hear this clever quip, but not one of us believes it for a moment. Rather, our chuckling and nodding are licensed by a serene certainty that the things we run after will, in fact, bring us far greater happiness than the things we run from. The research discussed in this chapter does not suggest that all ends are emotionally equivalent or that all desires are misdirected. Rather, it merely suggests that if we could know the future, we still might not know how much we would like it when we got there. The psychological mechanisms that keep us from this knowledge are many, and a better understanding of them seems well worth wanting.

ACKNOWLEDGMENTS

The writing of this chapter was supported by research grant RO1-MH56075 from the National Institute of Mental Health to Daniel T. Gilbert and Timothy D. Wilson. We thank Joe Forgas for his insightful comments on an earlier version of this chapter, and the other authors in [the book in which this chapter originally appeared] for helpful discussions of these issues.

31. Economic Preferences or Attitude Expressions? An Analysis of Dollar Responses to Public Issues

Daniel Kahneman, Ilana Ritov, and David A. Schkade

INTRODUCTION

Economics and psychology offer contrasting perspectives on the question of how people value things. The economic model of choice is concerned with a rational agent whose preferences obey a tight web of logical rules, formalized in consumer theory and in models of decision making under risk. The tradition of psychology, in contrast, is not congenial to the idea that a logic of rational choice can serve double duty as a model of actual decision behavior. Much behavioral research has been devoted to illustrations of choices that violate the logic of the economic model. The implied claim is that people do not have preferences, in the sense in which that term is used in economic theory (Fischhoff, 1991; Payne, Bettman, & Johnson, 1992; Slovic, 1995). It is therefore fair to ask: If people do not have economic preferences, what do they have instead? Does psychology provide theoretical notions that can, at least in some contexts, account for both apparent violations of the rational model of preference and the regularities of observed choices? Behavioral research has documented several psychological processes that provide partial answers to this question, including concepts such as mental accounting, loss aversion, and hyperbolic discounting. To this set of conceptual tools the present treatment adds the concept of *attitude*, which we borrow from social psychology, and the core process – we label it *affective valuation* – which determines the sign and the intensity of the emotional response to objects.

The main topic that we discuss in this chapter – the valuation of environmental public goods – is far from the core of economic discourse. It is an unusual case in which some economists have proposed to use responses to hypothetical questions as a measure of economic preference. In the contingent valuation method (CVM), survey respondents are asked to indicate a stated willingness to pay (SWTP) for public goods, including goods from which they derive no personal benefit, such as the continued existence of obscure species and the maintenance of pristine lakes in inaccessible areas. The proponents of CVM have argued that properly elicited statements of WTP reveal genuine economic preferences, to

Originally published in the *Journal of Risk and Uncertainty*, vol. 19, pp. 203–235. Copyright © 1999 by Kluwer Academic Publishers. Reprinted with permission.

which consumer theory applies (Hoehn & Randall, 1989; Mitchell & Carson, 1989; V. K. Smith, 1992).

We develop here an argument made earlier (Kahneman & Ritov, 1994) that statements of WTP are better viewed as expressions of attitudes than as indications of economic preferences. The conflicting views of the nature of SWTP lead to different interpretations of apparently anomalous features of CVM results, such as the low sensitivity to variations of scope and the discrepancy between the estimates of SWTP derived from open-ended and from referendum questions. The supporters of CVM have sometimes dismissed these anomalies as artifacts of poor technique (Carson & Mitchell, 1993; V. K. Smith, 1992) or explained them in terms of standard economic concepts, such as incentive compatibility and substitution and income effects (Hanemann, 1994; Randall & Hoehn, 1996; V. K. Smith, 1992). In contrast, the thesis of the present chapter is that the anomalies of contingent valuation (CV) are inevitable manifestations of known characteristics of attitudes and attitude expressions.

To demonstrate the generality of the analysis of SWTP in terms of attitudes, we draw on an experimental study of the setting of punitive damages in product liability cases (Kahneman, Schkade, & Sunstein, 1998). The tasks faced by a respondent to a CV survey and by a juror have little in common in the context of an economic analysis; consumer theory may apply to the former but surely not to the latter. In the framework that we propose, however, the two tasks are very similar. Both require the individual to express an attitude – to an environmental problem or to a defendant's actions – by using a dollar scale. The striking parallels between the findings in the two situations strongly support the attitude model.

The evidence that we present is drawn exclusively from studies of verbal answers to hypothetical questions about public issues. It is perhaps not surprising that, on this favorable terrain, the concepts of attitude and affective valuation provide a useful account of the data. It is early to say whether these concepts will prove equally useful in other domains to which the theory of economic preference is usually applied. On current evidence, it is possible to accept an attitude model for hypothetical CV responses while retaining the idea that the standard model of rational choice applies to more consequential decisions. This appears to be the position of economists who have criticized CVM (e.g., Diamond & Hausman, 1994). We believe, however, that the idea that actions are often interpretable as relatively direct expressions of an affective valuation is likely to prove useful in the analysis of many economically significant behaviors.

This chapter is organized in two parts. The first part, which includes four sections, introduces the concepts of attitude and affective valuation and explores some contrasts between attitudes and economic preferences, with examples from studies of CV and of punitive damages. The next two sections apply a psychophysical analysis of dollar responses to explain both the unpredictability of jury awards and some important results of CV research. Next, implications are discussed, and the final section presents the conclusion.

This chapter covers much ground and asserts many claims with relatively little documentation. To facilitate a separate assessment of the claims and of their associated evidence, we present our argument in the form of a series of propositions, with brief discussion of each proposition in turn.

INTRODUCTION TO VALUATION

The concept of attitude has been defined as "a psychological tendency that is expressed by evaluating a particular entity with some degree of favor or disfavor" (Eagly & Chaiken, 1998, p. 269). The core of an attitude is a valuation, *which assigns to the entity an* affective value *that can range from extremely positive to extremely negative.*[1]

Affective values vary in sign (positive or negative) and in intensity. The intensity of valuation is relative: An attitude object considered on its own is implicitly compared with a set of objects of the same general kind.

The concept of attitude has a considerably broader range of application than the standard concept of economic preferences. In contrast to economic preferences, which are about commodity bundles (Varian, 1984), objects of attitudes include anything that people can like or dislike, wish to protect or to harm, want to acquire or to reject. People have attitudes toward abstract concepts, individual persons and social groups, events in their personal past, and historical figures. Expressions of attitude are also diverse: They include smiles and frowns, verbal statements of approval or abuse, physical assault, charitable contributions, answers to survey questions, and many others. The valuation component of attitudes is assumed to be automatic and to facilitate a broad range of responses that express positive or negative affect (Fazio, Sanbonmatsu, Powell, & Kardes, 1986; Pratto, 1994; Tesser & Martin, 1996).

People's attitudes to objects and to activities that affect these objects are usually consistent. For example, a positive affective response to dolphins is likely to be associated with a positive valuation of actions that protect members of this species. The link between attitudes and actions is often far from perfect, however (Eagly & Chaiken, 1993).

The objects of attitudes and valuations are mental representations, not objective states of affairs. Valuations are therefore subject to framing effects and violate the logic of extensionality. In an example much discussed by philosophy students, an individual may have different attitudes to the evening star and to the morning star, although they are the same star. People can also have different attitudes to the same packaged meat depending on whether it is described as containing 5% fat or as being 95% fat-free. The latter example is a *framing effect*, in which two descriptions evoke different valuations although they are transparently co-extensional – they refer to the same state of the world. Many large and robust framing effects have been identified by students of individual decision making

---

[1] The terms "valuation" and "affective value" are not standard in the attitude literature, but the position we take is widely shared.

(e.g., Tversky & Kahneman, 1986) and students of political attitudes (Bartels, 1998; Quattrone & Tversky, 1984; Zaller, 1992). Framing effects violate a condition of extensionality (Arrow, 1982) or invariance (Tversky & Kahneman, 1986), which is commonly taken for granted in economic analyses of preference. The psychological analysis of attitudes and valuations explicitly rejects the extensionality assumption.

The following is a partial list of the properties of attitudes and of the ways they differ from preferences. (a) Attitudes are defined by the affective value of objects considered one at a time, not by choices. (b) Attitudes violate extensionality. The same object may evoke different valuations depending on its description and on the context in which it is evaluated. (c) The separate attitudes to two objects do not necessarily predict the outcome of a choice or direct comparison between them: Reversals can occur when the comparison alters the relative salience of some attributes (Hsee, 1996a) or when the objects belong to different categories. (d) The attitude to a set of similar objects is often determined by the affective valuation of a prototypical member of that set. The size of the set is neglected in this mode of valuation, which violates the logic of preferences. Alternative measures of attitudes differ in their precision, statistical efficiency, and susceptibility to biasing influences. Dollar measures are inferior on all three counts.

THE EVALUATION FACTOR

A central claim of the present treatment is that diverse responses to an object often express the same affective valuation. Consequently, the answers to ostensibly different questions are expected to yield similar rankings of attitude objects. The present section provides some evidence for this hypothesis. The data that we consider for each object are *averages* of attitude measures obtained from different samples of respondents. The correlations that we discuss in this section answer the following question: Do different ways of probing average attitudes to a set of objects yield similar attitude orders?

The affective value of an object is the major determinant of many responses to it, which are called attitude expressions. *A correlational analysis of the responses to a set of objects normally yields a strong* evaluation factor, *which captures the commonality among diverse expressions of the same attitude.* The classic set of studies that introduced the semantic differential technique (Osgood, Suci, & Tannenbaum, 1957) still provides the best illustration of this proposition. Participants in seimantic differential studies are presented with a series of objects or concepts. Their task is to rate each object in turn on a set of 7-point scales defined by bipolar adjectives, such as GOOD–BAD, KIND–CRUEL, BEAUTIFUL–UGLY, LARGE–SMALL, STRONG–WEAK, MASCULINE–FEMININE, IMPORTANT–UNIMPORTANT, and others. The range of objects to which this technique can be applied is hardly constrained: It includes particular objects, events, abstract ideas, activities, and nonsense figures. The participants are instructed to work quickly and to rate each object on every scale, regardless of whether or not it applies literally. Thus, "wisdom" and "Paris" could both be rated on the scales LARGE–SMALL and HOT–COLD – most people will rate wisdom as larger and colder than Paris.

For our purposes here, the most important conclusion of studies of the semantic differential is that the factorial structure of semantic differential data is surprisingly simple. The same structure has been confirmed in many studies. The largest factor to emerge is invariably an *evaluation factor*, so labeled because the highest loadings are on scales such as GOOD–BAD, KIND–CRUEL, and BEAUTIFUL–UGLY. The evaluation factor typically accounts for about 50% of the variance in scale responses. The scales that define the evaluation factor are not perfectly correlated, of course, and the differences among them are meaningful. For example, "justice" is likely to be rated higher on the GOOD–BAD scale than on the KIND–CRUEL scale. Large discrepancies are rare, however, and the different evaluation scales generally yield similar orderings of the objects of judgment.

Attitudes can be expressed on a scale of dollars, as well as on rating scales. Valuations expressed in dollars are highly correlated with those expressed on rating scales. Willingness to pay for environmental goods – for example, the maintenance of species – is one possible expression of attitudes to these goods and to interventions that affect them. Similarly, attitudes to defendants in civil trials can be expressed by an amount of punitive damages. Studies in both domains have examined the following two hypotheses: (a) different measures of the valuation of issues are highly correlated, as in the semantic differential, and (b) dollar measures belong to the cluster of attitude measures.

Kahneman and Ritov (1994) studied the valuation of 37 topics, including a wide array of environmental problems and other public issues. The issues were presented as headlines, in which a brief description of a problem was followed by a single sentence describing a proposed intervention. An example was "THE PEREGRINE FALCON IS THREATENED BY POLLUTION. Intervention: Support special program to protect the Peregrine falcon." Several measures were used: SWTP for the proposed intervention, degree of political support for the intervention, personal satisfaction expected from making a voluntary contribution (both on a 0–4 rating scale), and a rating of the importance of the problem as a public issue, on a 0–6 rating scale. The participants in the study were visitors at the San Francisco Exploratorium. Each participant used only one of these four response scales to evaluate anywhere from 9 to 19 of the assigned problems. The total sample was 1,441, and the number of respondents to any particular version of a problem was 50 to 115.

The 37 problems were ranked by the sample means for each of the response measures. Rank correlations between these means are shown in Table 31.1. The numbers on the diagonal represent measures of reliability, obtained by a bootstrapping procedure. Table 31.1 indicates that the rankings of the issues by the different measures were quite similar. Indeed, the correlations between orders derived from different measures were not substantially lower than the reliabilities of the individual measures.

570 D. Kahneman, I. Ritov, and D. A. Schkade

Table 31.1. Rank Correlations Between Mean Evaluations of 37 Issues

	SWTP	Support	Importance	Satisfaction
SWTP	(.87)			
Support	.84	(.85)		
Importance	.76	.84	(.88)	
Satisfaction	.84	.87	.85	(.90)

Note: Adapted from D. Kahneman and I. Ritov "Determinants of Stated Willingness to Pay for Public Goods: A Study in the Headline Method," *Journal of Risk and Uncertainty,* vol. 9, p. 15. Copyright © 1994 by Kluwer Academic Publishers. Reprinted with permission.

What do ratings of importance, predictions of moral satisfaction, statements of political support, and indications of WTP have in common? Our answer is that these expressions share a common affective core, which is so prominent that it allows the public attitude order over objects to be measured almost interchangeably by ostensibly diverse responses.

Payne, Schkade, Desvousges, and Aultman (2000) observed a similar result in a study of 190 citizens who responded to five CV surveys of realistic length and detail. The topics were air quality in the Grand Canyon, oil spill prevention, and preservation of wolves, salmon, and migratory waterfowl. Each respondent expressed an evaluation of each commodity in SWTP and on four 0 to 10 rating scales – importance compared with other problems in society, seriousness compared with other environmental problems, use value, and existence value. Respondents came for two separate 2-hour sessions, scheduled 2 weeks apart. In the first session a given participant responded to all five commodities on either SWTP or the four rating scales. In the second, they again responded to all five surveys, but using the response mode(s) they did not use in the first session. The results showed rank correlation levels between response modes similar to those of Table 31.1 (ranging from .67 to 1.00), despite the many differences in stimuli and procedure from the Kahneman and Ritov study.

Our next example is drawn from a study that employed a similar design to study the psychology of punitive damages. Kahneman et al. (1998) constructed 28 vignettes of cases in which a firm was found liable for compensatory damages in a product liability case. Each participant responded to a subset of 10 of these cases. Separate groups of respondents were asked to answer one of three questions about each scenario: "How outrageous was the defendant's behavior?" (on a 7-point scale), "How severely should the defendant be punished?" (on a 7-point scale), or "How much should the defendant be required to pay in punitive damages?" (in dollars). The respondents were 899 jury-eligible adults. An average of 107 participants responded to each different case-question combination. The 28 cases were ranked by the mean ratings of outrage and punitive intent, and by the median dollar award. The correlations between these rankings are shown in Table 31.2.

Table 31.2. Rank Correlations Between Mean Evaluations of 28 Cases

	$ Awards	Outrage	Punishment
$ Awards (median)	(.89)		
Outrage	.80	(.96)	
Punishment	.92	.86	(.98)

Note: From Kahneman, Schkade, and Sunstein, 1998.

Here again, we may ask what the three responses have in common that results in such high correlations. The outrage rating appears to be a rather direct measure of the affect evoked by cases of personal injury. The high correlations indicate that the same affective valuation also dominates ratings of punitive intent and judgments of punitive damages in dollars. The hypothesis that expressions of attitude are dominated by a shared affective reaction – in this case, by a degree of outrage – is again strongly supported.

The results shown in Tables 31.1 and 31.2 are correlations between averages of large samples, computed over objects. It is important to note that these correlations are not necessarily representative of the results that would be obtained within the data of individual respondents (Nickerson, 1995). As in the case of other summary statistics, it is possible for group results to be dominated by a few individuals who (a) produce more variance than others, and (b) have an atypical pattern of responses. These hypotheses are readily testable (e.g., by examining the effects of standardizing the data of each individual), and we are satisfied that they did not apply to the data reported in this section.[2]

Each expression of attitude also has its specific and distinctive determinants, but these account for less variance than the core affective value. The example of justice being GOOD but not necessarily KIND was used earlier to show that different expressions of the evaluation factor in the semantic differential are not interchangeable. The same conclusion applies to the factor of affective valuation that could be extracted from diverse responses in the data of Tables 31.1 and 31.2. It is convenient to analyze an expression of affective valuation as the sum of three separable components:

$$X = A + S + e \tag{1}$$

where A is the shared affective valuation, S is a response-specific component, and e is an error term. The high correlations shown in the previous section indicate that the first of these components accounts for much more variance than the second. The shared affective value dominates the diverse expressions of attitudes. As the following examples illustrate, however, the specific content associated with different responses is both interesting and important.

---

[2] Within-subject correlations were computed in the study of Payne, Schkade, et al. (2000) and they were quite high: The median correlation between rating scales was .69, and the median correlation between rating scales and individual SWTP was .51. The lower value of the correlations with SWTP is due to the high degree of noise in dollar responses.

Kahneman et al. (1998) offered an *outrage model* to account for both the similarities and the differences between the measures of outrage, punitive intent, and punitive awards. They examined the differences in two experiments. The first experiment demonstrated that rated outrage was the same regardless of whether harm was severe or mild. This result is intuitively plausible: A behavior can be judged as more or less outrageous without knowing its consequences. In contrast, ratings of punitive intent and assessments of punitive damages were both sensitive to the severity of harm. Punishment involves a retributive intent, which depends on the consequences of the act that is to be punished; this is the intuition that justifies treating murder and attempted murder as distinct crimes. A second experiment showed that the size of the defendant firm had a large effect on the amount awarded in punitive damages, but no effect whatsoever on either outrage or punitive intent. This result is also plausible: A payment that constitutes "very severe" punishment for a small firm may be quite insignificant for a larger one. As in the early studies of the semantic differential, we observe a pattern of meaningful differences among highly correlated expressions of the same affective valuation. Detailed examinations of responses to public goods also reveal systematic discrepancies between highly correlated measures (Kahneman & Knetsch, 1992). As the high correlations in these studies suggest, however, the discrepancies between measures are small in magnitude, relative to the large common influence of the underlying affective valuation.

VALUATION BY PROTOTYPE AND THE SCOPE PROBLEM

The evidence reviewed in the preceding section confirmed the similarity between the rankings of objects by different measures of attitude and provided suggestive evidence that the core of attitude is an affective valuation. In this section we argue that the affective valuation of a prototypical exemplar often determines the global attitude to sets of objects. We show that this process can explain an important finding of contingent valuation research: the inadequate sensitivity of SWTP to the quantitative aspects of problems and solutions.

People hold stored prototypes of many categories. They also form prototypes or representative exemplars of new categories and sets that they encounter. The prototypes of tables, of birds, and of Harvard MBAs are widely shared among members of the relevant culture. People also form ad hoc representations of a typical day of a seaside vacation or of a typical resident of a city they visit. These representations of prototypes are evoked in the service of thinking about concepts and classes (Barsalou, 1992).

In judgment by prototype, *a global judgment of a category or set is determined primarily by the relevant properties of its prototype.* The principle of judgment by prototype extends the older idea that a representativeness heuristic is involved in many intuitive judgments about uncertain events (Kahneman & Tversky, 1972, 1973; Tversky & Kahneman, 1971, 1983).

When the size of the set is logically relevant to its valuation, judgment by prototype leads to a bias of extension neglect: *Unless attention is specifically directed to it, the size of the set has little or no influence on its valuation. This pattern has been observed in different contexts, in which extension neglect takes different forms (Kahneman, 2003c).* To illustrate the generality of the phenomenon of extension neglect, we briefly describe three examples:

(a) Intuitive statistical inferences are often made by assessing the similarity between the statistic of a sample and the parameter of a population. The sample and the population are both ensembles, but the judgment about them is based mainly on the relation between the prototypes that represent them. Intuitive inferences based on such reasoning are characterized by extreme lack of sensitivity to sample size, which is the form that extension neglect takes in this task (Griffin & Tversky, 1992; Kahneman & Tversky, 1972; Tversky & Kahneman, 1971).

(b) In a familiar paradigm for the study of intuitive prediction, subjects judge the probability that an individual is a member of a specified social category (defined by a profession or an avocation) on the basis of a personality sketch (Kahneman & Tversky, 1973; Tversky & Kahneman, 1982). Probability is judged by the similarity of the individual's personality to the stereotype of the target category. For example, an individual described as "argumentative, flashy, self-confident, and competitive" will be judged more likely to be a lawyer than to be an engineer, because the description resembles the stereotype of the former profession more than that of the latter. In this paradigm, extension neglect takes the form of inadequate sensitivity to the base rates of outcomes (Kahneman & Tversky, 1973; see also Koehler, 1996; Novemsky & Kronzon, 1999).

(c) Extension neglect has also been observed in a paradigm in which participants are exposed for some time to an unpleasant experience. The participants provide a continuous report of current discomfort, using an "affect meter." Later, they provide a global judgment of the entire episode. Various experiences have been studied, including unpleasant films (e.g., of an amputation), immersion of the hand in cold water, exposure to loud noise, and painful medical procedures (see Kahneman, Wakker, & Sarin, 1997, for a review). For our purposes, an episode of discomfort can be construed as a set of unpleasant moments. The duration of the episode is the measure of extension. Valuation by prototype implies that participants will construct or remember a typical moment of the episode and evaluate the episode as a whole by the level of unpleasantness associated with the prototypical moment – the duration of the episode will be neglected. The hypothesis of duration neglect has been confirmed in several experiments, with both ratings and choices as dependent variables (Kahneman et al., 1997).

In all three situations, judgment by prototype and extension neglect can cause violations of monotonicity. People commonly underestimate the strength of evidence provided by "weak" results in a large sample, compared with stronger results in a small sample (Tversky & Kahneman, 1971). They assign a higher probability to the statement "Linda is a bank teller and a feminist" than to the statement "Linda is a bank teller," if the description of Linda resembles the stereotype of a feminist but not the stereotype of a bank teller (Tversky & Kahneman, 1982). Because the prototypical moment of an episode of discomfort is strongly influenced by how the episode ends, adding a period of diminishing pain to an episode makes it less aversive, in violation of dominance (Kahneman, Fredrickson, Schreiber, & Redelmeier, 1993).

In some applications of contingent valuation, a problem or a solution is specified by the quantity of a homogeneous good. In such cases, extension neglect takes the form of insensitivity to scope: *The quantitative attribute has little weight in the valuation, which is determined mainly by the affective response to a prototypical instance of the good.* Economic theory imposes stringent constraints on the response to variations in the quantities of a good. Diamond and his colleagues (Diamond, 1996; Diamond, Hausman, Leonard, & Denning, 1993) have formulated these constraints as a simple add-up test for SWTP in CV surveys: After allowing for an income effect, SWTP for the conjunction of two parts should equal the sum of SWTP for one part, plus SWTP for the second part conditional on already having the first part. It is generally agreed that adequate sensitivity to scope is essential to the acceptability of CVM (Arrow et al., 1993).

Sensitivity to scope has been studied in several research paradigms. We are concerned here with a particular variant, the *quantity design*, in which participants indicate their willingness to pay for a specified amount of a relatively homogeneous good.[3] The amount of the good is varied across groups of respondents. A well-known example of this experimental design was provided by Desvousges et al. (1992). The question these authors put to their respondents can be paraphrased as follows: "(2,000, or 20,000, or 200,000) migrating birds die each year by drowning in uncovered oil ponds, which the birds mistake for bodies of water. These deaths could be prevented by covering the oil ponds with nets. How much money would you be willing to pay to provide the needed nets?"

The principle of valuation by prototype applies in straightforward fashion to this example. The story constructed by Desvousges et al. (1992) probably evokes for many readers a mental representation of a prototypical incident, perhaps an image of an exhausted bird, its feathers soaked in black oil, unable to escape. The hypothesis of valuation by prototype asserts that the affective value of this image will dominate expressions of the attitude to the problem – including the willingness to pay for a solution. Valuation by prototype implies extension neglect. Although the number of birds that die in oil ponds is surely a relevant consideration, we would expect that – unless the respondents' attention

[3] In the currently most popular variant of CVM, known as the referendum format, respondents are not required to state their maximal SWTP, but only to answer a yes–no question about their willingness to pay a specified amount. The distribution of SWTP is then inferred from the responses to various amounts. We discuss the referendum method in a later section.

is specifically directed to it – the number of bird deaths will have little effect on SWTP or on other measures of attitudes. Indeed, mean SWTP was $80, $78, and $88, respectively, for saving 2,000 birds, 20,000 birds, or 200,000 birds annually (Desvousges et al., 1992).

Similar results have been obtained in other applications of the quantity design. In an early study using this design, Kahneman and Knetsch (see Kahneman, 1986) found that Toronto residents were willing to pay only a little more to clean up all the polluted lakes in Ontario than to clean up polluted lakes in a particular region of Ontario. McFadden and Leonard (1993) reported that residents in four Western states were willing to pay only 28% more to protect all 57 wilderness areas in those states than to protect a single area. Jones-Lee, Loomes, and Philips (1995) found that the SWTP of U.K. respondents for a program to reduce the risk of nonfatal road injuries increased by only 29% when the number of prevented injuries was increased by a factor of three. Laboratory studies show similar insensitivity to the quantity of the good. Baron and Greene (1996, Experiment 8), for instance, found no effect on SWTP of varying the number of lives saved by a factor of 10.

There is research in which the effects of quantitative variations appear to be larger, though certainly not enough to satisfy economic theory. For example, Carson and Mitchell (1995) describe an unpublished study of the value of reducing the risk associated with chlorination of drinking water. They report that an increase of risk from .004 to 2.43 annual deaths per 1,000 (a factor of 600) yielded an increase of SWTP from $3.78 to $15.23 (a factor of 4). This result does not contradict the general conclusion of other research in this area: The response to variations of scope is so slight that it is not explicable in the standard terms of economic analysis.

Explanations of insensitivity to scope in terms of an income effect are implausible, because the amounts are so small. Explanations in terms of substitution effects are equally unattractive. Several studies have shown that reminding subjects of substitutes or of their prior endowment does not substantially change their response (Loomis, Gonzales-Caban, & Gregory, 1994; Neill, 1995; Ritov, Baron, & Hershey, 1993). An interpretation in terms of substitution effects, if it were taken seriously, would be potentially disastrous for the environment. It would indeed be good news for polluters if the public's demand for clean lakes in Ontario could be satisfied by cleaning up a small subset of its lakes.

Our aim in this section was not to deal with the details of the heated controversy concerning sensitivity to scope (see, e.g., Carson & Mitchell, 1995; Frederick & Fischhoff, 1998). Our goal is both simpler and more ambitious: We hope to have shown that inadequate sensitivity to scope in CV surveys that employ the quantity design is *inevitable*, because this phenomenon is an instance of a broad class of similar effects that have been observed in diverse contexts and are explained by a single psychological principle.

Extension neglect is neither universal nor absolute. When extension information is both salient and readily interpretable an additive extension effect is observed: The effects of the valuation of the prototype and of the size of the relevant set are additive. This pattern violates normative rules that require nonlinear combination of the two types of information. In the situations we have discussed, the relevance of extension may be obvious if the quantity mentioned in the problem is readily classified as high or low. Under such circumstances, responses will show some sensitivity to extension. For example, even naïve respondents will appreciate that an annual death rate of .0004% from chlorinated water is very low, because of the impressively large number of leading zeros. However, there are situations in which the quantitative information is less easily interpreted: Unless the two numbers are seen together, for example, the subjective difference between two large quantities such as 20,000 or 200,000 birds dying in oil ponds is not very impressive (Hsee, 1996a). These are the conditions under which complete neglect of scope may be observed.

Studies of extension neglect in other domains have shown that multitrial experiments in which extension varies from trial to trial have two effects: They draw attention to extension as a relevant feature, and they provide a standard that helps the subject assess values of the extensional attribute as high or low. Extension is not completely neglected under these conditions. Indeed, significant effects of extension have been found in within-subject experiments in all the domains we have mentioned. When the base rate of outcomes is varied from trial to trial, people pay attention to it (Novemsky & Kronzon, 1999). When the duration of episodes that are to be evaluated varies from trial to trial, duration neglect is imperfect (Schreiber & Kahneman, 2000; Varey & Kahneman, 1992). Sample size also affects judgments in within-subject experiments (Griffin & Tversky, 1992).

A remarkable regularity appears in these experiments: The valuation of the prototype and the extension of the set (base rate or duration) contribute in strictly additive fashion to the global judgment (see also Anderson, 1996, p. 253). The participants in these experiments appear to reason as follows: "This medical procedure is quite painful, but it is short" or "This medical procedure is quite painful, and it is also long." In contrast to the logic of global evaluation, which requires multiplicative or quasi-multiplicative effects of extension, the size of the set is used as an extra feature in this reasoning.

The additive extension effect is also found in the valuation of environmental goods. Kahneman and Ritov (unpublished research) presented several groups of respondents messages such as the following: "The population of Dolphins in a coastal preserve has declined by 50%." The species mentioned ranged widely in emotional appeal, and the population decline was also varied. Some respondents rated the importance of the problem. Others indicated, for each species, how much of a contribution of $40 to a general environmental fund they would divert to restore the population of the species in the nature preserve. Figure 31.1 presents the results for both response measures. The striking feature of these data is that both the dollar measure and the rating of importance exhibit nearly perfect additivity of the effects of species popularity and size of population decline. Precisely the same pattern of results has been observed in studies of

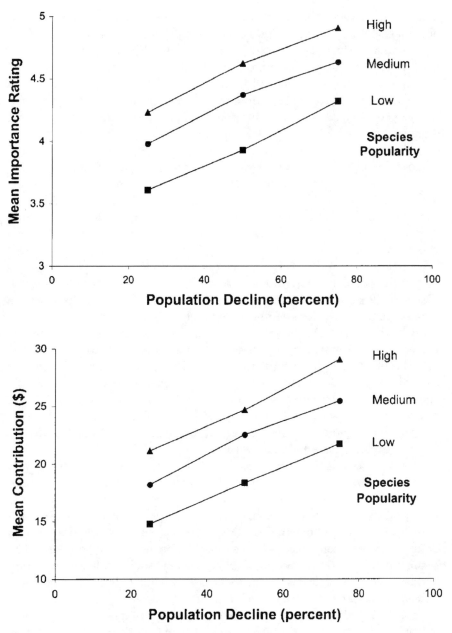

Figure 31.1. (Top) Mean importance ratings, by species popularity and degree of population decline. (Bottom) Mean contributions, by species popularity and degree of population decline.

individual prediction (Novemsky & Kronzon, 1999) and of the global evaluation of episodes (Schreiber & Kahneman, 2000). A related result was obtained
by DeKay and McClelland (1996), who found that the species attributes and
the probability of survival were combined additively in people's ranking of
programs to preserve endangered species.

We draw several conclusions from this research. First, some effect of extension can be obtained by a procedure, such as the within-subject experimental
design, which simultaneously draws attention to the quantitative variable and
provides a frame of reference for responding to it. Second, a demonstration
that people can be responsive to extension and scope under some conditions is
not sufficient to support the conclusion that they always use extension in accordance with the relevant logic. Third, and most important, we again find that the
anomalies observed in studies of the value of public goods do not remain either
puzzling or unique when they are viewed in the context of similar phenomena
in other domains.

*Several different designs have been used to test sensitivity to scope. The designs
are psychologically different, but the normative pattern defined by the add-up test
(Diamond, 1996) is unlikely to be satisfied in any of them.* Sensitivity to scope has
been examined in two designs other than the quantity design that was discussed
in previous sections. (a) In the *explicit list* design, respondents in different groups
value nested lists of heterogeneous goods. For example, one group may assess
the value of saving both the birds and the fish in a region, whereas other groups
value the birds or the fish in isolation. (b) In the *embedding* design, SWTP for a
good (e.g., saving dolphins) is obtained in two ways: by a direct question and
by a sequence of questions, first eliciting SWTP for an inclusive good, then the
fraction of that amount that should be allocated to a specified good (e.g., SWTP
for saving marine mammals, then an allocation to dolphins).

The various tests of scope are equivalent in an economic analysis, and
Diamond's add-up test is applicable to all three. In a psychological analysis,
however, the designs differ in important ways. The quantity design involves
a set or category of elements that are similar in essential respects (e.g., polluted lakes or different members of the same species). In contrast, the two other
designs involve heterogeneous elements, which are not readily represented by
a single prototype (Rosch & Lloyd, 1978). There is some evidence that a process of *judgment by maximum* operates in the valuation of heterogeneous categories and lists (Levav, 1996). A related result was reported by Rottenstreich and
Tversky (1997) in a study of judgments of frequency for explicit lists (e.g., "How
many Stanford students major in either English or Geography?"). Judgment of
the total frequency of an explicit disjunction were barely higher than judgments of its maximum. Judgment by maximum, of course, violates the add-up
rule.

Carson et al. (1994) reported a study using an explicit list design, which they
described as a demonstration of sensitivity to scope. Unfortunately, a basic
flaw of their study invalidates their conclusions. The study was concerned with

the valuation of the damage that deposits of DDT in the soil of Los Angeles Harbor has caused to the reproductive ability of two salient species of birds (Peregrine Falcon, American Bald Eagle) and two relatively obscure species of fish (White Croaker, Kelp Bass). The authors observed higher SWTP when the description of the problem involved all four species than when it involved only the fish. Of course, the results are equally consistent with the hypothesis that WTP to restore two important species of endangered birds is higher than WTP to restore two relatively obscure species of fish. The hypothesis of judgment by maximum suggests that the value attached to the four species would not be much higher than the value attached to the most important of these species. The results of an informal replication of the Los Angeles Harbor study, using ratings of importance, were generally consistent with this hypothesis (Levav, 1996). There is no reason to expect that the results of CV using explicit lists will satisfy the add-up test (see also Frederick & Fischhoff, 1998).

The findings obtained in the embedding design unequivocally violate the add-up rule. For example, Kemp and Maxwell (1993) found that SWTP for protection from oil spills off the coast of Alaska was $85 when the good was considered on its own, but only $0.29 when it was derived as an allocation of SWTP for a more inclusive category (environmental protection programs). Kahneman and Knetsch (1992) reported similar findings.

The central point of this section has been that inadequate sensitivity to scope is not a surprise. On the contrary, it would be a major surprise to observe measures of SWTP that reliably conform to the add-up test. This conclusion is relevant to the frequently expressed hope that the scope problem might be overcome by improved instructions, exhortation, or added information. Insensitivity to scope is the inevitable result of general rules that govern human judgment. It is naïve to expect broad psychological laws to be overcome by minor methodological adjustments.

CONTEXT-DEPENDENCE AND VALUATION REVERSALS

A preference reversal is said to exist when two strategically equivalent methods for probing the preference between objects yield conflicting results (see, e.g., Hsee, 1996a; Tversky & Thaler, 1990). Preference reversals simultaneously challenge two basic tenets of the standard economic analysis of choice: The existence of a preference order and the assumption of extensionality. One of the crucial differences between the concepts of economic preference and attitude is that preference reversals are anomalous only for the former, not for the latter. In this section we discuss preference reversals that arise from the context dependence of attitudes and affective valuations. Norm theory (Kahneman & Miller, 1986) provides the theoretical background for this discussion.

An object that is considered in isolation evokes a comparison set of similar objects. The valuation of the object is relative to the set that it evoked. Features that are common to the evoked set play no role in relative judgments and valuations. For an illustration of the relativity of judgment to an evoked set, consider the following two questions: "Is a subcompact car BIG or SMALL?" and "Is a bald eagle BIG or SMALL?" The plausible answers are that a subcompact is small and a bald eagle is big. The categories of cars and birds are spontaneously evoked by the mere mention of their members, and these categories provide the norm for a relative judgment of size. The conventions of language allow the entire range of size adjectives, from "tiny" to "enormous" to be applied to cars and to birds, to countries and to bacteria.

As we show later, expressions of attitudes show a similar relativity. Furthermore, casual observation indicates that affective values – not only the words used to describe them – are themselves relative. Thus, a guest's rude behavior at a party can arouse intense outrage and anger. Murder is much worse than rudeness, of course, but murder is not part of the evoked context that determines the emotional response to a rude remark. The relativity of affective value explains why people often seem to care intensely about matters that they can also view as trivial when the context changes.

Explicit comparison of several objects imposes a shared context for their judgment and valuation. When the objects belong to different categories, comparisons and isolated valuations can yield discrepant results. Differences between the modes of valuation are found both in dollar measures and in ratings. Table 31.3 presents preliminary tests of this hypothesis, drawn from two different studies. The same pair of issues was used in both studies: damage to coral reefs caused by cyanide fishing in Asia and increased incidence of multiple myeloma among the elderly. We surmised that the latter issue would be perceived as a fairly minor public health problem, whereas a threat to coral reefs would appear significant in an ecological context. We also surmised that public health problems would be assigned a higher general priority than ecological problems, but that this priority would become relevant only in a direct comparison.

Table 31.3. Responses to an Ecological and a Public Health Problem, by Presentation Order

Study 1

	Moral Satisfaction		Importance	
	First	Second	First	Second
Coral reefs	3.54	3.24	3.78	3.62
Myeloma	2.84	4.18	3.24	4.26

Study 2

	Moral Satisfaction		SWTP[a]	
	First	Second	First	Second
Coral reefs	3.47	3.05	$45	$59
Myeloma	2.98	3.76	$69	$109

[a] All values of WTP in excess of $500 were adjusted to $500.

The procedure of the two studies was similar. The participants were first asked to evaluate one problem; they were then shown the other problem and were asked to respond to it, with an explicit instruction to consider both problems before responding. The independent variable was the order of presentation of the two problems. The participants in Study 1 were 100 visitors at the San Francisco Exploratorium. They were asked to rate the importance of each problem and the satisfaction they would expect to get from making a contribution to its solution (both on a 0–6 scale). The data for Study 2 are drawn from a larger study, in which participants were jury-eligible residents of Austin. Some participants (N = 130) provided ratings of satisfaction as in Study 1. Others (N = 261) indicated their WTP to contribute to a solution; when they encountered the second problem they were instructed to treat it as the only cause to which they would be asked to contribute.

Our hypothesis about the role of context in judgments predicts a statistical interaction effect in each of the panels of Table 31.3: The difference between the valuations of the myeloma and coral reefs problems is expected to be larger when these items appear in the second position than in the first. The rationale for this prediction is that the difference between the categories of ecological and human problems is salient only when the issues are directly compared, not when they are valued in isolation. The predicted interaction is highly significant ($p < .001$) in each of the four panels of Table 31.3.

The context effect observed in SWTP is especially noteworthy, because the linguistic convention that allows words such as "important" or "satisfying" to be understood in a relative sense does not apply to the dollar scale. To appreciate the difference between scales that allow relativity and scales that do not, consider the questions: "What is the size of an eagle, in meters?" and "What is the size of a subcompact, in meters?" Of course, there is no reason to expect any effect of category on answers to this question. A context effect on a size judgment expressed in absolute units indicates a visual illusion – a change in the underlying perception, not in the language used to describe it. By the same logic, the finding of a context effect on a dollar measure implies that the evaluation itself, not only the expression of it, is altered by the comparison.

Kahneman, Schkade, and Sunstein (unpublished data) investigated the effects of a comparison context on punitive damage awards. The study was motivated by the observation that the highest punitive awards are commonly found in cases involving large financial harm, probably because the size of the compensatory damages provides a high anchoring value. Punitive damages are generally lower in cases of personal injury, where compensatory damages are also lower. We surmised, however, that cases that result in personal injury are, as a class, more outrageous than cases in which the only losses involve money. Of course, no jury ever considers cases of the two types at the same time, but we predicted that forcing jurors to do so in an experiment would alter or reverse the usual pattern of punitive awards. A sample of 114 jury-eligible citizens provided a punitive damage assessment for either a personal injury case adapted from

Kahneman et al. (1998; a child seriously hurt because of a flawed child-safety cap) or a financial harm case (business fraud), or both. Participants were told that compensatory damages had already been awarded, in the amount of $500,000 for the personal injury and $10 million for the financial harm. As predicted, respondents who judged only one case assessed greater punitive damages in the financial case (median = $5 million) than in the personal injury case (median = $2 million). However, a strong majority (75%) of respondents who judged the two cases together assessed larger awards in the personal injury case, resulting in a striking reversal of median awards ($2.5 million for the personal injury; $0.5 million for the financial harm). More recent data indicate similar effects in ratings of outrage and punitive intent. The same interpretation applies to these results and to the findings summarized in Table 31.3. Cases of personal injury and of financial harm, when considered in isolation, are apparently compared with very different evoked contexts. Here again, the conclusion that the context alters the underlying emotion is justified by the finding of an effect on a dollar measure. A financial transgression that appears outrageous on its own apparently arouses much less outrage when directly compared with an action that causes a child to suffer a severe injury (Kahneman, Schkade, Ritov, & Sunstein, 1999).

Choice is a special case of comparative valuation, whereas pricing (or the setting of WTP) is normally done by considering a problem in isolation. The different contexts of choice and pricing explain some preference reversals between the two tasks. The analysis of context effects in the preceding section helps explain preference reversals between choice and SWTP that were reported by Kahneman and Ritov (1994). Seven critical pairs of items were constructed, each including one ecological issue and one public health problem. The responses of two groups of respondents were compared. One group encountered both items in a questionnaire that elicited statements of WTP for interventions to alleviate each of several (12–14) problems, which the respondents were instructed to consider independently. Other respondents were asked to make a choice between two items from the same list. They were told that "it sometimes happens that budget constraints force a choice between two desirable projects. One has to be given up, at least for now, so that the other can go forward." The respondents were then asked which of the two interventions they would retain, if they had to make this choice.

Robust reversals of preference were obtained. On average, only 41% of the respondents who stated different WTP for the two items indicated greater willingness to pay for the public health problem.[4] However, 66% of responses favored the public health issues in the choice condition. The difference between the two conditions was statistically significant separately for each of the seven pairs of items. A different pattern was observed in five other pairs of issues, in which the two issues were drawn from the same category. In these control

---

[4] SWTP was the same for the two issues in about 40% of the cases – most often because both responses were zero.

pairs, the proportions favoring one issue over another were quite similar in choice and in SWTP.

The context dependence of valuations suggests three observations: (a) the hope of measuring preferences by SWTP is unrealistic, (b) a suitable choice of context may help improve the rationality of elicited preferences, and (c) there is no general attitude order, but modeling context-dependent affective valuations is feasible in principle. The finding of preference reversals between SWTP and choice implies that WTP does not provide a stable measure of the position of an object in a preference order – in our view, because there is no stable preference order to be measured. Like the scope problem that was discussed in the preceding section, the context dependence of SWTP is an unavoidable consequence of basic cognitive and evaluative processes. It is not a result of defective procedures, and it will not be eliminated by improved survey methods.

The reversals of valuation that we have observed in both SWTP and punitive damages raise a significant prescriptive question: When different methods for eliciting attitudes yield conflicting results, which method should be used? In general, of course, decisions that are based on a richer set of considerations and on a broader context are more likely to be stable and to satisfy standards of rationality. This principle suggests that asking people for choices may be better than asking them to consider issues in isolation. We have seen, for example, that the priority of public health over ecological concerns is effectively suppressed in the SWTP measure and becomes evident only when respondents must compare items from the two categories. Similarly, the difference in the outrageousness of actions that cause physical or financial damage was suppressed when cases were considered in isolation and revealed only by a direct comparison. The benefits of improved rationality are more likely to be achieved if the context of comparison is truly broad and if it has been selected impartially. Mere exhortations to consider many possibilities (Arrow et al., 1993) are not likely to be effective.

Our findings provided further evidence for a simple negative conclusion: There is no comprehensive and coherent "attitude order." This is not a message of despair. The phrase "Individual *I* likes/dislikes to extent *X* the description *D* of object *O*, considered in context *C*" is, at least in principle, subject to measurement, verification, and modeling. We already know, for example, that different measures of liking will yield similar estimates of *X* and that if two objects spontaneously evoke the same context *C*, measurements of their relative preference by liking and by choice will probably be consistent. Attitudes do not lack structure, but their structure is vastly more complex than the structure that economic analysis attributes to human preferences.

THE PSYCHOPHYSICS OF VALUATION

The results of the Evaluation Factor section demonstrated that average dollar responses for large groups yield much the same ranking of attitude objects as do other measures of attitudes. To the proponents of contingent valuation or to

584   D. Kahneman, I. Ritov, and D. A. Schkade

the supporters of the jury system this is faint praise, because they need much more than a ranking of objects. The goal of asking survey respondents to assess a public good or of asking jurors to assess punitive damages is to obtain a dollar value that is meaningful in absolute terms, not only in relation to other objects. Can this goal of absolute measurement be realized? In this section we draw on psychophysical research to examine the measurement properties of the dollar scale and to compare it with other measures of affective valuation.

The attitude expressions elicited in surveys can be classified as category scales *or* magnitude scales. These terms are borrowed from the field of psychophysics, the study of the functions that relate quantitative expressions of subjective reactions to physical variables. For example, the perceived loudness of tones that vary in amplitude can be measured on a bounded category scale (e.g., from "not loud at all" to "very very, loud"). Loudness can also be measured on a magnitude scale by presenting the subject with a series of tones, with the instruction to assign a given number (known as the *modulus*) to a specified standard tone and to assign numbers to other tones relative to this common modulus. The defining characteristics of a magnitude scale are that it is unbounded, has a meaningful zero, and expresses the ratios of the relevant underlying variable.

In terms of this classification of scales, the normal practice of survey research is to use category scales, such as numerical ratings on a bounded scale. However, attitudes can also be measured using magnitude scales (Lodge, 1981; Stevens, 1975). For example, Stevens (1975) reported judgments of the severity of crimes and also of the severity of different legal punishments, using an unbounded magnitude scale.

Studies of magnitude scaling in the context of psychophysical measurement have yielded several generalizations, which apply as well to the domain of attitude measurement (Stevens, 1975). (a) There is a fair degree of agreement among observers on the *ratios* of the magnitudes that they assign to the sensations evoked by particular stimuli. (b) In the absence of a designated common modulus, there are large individual differences in the mean values of judgments: Some observers assign generally high numbers to all stimuli; others assign low numbers. (c) The distribution of responses to any stimulus is positively skewed; a log-normal distribution often provides an adequate fit. (d) The standard deviation of the judgments of different stimuli is approximately proportional to their means; this relationship holds both when the same individual judges each stimulus several times and when the judgments are contributed by different observers. In contrast, category scales are characterized by a negligible correlation between the mean and the standard deviation of judgments. (e) In general, magnitude judgments of sensory intensity are a power function of the relevant physical variable: For example, brightness is a power function of luminance, and loudness is a power function of sound amplitude (both with an exponent of approximately 1/3). (f) Magnitude scales are generally related by a power function to category scales of the same stimuli.

The elicitation of dollar responses is a special case of magnitude scaling without a modulus. The scale of dollars is unbounded and its zero is a meaningful response; the respondents (participants in CV surveys or jurors in civil cases) are not provided with a standard problem to which a specified dollar amount must be assigned (i.e., a modulus). The defining characteristics of scaling without a modulus are therefore satisfied. The results obtained with dollar scales are similar to the results that are observed with magnitude scales in psychophysical studies. In particular, the distribution of dollar responses is positively skewed, both within the responses of each individual and within the responses to any given problem. The distribution of the mean dollar judgments of individual respondents is also highly skewed. Finally, the high correlation between the mean and the standard deviation of individuals, which is expected for magnitude scales, was observed both by Kahneman and Ritov (1994; $r = .93$) and by Kahneman et al. (1998; $r = .90$).

As expected for an application of magnitude scaling without a common modulus, dollar responses are statistically less efficient than category scale measures of the same attitudes. We have seen that the averages of different attitude expressions in large samples yield similar rankings of objects (see Tables 31.1 and 31.2). However, dollar responses produce much lower signal-to-noise ratios than do rating scales. Tables 31.4 and 31.5 present results from separate analyses of variance for each of the response measures used in the two studies. The analysis partitions the variance of responses into three components: (a) *Object (signal)*: the variance associated with differences among objects of judgments (e.g., public goods that differ in value, personal injury cases that vary in the outrageousness of the defendant's actions). (b) *Respondents*: the variance associated with individual differences in the mean level of responses, over objects (e.g., some respondents state generally higher WTP than others, some experimental jurors are generally more severe than others). (c) *Noise*: the residual variance, which combines the effects of individual differences in variability, idiosyncratic responses of some respondents to some objects or topics, and various sources of measurement error.

Tables 31.4 and 31.5 document a striking discrepancy in the strength of the signal (as indicated by the proportion of variance explained) between dollar measures and attitude expressions measured on standard bounded scales. The proportion of Object variance (i.e., signal) was 2 to 4 times larger for rating scales than for SWTP in Kahneman and Ritov (1994). The advantage of the rating scales was even more pronounced in responses to product liability cases, where the amount of Object variance was 5 to 8 times higher for ratings than for dollar responses (Kahneman et al., 1998).

Table 31.4. Proportion of Variance Explained by Problems

	Raw	Ranks
Support	.08	.26
Importance	.16	.28
Satisfaction	.12	.26
SWTP	.04	.23

Note: From Kahneman and Ritov, 1994.

Table 31.5. Proportion of Variance Explained by Scenarios

	Raw	Ranks
Outrage	.29	.42
Punishment	.49	.58
$ Awards	.06	.51

Note: Adapted from D. Kahneman, D. Schkade, and C. R. Sunstein, "Shared Outrage and Erratic Awards: The Psychology of Punitive Damages," *Journal of Risk and Uncertainty*, vol. 16, p. 66. Copyright © 1998 by Kluwer Academic Publishers. Reprinted with permission.

The low signal-to-noise ratio of dollar awards implies poor agreement among individuals, and even among juries. Kahneman et al. (1998) used Monte Carlo techniques to assess the average rank-correlation between dollar awards across cases for simulated "juries" of size 12: The estimated reliability (.42) appears unacceptably low.[5]

Some transformations of dollar responses improve statistical efficiency by reducing the effects of the skewness of magnitude scales and of the large individual differences in moduli. For example, logarithmic and rank transformations of each individual's dollar responses both yield substantial improvements of signal-to-noise ratio. Transforming SWTP responses to a logarithmic scale doubled the percentage of Object variance (from 4% to 8%), to a level comparable with the other measures. Logarithmic transformation of punitive awards yielded even more dramatic improvement (Object variance increased from 6% to 42%). As shown in Tables 31.4 and 31.5, a ranking transformation also yielded a substantial increase in the relative amount of Object variance in both studies. The success of these transformations is due to the fact that the effect of individual differences in the use of the dollar scale is reduced by the logarithmic transformation and eliminated by the ranking transformation. The good performance of the transformed measures also demonstrates that the dollar response contains useful information about respondents' attitudes. If the objective of research is to rank order a set of objects, the dollar response – suitably transformed, and with a sufficiently large sample – provides as much information as other expressions of affective evaluation. Of course, the proponents of CV and of the current jury system hope for much more, because their goal is to obtain an exact dollar amount.

Individual differences in the use of the dollar scale are large and may be arbitrary to a substantial extent. In psychophysical research, magnitude scaling without a common modulus yields large individual differences in the responses to stimuli, because subjects spontaneously adopt quite different moduli. If two subjects who share the same underlying psychophysical function adopt different moduli, their responses to all stimuli will differ by a constant of proportionality, which is the ratio of their individual moduli.

In the psychophysical laboratory, differences in moduli are usually considered to be entirely arbitrary, a mere source of statistical noise. Except for very unusual circumstances (e.g., deafness), there is little reason to believe that an

[5] The higher value shown in Table 31.2 (.89) was obtained with "juries" of 107 members.

individual who consistently assigns low numbers to the loudness of tones actually experiences less loudness than an individual who assigns higher numbers. Are the moduli that CV respondents and jurors apply in assigning dollar responses also arbitrary? A positive answer to this question would remove the rationale for any procedure in which the absolute values that people state are taken seriously, including contingent valuation and the setting of monetary punishments by juries.

There are several ways of testing whether individual differences in the use of the dollar scale are meaningful or arbitrary. (a) *Prediction of behavior.* Several studies have examined the correlation between hypothetical responses to WTP questions and actual behavior (e.g., Cummings, Harrison, & Rutstrom, 1995; Foster, Bateman, & Harley, 1997; Seip & Strand, 1992). The data indicate a substantial upward bias in hypothetical responses. (b) *Search for correlated variables.* If the difference between high-SWTP and low-SWTP respondents is real, it should be correlated with other characteristics of these individuals, such as income, or other indications of involvement in environmental issues. These correlations have been examined in some studies and are usually low or nonexistent. Kahneman et al. (1998) also failed to find significant correlations between the average size of the awards set by individual respondents and several relevant predictors, including demographic attributes and individuals' ratings of the importance that they attached to different features of the cases, such as the degree of malice or the amount of harm suffered by the plaintiff. (c) *Susceptibility to anchoring.* The large anchoring effects that we discuss in the next section indicate that dollar responses are very labile, both in CV surveys and in punitive awards. Arbitrary numbers that are mentioned in a question have considerable influence on responses – much as arbitrary moduli do.

We do not yet have the data needed to evaluate the relative size of the arbitrary and of the meaningful components in the variability of dollar responses. The available evidence, however, hardly justifies reliance on the absolute values of judgments denominated in dollars. There is at present no reason to believe that dollar responses contain useful information that cannot be obtained more simply and accurately by using other expressions of attitudes.

ANCHORING EFFECTS

The procedure of asking people to state their maximal WTP for a good has been largely supplanted in CV practice by a protocol in which respondents are asked how they would vote in a hypothetical referendum that would guarantee the provision of public good at a specified cost to the household. Different groups of respondents face different proposed payments, and the cumulative frequency distribution of positive responses is used to estimate the parameters of the underlying distribution of WTP. The estimates of WTP that are generated by this estimation technique are substantially higher than the estimates obtained by an open-ended question, such as "What is the maximum amount of payment for which you would still support the proposition?" (Desvousges et al., 1992; McFadden, 1994). The referendum format has been defended on grounds of its supposedly superior incentive compatibility (Hanemann, 1994; Hoehn & Randall, 1989). We do not directly debate this claim here (see Green, Jackowitz, Kahneman, & McFadden, 1998). Following the broad strategy of this chapter, we show instead that the discrepancy between the two types of WTP questions can be parsimoniously explained by a well-understood process of anchoring, which produces similar effects in contexts to which the incentive compatibility idea does not apply.

Tasks in which respondents indicate a judgment or an attitude by producing a number are susceptible to an anchoring effect*: The response is strongly biased toward any value, even if it is arbitrary, that the respondent is induced to consider as a candidate answer.* Anchoring effects are among the most robust observations in the psychological literature. In a striking demonstration, Wilson and his collaborators induced an anchoring effect by the following procedure: They required subjects to write the last four digits of their Social Security numbers, then to state whether they thought that the number of physicians and surgeons listed in the local Yellow Pages was higher or lower than that number. Finally, the subjects provided an open-ended estimate of the number of physicians and surgeons. The estimates that different subjects offered were strongly correlated with their Social Security numbers (Wilson, Houston, Etling, & Brekke, 1996). The necessary and apparently sufficient conditions for the emergence of anchoring effects are: (a) the presence of some uncertainty about the correct or appropriate response and (b) a procedure that causes the individual to consider a number as a candidate answer. A vast literature has documented anchoring effects in estimation tasks (see, e.g., Strack & Mussweiler, 1997; Wilson et al., 1996), as well as in other settings, including negotiations (Ritov, 1996), and the setting of both compensatory (Chapman & Bornstein, 1996) and punitive awards (Hastie, Schkade & Payne, 1999).

Jacowitz and Kahneman (1995) proposed an index of the size of anchoring effects, which they applied to estimation tasks. They first obtained a distribution of answers to open-ended questions about quantities such as the length of the Amazon or the height of the tallest redwood, and observed the 15th and 85th percentiles of the estimates for each quantity. These values were used as anchors for two additional groups. Respondents in these anchored groups first answered a binary question, such as "Is the height of the tallest redwood more or less than X?" where the value of X was either the high or the low anchor for that problem. The anchoring index was defined as a ratio. The numerator is the difference between the median estimates of the anchored groups; the denominator is the difference between the high and low anchors. By this measure, the anchoring effects were very large: The median anchoring index in a set of 20 problems was .49.

Anchors have a suggestive effect on the answers to binary questions. With scales bounded on one side (such as the dollar scale) this effect causes an upward bias in binary

*answers, relative to corresponding open-ended responses. In the context of CV sur-
veys, this bias explains the discrepancy previously observed between estimates of WTP
from referendum questions and from open-ended questions.* The design employed by
Jacowitz and Kahneman (1995) allows a comparison between two proportions:
(a) the proportion of respondents in the original group (unanchored) who spontaneously offered an estimate higher than an anchor, and (b) the proportion of
respondents in the anchored group who stated that the same anchor was lower
than the true value of the quantity. In the absence of bias, the two proportions
should be the same. However, the results showed a pronounced bias: On average, respondents in the anchored group judged the high anchor to be lower
than the true value on 27% of occasions, very significantly more than the 15%
expected from the responses of the unanchored group. Furthermore, there was
a pronounced asymmetry in the bias: The low anchors were judged to be too
high on only 14% of occasions. The asymmetry was due to the prevalence of
estimation problems in which the range of possible answers is bounded by
zero, for example, the height of the tallest redwood. The result of this bias, of
course, is that the estimates inferred from the binary question were generally
much higher than the estimates obtained directly from open-ended questions.
The discrepancy between the two response modes is similar to the discrepancy observed in CV research between estimates of WTP derived from open-
ended and from referendum questions (Desvousges et al., 1992; McFadden,
1994).

The similarity between the effects of anchors on estimates of uncertain quantities and on SWTP were explored in a study reported by Green et al. (1998).
Visitors at the San Francisco Exploratorium were recruited to answer five questions, including estimates of three quantities (height of the tallest redwood in
California, average monthly gasoline used by car owners, annual rainfall in the
wettest spot on earth) and two WTP questions (save 50,000 off-shore seabirds
each year from dying in oil spills, reduce auto accidents in California by 20%).
The first and the last questions in each questionnaire were WTP questions.
As in the Jacowitz and Kahneman (1995) study, a calibration group provided
open-ended answers to all five questions. Five anchored groups answered a
binary question about each quantity before estimating it. The anchors used in
the binary question were chosen to be at the percentiles 25, 50, 75, 90 and 95 of
the distribution of open-ended responses.

As expected, comparison of the anchored open-ended responses with the
responses of the unanchored groups revealed a large anchoring effect in both
estimation and WTP questions. For example, the mean estimate of the height of
a tallest redwood ranged from 282 ft (with 180 ft as an anchor) to 844 ft (with an
anchor of 1,200 ft). Similarly, mean SWTP to save 50,000 birds annually ranged
from $20.30 (with a $5 anchor) to $143.12 (with a $400 anchor).

An anchoring effect was also observed in answers to binary questions, for
both estimates and SWTP. On average, there were 4.3% of answers exceeding
the highest anchor in the calibration group, but 21.6% of respondents in the
anchoring condition judged the same anchor to be too low. The pattern for low

anchors was quite different: 21.5% of unanchored answers were lower than the low anchor, but the same anchor was judged to be too high on only 15.8% of occasions. As in the earlier study, high anchors induced a much larger bias. As a consequence of this asymmetric anchoring effect, the cumulative distribution derived from binary questions stochastically dominated the distribution of open-ended answers. Over the five questions, the average ratio of the mean of the distribution inferred from binary questions to the unanchored mean was 3.43 (2.97 for the three estimation questions, 4.13 for the two WTP questions).[6]

This study again illustrates the benefits of searching for parallel phenomena across domains. The psychological analysis reveals that the tasks of estimating positive quantities and of determining a WTP are deeply similar to each other, in both their open-ended and binary versions. They yield similarly skewed distributions of responses, are susceptible to similarly asymmetric anchoring effects, and therefore produce the same discrepancy between the parameters estimated from open-ended and from binary questions. In light of these observations, an explanation of the discrepancy in estimates of WTP in terms of incentive compatibility has little appeal, because it cannot be applied to the identical finding in another task.

APPLICATIONS

The central claim of this chapter has been that people are better described as having attitudes than preferences – perhaps in every domain, but certainly in the domain of public concerns. In contrast, CVM is rooted in the assumption that conventional consumer theory applies to public goods, including nonuse goods such as the continued existence of the whooping crane. At least in principle, the dollar value of such a good could be read off an individual's preference order. The assumption of an inclusive preference order appears to be widely shared among economists, including critics of CVM (e.g., Diamond & Hausman, 1994) and among rational-agent theorists in political science (see Bartels, 1998, for a discussion). In this theoretical framework, the main question to be asked about contingent valuation is the accuracy of measurement that it provides.

The problem with CVM, in our view, is not imprecise measurement but an incorrect theory. If consumer theory does not capture the nature of people's value for environmental goods, there can be no more hope of measuring the economic value of the whooping crane than there is of measuring the physical properties of the ether. Of course, many people do value the whooping crane and will even pay to preserve it. We have described these people as having a positive affective valuation of whooping cranes, which induces a positive attitude to interventions that will preserve this species. These valuations can be

[6] These results are based on a parametric estimation procedure described in detail by Green et al. (1998). A nonparametric estimation procedure yielded similar ratios: 2.14 for uncertain quantities, 2.22 for SWTP.

expressed in many ways, including statements of WTP, actual payments, and votes in both simulated and real referenda. Attitude objects can be ordered reliably by sample averages of diverse expressions of valuation, including SWTP. As we have seen, however, these valuations lack some of the essential properties that economic theory requires of preferences. In particular, expressions of affective valuation are susceptible to framing effects (Bartels, 1998; Zaller, 1992), inadequately sensitive to scope, and severely context dependent. Moreover, dollar measures of valuation are especially susceptible to the effects of anchors and of arbitrary moduli.

The extreme context dependence of attitudes undermines the most compelling rationale that has been offered for the CVM. As Hanemann (1994) pointed out, the referendum question presents the respondent with a realistic task of formulating a voting intention, and answers to such survey questions have often been found to predict voting outcomes with fair accuracy. However, the only permissible inference from this argument is that CVM results predict the outcome of a real referendum that precisely mimics the context and framing of the survey question (Payne, Bettman, & Schkade, 1999). The results do not provide reliable information about the voting outcomes that would be obtained with different wording of the question or if the target proposition were embedded in a particular list of propositions. The evidence that SWTP diminishes steadily when several causes are considered in sequence (Carson & Mitchell, 1995; Payne et al., 2000) is another illustration of context dependence and another demonstration that CVM results are not sufficiently robust to provide a basis for policy.

Our pessimism about the validity of CVM does not imply despair about the possibility of using public attitudes as an aid to policy making. The affective value that people attach to issues probably conveys useful information about their possible reactions to policy proposals or to actual outcomes. More formal approaches to the elicitation of priorities are also possible, if they are developed with adequate respect for the psychology of valuation. For example, a scale of value for environmental damage could be developed by constructing a small set of hypothetical benchmark scenarios, covering a broad range of damage magnitude and commodity importance. Two criteria for including scenarios in the scale would be: (a) high consensus in the attitudes of the public to the scenario, and (b) a hope of achieving professional and political consensus on appropriate dollar values. Public attitudes would be one input into this process, but probably not the only one. We expect that experts would bring in relevant considerations that lay judgment is prone to neglect, such as the scope and duration of the damage. The objective of the scaling effort would be to provide a mapping from attitudes and other relevant factors to dollar values for a particular class of environmental commodities.

Once a scale is established, a real issue that arises could be valued by a survey in which respondents would explicitly compare the current problem to the benchmark scenarios. The measures of attitude used in this comparison would be chosen by psychometric criteria: Measures of judged importance and political support would probably be preferred to SWTP. A dollar value would be assigned based on the rank of the target issue among the benchmark scenarios of the standard scale. One advantage of this proposal is that the difficult conceptual problems of anchoring the dollar value of public goods in the preferences and opinions of the citizenry would be addressed just once, in the process of constructing the initial scale linking monetary value to attitude. Clearly, professional and political consensus is more likely to be achieved in dealing with hypothetical questions constructed for this purpose than in evaluating real goods in the context of litigation. Rutherford, Knetsch, and Brown (1998) make a similar argument and propose that damage schedules be developed to replace ad hoc valuation based on SWTP responses.

The other domain that we have discussed, the setting of punitive damages, is a descendant of an old tradition that requires a small group of citizens to express their attitudes in dollars. It is remarkable that the jury system appears designed to enhance rather than minimize the deficiencies of human judgment: Juries are instructed to consider cases one at a time, using a dollar measure without a modulus. Not surprisingly, dollar awards are erratic, in spite of a high level of agreement on ratings of outrage and punitive intent. Sunstein, Kahneman, and Schkade (1998) provide a detailed analysis of possible reforms of the jury's task, which would require jurors to do what they can do well, not what they can do poorly. The determination of what jurors can do well combines normative evaluations with empirical facts. For example, if a normative analysis concludes that jurors' intuitions about appropriate severity of punishment are valid, but their ability to translate these intuitions into dollars is weak – a plausible conclusion in view of the data reported here – the system could be reformed by requiring jurors to provide graded verbal statements of the severity of punishment that they consider just, leaving to the judge the task of translating this intent into a dollar amount.

Taken together, the examples of CV and punitive damages show that the debate about the nature of preferences and about the rationality of agents is not merely theoretical. The procedures that lead to some significant societal decisions may take different forms, depending on whether the decisions of individual citizens are best understood as a reflection of attitudes or of standard economic preferences.

CONCLUDING REMARKS

The stereotyped role of the psychologist in the interdisciplinary conversation about the nature of human choice is that of a critic, engaged in the construction of counterexamples to the economist's rational models. We have attempted to expand this role here by focusing on the power and generality of psychological principles, rather than on the limitations of rational choice theory. Our theme has been that phenomena that appear anomalous from the perspective of standard preference models are in fact predictable – indeed, inevitable – consequences of well-established rules of judgment and valuation, which apply in domains that are beyond the reach of choice theory. The alternative to rational choice as a descriptive model is neither chaos nor an endless list of ad hoc claims. It is a manageable set of concepts and testable propositions, which often predict surprising parallels between ostensibly different behaviors in different domains.

The evidence that we have discussed in this chapter was restricted to hypothetical questions. However, the progression of ideas from the explanation of hypothetical questions to the understanding of economically consequential behavior has an encouraging history, albeit a brief one (much of it is collected by Thaler, 1992). An example is the notion of loss aversion (Tversky & Kahneman, 1991), which was originally formulated in the context of hypothetical choices between gambles, further developed in market experiments with real stakes, and eventually extended to significant economic phenomena. The idea that some actions are expressions of affective valuations is, in our view, a candidate for a similar trajectory.

ACKNOWLEDGMENTS

The U.S.–Israel Binational Science Foundation, the National Science Foundation, and the Environmental Protection Agency provided support for the preparation of this chapter. Shelley Chaiken, Jack Knetsch, Kristine Kuhn, and Barbara Mellers provided valuable comments.

32. Music, Pandas, and Muggers: On the Affective Psychology of Value

Christopher K. Hsee and Yuval Rottenstreich

How long would someone who is willing to work 3 hr for $30 be willing to work for $60? How much would someone who is willing to donate $10 to save one endangered animal be willing to donate to save four endangered animals? Such questions concern the relationship between the quantitative aspect or "scope" of a stimulus (e.g., the amount of financial reward, the number of endangered creatures) and a person's subjective value of that stimulus.

To elucidate the notion of subjective value, note that to gauge how much longer someone would work for $60 rather than $30, one must assess how much satisfaction or value the person accrues from either amount. If the satisfaction accrued from $60 is not much larger than that from $30, the individual will not work appreciably longer for the larger amount. Among other considerations, making a charitable donation presumably gives one moral satisfaction (e.g., Kahneman & Knetsch, 1992). Thus, to estimate how much more someone would donate to save four endangered animals rather than one, one must assess the extent to which an increase in the number of animals saved increases the amount of moral satisfaction.

As our disparate examples suggest, the notion of subjective value is very general and may be applied to just about any stimulus. The notion of scope is very general as well: Any quantitative aspect of a stimulus may form a scope variable. Perhaps not surprisingly then, the relationship between scope and value is of long-standing theoretical interest. For example, both the standard economic theory of consumption and prospect theory (Kahneman & Tversky, 1979) involve intricate analyses of this relationship.

In what follows, we examine the relationship between scope and value by using a process-based account of the determination of value. Recent literature identifies two distinct modes of thought, one deliberate and rule-based, the other associative and affect-based (e.g., Chaiken & Trope, 1999; Epstein, 1994; Kahneman & Frederick, 2002; Sloman, 1996). Building on such dual-process models, we distinguish between two psychological processes by which people might assess the value of a particular target: valuation by calculation and valuation by feeling.

We suggest that these two processes yield different relationships between scope and value, as depicted in Figure 32.1. Specifically, we suggest that under valuation by calculation, changes in scope have relatively constant influence on value throughout the entire range. The corresponding value function is relatively steep throughout (the dotted line). However, we suggest that under valuation by feeling, value is highly sensitive to the presence or absence of a stimulus (i.e., a change from 0 to some scope) but is largely insensitive to further variations in scope. The corresponding value function is relatively flat except for an initial rise (the solid line). We next provide examples and definitions of valuation by calculation and valuation by feeling.

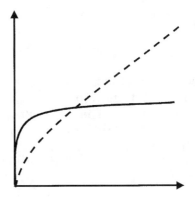

Figure 32.1. Value functions based on calculation (dotted line) and based on feeling (solid line). The *x*-axis of the function is the scope of a stimulus, and the *y*-axis is subjective value.

Consider decisions of how much to pay for a secondhand boxed set of either 5 or 10 Madonna compact discs (CDs). Valuation by calculation might appeal to the typical cost or worth of a single used CD (e.g., $3) and then account for the number of discs, perhaps leading to a willingness to pay of approximately $15 for the 5-CD set and $30 for the 10-CD set. In contrast, valuation by feeling might focus on feelings evoked by Madonna songs and images. Because such feelings should be independent of the number of discs available, using them as a cue for value might lead to roughly equal willingness to pay for either set.

More generally, we use the term *valuation by calculation* for determinations of preference on the basis of some algorithm (e.g., involving the typical cost of a disc) that takes into account both the nature of the stimulus (e.g., the boxed set consists of Madonna discs) and its scope (e.g., there are five discs in the collection). We use the term *valuation by feeling* for determinations of preference on the basis of one's feelings toward the stimulus (e.g., one's liking of Madonna). In essence, feelings depend on the nature of a stimulus but not on its scope, whereas calculations explicitly consider scope. Feelings are relatively qualitative; calculations are relatively quantitative. Thus, feelings yield marked sensitivity to the presence or absence of a stimulus (i.e., the change from 0 to some scope) but yield little sensitivity to subsequent increments of scope. In contrast, calculations yield relatively constant sensitivity throughout the entire range. For the sake of brevity, we henceforth say that feeling yields scope-insensitivity and calculation yields scope-sensitivity.

We emphasize that at any given scope level, feeling may generate either greater or lesser value than calculation, depending on the intensity of the relevant affect. For instance, someone who loves Madonna may establish a higher willingness to pay under feeling than under calculation for either the 5- or 10-disc collection, whereas someone who dislikes Madonna may establish a lower willingness to pay under feeling than calculation for either collection. A *crossover*, wherein feeling yields greater value at low scope but calculation yields greater value at high scope, emerges if valuation by feeling taps affect of intermediate intensity.

We later detail how our notion of valuation by feeling is closely connected to the works of Kahneman, Ritov, and Schkade (1999); Finucane, Alhakami, Slovic, and Johnson (2000); and Slovic, Finucane, Peters, and MacGregor (2002) and to a recent research trend that highlights the use of affect as a cue for value (e.g., Frederick, 2002). For now, we note only that we build on such analyses by explicitly juxtaposing feeling with calculation to provide a process-based account of the determination of value.

STUDY 1: MADONNA

Method
In this study, we attempted to manipulate participants' tendency to engage in either valuation by calculation or valuation by feeling, using an ostensibly unrelated priming task. The context of the study was similar to that of the Madonna CD example.

University of Chicago students ($N = 115$) were recruited in a public place on campus, where they individually completed a short questionnaire packet in exchange for payments varying between $2 and $4. Participants were told that the questionnaires in the packet were unrelated to one another. Most were indeed unrelated, but two formed the current study. One constituted a priming task; the second immediately followed the first and presented our main dependent measure.

Respondents were randomly assigned to one of four conditions of a 2 (scope) × 2 (priming) between-subjects design. The priming questionnaire attempted to encourage either valuation by calculation or valuation by feeling. In the calculation-priming condition, participants answered five questions requiring conscious and deliberate calculations. Two of the questions were as follows:

> If an object travels at five feet per minute, then by your calculations how many feet will it travel in 360 seconds?
> If a consumer bought 30 books for $540, then, by your calculations, on average, how much did the consumer pay for each book?

In the feeling-priming condition, participants answered five questions that required them to examine and report their feelings. Two of the questions were as follows:

> When you hear the name "George W. Bush," what do you feel? Please use one word to describe your predominant feeling.

When you hear the word "baby," what do you feel? Please use one word to describe your predominant feeling.

The main questionnaire asked participants to assume that, for family reasons, a friend of theirs who was from a foreign country had to unexpectedly leave the United States. They were told that the friend was a Madonna fan, owned a number of Madonna CDs, and wanted to sell the CDs to them as a bundle. Participants' responses to the question "What is the maximum you would be willing to pay for the bundle of CDs?" formed the study's dependent measure. Note that participants were not explicitly instructed to rely on calculations or on feelings when indicating the maximum they would be willing to pay. The number of CDs in the bundle formed the scope variable. In one version of the questionnaire, the bundle contained 5 CDs; in another version, 10 CDs.

We predicted that participants primed to calculate would decide how much to pay for the bundle of CDs by essentially counting the number of discs available and multiplying that count by a monetary figure reflecting the typical cost or worth of a single used disc. We further predicted that participants primed to feel would be less likely to count and would instead focus on their feelings for Madonna. Reliance on a calculation involving a count should yield relative scope-sensitivity, but because one's feelings for Madonna should be independent of the number of discs available, reliance on feelings should yield relative scope-insensitivity.

Results and Discussion

The results are consistent with our predictions. When primed to calculate, participants were willing to pay significantly more for the 10-CD set than for the 5-CD set ($M = 28.81$, $SD = 25.21$ for the 10-CD set, and $M = 15.10$, $SD = 11.43$ for the 5-CD set), $t(55) = 2.69$, $p < .01$. However, when primed to feel, participants were essentially insensitive to the number of CDs available ($M = 19.77$, $SD = 18.07$ for the 10-CD set and $M = 22.64$, $SD = 18.14$ for the 5-CD set), $t(54) < 1$, *not significant (ns)*. Analysis of variance (ANOVA) revealed a significant Scope × Priming interaction effect, $F(1, 109) = 5.57$, $p < .05$, $MSE = 348$, $\eta^2 = 0.05$, but no significant main effect of either scope or priming, $F(1, 109) < 1$, *ns*; $F(1, 109) = 2.32$, *ns*.[1]

The data also yield a crossover effect. At the 5-CD level, participants were willing to pay more when primed to feel than when primed to calculate ($22.64 vs. $15.10), $t(56) = 1.91$, $p = .06$. In contrast, at the 10-CD level, participants were actually willing to pay less when primed to feel ($19.77 vs. $28.81), $t(53) = 1.51$, *ns*. As we have mentioned, a crossover suggests that the feelings engendered by Madonna were on average of moderate intensity. Had these

---

[1] We excluded two respondents from our analysis: One indicated a negative willingness to pay, and the other indicated a willingness to pay of $200, twice as much as the next largest value across all conditions.

feelings been more positive, mean willingness to pay may have been greater in the feeling conditions at both scope levels. Conversely, had these feelings been less positive, mean willingness to pay may have been lower in the feeling conditions at both scope levels.

We emphasize that the main questionnaire in this study was identical across the feeling and calculation conditions. An ostensibly unrelated questionnaire was the sole instrument used to prime one or the other valuation process. Such a priming manipulation is by its nature quite subtle. Because it does not require participants to rely on either feelings or calculations, it avoids potential pitfalls associated with demand characteristics. At the same time, despite its subtlety, priming presumably influences the actual process used to assess value. As such, the present priming manipulation provides an operational definition of valuation by calculation and valuation by feeling.

Manipulations targeted directly at the valuation process itself, as used in Study 1, have certain experimental advantages. However, most real-world situations involve indirect manipulation of the valuation process: Whether people rely on calculation or feeling typically varies with (a) the target being valued and (b) the manner in which that target is presented. That is, varying the target being valued or the manner in which that target is presented (indirectly) influences which valuation process predominates, because certain targets and presentations may encourage valuation by calculation, whereas others may encourage valuation by feeling.

In particular, we suggest that relatively affect-rich targets and presentations engender more valuation by feeling, leading to scope-insensitivity, whereas relatively affect-poor targets and presentations engender more valuation by calculation, leading to scope-sensitivity. We next present three studies examining this hypothesis. Study 2 examines (a) the valuation of two different targets, one affect-rich, the other affect-poor, and Studies 3 and 4 examine (b) the valuation of a given target presented in either an affect-rich or an affect-poor manner.

STUDY 2: MUSIC BOOK VERSUS CASH

Method

University of Chicago undergraduates ($N = 331$) were recruited in a public place on campus, where they individually completed a short packet containing several unrelated studies in exchange for payments varying between $2 and $4. They were asked to imagine that they could work temporarily at the campus bookstore and to indicate how long they would work for a certain reimbursement, using a scale from 0 to 10 hr.

Participants were randomly assigned to one of four conditions of a 2 (scope) × 2 (target) between-subjects design. The two targets were a music book and cash. Participants in the music book condition were asked to imagine that they would be reimbursed with a copy of a book that was required for a music course they would soon take. They were instructed to imagine that they loved music and that they expected the book to be one of the most enjoyable works they would ever read. Participants in the cash condition were simply told that they would be reimbursed in cash (but were given no further instructions about how to consider this form of reimbursement).

We suggest that the music book is relatively affect-rich and that the cash is relatively affect-poor. To confirm this claim, we later asked a separate group of participants (recruited in a similar place and manner) "Which form of reimbursement would be emotionally more appealing?" A large majority, 76%, indicated that the music book was more emotionally appealing ($N = 49$, $p < .01$ by binomial test).

The financial value of the reimbursement formed the scope variable. Participants in the book conditions were told that the list price of the book was either $30 or $60. Participants in the cash conditions were told they would be paid either $30 or $60.

If the affect-poor cash encourages valuation by calculation, whereas the affect-rich music book encourages valuation by feeling, then the cash should yield relative scope-sensitivity, and the music book should yield relative scope-insensitivity. In the cash conditions, participants may appeal to a reference wage of $10 per hr. Using this modulus, calculations suggest working approximately 3 hr for $30 or approximately 6 hr for $60. Even allowing for adjustments from these anchors, responses in the cash condition should be scope-sensitive. In contrast, one may feel just as fond of a $30 book as of a $60 book; indeed, participants in the music book conditions had essentially been instructed to do so. If participants in the music book condition decided how long to work by consulting their feelings for the book, then responses in this condition should show little scope-sensitivity.

Results and Discussion

As expected, participants in the affect-poor cash conditions were willing to work much longer for $60 than for $30 ($M = 5.39$, $SD = 1.93$ for $60, and $M = 3.23$, $SD = 1.46$ for $30), $t(162) = 8.06$, $p < .01$, whereas participants in the affect-rich music book condition were less sensitive to the list price of the book ($M = 5.33$, $SD = 2.63$ for the $60 book, and $M = 4.40$, $SD = 2.03$ for the $30 book), $t(165) = 2.54$, $p < .05$. ANOVA revealed a significant Scope $\times$ Target interaction effect, $F(1, 327) = 7.48$, $p = .01$, $MSE = 4.26$, $\eta^2 = 0.02$, indicating less scope-sensitivity in the music book than cash conditions. Although they are not of theoretical interest here, ANOVA also revealed significant main effects of Scope, $F(1, 327) = 46.33$, $p < .01$, $\eta^2 = 0.12$, and Target, $F(1, 327) = 5.92$, $p < .01$, $\eta^2 = 0.02$.

Furthermore, the data again yielded a crossover. At $30, participants were willing to work more for the affect-rich music book than for the affect-poor cash (4.4 hr vs. 3.2 hr), $t(158) = 4.19$, $p < .01$. In contrast, at $60, participants were willing to work slightly (but not significantly) less for the music book (5.3 hr vs. 5.4 hr), $t(169) < 1$, ns.

We recognize that this study is somewhat stylized and that the cash and the music book differ in many potentially important ways. Despite these drawbacks, we feel that contrasting the cash and music book holds an important advantage of ecological validity: There are many real-world situations in which the valuation process that predominates will depend on the nature of the target being valued. Juxtaposition of the cash and music book is instructive to the extent that it mimics these types of real-world circumstances.

Our next studies adopt the general approach of Study 2, yet circumvent some of its limitations. Study 2 indirectly manipulated the valuation process, encouraging either calculation or feeling by changing the target being valued. The following studies also indirectly manipulate the valuation process; however, these studies hold constant the target being valued and encourage one or the other valuation process by changing the presentation of the target.

STUDY 3: SAVING PANDAS

Method

University of Chicago undergraduates ($N = 137$) were recruited in a public place on campus and individually completed a short questionnaire for $1. They were asked to imagine that a team of Chicago zoology students had discovered a number of pandas in a remote Asian region; the team intended to save these endangered animals and was soliciting donations for the rescue effort.

Respondents were randomly assigned to one of four conditions of a 2 (scope) × 2 (presentation) between-subjects design. The scope variable concerned the number of pandas discovered. Participants were told that the team had found either one or four pandas.

Presentation was either affect-poor or affect-rich. Participants were shown a table indicating the number of pandas found. In the affect-poor conditions, the table depicted each panda by a large dot. That is, in the affect-poor conditions the table included either one or four dots. In the affect-rich conditions, the table depicted each panda with a cute picture, reproduced in Figure 32.2. That is, in the affect-rich conditions, the table contained either one cute picture or four copies of the same cute picture.

Manipulation checks, conducted after completion of the study and using a new pool of participants recruited in a similar place and manner, confirmed that the pictures evoked considerably greater affective reactions than the dots. Participants were asked, "How much emotion is evoked when you look at the dot(s) (picture[s])?" On a 10-point scale ranging from 1 (*a little*) to 10 (*a lot*), mean responses were 3.8 for the dots versus 7.0 for the pictures ($N = 25$ in each condition), $t(48) = 4.95$, $p < .01$. Participants were also asked, "How strong of an emotional appeal is the team's request for donations?" On a 10-point scale ranging from 1 (*very weak*) to 10 (*very strong*), mean responses were 4.5 for the dots versus 5.9 for the pictures ($N = 25$ in each condition), $t(48) = 1.95$, $p = .06$.

Figure 32.2. Picture used in the affect-rich condition of Study 3 (saving pandas). Copyright © Samkee. Image from BigStock Photo.com.

The study's dependent measure asked participants to indicate "the most you would be willing to donate" by having them circle either $0, $10, $20, $30, $40, or $50. The response scale was placed just above the table, so that the $10 option was above the first dot or picture, the $20 option was above the second dot or picture, and so forth. This placement was meant to make salient a "one panda merits $10" modulus.

We predicted that participants encountering the affect-poor dots would be relatively likely to base their donation on a calculation or, to be specific, on a count of the number of pandas and an appeal to the suggested modulus. On the other hand, we predicted that participants encountering the affect-rich pictures would be relatively unlikely to count and would instead consider feelings engendered by the pictures. Reliance on a count and modulus should yield relative scope-sensitivity. In contrast, feelings concerning one cute picture should essentially match feelings concerning four cute pictures, yielding scope-insensitivity.

Results and Discussion

The results are consistent with our analysis. The dots yielded a fair degree of scope-sensitivity; mean donations were greater given four pandas rather than one ($M = 22.00$, $SD = 16.48$ for four pandas, and $M = 11.67$, $SD = 11.47$ for one panda), $t(58) = 2.82$, $p < .01$. In contrast, the pictures revealed dramatic scope-insensitivity; mean donations were virtually identical across the two scope levels ($M = 18.95$, $SD = 15.21$ for four pandas, and $M = 19.49$, $SD = 14.13$ for one panda), $t(75) < 1$, ns. The data revealed a significant Scope × Presentation interaction, $F(1, 133) = 4.76$, $p < .05$, $MSE = 209$, $\eta^2 = 0.03$, and a significant main effect of scope, $F(1, 133) = 3.86$, $p = .05$, $\eta^2 = 0.03$, but not of presentation, $F(1, 133) < 1$, ns.

Once more, the data revealed a crossover. Given one panda, participants donated more in the picture than in the dot condition (\$19.49 vs. \$11.67), $t(67) = 2.47$, $p < .05$, but given four pandas, participants donated slightly (but not significantly) less in the picture condition (\$18.95 vs. \$22.00), $t(66) < 1$, ns. Again, a crossover suggests that feelings engendered by the picture were of moderate intensity. Had the picture been even cuter (e.g., a mother panda caressing her young), affect-rich donations may have been greater at both scope levels. On the other hand, had the picture been aversive (e.g., an ugly panda biting a snake), affect-rich donations may have been smaller at both scope levels.

STUDY 4: SENTENCING A MUGGER

In Study 3, the affective intensity of the presentation was varied by the introduction of either an affect-rich or affect-poor cue (pictures vs. dots). In Study 4, exactly the same cues were provided to all participants, and the affective intensity of the presentation was manipulated using an empathy instruction that required participants to generate affect on their own.

Method
University of Chicago undergraduates ($N = 274$) were recruited in a public place on campus and individually completed a short questionnaire for \$1. They were asked to recommend a prison sentence of up to 10 years for an individual convicted of mugging a fellow student at night.

Respondents were randomly assigned to one of four conditions of a 2 (Scope) × 2 (Empathy) between-subjects design. Scope was manipulated by varying the number of previous mugging convictions attributed to the offender – zero or four. Empathy consisted of two conditions: empathy (affect-rich) and no empathy (affect-poor). In the empathy condition, prior to recommending a sentence, participants were told to "Put yourself in the position of the victim(s) and think about how you would feel when being mugged at night. Please write a sentence below to describe your feelings." In the no-empathy condition, these instructions were omitted.

Besides holding external cues constant, two additional aspects of the present methodology merit mention. First, in our previous studies, the targets being valued – CD bundles, reimbursement for work performed, endangered pandas to be saved – were all affectively positive. In the present study, the target being valued – crimes committed by a mugger – was affectively negative. We expected that our results in the positive domain would generalize to the negative domain. Second, unlike Studies 2 and 3, which facilitated calculation by making salient some modulus (i.e., \$10 for an hour, \$10 for one panda), the present study provided no explicit modulus and thus required that participants establish a calculative rule by their own initiative (e.g., "Four prior offenses merits many years in prison").

People often base punitive decisions largely on feelings, even without explicit instructions to do so (e.g., Sunstein, Kahneman, & Schkade, 1998). We predicted that this tendency would be especially pronounced in the affect-rich conditions. Compared with participants in the no-empathy conditions, participants in the empathy conditions should be even less likely to count offenses and more likely to base their sentence on the feelings they were asked to generate. These feelings should be essentially equivalent given either four or zero prior offenses.

Results and Discussion

The results accord with our analysis. In the no-empathy conditions, recommended sentences were highly sensitive to scope ($M = 2.56$, $SD = 2.49$, given no previous offense, and $M = 5.78$, $SD = 3.39$, given four previous offenses), $t(136) = 6.37$, $p < .01$. In contrast, in the empathy conditions, recommended sentences were less sensitive to scope ($M = 3.43$, $SD = 2.84$, given no previous offense, and $M = 4.65$, $SD = 3.39$, given four previous offenses), $t(134) = 2.17$, $p < .05$. ANOVA revealed a significant Scope × Empathy interaction, $F(1, 270) = 7.72$, $p < .01$, $MSE = 9.35$, $\eta^2 = 0.02$. The ANOVA found a significant main effect of scope, $F(1, 270) = 35.35$, $p < .01$, $\eta^2 = 0.11$, but not of empathy, $F(1, 270) < 1$, ns. As in the previous studies, there is a crossover. Given no prior offenses, the empathy instruction yielded longer sentences (3.4 vs. 2.6 years), $t(132) = 1.99$, $p < .05$, but given four prior offenses, the empathy instruction yielded shorter sentences (4.7 vs. 5.8 years), $t(138) = 1.99$, $p < .05$.

GENERAL DISCUSSION

Across a diverse set of scope variables and dependent measures, we observed a consistent pattern of results: relative scope-insensitivity when valuation by feeling is encouraged and relative scope-sensitivity when valuation by calculation is encouraged. We next discuss (a) the relationship between the present research and the existing literature on scope neglect, (b) other factors that may influence valuation, (c) the relationship between scope-insensitivity and probability weighting, and (d) implications of the present research for interpretations of the concavity revealed by most real-world value functions.

Relationship With Prior Research on Scope Neglect

Researchers interested in people's preferences for nonmarket goods – such as the rescue of endangered species – have conducted studies closely related to ours. In a representative experiment, Desvousges et al. (1993) asked separate groups of participants how much they would donate to save 2,000, 20,000, or 200,000 migrating birds from drowning in oil ponds. The mean responses, $80, $78, and $88, respectively, showed astounding neglect of scope (for similar findings, see Baron & Greene, 1996; Boyle, Desvousges, Johnson, Dunford, & Hudson, 1994; Carson & Mitchell, 1993; Fetherstonhaugh, Slovic, Johnson, & Friedrich, 1997; Frederick & Fischhoff, 1998).

Kahneman, Ritov, and Schkade (1999) explained these results by arguing that Desvousges et al.'s (1993) questions evoked "a mental representation of a prototypical incident, perhaps an image of an exhausted bird, its feathers soaked in black oil, unable to escape" (p. 652) and that participants decided how much to donate on the basis of their affective reactions to this image. More generally, Kahneman, Ritov, and Schkade (1999) used the term *affective valuation* to refer to assessments of preference on the basis of "the sign and intensity of the emotional response to objects" (p. 643) and stressed that affective valuations are scope-insensitive because "the attitude to a set of similar objects is often determined by the affective valuation of a prototypical member of that set" (p. 645).

Our notion of valuation by feeling is taken from the work of Kahneman, Ritov, and Schkade (1999). It also follows Slovic et al.'s (2002) and Finucane et al.'s (2000) investigation of affect as a cue for value (see also Frederick, 2002; Zajonc, 1980). We build on these analyses by explicitly juxtaposing valuation by feeling with valuation by calculation. In demonstrating that factors affecting the relative salience of these two processes moderate the degree of scope-sensitivity, we offer a process-based account of the determination of value.

In another related study, Dhar and Wertenbroch (2000) found that "hedonic" goods reveal greater loss aversion than "utilitarian" goods. This observation may provide a parallel to our findings: Hedonic goods may be thought of as affect-rich and utilitarian goods as affect-poor, and affect may influence not only scope-sensitivity, but loss aversion as well.

Complexity of Valuation Processes

Although we have offered an account that juxtaposes calculation and feeling, we emphasize that valuation is a complex process open to the influence of many variables. For instance, we speculate that joint valuations of multiple targets will yield greater scope-sensitivity than separate valuations of the same targets. To illustrate, consider a hypothetical modification of Desvousges et al's. (1993) study in which each participant makes three responses, indicating in turn a donation to save 2,000, 20,000, and 200,000 endangered birds. It seems likely that such joint valuations will yield pronounced scope-sensitivity. Hsee (1996a; Hsee et al., 1999; Hsee & Zhang, 2004) provided detailed analysis of the distinction between joint and separate evaluations.

In a slightly different vein, it is clear that valuations are often influenced by diverse considerations such as "What can I use this for?" or "What am I supposed to do?" that fall neatly into neither the category of calculation nor that of feeling. Gilbert, Gill, and Wilson (2002) provided an especially compelling example that contrasts preferences constructed by feeling with preferences constructed with an eye toward what one is supposed to do. These authors had grocery shoppers list the items they intended to purchase. Only some shoppers were allowed to retain their list during their actual shopping trip. Furthermore, some shoppers were asked to eat a quarter-pound of muffins before shopping. Among list-less shoppers, those who were unfed bought more unlisted items than those who were well fed. However, among shoppers retaining their lists, those who were unfed did not buy more unlisted items. Presumably, list-less shoppers experienced more positive affective reactions to unlisted items when unfed ("Those cookies look delicious!") than when well fed ("I never want to eat again"). Shoppers with lists surely had the same affective reactions but evidently decided whether to purchase an appealing item by checking their list to see if they were supposed to buy it rather than by following their affective reactions.

The conclusions we have drawn about how feeling and calculation yield different reactions to scope are not meant to deny the importance of other influences on valuation nor the inherent complexity of valuation. On the contrary, in our opinion the finding that systematic differences arise between valuation by feeling and calculation even though many factors might dilute such differences demonstrates the importance of distinguishing between these valuation processes.

Implications for Probability Weighting

Rottenstreich and Hsee (2001) observed probability by affect-richness interactions that parallel the scope by affect-richness interactions we report. In one experiment, participants were asked for their willingness to pay for either a 1% or 99% chance of winning a $500 coupon. The coupon could be used either for tuition payments (affect-poor) or toward expenses associated with a vacation to Paris, Venice, and Rome (affect-rich). At 1%, people were willing to pay more for the vacation coupon, but at 99%, people were willing to pay more for the tuition coupon. In other words, people were more sensitive to variation in probability between 1% and 99% when the prize was affect-poor than when it was affect-rich. These results parallel the Scope × Affect-Richness interaction we have observed, with probability in the role of scope.

The distinction between calculation and feeling may explain probability by affect-richness interactions much as it explains scope by affect-richness interactions. Rottenstreich and Hsee's (2001) results suggest that the value of affect-poor prospects reveals relatively constant sensitivity to probability throughout the entire range of probability, from 0 to 1 (see the dotted line in Figure 32.3). Relatively constant sensitivity is consistent with the notion that affect-poor prospects engender valuation by calculation. Furthermore, Rottenstreich and Hsee's results suggest that the value of affect-rich prospects is hypersensitive to the presence or absence of uncertainty (i.e., a change from a probability of 0 or 1 to some intermediate probability) but largely insensitive to further variations in probability (see the solid line in Figure 32.3). This pattern is consistent with the notion that affect-rich prospects engender valuation by feeling.

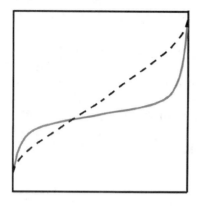

Figure 32.3. Probability weighting functions based on calculation (dashed line) and based on feeling (solid line). The *x*-axis of the function is stated probability, and the *y*-axis is the weight or impact of this probability on value.

Most real-world valuations consist of a mix of calculations and feelings. The resulting probability weighting function is more regressive than the nearly linear dotted line in Figure 32.3 but is less regressive than the nearly step-function solid line in Figure 32.3. Many researchers have observed exactly this pattern of probability weighting (Tversky & Kahneman, 1992; see also Abdellaoui, 2000; Bleichrodt & Pinto, 2000; Camerer & Ho, 1994; Gonzalez & Wu, 1999; Kilka & Weber, 2001; Wu & Gonzalez, 1996, 1998).

To appreciate why valuation by feeling may yield hypersensitivity near the end-points of the probability scale and insensitivity at intermediate probabilities, consider a thought experiment by Elster and Loewenstein (1992). Picture a fatal car crash involving your closest friend. This harrowing image might make you drive more carefully. In other words, the possibility of a terrible crash may lead to an affective reaction to a salient image, and this feeling (not explicit consideration of the scenario's probability) may guide behavior. Such feelings will be hypersensitive to departures from a probability of 0 or 1, because the difference between no chance and some chance or between some chance and certainty activates either an image of the potential outcome or a counterimage accentuating its absence. In contrast, such feelings will be independent of intermediate probability variations (whether the chances of a crash are 1 in 1,000 or 100,000), because intermediate variations will not alter the associated image. (For related hypotheses concerning how affect influences probability weighting, see Wu, 1999, and Brandstätter, Kühberger, & Schneider, 2002.)

Accounting for Concavity

Real-world value functions are typically concave – constant increments of scope yield successively smaller increments of value. Although our experimental data do not directly address this issue, we speculate that concavity arises in part because most real-world valuations mix calculation and feeling. Indeed, appropriate mathematical combinations of the two extreme functional forms previously mentioned (the linear and step functions in Figure 32.1) yield a concave function. In such mixes, greater reliance on feeling yields greater concavity.

Consider the family of functions $V = A^\alpha S^{1-\alpha}$. Here, V denotes subjective value, A the affective intensity of the target, S its scope, and α an affective focus coefficient bound by 0 and 1. When α is small, value depends mostly on scope rather than affect; when α is large the reverse is true. This form is equivalent to the Cobb–Douglas utility function often invoked in economics; for a given (A, α) pair, it reduces to the power law of psychophysics (Stevens, 1975).

To see how this family of functions captures the data from our experiments, let us apply it to the results of the panda study. In that experiment, S may be either 1 or 4 (the number of pandas), and A is larger in the picture than dot conditions (denote the particular values of A by $A_{picture} > A_{dot}$). For simplicity, suppose affect-poor presentations focus participants entirely on scope, yielding $\alpha = 0$, and affect-rich presentations focus participants entirely on feelings, yielding $\alpha = 1$. Then, the subjective value of the pandas will equal 1 and 4 in the two dot conditions but will be constant, equal to $A_{picture}$, across the two picture conditions. Thus, the model generates pronounced scope-insensitivity when feeling predominates and generates marked scope-sensitivity when calculation predominates. If $1 < A_{picture} < 4$, it yields the empirically observed crossover.

The preceding illustrations set α equal to either 0 or 1, making V either a step function or a linear function. Intermediate values of α yield a concave value function. As we mentioned, most real-world value functions are concave. Previous theoretical analyses explain concavity by the principle of satiation, according to which the more units of a good an individual consumes (e.g., reimbursement from work, pandas saved, steaks for dinner, anything else), the less one desires (and thus the less one values) additional units of this good. By this view, the faster the rate of satiation, the more concave is the value function. Although satiation is surely an important influence on value, the present analysis suggests another interpretation of concavity. The value function may be highly concave when feeling predominates (α approaches 1) and less concave when calculation predominates (α approaches 0). In other words, the extent to which different processes are used to assess value, not just the nature of consumption and satiation, may be an important determinant of the shape of the value function.

We close by noting that the model $V = A^\alpha S^{1-\alpha}$ highlights two mechanisms that might contribute to the influence of feelings on preferences. First, as captured by A, affect may be a source of value. Second, as captured by α, a person may focus on either affect or scope. Presumably, higher values of A will often coincide with higher values of α, because pronounced affect typically draws attention to itself (e.g., we have presumed that a cute panda picture is captivating or that strong empathy for a mugging victim is engrossing). The notion that affect tends to focus attention on certain attributes and draws attention away from others is consistent with the findings of Wright and Lynch (1995) and the accessibility–diagnosticity framework of Feldman and Lynch (1988). Nevertheless, A and α need not be perfectly correlated and could in principle operate independently. Indeed, in Gilbert, Gill, and Wilson's (2002) example, shoppers who retain their lists appear not to focus on their strong affective reactions.

Our experiments aimed to provide guidelines for predicting when people will be either scope-sensitive or scope-insensitive. Thus, they merely corroborate differences in the assessment of subjective value under affect-rich and affect-poor presentations. We hope that future work more carefully investigates the specific mechanisms contributing to such differences.

ACKNOWLEDGMENTS

This project has benefited greatly from discussions with many colleagues. We are especially indebted to Reid Hastie, Danny Kahneman, John Lynch, and Paul Slovic. We thank the University of Chicago Graduate School of Business and the China Europe International Business School, where Christopher K. Hsee visited during part of this research project, for their support.

33. Valuing Environmental Resources: A Constructive Approach

Robin Gregory, Sarah Lichtenstein, and Paul Slovic

INTRODUCTION

Contingent valuation (CV) has been used by economists to value public goods for about 25 years. The approach posits a hypothetical market for an unpriced good and asks individuals to state the dollar value they place on a proposed change in its quantity, quality, or access. Development of the CV concept has been described in reviews by Cummings, Brookshire, and Schulze (1986) and Mitchell and Carson (1989). The approach is now widely used to value many different goods whose quantity or quality might be affected by the decisions of a public agency or private developer. Environmental goods have received particular attention, because they are highly valued by society and entail controversial tradeoffs (e.g., manufacturing costs vs. pollution, urban development vs. wetlands protection) but are not usually sold through markets (Bromley, 1986).

The visibility of CV methods[1] has greatly increased following the 1989 interpretation of the Comprehensive Environmental Response, Compensation, and Liability Act of 1986 (CERCLA) by the District of Columbia Circuit Court of Appeals (in *Ohio v. United States Department of the Interior*). This decision (a) granted equal standing to expressed and revealed preference evaluation techniques (with willingness to pay measures preferred in all cases), (b) accepted nonuse values as a legitimate component of total resource value, and (c) recognized a "distinct preference" in CERCLA for restoring damaged natural resources, rather than simply compensating for the losses (Kopp, Portney, & Smith, 1990). The court's opinion on these three issues will likely lead to a substantial redrafting of the Department of Interior's rules for natural resource damage assessments.

Interest in CV applications has given rise to much research. Recent studies, for example, have used CV to estimate the value of wetlands protection (Loomis, Hanemann, Kanninen, & Wegge, 1991), water quality improvements

---

[1] Despite the many references in the literature to "the Contingent Valuation Method" (e.g., Mitchell & Carson, 1989), CV is a conceptual approach which, in application, employs a variety of methods.

Originally published in *Journal of Risk and Uncertainty*, vol. 7, pp. 177–197. Copyright © 1993 Kluwer Academic Publishers.

(Desvousges, Smith, & Fisher, 1987), groundwater (Mitchell & Carson, 1989), and forest wildlife resources (Walsh, Bjonback, Aiken, & Rosenthal, 1990).[2] On the other hand, much has been written about problems with CV techniques. They capture attitudinal intentions rather than behavior (Ajzen & Peterson, 1988), important information is omitted from CV questionnaires (Fischhoff & Furby, 1988), and their results are susceptible to influence from cognitive and contextual biases (Brown & Slovic, 1988).

One response to these criticisms is to argue that CV methods can provide valid estimates of resource values if studies are done carefully. This is the position taken by many practitioners of CV methods (e.g., Brookshire & Coursey, 1987; Randall, Hoehn, & Brookshire, 1983) and by the National Oceanic and Atmospheric Administration panel on Contingent Valuation (Arrow et al., 1993). Several prominent critics of current CV methods also argue for greater care in application; for example, Fischhoff and Furby (1988) provided detailed listings of the information needed to inform CV participants sufficiently about the assigned payment task, the social context for evaluation, and the good under consideration.

In contrast, others view these problems as casting doubt on the accuracy of CV responses and the usefulness of even the most carefully conducted CV results in litigation and damage assessments. Indeed, some reject CV as a method for obtaining monetary values of unpriced environmental goods. For example, Phillips and Zeckhauser (1989) questioned whether any CV study will be able to meet standard criteria of reliability and validity. Kahneman and Knetsch (1992) have argued that CV responses denote moral sentiments rather than economic values.

We believe there is a need for monetary assessments of environmental damages and that an evaluation approach based on an individual's expressed preferences is appropriate for this purpose. However, we believe that the holistic measures of monetary value used in current CV methods are flawed because they impose unrealistic cognitive demands on respondents. In our view, improved methods for valuing nonmarket natural resources can be found by paying closer attention to the multidimensional nature of environmental values and to the constructive nature of human preferences (Gregory & McDaniels, 1987). The underlying assumption of the approach to be discussed in this chapter is that people have strong feelings, beliefs, and values for many things that are not sold through markets (Brown, 1984). However, people's cognitive beliefs about these values typically are not numerically quantified and, most importantly for CV, are not represented monetarily.

The fact that people are not used to thinking about environmental goods in monetary units suggests that a CV approach must function as a kind of

---

[2] WTP techniques also are used to value human health and safety (Jones-Lee, Hammerton, & Phillips, 1985; Viscusi & Magat, 1987); however, this chapter focuses on the evaluation of environmental resources rather than the WTP research on health and safety issues.

tutorial, building the monetary value as it elicits it. We therefore view a CV survey as an active process of value construction (Tversky, Sattath, & Slovic, 1988), rather than as a neutral process of value discovery. Thus, we believe, the designers of a CV study should function not as archaeologists, carefully uncovering what is there, but as architects, working to build a defensible expression of value.

In this chapter, we first argue that CV methods need to be changed to accommodate the constructive nature of environmental preferences. We then propose criteria to guide the selection of a defensible environmental-values-elicitation method. Next, we examine the possibility of developing a new CV method based on techniques derived from multiattribute utility theory and decision analysis. Finally, we explain why we believe this new approach will help to solve several of the most vexing problems confronting practitioners and interpreters of environmental policy and valuation studies.

THE CONSTRUCTIVE NATURE OF ENVIRONMENTAL PREFERENCES

Almost 4 decades ago, a seminal article by Edwards (1954c) introduced psychologists and other behavioral scientists to theories of decision making and empirical methods for quantifying individuals' preferences. This intellectual enterprise has burgeoned into *behavioral decision theory* (Edwards, 1961; Einhorn & Hogarth, 1981) or *behavioral decision research* (Payne, Bettman, & Johnson, 1992). A major objective of researchers in this field has been to understand the nature of human preferences and values and to develop defensible ways to measure them.

One focus of behavioral decision research has been to clarify the role of judgmental rules of thumb, or heuristics, which are used to simplify complex judgments. These heuristics, such as anchoring on a starting point or relying on easily imaginable information, can be useful and even necessary, but also can lead to systematic biases and errors in judgment (Kahneman, Slovic, & Tversky, 1982). Another focus of this work has been to demonstrate the strong influence of context on measures of preference and value. As a result, decision scientists seeking to elicit values have recognized that order effects, the range and mixture of items being evaluated, the amount and nature of information provided about each item, the method of elicitation, and many other contextual factors can affect the results of any serious elicitation attempt.

This research has led to a perspective that we shall call the *constructive nature of preference*. This perspective has strong implications for the theory and practice of CV.

Consider, for example, the phenomenon of preference reversal, which has been studied by psychologists and economists for more than 20 years (Grether & Plott, 1979; Lichtenstein & Slovic, 1971; Tversky, Slovic, & Kahneman, 1990). Dozens of empirical studies, using gambles as well as many other stimuli (Slovic, Griffin, & Tversky, 1990), have demonstrated preference reversals:

Object A is clearly preferred over Object B under one method of measurement, whereas B is clearly preferred under a different but presumably equivalent measurement procedure.

Reversals of preference induced by changes in response mode have begun to appear in CV studies. Brown (1984) examined dollar and rating responses of subjects' willingness to pay (WTP) for environmental amenities (air quality and forest scenic quality) and commodities (cameras, cars, stereos, and bicycles). Most subjects were willing to pay more for the commodities than for the amenities when giving their answers in dollars, but most rated their WTP for the amenities higher than their WTP for the commodities. Similarly, Viscusi, Magat, and Huber (1986) found that people's values for reducing the risks from chemical products were higher when they were given paired comparisons (i.e., choices) than when they were asked to provide WTP values. Irwin, Slovic, Lichtenstein, and McClelland (1993) conducted several studies showing preference reversals in WTP. These studies involved comparisons of improvements in consumer goods, such as a better camera or a better VCR, with improvements in air quality. Their successful prediction of preference reversals, whereby WTP based on a single-stimulus response favored improvements in consumer goods and WTP based on a choice response favored improvements in air quality, was based on two judgment effects found in the decision-making literature: the compatibility effect (Slovic et al., 1990) and the prominence effect (Tversky et al., 1988).

Findings of preference reversals involving environmental values provide strong evidence for the constructive nature of preference. As Tversky et al. (1988) observed:

In the classical analysis, the relation of preference is inferred from observed responses and is assumed to reflect the decision maker's underlying utility or value. But if different elicitation procedures produce different orderings of options, how can preferences and values be defined? And in what sense do they exist? (p. 383)

The significance of changes in context on a person's expressed preferences supports this constructive view of values. For example, an attribute that would otherwise be of minor importance is more heavily weighed if all the objects are clearly described in terms of that attribute, when other attribute descriptions are incomplete (Slovic & McPhillamy, 1974). Huber (1980) showed that decision processes were influenced by whether information was presented in numerical or verbal form. Gaeth and Shanteau (1984) showed that inclusion of irrelevant information impaired judgment. Many context effects are grouped under the label *framing effects* (Hogarth, 1982; Tversky & Kahneman, 1981). For example, calling a sure loss "insurance" makes it more palatable (Slovic, Fischhoff, & Lichtenstein, 1982). Tversky and Kahneman's oft-cited "Asian disease" problem (1981) showed a reversal of preference when the wording of two public-health problems was framed in terms of "saving lives" versus a "loss of life" framing.

Not all the research on context effects applies directly to CV. All, however (and we have cited only a sampling earlier), reinforce the view that people are not just reporting their values or preferences. Instead, they are constructing them with whatever help or cues the circumstances provide.

The economists' prevailing response to preference construction is that holistic measures of value can be trusted but separate values for components cannot (e.g., Freeman, 1993b, Randall, 1986). Yet, this view, that people can aggregate values but cannot partition them, flies in the face of the decision-making literature. This literature tells us that, when faced with complex values, people often resort to simplifying strategies; Payne et al. (1992) have oriented their extensive review around this theme. Moreover, simplifying strategies increase when the complexity of the stimuli increases (Johnson, Meyer, & Ghose, 1989). Studies have found that people typically are unaware of their simplifications, and that when people are asked to make holistic judgments about multidimensional stimuli, they typically make use of fewer cues than they say they do (Slovic & Lichtenstein, 1971). In short, the more complex a decision problem, the more likely that expressions of value will be constructed based on only a subset of the available information. Dawes (1977), for example, reviewed both this literature and the findings that simple combinations of judged parts accurately predict known wholes and recommended just the opposite – namely, trust the values obtained from decomposition procedures more than those obtained from holistic judgments.

An important corollary of the constructive view is that the strong values that people hold for environmental goods are not represented in their minds in monetary form. Consider all the goods that we might want to value in dollar terms. These could be arrayed on a continuum according to the level of market experience that we have with them. At one extreme would be goods such as groceries, for which market experience is great and the strength of our values or preferences can be relatively easily represented by a market price. As we move from groceries to appliances, automobiles, and homes, market experience lessens and the ease of representing our preferences monetarily declines as well. For goods such as air or water quality, wilderness areas, endangered species, and many other elements of the natural environment, the market no longer applies, and the link between values and money becomes tenuous – so tenuous that it may not exist. Thus, we can have strongly held values that are not at all coded mentally in terms of dollars. Attempts to translate such values into monetary equivalents must take special cognizance of this problem.

One demonstration of the absence of a monetary representation for values comes from a study by Slovic, Lichtenstein, and Fischhoff (1979) that asked people to evaluate the social seriousness of a death from specified causes (e.g., smoking, alcoholism, nuclear-power accidents) by equating each death with a monetary loss. This was done by asking the respondents to compare a death from each cause to a standard unit of loss to society. In one condition, this standard loss was $1,000,000; in a second condition (with a new group of respondents) this standard loss was $10,000. Respondents were asked to provide a multiplying or dividing factor to indicate how many times greater (or smaller) the specified death (e.g., a cancer death) was in comparison to the standard.

The geometric-mean responses ranged in orderly fashion from smoking and alcohol-caused deaths at the low end, judged less serious than the standard, to death from pesticides and nuclear-power accidents at the extreme high end of the distribution. The correlation between the means in the two conditions, across 34 causes of death, was .94.

Notably, the mean responses (i.e., the multiplying factors) were almost identical in the two groups, despite the 100-fold difference in the comparison standard. For example, the mean for an alcohol-caused death was .91 for the 10^6 standard, and .89 for the 10^4 standard. In other words, the responses were almost perfectly consistent across the 34 items, but the dollar values implied by the responses differed by a factor of 100. Although there may be other explanations, these results can be interpreted as indicating that the seriousness of deaths from specified causes differed reliably across causes but was not represented monetarily in our respondents' minds.

We believe that the absence of any monetary representation is a principal cause of the *embedding* (or *part/whole*) effect observed by both CV proponents (e.g., Mitchell & Carson, 1989) and critics (Kahneman & Knetsch, 1992), whereby the same good is assigned a lower value when it is inferred from WTP for a more inclusive good than if the good is evaluated on its own. For example, Kahneman and Knetsch report that the willingness of Toronto residents to pay to maintain fishing by cleaning up the lakes in a small area of Ontario was almost as great as their willingness to pay to maintain fishing in all Ontario lakes. They replicated this finding for a diverse set of public goods. Kahneman and Knetsch interpreted their findings as indicating that the "good" that subjects are willing to pay for in these studies is a "sense of moral satisfaction," which exhibits an embedding effect – the satisfaction associated with contributing to an inclusive cause extends with little loss to any significant subset of that cause. Alternative explanations are that the subjects in these studies were not sensitive to the differences in the descriptions of the goods or that the subjects had no well-defined monetary representation of value for the goods.

DESIRABLE FEATURES OF AN ENVIRONMENTAL-VALUES-ELICITATION APPROACH

What are the characteristics of a good, defensible method for eliciting environmental values? The ultimate criterion is validity: A method clearly measures only what it is supposed to measure. Cronbach and Meehl (1955), in an article that has become a classic to psychologists, discussed four types of validity of which three are relevant to CV methods, namely, predictive, concurrent, and constructive validity.[3] *Predictive* and *concurrent* validity refer to the close relationships between the measure and a criterion of known validity (they differ only in timing; predictive validity involves comparison with a future criterion; concurrent validity involves a present criterion). Economic theory posits just such a criterion of known validity, that is unrestrained market prices at equilibrium. Unfortunately, CV methods are intended for use precisely in those situations for which no market exists.

Construct validity is thus the concept underlying tests of CV's validity. "A construct is defined implicitly by a network of associations or propositions in which it occurs. . . . Construct validation is possible only when some of the statements in the network lead to predicted relations among observables" (Cronbach & Meehl, 1955, pp. 299–300). Economic theory, in which the construct of contingent valuation is embedded, generously satisfies these requirements.

Construct validity is not sought via one definitive study but in the integration of evidence from many different sources. The finding that CV methods roughly match market values when they are applied, experimentally, to situations in which market values exist (Bishop & Heberlein, 1979; Dickie, Fisher, & Gerking, 1987) is one such piece of evidence favoring construct validity. Other evidence comes from comparisons of different assessment methods, such as comparing risk/risk to risk/money tradeoffs (Viscusi, Magat, & Huber, 1991) or comparing direct WTP responses to results from travel cost or hedonic (indirect) techniques (e.g., Brookshire, Thayer, Schulze, & d'Arge, 1982; Smith, Desvousges, & Fisher, 1986). Such studies have shown agreement among measures within a range of about ± 50% (Cummings, et al., 1986). Although a 50% margin of error might appall a polluter presented with a bill for damages under CERCLA, such findings do help to build the case for construct validity.

But construct validity also requires negative findings. If the method is valid, variables that *should not* affect the results *do not*. Here, conventional CV methods fare poorly. First, there is a widely observed disparity between the maximum amount that people are willing to pay to acquire a good and the minimum amount that they are willing to accept (WTA) to give it up. The observed difference between WTP and WTA is not, as economic theory would predict, small (most persuasively shown by Kahneman, Knetsch, & Thaler, 1990; see also Bishop & Heberlein, 1979; Knetsch & Sinden, 1984). Moreover, as noted earlier, the change from a WTP to a choice–response mode induces reversals in the preference ordering of an environmental improvement versus a market-commodity improvement (Irwin et al., 1993). Such findings contradict economic theory and thus seriously threaten the construct validity of WTP-based CV methods.

We are not surprised by these validity-threatening findings, for underlying the search for validity are the assumptions that monetary values for nonmarket

---

[3] The fourth, *content* validity, applies only to testing situations. To assess the content validity of a typing test, for example, one would show that the test is an appropriate sample of the universe of typing skills.

goods really do exist and that researchers can find appropriate ways to measure them. In contrast, we hold that such values do *not* exist in monetary form. Instead, they are created during the elicitation process. Thus, value formation is intimately tied to the specifics of the elicitation procedures. Following Simon's well-known distinction between procedural and substantive rationality (1978), we therefore present five process criteria that, if satisfied, can be used to defend the goodness of a CV method.[4]

Criterion 1: Accommodate the Multidimensionality of Value

Early work in behavioral decision research provides abundant evidence that people form judgments on the basis of multiple attributes and dimensions (Hammond, McClelland, & Mumpower, 1980). Moreover, there is a robust basis, in both economics and decision theory, for this perspective (Keeney & Raiffa, 1976; Lancaster, 1966). The multidimensionality of values for environmental goods is symbolized by the "multiple use" concept that guides the resource-management policies of federal agencies such as the U.S. Forest Service. Bishop (1986) presents categories of economic benefits from the environment that include both consumptive and nonconsumptive user benefits, as well as several classes of nonuser values. Environmental philosophers (e.g., Rolston, 1981) have distinguished a large number of dimensions that can be used to characterize environmental goods, including scientific, aesthetic, biodiversity, religious, symbolic, and life-support values, in addition to economic and recreational values.

The complexity and multidimensionality of environmental values necessitate that a value-elicitation method be sensitive to this diversity of values. Yet, a good CV method also must recognize the difficulties people have in thinking about such complexities. The experimental evidence previously described indicates that even when all aspects of all alternatives are fully described, people find it difficult to make explicit tradeoffs and typically rely on cognitive strategies that result in discounting or neglecting some important aspects.

The typical CV task goes one step further, that is, a holistic response is requested for a single stimulus presented, without either an explicit listing of the relevant dimensions of value or a description of the stimulus on each dimension. Because what is out of sight may be out of mind (Fischhoff, Slovic, & Lichtenstein, 1978), this situation can be expected to lead to the greatest distortions in the expression of multidimensional values. Gregory, MacGregor, and Lichtenstein (1992) have shown that open-ended, holistic WTP responses were poorly correlated, across a number of market and nonmarket goods, with several value-relevant attributes. Is this so surprising? In most elicitation settings,

---

[4] We do not claim that these are the only criteria to be considered. Several nonprocess criteria also merit consideration, such as legitimacy, standardization (are the same techniques used every time?), and consistency (do similar people respond similarly?). However, our focus in this chapter is on the key process criteria that will help people to construct their values.

people have had no experience in thinking about the structure – the multiple dimensions or attributes – of their values. How can people think clearly about the big picture when they cannot distinguish clearly among the components?

We realize that some recent CV studies have used focus groups to examine the multiple attributes of value. Recent CV booklets typically also extensively describe the proposed project or even present two possible projects, not only described in the text but also shown in a paired-comparison chart of attributes (thus aiding the respondent to make a richer consideration). We applaud these improvements. However, the central problem remains: Holistic responses to complex stimuli are not sufficiently sensitive to multidimensionality, because they require respondents to make difficult, unaided tradeoffs across attributes.

Criterion 2: Minimize Response Refusals

Response refusals are a common problem in CV studies (Mitchell & Carson, 1989). Stevens, Echeverria, Glass, Hager, and More (1991), for example, reported that over 80% of the participants in their recent CV survey in Massachusetts said that bald eagles, wild turkeys, and Atlantic salmon are very or somewhat important to them, but a majority of respondents (62%–64%) would not pay any money to maintain these same populations. Forty percent of the refusers protested the payment vehicle, and 25% refused to pay for ethical reasons. Irwin et al. (1990) and other researchers have reported similar findings. Elegant methods have been proposed for estimating the missing WTP values (Schulze, McClelland, Waldman, & Lazo, 1996). However, a better CV approach should avoid this vexing problem.

Criterion 3: Exclude Irrelevancies

If a CV study were intended to predict, for example, the results of a public vote on funding for a project, then any attribute value that will affect how people vote should properly be expressed in the study. However, contingent valuations are often needed for situations in which some aspects of value, even if strongly held, are legally or ethically irrelevant. For example, we conjecture that an individual's WTP to restore a damaged habitat or to accept compensation for an environmental loss will be strongly affected by the source of the damage (e.g., a natural cause vs. a careless spill by a detested chemical company). Legally, however, this attribute (who is to blame) is irrelevant under CERCLA. A good CV method should allow the exclusion of such attributes. This is difficult, if not impossible, for holistic-response methods like WTP or WTA.

Criterion 4: Separate Facts From Values

Defensible measures of value require respondents who have knowledge of the good under consideration, as well as knowledge of their preferences with regard to the good. For simple goods or for activities with which people have extensive experience, it makes sense to assume that the respondents are competent to assess both facts and values. However, many of the proposed environmental changes that form the subject of CV studies are scientifically complex. In such cases, a good CV method should not require that respondents have a thorough understanding of the scientific complexities to express their preferences.

For example, people may value species preservation. Suppose a proposed project will save 100 pairs of a threatened bird species. It is the experts who must provide the translation from the fact of saving 100 pairs of birds to the value-relevant scientific estimate of the associated change in the probability that the bird species will not become extinct. It is not reasonable to assume that respondents will know how to make such translations.

Criterion 5: Ask the Right Question

The usual CV study asks a WTP question, such as "How much would you be willing to pay each year in higher prices or increased taxes for . . . ?" or "Would you be willing to pay $X each year in higher prices or increased taxes for . . . ?" (with $X varied across respondents). Questions based on WTA payment for some loss are less common, because refusal rates are considerably higher and because average responses seem unduly large (Cummings et al., 1986; Kahneman et al., 1990).

Consider the case where a factory discharges pollutants into a lake, causing environmental damage. The relevant question under CERCLA is: How much should the damager pay? The general answer is that the damager is required under CERCLA to pay that amount necessary to restore or replace the lost resources (Kopp et al., 1990). Let us suppose that this is done to the extent reasonably possible, but that the repair takes some time and is not complete. Then the damager is liable both for losses from the time the damage occurs until the time the repair (whether by nature or by humans) is finished and for losses that cannot be repaired. How should a CV study assess the value of these losses?

This is a typical question and an important one for environmental policy analysis. However, WTP or WTA seems to us inappropriate for this question because it is not the responsibility of the respondent to pay for the damage. There are two separate points here. First, the request to pay for damages to the natural environment brings up the question of an individual's entitlement. If ownership of the resource (e.g., good water quality) forms part of a people's status quo assets, then why should they pay for what they already have a right to? The appropriate response is a refusal to pay. Second, under CERCLA, payment is the responsibility of the damager. Clearly, for some types of environmental damage, such as a widespread degradation of water quality caused by many damagers, the responsibility may effectively fall on us all. Whether we like it or not, consumer prices or taxes will pay for the clean-up. But even in such cases, it is likely that many people will deny the responsibility. This denial seems to underlie the large percentage of refusals in many CV studies of damaged resources.

In the factory discharge considered here, the damager is clearly liable. Thus, we must consider WTA. However, if you, the respondent, ask for too much money – so that your demand is refused – what will happen? The essence of any WTP or WTA question is a tradeoff of some sort between money and a good. But here we are evaluating unrestorable losses. If you are not paid, there will still be a loss; there is no compensating event in the no-exchange alternative that provides a balance against which you can weigh your WTA. Lacking such restraint, why not go for the moon?

It is tempting, in such cases, to ask a different question, such as, "How much would you pay to avoid a future spill like this one?" But this is, indeed, the wrong question, not only because it denies the true structure of the problem, but also because the respondents are thereby limited by their own ability to pay, whereas the real situation depends on the damager's ability to pay.

We have now trapped ourselves inside an uncomfortable box. WTP forms of CV questions are inappropriate for CERCLA cases, because they lack the proper structure. WTA forms of CV questions are inappropriate for practical reasons. The usual way out of this conundrum for CV practitioners is to employ WTP questions anyway, perhaps with an apology. However, this apologetic stance strikes us as unfortunate, because there is no reason why *any* measure of people's WTP needs to be obtained directly. Rather, what needs to be known for purposes of CERCLA is the monetary value people place on the damaged good.

This brings us to the central argument for a new approach to eliciting values for environmental resources. If values are constructed during the elicitation process in a way that is strongly determined by context and has profound effects on the resultant evaluations, we should take a deliberate approach to value construction in a manner designed to rationalize the process.

USING MULTIATTRIBUTE UTILITY THEORY IN RESOURCE VALUATIONS

We believe that there already exists a sound, formal approach to value construction that can provide the basis for an improved CV method. This approach draws on the techniques and practices of multiattribute utility theory (MAUT).

MAUT underlies the practice of decision analysis and specifies, axiomatically, the conditions under which one can sensibly attach numbers to values. MAUT and decision analysis are systematic procedures designed to assist people in making choices in the presence of conflicting objectives and uncertainty. They are "a formalization of common sense for decision problems that are too complex for informal use of common sense" (Keeney, 1982). Detailed descriptions of MAUT and decision analysis are given by Keeney (1980) and by von Winterfeldt and Edwards (1986).

MAUT is essentially a set of axiomatic theories of preference (Keeney & Raiffa, 1976). The central theorem of each theory says that if people can make choices based on their preferences and if these choices satisfy the axioms, then one can (a) assign numbers to utilities or values (we will use these terms as synonymous), and (b) specify a rule for combining the numbers into a summary measure, such that an object with a larger summary measure is preferred over an object with a smaller summary measure. The measurement scale underlying these utilities is not cardinal; it does not have an invariant zero point. But it is stronger than ordinal, because the ordering of differences between the measures, as well as the ordering of the measures, is invariant. Psychologists call such a scale an *interval* scale (Stevens, 1951).

The most helpful aspect of decision analysis is its ability to formally express subjective judgments in the assessment of alternatives and to establish an explicit framework for integrating the multidimensional components of complex values. However, some further development of these techniques will be needed to use decision analysis as the basis for improvements in CV methods. This is because the purpose of MAUT and decision analysis is to promote insight to help decision makers make choices among alternative plans of action. The purpose of a MAUT-based approach to CV would be more specific – namely, to provide dollar-based evaluations of specific nonmarket goods or programs.

Proposed Approach

The general approach required in a multiattribute CV (MAUT/CV) analysis can be described as a sequence of four steps: Structure the problem, assess utilities, calculate the total value, and perform sensitivity analysis.

Structure the Problem. In this step, the analyst collects, lists, and organizes a description of the problem, identifying all the attributes (that is, all the aspects of the problem that have value to people). The goal is to develop an explicit, comprehensive picture of all factors that contribute significantly to the value of the good or activity. To do so, the analyst will consult both technical experts to get the facts and the affected citizenry to find the link between the facts and the values.

This structuring process differs in two respects from the usual practice of CV. First, the value attributes are made explicit. The usual CV study, in contrast, describes the situation to be evaluated without such an explicit listing. The respondent is assumed to know all attributes of value or to infer them from descriptions in the questionnaire booklet. Second, a MAUT/CV would rely on the affected citizenry to elucidate the attributes of value. This step, which precedes the elicitation of values, has typically been omitted in CV. The value attributes implicit in the usual CV study come from experts in the topic of concern or from the study authors, rather than directly from the affected citizenry (although, recently, the increasing use of focus groups is mitigating this problem).

In MAUT/CV, diverse groups of people should be consulted to select the value attributes. These *stakeholders* are defined in an operational sense as groups of people who, for any reason (e.g., place of residence, occupation, favored activities), share common values or opinions regarding a proposed action (Edwards & von Winterfeldt, 1987). The MAUT/CV analyst might convene 3 to 10 stakeholder groups, each composed of three to seven people; from each group, a values structure is elicited. Careful selection of stakeholder groups ensures that the full range of views is adequately covered. For example, the representatives of an environmental advocacy organization might be expected to present a somewhat different list of attributes than would members of the local Chamber of Commerce, but the views of these two groups are likely to encompass those of many other citizens.

In a complex problem, the expressed attributes will vary in level of generality, and, therefore, often can be structured hierarchically into a value "tree." The eventual goal is to find a single hierarchy of values that all the shareholders can agree is complete. This values hierarchy must also be built with due concern for the form of the utility combination rule. The simplest such rule is additive; one adds all the utilities of the lowest-level scales to find the total utility. This combination rule requires value independence: The value of one level of one attribute must not depend on what the levels are on the other attributes. The decision analyst must probe frequently for value independence; lack of independence may signal an additional, unreported attribute of value.

The finished values hierarchy may have components using causal models, economic models, influence or means/ends diagrams, and so forth, showing the linkages between specific measures at the bottom and the abstract attributes at the top. Depending on the situation, some components may have probabilities explicitly built into the model, so that the final utility calculation will be an expected utility.

Suppose that someone wanted to do a MAUT/CV study of the monetary value of the damage resulting from a specific pollutant dumped into Lake Michigan. Technical experts can provide information describing the lake before and after the damage. These descriptions then can be presented to representatives of the people affected by the damage to identify the value attributes. For example, the physical event of the death of a large number of fish might imply aesthetic loss (when the dead fish wash up on the shore), loss of genetic diversity, and loss of commercial fishing jobs and profits. These losses indicate the value attributes.

Generic attributes for the lake problem might be Effects on Scenic Beauty, Effects on Genetic Diversity, Human Health Effects, Effects on Commerce, and so forth. Each attribute would have subattributes. For example, subattributes influencing Effects on Commerce might be Real Estate Values (the price of vacation homes would go down if the shoreline becomes ugly), Tourist Values, and Entitlement (expressing the general public's nonuse value for a beautiful lake). Some or all of these subattributes might be further broken down into sub-subattributes, and so forth, until all relevant values have been listed and organized. At the lowest level, each attribute is described in terms of some specific measure. For example, one subcomponent of Scenic Beauty concerned with shoreline attractiveness might have as its bottom-level measure the number of dead fish per acre of beach.

Assess Utilities. A typical CV study elicits values from a random sample of the affected citizenry; WTP responses are given by hundreds or thousands of people. In contrast, an approach based in decision analysis would elicit utilities (values) from the stakeholder groups, fewer than 100 people. Depth of value analysis is substituted for breadth of population sampling.

Utilities are assessed for every lowest-level value scale. To start with, it is convenient to assess every utility on a common scale, say, from 0 to 100. For example, the maximum number of dead fish per acre on Lake Michigan beaches as a result of our hypothetical pollutant spill might be assigned a utility score of 100, and the minimum impact level, perhaps 0 dead fish per acre, would be assigned a score of 0. It is essential that this range of outcomes be carefully specified, that the range encompasses all reasonably possible values for the attribute measure, and that this range, once chosen, remains fixed throughout the analysis. Tradeoffs are then assessed, using weights or multiplicative factors that rescale the utilities in recognition that not all attributes of value are equally important.

All these value elicitations would be done with numerous consistency checks. If you have told the analyst that a change from 0 to 100 on scale A is twice as good as a change from 0 to 100 on scale B, and that a change from 0 to 100 on scale B is four times as good as such a change on scale C, the analyst will then check to see that you do, indeed, believe that the scale A change is eight times as good as the scale C change.

Calculate the Total Value. Once all the pieces are in place, the combination rule specifies how to calculate the total utility for any particular plan, program, or scenario. This total utility will be expressed using a single arbitrary "utile" unit of measurement. For contingent valuation, these units must be converted to dollars. In theory, this conversion need only be made at one place in the model. For example, one such conversion might be made in the Lake Michigan pollution example by noting the monetary value and the utility (or, here, disutility) of the loss of 1 ton of fish to one fishery. Because all utilities, including this one, are measured on a common scale, the monetary worth of all utilities, including the total utility, can be computed from this one conversion. In practice, of course, one would want to find several parts of the model for which both utilities and their monetary equivalents are known (e.g., real estate values, perhaps even the value of a life).

Perform Sensitivity Analysis. The final step required in performing a MAUT/CV analysis would be to recalculate the final utility, using variations in the utilities and tradeoffs, to see how sensitive the final answer is to such variations (Merkhofer & Keeney, 1987). Sensitivity analyses performed on a first-draft MAUT/CV might be used to show which aspects should, because of their strong effect on the total, be subjected to additional stakeholder elicitations or to large-scale sampling of public values.

Different stakeholder groups can be expected to produce different utilities and tradeoffs; thus, the total monetary value may differ across groups. Sensitivity analysis will reveal the most important causes of these disagreements. The analyst can then return to each of the stakeholder groups to explore the possibility that small changes in their utilities and tradeoffs would be acceptable to the group, yet produce a total value more similar to the total value calculated for other groups. Although there is some encouraging evidence (Gardiner & Edwards, 1975) that the use of MAUT diminishes the disagreement between highly polarized groups, further research is needed to explore the conditions under which a single monetary value can be found that adequately expresses the values of all stakeholders.

Advantages and Disadvantages of MAUT/CV

The linkage of MAUT to contingent-valuation approaches will not be an all-purpose panacea. However, we believe that use of a MAUT-based approach to CV offers some strong advantages and possible solutions to several of the most troubling problems confronting environmental researchers. We start by discussing MAUT/CV in terms of the five evaluative criteria discussed earlier. We then comment on other advantages and disadvantages of a multiattribute CV approach.

Accommodates the Multidimensionality of Value. The judgments required as inputs to a MAUT/CV model will not be easy ones to make. But they are not holistic judgments, requiring the simultaneous integration of many dimensions of value. Thus, it is less likely that important aspects of value will be lost because of cognitive overload. Most importantly, the values that guide a MAUT/CV study will be elicited from a wide range of the potentially affected stakeholders. These stakeholders have a right to express their values as part of an open, constructive decision-aiding process.

Minimizes Response Refusals. MAUT measures value without regard to the problem of who must pay, an issue that can be decided in the voting booth or by the courts. To the extent that this problem underlies response refusals, a multiattribute CV procedure should reduce or eliminate the problem.

One obstacle to incorporating MAUT techniques is an ethical concern, stemming from the quantification of utilities for various goods and activities. Recognizing distinctions among value components and putting numbers on values is not easy, and, to some members of the public, it may be repugnant (MacGregor & Slovic, 1986). The argument can be made that the assignment of numerical values only makes clear the tradeoffs that otherwise would be made implicitly rather than explicitly. For some, this logic will be soothing; for others, however, any process requiring quantification is likely to remain questionable.

A further source of response refusals may arise from the extreme stances taken by different groups of stakeholders in a politically potent CV situation. Some stakeholder groups may refuse to participate for political or strategic reasons or because they distrust the agency conducting the study. In such situations, success may rest on the analyst's ability to convince respondents that cooperation in expressing their values will have a genuine impact on the results and that response refusals unfortunately may lead to the omission of their point of view.

Excludes Irrelevancies. A MAUT/CV model would explicitly list the sources of value. Thus, a MAUT-based CV approach would address the real issues in the problem and permit in-depth examination of the factual and values bases for concern. If irrelevant attributes are proposed in the problem-structuring stage, the analyst can either completely exclude them from the model or include them as separate aspects whose effects on the total value can later be calculated.

Separates Facts From Values. Conducting a multiattribute CV study requires extensive knowledge about the facts of a problem and detailed elicitations of people's values. But the method allows the analyst to distinguish facts from values; stakeholders are asked to determine the components of value; experts then make the factual contributions to understand impact pathways and magnitudes. Thus, the people whose values are sought do not need to understand scientific complexities to express their values. Instead, their values are expressed in numerous pieces, with each piece selected to be a readily understandable measure.

Asks the Right Question. There are many occasions when the financial ability of a population of people provides an appropriate and sensible limit on their WTP and thus on their CV for some situation. This occurs, for example, when tax monies will be dedicated to a specific project. But often people's ability to pay is irrelevant to the CV problem. One prominent example is CERCLA cases, in which the goal of the valuation enterprise is to determine the monetary payment that must be made by a polluter. Here, MAUT has a distinct advantage in avoiding WTP as a measure of value; it asks the right question: How valuable is this?

Other Advantages and Disadvantages

Integrates Market and Nonmarket Values. Neither values for which extensive, competitive markets exist nor diffuse, vague, but strongly held values get an advantage in a MAUT model. Economic models can be subsumed into the model where appropriate. Explicit and simple measures can be sought for vague and diffuse nonmarket values. The strength of the approach is that the model can integrate these different kinds of values.

Lessens the Embedding Problem. There may be several causes of the embedding problem. Earlier in this chapter, we suggested that the absence of a monetary representation for a good may be a principal reason for embedding.

In this case, the use of a MAUT-based approach to CV should help, because it will assist people to structure their monetary values in a defensible manner. Kahneman and Knetsch (1992) suggest a second cause, which is that people are not really responding to the specific problem but are reporting a general willingness to donate money to good causes. Because spending money is not directly the focus of MAUT elicitations, this source of embedding would not occur.

A third cause for embedding is that people may be trying to respond to the given problem, but are unable to be sufficiently sensitive to its specifications (e.g., 2,000 dead fish, not 4,000 dead fish) because of its complexity (see Fischhoff et al., 1993, or Loomis, Lockwood, & DeLacy, 1993). Two characteristics of a MAUT/CV method should increase such sensitivity. First, MAUT elicitation methods are decompositional and therefore do not require people to juggle many aspects of value at the same time. Second, the utility for each attribute is elicited across an entire range; respondents are, for example, asked to provide scale values separately for 2,000 fish and for 4,000 fish. It is hardly credible that in such a situation the respondents would give the same utility regardless of the number.

Irwin et al. (1990) have described a related form of the embedding problem that seems to derive from people's beliefs about nonindependence. They report approximately the same WTP for *health* improvements due to cleaner air, *visibility* improvements, and all improvements, apparently because the respondents assumed that any air cleaning leading to better health inevitably would also lead to better visibility, even though the researchers did not mention it. In the MAUT method, any such beliefs about nonindependence would be discovered in the structuring stage; the model would be adjusted to accommodate them.

Flexible in Changing Circumstances. A MAUT/CV model would elicit a broad range of values for each attribute. As a result, the information would be available, so that the calculations could be redone if the circumstances changed. Changing circumstances that add new elements to the problem, of course, would require further modeling and new elicitations. But in most cases, such changes would involve a small portion of the whole analysis, most of which would not need redoing.

Suitable for Construction. We have presented the view that people have not formed monetary values for many complex, nonmarket goods such as environmental improvements. Thus, a successful CV method should help the respondents to think carefully and thoroughly about what they value to *form* their values. A MAUT/CV approach would provide the setting for such extensive consideration, in both its structuring and its valuing phases.

Every value-elicitation method affects the values being elicited. So a MAUT-based method surely will. We cannot know the exact effects it would exert on people's values. But the process and results of a MAUT/CV would be explicitly recorded and thus open to scrutiny. In contrast to a WTP or a WTA study, one would be far less troubled by wondering what the respondents were and were not taking into consideration when expressing their values.

Cost. As far as we know, MAUT never has been used for contingent valuation of environmental resources. The first few exemplars might cost more than WTP studies now do, because MAUT techniques would have to be adjusted and developed to meet CV applications, whereas WTP techniques already have been extensively developed. After that, we do not know. Recent developments in CV practice (e.g., the use of focus groups and avoidance of collecting data by mail, as urged by Arrow et al., 1993) suggest that the cost of WTP assessments is increasing; this trend may eliminate any cost difference between WTP and MAUT approaches to CV.

A related concern derives from the required expertise: a MAUT/CV analysis would require the analyst to participate in the entire elicitation procedure with each stakeholder group. One of the criticisms often leveled at MAUT techniques is that their application requires as much art as science at a time when resources are scarce and there are few accomplished practitioners. However, the practice of a MAUT/CV effort strikes us as no more demanding or subjective than the practice of conventional CV or, for that matter, cost–benefit analysis (Gregory, Keeney, & von Winterfeldt, 1992).

CONCLUSION

Recent evidence from behavioral decision research casts a perspective on contextual effects that goes beyond bias and challenges traditional views of the nature and stability of environmental preferences and values. According to this view, preferences and values for objects that are unfamiliar and complex are often constructed, rather than revealed, in the elicitation process.

We believe that the concept of constructed preferences has important implications for the dollar-based measurement of environmental values. Environmental resources typically are complex goods that are valued across a number of diverse dimensions and that have not been thought about in quantitative terms, let alone dollar terms. Holistic measures of monetary value, as have been used in most CV studies, ignore these cognitive realities and require people to engage in a task that exceeds their capabilities. We propose that practitioners, rather than giving up on the attempt, adopt explicit value-structuring techniques that will link CV efforts with MAUT and decision analysis. This new CV method has the potential to eliminate many of the most vexing problems of conventional CV approaches and provide defensible monetary measures of environmental values.

ACKNOWLEDGMENTS

The authors gratefully acknowledge that this material is based on work supported by the Decision, Risk, and Management Science Program of the National

Science Foundation under Grant Nos. SES 88-12707 and SES 90-22952 to Decision Research. We thank Ward Edwards, Charles Howe, John Kadvany, Ralph Keeney, Julie Irwin, John Payne, and Detlof von Winterfeldt for their insightful comments on an earlier draft of this manuscript. Any opinions, findings, and conclusions or recommendations expressed in this article are those of the authors and do not necessarily reflect the views of the National Science Foundation.

34. Measuring Constructed Preferences: Towards a Building Code

John W. Payne, James R. Bettman, and David A. Schkade

INTRODUCTION

Imagine that you are a member of a management team at the Environmental Protection Agency (EPA) charged with allocating scarce resources to alternative environmental management interventions. As part of your efforts, you need to establish the value of potential natural resource benefits achieved from different proposed interventions. To help in that valuation exercise you seek information about public values for different levels of these natural resources; obtaining citizen inputs is a natural extension of the principles of democratic governance (see Gregory et al., 1997, for a discussion of this position). One method that you consider for getting such information about public values is to conduct a contingent valuation (CV) study of peoples' preferences for different levels of an environmental resource (for a general review of CV studies, see Mitchell & Carson, 1989). Those expressions of preferences will be used as inputs to *design* and select among alternative environmental management interventions.

Alternatively, imagine that you are the marketing manager for a new product and have been asked to generate a *prediction* regarding the likely sales of that product. The need to make such predictions is becoming both more important and more difficult because of rapid changes in technology and shortened product lives. You consider asking a sample of consumers to express their preference for your product in comparison with other competitor products that are, or might be, in the marketplace. Those expressions of preference will be used to predict future sales of your product.

How the EPA administrator or market manager approaches the measurement of preferences depends on the assumptions made about those preferences. One common viewpoint is that well-defined preferences exist for most objects, and therefore the task is to uncover (reveal) those preferences. Gregory, Lichtenstein, and Slovic (1993) have likened this task to an archaeological project, that is, uncovering values that may be hidden but are assumed to exist. An alternative viewpoint is that preferences are generally constructed – not revealed – at the time a valuation question is asked. The measurement of

Originally published in *Journal of Risk and Uncertainty*, vol. 19, pp. 243–270. Copyright © 1999 by Kluwer Academic Publishers. Reprinted with permission.

constructive preferences is then more like a form of architecture, that is, building a sturdy and "defensible" value or set of values, than archaeology (Gregory et al., 1993).[1] We argue later that a constructive view of preference expression requires a fundamentally different approach to the measurement of preferences than that implied by the view of preference expression as revealing well-defined values. That is, it matters greatly whether preference measurement is seen as a form of archaeology, uncovering values that are already there, or as a form of architecture, building some defensible set of values.

We believe that enough knowledge has been gained about decision processes to begin to develop a set of guidelines (a "building code") for measuring constructed preferences. These building code guidelines should help avoid (or at least mitigate) some of the common faults that can occur in preference construction. In illustrating the development of such a code, we consider both the nature of the information that might be provided to the decision maker (the construction materials) and useful tools for thinking (the construction procedures). We also consider how these "building code" guidelines should vary depending on whether the purpose of the exercise is to *guide* (*design*) future decisions (e.g., the EPA manager's task) or to *predict* individuals' future responses (e.g., the marketing manager's task).

The remainder of this chapter is organized as follows. First, we briefly discuss the two perspectives on preferences. Then we consider how to define a well-constructed preference and principles for good preference construction. Next, we discuss the stages of constructing a preference, outline the types of "faults" that are likely to occur in each stage, and provide guidelines for measuring constructed preferences that seek to mitigate these common faults at each stage. We initially focus on design tasks and then consider prediction situations. Finally, we discuss when our suggested remedies are most likely to be needed and provide some words of caution about developing a "building code" for measuring constructed preferences.

EXPRESSIONS OF PREFERENCE

Stable, Coherent, and Known Preferences

Although it is clear that economists vary in terms of the degree to which they believe well-defined preferences exist (McFadden, 1999), a common assumption in economics is that "each individual has stable and coherent preferences" (Rabin, 1998, p. 11). In addition, it is often assumed that "people know their preferences" (Freeman, 1993a, p. 7), that they have the ability or skill in computation

---

[1] The notion of constructed preferences is consistent with the "philosophy of basic values," which holds that people lack well-differentiated values for all but the most familiar evaluation tasks. The notion of well-defined preferences, on the other hand, is consistent with the "philosophy of articulated values," which assumes that people have values for all (most) valuation questions, and the trick is just to ask the question in the right way (Fischhoff, 1991).

to identify (calculate) the option that maximizes received value, and that they will choose accordingly.

Under such assumptions, the task involved in a valuation exercise is to uncover (reveal) these well-defined, preexisting preferences. However, there can be great difficulties in uncovering even such preexisting values. For example, a key problem is to be sure that the good to be valued has been defined properly, so that the "right" preferences are being uncovered. Mitchell and Carson (1989) provide an impressive list of the potential biases that may result when the respondent in a valuation study views the good in a way that was not intended by the researcher (sometimes called the problem of "scenario misspecification"). The researcher must also attempt to design the valuation study so that the respondent is motivated to research his or her preferences and respond truthfully (i.e., not strategically misrepresent his or her preferences).

This approach to preference measurement, which assumes a decision maker with existing, well-defined preferences, has contributed greatly to the prediction and understanding of decisions. However, an increasing number of researchers believe that the assumption of well-articulated preferences is tenable only when people are familiar and experienced with the preference object, and that an alternative, constructive view of preferences is needed in most situations.[2]

Constructive Preferences

Two major tenets of the constructive perspective on preferences are that (1) expressions of preference are generally constructed at the time the valuation question is asked, and (2) the construction process will be shaped by the interaction between the properties of the human information-processing system and the properties of the decision task (Payne, Bettman, & Johnson, 1992; Slovic, 1995), leading to highly contingent decision behavior. That is, we assume that people do not have existing well-defined values for many objects; in addition, when asked a valuation question, they will selectively use information that is part of the immediate task description, as well as information that is drawn selectively from memory, to construct a response on the spot. The constructive view also asserts that preferences are not necessarily generated by applying some invariant process, such as expected utility maximization; instead, a wide variety of heuristics (strategies) may be used in constructing a preferential response (Simon, 1955). Individuals may construct preferences because they lack the cognitive resources needed to compute and store well-defined preferences for many situations (March, 1978) or because they bring multiple, potentially conflicting processing goals to a decision problem (e.g., maximizing

---

[2] Lucas (1986) has argued that economists tend "to focus on situations in which the agent can be expected to 'know' or to have learned the consequences of different actions so that his observed choices reveal stable features of his underlying preferences" (p. S402). In a similar vein, Plott (1996) has argued that individuals have a consistent set of preferences but that such preferences only become known to the individual (are "discovered") through thought and experience.

accuracy, minimizing effort, minimizing negative emotion, or maximizing ease of justification; see Bettman, Luce, & Payne, 1998).[3]

The constructive viewpoint does not necessarily mean that there is no "true" value to be measured. Expressed preferences (measured values for decision objects), in our view, generally reflect *both* a decision maker's basic values for highlighted attributes (e.g., more money is preferred to less) *and* the particular (contingent) heuristics or processing strategies used to combine information selectively to construct the required response to a particular situation. That is, in addition to random error, expressed preferences include two different sources of systematic variance – stable values associated with the attributes of the object being evaluated that are relatively constant across situations and a situation-specific component that is the joint effect of the task and context contingencies that are present. We believe that the situational component will often be large, perhaps much larger than either the random error or stable value components. The focus of this chapter is on measuring preferences when the situational component is a major determinant of observed choice and judgment responses.

As suggested earlier, an important implication of the constructive nature of preferences (and evidence for such construction) is that decisions and decision processes are highly contingent on a variety of factors characterizing decision problems. The major findings from the past two decades of behavioral decision research support that conclusion. It is beyond the scope of the present chapter to review this evidence in detail; for reviews of the extensive evidence in support of the constructive view of decision behavior, see Payne, Bettman, and Johnson (1992, 1993), Bettman et al. (1998), Fischhoff (1991), Slovic (1995), and McFadden (1999). Instead, we briefly summarize some of the major conclusions of that research.

First, choice among options is context (or menu) dependent; the relative value of an option depends not only on the characteristics of that option, but also on characteristics of other options in the choice set. As noted by Tversky (1996), such context dependence indicates that "people do not maximize a pre-computed preference order, but construct their choices in light of the available options" (p. 17). Second, preference among options also depends on how the valuation question is asked; strategically equivalent methods for eliciting preferences can lead to systematically different preference orderings. Preference reversals due to response mode persist even in the face of substantial monetary incentives (see Grether & Plott, 1979). Third, choice among options depends on how the choice set is represented (framed) or displayed, even when the representations would be regarded as equivalent by the decision maker on reflection. As noted by Kahneman, Ritov, and Schkade (1999), "framing effects violate a condition of extensionality (Arrow, 1982), which is commonly taken for granted in economic analyses of preference" (p. 206). Finally, the process used to make a

---

[3] See Sen (1997) for a different but related discussion of how preferences are sensitive to choice processes and the goals evoked by those processes.

choice depends on the complexity of the decision task; the use of simple (heuristic) decision processes increases with task complexity. Thus, people construct preferences using a variety of methods (strategies), with such usage contingent on characteristics of the choice problem.

Clearly, not all expressions of preference are constructed at the time the valuation question is asked; at times, the expression of values reflects a reference to a well-defined value in memory. However, expressed preferences are likely to be constructed in a wide variety of situations in which we are interested in preference measurement. Therefore, a "building code" for measuring constructed preferences is likely to be widely applicable. We provide a more extensive discussion of the conditions leading to constructed preferences later in the chapter.

In the following sections of the chapter, we address issues in measuring constructive preferences. Our initial focus is on preference measurement for design purposes, that is, tasks similar to those facing the EPA administrator in our previous example. Later in the chapter we address assessing preferences for prediction problems such as those faced by the marketing manager in our example.

In design problems there is no obvious "correct" preference. Therefore, before we can address the measurement issues inherent in design problems, we first need to consider criteria for assessing the effectiveness of a preference construction and principles for good preference construction. Then we consider the process of preference construction, separating that process into several interrelated stages. For each stage we examine the possible "faults" in preference construction that might occur at that stage and suggest how those "faults" may be remedied or mitigated.

ASSESSING THE EFFECTIVENESS OF PREFERENCE CONSTRUCTION

Defining a Well-Constructed Preference

We believe that it is possible to judge the quality of a preference construction. For example, people express dismay when they learn that their preference orders vary as a function of how the question was asked (Tversky, Sattath, & Slovic, 1988). People also do not think it is a good idea to violate principles of coherent decision making, such as dominance or transitivity of choices. Beyond coherence in decisions, we believe that the *processes* (methods) leading to an expression of preference can, and should, be judged in terms of quality. That is, we accept that "truth ultimately resides in the process" of the decision (Slovic, 1995, p. 369). This tradition of evaluating human reasoning according to standards applied to the reasoning itself rather than to its conclusions can be traced back at least as far as Socrates, Aristotle, and Plato. It also has a long tradition in psychology (see Baron, 1988, for further discussion). Recently, Yankelovich (1991) has also argued that mindfulness of the consequences of an opinion should be a key component in judging the quality of an expressed opinion.

Sunstein (1990) makes a related argument about the importance of judging the quality of decision processes in the case of public decisions. He argues that not all preferences should be treated equally in a democracy and that more weight should be given to preferences that are reached "with a full and vivid awareness of available opportunities, with reference to all relevant information, and without illegitimate or excessive constraints on the process of preference formation" (p. 11).[4]

Obviously, quality must be defined in terms of the goals of a preference-measurement exercise such as measuring values as inputs to a public environmental protection decision or measuring values as a prediction of future market shares. In the latter case, the distinction between a better or more poorly constructed expression of preference may not matter as long as the measured preference corresponds to actual preferential behaviors such as buying a product. When measuring preferences for the purpose of designing better public or private decisions, however, we think that the focus should be on the processes leading to a well-constructed expression of preference. In part, this reflects the fact that the processes of preference construction are to some extent, at least, controllable ex ante.

What characteristics of the construction process should be used to assess effectiveness? Along with many others, we argue that a well-constructed expression of preference is based on thorough processing of information (reason and reflection) that is transparent and in proportion to the importance of the question at hand (e.g., Baron, 1988; Frisch & Clemen, 1994; Janis & Mann, 1977; Slovic, 1995; for an alternative view of the effects of increased thought, see Wilson and Schooler, 1991). Such processing should include consideration of a range of alternative courses of action, consideration of the full range of objectives to be fulfilled, thorough consideration of the information most critical to the individual, the making of tradeoffs, and careful review of responses to detect inconsistencies. Thus, we argue that an expression of preference based on highly selective use of information and avoidance of tradeoffs, and which is not endorsed on reflection, is not well constructed. Further, we believe that well-constructed expressions of preference should be sensitive to manipulations that should affect them, given the purposes of measurement (e.g., the quantity of the good provided) and should be insensitive to manipulations that should not affect them (e.g., framing effects, Baron, 1997a; Fischhoff, 1997; also see Hammond, 1996b, for a general discussion of how one judges the quality of a decision).[5]

---

[4] Clearly there are situations in which an individual's preferences must be given weight no matter how poorly constructed they may be. There are sometimes "rights" to preferences; see Sunstein (1990) for a further discussion of this point.

[5] Other properties of a well-constructed preference might include such things as high levels of test–retest reliability (stability); however, as noted by one reviewer, stability may result from the repeated use of similar information and processes in the construction process and should not be taken as a sufficient indicator of the retrieval of a well-defined preference (see Sudman, Bradburn, and Schwarz, 1996, for a related discussion).

Principles for Good Preference Construction

In the following sections of the chapter, we suggest some specific tools, pro-cedures, and tests that might be used to mitigate some of the faults in the con-struction of preferences. In other words, we outline some of the specifications in materials (information) and procedures (construction processes) that might make up a building code for the measurement of preferences. The procedures often involve greater work in the measurement of preferences, with a focus on doing more tasks with fewer respondents. This reflects the belief that it is sys-tematic effects (e.g., the effects of the choice context or complexity) rather than random error that have the greatest impact on most constructed expressions of preference. The procedures also require a greater sensitivity to the psychology of preference construction in our measurement efforts (e.g., requiring of people only those types of judgments that they can do well; Kahneman, Schkade, & Sunstein, 1998; Norman, 1988).

STAGES OF PREFERENCE CONSTRUCTION, THEIR FAULTS, AND PROPOSED REMEDIES

We are far from a complete theory of preferential decision making; however, there is general agreement that decision processes can usefully be viewed in terms of multiple, interacting stages (e.g., Hogarth, 1987). Generally, the stages include the initial cognitive representation of the decision problem, information acquisition and interpretation, information combination leading to an evalua-tion, and an expression or mapping of that valuation onto a response such as a choice or willingness-to-pay amount.

Next, we briefly describe and discuss the faults and building code implica-tions for each of these stages. Given space limitations, we only focus on what we believe are some of the most critical faults and possible remedies. For a summary of major faults and remedies at each stage, see Table 34.1.

Problem Representation

Our thought is controlled by mental models and frames, typically portrayed as associative networks of concepts interconnected by relationships of varying degrees of strength. Key components of a mental model for a decision (a decision frame) include the options to be considered, the states of nature to be evaluated, and the criteria used to measure the relative attractiveness of consequences. In addition, a decision frame affects both the boundaries one puts on a problem, such as whether prior costs (outcomes) are considered, and the reference points used to code a consequence as good or bad (Russo & Schoemaker, 1989).

When individuals construct mental models of a situation, they often make explicit as little information as possible to minimize the cognitive load. Such mental models affect what information we pay attention to and what we ignore. In particular, there is often a focusing phenomenon in which thoughts are restricted to what is explicitly represented in the mental model (Legrenzi, Girotto, & Johnson-Laird, 1993). At other times, the focal information will

Table 34.1. *Faults at Stages of the Preference-Construction Process and Proposed Remedies*

Stage	Fault	Remedies
Problem representation	Myopic decision frames	• Explicitly encourage consideration of multiple options, events, and objectives • Expand set of options, use value ladders • Encourage consideration of multiple futures • Construct a value tree • Clarify the distinction between fundamental and proxy values
	Using an inappropriate problem representation	• Use extensive pre-testing, focus groups • Use manipulation checks
Information acquisition and interpretation	Inappropriate selectivity and the focusing illusion	• Provide important information using formats that make it salient and easy to process
	Lack of comprehension of the information provided	• Use manipulation checks • Use common, anchored scale formats • Use common, anchored scale formats • Explicitly present range information
Information combination	Avoidance of tradeoffs	• Provide time and thinking tools, such as multiattribute utility analysis or judgment policy analysis • Assess swing weights • Decompose complex judgments • Use tools to help improve attribute weighting
Expression or mapping of preferences	Influences of scale compatibility	• Triangulation (ask questions in multiple ways) • Use lability as an asset – ask for reconciliation of inconsistencies
	Biases in scale usage	• Use explicit scale anchors, e.g., behaviorally anchored scales • Use less sensitive, more robust scales
All Stages		• Increased use of sensitivity analysis

depend on past experiences (knowledge) that an individual brings to the problem. In either case, the highlighting of some elements of a decision problem, while downplaying others, is very important in the context of a valuation exercise. For example, in assigning a value to "air quality," many evaluative dimensions of that concept can come to mind, such as visibility and health effects. Which components of air quality figure most strongly in the evaluation will depend on the mental frame adopted for the valuation exercise (Irwin et al., 1990). Finally, once a mental model has been constructed or retrieved that seems to work for the task at hand, people tend not to consider alternatives (Legrenzi et al., 1993).

As noted earlier, we believe that a well-constructed preference should be based on consideration of a range of options and those objectives most critical to the individual. Two major faults related to the problem representation stage concern failures to meet these standards. First, decision makers often focus on too narrow a range of options or objectives (often only one); that is, they adopt a myopic decision frame (problem representation). Second, decision makers may use an inappropriate representation, that is, they may try to solve the wrong problem using options or objectives that would not be most critical to them on reflection.

Myopic Decision Frames. Although simplification of decision problems is generally required, given limited information-processing capacity, the extent to which myopic problem representations are adopted is probably the major fault at the problem representation stage. For instance, people often focus on a single option, a single objective or attribute, or a single assumed state of the world when reasoning about a decision problem (Eisenhardt, 1989; Nutt, 1998; Shepard, 1964). This focusing is particularly acute when the decision is made under stressful conditions such as time pressure or heavy information load (e.g., Payne, Bettman, & Johnson, 1988). In the context of our example of the EPA administrator, the recent National Oceanic and Atmospheric Administration panel on CV studies (Arrow et al., 1993) highlighted this concern and emphasized being explicit about substitutes (i.e., multiple alternative courses of action) in well-designed CV studies. We believe that people generally will not consider alternative goods of the same type as the good evaluated unless explicitly reminded; see Baron (1997a) for a similar argument.

Remedies for Myopic Decision Frames. Remedies for this decision fault *explicitly* encourage people to think of multiple alternatives, multiple states of nature, and multiple attributes or objectives. First, it is important to expand the set of options considered. There should be at least two or more viable options considered when solving any decision problem if the goal is to make better decisions. Bazerman and Neale (1992, p. 69) capture this idea with their advice about house hunting: "Fall in love with three, not with one." In group decision making, there is a similar recommendation that each individual in a group be responsible for thinking of at least two valid solutions to the problem early in the process; this encourages critical thinking about the decision problem.

Keeney (1996) suggests making explicit how much money is spent on alternative public goods to encourage people to recognize alternatives in the context of a valuation of a specific public policy option, such as putting money into an environmental protection project. This technique might be thought of as a "value" ladder in the same way that "risk" ladders have been used to help communicate risks to people (Smith & Desvousges, 1987). A related idea in the CV literature is the use of "benchmark" amounts intended to "remind respondents that they are already paying for many public goods and to provide a general idea of the magnitude of those payments" (Mitchell & Carson, 1989, p. 243). Although there is an obvious danger that explicit benchmark amounts will provide an anchor for responses, we believe that the need to encourage consideration of alternative uses of resources when making decisions argues for making options as explicit as possible. This is particularly true when it is unlikely that people will retrieve options from memory in the normal course of solving a novel or complex valuation problem.

Does increasing the mental availability of options help in valuation? Although limited in quantity, research suggests that the answer is yes. For example, Baron and Greene (1996) found that explicitly reminding people of other goods helped reduce such problematic valuation effects as the adding up effect, where the value of good A assessed separately plus the value of good B assessed separately often exceeds the value of goods A and B when valued together. Another study by Posavac, Sanbonmatsu, and Fazio (1997) shows that the consistency between attitudes and decisions is higher when alternatives are made salient (explicit) in the decision context. This is most important when people are unlikely to generate (retrieve from memory) the complete set of options on their own. Finally, Nutt (1998) reports that consideration of more than one alternative course of action is associated with greater success in strategic decision making.

A second recommendation is to encourage consideration of multiple futures, because it is clear that people often fail to consider multiple uncertain futures when assessing preferences. One technique that can be used to address this problem is scenario generation (Schoemaker, 1991). The focus of most scenario exercises is not to list all possible futures but to generate at least two, three, or four different future states of the world so that people will be more cognizant of the possible range of uncertainties when making decisions.

Third, individuals should develop a multiattribute problem representation. One of the basic tools used in decision analysis to help people consider multiple objectives or attributes when making a decision is the construction of a value tree (Keeney, 1992), particularly as an early step in a decision process. A critical issue related to such a representation of objectives is the distinction between fundamental and means objectives or between fundamental values and proxy values (Keeney, 1992). Proxy values reflect means to an end and reflect beliefs about the extent to which satisfying the proxy value will satisfy more fundamental values. Baron (1997a, p. 83) suggests that "the failure to make respondents consult their fundamental values seriously may be the largest source of error in valuation of natural resources, as practiced." One solution to this problem mentioned by Baron is to provide respondents with expert opinions regarding which dimensions should be considered in assessing a value for an object (see DeKay & McClelland, 1996).

Inappropriate Decision Frames. A second class of faults at the problem representation stage is using an inappropriate representation. For example, a person may use an inappropriate analogy in generating a representation. One type of inappropriate problem representation is from the perspective of the decision maker himself or herself; that is, a person may construct a preference (answer) for a different problem than that which he or she would endorse on reflection. Inappropriate can also mean that a person is using a different frame than that intended by the researcher, that is, the problem of scenario misspecification. More generally, use of a frame different from that intended by the researcher is a critical problem in any form of attitude research.

As an example, individuals sometimes use the analogy of charitable giving in constructing an answer to a CV task (Schkade & Payne, 1994). As a result, the willingness to pay (WTP) amounts that are expressed are often similar to the amounts given by the respondent to charities, such as $25 or $50 for a "worthwhile" cause. Clearly, the retrieval and use of a response to a situation perceived to be similar can be an efficient solution to a difficult problem. However, there can be costs associated with such solutions. For example, in solving a decision problem through the use of analogies, respondents may not be properly sensitive to important characteristics of the good being valued, such as the quantity of the good (Baron & Greene, 1996). Also, as noted earlier, once a mental model has been retrieved that seems to work for the task at hand, people may not consider alternatives (Legrenzi et al., 1993) and therefore not appreciate what is omitted from the particular problem representation that they are using.

Remedies for Inappropriate Decision Frames. Mitchell and Carson (1989) suggest that the use of inappropriate representations can be minimized in a CV study by an intensive program of questionnaire development, including the use of focus groups. In their words, "If the study is well designed and carefully pretested, the respondents' answers to the valuation questions should represent valid WTP responses" (p. 3).

We believe that in addition to careful pre-testing, manipulation checks should be used to confirm the representation respondents are using. In fact, we feel that one obvious property of a well-designed preference measurement process is the use of manipulation checks to ensure that the information presented was understood by the respondent in sufficient detail to have confidence in his or her responses. Fischhoff et al. (1993) provide an example of the manipulation checks used in answering questions about the value of cleaning up rivers near Pittsburgh. Unfortunately, as noted by Fischhoff et al. (1993), the use of manipulation checks is not as common as it should be among valuation researchers. We argue that a minimum standard for a building code dealing with the measurement of preferences should be the use of manipulation checks (for a discussion of probing procedures developed by survey researchers, see DeMaio & Rothgeb, 1996).

Other methods for probing respondents' thought processes can also be useful as manipulation checks. For example, the researcher can take a verbal protocol from the respondent during the construction of a preference (e.g., Schkade & Payne, 1994). The reasoning processes used by the respondent can then be checked to see if the respondent was answering the question as the researcher understood it.

Information Acquisition and Interpretation

In most situations of importance to an individual, a great deal of information may be available from many sources. Some of these sources are external to the individual (e.g., catalogs and brochures, special magazine issues, guidebooks, or opinions from friends for a college choice), and some information is internal, in the individual's memory. Once acquired, information is then interpreted in light of the representation that has been adopted for the decision task. One key component of this interpretation is the coding of potential outcome information in terms of a gain or loss relative to some reference value.

Even though a great deal of information may be available, human processing limitations require selectivity. That is, only a subset of the available information will be examined. Aspects of the individual's information environment can influence selectivity by affecting the salience of various pieces of information. For example, the organization of an information display can make some piece of information either more salient or easier to process (e.g., Bettman, Payne, & Staelin, 1986; Kleinmuntz & Schkade, 1993; Russo, 1977). There is a general "concreteness principle" in information acquisition (Slovic, 1972): People will tend to use only explicitly displayed information and will use it untransformed from the form in which it is displayed. A related point is that respondents may use conversational norms to infer that the information presented (and not other, unmentioned information) is the appropriate focus (Schwarz, 1996). Thus, individuals will of necessity be selective; the important issue is how the individual chooses to be selective.

We have stated earlier that a well-constructed preference should be based on thorough consideration of the range of information most critical to the individual. Two of the major faults at the information acquisition and interpretation stage that impede attaining this objective are inappropriate selectivity and lack of information comprehension.

Inappropriate Selectivity. Selective acquisition of information is related to the focusing phenomenon in constructing mental representations of problems, and therefore many of the faults of these two stages are similar. Thus, one of the major faults of the information acquisition stage is that individuals are too selective and do not acquire and consider enough relevant information.

This problem can be compounded by the fact that the information that is most salient (the focus of attention) in a task environment can be uncorrelated or even negatively correlated with the diagnosticity or importance of the information for the individual's goals. Of course, it is also possible that individuals may seek to examine too much information, while not paying enough attention to the subset of information that is most important. A similar problem can occur when a decision maker is overloaded with too much information.

Remedies for Inappropriate Selectivity. One approach for generating well-constructed preferences, therefore, is to give people high-quality information to be used in constructing a preference. For example, many CV researchers argue for the use of in-person interviews, at least in part because it is easier to convey a good deal of high-quality information, such as pictures and other visual aids, in such interviews. Urban et al. (1997) have also emphasized the use of various multimedia tools to accelerate the learning of preferences about novel products through extensive, and hopefully more realistic, information provision.

However, as noted by Fischhoff and Furby (1988), the provision of information is not as straightforward a task as might be imagined. Although one does not want to leave out important information from the description of the valuation problem given to a respondent, providing all the relevant information for a valuation task can be a formidable task in itself. For example, Fischhoff and Furby give a checklist of the many components of a CV task that may need to be explained to the respondent for the respondent to generate a well-defined preference. As previously noted, it is also clearly possible to overload the respondent with too much information; consequently, comprehension may be affected and various simplifying heuristics may be used as a way to deal with the stress caused by the information load (Payne, 1976). As noted later, we generally need to provide cognitive reasoning tools to help individuals cope with such information load problems.

Given the tension between providing too much information and too little, it is important to consider how one might make information easier to process so that individuals are more likely to examine the information most critical to them. There is a good deal of research suggesting that careful design of information display formats can be extremely useful. A classic example of such an information format effect is Russo's (1977) demonstration that the use of unit price information by consumers was affected by simple changes in how information was made available to the consumer (by presenting unit prices ranked in a list instead of on individual shelf tags). Guidelines also have been developed for such tasks as providing warnings on product labels (e.g., Bettman et al., 1986).

Lack of Information Comprehension. A second major fault at the information acquisition and interpretation stage is that individuals simply may not comprehend the information available or comprehend it in ways not intended by the researcher. Comprehension failures can be due to confusing presentation, lack of knowledge, or other factors (Fischhoff, Welch, & Frederick, 1999). For example, Hsee, Loewenstein, Blount, and Bazerman (1999) review a growing body of research demonstrating that it is more difficult for individuals to evaluate the desirability of values on some attributes than on others. Hsee et al. also make clear that a more difficult to evaluate attribute will be given *less* weight when options are evaluated separately than when these options are evaluated jointly, which can lead to preference reversals. More generally, if the individual does not understand the object of the preference assessment, then we cannot expect meaningful responses (Fischhoff et al., 1993).

Remedies for Lack of Information Comprehension. We can attempt to ensure that individuals understand the information presented by using manipulation checks and by attempting to make the meaning of the information clear. As stressed earlier, one feature of a well-designed preference measurement process for design purposes should be the use of manipulation checks to ensure that the information presented was understood by the respondent in sufficient detail to have confidence in his or her responses.

Selective attention and comprehension faults due to information format also can be avoided by making the formats of the information as comparable as possible (e.g., using a common format to the extent possible) and by making the meaning of the information as clear as possible. In addition, decision analysts often attempt to make information more easily interpretable by explicitly presenting range information, such as mileage ranges for cars. They often do this by using a common scale, such as 0 to 100, for the values of various attributes and anchoring the end-points of the scales for each attribute by the worst (0) and best (100) attribute values provided by the alternatives in the choice set. Thus, the car in a choice set offering the best gas mileage (e.g., 30 miles per gallon [mpg]) would be given a value of 100, whereas the car offering the poorest gas mileage (e.g., 14 mpg) would be given a value of 0. The use of both absolute scale information, that is, mpg numbers and relative scale information (0 to 100) in combination, may help in interpreting attribute information. The use of meaningful end-points for scales also helps in the expression stage of preference construction, discussed later.

Information Combination

How people combine information and make tradeoffs has been a focal point of research on preferences. For many, this stage is the heart of the preferential decision-making process. It is in making tradeoffs between more of one thing and less of another that one's values are most often revealed to oneself and to outside observers; according to Freeman (1993a), the tradeoff ratios between pairs of goods that matter to people are at the core of the economist's concept of value. Many have argued that making tradeoffs is a crucial aspect of high-quality, rational decision making (e.g., Frisch & Clemen, 1994).

It is clear that people do make tradeoffs. Much of market research, for example, has been aimed at measuring tradeoffs using a variety of techniques, such as conjoint analysis (e.g., Green & Srinivasan, 1990) and direct methods for assessing exchange rates between attributes (e.g., Aaker, 1991). Similarly, asking people to make tradeoffs explicitly is a key part of decision analysis techniques (e.g., Clemen, 1996). However, the major fault of the information combination stage is that decision makers often avoid making explicit tradeoffs, relying instead on an array of noncompensatory decision heuristics.

Tradeoff Avoidance. The avoidance of tradeoffs by individuals is reflected in behaviors such as the selection of the status quo option, the expression of a "protest" zero in CV studies, delaying choice, or selection based on choice set context, violating menu independence (Luce, 1998). As noted earlier, the major fault of the information combination stage clearly is avoidance of tradeoffs.

Decision makers may avoid tradeoffs for several reasons. One explanation for tradeoff avoidance is simply that making tradeoffs is a cognitively demanding task that people will try to minimize (Payne et al., 1993). Thus, one observes frequent use of decision heuristics that emphasize comparing alternatives on just one (or a few) attributes as tasks become more complex (i.e., lexicographic-type heuristics; Payne, 1976).

Another explanation is that tradeoffs can be difficult for emotional as well as cognitive reasons (Hogarth, 1987; Luce, Payne, & Bettman, 1999). It can be emotionally trying to think about giving up something one values. Values that people are relatively unwilling to trade off have been called "protected" values (Baron & Spranca, 1997), and decisions involving such difficult tradeoffs have been termed "cruel choices" (Russell, 1990). Keeney (1996) suggests that public policy decision makers "rarely" make explicit tradeoffs between costs and the noneconomic impacts of programs.

Remedies for Tradeoff Avoidance. We believe that multiple approaches should be used to help individuals make explicit tradeoffs. Because thinking about tradeoffs is difficult for people, providing more information may be necessary, but not sufficient, for helping people think more deeply about their tradeoffs. As a general building code principle, we suggest that providing cognitive tools can help a respondent think about tradeoffs.

Some simple cognitive techniques for improving the making of tradeoffs have already been mentioned. For instance, expanding the set of options and thinking in terms of two or more alternatives helps people to appreciate that every option is likely to have some advantages and disadvantages. However, there are even more sophisticated thinking tools to facilitate making explicit tradeoffs, such as multiattribute utility analysis (MAUA) and judgment policy analysis.

Thinking tools like MAUA incorporate ways to avoid, or at least minimize, some of the more common faults in thinking about tradeoffs. For example, one of the most important errors identified by decision analysts is the failure to consider an adequate range of levels for particular attributes when deciding tradeoffs. A simple technique for helping people to do a better job of considering attribute ranges is the assessment of swing weights. Typically, the respondent compares alternatives that "swing" between the worst and best levels represented in the given (or plausible) set of alternatives for each attribute and assesses the extent to which the swings in each attribute contribute to overall value differences.

Another feature or characteristic of thinking aids for the making of tradeoffs is the decomposition of complex value judgments into a series of less complex judgments. A simple model like the additive model of preferences is then used to combine the simpler judgments into an overall valuation. Consistent with the idea that cognitive capacity constraints are a source of error in value construction, decomposing a complex judgment into a series of smaller judgments and then combining those judgments mechanically can improve judgment performance (see Einhorn, 1972; Jako & Murphy, 1990; Kleinmuntz, 1990).

Other thinking tools are available that may help in the construction of preferences through improving attribute weighting. Social judgment theory (Hammond, Stewart, Brehmer, & Steinmann, 1975), for instance, provides feedback to an individual about his or her judgment policy and the relative weights apparently placed on various attributes of value. The individual can then use that knowledge to decide how much, if at all, to change the weighting of attributes. Harris, Tinsley, and Donnelly (1988) discuss how judgment policy analysis might be applied to the valuation of natural resources.

However, as noted earlier, tradeoffs may be avoided for emotional as well as cognitive reasons. Even providing cognitive tools may not be sufficient to overcome individuals' emotional and moral reasons for avoidance. Therefore, an important area for future research is understanding the emotional costs of making tradeoffs and developing techniques that help to both alleviate such costs and encourage reasoned tradeoffs. For example, one advantage of the judgment, feedback, learn, and respond procedure of judgment policy analysis is that it might help overcome the emotional reaction to making even more explicit tradeoffs, although this needs to be investigated.

Expression or Mapping of Preferences

The essence of the expression or mapping stage is that an individual must take an internal preferential response and express that response using some specified response mode (e.g., a choice or a scale). However, even when a person has in mind a well-constructed preference, it is not always the case that he or she will be able to translate that preference or value easily and without error (bias) into the response called for in a valuation task (Kahneman, Ritov, & Schkade, 1999). The outcome of the expression or mapping stage should be a response that best reflects the individuals' values and is free of inconsistencies. Two major faults that hinder reaching this goal are influences of scale compatibility and biases in scale usage.

Influences of Scale Compatibility.   One major fault at the preference expression stage is the influence of scale compatibility. Expressions of preference are likely to be overly influenced by the compatibility between an attribute of the stimulus and the response scale or mode. For example, the weight of an attribute whose values are expressed in monetary terms is generally enhanced if the required response is also in monetary terms (Tversky et al., 1988). Similarly, Gregory et al. (1993) have suggested that although a person may hold a strong value for an environmental resource, that value is unlikely to be represented in memory in dollar terms. Consequently, in attempting to translate such a value into a monetary equivalent, the person may exhibit systematic errors.

Remedies for Influences of Scale Compatibility. We can attempt to overcome scale compatibility effects via triangulation of responses. When the goal of preference measurement is design, one important building code principle is that a preference question should not be asked in just one way; instead, questions about values that are likely to be the result of a constructive process should be asked in multiple ways (see Huber, Wittink, Fiedler, & Miller, 1993, for evidence of the effectiveness of such an approach). Differences in responses to different but strategically equivalent forms of a value question provide insight into the extent to which the expressed preference is constructed. In addition, one can then ask the respondent to consider the inconsistencies implied by his or her responses. Thus, lability of responses can provide an opportunity for the decision maker to think carefully about the inconsistencies and thereby gain greater insight into the decision (von Winterfeldt & Edwards, 1986). A related point is that asking for multiple types of responses allows different task orders; as suggested by a reviewer, different task orders should in fact be used, and any resultant order effects can be used as a source of insight into the construction process.

Biases in Scale Usage. A second set of expression or mapping faults is due to a number of classic psychophysical phenomena. For example, there are biases such as the tendency to use the center of the scale. It is also likely that any response scale will suffer from anchoring effects. Finally, scale use is affected by the meaningfulness of the scale's labels. If scale labels are vague and do not provide a context for the evaluation, expressed preferences may have little stability. For example, in a study that has implications for an area of debate in public policy, Kahneman et al. (1998) have shown that unpredictability in punitive damage awards may result from the difficulty that people have in mapping their preference for the degree of severity of punishment onto an unbounded dollar scale. This difficulty can be traced to the well-known difficulties people have with magnitude estimation scales in psychophysics. Kahneman, Ritov, and Schkade (1999) provide further discussion of psychophysical phenomena related to valuation tasks.

Remedies for Biases in Scale Usage. A general principle of our proposed building code for the measurement of preferences is that it is better to be explicit about anchors rather than leave the anchors implicit; this helps avoid large individual differences in the implicit anchors used by respondents. Scale usage and the ease of interpretation of a scale can also be improved by using meaningful anchors. For instance, it is recommended in performance appraisal that scales be behaviorally anchored. That is, rather than simply using the term "excellent" on a performance rating scale, one would provide an explicit example of excellent task performance, such as responding to a customer's service complaint.

There also may be times when it is better to use a less sensitive, but more robust, response scale. Kahneman et al. (1998) have suggested that one solution for the problem of unpredictability in punitive damage awards is for jurors to use a less sensitive category-type scale (e.g., a seven-category scale ranging from no punishment to extremely severe punishment) on which jurors can make more reliable and robust judgments. Those responses might then be converted into punitive damage amounts using a formula. This suggestion of Kahneman et al. is consistent with the general building code principle of asking people to do only those things that they can do well (Norman, 1988).

A More Prominent Role for Sensitivity Analysis

A final suggestion for better measurement cuts across the various stages of the preference construction process. Sensitivity analysis provides insight into the robustness of a decision to changes in the parameters and values used to define it. In our experience, one of the major factors in the increasing use of decision aiding techniques to solve real-world problems has been the ability of computer-based decision support tools to easily do, and display, the results of sensitivity analyses. The presence of an irreducible arbitrariness in measured preferences makes sensitivity analysis an essential tool in the construction of a defensible expression of value, particularly when the value is going to be used as an input for the design and selection of a public policy option.

Typically, sensitivity analysis is done after the problem structuring and valuation stages of a decision. However, given that expressed values may be constructed, we propose that in some cases it may be useful to start the analysis of a decision with a sensitivity analysis. For example, in looking for public values to be used as inputs into a policy decision about environmental protection levels, the decision maker might start by asking under what values a decision would shift. If the value of a natural resource must be above $X to warrant the cost of some action to improve or protect the environment, then the decision maker might use that knowledge to directly ask whether the constructed value is likely to be above or below $X. Of course, there is a danger that the values assessment could be directed by the decision maker to either support or not support an expression of value greater or less than $X; however, we suggest that the danger can be ameliorated by making the assessment process as explicit as possible and by including other anchors that are above or below $X.

Until now, when reviewing construction faults and possible remedies for those faults, we have emphasized situations in which the goal of the measurement task is to design or select a future course of action, particularly in the public domain. When the task is to predict rather than design preferences, another set of construction guidelines is called for, presented next.

MEASURING PREFERENCES FOR PREDICTION: CONTEXT MATCHING OF INFORMATION ENVIRONMENTS

When the goal of measurement is prediction, the "quality" of the measurement is determined by how well the measured preference corresponds to preferential behaviors of interest (e.g., buying a product). The basic building code principle for achieving such correspondence is context matching. That is, one attempts to match the task environment (the context) presented to the respondent for purposes of preference measurement as closely as possible to the task environment that the decision maker will actually face. In implementing context matching, the analyst attempts to determine the relevant factors that might influence preferences in the individual's environment and then matches the values of those factors in the measurement environment (Simmons, Bickart, & Lynch, 1993; Wright & Kriewall, 1980). For example, we now know from behavioral decision research that such factors as the response mode, the number of options and attributes, time pressure, information display, the context provided by competing options (choice set), and others can affect choices (Payne et al., 1992). The environment in which preferences are elicited should attempt to approximate the individual's environment on all these factors, particularly if the individual has little familiarity with the decision. The predictive validity of the preference data supplied by respondent depends crucially on his or her constructing the same preference during the staged measurement episode as he or she will when coming to grips with the real choice (Wright & Weitz, 1977; see also Marder, 1997, for a similar idea, the congruence principle). In sum, the measurement situation should attempt to mimic to the extent possible the major factors that affect how people deal with the actual decision problems that are the predictive focus.

Context matching thus demands a thorough knowledge of the properties of choice environments, which requires a fairly complete task analysis of the situations an individual will face when making the actual marketplace or public policy choice. This may not be an easy task to accomplish (see Huber, 1997, however, for an attempt to relate properties of market environments to properties of evaluation tasks). First, individuals may not have detailed knowledge of the situations for which they are predicting (Fischhoff, 1991). In addition, in some cases, factors may differ systematically across choice environments (e.g., the set of available options may vary). In that case, measurements may need to be taken for each of the major variants of the choice environment and then aggregated based on the relative frequency of those variants. This will be more difficult to the extent that these variants change over time and hence must also be predicted. Finally, it may be virtually impossible to match on all aspects of the environment. How can we determine which dimensions are most important to match on? As noted earlier, behavioral decision research has provided evidence for a set of plausible candidate properties (e.g., response mode); perhaps effect sizes from this prior research could be used as broad guidelines for selecting the most critical aspect of the environment on which to match.

DISCUSSION

Fischhoff (1997) notes that psychology "is still grappling with how to handle situations in which people might not know what they want" (p. 209). We would extend that view and say that researchers interested in the measurement of preferences are grappling with what it means to measure values in a world of constructed preferences. The purpose of this chapter is to begin a dialogue that will hopefully lead to agreement on at least some elements of a building code for the measurement of preferences. We believe that enough research now exists to identify some common "faults" in the construction of preferences that can, and should be, addressed. As noted earlier, many of our suggestions for addressing preference construction faults involve the provision of tools as well as information (i.e., the materials) for thinking about values. Our suggestions also involve greater effort devoted to the measurement of preferences, with a focus on doing more tasks with fewer respondents. In the next section we consider the conditions under which such efforts should be undertaken.

When Is a Building Code Needed?

Given that our guidelines often involve substantial effort on the part of respondents, it is important to consider when such guidelines are necessary. Just as housing construction codes often vary depending on the type or purpose of a building (e.g., whether for a high-rise office, a residence, a school, or a hospital) and the location of the building (e.g., whether the area is prone to earthquakes), we believe that the application of our building code should be contingent on characteristics of the measurement situation. In particular, we believe that the building code should be applied when preferences are more likely to be constructive and to the degree that the decision for which the preferences are relevant is more critical or important. We consider each of these two aspects of a measurement situation next.

When Are Preferences Likely to Be Constructed? Clearly, not all expressions of preference are constructed at the time the valuation question is asked. There are occasions when the expression of values reflects a reference to a well-defined value in memory. For example, for the first two authors of this chapter, asking for the name of their favorite college basketball team would yield a quick preferential response from memory – Duke. In Bayesian terms, there are times when individuals have strong priors.

Fischhoff, Slovic, and Lichtenstein (1980) argue that "people are most likely to have clear preferences regarding issues that are familiar, simple, and directly experienced" (p. 118). Experience allows a person to obtain feedback on the outcomes of prior judgments and choices and thus to learn preferences. In the field of attitude research, clear preferences have been called "crystallized" values (Schuman & Presser, 1981). Crystallized values are more likely when a person has had the opportunity to think about and/or obtain experience with a good prior to being asked a valuation question (Irwin et al., 1990). Thus, when the objects to be valued are ones with which the respondent is familiar and has directly experienced, the common assumptions of economics are more likely to be justified, that is, preferences exist to be uncovered.[6]

However, even if a preference is stored in memory, it may not always be retrieved; thus, preferences may be partially constructed even when there has been prior experience. The likelihood that a particular prior preference or value will be retrieved from memory is a positive function of (a) the accessibility in memory (i.e., ease of retrieval) of the prior valuation, and (b) the perceived diagnosticity of the prior valuation (i.e., the perceived degree to which that prior value aids the person in achieving his or her goals). On the other hand, the probability of a particular value's being retrieved will be a negative function of the (c) accessibility and (d) diagnosticity of alternative values available in memory (Feldman & Lynch, 1988). Accessibility can be influenced by a variety of factors, including various priming effects, information format, prior usage of the information, and so on (e.g., Alba & Chattopadhyay, 1985; Simmons et al., 1993).

When the object to be valued has any novelty or complexity, such as valuing a change in an environmental resource, a retrieved value or preference may simply serve as a starting point or anchor for a more elaborate inferential process in which existing values are related to the problem at hand (Fischhoff & Furby, 1988). The more the valuation exercise requires inferences to be drawn from past situations to a current problem and the more unfamiliar the terms and issues (e.g., the sustainability of an ecological system), the more the expression of preference is likely to reflect a constructive process. Also, the greater the conflict among existing values that might exist (e.g., environmental protection versus economic development), the greater the uncertainties about the future, and larger the number of options to be considered, the more the expression of preferences is likely to reflect a constructive process. Thus, expressed preferences are likely to be constructed in a wide variety of situations.

When Does a Decision Problem Warrant Use of the Guidelines? We have only begun to examine how the building code guidelines should vary according to properties of the measurement situation, such as the purpose of the valuation exercise. We have characterized the differences between the measurement of preferences for the two different purposes of decision design and prediction. However, as suggested in several places in this chapter, one might also want different "building code" guidelines for different situations involving decision design. Obviously, one would want to make more extensive use of the guidelines the more important the decision. One might also want to use the guidelines more extensively the greater the degree to which the expression of preference by one individual might affect the consequences experienced by another. The problem

[6] However, even such crystallized values can still be subject to task and context effects (Krosnick & Schuman, 1988). For a further discussion of such effects, see Kahneman et al. (1998).

of the EPA administrator clearly fits into the category of situations in which we think a more complete building code approach is needed. The characterization of when the guidelines should be used to a greater or lesser extent is a major topic for future research.

One final issue to be addressed is which guidelines are the most critical to implement when a decision to use the building code has been made. We believe that the following guidelines are the most critical: ensuring consideration of multiple decision frames and options, using manipulation checks to ensure understanding, encouraging explicit tradeoffs, use of more than one response mode, and the use of sensitivity analysis.

In the next section we consider a learning perspective on the construction of preferences that presents another view of the guidelines. Then we provide some words of caution for using the building code.

A Learning Perspective on the Construction of Preferences

One way to view the construction of preferences is from a learning perspective. That is, one could view the construction of a preference as a process by which a decision maker comes to "learn" his or her value for an object (see Plott, 1996, for a somewhat similar view). From such a perspective, a building code guideline can be seen as a method to encourage more effective learning. For example, facilitating explicit tradeoffs through the use of matching tasks (Tversky et al., 1988) can be viewed as a method for encouraging people to think (learn) about values through the making of tradeoffs. Similarly, the use of multimedia tools to provide complex information (e.g., Urban et al., 1997) is a way to accelerate the learning of preferences. Finally, we argue that helping people learn and consider the distinction between means and fundamental objectives is a critical learning step in the construction of a well-formed preference. However, the contingencies of decision making make clear that the learning of preferences can be highly path-dependent, that is, what is learned can depend on initial anchor values. Further, convergence on a preference may, at best, be a slow process. Thus, the building code guidelines suggested earlier represent suggestions for helping people to follow better and perhaps quicker paths in learning their preferences.

Words of Caution

A number of cautions need to be expressed. First, we are sensitive to the danger of overreaching when one talks about differentially treating better and more poorly constructed preferences. However, we argue that the more that measured preferences are to play a role in an important decision, for example, a public policy decision, the greater the weight that should be given to the better constructed preferences. As noted earlier in the chapter, we make this argument cognizant that there are situations in which an individual's preferences must be given weight, no matter how poorly constructed they may be.

A related point is that some of the suggestions for improving preference measurement appear paternalistic. We do not intend to imply that the analyst should impose values on the individual. Nevertheless, we believe that providing procedures and tools that help individuals discover their own preferences is in the best interests of those individuals, even though this may also influence those preferences. A reviewer made the cogent and related point that the influence of the measurement process on values may be subtle enough that it does not arouse respondents' defenses and hence may lead to "persuading" the respondents.

Second, not all examples of contingencies in decision making should necessarily be viewed as faults in the construction of preferences. For instance, coding an outcome as a gain or a loss relative to a particular reference value may reflect how that outcome in fact will be experienced by the decision maker and hence need not be a fault. Again, however, we argue that clarity in the use of a reference value should be a principle of a building code for preference measurement.

Third, to the extent that a measured preference today is really a prediction about a future preference, there is some research suggesting that people often get it wrong when predicting future preferences (Huber et al., 1997; Kahneman, 1994; Loewenstein & Schkade, 1999). People fail to fully appreciate, for example, the impact of adaptation on the experience of outcomes over time. One implication of a more dynamic view of preferences is that the closer the measurement of preferences is to the likely consumption experience the better. Another implication is that special instructions may be needed to help make the salience of time intervals greater (e.g., Read & Loewenstein, 1995). More generally, the guidelines for what constitutes a well-constructed preference may need to be modified when preferences develop substantially over time and people have great deficiencies in their ability to predict how future outcomes will be experienced.

Fourth, one reviewer expressed a caution about "protected" values or preferences (Baron & Spranca, 1997). Is it appropriate to even try to cause people to rethink such values during a design process? We argue that the importance of considering explicit tradeoffs must be very carefully weighed against the possible emotional costs that may be incurred by the respondent. We suspect that in at least some cases the benefits from making the tradeoffs will in fact outweigh these emotional costs.

Finally, we have suggested a number of ways in which preferences might be better constructed. Each of the suggested methods for improvement has a foundation in the research on human judgment and choice; however, some of the suggested methods reflect much more research than do others. Thus, there is much need for research that would verify that the methods we suggest for improving the construction of preferences are in fact likely to lead to better expressions of values.

CONCLUSION

We argue that there is a need for a "building code" for preference measurement in a world in which many expressions of preference are constructed by people at the time they are asked a valuation question. As in the case of the historical development of building codes, much of the impetus for a building code for constructed preferences comes from an awareness of faults in the processes typically used in preference construction. We have sought to begin the development of a building code for preference measurement by identifying some principles and techniques for preference construction and measurement that should mitigate some of the most common and important construction faults. Many of our suggestions for addressing preference construction faults build on the work of others and involve the provision of tools for thinking about values as well as providing information (i.e., the materials) for thinking about a given expression of preference. This reflects our belief that many construction faults and associated difficulties in the measurement of preferences are frequently due to cognitive limitations interacting with novel and complex task demands. We have also tried to begin a discussion of how a building code's guidelines should vary as a function of the purposes of the valuation exercise. Clearly, an architectural, constructive view of expressed preferences requires a fundamentally different approach to the measurement of preferences than that which is implied by an archaeological, well-defined existing preferences view.

ACKNOWLEDGMENTS

Preparation of this chapter was supported by grants from the National Science Foundation and from the Environmental Protection Agency.

35. Constructing Preferences From Labile Values

Baruch Fischhoff

People cannot know what they want in all possible situations. Rather, they must construct specific preferences from more basic values. In making these inferences, people must seek cues in a world that might be indifferent, helpful, or manipulative. The better they understand the factors shaping their inferences, the better their chance of learning what they want. An analogous challenge faces researchers, decision analysts, counselors, and others seeking to elicit people's values. It also faces those (advertisers, politicians, pundits, etc.) hoping to manipulate those factors and get people to convince themselves that they want a particular product, candidate, ideology, or lifestyle.

Identifying the factors shaping behavior is psychology's central challenge. To study theoretically relevant factors, researchers must control irrelevant ones. Over time, those nuisance factors often prove important in their own right. McGuire (1969) has depicted the history of psychology in terms of turning "artifacts into main effects." Table 35.1 assembles parts of this history in terms of the four essential elements of any behavior: the organism whose preferences matter, the stimulus intended for evaluation, the response mode for expressing preferences, and potentially distracting contextual elements.

In the 25 years since Table 35.1 was created, the attention paid to its various topics has varied, reflecting researchers' sensitivity to them as artifacts and interest in them as main effects. For example, affective influences on preferences are better understood now, partly due to advances in psychophysiology (Slovic, Finucane, Peters, & MacGregor, 2002). Whatever researchers' current interests, all the factors are still "out there" as potential confounds when eliciting preferences and potential opportunities when shaping them. What matters is each factor's strength, in specific contexts. Statistically reliable and theoretically informative effects may have limited practical importance, if they have been studied in settings fine-tuned to reveal them.

This chapter considers the implications of this complex body of research for preference elicitation. After sketching the circumstances requiring a constructive process, it identifies two converging streams of research. It then offers an elicitation approach that integrates the normative perspectives of decision theory and the descriptive results of psychology. Its application requires a philosophy of science for *reactive measurement* – by which people change through the construction process. Its touchstone is deepening people's understanding

Table 35.1. From Artifact to Main Effect

Liability in Judgment Due to	Led to
Organism	
Inattention, laziness, fatigue, habituation, learning, maturation, physiological limitations, natural rhythms, experience with related tasks	Repeated measures; professional subjects; stochastic response models; psychophysiology; proactive and retroactive inhibition research
Stimulus Presentation	
Homogeneity of alternatives, similarity of successive alternatives (especially first and second), speed of presentation, amount of information, range of alternatives, place in range of first alternative, distance from threshold, order of presentation, areal extent, ascending or descending series	Classic psychophysical methods; the new psychophysics; attention research; range-frequency theory; order-effects research; regression effects; anticipation
Response Mode	
Stimulus-response compatibility, naturalness of response, set, number of categories, halo effects, anchoring, very small numbers, response category labeling, use of end-points	Ergonomics research; set research; attitude measurement; assessment techniques; contrasts of between- and within-subject designs; response-bias research; use of blank trials
"Irrelevant" Context Effects	
Perceptual defenses, experimenter cues, social pressures, presuppositions, implicit payoffs, social desirability, confusing instructions response norms, response priming, stereotypic responses, second-guessing	New look in perception; verbal conditioning; experimenter demand; signal-detection theory; social pressure, comparison, and facilitation research

Source: Adapted from Fischhoff, Slovic, and Lichtenstein (1980). © 1980 by Lawrence Erlbaum Associates, Inc. Reprinted with permission.

of what they want regarding well-specified prospects. It is illustrated in three brief case studies, involving preferences with public policy implications.

NOT KNOWING WHAT YOU WANT

People are most likely to have clear preferences for choices that are familiar, simple, and directly experienced – properties that provide opportunities for trial-and-error learning. Individuals enjoying them have a better chance of developing stable habits. Groups enjoying them have a better chance of developing traditions that work for people sharing their core values. Personal or collective acceptance can itself stabilize preference, by adding the rewards of consistency and social approval.

These conditions are most likely to be met in a simple, unchanging society, with consistently presented, recurrent choices. Preferences are, then, not so much constructed as shaped, through operant conditioning or direct instruction. However, even when people have learned what they want, actual choices must be decoded to reveal the value issues embedded in them. As stability unravels, the old rules become untested, and perhaps untestable – if change outpaces chances to learn. That may often be the lot of people forced to choose jobs and investments, evaluate technologies and social policies, consider medical treatments for themselves and loved ones, and so on. They may be unfamiliar with the issues (e.g., discount rates, minuscule probabilities, megadeaths). They may have seemingly contradictory values (a desire to avoid catastrophic losses *and* greater concern for a single known victim than a large group of statistical ones). They may occupy roles (parents, workers, children, voters) with competing demands. They may waver between strongly held values (freedom of speech is inviolate, but should be denied to authoritarian movements). They may not even know how to begin thinking about some issues (e.g., what it means to give, or exercise, a living will). Their views may change predictably over time (as they age or the hour of decision approaches), without an obvious way to reconcile them. They may see things differently in theory and in reality. They may lack the cognitive capacity to keep everything in mind, adding noise to their choices.

This is the human condition that researchers have labored to understand. The research serves the public interest if it is presented with sympathy (for what people are up against), if it is used to help citizens learn what they want, and if it prompts needed protection (e.g., regulation) from those seeking to exploit value uncertainty. To these ends, old results, as well as current hot topics, might prove useful – hence, the historical perspective of the next section. It looks at two streams of research into the factors shaping preferences, each of which compares behavior with a normative standard, then seeks the psychological processes shaping (and limiting) the observed performance.

TWO RESEARCH STREAMS

Psychophysics Stream

History. Evaluation has been a central topic in experimental psychology since its inception in the mid-1800s. Emerging from the physical sciences, early psychology focused on *psychophysics*, assessing the sensory equivalent of physical stimuli. They saw internal mechanisms as translating external stimuli into states of arousal. They asked people to report on those states, with a word, number, or action (e.g., squeezing a handgrip, adjusting an illumination level to be as intense as the acridity of a smell).

From early on, psychophysicists discovered how complex these ostensibly simple processes are (Woodworth & Schlosberg, 1954). For example, a detection threshold might depend on whether stimuli (e.g., tones, weights, prices) appear in ascending or descending order. The basic (main effect) research examining such experimental artifacts is typically known only by specialists (e.g., in hearing). Unless these specialties are consulted, research might unwittingly carry a systematic bias. For example, years of experiments preceded awareness of experimenter effects, even though nonverbal communication had long been studied elsewhere in the social sciences (Rosenthal & Rosnow, 1969). Knowing about such effects allows the creation of studies with desired features, matching the contexts to which results will be extrapolated – in situations where subjects need to assume something about a feature, to give a task meaning.

After processing stimuli, subjects must translate their perceptions into numerical judgments. Poulton (1989) identified six "laws" for how procedural details shape those judgments, based on secondary analyses of studies estimating the rate of decreasing marginal sensitivity, for various sensory modalities. For example, two stimuli receive more different ratings when embedded in a narrower stimulus range than in a larger one. Ratings for larger stimuli get cramped if the initial (or standard) stimulus is relatively large (and spread out if it is relatively small).

These effects occur because, however well subjects understand their feelings about a stimulus, they must translate it into the researcher's terms. Where those terms differ from their natural mode of expression (or where nothing is natural, because the task is so novel), they rely on general heuristics for using scales. For example, people try to use the entire response scale, look for patterns in randomly ordered stimuli, and deduce an expected level of precision (Tune, 1964). Thus, responses are shaped by a task's form as well as by its substance, when people are unsure how to communicate their feelings – and must seek clues in task details, lending artifactual consistency to their responses.

The importance of these effects depends on how responses are used. For example, the contextual effects captured in Poulton's laws maintain response order, meaning that these design issues can be ignored in situations requiring just ordinal information. When stronger metric properties are needed, study conditions must match those of the analogous real-world context (e.g., avoiding fractional responses, if people rarely use them; showing the full stimulus range, so that subjects need not infer it). When there has been a mismatch, the laws allow extrapolating from the studied context to the focal one. For example, if a study used a restricted stimulus range, then its largest members would receive lower values if embedded in a larger range. Such research directs research design by providing an orderly, empirical foundation for identifying the (perhaps few) features that really matter. Ignoring such features forces consumers of research to disentangle their effects.

Evaluative Extensions. As attitude research developed, the psychophysical paradigm held great appeal. It had a strong pedigree, with distinguished researchers contributing theories, procedures, results, and analytical methods. It had been applied to diverse domains. It seemed relatively straightforward: Pose a clear question, offer clear response options, and report what people say. Moreover, attitude questions can use terms that seem consensually interpreted (e.g., strongly agree – strongly disagree; very happy – very unhappy), while avoiding unfamiliar units of physical stimuli (lumens, decibels).

However, here, too, subjects seek contextual cues for interpreting their task. In effect, "there's 'very happy' and then there's 'very happy'"(Turner & Krauss, 1978). Cues might be found in the wording, preceding topics, sponsor, consent form, and response options, among other places. For example, Schwarz (1999) found that subjects evaluate their lives more positively when a scale goes from [–5, + 5], rather than [0, 10], even when both versions use the same verbal anchors: [not at all successful, extremely successful]. Negative numbers may suggest the possibility of abject failure, whereas 0 suggests lack of success as the worst possible outcome. Other cues could signal whether to evaluate success relative to a comparison group (and, if so, which) or relative to one's dreams (or expectations).

Six laws might capture the key procedural cues determining quantitative scale use. No such summary is available, or perhaps even possible, for the myriad of possible verbal cues, for reading between the lines of questions and answers. One approach assumes that people interpret questions, including those on surveys, according to conversational norms – and respond in kind. Grice (1975) offers four *maxims*, expressing these norms. They require speech to be *relevant*, *concise*, *complete*, and *honest*. An investigator following them would ensure that a question (including its answer options) contains no irrelevant details, says nothing that could go without saying, omits nothing that subjects could confidently infer, nor has anything that misleads (or suggests dishonesty). The maxims are harder to apply when the parties lack a common culture, either in general or for the specific topic.

Decision Theory Stream

Von Neumann and Morgenstern's (1947) landmark formulation of decision theory prompted two interrelated lines of behavioral studies. *Behavioral decision research* examines the decision theory axioms' descriptive validity (Hastie & Dawes, 2002). It might directly test adherence, characterize the cognitive skills that facilitate (and constrain) rationality, or identify efficient (heuristic) approaches to imperfect decision making. *Decision analysis* seeks to increase the axioms' descriptive validity by helping people to make more rational choices (von Winterfeldt & Edwards, 1986). Decision analysts elicit their clients' probabilities and utilities for possible consequences of actions, hoping to overcome known judgmental limitations in three ways: (a) structuring the elicitation process, so that people make systematic use of what they know about themselves and their world; (b) focusing people's limited attention on the most critical issues, as identified by sensitivity and value-of-information analyses; and (c) computing expected utility of options, avoiding the vagaries of mental arithmetic.

The success of this enterprise hinges on participants' ability to express their beliefs and values in the required form: probabilities and utilities. The clear structure of these tasks should reduce the ambiguity endemic to attitude measurement and avoid the vagueness of verbal quantifiers (e.g., rare, likely), terms whose meaning can vary across people and contexts (Lichtenstein & Newman, 1967). The client–analyst interaction is a real (if stilted) conversation. It allows identifying and resolving miscommunications, unlike the "conversations" of surveys. Exploiting these opportunities requires analysts to "look for trouble," presenting multiple perspectives, to ensure mutual understanding (Fischhoff, 1991; Keeney, 1992).

As a result, in decision analysis, elicitation is inherently *reactive*, potentially changing participants as they reflect on their beliefs and values in a specific context. The process assumes that people may need help in understanding what they believe and want. It tries to deepen their thinking, without imposing any external views. It tries to reduce random error, without adding systematic error. It succeeds when clients have had a fair opportunity to consider any perspective that they might consider relevant. Its success depends on decision analysts' ability to identify those perspectives.

Prospect theory (Kahneman & Tversky, 1979) offers a way to generate alternative perspectives for people to use when triangulating on their values (e.g., "Think about both how many salmon will be left and how many will be lost"). Sensitivity to framing effects shows the coherence of those values. When framing effects exist, one needs a substantive theory of how people choose the reference points, defining their frames (e.g., whether people view a raise relative to the ones received in past years or by fellow workers; Fischhoff, 1983). Triangulation can be based on any context effect. For example, making a number salient draws responses toward it (Tversky & Kahneman, 1974). Such *anchoring* can have two (nonexclusive) effects: (a) directly priming that response, making it more available when people look for what to say, and (b) prompting people to evaluate its appropriateness, priming reasons that justify it. Contrasting anchors reduce the first effect, while taking advantage of the second.

A Philosophy of Science for Reactive Measurement

Decision analysts' hope for reflective responses contrasts with attitude researchers' quest for immediate, "natural" ones. The desire to have preexisting attitudes emerge through a neutral conduit leads to surveys with impassive interviewers, standardized questions, minimal clarification, and limited time to think. This could hardly be more different than intense interactions with decision analysts, reviewing alternative perspectives, returning to critical issues, and using converging measures.

The philosophies of science underlying these two elicitation strategies place different weights on sins of commission (inappropriately influencing people) and sins of omission (letting people misunderstand their own positions). Fearing the former discourages interaction; fearing the latter may require it. The proper degree of interaction depends on the risk that people will say later, "I wish that I had thought of that perspective," "I wish that I had been able to keep it all in my head," or "How could I have forgotten that?" That risk should be small with tasks having familiar substance *and* form, so that people have had a chance to learn just what they want, on that exact question.

Despite their different emphases, both streams recognize common steps toward formulating meaningful values, whether done by researchers, decision counselors, or individuals trying to fend for themselves.

1. Encode the task – ensuring that the choice is understood.
2. Access relevant personal values – structuring the evaluation process.
3. Interpret those values in the specific context – constructing a preference.
4. Translate that preference into suitable terms – stating that preference.

Researchers' aspirations can be arrayed along a continuum ranging from *gist* to *contractual* studies. *Gist* studies claim to elicit general answers to general questions, such as how much people tend to support the environment, worry about pollution, trust industry, or dislike regulation. *Contract* studies claim to elicit valuations for specific transactions, such as "willingness to pay 7% for 'green' products" (with "green" suitably defined) or "to incur a 0.2% rise in unemployment to meet Kyoto obligations."

Researchers must provide their subjects with the conditions needed to produce the valuations they seek (Fischhoff, 1980, 2005), lest they (and those who use their work) misrepresent the responses. Gist studies should provide only vague direction. Subjects haven't said very much; no one should read too much into their responses. Inferring more is akin to politicians claiming specific mandates based on diffuse electoral indicators. Gist researchers should oppose misuse of their work, in terms like, "All that they said was that they wanted cleaner cars; they didn't call for mandating that specific fuel system." Or, "General support for 'free trade' does not imply knowledge and advocacy of all World Trade Organization environmental provisions." Contractual claims bear a much greater burden of proof, showing that participants have accomplished all four tasks – hence, really understand the agreement they are endorsing. With a fixed budget, doing so will mean fewer subjects, achieving statistical power through better measurement, rather than larger samples.

The success of an evaluation process is an empirical question, with two parts: (a) have people understood the choice, and (b) have they understood themselves in that context? The gold standard for the former question is manipulation checks, comparing subjects' and elicitors' interpretations of the task. For the latter, it is whether people are sensitive to relevant task changes and insensitive to irrelevant ones – using their definition of relevance. Eliciting consistent responses with one procedure is necessary, but not sufficient, for demonstrating articulated values (Ariely, Loewenstein, & Prelec, 2003). Such consistency may just reflect an efficient ad hoc strategy, devised to get through a task (e.g., "They're varying the price of the fictitious apartments 'offered' in this study. I'll focus on that."). Even when those strategies reflect real concerns (e.g., price does matter), that consistency could fragment in more realistic contexts. Part of psychology's lore is how easily people find some way to answer any question, as seen in the low nonresponse rates when asked about fictitious issues (Plous, 1993). As a result, multiple methods are needed, looking for appropriate (in)sensitivity.

Even a clear specification, diligent presentation, and sensitive construction process will leave imperfections. There are three ways to deal with the residual uncertainty and incoherence in preferences. (a) *Disqualify* people whose preferences are insufficiently well constructed (failing the "building code"; Payne, Bettman, & Schkade, 1999). Deciding that they cannot represent their population (in research) or themselves (in life) means that surrogates are needed or the choice defies human capability. (b) *Adjust* preferences to undo suspected bias. For example, reduce the value assigned to future options when people have neglected, or not been told, the chance of the promised outcomes not being realized (Frederick, 2003). Or, reduce the value assigned to large gains (e.g., lottery wins), knowing that they typically have less utility than people expect – or preserve those false expectations, if that's how people want their lives to be guided (Kahneman, 2003b; Loewenstein, O'Donoghue, & Rabin, 2003). (c) *Accommodate* imperfectly constructed preferences when reporting studies or reflecting back to decision makers. Not knowing what one wants can be part of the human condition. Recognizing that allows people, and those depending on their preferences (e.g., doctors, policy makers), to prepare for surprises or defer choices.

The next section offers three examples of the empirical and philosophical issues involved with constructing preferences.

THREE CASE STUDIES

Evaluating Environmental Change, in Which Behavioral Decision Research Appears to Win Many of the Battles Without Winning the War

Environmental decisions with contractual implications often pose challenging preference tasks. They require people to weigh many outcomes, both for private choices (e.g., buying a vehicle, selecting a neighborhood, choosing paper or plastic) and public ones (e.g., fuel efficiency standards, land-use regulations, recyclability requirements). Even when the general issues are familiar, the specific formulation may not be. Having many technical details to master increases the cognitive load. Thus, decision makers may neglect critical issues, even when those posing the choices state them clearly.

The first step to ensuring shared understanding is creating a full task specification, addressing each feature potentially important to the researchers and respondents. In response to the ad hoc nature of many tasks, Fischhoff and Furby (1988) offered a general framework for contractual choices, conceptualized as transactions with a *good*, a *payment*, and a *social context*. These elements have both formal features, which should matter (e.g., how long before the good or payment is delivered), and substantive ones (e.g., whether natural or human processes cause a change), which might, depending on what respondents value. Unless all parties interpret each feature similarly, respondents are not answering the question being asked. For example, respondents could believe that they are less likely to receive a good at a later time, investigators' reassurances notwithstanding. If so, then they should value the future prospect less, even if the good itself would have equal utility at either time. Unfortunately, few studies offer full specifications – as Frederick (2003) showed for tasks involving time preferences and Fischhoff (1993) showed for ones involving protective measures. There is, of course, some circularity in needing to know which features matter before evaluating a transaction. That circle can be broken if there is an empirical record of how much various features have typically mattered. Absent such independent evidence, elicitation products must be evaluated in terms of their internal validity (reliability, manipulation checks, etc.).

The effort needed to convey a task depends on how familiar respondents are with its specific formulation. By election time, citizens might know the contractual commitment of a widely publicized referendum well enough to identify the personally relevant value issues and construct preferences from them. Contingent valuation (CV) studies often use a referendum metaphor when eliciting values for environmental goods – by asking people how much they would pay to prevent a negative environmental change or accept to allow it. The referendum metaphor provides a familiar social context. If it reflects legal, social, and political realities, the metaphor might efficiently communicate many task details. If not, then it might unfairly imply the legitimacy of "buying (or selling) nature" in that way. However, even where it passes that test, invoking the metaphor does not re-create the referendum process – unless subjects have a chance to absorb the details, evoke their relevant values, construct preferences, and articulate them in a way that captures their nuances.

Failure to meet these conditions, as in the typical CV study, should create vulnerability to incoherent preferences. Indeed, early CV studies showed a "starting point bias" that looked like a typical anchoring effect: Subjects expressed greater willingness to pay with higher suggested values (e.g., "Will you pay $100 [vs. $10]?"). The higher value both primes higher responses and suggests that they might be justified. Psychologists took note of these studies, which replicated their own findings, often with engaging, policy-relevant stimuli, and larger, more representative samples (Fischhoff, Slovic, & Lichtenstein, 1980). Kahneman, Ritov, and Schkade (1999) and others have shown the fertile field that CV studies provide for demonstrating incompletely constructed preferences.

These attentions have typically been greeted with skepticism and hostility. To some extent, that reflected CV practitioners' feeling that some psychologists had an incompatible agenda, seeing such anomalies as main effects, revealing factors shaping judgments. In contrast, CV practitioners see the anomalies as artifacts, interfering with their mission of producing the monetary valuations needed to keep environmental changes from being neglected in cost–benefit analyses (and the like). Natural processes lead each group to see what it expects in terms of which patterns predominate (Fischhoff, 1991).

The practical need for CV estimates is so great that explicit recognition of deep problems is unlikely. As a result, one can at best hope to find ways in which the practice has subtly shifted to incorporate psychological results. One possible shift is an increasing awareness of task specification. Psychologists typically use gist stimuli (the "headline method"; Kahneman, Ritov, & Schkade, 1999). Such studies show features that can matter to subjects and, hence, belong in contractual task specifications. They do not, however, engage the challenge of creating and communicating contractual tasks, addressing policy questions. Fischhoff and Furby's (1998) framework sought to bridge the gap by showing how to use psychology in CV studies. I think that it has had some influence on CV practice. For a time, the Environmental Protection Agency (EPA) gave it to CV contractors; it has been evoked in the "scope-insensitivity" battles over why subjects sometimes express the same value for different amounts of a good.

A second bridge is modest growth in CV studies' use of *manipulation checks*. Further adoption seems limited by legal factors. Sponsors do not want to document their subjects' imperfect understanding of task features, especially absent regulatory guidance on how to handle failures (disqualification, adjustment, accommodation).

Finally, there has been some modest adoption of constructive valuation processes. It seems to reflect some (a) weakening in economists' overall faith that people have ready values for all possible transactions; (b) realization that CV's nonreactive philosophy was, partly, a historical accident of turning to survey researchers (rather than decision analysts) for data collection; (c) growth in studies, involving economists, using disciplined reactive measurement (Beattie et al., 1998); and (d) an awareness that most analyses are advisory anyway, rather than being taken literally. Still, publications in the psychophysical, attitude research stream far outnumber those in the constructive, decision analysis stream. Their impacts on policy making are less clear. A senior U.S. government economist recently told me that he knew of only one official use of CV – in a case where all parties agreed on the policy, but needed a dollar value for legal purposes. ("Had the CV result been challenged, we would have found a travel-cost one.")

Ranking Risks, in Which Psychological Research May Have Created a Workable Alternative

In a seminal article, Starr (1969) tried to clarify the preferences revealed in society's responses to hazardous technologies. He found that economic benefit estimates explained some of the variance in estimated mortality risks, as though societal processes (markets, regulation) had tolerated greater risk in return for greater benefit. He found that predictive validity improved when he added a "qualitative" aspect of the risks: Tolerable risk levels were much higher for voluntarily incurred risks than for involuntarily imposed ones.

The plausibility of any such "revealed preference" study depends on whether people agree with the statistical risk and benefit estimates (hence, might see them as having guided society to that tradeoff). Fischhoff, Slovic, Lichtenstein, Read, and Combs (1978) found this not to be the case. Their subjects neither agreed with Starr's estimates nor saw a tradeoff. However, they were willing, in principle, to accept greater risk for greater benefit – and higher risks for more voluntary technologies. Subjects were also willing to accept a double standard for many other risk attributes (e.g., how well risks are understood, how controllable they seem).

Dealing with many attributes is unwieldy, cognitively and analytically. As a result, the study looked for redundancy in ratings of its nine attributes. Simple factor analysis found that two factors accounted for much of the variance. For one factor, the central concept was something like how well risks are known; for the second, something like how much the risks are dreaded. Uncertainty and catastrophic potential loaded heavily on the former, as did voluntariness. Catastrophic potential and dread loaded on the second. Many studies have examined these relationships, with many attributes, elicitation procedures, data reduction methods, respondent populations, and target technologies (Slovic, 1987). They have usually found something like the same two factors. An occasional third factor seems to center on catastrophic potential (pulling that attribute out of the other factors).

These results imply that evaluating technologies requires a multiattribute view of their risks. Fischhoff, Watson, and Hope (1984) showed how the relative riskiness of energy technologies could depend on how one weighted these factors as well as more conventional morbidity and mortality measures. Within experimental psychology, a weakly reactive way of assessing those weights is asking subjects to consider individual features after suggesting ways to think about the weights. Slovic, Lichtenstein, and Fischhoff (1984) pursued this strategy and found that catastrophic potential per se was less important than its signal value regarding how well technologies are managed. That aspect of uncertainty represents a much different principle than caring about how deaths are aggregated.

However, because importance is context dependent, isolated evaluations can inform policy, but not set it. The U.S. Environmental Protection Agency (1993) adopted a multiple-attribute perspective in a program of risk-ranking exercises during the early 1990s. That effort led to consensus rankings for most of the United States (and some regions and other countries). For the rankings, diverse stakeholders chose the attributes, in terms of which technical staff then characterized the options. Letting stakeholders choose the attributes increased credibility while reducing comparability across panels. One compromise is characterizing all risks in terms of criteria selected to represent the dimensions of risk. Stakeholders can choose attributes representing each factor. For example, because catastrophic potential and uncertainty are correlated, valuing one would mean valuing the other. However, the two criteria

Table 35.2. A General Framework for Characterizing Environmental Risks

Number of People Affected	Degree of Environmental Impact	Knowledge	Dread
Annual expected number of fatalities:	Area affected by ecosystem stress or change:	Degree to which impacts are delayed:	Catastrophic potential:
0–**450**–600 (10% chance of zero)	**50** km^2	**1–10** years	**1,000** times expected annual fatalities
Annual expected number of person-years lost:	Magnitude of environmental impact:	Quality of scientific understanding:	Outcome equity:
0–**9,000**–18,000 (10% chance of zero)	**modest** (15% chance of large)	**medium**	**medium** (ratio = 6)

Note: Each column includes two markers for a dimension of risk, found to affect overall judgments of riskiness, desire for regulation, and other evaluative judgments (Slovic, 1987, 2000b). For example, catastrophic potential and outcome equity are two attributes that tend to be correlated with one another, with judgments of the dread that a hazard evokes, and with other attributes often described as representing a dimension called "dread."
Source: Adapted from Florig et al. (2001).

raise different issues and, hence, evoke a broader consideration of that risk dimension.

Prompted by a request from the (White House) Office of Science and Technology Policy, we developed and evaluated such a procedure for constructing preferences in two domains, risks to children and to ecosystems (Florig et al., 2001). It adopts a standard representation, allowing users to choose the attributes most relevant to them (one version of which is shown in Table 35.2). The elicitation method uses two pairs of triangulating operations to help users understand the issues and their positions on them. One pair has users perform holistic rankings and provide attribute weights, from which their implicit priorities are computed. The second pair alternates self-study and group discussion. Users can reconcile differences as they see fit. We found that the method increased agreement between holistic and attribute-weight rankings and between public and private preferences. It also increased within-group agreement – although a valid procedure could also reveal and clarify disagreements.

In 2004, the British government proposed a standard multiattribute characterization of risk, complementing its guidance documents on economic analyses and public involvement in policy making (HM Treasury, 2004). Six attributes were chosen to: (a) span the risk space, (b) express common concerns, (c) be communicated easily, and (d) be assessed readily by technical staff. As with our approach, it leaves the criteria in a vector form, reflecting its goal of informing deliberations rather than producing summary valuations. It seeks the conceptual clarity needed to allow applying multiattribute utility theory procedures, but without actually pursuing that end.

After a period of public comment, the proposal was adopted as government policy, clearly recognizing constructive preferences based on behavioral decision research. That adoption involved acceptance, by economists and others, of these arguments: (1) the attributes express political–ethical values, whose importance is a matter for informed public debate; (2) the attributes involve "tangible" effects in the sense of potentially having real effects, even if they are not readily monetized (e.g., "dread" captures public concern whose physical consequences might be seen in stress-related health effects, as well as in reduced quality of life, from having the issue on one's mind); and (3) even when attributes have formal representations (e.g., economic metrics for distributional effects, uncertainty, and discounting), the issues may be harder to see and understand when embedded in analyses rather than considered separately. The six attributes are familiarity and experience of the risk, understanding of the cause–effect mechanism, equity of the consequences of the risk, fear of the risk consequences, control of the risk, and trust in risk management.

Adolescent Sexuality, in Which Behavioral Research Helps to Create Options in Which Preferences Could Be Constructed and Expressed

Many public policies depend on whether citizens are deemed competent to make choices in their own best interests or require paternalistic interventions. When people seem to choose poorly, misunderstanding is often the diagnosis – leading to extensive research into risk perception and communication (Morgan, Fischhoff, Bostrom, & Atman, 2002; Slovic, 2000b). However, it is not enough to understand the facts when one cannot get a fix on value issues.

One arena in which ineffective decision making has particular interest is adolescents. Teens' choices evoke such concern and disrespect that "adolescent decision making" is often considered an oxymoron. Nonetheless, by midadolescence, young people have a repertoire of cognitive skills like that of adults (Beyth-Marom & Fischhoff, 1997). They may know more or less than adults, depending on their interests and access to information. Unfortunately, that access is limited by social processes encouraging erroneous beliefs and overconfidence. For example, advertisers misrepresent the risks (and benefits) of smoking, whereas health educators may avoid issues for ideological reasons (e.g., the risks of oral and anal sex, alternatives to abstinence) or use terms vaguely (e.g., safe sex), creating an illusion of fluency. Nonetheless, misunderstanding risks is not a full account of teens' challenge.

One part of that challenge is the number of novel choices that teens must make, each requiring preference construction (e.g., what to do about smoking, drinking, drugs, sex, intimacy). Even if teens could make hard choices as well as adults, they would still have more errors. Moreover, their choices are part of a global preference-construction process, as they learn what they like, who they are, and which social conventions to adopt.

Learning from their complex experiences would be hard enough, if teens were testing well-formulated decisions. However, teens tend to describe their choices in terms of a focal option, "Should I do X?" perhaps with a vaguely described complement, "Should I do X or not?" (Fischhoff, 1996). Unfortunately, fewer outcomes come to mind when competing options are considered only indirectly, even when they are formal complements such as go versus stay (Beyth-Marom & Fischhoff, 1997). Neglecting nonfocal options leads to neglecting opportunity costs and honoring sunk costs, often observed with adults.

A further constraint on acting consistently with one's preferences is a perceived lack of control. Teens often describe feeling bound to particular scripts (e.g., sexual behavior expected in parties with drinking). As a possible remedy, we created an interactive DVD showing young women how to identify opportunities to make choices about sexual relations. Using self-efficacy theory (Bandura, 1997), we showed teens how they could create options consistent with their preferences at any time in an encounter. The DVD also conveys critical risk facts (about sexually transmitted illnesses, condoms, etc.), along with modeling how to get and share medical information, through a dramatized pelvic exam. In a randomized control trial, it increased knowledge and self-reported condom use, while decreasing condom problems and chlamydia reinfection rates (Downs et al., 2004).

Although the intervention was very accepting of teens' sexual behavior preferences, it did not increase their rate of self-reported sex. One possible explanation is that young women want less sex than they have, but can express that preference only when they have viable options. A second possible explanation is that impulsivity can be an effect, as well as a cause, of poor decision making: Being unable to construct clear preferences can cause frustration, leading, in turn, to more impulsive choices (e.g., anger, pleasure seeking) or indecision, so that choices are made under circumstantial pressure. In another study, teens who performed worst on a battery of behavioral decision research tasks also scored higher on measures of polarized thinking and oppositional defiance disorder – after controlling for differences in verbal and nonverbal intelligence. Thus, having basic decision-making skills may be protective (Parker & Fischhoff, 2005).

Although the DVD rarely cites decision-making constructs, it leads users through the four component tasks of preference construction. It shows teens the consequences of their choices, the general value issues involved, the expression of those issues in specific contexts, and the connections between possible actions and things they value. The DVD evaluation study raises three questions regarding the right balance of paternalism and autonomy for teens' sexual behavior: (a) How well have teens understood their options and articulated their preferences, under the intervention's favored conditions? (b) What conditions can they expect in life? (c) Who is responsible when those conditions are lacking?

CONCLUSIONS

Decision researchers have profited from other researchers' problems by turning experimental artifacts into theoretical main effects. If the process ends there, then the main-effects research threatens other fields, whose artifacts it has documented. One response is to specify tasks fully to elicit the most relevant preferences. That should be no problem for contractual studies, which have a real-world touchstone for that specification. The complexity of the resulting task may, however, be too much for many respondents to handle without help in constructing their preferences.

Decision analysis sets the philosophical standards for providing such help: deepening, but not biasing preferences; decreasing random error, without introducing systematic error; eliminating the effects of meaningless contextual changes, while heightening the effects of meaningful ones. Critical to this enterprise is "looking for trouble," presenting alternative perspectives, so that clients are not manipulated by the reactive measurement procedure and observers can see if there is a proper pattern of sensitivity and insensitivity (to relevant and irrelevant features). The elicitor's repertoire of alternative perspectives depends on substantive insight into a particular problem and methodological insight into potential artifacts (Table 35.1). In private counseling, analyst and client can decide how adequate the process is. External consumers (e.g., policy makers relying on CV estimates) may demand independent evidence. It could come from dedicated validity studies or from the cumulative record of which factors seem to matter. That record should reduce design costs by producing robust solutions (e.g., how to convey the time period for a payment or the magnitude of a change, how to convince respondents that a change will really happen, which features can go without saying or need no explanation).

That research may also reveal researchers to be victims of a *curse of cleverness*. They prize novel tasks, capturing nuances that eluded their colleagues, or addressing new policy issues. Such tasks are necessarily novel for respondents. The greater the novelty, the greater is the need for exposition and constructive elicitation. Like life, researchers present an unceasing stream of unfamiliar choices. As a result, there is an element of gist in all but the most overlearned choices in the most stable environments. Researchers can respond to that reality by taking expressed preferences less seriously. People do not have that luxury. That is the human predicament revealed by studies showing the need for constructed preferences and addressed by studies guiding the construction process.

36. Informed Consent and the Construction of Values

Douglas MacLean

Informed consent is a fundamental component of moral justification. It distinguishes love-making from rape, employment from servitude, and life-saving surgery from felonious assault with a deadly weapon, to mention just a few examples. At a more general level, consent distinguishes democratic from authoritarian governments, and it justifies a capitalist economic system. Efficiency is important, but freedom is what makes capitalism most appealing, as producers choose what to produce, and consumers choose what to buy. Consent is required to justify activities that impose a risk of harm or death on others. This is true of dramatic and newsworthy instances, such as trying to site a nuclear waste disposal facility, but it may also be true of activities as mundane as driving cars. When I drive a car in a city, I impose a risk of injury or death on innocent pedestrians. I also contribute to pollution and climate change, which imposes further risks on others. I do not know how the consent process works that permits me to engage in this kind of risk-imposing activity, but it seems reasonable to think that some sort of tacit consent must be at work to justify our using automobiles.

When disparities of power or the effects of new technologies threaten the effectiveness of consent, democratic governments intervene with regulations aimed at reinforcing the conditions of consent or establishing procedures for obtaining it. Laws that give citizens and consumers access to information, or that protect a variety of freedoms of expression, are examples of government activities aimed at making consent more effective.

How consent operates in different contexts is often puzzling and the subject of much analysis and theorizing. I will address some of these puzzles here, but my primary aim is to focus on a more fundamental question. What gives consent its transforming and justifying power? Perhaps this question has not received much attention because the answer seems obvious though difficult to articulate clearly. I will argue that the value of consent is less obvious than it is often taken to be. This fact has some important implications for determining policies and regulations that make the consent of those on whom risks are imposed more effective.

THE VALUE OF CONSENT IN PROMOTING WELL-BEING AND IN PROMOTING FREEDOM

Consent requirements have obvious *instrumental* value (Scheffler, 1985). If we assume that people generally know their own interests better than others know them, then consent requirements can be effective means for ensuring that the interests of those affected by decisions are given due weight in making those decisions. If we also assume that people are generally less willing to be treated in morally unacceptable ways themselves than they are to treat others unacceptably, then consent requirements also have value as an effective tool for deterring morally unacceptable behavior. You will be less likely to trample my interests in pursuit of your own if you need my consent before you act.

Consent requirements may also have a more direct and noninstrumental value in promoting well-being. In some settings, consent procedures may reduce alienation, hostility, and other destructive attitudes stemming from lack of inherent trust. The result may be to make cooperation more likely or, for example in clinical medical settings, to improve the prospects of a good outcome. Giving consent may promote a person's self-esteem, his sense of personal responsibility for his own recovery, and his feelings of identification and solidarity with those trying to help him. Being given a voice in the choice of actions that will affect one may also contribute directly to a person's well-being in a more general way, for a life deprived of such a voice would be deficient or servile in important ways that would affect a person's happiness.

But neither the instrumental value of consent in promoting well-being, nor the direct value it may have as a constituent of a person's well-being, can be the whole story of its justification. At least part of that story must appeal to a different kind of consideration altogether. The act of giving consent is a way of incorporating a person's will into decisions that affect her personally and into collective actions of which she is a part. Consider the fact that sometimes people really don't know what is good for them, and others may be able to intervene or act more effectively to protect them or make them better off. In many such situations, however, we tend nevertheless to insist that a free and rational person be given the right to consent to actions that will affect her. It is often important to let people choose, even if we have good reason to expect that they will make bad, harmful, or simply nonoptimal choices. Consent matters in these contexts not only as an effective means for getting our interests promoted and desires satisfied, but also to give us a voice in decisions that affect us or are made in our name. We cannot fully comprehend this aspect of the value of consent by appealing to the various ways that consent promotes happiness or well-being. Rather, part of the value of consent has to do with autonomy. Both at an individual level and in collective decision making, it is through consent that we realize our nature as free agents. If this is correct, then consent procedures must be designed not only to promote well-being but also to protect and enable us to realize our freedom. In what follows, I try to explain these remarks and explore their implications.

INFORMED CONSENT IN THE PHYSICIAN–PATIENT RELATIONSHIP

To help fix intuitions, I will focus on medical or health care decisions, although the claims I will be defending are meant to be general and not tied in any essential way to this domain. This is an area, however, in which the value of informed consent has received much thought and discussion. One standard view sees consent as having two components: informing and consenting. The health care professional is responsible for the former and the patient for the latter. This view of the value of consent has been clearly stated by Gorovitz (1982):

The doctrine of informed consent is simple and clear on the surface. Physicians do the sorts of things to their patients that people in general cannot justifiably do to one another. If the patient understands what the physician proposes to do and, thus informed, consents to its being done, then the medical intervention is not imposed on the patient in violation of the patient's autonomy; rather, that medical intervention is properly viewed as a service provided to the patient at the patient's request. Not only does this procedure of gaining informed consent respect the patient's autonomy, but it also protects the physician against the charge of imposing treatment on a patient who did not want that treatment – it protects the physician, in other words, against the charge of assault. On the face of it, the requirement should be applauded on all sides. (p. 38)

Gorovitz (1982) is aware that informing patients about their alternatives can be difficult and costly, and he is also sensitive to the kinds of duress and pressures that can undermine the value of a patient's consent. He allows that paternalistic actions can sometimes be justified, but he argues that the threshold must be high before we allow the principle of benevolence to override the principle of autonomy. "Respect for persons – for their liberty and their right to express their individuality by pursuing a freely chosen course of action – supports the Principle of Autonomy" (p. 42).

Only recently has this view of the value of informed consent in medical decision making become standard. There is a long tradition in medicine of authoritarian decision making, in which the physician took it upon himself to determine what was best for the patient and more or less informed the patient about what was going to happen, if he informed the patient at all. Over the past 40 years, this tradition of delegated decision making has been replaced in the United States and in other countries by a model of shared decision making. Many reasons account for this important change in the culture of health care, but one of them is due to advances in medical technologies, which allow us today to keep people alive in conditions that they could not have survived a half-century ago. The quality of a patient's life is an important concern, and physicians can no longer assume to know, without much discussion, the relevant values of their patients.

The standard model of informed consent described by Gorovitz (1982) nevertheless presupposes that at least the patient is aware of her values and preferences, but we have reasons to doubt this assumption as well. Patients may be confronting a decision under considerable stress, and they may also face a variety of complex prospects about conditions that are difficult to imagine or compare. In an excellent article that explores different models of the physician–patient relationship, Emanuel and Emanuel (1992) consider a common clinical case. A 43-year-old premenopausal woman, recently divorced and gone back to work, discovers a breast mass, which surgery reveals to be "a 3.5-cm ductal carcinoma with no lymph node involvement that is estrogen receptor positive" (p. 2223). What are her options? Mastectomy or lumpectomy with radiation have identical 80% 10-year survival rates, and lumpectomy without radiation results in a 30% to 40% risk of tumor recurrence. Lumpectomy with chemotherapy prolongs survival for premenopausal women who have axillary nodes involved in the tumor, but the effects of chemotherapy on women with node-negative breast cancer is unclear. Individual studies suggest that there is no benefit from chemotherapy, but the National Cancer Institute believes that there may be a positive impact. A clinical trial is under way to study the issue further, which this woman is eligible to enter. Chemotherapy would prolong treatment by many months, but it would also bring the benefits of receiving the best medical care for the duration of the trial and contributing to the advance of scientific knowledge about breast cancer and its treatments. How should this woman incorporate this information into a decision about which treatment she will consent to receive?

We can assume that she values her health, but she also cares about her appearance, self-image, and life outside the hospital. The idea of separating fact from value in the presentation of the alternatives seems unhelpful if not impossible. A more reasonable consent process would involve the physician in a discussion that would help the patient articulate her values and apply them to the facts and prospects that a good decision would have to take into account.

Emanuel and Emanuel (1992) thus describe four different models of a physician–patient relationship that define four different views of the nature of informed consent. The "paternalistic" and "informative" models are similar, respectively, to the authoritarian tradition and the alternative to it described by Gorovitz (1982), in which the physician's role is primarily that of an expert advisor. In the "interpretive model," the physician takes on the role of a counselor. She tries to help her patient elucidate or articulate her values in a way that can lead her to select the intervention that best realizes her aims. Finally, in the "deliberative model" the physician's role is described as "teacher or friend." The physician and patient together judge the worthiness and importance of health-related values. The dialectic of these models is to move from a delegated decision-making paradigm expressed in the paternalistic model to a direct decision-making paradigm in the informative model and beyond that to increasingly robust shared decision-making paradigms in the interpretive and deliberative models.

In assessing the strengths and weaknesses of these four models, Emanuel and Emanuel (1992) point out, obviously enough, that shared decision making can make considerable demands on a physician's time and requires skills that may be beyond a physician's expertise. In the end, however, they defend shared decision making in general and the deliberative model in particular for normal situations. This is a bold step in the literature on informed consent, with which I find myself mostly sympathetic. But my interest here is not in their defense of the deliberative model; rather, it is in the way they characterize objections and replies to it. They consider two objections: first, that in the deliberative model physicians judge their patients' values and promote the physicians' own health-related values; and second, that the deliberative process thus risks lapsing back into an unintended paternalism, which consent procedures were designed to avoid. Their reply is that autonomy requires "that individuals critically assess their own values and preferences; determine whether they are desirable; affirm, upon reflection, these values as ones that should justify their actions; and then be free to initiate action to realize the values" (p. 2226). Physicians should help their patients to do this. Emanuel and Emanuel boldly conclude that indeed physicians should not only help fit therapies to their patients' elucidated values, but they should also "promote health-related values" (p. 2226) themselves, such as not smoking, safe sex, and limited use of alcohol.

A CHALLENGE TO THE ASSUMPTION OF EXISTING PREFERENCES

Although the deliberative model that Emanuel and Emanuel (1992) defend is very different from the informative model described by Gorovitz (1982), both models in the end (although to varying degrees) share what I shall call the assumption of existing preferences. If patients do not have values that they can apply directly, almost mechanically, to the information they receive, they at least have deeper or more general values that can be mined, interpreted, and fitted to the alternatives they confront to generate preferences or choices that reflect those values. Surely we can safely assume that most 43-year-old women who learn that they have breast cancer want to survive and live an active life. The point I want to challenge is not whether people have any underlying values that they bring to their decisions, but the extent to which their values can be regarded as preexisting and thus independent of the descriptions of their prospects. The assumption of existing preferences presupposes a strong degree of independence. If we have reason to doubt this independence, as I believe we do, then the value of consent and the deliberative model will have to be seen in a different light.

The strongest reasons for doubting the assumption of existing prefer-ences comes from psychological research in behavioral decision theory, which explores the empirical bases of human judgment and choice. I want to focus on a particular aspect of this research, but to do this I must first describe briefly the broader context into which it fits.

Some of the most interesting research in behavioral decision theory shows how preferences are causally influenced in predictable but nonrational ways, with the implication that most of us can be led to make choices that we would also admit are not rationally justifiable. These predictable but nonrational determinants of preference track descriptions of choice situations that do not correspond to any features of the situation that most people would regard as relevant to their goals or interests. Psychologists call these influences *framing effects* (see Kahneman & Tversky, 2000). Some evolutionary story can probably be told to explain this tendency and show that it helped us survive the competition of natural selection, but this fact provides limited comfort when compared with the overall consequences of our susceptibility to framing effects.

The standard (but not uncontroversial) theory of rational choice – utility theory – consists of a set of axioms that define existence and coherence conditions for preferences. The main theorem of utility theory says that rational preferences maximize expected utility. This means that if an individual has preferences that are coherent, in the sense defined by the axioms, then it is possible to assign utilities and probabilities to the alternative possible outcomes so that the most preferred alternative is the one that maximizes expected utility. Utility theory sees rationality, therefore, in terms of preferences for *outcomes* or states.

Now consider the following experiment (Kahneman & Tversky, 1979):

Example 1: The isolation effect:

> **Problem 1:** Assume yourself richer by $300 than you are today.
> You have to choose between
>> A sure gain of $100
>> 50% chance to gain $200 and 50% chance to gain nothing.
>
> **Problem 2:** Assume yourself richer by $500 than you are today.
> You have to choose between
>> A sure loss of $100
>> 50% chance to lose nothing and 50% chance to lose $200.

These two problems offer equivalent prospects in terms of wealth. Each offers a choice between a sure gain of $400 and a gamble with an equal chance to gain either $300 or $500. If wealth completely defines the outcomes in these problems, then a rational person should choose the same option in both of them. But, in fact, most people choose the sure gain in *Problem 1* and the gamble in *Problem 2*. This is a framing effect. We are led to see the prospect in *Problem 1* as a choice among gains and the prospect in *Problem 2* as a choice among losses, and most people tend to value perceived gains and losses differently.

Utility theory cannot easily explain this popular pair of choices, though many theorists have attempted to do so (e.g., Bell, 1982; Loomes & Sugden, 1982). One attempt at an explanation goes as follows. Suppose we assume that a person actually reaches the stage described in the opening line of either problem and then confronts the prospect from one or another of these wealth positions. The person facing a choice in *Problem 1* has already realized a gain and must now decide whether to accept an additional $100 with certainty or take a risk to gain $200 or nothing. If he takes the risk and wins, he will indeed be happy, but if he gambles and loses, he will regret not having chosen the certain gain, and his feelings of regret at losing might be far stronger than the joy he will feel if he gambles and wins. Thus, he chooses to avoid the gamble and the possibility of regret. The person in *Problem 2*, however, seems to be in a different situation. Either he will lose $100 for sure, or he can gamble on losing $200 or nothing. Because he may lose in any event, he might reasonably believe that he would feel little additional regret if he gambles and loses more, so he is willing to take a chance at losing nothing. The outcomes in the two problems would then turn out to be different after all, for one has a potential to cause regret that is lacking in the other. The worse outcome in *Problem 1* is different from and worse than the worse outcome in *Problem 2*, although the positions are identical in terms of wealth. If the outcomes are indeed different, then no preference reversal has occurred, and the choices can be represented as rational by utility theory.

The problem with this explanation is that it fails to show an understanding of how framing effects work. Most people can be led to adopt either of the positions as a reference point, even when they are not richer than they are by $300 or $500 and have no good reason to assume that either position is the status quo. Seeing the prospect as a gain or a loss is merely a framing effect. The regret that attaches to one decision frame may be real, but it is a consequence of adopting the frame, not of the options or the context of choice. Utility theory can accommodate differences like these (and the myriad others that have been demonstrated in similar experiments) only if we are willing to individuate outcomes in a way that includes their descriptions along with their other properties. But the result of individuating outcomes in such a way would be to make the theory of rational choice vacuous. No set of preferences would ever be incoherent, because some description is always available that could distinguish alternatives in a way that eliminates any inconsistencies among preferences. A theory of choice that is so open-ended that it makes no set of preferences incoherent is not a theory of anything.

FRAMING EFFECTS AND METHODS
FOR ELICITING PREFERENCES

Preference reversals like the one demonstrated earlier are better explained by prospect theory, which is a behavioral theory of choice that is incompatible with utility theory (Kahneman & Tversky, 1979; Kahneman, 1994). First, prospect theory assigns values to changes in one's situation, which are perceived as gains or losses from a reference point. It thus assigns values to *events*, not *outcomes*. Second, prospect theory claims that people are loss averse, which means that we tend to weigh perceived losses more heavily than equivalent perceived gains, and we are risk seeking to avoid losses and risk averse with gains. Third, the reference point from which changes are perceived as gains or losses is subject to framing effects. It can be determined by the way a prospect is described.

Prospect theory, if correct, shows one way in which preferences and values are not independent of descriptions, but prospect theory by itself does not give a full or adequate account of framing effects. Other experiments demonstrate that preference reversals can also be generated by varying the procedure or method used to elicit preferences for a prospect. For example, consider one of the best-known instances of a preference reversal (Slovic, Griffin, & Tversky, 1990):

Example 2: The response mode effect:
Subjects are asked to express their preference between two gambles that have similar expected monetary outcomes. One gamble (the P bet) offers a high probability of a modest payoff, while the other gamble (the $ bet) offers a lower probability of a larger payoff. For instance:

> P bet: 29/36 chance to win $2
> $ bet: 7/36 chance to win $9

When asked which of the gambles they would prefer to play, most people choose the P bet, but when asked to evaluate the gambles independently by indicating how much money they would be willing to pay for the right to play either one, most people assign a higher value to the $ bet. A large majority of those who prefer to play the P bet in the direct comparison, moreover, indicate a willingness to pay more to play the $ bet, thus reversing their preferences with the different elicitation method.

Apparently, when people are asked to express their preferences by directly comparing these two gambles, the probability of winning weighs more heavily than the value of the prize. But when they are asked to express their preferences for each prospect independently using a willingness-to-pay metric, the prizes weigh more heavily than the probabilities. This result has been the subject of a great deal of research, the results of which make the phenomenon of preference reversals seem more robust and challenging (Tversky, Slovic, & Kahneman, 1990). For example, when subjects are asked to rate the prospects independently using a nonmonetary scale, the P bet is again preferred to the $ bet. However, when a small loss is added to the $ bet, that is,

> $' bet: 7/36 chance to win $9; 29/36 chance to lose $.05,

$' receives far higher ratings than $ on both the monetary and nonmonetary scales (Slovic, Finucane, Peters, & MacGregor, 2002). Of course, when $' is directly compared with $, nearly everyone prefers to play $.

It is not irrational of course to prefer either the P bet or the $ bet to the other, but reversing one's preferences as a result of a change in the elicitation process surely is irrational. In the words of Kenneth Arrow (1982), such changes violate "a fundamental element of rationality, so elementary that we hardly notice it"

(p. 1). No theory of rational choice can accommodate such violations. This violation has been illustrated with an analogy to using different methods for comparing the weights of physical objects. Suppose we wanted to determine which of two objects was heavier. We could place them on either side of a balance scale, which is a method of direct comparison, or we could weigh them independently on a spring scale that registers the weight of each and use that comparison to determine which is heavier. The ordering of the objects according to weight should be the same either way. It doesn't matter for this purpose what metric is used or whether the scales are accurate.

Now suppose that the weighings produced a different result, such that Object *A* was heavier when put on the balance scale, but Object *B* registered a greater weight on the spring scale. What would we think? We would probably think that something was wrong with one of the scales, and we'd look around for another one to determine which object was really heavier. But suppose now that further weighings produced the same result. Every balance scale we could find indicated that *A* was heavier than *B*, but *B* registered more kilos or pounds than *A* on every spring scale. We would be deeply puzzled. This result would upset a basic assumption we make about the physical world, that the relative weights of two objects do not vary with the kind of scale we use to determine those weights. With no other hypotheses available to explain these results, we would be forced to conclude that the weights of (at least these) objects was not independent of the scales used to measure or compare those weights. But, we might continue to wonder, which object is really, objectively heavier? It seems that this question has no answer. Surely it does no good to run off to a hundred scales to see what a majority of them tell us. The concept "heavier than" would seem not to be independent of the process of measurement. It is, we might say, constructed out of the measurement process and thus relative to it.

Now this fantasy about the relative weights of physical objects and the meaning of "heavier than" strains credibility from the start. Indeed, our experience convinces us that the basic properties of the physical world (or at least the common-sense physical world of medium-sized objects) are independent of our acts of perceiving and measuring them. But the psychological evidence indicates that preferences are not like this and that the assumption of existing preferences is simply not true.

Why should it be otherwise? There is little intuitive reason to think that preferences should simply be an ordering of objective states of the world. Our desires and values, after all, are to a considerable degree determined by how we describe and conceive things and by their relation to our subjective position in the world. It is not unreasonable to think that to have a preference for a prospect, we have to perceive our relationship to it in some way and that coming to see our relationship to it differently will affect our preferences.

We can now begin to appreciate the implication of these thoughts for the value of informed consent. We express our freedom when we consent to activities that affect us because we construct our values and preferences in ways that incorporate those activities into states of affairs that we endorse or reject. This is what the value of autonomy means in this context. Consent is part of a process of preference or value construction, which explains why it has the power to justify what happens to us.

A deliberative model of shared decision making should be the goal of the physician–patient relationship as well as other consent-giving relationships, therefore, because this is the only model that is suitable for constructing preferences and values. The kind of deliberative model I have in mind, however, differs from the one described by Emanuel and Emanuel (1992) in at least one significant respect: It does not rely on an assumption of existing preferences. Physician and patient work together to construct values in a deliberative process leading to consent. Getting information about the prospects we face is an important component of that process, but there is simply no neutral way in which to package, deliver, and integrate that information into an expression of consent. The act of informing is part of the value construction process, not merely a pre-condition of it.

PERFECT, IMPERFECT, AND PURE PROCEDURAL VALUES

Earlier I claimed that neither the instrumental value of consent in promoting well-being nor the direct value of consent as a constituent of well-being was the whole story of the value of informed consent. I then argued that consent should be understood to require a deliberative process of value construction. At least part of the value of consent, therefore, is procedural. What are the implications of this conclusion for how we make decisions and policies that express the consent of those who are affected by them?

In *A Theory of Justice*, John Rawls (1971) makes a distinction between perfect and pure procedural values. Suppose we have a goal in mind, and we must figure out a process or way to achieve that goal. A perfect procedure is one that ideally or unerringly achieves that goal. Such a procedure thus has instrumental value. In most cases, of course, we have to settle for imperfect procedures, and these are valuable to the extent that they come close to achieving the desired end. The scientific method may be the best process we have devised to discover truths about the world, and a market economy may be the best way to allocate scarce resources and match what is produced to what consumers want, but neither of these procedures is perfect. Each has procedural value of an instrumental but imperfect kind.

Pure procedural value is different. Rather than tracking what is good, some procedures confer value on outcomes. Suppose, for example, that Solomon has to give an indivisible good to one of two equally deserving mothers. He decides to flip a coin, which comes up heads, and he gives the good to the first mother. The procedure makes the outcome right. Had Solomon decided to give the prize to the first mother for some other reason, or for no reason at all, it would have been unfair and wrong. The coin flip gives each of the mothers an equal chance of getting the good, and it is because the outcome was determined by this (or some other) randomizing procedure that it is right.

Procedures can have other kinds of value, and many situations are complex in ways that make the value of some procedure complex as well. Consider, for example, the procedure of voting to elect members of Congress. Some might argue that the goal is to select the person who is best qualified to represent fairly and effectively his or her constituents. Voting is an imperfect procedure for determining who is best, but given the uncertainties of what counts as expertise in determining qualifications, as well as the biases of those who would make such determinations, leaving the decision to the will of the majority might be the best of the alternatives. Others might argue instead that voting has pure procedural value. The goal of voting is to give citizens a voice in determining who will represent them in government and to ensure that those representatives are directly accountable in some way to the citizens. The candidate who is elected through a fair voting process is the right candidate for the job precisely because she was chosen in this way. We might urge that voters should attend to the qualifications of the candidates in deciding how to cast their votes, but these qualifications are irrelevant to deciding the rightness of the outcome. Still others might call attention to different values of voting. Going to the polls on election day to cast one's vote can be seen as an expression of citizenship and community participation. This kind of value is often mentioned when people consider changing the voting procedure in ways that would make it less of a public event, for example, by letting people cast votes at home via the Internet over a period of weeks.

The expressive value of a procedure like voting is a kind of intrinsic value, because the value is directly realized through the act of voting. In this way, the expressive value of voting can be distinguished from the instrumental value of the procedure as an imperfect process for selecting the candidate whom we might determine by some independent criteria to be best qualified. Both of these kinds of procedural value should be distinguished in turn from the pure procedural value voting has in virtue of its ability to confer rightness on the results of fair elections. We should thus distinguish the value-conferring property of pure procedural value from both the intrinsic and instrumental values of a procedure.[1]

This is an important point, which I will try to illustrate with a different example. Suppose a physician has five units of a rare life-saving drug. One of his patients needs all five units to survive, and five other patients need one unit each to survive. Some people would argue that absent any other relevant considerations (e.g., the one patient who needs five units does not own the drug, does not have a special contractual relationship with the physician, etc.),

---

[1] Because of limitations of space, I am giving a very brief argument here for distinguishing different kinds of procedural values involved in informed consent. For a fuller treatment, see MacLean (1994); also Scheffler (1985).

the physician should use the drug to save five lives instead of saving one. John Taurek (1977) has argued, however, that this is the wrong decision because it is unfair to the patient who needs five units. In deciding to save the greater number of lives, the physician gives this patient no chance to survive. Taurek argues that something has value only if it has value for someone, from which it follows that saving the greater number of lives has no value at all. Saving five lives is better for each of the five who survive, but it is worse for the one who dies, just as saving the one patient is better for him but worse for each of the other five. Saving a greater number of lives has no value because it is not good for anyone. Thus, according to Taurek, a better and perhaps the only morally acceptable way for the physician to decide what to do in this situation is to flip a coin to determine whether to save one or five lives. In this way, each patient gets an equal chance at survival.

Ralph Keeney (1984), who believes that saving more lives is better than saving fewer lives, proposes nevertheless a way to accommodate Taurek's concerns within a decision analytic framework. Keeney argues that we should see this prospect as a choice between four possible outcomes. The best outcome would be to flip a coin and as a result save the five lives. The worst outcome would be simply to choose to save the one life. We would then have to figure out how to rank the two remaining possibilities: either simply to choose to save the five lives or to flip a coin and as a result save one life. Once we individuate the possible outcomes in this way and evaluate each outcome, we can then figure out which choice maximizes expected value. Keeney thus interprets Taurek's (1977) argument as claiming that flipping a coin has some kind of intrinsic value as a procedure for deciding what to do. He argues that we should weigh this value along with the intrinsic value of saving one life and the greater intrinsic value of saving five lives. But this is to misinterpret Taurek, for whom flipping a coin could have no more intrinsic value than saving a greater number of lives. Flipping a coin is not a good, in Taurek's view, because it is not good for anyone. Rather, it is the right thing to do because it gives everyone a fair chance at what is good for them, that is, their survival. Taurek is arguing that flipping a coin has pure procedural value. It is not an intrinsic good, but it confers rightness on the outcome that results, because it is fair.

Let me emphasize that I am not suggesting that we accept Taurek's (1977) general argument about goodness or the irrelevance of greater numbers. The point of this example is to illustrate that pure procedural value differs from both instrumental and intrinsic goodness.

If consent procedures were good because they enable us to uncover a person's existing values and use them to determine whether actions or policies that affect her are in her interest, then consent procedures would have perfect or imperfect value. But I have argued that it is more plausible to claim that we construct preferences and values in the consent process. The goal of a consent procedure, therefore, is more to enable a person to realize her autonomy than it is to assist her in promoting her well-being. Effective consent procedures thus have pure procedural value. Whether or not the process of gaining a person's consent promotes her well-being, the basic justification for consent lies elsewhere. The aim of a deliberative and interactive process of framing a decision problem and constructing preferences in response to it is to help us achieve our nature as free and rational beings. Through such processes, when they are fair and well designed, we confer rightness on the chosen prospects and thus on their outcomes.

PROCEDURAL VALUES, PREFERENCE CONSTRUCTION, AND CONTINGENT VALUATION METHODS

I will end with some brief remarks about the use of revealed preference techniques and contingent valuation methods to help determine and justify regulatory decisions in areas like environmental protection, workplace or consumer product safety, and others. These methods can be interpreted as attempts to base regulatory decisions on the informed consent of stakeholders or those who are most directly affected by these decisions.

Revealed preference techniques examine economic behavior in areas that would allow decision makers to infer preferences for making risk, cost, and benefit tradeoffs. They attempt to reveal, for example, how much people are willing to pay to reduce some increment of risk of death, to live in less polluted areas, or to fish or hike in undeveloped areas. Contingent valuation methods attempt to discover people's preferences for different combinations of risk, cost, and benefit especially in areas in which goods are not marketed or in areas where economic behavior does not reveal such preferences. These methods aim to discover, for example, how people value things like knowing that a wilderness area exists and is protected or ensuring that we are contributing our fair share to solving some global environmental problem. Contingent valuation methods (see, e.g., Freeman, 2003) typically inform people about alternative choices and ask them to state what they are willing to pay for some good or what they would accept as compensation for accepting some loss or risk of loss.

People who are asked these questions, as well as other critics of these methods, sometimes object to what they perceive as crass attempts to put monetary values on things that many people regard as priceless or sacred (see Ackerman & Heinzerling, 2004), but this is not the issue that concerns me here. These attempts to bring informed consent to bear in justifying regulatory decisions are controversial for other reasons as well. One issue involves the challenge of determining whether and to what extent we are justified in taking economic preferences, especially preferences revealed in behavior, as expressing our sincere and considered values for different goods, and especially the values that many people believe should be expressed and promoted in government actions. Our economic choices are not always well informed, and they are every bit as capable of revealing weakness of will as other kinds of choices that we are capable of making. We do not always behave or choose in ways that we would endorse on reflection. We don't always put our best foot – or our best selves – forward in our behavior, even when that behavior reveals our willingness to pay for something.

The argument that I have presented in this chapter about the value of informed consent raises a different issue, however, about the justification of using revealed preference techniques or contingent valuation methods to justify regulatory decisions. I am suggesting that these methods can be justified as basing decisions on informed consent only if they can be shown to be effective and fair methods for helping people to construct preferences about regulatory decisions. Whether they can meet this standard remains an open question.

37. Do Defaults Save Lives?

Eric J. Johnson and Daniel G. Goldstein

INTRODUCTION

What drives the decision to become a potential organ donor? Since 1995 over 45,000 people in the United States have died waiting for a suitable donor organ. Although an oft-cited poll (The Gallup Organization, Inc., 1993) has shown that 85% of Americans approve of organ donation, less than half had made a decision about donating, and fewer still (28%) had granted permission by signing a donor card. Given the shortage of donors, the gap between approval and action is a matter of life and death. To learn more about what causes people to become donors, looking at differing organ donation rates between countries might provide a clue. Even across neighbor states, organ donation rates vary widely. Within the European Union, for example, donation rates vary by nearly an order of magnitude across countries, and these differences are stable from year to year. Factors such as transplant infrastructure, economic and educational status, and religion all explain part of the difference (Gimbel, Strosberg, Lehrman, Gefenas, & Taft, 2003). However, even when these variables are controlled for, large differences in donation rates persist. Why?

Most public policy choices have a *no-action default*, that is, an assignment to a condition that is imposed when an individual fails to make a decision (Camerer, Issacharoff, Loewenstein, O'Donoghue, & Rabin, 2003; Sunstein & Thaler, 2003). For example, in the case of organ donation, European countries have one of two default policies. In *presumed consent* states, people are organ donors unless they register *not* to be, and in *explicit consent* countries, nobody is an organ donor unless they register to be. A standard economic analysis, according to which individuals know their preferences, would suggest that defaults would have a limited effect: When defaults are not consistent with preferences, people would switch and choose an appropriate alternative.

A different hypothesis arises from research depicting preferences as *constructed*, that is, not yet articulated in the minds of those who have not been asked (Kahneman & Tversky, 2000; Payne, Bettman, & Johnson, 1992; Slovic,

This article has been revised by the authors, reprinted with permission from *Science*, vol. 302, pp. 1338–1339, and www.sciencemag.org/cgi/content/full/302/5649/1338/DC1. Copyright © 2003 AAAS.

1995). Because many people may not yet have thought about whether to be an organ donor, is it possible that the default might make a difference?

If preferences for being an organ donor are constructed, defaults can influence choices in three ways: First, decision makers might believe that defaults are recommendations from the policy maker. Second, making a decision often involves effort, whereas accepting the default is effortless. Many people would rather avoid making an active decision about donation, because it can be unpleasant and stressful (Baron & Ritov, 1994). Physical effort, such as filling out a form and tracking down a postage stamp, may also increase acceptance of the default (Samuelson & Zeckhauser, 1988). Finally, defaults often represent the existing state or status quo, and change usually involves a tradeoff, giving up one thing for another. For example, respondents in our research often suggest that becoming a donor yields satisfaction, which they think of as a gain, and contemplate how their gift might benefit others. However, they also often mention a loss, imagining what will happen to their corpse. Because psychologists have shown that losses loom larger than the equivalent gains, a phenomenon known as *loss aversion* (Tversky & Kahneman, 1991), changes in the default may result in a change of choice. For current nondonors, changing status (becoming a donor) involves the tradeoff between a gain (satisfaction) and a loss (disturbing imagery). For donors, changing status changes the tradeoff: losing the satisfaction, while gaining freedom from negative imagery. In each case, loss aversion suggests an increased weighting of what is foregone, making the default seem more attractive.

The constructed preferences view stands in stark contrast to the classical economics view, that preferences exist and are easily accessible to the decision maker, and that people simply find too little value in organ donation. This view has led to calls for the establishment of a regulated market for the organs of the deceased (Clay & Block, 2002; "An ethically defensible market in organs," 2002), for the payment of donors or donors' families (Harris & Alcorn, 2001), and even for suggestions that organs should become public property on death (Harris, 2003). Calls for campaigns to change public attitudes (Wolf, Servino, & Nathan, 1997) are widespread. The existence of these proposals would make it seem that people require financial incentives to donate, are opposed to donation, or need to be convinced of the benefits of donation; the implication in each case is that people know their preferences and prefer not to donate. But how stable are preferences to become an organ donor? Do they stand up in the face of differing defaults?

EXISTING EVIDENCE

Quite inadvertently, governments, companies, and public agencies run several "natural experiments" testing the power of defaults. Consider the numerous real-world situations in which people are randomly assigned to one program and then given the chance to choose among a set of alternative ones – examples include assignment to health care plans (Samuelson & Zeckhauser, 1988) and the adoption of privacy policies (Bellman, Johnson, & Lohse, 2001; Johnson, Bellman, & Lohse, 2002). Without exception, these experiments show that random assignment to a default has a substantial role in determining what is chosen. In most cases, the majority of people choose the default option to which they were assigned, in violation of the Coase theorem from economics, which suggests that initial assignment does not determine final states (Coase, 1960). Two examples illustrate the point with significant economic consequences.

The States of New Jersey and Pennsylvania both attempted to deal with increased auto insurance costs, caused in part by fraud, by giving buyers of auto insurance a choice between a more expensive full tort plan, which provided the right to sue for pain and suffering, and a significantly less expensive limited tort plan, which covered the medical costs of the insured but removed the right to sue for difficult-to-prove "pain and suffering" claims. The idea behind the policy was that "honest" drivers would have more incentive to choose the limited tort plan both because it was cheaper and because they were less likely to use the pain and suffering option. Less honest (and therefore more expensive to cover) drivers, among others, would tend to choose the full tort plan, constructing what economists call a separating equilibrium: These drivers' choices of the more expensive policy would increase its cost further (reflecting their fraudulent claims), while not affecting the limited tort drivers. However, reality and economic theory did not match. This was confirmed by a natural experiment: New Jersey and Pennsylvania adopted different no-action defaults. New Jersey drivers were given the limited right to sue by default, whereas Pennsylvania drivers had the opposite default, the full right to sue. Interestingly, 79% of New Jersey drivers "preferred" the limited right to sue, whereas in Pennsylvania, 70% "preferred" the opposite plan! Given that Pennsylvania has about 8.2 million licensed drivers and that this participation rate has been stable, this conservatively suggests additional annual sales around $450 million of full tort coverage generated by the choice of default, or a total of about $5 billion since the law's inception.[1] A psychological study in which people were assigned one of the two tort plans by default confirmed this: The full right to sue was chosen 53% of the time when it was the default, but only 23% of the time when it was not (Johnson, Hershey, Meszaros, & Kunreuther, 1993).

Our second example involves retirement savings plans, particularly 401k plans. Allocation to these plans, which held $1.776 trillion in 2000, is perhaps the most important financial decision most Americans will ever make. In the United States, many workers are covered by a defined contribution plan in which people elect to save between 0% and 12% of their income for retirement. The plans are attractive: The contributions are in pre-tax dollars, the money

[1] This assumes that a figure near the New Jersey rate of participation (20%) would hold in Pennsylvania and that the savings due to limited tort is 15% of an annual premium (1996) of $687.42.

compounds tax-free, and the first 6% is often matched by an employer. Consistent with observations that Americans are not saving sufficiently toward retirement, many initially contribute the default, that is, nothing. However, as shown in recent studies (Madrian & Shea, 2001), when the default was changed, there was a marked increase in savings. One firm raised the default contribution from 0% to 3% and saw the percentage of new employees saving *anything* towards retirement rise from 31% to 86%. However, the effect was almost too powerful – the 3% default surprisingly decreased the number of people electing to save more than 3%. This result has been replicated in several firms (Choi, Laibson, Madrian, & Metrick, 2004), raising questions about what default is optimal. Could this be rational inaction? This seems unlikely because the economic stakes are simply too large (Samuelson & Zeckhauser, 1988). An alternative explanation may be that preferences for retirement savings options are constructed at the time of decision and are therefore influenced by implied endorsement, myopic laziness, or loss aversion.

DEFAULTS AND ORGAN DONATIONS

A number of European countries have been running similar natural experiments with organ donation spanning the last two decades. Different countries have different default options for individuals' decisions to become organ donors. Some countries require that one must give explicit consent and opt in to become a donor, whereas others presume consent, and individuals must opt out if they do not want to be donors. We can examine the role of defaults by looking at opt in, opt out, and actual donation rates in various countries.

ONLINE SURVEY

We investigated the effect of defaults on donation agreement rates using an online experiment. We asked 161 respondents whether they would be donors, using one of three questions with varying defaults. In the opt-in condition, participants were told to assume that they had just moved to a new state where the default was to *not be* an organ donor, and they were given a choice to confirm or change that status. The opt-out condition was identical, except the default was *to be* a donor. The third, neutral condition simply required them to choose with no prior default. Respondents could change their choice with a mouse click, largely eliminating effort explanations.

Respondents were recruited from our online subject pool, which consists of thousands of geographically diverse adults in North America, by offering $4.00 for filling out a brief questionnaire. Although this was not intended to be a representative sample, it did include a broad range of demographics. To minimize the effects of careless responses or multiple responding, before analyzing the data we deleted from our data any instances of multiple responses from the same IP address and any responses that were made unreasonably quickly,

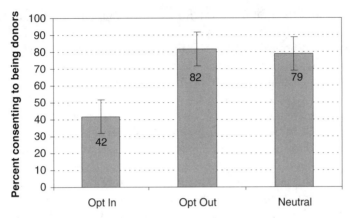

Figure 37.1. Effective consent rates, online experiment, by default.

yielding a total of 161 respondents. As can be seen in Figure 37.1, the form of the question had a dramatic effect, with revealed donation rates being about twice as high when opting out as when opting in. The opt-out condition did not differ significantly from the neutral condition, which required a choice without a default option. Only the opt-in condition, the current practice in the United States, was significantly lower.

Although these results appear dramatic, is it possible that we would see such effects in the actual decision to become an organ donor? Such decisions may be affected by governmental educational programs, the efforts of public health organizations, and cultural and infrastructural factors. We examined the rate of agreement to become a donor across European countries with explicit and presumed consent laws. We supplemented the data reported by Gäbel (2002) by contacting the central registries for several countries, allowing us to estimate the effective consent rate, that is, the number of people who had opted in (in explicit consent countries) or the number who had not opted out (in presumed consent countries). If preferences concerning organ donation are strong, we would expect defaults to have little or no effect. However, as can be seen in Figure 37.2, defaults appear to make a large difference, with the four opt-in countries on the left having lower rates than the six opt-out countries on the right. The result is surprisingly strong: The two distributions have no overlap, and nearly 60 percentage points separate the two groups. One reason these results appear to be greater than those in our laboratory study is that the cost of changing from the default is higher, involving filling out forms, making phone calls, and sending mail. These low rates of agreement to become a donor come, in some cases, despite marked efforts to increase donation rates. In the Netherlands, for example, the 1998 creation of a national donor registry was accompanied by an extensive educational campaign and a mass mailing (of more than 12 million letters in a country of 15.8 million people) asking citizens

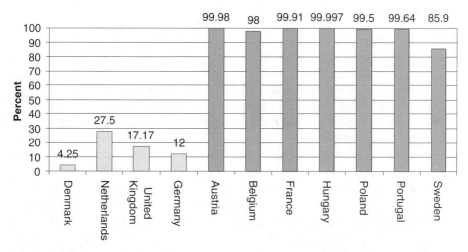

Figure 37.2. Effective consent rates, by country; the four leftmost light bars are explicit consent (opt in); the seven rightmost dark bars are presumed consent (opt out).

to register. This effort failed to change the effective consent rate (Oz et al., 2003).

Do increases in agreement rates result in increased rates of donation? There are many reasons preventing registered potential donors from actually donating. These include families' objections to a loved one's consent, doctors' hesitancy to use a default option, a mismatch with potential recipients, and differences in religion, culture, and infrastructure. These factors may influence the role of the differences in Figure 37.2 in determining the number of donors in various countries.

To examine this we analyzed the actual number of caderveric donations made per million on a slightly larger list of countries, here using a time series of data from 1991 to 2001. We analyzed these data using a multiple regression analysis with the actual donation rates as dependent measures and the default as a predictor variable. To control for other differences in the countries' propensities toward donation, transplant infrastructure, educational level, and religion, we include variables known to serve as proxies for these constructs (see Gimbel et al., 2003) and an indicator variable representing each year.[2]

This analysis presents a strong conclusion. Although there are no differences across years, there is a strong effect of the default: When donation is the default, there is a significant ($p < .02$) increase in donation, increasing from 14.1 to 16.4, a 16.3% increase. Using similar techniques, but looking only at 1999 for a broader set of countries, including many more from Eastern Europe, Gimbel et al. (2003) reported an increase from 10.8 to 16.9, a 56.5% increase.

[2] Details of the statistical analysis can be found in the original article's online supporting material at http://www.sciencemag.org/cgi/content/full/302/5649/1338/DC1.

CONCLUSION

Both our correlational and experimental data suggest that the default has a significant effect on organ donation. What is the correct default? Several factors should influence the answer to this question.

First, every policy must have a no-action default, and defaults impose physical, cognitive, and, in the case of donation, emotional costs on those who must change their status. As noted earlier, both national surveys and the no-default condition in our experiment suggest that most Americans favor organ donation. This implies that explicit consent policies impose the costs of switching on the apparent majority.[3]

Second, defaults can lead to two kinds of misclassification: (1) willing donors who are not identified or (2) people who become donors against their wishes. Balancing these errors with the good done by the lives saved through organ transplantation is a delicate ethical and psychological question, to say the least. These decisions should be informed by further research examining the role of the three causes of default effects. For example, one might draw very different conclusions if the effect of defaults on donation rates is due primarily to physical costs of responding than if they were due to loss aversion.

The tradeoff between errors of classification and physical, cognitive, and emotional costs must be made with the knowledge that defaults make a large difference in lives saved through transplantation. Our data and those of Gimbel et al. (2003) suggest that changes in defaults could increase donations by between 16% and 56%, resulting in a potential increase in the United States of thousands of donors a year. Rates of agreement show an even larger effect, increasing from between 100% and 300% in our studies. Because each donor can result in about three transplants, the consequences are substantial in lives saved.

Our results stand in contrast to the suggestion that defaults do not matter (Caplan, 1994). We find that they do, both in survey evidence and in natural experiments of the effects of defaults in European countries. Policy makers, through the election of defaults, can influence the fate of the thousands of people who die each year for want of organs.

---

[3] An alternative advocated by the American Medical Association (1993) is mandated choice, imposing the cost of making an active decision on all. This practice is currently employed in the state of Virginia, but, consistent with the constructive preferences perspective, about 24% of the first million Virginians asked said they were undecided (Klassen & Klassen, 1996).

38. Libertarian Paternalism Is Not an Oxymoron

Cass R. Sunstein and Richard H. Thaler

Consider two studies of savings behavior:

- Hoping to increase savings by workers, several employers have adopted a simple strategy. Instead of asking workers to elect to participate in a 401(k) plan, workers will be assumed to want to participate in such a plan, and hence they will be enrolled automatically unless they specifically choose otherwise. This simple change in the default rule has produced dramatic increases in enrollment (Choi, Laibson, Madrian, & Metrick, 2002; Madrian & Shea, 2001).
- Rather than changing the default rule, some employers have provided their employees with a novel option: *Allocate a portion of future wage increases to savings.* Employees who choose this plan are free to opt out at any time. A large number of employees have agreed to try the plan, and only a few have opted out. The result has been significant increases in savings rates (Thaler & Benartzi, 2004).

Libertarians embrace freedom of choice, and so they deplore paternalism. Paternalists are thought to be skeptical of unfettered freedom of choice and to deplore libertarianism. According to the conventional wisdom, libertarians cannot possibly embrace paternalism, and paternalists abhor libertarianism. The idea of libertarian paternalism seems to be a contradiction in terms.

Generalizing from the two studies just described, we propose a form of paternalism, libertarian in spirit, that should be acceptable to those who are firmly committed to freedom of choice on grounds of either autonomy or welfare. Indeed, we urge that libertarian paternalism provides a basis for both understanding and rethinking a number of areas of contemporary law, including those aspects that deal with worker welfare, consumer protection, and the family. In the process of defending these claims, we intend to make some objections to widely held beliefs about both freedom of choice and paternalism. Our emphasis is on the fact that in many domains, people lack clear, stable, or well-ordered

This article has been abridged by the authors. The complete version appeared in the *University of Chicago Law Review*, vol. 70, pp. 1159–1202. Copyright © 2003 by the University of Chicago Law School. Reproduced with permission of the University of Chicago Law School in the format Trade Book via Copyright Clearance Center.

preferences. What they choose is strongly influenced by details of the context in which they make their choices, for example default rules, framing effects (that is, the wording of possible options), and starting points. These contextual influences render the very meaning of the term "preferences" unclear.

Consider the question whether to undergo a risky medical procedure. When people are told, "Of those who undergo this procedure, 90% are still alive after five years," they are far more likely to agree to the procedure than when they are told, "Of those who undergo this procedure, 10% are dead after five years" (Redelmeier, Rozin, & Kahneman, 1993, p. 73). What, then, are the patient's "preferences" with respect to this procedure? Repeated experiences with such problems might be expected to eliminate this framing effect, but doctors too are vulnerable to it. This simple example can be extended to many situations involving the behavior of workers and consumers.

As the savings problem illustrates, the design features of both legal and organizational rules have surprisingly powerful influences on people's choices. We urge that such rules should be chosen with the explicit goal of improving the welfare of the people affected by them. The libertarian aspect of our strategies lies in the straightforward insistence that, in general, people should be free to opt out of specified arrangements if they choose to do so. To borrow a phrase, libertarian paternalists urge that people should be "free to choose" (Friedman & Friedman, 1980). Hence, we do not aim to defend any approach that blocks individual choices.

The paternalistic aspect consists in the claim that it is legitimate for private and public institutions to attempt to influence people's behavior even when third-party effects are absent. In other words, we argue for self-conscious efforts, by private and public institutions, to steer people's choices in directions that will improve the choosers' own welfare. In our understanding, a policy therefore counts as "paternalistic" if it attempts to influence the choices of affected parties in a way that will make choosers better off (see also VanDeVeer, 1986, p. 22). Drawing on some well-established findings in behavioral economics and cognitive psychology, we emphasize the possibility that in some cases individuals make inferior decisions in terms of their own welfare – decisions that they would change if they had complete information, unlimited cognitive abilities, and no lack of self-control (Jolls, Sunstein, & Thaler, 1998).

Libertarian paternalism is a relatively weak and nonintrusive type of paternalism, because choices are not blocked or fenced off. In its most cautious forms, libertarian paternalism imposes trivial costs on those who seek to depart from the planner's preferred option. But the approach we recommend nonetheless counts as paternalistic, because private and public planners are not trying to track people's anticipated choices, but are self-consciously attempting to move people in welfare-promoting directions. It follows that one of our principal targets is the dogmatic antipaternalism of numerous analysts of law and policy. We believe that this dogmatism is based on a combination of a false assumption and two misconceptions.

The false assumption is that almost all people, almost all of the time, make choices that are in their best interests or at the very least are better, by their own lights, than the choices that would be made by third parties. This claim is either tautological, and therefore uninteresting, or testable. We claim that it is testable and false, indeed obviously false. In fact, we do not think that anyone believes it on reflection. Suppose that a chess novice were to play against an experienced player. Predictably, the novice would lose precisely because he made inferior choices – choices that could easily be improved by some helpful hints. More generally, how well people choose is an empirical question, one whose answer is likely to vary across domains. As a first approximation, it seems reasonable to say that people make better choices in contexts in which they have experience and good information (say, choosing ice cream flavors) than in contexts in which they are inexperienced and poorly informed (say, choosing among medical treatments or investment options).

The first misconception is that there are viable alternatives to paternalism. In many situations, some organization or agent *must* make a choice that will affect the behavior of some other people. There is, in those situations, no alternative to a kind of paternalism – at least in the form of an intervention that affects what people choose. We are emphasizing, then, the possibility that people's preferences, in certain domains and across a certain range, are influenced by the choices made by planners.

As a simple example, consider the cafeteria at some organization. The cafeteria must make a multitude of decisions, including which foods to serve, which ingredients to use, and in what order to arrange the choices. Suppose that the director of the cafeteria notices that customers have a tendency to choose more of the items that are presented earlier in the line. How should the director decide in what order to present the items? To simplify, consider some alternative strategies that the director might adopt in deciding which items to place early in the line:

1. She could make choices that she thinks would make the customers best off, all things considered.
2. She could make choices at random.
3. She could choose those items that she thinks would make the customers as obese as possible.
4. She could give customers what she thinks they would choose on their own.

Option 1 appears to be paternalistic, but would anyone advocate options 2 or 3? Option 4 is what many antipaternalists would favor, but it is much harder to implement than it might seem. Across a certain domain of possibilities, consumers will often lack well-formed preferences, in the sense of preferences that are firmly held and preexist the director's own choices about how to order the relevant items. If the arrangement of the alternatives has a significant effect on the selections the customers make, then their true "preferences" do not formally exist.

Although some libertarians will happily accept this point for private institutions, they will object to government efforts to influence choice in the name of welfare. We agree that for government, the risks of mistake and overreaching are real and sometimes serious. But governments, no less than cafeterias (which governments frequently run), have to provide starting points of one or another kind; this is not avoidable. As we shall emphasize, they do so every day through the rules of contract and tort, in a way that inevitably affects some preferences and choices. In this respect, the antipaternalist position is unhelpful – a literal nonstarter.

The second misconception is that paternalism always involves coercion. As the cafeteria example illustrates, the choice of the order in which to present food items does not coerce anyone to do anything, yet one might prefer some orders to others on grounds that are paternalistic in the sense that we use the term. Would anyone object to putting the fruit and salad before the desserts at an elementary school cafeteria if the result were to increase the consumption ratio of apples to Twinkies? Is this question fundamentally different if the customers are adults? Because no coercion is involved, we think that some types of paternalism should be acceptable to even the most ardent libertarian.

The thrust of our argument is that the term "paternalistic" should not be considered pejorative, just descriptive. Once it is understood that some organizational decisions are inevitable, that a form of paternalism cannot be avoided, and that the alternatives to paternalism (such as choosing options to make people worse off) are unattractive, we can abandon the less interesting question of whether to be paternalistic or not and turn to the more constructive question of how to choose among the possible choice-influencing options.

THE RATIONALITY OF CHOICES

The presumption that individual choices should be respected is usually based on the claim that people do an excellent job of making choices, or at least that they do a far better job than third parties could possibly do.[1] As far as we

---

[1] It is usually, but not always, based on this claim. Some of the standard arguments against paternalism rest not on consequences but on autonomy – on a belief that people are entitled to make their own choices even if they err. Thus, Mill (1974) advances a mix of autonomy-based and consequentialist claims. Our principal concern here is with welfare and consequences, though as we suggest later, freedom of choice is sometimes an ingredient in welfare. We do not disagree with the view that autonomy has claims of its own, but we believe that it would be fanatical, in the settings that we discuss, to treat autonomy, in the form of freedom of choice, as a kind of trump not to be overridden on consequentialist grounds. In any case, the autonomy argument is undermined by the fact, discussed earlier, that sometimes preferences and choices are a function of given arrangements. Most importantly, we think that respect for autonomy is adequately accommodated by the libertarian aspect of libertarian paternalism, as discussed later.

can tell, there is little empirical support for this claim, at least if it is offered in this general form. Consider the issue of obesity. Rates of obesity in the United States are now approaching 20%, and over 60% of Americans are considered either obese or overweight (Centers for Disease Control and Prevention, 2003). There is a great deal of evidence that obesity causes serious health risks, frequently leading to premature death (Calle, Thun, Petrelli, Rodriguez, & Heath, 1999; National Institute of Diabetes and Digestive and Kidney Diseases, 2001). It is quite fantastic to suggest that everyone is choosing the optimal diet or a diet that is preferable to what might be produced with third-party guidance.

Of course, rational people care about the taste of food, not simply about health, and we do not claim that everyone who is overweight is necessarily failing to act rationally. It is the strong claim that all or almost all Americans are choosing their diet *optimally* that we reject as untenable. What is true for diets is true as well for much other risk-related behavior, including smoking and drinking, which produce many thousands of premature deaths each year (Sunstein, 2002a, pp. 8–9). In these circumstances, people's independent choices cannot reasonably be thought, in all domains, to be the best means of promoting their well-being.

On a more scientific level, research by psychologists and economists over the past three decades has raised questions about the rationality of many judgments and decisions that individuals make. People fail to make forecasts that are consistent with Bayes's rule (Grether, 1980); use heuristics that can lead them to make systematic blunders (Kahneman & Frederick, 2002; Tversky & Kahneman, 1973, 1974); exhibit preference reversals (that is, they prefer A to B *and* B to A; Sunstein, Kahneman, Schkade, & Ritov, 2002; Tversky & Thaler, 1990); suffer from problems of self-control (Frederick, Loewenstein, & O'Donoghue, 2002); and make different choices depending on the framing of the problem (Camerer, 2000; Johnson, Hershey, Meszaros, & Kunreuther, 1993). Studies of actual choices reveal many of the same problems, even when the stakes are high (Camerer & Hogarth, 1999; De Bondt & Thaler, 1990; Shiller, 2000, pp. 135–147).

We do not intend to outline all of the relevant evidence here, but consider an illustration from the domain of savings behavior. Benartzi and Thaler (2002) have investigated how much investors like the portfolios they have selected in their defined contribution savings plans. Employees volunteered to share their portfolio choices with the investigators by bringing a copy of their most recent statement to the lab. They were then shown the probability distributions of expected retirement income for three investment portfolios simply labeled A, B, and C. Unbeknownst to the subjects, the three portfolios were their own and portfolios mimicking the average and median choices of their fellow employees. The distributions of expected returns were computed using the software of Financial Engines, the financial information company founded by William Sharpe. On average, the subjects rated the average portfolio equally with their own portfolio and judged the median portfolio to be significantly more attractive than their own. Indeed, only 20% of the subjects preferred their own portfolio to the median portfolio. Apparently, people do not gain much, by their own lights, from choosing investment portfolios for themselves.

Or consider people's willingness to take precautions. In general, the decision to buy insurance for natural disasters is a product not of a systematic inquiry into either costs or benefits, but of recent events. If floods have not occurred in the immediate past, people who live on flood plains are far less likely to purchase insurance (Kunreuther, 1996). In the aftermath of an earthquake, the level of insurance coverage for earthquakes rises sharply – but it declines steadily from that point, as vivid memories recede (Kunreuther, 1996; Slovic, Kunreuther, & White, 1974). Findings of this kind do not establish that people's choices are usually bad or that third parties can usually do better. But they do show that some of the time, people do not choose optimally even when the stakes are high.

IS PATERNALISM INEVITABLE?

A few years ago, the tax law was changed so that employees could pay for employer-provided parking on a pre-tax basis (Qualified Transportation Fringe Benefits, 2001). Previously, such parking had to be paid for with after-tax dollars. Our employer, and the employer of some of our prominent antipaternalist colleagues, sent around an announcement of this change in the law and adopted the following policy: Unless the employee notified the payroll department, deductions for parking would be taken from pre-tax rather than post-tax income. In other words, the University of Chicago decided that the default option would be to pay for parking with pre-tax dollars, but employees could opt out of this arrangement and pay with after-tax dollars. Call this choice Plan A. An obvious alternative, Plan B, would be to announce the change in the law and tell employees that if they want to switch to the new pre-tax plan they should return some form electing this option. The only difference between the two plans is the default. Under Plan A the new option is the default, whereas under Plan B the status quo is the default. We will refer to the former as an "opt-out" strategy and the latter as an "opt-in" strategy.

How should the university choose between opt in and opt out? In the parking example, it seems to be the case that every employee would prefer to pay for parking with pre-tax dollars rather than after-tax dollars. Because the cost savings are substantial (parking costs as much as $1,200 per year) and the cost of returning a form is trivial, standard economic theory predicts that the university's choice will not really matter. Under either plan, all employees would choose (either actively under Plan B or by default under Plan A) the pre-tax option. In real life, however, had the university adopted Plan B, we suspect that many employees, especially faculty members (and probably including the present authors), would still have that form buried somewhere in their offices and would be paying substantially more for parking on an after-tax basis. In short, the default plan would have had large effects on behavior. Throughout, we shall be drawing attention to the effects of default plans on choices. Often, those plans will be remarkably "sticky."

SAVINGS AND EMPLOYERS

Data and Default Rules

Our conjecture that default plans affect outcomes is supported by the results of numerous experiments documenting a "status quo" bias (Kahneman, Knetsch, & Thaler, 1991; Samuelson & Zeckhauser, 1988). The existing arrangement, whether set out by private institutions or by government, is often robust. One illustration of this phenomenon comes from studies of automatic enrollment in 401(k) employee savings plans (Choi et al., 2002; Madrian & Shea, 2001), and we now elaborate the brief account with which we began. Most 401(k) plans use an opt-in design. When employees first become eligible to participate in the 401(k) plan, they receive some plan information and an enrollment form that must be completed to join. Under the alternative of automatic enrollment, employees receive the same information but are told that unless they opt out, they will be enrolled in the plan (with default options for savings rates and asset allocation). In companies that offer a "match" (the employer matches the employee's contributions according to some formula, often a 50% match up to some cap), most employees eventually do join the plan, but enrollments occur much sooner under automatic enrollment. For example, Madrian and Shea (2001) found that initial enrollments jumped from 49% to 86%, and Choi et al. (2002) found similar results.[2]

Should the adoption of automatic enrollment be considered paternalistic? And if so, should it be seen as a kind of officious meddling with employee preferences? We answer these questions yes and no, respectively. If employers think (correctly, we believe) that most employees would prefer to join the 401(k) plan if they took the time to think about it and did not lose the enrollment form, then by choosing automatic enrollment, they are acting paternalistically by our

---

[2] In a separate phenomenon, the default rule also had a significant effect on the chosen contribution rate (Madrian & Shea, 2001). The default contribution rate (3%) tended to stick; a majority of employees maintained that rate even though this particular rate was chosen by around 10% of employees hired before the automatic enrollment. The same result was found for the default allocation of the investment: Although less than 7% of employees chose a 100% investment allocation to the money market fund, a substantial majority (75%) of employees stuck with that allocation when it was the default rule. The overall default rate (participation in the plan, at a 3% contribution rate, investing 100% in the money market fund) was 61%, but only 1% of employees chose this set of options prior to their adoption as defaults.

definition of the term. Because no one is forced to do anything, we think that this steering should be considered unobjectionable, even to committed libertarians. No law of nature says that in the absence of an affirmative election by employees, 0% of earnings will go into a retirement plan. Because any plan alters choices, neither one can be said, more than the other, to count as a form of objectionable meddling.

Skeptics

Skeptical readers, insistent on freedom of choice, might be tempted to think that there is a way out of this dilemma. Employers could avoid choosing a default if they *required* employees to make an active choice, either in or out. Call this option *required active choosing*. Undoubtedly, required active choosing is attractive in some settings, but a little thought reveals that this is not at all a way out of the dilemma. On the contrary, required active choosing is simply another option among many that the employer can elect. In fact, the very requirement that employees make a choice has a strong paternalistic element. Some employees may not want to have to make a choice (and might make a second-order choice not to have to do so). Why should employers force them to choose?

Required active choosing honors freedom of choice in a certain respect, but it does not appeal to those who would choose not to choose, and indeed it will seem irritating and perhaps unacceptably coercive by their lights. In some circumstances, required choosing will not even be feasible. In any case, an empirical question remains: What is the effect of forced choosing? Choi et al. (2002) found that required active choosing increased enrollments relative to the opt-in rule, though not by as much as automatic enrollment (opt out).

Other skeptics might think that employers should avoid paternalism by doing what most employees would want employers to do. On this approach, a default rule can successfully avoid paternalism if it tracks employees' preferences. Sometimes this is a plausible solution. But what if many or most employees do not have stable or well-formed preferences, and what if employee choices are inevitably a product of the default rule? In such cases, it is meaningless to ask what most employees would do. The choices employees will make depend on the way the employer frames those choices. Employee "preferences," as such, do not exist in those circumstances.

GOVERNMENT

Some enthusiasts for free choice might be willing to acknowledge these points and hence to accept private efforts to steer people's choices in what seem to be the right directions. But our emphasis has been on the inevitability of paternalism, and on this count, the same points apply to some choices made by governments in establishing legal rules.

Default Rules

Default rules of some kind are inevitable, and much of the time those rules will affect preferences and choices (Korobkin, 1998; Sunstein, 2002b). In the neglected words of a classic article (Calabresi & Melamed, 1972):

> [A] minimum of state intervention is always necessary.... When a loss is left where it falls in an auto accident, it is not because God so ordained it. Rather it is because the state has granted the injurer an entitlement to be free of liability and will intervene to prevent the victim's friends, if they are stronger, from taking compensation from the injurer. (pp. 1090–1091)

If the entitlement-granting rules seem invisible and seem to be a simple way of protecting freedom of choice, it is because they appear so sensible and natural that they are not taken to be a legal allocation at all. But this is a mistake. What we add here is that when a default rule affects preferences and behavior, it has the same effect as employer presumptions about savings plans. This effect is often both unavoidable and significant. So long as people can contract around the default rule, it is fair to say that the legal system is protecting freedom of choice, and in that sense, complying with libertarian goals.

Consumers, workers, and married people,[3] for example, are surrounded by a network of legal allocations that provide the background against which agreements are made. As a matter of employment law, and consistent with freedom of contract, workers might be presumed subject to discharge "at will," or they might be presumed protected by an implied right to be discharged only "for cause." They might be presumed to have a right to vacation time, or not. They might be presumed protected by safety requirements, or the employer might be free to invest in safety as he wishes, subject to market pressures. In all cases, the law must establish whether workers have to "buy" certain rights from employers or vice versa (Sunstein, 2001). Legal intervention, in this important sense, cannot be avoided. The same is true for consumers, spouses, and all others who are involved in legal relationships. Much of the time, the legal background matters, even if transaction costs are zero, because it affects choices and preferences, as demonstrated by Korobkin (1998) and Kahneman et al. (1991). Here, as in the private context, a form of paternalism is unavoidable.

In the context of insurance, an unplanned, natural experiment showed that the default rule can be very "sticky" (Johnson, Hershey, et al., 1993). New Jersey created a system in which the default insurance program for motorists included a relatively low premium and limited right to sue; purchasers were allowed to deviate from the default program and to purchase the right to sue by choosing a program with that right and also a higher premium. By contrast, Pennsylvania offered a default program containing a full right to sue and a relatively high premium; purchasers could elect to switch to a new plan by "selling" the more

---

[3] Okin (1989) is a good source of general information on marriage and legal rules.

ample right to sue and paying a lower premium. In both cases, the default rule tended to stick. A strong majority accepted the default rule in both states, with only about 20% of New Jersey drivers acquiring the full right to sue, and 75% of Pennsylvanians retaining that right. There is no reason to think that the citizens of Pennsylvania have systematically different preferences from the citizens of New Jersey. The default plan is what produced the ultimate effects. Indeed, controlled experiments (Johnson, Hershey, et al., 1993) find the same results, showing that the value of the right to sue is much higher when it is presented as part of the default package.

In another example, a substantial effect from the legal default rule was found in a study of law student reactions to different state law provisions governing vacation time from firms (Sunstein, 2002b). The study was intended to be reasonably realistic, involving as it did a pool of subjects to whom the underlying issues were hardly foreign. Most law students have devoted a good deal of time to thinking about salaries, vacation time, and the tradeoffs between them. The study involved two conditions. In the first, state law guaranteed two weeks of vacation time, and students were asked to state their median willingness to pay (WTP; in reduced salary) for 2 extra weeks of vacation. In this condition, the median WTP was $6,000. In the second condition, state law provided a mandatory, nonwaivable 2-week vacation guarantee, but it also provided employees (including associates at law firms) with the right to 2 additional weeks of vacation, a right that could be "knowingly and voluntarily waived." Hence, the second condition was precisely the same as the first, except that the default rule provided the 2 extra weeks of vacation. In the second condition, students were asked how much employers would have to pay them to give up their right to the 2 extra weeks. All by itself, the switch in the default rule more than doubled the students' responses, producing a median willingness to accept of $13,000.

Anchors

In emphasizing the absence of well-formed preferences, we are not speaking only of default rules. Consider the crucial role of "anchors," or starting points, in contingent valuation studies, an influential method of valuing regulatory goods such as increased safety and environmental protection (Bateman & Willis, 1999). Such studies, used when market valuations are unavailable, attempt to ask people their WTP for various regulatory benefits. Contingent valuation has become prominent in regulatory theory and practice. Because the goal is to determine what people actually want, contingent valuation studies are an effort to elicit, rather than to affect, people's values. Paternalism, in the sense of effects on preferences and choices, is not supposed to be part of the picture. But it is extremely difficult for contingent valuation studies to avoid constructing the very values that they are supposed to discover (Payne, Bettman, & Schkade, 1999). The reason is that in the contexts in which such studies are used, people do not have clear or well-formed preferences, and hence it is unclear that people have straightforward "values" that can actually be found. Hence, some form of paternalism verges on the inevitable: Stated values will often be affected, at least across a range, by how the questions are set up.

Perhaps the most striking evidence of this effect comes from a study of willingness to pay to reduce annual risks of death and injury in motor vehicles (Jones-Lee & Loomes, 2001). The authors of that study attempted to elicit both maximum and minimum willingness to pay for safety improvements. People were presented with a statistical risk and an initial monetary amount, and asked whether they were definitely willing or definitely unwilling to pay that amount to eliminate the risk, or if they were "not sure." If they were definitely willing, the amount displayed was increased until they said that they were definitely unwilling. If they were unsure, the number was moved up and down until people could identify the minimum and maximum.

The authors were not attempting to test the effects of anchors; on the contrary, they were alert to anchoring only because they "had been warned" of a possible problem with their procedure, in which people "might be unduly influenced by the first amount of money that they saw displayed" (Jones-Lee & Loomes, 2001, p. 210). To solve that problem, the study allocated people randomly to two subsamples, one with an initial display of £25, the other with an initial display of £75. The authors hoped that the anchoring effect would be small, with no significant consequences for minimum and maximum values. But their hope was dashed. *For every level of risk, the minimum willingness to pay was higher with the £75 starting point than the maximum willingness to pay with the £25 starting point!* For example, a reduction in the annual risk of death by 4 in 100,000 produced a *maximum* willingness to pay of £149 with the £25 starting value, but a *minimum* willingness to pay of £232 with the £75 starting value (and a maximum, in that case, of £350). The most sensible conclusion is that people are sometimes uncertain about appropriate values, and whenever they are, anchors have an effect – sometimes a startlingly large one.

It is not clear how those interested in eliciting (rather than affecting) values might respond to this problem. What is clear is that in the domains in which contingent valuation studies are used, people often lack well-formed preferences, and starting points have important consequences for behavior and choice.

Framing

We have suggested that in the important context of medical decisions, framing effects are substantial (Redelmeier et al., 1993). Apparently, most people do not have clear preferences about how to evaluate a procedure that leaves 90% of people alive (and 10% of people dead) after a period of years. A similar effect has been demonstrated in the area of obligations to future generations (Frederick, 2003), a much-disputed policy question (Morrison, 1998; Revesz, 1999). This question does not directly involve paternalism, because those interested in the valuation of future generations are not attempting to protect people from their own errors. But a regulatory system that attempts to track people's preferences would try to measure intergenerational time preferences, that is, to elicit people's judgments about how to trade off the protection of current lives and future lives (Revesz, 1999).

Hence, an important question, asked in many debates about the issue, is whether people actually make such judgments and whether they can be elicited. From a series of surveys, Maureen Cropper and her coauthors (Cropper, Aydede, & Portney, 1994) suggested that people were indifferent between saving 1 life today and saving 44 lives in 100 years. They made this suggestion on the basis of questions asking people whether they would choose a program that saves "100 lives now" or a program that saves a substantially larger number "100 years from now."

But it turns out that other descriptions of the same problem yield significantly different results (Frederick, 2003). Here, as in other contexts, it is unclear whether people actually have well-formed preferences with which the legal system can work. The most sensible conclusion is that people do not have robust, well-ordered intergenerational time preferences. If so, it is not possible for government to track those preferences, because they are an artifact of how the question is put. The point applies in many contexts. For example, people are unlikely to have context-free judgments about whether government should focus on statistical lives or statistical life-years in regulatory policy; their judgments will be much affected by the framing of the question (Sunstein, 2004).

WHY EFFECTS ON CHOICE CAN BE HARD TO AVOID

Explanations

Why, exactly, do default rules, starting points, and framing effects have such large effects?

Suggestion. In the face of uncertainty about what should be done, people might rely on one of two related heuristics: Do what most people do, or do what informed people do. Choosers might think that the default plan or value captures one or the other. In many settings, any starting point will carry some informational content and will thus affect choices. When a default rule affects behavior, it might well be because it is taken to carry information about how sensible people usually organize their affairs.

Inertia. A separate explanation points to inertia. Any change from the default rule or starting value is likely to require some action. Even a trivial action, such as filling in some form and returning it, can leave room for failures due to memory lapses, sloth, and procrastination. Many people wait until the last minute to file their tax returns, even when they are assured of getting a refund. Madrian and Shea (2001, p. 1171) noted that, under automatic enrollment, individuals become "passive savers" and "do nothing to move away from the default contribution rate."

Endowment Effect. A default rule might create a "pure" endowment effect. It is well known that people tend to value goods more highly if those goods have been initially allocated to them than if those goods have been initially allocated elsewhere (Korobkin, 1998; Thaler, 1991). And it is well known that, in many cases, the default rule will create an endowment effect (Kahneman et al., 1991; Samuelson & Zeckhauser, 1988). When an endowment effect is involved, the initial allocation, by private or public institutions, affects people's choices simply because it affects their valuations.

Ill-Formed Preferences. In the cases we have discussed, people's preferences are ill formed and murky. Suppose, for example, that people are presented with various payouts and risk levels for various pension plans. They might be able to understand the presentation; there might be no confusion. But people might not have a well-defined preference for, or against, a slightly riskier plan with a slightly higher expected value. In these circumstances, their preferences might be endogenous to the default plan simply because they lack well-formed desires that can be accessed to overrule the default starting points. In unfamiliar situations, it is especially unlikely that well-formed preferences will exist.

Because framing effects are inevitable, it is hopelessly inadequate to say that when people lack relevant information the best response is to provide it. To be effective, any effort to inform people must be rooted in an understanding of how people actually think. Presentation makes a great deal of difference: The behavioral consequences of otherwise identical pieces of information depend on how they are framed.

Consider one example from the realm of retirement savings. Benartzi and Thaler (1999) asked participants in a defined contribution savings plan to imagine that they had only two investment options, Fund A and Fund B, and asked them how they would allocate their investments between these two funds. (The two funds were, in fact, a diversified stock fund and an intermediate term bond fund.) All subjects were given information about the historic returns on these funds. However, one group was shown the distribution of annual rates of return, whereas another group was shown simulated 30-year rates of return. The long-term rates of return were derived from the annual rates of return (by drawing years at random from history), and so the two sets of information were, strictly speaking, identical. Nevertheless, participants elected to invest about 40% of their money in equities when shown the annual returns and 90% when shown the long-term rates of return. The lesson from this example is that plan sponsors cannot avoid influencing the choices their participants make simply by providing information. The way they display the information will, in some situations, strongly alter the choices people make.

BEYOND THE INEVITABLE (BUT STILL LIBERTARIAN)

The inevitability of paternalism is most clear when the planner has to choose starting points or default rules. But if the focus is on welfare, it is reasonable to ask whether the planner should go beyond the inevitable and whether such a planner can also claim to be libertarian.

In the domain of employee behavior, there are many imaginable illustrations. Employees might be automatically enrolled in a 401(k) plan, with a right to opt out, but employers might require a waiting period, and perhaps a consultation with an adviser, before the opt-out could be effective. Thaler and Benartzi (2004) have proposed a method of increasing contributions to 401(k) plans that also meets the libertarian test. Under the Save More Tomorrow plan, briefly described in the introduction, employees are invited to sign up for a program in which their contributions to the savings plan are increased annually whenever they get a raise. Once employees join the plan, they stay in until they opt out or reach the maximum savings rate. In the first company to use this plan, the employees who joined increased their savings rates from 3.5% to 11.6% in a little over 2 years (three raises). Very few of the employees who join the plan drop out.

It should now be clear that the difference between libertarian and nonlibertarian paternalism is not simple and rigid. The libertarian paternalist insists on preserving choice, whereas the nonlibertarian paternalist is willing to foreclose choice. But in all cases, a real question is the cost of exercising choice, and here there is a continuum rather than a sharp dichotomy. A libertarian paternalist who is especially enthusiastic about free choice would be inclined to make it relatively costless for people to obtain their preferred outcomes. (Call this a *libertarian* paternalist.) By contrast, a libertarian paternalist who is especially confident of his welfare judgments would be willing to impose real costs on workers and consumers who seek to do what, in the paternalist's view, would not be in their best interests. (Call this a libertarian *paternalist*.)

HOW TO CHOOSE: THE TOOLBOX OF THE LIBERTARIAN PATERNALIST

How should sensible planners choose among possible systems, given that some choice is necessary? We suggest two approaches to this problem. If feasible, a comparison of possible rules should be done using a form of cost–benefit analysis, one that pays serious attention to welfare effects. In many cases, however, such analyses will be both difficult and expensive. As an alternative, we offer some rules of thumb that might be adopted to choose among various options.

COSTS AND BENEFITS

The goal of a cost–benefit study would be to measure the full ramifications of any design choice. In the context at hand, the cost–benefit study cannot be based on WTP, because WTP will be a function of the default rule (Kahneman et al., 1991; Korobkin, 1998). It must be a more open-ended (and inevitably somewhat subjective) assessment of the welfare consequences. To illustrate, take the example of automatic enrollment. Under automatic enrollment, some employees, who otherwise would not join the plan, will now do so. Presumably, some are made better off (especially if there is an employer match), but some may be made worse off (for example, those who are highly liquidity-constrained and do not exercise their right to opt out). A cost–benefit analysis would attempt to evaluate these gains and losses.

If the issue were only enrollment, we think it highly likely that the gains would exceed the losses. Because of the right to opt out, those who need the money immediately are able to have it. In principle one could also compare the costs of foregone current consumption and the benefits of increased consumption during retirement, though this is, admittedly, difficult to do in practice. It is also possible to make inferences from actual choices about welfare. For example, most employees do join the plan eventually, and very few drop out if automatically enrolled (Choi et al., 2002; Madrian & Shea, 2001). These facts suggest that, at least on average, defaulting people into the plan will mostly hasten the rate at which people join the plan and that the vast majority of those who are so nudged will be grateful.

Once the other effects of automatic enrollment are included, the analysis becomes cloudier. Any plan for automatic enrollment must include a specified default savings rate. Some of those automatically enrolled at a 3% savings rate – a typical default in automatic enrollment – would have chosen a higher rate if left to their own devices (Choi et al., 2002). If automatic enrollment leads some or many people to save at a lower rate than they would choose, the plan might be objectionable for that reason. Hence, we are less confident that this more complete cost–benefit analysis would support the particular opt-out system, though a higher savings rate might well do so.

RULES OF THUMB

In many cases, the planner will be unable to make a direct inquiry into welfare, either because too little information is available or because the costs of conducting the analysis are not warranted. The committed antipaternalist might say, in such cases, that people should simply be permitted to choose as they see fit. We hope that we have said enough to show why this response is unhelpful. What people choose often depends on the starting point, and hence the starting point cannot be selected by asking what people choose. In these circumstances, the libertarian paternalist would seek indirect proxies for welfare – methods that test whether one or another approach promotes welfare without relying on guesswork about that question. We suggest three possible methods.

First, the libertarian paternalist might select the approach *that the majority would choose if explicit choices were required and revealed*. In the context of contract law, this is the most familiar inquiry in the selection of default rules (Ayres & Gertner, 1989) – provisions that govern contractual arrangements in the absence of express decisions by the parties. Useful though it is, this market-mimicking approach raises its own problems. Perhaps the majority's choices would be insufficiently informed or a reflection of bounded rationality or bounded self-control. Perhaps those choices would not, in fact, promote the majority's welfare. At least as a presumption, however, it makes sense to follow those choices if the planner knows what they would be.

Second, the libertarian paternalist might select the approach that we have called required active choices, one *that would force people to make their choices explicit*. This approach might be chosen if the market-mimicking strategy fails, either because of the circularity problem or because the planner does not know which approach would in fact be chosen by the majority.

Here, too, however, there is a risk that the choices that are actually elicited will be inadequately informed or will not promote welfare. The only suggestion is that where social planners are unsure how to handle the welfare question, they might devise a strategy that requires people to choose.

Third, the libertarian paternalist might select the approach *that minimizes the number of opt-outs*. Suppose, for example, that when drivers are presumed to want to donate their organs to others, only 10% opt out, but that when drivers are required to signal their willingness to donate their organs to others, 30% opt in. This is an ex post inquiry into people's preferences, in contrast to the ex ante approach favored by the market-mimicking strategy. With those numbers, there is reason to think that the presumption in favor of organ donation is better, if only because more people are sufficiently satisfied to leave it in place.

HOW MUCH CHOICE SHOULD BE OFFERED?

It is far beyond our ambition here to venture a full analysis of the question of how much choice to offer individuals in various domains (Dworkin, 1988, pp. 62–81; Loewenstein, 2000). Instead, we identify some questions that a libertarian paternalist might ask to help decide how much (reasonable) choice to offer.

DO CHOOSERS HAVE INFORMED PREFERENCES?

In some domains, consumers and workers are highly informed – so much so that they will not even be influenced by default rules. Most adults have experimented enough over the course of their lives to have a good sense of what flavors of ice cream they like. They can do a decent job of picking even in a shop offering dozens of flavors. If the default option is asparagus-flavored ice cream, they will be unlikely to choose it and might well be annoyed. But when faced with a menu listing many unfamiliar foods in a foreign country, customers would be unlikely to benefit from being required to choose among them, and they might prefer a small list or ask the waiter for a default suggestion (for example, what do other tourists like?). In such settings, clever restaurants catering to tourists often offer a default "tourist menu." Many actual choices fall between the poles of ice cream flavors and foreign menus. When information is limited, a menu of countless options increases the costs of decisions without increasing the likelihood of accuracy. But when choosers are highly informed, the availability of numerous options decreases the likelihood of error and does not greatly increase decision costs, simply because informed choosers can more easily navigate the menu of options.

Is the Mapping From Options to Preferences Transparent?

If we order a coffee ice cream cone, we have a pretty good idea what we will consume. If we invest $10,000 in a mix of mutual funds, we have little idea (without the aid of sophisticated software) what a change in the portfolio will do to our distribution of expected returns in retirement. When we choose between health plans, we may not fully understand all the ramifications of our choice. If I get a rare disease, will I be able to see a good specialist? How long will I have to wait in line? When people have a hard time predicting how their choices will end up affecting their lives, they have less to gain from having numerous options from which to choose. If it is hard to map from options to preferences, a large set of choices is likely to be cognitively overwhelming, and thus to increase the costs of decisions without also increasing welfare by reducing errors.

How Much Do Preferences Vary Across Individuals?

Some people smoke; others hate the smell of smoke. Some people like hard mattresses; others like soft ones. How do hotels deal with this problem? Most choose to cater to differences in tastes with respect to smoking but not with respect to mattresses. The mattress that appeals to the median hotel guest seems to be good enough to satisfy most customers, but the threat of a smoky room (or a night without cigarettes) is enough to scare customers away. Here is a case in which many people have well-formed preferences that trump default rules. Many planners, both private and public, must make similar tradeoffs. Because offering choice is costly, sensible planners make multiple choices available when people's preferences vary most. The argument for a large option set is thus strongest in cases of preferences that are both clear and heterogeneous. In such cases, people's welfare is likely to be promoted if each can choose as he sees fit, and homogeneity will lead to inaccuracy and thus widespread error costs.

Do Consumers Value Choosing for Themselves, Per Se?

Freedom of choice is itself an ingredient in welfare. In some situations people derive welfare from the very act of choosing. But sometimes it is a chore to have to choose, and the relevant taste can differ across individuals. (One of us derives pleasure from reading and choosing from a wine list; the other finds that enterprise basically intolerable.) A more serious example comes from evidence that many patients do not want to make complex medical decisions and would prefer their doctors to choose for them (Schneider, 1998). The point very much bears on the decision whether to force explicit choices or instead to adopt a default rule that reflects what the majority wants. If making choices is itself a subjective good, the argument for forced choices is strengthened. But much of the time, especially in technical areas, people do not particularly enjoy the process of choice, and a large number of options becomes a burden. By contrast, a thoughtfully chosen default rule, steering them in sensible directions, is a blessing.

OBJECTIONS

The argument for libertarian paternalism seems compelling to us, even obvious, but we suspect that hard-line antipaternalists, and possibly others, will have objections.

The first objection is that by advocating libertarian paternalism, we are starting down a very slippery slope. Once one grants the possibility that default rules for savings or cafeteria lines should be designed paternalistically, it might seem impossible to resist highly nonlibertarian interventions. In the face of the risk of overreaching, might it not be better to avoid starting down the slope at all?

There are three responses. First, in many cases there is simply no viable alternative to paternalism in the weak sense, and hence planners are forced to take at least a few tiny steps down that slope. Recall that paternalism, in the form of effects on behavior, is frequently inevitable. In such cases, the slope cannot be avoided. Second, the libertarian condition, requiring opt-out rights, sharply limits the steepness of the slope. So long as paternalistic interventions can be easily avoided by those who seek to adopt a course of their own, the risks emphasized by antipaternalists are minimal. Third, those who make the slippery slope argument are acknowledging the existence of a self-control problem, at least for planners. But if planners, including bureaucrats and human resource managers, suffer from self-control problems, then it is highly likely that other people do, too.

A second and different sort of objection is based on a deep mistrust of the ability of the planner (especially the planner working for the government) to make sensible choices. Even those who normally believe that everyone chooses rationally treat with deep skepticism any proposal that seems to hinge on rational choices by bureaucrats. We happily grant that planners are human and thus are both boundedly rational and subject to the influence of objectionable pressures (Jolls et al., 1998). Nevertheless, as we have stressed, these human planners are sometimes forced to make choices, and it is surely better to have them trying to improve people's welfare rather than the opposite.

A third objection would come from the opposite direction. Enthusiastic paternalists, emboldened by evidence of bounded rationality and self-control problems, might urge that in many domains, the instruction to engage in only libertarian paternalism is too limiting. At least if the focus is entirely or mostly on welfare, it might seem clear that in certain circumstances, people should not be given freedom of choice for the simple reason that they will choose poorly. In those circumstances, why should anyone insist on libertarian paternalism, as opposed to unqualified or nonlibertarian paternalism?

This objection raises complex issues of both value and fact, and we do not intend to venture into difficult philosophical territory here. Our basic response is threefold. First, we reiterate our understanding that planners are human, and so the real comparison is between boundedly rational choosers with self-control problems and boundedly rational planners facing self-control problems of their own (Jolls et al., 1998). It is doubtful that the comparison can sensibly be made in the abstract. Second, an opt-out right operates as a safeguard against confused or improperly motivated planners, and in many contexts, that safe-guard is crucial even if it potentially creates harm as well. Third, nothing we have said denies the possibility that in some circumstances it can be advisable to impose significant costs on those who reject the proposed course of action, or even to deny freedom of choice altogether. Our only qualification is that when third-party effects are not present, the general presumption should be in favor of freedom of choice, and that presumption should be rebutted only when individual choice is demonstrably inconsistent with individual welfare.

CONCLUSION

Our goal here has been to describe and to advocate libertarian paternalism – an approach that preserves freedom of choice but that encourages both private and public institutions to steer people in directions that will promote their own welfare. Some kind of paternalism is likely whenever such institutions set out default plans or options. Our central empirical claim has been that in many domains, people's preferences are labile and ill formed, and hence starting points and default rules are likely to be quite sticky. In these circumstances, the goal should be to avoid random, inadvertent, arbitrary, or harmful effects and to produce a situation that is likely to promote people's welfare, suitably defined. Indeed, many current social outcomes are, we believe, both random and inadvertent, in the sense that they are a product of default rules whose behavior-shaping effects have never been a product of serious reflection.

In our view, libertarian paternalism is not only a conceptual possibility; it also provides a foundation for rethinking many areas of private and public law. We believe that policies rooted in libertarian paternalism will often be a big improvement on the most likely alternative: inept neglect.

References

The numbers at the end of each reference show which chapters in this volume cite the reference. For a reference that is a chapter in this volume, the chapter number appears in **bold**.

Aaker, D. A. (1991). *Managing brand equity*. New York: The Free Press. [10, 34]

Abdellaoui, M. (2000). Parameter-free elicitation of utility and probability weighting functions. *Management Science, 46*, 1497–1512. [32]

Abelson, R. P., & Levi, A. (1985). Decision making and decision theory. In G. Lindzey & E. Aronson (Eds.), *Handbook of social psychology* (pp. 231–309). New York: Random House. [7, 19]

Ackerman, F., & Heinzerling, L. (2004). *Priceless: On knowing the price of everything and the value of nothing*. New York: The New Press. [36]

Ainslie, G. (1975). Specious reward: A behavioral theory of impulsiveness and impulse control. *Psychological Bulletin, 82*, 463–496. [20]

Ainslie, G. (1992). *Picoeconomics: The strategic interaction of successive motivational states within the person*. New York: Cambridge University Press. [20]

Ainslie, G., & Haslam, N. (1992). Self-control. In G. Loewenstein & J. Elster (Eds.), *Choice over time* (pp. 177–209). New York: Russell Sage Foundation. [20]

Ajzen, I., & Peterson, G. L. (1988). Contingent value measurement: The price of everything and the value of nothing? In G. L. Peterson, B. L. Driver, & R. Gregory (Eds.), *Amenity resource valuation: Integrating economics with other disciplines* (pp. 65–76). State College, PA: Venture. [33]

Alba, J. W., & Chattopadhyay, A. (1985). Effects of context and part-category cues on recall of competing brands. *Journal of Marketing Research, 22*, 340–349. [34]

Alba, J. W., & Hutchinson, J. W. (1987). Dimensions of expertise. *Journal of Consumer Research, 13*, 411–454. [15, 17]

Alba, J. W., Hutchinson, J. W., & Lynch, J. G., Jr. (1991). Memory and decision making. In T. S. Robertson & H. H. Kassarjian (Eds.), *Handbook of consumer behavior* (pp. 1–49). Englewood Cliffs, NJ: Prentice-Hall. [10]

Alba, J. W., Lynch, J. G., Weitz, B., Janiszweki, C., Lutz, R. J., Sawyer, A. G., et al. (1997). Interactive home shopping: Consumer, retailer, and manufacturer incentives to participate in electronic marketplaces. *Journal of Marketing, 61*, 38–53. [17]

Alba, J. W., & Marmorstein, H. (1987). The effects of frequency knowledge on consumer decision making. *Journal of Consumer Research, 14*, 14–26. [17]

Alhakami, A. S., & Slovic, P. (1994). A psychological study of the inverse relationship between perceived risk and perceived benefit. *Risk Analysis, 14*, 1085–1096. [23, 24]

Allais, M. (1953). Le comportement de l'homme rationnel devant le risque: Critique des postulate et axioms de l'école americaine [The behavior of rational man in risk situations: A critique of the axioms and postulates of the American school]. *Econometrica, 21,* 503–546. [1, 2, 9, 19, 27]

Allison, G. T. (1971). *Essence of decision: Explaining the Cuban missile crisis.* Boston: Little Brown. [22]

American Medical Association. (1993). *Strategies for cadaveric organ procurement: Mandated choice and presumed consent.* Chicago: American Medical Association. [37]

Ames, D. R., Flynn, F. J., & Weber, E. U. (2004). It's the thought that counts: On perceiving how helpers decide to lend a hand. *Personality and Social Psychology Bulletin, 30,* 461–474. [21]

Amiel, Y., Cowell, F. A., Davidovitz, L., & Plovin, A. (2003). *Preference reversals and the analysis of income distributions* (No. DARP 66). Retrieved April 20, 2005, from London School of Economics, Suntory and Toyota International Centres for Economics and Related Disciplines Web site: http://sticerd.lse.ac.uk/publications/darp.asp. [1]

Amir, O., & Ariely, D. (in press). Decisions by rules: The case of unwillingness to pay for beneficial delays. *Journal of Marketing Research.* [28, 29]

Anderson, J. R. (1983). *The architecture of cognition.* Cambridge, MA: Harvard University Press. [21]

Anderson, J. R., & Reder, L. M. (1999). The fan effect: New results and new theories. *Journal of Experimental Psychology: General, 128,* 186–197. [21]

Anderson, M. C., & Neely, J. H. (1996). Interference and inhibition in memory retrieval. In E. L. Bjork & R. A. Bjork (Eds.), *Memory* (2nd ed., pp. 237–313). San Diego, CA: Academic Press. [21]

Anderson, M. C., & Spellman, B. A. (1995). On the status of inhibitory mechanisms in cognition: Memory retrieval as a model case. *Psychological Review, 102,* 68–100. [21]

Anderson, N. (1996). *A functional theory of cognition.* Mahwah, NJ: Lawrence Erlbaum Associates. [31]

Anderson, N. D., & Craik, F. I. M. (2000). Memory in the aging brain. In E. Tulving & F. I. M. Craik (Eds.), *The Oxford handbook of memory* (pp. 411–425). Oxford, UK: Oxford University Press. [21]

Argyle, M. (1987). *The psychology of happiness.* London: Methuen. [28]

Ariely, D. (1998). Combining experiences over time: The effects of duration, intensity changes and on-line measurements on retrospective pain evaluations. *Journal of Behavioral Decision Making, 11,* 19–45. [9, 13, 29]

Ariely, D., & Carmon, Z. (2003). Summary assessment of experiences: The whole is different from the sum of its parts. In G. Loewenstein, D. Read, & R. F. Baumeister (Eds.), *Time and decision: Economic and psychological perspectives on intertemporal choice* (pp. 323–349). New York: Russell Sage Foundation. [14]

Ariely, D., & Levav, J. (2000). Sequential choice in group settings: Taking the road less traveled and less enjoyed. *Journal of Consumer Research, 27,* 279–290. [29]

Ariely, D., & Loewenstein, G. (2000). The importance of duration in ratings of and choices between sequences of outcomes. *Journal of Experimental Psychology: General, 129,* 508–523. [13]

Ariely, D., Loewenstein, G., & Prelec, D. (2002). *Determinants of anchoring effects* (Working paper). [13]

Ariely, D., Loewenstein, G., & Prelec, D. (2003). Coherent arbitrariness: Stable demand curves without stable preferences. *The Quarterly Journal of Economics, 118,* 73–105. [1, **13**, 14, 21, 35]

Ariely, D., Loewenstein, G., & Prelec, D. (2006). Tom Sawyer and the myth of fundamental value. *Journal of Economic Behavior & Organization, 60,* 1–10. [1, **14**]

Ariely, D., & Wallsten, T. (1995). Seeking subjective dominance in multidimensional space: An explanation of the asymmetric dominance effect. *Organizational Behavior and Human Decision Processes, 63*, 223–232. [18]

Ariely, D., & Zauberman, G. (2000). On the making of an experience: The effects of breaking and combining experiences on their overall evaluation. *Journal of Behavioral Decision Making, 13*, 219–232. [13]

Arkes, H. R. (2001). *The attribution of cues, implicit memory, and human judgment.* Columbus, OH: Department of Psychology, Ohio State University. [21]

Arkes, H. R., & Ayton, P. (1999). The sunk cost and Concorde effects: Are humans less rational than lower animals? *Psychological Bulletin, 125*, 591–600. [29]

Arkes, H. R., & Blumer, C. (1985). The psychology of sunk cost. *Organizational Behavior and Human Decision Processes, 35*, 124–140. [29]

Arrow, K. J. (1982). Risk perception in psychology and economics. *Economic Inquiry, 20*, 1–9. [6, 27, 31, 34, 36]

Arrow, K. J., Solow, R., Portney, P. R., Leamer, E. E., Radner, R., & Schuman, H. (1993). *Report of the NOAA Panel on Contingent Valuation.* Washington, DC: National Oceanic and Atmospheric Administration. [31, 33, 34]

Axelrod, P. (1976). *Structure of decision: The cognitive maps of political elites.* Princeton, NJ: Princeton University. [18]

Ayres, I., & Gertner, R. (1989). Filling gaps in incomplete contracts: An economic theory of default rules. *Yale Law Journal, 99*, 87–130. [38]

Baddeley, A. D. (1986). *Working memory.* Oxford, UK: Oxford University Press. [20]

Bandura, A. (1997). *Self-efficacy: The exercise of control.* New York: W. H. Freeman. [35]

Barber, B., Heath, C., & Odean, T. (2002). *Good rationales sell: Reason-based choice among group and individual investors in the stock market.* (Working paper). Stanford, CA: Stanford University. [29]

Bar-Gad, I., & Bergman, H. (2001). Stepping out of the box: Information processing in the neural networks of the basal ganglia. *Current Opinion in Neurobiology, 11*, 689–695. [11]

Bargh, J. A., Chen, M., & Burrows, L. (1996). Automaticity of social behavior: Direct effects of trait construct and stereotype activation on action. *Journal of Personality and Social Psychology, 71*, 230–244. [21]

Baron, J. (1988). *Thinking and deciding.* New York: Cambridge University Press. [9, 34]

Baron, J. (1997a). Biases in the quantitative measurement of values for public decisions. *Psychological Bulletin, 122*, 72–88. [34]

Baron, J. (1997b). Confusion of relative and absolute risk in valuation. *Journal of Risk and Uncertainty, 14*, 301–309. [9, 23]

Baron, J. (2000). *Thinking and deciding* (3rd ed.). New York: Cambridge University Press. [12]

Baron, J., & Greene, J. (1996). Determinants of insensitivity to quantity in valuation of public goods: Contribution, warm glow, budget constraints, availability, and prominence. *Journal of Experimental Psychology: Applied, 2*, 107–125. [31, 32, 34]

Baron, J., & Ritov, I. (1994). Reference points and omission bias. *Organizational Behavior and Human Decision Processes, 59*, 475–498. [37]

Baron, J., & Spranca, M. (1997). Protected values. *Organizational Behavior and Human Decision Processes, 70*, 1–16. [34]

Baron, R. M., & Kenny, D. A. (1986). The moderator-mediator variable distinction in social-psychological research: Conceptual, strategic, and statistical considerations. *Journal of Personality and Social Psychology, 51*, 1173–1182. [15]

Barsalou, L. W. (1992). *Cognitive psychology: An overview for cognitive scientists.* Hillsdale, NJ: Lawrence Erlbaum Associates. [31]

Bartels, L. M. (1998, September). *Democracy with attitudes.* Paper presented at the annual meeting of American Political Science Association, Boston. [31]

Bartlett, F. C. (1932). *A study in experimental and social psychology.* Cambridge, UK: Cambridge University Press. [1]

Bateman, I. A., Carson, R., Day, R., Hanemann, M., Hanley, N., Hett, T., et al. (2002). *Economic valuation with stated preference techniques: A manual.* Cheltenham, UK: Edward Elgar Publishing. [1]

Bateman, I. A., Dent, S., Peters, E., Starmer, C., & Slovic, P. (2006). *The affect heuristic and the attractiveness of simple gambles.* (Report No. 06-06). Eugene, OR: Decision Research. [1, 23]

Bateman, I. A., & Willis, K. G. (1999). *Valuing environmental preferences.* New York: Oxford University Press. [38]

Bazerman, M. H., Loewenstein, G., & White, S. B. (1992). Reversals of preference in allocation decisions: Judging an alternative versus choosing among alternatives. *Administrative Science Quarterly, 37,* 220–240. [9, 10, 28]

Bazerman, M. H., Moore, D. A., Tenbrunsel, A. E., Wade-Benzoni, K. A., & Blount, S. (1999). Explaining how preferences change across joint versus separate evaluation. *Journal of Economic Behavior & Organization, 39,* 41–58. [29]

Bazerman, M. H., & Neale, M. A. (1992). *Negotiating rationally.* New York: The Free Press. [34]

Bazerman, M. H., Schroth, H. A., Shah, P. P., Diekmann, K. A., & Tenbrunsel, A. E. (1994). The inconsistent role of comparison others and procedural justice in reactions to hypothetical job descriptions: Implications for job acceptance procedures. *Organizational Behavior and Human Decision Processes, 60,* 326–352. [9]

Bazerman, M. H., Tenbrunsel, A. E., & Wade-Benzoni, K. A. (1998). Negotiating with yourself and losing: Understanding and managing competing internal preferences. *Academy of Management Review, 23,* 225–241. [9]

Bazerman, M. H., White, S. B., & Loewenstein, G. (1995). Perceptions of fairness in interpersonal and individual choice situations. *Current Directions in Psychological Science, 4,* 39–43. [1]

Beach, L. R. (1990). *Image theory: Decision making in personal and organizational contexts.* Chichester, UK: Wiley. [17, 18, 19]

Beach, L. R., & Lipshitz, R. (1993). Why classical decision theory is an appropriate standard for evaluating and aiding most human decision making. In G. A. Klein, J. Orasanu, R. Calderwood, & C. E. Zsambok (Eds.), *Decision making in action: Models and methods* (pp. 21–35). Norwood, NJ: Ables. [18]

Beach, L. R., & Mitchell, T. R. (1978). A contingency model for the selection of decision strategies. *Academy of Management Review, 3,* 439–449. [19]

Beach, L. R., & Mitchell, T. R. (1987). Image theory: Principles, goals, and plans in decision making. *Acta Psychologica, 66,* 201–308. [21]

Beattie, J., & Baron, J. (1991). Investigating the effect of stimulus range on attribute weight. *Journal of Experimental Psychology: Human Perception and Performance, 17,* 571–585. [9]

Beattie, J., Baron, J., Hershey, J. C., & Spranca, M. D. (1994). Psychological determinants of decision attitude. *Journal of Behavioral Decision Making, 7,* 129–144. [16]

Beattie, J., Covey, J., Dolan, P., Hopkins, L., Jones-Lee, M., Loomes, G., et al. (1998). On the contingent valuation of safety and the safety of contingent valuation. *Journal of Risk and Uncertainty, 17*, 5–25. [35]

Bechara, A., Damasio, A. R., Damasio, H., & Anderson, S. W. (1994). Insensitivity to future consequences following damage to human prefrontal cortex. *Cognition, 50*, 7–15. [24]

Becker, G. M., DeGroot, D. H., & Marschak, J. (1963). An experimental study of some stochastic models for wagers. *Behavioral Science, 8*, 41–55. [13]

Becker, G. M., DeGroot, M. H., & Marschak, J. (1964). Measuring utility by a single-response sequential method. *Behavioral Science, 9*, 226–232. [1, 2, 3, 4, 5, 8]

Becker, G. S. (1962). Irrational behavior and economic theory. *Journal of Political Economy, 70*, 1–13. [13]

Becker, G. S. (1968). Crime and punishment: An economic approach. *Journal of Political Economy, 76*, 169–217. [5]

Becker, G. S. (1973). A theory of marriage: Part I. *Journal of Political Economy, 81*, 813–846. [5]

Becker, G. S. (1974). A theory of marriage: Part II. *Journal of Political Economy, 82*, 511–526. [5]

Beckmann, J., & Kuhl, J. (1984). Altering information to gain action control: Functional aspects of human information processing in decision making. *Journal of Research in Personality, 18*, 224–237. [18]

Belk, R. W. (1988). Possessions and the extended self. *Journal of Consumer Research, 15*, 139–168. [17]

Bell, B. E., & Loftus, E. F. (1989). Trivial persuasion in the courtroom: The power of (a few) minor details. *Journal of Personality and Social Psychology, 56*, 669–679. [21]

Bell, D. E. (1982). Regret in decision making under uncertainty. *Operations Research, 30*, 961–981. [36]

Bellah, R., Madsen, R., Sullivan, W., Swindler, A., & Tipton, S. (1985). *Habits of the heart.* Los Angeles: University of California Press. [16]

Bellman, S., Johnson, E. J., & Lohse, G. L. (2001). To opt-in or opt-out? It depends on the question. *Communications of the ACM, 44*(2), 25–27. [37]

Bellman, S., Lohse, G. L., & Johnson, E. J. (1999). Predictors of online buying behavior. *Communications of the ACM, 42*(12), 32–38. [15]

Bem, D. J. (1972). Self-perception theory. In L. Berkowitz (Ed.), *Advances in experimental social psychology* (Vol. 6, pp. 2–62). New York: Academic Press. [22]

Benartzi, S., & Thaler, R. H. (1995). Myopic loss aversion and the equity premium puzzle. *The Quarterly Journal of Economics, 110*, 73–92. [20]

Benartzi, S., & Thaler, R. H. (1999). Risk aversion or myopia? Choices in repeated gambles and retirement investments. *Management Science, 45*, 364–381. [38]

Benartzi, S., & Thaler, R. H. (2002). How much is investor autonomy worth? *Journal of Finance, 57*, 1593–1616. [38]

Benson, L. (1993). *Studies in human decision making: On the effects of experimental instructions, framing, and time constraints.* Unpublished doctoral dissertation, Lund University, Lund, Sweden. [19]

Benson, L., & Svenson, O. (1992). Post-decision consolidation following the debriefing of subjects about experimental manipulations affecting their prior decisions. *Lund University, Psychological Research Bulletin, 32*(3). [19]

Bentham, J. (1996). *An introduction to the principles of morals and legislation* (J. H. Burns & H. L. A. Hart, Eds.). New York: Oxford University Press (Original work published in 1823). [27]

Benthin, A., Slovic, P., Moran, P., Severson, H., Mertz, C. K., & Gerrard, M. (1995). Adolescent health-threatening and health-enhancing behaviors: A study of word association and imagery. *Journal of Adolescent Health, 17*, 143–152. [23]

Benthorn, L. (1994). *On post-decision processes.* Unpublished doctoral dissertation, Lund University, Lund, Sweden. [19]

Berg, J. E., Dickhaut, J. W., & O'Brien, J. R. (1985). Preference reversal and arbitrage. In V. L. Smith (Ed.), *Research in experimental economics* (pp. 31–72). Greenwich, CT: JAI Press. [8]

Berg, J. E., Dickhaut, J. W., & Rietz, T. A. (2003). Preference reversals and induced risk preferences: Evidence for noisy maximization. *Journal of Risk and Uncertainty, 27*, 139–170. [1]

Berman, L. (1982). *Planning a tragedy.* New York: Norton. [22]

Bernoulli, D. (1954). Exposition of a new theory on the measurement of risk (L. Sommer, Trans.). *Econometrica, 22*, 23–36 (Reprinted from *Commentarii Academiae Scientiarum Imperialis Petropolitanae, 1738*, 5, 175–192). [2]

Bettman, J. R. (1979). *An information processing theory of consumer choice.* Reading, MA: Addison-Wesley. [1, 17]

Bettman, J. R., Johnson, E. J., & Payne, J. W. (1991). Consumer decision making. In T. S. Robertson & H. H. Kassarjian (Eds.), *Handbook of consumer behavior* (pp. 50–84). Englewood Cliffs, NJ: Prentice-Hall. [19]

Bettman, J. R., & Kakkar, P. (1977). Effects of information presentation format on consumer information acquisition strategies. *Journal of Consumer Research, 3*, 233–240. [7]

Bettman, J. R., Luce, M. F., & Payne, J. W. (1998). Constructive consumer choice processes. *Journal of Consumer Research, 25*, 187–217. [1, **17**, 29, 34]

Bettman, J. R., & Park, C. W. (1980). Effects of prior knowledge and experience and phase of the choice process on consumer decision processes: A protocol analysis. *Journal of Consumer Research, 7*, 234–248. [17]

Bettman, J. R., Payne, J. W., & Staelin, R. (1986). Cognitive considerations in designing effective labels for presenting risk information. *Journal of Marketing and Public Policy, 5*, 1–28. [34]

Bettman, J. R., & Sujan, M. (1987). Effects of framing on evaluation of comparable and noncomparable alternatives by expert and novice consumers. *Journal of Consumer Research, 14*, 141–154. [15, 17]

Bettman, J. R., & Zins, M. A. (1979). Information format and choice task effects in decision making. *Journal of Consumer Research, 6*, 141–153. [7]

Betts, R., & Gelb, L. (1979). *The irony of Vietnam: The system worked.* Washington, DC: Brookings Institution. [22]

Bewley, T. F. (1998). Why not cut pay? *European Economic Review, 62*, 459–490. [13]

Beyth-Marom, R., & Fischhoff, B. (1997). Adolescent decisions about risk. In J. Schulenberg, J. Maggs, & K. Hurnelmans (Eds.), *Health risks and developmental transactions during adolescence* (pp. 110–135). New York: Cambridge University Press. [35]

Biehal, G., & Chakravarti, D. (1983). Information accessibility as a moderator of consumer choice. *Journal of Consumer Research, 10*, 1–14. [10]

Biehal, G., & Chakravarti, D. (1986). Consumers' use of memory and external information on choice: Macro and micro perspectives. *Journal of Consumer Research, 12*, 382–405. [15]

Biel, A., & Montgomery, H. (1986). Scenarios in energy planning. In B. Brehmer, H. Jungermann, P. Lourens, & G. Sevon (Eds.), *New directions in research on decision making* (pp. 205–218). Amsterdam: North-Holland. [18]

Bigelow, J. (Ed.). (1887). *The complete works of Benjamin Franklin* (Vol. 4). New York: Putnam. [22]

Billig, M. (1987). *Arguing and thinking: A rhetorical approach to social psychology.* New York: Cambridge University Press. [22]

Billig, M. (1991). *Ideology and opinions.* London: Sage. [18]

Billings, R. S., & Scherer, L. L. (1988). The effect of response mode and importance on decision-making strategies: Judgment versus choice. *Organizational Behavior and Human Decision Processes, 41*, 1–19. [10]

Birnbaum, M. H. (1982). Controversies in psychological measurement. In B. Wegener (Ed.), *Social attitudes and psychophysical measurement* (pp. 401–485). Hillsdale, NJ: Lawrence Erlbaum Associates. [1]

Birnbaum, M. H. (1992). Issues in utility measurement. *Organizational Behavior and Human Decision Processes, 52*, 319–330. [9]

Birnbaum, M. H., & Mellers, B. A. (1979). Stimulus recognition may mediate exposure effects. *Journal of Personality and Social Psychology, 37*, 1090–1096. [25]

Birnbaum, M. H., & Stegner, S. E. (1979). Source credibility in social judgment: Bias, expertise, and the judge's point of view. *Journal of Personality and Social Psychology, 37*, 48–74. [21]

Birnbaum, M. H., & Sutton, S. E. (1992). Scale convergence and utility measurement. *Organizational Behavior and Human Decision Processes, 52*, 183–215. [1, 11]

Bishop, R. C. (1986). Resource valuation under uncertainty: Theoretical principles for empirical research. In V. K. Smith (Ed.), *Advances in applied micro-economics* (Vol. 4, pp. 133–152). Greenwich, CT: JAI Press. [33]

Bishop, R. C., & Heberlein, T. A. (1979). Measuring values of extramarket goods: Are indirect measures biased? *American Journal of Agricultural Economics, 61*, 926–930. [33]

Bizer, G. Y., & Krosnick, J. A. (2001). Exploring the structure of strength-related attitude features: The relation between attitude importance and attitude accessibility. *Journal of Personality and Social Psychology, 81*, 566–586. [15]

Blattberg, R. C., & Neslin, S. A. (1990). *Sales promotion: Concepts, methods, and strategies.* Englewood Cliffs, NJ: Prentice-Hall. [22]

Bleichrodt, H., & Pinto, J. (2000). A parameter-free elicitation of the probability weighting function in medical decision analysis. *Management Science, 46*, 1485–1497. [32]

Blom Kemdal, A., & Montgomery, H. (1997). Perspectives and emotions in personal decision making. In R. Ranyard, W. R. Crozier, & O. Svenson (Eds.), *Decision making: Cognitive models and explanations* (pp. 72–89). London: Routledge. [18]

Blount, S., & Bazerman, M. H. (1996). The inconsistent evaluation of absolute versus comparative payoffs in labor supply and bargaining. *Journal of Economic Behavior & Organization, 30*, 227–240. [9]

Bockenholt, U., Albert, D., Aschenbrenner, M., & Schmalhofer, F. (1991). The effects of attractiveness, dominance, and attribute differences on information acquisition in multiattribute binary choice. *Organizational Behavior and Human Decision Processes, 49*, 258–281. [18]

Bohm, P. (1994). Behavior under uncertainty without preference reversals: A field experiment. *Empirical Economics, 19*, 185–200. [1]

Bohm, P., & Lind, H. (1993). Preference reversal, real-world lotteries, and lottery-interested subjects. *Journal of Economic Behavior & Organization, 22*, 327–348. [1]

Bornstein, R. F. (1989). Exposure and affect: Overview and meta-analysis of research, 1968–1987. *Psychological Bulletin, 106*, 265–289. [23]

Bostic, R., Herrnstein, R. J., & Luce, R. D. (1990). The effect on the preference-reversal phenomenon of using choice indifferences. *Journal of Economic Behavior & Organization, 13*, 193–212. [1, 8]

Bovie, P. (Ed.). (1992). *Terence: The comedies.* Baltimore: Johns Hopkins University Press. [16]

Bower, G. (1981). Mood and memory. *American Psychologist, 36*, 129–148. [24]

Boyle, K., Desvousges, W., Johnson, F., Dunford, R., & Hudson, S. (1994). An investigation of part-whole biases in contingent valuation studies. *Journal of Environmental Economics and Management, 27*, 64–83. [32]

Bradley, M. M., & Lang, P. J. (1994). Measuring emotion: The Self-Assessment Manikin and the semantic differential. *Journal of Behavior Therapy and Experimental Psychiatry, 25*, 49–59. [24]

Braga, J., & Starmer, C. (2004). *Does market experience eliminate preference reversal?* Unpublished manuscript. [1]

Brandstätter, E., Kühberger, A., & Schneider, F. (2002). A cognitive-emotional account of the shape of the probability weighting function. *Journal of Behavioral Decision Making, 15*, 79–100. [32]

Brehm, J. W. (1956). Post-decision changes in desirability of alternatives. *Journal of Abnormal and Social Psychology, 52*, 384–389. [19, 26]

Brehm, J. W. (1966). *A theory of psychological reactance.* New York: Academic Press. [16]

Brehmer, B. (1990). Strategies in real-time dynamic decision making. In R. Hogarth (Ed.), *Insights in decision making: A tribute to Hillel J. Einhorn* (pp. 262–279). Chicago: University of Chicago Press. [18]

Brickman, P., Coates, D., & Janoff-Bulman, R. J. (1978). Lottery winners and accident victims: Is happiness relative? *Journal of Personality and Social Psychology, 36*, 917–927. [27, 28, 30]

Bromley, D. (Ed.). (1986). *National resource economics: Policy problems and contemporary analysis.* Boston: Kluwer/Nijhoff Publishing. [33]

Brookshire, D. S., & Coursey, D. (1987). Measuring the value of a public good: An empirical comparison of elicitation procedures. *American Economic Review, 77*(4), 554–566. [33]

Brookshire, D. S., Thayer, M. A., Schulze, W. D., & D'Arge, R. C. (1982). Valuing public goods: A comparison of survey and hedonic approaches. *American Economic Review, 72*(1), 165–177. [33]

Brown & Williamson Tobacco Company. (1999). *Kool Natural Lights* [Advertisement]. [23]

Brown, C., & Feinberg, F. (2002). How does choice affect evaluations? *Advances in Consumer Research, 29*, 331–332. [28]

Brown, T. C. (1984). The concept of value in resource allocation. *Land Economics, 60*, 231–246. [33]

Brown, T. C., & Slovic, P. (1988). Effects of context on economic measures of value. In G. L. Peterson, B. L. Driver, & R. Gregory (Eds.), *Integrating economic and psychological knowledge in valuations of public amenity resources* (pp. 23–30). State College, PA: Venture. [33]

Brownstein, A. (2003). Biased pre-decision processing. *Psychological Bulletin, 129,* 545–568. [12, 19]

Brucks, M. (1985). The effects of product class knowledge on information search behavior. *Journal of Consumer Research, 11,* 1–16. [15]

Brucks, M. (1988). Search monitor: An approach for computer-controlled experiments involving consumer information search. *Journal of Consumer Research, 15,* 117–121. [15]

Bruner, J. S. (1957). On perceptual readiness. *Psychological Review, 64,* 123–152. [15]

Bruner, J. S., Goodnow, J. J., & Austin, G. A. (1956). *A study of thinking.* New York: Wiley. [2]

Busemeyer, J. R., & Diederich, A. (2002). Survey of decision field theory. *Mathematical Social Sciences, 43,* 345–370. [11]

Busemeyer, J. R., & Goldstein, D. G. (1992). Linking together different measures of preference: A dynamic model of matching derived from decision field theory. *Organizational Behavior and Human Decision Processes, 52,* 370–396. [11]

Busemeyer, J. R., Hastie, R., & Medin, D. L. (1995). *Decision making from a cognitive perspective.* San Diego, CA: Academic. [23]

Busemeyer, J. R., & Townsend, J. T. (1992). Fundamental derivations for decision field theory. *Mathematical Social Sciences, 23,* 255–282. [11]

Busemeyer, J. R., & Townsend, J. T. (1993). Decision field theory: A dynamic cognition approach to decision making. *Psychological Review, 100,* 432–459. [11, 12, 19]

Busemeyer, J. R., Townsend, J. T., & Stout, J. C. (2002). Motivational underpinnings of utility in decision making: Decision Field Theory analysis of deprivation and satiation. In S. C. Moore & M. Oaksford (Eds.), *Advances in consciousness research: Vol. 44. Emotional cognition: From brain to behaviour* (pp. 197–219). Amsterdam: John Benjamins. [11]

Cabanac, M. (1992). Pleasure: The common currency. *Journal of Theoretical Biology, 155,* 173–200. [24]

Calabresi, G., & Melamed, A. D. (1972). Property rules, liability rules, and inalienability: One view of the cathedral. *Harvard Law Review, 85,* 1089–1128. [38]

Caldwell, C. (2004, March 1). Select all: Can we have too many choices? *The New Yorker,* pp. 91–93. [1]

Calle, E. E., Thun, M. J., Petrelli, J. M., Rodriguez, C., & Heath, C. W., Jr. (1999). Body-mass index and mortality in a prospective cohort of U.S. adults. *New England Journal of Medicine, 341,* 1097–1105. [38]

Camerer, C. F. (2000). Prospect theory in the wild: Evidence from the field. In D. Kahneman & A. Tversky (Eds.), *Choices, values, and frames* (pp. 288–300). Cambridge, UK: Cambridge University Press. [38]

Camerer, C. F., Babcock, L., Loewenstein, G., & Thaler, R. H. (1997). Labor supply of New York City cab drivers: One day at a time. *The Quarterly Journal of Economics, 112,* 407–441. [20]

Camerer, C. F., & Ho, T. (1994). Violations of the betweenness axiom and nonlinearity in probabilities. *Journal of Risk and Uncertainty, 8,* 167–196. [32]

Camerer, C. F., & Hogarth, R. M. (1999). The effects of financial incentives in experiments: A review and capital-labor-production framework. *Journal of Risk and Uncertainty, 19,* 1–3, 7–42. [38]

Camerer, C. F., Issacharoff, S., Loewenstein, G., O'Donoghue, T., & Rabin, M. (2003). Regulation for conservatives: Behavioral economics and the case for "asymmetric paternalism." *University of Pennsylvania Law Review, 151*, 2111–2154. [37]

Camerer, C. F., Loewenstein, G., & Weber, M. (1989). The curse of knowledge in economic settings: An experimental analysis. *Journal of Political Economy, 117*, 1232–1254. [13]

Caplan, A. L. (1994). Current ethical issues in organ procurement and transplantation. *Journal of the American Medical Association, 272*, 1708–1709. [37]

Card, S. K., Moran, T. P., & Newell, A. (1983). *The psychology of human computer interaction.* Hillsdale, NJ: Lawrence Erlbaum Associates. [7]

Carlson, K. A., & Klein Pearo, L. (2004). Limiting predecisional distortion by prior valuation of attribute components. *Organizational Behavior and Human Decision Processes, 94*, 48–59. [19]

Carlson, K. A., & Russo, J. E. (2001). Biased interpretation of evidence by mock jurors. *Journal of Experimental Psychology: Applied, 7*, 91–103. [21]

Carroll, J. D. (1972). Individual differences and multidimensional scaling. In R. N. Shepard, A. K. Romney, & S. Neriove (Eds.), *Multidimensional scaling: Theory and applications in the behavioral sciences: Vol. 1. Theory* (pp. 105–155). New York: Seminar Press. [6]

Carson, R. T., Hanemann, M., Kopp, R., Krosnick, J., Mitchell, R., Presser, S., et al. (1994). *Prospective interim lost use value due to DDT and PCB contamination in the Southern California Bight.* La Jolla, CA: Natural Resource Damage Assessment. [31]

Carson, R. T., & Mitchell, R. C. (1993). The issue of scope in contingent valuation studies. *American Journal of Agricultural Economics, 75*, 1263–1267. [31, 32]

Carson, R. T., & Mitchell, R. C. (1995). Sequencing and nesting in contingent valuation surveys. *Journal of Environmental Economics and Management, 28*, 155–173. [31]

Casey, J. T. (1991). Reversal of the preference reversal phenomenon. *Organizational Behavior and Human Decision Processes, 48*, 224–251. [1]

Centers for Disease Control and Prevention. (2003). *1991–2001 prevalence of obesity among U.S. adults, by characteristics.* Retrieved May 6, 2004, from http://www.cdc.gov/nccdphp/dnpa/obesity/trend/prev_char.htm. [38]

Chaiken, S., & Trope, Y. (1999). *Dual-process theories in social psychology.* New York: Guilford Press. [1, 32]

Chapman, G. B., & Bornstein, B. (1996). The more you ask the more you get: Anchoring in personal injury verdicts. *Applied Cognitive Psychology, 10*, 519–540. [31]

Chapman, G. B., & Johnson, E. J. (1994). The limits of anchoring. *Journal of Behavioral Decision Making, 7*, 223–242. [21]

Chapman, G. B., & Johnson, E. J. (1999). Anchoring, activation, and the construction of values. *Organizational Behavior and Human Decision Processes, 79*, 115–153. [13, 14, 15, 21]

Chapman, G. B., & Johnson, E. J. (2002). Incorporating the irrelevant: Anchors in judgments of belief and value. In T. Gilovich, D. Griffin, & D. Kahneman (Eds.), *Intuitive judgment: Heuristics and biases* (pp. 120–138). Cambridge, UK: Cambridge University Press. [21]

Chen, M., & Bargh, J. A. (1999). Consequences of automatic evaluation: Immediate behavioral predispositions to approach or avoid the stimulus. *Personality and Social Psychology Bulletin, 25*, 215–224. [24]

Cherry, T. L., Crocker, T. D., & Shogren, J. F. (2003). Rationality spillovers. *Journal of Environmental Economics and Management, 45*, 63–84. [1]

Chitturi, R., Raghunathan, R., & Mahajan, V. (2003). *Form vs. function: Emotional and behavioral consequences of trading off hedonic vs. utilitarian attributes* (Working paper). University of Texas, Austin. [29]

Choi, J. J., Laibson, D., Madrian, B. C., & Metrick, A. (2002). Defined contribution pensions: Plan rules, participant decisions, and the path of least resistance. In J. M. Poterba (Ed.), *Tax policy and the economy* (Vol. 16, pp. 67–113). Cambridge, MA: MIT Press. [38]

Choi, J. J., Laibson, D., Madrian, B. C., & Metrick, A. (2004). For better or for worse: Default effects and 401(k) savings behavior. In D. Wise (Ed.), *Perspectives in the economics of aging* (pp. 81–121). University of Chicago. [37]

Christensen-Szalanski, J. J. J. (1978). Problem-solving strategies: A selection mechanism, some implications, and some data. *Organizational Behavior and Human Performance, 22*, 307–323. [16]

Christensen-Szalanski, J. J. J. (1980). A further examination of the selection of problem-solving strategies: The effects of deadlines and analytic aptitudes. *Organizational Behavior and Human Performance, 25*, 107–122. [16]

Christensen-Szalanski, J. J. J. (1984). Discount functions and the measurement of patients' values: Women's values during childbirth. *Medical Decision Making, 4*, 47–58. [27]

Chu, Y. P., & Chu, R. L. (1990). The subsidence of preference reversals in simplified and marketlike experimental settings: A note. *American Economic Review, 80*(4), 902–911. [1]

Cicchetti, C., & Dubin, J. (1994). A microeconomic analysis of risk aversion and the decision to self-insure. *Journal of Political Economy, 102*, 169–186. [20]

Clay, M., & Block, W. (2002). A free market for human organs. *Journal of Social, Political, and Economic Studies, 27*, 227–236. [37]

Clemen, R. T. (1996). *Making hard decisions: An introduction to decision analysis*. Belmont, CA: Duxbury. [34]

Coase, R. H. (1960). The problem of social cost. *Journal of Law and Economics, 3*, 1–44. [37]

Cohen, M. S. (1993). The naturalistic basis of decision biases. In G. A. Klein, J. Orasanu, R. Calderwood, & C. E. Zsambok (Eds.), *Decision making in action: Models and methods* (pp. 51–99). Norwood, NJ: Ables. [18]

Cohen, M. S., Freeman, J. P., & Wolf, S. (1996). Metarecognition in time-stressed decision making: Recognizing, critiquing, and correcting. *Human Factors, 38*, 206–219. [18]

Collins, A. M., & Loftus, E. F. (1975). A spreading activation theory of semantic processing. *Psychological Review, 82*, 407–428. [15, 21]

Collins, B. E., & Hoyt, M. G. (1972). Personal responsibility for consequences: An integration and extension of the "forced compliance" literature. *Journal of Experimental Social Psychology, 8*, 558–593. [16]

Connolly, T., & Zeelenberg, M. (2002). Regret in decision making. *Current Directions in Psychological Science, 11*, 212–215. [24]

Constans, J. I., & Mathews, A. M. (1993). Mood and the subjective risk of future events. *Cognition & Emotion, 7*, 545–560. [24]

Coombs, C. H. (1958). On the use of inconsistency of preference in psychological measurement. *Journal of Experimental Psychology, 55*, 1–7. [19]

Coombs, C. H., Bezembinder, T. G., & Goode, F. M. (1967). Testing expectation theories of decision making without measuring utility or subjective probability. *Journal of Mathematical Psychology, 4,* 72–103. [2, 3, 6]

Coombs, C. H., & Pruitt, D. G. (1960). Components of risk in decision making: Probability and variance preferences. *Journal of Experimental Psychology, 60,* 265–277. [1, 2]

Cooper, J., & Fazio, R. H. (1984). A new look at dissonance theory. In L. Berkowitz (Ed.), *Advances in experimental social psychology* (Vol. 17, pp. 229–266). Orlando, FL: Academic Press. [16]

Cordova, D. I., & Lepper, M. R. (1996). Intrinsic motivation and the process of learning: Beneficial effects of contextualization, personalization, and choice. *Journal of Educational Psychology, 88,* 715–730. [16]

Cortese, A. E., & Stepanek, M. (1998, May 4). Goodbye to fixed pricing? How electronic commerce could create the most efficient market of them all. *Business Week,* pp. 70–71. [15]

Coupey, E. (1994). Restructuring: Constructive processing of information displays in consumer choice. *Journal of Consumer Research, 21,* 83–99. [17, 19]

Coupey, E., Irwin, J. R., & Payne, J. W. (1998). Product category familiarity and preference construction. *Journal of Consumer Research, 24,* 459–467. [9, 15]

Coursey, D. L., Hovis, J. J., & Schulze, W. D. (1987). The disparity between willingness to accept and willingness to pay measures of value. *The Quarterly Journal of Economics, 102,* 679–690. [9]

Cox, J. C., & Epstein, S. (1989). Preference reversals without the independence axiom. *American Economic Review, 79*(3), 408–426. [1, 8]

Cox, J. C., & Grether, D. M. (1996). The preference reversal phenomenon: Response mode, markets, and incentives. *Economic Theory, 7,* 381–405. [1, 13]

Cronbach, L. J., & Meehl, P. M. (1955). Construct validity in psychological tests. *Psychological Bulletin, 52,* 281–302. [33]

Cropper, M. L., Aydede, S. K., & Portney, P. R. (1994). Preferences for life-saving programs: How the public discounts time and age. *Journal of Risk and Uncertainty, 8,* 243–265. [38]

Cubitt, R. P., Munro, A., & Starmer, C. (2004). Testing explanations of preference reversal. *The Economic Journal, 114,* 709–726. [1]

Cummings, R. G., Brookshire, D. S., & Schulze, W. D. (1986). *Valuing environmental goods: Assessment of the contingent valuation method.* Totowa, NJ: Rowman and Allanheld. [1, 33]

Cummings, R. G., Harrison, G. W., & Rutstrom, E. E. (1995). Homegrown values and hypothetical surveys: Is the dichotomous choice approach incentive-compatible? *American Economic Review, 85*(1), 260–266. [31]

Dahlstrand, U., & Montgomery, H. (1984). Information search and evaluative processes in decision making: A computer-based process tracing study. *Acta Psychologica, 56,* 113–123. [18]

Dale, H. C. A. (1959). A priori probabilities in gambling. *Nature, 183,* 842–843. [2]

Damasio, A. R. (1994). *Descartes' error: Emotion, reason, and the human brain.* New York: Avon. [1, 23, 24]

Damasio, A. R., Tranel, D., & Damasio, H. (1990). Individuals with sociopathic behavior caused by frontal damage fail to respond autonomically to social stimuli. *Behavioural Brain Research, 41,* 81–94. [23]

Darley, J. M., & Berscheid, E. (1967). Increased liking caused by the anticipation of interpersonal contact. *Human Relations, 10*, 29–40. [30]

Davidson, A. R., Yantis, S., Norwood, M., & Montano, D. E. (1985). Amount of information about the attitude object and attitude-behavior consistency. *Journal of Personality and Social Psychology, 49*, 1184–1198. [26]

Davidson, D., & Marschak, J. (1959). Experimental tests of a stochastic decision theory. In C. W. Churchman & P. Ratoosh (Eds.), *Measurement: Definitions and theories* (pp. 233–269). New York: Wiley. [2]

Dawes, R. M. (1977). Predictive models as a guide to preference. *IEEE Transactions on Systems, Man and Cybernetics, SMC-7*, 355–358. [33]

Dawes, R. M. (1979). The robust beauty of improper linear models in decision making. *American Psychologist, 34*, 571–582. [17]

Dawes, R. M. (1998). Behavioral decision making, judgment, and inference. In D. Gilbert, S. Fiske, & G. Lindzey (Eds.), *Handbook of social psychology* (pp. 589–597). Boston: McGraw-Hill. [19]

De Bondt, W. F. M., & Thaler, R. H. (1990). Do security analysts overreact? *American Economic Review, 80*(2), 52–57. [38]

de Charms, R. (1968). *Personal causation.* New York: Academic Press. [16]

de Tocqueville, A. (1969). *Democracy in America.* New York: Harper & Row (Original work published 1830). [16]

Deci, E. L. (1975). *Intrinsic motivation.* New York: Plenum Press. [16]

Deci, E. L. (1981). *The psychology of self-determination.* Lexington, MA: Heath. [16]

Deci, E. L., & Ryan, R. M. (1985). *Intrinsic motivation and self-determination in human behavior.* New York: Plenum Press. [16]

DeKay, M., & McClelland, G. (1996). Probability and utility components of endangered species preservation programs. *Journal of Experimental Psychology: Applied, 2*, 60–83. [31, 34]

Delucchi, K. L. (1983). The use and misuse of chi-square: Lewis and Burke revisited. *Psychological Bulletin, 94*, 166–176. [16]

DeMaio, T. J., & Rothgeb, J. M. (1996). Cognitive interviewing techniques: In the lab and in the field. In N. Schwarz & S. Sudman (Eds.), *Answering questions: Methodology for determining cognitive and communication processes in survey research* (pp. 177–195). San Francisco: Jossey-Bass. [34]

Dember, W. N., Galinsky, T. L., & Warm, J. S. (1992). The role of choice in vigilance performance. *Bulletin of the Psychonomic Society, 30*, 201–204. [16]

Dembo, T. (1931). Der Ärger als dynamisches Problem [Anger as a dynamic problem]. *Psychologische Forschung, 15*, 1–144. [19]

Denes-Raj, V., & Epstein, S. (1994). Conflict between intuitive and rational processing: When people behave against their better judgment. *Journal of Personality and Social Psychology, 66*, 819–829. [23]

Desvousges, W. H., Johnson, F. R., Dunford, R. W., Boyle, K. J., Hudson, S. P., & Wilson, K. N. (1992). *Measuring nonuse damages using contingent valuation: An experimental evaluation of accuracy* (Research Triangle Institute Monograph 92–1). Research Triangle Park, NC: Research Triangle Institute. [1, 9, 31]

Desvousges, W. H., Johnson, F. R., Dunford, R. W., Boyle, K. J., Hudson, S. P., & Wilson, K. N. (1993). Measuring natural resource damages with contingent valuation: Tests of validity and reliability. In J. A. Hausman (Ed.), *Contingent valuation: A critical assessment* (pp. 91–164). Amsterdam: North-Holland. [32]

Desvousges, W. H., Smith, V. K., & Fisher, A. (1987). Option price estimates for water quality improvements: A contingent valuation study for the Monongahela River. *Journal of Environmental Economics and Management, 14,* 248–267. [33]

Devine, P. C. (1989). Stereotypes and prejudice: Their automatic and controlled components. *Journal of Personality and Social Psychology, 56,* 5–18. [15]

Dhar, R. (1997). Consumer preference for a no-choice option. *Journal of Consumer Research, 24,* 215–231. [10, 16]

Dhar, R., & Nowlis, S. M. (1999). The effect of time pressure on consumer choice deferral. *Journal of Consumer Research, 25,* 369–384. [16]

Dhar, R., Nowlis, S. M., & Sherman, S. J. (1999). Comparison effects on preference construction. *Journal of Consumer Research, 26,* 293–306. [28]

Dhar, R., Nowlis, S. M., & Sherman, S. J. (2000). Trying hard or hardly trying: An analysis of context effects in choice. *Journal of Consumer Psychology, 9,* 189–200. [11]

Dhar, R., & Simonson, I. (2003). The effect of forced choice on choice. *Journal of Marketing Research, 40,* 146–160. [11]

Dhar, R., & Wertenbroch, K. (2000). Consumer choice between hedonic and utilitarian goods. *Journal of Marketing Research, 27,* 60–71. [32]

Diamond, P. A. (1996). Testing the internal consistency of contingent valuation surveys. *Journal of Environmental Economics and Management, 30,* 337–347. [31]

Diamond, P. A., & Hausman, J. A. (1994). Contingent valuation: Is some number better than no number? *The Journal of Economic Perspectives, 8*(4), 45–64. [31]

Diamond, P. A., Hausman, J. A., Leonard, G., & Denning, M. (1993). Does contingent valuation measure preferences? Experimental evidence. In J. A. Hausman (Ed.), *Contingent valuation: A critical assessment* (pp. 41–85). Amsterdam: North-Holland. [31]

Dickens, W. T., & Katz, L. F. (1987). Inter-industry wage differences and industry characteristics. In K. Lang & J. S. Leonard (Eds.), *Unemployment and the structure of labor markets* (pp. 48–89). Oxford, UK: Basil Blackwell. [13]

Dickie, M., Fisher, A., & Gerking, S. (1987). Market transactions and hypothetical demand data: A comparative study. *Journal of the American Statistical Association, 82,* 69–75. [33]

Diederich, A. (1997). Dynamic stochastic models for decision making under time constraints. *Journal of Mathematical Psychology, 41,* 260–274. [11]

Diederich, A., & Busemeyer, J. R. (2003). Simple matrix methods for analyzing diffusion models of choice probability, choice response time, and simple response time. *Journal of Mathematical Psychology, 47,* 304–322. [11]

Diener, E. (2000). Subjective well-being: The science of happiness and a proposal for a national index. *American Psychologist, 55,* 34–43. [28]

Diener, E., Scollon, C. N., & Lucas, R. E. (2003). The evolving concept of subjective well-being: The multifaceted nature of happiness. In P. T. Costa & I. C. Siegler (Eds.), *Advances in cell aging and gerontology: Vol. 15. Relevant advances in psychology and aging* (pp. 187–219). Amsterdam: Elsevier. [28]

Diener, E., Suh, E. M., Lucas, R. E., & Smith, H. L. (1999). Subjective well-being: Three decades of progress. *Psychological Bulletin, 125,* 276–302. [28]

Dougherty, M. R. P., Gettys, C. F., & Ogden, E. E. (1999). MINERVA-DM: A memory processes model for judgments of likelihood. *Psychological Review, 106,* 180–209. [21]

Dougherty, M. R. P., Gronlund, S. D., & Gettys, C. F. (2003). Memory as a fundamental heuristic for decision making. In S. L. Schneider & J. Shanteau (Eds.), *Emerging perspectives on judgment and decision making* (pp. 125–164). Cambridge, UK: Cambridge University Press. [21]

Downs, J. S., Murray, P. J., Bruine de Bruin, W., White, J. P., Palmgren, C., & Fischhoff, B. (2004). An interactive video program to reduce adolescent females' STD risk: A randomized controlled trial. *Social Science and Medicine, 59*, 1561–1572. [35]

Doyle, J. R., O'Connor, D. J., Reynolds, G. M., & Bottomley, P. A. (1999). The robustness of the asymmetrically dominated effect: Buying frames, phantom alternatives, and in-store purchases. *Psychology & Marketing, 16*, 225–243. [1]

Drolet, A. (1997). *Generic preferences*. Unpublished doctoral dissertation, Stanford University, Stanford, CA. [17]

Drolet, A., Simonson, I., & Tversky, A. (2000). Indifference curves that travel with the choice set. *Marketing Letters, 11*, 199–209. [13]

Dunn, E. W., Wilson, T. D., & Gilbert, D. T. (2003). Location, location, location: The misprediction of satisfaction in housing lotteries. *Personality and Social Psychology Bulletin, 29*, 1421–1432. [28]

Dunning, D., Griffin, D. W., Milojkovoc, J., & Ross, L. (1990). The overconfidence effect in social predication. *Journal of Personality and Social Psychology, 58*, 568–581. [30]

Dutton, D. G., & Aron, A. P. (1974). Some evidence for heightened sexual attraction under conditions of high anxiety. *Journal of Personality and Social Psychology, 30*, 510–517. [30]

Dworkin, G. (1988). *The theory and practice of autonomy*. Cambridge, UK: Cambridge University Press. [38]

Eagly, A. H., & Chaiken, S. (1993). *The psychology of attitudes*. Fort Worth, TX: Harcourt Brace Jovanovich College. [31]

Eagly, A. H., & Chaiken, S. (1998). Attitude structure and function. In D. T. Gilbert, S. T. Fiske, & G. Lindzey (Eds.), *The handbook of social psychology* (4th ed., Vol. 1, pp. 269–322). Boston: McGraw-Hill. [31]

Easterlin, R. A. (1974). Does economic growth improve the human lot? In P. A. David & M. W. Reder (Eds.), *Nations and households in economic growth: Essays in honor of Moses Abramovitz* (pp. 89–125). New York: Academic Press. [28]

Easterlin, R. A. (2001). Income and happiness: Towards a unified theory. *The Economic Journal, 111*, 465–484. [28]

Easterlin, R. A. (2003). *Building a better theory of well-being* (IZA discussion paper). Bonn, Germany: Institute for the Study of Labor. [28]

Edwards, A. L. (1957). *Techniques of attitude scale construction*. New York: Appleton-Century-Croft. [23]

Edwards, W. (1953). Probability-preferences in gambling. *American Journal of Psychology, 66*, 349–364. [1, 2]

Edwards, W. (1954a). Probability-preferences among bets with differing expected values. *American Journal of Psychology, 67*, 56–67. [1, 2]

Edwards, W. (1954b). The reliability of probability-preferences. *American Journal of Psychology, 67*, 68–95. [1, 2]

Edwards, W. (1954c). The theory of decision making. *Psychological Bulletin, 51*, 380–417. [1, 18, 19, 33]

Edwards, W. (1954d). Variance preferences in gambling. *American Journal of Psychology, 67*, 441–452. [2]

Edwards, W. (1955). The prediction of decisions among bets. *Journal of Experimental Psychology, 51*, 201–214. [2, 3]

Edwards, W. (1961). Behavioral decision theory. *Annual Review of Psychology, 12*, 473–498. [1, 33]

Edwards, W. (1962). Subjective probabilities inferred from decisions. *Psychological Review, 69*, 109–135. [2]

Edwards, W., & Fasolo, B. (2001). Decision technology. *Annual Review of Psychology, 52*, 581–606. [12]

Edwards, W., & Newman, J. R. (1982). *Multiattribute evaluation.* Beverly Hills, CA: Sage. [12]

Edwards, W., & von Winterfeldt, D. (1987). Public values in risk debates. *Risk Analysis, 7*, 141–158. [33]

Einhorn, H. J. (1972). Expert measurement and mechanical combination. *Organizational Behavior and Human Decision Processes, 7*, 86–106. [34]

Einhorn, H. J. (1980). Learning from experience and suboptimal rules in decision making. In T. S. Wallsten (Ed.), *Cognitive processes in choice and decision behavior* (pp. 1–20). Hillsdale, NJ: Lawrence Erlbaum Associates. [17]

Einhorn, H. J., & Hogarth, R. M. (1981). Behavioral decision theory: Processes of judgment and choice. *Annual Review of Psychology, 32*, 53–88. [19, 33]

Eisele, P. (2000). Post-decision consolidation: Group members in different social settings compared to individual decision makers. *Scandinavian Journal of Psychology, 41*, 275–282. [19]

Eisenhardt, K. M. (1989). Making fast strategic decisions in high velocity environments. *Academy of Management Journal, 32*, 543–576. [34]

Ellickson, R. C. (1989). Bringing culture and human frailty to rational actors: A critique of classical law and economics. *Chicago-Kent Law Review, 65*, 23–55. [27]

Elliott, R., & Dolan, R. J. (1998). Neural response during preference and memory judgments for subliminally presented stimuli: A functional neuro-imaging study. *Journal of Neuroscience, 18*, 4697–4704. [1, 25]

Ellsberg, D. (1961). Risk ambiguity and the Savage axioms. *The Quarterly Journal of Economics, 75*, 643–669. [27]

Elster, J., & Loewenstein, G. (1992). Utility from memory and anticipation. In J. Elster & G. Loewenstein (Eds.), *Choice over time* (pp. 213–224). New York: Russell Sage Foundation. [27, 32]

Emanuel, E. E., & Emanuel, L. L. (1992). Four models of the physician-patient relationship. *Journal of the American Medical Association, 267*, 2221–2226. [36]

Epley, N., & Gilovich, T. (2001). Putting adjustment back in the anchoring and adjustment heuristic: Differential processing of self-generated and experimenter-provided anchors. *Psychological Science, 12*, 391–396. [13, 21]

Epstein, S. (1994). Integration of the cognitive and the psychodynamic unconscious. *American Psychologist, 49*, 709–724. [1, 23, 32]

Erber, M. W., Hodges, S. D., & Wilson, T. D. (1995). Attitude strength and attitude stability. In R. E. Petty & J. A. Krosnick (Eds.), *Attitude strength: Antecedents and consequences* (pp. 433–454). Hillsdale, NJ: Lawrence Erlbaum Associates. [26]

Ericsson, K. A., & Simon, H. A. (1980). Verbal reports as data. *Psychological Review, 87*, 215–251. [10, 18]

Eriksen, C. W. (1980). Discrimination and learning without awareness: A methodological survey and evaluation. *Psychological Review, 67*, 279–300. [25]

Erwin, P. G., & Calev, A. (1984). The influence of Christian name stereotypes on the marking of children's essays. *British Journal of Educational Psychology, 54*, 223–227. [23]

Estes, W. K. (1994). *Classification and cognition.* New York: Oxford University Press. [19]

An ethically defensible market in organs [Editorial]. (2002). *British Medical Journal, 325*, 114–115. [37]

Fair, R. C. (1978). A theory of extramarital affairs. *Journal of Political Economy, 86*, 45–61. [5]

Falmagne, J.-C. (1985). *Elements of psychophysical theory.* New York: Oxford University Press. [6]

Fazio, R. H. (1995). Attitudes as object-evaluation associations: Determinants, consequences, and correlates of attitude accessibility. In R. E. Petty & J. A. Krosnick (Eds.), *Attitude strength: Antecedents and consequences* (pp. 247–282). Mahwah, NJ: Lawrence Erlbaum Associates. [23]

Fazio, R. H., Sanbonmatsu, D. M., Powell, M. C., & Kardes, F. R. (1986). On the automatic activation of attitudes. *Journal of Personality and Social Psychology, 50*, 229–238. [31]

Feldman, J. M., & Lynch, J. G., Jr. (1988). Self-generated validity and other effects of measurement on belief, attitude, intention, and behavior. *Journal of Applied Psychology, 73*, 421–435. [17, 32, 34]

Feldman-Stewart, D., Brundage, M. D., Van Manen, L., & Svenson, O. (2004). Patient-focused decision making in early-stage prostate cancer: Insights from a cognitively based decision aid. *Health Expectations, 7*, 126–141. [19]

Festinger, L. (1957). *A theory of cognitive dissonance.* Stanford, CA: Stanford University Press. [18, 19, 30]

Festinger, L. (1964). *Conflict, decision, and dissonance.* Stanford, CA: Stanford University Press. [12, 19]

Fetherstonhaugh, D., Slovic, P., Johnson, S. M., & Friedrich, J. (1997). Insensitivity to the value of human life: A study of psychophysical numbing. *Journal of Risk and Uncertainty, 14*, 283–300. [9, 23, 32]

Finucane, M. L., Alhakami, A., Slovic, P., & Johnson, S. M. (2000). The affect heuristic in judgments of risks and benefits. *Journal of Behavioral Decision Making, 13*, 1–17. [23, 32]

Fischer, G. W. (1995). Range sensitivity to attribute weights in multiattribute value models. *Organizational Behavior and Human Decision Processes, 63*, 252–266. [10]

Fischer, G. W., Carmon, Z., Ariely, D., & Zauberman, G. (1999). Goal-based construction of preferences: Task goals and the prominence effect. *Management Science, 45*, 1057–1075. [1, 21, 28, 29]

Fischer, G. W., Damodaran, N., Laskey, K. B., & Lincoln, D. (1987). Preferences for proxy attributes. *Management Science, 33*, 198–214. [6, 9]

Fischer, G. W., & Hawkins, S. (1993). Strategy compatibility, scale compatibility, and the prominence effect. *Journal of Experimental Psychology: Human Perception and Performance, 19*, 580–597. [1, 9, 10, 18, 29]

Fischer, G. W., Jia, J., & Luce, M. F. (2000). Attribute conflict and preference uncertainty: The Rand MAU model. *Management Science, 46*, 669–684. [11]

Fischer, P. M. (1991). Brand logo recognition by children ages 3 to 6 years: Mickey Mouse and Old Joe the Camel. *Journal of the American Medical Association, 266*, 3145. [23]

Fischhoff, B. (1975). Hindsight ≠ foresight: The effect of outcome knowledge on judgment under uncertainty. *Journal of Experimental Psychology: Human Perception and Performance, 1*, 288–299. [19]

Fischhoff, B. (1980). Clinical decision analysis. *Operations Research, 28*, 28–43. [35]

Fischhoff, B. (1983). Predicting frames. *Journal of Experimental Psychology: Learning, Memory, and Cognition, 9*, 113–116. [1, 21, 35]

Fischhoff, B. (1991). Value elicitation: Is there anything in there? *American Psychologist, 46*, 835–847. [15, 19, 21, 31, 34, 35]

Fischhoff, B. (1993). Transaction analysis: A framework and an application to insurance decisions. *Journal of Risk and Uncertainty, 7*, 53–69. [35]

Fischhoff, B. (1996). The real world: What good is it? *Organizational Behavior and Human Decision Processes, 65*, 232–248. [19, 35]

Fischhoff, B. (1997). What do psychologists want? Contingent valuation as a special case of asking questions. In R. J. Kopp, W. W. Pommerehne, & N. Schwartz (Eds.), *Determining the value of non-marketed goods: Economic, psychological, and policy relevant aspects of contingent valuation methods* (pp. 189–217). Boston: Kluwer Academic Publishing. [34]

Fischhoff, B. (2005). Cognitive issues in stated preference methods. In K.-G. Mäler & J. R. Vincent (Eds.), *Handbook of environmental economics: Vol. 2. Valuing environmental changes* (pp. 937–968). Amsterdam: Elsevier. [35]

Fischhoff, B., & Furby, L. (1988). Measuring values: A conceptual framework for interpreting transactions with special reference to contingent valuation of visibility. *Journal of Risk and Uncertainty, 1*, 147–184. [33, 34, 35]

Fischhoff, B., Quadrel, M. J., Kamlet, M., Loewenstein, G., Dawes, R. M., Fischbeck, P., et al. (1993). Embedding effects: Stimulus representation and response mode. *Journal of Risk and Uncertainty, 6*, 211–234. [33, 34]

Fischhoff, B., Slovic, P., & Lichtenstein, S. (1978). Fault trees: Sensitivity of estimated failure probabilities to problem representation. *Journal of Experimental Psychology: Human Perception and Performance, 4*, 330–344. [33]

Fischhoff, B., Slovic, P., & Lichtenstein, S. (1980). Knowing what you want: Measuring labile values. In T. Wallstein (Ed.), *Cognitive processes in choice and decision behavior* (pp. 117–141). Hillsdale, NJ: Lawrence Erlbaum Associates. [6, 19, 34, 35]

Fischhoff, B., Slovic, P., Lichtenstein, S., Read, S., & Combs, B. (1978). How safe is safe enough? A psychometric study of attitudes toward technological risks and benefits. *Policy Sciences, 9*, 127–152. [23, 35]

Fischhoff, B., Watson, S., & Hope, C. (1984). Defining risk. *Policy Sciences, 17*, 123–139. [35]

Fischhoff, B., Welch, N., & Frederick, S. (1999). Construal processes in preference assessment. *Journal of Risk and Uncertainty, 19*, 139–176. [34]

Fishburn, P. C. (1984). SSB utility theory: An economic perspective. *Mathematical Social Sciences, 8*, 63–94. [6, 8]

Fishburn, P. C. (1985). Nontransitive preference theory and the preference reversal phenomenon. *Rivista Internazionale di Scienze Economiche e Commerciali, 32*, 39–50. [1, 6, 8]

Fisher, I. (1906). *The nature of capital and income.* New York: Macmillan. [2]

Fisher, I. (1968). Is 'utility' the most suitable term for the concept it is used to denote? In A. N. Page (Ed.), *Utility theory: A book of readings* (pp. 49–51). New York: Wiley (Reprinted from *American Economic Review, 8*, 335–337, 1918). [27]

Fisher, R. (1969). *Basic negotiating strategy: International conflict for beginners*. London: Allen Lane. [20]

Fiske, S. T. (1980). Attention and weight in person perception: The impact of negative and extreme behavior. *Journal of Personality and Social Psychology, 38*, 889–906. [7]

Fiske, S. T., & Pavelchak, M. A. (1986). Category-based versus piecemeal-based affective responses: Developments in schema-triggered affect. In R. M. Sorrentino & E. T. Higgins (Eds.), *The handbook of motivation and cognition: Foundations of social behavior* (pp. 167–203). New York: Guilford Press. [19]

Fitts, P. M., & Seeger, C. M. (1953). S-R compatibility: Spatial characteristics of stimulus and response codes. *Journal of Experimental Psychology, 46*, 199–210. [6]

Fitzsimons, G. J., & Morwitz, V. G. (1996). The effect of measuring intent on brand-level purchasing behavior. *Journal of Consumer Research, 23*, 1–11. [21]

Florig, H. K., Morgan, M. G., Morgan, K. M., Jenni, K. E., Fischhoff, B., & Fischbeck, P. S., et al. (2001). A test bed for studies of risk taking. *Risk Analysis, 21*, 913–922. [35]

Ford, J. K., Schmitt, N., Schechtman, S. L., Hults, B. M., & Doherty, M. L. (1986). Process tracing methods: Contribution, problems, and neglected research questions. *Organizational Behavior and Human Decision Processes, 43*, 75–117. [19]

Forgas, J. P. (1995). Mood and judgment: The affect infusion model (AIM). *Psychological Bulletin, 117*, 39–66. [21, 30]

Foster, V., Bateman, I. J., & Harley, D. (1997). Real and hypothetical willingness to pay for environmental preservation: A non-experimental comparison. *Journal of Agricultural Economics, 48*, 123–138. [31]

Fox, C. R., & Tversky, A. (1995). Ambiguity aversion and comparative ignorance. *The Quarterly Journal of Economics, 110*, 585–603. [9, 13, 14]

Franciosi, R., Kujal, P., Michelitsch, R., & Smith, V. (1993). *Experimental tests of the endowment effect* (Working paper). Tucson: University of Arizona, Department of Economics. [27]

Frank, R. H. (1992). The role of moral sentiments in the theory of intertemporal choice. In J. Elster & G. Loewenstein (Eds.), *Choice over time* (pp. 265–286). New York: Russell Sage Foundation. [27]

Frank, R. H. (1997). The frame of reference as public good. *Economic Journal, 107*, 1832–1847. [28]

Franklin, B. (1950). *The autobiography of Benjamin Franklin*. New York: Pocket Books. [26]

Frederick, S. (2002). Automated choice heuristics. In T. Gilovich, D. Griffin, & D. Kahneman (Eds.), *Heuristics and biases: The psychology of intuitive judgment* (pp. 548–558). Cambridge, UK: Cambridge University Press. [29, 32]

Frederick, S. (2003). Measuring intergenerational time preference: Are future lives valued less? *Journal of Risk and Uncertainty, 26*, 39–53. [35, 38]

Frederick, S., & Fischhoff, B. (1998). Scope (in)sensitivity in elicited valuations. *Risk Decision and Policy, 3*, 109–123. [9, 13, 14, 31, 32]

Frederick, S., & Loewenstein, G. (1999). Hedonic adaptation. In D. Kahneman, E. Diener, & N. Schwarz (Eds.), *Well-being: The foundations of hedonic psychology* (pp. 302–329). New York: Russell Sage Foundation. [28]

Frederick, S., Loewenstein, G., & O'Donoghue, T. (2002). Time discounting and time preference: A critical review. *Journal of Economic Literature, 40*, 351–401. [38]

Fredrickson, B. L., & Kahneman, D. (1993). Duration neglect in retrospective evaluations of affective episodes. *Journal of Personality and Social Psychology, 65*, 45–55. [27]

Freeman, A. M., III. (1993a). *The measurement of environmental and resource values: Theory and methods.* Washington, DC: Resources for the Future. [34]

Freeman, A. M., III. (1993b). Nonuse values in natural resource damage assessments. In R. Kopp & V. K. Smith (Eds.), *Valuing natural assets: The economics of natural resource damage assessment* (pp. 264–303). Washington, DC: Resources for the Future. [33]

Freeman, A. M., III. (2003). *The measurement of environmental and resource values: Theory and methods* (2nd ed.). Washington, DC: Resources for the Future. [36]

Freud, A. (1937). *The ego and the mechanisms of defense.* London: Hogarth Press. [30]

Frey, B. S., & Stutzer, A. (2000). Happiness, economy, and institutions. *Economic Journal, 110*, 918–938. [28]

Frey, B. S., & Stutzer, A. (2002a). *Happiness and economics.* Princeton, NJ: Princeton University Press. [28]

Frey, B. S., & Stutzer, A. (2002b). What can economists learn from happiness research? *Journal of Economic Literature, 40*, 402–435. [28]

Frey, B. S., & Stutzer, A. (2003). *Economic consequences of mispredicting utility.* Unpublished manuscript. [28]

Frey, D. (1981). Postdecisional preference for decision-relevant information as a function of its source and the degree of familiarity with its information. *Journal of Experimental Social Psychology, 17*, 51–67. [19]

Frey, D. (1986). Recent research on selective exposure to information. *Advances in Experimental Social Psychology, 19*, 41–80. [19]

Friedman, M., & Friedman, R. (1980). *Free to choose: A personal statement.* New York: Harcourt Brace Jovanovich. [38]

Friedrich, J., Barnes, P., Chapin, K., Dawson, I., Garst, V., & Kerr, D. (1999). Psychophysical numbing: When lives are valued less as the lives at risk increase. *Journal of Consumer Psychology, 8*, 277–299. [23]

Frijda, N. H. (1986). *The emotions: Studies in emotion and social interaction.* New York: Cambridge University Press. [24]

Frisch, D., & Clemen, R. T. (1994). Beyond expected utility: Rethinking behavioral decision research. *Psychological Bulletin, 116*, 46–54. [17, 34]

Frisch, D., & Jones, S. K. (1993). Assessing the accuracy of decisions. *Theory and Psychology, 3*, 115–135. [9]

Gäbel, H. (2002). *Donor and non-donor registries in Europe.* Stockholm, Sweden: On behalf of the committee of experts on the Organizational Aspects of Co-operation in Organ Transplantation of the Council of Europe. [37]

Gaeth, G. J., & Shanteau, J. (1984). Reducing the influence of irrelevant information on experienced decision makers. *Organizational Behavior and Human Performance, 33*, 263–282. [33]

Gallhofer, L., & Saris, W. (1989). Decision trees and decision rules: The empirical decision analysis procedure. In H. Montgomery & O. Svenson (Eds.), *Process and structure in human decision making* (pp. 293–311). Chichester, UK: Wiley. [18]

The Gallup Organization, Inc. (1993). *The American public's attitude toward organ donation and transplantation.* Boston: Author. [37]

Ganzach, Y. (1995). Attribute scatter and decision outcome: Judgment versus choice. *Organizational Behavior and Human Decision Processes, 62*, 113–122. [10]

Ganzach, Y. (1996). Preference reversals in equal-probability gambles: A case for anchoring and adjustment. *Journal of Behavioral Decision Making, 9*, 95–109. [11]

Gardiner, P. C., & Edwards, W. (1975). Public values: Multiattribute-utility measurement for social decision making. In M. F. Kaplan & S. Schwartz (Eds.), *Human judgment and decision processes* (pp. 1–37). New York: Academic Press. [33]

Garvil, J., Gärling, T., Lindberg, E., & Montgomery, H. (1991, August). In search of evidence for dominance structuring in decision making. Paper presented at the 13th European Research Conference of Subjective Probability, Utility, and Decision Making, Fribourg, Switzerland. [18]

Gertner, J. (2003, September 7). The futile pursuit of happiness. *The New York Times,* Sec. 6, p. 44. [1]

Gettys, C. F., Pliske, R. M., Manning, C., & Casey, J. T. (1987). An evaluation of human act generation performance. *Organizational Behavior and Human Decision Processes, 39*, 23–51. [9]

Gigerenzer, G., & Selten, R. (2001). Rethinking rationality. In G. Gigerenzer & R. Selten (Eds.), *Bounded rationality: The adaptive toolbox* (pp. 1–12). Cambridge, MA: The MIT Press. [1]

Gigerenzer, G., Todd, P. M., & The ABC Group. (1999). *Simple heuristics that make us smart.* New York: Oxford University Press. [21]

Gilbert, D. T., Driver-Linn, E., & Wilson, T. D. (2002). The trouble with Vronsky: Impact bias in the forecasting of future affective states. In L. F. Barrett & P. Salovey (Eds.), *The wisdom in feeling: Psychological processes in emotional intelligence* (pp. 114–143). New York: Guilford Press. [28]

Gilbert, D. T., & Ebert, J. E. J. (2002). Decisions and revisions: The affective forecasting of changeable outcomes. *Journal of Personality and Social Psychology, 82*, 503–514. [30]

Gilbert, D. T., Gill, M. J., & Wilson, T. D. (2002). The future is now: Temporal correction in affective forecasting. *Organizational Behavior and Human Decision Processes, 88*, 430–444. [28, 29, 30, 32]

Gilbert, D. T., Lieberman, M. D., Morewedge, C. K., & Wilson, T. D. (2004). The peculiar longevity of things not so bad. *Psychological Science, 15*, 14–19. [30]

Gilbert, D. T., Pinel, E. C., Wilson, T. D., Blumberg, S. J., & Wheatley, T. P. (1998). Immune neglect: A source of durability bias in affective forecasting. *Journal of Personality and Social Psychology, 75*, 617–638. [28, 30]

Gilbert, D. T., Pinel, E. C., Wilson, T. D., Blumberg, S. J., & Wheatley, T. P. (2002). Durability bias in affective forecasting. In T. Gilovich, D. Griffin, & D. Kahneman (Eds.), *Heuristics and biases: The psychology of intuitive judgment* (pp. 292–312). Cambridge, UK: Cambridge University Press. [28]

Gilbert, D. T., & Wilson, T. D. (2000). Miswanting: Some problems in the forecasting of future affective states. In J. P. Forgas (Ed.), *Feeling and thinking: The role of affect in social cognition* (pp. 178–197). Cambridge, UK: Cambridge University Press. [1, 28, 30]

Gilboa, I., & Schmeidler, D. (1995). Case-based decision theory. *The Quarterly Journal of Economics, 110*, 605–639. [13]

Gilovich, T., & Medvec, V. H. (1995). The experience of regret: What, when, and why. *Psychological Review, 102*, 379–395. [16]

Gimbel, R. W., Strosberg, M. A., Lehrman, S. E., Gefenas, E., & Taft, F. (2003). Presumed consent and other predictors of cadaveric organ donation in Europe. *Progress in Transplantation, 13*, 5–15. [37]

Glass, D. C., & Singer, J. E. (1972a). *Stress and adaptation: Experimental studies of behavioral effects of exposure to aversive events.* New York: Academic Press. [16]

Glass, D. C., & Singer, J. E. (1972b). *Urban stress.* New York: Academic Press. [16]

Glimcher, P. W., & Rustichini, A. (2004). Neuroeconomics: The consilience of brain and decision. *Science, 306*, 447–452. [1]

Gneezy, U., & Potters, J. (1997). An experiment on risk taking and evaluation periods. *The Quarterly Journal of Economics, 112*, 631–645. [20]

Gold, J. I. (2003). Linking reward expectation to behavior in the basal ganglia. *Trends in Neurosciences, 26*, 12–14. [11]

Gold, J. I., & Shadlen, M. N. (2001). Neural computations that underlie decisions about sensory stimuli. *Trends in Cognitive Science, 5*, 10–16. [11]

Goldstein, W. M. (1984). The relationship between judgment and choice. *Dissertation Abstracts International, 45*(07B), 2341. [7]

Goldstein, W. M., & Einhorn, H. J. (1987). Expression theory and the preference reversal phenomena. *Psychological Review, 94*, 236–254. [1, 6, 7, 8, 9, 10, 11]

Gollwitzer, P. M. (1990). Action phases and mind-sets. In E. T. Higgins & R. M. Sorrentiono (Eds.), *Handbook of motivation and cognition: Foundations of social behavior* (Vol. 2, pp. 53–92). New York: Guilford Press. [18]

Gollwitzer, P. M., & Bayer, U. (1999). Deliberative versus implementational mindsets in the control of action. In S. Chaiken & Y. Trope (Eds.), *Dual-process theories in social psychology* (pp. 403–422). New York: Guilford Press. [12]

Gollwitzer, P. M., Heckhausen, H., & Ratajczak, H. (1990). From weighting to willing: Approaching a change decision through pre- or postdecisional mentation. *Organizational Behavior and Human Decision Processes, 45*, 41–65. [18]

Gollwitzer, P. M., Heckhausen, H., & Steller, B. (1990). Deliberative and implementational mind mind-sets: Cognitive turning toward congruous thoughts and information. *Journal of Personality and Social Psychology, 59*, 1119–1127. [19]

Gonzalez, R., & Wu, G. (1999). On the shape of the probability weighting function. *Cognitive Psychology, 38*, 129–166. [32]

González-Vallejo, C., Erev, I., & Wallsten, T. S. (1994). Do decision quality and preference order depend on whether probabilities are verbal or numerical? *American Journal of Psychology, 107*, 157–172. [29]

González-Vallejo, C., & Moran, E. (2001). The evaluability hypothesis revisited: Joint and separate preference reversal as a function of attribute importance. *Organizational Behavior and Human Decision Processes, 86*, 216–233. [28]

Gorovitz, S. (1982). *Doctors' dilemmas: Moral conflict and medical care.* New York: Macmillan. [36]

Gourville, J. T. (1998). Pennies-a-day: The effect of temporal re-framing on transaction evaluation. *Journal of Consumer Research, 24*, 395–408. [20]

Green, D., Jacowitz, K., Kahneman, D., & McFadden, D. (1998). Referendum contingent valuation, anchoring, and willingness to pay for public goods. *Resource and Energy Economics, 20*, 85–116. [13, 31]

Green, P. E., & Srinivasan, V. (1990). Conjoint analysis in marketing: New developments with implications for research and practice. *Journal of Marketing, 45*, 33–41. [34]

Greenwald, A. G. (1980). The totalitarian ego: Fabrication and revision of personal history. *American Psychologist, 35*, 603–618. [19]

Greenwald, A. G., Carnot, C. G., Beach, R., & Young, B. (1987). Increasing voting behavior by asking people if they expect to vote. *Journal of Applied Psychology, 72*, 315–318. [21]

Gregory, R., Flynn, J., Johnson, S. M., Satterfield, T. A., Slovic, P., & Wagner, R. (1997). Decision pathway surveys: A tool for resource managers. *Land Economics, 73*, 240–254. [34]

Gregory, R., Keeney, R., & von Winterfeldt, D. (1992). Adapting the environmental impact statement process to inform decision makers. *Journal of Policy Analysis and Management, 1*, 58–75. [33]

Gregory, R., Lichtenstein, S., Brown, T. C., Peterson, G. L., & Slovic, P. (1995). How precise are monetary representations of environmental improvements? *Land Economics, 71*, 462–473. [1]

Gregory, R., Lichtenstein, S., & Slovic, P. (1993). Valuing environmental resources: A constructive approach. *Journal of Risk and Uncertainty, 7*, 177–197. [1, 17, **33**, 34]

Gregory, R., MacGregor, D. G., & Lichtenstein, S. (1992). Assessing the quality of expressed preference measures of value. *Journal of Economic Behavior & Organization, 17*, 277–292. [33]

Gregory, R., & McDaniels, T. (1987). Valuing environmental losses: What promise does the right measure hold? *Policy Sciences, 20*, 11–26. [33]

Grether, D. M. (1980). Bayes rules as a descriptive model: The representativeness heuristic. *The Quarterly Journal of Economics, 95*, 537–557. [38]

Grether, D. M., & Plott, C. R. (1979). Economic theory of choice and the preference reversal phenomenon. *American Economic Review, 69*(4), 623–638. [1, **5**, 6, 7, 8, 9, 11, 33, 34]

Grice, H. P. (1975). Logic and conversation. In D. Davidson & G. Harman (Eds.), *The logic of grammar* (pp. 64–75). Encino, CA: Dickenson. [35]

Griffin, D. W., Dunning, D., & Ross, L. (1990). The role of construal processes in overconfident predictions about the self and others. *Journal of Personality and Social Psychology, 59*, 1128–1139. [30]

Griffin, D. W., & Ross, L. (1991). Subjective construal, social interference, and human misunderstanding. In M. Zanna (Ed.), *Advances in experimental social psychology* (Vol. 24, pp. 319–356). New York: Academic Press. [30]

Griffin, D. W., & Tversky, A. (1992). The weighing of evidence and the determinants of confidence. *Cognitive Psychology, 24*, 411–435. [31]

Grossberg, S. (1982). Associative and competitive principles of learning and development: The temporal unfolding and stability of STM and LTM patterns. In S. I. Amari & M. Arbib (Eds.), *Competition and cooperation in neural networks* (pp. 448–485). New York: Springer-Verlag. [11]

Grossberg, S. (1988). *Neural networks and natural intelligence.* Cambridge, MA: MIT Press. [11]

Grossberg, S., & Gutowski, W. E. (1987). Neural dynamics of decision making under risk: Affective balance and cognitive-emotional interactions. *Psychological Review, 94*, 300–318. [11]

Guadagni, P. M., & Little, J. D. C. (1983). A logit model of brand choice calibrated on scanner data. *Marketing Science, 2*, 203–238. [10]

Guala, F. (2000). Artefacts in experimental economics: Preference reversals and the Becker-deGroot-Marschak mechanism. *Economics and Philosophy, 16*, 47–75. [1]

Guo, F. Y., & Holyoak, K. J. (2002, August). *Understanding similarity in choice behavior: A connectionist model*. Poster presented at the Cognitive Science Society Meeting, Fairfax, VA. [11]

Hamm, R. M. (1984). *The conditions of occurrence of the preference reversal phenomenon* (ICS Publication #90–11). Boulder: University of Colorado, Center for Research on Judgment and Policy. [8]

Hammarberg, A., & Svenson, O. (2000). Individual postdecisional processes in group settings. *Scandinavian Journal of Psychology, 41*, 145–158. [19]

Hammermesh, D., & Soss, D. (1978). An economic theory of suicide. *Journal of Political Economy, 82*, 83–98. [5]

Hammond, J. S., Keeney, R. L., & Raiffa, H. (1999). *Smart choices: A practical guide to making better decisions*. Boston: Harvard Business School Press. [1]

Hammond, K. R. (1990). Functionalism and illusionism: Can integration be usefully achieved? In R. M. Hogarth (Ed.), *Insights in decision making: A tribute to Hillel J. Einhorn* (pp. 227–261). Chicago: University of Chicago Press. [21]

Hammond, K. R. (1996a). How convergence of research paradigms can improve research on diagnostic judgment. *Medical Decision Making, 16*, 216–233. [28]

Hammond, K. R. (1996b). *Human judgment and social policy: Irreducible uncertainty, inevitable error, unavoidable injustice*. New York: Oxford University Press. [34]

Hammond, K. R., Hursch, C., & Todd, F. J. (1964). Analyzing the components of clinical inference. *Psychological Review, 72*, 215–224. [1, 2]

Hammond, K. R., McClelland, G. H., & Mumpower, J. (1980). *Human judgment and decision making: Theories, methods, and procedures*. New York: Praeger. [33]

Hammond, K. R., Stewart, T. R., Brehmer, B., & Steinmann, D. O. (1975). Social judgment theory. In M. F. Kaplan & S. Schwartz (Eds.), *Human judgment and decision processes*. New York: Academic Press. [34]

Hammond, P. (1985). *Consequential behavior in decision trees and expected utility* (Working Paper No. 112). Stanford, CA: Stanford University, Institute for Mathematical Studies in the Social Sciences. [27]

Hanemann, W. M. (1994). Valuing the environment through contingent valuation. *The Journal of Economic Perspectives, 8*(4), 19–43. [31]

Hansen, F. (1972). *Consumer choice behavior: A cognitive theory*. New York: The Free Press. [17]

Hanson, J. D., & Kysar, D. A. (1999a). Taking behavioralism seriously: Some evidence of market manipulation. *Harvard Law Review, 112*(7), 1420–1572. [1, 23]

Hanson, J. D., & Kysar, D. A. (1999b). Taking behavioralism seriously: The problem of market manipulation. *New York University Law Review, 74*(3), 630–749. [1, 23]

Hanson, J. D., & Kysar, D. A. (2001). The joint failure of economic theory and legal regulation. In P. Slovic (Ed.), *Smoking: Risk, perception, & policy* (pp. 229–276). Thousand Oaks, CA: Sage. [23]

Harari, H., & McDavid, J. W. (1973). Name stereotypes and teachers' expectations. *Journal of Educational Psychology, 65*, 222–225. [23]

Hardie, B. G. S., Johnson, E. J., & Fader, P. S. (1993). Modeling loss aversion and reference dependence effects on brand choice. *Marketing Science, 12*, 378–394. [27]

Hare, R. D. (1965). Psychopathy, fear arousal, and anticipated pain. *Psychological Reports, 16*, 499–502. [23]

Harris, C. C., Tinsley, H. E. A., & Donnelly, D. M. (1988). Research methods for public amenity resource valuation: Issues and recommendations. In G. L. Peterson, B. L.

Driver, & R. Gregory (Eds.), *Amenity resource valuation: Integrating economics with other disciplines* (pp. 201–218). State College, PA: Venture. [34]

Harris, C. E., & Alcorn, S. P. (2001). To solve a deadly shortage: Economic incentives for human organ donation. *Issues in Law and Medicine, 3*, 213–233. [37]

Harris, J. (2003). Organ procurement: Dead interests, living needs. *Journal of Medical Ethics, 29*, 130–134. [37]

Harte, J. M., Westenberg, R. M., & van Someren, M. (1994). Process models in decision making. *Acta Psychologica, 87*, 95–120. [19]

Hastie, R., & Dawes, R. M. (2002). *Rational choice in an uncertain world* (2nd ed.). Thousand Oaks, CA: Sage. [35]

Hastie, R., & Park, B. (1986). The relationship between memory and judgment depends on whether the judgment task is memory-based or on-line. *Psychological Review, 93*, 258–268. [15]

Hastie, R., Schkade, D., & Payne, J. (1999). Juror judgments in civil cases: Effects of plaintiff's request and plaintiff's identity on punitive damage awards. *Law and Human Behavior, 23*, 445–470. [31]

Hauser, J. R., Simester, D. I., & Wernerfelt, B. (1994). Customer satisfaction incentives. *Marketing Science, 13*, 327–350. [10]

Hauser, J. R., & Wernerfelt, B. (1990). An evaluation cost model of consideration sets. *Journal of Consumer Research, 16*, 393–408. [16]

Hausman, D. M. (1991). On dogmatism in economics: The case of preference reversals. *Journal of Socio-Economics, 20*, 205–225. [1]

Hays, W. L. (1963). *Statistics for psychologists*. New York: Holt, Rinehart & Winston. [2]

Heath, C., & Soll, J. (1996). Mental budgeting and consumer decisions. *Journal of Consumer Research, 23*, 40–52. [20]

Heeler, R. M., Okechuku, C., & Reid, S. (1979). Attribute importance: Contrasting measurements. *Journal of Marketing Research, 16*, 60–63. [10]

Heider, F. (1980). *The psychology of interpersonal relations*. New York: Wiley. [22]

Helson, H. (1933). The fundamental functions of gestalt psychology. *Psychological Review, 40*, 13–22. [19]

Hendrick, C., Mills, M., & Kiesler, C. A. (1968). Decision time as a function of number and complexity of equally attractive alternatives. *Journal of Personality and Social Psychology, 8*, 313–318. [16]

Hendrickx, L., Vlek, C., & Oppewal, H. (1989). Relative importance of scenario information and frequency information in the judgment of risk. *Acta Psychologica, 72*, 41–63. [23]

Herman, L. M., & Bahrick, H. P. (1966). Information encoding and decision time as variables in human choice behavior. *Journal of Experimental Psychology, 71*, 718–724. [2]

Herr, P. M. (1986). Consequences of priming: Judgment and behavior. *Journal of Personality and Social Psychology, 19*, 323–340. [15]

Herr, P. M. (1989). Priming price: Prior knowledge and context effects. *Journal of Consumer Research, 16*, 67–75. [15]

Herr, P. M., Sherman, S. J., & Fazio, R. H. (1983). On the consequences of priming: Assimilation and contrast effects. *Journal of Experimental Social Psychology, 19*, 323–340. [15]

Herrnstein, R. J. (1982). Stimuli and the texture of experience. *Neuroscience & Biobehavioral Reviews, 6*, 105–117. [20]

Herrnstein, R. J., Loewenstein, G., Prelec, D., & Vaughan, W. (1993). Utility maximization and melioration: Internalities in individual choices. *Journal of Behavioral Decision Making, 6*, 149–185. [20]

Herrnstein, R. J., & Prelec, D. (1992a). Melioration. In G. Loewenstein & J. Elster (Eds.), *Choice over time* (pp. 235–263). New York: Russell Sage Foundation. [20]

Herrnstein, R. J., & Prelec, D. (1992b). A theory of addiction. In G. Loewenstein & J. Elster (Eds.), *Choice over time* (pp. 331–360). New York: Russell Sage Foundation. [20]

Hershey, J., & Schoemaker, P. J. (1985). Probability vs. certainty equivalence methods in utility measurement: Are they equivalent? *Management Science, 31*, 1213–1231. [1, 6]

Heyman, G. M. (1996). Resolving the contradictions of addiction. *Behavioral and Brain Sciences, 19*, 561–610. [20]

Higgins, E. T. (1996). Knowledge activation: Accessibility, applicability, and salience. In E. T. Higgins & A. W. Kruglanski (Eds.), *Social psychology: Handbook of basic principles* (pp. 133–168). New York: Guilford Press. [15]

Higgins, E. T., & Kruglanski, A. W. (1996). *Social psychology: Handbook of basic principles*. New York: Guilford Press. [21]

Hirt, E. R., & Markman, K. D. (1995). Multiple explanations: A consider-an-alternative strategy for debiasing judgments. *Journal of Personality and Social Psychology, 69*, 1069–1086. [28]

Hirt, E. R., & Sherman, S. J. (1985). The role of prior knowledge in explaining hypothetical events. *Journal of Experimental Social Psychology, 21*, 519–543. [21]

HM Treasury. (2004). *Managing risks to the public: Appraisal guidance*. London: Author. [35]

Hoch, S. J. (1984). Availability and interference in predictive judgment. *Journal of Experimental Psychology: Learning, Memory, and Cognition, 10*, 649–662. [21]

Hoch, S. J. (1985). Counterfactual reasoning and accuracy in predicting personal events. *Journal of Experimental Psychology: Learning, Memory, and Cognition, 11*, 719–731. [21]

Hoch, S. J., & Loewenstein, G. (1991). Time-inconsistent preferences and consumer self-control. *Journal of Consumer Research, 17*, 492–507. [17]

Hoeffler, S., & Ariely, D. (1999). Constructing stable preferences: A look into dimensions of experience and their impact of preference stability. *Journal of Consumer Psychology, 11*, 113–139. [13]

Hoehn, J. P., & Randall, A. (1989). Too many proposals pass the benefit cost test. *American Economic Review, 79*(3), 544–551. [31]

Hoffman, D. L., & Novak, T. P. (1996). Marketing in hypermedia computer-mediated environments: Conceptual foundations. *Journal of Marketing, 60*, 50–68. [15]

Hoffman, P. J. (1960). The paramorphic representation of clinical judgment. *Psychological Bulletin, 57*, 116–131. [1, 2]

Hogarth, R. M. (Ed.). (1982). *New directions for methodology of social and behavioral science: No. 11. Question framing and response consistency*. San Francisco, CA: Jossey-Bass. [33]

Hogarth, R. M. (1987). *Judgment and choice*. New York: Wiley. [34]

Hollerman, J. R., & Shultz, W. (1998). Dopamine neurons report an error in the temporal prediction of reward during learning. *Nature Neuroscience, 1*, 304–309. [11]

Holt, C. A. (1986). Preference reversals and the independence axiom. *American Economic Review, 76*(3), 508–515. [1, 8]

Holyoak, K. J., & Simon, D. (1999). Bidirectional reasoning in decision making by constraint satisfaction. *Journal of Experimental Psychology: General, 128*, 3–31. [11, 12, 19]

Holyoak, K. J., & Thagard, P. (1989). Analogical mapping by constraint satisfaction. *Cognitive Science, 13*, 295–355. [12]

Holzberg, J. D. (1957). The clinical and scientific method: Synthesis or antithesis? *Journal of Projective Techniques, 21*, 227–242. [2]

Hong, S.-T., & Wyer, R. S. (1990). Determinants of product evaluation: Effects of the time interval between knowledge of products' country of origin and information about its specific attributes. *Journal of Consumer Research, 17*, 277–288. [10]

Horsky, D., & Nelson, P. (1992). New brand positioning and pricing in an oligopolistic market. *Marketing Science, 11*, 133–153. [10]

Houston, D. A., & Sherman, S. J. (1995). Cancellation and focus: The role of shared and unique features in the choice process. *Journal of Experimental Social Psychology, 31*, 357–378. [28]

Hovenkamp, H. (1991). Legal policy and the endowment effect. *Journal of Legal Studies, 20*, 225–247. [27]

Howard, J. A., & Sheth, J. N. (1969). *The theory of buyer behavior*. Reading, MA: Addison-Wesley. [17]

Hsee, C. K. (1993). *When trend of monetary outcomes matters: Separate versus joint evaluation and judgment of feelings versus choice*. Unpublished manuscript, The University of Chicago. [9]

Hsee, C. K. (1995). Elastic justification: How tempting but task-irrelevant factors influence decisions. *Organizational Behavior and Human Decision Processes, 62*, 330–337. [9, 29]

Hsee, C. K. (1996a). The evaluability hypothesis: An explanation for preference reversals between joint and separate evaluations of alternatives. *Organizational Behavior and Human Decision Processes, 67*, 247–257. [1, 9, 10, 20, 23, 28, 29, 31, 32]

Hsee, C. K. (1996b). Elastic justification: How unjustifiable factors influence judgments. *Organizational Behavior and Human Decision Processes, 66*, 122–129. [9, 23]

Hsee, C. K. (1998). Less is better: When low-value options are valued more highly than high-value options. *Journal of Behavioral Decision Making, 11*, 107–121. [1, 9, 23, 28]

Hsee, C. K. (1999). Value-seeking and prediction-decision inconsistency: Why don't people take what they predict they'll like the most? *Psychonomic Bulletin and Review, 6*, 555–561. [29]

Hsee, C. K. (2000). Attribute evaluability and its implications for joint-separate evaluation reversals and beyond. In D. Kahneman & A. Tversky (Eds.), *Choices, values and frames* (pp. 543–563). Cambridge, UK: Cambridge University Press. [28]

Hsee, C. K., & Abelson, R. P. (1991). Velocity relation: Satisfaction as a function of the first derivative of outcome over time. *Journal of Personality and Social Psychology, 60*, 341–347. [9, 29]

Hsee, C. K., Abelson, R. P., & Salovey, P. (1991). The relative weighting of position and velocity in satisfaction. *Psychological Science, 2*, 263–266. [1]

Hsee, C. K., & Kunreuther, H. (2000). The affection effect in insurance decisions. *Journal of Risk and Uncertainty, 20*, 141–159. [23, 29]

Hsee, C. K., & Leclerc, F. (1998). Will products look more attractive when evaluated jointly or when evaluated separately? *Journal of Consumer Research, 25*, 175–186. [9, 28]

Hsee, C. K., Loewenstein, G., Blount, S., & Bazerman, M. H. (1999). Preference reversals between joint and separate evaluations of options: A review and theoretical analysis. *Psychological Bulletin, 125*, 576–590. [1, **9**, 10, 13, 14, 20, 28, 29, 32, 34]

Hsee, C. K., & Menon, S. (1999). *Affection effect in consumer choices.* Unpublished study, University of Chicago. [23]

Hsee, C. K., & Rottenstreich, Y. (2004). Music, pandas, and muggers: On the affective psychology of value. *Journal of Experimental Psychology: General, 133*, 23–30. [1, 28, 29, **32**]

Hsee, C. K., Salovey, P., & Abelson, R. P. (1994). The quasi-acceleration relation: Satisfaction as a function of the change in velocity of outcome over time. *Journal of Experimental Social Psychology, 30*, 96–111. [9]

Hsee, C. K., & Weber, E. U. (1997). A fundamental prediction error: Self-other discrepancies in risk preference. *Journal of Experimental Psychology: General, 126*, 45–53. [28]

Hsee, C. K., Yu, F., Zhang, J., & Zhang, Y. (2003). Medium maximization. *Journal of Consumer Research, 30*, 1–14. [28, 29]

Hsee, C. K., & Zhang, J. (2003). *Inconsistency between choice and consumption experience.* Unpublished manuscript. [28]

Hsee, C. K., & Zhang, J. (2004). Distinction bias: Misprediction and mischoice due to joint evaluation. *Journal of Personality and Social Psychology, 86*, 680–695. [1, **28**, 32]

Hsee, C. K., Zhang, J., & Chen, J. (2004). Internal and substantive inconsistencies in decision-making. In D. J. Koehler & N. Harvey (Eds.), *Blackwell handbook of judgment and decision making* (pp. 360–378). Oxford, UK: Blackwell. [1, 28]

Hsee, C. K., Zhang, J., Yu, F., & Xi, Y. (2003). Lay rationalism and inconsistency between predicted experience and decision. *Journal of Behavioral Decision Making, 16*, 257–272. [1, 28, **29**]

Huber, J. (1997). What we have learned from 20 years of conjoint research: When to use self-explicated, graded pairs, full profiles, or choice experiments. In *1997 Sawtooth Conference Proceedings.* Sequim, WA: Sawtooth Software. [34]

Huber, J., Lynch, J. G., Corfman, K. P., Feldman, J., Holbrook, M. C., Lehman, D. R., et al. (1997). Thinking about values in prospect and retrospect: Maximizing experienced utility. *Marketing Letters, 8*, 323–334. [34]

Huber, J., Payne, J. W., & Puto, C. (1982). Adding asymmetrically dominated alternatives: Violations of regularity and the similarity hypothesis. *Journal of Consumer Research, 9*, 90–98. [1, 10, 11, 17, 18, 22]

Huber, J., Wittink, D. R., Fiedler, J. A., & Miller, R. (1993). The effectiveness of alternative preference elicitation procedures in predicting choice. *Journal of Marketing Research, 30*, 105–114. [10, 17, 34]

Huber, O. (1980). The influence of some task variables on cognitive operations in an information-processing decision model. *Acta Psychologica, 45*, 187–196. [10, 33]

Huber, O. (1989). Information-processing operators in decision making. In H. Montgomery & O. Svenson (Eds.), *Process and structure in human decision making* (pp. 3–21). Chichester, UK: Wiley. [19]

Irwin, J. R. (1994). Buying/selling price preference reversals: Preference for environmental changes in buying versus selling modes. *Organizational Behavior and Human Decision Processes, 60*, 431–457. [9, 28]

Irwin, J. R., Schenk, D., McClelland, G. H., Schulze, W. D., Stewart, T., & Thayer, M. (1990). Urban visibility: Some experiments on the contingent valuation method. In

C. V. Mathei (Ed.), *Visibility and fine particles* (pp. 647–658). Pittsburgh, PA: Air and Waste Management Association. [33, 34]

Irwin, J. R., Slovic, P., Lichtenstein, S., & McClelland, G. H. (1993). Preference reversals and the measurement of environmental values. *Journal of Risk and Uncertainty, 6*, 5–18. [1, 9, 33]

Isen, A. M. (1993). Positive affect and decision making. In M. Lewis & J. M. Haviland (Eds.), *Handbook of emotions* (pp. 261–277). New York: Guilford Press. [23]

Isen, A. M. (2000). Some perspectives on positive affect and self-regulation. *Psychological Inquiry, 11*, 184–187. [24]

Iyengar, S. S., & Lepper, M. R. (2000). When choice is demotivating: Can one desire too much of a good thing? *Journal of Personality and Social Psychology, 79*, 995–1006. [1, **16**]

Jacowitz, K., & Kahneman, D. (1995). Measures of anchoring in estimation tasks. *Personality and Social Psychology Bulletin, 21*, 1161–1166. [13, 31]

Jako, R. A., & Murphy, K. R. (1990). Distributional ratings, judgment decomposition, and their impact on interrater agreement and rating accuracy. *Journal of Applied Psychology, 75*, 500–505. [34]

James, W. (1981). *The principles of psychology* (Vol. 2). Cambridge, MA: Harvard University Press (Original work published 1890). [22]

Janis, I. L., & Mann, L. (1977). *Decision making: A psychological analysis of conflict, choice, and commitment.* New York: The Free Press. [9, 12, 19, 26, 28, 34]

Jenni, K., & Loewenstein, G. (1997). Explaining the "identifiable victim effect." *Journal of Risk and Uncertainty, 14*, 235–257. [9, 23]

John, D. R., & Whitney, J. C. (1986). The development of consumer knowledge in children: A cognitive structure approach. *Journal of Consumer Research, 12*, 406–417. [17]

Johnson, E. J. (2001). Digitizing consumer research. *Journal of Consumer Research, 28*, 331–336. [15]

Johnson, E. J., Bellman, S., & Lohse, G. L. (2002). Defaults, framing and privacy: Why opting in-opting out. *Marketing Letters, 13*, 5–15. [37]

Johnson, E. J., & Goldstein, D. G. (2003). Do defaults save lives? *Science, 302*, 1338–1139. [1, **37**]

Johnson, E. J., Hershey, J., Meszaros, J., & Kunreuther, H. (1993). Framing, probability distortions, and insurance decisions. *Journal of Risk and Uncertainty, 7*, 35–51. [37, 38]

Johnson, E. J., Meyer, R. M., & Ghose, S. (1989). When choice models fail: Compensatory representations in negatively correlated environments. *Journal of Marketing Research, 26*, 255–270. [33]

Johnson, E. J., Payne, J. W., & Bettman, J. R. (1988). Information displays and preference reversals. *Organizational Behavior and Human Decision Processes, 42*, 1–21. [7]

Johnson, E. J., Payne, J. W., & Bettman, J. R. (1993). Adapting to time constraints. In O. Svenson & A. J. Maule (Eds.), *Time pressure and stress in human judgment and decision making* (pp. 103–116). New York: Plenum. [15]

Johnson, E. J., Payne, J. W., Schkade, D. A., & Bettman, J. R. (1988). *Monitoring information acquisitions and decisions: Mouse decision laboratory software* [Mouselab users manual]. Durham, NC: Duke University, Fuqua School of Business. [7]

Johnson, E. J., & Russo, J. E. (1984). Product familiarity and learning new information. *Journal of Consumer Research, 11*, 542–550. [15]

Johnson, E. J., & Schkade, D. A. (1989). Bias in utility assessments: Further evidence and explanations. *Management Science, 35,* 406–424. [7, 13, 14]

Johnson, E. J., & Tversky, A. (1983). Affect, generalization, and the perception of risk. *Journal of Personality and Social Psychology, 45,* 20–31. [21, 23, 24]

Johnson, E. J., & Weber, E. U. (2000, November). *Preferences as memory.* Paper presented at the meetings of the Judgment and Decision Making Society, New Orleans, LA. [21]

Johnson, J. G., & Busemeyer, J. R. (2005). A dynamic, stochastic, computational model of preference reversal phenomena. *Psychological Review, 112,* 841–861. [1, 11]

Johnson, M. D. (1984). Consumer choice strategies for comparing noncomparable alternatives. *Journal of Consumer Research, 11,* 741–753. [10, 17]

Jolls, C., Sunstein, C. R., & Thaler, R. H. (1998). A behavioral approach to law and economics. *Stanford Law Review, 50,* 1471–1550. [38]

Jones-Lee, M., Hammerton, M., & Phillips, R. (1985). The value of safety: Results from a national survey. *Economic Journal, 95,* 49–72. [33]

Jones-Lee, M., & Loomes, G. (2001). Private values and public policy. In E. U. Weber, J. Baron, & G. Loomes (Eds.), *Conflict and tradeoffs in decision making* (pp. 205–230). Cambridge, UK: Cambridge University Press. [38]

Jones-Lee, M., Loomes, G., & Philips, P. (1995). Valuing the prevention of non-fatal road injuries: Contingent valuation vs. standard gambles. *Oxford Economic Papers, 47,* 676–695. [31]

Joseph, R. A., Larrick, R. F., Steele, C. M., & Nisbett, R. E. (1992). Protecting the self from negative consequences of risky decisions. *Journal of Personality and Social Psychology, 62,* 26–37. [19]

Just, M. A., & Carpenter, P. A. (1976). Eye fixations and cognitive processes. *Cognitive Psychology, 8,* 441–480. [7]

Kagel, J. H., & Battalio, R. C. (1975). Experimental studies of consumer demand behavior using laboratory animals. *Economic Inquiry, 13,* 22–38. [5]

Kagel, J. H., & Battalio, R. C. (1976). *Demand curves for animal consumers* [Mimeo]. St. Louis, MO: Washington University. [5]

Kahneman, D. (1973). *Attention and effort.* Cliffs, NJ: Prentice-Hall. [17, 20]

Kahneman, D. (1986). Valuing environmental goods: An assessment of the contingent valuation method. In R. Cummings, D. Brookshire, & W. Schulze (Eds.), *Valuing environmental goods: An assessment of the contingent valuation method* (pp. 185–194). Totowa, NJ. [31]

Kahneman, D. (1994). New challenges to the rationality assumption. *Journal of Institutional and Theoretical Economics, 150,* 18–36. [1, 17, 23, **27**, 28, 29, 34, 36]

Kahneman, D. (1995). Varieties of counterfactual thinking. In N. J. Roese & J. M. Olson (Eds.), *What might have been: The social psychology of counterfactual thinking* (pp. 375–396). Mahwah, NJ: Lawrence Erlbaum Associates. [28]

Kahneman, D. (2000). Experienced utility and objective happiness: A moment-based approach. In D. Kahneman & A. Tversky (Eds.), *Choices, values and frames* (pp. 673–692). Cambridge, UK: Cambridge University Press. [28]

Kahneman, D. (2003a). Experiences of collaborative research. *American Psychologist, 58,* 723–730. [1]

Kahneman, D. (2003b). Maps of bounded reality. *American Economic Review, 93*(5), 1449–1475. [35]

Kahneman, D. (2003c). A perspective on judgment and choice: Mapping bounded rationality. *American Psychologist, 58,* 697–720. [24, 31]

Kahneman, D., Diener, E., & Schwarz, N. (Eds.). (1999). *Well-being: The foundations of hedonic psychology.* New York: Russell Sage Foundation. [28]

Kahneman, D., & Frederick, S. (2002). Representativeness revisited: Attribute substitution in intuitive judgment. In T. Gilovich, D. Griffin, & D. Kahneman (Eds.), *Heuristics of intuitive judgment: Extensions and applications* (pp. 49–81). New York: Cambridge University Press. [32, 38]

Kahneman, D., Fredrickson, B. L., Schreiber, C. A., & Redelmeier, D. (1993). When more pain is preferred to less: Adding a better end. *Psychological Science, 4,* 401–405. [9, 27, 29, 31]

Kahneman, D., & Knetsch, J. L. (1992). Valuing public goods: The purchase of moral satisfaction. *Journal of Environmental Economics and Management, 22,* 57–70. [1, 13, 20, 31, 32, 33]

Kahneman, D., & Knetsch, J. L. (1993). *Anchoring or shallow inferences: The effect of format.* University of California, Berkeley. [13]

Kahneman, D., Knetsch, J. L., & Thaler, R. H. (1986). Fairness and the assumptions of economics. *Journal of Business, 59,* 285–300. [28]

Kahneman, D., Knetsch, J. L., & Thaler, R. H. (1990). Experimental tests of the endowment effect and the Coase theorem. *Journal of Political Economy, 98,* 1325–1348. [1, 9, 19, 27, 33]

Kahneman, D., Knetsch, J. L., & Thaler, R. H. (1991). Anomalies: The endowment effect, loss aversion, and status quo bias. *The Journal of Economic Perspectives, 5(1),* 193–206. [27, 31, 38]

Kahneman, D., & Lovallo, D. (1993). Timid choices and bold forecasts: A cognitive perspective on risk taking. *Management Science, 39,* 17–31. [20]

Kahneman, D., & Miller, D. T. (1986). Norm theory: Comparing reality with its alternatives. *Psychological Review, 93,* 136–153. [9, 13, 31]

Kahneman, D., & Ritov, I. (1994). Determinants of stated willingness to pay for public goods: A study in the headline method. *Journal of Risk and Uncertainty, 9,* 5–38. [9, 13, 20, 23, 31]

Kahneman, D., Ritov, I., & Schkade, D. (1999). Economic preferences or attitude expressions? An analysis of dollar responses to public issues. *Journal of Risk and Uncertainty, 19,* 203–235. [1, 9, 13, 14, 28, **31**, 32, 34, 35]

Kahneman, D., Schkade, D., Ritov, I., & Sunstein, C. R. (1999). *Reversals of judgement: The effect of cross-category comparisons on intendedly absolute scales.* Unpublished manuscript. [31]

Kahneman, D., Schkade, D., & Sunstein, C. R. (1998). Shared outrage and erratic awards: The psychology of punitive damages. *Journal of Risk and Uncertainty, 16,* 49–86. [13, 23, 24, 29, 31, 34]

Kahneman, D., Slovic, P., & Tversky, A. (Eds.). (1982). *Judgment under uncertainty: Heuristics and biases.* New York: Cambridge University Press. [1, 23, 33]

Kahneman, D., & Snell, J. (1990). Predicting utility. In R. M. Hogarth (Ed.), *Insights in decision making: A tribute to Hillel J. Einhorn* (pp. 295–311). Chicago: University of Chicago Press. [1, 9, 21, 27, 28, 29]

Kahneman, D., & Snell, J. (1992). Predicting a change in taste. *Journal of Behavioral Decision Making, 5,* 187–200. [9, 19, 23, 27, 28, 29, 30]

Kahneman, D., & Tversky, A. (1972). Subjective probability: A judgment of representativeness. *Cognitive Psychology, 3,* 430–454. [31]

Kahneman, D., & Tversky, A. (1973). On the psychology of prediction. *Psychological Review, 80,* 237–251. [31]

Kahneman, D., & Tversky, A. (1979). Prospect theory: An analysis of decision under risk. *Econometrica, 47,* 263–291. [1, 8, 17, 18, 19, 20, 21, 22, 27, 28, 32, 35, 36]

Kahneman, D., & Tversky, A. (1982). The simulation heuristic. In D. Kahneman, P. Slovic, & A. Tversky (Eds.), *Judgment under uncertainty: Heuristics and biases* (pp. 509–520). New York: Cambridge University Press. [28]

Kahneman, D., & Tversky, A. (1984). Choices, values, and frames. *American Psychologist, 39,* 341–350. [1, 6, 17]

Kahneman, D., & Tversky, A. (Eds.). (2000). *Choices, values, and frames.* Cambridge, UK: Cambridge University Press. [36, 37]

Kahneman, D., & Varey, C. A. (1991). Notes on the psychology of utility. In J. Roemer & J. Elster (Eds.), *Interpersonal comparisons of well-being* (pp. 127–163). New York: Cambridge University Press. [27]

Kahneman, D., Wakker, P. P., & Sarin, R. (1997). Back to Bentham? Explorations of experienced utility. *The Quarterly Journal of Economics, 112,* 375–405. [13, 20, 28, 31]

Kant, I. (1785/1959). *Foundations of the metaphysics of morals.* New York: Bobbs-Merrill. [18]

Karni, E., & Safra, Z. (1987). "Preference reversal" and the observability of preferences by experimental methods. *Econometrica, 55,* 675–685. [1, 8]

Keeney, R. L. (1980). *Siting energy facilities.* New York: Academic. [33]

Keeney, R. L. (1982). Decision analysis: An overview. *Operations Research, 30,* 803–838. [33]

Keeney, R. L. (1984). Ethics, decision analysis, and public risk. *Risk Analysis, 4,* 117–129. [36]

Keeney, R. L. (1992). *Value-focused thinking: A path to creative decisionmaking.* Cambridge, MA: Harvard University. [19, 34, 35]

Keeney, R. L. (1996). Valuing billions of dollars. In R. J. Zeckhauser, R. L. Keeney, & J. K. Sebenius (Eds.), *Wise choices: Decisions, games, and negotiations* (pp. 63–80). Boston: Harvard Business School Press. [34]

Keeney, R. L., & Raiffa, H. (1976). *Decisions with multiple objectives: Preferences and value tradeoffs.* New York: Wiley. [12, 33]

Keller, K. (1993). Conceptualizing, measuring, and managing customer-based brand equity. *Journal of Marketing, 57,* 1–22. [10]

Keller, L. R., & Ho, J. L. (1988). Decision problem structuring: Generating options. *IEEE Transactions on Systems, Man and Cybernetics, 18,* 715–728. [19]

Kelley, H. H. (1967). Attribution theory in social psychology. In D. Levine (Ed.), *Nebraska Symposium on Motivation* (Vol. 15, pp. 192–240). Lincoln: University of Nebraska Press. [16]

Kelley, H. H. (1973). The process of causal attribution. *American Psychologist, 28,* 107–128. [16]

Kemp, M., & Maxwell, C. (1993). Exploring a budget context for contingent valuation. In J. A. Hausman (Ed.), *Contingent valuation: A critical assessment* (pp. 217–265). Amsterdam: North-Holland. [31]

Keren, G. (1991a). Additional tests of utility theory under unique and repeated conditions. *Journal of Behavioral Decision Making, 4,* 297–304. [19]

Keren, G. (1991b). Calibration and probability judgments: Conceptualization and methodological issues. *Acta Psychologica, 77,* 217–273. [20]

Keren, G. (1999). The explanatory power of choice bracketing: A commentary on Read et al., "Choice bracketing." *Journal of Risk and Uncertainty, 19,* 199–200. [1]

Keren, G., & Raaijmakers, J. B. (1988). On between-subjects versus within-subjects comparisons in testing utility theory. *Organizational Behavior and Human Decision Processes*, 4, 233–247. [13, 14]

Keren, G., & Wagenaar, W. A. (1987). Violation of utility theory in unique and repeated gambles. *Journal of Experimental Psychology: Learning, Memory, and Cognition*, 13, 387–391. [19, 20]

Keselman, H. J., Lix, L. M., & Kowalchuk, R. K. (1998). Multiple comparison procedures for trimmed means. *Psychological Methods*, 3, 123–141. [15]

Kiesler, C. A. (1966). Conflict and number of choice alternatives. *Psychological Reports*, 18, 603–610. [16]

Kiesler, C. A. (1971). *The psychology of commitment: Experiments linking behavior to belief.* New York: Academic Press. [12]

Kilka, M., & Weber, M. (2001). What determines the shape of the probability weighting function? *Management Science*, 47, 1712–1726. [32]

Kim-Prieto, C., Diener, E., Tamir, M., Scollon, C., & Diener, M. (2005). Integrating the diverse definitions of happiness: A time-sequential framework of subjective well-being. *Journal of Happiness Studies*, 6, 261–300. [28]

Kirby, K. N. (1997). Bidding on the future: Evidence against normative discounting of delayed rewards. *Journal of Experimental Psychology: General*, 126, 54–70. [20]

Klassen, A. C., & Klassen, D. K. (1996). Who are the donors in organ donation? The family's perspective in mandated choice. *Annals of Internal Medicine*, 125, 70–73. [37]

Klayman, J., & Brown, K. (1993). Debias the environment instead of the judge: An alternative approach to improving diagnostic (and other) judgment. *Cognition*, 49, 97–122. [29]

Klein, G. A. (1989). Recognition-primed decisions. In W. B. Rouse (Ed.), *Advances in man-machine system research* (Vol. 5, pp. 47–92). Greenwich, CT: JAI Press. [19]

Klein, G. A. (1993a). A recognition primed decision (RPD) model of rapid decision making. In G. A. Klein, J. Orasanu, R. Calderwood, & C. E. Zsambok (Eds.), *Decision making in action: Models and methods* (pp. 138–147). Norwood, NJ: Ablex. [18]

Klein, G. A. (1993b). Twenty questions: Suggestions for research in naturalistic decision making. In G. A. Klein, J. Orasanu, R. Calderwood, & C. E. Zsambok (Eds.), *Decision making in action: Models and methods* (pp. 389–403). Norwood, NJ: Ablex. [18]

Klein, G. A., Orasanu, J., Calderwood, R., & Zsambok, C. E. (Eds.). (1993). *Decision making in action: Models and methods*. Norwood, NJ: Ablex. [18, 21]

Kleindorfer, P. R., Kunreuther, H. C., & Schoemaker, P. J. H. (1993). *Decision sciences: An integrative perspective.* New York: Cambridge University Press. [19]

Kleinmuntz, B. (1963). Profile analysis revisited: A heuristic approach. *Journal of Counseling Psychology*, 70, 315–324. [19]

Kleinmuntz, D. N. (1990). Decomposition and the control of error in decision-analytic models. In R. M. Hogarth (Ed.), *Insights in decision making: A tribute to Hillel J. Einhorn* (pp. 107–126). Chicago: University of Chicago Press. [34]

Kleinmuntz, D. N., & Schkade, D. A. (1993). Information displays and decision processes. *Psychological Science*, 4, 221–227. [28, 34]

Knetsch, J. L., & Sinden, J. A. (1984). Willingness to pay and compensation demanded: Experimental evidence of an unexpected disparity in measures of value. *The Quarterly Journal of Economics*, 99, 507–521. [9, 33]

Knez, M., & Smith, V. L. (1991). Hypothetical valuations and preference reversals in the context of asset trading. In V. L. Smith (Ed.), *Papers in experimental economics* (pp. 315–338). Cambridge, UK: Cambridge University Press. [8]

Koehler, J. (1996). The base-rate fallacy reconsidered: Descriptive, normative, and methodological challenges. *Behavioral and Brain Sciences, 19*, 1–53. [31]

Kopp, R., Portney, P., & Smith, V. K. (1990). Natural resource damages: The economics have shifted after Ohio v. United States Department of the Interior. *Environmental Law Reporter, 4*, 10127–10131. [33]

Koriat, A., Lichtenstein, S., & Fischhoff, B. (1980). Reasons for confidence. *Journal of Experimental Psychology: Human Learning and Memory, 6*, 107–118. [21, 26]

Korobkin, R. (1998). The status quo bias and contract default rules. *Cornell Law Review, 83*, 608–687. [38]

Krantz, D. H. (1991). From indices to mappings: The representational approach to measurement. In D. R. Brown & J. E. K. Smith (Eds.), *Frontiers of mathematical psychology* (pp. 1–52). New York: Springer-Verlag. [1]

Krantz, D. H., Luce, R. D., Suppes, P., & Tversky, A. (1971). *Foundations of measurement* (Vol. 1). New York: Academic Press. [6]

Kray, L. (2000). Contingent weighting in self-other decision making. *Organizational Behavior and Human Decision Processes, 83*, 82–106. [29]

Kray, L., & Gonzales, R. (1999). Differential weighting in decision versus advice: I'll do this, you do that. *Journal of Behavioral Decision Making, 12*, 207–217. [29]

Kreuger, J., & Rothbart, M. (1990). Contrast and accentuation effects in category learning. *Journal of Personality and Social Psychology, 59*, 651–663. [19]

Krosnick, J. A., & Schuman, H. (1988). Attitude intensity, importance, and certainty and susceptibility to response effects. *Journal of Personality and Social Psychology, 54*, 940–952. [34]

Krueger, A. B., & Summers, L. H. (1988). Efficiency wages and inter-industry wage structure. *Econometrica, 56*, 259–293. [13]

Kudajie-Gyambi, E., & Rachlin, H. (1996). Temporal patterning choice among delayed outcomes. *Organizational Behavior and Human Decision Processes, 65*, 61–67. [20]

Kuhl, J. (1992). A theory of self-regulation: Action versus state orientation, self-discrimination, and some applications. *Applied Psychology: An International Review, 41*, 97–129. [18]

Kuhl, J., & Beckmann, J. (1994). *Volition and personality: Action versus state orientation.* Seattle, WA: Hogrefe and Huber. [19]

Kunda, Z. (1990). The case for motivated reasoning. *Psychological Bulletin, 108*, 480–498. [17, 19, 29]

Kunreuther, H. (1996). Mitigating disaster losses through insurance. *Journal of Risk and Uncertainty, 12*, 171–187. [38]

Kunreuther, H., & Hogarth, R. (1993, August). *Decision making under ignorance: Arguing with yourself* (Center for Decision Research Report). University of Chicago, Graduate School of Business. [19]

La France, M., & Hecht, M. A. (1995). Why smiles generate leniency. *Personality and Social Psychology Bulletin, 21*, 207–214. [23]

Laibson, D. (1994). *Hyperbolic discounting and consumption.* Unpublished doctoral dissertation, Massachusetts Institute of Technology, Cambridge. [20]

Laibson, D. (1997). Golden eggs and hyperbolic discounting. *The Quarterly Journal of Economics, 112*, 443–477. [20]

Laibson, D. (1999). Commentary on "Choice bracketing" by Read, Loewenstein and Rabin. *Journal of Risk and Uncertainty, 19*, 201–202. [1]

Lancaster, K. (1966). A new approach to consumer theory. *Journal of Political Economy, 74*, 132–157. [33]

Langer, E. J. (1975). The illusion of control. *Journal of Personality and Social Psychology*, 32, 311–328. [16]

Langer, E. J. (1978). Rethinking the role of thought in social interaction. In J. H. Harvey, W. J. Ickes, & R. F. Kidd (Eds.), *New directions in attribution research* (Vol. 2, pp. 35–58). Hillsdale, NJ: Lawrence Erlbaum Associates. [26]

Langer, E. J. (1989). Minding matters: The consequences of mindlessness-mindfulness. In L. Berkowitz (Ed.), *Advances in experimental social psychology* (Vol. 22, pp. 137–173). San Diego, CA: Academic Press. [26]

Langer, E. J., & Rodin, J. (1976). The effects of choice and enhanced personal responsibility for the aged: A field experiment in an institutional setting. *Journal of Personality and Social Psychology*, 34, 191–198. [16]

Lazarus, R. S. (1982). Thoughts on the relations between emotion and cognition. *American Psychologist*, 46, 352–367. [25]

LeDoux, J. E. (1996). *The emotional brain: The mysterious underpinnings of emotional life.* New York: Simon & Schuster. [1, 25]

Lefcourt, H. M. (1973). The function of the illusions of control and freedom. *American Psychologist*, 28, 417–425. [16]

Legrenzi, P., Girotto, V., & Johnson-Laird, P. N. (1993). Focusing in reasoning and decision making. *Cognition*, 49, 37–66. [9, 17, 34]

Lehman, D. R., Davis, C. G., Delongis, A., Wortman, C. B., Bluck, S., Mandel, D. R., et al. (1993). Positive and negative life changes following bereavement and their relations to adjustment. *Journal of Social and Clinical Psychology*, 12, 90–112. [30]

Lepper, M. R. (1983). Social control processes and the internalization of social values: An attributional perspective. In E. T. Higgins, D. N. Ruble, & W. W. Hartup (Eds.), *Social cognition and social development* (pp. 294–330). New York: Cambridge University Press. [16]

Lerner, J. S., Gonzalez, R. M., Small, D. A., & Fischhoff, B. (2003). Effects of fear and anger on perceived risks of terrorism: A national field experiment. *Psychological Science*, 14, 144–150. [24]

Lerner, J. S., & Keltner, D. (2000). Beyond valence: Toward a model of emotion-specific influences on judgment and choice. *Cognition & Emotion*, 14, 473–493. [24]

Lerner, J. S., Small, D. A., & Loewenstein, G. (2004). Heart strings and purse strings: Carryover effects of emotions on economic decisions. *Psychological Science*, 15, 337–341. [21, 24]

Lerner, J. S., & Tetlock, P. E. (1999). Accounting for the effects of accountability. *Psychological Bulletin*, 125, 255–275. [29]

Levav, J. (1996). *Questioning contingent valuation: Maximality and violations of monotonicity in willingness-to-pay for public goods.* Unpublished undergraduate thesis, Princeton University, Princeton, NJ. [31]

Levin, I. P. (1999, November). *Why do you and I make different decisions? Tracking individual differences in decision making.* Presidential address to the Society for Judgment and Decision Making, Los Angeles, CA. [1]

Levin, I. P., & Gaeth, G. J. (1988). How consumers are affected by the framing of attribute information before and after consuming the product. *Journal of Consumer Research*, 15, 374–378. [17, 21]

Levin, I. P., & Hart, S. S. (2003). Risk preferences in young children: Early evidence of individual differences in reaction to potential gains and losses. *Journal of Behavioral Decision Making*, 16, 397–413. [1]

Levin, I. P., & Jasper, J. D. (1993, November). *Identifying compensatory and non-compensatory processes in phased decision making.* Paper presented at the meeting of the Judgment and Decision Making Society, Washington, DC. [19]

Levin, S. J., & Levine, D. S. (1996). Multiattribute decision making in context: A dynamic neural network methodology. *Cognitive Science, 20,* 271–299. [11]

Lewicka, M. (1997). Rational or uncommitted? Depression and indecisiveness in interpersonal decision making. *Scandinavian Journal of Psychology, 38,* 227–236. [18]

Lewin, K. (1952). Group decision and social change. In G. E. Swanson, T. M. Newcomb, & E. L. Hartley (Eds.), *Readings in social psychology* (pp. 459–473). New York: Henry Holt. [16]

Lewin, K., Dembo, T., Festinger, L. A., & Sears, P. S. (1944). Levels of aspiration. In J. M. Hunt (Ed.), *Personality and behavior disorders* (Vol. 1, pp. 333–378). New York: Ronald. [19]

Lichtenstein, S. (1965). Bases for preferences among three-outcome bets. *Journal of Experimental Psychology, 69,* 162–169. [2, 3]

Lichtenstein, S., & Newman, J. R. (1967). Empirical scaling of common verbal phrases associated with numerical probabilities. *Psychonomic Science, 9,* 563–564. [35]

Lichtenstein, S., & Slovic, P. (1971). Reversals of preference between bids and choices in gambling decisions. *Journal of Experimental Psychology, 89,* 46–55. [1, 3, 4, 5, 6, 7, 8, 9, 10, 11, 12, 18, 21, 29, 33]

Lichtenstein, S., & Slovic, P. (1973). Response-induced reversals of preference in gambling: An extended replication in Las Vegas. *Journal of Experimental Psychology, 101,* 16–20. [1, 4, 5, 6, 7, 8, 11]

Lichtenstein, S., Slovic, P., Fischhoff, B., Layman, M., & Combs, B. (1978). Judged frequency of lethal events. *Journal of Experimental Psychology: Human Learning and Memory, 4,* 551–578. [23]

Lifton, R. J. (1990). *The Nazi doctors: Medical killings and the psychology of genocide.* New York: Basic Books. [20]

Lindberg, E., Gärling, T., & Montgomery, H. (1988). People's beliefs and values as determinants of housing preferences and simulated choices. *Scandinavian Housing and Planning Research, 5,* 181–197. [18]

Lindberg, E., Gärling, T., & Montgomery, H. (1989a, August). *Decision with incompletely described alternatives.* Paper presented at the 12th European Research Conference on Subjective Probability, Utility, and Decision Making, Moscow. [18]

Lindberg, E., Gärling, T., & Montgomery, H. (1989b). Differential predictability of preferences and choices. *Journal of Behavioral Decision Making, 2,* 205–219. [10, 18]

Lindberg, E., Gärling, T., & Montgomery, H. (1989c). Belief-value structures as determinants of consumer behavior: A study of housing preferences and choices. *Journal of Consumer Policy, 12,* 119–137. [18]

Lindberg, E., Gärling, T., & Montgomery, H. (1990). *Intra-urban residential mobility: Subjective belief-value structures as determinants of residential preferences and choices* (Umea Psychological Reports, No. 197). Umea, Sweden: Department of Psychology, University of Umea. [18]

Lindecrantz, M. (2001). *Individuella skillnader vid beslutsfattande: Beslutsprocesser hos staterespektive actionorienterade individer* [Individual differences in decision making: Decision processes in state- versus action-oriented individuals]. Unpublished masters thesis, Stockholm University, Stockholm. [19]

Linder, D. E., Cooper, J., & Jones, E. E. (1967). Decision freedom as a determinant of the role of incentive magnitude in attitude change. *Journal of Personality and Social Psychology, 6*, 245–254. [16]

Lindman, H. R. (1965). *The measurement of utilities and subjective probabilities.* Unpublished doctoral dissertation, University of Michigan, Ann Arbor. [1, 2]

Lindman, H. R. (1971). Inconsistent preferences among gambles. *Journal of Experimental Psychology, 89*, 390–397. [1, 3, 4, 5, 8, 11]

Linville, P., & Fischer, G. W. (1991). Preferences for separating or combining events. *Journal of Personality and Social Psychology, 60*, 5–23. [20]

Lipshitz, R. (1993). Converging themes in the study of decision making in realistic settings. In G. A. Klein, J. Orasanu, R. Calderwood, & C. E. Zsambok (Eds.), *Decision making in action: Models and methods* (pp. 103–137). Norwood, NJ: Ablex. [18]

Littig, L. W. (1962). Effects of skill and chance orientations on probability preferences. *Psychological Reports, 10*, 67–70. [2]

Lodge, M. (1981). *Magnitude scaling: Quantitative measurement of opinions.* Beverly Hills, CA: Sage. [31]

Loewenstein, G. (1987). Anticipation and the valuation of delayed consumption. *Economic Journal, 97*, 666–684. [23]

Loewenstein, G. (1988). Frames of mind in intertemporal choice. *Management Science, 34*, 200–214. [21]

Loewenstein, G. (1996). Out of control: Visceral influences on behavior. *Organizational Behavior and Human Decision Processes, 65*, 272–292. [9, 28, 29]

Loewenstein, G. (2000). How people make decisions: Costs and benefits of health- and retirement-related choice. In S. Burke, E. Kingson, & U. Reinhardt (Eds.), *Social Security and Medicare: Individual versus collective risk and responsibility* (pp. 87–113). Washington, DC: National Academy of Social Insurance. [38]

Loewenstein, G., & Adler, D. (1995). A bias in the prediction of tastes. *Economic Journal, 105*, 929–937. [27]

Loewenstein, G., Blount, S., & Bazerman, M. H. (1993). *Reversals of preference between independent and simultaneous evaluation of alternatives.* Unpublished manuscript, Carnegie Mellon University, Pittsburgh, PA. [9]

Loewenstein, G., & Frederick, S. (1997). Predicting reactions to environmental change. In M. Bazerman, D. Messick, A. Tenbrunsel, & K. Wade-Benzoni (Eds.), *Environment, ethics, and behavior* (pp. 52–72). San Francisco: New Lexington Press. [9, 29]

Loewenstein, G., O'Donoghue, T., & Rabin, M. (2003). Projection bias in predicting future utility. *The Quarterly Journal of Economics, 118*, 1209–1248. [35]

Loewenstein, G., & Prelec, D. (1992). Anomalies in intertemporal choice: Evidence and an interpretation. *The Quarterly Journal of Economics, 107*, 573–597. [20]

Loewenstein, G., & Prelec, D. (1993). Preferences for sequences of outcomes. *Psychological Review, 100*, 91–108. [9, 20, 29]

Loewenstein, G., & Schkade, D. (1999). Wouldn't it be nice? Predicting future feelings. In E. Diener, N. Schwartz, & D. Kahneman (Eds.), *Well-being: The foundations of hedonic psychology* (pp. 85–105). New York: Russell Sage Foundation. [23, 28, 29, 30, 34]

Loewenstein, G., & Sicherman, N. (1991). Do workers prefer increasing wage profiles? *Journal of Labor Economics, 9*, 67–84. [9, 27]

Loewenstein, G., & Thaler, R. H. (1989). Anomalies: Intertemporal choice. *The Journal of Economic Perspectives, 3*(4), 181–193. [13]

Loewenstein, G., Weber, E. U., Hsee, C. K., & Welch, E. S. (2001). Risk as feelings. *Psychological Bulletin, 127*, 267–286. [21, 23, 24, 29]

Loftus, E. F., & Pickrell, J. E. (1995). The formation of false memories. *Psychiatric Annals, 25*, 720–725. [21]

Loomes, G., Starmer, C., & Sugden, R. (1989). Preference reversal: Information-processing effect or rational nontransitive choice. *Economic Journal, 99*, 140–151. [8]

Loomes, G., & Sugden, R. (1982). Regret theory: An alternative theory of rational choice under uncertainty. *Economic Journal, 92*, 805–824. [6, 8, 19, 36]

Loomes, G., & Sugden, R. (1983). A rationale for preference reversal. *American Economic Review, 73*(3), 428–432. [1, 6, 7, 8]

Loomis, J. B., Gonzalez-Caban, A., & Gregory, R. (1994). Do reminders of substitutes and budget constraints influence contingent valuation estimates? *Land Economics, 70*, 499–506. [31]

Loomis, J. B., Hanemann, W. M., Kanninen, B., & Wegge, T. (1991). Willingness to pay to protect wetlands and reduce wildlife contamination from agricultural damage. In A. Dinar & D. Zilberman (Eds.), *The economics and management of water and drainage in agriculture* (pp. 411–429). Boston: Kluwer Academic. [33]

Loomis, J. B., Lockwood, M., & DeLacy, T. (1993). Some empirical evidence on embedding effects in contingent valuation of forest protection. *Journal of Environmental Economics and Management, 25*, 45–55. [33]

Lopes, L. L. (1981). Decision making in the short run. *Journal of Experimental Psychology: Human Learning and Memory, 7*, 377–385. [19, 20]

Lopes, L. L. (1982, December). *Toward a procedural theory of judgment* (Technical Report No. WHIPP 17). Madison: Wisconsin Human Information Processing Program. [7]

Lopes, L. L. (1996). When time is of the essence: Averaging, aspiration, and the short run. *Organizational Behavior and Human Decision Processes, 65*, 179–189. [20]

Lord, C. G., Lepper, M. R., & Mackie, D. (1984). Attitude prototypes as determinants of attitude-behavior consistency. *Journal of Personality and Social Psychology, 46*, 1254–1266. [30]

Lowenthal, D. (1993). *Preference reversals in candidate evaluation* (Working paper). Pittsburgh, PA: Carnegie Mellon University. [9]

Lucas, R. E. (1986). Adaptive behavior and economic theory. *Journal of Business, 59*, S401–S426. [17, 34]

Luce, M. F. (1998). Choosing to avoid: Coping with negatively emotion-laden consumer decisions. *Journal of Consumer Research, 24*, 409–423. [34]

Luce, M. F., Payne, J. W., & Bettman, J. R. (1999). Emotional trade-off difficulty and choice. *Journal of Marketing Research, 36*, 143–159. [17, 29, 34]

Luce, R. D. (1986). *Response times: Their role in inferring elementary mental organization.* New York: Oxford University Press. [15]

Lundberg, C. G., & Svenson, O. (2000). Postdecision consolidation in a trend prediction task. *Scandinavian Journal of Psychology, 41*, 159–168. [19]

Lusk, C. M., & Judd, C. M. (1988). Political expertise and the structural mediators of candidate evaluations. *Journal of Experimental Social Psychology, 24*, 105–126. [26]

Lustig, C., & Hasher, L. (2001). Implicit memory is not immune to interference. *Psychological Bulletin, 127*, 618–628. [21]

Lynch, J. G., Chakravarti, D., & Mitra, A. (1991). Contrast effects in consumer judgments: Changes in mental representations or in the anchoring of rating scales? *Journal of Consumer Research, 18*, 284–297. [17]

Lynch, J. G., Marmorstein, H., & Weigold, M. F. (1988). Choices from sets including remembered brands: Use of recalled attributes and prior overall evaluations. *Journal of Consumer Research, 15*, 169–184. [10]

MacGregor, D. G., & Slovic, P. (1986). Perceived acceptability of risk analysis as a decision-making approach. *Risk Analysis, 6*, 245–256. [33]

MacGregor, D. G., Slovic, P., Dreman, D., & Berry, M. (2000). Imagery, affect, and financial judgment. *Journal of Psychology and Financial Markets, 1*, 104–110. [23]

Machina, M. J. (1987). Choice under uncertainty: Problems solved and unsolved. *Economic Perspectives, 1*, 121–154. [8]

MacLean, D. (1994). Cost-benefit analysis and procedural values. *Analyse & Kritik, 2*, 166–180. [36]

Madrian, B. C., & Shea, D. F. (2001). The power of suggestion: Inertia in 401(k) participation and savings behavior. *The Quarterly Journal of Economics, 116*, 1149–1187. [37, 38]

Malone, T. W., & Lepper, M. R. (1987). Making learning fun: A taxonomy of intrinsic motivations for learning. In R. E. Snow & M. J. Farr (Eds.), *Aptitude, learning and instruction: Vol. 3. Conative and affective process analysis* (pp. 223–253). Hillsdale, NJ: Lawrence Erlbaum Associates. [16]

Mandel, N., & Johnson, E. J. (2002). When Web pages influence choice: Effects of visual primes on experts and novices. *Journal of Consumer Research, 29*, 235–245. [1, **15**, 21]

Mann, L., Janis, I. L., & Chaplin, R. (1969). The effects of anticipation of forthcoming information on predecisional processes. *Journal of Personality and Social Psychology, 11*, 10–16. [18]

March, J. (1978). Bounded rationality, ambiguity, and the rationality of choice. *Bell Journal of Economics, 9*, 587–608. [1, 6, 9, 17, 27, 29, 34]

March, J. (1994). *A primer on decision making: How decisions happen.* New York: The Free Press. [28, 29]

Marder, E. (1997). *The laws of choice.* New York: The Free Press. [34]

Markman, A. B., & Medin, D. L. (1995). Similarity and alignment in choice. *Organizational Behavior and Human Decision Processes, 63*, 117–130. [10]

Markman, A. B., Zhang, S., & Moreau, C. P. (2000). Representation and the construction of preferences. In E. Dietrich & A. Markman (Eds.), *Cognitive dynamics: Conceptual and representational change in humans and machines* (pp. 343–365). Mahwah, NJ: Lawrence Erlbaum Associates. [12]

Markman, K. D., & Hirt, E. R. (2002). Social prediction and the allegiance bias. *Social Cognition, 20*, 58–86. [28]

Markowitz, H. (1952). The utility of wealth. *Journal of Political Economy, 60*, 151–158. [20]

Marsh, H. W. (1984). Students' evaluations of university teaching: Dimensionality, reliability, validity, potential biases, and utility. *Journal of Educational Psychology, 76*, 707–754. [9]

Martin, L. L., & Tesser, A. (Eds.). (1992). *The construction of social judgments.* Hillsdale, NJ: Lawrence Erlbaum Associates. [1]

Martin, L. M. (1986). Set/reset: Use and disuse of concepts in impression formation. *Journal of Personality and Social Psychology, 51*, 493–504. [15]

May, K. O. (1954). Intransitivity, utility, and the aggregation of preference patterns. *Econometrica, 22*, 1–3. [1, 9, 19]

McClure, S. M., Li, J., Tomlin, D., Cypert, K. S., Montague, L. M., & Montague, R. P. (2004). Neural correlates of behavioral preference for culturally familiar drinks. *Neuron, 44*, 379–387. [1]

McFadden, D. (1994). Contingent valuation and social choice. *American Journal of Agricultural Economics, 76*, 689–703. [31]

McFadden, D. (1999). Rationality for economists. *Journal of Risk and Uncertainty, 19*, 73–106. [17, 34]

McFadden, D., & Leonard, G. (1993). Issues in The contingent valuation of environmental goods: Methodologies for data collection and analysis. In J. A. Hausman (Ed.), *Contingent valuation: A critical assessment* (pp. 165–208). Amsterdam: North-Holland. [31]

McGuire, W. J. (1969). Suspiciousness of experimenter's intent. In R. Rosenthal & R. L. Rosnow (Eds.), *Artifact in behavioral research* (pp. 13–57). New York: Academic Press. [35]

McKenzie, C. R. M., & Nelson, J. D. (2003). What a speaker's choice of frame reveals: Reference points, frame selection, and framing effects. *Psychonomic Bulletin and Review, 10*, 596–602. [21]

McKoon, G., & Ratcliff, R. (1995). Conceptual combinations and relational contexts in free association and in priming in lexical decision and naming. *Psychonomic Bulletin and Review, 2*, 527–533. [15]

McLanahan, S. S., & Sorensen, A. B. (1984). Life events and psychological well-being: A reexamination of theoretical and methodological issues. *Social Science Research, 13*, 111–128. [28]

McNamara, T. P. (1992). Priming and constraints it places on theories of memory and retrieval. *Psychological Review, 99*, 650–662. [15]

McNeil, B. J., Pauker, S. G., Sox, H. C., Jr., & Tversky, A. (1982). On the elicitation of preferences for alternative therapies. *New England Journal of Medicine, 306*, 1259–1262. [1]

Mellers, B. A., Chang, S., Birnbaum, M. H., & Ordóñez, L. D. (1992). Preferences, prices, and ratings in risky decision making. *Journal of Experimental Psychology: Human Perception and Performance, 18*, 347–361. [9, 10, 28]

Mellers, B. A., & Cooke, A. D. J. (1994). Trade-offs depend on attribute range. *Journal of Experimental Psychology: Human Perception and Performance, 20*, 1055–1067. [9]

Mellers, B. A., & Cooke, A. D. J. (1996). The role of task and context in preference measurement. *Psychological Science, 7*, 76–82. [10]

Mellers, B. A., Ordóñez, L., & Birnbaum, M. H. (1992). A change-of-process theory for contextual effects and preference reversals in risky decision making. *Organizational Behavior and Human Decision Processes, 52*, 331–369. [1, 9]

Mellers, B. A., Richards, V., & Birnbaum, M. H. (1992). Distributional theories of impression formation. *Organizational Behavior and Human Decision Processes, 51*, 313–343. [23]

Mellers, B. A., Schwartz, A., & Cooke, A. D. J. (1998). Judgment and decision making. *Annual Review of Psychology, 49*, 447–477. [17]

Mellers, B. A., Schwartz, A., Ho, K., & Ritov, I. (1997). Elation and disappointment: Emotional reactions to risky options. *Psychological Science, 8*, 423–429. [24, 29]

Mellers, B. A., Schwartz, A., & Ritov, I. (1999). Emotion-based choice. *Journal of Experimental Psychology: General, 128*, 332–345. [29]

Merkhofer, M. W., & Keeney, R. L. (1987). A multiattribute utility analysis of alternative sites for the disposal of nuclear waste. *Risk Analysis, 7*, 173–194. [33]

Middleton, F. A., & Strick, P. L. (2000). A revised neuroanatomy of frontal-subcortical circuits. In D. G. Lichter & J. L. Cummings (Eds.), *Frontal-subcortical circuits in psychiatric and neurological disorders* (pp. 44–58). New York: Guilford Press. [11]

Mill, J. S. (1974). *On liberty*. London: Penguin. [38]

Millar, M. G., & Tesser, A. (1986). Effects of affective and cognitive focus on the attitude-behavior relationship. *Journal of Personality and Social Psychology, 51*, 270–276. [26]

Millar, M. G., & Tesser, A. (1989). The effects of affective-cognitive consistency and thought on the attitude-behavior relation. *Journal of Experimental Social Psychology, 25*, 189–202. [26]

Miller, G. A. (1956). The magical number seven, plus or minus two: Some limits on our capacity for processing information. *Psychological Review, 63*, 81–97. [19, 20]

Miller, J. G. (1961). Sensory overloading. In B. E. Flaherty (Ed.), *Psychophysiological aspects of space flight* (pp. 215–237). New York: Columbia University Press. [2]

Miller, L., & Meyer, D. E. (1966). Decision effectiveness as a function of the structure and number of alternatives at a choice point. *Proceedings of the 74th Annual Convention of the American Psychological Association, 1*, 25–26. [2]

Milliken, B., Joordens, S., Merikle, P. M., & Seiffert, A. E. (1998). Selective attention: A reevaluation of the implications of negative priming. *Psychological Review, 105*, 203–229. [21]

Mills, J., Meltzer, R., & Clark, M. (1977). Effect of number of options on recall of information supporting different decision strategies. *Personality and Social Psychology Bulletin, 3*, 213–218. [16]

Mintzberg, H., Raisinghani, D., & Thoret, A. (1976). The structure of unstructured decisions. *Administrative Science Quarterly, 21*, 246–275. [19]

Mitchell, R. C., & Carson, R. T. (1989). *Using surveys to value public goods: The contingent valuation method*. Washington, DC: Resources for the Future. [31, 33, 34]

Monahan, J. L., Murphy, S. T., & Zajonc, R. B. (2000). Subliminal mere exposure: Specific, general, and diffuse effects. *Psychological Science, 11*, 462–466. [25]

Montague, R. P. (2002, October). *Neural economics and the biological substrates of valuation* [Lecture notes]. Paper presented at the University of California Conference on Recent Research in Behavioral Finance, Monterey, CA. [1]

Montague, R. P., & Berns, G. S. (2002). Neural economics and the biological substrates of valuation. *Neuron, 36*, 265–284. [1, 24]

Montgomery, H. (1983). Decision rules and the search for a dominance structure: Towards a process model of decision making. In P. C. Humphreys, O. Svenson, & A. Vari (Eds.), *Analysing and aiding decision processes* (pp. 343–369). Amsterdam/ Budapest: North-Holland and Hungarian Academic Press. [1, 6, 12, 18, 19, 22, 23]

Montgomery, H. (1989). From cognition to action: The search for dominance in decision making. In H. Montgomery & O. Svenson (Eds.), *Process and structure in human decision making* (pp. 23–49). Chichester, England: Wiley. [18]

Montgomery, H. (1993). The choice of a home seen from the inside: Psychological contributions to the study of decision making in housing markets. In T. Gärling & R. G. Golledge (Eds.), *Behavior and environment* (pp. 317–341). Amsterdam: Elsevier. [18]

Montgomery, H. (1994). Towards a perspective theory of decision making and judgment. *Acta Psychologica, 87*, 155–187. [18, 19]

Montgomery, H. (1997). Surrender at Perevolochna: A case study of perspective and action control in decision making under stress. In R. Flin, E. Salas, M. Strub,

& L. Martin (Eds.), *Decision making under stress: Emerging themes and applications* (pp. 193–204). Aldershot, England: Ashgate. [18]

Montgomery, H. (1998). Decision making and action: The search for a dominance structure. In M. Kofta, G. Weary, & G. Sedek (Eds.), *Personal control in action: Cognitive and motivational mechanisms* (pp. 279–298). New York: Plenum. [1, **18**]

Montgomery, H., Gärling, T., Lindberg, E., & Selart, M. (1990). Preference judgments and choice: Is the prominence effect due to information integration or to information evaluation? In K. Borcherding, O. I. Larichev, & D. Messick (Eds.), *Contemporary issues in decision making* (pp. 149–157). Amsterdam: North-Holland. [18]

Montgomery, H., & Hemlin, S. (1991). *Judging scientific quality: A cross-disciplinary investigation of professorial evaluation documents* (Göteborg Psychological Reports, Vol. 21, No. 4). Göteborg, Sweden: University of Göteborg, Department of Psychology. [18]

Montgomery, H., Selart, M., Gärling, T., & Lindberg, E. (1994). The judgment-choice discrepancy: Noncompatibility or restructuring? *Journal of Behavioral Decision Making, 7*, 145–155. [10, 18]

Montgomery, H., & Svenson, O. (1989). A think aloud study of dominance structuring in decision processes. In H. Montgomery & O. Svenson (Eds.), *Process and structure in human decision making* (pp. 135–150). Chichester, UK: Wiley. [18, 19]

Moore, D. (1999). Order effects in preference judgments: Evidence for context dependence in the generation of preferences. *Organizational Behavior and Human Decision Processes, 78*, 146–165. [28]

Morewedge, C. K., Gilbert, D. T., & Wilson, T. D. (2005). The least likely of times: How remembering the past biases forecasts of the future. *Psychological Science, 16*, 626–630. [1]

Morgan, M. G., Fischhoff, B., Bostrom, A., & Atman, C. J. (2002). *Risk communication: A mental models approach.* New York: Cambridge University Press. [35]

Morrison, E. R. (1998). Judicial review of discount rates used in regulatory cost-benefit analysis. *The University of Chicago Law Review, 65*, 1333–1359. [38]

Morrow, J., & Nolan-Hoeksema, S. (1990). Effects of responses to depression on the remediation of depressive affect. *Journal of Personality and Social Psychology, 58*, 519–527. [26]

Morwitz, V. G. (1997). Why consumers don't always accurately predict their own future behavior. *Marketing Letters, 8*, 57–60. [21]

Morwitz, V. G., Johnson, E. J., & Schmittlein, D. (1993). Does measuring intent change behavior? *Journal of Consumer Research, 20*, 46–61. [21]

Morwitz, V. G., & Pluzinski, C. (1996). Do polls reflect opinions or do opinions reflect polls? The impact of political polling on voters' expectations, preferences, and behavior. *Journal of Consumer Research, 23*, 53–67. [21]

Mowen, J. C., & Gentry, J. W. (1980). Investigation of the preference-reversal phenomenon in a new product introduction task. *Journal of Applied Psychology, 65*, 715–722. [1, 8]

Mowrer, O. H. (1960a). *Learning theory and behavior.* New York: John Wiley & Sons. [23]

Mowrer, O. H. (1960b). *Learning theory and the symbolic processes.* New York: John Wiley & Sons. [23]

Murphy, S. T., Monahan, J. L., & Zajonc, R. B. (1995). Additivity of nonconscious affect: Combined effects of priming and exposure. *Journal of Personality and Social Psychology, 69*, 589–602. [25]

Murray, K. B., & Häubl, G. (2005). Processes of preference construction in agent-assisted online shopping. In C. Haugtvedt, K. Machleit, & R. Yalch (Eds.), *Online consumer psychology: Understanding and influencing consumer behavior in the virtual world* (pp. 265–286). Mahwah, NJ: Lawrence Erlbaum Associates. [1]

Mussweiler, T., & Strack, F. (2001a). Considering the impossible: Explaining the effects of implausible anchors. *Social Cognition, 19*, 145–160. [13]

Mussweiler, T., & Strack, F. (2001b). The semantics of anchoring. *Organizational Behavior and Human Decision Processes, 86*, 234–255. [21]

Mussweiler, T., Strack, F., & Pfeiffer, T. (2000). Overcoming the inevitable anchoring effect: Considering the opposite compensates for selective accessibility. *Personality and Social Psychology Bulletin, 26*, 1142–1150. [21]

Myers, D. G. (1993). *The pursuit of happiness: Who is happy and why?* New York: Avon Books. [28]

National Institute of Diabetes and Digestive and Kidney Diseases. (2001). *Understanding adult obesity*. Retrieved May 4, 2005, from http://win.niddk.nih.gov/publications/understanding.htm. [38]

Neill, H. (1995). The context for substitutes in CVM studies: Some empirical observations. *Journal of Environmental Economics and Management, 29*, 393–397. [31]

Neisser, U. (1967). *Cognitive psychology*. New York: Appleton-Century-Crofts. [1]

Nelson, P. (1970). Information and consumer behavior. *Journal of Political Economy, 78*, 331–329. [10]

Nickerson, C. (1995). Does willingness-to-pay reflect the purchase of moral satisfaction? A reconsideration of Kahneman and Knetsch. *Journal of Environmental Economics and Management, 28*, 126–133. [31]

Nicosia, F. M. (1966). *Consumer decision processes: Marketing and advertising implications*. Englewood Cliffs, NJ: Prentice-Hall. [17]

Nisbett, R., & Ross, L. (1980). *Human inference: Strategies and shortcomings of social judgment*. Englewood Cliffs, NJ: Prentice-Hall. [1]

Nisbett, R. E., & Wilson, T. D. (1977). Telling more than we can know: Verbal reports on mental processes. *Psychological Review, 84*, 231–259. [22, 26]

Nogee, P., & Lieberman, B. (1960). The auction value of certain risky situations. *Journal of Psychology, 49*, 167–179. [2]

Norman, D. A. (1988). *The psychology of everyday things*. New York: Basic Books. [34]

North, A. C., Hargreaves, D. J., & McKendrick, J. (1999). The influence of in-store music on wine selections. *Journal of Applied Psychology, 84*, 271–276. [21]

Norwick, R. J., Gilbert, D. T., & Wilson, T. D. (2005). *Surrogation: An antidote for errors in affective forecasting*. Unpublished manuscript, Harvard University, Cambridge, MA. [1]

Novemsky, N., & Kronzon, S. (1999). How are base-rates used, when they are used: A comparison of additive and Bayesian models of base-rate use. *Journal of Behavioral Decision Making, 12*, 55–69. [31]

Novemsky, N., & Ratner, R. K. (2003). The time course and impact of consumers' erroneous beliefs about hedonic contrast effects. *Journal of Consumer Research, 29*, 507–516. [28]

Nowlis, S. M., & Simonson, I. (1994). *The context-dependency of attributes as a determinant of preference reversals between choices and judgments of purchase likelihood* (Working paper). Palo Alto, CA: Stanford University. [9, 10]

Nowlis, S. M., & Simonson, I. (1997). Attribute-task compatability as a determinant of consumer preference reversals. *Journal of Marketing Research, 34*, 205–218. [1, 9, **10**, 20, 28, 29]

Nutt, P. C. (1998). How decision makers evaluate alternatives and the influence of complexity. *Management Science, 44*, 1148–1166. [34]

O'Curry, S. (1995). *Income source effects* (Working paper). Chicago: DePaul University, Department of Marketing. [20]

O'Donoghue, E., & Rabin, M. (1997). *Incentives for procrastinators* (Working paper). University of California, Berkeley, Department of Economics. [20]

O'Donoghue, E., & Rabin, M. (1999). Doing it now or later. *American Economic Review, 89*(1), 103–124. [20]

Okin, S. M. (1989). *Justice, gender, and the family*. New York: Basic. [38]

Orasanu, J., & Connoly, T. (1993). The reinvention of decision making. In G. A. Klein, J. Orasanu, R. Calderwood, & C. E. Zsambok (Eds.), *Decision making in action: Models and methods* (pp. 3–20). Norwood, NJ: Ablex. [18]

Osgood, C. E., Suci, G. J., & Tannenbaum, P. H. (1957). *The measurement of meaning*. Urbana: University of Illinois. [23, 31]

Osnos, E. (1997, September 27). Too many choices? Firms cut back on new products. *Philadelphia Inquirer*, D1, D7. [16]

Oz, M. C., Kherani, A. R., Rowe, A., Roels, L., Crandall, C., Tournatis, L., et al. (2003). How to improve organ donation: Results of the ISHLT/FACT poll. *Journal of Heart and Lung Transplantation, 22*, 389–396. [37]

Pachella, R. G. (1974). The interpretation of reaction time in information processing research. In B. H. Kantowitz (Ed.), *Human information processing: Tutorials in performance and cognition* (pp. 41–82). Hillsdale, NJ: Lawrence Erlbaum Associates. [15]

Papandreou, A. G. (1953). An experimental test of an axiom in the theory of choice. *Econometrica, 21*, 477. [19]

Parfit, D. (1984). *Reasons and persons*. Oxford, UK: Oxford University Press. [27]

Parker, A. M., & Fischhoff, B. (2005). Decision-making competence: External validation through an individual-differences approach. *Journal of Behavioral Decision Making, 18*, 1–27. [1, 35]

Patrick, C. J. (1994). Emotion and psychopathy: Startling new insights. *Psychophysiology, 31*, 319–330. [23]

Payne, J. W. (1976). Task complexity and contingent processing in decision making: An information search and protocol analysis. *Organizational Behavior and Human Performance, 16*, 366–387. [7, 17, 19, 34]

Payne, J. W. (1982). Contingent decision behavior. *Psychological Bulletin, 92*, 382–401. [6, 10, 16, 17, 19]

Payne, J. W., Bettman, J. R., & Johnson, E. J. (1988). Adaptive strategy selection in decision making. *Journal of Experimental Psychology: Learning, Memory, and Cognition, 14*, 534–552. [1, 16, 34]

Payne, J. W., Bettman, J. R., & Johnson, E. J. (1990). The adaptive decision maker: Effort and accuracy in choice. In R. M. Hogarth (Ed.), *Insights in decision making: A tribute to Hillel J. Einhorn* (pp. 129–153). Chicago: University of Chicago Press. [21]

Payne, J. W., Bettman, J. R., & Johnson, E. J. (1992). Behavioral decision research: A constructive processing perspective. *Annual Review of Psychology, 43*, 87–131. [1, 9, 10, 12, 17, 19, 21, 22, 31, 33, 34, 37]

Payne, J. W., Bettman, J. R., & Johnson, E. J. (1993). *The adaptive decision maker.* New York: Cambridge University Press. [11, 13, 15, 16, 17, 19, 23, 34]

Payne, J. W., Bettman, J. R., & Schkade, D. A. (1999). Measuring constructed preferences: Towards a building code. *Journal of Risk and Uncertainty, 19*, 243–270. [1, 17, 24, 31, **34**, 35, 38]

Payne, J. W., & Braunstein, M. L. (1978). Risky choice: An examination of information acquisition behavior. *Memory & Cognition, 5*, 554–561. [7]

Payne, J. W., Braunstein, M. L., & Carroll, J. S. (1978). Exploring predecisional behavior: An alternative approach to decision research. *Organizational Behavior and Human Performance, 22*, 17–44. [7]

Payne, J. W., Schkade, D. A., Desvousges, W. H., & Aultman, C. (2000). Valuation of multiple environmental programs. *Journal of Risk and Uncertainty, 21*, 95–115. [31]

Pennington, N., & Hastie, R. (1988). Explanation-based decision making: Effects of memory structure on judgment. *Journal of Experimental Psychology: Learning, Memory, and Cognition, 14*, 521–533. [22]

Pennington, N., & Hastie, R. (1992). Explaining the evidence: Tests of the story model for juror decision making. *Journal of Personality and Social Psychology, 62*, 189–206. [22]

Pennington, N., & Hastie, R. (1993a). Reasoning in explanation-based decision making. *Cognition, 49*, 123–163. [18]

Pennington, N., & Hastie, R. (1993b). A theory of explanation-based decision making. In G. Klein, J. Orasano, R. Calderwood, & C. E. Zsambok (Eds.), *Decision making in action: Models and methods* (pp. 188–204). Norwood, NJ: Ablex. [23]

Peters, E., & Slovic, P. (1996). The role of affect and worldviews as orienting dispositions in the perception and acceptance of nuclear power. *Journal of Applied Social Psychology, 26*, 1427–1453. [23, 24]

Peters, E., & Slovic, P. (2000). The springs of action: Affective and analytical information processing in choice. *Personality and Social Psychology Bulletin, 26*, 1465–1475. [1, 23, 24]

Peters, E., & Slovic, P. (2006). *Affective asynchrony and development of the HUE affect scale.* (Report No. 06-04). Eugene, OR: Decision Research. [24]

Peters, E., Slovic, P., & Gregory, R. (2003). The role of affect in the WTA/WTP disparity. *Journal of Behavioral Decision Making, 16*, 309–330. [24]

Peters, E., Slovic, P., & Hibbard, J. (2004). *Evaluability manipulations influence the construction of choices among health plans.* (Report No. 04-02). Eugene, OR: Decision Research. [24]

Peters, E., Slovic, P., Hibbard, J., & Tusler, M. (2006). Why worry? Worry, risk perceptions, and willingness to act to reduce errors. *Health Psychology, 25*, 144–152. [24]

Peters, E., Västfjäll, D., & Starmer, C. (2006). *Feeling your way to the right price.* (Report No. 06-05). Eugene, OR: Decision Research. [24]

Pham, M. T. (1998). Representativeness, relevance, and the use of feelings in decision making. *Journal of Consumer Research, 25*, 144–159. [23]

Phillips, C., & Zeckhauser, R. (1989). Contingent valuation of damage to natural resources: How accurate? How appropriate? *Toxics Law Reporter, 4*, 520–529. [33]

Phillips, F. (2002). The distortion of criteria after decision-making. *Organizational Behavior and Human Decision Processes, 88*, 769–784. [12, 19]

Phillips, L. D. (1984). A theory of requisite decision models. *Acta Psychologica, 56*, 29–48. [1]

Phillips, L. D., & Edwards, W. (1966). Conservatism in a simple probability inference task. *Journal of Experimental Psychology, 72*, 346–354. [1]

Pidgeon, N., & Gregory, R. (2004). Judgment, decision making, and public policy. In D. J. Koehler & N. Harvey (Eds.), *Blackwell handbook of judgment and decision making* (pp. 604–623). Oxford: Blackwell. [1]

Plott, C. R. (1996). Rational individual behavior in markets and social choice processes: The discovered preference hypothesis. In K. J. Arrow, C. Colombatto, M. Perleman, & C. Schmidt (Eds.), *The rational foundations of economic behavior* (pp. 225–250). New York: St. Martin's. [1, 17, 34]

Plous, S. (1993). *The psychology of judgment and decision making.* New York: McGraw-Hill. [35]

Pommerehne, W. W., Schneider, F., & Zweifel, P. (1982). Economic theory of choice and the preference reversal phenomenon: A reexamination. *American Economic Review, 72*(3), 569–574. [8]

Posovac, S. S., Sanbonmatsu, D. M., & Fazio, R. H. (1997). Considering the best choice: Effects of the salience and accessibility of alternatives on attitude-decision consistency. *Journal of Personality and Social Psychology, 72*, 253–261. [34]

Postman, L., & Underwood, B. J. (1973). Critical issues in interference theory. *Memory & Cognition, 1*, 19–40. [21]

Poulton, E. C. (1989). *Bias in quantifying judgment.* Hillsdale, NJ: Lawrence Erlbaum Associates. [35]

Pratkanis, A. (1989). The cognitive representation of attitudes. In A. Pratkanis, S. J. Breckler, & A. G. Greenwald (Eds.), *Attitude structure and function* (pp. 71–98). Hillsdale, NJ: Lawrence Erlbaum Associates. [23]

Pratto, F. (1994). Consciousness and automatic evaluation. In P. M. Niedenthal & S. Kitayama (Eds.), *The heart's eye: Emotional influences in perception and attention* (pp. 115–143). San Diego, CA: Academic Press. [31]

Prelec, D., & Herrnstein, R. (1991). Preferences or principles: Alternative guidelines for choice. In R. J. Zeckhauser (Ed.), *Strategy and choice* (pp. 319–340). Cambridge, MA: MIT Press. [22, 28, 29]

Prelec, D., & Loewenstein, G. (1991). Decision making over time and under uncertainty: A common approach. *Management Science, 37*, 770–786. [21]

Premack, D., & Premack, A. J. (1983). *The mind of an ape.* New York: Norton. [26]

Preston, M. G., & Baratta, P. (1948). An experimental study of the auction-value of an uncertain outcome. *American Journal of Psychology, 61*, 183–193. [2]

Puto, C. P. (1987). The framing of buying decisions. *Journal of Consumer Research, 14*, 301–315. [17]

Qualified Transportation Fringe Benefits, 26 CFR Parts 1 and 602. (2001). [38]

Quattrone, G., & Tversky, A. (1984). Causal versus diagnostic contingencies: On self-deception and the voter's illusion. *Journal of Personality and Social Psychology, 46*, 237–248. [31]

Rabin, M. (1998). Psychology and economics. *Journal of Economic Literature, 36*, 11–46. [34]

Rachlin, H. (1995). Self-control: Beyond commitment. *Behavioral and Brain Sciences, 18*, 109–159. [20]

Rae, J. (1834/1905). *The sociological theory of capital.* London: Macmillan. [13]

Raiffa, H. (1968). *Decision analysis: Introductory lectures on choices under uncertainty.* Reading, MA: Addison-Wesley. [1, 3, 26]

Rajecki, D. W. (1974). Effects of prenatal exposure to auditory or visual stimulation on postnatal distress vocalizations in chicks. *Behavioral Biology, 11*, 525–536. [25]

Randall, A. (1986). Valuation in a policy context. In D. Bromley (Ed.), *Natural resource economics: Policy problems and contemporary analysis* (pp. 163–200). Boston: Kluwer/Nijhoff Publishing. [33]

Randall, A., & Hoehn, J. (1996). Embedding in market demand systems. *Journal of Environmental and Economic Management, 30*, 369–380. [31]

Randall, A., Hoehn, J., & Brookshire, D. (1983). Contingent valuation surveys for evaluating environmental assets. *Natural Resources Journal, 23*, 635–648. [33]

Ranyard, R. (1989). Structuring and evaluating simple monetary risks. In H. Montgomery & O. Svenson (Eds.), *Process and structure in human decision making*. Chichester, UK: Wiley. [19]

Rasmussen, J. (1993). Deciding and doing: Decision making in natural contexts. In G. A. Klein, J. Orasanu, R. Calderwood, & C. E. Zsambok (Eds.), *Decision making in action: Models and methods* (pp. 158–171). Norwood, NJ: Ablex. [18]

Ratcliff, R., Cherian, A., & Segraves, M. (2003). A comparison of macaque behavior and superior colliculus neuronal activity to predictions from models of two-choice decisions. *Journal of Neurophysiology, 90*, 1392–1407. [11]

Ratcliff, R., & McKoon, G. (1997). A counter model for implicit priming in perceptual word identification. *Psychological Review, 104*, 319–343. [21]

Ratner, R. K., Kahn, B., & Kahneman, D. (1999). Choosing less-preferred experiences for the sake of variety. *Journal of Consumer Research, 26*, 1–15. [28]

Ratneshwar, S., Warlop, L., Mick, D. G., & Seeger, G. (1997). Benefit salience and consumers' selective attention to product features. *International Journal of Research in Marketing, 14*, 245–259. [15]

Rawls, J. (1971). *A theory of justice*. Cambridge, MA: Harvard University Press. [36]

Read, D., & Loewenstein, G. (1995). Diversification bias: Explaining the discrepancy in variety seeking between combined and separate choices. *Journal of Experimental Psychology: Applied, 1*, 34–49. [17, 20, 30, 34]

Read, D., Loewenstein, G., & Kalyanaraman, S. (1999). Mixing virtue with vice: The combined effects of hyperbolic discounting and diversification. *Journal of Behavioral Decision Making, 12*, 257–273. [20]

Read, D., Loewenstein, G., & Rabin, M. (1999). Choice bracketing. *Journal of Risk and Uncertainty, 19*, 171–197. [1, **20**]

Read, D., Van den Ouden, L., Trienekens, H., & Antonides, G. (1999). *Diversification bias in choice for consecutive consumption* (Working paper). Leeds, UK: Leeds University Business School. [20]

Read, D., & van Leeuwen, B. (1998). Predicting hunger: The effects of appetite and delay on choice. *Organizational Behavior and Human Decision Processes, 76*, 189–205. [20, 28]

Read, S. J., & Marcus-Newhall, J. (1993). Explanatory coherence in social explanations: A parallel distributed processing account. *Journal of Personality and Social Psychology, 65*, 429–447. [12]

Read, S. J., Snow, C. J., & Simon, D. (2003, August). *Constraint satisfaction processes in social reasoning*. Paper presented at the annual meeting of the Cognitive Science Society, Boston. [12]

Read, S. J., Vanman, E. J., & Miller, L. C. (1997). Connectionism, parallel constraint satisfaction processes, and gestalt principles: (Re)introducing cognitive dynamics in social psychology. *Personality and Social Psychology Review, 1*, 26–53. [12]

Redelmeier, D., & Kahneman, D. (1996). Patients' memories of painful medical treatment: Real-time and retrospective evaluations of two minimally invasive procedures. *Pain, 116*, 3–8. [1, 27]

Redelmeier, D., Rozin, P., & Kahneman, D. (1993). Understanding patients' decisions: Cognitive and emotional perspectives. *Journal of the American Medical Association, 270*, 72–76. [38]

Redelmeier, D., & Shafir, E. (1993). *Medical decisions over multiple alternatives* (Working paper). Toronto, Canada: University of Toronto. [22]

Redelmeier, D., & Tversky, A. (1992). On the framing of multiple prospects. *Psychological Science, 3*, 191–193. [20]

Reder, L. M., & Anderson, J. R. (1980). A partial resolution of the paradox of interference: The role of integrating knowledge. *Cognitive Psychology, 12*, 447–472. [21]

Reilly, R. J. (1982). Preference reversal: Further evidence and some suggested modifications in experimental design. *American Economic Review, 72*(3), 576–584. [8]

Revesz, R. L. (1999). Environmental regulation, cost-benefit analysis, and the discounting of human lives. *Columbia Law Review, 99*, 941–1017. [38]

Reyna, V. F., & Lloyd, F. (1997). Theories of false memory in children and adults. *Learning and Individual Differences, 9*, 95–123. [21]

Reyna, V. F., Lloyd, F. J., & Brainerd, C. J. (2003). Memory, development, and rationality: An integrative theory of judgment and decision making. In S. L. Schneider & J. Shanteau (Eds.), *Emerging perspectives on judgment and decision research* (pp. 203–245). Cambridge, UK: Cambridge University Press. [21]

Ristau, C. A., & Robbins, D. (1982). Language in the great apes: A critical review. In J. S. Rosenblatt, R. A. Hinde, C. Beer, & M. Busnel (Eds.), *Advances in the study of behavior* (Vol. 12, pp. 141–255). New York: Academic Press. [26]

Ritov, I. (1996). Anchoring in a simulated competitive market negotiation. *Organizational Behavior and Human Decision Processes, 67*, 16–25. [31]

Ritov, I., Baron, J., & Hershey, J. (1993). Framing effects in the evaluation of multiple risk reduction. *Journal of Risk and Uncertainty, 6*, 145–159. [31]

Robinson, G. H. (1964). Continuous estimation of a time-varying probability. *Ergonomics, 7*, 7–21. [2]

Robinson, R. J., Keltner, D., Ward, A., & Ross, L. (1995). Actual versus assumed differences in construal: "Naive realism" in intergroup perception and conflict. *Journal of Personality and Social Psychology, 68*, 404–417. [30]

Roe, R. M., Busemeyer, J. R., & Townsend, J. T. (2001). Multi-alternative decision field theory: A dynamic connectionist model of decision-making. *Psychological Review, 108*, 370–392. [11]

Roedder, D. L. (1981). Age differences in children's responses to television advertising: An information-processing approach. *Journal of Consumer Research, 8*, 144–153. [17]

Roedder, D. L., Sternthal, B., & Calder, B. J. (1983). Attitude-behavior consistency in children's responses to television advertising. *Journal of Marketing Research, 20*, 337–349. [17]

Roedinger, H. L., & Guynn, M. J. (1996). Retrieval processes. In E. L. Bjork & R. A. Bjork (Eds.), *Memory* (pp. 197–236). San Diego, CA: Academic Press. [21]

Roese, N. J. (1997). Counterfactual thinking. *Psychological Bulletin, 121*, 133–148. [28]

Rohrmann, B., & Borcherding, K. (1988, August). *The cognitive structure of residential decisions: A longitudinal field study*. Paper presented at the XXIV International Congress of Psychology, Sydney, Australia. [18]

Rolston, H. (1981). Values in nature. *Environmental Ethics, 3*, 115–128. [33]

Rosch, E., & Lloyd, B. (1978). *Cognition and categorization.* Hillsdale, NJ: Lawrence Erlbaum Associates. [31]

Rosen, L. D., & Rosenkoetter, P. (1976). An eye fixation analysis of choice and judgement with multiattribute stimuli. *Memory & Cognition, 4*, 747–752. [7]

Rosenthal, R., & Rosnow, R. L. (1969). *Artifact in behavioral research.* New York: Academic Press. [35]

Ross, H. L. (1973). Law, science, and accidents: The British Road Safety Act of 1967. *Journal of Legal Studies, 2*, 1–78. [13]

Rottenstreich, Y., & Hsee, C. K. (2001). Money, kisses, and electric shocks: On the affective psychology of risk. *Psychological Science, 12*, 185–190. [23, 24, 29, 32]

Rottenstreich, Y., & Tversky, A. (1997). Unpacking, repacking, and anchoring: Advances in support theory. *Psychological Review, 104*, 406–415. [31]

Rotter, J. B. (1966). Generalized expectancies for internal versus external locus of control of reinforcement. *Psychological Monographs, 80*, 1–28. [16]

Royden, H. L., Suppes, P., & Walsh, K. (1959). A model for the experimental measurement of the utility of gambling. *Behavioral Science, 4*, 11–18. [2]

Rumelhart, D. E., & McClelland, J. L. (1986). *Parallel distributed processing: Explorations in the microstructure of cognition* (Vol. 1). Cambridge, MA: MIT Press. [11, 12]

Russell, J. A. (2002). Core affect and the psychological construction of emotion. *Psychological Review, 110*, 145–172. [21]

Russell, M. (1990). The making of cruel choices. In P. B. Hammond & R. Coppock (Eds.), *Valuing health risks, costs, and benefits for environmental decision making: Report of a conference* (pp. 15–22). Washington, DC: National Academy Press. [34]

Russo, J. E. (1977). The value of unit price information. *Journal of Marketing Research, 14*, 193–201. [17, 34]

Russo, J. E., & Dosher, B. A. (1983). Strategies for multiattribute binary choice. *Journal of Experimental Psychology: Learning, Memory, and Cognition, 9*, 676–696. [7, 9, 10, 17]

Russo, J. E., & Leclerc, F. (1991). Characteristics of successful product information programs. *Journal of Social Issues, 67*, 73–92. [13]

Russo, J. E., & Leclerc, F. (1994). An eye-fixation analysis of choice processes for consumer nondurables. *Journal of Consumer Research, 21*, 274–290. [1, 17]

Russo, J. E., Medvec, V. H., & Meloy, M. G. (1996). The distortion of information during decisions. *Organizational Behavior and Human Decision Processes, 66*, 102–110. [12, 17, 19]

Russo, J. E., Meloy, M. G., & Medvec, V. H. (1998). Predecisional distortion of product information. *Journal of Marketing Research, 35*, 438–452. [12, 19, 21]

Russo, J. E., Meloy, M. G., & Wilks, T. J. (2000). Predecisional distortion of information by auditors and salespersons. *Management Science, 46*, 13–27. [19, 21]

Russo, J. E., & Rosen, L. D. (1975). An eye fixation analysis of multialternative choice. *Memory & Cognition, 3*, 267–276. [7]

Russo, J. E., & Schoemaker, P. J. H. (1989). *Decision traps.* New York: Fireside. [34]

Rutherford, M., Knetsch, J. L., & Brown, T. (1998). Assessing environmental losses: Judgments of importance and damage schedules. *Harvard Environmental Law Review, 22*, 51–101. [31]

Ryan, R. M., & Deci, E. L. (2001). On happiness and human potentials: A review of research on hedonic and eudaimonic well-being. *Annual Review of Psychology, 52*, 141–166. [28]

Sabini, J., & Silver, M. (1982). *Moralities of everyday life*. Oxford, UK: Oxford University Press. [20]

Salancik, G. R. (1974). Inference of one's attitude from behavior recalled under linguistically manipulated cognitive sets. *Journal of Experimental Social Psychology, 10*, 415–427. [26]

Salo, I. (2000). *A psychological process approach to decision making: Postdecision restructuring of value conflicts*. Unpublished doctoral dissertation, Lund University, Lund, Sweden. [19]

Salo, I., & Svenson, O. (2001). Constructive psychological responses before and after a real-life choice. In C. M. Alwood & M. Selart (Eds.), *Decision making: Social and creative dimensions* (pp. 137–151). Dordrecht, Germany: Kluwer. [19]

Salthouse, T. A. (1992). Why do adult age differences increase with task complexity? *Developmental Psychology, 28*, 905–918. [24]

Samuelson, P. (1963). Risk and uncertainty: A fallacy of large numbers. *Scientia, 98*, 108–113. [20]

Samuelson, W., & Zeckhauser, R. (1988). Status quo bias in decision-making. *Journal of Risk and Uncertainty, 1*, 7–59. [19, 37, 38]

Sanbonmatsu, D. M., & Fazio, R. H. (1990). The role of attitudes in memory-based decision making. *Journal of Personality and Social Psychology, 59*, 614–622. [10]

Sanbonmatsu, D. M., Kardes, F. R., & Gibson, B. D. (1991). The role of attribute knowledge and overall evaluations in comparative judgment. *Organizational Behavior and Human Decision Processes, 48*, 131–146. [10]

Sanfey, A., & Hastie, R. (1998). Does evidence presentation format affect judgment? An experimental evaluation of displays of data for judgments. *Psychological Science, 9*, 99–103. [23]

Savage, L. J. (1954). *The foundations of statistics*. New York: Wiley. [1, 22]

Scheffler, S. (1985). The role of consent in the legitimation of risky activities. In M. Gibson (Ed.), *To breathe freely* (pp. 75–88). Totowa, NJ: Rowman and Littlefield. [36]

Schelling, T. C. (1978). *Micromotives and macrobehavior*. New York: Norton. [14]

Schelling, T. C. (1984a). *Choice and consequence: Perspectives of an errant economics*. Cambridge, MA: Harvard University Press. [27]

Schelling, T. C. (1984b). Self-command in practice, in policy, and in a theory of rational choice. *American Economic Review, 74*(2), 1–11. [29]

Schick, F. (1991). *Understanding action: An essay on reasons*. New York: Cambridge University Press. [22]

Schkade, D. A., & Johnson, E. J. (1989). Cognitive processes in preference reversals. *Organizational Behavior and Human Performance, 44*, 203–231. [1, 6, **7**, 8, 9, 10, 11]

Schkade, D. A., & Kahneman, D. (1998). Does living in California make people happy? A focusing illusion in judgments of life satisfaction. *Psychological Science, 9*, 340–346. [21, 28, 29, 30]

Schkade, D. A., & Payne, J. W. (1994). How people respond to contingent valuation questions: A verbal protocol analysis of willingness to pay for an environmental regulation. *Journal of Environmental Economics and Management, 26*, 88. [20, 34]

Schmidt, U., & Hey, J. D. (2004). Are preference reversals errors? *Journal of Risk and Uncertainty, 29*, 207–218. [1]

Schneider, C. E. (1998). *The practice of autonomy: Patients, doctors, and medical decisions*. New York: Oxford University Press. [38]

Schoemaker, P. J. H. (1982). The expected utility model: Its variants, purposes, evidence, and limitations. *Journal of Economic Literature, 20*, 529–563. [7]

Schoemaker, P. J. H. (1991). When and how to use scenario planning: A heuristic approach with illustration. *Journal of Forecasting, 10*, 549–564. [34]

Schooler, J. W., & Engstler-Schooler, T. Y. (1990). Verbal overshadowing of visual memories: Some things are better left unsaid. *Cognitive Psychology, 22*, 36–71. [26]

Schooler, J. W., Ohlsson, S., & Brooks, K. (1993). Thoughts beyond words: When verbalization overshadows insight. *Journal of Experimental Psychology: General, 122*, 166–183. [26]

Schreiber, C. A., & Kahneman, D. (2000). Determinants of the remembered utility of aversive sounds. *Journal of Experimental Psychology: General, 129*, 27–42. [31]

Schultz, W., Romo, R., Ljungberg, T., Mirenowicz, J., Hollerman, J. R., & Dickinson, A. (1995). Reward-related signals carried by dopamine neurons. In J. C. Houk, J. L. Davis, & D. G. Beiser (Eds.), *Models of information processing in the basal ganglia* (pp. 233–248). Cambridge, MA: MIT Press. [11]

Schulz, R. (1976). Effects of control and predictability on the physical and psychological well-being of the institutionalized aged. *Journal of Personality and Social Psychology, 33*, 563–573. [16]

Schulz, R., & Hanusa, B. H. (1978). Long-term effects of control and predictability-enhancing interventions: Findings and ethical issues. *Journal of Personality and Social Psychology, 36*, 1194–1201. [16]

Schulze, W., McClelland, G. H., Waldman, D., & Lazo, J. (1996). Sources of bias in contingent valuation. In D. J. Bjornstad & J. R. Kahn (Eds.), *The contingent valuation of environmental resources: Methodological issues and research needs* (pp. 97–116). Brookfield, VT: Edward Elgar. [33]

Schuman, H., & Presser, S. (1981). *Questions and answers in attitude surveys: Experiments on question form, wording, and context.* New York: Academic Press. [34]

Schwartz, B. (1994). *The costs of living: How market freedom erodes the best things in life.* New York: W. W. Norton & Company. [16]

Schwartz, B. (2000). Self-determination: The tyranny of freedom. *American Psychologist, 55*, 79–88. [16]

Schwartz, B. (2004). *The paradox of choice: Why more is less.* New York: HarperCollins. [1]

Schwarz, N. (1990). Feelings as information: Informational and motivational functions of affective states. In E. T. H. R. Sorrentino (Ed.), *Handbook of motivation and cognition: Foundations of social behavior* (Vol. 2, pp. 527–561). New York: Guilford Press. [30]

Schwarz, N. (1996). *Cognition and communication: Judgmental biases, research methods, and the logic of conversation.* Mahwah, NJ: Lawrence Erlbaum Associates. [34]

Schwarz, N. (1999). Self-reports: How the questions shape the answers. *American Psychologist, 54*, 93–105. [35]

Schwarz, N., & Clore, G. L. (1983). Mood, misattribution, and judgments of well-being: Information and directive functions of affective states. *Journal of Personality and Social Psychology, 45*, 513–523. [21, 24, 30]

Schwarz, N., & Clore, G. L. (1988). How do I feel about it? Informative functions of affective states. In K. Fiedler & J. Forgas (Eds.), *Affect, cognition, and social behavior* (pp. 44–62). Toronto: Hogrefe International. [23]

Schwarz, N., & Clore, G. L. (2003). Mood as information: 20 years later. *Psychological Inquiry, 14*, 294–301. [24]

Schweitzer, M. (1994). Disentangling status quo and omission effects: An experimental analysis. *Organizational Behavior and Human Decision Processes, 58*, 457–476. [19]

Scitovsky, T. (1976). *The joyless economy*. New York: Oxford University Press. [27, 28]

Sedeck, G., Kofta, M., & Tyszka, T. (1993). Effects of uncontrollability on subsequent decision making: Testing the cognitive exhaustion hypothesis. *Journal of Personality and Social Psychology, 6*, 1270–1281. [18]

Segal, U. (1988). Does the preference reversal phenomenon necessarily contradict the independence axiom? *American Economic Review, 78*(1), 233–236. [1, 8]

Seidl, C. (2002). Preference reversal. *Journal of Economic Surveys, 16*, 621–655. [1]

Seip, K., & Strand, J. (1992). Willingness to pay for environmental goods in Norway: A contingent valuation study with real payment. *Environmental and Resource Economics, 2*, 91–106. [31]

Selart, M. (1996). Structure compatibility and restructuring in judgment and choice. *Organizational Behavior and Human Decision Processes, 65*, 106–116. [18]

Selart, M., Montgomery, H., Romanus, J., & Gärling, T. (1994). Violations of procedural invariance in preference measurement: Cognitive explanations. *European Journal of Cognitive Psychology, 6*, 417–436. [18]

Seligman, C., Fazio, R. H., & Zanna, M. P. (1980). Effects of salience of extrinsic rewards on liking and loving. *Journal of Personality and Social Psychology, 38*, 453–460. [26]

Seligman, M. E. P. (2002). *Authentic happiness: Using the new positive psychology to realize the potential for lasting fulfillment*. New York: The Free Press. [28]

Seligman, M. E. P., & Csikszentmihalyi, M. (2000). Positive psychology: An introduction. *American Psychologist, 55*, 5–14. [28]

Sen, A. (1982). *Choice, welfare, and measurement*. Cambridge, MA: MIT Press. [13]

Sen, A. (1987). *On ethics and economics*. Blackwell, UK: Oxford. [27]

Sen, A. (1990). Rational behavior. In J. Eatwell, M. Milgate, & P. Newman (Eds.), *The new Palgrave: Utility and probability* (pp. 198–216). New York: W. W. Norton. [27]

Sen, A. (1993). Internal consistency of choice. *Econometrica, 61*, 495–521. [27, 28]

Sen, A. (1997). Maximization and the act of choice. *Econometrica, 65*, 745–779. [34]

Shafer, G., & Tversky, A. (1985). Language and designs for probability judgment. *Cognitive Science, 9*, 309–339. [6]

Shafir, E. (1993). Choosing versus rejecting: Why some options are both better and worse than others. *Memory & Cognition, 21*, 546–556. [1, 9, 19, 22]

Shafir, E. (2002). Cognition, intuition, and policy guidelines. In R. Gowda & J. Fox (Eds.), *Judgments, choices, and public policy* (pp. 71–88). Cambridge, UK: Cambridge University Press. [9, 28]

Shafir, E., & LeBoeuf, R. A. (2002). Rationality. *Annual Review of Psychology, 53*, 491–517. [19]

Shafir, E., Osherson, D. N., & Smith, E. E. (1989). An advantage model of choice. *Journal of Behavioral Decision Making, 2*, 1–23. [17, 23]

Shafir, E., Osherson, D. N., & Smith, E. E. (1993). The advantage model: A comparative theory of evaluation and choice under risk. *Organizational Behavior and Human Decision Processes, 55*, 325–378. [17, 23]

Shafir, E., Simonson, I., & Tversky, A. (1993). Reason-based choice. *Cognition, 49*, 11–36. [1, 12, 16, 18, 21, **22**, 23, 29]

Shafir, E., & Tversky, A. (1992). Thinking through uncertainty: Nonconsequential reasoning and choice. *Cognitive Psychology, 24*, 449–474. [16, 19, 22]

Shamoun, S. (2004). *Post-decisional processes: Consolidation and value conflicts in decision making*. Unpublished doctoral dissertation, Stockholm University, Stockholm. [19]

Shamoun, S., & Svenson, O. (2002). Value conflict and post-decisional consolidation. *Scandinavian Journal of Psychology, 43*, 325–333. [19]

Shepard, R. N. (1964). On subjectively optimum selection among multiattribute alternatives. In M. W. Shelley, II, & G. L. Bryan (Eds.), *Human judgments and optimality* (pp. 257–281). New York: Wiley. [2, 19, 34]

Sherman, D. A., Kim, H., & Zajonc, R. B. (1998, August). *Affective perseverance: Cognitions change but preferences stay the same*. Paper presented at the annual meeting of the American Psychological Society, San Francisco. [23]

Sherman, L. W. (1990). Police crackdowns: Initial and residual deterrence. In M. Tonry & N. Morris (Eds.), *Crime and justice: An annual review of research* (Vol. 12, pp. 1–48). Chicago: University of Chicago Press. [13]

Sherman, S. J. (1980). On the self-erasing nature of errors of prediction. *Journal of Personality and Social Psychology, 39*, 211–221. [28]

Sherman, S. J., McMullen, M. N., & Gavanski, I. (1992). Natural sample spaces and the inversion of conditional judgments. *Journal of Experimental Social Psychology, 28*, 401–421. [21]

Shiffrin, R. M., & Schneider, W. (1977). Controlled and automatic human information processing: II. Perceptual learning, automatic attending, and a general theory. *Psychological Review, 84*, 127–190. [19]

Shiller, R. J. (1998). Human behavior and the efficiency of the financial system. In J. B. Taylor & M. Woodford (Eds.), *Handbook of macroeconomics* (Vol. 1, pp. 1305–1340). Amsterdam: Elsevier. [13, 14]

Shiller, R. J. (2000). *Irrational exuberance*. Princeton, NJ: Princeton University Press. [1, 38]

Shiv, B., Edell, J. A., & Payne, J. W. (1997). Factors affecting the impact of negatively and positively framed ad messages. *Journal of Consumer Research, 24*, 285–294. [17]

Shuford, E. H. (1961). Percentage estimation of proportion as a function of element type, exposure time, and task. *Journal of Experimental Psychology, 61*, 430–436. [2]

Siegel, S. (1956). *Nonparametric statistics for the behavioral sciences*. New York: McGraw-Hill. [16]

Siegel, S., Krank, M. D., & Hinson, R. E. (1987). Anticipation of pharmacological and nonpharmacological events: Classical conditioning and addictive behavior. *Journal of Drug Issues, 17*, 83–110. [21]

Simmons, C. J., Bickart, B. A., & Lynch, J. G., Jr. (1993). Capturing and creating public opinion in survey research. *Journal of Consumer Research, 20*, 316–329. [17, 34]

Simon, D., & Holyoak, K. J. (2002). Structural dynamics of cognition: From consistency theories to constraint satisfaction. *Personality and Social Psychology Review, 6*, 283–294. [1, 12, 19]

Simon, D., Krawczyk, D. C., & Holyoak, K. J. (2004). Construction of preferences by constraint satisfaction. *Psychological Science, 15*, 331–336. [1, **12**,19]

Simon, D., Pham, L. B., Le, Q. A., & Holyoak, K. J. (2001). The emergence of coherence over the course of decision making. *Journal of Experimental Psychology: Learning, Memory, and Cognition, 27*, 1250–1260. [12, 19]

Simon, D., Snow, C. J., & Read, S. J. (2004). The redux of cognitive consistency theories: Evidence judgments by constraint satisfaction. *Journal of Personality and Social Psychology, 86*, 814–837. [12]

Simon, H. A. (1955). A behavioral model of rational choice. *The Quarterly Journal of Economics, 59*, 99–118. [1, 16, 17, 19, 27, 34]

Simon, H. A. (1956). Rational choice and the structure of the environment. *Psychological Review, 63*, 129–138. [1, 16, 23]

Simon, H. A. (1957). *Models of man: Social and rational.* New York: Wiley. [2, 20]

Simon, H. A. (1978). Rationality as process and as product of a thought. *American Economic Review, 68*(2), 1–16. [33]

Simon, H. A. (1990). Invariants of human behavior. *Annual Review of Psychology, 41*, 1–19. [17, 19]

Simonson, I. (1989). Choice based on reasons: The case of attraction and compromise effects. *Journal of Consumer Research, 16*, 158–174. [1, 11, 22, 29]

Simonson, I. (1990). The effect of purchase quantity and timing on variety seeking behavior. *Journal of Marketing Research, 27*, 150–162. [17, 20, 27, 28, 29, 30]

Simonson, I. (1992). The influence of anticipating regret and responsibility on purchase decisions. *Journal of Consumer Research, 19*, 105–118. [17]

Simonson, I., Carmon, Z., & O'Curry, S. (1994). Experimental evidence on the negative effect of product features and sales promotions on brand choice. *Marketing Science, 13*, 23–40. [22]

Simonson, I., Huber, J., & Payne, J. W. (1988). The relationship between prior brand knowledge and information acquisition order. *Journal of Consumer Research, 14*, 566–578. [10]

Simonson, I., & Nowlis, S. M. (2000). The role of explanations and need for uniqueness in consumer decision making: Unconventional choices based on reasons. *Journal of Consumer Research, 27*, 150–162. [28, 29]

Simonson, I., Nowlis, S. M., & Lemon, K. (1993). The effect of local consideration sets on global choice between lower price and higher quality. *Marketing Science, 12*, 357–377. [10]

Simonson, I., Nowlis, S. M., & Simonson, Y. (1993). The effect of irrelevant preference arguments on consumer choice. *Journal of Consumer Psychology, 2*, 287–306. [22]

Simonson, I., & Tversky, A. (1992). Choice in context: Tradeoff contrast and extremeness aversion. *Journal of Marketing Research, 29*, 281–295. [10, 17, 22]

Simonson, I., & Winer, R. S. (1992). The influence of purchase quantity and display format on consumer preference for variety. *Journal of Consumer Research, 19*, 133–138. [20]

Sloman, S. A. (1996). The empirical case for two systems of reasoning. *Psychological Bulletin, 119*, 3–22. [1, 23, 32]

Slovic, P. (1972). From Shakespeare to Simon: Speculation – and some evidence – about man's ability to process information. *Oregon Research Institute Research Monograph, 12*(2). [34]

Slovic, P. (1975). Choice between equally valued alternatives. *Journal of Experimental Psychology: Human Perception and Performance, 1*, 280–287. [5, 6, 18, 19, 22]

Slovic, P. (1987). Perception of risk. *Science, 236*, 280–285. [23, 35]

Slovic, P. (1990). Choice. In D. N. Osherson & E. E. Smith (Eds.), *An invitation to cognitive science* (Vol. 3, pp. 89–116). Cambridge, MA: MIT Press. [22]

Slovic, P. (1995). The construction of preference. *American Psychologist, 50*, 364–371. [12, 13, 14, 15, 17, 19, 21, 23, 24, 31, 34, 37]

Slovic, P. (2000a). Rational actors and rational fools: The influence of affect on judgment and decision-making. *Roger Williams University Law Review, 6*, 163–212. [23]

Slovic, P. (Ed.). (2000b). *The perception of risk.* London: Earthscan. [35]

Slovic, P. (2001). Cigarette smokers: Rational actors or rational fools? In P. Slovic (Ed.), *Smoking: Risk, perception, & policy* (pp. 97–124). Thousand Oaks, CA: Sage. [23]

Slovic, P., Finucane, M. L., Peters, E., & MacGregor, D. G. (2002). The affect heuristic. In T. Gilovich, D. Griffin, & D. Kahneman (Eds.), *Heuristics and biases: The psychology of intuitive judgment* (pp. 397–420). New York: Cambridge University Press. [1, **23**, 24, 29, 32, 35, 36]

Slovic, P., Fischhoff, B., & Lichtenstein, S. (1977). Behavioral decision theory. *Annual Review of Psychology, 28*, 1–39. [19]

Slovic, P., Fischhoff, B., & Lichtenstein, S. (1982). Response mode, framing, and information-processing effects in risk assessment. In R. M. Hogarth (Ed.), *New directions for methodology of social and behavioral science: No. 11. Question framing and response consistency* (pp. 21–36). San Francisco: Jossey-Bass. [33]

Slovic, P., Griffin, D., & Tversky, A. (1990). Compatibility effects in judgment and choice. In R. M. Hogarth (Ed.), *Insights in decision making: A tribute to Hillel J. Einhorn* (pp. 5–27). Chicago: University of Chicago. [1, 6, 8, 9, 10, 11, 19, 23, 33, 36]

Slovic, P., Kunreuther, H., & White, G. F. (1974). Decision processes, rationality and adjustment to natural hazards. In G. F. White (Ed.), *Natural hazards: Local, national, global* (pp. 187–205). New York: Oxford University Press. [38]

Slovic, P., Layman, M., Kraus, N., Flynn, J., Chalmers, J., & Gesell, G. (1991). Perceived risk, stigma, and potential economic impacts of a high-level nuclear waste repository in Nevada. *Risk Analysis, 11*, 683–696. [23]

Slovic, P., & Lichtenstein, S. (1968). Relative importance of probabilities and payoffs in risk-taking. *Journal of Experimental Psychology Monograph, 78*(3, Pt. 2), 1–18. [1, **2**, 3, 4, 6, 7, 8, 29]

Slovic, P., & Lichtenstein, S. (1971). Comparison of Bayesian and regression approaches to the study of information processing in judgment. *Organizational Behavior and Human Performance, 6*, 649–744. [1, 6, 33]

Slovic, P., & Lichtenstein, S. (1983). Preference reversals: A broader perspective. *American Economic Review, 73*(4), 596–605. [1, 6, 7, 8, 18]

Slovic, P., Lichtenstein, S., & Edwards, W. (1965). Boredom-induced changes in preferences among bets. *American Journal of Psychology, 78*, 208–217. [1, 2]

Slovic, P., Lichtenstein, S., & Fischhoff, B. (1979). Images of disaster: Perception and acceptance of risks from nuclear power. In G. Goodman & W. Rowe (Eds.), *Energy risk assessment* (pp. 223–245). London: Academic Press. [33]

Slovic, P., Lichtenstein, S., & Fischhoff, B. (1984). Modeling the societal impact of fatal accidents. *Management Science, 30*, 464–474. [35]

Slovic, P., & MacPhillamy, D. J. (1974). Dimensional commensurability and cue utilization in comparative judgment. *Organizational Behavior and Human Performance, 11*, 172–194. [1, 10, 33]

Slovic, P., Monahan, J., & MacGregor, D. G. (2000). Violence risk assessment and risk communication: The effects of using actual cases, providing instructions, and employing probability vs. frequency formats. *Law and Human Behavior, 24*, 271–296. [23]

Slovic, P., & Tversky, A. (1974). Who accepts Savage's axiom? *Behavioral Science, 19*, 368–373. [27]

Smith, E. R. (1992). The role of exemplars in social judgment. In L. L. Martin & A. Tesser (Eds.), *The construction of social judgments* (pp. 107–132). Hillsdale, NJ: Lawrence Erlbaum Associates. [19]

Smith, G. (1997). *The political impact of name sounds.* Unpublished manuscript, Eastern Washington University, Ellensburg, WA. [23]

Smith, V. K. (1992). Arbitrary values, good causes, and premature verdicts. *Journal of Environmental Economics and Management, 22,* 71–89. [31]

Smith, V. K., & Desvousges, W. (1987). An empirical analysis of the economic value of risk changes. *Journal of Political Economy, 95,* 89–114. [34]

Smith, V. K., Desvousges, W., & Fisher, A. (1986). A comparison of direct and indirect methods for estimating environmental benefits. *American Journal of Agricultural Economics, 68,* 280–290. [33]

Soelberg, P. (1967). Unprogrammed decision making. *Management Review, 3,* 19–29. [18]

Soman, D., & Cheema, A. (2001). The effects of windfall gains on the sunk-cost effect. *Marketing Letters, 12,* 51–62. [29]

Spangenberg, E. R., & Greenwald, A. G. (1999). Social influence by requesting self-prophecy. *Journal of Consumer Psychology, 8,* 61–89. [28]

Spellman, B. A., & Holyoak, K. J. (1992). If Saddam is Hitler then who is George Bush? Analogical mapping between systems of social roles. *Journal of Personality and Social Psychology, 62,* 913–933. [12]

Spellman, B. A., Ullman, J. B., & Holyoak, K. J. (1993). A coherence model of cognitive consistency: Dynamics of attitude change during the Persian Gulf War. *Journal of Social Issues, 49,* 147–165. [12]

Stanovich, K. E. (1999). *Who is rational? Studies of individual differences in reasoning.* Mahwah, NJ: Lawrence Erlbaum Associates. [1]

Stanovich, K. E., & West, R. F. (1998). Individual differences in rational thought. *Journal of Experimental Psychology: General, 127,* 161–188. [17]

Stanovich, K. E., & West, R. F. (2000). Individual differences in reasoning: Implications for the rationality debate? *Behavioral and Brain Sciences, 23,* 645–726. [1]

Starr, C. (1969). Social benefit versus technological risk. *Science, 165,* 1232–1238. [35]

Steele, C. M. (1988). The psychology of self-affirmation: Sustaining the integrity of self. In L. Berkowitz (Ed.), *Advances in experimental social psychology* (Vol. 21, pp. 261–302). New York: Academic Press. [30]

Stevens, S. S. (1951). Mathematics, measurement, and psychophysics. In S. S. Stevens (Ed.), *Handbook of experimental psychology* (pp. 1–49). New York: Wiley. [33]

Stevens, S. S. (1975). *Psychophysics.* New York: Wiley. [13, 31, 32]

Stevens, S. S., & Galanter, E. H. (1957). Ratio scales and category scales for a dozen perceptual continua. *Journal of Experimental Psychology, 54,* 377–411. [2]

Stevens, T. H., Echeverria, J., Glass, R. J., Hager, T., & More, T. A. (1991). Measuring the existence value of wildlife: What do CVM estimates really show? *Land Economics, 67,* 390–400. [1, 33]

Strack, F., Argyle, M., & Schwarz, N. (Eds.). (1991). *Subjective well-being: An interdisciplinary perspective.* New York: Pergamon Press. [28]

Strack, F., & Mussweiler, T. (1997). Explaining the enigmatic anchoring effect: Mechanisms of selective accessibility. *Journal of Personality and Social Psychology, 73,* 437–446. [13, 21, 31]

Sudman, S., Bradburn, N. M., & Schwarz, N. (1996). *Thinking about answers: The application of cognitive processes to survey methodology.* San Francisco: Jossey-Bass. [34]

Suh, E., Diener, E., & Fujita, F. (1996). Events and subjective well-being: Only recent events matter. *Journal of Personality and Social Psychology, 70,* 1091–1102. [30]

Sujan, M. (1985). Consumer knowledge: Effects of evaluation strategies mediating consumer judgments. *Journal of Consumer Research, 12,* 16–31. [10]

Summers, L. H. (1986). Does the stock market rationally reflect fundamental values? *Journal of Finance, 41,* 591–602. [13, 14]

Sunstein, C. R. (1990). Preferences and politics. *Philosophy and Public Affairs, 20,* 3–34. [34]

Sunstein, C. R. (2001). Human behavior and the law of work. *Virginia Law Review, 87,* 205–276. [38]

Sunstein, C. R. (2002a). *Risk and reason: Safety, law, and the environment.* Cambridge, UK: Cambridge University Press. [38]

Sunstein, C. R. (2002b). Switching the default rule. *New York University Law Review, 77,* 106–134. [38]

Sunstein, C. R. (2004). Lives, life-years, and willingness to pay. *Columbia Law Review, 104,* 205–252. [38]

Sunstein, C. R., Kahneman, D., & Schkade, D. (1998). Assessing punitive damages. *Yale Law Journal, 107,* 2071–2153. [31, 32]

Sunstein, C. R., Kahneman, D., Schkade, D., & Ritov, I. (2002). Predictably incoherent judgments. *Stanford Law Review, 54,* 1153–1215. [13, 14, 28, 38]

Sunstein, C. R., & Thaler, R. H. (2003). Libertarian paternalism is not an oxymoron. *The University of Chicago Law Review, 70,* 1159–1202. [1, 37, **38**]

Svenson, O. (1973). *Analysis of strategies in subjective probability inferences as evidenced in continuous verbal reports and numerical responses.* (Reports from the Psychological Laboratories, No. 396.) Sweden: University of Stockholm. [19]

Svenson, O. (1974). *A note on think aloud protocols obtained during the choice of a home.* (Reports from the Psychological Laboratories, No. 421.) Sweden: University of Stockholm. [19]

Svenson, O. (1979). Process descriptions of decision making. *Organizational Behavior and Human Decision Processes, 23,* 86–112. [1, 18, 19]

Svenson, O. (1983). Cognitive processes in judging cumulative risk over different periods of time. *Organizational Behavior and Human Performance, 33,* 22–41. [19]

Svenson, O. (1985). Cognitive strategies in a complex judgment task: Analysis of concurrent verbal reports and judgments of cumulated risk over different exposure times. *Organizational Behavior and Human Decision Processes, 36,* 1–15. [19]

Svenson, O. (1990). Some propositions for the classification of decision situations. In K. Borcherding, O. I. Larichev, & D. M. Messick (Eds.), *Contemporary issues in decision making* (pp. 17–31). Amsterdam: Elsevier. [19]

Svenson, O. (1992). Differentiation and Consolidation Theory of human decision making: A frame of reference for the study of pre- and post-decision processes. *Acta Psychologica, 80,* 143–168. [12, 18, 19]

Svenson, O. (1996). Decision making and the search for fundamental psychological realities: What can be learned from a process perspective? *Organizational Behavior and Human Decision Processes, 65,* 252–267. [1, 18, **31**]

Svenson, O. (2003). Values, affect, and processes in human decision making: A Differentiation and Consolidation Theory perspective. In S. L. Schneider & J. Shanteau (Eds.), *Emerging perspectives on judgment and decision making* (pp. 287–326). Cambridge, UK: Cambridge University Press. [19]

Svenson, O., & Benthorn, L. (1992). Consolidation processes in decision making: Post-decision changes in attractiveness of alternatives. *Journal of Economic Psychology, 13,* 1–13. [19]

Svenson, O., & Edland, A. (1987). Change of preferences under time pressure: Choices and judgments. *Scandinavian Journal of Psychology, 29*, 322–330. [1]

Svenson, O., & Fischhoff, B. (1985). Levels of environmental decisions: A case study of radiation in Swedish homes. *Journal of Environmental Psychology, 5*, 55–67. [19]

Svenson, O., & Hill, T. (1997). Turning prior disadvantages into advantages: Decision making through the glass of differentiation and consolidation theory. In R. Ranyard, W. R. Crozier, & O. Svenson (Eds.), *Decision making: Cognitive models and explanations* (pp. 218–232). London: Routledge. [18, 19]

Svenson, O., & Malmsten, N. (1991). Post-decision consolidation processes in human decision making. *Journal of Scientific Contributions to Human Decision Making (Italy), 6*, 109–120. [19]

Svenson, O., & Malmsten, N. (1996). Post-decision consolidation overtime as a function gain or loss of an alternative. *Scandinavian Journal of Psychology, 37*, 302–311. [19]

Svenson, O., Ortega Rayo, A., Sandberg, A., Svahlin, I., & Andersen, M. (1994). Post-decision consolidation as a function of the instructions to the decision maker and of the decision problem. *Acta Psychologica, 87*, 181–197. [19]

Svenson, O., & Shamoun, S. (1997). Predecision conflict and different patterns of post-decision attractiveness restructuring: Empirical illustrations from an important real-life decision. *Scandinavian Journal of Psychology, 38*, 243–251. [19]

Swagler, R. M., & Wheeler, P. (1989). Rental-purchase agreements: A preliminary investigation of consumer attitudes and behaviors. *Journal of Consumer Affairs, 23*, 145–160. [20]

Swann, W. B., & Pittman, T. S. (1977). Initiating play activity of children: The moderating influence of verbal cues on intrinsic motivation. *Child Development, 48*, 1128–1132. [16]

Taurek, J. (1977). Should the numbers count? *Philosophy and Public Affairs, 6*, 293–316. [36]

Taylor, K. F., & Sluckin, W. (1964). Flocking in domestic chicks. *Nature, 201*, 108–109. [25]

Taylor, S. E. (1983). Adjustment to threatening events: A theory of cognitive adaptation. *American Psychologist, 38*, 1161–1173. [30]

Taylor, S. E. (1989). *Positive illusions: Creating self-deception and the healthy mind.* New York: Basic Books. [16]

Taylor, S. E., & Armor, D. A. (1996). Positive illusions and coping with adversity. *Journal of Personality, 64*, 873–898. [30]

Taylor, S. E., & Brown, J. D. (1988). Illusion and well-being: A social-psychological perspective on mental health. *Psychological Bulletin, 103*, 193–210. [16, 30]

Taylor, S. E., & Fiske, S. T. (1981). Getting inside the head: Methodologies for process analysis. In J. H. Harvey, W. J. Ickes, & R. F. Kidd (Eds.), *New directions in attribution research* (Vol. 3, pp. 459–524). Hillsdale, NJ: Lawrence Erlbaum Associates. [7]

Taylor, S. E., & Gollwitzer, P. M. (1996). Effects of mindset on positive illusions. *Journal of Personality and Social Psychology, 69*, 213–226. [18]

Telhami, S. (1990). *Power and leadership in international bargaining: The path to the Camp David Accords.* New York: Columbia University Press. [22]

Tesser, A. (1978). Self-generated attitude change. In L. Berkowitz (Ed.), *Advances in experimental social psychology* (Vol. 11, pp. 289–338). New York: Academic Press. [1]

Tesser, A., Leone, C., & Clary, G. (1978). Affect control: Process constraints versus catharsis. *Cognitive Therapy and Research, 2*, 265–274. [26]

Tesser, A., & Martin, L. (1996). The psychology of evaluation. In E. T. Higgins & A. W. Kruglanski (Eds.), *Social psychology: Handbook of basic principles* (pp. 400–432). New York: Guilford Press. [31]

Tetlock, P. E. (1992). The impact of accountability on judgment and choice: Toward a social contingency model. In M. P. Zanna (Ed.), *Advances in experimental social psychology* (Vol. 25, pp. 331–376). New York: Academic Press. [22]

Tetlock, P. E., & Boettger, R. (1989). Accountability: A social magnifier of the dilution effect. *Journal of Personality and Social Psychology, 57*, 388–398. [29]

Thagard, P. (1989). Explanatory coherence. *Behavioral and Brain Sciences, 12*, 435–502. [12]

Thaler, R. H. (1980). Toward a positive theory of consumer choice. *Journal of Economic Behavior & Organization, 1*, 39–60. [27]

Thaler, R. H. (1985). Mental accounting and consumer choice. *Marketing Science, 4*, 199–214. [20, 29]

Thaler, R. H. (1991). *Quasi-rational economics*. New York: Russell Sage. [38]

Thaler, R. H. (1992). *The winner's curse: Paradoxes and anomalies of economic life*. New York: The Free Press. [31]

Thaler, R. H. (1999). Mental accounting matters. In D. Kahneman & A. Tversky (Eds.), *Choices, values and frames* (pp. 241–268). Cambridge, UK: Cambridge University Press. [20, 21, 29]

Thaler, R. H., & Benartzi, S. (2004). Save More Tomorrow™: Using behavioral economics to increase employee saving. *Journal of Political Economy, 112*, S164–S187. [38]

Thaler, R. H., & Shefrin, H. M. (1981). An economic theory of self-control. *Journal of Political Economy, 89*, 392–406. [20, 29]

Thaler, R. H., Tversky, A., Kahneman, D., & Schwartz, A. (1997). The effect of myopia and loss aversion on risk taking: An experimental test. *The Quarterly Journal of Economics, 112*, 647–661. [20]

Thorngate, W. (1980). Efficient decision heuristics. *Behavioral Science, 25*, 219–225. [1]

Thurstone, L. L. (1928). Attitudes can be measured. *American Journal of Sociology, 33*, 529–554. [23]

Timmermans, D. (1993). The impact of task complexity on information use in multi-attribute decision making. *Journal of Behavioral Decision Making, 6*, 95–111. [16]

Toda, M. (1962). The design of a fungus-eater: A model of human behavior in an unsophisticated environment. *Behavioral Science, 7*, 164–183. [2]

Toulmin, S. (1950). *An examination of the place of reason in ethics*. New York: Cambridge University Press. [22]

Townsend, J. T., & Busemeyer, J. R. (1995). Dynamic representation of decision-making. In R. F. Port & T. Van Gelder (Eds.), *Mind as motion* (pp. 101–120). Cambridge, MA: MIT Press. [11]

Trafimow, D., & Sheeran, P. (2004). A theory about the translation of cognition into affect and behavior. In G. R. Maio & G. Haddock (Eds.), *Contemporary perspectives in the psychology of attitudes: The cardoff symposium* (pp. 57–75). London: Psychology Press. [24]

Trollope, A. (1883/1980). *An autobiography*. Oxford, UK: Oxford University Press. [20]

Tune, G. S. (1964). Response preferences: A review of some relevant literature. *Psychological Bulletin, 61*, 286–302. [35]

Turner, C. F., & Krauss, E. (1978). Fallible indicators of the subjective state of the union. *American Psychologist, 33*, 456–470. [35]

Tversky, A. (1967a). Additivity, utility and subjective probability. *Journal of Mathematical Psychology, 4*, 175–201. [2]

Tversky, A. (1967b). Utility theory, additivity analysis, and decision making under risk. *Journal of Experimental Psychology, 75*, 27–36. [2, 3]

Tversky, A. (1969). Intransitivity of preferences. *Psychological Review, 76*, 31–48. [1, 3, 5, 6, 7, 8, 9, 11, 17, 28]

Tversky, A. (1972). Elimination by aspects: A theory of choice. *Psychological Review, 79*, 281–299. [1, 5, 11, 17, 19, 23]

Tversky, A. (1977). Features of similarity. *Psychological Review, 84*, 327–352. [6, 17]

Tversky, A. (1996). Contrasting rational and psychological principles of choice. In R. J. Zeckhauser, R. L. Keeney, & J. K. Sebenius (Eds.), *Wise choices: Decisions, games, and negotiations* (pp. 5–21). Boston: Harvard Business School Press. [17, 34]

Tversky, A., & Bar-Hillel, M. (1983). Risk: The long and the short. *Journal of Experimental Psychology: Learning, Memory, and Cognition, 9*, 713–717. [20]

Tversky, A., & Gati, I. (1978). Studies of similarity. In E. Rosch & B. Lloyd (Eds.), *Cognition and categorization* (pp. 79–98). Hillsdale, NJ: Lawrence Erlbaum Associates. [6]

Tversky, A., & Griffin, D. (1991). Endowment and contrast in judgments of well-being. In F. Strack, M. Argyle, & N. Schwarz (Eds.), *Subjective well-being: An interdisciplinary perspective* (Vol. 12, pp. 101–118). Oxford, UK: Pergamon Press. [9, 29]

Tversky, A., & Kahneman, D. (1971). Belief in the law of small numbers. *Psychological Bulletin, 76*, 105–110. [31]

Tversky, A., & Kahneman, D. (1973). Availability: A heuristic for judging frequency and probability. *Cognitive Psychology, 5*, 207–232. [38]

Tversky, A., & Kahneman, D. (1974). Judgment under uncertainty: Heuristics and biases. *Science, 185*, 1124–1131. [1, 6, 7, 13, 21, 23, 35, 38]

Tversky, A., & Kahneman, D. (1981). The framing of decisions and the psychology of choice. *Science, 211*, 453–458. [1, 17, 19, 20, 33]

Tversky, A., & Kahneman, D. (1982). Evidential impact of base rates. In D. Kahneman, P. Slovic, & A. Tversky (Eds.), *Judgment under uncertainty: Heuristics and biases* (pp. 153–160). New York: Cambridge University Press. [31]

Tversky, A., & Kahneman, D. (1983). Extensional versus intuitive reasoning: The conjunction fallacy in probability judgment. *Psychological Review, 90*, 293–315. [31]

Tversky, A., & Kahneman, D. (1986). Rational choice and the framing of decisions. *Journal of Business, 59*, S251–S278. [1, 6, 8, 12, 17, 22, 27, 31]

Tversky, A., & Kahneman, D. (1991). Loss aversion in riskless choice: A reference-dependent model. *The Quarterly Journal of Economics, 106*, 1039–1061. [17, 21, 27, 31, 37]

Tversky, A., & Kahneman, D. (1992). Advances in prospect theory: Cumulative representation of uncertainty. *Journal of Risk and Uncertainty, 5*, 297–323. [19, 27, 32]

Tversky, A., Sattath, S., & Slovic, P. (1988). Contingent weighting in judgment and choice. *Psychological Review, 95*, 371–384. [1, 6, 7, 8, 9, 10, 11, 17, 18, 21, 22, 28, 29, 33, 34]

Tversky, A., & Shafir, E. (1992a). Choice under conflict: The dynamics of deferred decision. *Psychological Science, 3*, 358–361. [22]

Tversky, A., & Shafir, E. (1992b). The disjunction effect in choice under uncertainty. *Psychological Science, 3*, 305–309. [22]

Tversky, A., & Simonson, I. (1993). Context-dependent preferences. *Management Science, 39*, 1179–1189. [11, 17, 22]

Tversky, A., Slovic, P., & Kahneman, D. (1990). The causes of preference reversal. *American Economic Review, 80*(1), 204–217. [1, 6, 7, **8**, 27, 33, 36]

Tversky, A., & Thaler, R. H. (1990). Anomalies: Preference reversals. *The Journal of Economic Perspectives, 4*(2), 201–211. [Frontispiece, 1, 31, 38]

Tyszka, T. (1983). Contextual multiattribute decision rules. In L. Sjöberg, T. Tyszka, & J. A. Wise (Eds.), *Human decision making* (pp. 243–256). Bodafors, Sweden: Bokförlaget Doxa. [18]

Tyszka, T. (1985). Variability of predecisional information seeking behavior. *Polish Psychological Bulletin, 16*, 275–282. [19]

Tyszka, T., & Wielochovski, M. (1991). Must boxing verdicts be partial? *Journal of Behavioral Decision Making, 4*, 283–295. [18, 19]

Urban, G. L., & Hauser, J. R. (1993). *Design and marketing of new products* (2nd ed.). Englewood Cliffs, NJ: Prentice-Hall. [10]

Urban, G. L., Hauser, J. R., Qualls, W. J., Weinberg, B. D., Bohlmann, J. D., & Chicos, R. A. (1997). Information acceleration: Validation and lessons from the field. *Journal of Marketing Research, 34*, 143–153. [34]

U.S. Environmental Protection Agency. (1993). *Comparative risk*. Washington, DC: Author. [35]

Usher, M., & McClelland, J. L. (2004). Loss aversion and inhibition in dynamic models of multi-alternative choice. *Psychological Review, 111*, 757–769. [11]

Vaillant, G. (1993). *The wisdom of the ego*. Cambridge, MA: Harvard University Press. [30]

Van der Meer, H. C. (1963). Decision-making: The influence of probability preference, variance preference, and expected value on strategy in gambling. *Acta Psychologica, 21*, 231–259. [2]

Van Gelder, L. (1996, January 7). Remembering the road not taken. *The New York Times*, p. F7. [30]

van Praag, B. M. S. (2003). *The connection between old and new approaches to financial satisfaction*. Unpublished manuscript. [28]

van Raaij, W. F. (1977). Consumer information processing for different information structures and formats. In W. D. Perrault (Ed.), *Advances in consumer research* (pp. 176–184). Chicago: Association for Consumer Research. [19]

Vanderplas, J. M. (1960). Some tests of significance of multivariate data. *Journal of General Psychology, 62*, 257–268. [2]

VanDeVeer, D. (1986). *Paternalistic intervention: The moral bounds of benevolence*. Princeton, NJ: Princeton University Press. [38]

Varey, C. A., & Kahneman, D. (1992). Experiences extended across time: Evaluation of moments and episodes. *Journal of Behavioral Decision Making, 5*, 169–185. [27, 31]

Varian, H. R. (1984). *Microeconomic analysis*. New York: Norton. [6, 31]

Varian, H. R. (1999). *Intermediate microeconomics: A modern approach* (5th ed.). New York: Norton. [21]

Verplanken, B., Hofstee, G., & Janssen, H. J. W. (1998). Accessibility of affective versus cognitive components of attitudes. *European Journal of Social Psychology, 28*, 23–36. [24]

Verplanken, B., & Svenson, O. (1997). Personal involvement in human decision making: On conceptualization and effects on decision process. In R. Ranyard, W. R. Crozier, & O. Svenson (Eds.), *Decision making: Cognitive models and explanations* (pp. 41–57). London: Routledge. [19]

Viscusi, W. K. (1992). *Smoking: Making the risky decision*. New York: Oxford University Press. [23]

Viscusi, W. K., & Magat, W. A. (1987). *Learning about risk: Consumer and worker responses to hazard warnings*. Cambridge, MA: Harvard University Press. [33]

Viscusi, W. K., Magat, W. A., & Huber, J. (1986). Informational regulation of consumer health risks: An empirical evaluation of hazard warnings. *Rand Journal of Economics, 17*, 351–365. [33]

Viscusi, W. K., Magat, W. A., & Huber, J. (1991). Pricing environmental health risks: Survey assessments of risk-risk and risk-dollar trade-offs for chronic bronchitis. *Journal of Environmental Economics and Management, 21*, 32–51. [33]

Viswanathan, M., & Narayanan, S. (1994). Comparative judgments of numerical and verbal attribute labels. *Journal of Consumer Psychology, 3*, 79–102. [10, 29]

von Clausewitz, C. (1992). *On war*. Harmandsworth, UK: Penguin Books (Original work published 1832). [20]

von Neumann, J., & Morgenstern, O. (1947). *Theory of games and economic behavior* (2nd ed.). Princeton, NJ: Princeton University Press. [21, 22, 35]

von Winterfeldt, D. (1999). On the relevance of behavioral decision research for decision analysis. In J. Shanteau, B. Mellers, & D. Schum (Eds.), *Decision science and technology: Reflections on the contributions of Ward Edwards* (pp. 133–154). Boston: Kluwer. [1]

von Winterfeldt, D., & Edwards, W. (1986). *Decision analysis and behavioral research*. New York: Cambridge University Press. [33, 34, 35]

Wald, A. (1950). *Sequential analysis*. New York: Wiley. [19]

Walden, M. L. (1990). The economics of rent-to-own contracts. *Journal of Consumer Affairs, 24*, 326–337. [20]

Walsh, R. G., Bjonback, R. D., Aiken, R. A., & Rosenthal, D. H. (1990). Estimating the public benefits of protecting forest quality. *Journal of Environmental Management, 30*, 175–189. [33]

Watkins, M. J., & Tulving, E. (1978). When retrieval cueing fails. *British Journal of Psychology, 69*, 443–450. [21]

Watkins, O. C., & Watkins, M. J. (1975). Buildup of proactive inhibition as a cue-overload effect. *Journal of Experimental Psychology: Human Learning and Memory, 1*, 442–452. [21]

Watterson, B. (1996). *It's a magical world*. Kansas City, MO: Andrews and McNeel. [16]

Weber, E. U., Ames, D. R., & Blais, A.-R. (2005). "How do I choose thee? Let me count the ways": A textual analysis of similarities and differences in modes of decision-making in China and the United States. *Management and Organization Review, 1*, 87–118. [21]

Weber, E. U., Goldstein, W. M., & Barlas, S. (1995). And let us not forget memory: The role of memory processes and techniques in the study of judgment and choice. In J. R. Busemeyer, R. Hastie, & D. L. Medin (Eds.), *Decision making from the perspective of cognitive psychology* (Vol. 32, pp. 33–82). San Diego: Academic Press. [17, 21]

Weber, E. U., & Hsee, C. K. (2000). Culture and individual judgment and decision making. *Applied Psychology: An International Review, 49*, 32–61. [21]

Wedell, D. H. (1991). Distinguishing among models of contextually induced preferences reversals. *Journal of Experimental Psychology, 17,* 767–778. [22]

Wedell, D. H., & Bockenholt, U. (1990). Moderation of preference reversals in the long run. *Journal of Experimental Psychology: Human Perception and Performance, 16,* 429–438. [1, 20]

Wedell, D. H., & Bockenholt, U. (1994). Contemplating single versus multiple encounters of a risky prospect. *American Journal of Psychology, 107,* 499–518. [20]

Wertenbroch, K. (1998). Segmentation and pricing under consumption self-control via purchase quantity rationing. *Marketing Science, 17,* 317–337. [17]

West, P. M., Brown, C. L., & Hoch, S. J. (1996). Consumption vocabulary and preference formation. *Journal of Consumer Research, 23,* 120–135. [17]

Westen, D. (1994). Toward an integrative model of affect regulation: Applications to social psychological research. *Journal of Personality, 62,* 641–667. [30]

Wickens, C. D. (1984). *Engineering psychology and human performance.* Columbus, OH: Merrill. [6]

Wickens, J. R., & Oorschot, D. E. (2000). Neuronal dynamics and surround inhibition in the neostriatum: A possible connection. In R. Miller & J. R. Wickens (Eds.), *Brain dynamics and the striatal complex* (pp. 141–150). Amsterdam: Harwood Academic. [11]

Wicklund, R. A., & Brehm, J. W. (1976). *Perspectives on cognitive dissonance.* Hillsdale, NJ: Lawrence Erlbaum Associates. [12, 22]

Wilde, O. (1893). *Lady Windermere's fan: A play about a good woman.* London: Mathews and Lane. [30]

Willemsen, M. C., & Keren, G. (2002). Negative-based prominence: The role of negative features on matching and choice. *Organizational Behavior and Human Decision Processes, 88,* 643–666. [28]

Willemsen, M. C., & Keren, G. (2004). The role of negative features in joint and separate evaluation. *Journal of Behavioral Decision Making, 17,* 313–329. [28]

Willén, H. (1994). *How do couples decide about having their first child? An explorative study* (Göteborg Psychological Reports, Vol. 24, No. 1). Göteborg, Sweden: Göteborg University, Department of Psychology. [18]

Wilson, T. D. (1990). Self-persuasion via self-reflection. In J. M. Olson & M. P. Zanna (Eds.), *Self-inference processes: The Ontario Symposium* (Vol. 6, pp. 43–67). Hillsdale, NJ: Lawrence Erlbaum Associates. [26]

Wilson, T. D., & Brekke, N. (1994). Mental contamination and mental correction: Unwanted influences on judgments and evaluations. *Psychological Bulletin, 19,* 117–142. [30]

Wilson, T. D., & Dunn, D. S. (1986). Effects of introspection on attitude-behavior consistency: Analyzing reasons versus focusing on feelings. *Journal of Experimental Social Psychology, 22,* 249–263. [26]

Wilson, T. D., Dunn, D. S., Kraft, D., & Lisle, D. J. (1989). Introspection, attitude change, and attitude-behavior consistency: The disruptive effects of explaining why we feel the way we do. *Advances in Experimental Social Psychology, 22,* 287–343. [26, 29]

Wilson, T. D., & Gilbert, D. T. (2003). Affective forecasting. In M. Zanna (Ed.), *Advances in experimental social psychology* (pp. 345–411). New York: Elsevier. [28]

Wilson, T. D., & Hodges, S. D. (1992). Attitudes as temporary constructions. In A. Tesser & L. Martin (Eds.), *The construction of social judgment* (pp. 37–65). Hillsdale, NJ: Lawrence Erlbaum Associates. [1, 26]

Wilson, T. D., Hodges, S. D., & LaFleur, S. J. (1995). Effects of introspecting about reasons: Inferring attitudes from accessible thoughts. *Journal of Personality and Social Psychology, 68*, 16–28. [29]

Wilson, T. D., Houston, C. E., Etling, K. M., & Brekke, N. (1996). A new look at anchoring effects: Basic anchoring and its antecedents. *Journal of Experimental Psychology: General, 125*, 387–402. [31]

Wilson, T. D., & Kraft, D. (1993). Why do I love thee? Effects of repeated introspections about a dating relationship on attitudes toward the relationship. *Personality and Social Psychology Bulletin, 19*, 409–418. [26]

Wilson, T. D., Kraft, D., & Dunn, D. S. (1989). The disruptive effects of explaining attitudes: The moderating effect of knowledge about the attitude object. *Journal of Experimental Social Psychology, 25*, 379–400. [26, 28]

Wilson, T. D., & LaFleur, S. J. (1993). [Effects of analyzing reasons on the accuracy of self-predictions]. Unpublished data, University of Virginia. [26]

Wilson, T. D., LaFleur, S. J., & Lindsey, J. S. (1995). *Expertise and introspection: Analyzing the reasons for one's attitudes.* Unpublished manuscript. [1]

Wilson, T. D., Lisle, D. J., Schooler, J. W., Hodges, S. D., Klaaren, K. J., & LaFleur, S. J. (1993). Introspecting about reasons can reduce post-choice satisfaction. *Personality and Social Psychology Bulletin, 19*, 331–339. [1, **26**, 30]

Wilson, T. D., & Schooler, J. W. (1991). Thinking too much: Introspection can reduce the quality of preferences and decisions. *Journal of Personality and Social Psychology, 60*, 181–192. [1, 22, 26, 28, 29, 34]

Wilson, T. D., Wheatley, T., Meyers, J. M., Gilbert, D. T., & Axsom, D. (2000). Focalism: A source of durability bias in affective forecasting. *Journal of Personality and Social Psychology, 78*, 821–836. [28, 30]

Wilson, W. R. (1979). Feeling more than we can know: Exposure effects without learning. *Journal of Personality and Social Psychology, 37*, 811–821. [25]

Winer, B. J. (1971). *Statistical principles in experimental design.* New York: McGraw-Hill. [7]

Winkielman, P., Zajonc, R. B., & Schwarz, N. (1997). Subliminal affective priming resists attributional interventions. *Cognition & Emotion, 11*, 433–465. [23]

Wolf, J. S., Servino, E. M., & Nathan, H. N. (1997). National strategy to develop public acceptance of organ and tissue donation. *Transplantation Proceedings, 29*, 1477–1478. [37]

Wood, W. (1982). Retrieval of attitude-relevant information from memory: Effects on susceptibility to persuasion and on intrinsic motivation. *Journal of Personality and Social Psychology, 42*, 798–810. [26]

Woodworth, R. S., & Schlosberg, H. (1954). *Experimental psychology.* New York: Holt. [35]

Wortman, C. B., & Silver, R. C. (1989). The myths of coping with loss. *Journal of Consulting and Clinical Psychology, 57*, 349–357. [30]

Wright, A. A., & Lynch, J. G. (1995). Communication effects of advertising versus direct experience when both search and experience attributes are present. *Journal of Consumer Research, 21*, 708–718. [29, 32]

Wright, P. L. (1975). Consumer choice strategies: Simplifying vs. optimizing. *Journal of Marketing Research, 12*, 60–67. [16, 17, 23]

Wright, P. L., & Kriewall, M. A. (1980). State-of-mind effects on the accuracy with which utility functions predict marketplace choice. *Journal of Marketing Research, 17*, 277–293. [17, 34]

Wright, P. L., & Rip, P. D. (1980). Product class advertising effects on first time buyers' decision strategies. *Journal of Consumer Research, 7*, 176–188. [15]

Wright, P. L., & Weitz, B. (1977). Time horizon effects on product evaluation strategies. *Journal of Marketing Research, 14*, 429–443. [34]

Wright, W., & Bower, G. H. (1992). Mood effects on subjective probability assessment. *Organizational Behavior and Human Decision Processes, 52*, 276–291. [24]

Wu, G. (1999). Anxiety and decision making with delayed resolution of uncertainty. *Theory and Decision, 46*, 159–198. [32]

Wu, G., & Gonzalez, R. (1996). Curvature of the probability weighting function. *Management Science, 42*, 1676–1690. [32]

Wu, G., & Gonzalez, R. (1998). Common consequence effects in decision making under risk. *Journal of Risk and Uncertainty, 16*, 113–135. [32]

Yaari, M., & Bar-Hillel, M. (1984). On dividing justly. *Social Choice and Welfare, 1*, 1–24. [20]

Yalch, R. F., & Yalch, R. E. (1984). The effect of numbers on the route to persuasion. *Journal of Consumer Research, 11*, 522–527. [29]

Yamagishi, K. (1997). When a 12.86% mortality is more dangerous than 24.14%: Implications for risk communication. *Applied Cognitive Psychology, 11*, 495–506. [23]

Yankelovich, D. (1991). *Coming to public judgment: Making democracy work in a complex world*. Syracuse, NY: Syracuse University Press. [34]

Yates, J. F. (1990). *Judgment and decision making*. Englewood Cliffs, NJ: Prentice-Hall. [19]

Yi, Y. (1990). The effects of contextual priming in print advertisements. *Journal of Consumer Research, 17*, 215–222. [15]

Zajonc, R. B. (1968). Attitudinal effects of mere exposure. *Journal of Personality and Social Psychology Monograph, 9*(2, Pt. 2), 1–27. [23, 25]

Zajonc, R. B. (1980). Feeling and thinking: Preferences need no inferences. *American Psychologist, 35*, 151–175. [1, 19, 22, 23, 25, 27, 32]

Zajonc, R. B. (2000). Feeling and thinking: Closing the debate over the independence of affect. In J. P. Forgas (Ed.), *Feeling and thinking: The role of affect in social cognition* (pp. 31–58). Cambridge, UK: Cambridge University Press. [25]

Zajonc, R. B. (2001). Mere exposure: A gateway to the subliminal. *Current Directions in Psychological Science, 10*, 224–228. [1, **25**]

Zakay, D., & Tsal, Y. (1993). The impact of using forced decision making strategies on post-decision confidence. *Journal of Behavioral Decision Making, 6*, 53–68. [19]

Zaller, J. (1992). *The nature and origins of mass opinion*. Cambridge, UK: Cambridge University Press. [31]

Zinbarg, R. E., & Mohlman, J. (1998). Individual differences in the acquisition of affectively-valenced associations. *Journal of Personality and Social Psychology, 74*, 1024–1040. [24]

Zola-Morgan, S., Squire, L. R., Alvarez-Royo, P., & Clower, R. P. (1991). Independence of memory functions and emotional behavior. *Hippocampus, 1*, 207–220. [25]

Zuckerman, M., Porac, J., Lathin, D., Smith, R., & Deci, E. L. (1978). On the importance of self-determination for intrinsically motivated behavior. *Personality and Social Psychology Bulletin, 4*, 443–446. [16]

Index